THE PENINSULAR WAR
ATLAS

THE
PENINSULAR WAR
ATLAS

NICK LIPSCOMBE

OSPREY
PUBLISHING

First published in Great Britain in 2010 by Osprey Publishing,
Midland House, West Way, Botley, Oxford, OX2 0PH, UK
44-02 23rd Street, Suite 219, Long Island City, NY 11101, USA

E-mail: info@ospreypublishing.com

A CIP catalogue record for this book is available from the British Library

ISBN: 978 1 84908 364 5

Page layout by Myriam Bell Design, France
Cartography by Peter Bull Art Studio
Typeset in Baskerville
Originated by PDQ media, Bungay, UK
Printed in China through Worldprint Ltd

10 11 12 13 14   10 9 8 7 6 5 4 3 2 1

Front Cover: Wellington in Spain (oil on panel) by Robert Alexander Hillingford. (The Bridgeman Art Library)

Osprey Publishing is supporting the Woodland Trust, the UK's leading woodland conservation charity, by funding
the dedication of trees.

NOTE ON THE TEXT: The great variety of historical, national and local spellings of certain
place names means that they may vary within the text according to the source and context in
which they are used.

EDITOR'S NOTE:
Maps 73 and 89: Sarrut's order of battle shows 1/36e, 2/36e, 3/36e, 4/36e Léger, however,
both should be 1/36e, 2/36e, 3/36e, 4/36e Ligne.
Appendix 3:
The French Army in Spain, 15 January 1810. In addition to the figures shown here, the army
had a further 10,933 artillery, 1,023 detached troops, 674 staff, 5,401 garrison troops,
14,778 troops on their way to join the battle and 820 HQ Guard.
Masséna's Army of Portugal. In addition, Masséna also commanded 2,608 artillery,
Gendarmerie and staff.
Wellington's Army within the Lines of Torres Vedras. Wellington's army had an extra
938 unattached infantry, 1,514 artillery and 505 engineers, train and staff.
In addition to the Portuguese troops listed under Wellington's army, the 1st and 3rd Caçadores
(numbering 964) were attached to the Light Division, and the 12th line (contributing
1,213 troops) was attached to Lecor's Militia.

CONTENTS

FOREWORD ⚜

by His Grace The Duke of Wellington KG, LVO, OBE, MC, DL

No one would dispute that maps are essential for the prosecution and subsequent study of battles, sieges, campaigns and wars. The Peninsular War was a defining moment in British military history; amongst the many improvements that the campaign brought was the transformation of British military mapmaking and the flowering of a cartographical department within the newly formed Royal Staff Corps. By 1808 the new Corps was fully operational, but it was not in time for Arthur Wellesley's first engagements at Roliça and Vimeiro. Wellesley commented, 'I should have pushed the advanced guard as far as the heights of Mafra, and should have halted the main body about four or five miles from that place. By this movement the enemy's position at Torres Vedras would have been turned and I should have brought the army into a country of which I had an excellent map and topographical accounts…'

Portuguese and Spanish mapping of the period was small-scale and lacking in the sort of topographical detail that enabled commanders to make informed decisions on the practicality of movement and of the suitability of terrain for tactical purposes. Under the Duke of Wellington's instructions his Quartermaster General, Colonel George Murray, issued orders for these new cartographic officers to embark on a programme of sketching large parts of the Peninsula. At the end of the war, Murray proposed to the Duke of Wellington a programme of retrospective mapping of the battlefields to illustrate the operations of the British forces. The British government approved the idea and Lieutenant Thomas Mitchell was returned to Iberia charged with the task. But by 1819 funding was withdrawn and Mitchell returned, his task uncompleted. There the matter lay for nearly two centuries.

That no dedicated and complete atlas has ever been produced of the epic conflict in Iberia and Southern France between 1808 and 1814 is quite remarkable. Colonel Lipscombe's work has, at last, concluded (and indeed enhanced) what Colonel Murray set out to achieve nearly two hundred years ago. This atlas is comprehensive; it covers not just the battles and conflicts of the British and Anglo-Portuguese armies but also of all the major engagements that the Spanish and Portuguese armies fought against the French. It is a fitting academic contribution in this bicentenary commemorative period.

Wellington

January 2010

PREFACE

As for geography, Trim, (said my Uncle Toby), 'tis of absolute use to a soldier... He should know...
if it is required... to give thee an exact map of all the plains and defiles, the forts, the acclivities,
the woods, the morasses, through and by which his army is to pass.

Laurence Stern, *Tristram Shandy* (1760)

Two hundred years on, with satellites, high-altitude 'spy' platforms, remotely piloted vehicles and four-dimensional mapping, it is easy to forget the plight of military commanders of the Napoleonic era who yearned to know what lay on the other side of the hill. Nowhere was this more apposite than in the Iberian Peninsula where the only available mapping was small in scale and grossly lacking in accuracy. In consequence, the Peninsular War marked a turning point for British military cartography. Although the need for detailed mapping based on 'reconnaissance-survey' had been spawned at the Frederick the Great's Ritter Akademie des Nobles in Berlin in the 1760s, the British had been comparatively slow on the uptake. This was not so much due to any ambivalence in recognising the significance of military survey, but instead, it was largely the result of the command and control structure of the army at the time. Throughout the 18th century, survey and mapping had been in the hands of the Board of Ordnance. This Board – created by Henry VIII and initially concerned with the manufacture and supply of guns to the army and navy – controlled the Ordnance Corps which embraced the Royal Artillery and the Royal Engineers, and was independent from the army's general staff Horse Guards. In the last years of the 18th century, Lieutenant Colonel Charles Vallancey, the Director of Engineers responsible for the survey of Ireland, had acknowledged the need for tactical maps, but had concluded that, 'the engineer, from the nature of his duties in our service is a stranger to the movements and manoeuvres of an army and ill qualified for a duty of this kind'. Given the lack of any formal military staff training, meanwhile, this was even truer of the rest of the army. However, the establishment of the Royal Military College (the brainchild of a cavalry colonel, John Gaspard le Marchant) at High Wycombe in 1798 provided the basis for a staff training that included the elaboration of sketch maps in the field.[1] Then in 1800 came a further development with the formation of a department that took up and trained field cartographers for service in a unit known as the Royal Staff Corps – more colloquially, the Staff Corps Cavalry – that was to provide many of the principal topographers in the Peninsular War.

Wellington, of course, had completed his military education some years prior to the opening of the first Royal Military College. Unlike many army officers, he had at least attended a military

academy – the famous Académie Royale d'Equitation at Angers, France – but it is not clear whether he received any instruction in mapping or sketching. At all events, it was certainly not an area of staff-work with which he felt comfortable. As he wrote to the Secretary of State for War and the Colonies, Lord Castlereagh, in 1808, 'In respect to your wish that I should go into the Asturias to examine the country, and form a judgement of its strength, I have to mention to you that I am not a draftsman and but a bad hand at description.'[2] That said, he was certainly aware of the importance of the subject. Within two years, Wellington's Quartermaster-General (i.e. chief of staff), Colonel George Murray, had created, *inter alia*, a most efficient topographical department and embarked on a programme to map the entire Peninsula for military purposes. The result was an 'ordnance survey' map that eventually covered the whole of Spain and Portugal, but it was not long before recognition dawned that in the years following the war an entirely different set of maps would be needed.

In brief, if the operations of Sir John Moore and the Duke of Wellington were not to be forgotten, and if, too, future army officers were to derive some profit from their study, there would have to be some sort of visual record of Salamanca, Vitoria and the rest. As early as the fall of Toulouse in 1814, then, Murray made recommendations to Wellington for the compilation of a set of maps to illustrate the history of the war, or at least Britain's part therein. The scheme was warmly supported by the Depot of Military Knowledge at Horse Guards where there was now a well established opinion that the study of military history was essential to an officer's education and, further, that mapping was vital to the planning, prosecution and subsequent analysis of military operations at every level, whether strategic, operational or tactical.[3]

Lieutenant Thomas Mitchell[4] was therefore sent back to the Peninsula in 1814 to complete unfinished sketches and map other areas where insufficient detail had been recorded, in an attempt to compile a complete atlas of the operations of the British Forces. Alas, his work was cut short in 1819 when government funding dried up, and Mitchell's work lay unfinished and unpublished until 1840 when James Wyld (Geographer to Her Majesty Queen Victoria) published the fruits of Mitchell's labour.[5] The work that resulted is absolutely marvellous, but, sadly, it is not widely available. It also only covers the operations of Moore and Wellington and is therefore less than adequate as a record of the Peninsular War as a whole. If any doubt exists as to this point, consider the following statistic: not counting subsequent operations in France, which really form part of a separate campaign, but are here included for the sake of completeness, the British army was involved in fifteen field battles and four major sieges. If the campaigns of the Spaniards and the Portuguese are included, the total for the war as a whole rises to forty of the former and nineteen of the latter.

---

2   Wellington to Lord Castlereagh, 5 September 1808, WD, IV, p.139.

3   A copy of the 'ordnance survey' map of Spain and Portugal may be viewed in the Department of Special Collections in the University of Liverpool's Sydney Jones Library.

4   Major Sir Thomas Livingstone Mitchell (1792–1855) took up the post as Surveyor-General, New South Wales, Australia in 1827.

5   Cf. J. Wyld, *Maps and Plans showing the Principal Movements, Battles and Sieges in which the British Army was engaged during the war from 1808 to 1814 in the Spanish* [sic] *Peninsula and the South of France* (London, 1840).

---

1   This college moved to Great Marlow in 1802 and then to Sandhurst in 1812. Gunner and Engineer officer cadets were trained at the older Royal Military Academy, Woolwich ('The Shop') founded in 1741; the two institutions were merged in 1947 to establish the present Royal Military Academy, Sandhurst.

The need, therefore, has remained for a more complete, comprehensive and readily available set of maps to assist the study of the epic confrontation known in the English language as the Peninsular War.[6] Hence this atlas, which, despite the omission of some of the smaller skirmishes and engagements to avoid elevating costs to prohibitive levels, is the most complete ever produced. Every map is supported by explanatory text which forms the concise history of the conflict. Here, however, there is an important distinction from standard histories of the war, in that the text supports the maps and not vice versa. This in turn restricts the amount of text, and that was perhaps one of the greatest difficulties of this work. Trying to slim down to a single volume a historical account which took Southey three volumes, Napier six, Oman seven and the Spaniard, Gómez de Arteche, no fewer than fourteen, has presented a considerable challenge: there was so much more that could have been included and so many other sources that could have been quoted. Indeed, deciding what *not* to include posed a far greater dilemma than deciding what to incorporate.

As to the solutions that were adopted, it will be found that there is, perforce, a concentration on the military aspects of the struggle: the text only touches on matters political and strategic where it is necessary to facilitate the flow of the narrative. Also missing are debates on numbers of casualties (killed, wounded or missing in action). As a history of the Peninsular War, therefore, this work cannot be regarded as anything more than a beginning. Yet it was never intended to emulate or replicate the efforts of earlier scholars; rather, it was designed to assist the process of understanding events in Iberia and southern France between October 1807 and April 1814 in recognition of the fact that many excellent accounts that have been written of the struggle have been spoiled by a lack of supporting maps that would enable the reader to resolve what, how and, in some cases, even where events took place.

What, though, of the maps themselves? In brief, the overriding aim has been to produce a set of national, regional and battle/siege maps in a common style in which precedence is given to the military detail (the topographical detail, then, has been kept to a minimum). Where space permits a detailed order of battle (ORBAT) has been included with the appropriate map; where not, this is included in the appropriate appendix. Some ORBATs are impossible to determine, and in these cases the reader will find no more than a list of participating forces, with their chain of command. Within this system – and unusually so – artillery batteries have been listed as separate units (although this is an area where far greater research needs to be undertaken, and especially so in respect of the French artillery), whilst, in recognition of the significant role played by the maritime forces and the unquestionable advantage this provided the allies, some attempt has also been made to include details of the various Royal Navy commands and their

commanders. Names and place names are an incessant challenge as they change in national usage (Corunna, La Coruña), or can be rendered with or without accents (Cadiz, Cádiz) or have different spellings in the various languages of Spain (Vich, Vic), or have been recorded differently in different sources (Ballasteros, Ballesteros), or have sometimes acquired modern alternatives (San Sebastián, Donosti). To deal with this, a simple rule of thumb has been used: all place names are in the national languages of Spain and Portugal, and all regional and national titles are in English (i.e. Spain not España). Where some confusion might creep in, both names have been used (i.e. Buçaco, Bussaco). The only exceptions are Lisbon (vice Lisboa) and Oporto (vice Porto), where the English spellings are too well known to adhere to the rule. As for the names of individuals, the versions opted for are those most commonly used in historical texts and previous publications.

Recording the history of the war in Iberia has always been a complex business, but the task of doing so has over the years been further burdened by a great weight of nationalism and, still worse, xenophobia. Sadly, this has been at its most visible in the accounts of nations allied during the struggle. With many British officers and men either out of work or on half pay following Napoleon's final defeat at Waterloo, the conditions were ripe for an explosion of personal narratives of the Revolutionary and Napoleonic Wars, and in these the Peninsular War often figured very strongly. Much the same was also true of France, but in Spain and Portugal alike the absence of an adequate market – the product of a level of social and economic development that was much lower – ensured that few such memoirs were ever published. Many of these narratives were necessarily marked by bias and prejudice of various sorts, but, unfortunately, it was not long before these defects had penetrated the more formal historiography of the conflict.

Taking Britain as our chief example, matters actually began quite well in that the first man to embark on a full-length history of the war was Robert Southey, who was not only the Poet Laureate, but a deep admirer of Spain who had acquired the distinction of membership of Spain's Royal Academy and the Royal Academy of History. When it appeared in 1821, the first volume of his work (which covers the story of the war up until the death of Sir John Moore at La Coruña) gave much prominence to the Spanish war effort, whilst it is very clearly heavily based on Spanish sources. As an account of the events of 1808 it is actually deeply flawed, but, even so, left to himself, Southey might have been able to give an entirely different cast to the British historiography of the Peninsular War.[7] The fact that he did not do so was the responsibility of one man and one man only. In brief, Southey was not the only British writer who had decided to embark on a history of the Peninsular War.

Also at work was William Napier, a half-pay veteran of the Forty-Third Foot who had fallen on hard times, and was in 1823 invited to produce such a work himself on the strength of little more than one or two contributions to such publications as the *Edinburgh Review*. Unfortunately, however, backed though he was by considerable patronage on both sides of the English Channel, Napier was not the happiest of choices for such a task. As a veteran of the campaigns of La Coruña, Buçaco, Salamanca, the Pyrenees and the invasion of France, he certainly had much

---

6   The issue of what the war should be called is far from straightforward. In England it is known as the Peninsular War; in most of Spain – albeit not without increasing levels of argument – the War of Independence; in Catalonia the War of the French; in Portugal the War of the French Invasions; and in France the Campaign in Spain. If the term 'Peninsular War' has been used here, it is not just because it accords with English usage, but also because it both embraces the whole of Iberia and avoids the political controversy that attaches to some of the other terms. Note, however, that even Peninsular War has its problems, and particularly when it is extended to cover the entirely separate campaigns in south-western France; in this respect it is interesting to note that Napier entitled his work not *A History of the Peninsular War*, but *A History of the War in the Peninsula and the South of France*.

7   For the full work, cf. R. Southey, *History of the Peninsular War* (London, 1823–1832).

experience of the fighting, but his broader view of the war was coloured first by an attitude to Wellington and, particularly, Moore, that bordered on hero worship, and, secondly, by the strong Whig influence ensured by the fact that he was married to the niece of the erstwhile prime minister, Charles James Fox. Put together, these two factors did not make for a happy mix.

On the one hand, Napier's heroes could do no wrong, whilst on the other nothing could disabuse him of a naïve belief that Napoleon, whom Napier admired nearly as much as he did Moore and Wellington, was the personification of the principles of the French Revolution and, more than that, a reluctant warrior who had been forced to take up arms by the hatred of a vengeful *ancien régime*. From all this there stemmed a most unfortunate consequence. For Napier it was axiomatic that Spain and Portugal were mediaeval relics dominated by the Catholic Church – the real cause, in his eyes, of their opposition to Napoleon – whilst, precisely because of their Catholicism, they were also necessarily as incompetent as they were inefficient, and therefore little use as allies. With the author also in constant pain due to the many wounds he had received in the war, the result was a view of the war that was skewed in the extreme. Openly proclaiming his intention to concentrate solely on the operations of the British army, Napier in effect only mentioned the Spaniards in order to denigrate them (thanks to their decision to place themselves at British orders, the Portuguese come off less badly): so far as he was concerned, indeed, Spain's generals were fools; Spain's people cowardly, miserable, shameful and deceitful; and Spain's politicians were incompetent and corrupt.[8]

Thus the scene was set for what has ever since been a dialogue of the deaf. As a soldier, and a very fine one at that, Napier is to be forgiven: any soldier sent to assist an invaded nation or persecuted people can be excused for feeling that they should do as much as possible to help themselves and show adequate gratitude to boot. At the same time, too, there was a story to tell of the Spanish war effort that very much flew in the face of the heroic myth. However, Napier went too far, and injected a level of venom into the debate from which it has never really recovered, the reason for this being, above all, that he simply swept the board. A writer of considerable power whose style very much captures the imagination, he was lent added authority by his access to the correspondence of such figures as Wellington, Soult and Joseph Bonaparte. With the British public eager to hear the tale of heroism and glory that he retailed, the result was that he carried all before him.

Completely outflanked by the publication of his first volume in 1828, Southey – a man who lived by his pen and was therefore particularly vulnerable to the vagaries of the market – had no option but to abandon his story of an Iberian war and adopt a style that was much more Anglocentric, while his work, like other histories of the war that appeared at about the same time (the best example is the one written by the Marquis of Londonderry[9]), in any case sank without trace. With Napier triumphant, what followed was inevitable. On the one hand, British authors felt constrained to follow Napier's example and, indeed, in many cases knew no better than to do so – whilst adding greater detail to the story and, in the latter case, making a genuine

attempt to extend to cover the war as a whole; even the great experts, Fortescue and Oman, did little to dispel the idea that Britain's allies were backward and despicable.[10]

The Spaniards responded with fury and in general withdrew into ever-increasing levels of pride and Anglophobia.[11] Nor, meanwhile, was their own historiography productive of a more balanced approach. Although actually quite generous in respect of the British, the great history of the war produced in the 1830s by the Conde de Toreno – another participant in the struggle – was inclined to obscure the issue by its constant stress on the supposed determination of the Spanish people to recover their liberty, whilst the interminable blow-by-blow account of the fighting written from the 1860s onwards by General José Gómez de Arteche y Moro was so anxious to recount the story of every minor skirmish that its chief effect is to cause the reader completely to lose sight of the big picture, and, in particular, the importance of the operations of Sir John Moore and the Duke of Wellington.[12] Hence the anti-British theme that was, sadly but predictably, to persist up to and beyond the bicentenary commemorations in 2008, and also the complete absence amongst most Spaniards of any recognition, or even knowledge, of the efforts made by the British army in Spain's defence. It is very sad that in 2009 the one thing that all Spaniards can be guaranteed to 'know' about British operations is the decision to destroy the royal porcelain factory in Madrid in October 1812 in a supposed bid to forestall a Spanish industrial revolution.[13]

Denigration of the Portuguese in the British historiography, whilst extant, pales into insignificance against vilification of the Spanish. Militarily speaking, Portugal may have assumed a subordinate role in the struggle, but the unquestionable courage of the Portuguese soldiers was established on the ridge at Buçaco and confirmed at Vitoria, where they earned Wellington's endorsement as his 'fighting cocks'.[14] From 1809 to the end of the war, the British commander's army was an Anglo-Portuguese one, and it should be recognised that the 6,000 men or so Portuguese who died under his command represented a disproportionate share of Allied

10 Cf. J. Fortescue, *A History of the British Army from the Norman Conquest to the First World War* (London, 1899–1930); C. Oman, *A History of the Peninsular War* (Oxford, 1902–1930). For Fortescue's coverage of matters Peninsular, cf. volumes VI–X.

11 The general tone of the Spanish response was set by J. Canga Argüelles, *Observaciones sobre la historia de la guerra de España que escribieron los Señores Clarke, Southey, Londonderry y Napier* (Madrid, 1833–36).

12 Cf. Conde de Toreno, *Historia del levantamiento, guerra y revolución de España* (Madrid, 1835–37), and J. Gómez de Arteche y Moro, *Guerra de la Independencia: historia militar de España de 1808 a 1814* (Madrid, 1868–1903). It is, of course, easy to criticise these works, but it should be stressed that they remain fundamental to any serious study of Spain in the Peninsular War.

13 This story is worth re-telling as an example of the way facts can get twisted. That the royal porcelain factory – an establishment set up by King Charles III in the 1770s in the gardens of the Buen Retiro palace in Madrid – was blown up by the British is true enough, but, as normally told in Spain, the story contains only a fragment of the truth. In brief, the venture was a failure in economic terms and by 1808 the building was a mere shell. Indeed, the only thing of importance about it was its site, the gardens on which it was built standing on high ground overlooking the city, and thus it was that, when the French decided to build a citadel from which to hold down Madrid, it soon found itself enclosed in a ring of fortifications and pressed into service as a magazine. When, having first re-taken the city in the wake of the battle of Salamanca, the Anglo-Portuguese forces were forced to evacuate the capital in October 1812, the whole complex was slighted rather than allow it to fall into the hands of the enemy, and this in turn led to the destruction of the building in which the factory had been housed, but this is clearly a rather different matter than the traditional version of events.

14 Wellington to Lord Liverpool, 25 July 1813, WD, X, p.569.

8 Cf. W. Napier, *History of the War in the Peninsula and the South of France from 1807 to 1814* (London, 1828–1840).

9 Marquis of Londonderry, *Narrative of the Peninsular War from 1808 to 1813* (London, 1828).

casualties (the number of British dead in Wellington's battles was only about 10,000). To say that this has gone insufficiently noted in Britain would be unfair, but what is true is that British and American readers have access to comparatively little information on the Portuguese war effort, the reasons for this being two-fold: in the first place, Portuguese accounts such as that by Luz Soriano – the Portuguese Napier or Toreno – have never been translated into English, and, in the second, few Anglophone specialists have ever engaged with the Portuguese archives.[15] Given that accessibility will always remain a problem, let us hope, then, both that publishers such as Osprey will consider publishing translations of the many interesting works produced by Portuguese publishers, and also that British and American scholars will engage with the subject of the Portuguese war effort (of course, Spanish histories of the war such as those by the Conde de Toreno and Gómez de Arteche have not appeared in translation either, but at least Spain has had the attention of Charles Esdaile, a professional hispanist of great distinction who has struggled without cease to convince British audiences of the need to integrate the story of Spain's struggle against Napoleon into the standard account of the Peninsular War. Though Esdaile has never been content to accept the traditional Spanish version of events at face value either, Spanish readers would do well to recognise that their country has rarely had so loyal and devoted a friend).[16]

What, then, does this atlas represent? In brief, in line with Esdaile's argument that the Peninsular War was, above all, an Iberian struggle, it tries to place the operations of the British army, and later the Anglo-Portuguese army, in their Spanish and Portuguese context, and in the process to show Britons, Spaniards and Portuguese alike that their histories are inter-linked and cannot be viewed in isolation from one another, or, to put it another way, that their struggle was a common one waged in a common cause. Obtained in the face of extraordinary difficulties, their defeat of the French was very much a victory for coalition diplomacy and coalition generalship, and it is hoped that presenting matters in this fashion will serve as a lesson to those in England, France, Portugal and Spain alike whose xenophobia and ignorance serve only to perpetuate the myths of the past and deter more serious scholars from devoting themselves to perhaps the most fascinating aspect of the whole of the Napoleonic Wars.

Finally, if the expulsion of the French from Spain was very much a coalition effort, so was this atlas: indeed, this atlas would certainly have failed had it not been for the enormous amount of help I have received over the course of the eight years that I spent compiling the maps, gathering the information and visiting (most of) the battle and siege sites. In England I am extremely grateful to His Grace, the Duke of Wellington, KG, LVO, OBE, MC, DL, for penning the foreword, and to Professor Charles Esdaile, FRHistS, for his help, friendship and guidance throughout and for his excellent introduction.

In Spain I am in the first place deeply indebted to José Luis Arcón Domínguez, who has become a good friend and whose work on events on the east coast, and the battle for Valencia in particular, is ground breaking; his knowledge is encyclopaedic and eye for factual detail quite breathtaking: his assistance in confirming Spanish organisations for battle has been inimitable.[17] Also important in Spain have been the help and guidance I received from the Foro para el Estudio de la Historia Militar de España, in particular Jesús Maroto de las Heras and José Maria Espinosa de los Monteros.

Last but not least, we come to Portugal. Here I am extremely thankful for the help and direction I received from Professor Mendo Castro Henriques of the Universidade Católica Portuguesa and Pedro de Avillez from Tribuna da História, both of whom have considerable knowledge and a shared and justifiable desire to raise the Portuguese profile within the Peninsular War debate. Alongside Mendo and Pedro is Tenente Coronel Nuno Lemos Pires who is an accomplished historian and excellent officer who (as I pen this Preface) is leading the Portuguese Military Liaison Team in Kabul, Afghanistan; other names to mention here being the British Historical Society of Portugal and, in particular, Clive Gilbert, Mark Crathorne and Colonel Gerald Napier; the last named having proved especially helpful in respect of the mapping of the Lines of Torres Vedras.

Staying with the theme of coalition campaigning, much assistance has been received from the armed forces of Spain and Portugal alike. This having proving invaluable, in this regard I would particularly like to thank Teniente José Antonio Montenegro Falcón and Brigada Jesús Barrón Campo from Spain's Centro Geográfico del Ejército, Teniente Coronel Horacio Lopes of Portugal's Instituto Geográfico do Exército and Sargento Ajudante Antonio Vieira Cardoso of da força aérea Portuguesa.

In the course of my travels I owe so much for the help and hospitality I received on the road. To Coronel José Navas Ramírez-Cruzado, Teniente Coronel Francisco Gómez-Cobas and Manuel Santiago Arenas Roca at La Coruña; to Jaime Aragón, Luis Sola Bartina and Admiral Francisco Hernández Moreno at Cádiz; to Juan Soriano Izquierdo at Bailén; to Coronel Manuel José Marques Ribero de Faria at Buçaco; to Dr. Sérgio Veludo Coelho at Oporto; to Colonel Jean-Luis Reynaud of the Department of Strategy and History at the Ecole Supérieure de Guerre; to Miguel Martín Más and the Asociación Histórico Cultural de Salamanca; to Miguel Angel Gómez Madera of the Asociación Napoleonica at La Albuera; to Joan Manuel Alfaro i Guixot and Pablo de la Fuente in Cataluña, and to Dr Xavier Rubio from the Universitat de Barcelona; and, finally, to Antonio Martínez de Medinilla Moro, Jose Manuel Rodriguez, Sergio de la Llave Muñoz, Francisco Castaño and Carlos Gil Sanz at Talavera.

---

15   Luz Soriano's work is contained in a general history of the establishment of constitutional monarchy in Portugal, and, as such, does not amount to an account of the Peninsular War *per se*. That said, it is replete with useful information, and should not be overlooked. Cf. S.J da Luz Soriano, *Historia da Guerra Civil e do establecimento do governo partalmentarem Portugal, comprehedendo a historia d'este reino desde 1777 até 1834* (Lisbon, 1866–93).

16   Esdaile is the author of numerous works on the Peninsular War, but his *magnum opus* is *The Peninsular War: a New History* (London, 2002).

17   See Chapter 36. The version of the battle of Sagunto differs from the hitherto accepted accounts of the battle. It is based on extensive research by Arcón Dominguez, during which he has unquestioningly confirmed, that Blake's objectives were entirely to the south and east of Montenegro and not through the mountains of Calderona. Although there is evidence that it had been Blake's original intention of turning the French right, he changed his plans at some stage prior to the 24 October 1811. Oman admits that, 'There are terrible difficulties as to the timing of the battle of Saguntum' (vol. V. p.36, note 1). Oman interprets Arteche and uses Suchet and Schepeler as his principal sources but not the battle reports of O'Donnell, Miranda, San Juan, Obispo and Lardizabal as well as three other official Spanish diaries all of which (unanimously) confirm that Blake's objectives were confined to the valley floor between the Montenegro and the Mediterranean Sea.

Additionally, I have received help for which I am extremely grateful from Lady Jane Wellesley, Major General Sir Evelyn Webb-Carter KCVO. OBE and Lieutenant Colonel Fabrice Delaître whose relative, General Baron Charles Delaître, commanded the Mamelukes at Austerlitz, the Polish Light Horse in the Peninsula and the 30e Brigade of cavalry during the Russian Campaign. I would like to thank Her Majesty's Ambassadors to Spain and Portugal, Dame Denise Holt and Alex Ellis respectively and to the defence attachés Captain (now Commodore) David Wolfe RN, Captain Freddie Price RN OBE and Commander David Fields RN; from the Portuguese Ministry of Defence/Commission of Military History, Lieutenant General Alexandre de Sousa Pinto and Coronel José Banazol; and from the Spanish Ministry of Defence, Santos Castro Fernández (Director General de Relaciones Institucionales), Teniente Coronel Carlos Medina Ávila (Director de Protocolo) and Capitán Germán Segura; the latter in particular for his work with Peninsular War 200. I am very grateful to General Alfredo Cardona for providing me the opportunity to pursue my studies and research during my time at the Spanish High Readiness Force Headquarters. To many of my Spanish military colleagues I owe special thanks for their help in translating work; especially deserving of notice here are Teniente Coronel Antonio Carrión, Teniente Coronel Joaquin Rosique, Comandante Francisco Izquierdo, Comandante Federico Clemente, Comandante Pedro Latorre and Capitán Francisco González-Mártinez.

I am also indebted to Lieutenant Colonel Bob Napier for his help in proof reading the text; to Paul Evans and Major Dennis Rollo at the James Clavell Library, Woolwich; and finally to Richard Sullivan, Ruth Shepherd and Jon Jackson at Osprey Publishing: thank you for your support and encouragement and, more especially, the confidence you have placed in me.

Finally, some special thanks. Firstly to Lieutenant General Sir Nick Parker KCB, CBE, who, without hesitation, assumed the mantle as President of Peninsular War 200; secondly, and – well deservedly! – for a second time, to Professor Charles Esdaile who has worked tirelessly beside me to ensure that the United Kingdom plays a full and leading role in the ongoing bicentenary commemorations; and finally to Sarah King who continues to manage the *Peninsular War 200* web site www.peninsularwar200.org with considerable passion and dedication. And then two special mentions in conclusion: to Yolande Hodson whose interest in British military map making in the Peninsular War produced the catalyst for this atlas and to my good friend Teniente Colonel Jesús Gil Ruiz who cajoled me to continue and supported me in tackling some of the more extraordinary Spanish obstacles that cropped up along the way.

Nick Lipscombe,
Lisbon, December 2009

Chronology of Events in the Peninsular War 1807–1814

Note: The country in red denotes the victor.

1807

7 Jul	Treaty of Tilsit between Napoleon and Tsar Alexander I
2 Aug	Junot assumes command of 'Corps of Observation of Gironde'
11 Oct	Ferdinand, Prince of Asturias, requests Napoleon's help against his father, King Carlos IV
18 Oct	French troops cross Franco-Spanish border (28,000 men under Junot)
27 Oct	Treaty of Fontainebleau – Napoleon agrees with Spain to invade Portugal
19 Nov	French troops begin crossing into Portugal
22 Nov	Second Corps of Observation of Gironde under Dupont crosses Pyrenees
27–29 Nov	Prince Regent Joao VI and his court sail from Lisbon (to Brazil)
30 Nov	Lisbon occupied by the French without struggle
Dec	General Junot disbands the Portuguese Army

1808

Early months	Additional 75,000 French Troops cross Pyrenees
19 Jan	The Prince Regent and court land in Brazil
1 Feb	Junot appointed governor of Portugal
16 Feb	Seizure of Pamplona
20 Feb	Murat appointed commander of all French forces in Spain
29 Feb	Seizure of Barcelona
5 Mar	San Sebastián surrenders under threat of French assault
10 Mar	Murat crosses into Spain
18 Mar	Seizure of Figueras
19 Mar	Abdication of Spanish king, Carlos IV
23 Mar	Madrid occupied by the French without struggle
24 Mar	Murat enters Madrid
10 Apr	Ferdinand departs for Bayonne to meet up with Napoleon
20 Apr	Ferdinand arrives at Bayonne
30 Apr	Carlos and Queen Maria Luisa join Ferdinand at Bayonne
2 May	Madrid 'El Dos de Mayo' uprising
6–10 May	Ferdinand forced to relinquish his throne
25 May	Province of Asturias declares war on French
May–Jun	Insurrections against the French throughout Spain and Portugal
6 Jun	Insurrection starts in Portugal and Galicia
6 Jun	Supreme Junta in Sevilla declares war on France and Spanish War of Independence officially commences
6 Jun	Combat at pass of Bruch (France ✕ Spain)
7 Jun	Combat at Alcolea (France ✕ Spain)
8–14 Jun	Combat at Tudela, Mallen & Alagon (France ✕ Spain)
12 Jun	Combat at Cabezon (France ✕ Spain)
14 Jun	Second combat at pass of Bruch (France ✕ Spain)
14 Jun	Spanish garrison and fleet at Cádiz capture French squadron
15 Jun	First siege of Zaragoza starts (France ✕ Spanish)
18 Jun	Fortress of Faro falls to the Portuguese
19 Jun	Portuguese Supreme Junta organized by the Bishop of Oporto
20 Jun	French assault on Girona fails (France ✕ Spain)
24 Jun	Combat at Epila (France ✕ Spain)
26 Jun	French take and sack the Portuguese towns of Vila Visoza and Beja
26–28 Jun	French assault on Valencia fails (France ✕ Spain)
27 Jun	Portuguese take the fort of Santa Caterina at Figueira da Foz
30 Jun	Combat on the Llobregat (France ✕ Spain)
5 Jul	Spain and Britain officially declare peace, having been at war since 1804
6 Jul	French take and sack Leiria but later fall back on Lisbon
9 Jul	Joseph Bonaparte, 'King of Spain', crosses Pyrenees
11 Jul	Investment of Roses (France ✕ Spain)
12 Jul	Wellesley and his troops set sail from Cork
14 Jul	Battle of Medina de Ríóseco (France ✕ Spain)
16 Jul	Combat at Mengibar (France ✕ Spain)
16 Jul	Portuguese levies surround and blockade the fortress at Almeida
20 Jul	King Joseph enters Madrid
20 Jul	Dupont capitulates at Bailén (France ✕ Spain) for the greatest Spanish victory of the war
24 Jul	Preparations begin for siege of Girona (France ✕ Spain)
29 Jul	Loison engages Portuguese at Evora (France ✕ Portugal & Spain)
Early Aug	Napoleon orders 130,000 men to be withdrawn from Germany and redeployed to Peninsula – Ney, Lannes, Soult, St Cyr and Victor under orders to join them
Aug–Oct	French and Spanish preparations along the river Ebro
1 Aug	King Joseph evacuates Madrid – retires north of river Ebro
5 Aug	Combat at Aranjuez (France ✕ Spain)
1–8 Aug	Wellesley's British army lands at Mondego Bay, Portugal
12 Aug	Wellesley meets Portuguese leaders – Portuguese contingent joins British army
14 Aug	First siege of Zaragoza ends (France ✕ Spain)
16 Aug	Siege of Girona defeated (France ✕ Spain)
17 Aug	Combat at Roliça (France ✕ Britain & Portugal)

21 Aug	Battle of Vimeiro (France × Britain & Portugal)
22 Aug	Sir Harry Burrard arrives and assumes command of British army in Portugal
22 Aug	Sir Hew Dalrymple arrives and takes over command from Burrard
24 Aug	Sir John Moore arrives in Portugal
25 Aug	Jourdan arrives in Miranda and assumes command of French armies
31 Aug	Convention of Cintra ratified – French agree to leave Portugal
15 Sep	Last French troops leave Portugal
25 Sep	Orders despatched to Portugal for Moore to assume command and to cooperate with the Spanish in the expulsion of the French from Spain. (Received on 6 October)
18 Oct	Bulk of Moore's army en route for Salamanca
25–26 Oct	Combat at Logroño and Lerin (France × Spain)
27 Oct	Moore leaves Lisbon
31 Oct	Battle of Zornoza (France × Spain)
3 Nov	Napoleon arrives in-theatre at Bayonne
5 Nov	Combat at Valmaceda (Balmaceda) (France × Spain)
8 Nov	Combat at Guenes (France × Spain)
10 Nov	Battle of Espinosa (France × Spain)
10 Nov	Battle of Burgos ó de Gamonal (France × Spain)
23 Nov	Battle of Tudela (France × Spain) – Castaños routed and relieved of command
23 Nov	Moore's advance guard arrives at Salamanca
30 Nov	Combat at the Pass of Somosierra (France × Spain)
2 Dec	Napoleon arrives at the gates of Madrid
3 Dec	Madrid capitulates
5 Dec	Siege of Roses ends. (France × Spain) Spanish supported by Royal Navy
10 Dec	Moore's British Army advances from Salamanca
16 Dec	Battle of Cardedeu (France × Spain)
20 Dec	Second siege of Zaragoza commences
21 Dec	Combat at Sahagún (France × Britain)
21 Dec	Battle of Molins de Rey (France × Spain)
24 Dec	Moore retreats from Sahagún to La Coruña
29 Dec	Combat at Benavente (France × Britain) fighting withdrawal, attributed as a British victory
30 Dec	Combat at Mansilla (France × Spain)
31 Dec	Moore refuses to fight and evacuates Astorga

1809

1 Jan	Napoleon decides to return to France – but remained at Valladolid from 6–17 Jan
3 Jan	Combat at Cacabellos (France × Britain) fighting withdrawal, attributed as a British victory
5 Jan	Rearguard action at Constantino (France × Britain)
6 Jan	Moore offers battle at Lugo, Soult declines
8 Jan	Night of, Moore continues retreat
11 Jan	Moore and bulk of army reach La Coruña
13 Jan	Battle of Uclés (France × Spain)
16 Jan	Battle of La Coruña (France × Britain). Claimed as a victory by both sides. The majority of the British army was evacuated
17 Jan	Napoleon leaves Spain
22 Jan	King Joseph re-established in Madrid
End Jan	Soult plans second French invasion of Portugal
Early Feb	British Major General Beresford appointed commander of Portuguese army
18 Feb	Combat at Igualada (France × Spain)
20 Feb	Second siege of Zaragoza ends (France × Spain)
25 Feb	Battle of Valls (France × Spain)
9 Mar	Soult's vanguard enters Portugal
14 Mar	Combat at Chaves (France × Portugal)
17 Mar	Combat at Mesa de Ibor (France × Spain)
20 Mar	Battle of Braga (Lanhozo) (France × Portugal)
21 Mar	Combat at Miajadas (France × Spain)
27 Mar	Rout of General Cartaojal at Ciudad Real (France × Spain)
29 Mar	Battle of Medellin (France × Spain)
29 Mar	Storming of Oporto (France × Portugal)
2 Apr	Wellesley given command of army in 'Defence of Portugal'
22 Apr	Wellesley arrives back in Lisbon – commanding both British & Portuguese
18 Apr	Rearguard at D'Amarante commences (France × Portugal)
3 May	Rearguard at D'Amarante completed (France × Portugal)
11 May	Combat at Gijón (France × Britain & Portuguese)
12 May	Wellesley takes Oporto (France × Britain & Portugal)
18 May	Pursuit of Soult abandoned – Portugal liberated for second time
22 May	Wellesley approaches Spanish General Cuesta regarding combined operations against the French in Spain
22 May	Combat near Santiago (France × Spain)
23 May	Battle of Alcañiz (France × Spain)
24 May	Second siege of Girona commences
8 Jun	Combat at river Oitaben (France × Spain)
15 Jun	Battle of Maria (France × Spain). Spanish conducted themselves well at the battle but were routed the next day at Belchite
Mid Jun	Victor withdraws from Estremadura – arrives at Talavera on 26 June
End Jun	Soult abandons Galicia
3 July	The British army enters Spain
28 Jul	Battle of Talavera (France × Britain & Spain)
8 Aug	Combat at Arzobispo (France × Spain)
11 Aug	Battle of Almonacid (France × Spain)
26 Aug	Wellesley elevated to peerage as Viscount Wellington of Talavera
1 Sep	Combat at Salt (France × Spain)
18 Oct	Battle of Tamames (France × Spain)
19 Nov	Battle of Ocaña (France × Spain)

20 Oct	Work commences of the Lines of Torres Vedras
20 Nov	Wellington issues orders for the withdrawal to Portugal
28 Nov	Battle of Alba de Tormes (France ⚔ Spain)
11 Dec	Second siege of Girona completed (France ⚔ Spain). French victory at considerable cost
25 Dec	Wellington's Peninsular army in Portugal

1810

Early Jan	Joseph and Soult (now his COS) turn their attention to Andalusia
16 Jan	Siege of Hostalrich commences
29 Jan	Central Junta resigns in light of Spanish failures
5 Feb	Siege of Cádiz commences (lifted on 24 August 1812)
20 Feb	Battle of Vich (France ⚔ Spain)
21 Mar	Siege of Astorga commences
11 Apr	Siege of Lérida commences
15 Apr	Combat at Zalamena (France ⚔ Spain)
17 Apr	Imperial Decree announces Masséna's Army of Portugal
22 Apr	Siege of Astorga completed (France ⚔ Spain)
23 Apr	Combat at Margalef (France ⚔ Spain)
26 Apr	First siege of Ciudad Rodrigo commences
12 May	Siege of Hostalrich concluded (France ⚔ Spain)
13 May	Siege of Lérida concluded (France ⚔ Spain)
15 May	Siege of Mequinenza commences
26 May	Combat at Aracena (France ⚔ Spain)
5 Jun	Siege of Mequinenza completed (France ⚔ Spain)
10 Jul	Siege of Ciudad Rodrigo completed (France ⚔ Spain)
10 Jul	Combat at Barquilla (France ⚔ Britain & Portugal)
24 Jul	Combat on the Coa (at Almeida) (France ⚔ Britain & Portugal)
11 Aug	Combat at Villagarcia (France ⚔ Spain)
15 Aug	Siege of Almeida commences
27 Aug	Siege of Almeida completed (France ⚔ Britain & Portugal)
14 Sep	Combat at La Bispal (France ⚔ Spain)
27 Sep	Battle of Buçaco (France ⚔ Britain & Portugal)
29 Sep	Wellington's army retreats to Lines of Torres Vedras
13 Oct	Attempted siege of Fuengirola fails (France ⚔ Britain)
3 Nov	Rout of General Blake at Baza (France ⚔ Spain)
16 Dec	Siege of Tortosa commences

1811

2 Jan	Siege of Tortosa concluded (France ⚔ Spain)
11 Jan	Siege of Olivenza commences
15 Jan	Combat at Pla (France ⚔ Spain)

23 Jan	Siege of Olivenza concluded (France ⚔ Spain)
25 Jan	Combat at Villanueva (de los Castillejos) (France ⚔ Spain)
26 Jan	Siege of Badajoz commences (France ⚔ Spain)
19 Feb	Battle of Gevora (France ⚔ Spain & Portugal)
3 Mar	Masséna retreats from Santarem
5 Mar	Battle of Barrosa (France ⚔ Britain & Portugal & Spain)
11–15 Mar	Series of rearguard actions fought by the French as the 'Army of Portugal' retreats:
	11 Mar — Combat at Pombal (France ⚔ Britain & Portugal)
	12 Mar — Combat at Redinha (France ⚔ Britain & Portugal)
	13 Mar — Combat at Condeixa (France ⚔ Britain & Portugal)
	14 Mar — Combat at Casal Novo (France ⚔ Britain & Portugal)
	15 Mar — Combat at Foz d'Arouce (France ⚔ Britain & Portugal)
11 Mar	Siege of Badajoz concluded (France ⚔ Spain)
15 Mar	Siege of Campo Mayor commences
15–16 Mar	Siege of Alburquerque (France ⚔ Spain)
19 Mar	Spanish surprised during their attack on Monjuich – Barcelona (France ⚔ Spain)
21 Mar	Siege of Campo Mayor concluded (France ⚔ Spain)
25–26 Mar	Combat at Campo Mayor (France ⚔ Britain & Portugal) inconclusive
3 Apr	Combat at Sabugal (France ⚔ Britain & Portugal)
7 Apr	Siege of Almeida commences
9 Apr	Spanish capture fort and town of Figueras
9 Apr	Allied siege of Olivenza commences
10 Apr	Siege of Figueras commences
11 Apr	Masséna reaches Salamanca
12 Apr	Blockade of Almeida commences
15 Apr	Allied siege of Olivenza concluded (France ⚔ Britain & Portugal)
23 Apr	King Joseph departs Madrid, arrives Paris 15 May
3–5 May	Battle of Fuentes de Oñoro (France ⚔ Britain & Portugal) – Masséna retreats on morning of 6 May
3 May	Combat at Figueras (France ⚔ Spain)
4 May	Siege of Tarragona commences
6 May	First Allied Siege of Badajoz commences
10 May	Blockade of Almeida concludes when the French escape
11 May	Siege of Almeida concluded (France ⚔ Britain & Portugal)
11 May	Marmont assumes command of the Army of Portugal from Masséna
12 May	First Allied siege of Badajoz ends – raised due to French advances
16 May	Battle of Albuera (France ⚔ Britain & Portugal & Spain) victory with heavy Allied losses
19 May	Second Allied siege of Badajoz commences
25 May	Combat of Usagre (France ⚔ Britain & Portugal)
10 Jun	Second Allied siege of Badajoz ends – Wellington abandons siege
16 Jun	Marmont and Soult join forces and relieve Badajoz on 20 June
16 Jun	King Joseph departs Paris, arrives Madrid 16 July

23–25 Jun	Wellington offers battle on the Caia – Soult and Marmont decline
23 Jun	Combat at Benavides (France ✕ Spain)
28 Jun	Siege of Tarragona completed (France ✕ Spain)
2 Jul	Combat on the river Orbigo (France ✕ Spain)
25 Jul	Storming of Montserrat mountain (France ✕ Spain)
10 Aug	Wellington begins blockade of Ciudad Rodrigo
19 Aug	Siege of Figueras concluded (France ✕ Spain)
23 Sep	French arrive at Ciudad Rodrigo, Allies pull back
23 Sep	Siege of Saguntum (Sagunto) commences
25 Sep	Combat at El Bodón (France ✕ Britain & Portugal) probing action by the French
25 Sep	Combat at Carpio de Azaba (France ✕ Britain & Portugal)
27 Sep	Combat at Aldeia da Ponte (France ✕ Britain & Portugal)
28 Sep	Wellington offers battle in front of Sabugal – Marmont refuses to advance
25 Oct	Battle of Saguntum (Sagunto) (France ✕ Spain)
26 Oct	Siege of Saguntum (Sagunto) concluded (France ✕ Spain)
28 Oct	Action at Arroyo dos Molinos – Hill surprises Girard
29 Oct–2 Nov	Spanish irregular raids into southern France (Valley of Cerdagne)
5 Nov	Combat at Bornos (France ✕ Spain)
20 Dec	Siege of Tarifa commences
28 Dec	Siege of Valencia commences
29 Dec	Combat at Membrillo (France ✕ Britain & Portugal)

1812

4 Jan	Victor calls off the siege of Tarifa (France ✕ Britain & Spain)
8 Jan	Wellington commences siege of Ciudad Rodrigo
9 Jan	Siege of Valencia concluded (France ✕ Spain)
18 Jan	Combat at Villaseca (France ✕ Spain)
19 Jan	Wellington takes Ciudad Rodrigo (France ✕ Britain & Portugal)
20 Jan	Siege of Peñiscola commences
24 Jan	Combat at Altafulla (France ✕ Spain)
2 Feb	Siege of Peñiscola concluded without a fight (France ✕ Spain)
5 Mar	Combat at Roda (France ✕ Spain)
16 Mar	Third British siege of Badajoz commences
6 Apr	Wellington takes Badajoz (France ✕ Britain & Portugal)
11 Apr	Combat at Villagarcia (France ✕ Britain)
18 May	Hill's assaults on the forts at the Bridge of Almaraz (France ✕ Britain & Portugal)
1 Jun	Combat at Bornos (France ✕ Spain)
11 Jun	Combat at Maguilla (France ✕ Britain & Portugal)
15 Jun	Siege of Astorga commences
18 Jun	Siege of the three Salamanca forts commences
21 Jun	Storm of Lequeitio (Lekeitio) by Rear Admiral Home Popham
27 Jun	Salamanca forts surrender (France ✕ Britain & Portugal)

7–8 Jul	Siege and capture of Castro Urdiales (France ✕ Britain)
18 Jul	Combat at Castrejón (France ✕ Britain & Portugal)
18 Jul	Combat at Castrillo (France ✕ Britain & Portugal)
21 Jul	Battle of Castalla (France ✕ Spain)
22 Jul	Battle of Salamanca (France ✕ Britain & Portugal & Spain)
22 Jul–2 Aug	Rear Admiral Home Popham blockades and occupies Santander
23 Jul	Combat at Garcihernández (France ✕ Britain)
31 Jul	General Maitland lands at Palamos with an expeditionary force from Sicily
2 Aug	Port of Santander taken by the Allies (France ✕ Britain & Portugal & Spain)
11 Aug	Combat at Majadahonda (France ✕ Britain & Portugal)
11 Aug	King Joseph departs Madrid
12 Aug	Soult commences the evacuation of Andalusia
12–13 Aug	Madrid falls to the Allies – Wellington enters
13 Aug	Spanish take Bilbao
14 Aug	General Santocildes abandons Valladolid; French retake the city
18 Aug	Siege of Astorga concluded (France ✕ Spain)
24 Aug	Soult calls off Siege of Cádiz (since 5 Feb 1810) (France ✕ Britain & Spain)
18 Sep	Wellington commences the siege of Burgos
22 Sep	Wellington made *generalissimo* of Spanish armies by the Cortes
20 Oct	Wellington raises the siege of Burgos and retreats (France ✕ Britain & Portugal)
23 Oct	Spanish General Ballesteros attempts a coup d'état; it fails and he is arrested
23 Oct	Combat at Venta Del Pozo (France ✕ Britain & Portugal)
23 Oct	Combat at Villadrigo (France ✕ Britain)
25 Oct	Combat at Villa Muriel (France ✕ Britain & Portugal & Spain)
30 Oct	Combat at Puente Larga (France ✕ Britain & Portugal) inconclusive
10–11 Nov	Combat at Alba de Tormes (France ✕ Britain & Portugal)
15 Nov	Wellington offers battle at Salamanca
17 Nov	Combat at San Muñoz (or Huebra) (France ✕ Britain & Portugal) inconclusive
19 Nov	The Allied army retreats from Ciudad Rodrigo
23 Dec	Wellington arrives in Cádiz to discuss his plans for reorganization of Spanish armies

1813

10 Feb	Combat at Poza (France ✕ Spain)
20 Feb	Raid on Béjar (France ✕ Britain)
23 Mar	Joseph transfers his headquarters to Valladolid from Madrid
31 Mar	Combat at Lerín (France ✕ Spain)
11 Apr	Combat at Yecla (France ✕ Spain)
11–12 Apr	Siege of Villena (France ✕ Spain)
12 Apr	Combat at Biar (France ✕ Britain). Rearguard action
13 Apr	Battle of Castalla (France ✕ Britain & Spain)
29 Apr	Siege of Castro-Urdiales commences
12 May	Siege of Castro-Urdiales concluded (France ✕ Britain & Spain)

22 May	Wellington's final offensive in Spain commences
27 May	French evacuate Madrid
2 Jun	Combat at Morales (France ⚔ Britain & Portugal)
3 Jun	French evacuate Valladolid
3 Jun	Siege of Tarragona by General Murray commences
12 Jun	Joseph abandons Burgos and retreats
15 Jun	Siege of Tarragona lifted by General Murray (France ⚔ Britain & Spain)
18 Jun	Combat at Osma (France ⚔ Britain & Portugal)
18 Jun	Combat at San Millan (France ⚔ Britain & Portugal)
21 Jun	Battle of Vitoria (France ⚔ Britain & Portugal & Spain)
24 Jun	Combat at Villafranca (France ⚔ Britain & Portugal) inconclusive
25 Jun	Blockade around Pamplona commences
26 Jun	Combat at Tolosa (France ⚔ Britain & Portugal & Spain)
7 Jul	Combat at Maya (France ⚔ Britain & Portugal) inconclusive
8 Jul	Combat at La Salud (France ⚔ Spain)
10 Jul	Spanish irregulars under Mina capture Zaragoza
11 Jul	First siege of San Sebastián commences
25 Jul	First siege of San Sebastián ends in failure (French ⚔ Britain & Spain)
25 Jul–2 Aug	Battle of the Pyrenees
	25 Jul Combat at Roncesvalles (France ⚔ Britain) inconclusive
	25 Jul French force the Maya Pass (France ⚔ Britain)
	26 Jul Combat at Linzoain (France ⚔ Britain & Portugal)
	28 Jul First battle of Sorauren (France ⚔ Britain & Portugal & Spain)
	30 Jul Second battle of Sorauren (France ⚔ Britain & Portugal & Spain)
	30 Jul Combat at Beunza (France ⚔ Britain & Portugal)
	31 Jul Combat at Venta de Urroz (France ⚔ Britain & Portugal)
	1 Aug Combat at Sumbilla (France ⚔ Britain & Portugal)
	1 Aug Combat at Yanzi (France ⚔ Britain & Portugal)
	2 Aug Combat at Echalar (Elxalar) (France ⚔ Britain & Portugal)
30 Jul	Blockade of Tarragona by General Bentinck commences
1 Aug	Soult and the French army retreat into France
6 Aug	Second Siege of San Sebastián commences
15 Aug	Blockade of Tarragona lifted by General Bentinck (France ⚔ Britain & Spain)
19 Aug	Combat at Amposta (France ⚔ Spain)
31 Aug	San Sebastián falls to the Allies (France ⚔ Britain & Portugal)
31 Aug	Battle of San Marcial (France ⚔ Britain & Portugal & Spain)
1–8 Sep	Citadel of San Sebastián captured (France ⚔ Britain & Portugal)
13 Sep	Combat at Ordal (France ⚔ Britain & Spain)
14 Sep	Combat at Villafranca (France ⚔ Britain & Portugal & Spain) inconclusive

7–8 Oct	Wellington crosses Bidassoa and fights battle of Vera (France ⚔ Britain & Portugal & Spain)
31 Oct	Pamplona falls to the Allies (France ⚔ Britain & Portugal & Spain)
10 Nov	Battle of the Nivelle (France ⚔ Britain & Portugal & Spain)
21 Nov	Wellington sends his Spanish allies back to Spain
9–13 Dec	Battles on the Nive (France ⚔ Britain & Portugal)
9 Dec	Combat at Villafranca (France ⚔ Britain & Portugal)
9 Dec	Combat at Anglet (France ⚔ Britain & Portugal) inconclusive
10 Dec	Combat at Arcangues (France ⚔ Britain & Portugal) inconclusive
10 Dec	First combat at Barrouillet (France ⚔ Britain & Portugal) inconclusive
11 Dec	Second combat at Barrouillet (France ⚔ Britain & Portugal) inconclusive
13 Dec	Battle of St. Pierre (France ⚔ Britain & Portugal)

1814

16 Jan	Combat at Molins de Rey (France ⚔ Britain & Spain) inconclusive
2 Feb	The Cortes rejects Napoleon's Treaty of Valençay
12 Feb	Wellington's new offensive commences
15 Feb	Combat at Garris (France ⚔ Britain & Portugal & Spain)
16 Feb	Combat at Arriverayte (France ⚔ Britain & Portugal)
23 Feb	Blockade of Bayonne commences
27 Feb	St. Étienne stormed and captured (France ⚔ Britain & Portugal)
27 Feb	Battle of Orthez (France ⚔ Britain & Portugal)
2 Mar	Combat at Aire (France ⚔ Britain & Portugal)
12 Mar	Insurrection at Bordeaux: France welcome the allies and return of their 'King'
19 Mar	Combat at Vic-Bigorre (France ⚔ Britain & Portugal) inconclusive
20 Mar	Combat at Tarbes (France ⚔ Britain & Portugal) inconclusive
24 Mar	Ferdinand VII re-enters Spain
6 Apr	Combat at Étauliers (France ⚔ Britain & Portugal)
8 Apr	Combat at Croix D'Orade (France ⚔ Britain)
10 Apr	Battle of Toulouse (France ⚔ Britain & Portugal & Spain)
14 Apr	French sortie at St Étienne (France ⚔ Britain & Portugal & Spain)
16 Apr	Sortie from Barcelona (France ⚔ Spain)
11–16 Apr	French forces capitulate and end of the Peninsular War
26 Apr	Bayonne capitulates

INTRODUCTION

Next to the battle of Waterloo, the Peninsular War of 1808–14 is one of the most famous campaigns in the history of the British army prior to World War I, while also one of its longest and bloodiest. Only the War of American Independence was more prolonged, while, out of perhaps as few as 200,000 men who served in the campaigns in Spain, Portugal and Southern France, around 40,000 died. Precise comparisons are difficult, but this is a loss rate that is almost certainly comparable to that experienced in World War I. In the latter conflict, about one in every 13 of the 5,215,162 men who were mobilized for service with the army made the ultimate sacrifice; but the number of troops raised by Britain in the Napoleonic Wars was much smaller, and at no time did the regular army number more than about 330,000 men. Even including foreigners, the number of men who passed through the army's ranks probably amounted to no more than 500,000. Given that we have also to add in those who fell in other campaigns – most notably at Waterloo – it therefore seems possible that, not counting wounded – for the Peninsular War a figure estimated at another 40,000 men – losses might have reached a level of one in ten.

Similar comparisons may be made with regard to individual actions. At the battle of Le Cateau in 1914, for example, the British Expeditionary Force lost 7,812 men killed, wounded and taken prisoner out of some 40,000 men engaged, whilst at Neuve Chapelle in 1915 a similar number of men on the field lost 11,200 casualties.[1] These figures are bad enough – in the first instance they approximate to 19.5 per cent of those engaged and in the second 28 per cent, but consider the Peninsular battles of Talavera, Barrosa and Albuera. In the first of these, 4,594 men became casualties out of 20,194; in the second, 1,182 out of 4,885; and in the third 4,156 out of 10,449.

Losses, then, ranged between 23 and 30 per cent. The fact is that a 'Tommy' in Wellington's army had more or less the same chance of being killed or wounded as in the armies of Sir John French and Sir Douglas Haig. And, if the situation was bad on the battlefield, off it it was even worse – standards of health and medical care having enormously improved over the century that separated the battle of Mons from the battle of Waterloo. Men who were wounded or fell ill in the course of World War I had a reasonable chance of surviving, whereas in the Napoleonic Wars even relatively simple wounds were often followed by death from infection, and still more were caused by diseases such as typhus. Things were not quite as apocalyptic as has sometimes

been suggested – thanks to the dedication and professionalism of the chief of the Peninsular army's medical staff, Sir James McGrigor, between 1812 and 1814 the mortality rate in Wellington's hospitals was only some 5 per cent – while, thanks to the greater destructive power of modern weapons, death rates from wounds may actually have been significantly higher in World War I (in the latter conflict the chances of dying after being hit in battle were about 27 per cent, whereas in the Peninsula it was only about 18 per cent). Yet, even granted the great influenza epidemic of 1918 – something that actually led to the deaths of only about 7 per cent of the British soldiers who caught it – this statistic is countered by the fact that illness was a far greater scourge in the Napoleonic epoch than it was to be 100 years later. Statisics aside, the suffering of the sick and wounded also reached heights that were rarely equalled in World War I. Evacuation from the battlefield often took much longer; transport was more primitive; medical staff were in shorter supply and less well trained; operations were more agonizing (there were, of course, no anaesthetics); and hospitals were infinitely less comfortable and well-appointed.[2]

For the men who fought in the Peninsular War, there were other factors that made their experiences different from those of their successors of 1914–18. We think of the trenches as being a particularly dreadful environment in which men perpetually lived, in the words of the song, 'up to their waists in water and up to their eyes in slush' – and at their worst, they were indeed quite horrific. For months battle lines were wholly static with the result that, crowded together in the most claustrophobic conditions, men lived cheek by jowl with thousands of rotting corpses, not to mention hundreds of thousands of tons of human excrement. Subjected to just as many months of concentrated battering, meanwhile, the countryside through which the frontlines ran was stripped of all vestiges of beauty and turned into a wasteland marked only by flooded shell craters, splintered trees and fragments of shattered brickwork. Though other horrors of war were all too visible, such scenes were almost entirely absent from Spain and Portugal. Setting aside the fact that early 19th century artillery was far less devastating than the guns and howitzers of 1914–1918, thanks to the fact that the struggle was essentially one of manoeuvre, the principal theatre of operations was always changing position and therefore the destruction was more widely spread. Indeed, even in World War I, many stretches of the Western Front retained their bucolic character for much of the war: taking the battlefield of the Somme as an example, all eyewitness accounts agree that right up until 1 July 1916, the area remained one of great natural beauty.

It is possible, then, to have far too stereotypical a view of the environment of war in 1914–18, and, if this is so, this is even truer of the experience of the soldier. Thus, in the British army at least, most infantrymen spent comparatively little time in the trenches, battalions rather being rotated in and out of the front line on a regular basis. And, once out of the line, things were very different. Conditions might still be rather basic, but there was hot food, clean clothing, the chance of a bath or a shower and a dry billet, as well as the chance to enjoy wine, women and song, not

---

1   These actions have been selected because they are directly comparable to battles in the Napoleonic age and, more importantly, offer reasonable statistics in respect to the number of men actually engaged with the enemy. Later battles, of course, were far worse, but even on the first day of the battle of the Somme the 57,470 men who were killed, wounded or taken prisoner probably represented no more than 40 per cent of the troops in range of enemy fire, a figure that is roughly the same as the proportion of Wellington's British soldiers who fell at Waterloo. One may play all sorts of games with these statistics, of course – restrict the Somme calculation only to those men who actually went over the top and the loss rate rises to almost one in two, whilst add in the German, Dutch and Belgian contingents and their losses at Waterloo and the figure falls to about one in four, but the fact remains that for Britain's own soldiers 18 June 1815 was an experience that was directly comparable to 1 July 1916.

2   For a detailed comparison of the Peninsular War and World War I in terms of the experiences of the sick and wounded, cf. M. Crumplin, *Men of Steel: Surgery in the Napoleonic Wars* (Shrewsbury, 2007), pp.75–9. For some affecting accounts of the sufferings of the wounded, cf. C. J. Esdaile, *Peninsular Eyewitnesses: the Human Experience of War in Spain and Portugal, 1808–1814* (Barnsley, 2008), pp.212–14.

to mention egg and chips in some local *estaminet*. With all this often came hard labour as troops who were theoretically resting were frequently plundered as a cheap workforce, but there was also leisure and entertainment: men could attend concerts, take part in sports days or simply play football. Much more infrequently, there was also the opportunity to go on leave. Meanwhile, even in the trenches men regularly got letters and parcels from home and they very rarely went hungry, even if all that was available was ship's biscuit, corned beef and plum-and-apple jam.[3]

None of this is intended to minimise the misery from time to time endured by the British soldiers who fought on the Western Front, but consider the situation of Wellington's army. In winter the troops could generally – though not always – expect to be billeted in some village or small town, but otherwise they were for the most part exposed to the elements in all weathers: even tents were not issued to them until the autumn of 1813, and only then at the cost of stripping them of their greatcoats. Campaigning in the autumn and winter was therefore a nightmare, while, in contrast to the soldiers of World War I, Wellington's troops could regularly expect to march many hundreds of miles, averaging ten or 15 miles a day, but in an emergency marching up to 25 or even 30 miles a day. The most famous feat of endurance in this respect is the Light Division's famous march from Navalmoral de la Mata to Talavera de la Reina in July 1809, a distance of 43 miles in 22 hours. But the famous retreat to La Coruña was a more sustained performance: in eight days of actual marching, Sir John's army managed an average of some 17 miles a day. Such feats were exceptional, but, even so, over a long period the distances covered could be enormous. In the course of 1812, for example, the Coldstream Guards travelled some 1,700 miles. All this was done over roads that were frequently very poorly constructed, in the context of a level of material support that was utterly inadequate. If the rations due to the troops were issued in full – something that was generally honoured more in the breach than the observance, the men got the equivalent of no more than 2,400 calories a day, or in other words only two-thirds of what an active adult male needs to sustain himself. In World War I, by contrast, British army rations were set at about 3,400 calories (an allowance that was generally seen as being rather low in comparison to those favoured by France and Germany). As for the food that was issued, it consisted almost entirely of beef and biscuit and was frequently of poor quality, while much was wasted for want of means to cook and carry it properly. In short, Wellington's soldiers were frequently hungry, and sometimes desperately so.[4]

By comparison with all this, then, the soldiers of World War I were positively cherished. At the same time, they also had far more hope of reward. Decorations – the Victoria Cross, the Military Cross, the Distinguished Service Medal – were issued in some numbers, while men might also hope to be promoted from the ranks. At the same time, feted as heroes when they left for the front and loudly praised by a proud and an appreciative press, soldiers could hope that courage and endurance at the front would be rewarded by a warm welcome when finally they returned home – if not, indeed, new 'homes fit for heroes'. As for discipline, it was unbending – sometimes harsh, even – but there were strict limits on what even the toughest sergeant major could do. Finally, wives and children back home were cared for, albeit at a rather limited level, by the State, and pensions paid to the families of those killed in action.

Contrast all this, too, with the experience of the average 'redcoat'. Recruited on the whole from a despised underclass rather than the nation's manpower as a whole – other than a few boys of lower middle class birth, of few means but great hopes for adventure, the majority of the army's recruits were Irish or Scottish peasants, labourers of various kinds, artisans (especially weavers) who had fallen on hard times, and, finally, foreign deserters and prisoners of war. Soldiers were poorly paid and could only rarely expect material rewards of any kind, let alone medals or promotion (something that hardly extended as far as advancement into the ranks of the officer corps).[5] If they were wounded and invalided home, a lucky few might find jobs as doormen or places in Chelsea Hospital, but the rest would have to face life on the streets as vendors, buskers or even beggars.

Nor were their families given anything in the way of support: six wives per company were allowed to accompany each battalion sent on campaign, but the rest were turned loose to fend for themselves, something that in many cases presumably forced them to turn to prostitution. With all this came the scorn of much of a society which was deeply marked by prejudice against standing armies in general and soldiers in particular, this scorn being reinforced still further by the savage punishments to which the latter could be subjected for the slightest offence. In some regiments flogging was on its way out, or even had in practice been set aside, but in others sentences of up to 1,000 lashes were still a common occurrence. Though one or two men who enlisted were undoubtedly on the run from the law, in general few soldiers were actually convicted criminals – as Coss has recently pointed out, in the Napoleonic period there is almost no record of men being consigned to the army by magistrates' courts in lieu of being hanged or transported[6] – but there can be little doubt that the general public viewed them, if not as the proverbial scum of the earth, then at the very least as rogues and ne'er-do-wells.

Here and there among the army's recruits there may have been the odd plough-boy, eager for some desperate glory and swept up in the mood of Church-and-King loyalty that had gripped much of the country since the outbreak of the war with France in 1793; at all events, these were the triggers favoured by many recruiting parties. However, the reason why most men enlisted had nothing to do with either glory or patriotism: they were hungry and had no other means to support themselves other than to turn to crime. In an era of rapid population growth, burgeoning

---

3   The best general guide to the conditions experienced by the British army on the Western Front is undoubtedly R. Holmes, *Tommy: the British Soldier on the Western Front, 1914–1918* (London, 2004), while an interesting discussion of how World War I is remembered (and how memories of that struggle have become distorted) may be found in D. Todman, *The Great War: Myth and Modern Memory* (London, 2005).

4   For an excellent discussion of the dietary problems faced by the British forces, cf. E. Coss, *All for a Shilling a Day: the British Army under Wellington* (University of Oklahoma Press, 2010). A truly seminal work, Coss' study is likely to become the definitive study of the internal dynamics of the British army of the Napoleonic period.

5   For the recruitment of the rank and file of the British army, cf. P. Haythornthwaite, *The Armies of Wellington* (London, 1994), pp.43–50; T. H. McGuffie, 'Recruiting the ranks of the regular British army during the French Wars: recruiting, recruits and methods of enlistment,' *Journal of the Society of Army Historical Research*, XXXIV, No. 138 (June, 1956), pp.508, and *Ibid.*, No. 139 (September, 1956), pp.123–32.

6   Coss, *All for a Shilling a Day*.

social change, economic disruption and limited welfare support, the army at least offered something other than starvation and the gallows; there was a welcome, too, for men fleeing untenable situations in their home life or trying to redeem themselves in the wake of personal failure. In particular areas of the country, most notably the Scottish Highlands, particular patterns of landholding rendered the populace vulnerable to economic pressure on the part of propertied classes, eager to boost their social status by supporting the expansion of the army and establishing 'family' regiments.

In short, what we have is seemingly a classic army of professional soldiers, an army that was offered little by the society from which it sprang, and consequently could hardly be expected to exert itself very much in its defence. This was certainly the sort of theory that had encouraged the leaders of the French Revolution to declare war on Austria and Prussia in 1793; yet from the beginning, and in particular in the Peninsula, the British army proved one of the toughest opponents the French ever had to face. The fact is that there are stimuli other than patriotism or economic reward. On the one hand the army's highly developed regimental system provided recruits with a community that offered them acceptance and which they were loathe to alienate, and, on the other, poverty and despair did not preclude the existence of other feelings, including, most notably, the desire to better themselves or do credit to their families. It is notable, for example, that recruits began to show preference for units with good reputations, such as the so-called '95th Rifles', whilst it is also around this time that lasting patterns of family recruitment began to be established in Ireland, with successive generations of the same families enlisting in the same regiments. At the same time, there is some evidence that as Wellington's army won more and more success in Spain, so recruitment began to pick up on the home front.[7]

Whatever the reason, as is self-evident from any study of the Peninsular War, the British fought extremely well, whilst their self-confidence and willingness to sacrifice themselves for the common cause was boosted by a growing mood of confidence in their officers and the army of which they formed a part. In short, it naturally helped the morale of Britain's soldiers to be constantly on the winning side, but this was not just due to their courage and dedication. On the contrary, a series of internal developments, not least innovative tactical thinking on the part of the Duke of Wellington and the massive reinforcement of the army's ability to deploy skirmishers on the battlefield, turned the British army into a weapon to which the French had few answers. On occasion, certainly, it was forced to retreat by the emergence of unfavourable strategic situations, but it never lost a battle and at the same time demonstrated a versatility that was all but unmatched in the annals of the Napoleonic Wars. What is often forgotten is that the famous 'thin red line' was as often on the attack as it was on the defence.

As a record it is second to none in British military history – greater victories, perhaps, were won on the Western Front in 1918, but in the Peninsula there was no blood-soaked learning curve – and, given its importance in the history of Napoleonic Europe, it is certainly one that demands admiration and respect, while it is not going too far to suggest that Wellington's army was the best that Britain has ever fielded. Yet it is an army that, if not all but forgotten, has scarcely received its due. In Britain, Salamanca and Vitoria are eclipsed by Waterloo in the popular imagination, while in Spain and Portugal powerful nationalist resentments and – particularly in the former case – the manipulation of history for political purposes have ensured that Britain has been pushed to the sidelines. In some places – splendid examples are Salamanca and La Albuera – considerable attempts have been made by conscientious and enthusiastic local historians to revive the memory of the British presence, but elsewhere it remains unmarked and forgotten, while the bicentenary of the uprising of 1808 has in some cases been used as a platform by figures who wish actively to undermine perceptions of the role played by the forces of Moore and Wellington.

Hence in part the need for this atlas. In laying out each and every campaign of the Peninsular War in sequence, it cannot but demonstrate both the importance of Britain's contribution to the struggle and the intensity of the fighting in which her forces were engaged. As such, it is hoped that it will serve as a fitting memorial to the 'redcoats' who fought so hard and for so long, and, more particularly, the 40,000 men who lost their lives, men whose graves are marked by no neat Commonwealth War Graves Commission cemeteries and which for the most part do not even have a name. At the same time, too, perhaps historians engaged in the teaching of military history will find in it sufficient material to consider campaigns of the Napoleonic Wars other than just those of Napoleon himself.

In so doing, they will doubtless discover that the Peninsular War offers much food for thought. Armies operating in Germany and Italy were after all operating in parts of the Continent that were relatively densely populated, characterized by terrain that was easily accessible and possessed of reasonable communications in terms of roads and rivers. In Spain and Portugal, however, no such advantages were present, and the fact that the campaigns there were as mobile as they actually were suggests that the generalship displayed is worthy of closer attention than it has often been given. And, finally, with the battlefields of Spain and Portugal easily accessible to visitors, the Peninsular War is a conflict which particularly calls for the publication of a new atlas based on modern cartographical techniques, and all the more so as the only comparable work to date is one based largely on photographic reproductions of maps drawn up in the 19th century.[8]

Thus far we have spoken solely of the British army. However, neither Sir John Moore nor the Duke of Wellington ever operated in a vacuum, and it cannot be said too often that the Peninsular War was never solely an Anglo-French struggle. On the contrary, the Spaniards and the Portuguese also had a crucial role to play and great care has therefore been taken to include the many campaigns in which not a single British soldier was engaged. If only on the basis of remembrance, this is more than justified: the number of Portuguese who died in what they term the War of the French Invasions was probably at least 150,000, including some 22,000 military fatalities, while

---

7   For an interesting discussion of the motivations for enlistment, cf. R. Holmes, *Redcoat: the British soldier in the Age of Horse and Musket* (London, 2001), pp.135–156. Meanwhile, the particularly thorny issue of the Scottish Highlands is covered by R. Clyde, *From Rebel to Hero: the Image of the Highlander, 1745–1830* (East Linton, 1995), pp.165–72.

8   For the work concerned, cf. C. Worley (ed.), *Atlas of the Peninsular War* (Felling, 2000).

Spanish losses have been estimated at anything from 250,000 to half a million.[9] However, in Britain there has always been a strong tendency to play down or, at least, skate over the indigenous contribution to the defeat of Napoleon. Largely because from 1809 onwards the Portuguese army fought alongside Wellington's troops – indeed, it was fully incorporated into their ranks – and because of laziness in the use of language, there has been a tendency to lose sight of it as a separate force. (We constantly hear, for example, of British soldiers attacking here or defending there when in reality the men concerned were dressed both in British red and Portuguese blue.)

Indeed, there were major campaigns in Portugal – above all, that of March 1809 – in which no British troops were engaged, and these have not received much in the way of detailed attention. Yet few British commentators would downplay the role of the Portuguese in a general sense, and in this there is a massive difference from British perceptions of the Spanish war effort. Whilst lip-service is paid to the heroism of the Spanish people and, more particularly, the guerrilla bands which sprang up to oppose the French, there is little understanding of the general picture and a strong inclination to ignore the role of the Spanish regular army. However, to the very end of the war this was a force that always mattered; witness, for example, Wellington's horrified reaction to the fall of Valencia in 1812. It is therefore hoped that here too the atlas will draw readers' attention to episodes of the struggle that they may never have considered, including, not least, the largest cavalry-on-cavalry battle of the entire war (that of Ocaña: fought on 19 November 1809, this brought together some 82,000 men).[10]

Last but not least, one should, perhaps, give some thought to the 500,000 or more French troops who served in the war (a number that included significant numbers of Dutchmen, Germans, Italians and Poles). From this distance it is hard to feel much sympathy for the cause in which they fought – the idea that Napoleon intervened in Spain and Portugal to advance the cause of emancipation and enlightenment may, alas, be discarded from the outset – but their sufferings were great and their feats of arms considerable. As for their losses, these were substantial – an educated guess might suggest a minimum of 200,000 – and so it would be churlish indeed not to recognise their courage and dedication. Against this, of course, must be put down their record of slaughter and atrocity – one thinks here of such affairs as the capture of Oporto and the storm of Tarragona – but against these must be set the dreadful scenes witnessed at Ciudad Rodrigo, Badajoz and San Sebastián, and, in addition, the fact that the invaders were conditioned by a variety of factors to feel that, especially in areas that witnessed considerable irregular resistance, they were fighting an enemy who were somehow beyond the pale of civilization. In short, the French may have been the enemy, but they were not an enemy that was somehow uniquely evil, the consequence being that it does not seem inappropriate to let this atlas commemorate them as well. If the roads that led from Lisbon and Cádiz to the Pyrenees was long and hard, so were the roads that led from the Pyrenees to Lisbon and Cádiz.

At this point it is necessary to review the history of the Peninsular War.[11] A bloodbath that cost up to 750,000 lives, the Peninsular War was the fruit of overconfidence, folie de grandeur and miscalculation. In October 1807, with the permission and assistance of the Spanish government, French troops were sent by Napoleon to occupy Portugal in order to close it off to British trade. The royal family escaped to Brazil, but resistance was non-existent, and there seems little reason to believe that the French would have experienced more than minor local difficulties in the ordinary course of events. However, impelled by the looming prospect of war with the Ottoman Empire, early in 1808 Napoleon resolved on the overthrow of the Spanish Bourbons, his aim being to make Spain a more effective ally. This proved a disastrous mistake. In March 1808 a palace coup had replaced King Charles IV with the heir to the throne, Ferdinand VII. Thanks to the propaganda of powerful elements of the church and aristocracy bent on opposing Bourbon reformism, who had seized on the vacuous and malleable Ferdinand as a Trojan horse, the new king was seen as a 'Prince Charming' who would put all of Spain's many ills to rights. French intervention, and, more specifically, the invitation of the entire royal family to a 'conference' with Napoleon in Bayonne, therefore provoked unrest: there was, for example, a serious rising in Madrid on 2 May. In consequence, news that Ferdinand had been forced to abdicate in favour of Napoleon's brother, Joseph, was the catalyst for a series of revolts in the many parts of the country that had remained unoccupied by the French, and a similar wave of rebellion soon gripped Portugal.

The nature of this revolt has been widely misunderstood. The subject is a complex one, but in short it was not the unanimous uprising for God, king and fatherland of legend. Popular concern was not for the Bourbons or the Braganças, but rather land, bread and revenge on the propertied classes, whilst the leaders of the insurrection entertained a variety of conflicting interests, which they sought to pursue at the same time as channelling the people's energies into fighting the French. In consequence, the political history of the war is one of great complexity – its chief feature is the elaboration of a liberal constitution in Spain in 1812 – whilst the background to the struggle was everywhere one of desertion, banditry, agrarian unrest, and resistance to conscription. It is true that in those areas actually occupied by the French, much irregular resistance inconvenienced the invaders, but close analysis of this phenomenon has suggested that in most cases it bore little resemblance to the legend so beloved of the traditional historiography. On close inspection, indeed, much of the 'little war' proves to have been the work of forces of regular troops or local militias raised and controlled by representatives of the Patriot state. At the same time, such irregular bands as were formed were drawn in large part from men who had either already been bandits in 1808, or had been drawn into banditry since the start of the war (including many men who fled to the hills to avoid conscription into the Spanish army, or who deserted after being called up). With other men brought in by impressments of one sort or another, it is in consequence hard to see how the Spanish struggle against Napoleon can really merit the description of a 'people's war'; especially given that the

---

9   For a recent study of the demographic impact of the Peninsular War in Spain, cf. R. Fraser, *Napoleon's Cursed War: Spanish Popular Resistance in the Peninsular War* (London, 2008), pp.513–18.

10   To return to a point made earlier, there is, of course, a reverse side to this coin. With regard to Spain, in particular, the hope might be expressed that this atlas will open the eyes of general readers to the British and, indeed, Portuguese contribution to victory.

11   The text that follows is largely taken from the entry on the Peninsular War written by the author for G. Fremont-Barnes (ed.) *Encyclopaedia of the French Revolutionary and Napoleonic Wars: a Political, Social and Military History* (Santa Barbara, 2006). For a more detailed account, cf. C. J. Esdaile, *The Peninsular War: a New History* (London, 2002).

guerrilla bands – except those which were militarized in the style of the forces commanded by Juan Martín Díez and Francisco Espoz y Mina – did not follow the French as they evacuated their areas of operation in the latter part of the war, but rather battened upon civilian inhabitants and the baggage trains of the Allied armies.

Whether these reservations can also be applied to Portugal is a moot point. Here we do not have the same weight of detailed historical research available to us, while the situation was devoid of the complexities of the political and social situation that reigned across the frontier in Spain. In brief, however, revolt broke out in June 1808 following the news of the insurrection that had gripped Spain the previous month. Without access to Portuguese accounts, details are sketchy, but the prime movers in the disturbances appear to have been above all the crowd – in the north, the peasantry of such mountain districts as Tras-os-Montes, and in the south the fishermen of the Algarve. At all events, in such places as Oporto large masses of civilians appear to have come forward as volunteers, whilst in the rural districts the home guard known as the *ordenança* had soon taken to arms and thereafter done its best to harass the movements of the French as they struggled to concentrate their scattered forces. Infinitely better trained, armed and equipped – as many of the insurgents were armed only with pikes and fowling pieces – commanders such as Loison (a name hated in Portugal to this day) were able to inflict terrible damage upon the forces that sought to oppose them, but, unlike in Spain, popular enthusiasm for the struggle seems in the first instance to have remained very high.

Militarily speaking, the history of the war is much simpler. Initially, the French armies were roughly handled, the forces sent to Portugal being expelled by a British expeditionary force under Sir Arthur Wellesley (later Duke of Wellington) – aided, of course, by such troops as the Portuguese authorities could get together at this early stage – after a battle at Vimeiro (21 August 1808) and after another contingent was forced to surrender at Bailén by the Spaniards. Other forces, meanwhile, were repulsed from Valencia and Girona, whilst Zaragoza beat off a full-scale siege despite the fact that it was devoid of regular fortifications. Forced to draw back beyond the river Ebro, the invaders then received major reinforcements, and Napoleon himself came to Spain to take charge of operations. There followed a whirlwind campaign, which saw the Spaniards suffer major defeats at Espinosa de los Monteros, Gamonal, Tudela and Somosierra. With the Spanish armies in tatters, on 4 December the emperor recaptured Madrid. Meanwhile, the position had also been restored in Catalonia, where the French army of occupation had for the last few months been bottled up in Barcelona, the Spaniards having been routed by fresh forces dispatched from France at Cardedeu and Molins de Rei. Given this situation, it seemed entirely possible that the French would go on to overrun the entire Peninsula and end the war at a stroke. All possibility of this, however, was precluded by a last-minute intervention in the campaign on the part of the British. Having cleared the French from Portugal, the British expeditionary force had advanced into Spain under the command of Sir John Moore. For various reasons it had taken a long time for it to get ready for action, and for a while it looked as if Moore would have no option but to withdraw into Portugal. Eventually, however, Moore resolved on an offensive against the French communications in Old Castile. As this brought the full weight of the French armies in northern Spain against his 20,000 men, he was soon forced to retreat to the coast of Galicia in search of rescue by the Royal Navy, but so many troops were pulled after him that the French had effectively to abandon their plans for the immediate conquest of southern Spain. As for Moore and his army, almost all the troops were rescued after a rearguard action at La Coruña on 16 January 1809, but their commander was mortally wounded by a cannon ball at the moment of victory.

The campaign of November 1808 to January 1809 set the pattern of operations for the whole of the next year. In brief, the French controlled most of central and northern Spain, together with a separate area around Barcelona, whilst Spanish armies held southern Catalonia, the Levante, Andalusia and Extremadura. As for Portugal, it too was in Allied hands, with a British garrison in Lisbon and such few troops as the Portuguese could muster deployed to protect Elvas, Almeida and Oporto. Called away from Spain by growing fears of a new war with Austria, Napoleon had left instructions for the various commanders he had left in Spain – most notably, Soult, Ney and Victor – to crush Allied resistance by a series of powerful offensives, but this plan quickly foundered. The Spanish armies defending Andalusia proved unexpectedly aggressive, the British reinforced their presence in Portugal and, now commanded once again by Sir Arthur Wellesley, repelled a French invasion led by Marshal Soult that, coming from the north, had on 29 March 1809 got as far as the northern city of Oporto. The province of Galicia rose in revolt, and the cities of Zaragoza and Girona both put up desperate resistance (in the case of Girona, it did not fall until December). By the summer, then, the initiative had passed to the Allies, the rest of the year being dominated by two major attempts to recover Madrid. Of these, the first – an Anglo-Spanish offensive from the west and south – led merely to stalemate. Thus, a major triumph at Talavera was deprived of all effect, first, by the arrival of massive French reinforcements released by the fortuitous evacuation of Galicia one month earlier, and, second, serious divisions in the Allied command. The second offensive, however, was a far more serious affair. In the wake of Talavera, Wellesley – now Viscount Wellington – refused to engage in any further operations with the Spaniards, and pulled his men back to the Portuguese frontier. In consequence, the offensive was the work of the Spaniards alone. Operating on exterior lines from the northwest, the west and the south in terrain that greatly favoured the vastly superior French cavalry, however, they had no chance and were routed at the battles of Ocaña and Alba de Tormes with terrible losses.

The defeat of the main Spanish field armies and the British decision to concentrate on the defence of Portugal opened a new phase in the conflict. So serious had been the Spanish losses in the campaigns of 1809 that there was little left to put into the line. Nor could these losses be made up: although generous, the British supply of arms and uniforms was insufficient to the task of equipping whole new armies from scratch, while resistance to conscription amongst the populace was greater than ever. Meanwhile, with the new Austrian war fought and won, Napoleon was pouring large numbers of fresh troops into Spain, the result being that the initiative passed back to the French. With the Spaniards further emasculated by the outbreak of revolution in Latin America – by now their chief source of revenue – for the next two years the picture is one of constant French advances. City after city fell into the invaders' hands, while the Spaniards lost more and more of such troops and sinews of war as remained to them.

First to fall were Sevilla, Granada, Córdoba, Málaga and Jaén, all of which were overrun by a massive French offensive in January 1810, and these were followed by Oviedo, Astorga, Ciudad Rodrigo, Lérida, Tortosa, Badajoz and Tarragona. By late 1811 all that was left of Patriot Spain was Galicia, the Levante and the blockaded island city of Cádiz, which had in 1810 become the new capital. Penned up inside Portugal, the British could do nothing to arrest the march of French conquest, while much the same was true of the Spanish guerrillas, who at the same time were coming under more and more pressure. Indeed, it is clear that Napoleon's commanders could have crushed resistance in Spain and then marched against Portugal in such overwhelming force that even Wellington could not have overcome them. All that was needed was for the French armies in the Peninsula to receive a constant stream of replacements and reinforcements. Thanks to the impending invasion of Russia, however, in 1812 the supply of men dried up, and the Armée d'Espagne was even stripped of some troops. As was only to be expected, the result was that the French forces suddenly found themselves badly overextended, and all the more so as Napoleon insisted that they continue with the offensive against Valencia which they had begun in the autumn of 1811.

What saved the Allied cause in the Peninsula was therefore not Wellington's genius but rather Napoleon's errors. This, however, is not to decry the British commander's very real contribution to the Allied cause. Particular attention should be paid here to his defence of Portugal in 1810–1811. In accordance with France's resumption of the offensive in the Peninsula in 1810, the summer of that year saw some 65,000 men under Marshal Masséna move across the Portuguese frontier and besiege the fortress of Almeida. This fell very rapidly, thanks to the chance explosion of its main powder magazine and the consequent destruction of much of the town, and the French moved on towards Lisbon. Wellington, however, had anticipated such a move and put together a comprehensive plan for the defence of Portugal. From the beginning the countryside in the path of the invaders would be devastated and the French forces harassed by the irregular home guard known as the *ordenança*. If possible, the French would then be brought to battle and forced to retreat. To this end, the Portuguese army had been completely rebuilt under the direction of Sir William Beresford and the main routes toward Lisbon blocked by field works at a number of obvious defensive positions. Failing that, however, the countryside would continue to be devastated, whilst the Anglo-Portuguese army would continue to fall back on Lisbon, along with – so it was hoped – the bulk of the civilian population. Waiting for them would be probably the greatest single engineering feat in the entire Napoleonic era in the form of the so-called Lines of Torres Vedras – an impenetrable belt of fortifications stretching from one side of the peninsula on which Lisbon was built to the other. Whether this plan would have sufficed to hold off the French had they ever unleashed the sort of massive offensive that would have followed the final conquest of Spain is unclear – Wellington, for one, certainly had his doubts – but against the 65,000 men brought by Masséna, it was more than adequate. Despite achieving complete success on the battlefield itself, an attempt to turn the French back at Buçaco – an action in which the Portuguese army, now rebuilt with the aid of national conscription and thoroughly reorganized under the leadership of General Beresford, greatly distinguished itself – failed, due to the marshal's discovery of an unguarded track round Wellington's northern front. But when the French reached the Lines of Torres Vedras they found that they could go no further. In this situation Masséna did his best, but, deprived of adequate supplies and harassed without mercy by the *ordenança*, he could not continue to blockade the lines forever, and in March 1811 he abandoned his headquarters at Santarem and fell back on the Spanish frontier.

However, clearing Masséna from Portugal was one thing, and invading Spain quite another. For the whole of 1811, the situation on the Portuguese frontier was a stalemate. Authorized by the British government to enter Spain once more, Wellington soon found that this was easier said than done. The crucial border fortresses of Ciudad Rodrigo and Badajoz had been greatly strengthened by the French while every attempt to besiege them was met by massive French counter-offensives, as at Albuera and Fuentes de Oñoro. Repelled though these were, they cost Wellington heavy losses and dissuaded him from marching too far into Spain, while progress was in any case rendered still more difficult by the fact that the Anglo-Portuguese army lacked an adequate siege train. Of course, the French were in no better state. Twice, indeed, they refused battle rather than attack him in powerful defensive positions inside Portugal, whilst an attempt on Elvas or Almeida (now back in Allied hands again) would have been out of the question. But the French position regarding Portugal mattered far less than the fact that for the whole of 1811 the British were able to exert only the most marginal influence on the situation in Spain.

In the autumn of 1811, however, the situation changed dramatically. Firstly, Wellington took delivery of a powerful siege train, and secondly, the effect of Napoleon insisting that the French commanders in Spain should continue to expand the territory under their control, and in particular to continue with the offensive they had launched against Valencia, at the very time that he was pulling men out of Spain and cutting the supply of reinforcements, completely destabilized the position on the Portuguese frontier. The French no longer had the men they needed to contain Wellington. What followed was all too predictable. Seeing his chance, Wellington struck across the border and was quickly able to capture the fortresses of Ciudad Rodrigo and Badajoz, win a major victory at Salamanca and liberate Madrid. Due to a variety of problems, however, of which by far the greatest was the de facto collapse of government and society in Spain, in November 1812 Wellington was again forced to retreat to Portugal, but the French were never fully able to recover and were further weakened by the withdrawal of still more troops in the early months of 1813. Aided by the continued attempts of the French to hold more territory than they could garrison, in May 1813 Wellington was therefore able to launch a fresh offensive that led to the defeat of King Joseph's main field forces at Vitoria on 21 June, after which, Catalonia and a few scattered garrisons aside, most of what remained of his domains had to be evacuated. Bitter fighting continued in the Pyrenees, with the French vainly trying to relieve the besieged fortresses of San Sebastián and Pamplona, but they were repelled at Sorauren and San Marcial, while in October 1813 Wellington invaded France and, after several fierce battles, established himself in an unassailable position south of Bayonne. Though French troops stayed in part of Catalonia until the end of hostilities in April of the following year, to all intents and purposes the Peninsular War was over, the battles that Wellington went on to fight at Orthez and Toulouse really belonging more to the campaign of 1814.

The significance of the Peninsular War was considerable. British historians have, for obvious reasons, been inclined to emphasize the part that it played in the downfall of Napoleon, while the emperor also assigned it much importance, famously calling it his 'Spanish ulcer'. But in this respect its effects have probably been exaggerated. Whilst it inspired many German nationalists, for example, it did not inspire much popular participation in the campaigns of 1813 and 1814, and still less did it persuade the people of Germany to heed the various attempts to persuade them to rise against Napoleon that were made in the course of 1809. Nor did it do much to erode the emperor's war-making capacity, as it is hard, for instance, to see how the forces caught up in the Peninsular War would have made much difference in Russia in 1812. Nevertheless, the continued struggle in the Peninsula undoubtedly strengthened the credibility of British diplomacy in the period 1812–14, while the heavy losses suffered in Spain and Portugal certainly played their part in eroding support for the French ruler in the final crisis of the empire. In Spain and Portugal, by contrast, no one can doubt its importance. In both states it was the key to liberal revolution, loss of empire and a series of civil wars, whilst in Spain in particular it gave birth to a long tradition of military intervention in politics that culminated in the bloody conflict of 1936–39 and the subsequent dictatorship of General Franco.

It is important, however, that we do not end this introduction on a negative note so far as Spain and Portugal are concerned. In the former, especially, there is considerable reason to doubt popular commitment to the struggle against Napoleon, while even in Portugal the subject is one that cries out for detailed assessment. Whatever the attitude of the people, however, there can be no doubt either of the determined manner in which the political leadership of both countries held firm to the need to stand fast against Napoleon even in the face of great temptation; when Andalusia fell to the French in January 1810, for example, it would have been all too easy for the newly formed Spanish Regency to surrender to Joseph Bonaparte. There is also the heroism displayed by the Spanish army and the Portuguese army alike. Though the Spanish army was frequently beaten, it was not because its soldiers were cowards or its officers (with some glaring exceptions) incompetent, but rather because of serious structural problems that hampered its mobilization, equipment and training, not to mention the extremely difficult strategic conditions in which it was forced to operate. However, it played a full part – even the major part – in the 'little war' that did so much to harm the French. As for the Portuguese army, it was generally no more fortunate when it tried to take on the French in 1809, as witness the terrible defeat that it suffered at Lanhoso in the course of the French invasion of March of that year. Yet once given a fair chance, as was the case once it began to fight alongside the British army after 1810, its men proved themselves to be every bit as tough and dependable as Wellington's own soldiers and suffered heavy casualties in many of his battles.

To conclude, then, it is entirely appropriate that this atlas should consider all the campaigns of the struggle of 1808–14 rather than just the operations of the British army – indeed, that it should clearly and specifically make the point that a history of the campaigns of Sir John Moore and the Duke of Wellington is not the same as a history of the Peninsular War. Only the most extreme and unyielding Spanish and Portuguese nationalists would seek to deny that it was the British army that was the motor of the struggle – that without the men commanded by Moore and Wellington the Iberian Peninsula would have fallen into the hands of the French. Equally, only such observers would seek to maintain that it was not the Duke of Wellington who played the dominant role in finally driving the French back across the Pyrenees in 1813. Yet, by the same token, no serious British historian can possibly claim that Britannia ruled the *meseta* alone. Without his steadfast Portuguese auxiliaries, for example, Wellington could not have turned back Marshal Masséna in 1810, nor still less advanced to the Pyrenees. Beyond the Spanish frontier, he was also heavily dependent on the Spaniards who, by one means or another – the story is certainly not simply one of heroic bands of priests and peasants turned guerrillas – to the very end tied down large parts of an occupying force that never numbered less than four times the numbers of British and Portuguese troops Wellington had in Portugal. And, of course, if Britain's soldiers frequently endured dreadful conditions, they had no monopoly on suffering; even now, the story of the misery endured by the Army of the Left in the campaign of October 1808–January 1809 is awe-inspiring in its extremity. Victory, then, was above all, a coalition affair, and it is precisely as a coalition affair that we are proud to present this atlas.

Charles J. Esdaile, 24 September 2009

LEGEND TO MAPS

Military Symbols

British Forces
French Forces
Portuguese Forces
Spanish Forces

Infantry (British)
Cavalry (French)
Artillery (Portuguese)
Horse Artillery (Spanish)
Engineers (British)

Army (British)
Corps (French)
Division (Portuguese)
Brigade (Spanish)
Regiment (Spanish)
Battalion (French)
Company (Portuguese)

Army Headquarters (British)

Cavalry Division (French)
Cavalry Brigade (Portuguese)
Cavalry Regiment (Spanish)
Cavalry Squadron (British)

Artillery Brigade (French)
Artillery Battery (Portuguese)
Artillery Battery (Spanish)
Horse Artillery Battery (British)

Engineer Battalion (French)
Engineer Company (Portuguese)

Interpretation of Military Symbols

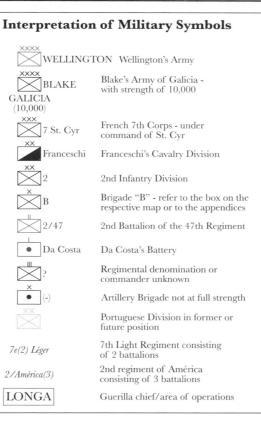

WELLINGTON Wellington's Army

BLAKE GALICIA (10,000) Blake's Army of Galicia - with strength of 10,000

7 St. Cyr French 7th Corps - under command of St. Cyr

Franceschi Franceschi's Cavalry Division

2 2nd Infantry Division

B Brigade "B" - refer to the box on the respective map or to the appendices

2/47 2nd Battalion of the 47th Regiment

Da Costa Da Costa's Battery

? Regimental denomination or commander unknown

(-) Artillery Brigade not at full strength

Portuguese Division in former or future position

7e(2) Léger 7th Light Regiment consisting of 2 battalions

2/América(3) 2nd regiment of América consisting of 3 battalions

LONGA Guerilla chief/area of operations

Miscellaneous Symbols

Battle
Siege
Naval
Transport or Baggage
Medical Facility
Camp or Laager Area
Artillery gun or unit
Redoubt or isolated fort
Signal Station
Fortified Line/Scarping
Fortified Line
Abattis
Infantry in Square
Occupied town/city
Siege parallels and trenches
Screening force
Skirmish/Tirailleur line

Arrows & Directional Symbols

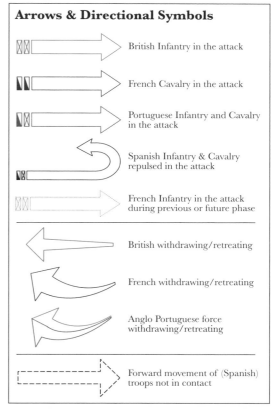

British Infantry in the attack
French Cavalry in the attack
Portuguese Infantry and Cavalry in the attack
Spanish Infantry & Cavalry repulsed in the attack
French Infantry in the attack during previous or future phase

British withdrawing/retreating
French withdrawing/retreating
Anglo Portuguese force withdrawing/retreating

Forward movement of (Spanish) troops not in contact

Topographical & Map Symbols

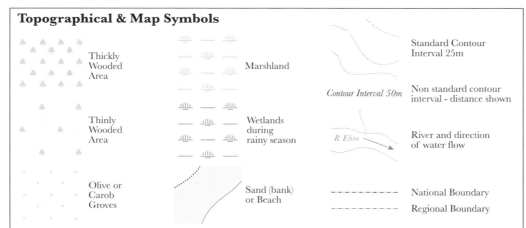

Thickly Wooded Area

Thinly Wooded Area

Olive or Carob Groves

Marshland

Wetlands during rainy season

Sand (bank) or Beach

Standard Contour Interval 25m

Contour Interval 50m Non standard contour interval - distance shown

R Ebro River and direction of water flow

National Boundary

Regional Boundary

Typical scale

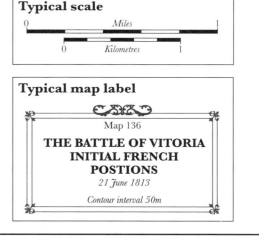

0   *Miles*   1

0   *Kilometres*   1

Typical map label

Map 136

THE BATTLE OF VITORIA INITIAL FRENCH POSTIONS

21 June 1813

Contour interval 50m

Chapter 1

JUNOT'S INVASION OF PORTUGAL

General Junot was one of Napoleon's favoured officers, who had attained his position through his undoubted bravery and unquestionable dedication to the Emperor. It was not surprising, therefore, that he was given command of an army of 25,000 men that was assembled around Bayonne in the autumn of 1807. Following the collapse of Napoleon's plans for cross-Channel invasion, these men had been withdrawn from home defence and security tasks in the northern French provinces, and in response to the uprising in Vendée and British operations near Bordeaux the army was named the Corps of Observation of the Gironde. While the diplomats delivered ultimatums to the Portuguese government, instructing them to declare war on England and seize English property, Junot was knocking his new army into shape.

On 30 September, despite the apparent compliance of the Portuguese Prince Regent regarding French demands, the French chargé d'affaires left Lisbon, quickly followed by the Spanish ambassador. Spanish accord to the French duplicity was beginning to surface and was soon sealed by the Treaty of Fontainebleau on 27 October, where the two nations confirmed their plans for the partition and eradication of the Portuguese nation. Twelve days prior to the meeting at Fontainebleau, Junot had received orders to commence operations. The Spanish forces earmarked to join this French corps took to the field a month or so later; a division assembled at Alcantara under Caraffa's command, a second division under Taranco was concentrated at Tui and poised to occupy the northern Portuguese provinces, while Solano's Division collected at Badajoz with the task of subjugating the southern provinces in the name of Godoy.[1]

Three weeks later Junot reached Salamanca, where the Spanish received their allies and prepared to install them in pre-prepared cantonments. Before the French had settled the diplomatic pretence had run its course, and Junot received orders to enter Portugal immediately. Napoleon's instructions were clear: 'the march of the army should not be delayed for a single day, under pretence of securing subsistence … twenty thousand men can live anywhere, even in a desert.'[2] Junot had to decide which of two available routes he should adopt to commence the invasion. The northern route was by far the most suitable to move a corps with artillery and baggage train, but the southern route was considerably shorter. From available mapping it was hard to gauge the difficulty of the terrain and, reminded of Napoleonic urgency, Junot chose the latter. He was soon to discover the enormity of his miscalculation. Indeed, had the Portuguese organized a determined military resistance against the Franco Spanish forces, Junot's mission would likely have ended in disaster.

The French and Spanish corps began leaving Salamanca on 12 November, a brigade each day accompanied by cavalry, artillery and baggage. The leading brigade was to reach Alcantara five days later, a day before the last brigade set off from Salamanca. The weather was atrocious and the roads and tracks quickly disintegrated; the artillery and baggage trains fell behind and blocked the route, and both men and horses suffered through lack of provisions. Many departed from the path in search of food but found only a few impoverished villages and settlements that were quickly plundered. Even before Junot set off down the Tagus valley, the Corps of Observation had already lost its semblance of order and discipline, ammunition cartridges were soaked and inoperable, many men had disappeared, many horses had perished, some guns were lost and the baggage train was some considerable distance to the rear. Junot took the opportunity to rest and reorganize his forces at Alcantara and, in the process, removed the meagre rations and dry cartridge cases from the Spanish battalions of Caraffa's Division who had managed to keep pace with their allies. On 19 November, the French corps crossed the border and, 'informed the Portuguese that the armies of Napoleon were entering their country, in order to make common cause with their beloved sovereign against the tyrant of the seas'.[3] Elements of the Spanish corps followed, but no explanation was provided for their presence.

It was immediately apparent that this road was even more demanding than that encountered in the initial leg from Salamanca. Having determined that the Portuguese had no intention of armed resistance, Junot decided to split the column at Castelo Branco, sending only Loison's Division and a few horse by the southern route, and Delaborde's Division, the balance of mainly dismounted cavalry, and the artillery by the upper road (Travot's Division was still far to the rear). The weather, terrain and lack of supplies took a heavy toll and in considerable disarray, and devoid of all artillery, except for a troop of Spanish horse artillery guns, the leading elements of these divisions began to gather at Abrantes on 23 November. José Barreto de Oliveira, the Prince Regent's representative, met them for dialogue; this was the signal for Junot to gather his more able troops and make a rapid dash for Lisbon, only 75 miles distant. At Abrantes the French had found supplies and the road to the capital was well established. On 30 November at the head of 1,500 exhausted and dishevelled men, Junot entered Lisbon and, on realizing that the Prince Regent had vacated his seat the previous day,[4] established himself as governor without a shot being fired. The first phase of Napoleon's plan was complete.

---

1   Manuel de Godoy, the first minister of the Spanish Bourbon King, Charles IV.

2   General Foy, *War in the Peninsular under Napoleon*, p.21.

3   *Ibid.* p.29.

4   The movement of the Prince Regent, the royal household and national artefacts was a well-organized affair. A Portuguese fleet of 16 men-of-war and 20 commercial ships evacuated 15,000 people. The Royal Navy assisted them in their task.

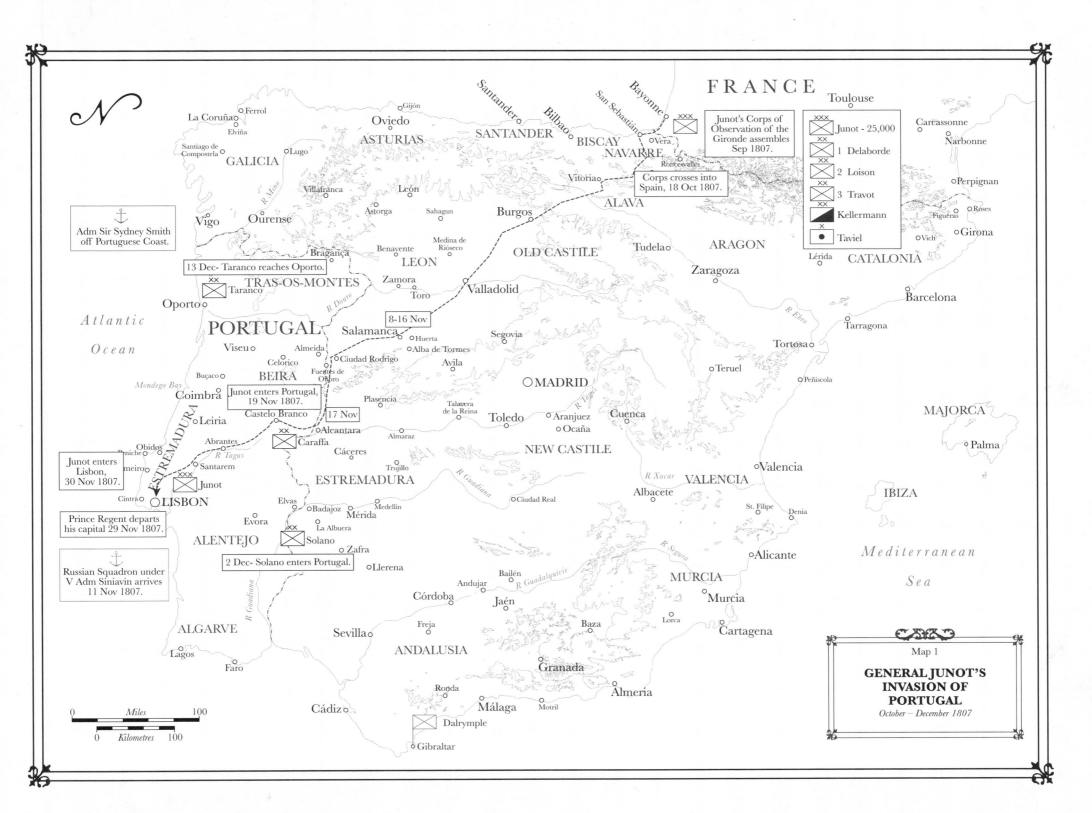

N

FRANCE

Junot's Corps of Observation of the Gironde assembles Sep 1807.

Corps crosses into Spain, 18 Oct 1807.

XXX	Junot - 25,000
XX	1 Delaborde
XX	2 Loison
XX	3 Travot
	Kellermann
•	Taviel

Adm Sir Sydney Smith off Portuguese Coast.

13 Dec- Taranco reaches Oporto.

8-16 Nov

Junot enters Portugal, 19 Nov 1807.

17 Nov

Junot enters Lisbon, 30 Nov 1807.

Prince Regent departs his capital 29 Nov 1807.

Russian Squadron under V Adm Siniavin arrives 11 Nov 1807.

2 Dec- Solano enters Portugal.

Atlantic Ocean

PORTUGAL

ESTREMADURA

ALENTEJO

ALGARVE

SPAIN place names: La Coruña, Ferrol, Elviña, Gijón, Oviedo, ASTURIAS, SANTANDER, Santander, Bilbao, BISCAY, San Sebastián, Bayonne, Toulouse, Carcassonne, Narbonne, Perpignan, Roses, Figueras, Girona, Vich, Barcelona, CATALONIA, Lérida, ARAGON, Zaragoza, Tortosa, Peñiscola, Teruel, NAVARRE, Vera, Roncesvalles, ALAVA, Vitoria, Burgos, OLD CASTILE, Tudela, Santiago de Compostela, GALICIA, Lugo, Ourense, Vigo, R Miño, Villafranca, Astorga, León, Sahagun, Medina de Ríoseco, Benavente, LEON, Bragança, TRAS-OS-MONTES, Zamora, Toro, Valladolid, Segovia, R Ebro, Tarragona, MAJORCA, Palma, IBIZA, Salamanca, Huerta, Alba de Tormes, Avila, MADRID, Cuenca, VALENCIA, Valencia, Viseu, Almeida, Celorico, Ciudad Rodrigo, Fuentes de Oñoro, Plaséncia, Talavera de la Reina, Toledo, Aranjuez, Ocaña, NEW CASTILE, Albacete, St. Filipe, Denia, Buçaco, BEIRA, Coimbra, Leiria, Castelo Branco, Alcantara, Almaraz, Cáceres, Trujillo, R Tagus, R Xucar, Alicante, Obidos, Peniche, Abrantes, Santarem, Cintra, LISBON, Evora, Elvas, Badajoz, Medellin, Mérida, La Albuera, Zafra, Llerena, Ciudad Real, R Guadiana, MURCIA, Murcia, R Segura, Lorca, Cartagena, Lagos, Faro, Cádiz, Sevilla, Freja, ANDALUSIA, Córdoba, Jaén, Andujar, Bailén, R Guadalquivir, Baza, Almería, Ronda, Málaga, Motril, Granada, Gibraltar, *Mediterranean Sea*, Mondego Bay

Taranco

Oporto

Caraffa

Junot

Solano

Dalrymple

Miles		100
0		
Kilometres		100
0		

Map 1

GENERAL JUNOT'S INVASION OF PORTUGAL

October – December 1807

Chapter 2

THE ROAD TO WAR – THE FIRST SIX MONTHS OF 1808

Godoy was unable to share Napoleon and Junot's jubilation at the speed and ease of the Portuguese capitulation. One of the terms of the Treaty of Fontainebleau allowed a further 40,000 Frenchmen to enter Spain in the event of British intervention in support of Portugal. Eight days before Junot's triumphant, if somewhat dishevelled, entrance into the Portuguese capital, General Dupont had crossed the Pyrenees with 25,000 men, and right behind him was another corps under Marshal Moncey numbering some 30,000. The sixth article of Fontainebleau required that prior notice be provided to the King of Spain, but none was forthcoming. Napoleon's intentions were becoming plain.[1]

In early January 1808 Moncey crossed into Spain and relieved Dupont's troops in the northern towns in Biscay and Navarre. This enabled the latter forces to forge south-west toward Valladolid and Burgos; purportedly poised to strike in support of Junot, but equally conveniently perched for advancement toward the Spanish capital. A month later another corps of 14,000 combined French and Italian troops under General Duhesme crossed the eastern Pyrenees into Catalonia. There was no disguising the fact that they were not destined for Portugal, but instead ambling toward Barcelona. The pretence was over and, on 16 February, Pamplona was seized by a somewhat farcical *coup de main*, which caught the Spanish garrison off-guard.

Charles IV and Godoy were at a loss as to how to respond, their proposal of a marital union between a Bonaparte princess and Ferdinand having been coldly cast aside, they reluctantly admitted that the game was up. Meanwhile, French exploits continued and on 29 February General Lecchi captured the fortress at Barcelona through a laughable deception operation.[2] A few days later the other frontier forts had also fallen: Figueras by a *coup de main* along similar

lines to Pamplona and San Sebastián through surrender, having received orders from Madrid not to resist. Godoy felt compelled to order the withdrawal of the three Spanish divisions in support of Junot[3] and he convinced the king and queen to seek refuge in Aranjuez, with plans to evacuate them further away if necessary.

With the royal family ensconced in the palaces at Aranjuez, Godoy's resolve was soon put to the test by the arrival of a new French personality. Joachim Murat was Napoleon's brother-in-law; unquestionably reckless, undeniably ambitious and categorically unintelligent, he arrived in southern France on 26 February to assume command of all French forces in Spain under the grand title of 'Lieutenant of the Emperor'. With control of a kingdom at stake, he was prepared to do whatever necessary to assert his claim. By 13 March he was at Burgos, closely followed by yet another corps, this one, 30,000 strong and commanded by Marshal Bessières. French forces in Spain now numbered over 100,000 men (see Appendix 1) and this formidable force was closing in on Madrid, forcing Godoy to execute his evacuation plan for the royal family. The normally mild inhabitants rallied to prevent the flight, firmly of the opinion that Godoy was in cahoots with Napoleon. The uprising that ensued only abated when Ferdinand announced that the king had dismissed his first minister. However, when Godoy resurfaced the following day the unrest resumed, and second time around, public and (certain) military opinion could only be appeased by the actual abdication of Charles in favour of his son.

Murat meanwhile continued toward Madrid and entered the city on 23 March. Ferdinand returned to the Spanish capital the following day, prepared to negotiate the Spanish position – firmly under the misapprehension that Napoleon's objective had purely been the removal of Godoy and not the conquest of Spain. The accession of the young and popular Ferdinand was a major spanner in Napoleon's works, and Bonaparte resolved to remove the Spanish Bourbon line and replace it with his older brother Joseph.[4] Through a series of Machiavellian enterprises, Ferdinand was lured to Bayonne and stripped of his crown. Murat brought matters to a head when he ordered the Junta to turn over the remaining members of the royal family: the *madrileños* rose as one and turned on their French invaders. The date was 2 May 1808, a date subsequently enshrined on the hearts and souls of the Spanish people. 'El Dos de Mayo' was a spontaneous, possibly overdue but predictably Spanish reaction, which provided the catalyst for the nationwide insurrection that followed. 'Grapeshot and the bayonet cleared the streets,' Murat wrote in his report.[5] Napoleon had just made an uncharacteristic miscalculation and the *Guerre de la Independencia* had just begun.

---

1   The disunity in the Spanish court, the ease of capitulation in the Portuguese campaign, and the misguided belief that Spain would follow suit, had led Napoleon to err, which was despite strong opposition from the cunning but able Talleyrand, his minister of foreign affairs. Talleyrand chose the moment to resign, to be succeeded by the far less capable Champagny. The point marked a distinct downward turn in the Emperor's skill as an international statesman.

2   See Oman, *History of the Peninsular War*, vol. I, p.36.

3   The divisions of Caraffa, Solano and Belesta – see Chapter 1 and Map 1.

4   Napoleon initially offered the throne to his younger brother, Louis who had the foresight to turn it down.

5   Sarrazin, *History of the War in Spain & Portugal 1807-1814*, p.33.

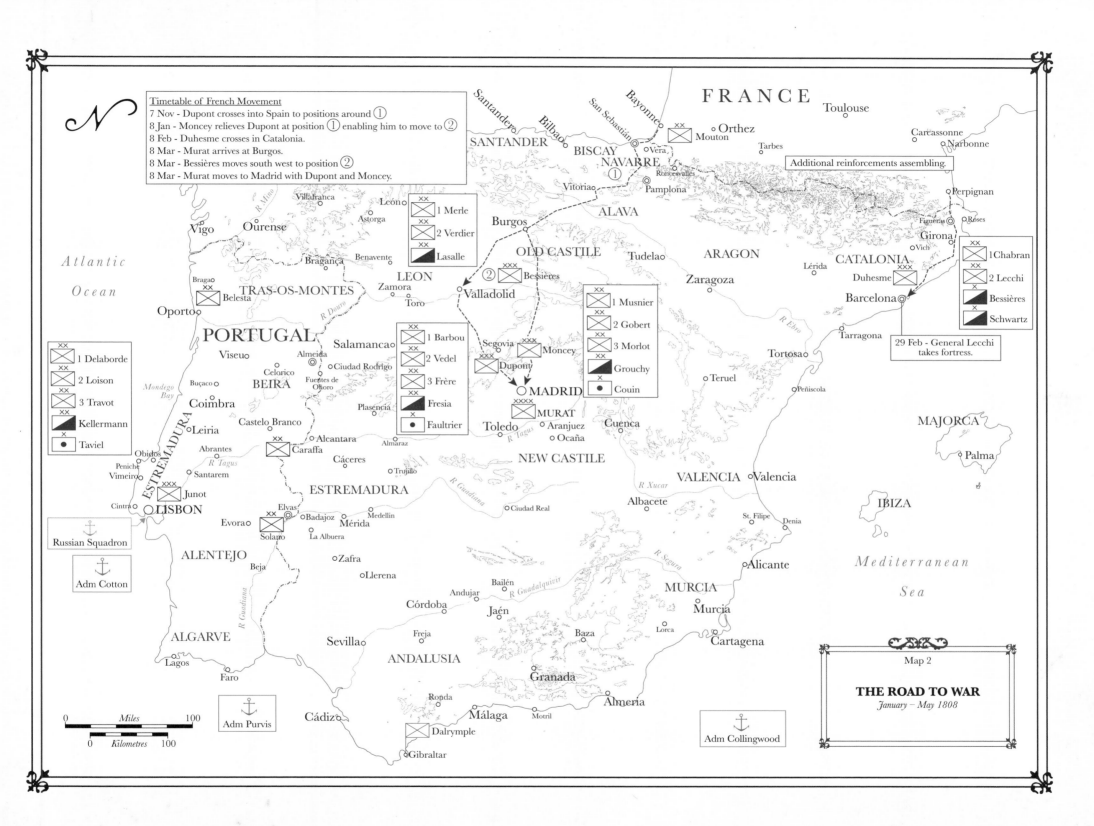

Timetable of French Movement
7 Nov - Dupont crosses into Spain to positions around ①
8 Jan - Moncey relieves Dupont at position ① enabling him to move to ②
8 Feb - Duhesme crosses in Catalonia.
8 Mar - Murat arrives at Burgos.
8 Mar - Bessières moves south west to position ②
8 Mar - Murat moves to Madrid with Dupont and Moncey.

FRANCE

Additional reinforcements assembling.

29 Feb - General Lecchi takes fortress.

Atlantic Ocean

Mediterranean Sea

XX	1 Delaborde
XX	2 Loison
XX	3 Travot
	Kellermann
•	Taviel

Russian Squadron

Adm Cotton

Adm Purvis

Adm Collingwood

XX	1 Merle
XX	2 Verdier
XX	Lasalle

XX	1 Barbou
XX	2 Vedel
XX	3 Frère
	Fresia
×	Faultrier

XX	1 Musnier
XX	2 Gobert
XX	3 Morlot
	Grouchy
•	Couin

XX	1 Chabran
XXX	2 Lecchi
	Bessières
	Schwartz

Map 2

THE ROAD TO WAR
January – May 1808

Chapter 3 ❦

THE SPANISH BACKLASH AND THE FRENCH RESPONSE: MAY–JUNE 1808

Within a week of 'El Dos de Mayo,' the news of insurrection had reached every corner of Spain; embellished at every passing, the event had translated into a massacre by Murat and the French invaders. Rumour of underhand dealings at Bayonne quickly followed, increasing the temperature, and yet it was to be many days before the backlash commenced. The reasons for this slow ignition were straightforward enough. Firstly, the majority of Spain had no physical French presence upon which to focus their anger, and secondly, Ferdinand, since his accession and before being lured to France, had insufficient time to populate La Junta de Gobierno[1], the provincial ministries and the military regions[2] with supporters loyal to his new regime. Factions faithful to Godoy, both civilian and military, still permeated the system and they felt inclined to wait for Napoleon to make the first move. These groups delayed, supposedly fearing a bloodbath; in reality their fears centred on their own future roles, power and prosperity. Consequently, the rising when it came had two objectives, removing the French and instigating political change. To complicate matters, the church followed the nation, and not the nation the church: indeed many of the spiritual hierarchy were among the most servile instruments of Murat[3].

On 25 May, the people of Oviedo, ignoring the apathy of their leadership, rose up and declared war on France. Within days the cities and towns in Galicia had followed suit, the Spanish regional military commander[4] was removed and killed (some time later) for trying to stand in their way. Generals in Badajoz, Cádiz, Cartagena and Valladolid were to meet a similar fate, along with officials, judges, mayors and clerks all deemed to be allied – in one way or another, and rightly or wrongly – with the *antiguo régimen*. During the first week of June the insurrection spread across the nation, but it remained rebellion and not revolution, with the

provincial Juntas being purged and the military mobilized, much against the judgement of many military commanders.[5]

In the areas under French military control, rebellion was sporadic, being quickly and ruthlessly dealt with by Murat's forces. From the existing military Juntas, five centres of gravity emerged. The first and most important was Andalusia, which was home to a series of large regular garrisons and a large fleet that had been bottled up in the harbour at Cádiz since the naval battle off Cape Trafalgar in 1805.[6] The second area was Galicia, which was also well served by standing forces and large arsenals at La Coruña and Ferrol. The third, Catalonia had fewer regulars (*miqueletes*); however, their smaller forces were quickly augmented with troops from the Balearic isles and more significantly by a number of *somatenes*. The Catalan struggle focused primarily on Barcelona and the vital French lines of communication in the eastern Pyrenees. Finally, there was the region of Aragon, which suffered occupation through much of the war; and Valencia (including Murcia), which, notwithstanding Moncey's brief interlude in 1808, evaded subjugation until the end of 1811.

Towards the end of May, Murat fell ill and took to his bed, within days he had handed over the reins of command to General Savary and departed for France to convalesce. Not however, before sending copious despatches to Napoleon at Bayonne, playing down the overall situation from one of national insurrection to that of localized riots. Based predominantly on the thrust of these reports, Napoleon penned and despatched a plan. In summary, the orders retained a large reserve at Madrid and provided a number of formations to the outlying areas in order to quell the unrest and restore order. Bessières was to keep open the lines of communication between France and Madrid, while at the same time sending a force to Zaragoza of about 4,000 men[7] and detaching a brigade to Merle's Division, which was tasked to subjugate Santander and Bilbao. Of the two corps in and around Madrid, Dupont was to head south with Barbou's infantry division and Fresia's cavalry division to subdue Andalusia while Moncey, with a force of 6,000 men, consisting of Musnier's infantry division and Wathier's cavalry brigade, set off to capture Valencia. The balance of Dupont and Moncey's corps was to remain in and around Madrid and act as a reserve in support of either commander, or to Bessières in the north. Finally, Duhesme was tasked to support both Moncey and Lefebvre-Desnouettes with his meagre force of 12,000, in executing their mission to garrison Barcelona and keep open the eastern lines of communication.

At this stage, Napoleon was convinced that 91,000 men in Spain were more than enough to stabilize the situation, and he saw no reason to include Junot's force in his plan. But even had he have done so, they would have been unable to offer assistance for on the same day, 6 June, an insurrection ignited in Portugal. Napoleon now had rebellions in two countries to contend with,

---

1   The provincial Juntas were in control until September 1808; however, in that month the obvious need for a new central government produced the formation of a provisional collective head of state drawn from all the provincial Juntas; this was known as the Junta Suprema Central de Gobierno, or more usually the Junta Central/Central Junta but sometimes known/titled as the Junta Suprema/Supreme Junta.

2   Spain was divided into 32 provinces and 14 military regions.

3   Oman, *History of the Peninsular War*, vol. I, p.67.

4   Captain General Filanghieri.

5   Notably General Cuesta, the Governor-General of Old Castile, who according to Oman (vol. 1, p.68.) only agreed to lead an army when the rope was actually around his neck.

6   The French squadron under Admiral Rosily, which had taken sanctuary at the same location, was to receive the first shots of the war.

7   For this task he utilized his Chief of Staff, General Lefebvre-Desnouettes.

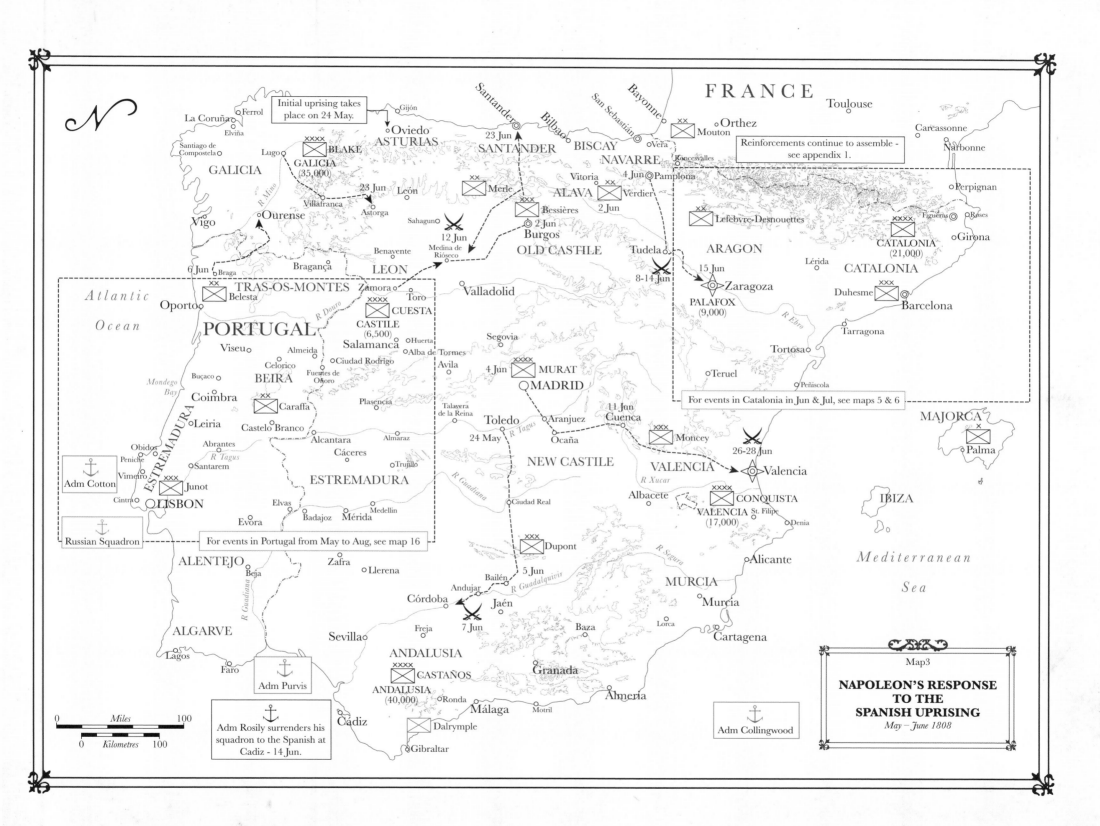

N

FRANCE
Toulouse

La Coruña Ferrol Gijón
Elviña Oviedo Santander Bilbao Bayonne Orthez Carcassonne
Santiago de Compostela ASTURIAS SANTANDER BISCAY San Sebastián Mouton Narbonne

Initial uprising takes place on 24 May.

23 Jun NAVARRE Vera Reinforcements continue to assemble - see appendix 1.
Lugo BLAKE Roncesvalles Perpignan
GALICIA GALICIA (35,000) Merle ALAVA Vitoria 4 Jun Pamplona
Vigo León Verdier 2 Jun Figueras Roses
23 Jun Bessières Lefebvre-Desnouettes Girona
Villafranca Astorga Sahagun 2 Jun ARAGON Lérida CATALONIA (21,000)
Ourense Benavente 12 Jun Medina de Ríoseco Burgos OLD CASTILE Tudela CATALONIA
6 Jun Braga Zamora 8-14 Jun 15 Jun Duhesme
TRAS-OS-MONTES Toro Valladolid Zaragoza Barcelona
Oporto Belesta CUESTA PALAFOX (9,000) R Ebro Tarragona
PORTUGAL CASTILE (6,500) Huerta Segovia Tortosa
Viseu Almeida Salamanca Alba de Tormes Teruel Peñiscola
Celorico Ciudad Rodrigo Avila MAJORCA
Buçaco BEIRA Fuentes de Oñoro Plasencia 4 Jun MURAT Palma
Coimbra Caraffa MADRID 11 Jun Cuenca
Leiria Castelo Branco Talavera de la Reina Aranjuez Moncey 26-28 Jun
Obidos Abrantes Alcantara Almaraz Toledo Ocaña Valencia
Peniche Santarem Cáceres 24 May R Tagus NEW CASTILE IBIZA
Adm Cotton Vimeiro R Tagus Trujillo VALENCIA R Xucar CONQUISTA
Junot ESTREMADURA Albacete VALENCIA St. Filipe
Cintra LISBON Elvas Medellin Ciudad Real (17,000) Denia
Russian Squadron Evora Badajoz Mérida Dupont Alicante Mediterranean Sea
For events in Portugal from May to Aug, see map 16 Zafra Llerena Bailén 5 Jun R Segura MURCIA
ALENTEJO Beja Andujar R Guadalquivir Murcia
Córdoba 7 Jun Jaén Baza Lorca
ALGARVE Freja Cartagena
Lagos Faro Sevilla ANDALUSIA Granada
Adm Purvis CASTAÑOS Almeria
Adm Rosily surrenders his squadron to the Spanish at Cadiz - 14 Jun. ANDALUSIA (40,000) Ronda Málaga Motril
Cadiz Dalrymple Adm Collingwood
Gibraltar

0 Miles 100
0 Kilometres 100

For events in Catalonia in Jun & Jul, see maps 5 & 6

Map3

NAPOLEON'S RESPONSE TO THE SPANISH UPRISING
May – June 1808

and a third country was soon to enter the fray. In late May, two emissaries from the newly appointed Asturian Junta arrived in London and were given an audience with Lord Canning, the Foreign Secretary. They were provided assurances of support by way of arms, munitions and money. In fact, on 25 May, Viscount Castlereagh, the Secretary of State for War, had already sent instructions to General Dalrymple (commanding Gibraltar) to support if at all possible the Spanish uprising in the south with his garrison force of 10,000. British eyes were also on Cádiz and the French fleet harboured there and orders were sent from the Admiralty, to both admirals Collingwood and Purvis, to capitalise upon any advantage the disorder in the region might offer with particular regard to the capture of Rosily's squadron. At about the same time the British Cabinet had suggested to King George III that there were distinct national benefits to armed intervention in Spain, and the force currently being assembled for operations in Central America was considered for re-tasking to the Iberian Peninsula. The command of this force had already been allocated to Arthur Wellesley.[8]

In executing Napoleon's plan, Dupont was the first to set off, departing Toledo with his force of 13,000 men on 24 May. His journey to Andujar (a few miles west of Bailén) attained a frosty but uneventful passage. He arrived on 5 June and soon received numerous reports of uprisings throughout the province, and, perhaps more disturbingly, of the assembly of two Spanish armies, one around Sevilla and the other near Granada. The situation was clearly far worse than anticipated and, despite being warned that he would not enter Córdoba without a fight, he resolved to push on and capture the great city located a few miles further west.[9] The defence of the city had been entrusted to Don Pedro Agostino de Echávarri, a retired lieutenant colonel, who boasted about 1,400 regular soldiers, a further 10,000 to 12,000 armed locals and eight rather antique artillery pieces.[10] He deployed his force on either side of the bridge at Alcolea, which he barricaded and covered with his eight guns on the home bank, from where he could enfilade the entire length of the bridge and its approaches. The regular battalions were deployed either side of the guns, and elements of the armed civilians were positioned to the flanks (map 4, positions 1 and 2); the balance, including the mounted elements, were deployed on the heights on the far bank to the south, which dominated the approaches (map 4, position 3). The task of this latter group was to 'threaten' to fall upon the flank of the French should they try and force passage across the bridge.

Dupont, on discovering the Spaniards deployed in a blocking position, called up a battery, and for a short while pounded the far side of the bridge, providing time and cover for Pannetier's Brigade to deploy into formation and storm the barricades. On cue, the armed civilians (some on horseback) began to show themselves on the heights to the French left. Unperturbed, Dupont ordered Fresia's cavalry, supported by the battalion of Marines of the Guard, to see off this

diversion while Pannetier continued his attack on the main objective. Both French manoeuvres were successful and the Spanish fled from the hill and bridge back toward the city. The vast majority continued rapidly westwards, making no attempt to stand in defence of the city or its inhabitants. Dupont's forces followed, expecting to find Echávarri's troops deployed in a second line of defence before the city. Instead he found the way open. The closed gates were quickly removed by round shot and the French troops poured into the city and committed 'dreadful scenes, for which no excuse was to be found in the loss sustained by the victors; since the attack on the city had not cost them ten men, and the success of the day only thirty killed and eighty injured'.[11] Dupont then lingered at Córdoba; he had left no detachments en route, none had been despatched from Madrid, and his lines of communication with Toledo were now severed. His position was becoming increasingly precarious and on 16 June, after nine days in the city, Dupont elected to retrace his steps towards Madrid.

Meanwhile Bessières was implementing his part in Napoleon's plan. On 2 June he had despatched two columns: the first under Verdier to subdue Logroño, which was achieved in a bloody but effective manner, and the second under Merle, to move from Burgos to Santander to quell the disturbances on the coast of Biscay. Merle was on the road to the coastal town and about to force a passage across the Cantabrian mountains when he received orders to return and assist in the suppression of a more pressing uprising in the plains of Castile. General Cuesta had gathered a considerable force of about of about 6,500 men[12] and was poised to cut the Burgos to Madrid road. Bessières tasked Lasalle (his cavalry commander) to link up with Merle and counter the threat. Lasalle, a resolute, talented but impetuous cavalry officer, did not wait for his infantry counterpart; setting off instantly, he sacked Torquemada, plundered Palencia and then made contact with Cuesta's forces at the bridge at Cabezon, where the main road from Burgos to Valladolid crosses the river Pisuerga. Merle joined him on 11 June at Dueñas and the following morning the combined force fell upon Cuesta at Cabezon, where he had (inexpertly) deployed his force in front of the bridge and river. Lasalle's chasseurs led the spirited assault and Spanish resolve immediately collapsed; the ranks broke and the French cavalry crossed the bridge, sabred the gunners on the far side and captured four guns. Many hundreds more were cut down as they fled westwards and a large number drowned in the river Pisuerga. Bessières's right flank was now secure and Merle once again turned his attention north, entering Santander on 23 June.

On Bessières's left flank, Verdier was firm in Logroño and, on 4 June, Lefebvre-Desnouettes departed from Pamplona with a small force of about 4,000 and a few artillery guns to move against the newly appointed Spanish Captain-General Palafox in Zaragoza. It was considered almost a routine mission, as it was thought that there were no regular Spanish forces in Aragon, and the likelihood of resistance by the population was not entertained. In fact Palafox, who had only been in command since 26 May, had raised and already trained seven regiments

8   There is some evidence that this proposal was first raised by Wellesley himself in his capacity as Chief Secretary for Ireland. Glover, *The Peninsular War 1807–1814: A Concise Military History*, p.57.

9   Foy, *History of the War in the Peninsula under Napoleon*, vol. II, p.218.

10 These are Oman's figures. Foy states 3,000–4,000 regular and 3,000–4,000 armed locals; Napier 3,000 regulars and 10,000 armed civilians; while De la Cierva, *Historia Militar de España*, vol. VII, p.54, quotes 2,100 regulars and 20,000 armed locals.

11 Foy, op. cit., p.222.

12 However, about 5,000 were poorly trained volunteers, his cavalry numbered a mere 300 and his artillery was in a terrible state of repair.

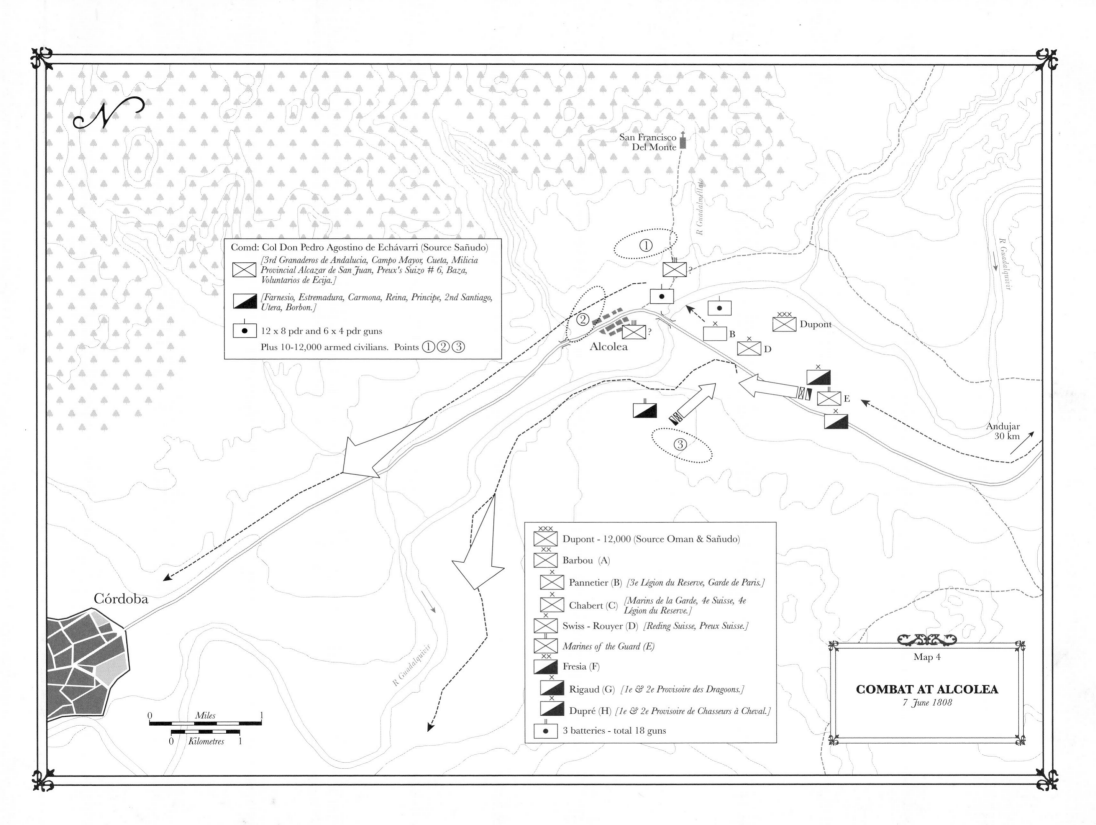

Map legend (top)

Comd: Col Don Pedro Agostino de Echávarri (Source Sañudo)

[3rd Granaderos de Andalucia, Campo Mayor, Cueta, Milicia Provincial Alcazar de San Juan, Preux's Suizo # 6, Baza, Voluntarios de Ecija.]

[Farnesio, Estremadura, Carmona, Reina, Principe, 2nd Santiago, Utera, Borbon.]

12 x 8 pdr and 6 x 4 pdr guns

Plus 10-12,000 armed civilians. Points ① ② ③

Map labels

San Francisco Del Monte

R Guadalmellato

R Guadalquivir

①

②

Alcolea

③

Dupont

B

D

E

Andujar 30 km

Córdoba

R Guadalquivir

Miles 0 — 1

Kilometres 0 — 1

Map legend (bottom)

Dupont - 12,000 (Source Oman & Sañudo)

Barbou (A)

Pannetier (B) *[3e Légion du Reserve, Garde de Paris.]*

Chabert (C) *[Marins de la Garde, 4e Suisse, 4e Légion du Reserve.]*

Swiss - Rouyer (D) *[Reding Suisse, Preux Suisse.]*

Marines of the Guard (E)

Fresia (F)

Rigaud (G) *[1e & 2e Provisoire des Dragoons.]*

Dupré (H) *[1e & 2e Provisoire de Chasseurs à Cheval.]*

3 batteries - total 18 guns

Map 4

COMBAT AT ALCOLEA
7 June 1808

and had the assistance of a few hundred former regulars. In total his force numbered about 9,000 men and numerous cannon, although they possessed little expertise in gunnery. On hearing of the advancing French force, Palafox despatched a small force from Zaragoza to meet them. The two sides met at Tudela on 8 June; the engagement was brief and the Spanish were quickly pushed back to Mallen where, on 13 June, they once again offered battle. The Spanish were again forced to retreat, on this occasion suffering severe losses, and they pulled back to a third position at Alagon, where Palafox and the balance of the force at Zaragoza rode out in support of them. The Spanish forces amounted to 6,500, numerically superior to the French, and expectations were high. The battle commenced early on 14 June and the outcome was swift; the French artillery outnumbered that of the Spanish by three to one and the poorly trained infantry were outclassed and outmanoeuvred by the agility and speed of the Polish light horse. Somewhat dejected, the Spanish withdrew within the walls of Zaragoza and the following day the French forces appeared before the city, confident of a quick submission. Their optimism was to be short lived.

On the same day that Lefebvre-Desnouettes had departed Pamplona, Moncey was completing his last-minute preparations for an advance on Valencia. With his 8,000 men he moved east via the northern and more mountainous route, a decision that took the Conde de Cervellon completely by surprise. Virtually his entire blocking force was deployed to the south, astride the more accessible route in the plains. Moncey, realizing his fortune, forced the bridge at Cabriel and continued his advance with haste, crossing the defile at Cabrillas two days later. By 26 June he was closing in on the city of Valencia, only to discover a large makeshift Spanish force that had deployed in defensive positions along the approaches. It took most of the subsequent day to dislodge the ad hoc group before he could present himself in front of the city gates and demand surrender. However, Valencian resolve was sterner than he had hitherto witnessed in the Cuenca mountains; they flatly refused to negotiate and Moncey was forced to attempt to take the city by storm. On 28 June he tried twice before realising that his forces and field artillery was no match for the Valencian fortitude and fortifications.[13] Moncey was now in a precarious situation as Cervellon's army, realizing their mistake, had turned and were now moving in his direction; his lines of retreat to Madrid were now cut and his supplies badly diminished. Unsure of the geography to the north and with a vague idea of Cervellon's whereabouts, Moncey elected to swing well south before heading back inland and returning to Madrid. Cervellon, aware that Moncey was on the move, anticipated that the French would move back the way they had come and gambled on the northern route. For a second time he erred, enabling Moncey to escape. On 8 July Moncey met up with Frère at San Clemente and a week later they were back in Madrid.[14]

Since the capture of Barcelona at the end of February, Duhesme's corps had remained within the confines of the city. The Catalan reaction to El Dos de Mayo was stifled by the presence of 12,000 Frenchmen in their capital. Rebellion was centred on Lérida, and somewhat localized,

but Catalonia more than any other part of Spain had reason to rebel against French occupation. They had suffered greatly through loss of trade inflicted by the continental system; they had lost their fight for regional independence following the Wars of the Spanish Succession; and they had been abandoned by the French following their revolt against the House of Castile in the 17th century. Catalan reaction was only a matter of time, and the presence of the two regular battalions of Spanish and Walloon Guards and the cavalry regiment of Bourbon, which were still intact within the walls of Barcelona, was a particular concern to Duhesme. Much to his relief they decided to disband in small groups following news of events in Madrid. However, while deliberating on how to deal with the mounting Catalan insurrection, Duhesme received fresh orders from Napoleon reducing his options considerably. He was to support Lefebvre-Desnouettes in Zaragoza, Moncey in Valencia and to hold open the lines of communication with France. Retaining control in Barcelona and regaining control in Catalonia were implied tasks. There can be little doubt that these orders confirmed Napoleon's lack of understanding of the scale of the uprising, a poor appreciation of the ground and a mistaken assessment of Spanish acquiescence.

Nonetheless, Duhesme did his level best to comply with Napoleon's requirements. General Schwartz led the move on Lérida and the link-up with Lefebvre-Desnouettes at Zaragoza with a force of 3,200, while Chabran commanded the move south with a slightly smaller force. Schwartz departed the confines of Barcelona on 4 June and two days later arrived at the pass of Bruch, where he discovered about 400 *somatenes*, drawn up, blocking the pass. He engaged and drove them back towards Manresa, where the local fighters were joined by several hundreds more of their countrymen flooding south from the upper Llobregat. Schwartz was taken by surprise at the tenacity of the Catalans and, fearing being cut off, ordered a slow retreat down the valley in formation. After drawing back about 10km, Schwartz's men lost cohesion and the orderly withdrawal became more of a flight. By nightfall the dispirited French force was back on the coastal plains and the next morning they re-entered Barcelona, having lost face and one of their four guns. Duhesme's second column under Chabran set off for Valencia on 4 June and moved along the coast road, reaching Tarragona three days later. The divisional commander occupied the citadel and seconded the Swiss Regiment[15] to join the French forces in their conquest of Valencia. However, the next day, news of Schwartz's defeat at Bruch came through along with orders from Duhesme to return at once. Leaving the Swiss in place, Chabran returned on 9 June, re-entering Barcelona three days later. (The Swiss immediately switched allegiance back to the new Junta at Lérida.)

Duhesme was disappointed, but satisfied that he had at least attempted to comply with Napoleon's interventions, and with his corps now reunited, he decided to instigate his own plans for the subjugation of upper Catalonia. However, the *somatenes* and *miqueletes* had grown in confidence following the rout of Schwartz at Bruch, and were now threatening Duhesme's communication with France. Accordingly, Chabran was assigned to punish the Catalans at Bruch and force the pass; he departed on 14 June with his entire division and Schwartz's combined Swiss and Italian Brigade. Once again the French were to be humiliated at Bruch by the

---

13   French losses numbered about 1,200: a sixth of the force.

14   Frère was commanding Dupont's 3rd Division – and was sent in search of Moncey once communications had been cut.

15   Wimpffen's Swiss Regiment, under Spanish pay, which garrisoned the city.

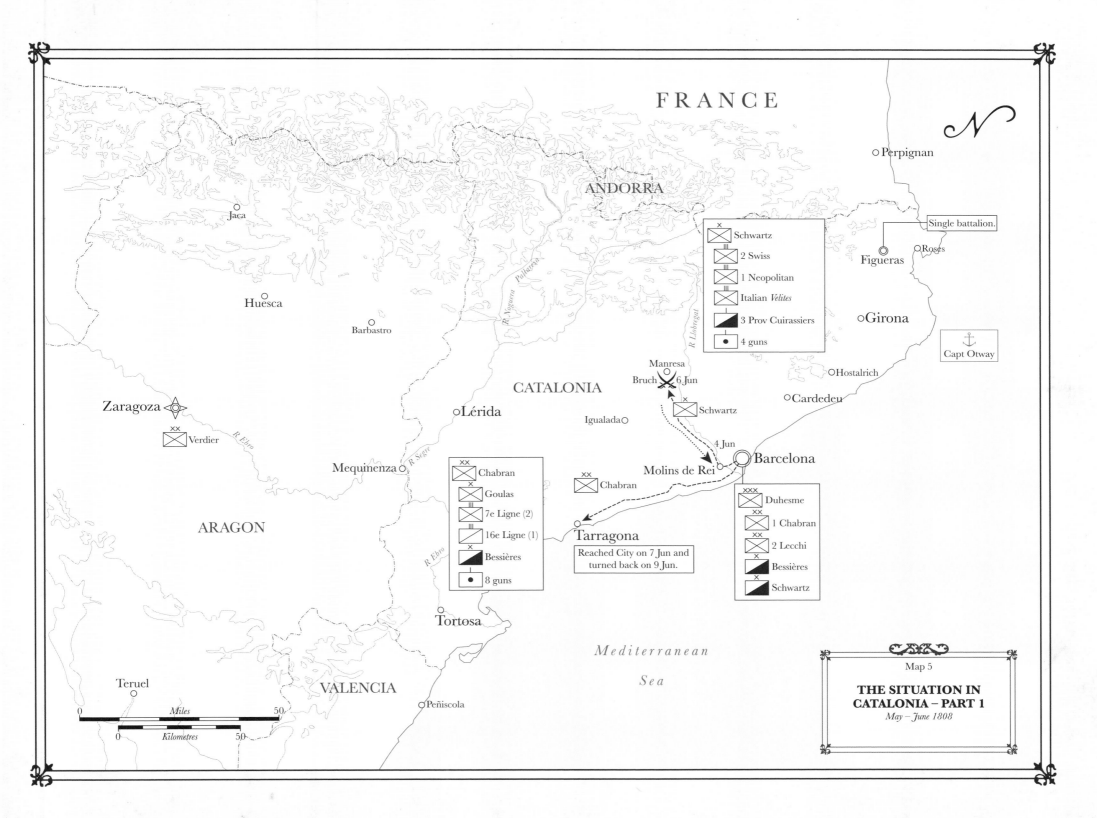

FRANCE

N

Perpignan

ANDORRA

Jaca

Single battalion.

Schwartz

2 Swiss

1 Neopolitan

Italian *Velites*

3 Prov Cuirassiers

4 guns

Figueras

Roses

Huesca

Barbastro

R. Niguera

Pallaresa

R. Llobregat

Girona

Capt Otway

Hostalrich

CATALONIA

Manresa

Bruch 6 Jun

Cardedeu

Zaragoza

Lérida

Igualada

Schwartz

Verdier

4 Jun

R. Ebro

R. Segre

Mequinenza

Barcelona

Molins de Rei

Chabran

Goulas

7e Ligne (2)

16e Ligne (1)

Bessières

8 guns

Chabran

Duhesme

1 Chabran

2 Lecchi

Bessières

Schwartz

R. Ebro

ARAGON

Tarragona

Reached City on 7 Jun and
turned back on 9 Jun.

Tortosa

Mediterranean

Sea

Map 5

**THE SITUATION IN
CATALONIA – PART 1**
May – June 1808

Teruel

Miles

0   50

VALENCIA

0   50

Kilometres

Peñiscola

determination and vigour of the *somatenes*, who were supported by a small force from Lérida and four guns. A somewhat mortified Chabran returned to Barcelona, the first part of Duhesme's plans having failed miserably.

As Chabran's force re-entered the city, Duhesme received confirmation that his lines of communication with Figueras were cut. The *somatenes* had driven in the French battalion within the citadel and they were besieging the place. Duhesme acted swiftly establishing a force of about 6,000, which he led personally; they departed Barcelona on 17 June and quickly encountered swarms of *somatenes* at Mongat, only 10km outside the city. These were swiftly swept aside and he pushed on, only to find his path blocked again at Mataro. This time a more deliberate attack was required by Milosewitz's Italian Brigade, which once successful provided the perfect excuse to sack the small town and murder a significant number of citizens. The next morning they moved on and were at the gates of Girona by 20 June. Duhesme had no siege artillery and could not hope to engage the city or begin to capture all the surrounding forts and redoubts (see map 13). Instead, he chose to send a small, almost token force, to the Capuchin Fort and assembled the balance of his men for a direct attack on one of the city gates. He rather disgracefully tried to trick the Spanish defenders into opening the gates under the pretence of a white flag, but the ploy failed along with the attack and the heavier garrison artillery mounted on the city walls soon silenced the French field guns. Unperturbed, that night Duhesme attempted to storm the city walls under the cover of darkness: Schwartz's Italian battalions tried to force entry with ladders at one of the bastions; a few reached the rampart but were soon driven back. A final attempt a few hours later received similar treatment prompting Duhesme to break camp and return to Barcelona. Within hours of arriving at the city his reconnaissance teams reported that about 8,000–10,000 *somatenes* had gathered to the south and were preparing to attack. On 30 June

Chabran, with Bessières's[16] cavalry, was sent out to deal with the threat; he succeeded in turning the flank of the Catalans, who fled to the nearby mountains having lost their artillery and many men. This brief success was the only glimmer of hope in a dismal month for the French commander in Catalonia. A subsequent foray a few days later to disperse another concentration of *somatenes* to the north once again ended in failure. Throughout the month, Duhesme had been sending despatches to Napoleon at Bayonne appealing for support; the latter despatches were unable to get through and Bonaparte had no idea about the fate of the garrison at Figueras.

Napoleon had greater concerns than the war in Catalonia; nevertheless he resolved to provide an additional division under one of his aides-de-camp, a certain General Reille whom he supplied with a force of about 8,000 men. None of these reinforcements were veterans; they were to be drawn together from south of the Alps and Piedmont, which was to take some time. By 5 July Reille had received only two regiments, but considered this sufficient to raise the siege of the French battalion at Figueras, which he achieved by 6 July. The additional reinforcements continued to arrive over the coming days and were sent forward to join Reille at Figueras. By 11 July, with about 3,500 men available, he decided to attack the fishing village of Roses, defended by no more than 400 *miqueletes* and a battery of guns. However, when the capable French commander deployed his forces he soon discovered that his rear was decidedly vulnerable to the 4,000–5,000 *somatenes* who had been assembled from the Catalan coast by a retired infantry captain, Don Juan Claros. In addition HMS *Montague*, which was operating off the Bay of Roses, landed a detachment of British marines directly into the citadel. Reille withdrew in haste, pursued by Claros and his ad hoc force, which proceeded to kill or capture about 200 of the mainly Italian and Swiss force. Communications with Duhesme remained cut and both French commanders were beginning to realize just how difficult it would be to crack the Catalan nut.

---

16   The brother of General Bessières, the Duke of Istria.

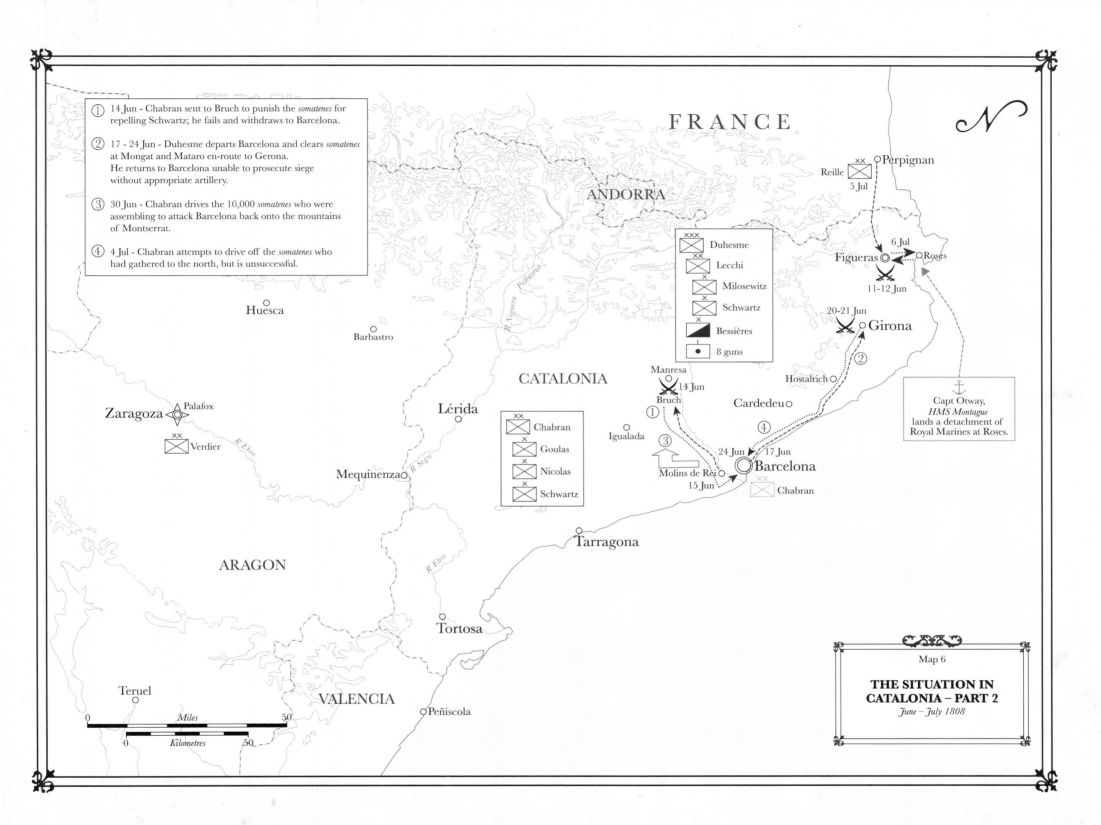

FRANCE

ANDORRA

① 14 Jun - Chabran sent to Bruch to punish the *somatenes* for repelling Schwartz; he fails and withdraws to Barcelona.

② 17 - 24 Jun - Duhesme departs Barcelona and clears *somatenes* at Mongat and Mataro en-route to Gerona. He returns to Barcelona unable to prosecute siege without appropriate artillery.

③ 30 Jun - Chabran drives the 10,000 *somatenes* who were assembling to attack Barcelona back onto the mountains of Montserrat.

④ 4 Jul - Chabran attempts to drive off the *somatenes* who had gathered to the north, but is unsuccessful.

N

Perpignan

Reille

5 Jul

6 Jul

Roses

Figueras

11-12 Jun

Duhesme

Lecchi

Milosewitz

Schwartz

Bessières

8 guns

20-21 Jun

Girona

Huesca

Barbastro

CATALONIA

Manresa

14 Jun

Bruch

Hostalrich

Lérida

Cardedeu

Capt Otway,
HMS Montague
lands a detachment of
Royal Marines at Roses.

Zaragoza

Palafox

Verdier

Chabran

Goulas

Nicolas

Schwartz

Igualada

①

③

④

24 Jun

17 Jun

R Ebro

Mequinenza

R Segre

Molins de Rei

15 Jun

Barcelona

Chabran

ARAGON

R Ebro

Tarragona

Teruel

VALENCIA

Peñiscola

Tortosa

Miles   50
0

0   Kilometres   50

Map 6

**THE SITUATION IN
CATALONIA – PART 2**

June – July 1808

Chapter 4

THE FIRST SIEGE OF ZARAGOZA, 15 JUNE–14 AUGUST 1808

Having driven away the Spanish outposts, Lefebvre-Desnouettes appeared before the city on 15 June. Possessing only a field battery, a formal siege was out of the question and with the gates wide open and thinly defended he elected to assault the city in much the same way that Moncey was to some days later at Valencia (see page 36). A simultaneous attack was undertaken on 16 June by one French brigade at the gates of Portillo and Carmen (map 7, point 1) while the Polish cavalry supported by one regiment of the Polish infantry[1] attacked the gate adjacent to the Convent of Santa Engracia (map 7, point 2). Despite some ingress into the city, both attacks were to fail. A second attempt later in the day produced a similar result despite the fact that the French had succeeded in joining forces within the walls. But once their momentum diminished, the Spanish rallied (at the bullring) and evicted the weary and dispirited attackers.

The determination and aggression of the local inhabitants had completely taken the French by surprise. Having swept aside the force under Palafox[2] at Alagon on 14 June, they expected to capture the city with ease. During the night of 14 June Palafox had retreated back to the city with the remnants of his beaten force, but departed quickly thereafter under the premise of raising a new force to cut the French lines of communication. The bulk of the recent recruits to the Army of Aragon remained within the city, and, combined with an additional 4,000–5,000 armed civilians, provided a conglomerate body of about 10,000 souls who paid little heed to orders or organization. Encouraged by the news of events on 16 June, Palafox linked up with the Baron de Versage who had raised two new regiments to the south and resolved to lift the siege of Zaragoza. Combined with his small regular force and the 2,000 or so armed locals,[3] he established a body of about 4,000 men; 350 of whom were mounted. Lefebvre-Desnouettes, on hearing of Palafox's force and intentions, preempted any offensive action by the Spanish by detaching Colonel Chlopicki with the Polish Regiment, a French battalion, a squadron of Polish light horse and four guns. They fell upon the unsuspecting Aragonese at Epila on the night of 23 June and completely routed them. Palafox was badly shaken by this second defeat in open battle and decided to return to the city with the remnants of his force, about 1,000 men, to reinforce the defence against the ongoing siege. This increased the number of defenders to 11,000, but more significantly provided

a leader and chain of command, which was to prove invaluable over the coming weeks. However, before Palafox reached to the city (on 1 July) the French reinforcements had already arrived and the situation had altered considerably. General Verdier had appeared at the end of June with about 3,000 men and, being the senior of the generals, assumed command of the siege operation. Most significantly, he had escorted a siege train that had been established at Pamplona and consisted of 46 pieces of ordnance. His first act was to remove the Spaniards from Monte Torrero, a hill feature to the south-west, which dominated the city and housed the city magazines. These subsequently proved an invaluable source of building materials for the parallels, gun pits and a bridge, which the French engineers constructed and deployed upstream some days later.

The initial breaching battery positions were dug in on the slopes of Monte Torrero and supported by a few more batteries to the west of the city near the Moorish castle of Aljafería (map 7, points 3–6). The batteries were started on 28 June and were armed two days later with all 46 guns. The French gunners opened the barrage at midnight and continued bombarding the city for the next 24 hours, causing considerable structural damage to the outer walls and to the castle of Aljafería. The following morning, somewhat impatiently, Verdier launched an all-out assault on the south and western approaches to the city with all his available infantry in six columns. About 10,000 men attacked the entry points, which had been badly damaged during the preliminary bombardment, but none managed to secure lodgement. The fiercest fighting was around the gates of Sancho and Portillo and it was at this latter point that Agustina Zaragoza (purportedly) ran forward to fire an artillery gun loaded with canister at the head of the French column a few feet away. The shock of the blast halted the French attack and rallied the defenders; Agustina's courage and example earned her an instant commission in the artillery and a place in the hearts and history books of the people of Aragon. 'Agustina demonstrated very similar prowess to [that] of María Pita in her action against the English at la Coruña in 1589; this action was also rewarded in a similar fashion, when Felipe II awarded her the rank and salary of a second lieutenant, Palafox provided similar remuneration in the guise of a military grade and a pension for life.'[4]

Verdier lost about 200 men in this failed assault and concluded, somewhat reluctantly, that the city would only fall through regular siege. He immediately gave orders to extend the parallels up to the city walls and to capture the outer fortifications of the convents of San José, Capuchin and Trinitarios. He had succeeded in capturing all three structures by 24 July and then began the task of linking them through a series of additional parallels and the construction of the breaching batteries (see map 8). The main battery positions were to the south, with a deception battery (and subsequent attack) planned at the Portillo gate. The heavy guns, mortars and howitzers began their unrelenting bombardment on 4 August; within hours the Spanish guns had been silenced and numerous breaches had been formed along the walls, particularly around the convent of Santa Engracia. Shortly after noon, Verdier gave the order for the three columns to attack, releasing the 13 battalions[5] to assault the three main breaches (points 1 to 3). All three attacks succeeded in penetrating the outer walls and made considerable ingress within the city

---

1   The 1st Regiment of the Vistula, two battalions.

2   He was wounded during the battle.

3   Which, according to Oman, included a company of 80 armed Capuchin friars and a body of mounted smugglers.

4   Toreno, *Guerra de la Independencia, El 2 de Mayo de 1808*, vol. II, p.100.

5   Nine French and four Polish.

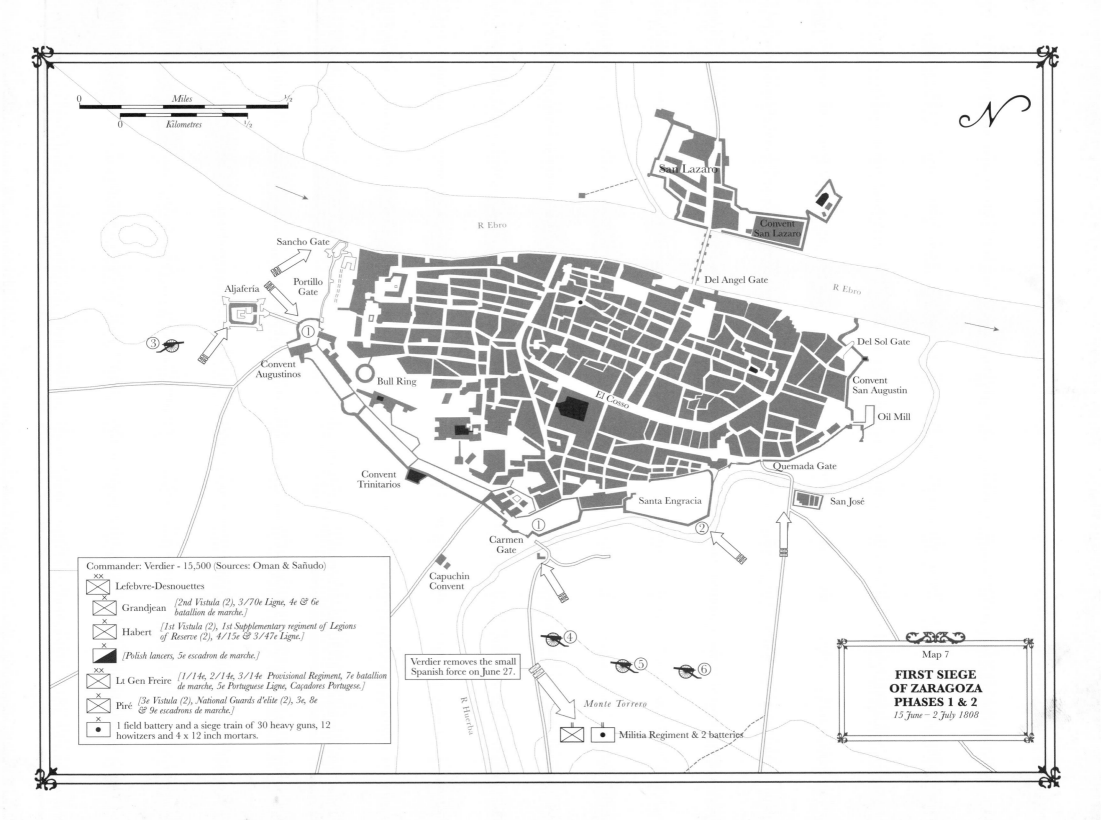

Miles
0 ½

Kilometres
0 ½

N

San Lazaro

Convent
San Lazaro

R Ebro

R Ebro

Del Angel Gate

Sancho Gate

Portillo
Gate

Aljaferia

③

Convent
Augustinos

Bull Ring

El Cosso

Del Sol Gate

Convent
San Augustin

Oil Mill

①

Convent
Trinitarios

Quemada Gate

Santa Engracia

②

San José

Carmen
Gate

①

Capuchin
Convent

Commander: Verdier - 15,500 (Sources: Oman & Sañudo)

Lefebvre-Desnouettes

Grandjean   *[2nd Vistula (2), 3/70e Ligne, 4e & 6e batallion de marche.]*

Habert   *[1st Vistula (2), 1st Supplementary regiment of Legions of Reserve (2), 4/15e & 3/47e Ligne.]*

[Polish lancers, 5e escadron de marche.]

Lt Gen Freire   *[1/14e, 2/14e, 3/14e Provisional Regiment, 7e batallion de marche, 5e Portuguese Ligne, Caçadores Portugese.]*

Piré   *[3e Vistula (2), National Guards d'elite (2), 3e, 8e & 9e escadrons de marche.]*

1 field battery and a siege train of 30 heavy guns, 12 howitzers and 4 x 12 inch mortars.

Verdier removes the small
Spanish force on June 27.

④

⑤   ⑥

R Huerba

Monte Torrero

Militia Regiment & 2 batteries

Map 7

**FIRST SIEGE
OF ZARAGOZA
PHASES 1 & 2**
15 June – 2 July 1808

itself, but they soon became embroiled in ferocious street-to-street and house-to-house fighting. These French troops had never experienced this form of combat before and they were soon taking considerable losses from Spanish muskets firing down on them from upper windows and rooftops. After some considerable time (at least) one column made it to the El Cosso (the city centre) but the French attacks had already lost momentum. Verdier tried to rally his men and push on to the gate Del Angel and the Puente de Piedra and thereby cut the city in half. In the process, he was wounded, and the French soldiers soon became diverted by the prospect of plunder and all manner of other distractions.

By nightfall the French had fallen back across the city and only retained a slim wedge running from El Cosso to the gates of Santa Engracia and Carmen. Losses on the French side were considerable: at least 500 killed and three times that number wounded, one-sixth of the force. Losses amongst the Zaragozanos were about the same but many of those casualties resulted from the preliminary bombardment and not from the street fighting that ensued. A restless night followed during which both sides prepared their defences, sometimes within a few metres of each other. Most of the buildings in the French-controlled area of the city were in ruins; in the area held by the local inhabitants, houses were 'mouse-holed' to provide communication and avoid exposure to the deadly musket and cannon fire that dominated the streets. Both sides were by now too exhausted to continue fighting and a standoff ensued, lasting a number of days during which conditions deteriorated rapidly on both sides of the divide.

Verdier's forces were overstretched and had been unable to effectively blockade the city leaving the suburb of San Lazaro open throughout the siege. On the day of the French assault a large relief column had arrived from Catalonia consisting of about 4,000 men[6] and some badly needed supplies. Palafox had ridden out to join this force and some supplies were brought back the next day, but Palafox remained outside the perimeter and elected to attack Piré's Brigade, which was functioning to the north of the river Ebro, and therefore posed a threat to Spanish lines of communication and operations in the area. On 8 August, Palafox attacked this inferior French force and drove it back to the river; at which point Verdier ordered Piré to vacate the northern bank. At this juncture news began to filter through of extraordinary events at Bailén, and both Verdier and Palafox knew that this reversal for the French would have national consequences. Lifting the siege at Zaragoza was only a matter of time. Verdier continued to relentlessly bombard the city but on 13 August the French destroyed their defensive positions inside the city, blew up their stockpiles of ammunition and spiked or destroyed a total of 54 guns, mortars and howitzers,[7] and the next day, Verdier marched the remnants of his force westwards.

Notwithstanding the incredible news from Bailén, the Zaragozanos 'had accomplished a rare feat: almost unaided by regular troops, almost destitute of trained artillerymen and engineers, they had held at bay, a force which Napoleon at the commencement of the siege would have supposed to be equal to the task of conquering not only Aragon, but the whole eastern side of the Iberian Peninsula.'[8] 'This series of reverses did much to soften the impact of Napoleon's initial success: already, indeed, patriot Spain's fecund propagandists were starting to claim that the heroic Spanish people had routed the veterans of Austerlitz and Jena. At this point nothing could have been more embarrassing for the emperor.'[9]

---

6   Two regular battalions and about 3,000 armed peasants.

7   Many of which were salvaged and repaired by the Spanish subsequently.

8   Oman, *History of the Peninsular War*, vol. I, p.162.

9   Esdaile, *The Peninsular War, A New History*, p.69.

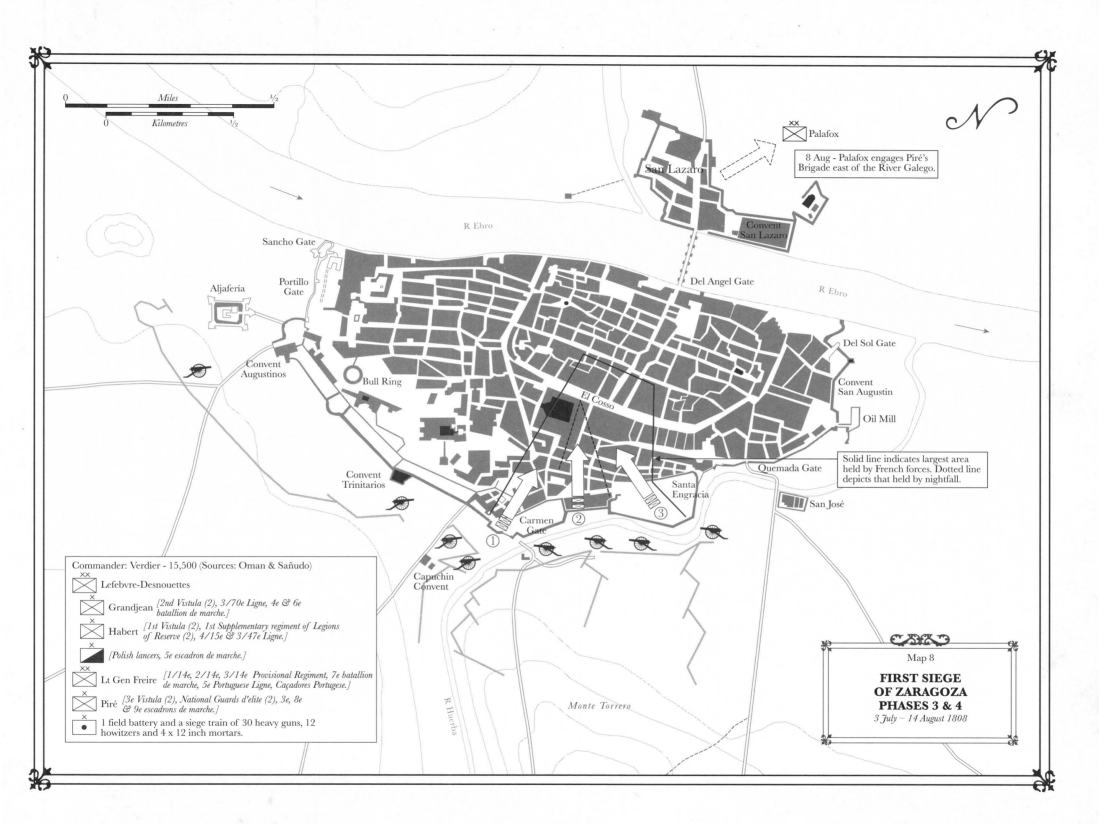

Miles
0 .... ½

Kilometres
0 .... ½

N

San Lazaro

XX
☒ Palafox

8 Aug - Palafox engages Piré's Brigade east of the River Galego.

Convent San Lazaro

R Ebro

R Ebro

Sancho Gate

Del Angel Gate

Aljafería

Portillo Gate

Del Sol Gate

Convent Augustinos

Bull Ring

Convent San Augustin

Oil Mill

El Cosso

Convent Trinitarios

Quemada Gate

Solid line indicates largest area held by French forces. Dotted line depicts that held by nightfall.

Santa Engracia

① Carmen Gate

②

③

San José

Capuchin Convent

Commander: Verdier - 15,500 (Sources: Oman & Sañudo)

XX
☒ Lefebvre-Desnouettes

X
☒ Grandjean *[2nd Vistula (2), 3/70e Ligne, 4e & 6e batallion de marche.]*

X
☒ Habert *[1st Vistula (2), 1st Supplementary regiment of Legions of Reserve (2), 4/15e & 3/47e Ligne.]*

X
◥ *[Polish lancers, 5e escadron de marche.]*

XX
☒ Lt Gen Freire *[1/14e, 2/14e, 3/14e Provisional Regiment, 7e batallion de marche, 5e Portuguese Ligne, Caçadores Portugese.]*

X
☒ Piré *[3e Vistula (2), National Guards d'elite (2), 3e, 8e & 9e escadrons de marche.]*

X
• 1 field battery and a siege train of 30 heavy guns, 12 howitzers and 4 x 12 inch mortars.

R Huerba

Monte Torrero

Map 8

FIRST SIEGE OF ZARAGOZA PHASES 3 & 4

3 July – 14 August 1808

Chapter 5

OPERATIONS IN THE NORTH: THE BATTLE OF MEDINA DE RIÓSECO

In Galicia, Filanghieri's[1] replacement was a young officer, Brigadier-General Joaquín Blake,[2] the grandson of a Scottish Jacobite who had joined the Spanish service. His rapid reorganization of the Galician army enabled him to put 25,000 men in the field[3] with another 10,000 in training. By 23 June, Blake had moved this force to the borders of Galicia and Leon with the purpose of establishing a defensive posture along the passes above Astorga. However, his intentions were to be transformed by the Galician Junta who had been pressurized by Cuesta into a union of Blake's force with that of his own. The Asturians had also been invited to participate but they, like Blake, were dubious of the union and provided just a single regiment.[4] The two armies joined at Villalpando on 10 July and Cuesta made it quite clear that his rank and seniority entitled him to overall command of the combined force. Blake was under clear orders from the Galician Junta not to second his position or his force and the two generals failed to resolve their differences on the issue. To his credit Cuesta, following his defeat at Cabezon, had not been deterred from taking the fight to the French, but Blake could not accept the sense in fighting a pitched battle on the plains of Leon. Much against Blake's judgement Cuesta proceeded to march east to Valladolid and, after much debate, they reached a compromise which consisted of detaching the Galician 3rd Division at Benavente to cover the approach to Galicia.[5] As it turned out, however, this decision achieved little more than to deprive the main force of its reserve at the impending battle.

In Madrid Savary had predicted just such an easterly move by Cuesta and had already directed reinforcements to move towards Burgos to assist Bessières, whose force was stretched to the limit covering the additional defensive tasks in Navarre, Aragon and Santander. These reinforcements consisted of Mouton's Division, which had arrived from Bayonne with ten veteran battalions fresh from Germany, as well as one regiment of the Imperial Guard and three cavalry squadrons from Madrid. Furthermore, elements of Merle's Division, including the commander himself, were withdrawn from their tasks in Santander and, on 9 July, they marched to Palencia where they linked up with Lasalle's Cavalry Brigade. This reorganization and subsequent concentration provided Bessières with a force of nearly 14,000 men; still well below the combined Spanish total of 22,000. The French nevertheless enjoyed considerable superiority in cavalry and artillery and, with the arrival of Mouton, a number of weathered veterans.

At last light on 13 July, Lasalle's light cavalry reconnaissance came into contact with some of the Spanish outposts deployed in advance of the town of Medina de Rióseco. It was not a strong position, as it offered no protection from flanking manoeuvre, and any retreat through the town of Medina was certain to be problematic. Cuesta's exact plans for the engagement at Medina are unclear and there is considerable confusion over the deployment of the Spanish forces.[6] 'Blake had not occupied the ground until after the initial skirmish line – the two vanguard half battalions and the Headquarters Guard – had encountered French tirailleurs. It was only then that the main body began, with painful slowness, to occupy the Páramo de Val de Cuevas, [see map 10]. The situation occurred, they believe, because Blake was marching on a different road to Cuesta and, like that general, had no earlier knowledge of Bessières's approach, thinking him to be nearer Valladolid. Thus his purported unanticipated occupation of the Páramo was due more to force of necessity than the inadequacies of his colleague.'[7] There is another 'logical explanation for the Spanish general's flagrant negligence in that he was concerned about the right flank being turned'.[8] Furthermore, 'we should not forget their enormous disinformation about the enemy troops and their approach routes, and it follows that there was a fear that the imperial forces could appear on the Valladolid road. At some stage, during Blake's redeployment, Cuesta requested support from the Galician commander who sent him the 4th Division.'[9] The result, irrespective of the circumstance, was that there was a gap of some 2km between the two groups of Spanish forces; arrangements that negated any mutual support, complicated communication and invited attack.

Bessières deployed Mouton to the right of the road and Merle to the left and then commenced his advance to probe the Spanish strengths and dispositions. Mouton pushed his cavalry forward and, from the northern heights of the Páramo, they were able to see Cuesta's force deployed in front of the town of Medina. The gap between the two forces was now clear to Bessières, who was quick to appreciate the geographical and tactical weakness of the Spanish

---

[1] Contrary to many British texts, Filanghieri was not murdered in May, but on 24 June 1808, after Blake had superseded him.

[2] Blake was promoted to Lieutenant General but as head of the Army of Galicia, was *ipso facto* the Captain-General of this province.

[3] However, as many as 9,000 were recent recruits from the countryside, with less than a month's training, poorly armed and with no uniforms.

[4] Regimiento de Corvadonga.

[5] The Galician Junta had already held back in the 2nd Galician Division at the Manzanal pass for the protection of the region.

[6] Oman is very critical of Cuesta's deployment while Esdaile, *The Peninsular War, A New History*, p.72, suggests that Cuesta had deployed initially to face the threat from the south, which is entirely possible. Partridge & Oliver, *Battle Studies in the Peninsula May 1808–January 1809*, state the position held by many modern Spanish researchers, and it is this version that it utilized.

[7] Partridge & Oliver, *Battle Studies in the Peninsula May 1808–January 1809*, p.48.

[8] Sañudo, Stampa & Arcón, *Batallas Campales de 1808*, p.34.

[9] Toreno, *Guerra de la Independencia, El 2 de Mayo de 1808*, vol II. p.63.

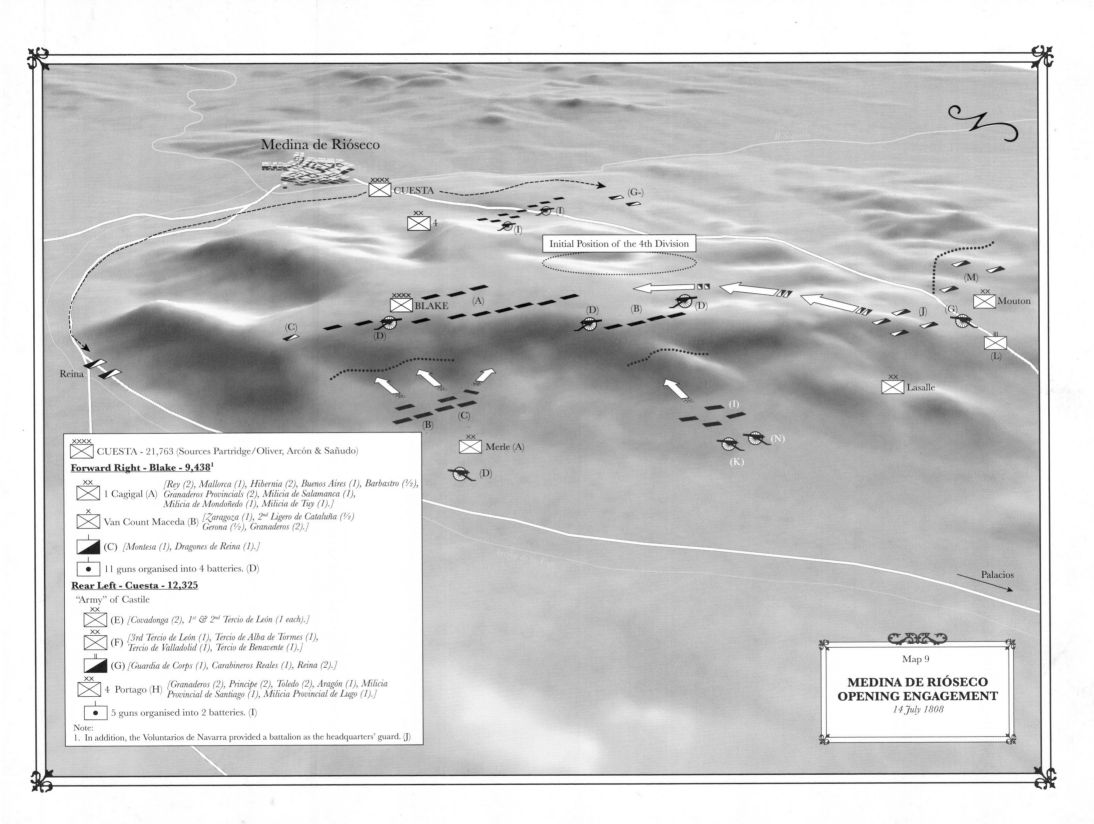

Medina de Rióseco

CUESTA

4

Initial Position of the 4th Division

(G-)

(I)

(I)

BLAKE (A) (D) (B) (M)

(C) (D) (D) (J) (G) Mouton

Reina (III) (L)

Lasalle

(B) (C) (I) (N)

Merle (A) (K)

(D)

(D)

Palacios

CUESTA - 21,763 (Sources Partridge/Oliver, Arcón & Sañudo)

Forward Right - Blake - 9,438[1]

1 Cagigal (A)   *[Rey (2), Mallorca (1), Hibernia (2), Buenos Aires (1), Barbastro (½), Granaderos Provincials (2), Milicia de Salamanca (1), Milicia de Mondoñedo (1), Milicia de Tuy (1).]*

Van Count Maceda (B)   *[Zaragoza (1), 2ⁿᵈ Ligero de Cataluña (½) Gerona (½), Granaderos (2).]*

(C)   *[Montesa (1), Dragones de Reina (1).]*

11 guns organised into 4 batteries. (D)

Rear Left - Cuesta - 12,325

"Army" of Castile

(E)   *[Covadonga (2), 1ˢᵗ & 2ⁿᵈ Tercio de León (1 each).]*

(F)   *[3rd Tercio de León (1), Tercio de Alba de Tormes (1), Tercio de Valladolid (1), Tercio de Benavente (1).]*

(G)   *[Guardia de Corps (1), Carabineros Reales (1), Reina (2).]*

4 Portago (H)   *[Granaderos (2), Principe (2), Toledo (2), Aragón (1), Milicia Provincial de Santiago (1), Milicia Provincial de Lugo (1).]*

5 guns organised into 2 batteries. (I)

Note:
1. In addition, the Voluntarios de Navarra provided a battalion as the headquarters' guard. (J)

Map 9

MEDINA DE RIÓSECO OPENING ENGAGEMENT
14 July 1808

position. He chose to contain Cuesta and envelop Blake. Infantry were sent in to clear the lower hills of Spanish skirmishers, and then Bessières moved two batteries of guns on to the forward edge of the Tesón de Monclín, support by Sabathier's Brigade, which was to provide protection to the French gunners and serve as a distraction for the movement of D'Armagnac and Ducos's brigades in the execution of their left flanking manoeuvre. The French guns ruthlessly pounded the Spanish positions despite being subject to intense and accurate counter-battery fire from the two Galician batteries positioned in front of Maceda's Vanguard Brigade. D'Armagnac had the farthest to move, having been allocated the left of line with Ducos in the centre. Sabathier's attack on Maceda's Vanguard Brigade and the fire of the French artillery reserve did little to mask their approach in the open ground to the front of Blake's position.

'The Spaniards made a brilliant defence. Although more than half the army was composed of new levies, their enthusiasm and courage, operating in lieu of instruction and experience, left victory a long time doubtful.'[10] For some time the two forces exchanged fire and both the Spanish infantry and artillery were holding their own, but as this exchange was playing out, Lasalle moved Colbert's Cavalry Brigade up the mule track undetected. Once Colbert was in position, Bessières ordered Merle and Lasalle to release their infantry and, once in motion, the order was given to Colbert to charge into the gap between the Spanish armies and to swing left behind Maceda and into Cagigal's flank. The shock of 22e Chasseurs crashing into the side of the preoccupied Spanish infantry was overwhelming and instant; the regiment of Buenos Aires broke, disrupting the regiment on their right, which in turn also lost cohesion and sought refuge on the next battalion. Before long the defence line, which had performed so well, had lost organization and with Merle's infantry pressing home their attack from the front, Blake was forced to retreat. The Headquarters Guard formed square and were able to cover the withdrawal but not without considerable loss. 'Additionally, the retreating Spanish battalions would likely have offered some resistance to pursuit even if only in an attempt at self-preservation … it is doubtful that there would have been quite so many still with the colours after a rout with cavalry pursuit had this not been so.'[11] 'Blake performed prodigies of valour and covered the retreat upon Benavente,'[12] and although it is true that some guns were lost, these were left at the back of the Páramo de Val de Cuevas for want of civilian drivers who had fled with their mounts. 'Blake himself states in his diary that the feebleness displayed by one unit (Buenos Aires), "that they were scared just looking at the approaching cavalry and transmitted that disorder and confusion to adjacent

battalions". However, this rather simplistic explanation is not very convincing and rather conveniently heaps the blame for the unfolding collapse and disaster on a single unit. By so doing it provides a convenient scapegoat.'[13]

Bessières left Lasalle and some of Sabathier's men to see off Blake while he turned his attention to Cuesta's force. While the attack on the Páramo de Val de Cuevas was playing out, Mouton had already advanced in dead ground towards Cuesta's lines, with two extended rows of tirailleurs (from the 4e Léger and 15e Ligne) who pushed well forward and exchanged bickering fire with the Spanish skirmishers deployed by Cuesta. Bessières quickly dispensed with this foreplay and redirected his troops. Mouton took the right, Merle moved to his left, and the Imperial Guard formed the reserve, with the three squadrons of Imperial Guard cavalry combining with the strong line of tirailleurs to lead the advance. No sooner had this second French attack begun to move forward when they were checked in astonishment at the sight of the Spanish advancing uphill to meet them. The four Spanish cavalry squadrons were sent ahead to clear the tirailleurs, which they achieved with considerable composure, but then gave way when engaged by the French cavalry. The 4th Galician Division, following behind the cavalry, fought with considerable valour and with some success[14] but the French reorganization subsequent to Blake's withdrawal, provided them a considerable numerical supremacy in this part of the field. A cavalry charge by the Gendarmes d'Elite, of the Guards Cavalry, finally broke the deadlock[15] and Portago's infantry began to fall back onto the Army of Castile formed up in front of the town. Cuesta ordered two battalions[16] to cover the Army's retreat, which was achieved with few losses. It appears that Bessières had been caught off guard by Cuesta's offensive action and when the Spanish elected to break contact they were able to do so almost intact: although it must be stated that the French soldiers were exhausted, many having been in combat continually for nearly five hours.

The two Spanish commanders met some miles to the west and parted on acrimonious terms; Cuesta's Castilian army having suffered little but Blake's force had been reduced by 3,000 men, lost ten field guns and several colours. Bessières had removed the threat to cut the vital lines of communication between Madrid and Bayonne, and Napoleon was content with the situation. He was however, unaware of events that were unfolding in Andalusia.

---

10 Sarrazin, *History of the War in Spain and Portugal*, p.39.

11 Partridge & Oliver, *Battle Studies in the Peninsula May 1808-January 1809*, p.55.

12 Sarrazin, *History of the War in Spain and Portugal*, p.39.

13 Sañudo, Stampa & Arcón, *Batallas Campales de 1808*, p.34.

14 At one stage they captured a half-battery of the Imperial Guard artillery.

15 This was a trend that was to be repeated continuously during the war in engagements between the Spanish and French. The superiority of the French cavalry mounts and troopers was a significant factor in virtually every engagement.

16 The 3rd Tercio de Voluntarios de Leon and a second unknown battalion.

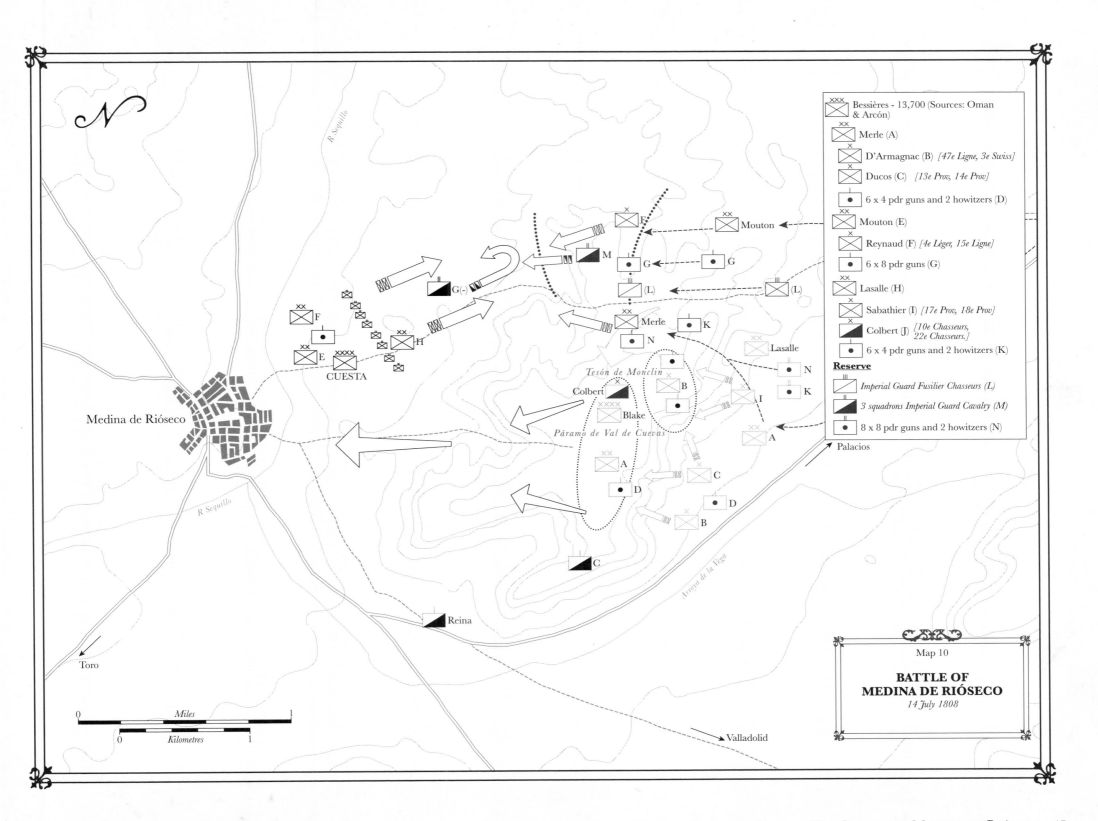

N

Bessières - 13,700 (Sources: Oman & Arcón)

Merle (A)

D'Armagnac (B) *[47e Ligne, 3e Swiss]*

Ducos (C) *[13e Prov, 14e Prov]*

6 x 4 pdr guns and 2 howitzers (D)

Mouton (E)

Reynaud (F) *[4e Léger, 15e Ligne]*

6 x 8 pdr guns (G)

Lasalle (H)

Sabathier (I) *[17e Prov, 18e Prov]*

Colbert (J) *[10e Chasseurs, 22e Chasseurs.]*

6 x 4 pdr guns and 2 howitzers (K)

Reserve

Imperial Guard Fusilier Chasseurs (L)

3 squadrons Imperial Guard Cavalry (M)

8 x 8 pdr guns and 2 howitzers (N)

R. Sequillo

Mouton

E

M

G(-)

G

G

(L)

(L)

F

H

Merle

K

N

E

CUESTA

Lasalle

N

K

Medina de Ríóseco

Tesón de Monclin

Colbert

Blake

Páramo de Val de Cuevas

B

I

A

A

D

C

D

B

Palacios

R. Sequillo

C

Arroya de la Vega

Reina

Toro

0   *Miles*   1

0   *Kilometres*   1

Map 10

BATTLE OF MEDINA DE RIÓSECO

14 July 1808

Valladolid

Chapter 6

CAPITULATION AT BAILÉN: THE GREATEST SPANISH VICTORY OF THE WAR

Having spent overly long at Córdoba, Dupont was now keen to return to the relative safety of the Sierra Morena and make contact with the French army in Madrid. He was however, loath to leave the area without appropriate orders, more especially as he had failed to accomplish his original mission. In Madrid, Savary had become increasingly concerned for Dupont's safety, and after three weeks he ordered Vedel to take his division south. The union of Vedel and Dupont had been achieved by 27 June; the arrival of an additional 6,000 men now reestablished Dupont's confidence and he decided to remain in the area, and began making plans to engage Castaños, who was massing the Army of Andalusia to the south. This Spanish army numbered some 34,000, with 2,600 cavalry, but many of the regiments were newly raised and their soldiers poorly trained. However, in the time it had taken Dupont to cross the Sierra Morena and complete his initial moves against Andalusia, Castaños had beaten his raw recruits into shape. They were organized into four divisions and two flying columns, one commanded by Colonel Cruz Murgeon, the second by the Conde de Valdecañas. Both columns were to move north and south respectively and outflank the French force and cut their lines of communication and retreat. As it transpired, neither actually achieved their aims; Cruz Murgeon fell upon Dupont's baggage train during the forthcoming battle and Valdecañas took and held Linares on 16 July.[1]

Dupont wanted to assert himself in the region but was guarded against resuming an offensive posture and commenced proceedings, somewhat tentatively, by ordering one of Vedel's brigades to move to Jaén, the provincial capital. Cassagnes was tasked with the mission and, after sacking the city on 1 July, the brigade returned north of the river and rejoined Vedel at Bailén. During this excursion the remainder of Dupont's forces had lingered in a defensive line along the river Guadalquivir, stretching from Andujar to Mengibar and, despite the arrival of Gobert's Division[2] from Madrid in the hiatus, the entire front was simply too long to defend effectively. Dupont

positioned his main force at Andujar, leaving Vedel at Bailén and ordered Gobert to remain at La Carolina, securing the passes to the Sierra Morena and the road to Madrid. Vedel later created an ad hoc brigade under Liger-Belair (with two battalions of the 1e Légion de Reserve) to cover the ferry crossing at Mengibar, fourteen kilometres south of the main position at Bailén.

On 11 July, at the small town of Porcuña, Castaños outlined his plan in response to this French deployment. He would undertake a diversionary attack with two divisions against Dupont at Andujar; Coupigny's 2nd Division was to cross the Guadalquivir by the ford at Villa Nueva while Reding, with the 1st Division,[3] was to seize the ferry at Mengibar. Once across the Guadalquivir both divisions were to march on Bailén. Manoeuvres commenced on 13 July with Castaños waiting for both his divisional commanders to be in position before stirring to attract and retain Dupont's attention. The next morning Reding appeared to the south of the village of Mengibar and drove in the outlying piquets of Liger-Belair, which withdrew north of the river. Reding then spent the rest of the day in reconnaissance of the area while Dupont, concerned at the news of Reding's Division, and the threat it posed to his southern flank, ordered Gobert to decamp from the passes at La Carolina and move his division down to Bailén in support of Vedel.

'Early on 15 July, Castaños occupied the heights overlooking Andujar, while the French artillery tried to impede them. At the same time, two French battalions from Villanueva de la Reyna sought to cut the lines of communication of the second division with those of Castaños and Reding.'[4] Coupigny had simultaneously descended on the lightly held ford at Villa Nueva, and Reding crossed the Guadalquivir with similar resolve at Mengibar. He was pushing back the infantry of Liger-Belair, when Vedel arrived from Bailén (map 11, point 1) in support of his subordinate. Engaged with a formation of similar strength, Reding decided to withdraw south of the river, giving up the ground he had already secured. All along the line the French were holding the Spanish but the defenders were about to make a costly mistake. Dupont, having been taken completely by Castaños's feint, ordered Vedel to send immediate reinforcements to his area. Vedel complied with the order, sending not just the two battalions as requested, but his entire division (map 11, point 2).

The next morning Reding, sensing that the French line had weakened, repeated his probing attacks across the river Guadalquivir, prompting Liger-Belair to despatch urgent requests for support from Gobert. However, Gobert was only able to come to his aid with three battalions and two squadrons of cavalry, and this force arrived too late in the day to make a substantial difference (map 11, point 3). Gobert was mortally wounded during the engagement and the entire group under Liger-Belair and Dufour[5] fell back in some disarray toward Bailén under pressure from Reding. However, Reding did not follow up his pursuit, but opted to return to the south bank of Guadalquivir, as he had received news that Coupigny had been less successful at Villa Nueva and had failed to secure a lodgement on the far bank despite being pitched against just a

---

1   The existence of this Spanish force at Linares played a significant role in reducing French options for manoeuvre and subsequent retreat and has not been given due recognition.

2   Only 12 of the original 17 battalions deployed from Madrid and of these only nine deployed beyond La Carolina, the other three remaining in key towns en route.

3   His was the strongest and best trained of all the forces.

4   Soriano, *Batalla de Bailén*, p.48.

5   Dufour was one of Gobert's brigade commanders who had assumed command on his death.

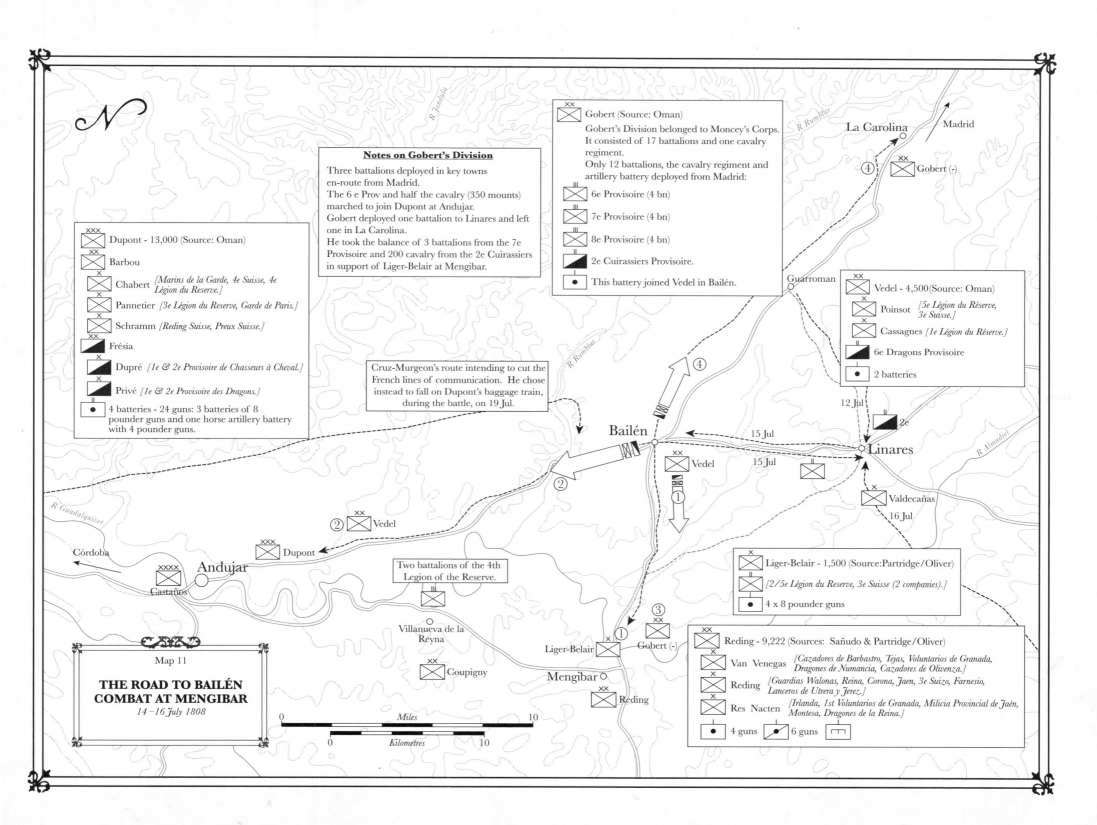

N

Notes on Gobert's Division

Three battalions deployed in key towns en-route from Madrid.
The 6e Prov and half the cavalry (350 mounts) marched to join Dupont at Andujar.
Gobert deployed one battalion to Linares and left one in La Carolina.
He took the balance of 3 battalions from the 7e Provisoire and 200 cavalry from the 2e Cuirassiers in support of Liger-Belair at Mengibar.

Gobert (Source: Oman)

Gobert's Division belonged to Moncey's Corps. It consisted of 17 battalions and one cavalry regiment.
Only 12 battalions, the cavalry regiment and artillery battery deployed from Madrid:

6e Provisoire (4 bn)

7e Provisoire (4 bn)

8e Provisoire (4 bn)

2e Cuirassiers Provisoire.

This battery joined Vedel in Bailén.

Dupont - 13,000 (Source: Oman)

Barbou

Chabert *[Marins de la Garde, 4e Suisse, 4e Légion du Reserve.]*

Pannetier *[3e Légion du Reserve, Garde de Paris.]*

Schramm *[Reding Suisse, Preux Suisse.]*

Frésia

Dupré *[1e & 2e Provisoire de Chasseurs à Cheval.]*

Privé *[1e & 2e Provisoire des Dragons.]*

4 batteries - 24 guns: 3 batteries of 8 pounder guns and one horse artillery battery with 4 pounder guns.

Vedel - 4,500 (Source: Oman)

Poinsot *[5e Légion du Réserve, 3e Suisse.]*

Cassagnes *[1e Légion du Réserve.]*

6e Dragons Provisoire

2 batteries

Cruz-Murgeon's route intending to cut the French lines of communication. He chose instead to fall on Dupont's baggage train, during the battle, on 19 Jul.

Liger-Belair - 1,500 (Source: Partridge/Oliver)

[2/5e Légion du Reserve, 3e Suisse (2 companies).]

4 x 8 pounder guns

Reding - 9,222 (Sources: Sañudo & Partridge/Oliver)

Van Venegas *[Cazadores de Barbastro, Tejas, Voluntarios de Granada, Dragones de Numancia, Cazadores de Olivenza.]*

Reding *[Guardias Walonas, Reina, Corona, Jaen, 3e Suizo, Farnesio, Lanceros de Utrera y Jerez.]*

Res Nacten *[Irlanda, 1st Voluntarios de Granada, Milicia Provincial de Jaén, Montesa, Dragones de la Reina.]*

4 guns   6 guns

La Carolina
Madrid
Gobert (-)
Guarroman
12 Jul
2e
Linares
Valdecañas
16 Jul
R Jándula
R Rumblar
R Rumblar
R Almudiel
R Guadalquivir

Bailén
Vedel
15 Jul
15 Jul

Vedel
Dupont
Córdoba
Andujar
Castaños

Two battalions of the 4th Legion of the Reserve.

Villanueva de la Reyna

Coupigny

Liger-Belair
Gobert (-)
Mengibar
Reding

Map 11

THE ROAD TO BAILÉN COMBAT AT MENGIBAR
14-16 July 1808

Miles
0   10

Kilometres
0   10

single French battalion. Nevertheless, Liger-Belair, expecting a follow-up, felt exposed at Bailén and elected to withdraw to La Carolina; a decision that was to have far-reaching consequences.

Dupont, on hearing that Reding had forced the crossing at Mengibar, immediately sent Vedel back to Bailén to support Liger-Belair. He logically concluded that Reding had, by now, advanced on the place. Accordingly, early on 17 July, Vedel set off with 6,000 men[6] and on arrival was surprised and confused to find the town devoid of any troops. He supposed that Reding had evicted the French from the area and was now in pursuit of them towards La Carolina; with time against him he conducted a hasty reconnaissance with his cavalry who failed to discover either Reding or Coupigny to the south. As evening approached, convinced of the accuracy of his earlier hypothesis, Vedel set off up the road to La Carolina[7] (map 11, point 4). Dupont's miscalculations in sending back elements of his main force and Vedel's failure to complete a reconnaissance of Spanish dispositions combined to split the French force: 13,000 with Dupont and 11,000 with Vedel.[8] The foundations had now been laid for the failure that was to follow.

On 18 July, Coupigny crossed the Guadalquivir, joined Reding, and the two divisions advanced north to attack Bailén. Much to their surprise they discovered the place empty, and believing Vedel to still be with Dupont at Andujar, drew up plans to advance west and come upon the French from behind. Reding however, thought it prudent to seek compliance from Castaños before moving. To the west, Dupont was now sandwiched between the two Spanish forces and dangerously exposed. He had already decided to vacate his defensive position on the river and pull back in order to link up his entire corps, and he elected to move under the cover of darkness in the hope of relinquishing his defensive positions without being seen. He needed to buy time, as he was still encumbered by large amounts of plunder from Córdoba which he knew would slow his progress considerably. Quite understandably, it never occurred to Dupont that Reding's force could be between him and that of Vedel. Accordingly, his order of march was arranged to meet the threat from behind, with a strong rearguard supported by all but one battery of artillery. Conversely, the vanguard was a weak guard force of one brigade followed by the large 600-wagon baggage train, which stretched 3km along the tracks.

At Bailén, the Spanish force, waiting for word from Castaños, had prepared defensive positions to the west of the town;[9] Venegas was holding the northern shoulder, Coupigny the southern and Reding, in overall command, positioned himself in the centre,[10] along with the combined artillery of 16 guns[11] facing down the road with the cavalry to their rear. Reding had also placed seven battalions and one cavalry squadron to the rear of the city to thwart any attack from the east. The French vanguard unexpectedly came upon the Spanish outposts at about 0300 hours on 19 July, and unsure of the size of the Spanish force, began to push in on the positions south of the road as dawn broke. Chabert was commanding the leading brigade, and when this arrived on the scene the general formed up his brigade in line supported by his battery[12] and made a spirited advance south of the road towards Coupigny's division. His battery was soon completely destroyed by the massed Spanish guns and his infantry quickly lost its momentum and was soon being pursued by the Spanish. As this attack was being repulsed, Dupont rode up to the crest of the hill to witness the massed Spanish lines across the road to his front. His worst fears were quickly realized.

He immediately ordered Schramm, Privé and Dupré up to the front, which they had great difficulty in achieving for the enormous convoy was blocking the entire road from the bridge across the river Rumblar to the area just behind Chabert's by now dispirited brigade. The French troops were exhausted, having marched through the night on poor roads, and were simply not mentally prepared for the fight ahead.[13] With hindsight, Dupont would have been wise to take stock of the situation and wait for his force to concentrate, using the interim time to undertake a thorough reconnaissance and determine the strengths and dispositions of the Spanish forces to his front. However, in the belief that Castaños was about to fall on his rear at any moment, he seemed to lose his sense of reasoning. Schramm pushed along the road and fell in with Chabert, who was trying to rally his men south of the road. Just behind Schramm's Swiss battalions, the cavalry brigades forced their way past the convoy and, once past the bridge, were able to make better speed over the more open ground. Pannetier, who had also been ordered forward, was still some way to the rear. The Marines of the Guard were left to cover the rear of the force, but Dupont despairingly accepted that the guns would take considerably longer to come forward. The cavalry moved up the road and Privé was despatched to Chabert's right, with the light cavalry of Dupré staying on the road in reserve. Dupont's appreciation was rushed and his orders were delivered hastily.

The second attack commenced at around 0800 hours (see map 12). Privé's heavy cavalry (on the right flank) advanced toward the Cerrajon with characteristic vitality and cut their way deep into the strong skirmish lines provided by the 3rd Guardias Walonas and the 1st Suizo, neither battalion being organized to form square to meet the threat. However, the momentum of the heavy cavalry soon ebbed and they were forced to withdraw, having outpaced the infantry which was only now beginning to advance in the centre and left. They advanced directly into the effective canister fire from the Spanish guns, which quickly checked their advance, shattered their cohesion and sapped their momentum; within minutes both Chabert and Schramm's infantry were pulling back. It was clear that the second attack had also failed and Dupont became increasingly agitated. In the heat of the moment, as Pannetier's exhausted men arrived to the

---

6   Consisting of his own division and the infantry and cavalry sent forward initially by Gobert.

7   This episode provides a good example of the difficulties facing the French in soliciting accurate information and intelligence on troop movement from the local population.

8   Adding the 6,000 from Andujar to Dufour and Liger-Belair's forces.

9   The position of the Spanish differs from that depicted in Oman and other earlier British works.

10   He subsequently moved to command the situation on the Spanish right against the French main effort.

11   Two guns had been lost at Mengibar.

12   The rest of the three batteries were part of the rearguard.

13   Partridge and Oliver, *Battle Studies in the Peninsula May 1808–January 1809*, p.107 support the possibility that the troops were suffering physically. A. F. Berlincourt, *The Battle of Bailén, A New Approach* – from the British Historical Society Papers following the International Congress on the Iberian Peninsula 1991 – states that the conditions around Andujar were appalling and that many of the French soldiers were not just exhausted, hungry and very thirsty but that as many as three-quarters were suffering from dysentery.

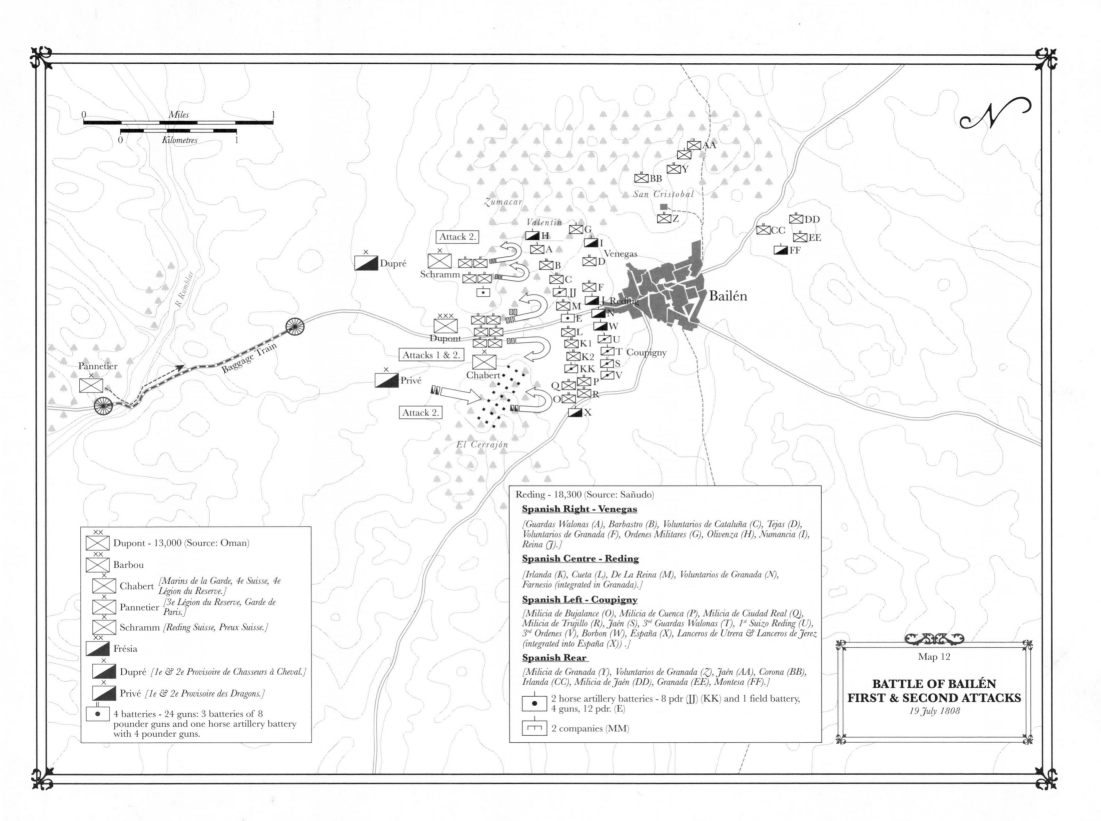

N

Miles
0 — 1

Kilometres
0 — 1

Attack 2.

Dupré

Schramm

Attack 2.

Zumacar

Valentín

H **G**
A **I**
B
C
JJ **F**
M
E
L
K1
K2
KK
Q
O
X

D **Venegas**

J Reding

N
W
U
T Coupigny
S
V
P
R

San Cristobal

AA
Y
BB
Z

DD
CC **EE**
FF

Bailén

Attacks 1 & 2.

Dupont

Attacks 1 & 2.

Chabert

Privé

Attack 2.

El Cerrajón

Pannetier

Baggage Train

R. Rumblar

Reding - 18,300 (Source: Sañudo)

Spanish Right - Venegas

[Guardas Walonas (A), Barbastro (B), Voluntarios de Cataluña (C), Tejas (D), Voluntarios de Granada (F), Ordenes Militares (G), Olivenza (H), Numancia (I), Reina (J).]

Spanish Centre - Reding

[Irlanda (K), Cueta (L), De La Reina (M), Voluntarios de Granada (N), Farnesio (integrated in Granada).]

Spanish Left - Coupigny

[Milicia de Bujalance (O), Milicia de Cuenca (P), Milicia de Ciudad Real (Q), Milicia de Trujillo (R), Jaén (S), 3rd Guardas Walonas (T), 1st Suizo Reding (U), 3rd Ordenes (V), Borbon (W), España (X), Lanceros de Utrera & Lanceros de Jerez (integrated into España (X)) .]

Spanish Rear

[Milicia de Granada (Y), Voluntarios de Granada (Z), Jaén (AA), Corona (BB), Irlanda (CC), Milicia de Jaén (DD), Granada (EE), Montesa (FF).]

⊡ 2 horse artillery batteries - 8 pdr (JJ) (KK) and 1 field battery, 4 guns, 12 pdr. (E)

⊟ 2 companies (MM)

Dupont - 13,000 (Source: Oman)

Barbou

Chabert *[Marins de la Garde, 4e Suisse, 4e Légion du Reserve.]*

Pannetier *[3e Légion du Reserve, Garde de Paris.]*

Schramm *[Reding Suisse, Preux Suisse.]*

Frésia

Dupré *[1e & 2e Provisoire de Chasseurs à Cheval.]*

Privé *[1e & 2e Provisoire des Dragons.]*

● 4 batteries - 24 guns: 3 batteries of 8 pounder guns and one horse artillery battery with 4 pounder guns.

Map 12

**BATTLE OF BAILÉN
FIRST & SECOND ATTACKS**
19 July 1808

rear, he threw them directly into the fray against the Spanish right. In utter desperation, Chabran's by now depleted and broken formation was rallied for a second time and, along with the Swiss infantry and cavalry, was pressed back to engage with the Spanish centre and left. The whole made little headway; engagements consisting of long-range bickering fire rather than concerted offensive action.

Dupont was now desperate and seems to have lost his composure completely. In a last, desperate attempt to break through he ordered up his Marines of the Guard and, positioning them in the centre with the quasi-rallied troops of Pannetier, Chabert and Schramm on either side, supported by Dupré's cavalry to the north. It was around noon when the marines pushed right up to the front of the Spanish batteries but they too were decimated by close-range canister. Dupré's light cavalry had some success but they lacked the numbers to force a passage. Dupré was shot dead[14] and, at about the same time, Dupont was also wounded; he rode to the rear and the fourth and final attack collapsed. The French rolled back and many of the Swiss surrendered. As Dupont paused to consider his predicament he began to hear firing from their rear. Colonel Cruz-Murgeon had appeared from the mountains to the north and fallen on the small force guarding the baggage train. Worse was to come; within minutes the Spanish vanguard, led by La Peña, emerged from the west. Dupont, still unaware of Vedel's whereabouts, sensed it was all over. Seeking terms, Dupont sent Captain Villoutreys (his aide-de-camp) to Reding, requesting a cessation of hostilities. It was about 1400 hours. He proposed a withdrawal of all French troops from Andalusia; terms that Reding was not prepared to accept but, unsure of how to proceed, he elected to defer the matter until the arrival of Castaños. In the interim he agreed to a suspension of fighting and detailed Colonel Copons[15] to escort the young French captain to the Spanish commander-in-chief. In fact, Castaños had not followed his vanguard with much urgency and was still at Andujar; the two officers met with him at around 1700 hours that evening.

At approximately the same time, Vedel emerged from the passes west of the town. Having realized his earlier mistake, he had collected his men and returned to Bailén.[16] As he approached the lower hills the sounds of gunfire dwindled and, on discovering Spanish troops to his front, he began to comprehend the enormity of that earlier error. Despite the appearance of a white flag and elucidation of the suspension of hostilities by its bearers, Vedel felt compelled to announce (for Dupont's benefit) his presence and attack, sending the Spanish officers back to Reding with this report. Fifteen minutes later, the 3e Suisse and the 5e Légion attacked San Cristobal and the 1e Légion and Boussard's dragoons attacked El Cerro del Ahorcado. A thousand prisoners were taken at the latter position without firing a shot but Vedel was prevented from executing a second attack by the appearance of a second white flag, accompanied by one of Dupont's aides-de-camp who carried a letter from his commander ordering Vedel to cease hostilities. Vedel reluctantly complied and withdrew 3km back up the road towards La Carolina.

Castaños read Dupont's proposals and rejected them out of hand. In return his demands were spelt out: Dupont's 'captured force' was to lay down its arms immediately, but a clause allowed them to return to France rather than go into captivity. By omitting mention of Vedel's force, Castaños seemed to accept that it would most likely extract itself and therefore form no part of the subsequent negotiation. Early on 20 July Captain Villoutreys returned to the outskirts of Bailén with these conditions and handed them to a dejected Dupont. During the previous night, the French commander had toured the bivouacs and campfires of his men; an undertaking that confirmed his force was spent. As Dupont cursed his luck and considered his predicament, Castaños strengthened his stranglehold by bringing up the balance of his force behind La Peña, who had moved forward of the bridge at Rumblar.

Dupont agreed to commence dialogue. The subsequent negotiations were complicated and prolonged. The release of the Spanish prisoners from Vedel's custody took some time to organize, and during the delay Dupont covertly instructed Vedel to extricate his force from the area as the Spanish were now reconsidering their position with regard to it. During the night of 20 July Vedel pulled back and, on 23 July, the remnants of Dupont's corps laid down their arms. A total of nearly 18,000 men were marched to the coast, from where they were to be repatriated to France courtesy of the Royal Navy; however Britain had not been privy to the terms of the agreement and refused to move the men.[17] No other European army had ever defeated an entire French army in open battle since the beginning of the Revolutionary Wars; it was an incredible military achievement, the repercussions of which were to be felt across Europe.

---

14   There is a small chapel in the town that purportedly houses Dupré's remains.

15   He became general and commander of the reorganized Spanish 1st Army of Catalonia in December 1812.

16   The subsequent French court martial into events surrounding the catastrophe at Bailén questioned Vedel at length as to why it took him so long to realize his mistake and why he had rested his men (at midday) for four hours when he could clearly hear the sounds of battle in the plains below. He had committed probably the greatest Napoleonic *faux pas* by not marching with all haste to the sound of the guns, particularly as he now realized Reding's force had not pursued Liger-Belair.

---

17   The story of what happened to these men is most regrettable. They spent some months on pontoons off Cádiz before some were despatched to the Isle of Cabrera, part of the Balearic isles, where more than half died.

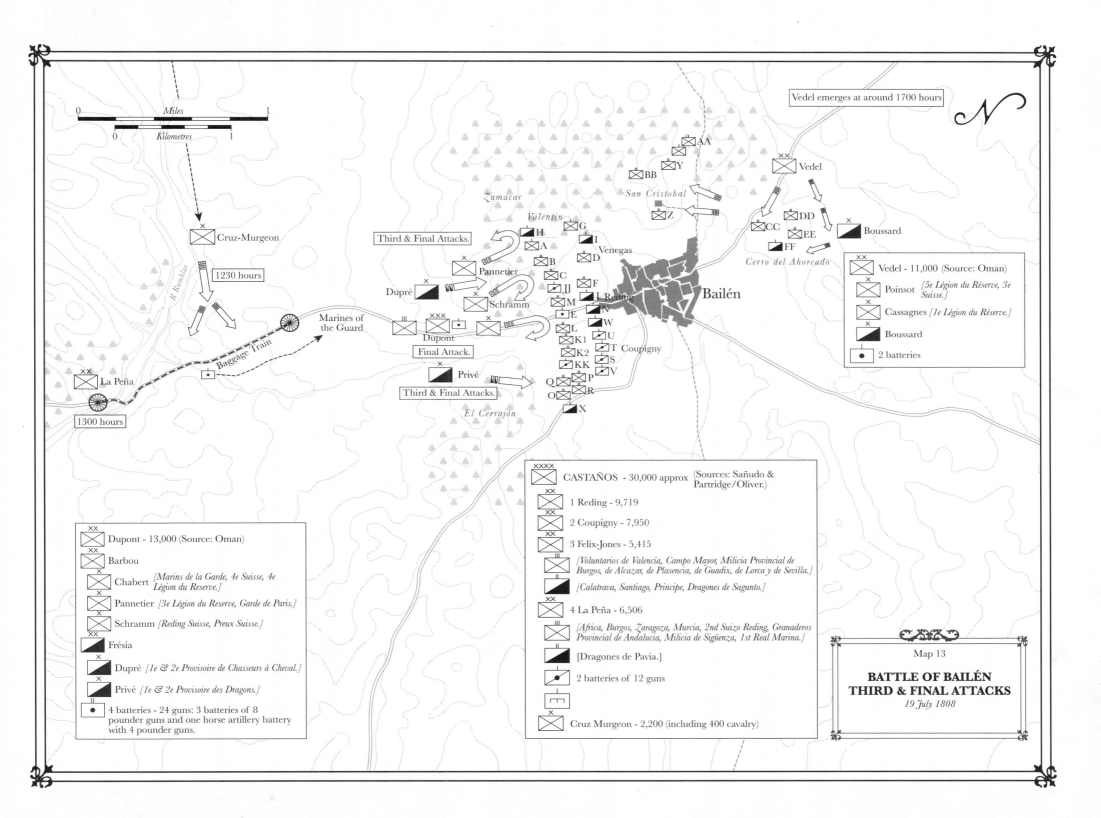

Vedel emerges at around 1700 hours

N

0   Miles   1

0   Kilometres   1

Cruz-Murgeon

1230 hours

R. Rumblar

Baggage Train

Marines of
the Guard

La Peña

1300 hours

Zumacar

Valentín

Third & Final Attacks.

H
A
B
C
JJ

G
I
D
F
M
E
L
K1
K2
KK

Pannetier

Dupré

Schramm

Dupont

Final Attack.

Privé

Third & Final Attacks.

El Cerrajón

San Cristóbal

Z

Venegas

Reding

N
W
U
T Coupigny
S
V
P
R
Q
O
X

J

Bailén

Cerro del Ahorcado

AA
Y
BB

Vedel

CC
DD
EE
FF

Boussard

Vedel - 11,000 (Source: Oman)

Poinsot   *[5e Légion du Réserve, 3e Suisse.]*

Cassagnes *[1e Légion du Réserve.]*

Boussard

2 batteries

Dupont - 13,000 (Source: Oman)

Barbou

Chabert   *[Marins de la Garde, 4e Suisse, 4e Légion du Réserve.]*

Pannetier   *[3e Légion du Réserve, Garde de Paris.]*

Schramm   *[Reding Suisse, Preux Suisse.]*

Frésia

Dupré   *[1e & 2e Provisoire de Chasseurs à Cheval.]*

Privé   *[1e & 2e Provisoire des Dragons.]*

4 batteries - 24 guns: 3 batteries of 8
pounder guns and one horse artillery battery
with 4 pounder guns.

CASTAÑOS - 30,000 approx (Sources: Sañudo & Partridge/Oliver.)

1 Reding - 9,719

2 Coupigny - 7,950

3 Felix-Jones - 5,415

[Voluntarios de Valencia, Campo Mayor, Milicia Provincial de Burgos, de Alcazar, de Plasencia, de Guadix, de Lorca y de Sevilla.]

[Calatrava, Santiago, Principe, Dragones de Sagunto.]

4 La Peña - 6,506

[Africa, Burgos, Zaragoza, Murcia, 2nd Suizo Reding, Granaderos Provincial de Andalucia, Milicia de Sigüenza, 1st Real Marina.]

[Dragones de Pavia.]

2 batteries of 12 guns

Cruz Murgeon - 2,200 (including 400 cavalry)

Map 13

**BATTLE OF BAILÉN
THIRD & FINAL ATTACKS**
19 July 1808

Chapter 7

French Failures and British Intervention

‘The battle of Rio Seco was not dishonourable to the Spaniards: they were more numerous, and they were beaten; but they disputed the victory. It was a specimen of the Old Spanish army, which showed what it might have done; it was a great deal for a new army trying its strength for the first time with troops inured to war.'[1] However, the victory at Medina de Rióseco provided a glimmer of French hope. Things had started well enough at Alcolea, Tudela, Cabezon and Epila but since the disaster at Bailén there was much to lament. The French squadron had been captured in Cádiz; the siege of Zaragoza was not proceeding according to French expectations, the assaults on Valencia, Girona and Roses had failed entirely, and Junot's occupying army in Portugal was stretched to the limit. Nonetheless, victory at Medina de Rióseco had removed the threat to the lines of communication from Madrid to Bayonne and opened the road for its future 'king'.

King Joseph had chosen to wait at Burgos until the threat from Cuesta had been neutralized before proceeding to Madrid. His state entry on 20 July was a stifled affair and visibly devoid of Spanish supporters, less for the handful of *Afrancesados* who embraced the new regime. Napoleon's brother was formally proclaimed as king four days later amidst rumours of catastrophe in Andalusia. Another four days passed before these rumours could be confirmed and on 1 August, just ten days after his arrival, Joseph fled his capital and headed north and relative safety. His flight was bitterly opposed by Savary who displayed considerably greater determination to hold the Spanish capital than the country's new king.

While this drama played out in central and southern Spain events were unfolding on the east coast in Catalonia. The military governor of the Balearic isles, Captain-General Vives, reluctantly agreed to send half his 10,000 men to support the Catalan cause. In the second half of July his second-in-command, Marquis Del Palacio, landed near Tortosa and marched towards Zaragoza. His arrival in the area coincided with that of several other regular elements from across Spain, and the struggle for Catalonia passed, to an extent, from the *somatenes* to the regular army. Their opportunity to engage the French was not long in coming. Duhesme, uplifted by the news of Reille's arrival in Figueras, resolved to try and take Girona a second time. He headed north on 10 July and collected additional troops from General Chabran, who had been motionless at Granollers following his abortive attempt to clear the concentration of *somatenes* north of Barcelona. His journey north was plagued by incessant attacks on the fringes of his column and he arrived, somewhat exhausted, in front of Girona on 21 July. He was relieved to discover the presence of Reille, who had arrived a few hours earlier in the day; the latter established his headquarters at Pontemayor and the former at Santa Eugenia. Duhesme personally assumed control of the siege operations and established his siege guns, howitzers and mortars as depicted (map 14, points 1 to 6). The tardiness with which the French completed the task was a clear indication that this rather ad hoc French Army of Catalonia was not well practised in the art of siege warfare; the batteries did not open in earnest until 12 August.

Before the French forces had sealed the approaches to the town, one of Del Palacio's battalions[2] slipped past the attackers and entered the city. Del Palacio, who was busy blockading Barcelona, was inspired by the joint news of victory at Bailén and of 'royal' withdrawal from Madrid, and decided to send additional troops[3] under General Caldagues to assist the *somatenes* in disrupting the besieging force at Girona. In addition, Del Palacio tightened the screws on Lecchi and his small defending force at Barcelona. He ensured that the Italian's appeals for support from Duhesme found their way through, in the hope that they would provoke a French response which, in turn, would entice the French to lift the siege at Girona. Amazingly, Caldagues was able to penetrate the (clearly incompetent) French cordon and enter Girona to meet with the two battalion commanders.[4] Together they planned an elaborate and daring attack on the French battery and trench positions, and delivered their assault soon after 0900 hours on 16 August. The two battalions charged from within the city up to the trenches on the heights above the town, drove off the battalion on guard duty, seized the guns and destroyed the battery positions and gun platforms (map 14, points 2, 3 and 4). The French battalions from Reille's Division were rushed to the scene but before they could establish themselves they were driven back down the hill towards Pontemayor. Reille rallied his men and was about to execute a counter-attack when Caldagues's Brigade appeared on the hill to his front and began advancing in four columns. Reille checked his counter move and drew back across the Ter; Duhesme who had witnessed events from near Santa Eugenia pulled his men and guns back to the village.

Caldagues wisely refrained from coming down onto the flatter ground; instead he established a defensive position on the hills and waited for a more coordinated counter-attack. It never materialized. Duhesme, demoralized by events of the previous days and by news from Barcelona, decided to lift the siege and send Reille back to Figueras while he made best speed back to Barcelona to assist Lecchi. Siege guns were spiked and buried, stores destroyed and any unnecessary baggage ditched in an attempt to speed the passage. Despite this, the *miqueletes* and *somatenes* were waiting and they pursued the French force mercilessly through the mountains. When the unhappy French column reached the coast road, in addition to the incessant attacks from the hills to the west, they were also bombarded by two Royal Navy frigates.[5] On 20 August, exhausted and destitute of all their military equipment, except for muskets and some ammunition,

---

1   Foy, *History of the War in the Peninsula under Napoleon*, vol. II, p.277.

2   The 2nd Voluntarios de Barcelona, which had formed part of the garrison in Minorca.

3   Four companies of regulars, 2,000 *miqueletes* and three light field guns.

4   La Valeta commanded the Barcelona Volunteers and Henry O'Donnell the Ultonia.

5   The *Impérieuse* and *Cambrian* under Captain Cochrane's command.

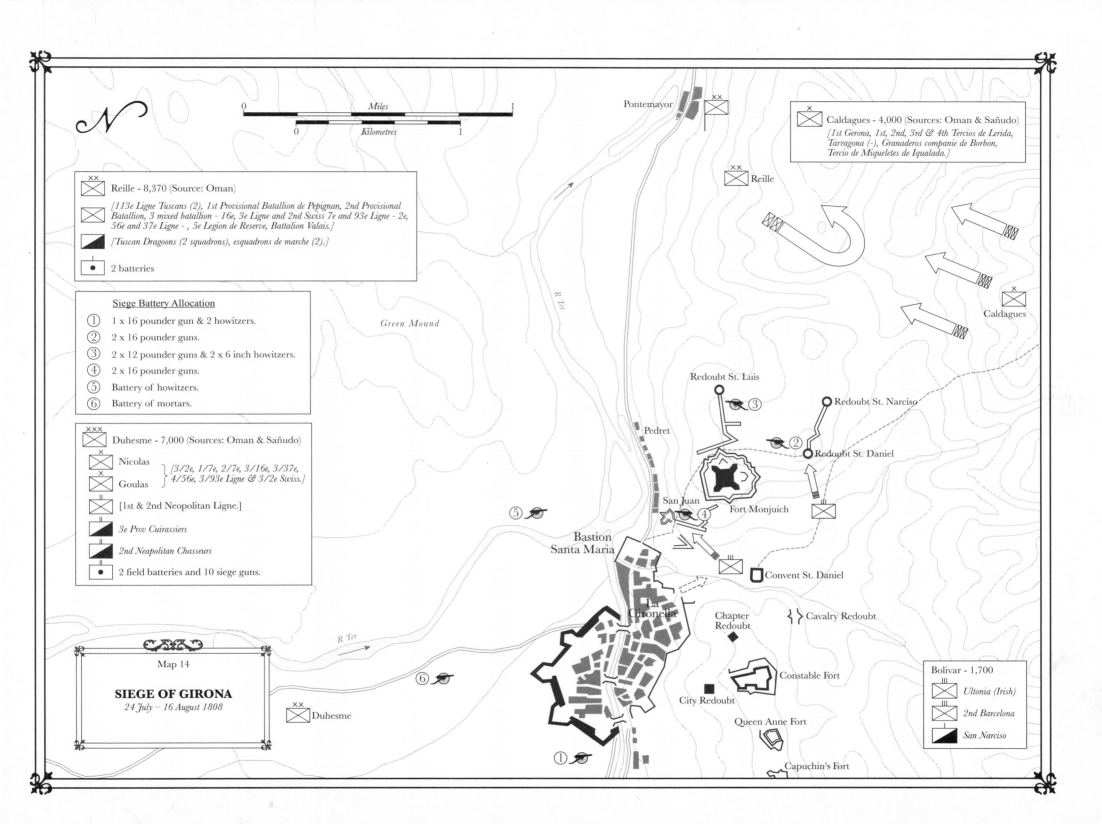

N

0   Miles   1

0   Kilometres   1

Reille - 8,370 (Source: Oman)

[113e Ligne Tuscans (2), 1st Provisional Batallion de Pepignan, 2nd Provisional Batallion, 3 mixed batallion - 16e, 3e Ligne and 2nd Swiss 7e and 93e Ligne - 2e, 56e and 37e Ligne - , 5e Legion de Reserve, Battalion Valais.]

[Tuscan Dragoons (2 squadrons), esquadrons de marche (2).]

2 batteries

Siege Battery Allocation

1. 1 x 16 pounder gun & 2 howitzers.
2. 2 x 16 pounder guns.
3. 2 x 12 pounder guns & 2 x 6 inch howitzers.
4. 2 x 16 pounder guns.
5. Battery of howitzers.
6. Battery of mortars.

Duhesme - 7,000 (Sources: Oman & Sañudo)

Nicolas

Goulas   [3/2e, 1/7e, 2/7e, 3/16e, 3/37e, 4/56e, 3/93e Ligne & 3/2e Swiss.]

[1st & 2nd Neopolitan Ligne.]

3e Prov Cuirassiers

2nd Neapolitan Chasseurs

2 field batteries and 10 siege guns.

Caldagues - 4,000 (Sources: Oman & Sañudo)

[1st Gerona, 1st, 2nd, 3rd & 4th Tercios de Lerida, Tarragona (-), Granaderos companie de Borbon, Tercio de Miqueletes de Iqualada.]

Pontemayor

Reille

Green Mound

R Ter

Caldagues

Redoubt St. Luis

③

Pedret

②

Redoubt St. Narciso

Redoubt St. Daniel

San Juan

④

Fort Monjuich

Bastion Santa Maria

⑤

Convent St. Daniel

La Gironella

Chapter Redoubt

Cavalry Redoubt

Constable Fort

City Redoubt

R Ter

⑥

Queen Anne Fort

Capuchin's Fort

Map 14

SIEGE OF GIRONA

24 July – 16 August 1808

Duhesme

①

Bolivar - 1,700

Ultonia (Irish)

2nd Barcelona

San Narciso

the beleaguered force arrived back in Mongat, just north of Barcelona, and had to be assisted by some of Lecchi's men over the last few kilometres.

Long before this latest misfortune had befallen the French Army in Catalonia, strategic and operational plans were being worked in Paris to remedy the situation in the region. On receiving the news of Bailén Napoleon was apoplectic with rage, stating in letters to his minister of war in Paris that the entire affair was a stupid, cowardly and idiotic business. 'Dupont has soiled our banners. What folly and what baseness!'[6] His mood was hardly placated a few days later when he heard that his brother had deserted Madrid – Napoleonic dignity was severely injured. Joseph had retired with a force of some 23,000, which had gone firm on the river Douro south of Burgos: Bessières was to hold the left flank with his 15,000 men at Valladolid while Verdier was ordered to lift the siege of Zaragoza and move with his force to Tudela to secure the right wing. However, even before these orders had reached their respective commanders, Joseph had decided to withdraw further north and relocate at Burgos. Bessières and Verdier, sensitive to Napoleon's aim of holding the forward line of the Douro, nevertheless realized that they must fall back in unison and establish a new line along the Ebro. By mid-August this combined force of some 70,000 men, composed of the entire French forces in Spain (less for the French Army of Catalonia), was established with a frontage of less than 150km. Despite months of misleading reports, Napoleon had begun to grasp the size and complexity of the mission in Spain and settled that a force of 98,000 was insufficient for the undertaking. He penned new orders for his Peninsular commanders and composed directives for massive reinforcements from France, Italy, Germany and the Confederation of the Rhine. An additional 130,000 soldiers were to head south, many of them veterans of the *Grande Armée*. Napoleon was determined to crush the insubordinate Spaniards once and for all.

The Spanish political and military reaction to the withdrawal of the French armies in central Spain was slow and indecisive. The French position on the Ebro was vulnerable to attacks from the flanks: Blake and Cuesta from the west and Palafox from the east. However, by the time offensive operations were in the planning stage it was already early September, and large numbers of French reinforcements were already arriving. Marshal Jourdan arrived at Miranda on 25 August and assumed command from Savary, and five days later Marshal Ney arrived at the Pyrenees bringing with him the spirit of *la glorie*, which had been distinctly lacking in Napoleon's Peninsular lieutenants in the early phase of the war. For the Spanish, to a great extent, the moment had passed.

It took the *madrileños* some days to comprehend that they were free from the shackles of French occupation. The Council of Castile, which had served Murat and Savary since May, tried to hang on to their senatorial power – much to the fury and in some cases amusement of the local Juntas. The nation, the church and the new army were divided on the best way to proceed. Juntas were reluctant to rally to the requirements of the nation, being more concerned and preoccupied with provincial anxieties. Cuesta had taken off into the Sierra de la Culebra in a huff; Blake had been restricted from further operations by the insular Junta; Galluzzo was

still embroiled in investing Elvas; Cervellon felt as though he had done his bit by sending the division of St March to assist Palafox who, along with the Catalan army were in effect manning the front line. It was not until early September that Castaños could muster 20,000 men in the capital and provide military support and influence to the political process. The entire month of August had been wasted from the political and military perspective; the initiative, so marvellously gained from victories in Andalusia, Catalonia and Aragon, had been thrown away. Eventually, agreement was sought and received from the provincial Juntas to establish a Central Junta, not in Madrid but in Aranjuez. A subsequent council of war penned a collective plan of operations but then spent many weeks tying up the detail and appeared completely unaware that Napoleon was preparing to strike.

Since Junot's arrival in Portugal in November 1807, life in the country had been relatively uneventful – other than a short-lived insurrection on 13 December in Lisbon – until news permeated of civil uprisings across Spain. Before Junot could comprehend the scale of rebellion, his communications with Madrid were severed. His last orders from Madrid called upon him to send 4,000 men in aid of Bessières and another 8,000 to Dupont, for operations in the south. To a lesser extent he complied with this decree[7] but soon after Junot lost the remaining two Spanish divisions, which had assisted him in invading the country six months previously,[8] leaving him inadequately resourced to deal with events as they now unfolded. Following the withdrawal of Belesta's Spanish Division from Oporto on 6 June insurrection in the area gathered pace. The province of Tras-os-Montes took up the mantle and soon the movement gained considerable momentum in the north of the country. With reports that the French were marching north from Almeida, the people took matters a step further and created a Supreme National Junta led by the Bishop of Oporto, D. Antonio de Castro. This new legislature set about establishing a regular body of troops. They were assisted in their task as the military magazines at Oporto had sufficient material to supply the new force,[9] equipping some 7,000 soldiers. Perhaps more significantly, they despatched two envoys to England to ask for military assistance and additional equipment and supplies for up to 40,000 men.

The south of Portugal took up the reins of rebellion on 16 June; Faro led the movement, which quickly spread the length of the southern coastline. Events in central Portugal also gathered pace, firstly at Coimbra and then at Leiria, edging ever closer to the capital. Lisbon was simmering, but the presence of the majority of Junot's army was enough to enable the beleaguered French commander to retain a semblance of control. However, his concerns were mounting, exacerbated

---

6   *Napoleonic Correspondence, 3 August 1808*, Napoleon to Clarke.

7   A brigade under Avril went to Andalusia and a second under Loison to open up communications with Bessières in Leon. Neither made it to their final destinations.

8   Solano had already returned to Andalusia, Taranco had died during the winter and been replaced by Belesta and Caraffa remained in the upper Tagus valley. The former withdrew to Galicia on 6 June, the latter was disarmed on 9 June and his 6,000 men placed in confinement on boats and pontoons in Lisbon harbour.

9   One of Junot's first actions had been to dissolve the Portuguese Army. He then pressed about 6,500 of them into 9 units and sent them to serve the *Imperial Armée*; they ended up in the Baltic States and Northern Germany. There were even some units left for the Moscow Campaign although they nearly all died during the retreat. Many of the more capable members of the officer corps had departed with the Prince Regent and Royal Court in 1807 so what was left, in terms of manpower and equipment was of questionable quality.

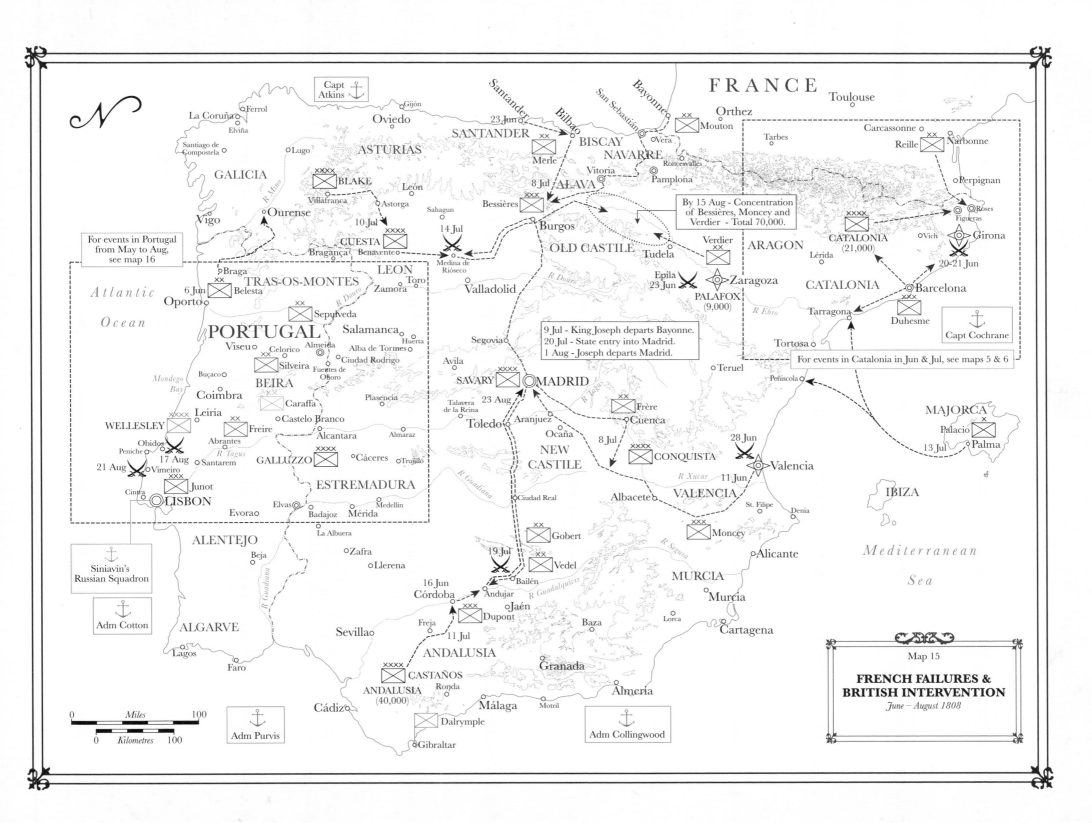

N

Capt Atkins ⚓

FRANCE

La Coruña · Ferrol · Gijón
Elviña
Santiago de Compostela · Lugo
Oviedo
GALICIA
ASTURIAS · SANTANDER · BISCAY
Vigo · Ourense
León
XXXX BLAKE
Villafranca · Astorga · Sahagun
10 Jul
CUESTA XXXX
14 Jul
Bragança · Benavente · Medina de Ríoseco
Braga · Belesta
6 Jun
TRAS-OS-MONTES · LEON
Oporto
Zamora · Toro
PORTUGAL
Sepúlveda XX
Viseu · Salamanca
Celorico · Huerta
Almeida · Alba de Tormes
Silveira XX
BEIRA · Ciudad Rodrigo
Fuentes de Oñoro
Coimbra · Plasencia
Leiria · Caraffa
WELLESLEY XXXX
Obidos · Castelo Branco
Peniche · Freire XX
17 Aug
21 Aug · Vimeiro
Abrantes · Alcantara · Almaraz
XXXX · Junot · GALLUZZO XXXX · Cáceres · Trujillo
Cintra · LISBON
Santarem
Evora · ESTREMADURA
ALENTEJO · Elvas
Beja · Badajoz · Mérida
Siniavin's Russian Squadron ⚓
Medellin
La Albuera
Zafra
Adm Cotton ⚓
Llerena
ALGARVE
Lagos · Sevilla
Faro
Córdoba
16 Jun
Freja
11 Jul
ANDALUSIA
XXXX CASTAÑOS
ANDALUSIA (40,000)
Ronda
Cádiz
Málaga · Motril
Dalrymple XX
Gibraltar

Santander
23 Jun · Bilbao
Merle XX
8 Jul · ALAVA
Bessières XXXX
Burgos
OLD CASTILE
Valladolid
San Sebastián · Bayonne
Vitoria · Orthez
Pamplona · Mouton XX
Roncesvalles
Vera
NAVARRE

By 15 Aug - Concentration of Bessières, Moncey and Verdier - Total 70,000.

Verdier XX
Tudela
ARAGON
Epila XXXX Zaragoza
23 Jun
PALAFOX (9,000)
R Ebro

Toulouse
Tarbes · Carcassonne
Narbonne XX Reille
Perpignan
CATALONIA XXXX (21,000)
Lérida · Vich
Roses · Figueras
Girona
20-21 Jun
CATALONIA
Barcelona
Tarragona
Duhesme XX
Capt Cochrane ⚓
Tortosa
Peñíscola

For events in Catalonia in Jun & Jul, see maps 5 & 6

Segovia
Avila
9 Jul - King Joseph departs Bayonne.
20 Jul - State entry into Madrid.
1 Aug - Joseph departs Madrid.
Teruel
SAVARY XXXX · MADRID
23 Aug
Talavera de la Reina
Toledo · Aranjuez
Frère XX · Cuenca
Ocaña
8 Jul
NEW CASTILE
R Guadiana
Ciudad Real
XXXX CONQUISTA
28 Jun
Valencia
11 Jun
VALENCIA
St. Filipe · Denia
Albacete
R Xucar
Moncey XXX
Alicante
MURCIA
Murcia
R Segura
Lorca
Baza
Cartagena
19 Jul
Gobert XX
Vedel XX
Bailén
Andujar · R Guadalquivir
Jaén
XXX Dupont
Granada
Almería

MAJORCA
Palacio XX
Palma
13 Jul
IBIZA
Mediterranean Sea

Adm Collingwood ⚓

Miles 0 — 100
Kilometres 0 — 100

Adm Purvis ⚓

Map 15

FRENCH FAILURES & BRITISH INTERVENTION

June – August 1808

For events in Portugal from May to Aug, see map 16

by a lack of information; he had received reports of a Spanish force near Badajoz threatening Elvas and, perhaps most disturbing, he had confirmation that General Spencer had sailed from Gibraltar with an undisclosed number of British troops.[10]

Following a council of war on 25 June, Junot issued orders to garrison Elvas, Almeida and Peniche and to withdraw all the remaining forces into the vicinity of the capital. Kellermann left a small force at Elvas and returned to Lisbon, collecting Avril en route. Loison left a similar garrison force at Almeida and Maransin returned from Mertola, sacking Beja on the way. By 11 July the concentration was complete and Junot felt more secure, but in reality this extraction had created a vacuum, allowing the nationwide insurrection to gather momentum unabated. As soon as the French vacated a town or valley the locals pledged their allegiance to the new Junta in Oporto and began to organize themselves in some form of armed resistance. The lack of any military equipment was to hamper the process, but not the enthusiasm. The students at Coimbra, led by Zagalo, succeeded in taking the coastal fort of Santa Catarina at Figueira da Foz. This success was quickly capitalized upon by the Junta at Oporto who immediately despatched approximately 5,000 regulars to the line of the Mondego. The north of Portugal was thus largely secured.

When similar events materialized further south at Leiria and Tomar, this was too close for comfort for Junot. He quickly despatched General Margaron with a brigade to both locations to restore some control. The Portuguese, lacking basic military equipment, were unable to maintain any sustained offensive and, after two weeks of inactivity Junot decided to try and reopen communications with Elvas and secure a possible line of withdrawal. On 25 July he despatched Loison with 7,000 men who reached Evora four days later. As Loison approached he was amazed to see a force of about 3,000 Portuguese and Spanish deployed to his front, ready to give battle.[11] Loison directed Margaron to engage the line on the left and Solignac to sweep right in an attempt to outflank the force south of the city. The defenders, who were poorly equipped, did not wait for the French to close before dispersing, they ran to the city for protection but a great number of the ill equipped and barley trained soldiers and many civilians were killed in the mêlée (numbers vary from two to eight thousand). Three days later, Loison moved on to Elvas where he quickly dismissed any opposition and was preparing to move on Badajoz when he received orders to return to the Portuguese capital immediately. The British intervention had begun.

A series of events had prompted British political support in aid of the Portuguese, and subsequently the Spanish, in their combined struggle against Bonaparte. Failed expeditions to Holland in 1799, Calabria in 1806 and Buenos Aires in 1807 had left a bitter taste and a yearning to notch up a military and foreign policy success. Excuses for these failures in the early years of the 19th century abounded, but principally they failed because they were (in some cases) badly led, undertaken piecemeal, with indistinct missions and end-states and with inadequate forces. In May, a force of about 9,000 was being assembled in Cork for possible operations in South America; this was easily redirected to the Peninsula. It was to be enhanced by two brigades from the south of England who were in training for an attack on Boulogne. Most significantly however, this new force destined for the Iberian Peninsula was to be bolstered by Lieutenant General Sir John Moore's force of 10,000, which had failed to establish common ground for combined operations with the King of Sweden and was being recalled. Adding General Spencer's force in Gibraltar and Cádiz, the combined army numbered 30,000.

Command of this new army proved a greater challenge to the British War Office; Wellesley, a junior lieutenant general, fresh from victories in India, was Castlereagh's favourite, while the Duke of York favoured other, more senior generals. Before the final decisions were made, Wellesley had been allowed to set sail from Cork on 12 July. He called into La Coruña and Oporto on the way, and agreed to rendezvous with the fleet off Mondego Bay, where they began to disembark on 1 August, to be greeted with the significant news of events at Bailén.

---

10   Spencer in fact turned around and returned to Cádiz when he discovered that Junot still had 15,000 troops in the Portuguese capital.

11   The force was headed by General Leite; he had about 1,250 infantry and 120 horse and had been joined by the Spanish Colonel Moretti with about the same number of infantry and a regiment of regular cavalry – the Hussars of Maria Luisa and two batteries, one horse and one field.

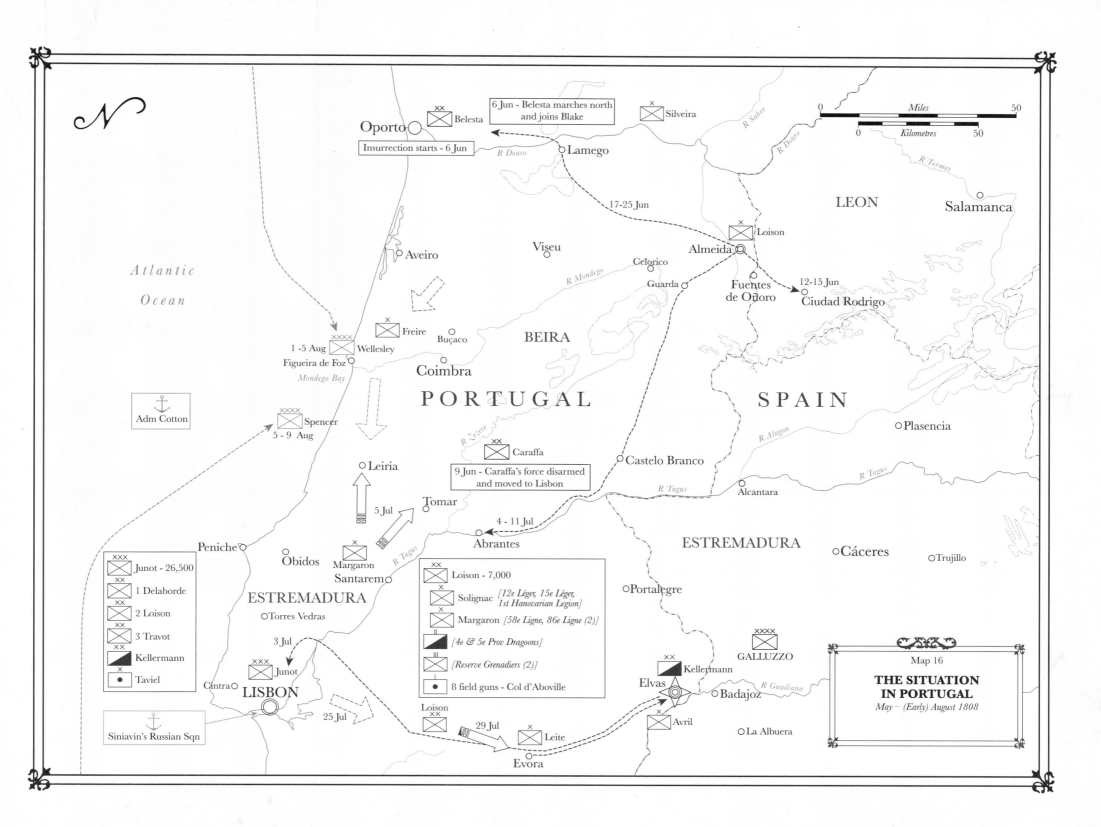

N

6 Jun - Belesta marches north and joins Blake

Oporto — Belesta

Insurrection starts - 6 Jun

R Douro — Lamego

Silveira

R Sabor

R Douro

0 — Miles — 50

0 — *Kilometres* — 50

17-25 Jun

LEON — Salamanca

R Tormes

Loison — Almeida

Viseu

R Mondego — Celorico

Guarda — Fuentes de Onoro

12-15 Jun — Ciudad Rodrigo

Atlantic Ocean

Aveiro

BEIRA

Freire — Buçaco

1 -5 Aug — Wellesley

Figueira de Foz

Mondego Bay

Coimbra

P O R T U G A L

S P A I N

⚓ Adm Cotton

Spencer

5 - 9 Aug

R Zezere

Caraffa

9 Jun - Caraffa's force disarmed and moved to Lisbon

Castelo Branco

R Alagon

Plasencia

Leiria

R Tagus

Tomar

5 Jul

4 - 11 Jul

Alcantara

R Tagus

Peniche

Óbidos

Margaron — Santarem

R Tagus

Abrantes

ESTREMADURA

Cáceres

Trujillo

ESTREMADURA

Torres Vedras

Portalegre

3 Jul

Cintra

Junot

LISBON

25 Jul

⚓ Siniavin's Russian Sqn

Loison

29 Jul

Leite

Evora

GALLUZZO

Kellermann

Elvas

Badajoz

Avril

La Albuera

R Guadiana

Key box (lower left):

XXX	Junot - 26,500
XX	1 Delaborde
XX	2 Loison
XX	3 Travot
◣	Kellermann
•	Taviel

Key box (centre):

XX Loison - 7,000	
X Solignac	*[12e Léger, 15e Léger, 1st Hanovarian Legion]*
X Margaron	*[58e Ligne, 86e Ligne (2)]*
◣	*[4e & 5e Prov Dragoons]*
X	*[Reserve Grenadiers (2)]*
•	8 field guns - Col d'Aboville

Map 16

THE SITUATION IN PORTUGAL

May – (Early) August 1808

Chapter 8 ⚬—✦——

THE LIBERATION OF PORTUGAL

Disappointingly for Wellesley, the report of events at Bailén was not the only news he received on landing at Mondego Bay. A dispatch from Downing Street, drafted on 15 July, informed the ambitious young general that he was to be superseded by no less than three other generals who were all en route. Command of the expeditionary army was to be given to Sir Hew Dalrymple[1] with Sir Harry Burrard as his second-in-command. Even Lieutenant General Sir John Moore was not to be provided with an independent command when he landed with his force from the Baltic, but his seniority ensured that he would at least supersede Wellesley.

Wellesley was ashore at the mouth of the river Mondego by 5 August, having suffered a few losses attributable to the Atlantic surf during disembarkation. His force numbered just over 9,000. As the last of his men clambered ashore, General Spencer's force, which had sailed from Gibraltar and Cádiz, rounded the headland and entered Mondego Bay. By 9 August these additional 4,500 troops were also ashore and Wellesley prepared to march on Lisbon, indignantly aware that Dalrymple was expected to arrive at any moment. His force was small, comprising only 400 cavalry and lacked adequate transport; indeed he was forced to leave Spencer's battery of light six-pounder guns at the landing site for lack of draught horses. Wellesley's discussions with the Bishop of Oporto were inconclusive; they were unable to agree terms for a combining of their forces, but he did receive the services of General Freire who was commanding a divisional-sized force of about 5,000 men, while another contingent would blockade Almeida and secure Wellington's left flank. Wellesley met up with the Portuguese general at Leiria on the 10th August and negotiated the use of Colonel Trant's brigade[2] and an ad hoc cavalry group, which accompanied Wellesley south.

Junot, aware of the British landings to the north and responsive to news that Spencer had set sail from Gibraltar, sent out Delaborde on 6 August with a small composite divisional force[3] to observe and if possible contain the British. He was told to expect Loison's force, returning from Elvas, to link up in a few days. Eventually after completing a reconnaissance of the area, Delaborde establish his force on the hill at Roliça with a forward defensive position within the walls at Obidos, a few kilometres further north. His intention was to give ground at both these locations and establish a main defensive position on the higher ground above Columbeira, about 2km to the rear. He hoped to buy sufficient time for Loison to reach him.

Late on 16 August, two battalions from Fane's Brigade drove in the French piquet north of Obidos, but the French still held the town that night. The following morning, it became apparent that the French had fallen back from Obidos to Roliça. With more open ground to his right and steeper hills to his left, Wellesley decided to push out on both flanks in an attempt to envelop the French and cut off their lines of retreat. Trant took the former and Ferguson, with Bowes's Brigade under command, assumed responsibility for the latter. Ferguson's force was stronger, to enable it to hold off Loison if necessary. The balance of the force moved directly towards the French position on the small rise to the west of the village of Roliça. From this position, Delaborde was able to observe the deployment of both enveloping forces and he waited until both Trant and Ferguson were well advanced before giving the order to fall back to his main defensive position on the wooded heights above Columbeira.

Wellesley retained the same formation for the subsequent advance, but instructed the main body to restrain from attacking the position until the flanking manoeuvres were fully developed. In addition, he instructed Lieutenant Colonel Robe, commanding the artillery, to deploy early and begin a preliminary barrage to soften the position and to distract French attention from Trant and Ferguson. Events did not turn out as ordered; the eager British infantry could not be restrained from the long-awaited opportunity to get to grips with Napoleon's forces, and when within sight of the French they pushed too far forwards, not waiting for the flanks to advance or for the gunners to soften the foe. The feature itself is about 250m high and is scarred by four gullies (facing north) up which the British infantry climbed. The 5th had the far right, then the 29th and 82nd the central two, and the 45th the far left. Lieutenant Colonel Lake, commanding the 29th, began to charge long before the other battalions were in place (map 17, point 1). It was a hot August day, the gully was steeper and longer than it appeared from the valley floor, and suddenly the 29th were being fired upon from three sides. Their attack quickly lost momentum and the French, realizing that Lake had overextended himself, fell on the red-coated soldiers, killing their commanding officer along with many other officers and men and capturing their colours.[4] By this stage the other battalion attacks had been hastened to commence and the remnants of the 29th were able to regroup and were soon joined by companies from the 9th. The attacks continued for at least two hours; Delaborde's position was strong and his troops repulsed each attack, but the British were able to gain ground and, in time, lodgements were secured at both ends of the ridge by the 5th and the 45th.

Three detached companies of the 70e Ligne, which they ultimately bypassed, had held up the flanking movement of Ferguson. His two brigades began to appear on the brow of the hill to the right rear of the French position and Delaborde now gave the order to pull back, leapfrogging by alternate battalions, and using his cavalry to cover both flanks to counter the British and Portuguese cavalry charges. Wellesley's men pursued the French as best they could after such a long march and engagement in the blistering August sun. They enjoyed some success, capturing three of the five French guns as they pressed through the defile at Azambujeira, but Wellesley did not prolong the chase and the next morning he received news of the arrival of

---

[1]   Currently commanding the garrison at Gibraltar.

[2]   Trant was a British officer in Portuguese service.

[3]   The actual size of this force is unclear: Thiébault states 1,900, Foy, 2,500, Wellington in his dispatches 6,000. Oman calculates 4,350 and this seems a reasonable figure given the force structure.

---

[4]   Which were subsequently recovered by the 9th and 29th when they executed a combined counter-attack.

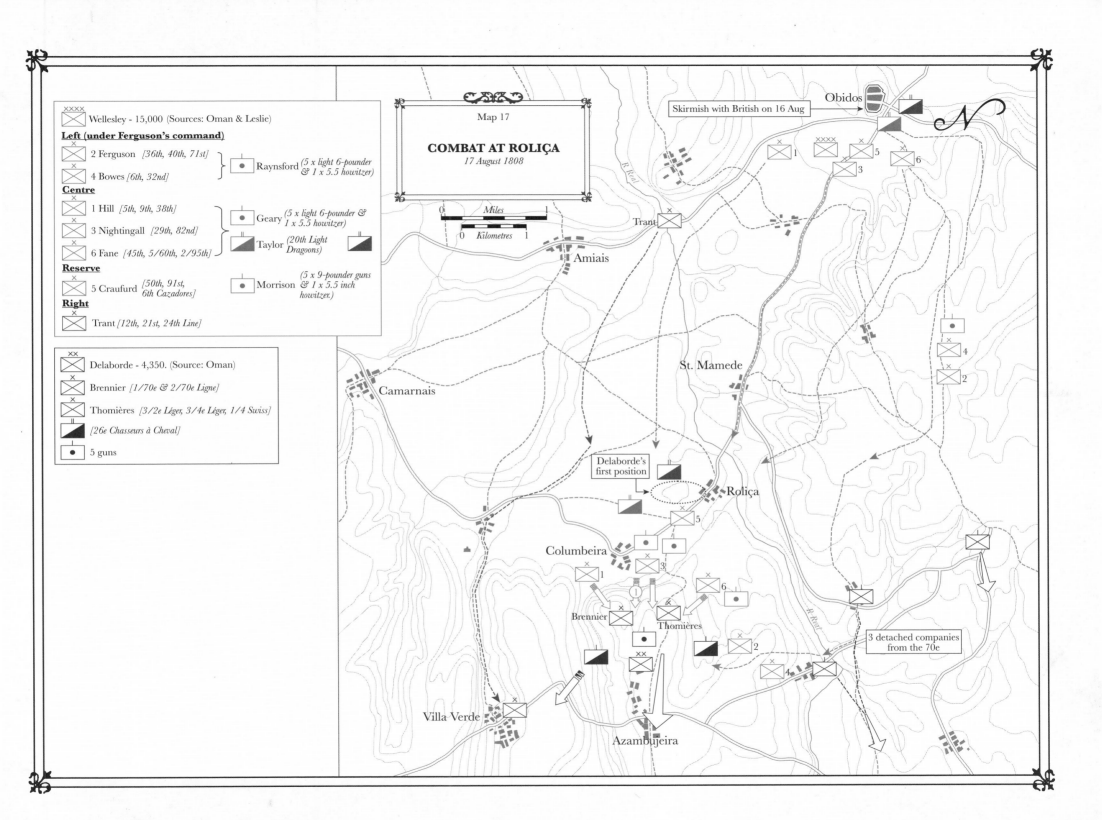

Map 17

COMBAT AT ROLIÇA
17 August 1808

Miles
0 _____ 1

Kilometres
0 _____ 1

Wellesley - 15,000 (Sources: Oman & Leslie)

Left (under Ferguson's command)

2 Ferguson *[36th, 40th, 71st]*

4 Bowes *[6th, 32nd]*

Raynsford *(5 x light 6-pounder & 1 x 5.5 howitzer)*

Centre

1 Hill *[5th, 9th, 38th]*

3 Nightingall *[29th, 82nd]*

Geary *(5 x light 6-pounder & 1 x 5.5 howitzer)*

6 Fane *[45th, 5/60th, 2/95th]*

Taylor *(20th Light Dragoons)*

Reserve

5 Craufurd *[50th, 91st, 6th Cazadores]*

Morrison *(5 x 9-pounder guns & 1 x 5.5 inch howitzer.)*

Right

Trant *[12th, 21st, 24th Line]*

Delaborde - 4,350. (Source: Oman)

Brennier *[1/70e & 2/70e Ligne]*

Thomières *[3/2e Léger, 3/4e Léger, 1/4 Swiss]*

[26e Chasseurs à Cheval]

5 guns

Obidos

Skirmish with British on 16 Aug

Trant

Amiais

Camarnais

St. Mamede

Delaborde's first position

Roliça

Columbeira

Brennier

Thomières

3 detached companies from the 70e

Villa Verde

Azambujeira

Acland and Anstruther's brigades from England, who were to disembark a day's march to the south-west. Wellesley marched south to link up with these additional forces and established a defensive position at Vimeiro.

Delaborde had withdrawn to Torres Vedras where, on 19 August, he joined forces with Junot who had marched north from Lisbon, and Loison who had finally arrived from Santarem.[5] Having debriefed Delaborde on the engagement at Roliça, and unaware that Wellesley had been reinforced in the interim, Junot was content that his force slightly outnumbered the British and on that basis he was keen to give battle.[6] That same day, Wellesley established his force in a defensive position around Vimeiro having covered, as planned, the disembarkation of Anstruther's Brigade at Paimogo and, the following day, Acland's Brigade at Porto Novo. His intentions to march to Lisbon had, however, been countermanded by General Burrard who had arrived offshore and reined in the ambitions of the younger Wellesley. Fortuitously, Burrard chose to spend another night in his more comfortable surroundings on board ship, before coming ashore to assume command of the army. By that time, the outcome of the subsequent day's events had already been decided.

At midnight on 20 August, the sounds of the approaching French force echoed through the still night air. Orders were given to stand-to an hour before first light and all eyes were trained south as dawn broke. In fact, Junot appeared later than expected and to the east, and proceeded to move past the Allied position continuing northwards until opposite Vimeiro, where he turned. Wellesley rapidly redeployed his force from the western to the eastern ridge to provide defence in depth against the threat now coming from this unexpected quarter. In addition, he pushed Craufurd and Trant, well north and out of sight, to block any French intentions of a right flanking nature on the eastern ridge. Junot completed a rapid, almost perfunctory reconnaissance and quickly chose to attack the hillock south of Vimeiro as his main effort while sending a strong divisional-sized force[7] to the north in a flanking manoeuvre. This, as it turned out, was to be a grave error.

Having swept back the British piquet line east of Vimeiro Hill, Junot deployed into attacking formation about 1.5km from the British main position. Charlot deployed front left, Thomières front right and Kellermann in a second line as reserve with the French cavalry to his rear. The Allied position at Vimeiro was strong despite having the sea at their backs; the quick reorganization by Wellesley was skilfully executed and immediately provided depth against the French attack from the east. It was an early glimmer of Wellesley's skill in the use of ground and in his sound tactical appreciation and foresight. Both Fane and Anstruther had deployed thick lines of skirmishers at the foot of the hill, hidden amongst the vineyards and scrub; the line of tirailleurs that preceded the French brigades began to push the British skirmishers back on their main lines. Their presence, however, was enough to slow the French advance, which was coming under accurate artillery fire from the two batteries with line of sight of the French advance.[8] They were firing shrapnel shells to great effect, as Foy recalled, 'the Shrapnel-shells at the first discharge struck down the files of a platoon, and then exploded in the platoon that followed'.[9] After some considerable time, the exhausted French infantry finally reached the crest of the hill, (map 18, point 1) and as they did so they were met with one final discharge of the guns, followed by a spirited charge by the British infantry. Both Thomières and Charlot's brigades broke immediately and fled, hotly pursued by the euphoric defenders who followed them well into the lower ground, and in so doing captured Prost's battery of seven guns that, due to the angle, had been unable to provide much by way of fire support.

Junot immediately called up his reserve brigade under Kellermann and the reserve battery under Foy. Colonel St Clair's Regiment was the first to be thrown into the fray, followed shortly thereafter by the balance of grenadier battalions under Colonel Maransin. Despite taking a different line of approach, between the two hills and into the village of Vimeiro (map 18, point 2), both formations were mauled by British musket and shrapnel fire in much the same way as the two first brigades. In fact, all Kellermann succeeded in doing was attracting attention from Acland and his guns on the southern end of the eastern ridge. This second attack quickly ground to a halt. There was some fierce hand-to-hand fighting in the village itself but finally the grenadiers gave way and Junot was forced to deploy a cavalry regiment to support their withdrawal. At the same moment, Wellesley chose to release the Light Dragoons to pursue the fleeing Frenchmen. The two forces met along the road, with the British Dragoons bursting through the smaller French cavalry and continuing to pursue the fleeing infantry. They wrought considerable havoc but overextended their pursuit, and were lucky to extract themselves with relatively small losses under the circumstances.[10]

To the north, events were also not going well for the French. Brennier's Brigade, with his 3e Provisional Dragoons leading, had taken a very long and circuitous route, which had separated it from Solignac's Brigade and the French main body. Solignac had turned west earlier than Brennier, in an attempt to cut the corner and reach the village of Ventosa, his intended target. He could see a line of British skirmishers, whom he mistook for flank piquets, on the hill to the south-west of the village. However, he was completely unaware of the three British brigades who were in the dead ground directly behind them. Somewhat fatigued from their exertions of the march and climb, from dragging three guns up the hill and from clearing the line of British skirmishers, the French infantry took their time forming up for the assault. During this laboured

---

5   Loison had been held up by the 24th Portuguese Infantry and *ordenança*.

6   As Rear Admiral Siniavin continued to refuse to patrol Lisbon, Junot felt compelled to leave 6,500 men behind to protect the capital from a Portuguese insurrection, whose leaders were in touch with Admiral Cotton. This was to prove a costly error and to solicit Napoleonic rebuke.

7   It is puzzling as to the choice of this force. At Torres Vedras, Junot had established two divisions; the first under Delaborde, consisting of the brigades of Brennier and Thomières, and the second under Loison, consisting the brigades of Solignac and Charlot, but he then broke up these groups when he task organized his force for the attacks at Vimeiro. The Swiss battalion in Thomières' brigade maybe the reason.

8   It is not possible to determine who commanded which battery (or brigade of guns) at the battle. Geary had been killed at Roliça and, given the ranks of the other officers, it is fair to assume that Raynsford and Morrison commanded the same brigades as they had at Roliça and that 2nd Capt Elliot had assumed command of the third. Lt Col Robe was still the CRA.

9   Foy, *History of the War in the Peninsula under Napoleon*, vol. II, p.521.

10   Their commanding officer, Lieutenant Colonel Taylor was killed.

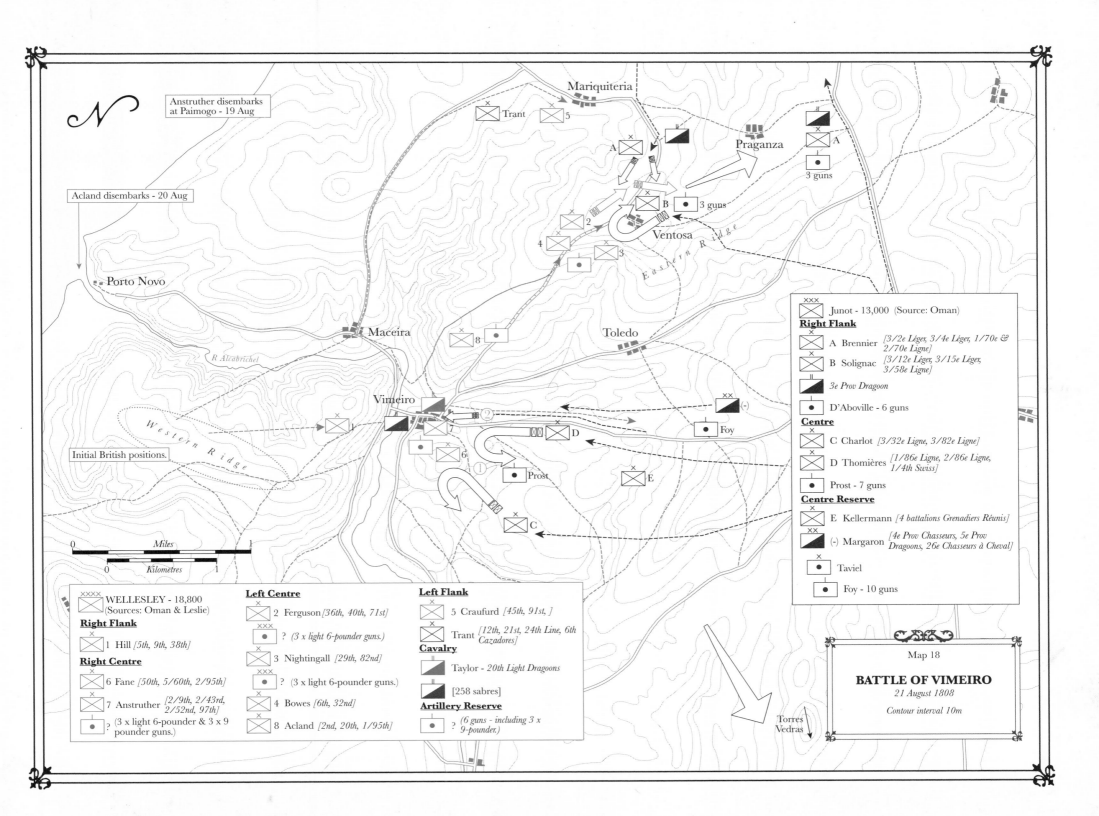

N

Anstruther disembarks
at Paimogo - 19 Aug

Acland disembarks - 20 Aug

Porto Novo

Maceira

R Alcabrichel

Initial British positions.

Western Ridge

Mariquiteria

Trant

5

A

B • 3 guns

Praganza

A

• 3 guns

2

Ventosa

4

3

Eastern Ridge

Vimeiro

8

Toledo

1

2

D

Foy •

6

Prost •

E

C

Junot - 13,000 (Source: Oman)

Right Flank

A Brennier *[3/2e Léger, 3/4e Léger, 1/70e & 2/70e Ligne]*

B Solignac *[3/12e Léger, 3/15e Léger, 3/58e Ligne]*

3e Prov Dragoon

• D'Aboville - 6 guns

Centre

C Charlot *[3/32e Ligne, 3/82e Ligne]*

D Thomières *[1/86e Ligne, 2/86e Ligne, 1/4th Swiss]*

• Prost - 7 guns

Centre Reserve

E Kellermann *[4 battalions Grenadiers Réunis]*

(-) Margaron *[4e Prov Chasseurs, 5e Prov Dragoons, 26e Chasseurs à Cheval]*

• Taviel

• Foy - 10 guns

Torres
Vedras

Map 18

BATTLE OF VIMEIRO
21 August 1808

Contour interval 10m

WELLESLEY - 18,800
(Sources: Oman & Leslie)

Right Flank

1 Hill *[5th, 9th, 38th]*

Right Centre

6 Fane *[50th, 5/60th, 2/95th]*

7 Anstruther *[2/9th, 2/43rd, 2/52nd, 97th]*

• ? *(3 x light 6-pounder & 3 x 9 pounder guns.)*

Left Centre

2 Ferguson *[36th, 40th, 71st]*

• ? *(3 x light 6-pounder guns.)*

3 Nightingall *[29th, 82nd]*

• ? *(3 x light 6-pounder guns.)*

4 Bowes *[6th, 32nd]*

8 Acland *[2nd, 20th, 1/95th]*

Left Flank

5 Craufurd *[45th, 91st,]*

Trant *[12th, 21st, 24th Line, 6th Cazadores]*

Cavalry

Taylor - *20th Light Dragoons*

[258 sabres]

Artillery Reserve

• ? *(6 guns - including 3 x 9-pounder.)*

deployment the four leading British battalions rose up and delivered a simultaneous volley at a range of less than 100 yards into the astonished French infantry. Before the French could recover the British infantry had reloaded and began their advance; the French wavered and then fled back down the hill. Two battalions pursued the retreating brigade north-westwards, while the other two battalions corralled the many prisoners and took possession of the three guns. As this was taking place, Brennier suddenly appeared from the north and immediately fell on the flanks of the four exposed British battalions. The French at once gained the upper hand and were able to release many of their recently captured comrades until Bowes's battalions arrived and, without delay, launched themselves at the French, forcing Brennier's men to retreat back up hill they way they had come.

Combat had commenced at about 0930 hours. It was now midday and the French were falling back at both ends of the battlefield. They fully expected the British to follow up their success, but to their surprise and relief, the Allies remained at their posts. Burrard had just assumed command and had prevented Wellesley from pursuit. Early on 22 August, Sir Hew Dalrymple arrived at Porto Novo and the British army had its third commander within 24 hours. He supported Burrard's decision to wait for Moore's reinforcements to join the army before continuing offensive operations, and the opportunity passed. It had been a disastrous engagement for Junot with the loss of thirteen guns, a number of prisoners (including Brennier) and the wounding of a significant number of general officers.[11] Later on 21 August, Kellermann[12] appeared under a flag of truce to discuss terms and was surprised to discover that the commander was Dalrymple, not Wellesley; he quickly grasped that Dalrymple was in a quandary, uneasy about his predicament and positive to suggestions of a convention. Kellermann proposed that Junot's army be allowed to return to France by sea, on British ships, without any form of capitulation and carrying military baggage and equipment. While the terms had some merit, as they rid the country of the occupying army and left the structures and wealth unharmed, they were, under the circumstances, far too lenient. Even Siniavin's men were returned to Russia and would have been able to so do on their own ships had it not been flatly refused by Admiral Cotton who had spent many months blockading the force and was not about to let it sail away under his very eyes.

The Convention of Cintra, as it became known, understandably received furious criticism from the Portuguese and British authorities. Within weeks Dalrymple, Burrard and Wellesley had been recalled to London to give an account. The court of inquiry published its findings just before Christmas; Wellesley was lucky to emerge unscathed but Dalrymple and Burrard were severely chastised and lost any hope of future field command. In the meantime, Moore had assumed command of the British army in Portugal. By mid-September, the French (and Russians) had all but left the country and the fury of the Portuguese gave way to celebration.

'Twenty two thousand returned to France. They departed from thence inexperienced conscripts; they came back well-trained, warlike soldiers: and they took their place in the columns of the *Grande Armée*, which was traversing France on its way back to the Spanish Peninsula, to retrieve the disasters of the campaign.'[13] It inspired Byron to pen the words:

> *Here folly dash'd to earth the victor's plume,*
> *And Policy regain'd what arms had lost:*
> *For chiefs like ours in vain may laurels bloom!*[14]

The Bishop of Oporto and General Freire were furious at their exclusion to the deliberations over the Convention. It was of little direct consequence. The Regency was reestablished in Lisbon and the emergency Juntas at Oporto, Algarve, Alentejo and Tras-os-Montes were disbanded. The nation had been liberated.

---

11 Namely, Delaborde Charlot, Brennier and Solignac as well as colonels Foy and Prost.

12 Kellermann was an accomplished officer who had served as an attaché in the French embassy in the United States in 1791.

13 Foy, *History of the War in the Peninsula under Napoleon*, vol. II, p.540.

14 *Childe Harold's Pilgrimage*, Canto I, XXV

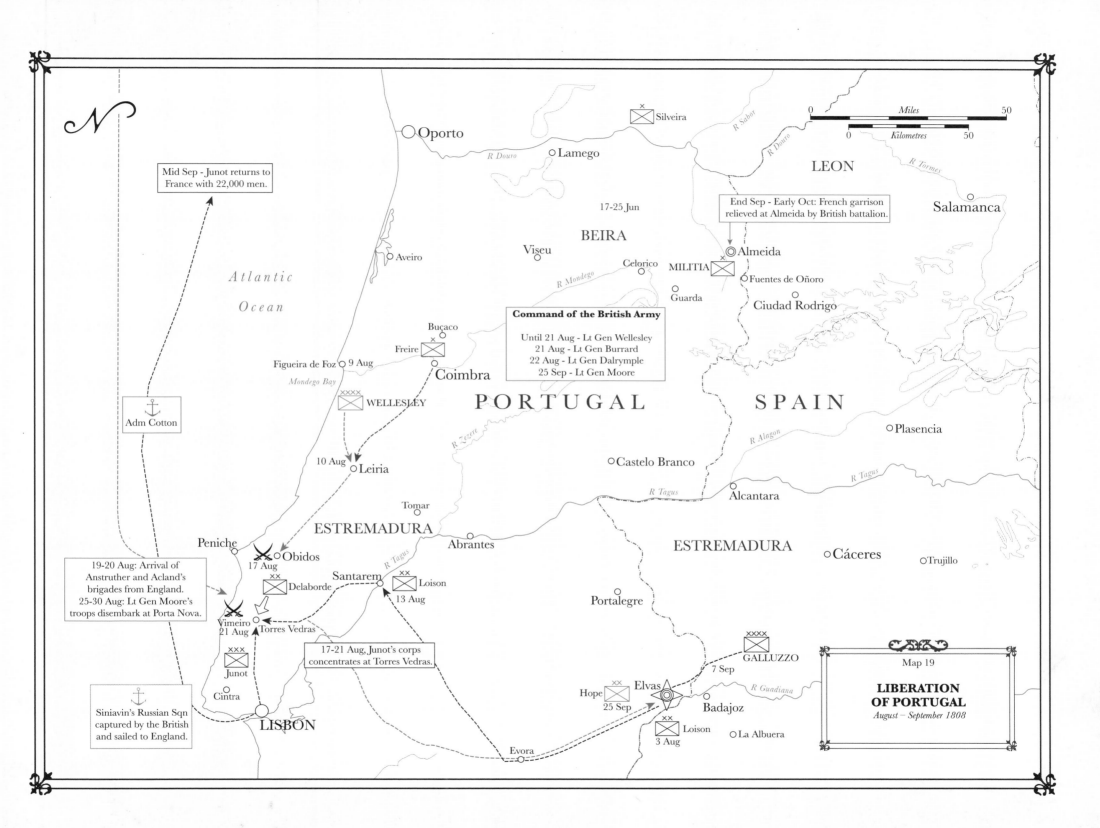

N

Oporto

Silveira

R Douro

Lamego

LEON

R Sabor

R Douro

R Tormes

Salamanca

Mid Sep - Junot returns to
France with 22,000 men.

17-25 Jun

BEIRA

End Sep - Early Oct: French garrison
relieved at Almeida by British battalion.

Viseu

Celorico

Almeida

MILITIA

Atlantic

Fuentes de Oñoro

R Mondego

Ocean

Guarda

Ciudad Rodrigo

Buçaco

Freire

Command of the British Army

Figueira de Foz

9 Aug

Coimbra

Mondego Bay

WELLESLEY

Until 21 Aug - Lt Gen Wellesley
21 Aug - Lt Gen Burrard
22 Aug - Lt Gen Dalrymple
25 Sep - Lt Gen Moore

PORTUGAL

SPAIN

Adm Cotton

Plasencia

R Alagon

10 Aug

Leiria

R Jezere

R Tagus

Tomar

Castelo Branco

R Tagus

Alcantara

ESTREMADURA

Abrantes

ESTREMADURA

Cáceres

Peniche

Obidos

R Tagus

17 Aug

19-20 Aug: Arrival of
Anstruther and Acland's
brigades from England.
25-30 Aug: Lt Gen Moore's
troops disembark at Porta Nova.

Delaborde

Santarem

Loison

13 Aug

Trujillo

Portalegre

Vimeiro
21 Aug

Torres Vedras

17-21 Aug, Junot's corps
concentrates at Torres Vedras.

GALLUZZO

7 Sep

R Guadiana

Junot

Hope

Elvas

25 Sep

Cintra

Loison

Badajoz

Siniavin's Russian Sqn
captured by the British
and sailed to England.

LISBON

3 Aug

La Albuera

Evora

Map 19

**LIBERATION
OF PORTUGAL**

August – September 1808

Chapter 9 ⊶—⊷

STRATEGIC MANOEUVRING: SEPTEMBER TO OCTOBER 1808

From mid-August to the end of October the Supreme Junta achieved little militarily. They failed to appoint a commander-in-chief, delayed the movement of the victorious army from Andalusia and made scant effort to raise new armies in Leon and Castile. This lethargy provided Bonaparte the breathing space he required for the complicated plans to transform the French Army of Spain, by transferring 130,000 men from Germany and France, which would take time and leave a void in his strategic capability. Vienna's immediate intentions were unclear and Napoleon made strong representation to Metternich[1] that he would, in time, replace these troops and could still more than hold his own in central Europe. Additionally, in late September, the French Emperor was to meet with Emperor Alexander of Russia under the pretext of discussing a proposal of peace with Britain, in fact he wanted to determine whether he could rely on Russian support in the event of Austrian aggression. He could, and his Iberian venture now received his full attention.

When the Spanish armies did finally advance to the line of the Ebro they did so piecemeal and, once there, failed to concentrate. The Spanish forces had been reorganized into three main armies in the first line and a series of smaller reserve units in the second line (see Appendix 1). Blake formed the Army of the Left with the Galicians and Asturians; this force included the division of La Romana.[2] Galluzzo and Castaños formed the Army of the Centre and Palafox and Vives (who had assumed command of the Catalan force) constituted the Army of the Right. The elaborate plan of operations had been drawn up on 5 September, but it was several weeks until the forces were in place. This was largely due to the lack of a single commander-in-chief to cajole the otherwise independent commanders into action; Castaños and Galluzzo were particularly sluggish. In the meantime Blake threatened the French line to the north by sending a reserve force to contain Bessières at Burgos and then marching with four divisions on Bilbao. The French had long anticipated a major Spanish offensive and believed this to be their opening move. Bessières fell back from Burgos and took a second line of defence around Vitoria, thereby releasing Ney to move on Blake at Bilbao. When Ney arrived in late September, the 4th Galician Division, that had hitherto contained the town, moved back and joined Blake's main body at

Valmaceda. Blake remained poised in this area, covering the left of the line. To his right should have been the Army of the Centre, but the 12,000 men of Galluzzo's army did not begin their march north until around mid October, and the reorganization of Castaños's large force (of over 50,000 men) took an inordinately long time. Much of the blame for this tardiness must be heaped on the Junta at Sevilla who were reluctant to release the Andalusian troops for the national cause.

In fact, with a total French force of only 100,000 men during much of this period, a third of whom were deployed in Catalonia alone, the French front line was extremely vulnerable. The Napoleonic decree of 7 September had completely restructured the French Army in Spain; there were to be eight corps (see Appendix 1). The bulk of the one hundred and thirty thousand reinforcements comprised of three veteran corps from the Elbe who were due in southern France by the end of October. Until then, Jourdan's aim was to contain the situation, leaving it to the Spanish to make the first move. Castaños endeavoured to commence proceedings but could not convince the Supreme Junta to empower him as the commander-in-chief, despite trying for a second time on 13 October. He left Madrid somewhat dejected and opened discussions for combined operations as an equal, rather than as a superior, but nevertheless managed to cobble together a plan of sorts.

Castaños would edge the balance of his army south along the Ebro to join forces with those of Palafox; together they would fall on Moncey's flank. Pignatelli and Grimarest's divisions would be left in place to contain Ney and Bessières. He hoped also to convince Blake to commence the offensive on Bilbao and thence to Tolosa, thereby cutting off Jourdan from France. However, before this plan was instigated the Spanish themselves were attacked. For some time, and unknown to Castaños, Pignatelli and Grimarest had been probing well forward across the Ebro. This action eventually provoked a response from Ney, who attacked Pignatelli while Moncey engaged Grimarest and Bessières sent a force to Logroño to cut off the Spanish retreat. Both Spanish divisions suffered badly; Ney had captured Logroño and Moncey secured Lodosa. The Spanish plans were thrown into confusion, the French had gained the initiative, Napoleon was a matter of days away and Castaños had taken to his bed with an attack of gout.

During the month of October, initially Merlin and subsequently Lefebvre engaged Blake. On 4 October, Ney arrived in the area with his composite group,[3] forcing Blake to withdraw the 4th Galician Division (under the Marquis of Portago) from Biscay and deploy with it to a defensive position at Valmaceda, approximately 30km to the west. Here he was joined by the 3rd Galician Division and with the force ratio tipped sufficiently against Ney, the French commander wisely elected to pause and wait for the arrival of Joseph's reserves. However, they never appeared, for the French higher command considered Blake's actions a mere feint and concluded that the greater threat lay at Burgos, where a large Spanish force still remained. Ney was consequently ordered back to his old positions around La Guardia and he retired, leaving General Merlin with 3,000 men in the Biscayan capital to observe the Galician force. In light of this development, Blake was quick to resume the offensive and on 11 October, drove Merlin

---

1 At that time he was the Austrian Ambassador to France.

2 This was the force of about 9,000 that had joined the *Grande Armée* in spring 1807 and been sent to the Baltic and scattered along the Danish isles. They were sprung by the British naval force and returned to Santander by 11 October 1808.

3 Consisting of two small infantry divisions.

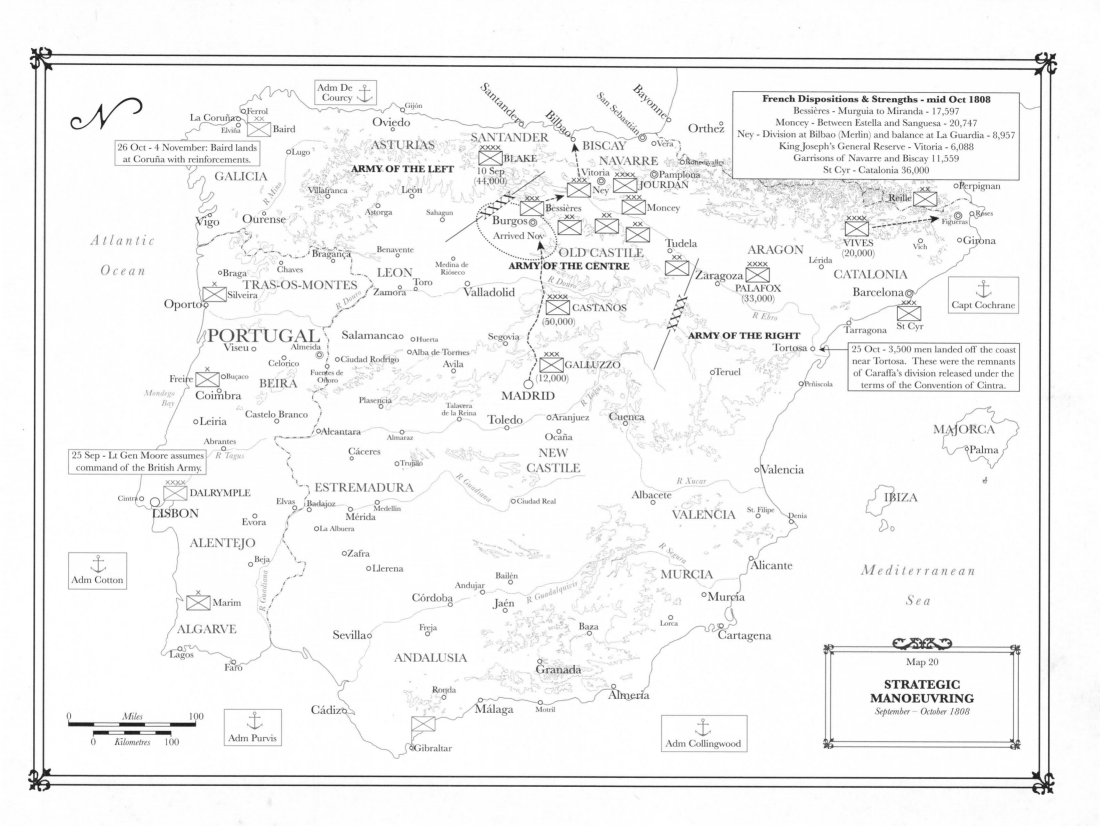

N

Adm De Courcy ⚓

26 Oct - 4 November: Baird lands at Coruña with reinforcements.

French Dispositions & Strengths - mid Oct 1808
Bessières - Murguia to Miranda - 17,597
Moncey - Between Estella and Sanguesa - 20,747
Ney - Division at Bilbao (Merlin) and balance at La Guardia - 8,957
King Joseph's General Reserve - Vitoria - 6,088
Garrisons of Navarre and Biscay 11,559
St Cyr - Catalonia 36,000

Gijón

La Coruña
Ferrol
Elviña
Baird

Oviedo

ASTURIAS

SANTANDER

Santander

Bilbao

BISCAY

San Sebastián

Bayonne

Vera

Orthez

Roncesvalles

Lugo

GALICIA

ARMY OF THE LEFT

BLAKE
10 Sep
(44,000)

Vitoria

NAVARRE

Pamplona

JOURDAN

Ney

Villafranca

León

Astorga

Sahagun

Bessières

Moncey

Perpignan

Vigo

Ourense

Benavente

Burgos
Arrived Nov

ARMY OF THE CENTRE

OLD CASTILE

Tudela

ARAGON

Lérida

VIVES
(20,000)

Reille

Rôses

Figueras

Vich

Girona

CATALONIA

Braga

Chaves

Bragança

TRAS-OS-MONTES

Zamora

Toro

LEON

R Douro

Valladolid

Zaragoza

PALAFOX
(33,000)

Barcelona

Oporto
Silveira

CASTAÑOS
(50,000)

St Cyr

Capt Cochrane ⚓

R Douro

Tarragona

PORTUGAL

Salamanca

Huerta

Alba de Tormes

Segovia

ARMY OF THE RIGHT

Tortosa

25 Oct - 3,500 men landed off the coast near Tortosa. These were the remnants of Caraffa's division released under the terms of the Convention of Cintra.

Viseu
Almeida

Celorico

Ciudad Rodrigo

Avila

GALLUZZO
(12,000)

Teruel

Peñiscola

Freire
Buçaco

BEIRA

Fuentes de Oñoro

Plasencia

Talavera
de la Reina

MADRID

R Tagus

MAJORCA

Palma

Coimbra

Mondego
Bay

Castelo Branco

Toledo

Ocaña

Cuenca

Leiria

Alcantara

Almaraz

Aranjuez

NEW
CASTILE

Valencia

IBIZA

25 Sep - Lt Gen Moore assumes command of the British Army.

Abrantes

R Tagus

Cáceres

Trujillo

R Xucar

Albacete

VALENCIA

St. Filipe

Denia

Mediterranean

Cintra

DALRYMPLE

ESTREMADURA

R Guadiana

Ciudad Real

LISBON

Elvas

Badajoz

Medellin

Mérida

Sea

Adm Cotton ⚓

Evora

La Albuera

ALENTEJO

Zafra

R Guadiana

Llerena

R Segura

MURCIA

Alicante

Beja

Marim

Andujar

Bailén

ALGARVE

Córdoba

Jaén

R Guadalquivir

Murcia

Lorca

Cartagena

Lagos

Faro

Freja

Baza

Sevilla

ANDALUSIA

Granada

Almería

Ronda

Adm Purvis ⚓

Cádiz

Málaga

Motril

Adm Collingwood ⚓

Gibraltar

Miles 0 — 100
Kilometres 0 — 100

Atlantic
Ocean

Map 20

STRATEGIC MANOEUVRING
September – October 1808

back out of Bilbao. The French commander took up a defensive position at Durango with outposts at Zornoza and waited for reinforcement, which arrived within hours in the form of General Verdier and 7,000 men.

Despite this reinforcement, Blake still outnumbered the French by two to one. However, he still erred on the side of caution and did not advance for another two weeks; by which time the two newly arrived corps of Lefebvre and Victor had been moved to the vicinity. Indeed, as early as 18 October, Lefebvre had relieved Merlin and Verdier and established three divisions[4] in the area around Durango. Meanwhile, Joseph and Jourdan had issued instructions for Victor to move north on the road to Bilbao in order to cut off Blake's retreat, and simultaneously tasked Bessières to move to Valmaceda, which Blake would have to pass if he eluded both the former French corps. As it transpired, neither Victor nor Bessières followed their orders, stating that they were contrary to Napoleon's wishes and with the Emperor only days away, their reluctance was not questioned further. Lefebvre, on the other hand, was desperate to prove himself and felt no such desire to wait for Napoleon. Furthermore, an inferior Spanish force lay tantalisingly to his front; nevertheless, he decided to cover his insubordination by provoking the Spanish to attack his outposts, and in this they obliged.

Blake deployed his Vanguard Brigade in two parts on the high ground astride the road from Durango. The 1st Division was located slightly to the rear on the high ground to the north of the road, and the 3rd and 4th divisions were in depth behind them (the latter in the village of Zornoza itself). The 4th Division had also deployed a detachment of troops onto the high ground to the south of the road. On 31 October Lefebvre took advantage of the early morning haze to close right up to Blake's vanguard. Villatte advanced south of the road and Sebastiani moved up the road itself, with Leval to the north. The vanguard was quickly driven in, and Blake immediately ordered them to fall back on both sides of the road and he sent the single battery back as far as Zornoza. Blake now had a better idea of the strength of the French force to his front and of the determination of their commander, and therefore reconsidered his original intent to stand firm. However, he wanted to test French resolve and at the very least make a point before pulling back and, accordingly, ordered the Vanguard Brigade to fall back with the 1st Division to the heights of Mont St Martin, where they were joined by the 3rd Division.

While Villatte pushed on south of the road, Lefebvre deployed his guns on the knoll to the south-east of Mont St Martin and opened on the concentrated Spanish position to his front (map 21, point 1). With Sebastiani and Villatte now well forward (in the centre and left), Blake was in danger of being cut off. He ordered an immediate retreat to Bilbao and Valmaceda. The divisions of Acevedo and Martinengo,[5] which were covering Blake's southern flank, were ordered to join him at Bilbao and retreat further into the Asturias as a formed body. However, these flanking formations received their orders too late to be effective. As they moved north they discovered that Lefebvre had already occupied Miravelles and cut the road to Bilbao. Acevedo pulled back and went to ground. Lefebvre seemed oblivious to his presence and was in full pursuit of Blake, whom he followed as far as Valmaceda before accepting that he was probably chasing a lost cause. He left Villatte's division at Valmaceda and retired to Bilbao with the other two divisions where his men were rested and allowed to recuperate.

Meanwhile, Acevedo and Martinengo had slipped passed Lefebvre but were still separated from their commander by the presence of Villatte's division. Worse still, Victor had ventured north with one division and was now bearing down on the Spanish from the other end of the defile. When he came upon the Spaniards he assumed it was Blake's entire army rather than an isolated group of 8,000 men. He stopped to appraise the situation and determine the whereabouts of Lefebvre. This provided the time that Blake required to move his force into position and, on 5 November, he fell on Villatte's force and forced them back. Acevedo capitalized on the opportunity to break clean across the hills and, fortuitously for the Spanish, Victor stayed put. As Villatte fell back, his advance guard came into contact with Acevedo's force at Guenes: the latter had deployed across the road and stream. Villatte formed up in a solid mass and burst through the makeshift defences and escaped at the expense of a gun and 300 men who were taken prisoner. Lefebvre, having received news of Villatte's predicament, moved in haste to succour his divisional commander and was greatly relieved to find the division intact. In anger, and hungry for revenge, he set off in pursuit of Blake and immediately recaptured Guenes. Blake was now in the most precarious position; his men were almost devoid of rations, short of ammunition and exhausted from five weeks of almost constant campaigning.

---

4   His own divisions of Sebastiani and Leval, as well as Villatte's division from the 1st Corps, to compensate for the lack of his third division, that of Valence, which was still some way to the rear.

5   The 2nd Galician and Asturian divisions respectively.

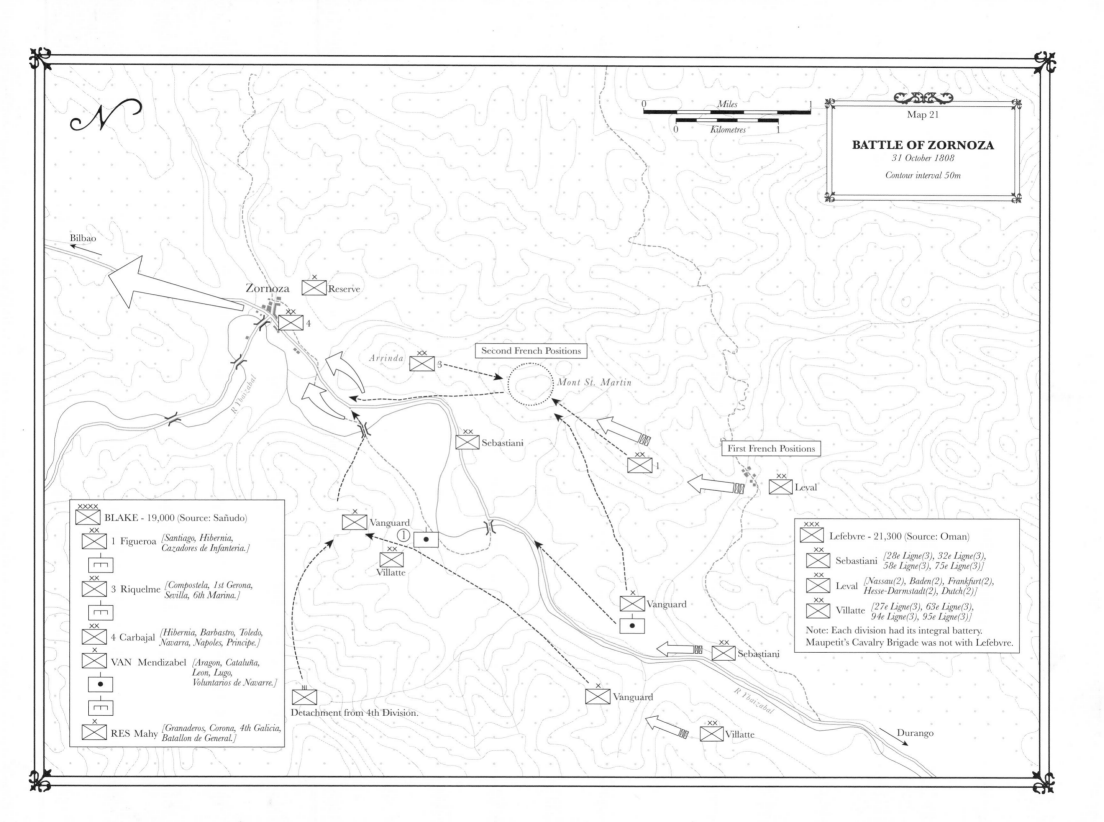

N

0 — Miles — 1

0 — Kilometres — 1

Map 21

BATTLE OF ZORNOZA

31 October 1808

Contour interval 50m

Bilbao

Zornoza

Reserve

4

Arrinda

3

Second French Positions

Mont St. Martin

First French Positions

Sebastiani

1

Leval

R. Yhaizabal

BLAKE - 19,000 (Source: Sañudo)

1 Figueroa *[Santiago, Hibernia, Cazadores de Infanteria.]*

3 Riquelme *[Compostela, 1st Gerona, Sevilla, 6th Marina.]*

4 Carbajal *[Hibernia, Barbastro, Toledo, Navarra, Napoles, Principe.]*

VAN Mendizabel *[Aragon, Cataluña, Leon, Lugo, Voluntarios de Navarre.]*

RES Mahy *[Granaderos, Corona, 4th Galicia, Batallon de General.]*

Vanguard

Villatte

Vanguard

Lefebvre - 21,300 (Source: Oman)

Sebastiani *[28e Ligne(3), 32e Ligne(3), 58e Ligne(3), 75e Ligne(3)]*

Leval *[Nassau(2), Baden(2), Frankfurt(2), Hesse-Darmstadt(2), Dutch(2)]*

Villatte *[27e Ligne(3), 63e Ligne(3), 94e Ligne(3), 95e Ligne(3)]*

Note: Each division had its integral battery. Maupetit's Cavalry Brigade was not with Lefebvre.

Detachment from 4th Division.

Vanguard

Sebastiani

Villatte

R. Yhaizabal

Durango

Chapter 10 ❧

Napoleonic Intervention: November 1808

In 1808, the Grande Armée numbered in excess of three hundred and fifty thousand men: a total of four hundred and seventeen battalions, eighty cavalry regiments and the capability to field a thousand cannon. Yet, faced with the unexpected turn of events in Spain, Napoleon needed to ensure the continued order in Central, Eastern and Southern Europe before committing additional men to the Iberian theatre. Since the Treaty of Tilsit, signed between Tsar Alexander and Napoleon on 7 July 1807, Franco-Russian relations had deteriorated sufficiently to convince the French Emperor of the need to rekindle conciliation to free his hands. The meeting was very different from that conducted on the purpose built raft of the River Niemen at Tilsit the previous year. An agreement of sorts was signed on 12 October; it fell well short of Napoleon's aspirations but it was considered sufficient to put the corps législatif in motion and commence the large scale reorganisation of forces destined for Spain.

Napoleon left Erfurt on 14 October and, after a ten-day stop in Paris, continued south, reaching Bayonne on 3 November. The corps of Victor and Lefebvre were already in Spain, and Mortier's corps, the divisions for Ney, the Imperial Guard and many extra divisions of cavalry were not far behind. Furthermore, Junot's corps had now landed at the ports of Quiberon and Rochefort[1] and was being quickly re-equipped and redirected to Spain via Bordeaux. Napoleon would soon have at his immediate disposal nearly 280,000 men (see Appendix 1) and was determined to put an end to Spanish defiance swiftly and decisively. Napoleon adroitly slipped from political statesman to military commander. His plan was simple but ingenious and predicated on his contempt for the Spanish generals and their armies. It prompted him to draw up plans not just to retake Madrid but also to capture and annihilate the armies of Blake, Castaños and Palafox by bursting through the centre and then enveloping left and right, trapping, surrounding and subsequently destroying them. As for the troublesome British force, it is apparent from his subsequent dispatches that he was aware of Moore's army, but at no juncture did he consider that they might move overland in support of Madrid.

In penning his plan, Napoleon knew Blake was in front of Zornoza, Castaños at Tudela and the majority of Palafox's Army of Aragon near Sanguesa. However he was unaware of Galluzzo's Army of Estremadura,[2] which was en route for Burgos to plug the very gap that was pivotal to Napoleon's plans. Having taken the three principal passages over the upper Ebro at Miranda,

Logroño and Lodosa during the preliminary operations in October, he sent explicit instructions that no further advances were to be made against the Spanish for fear of them withdrawing from their forward, more exposed positions and complicating any subsequent envelopment. Lefebvre's disobedience and the subsequent battle of Zornoza on 31 October (see Chapter 9) could so easily have derailed Napoleon's campaign had Blake fallen back on Reynosa and not Bilbao which, as it transpired, served Napoleon's purpose admirably.

On the French right, Lefebvre was to occupy Blake, while Moncey was to do likewise with his divisions against Castaños and Palafox on the French left. Victor was then to get in behind Blake at an early stage to prevent him breaking clean. In the centre, Napoleon, at the head of his main body, was to cross the Ebro at Miranda and exploit the purported gap left between the Spanish armies of the centre and left. Once at Burgos any hope of a link-up between the Spanish armies would be thwarted and then the encirclement would commence. Ney was to swing left and cut off Castaños and Palafox's retreat to Madrid, while simultaneously Soult[3] was to swing right and cut off Blake's retreat westwards – if Victor had not already succeeded in this respect. The two commanders would then link up and destroy the Gallegos and Asturians under Blake while on the French left, Ney would link up with Moncey and press Castaños and Palafox into the north-eastern corner of Catalonia. Napoleon, with the balance of the main body supported by Mortier's Corps, which was en route from France, would then march directly from Burgos to Madrid. Central to Napoleon's plans was the rapid capture of the nation's capital; he was completely confident the nation would then submit. The troublesome 'British leopard' hardly featured in his plans but once he had taken Madrid, he would drive it into the sea. He considered the war a military problem, it never occurred to him that despite losing their capital and their king that the people would fight on more determined than ever to remove the French invaders by low-level but effective resistance and spawn a new form of warfare: that of the guerrilla.

Lefebvre, having linked up with Villatte, was determined to punish Blake for taking the offensive while his back was turned. He retook the village of Guenes but was unable to tie Blake to battle; the Gallegos fought three rearguard actions on 7 and 8 November, falling back each time. The fact was that Blake's army was in a dreadful state, devoid of rations, short of ammunition and suffering from sickness. Lefebvre had been chastised for his disobedience in opening hostilities with Blake in advance of the Emperor's timetable, but Victor then received a similar rebuke for failing to take the offensive once Blake was on the run. He took up the chase and was ordered to gather Villatte's division, back under his rightful command, and execute his part of Napoleon's plan. Following his reprimand, he commenced the operation with some vigour and Blake's rearguard, formed on the Conde de San Roman's division[4] was harassed mercilessly by Victor's vanguard. Late on 9 November, Blake's force drew up at Espinosa; his losses had mounted and of his original force of 38,000,[5] he mustered less than

---

1 Having been repatriated from Portugal – see Chapter 8.

2 This force was long awaited but numbered only 12,000 and came under Castaños's command in the Army of the Centre.

3 Soult assumed command of the 2nd Corps on 9 November releasing Bessières to command the Reserve Cavalry of the Army consisting of five divisions.

4 This was part of La Romana's Army that had landed at Santander on 11 October 1808.

5 His army numbered some 44,000 in October but about 4,000 were otherwise deployed and 2,000 were from the element of the Galician 4th Division, which had been cut off and retreated to Santander.

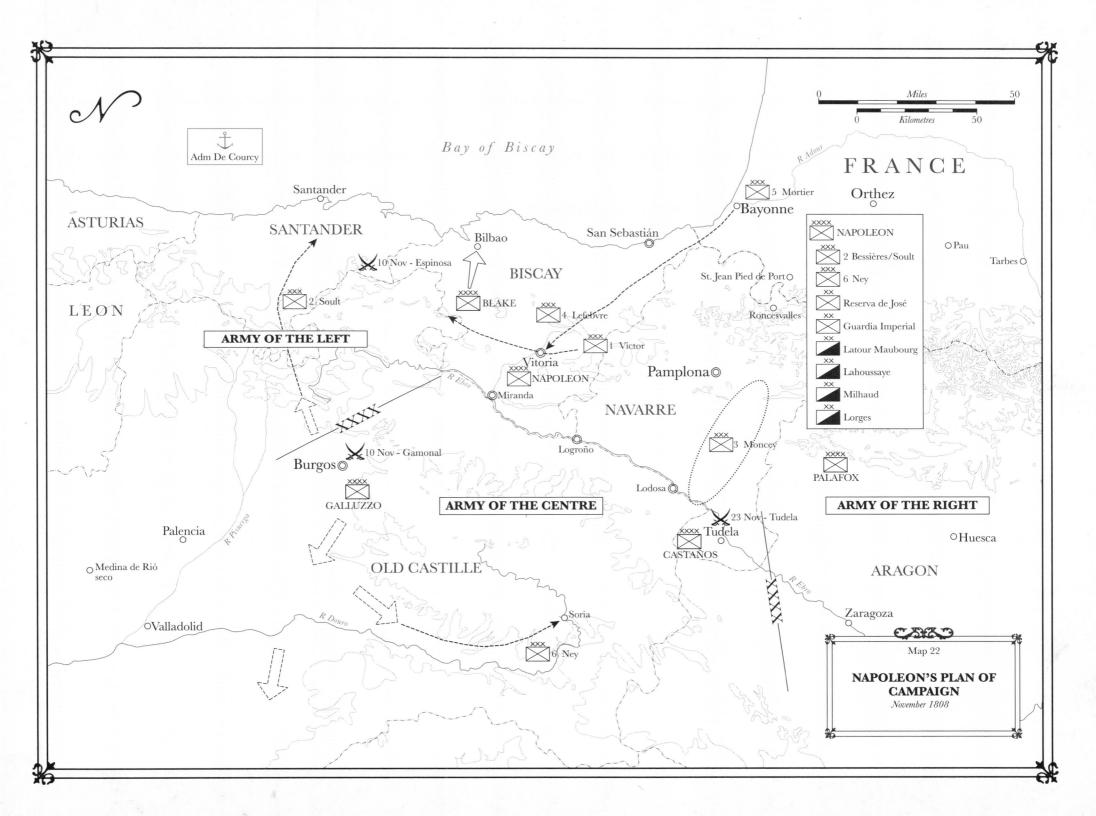

N

Bay of Biscay

FRANCE

Adm De Courcy

Santander

SANTANDER

ASTURIAS

Bilbao

BISCAY

San Sebastián

R Adour

Orthez

XXX
5 Mortier

Bayonne

Pau

Tarbes

LEON

10 Nov - Espinosa

XXX
2 Soult

ARMY OF THE LEFT

XXXX
BLAKE

XXX
4 Lefèbvre

St. Jean Pied de Port

XXX
1 Victor

Roncesvalles

XXXX
NAPOLEON

Vitoria

Miranda

R Ebro

Pamplona

NAVARRE

XXXX
NAPOLEON

XXX
2 Bessières/Soult

XXX
6 Ney

Reserva de José

Guardia Imperial

XX
Latour Maubourg

XX
Lahoussaye

XX
Milhaud

XX
Lorges

10 Nov - Gamonal

Burgos

Logroño

XXX
3 Moncey

XXXX
PALAFOX

XXXX
GALLUZZO

ARMY OF THE CENTRE

Lodosa

ARMY OF THE RIGHT

Palencia

23 Nov - Tudela

XXXX
CASTAÑOS

Tudela

Huesca

Medina de Rió
seco

OLD CASTILLE

ARAGON

Valladolid

R Douro

Soria

R Ebro

Zaragoza

XXX
6 Ney

Map 22

**NAPOLEON'S PLAN OF
CAMPAIGN**
November 1808

R Pisuerga

25,000 and six guns.[6] Blake recognized the protective attributes in front of the Espinosa and immediately directed the rearguard to take up defensive positions to the east of the town and then brought back the rest of his army to form up in a horseshoe formation on the hills that funnelled in on Espinosa itself.

Villatte came across the Spanish deployed for battle at around midday on 10 November. The position was undoubtedly strong, but Villatte considered the Galician army a spent force and besides, he had a personal score to settle. He wasted no time in deploying his entire division of 12 battalions; tasking the Vanguard Brigade to keep the Spanish occupied while ordering the other brigade, consisting of the 94e and 95e Ligne, left up the hill with the aim of dislodging the 5th Galician Division and turning the Spanish position. After two hours of hard fighting the French had made no headway, the elite forces from La Romana's troops held their positions and Villatte, somewhat frustrated, was forced to withdraw Puthod's Brigade. At about this time (1500 hours) Victor emerged at the head of his other two divisions. Following his chastisement for casualness, he too had a score to settle and rather hot-headedly emulated Villatte's earlier attempt to dislodge the Spanish. Dispensing with a proper reconnaissance and eager to get on with the task (as the winter evening beckoned) he committed nine new battalions to dislodge the 5th Galician Division from the same heights. This force consisted of a brigade from Ruffin's division and a regiment from Lapisse.[7]

Following another couple of hours of fierce fighting, the Conde de San Roman's troops were still in possession of the heights, but Blake had been forced to call up the entire 3rd Division and elements of the 2nd to assist them in their task. Nonetheless, the Spanish achievement had been most credible. The 5th Division numbered about 5,000 men and they had, over four hours of hard fighting, beaten off twice their number. As dusk fell Victor was compelled to recall his force and reconsider his options.

The next morning, following a full reconnaissance, Victor decided to feint against the Spanish right, hold the centre and attempt to turn the left. He calculated that Blake would have reinforced his right and he was correct; the 2nd Division and the balance of the 4th (the latter was just one regiment) were positioned directly behind the 5th, while the vanguard straddled the road and the 3rd were to their immediate right (see map 23). On the Spanish left, the 1st Galician and Asturias divisions were deployed covering the heights of Las Penuccas, strung out in a wide arc with no reserve. Ruffin moved to the left of the road and Villatte to the right, both divisions serving as a distraction for Lapisse's Division, which was now the main effort. Lapisse moved out from the village of Quintana and used the dead ground provided by the river gully of the same name to advance, virtually unseen, upon the Asturias Division. Acevedo's troops were largely new recruits; of his ten battalions, he possessed only one regular and one militia battalion. The strong French skirmish line was enough to cause panic, which Acevedo and his two brigade commanders, Quiros and Valdes, did their utmost to quell. Rallying their men repeatedly, all three were eventually struck

down. It was the catalyst for collapse and the Asturians broke and fled down the hill into Espinosa town. General de Brigade Maison, who had led the French attack, displayed great presence of mind by restraining his force from plunging headlong after the beaten division and instead wheeled them left and into the flank of the 1st Galician Division. At the same moment Victor ordered both Ruffin and Villatte to press home their attacks. The Spanish gave way across the front escaping over the river Trueba and south over the hills to Reynosa. 'They had to retire by a bridge over the Trueba and a defile; and instead of attempting to save the guns, which would necessarily have impeded the retreat of the army, Blake thought it better to employ them until the last moment; this was done with great effect, and they were spiked when the enemy was close to them.'[8]

Casualties were not high, about 3,000 Spanish, but when Blake rallied his men at Reynosa only 12,000 could be accounted for, with the balance scattered in the hills. There was more bad news; Malaspina's Brigade, which had provided the guard force to the depot at Villarcayo, had been intercepted by Lefebvre's Corps and had beaten a hasty retreat, abandoning the six guns they had brought to support Blake at Espinosa. 'Yet in justice to this ill-fated army it should be said, that no men ever behaved more gallantly, nor with more devoted patriotism. Without cavalry, half clothed, almost without food, they fought battle after battle against troops always their superior in number, and whose losses were always filled up with reinforcements.'[9] The Army of the Left had lived to fight another day but were unaware that another French corps, that of Soult, had joined the chase.

The day prior to the first engagement at Espinosa, Napoleon had set out from Vitoria. He had been there four days waiting for positive news from Victor and Lefebvre and similar indications that Bessières, who had set off on the 6th, had captured Burgos. Napoleonic patience was running thin and Soult, summoned earlier from command in Germany, was hastened to the front to assume command from Bessières and get on with the job of taking Burgos. The 24,500 men of the 2nd Corps and the cavalry divisions of Milhaud (dragoons) and Franceschi (light) constituted the French front line. The balance of the main body, another 44,000 – almost half of which were veterans from Germany – were not far behind. Napoleon had expected the city to be held by Pignatelli's Army of Castile but he had been relieved of his command by Castaños at the end of October and his troops dispersed into the Army of Andalusia.[10] Indeed, up until 7 November only two reserve battalions from Blake's Army held the city but, on that day, the Conde de Belvedere arrived from Madrid with the 1st Division of the Army of Estremadura. This force of 4,000 men and 400 cavalry was joined the next day by the greater part of the 2nd Division, adding another 3,000 infantry and two hussar regiments. Belvedere, a headstrong young aristocrat, was now commanding the Army of Estremadura by default. On 2 November, the 2nd Division's commander, Don Joseph Galuzzo, had been recalled to Aranjuez to answer charges brought by the Supreme Junta. No successor was nominated and this extraordinary turn of events led to the

---

6   Blake had chosen to leave 32 of his 38 guns at a depot at Villarcayo because of the difficulties in manoeuvring the ordnance over the terrain. It however, deprived him of any serious artillery at both Zornoza and Espinosa.

7   The 9e Léger, 24e Ligne and 54e Ligne.

8   Southey, R., History of the Peninsular War 1807–1811, vol. II, p.391.

9   Ibid, pp.393–4

10   Pignatelli had given up the principal crossing of the Ebro at Logroño without a fight on 25 October. Ney seized the vital point the next day.

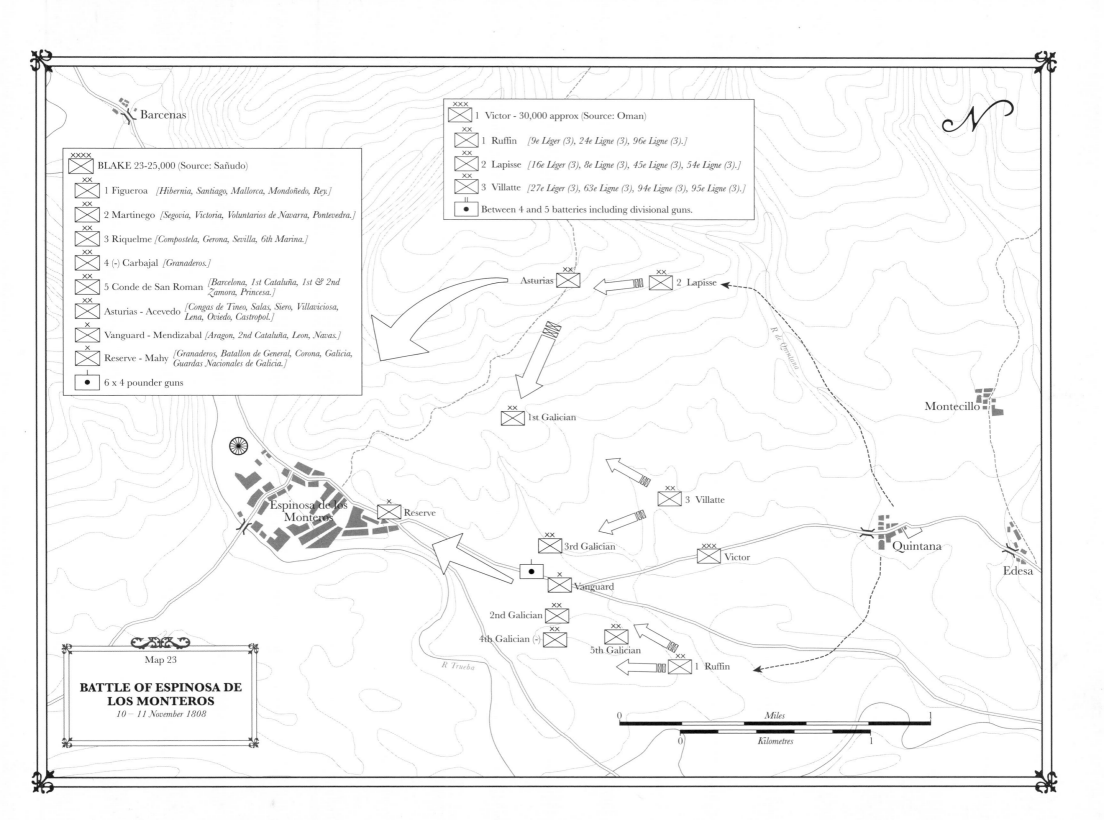

Barcenas

BLAKE 23-25,000 (Source: Sañudo)

1 Figueroa *[Hibernia, Santiago, Mallorca, Mondoñedo, Rey.]*

2 Martinego *[Segovia, Victoria, Voluntarios de Navarra, Pontevedra.]*

3 Riquelme *[Compostela, Gerona, Sevilla, 6th Marina.]*

4 (-) Carbajal *[Granaderos.]*

5 Conde de San Roman *[Barcelona, 1st Cataluña, 1st & 2nd Zamora, Princesa.]*

Asturias - Acevedo *[Congas de Tineo, Salas, Siero, Villaviciosa, Lena, Oviedo, Castropol.]*

Vanguard - Mendizabal *[Aragon, 2nd Cataluña, Leon, Navas.]*

Reserve - Mahy *[Granaderos, Batallon de General, Corona, Galicia, Guardas Nacionales de Galicia.]*

6 x 4 pounder guns

1 Victor - 30,000 approx (Source: Oman)

1 Ruffin *[9e Léger (3), 24e Ligne (3), 96e Ligne (3).]*

2 Lapisse *[16e Léger (3), 8e Ligne (3), 45e Ligne (3), 54e Ligne (3).]*

3 Villatte *[27e Léger (3), 63e Ligne (3), 94e Ligne (3), 95e Ligne (3).]*

Between 4 and 5 batteries including divisional guns.

Asturias

2 Lapisse

Montecillo

1st Galician

Espinosa de los Monteros

Reserve

3 Villatte

3rd Galician

Victor

Quintana

Vanguard

Edesa

2nd Galician

4th Galician (-)

5th Galician

1 Ruffin

R de Ormietana

R Trueba

Map 23

BATTLE OF ESPINOSA DE LOS MONTEROS

10 – 11 November 1808

0   Miles   1

0   Kilometres   1

3rd Division failing to move up in time to join Belvedere and the 1st and 2nd divisions at Burgos. Lacking his entire force and unaware of the strength and dispositions of the French force to his front, Belvedere would have been wise to exercise caution and utilize the significant defences afforded by the city. Instead he threw caution to the wind and advanced east through the city and out onto the plains north-east of the village of Gamonal. He deployed his nine battalions in a line along the front edge of a substantial wood and placed his cavalry on both flanks. The other two battalions were to the rear with the 2nd Hussars and the half battery of light guns.

At about 1000 hours on 10 November Soult rode up with Lasalle's Cavalry Division, and through the sparsely wooded terrain was able to pick out the line of Spanish troops deployed across the road in front of the wooded feature on the far side. The French marshal was on slightly higher ground than the Spanish and, with open ground either side of the Spanish lines, he was able to instantly determine their significant disadvantage in numbers and the questionable nature of their deployment. He did not hesitate for a moment. Hastening Mouton forward he ordered him to deploy using the trees as cover, sending a strong skirmish line ahead of the infantry. Lasalle's light cavalry swung south forming the centre and Milhaud's Dragoons manoeuvred to their left, crossed the river and deployed on the open ground. The flat but firm ground south of the woodland and north of the river Arlanzón was about 1.5km wide – a comfortable size for the 4,500 cavalry who were quick into formation, eagerly anticipating their first encounter since arriving in-theatre.

Belvedere had deployed the ten guns of the two horse artillery batteries on the road in the centre of the infantry and, as Mouton's tirailleurs emerged from the sparse tree line 500m to their front, they were heavily and effectively engaged with canister. However, such was the speed of the engagement that the unfortunate gunners only had time for three to four salvoes before the thunder of hooves and cacophony of battle cries revealed the massed French cavalry as it rounded the wood line to the south and smashed into the Spanish infantry on the right flank as Mouton's infantry simultaneously closed in. The single Spanish regiment of hussars on the southern flank was swept away and the infantry in the front line struggled to form into squares before the wave galloped over them. Four of the battalions were non-regulars[11] who stood little chance of being able to conduct such a complicated manoeuvre in time. To add to their confusion Mouton's infantry were now almost upon them – the result was unavoidable. The two guards battalions were able to form squares but their numbers were few, about 400 men each, and they fought gallantly against overwhelming odds before inevitably accepting the battle lost. Both regiments left the field with dignity, maintaining some form of defence against the elated French cavalry who robustly pursued the Spanish for 12km, breaking off the chase only to join their infantry colleagues, who by now were busy sacking the city of Burgos.

The events at Gamonal were a disaster for the Spanish; they lost about 3,000 men[12] killed, wounded or captured, all 16 of their guns and 12 colours. However, more importantly, the defensive line had been all too easily punctured and the way was now open to Madrid. Napoleon came up that night and stayed in Burgos and experienced firsthand the ill-discipline of his troops who set fire to the adjacent buildings, forcing him to find alternative accommodation. The next day he executed the first of the encircling movements; Soult departed the environs of Burgos with Debelle's Cavalry Brigade[13] in an attempt to get to Reynosa before Blake and cut off his retreat. Two days later Ney[14] was sent to the east with orders to eliminate Castaños who was reported in the area of Tudela. As Soult and Ney marched ever closer to their respective prey, Napoleon stayed at Burgos with the balance of his army, preparing for the move on Madrid. He issued strict instructions to this force that they were not to make the final assault on the capital until he was certain that Blake, Castaños and Palafox had been neutralized.

Soult's force made extraordinary speed, covering 90km in three days over difficult terrain, and arrived on the outskirts of Reynosa in the evening of 13 November. Blake, conscious that both Victor and Lefebvre were pursuing him, had already despatched the artillery and baggage on the León road but calculated he had another couple of days to rest and recoup his exhausted infantry. It was a rude shock, therefore, when Soult's advance cavalry guard caught the tail end of this convoy. With Lefebvre and Victor closing in from the north, and the only road to the south and west now blocked, his alternatives were limited. He instructed his dispirited army to abandon all their stores, horses and carriages and make off into the mountains to the north. Their retreat was gruelling and the route demanding in the extreme, with snow lying thick on some of the highest mountains in Spain, but after two days the force had broken clean from French pursuit. Barely half of the original numbers made León and those who succeeded were unarmed, starved, impoverished and wracked with disease. Blake's reward was notification from the Junta that, following his failure at Zornoza, he was relieved of command and was to hand over the army to La Romana. Soult had to console himself with the mass of plunder in Reynosa, which included 15,000 new British muskets and 35 field guns. Victor and Lefebvre joined Soult at Reynosa on 15 November and received rapid notification from a slightly disgruntled Napoleon to break up this superfluous assembly of 50,000 men. Victor was recalled to Burgos and Lefebvre sent south to Carrion, Soult was sent to Santander and charged with continuing the pursuit of the Galician Army. As he arrived at the port he caught sight of 17 British transports sailing out of the harbour laden with stores and munitions. Soult gratefully acquired the remainder of the army's stores, which had been abandoned. Bonnet's division was left in Santander[15] and Soult set off westwards.

Meanwhile, Moncey continued to contain Castaños and Palafox's respective armies of the centre and right. Moncey's enhanced corps numbered about 31,500[16] and was facing the two

---

11   The two battalions from the Volunteers of Badajoz and the two Galician battalions of Tui and Benavente.

12   Oman states 2,500 killed and 900 prisoners, Napoleon in his *Bulletin* 3,000 killed and 3,000 prisoners, but most Spanish accounts agree with a total of about 3,000.

13   Lasalle's Division, from Soult's Corps, had been dispatched to Lerma following the remnants of the Army of Estremadura. Milhaud was sent to Palencia and Franceschi to Urbel and Odra.

14   With Marchand's Division from his own corps, four regiments from the central reserve and Beaumont's Cavalry Brigade – originally task-organized with Victor's Corps.

15   Where he stayed until 1812 before being called to join Marmont at Salamanca.

16   In addition to his own corps he received Colbert's Brigade from Ney's Corps, and Digeon's Dragoon Brigade from the cavalry reserve.

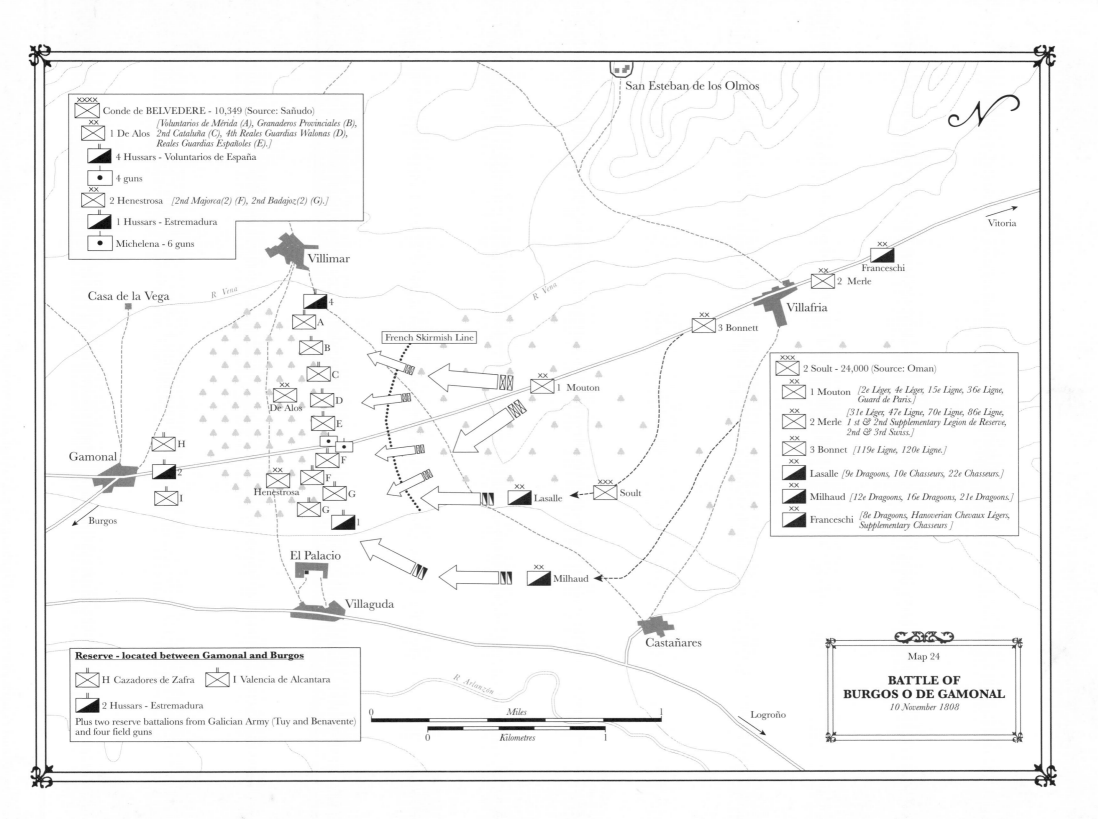

San Esteban de los Olmos

Conde de BELVEDERE - 10,349 (Source: Sañudo)
[Voluntarios de Mérida (A), Granaderos Provinciales (B),
1 De Alos   *2nd Cataluña (C), 4th Reales Guardias Walonas (D),*
Reales Guardias Españoles (E).]

4 Hussars - Voluntarios de España

4 guns

2 Henestrosa   *[2nd Majorca(2) (F), 2nd Badajoz(2) (G).]*

1 Hussars - Estremadura

Michelena - 6 guns

Vitoria

Villimar

Franceschi

2 Merle

Villafria

Casa de la Vega

R. Vena

R. Vena

3 Bonnett

French Skirmish Line

A

B

C

1 Mouton

2 Soult - 24,000 (Source: Oman)

1 Mouton   *[2e Léger, 4e Léger, 15e Ligne, 36e Ligne,*
Guard de Paris.]

[31e Léger, 47e Ligne, 70e Ligne, 86e Ligne,
2 Merle   *1 st & 2nd Supplementary Legion de Reserve,*
2nd & 3rd Swiss.]

3 Bonnet   *[119e Ligne, 120e Ligne.]*

Lasalle   *[9e Dragoons, 10e Chasseurs, 22e Chasseurs.]*

Milhaud   *[12e Dragoons, 16e Dragoons, 21e Dragoons.]*

Franceschi   *[8e Dragoons, Hanoverian Chevaux Légers,*
Supplementary Chasseurs]

De Alos

D

E

Gamonal

H

F

2

F

Henestrosa

G

I

G

1

Soult

Lasalle

Burgos

El Palacio

Milhaud

Villaguda

Castañares

R. Arlanzón

Reserve - located between Gamonal and Burgos

H Cazadores de Zafra   I Valencia de Alcantara

2 Hussars - Estremadura

Plus two reserve battalions from Galician Army (Tuy and Benavente)
and four field guns

Logroño

Map 24

**BATTLE OF
BURGOS O DE GAMONAL**
10 November 1808

0   Miles   1

0   Kilometres   1

(combined) Spanish armies – which totalled twice the French strength – but once again the Spanish did not make use of their advantage. As October passed so did the opportunity to attack and, by early November, massed French arrivals rendered any offensive most unwise. Furthermore, the Spanish troops were suffering terribly through lack of suitable clothing. 'An English observer, who passed through the camps of Palafox and Castaños at this moment, reports that while the regulars and Valencian troops seem fairly well clad, the Aragonese, the Castilians and the Murcians were suffering terribly from exposure.'[17] An epidemic of dysentery thinned the Spanish ranks and by the time Castaños engaged the French his combined army numbered no more than 49,000. It was early November when the Spanish commander finally elected to engage Moncey's corps and issued orders accordingly, but on the 11th he was taken ill and during his absence his deputy, Francisco Palafox,[18] changed Castaños's original instructions and ordered a general advance across the entire frontage. Over the coming days this rather hasty decision succeeded in splitting the two armies on either side of the Ebro with the bridge at Tudela the only means of reuniting the force.

By 21 November Castaños was back on his feet just in time to receive the news of Ney's flanking manoeuvre. He was now in the most precarious position and issued immediate orders to pull back to the line of Tudela–Tarazona, whilst at the same time requesting Joseph Palafox to bring his Army of Aragon down from Caparrosa in an attempt to increase his constantly dwindling force. Palafox remained uncommitted to the idea until 22 November when he finally agreed to send O'Neille and the two divisions to Tudela. They arrived on the east bank that evening, but elected to remain there for the night. It was to be a costly mistake. Castaños's plan allocated the left of the line (from Tarazona to Cascante) to his own army and that from Cascante to Tudela to the Army of the Left and the Murcian Division from the Army of Andalusia. The Spanish were therefore deployed with Roca north of Tudela; the divisions of Saint March and O'Neille, from the Army of Aragon, on the hills to the south west of the town; La Peña five kilometres further south at Cascante and finally Grimarest and Villariezo at Tarazona. The resulting line was 16km long and, with only 48,500 men, was insufficient to hold an advancing army of some 34,000 who could concentrate at any number of points. Castaños's defensive plan was ambitious and relied on an early indication of the French axis of attack, but having kept his considerable cavalry force to the rear of the infantry, he denied himself this intelligence, and with it the time to react. Furthermore, O'Neille's lethargy at getting into position early on 23 November resulted in the French attacking before the Spanish line had been fully formed. La Peña was at Cascante and Roca on the Cerro de Santa Barbara north of the city of Tudela, while the Army of Aragon moved to the heights of Cabeza Malla and Santa Quiteria, leaving a large gap between O'Neille on the former feature and La Peña to the south.

Much to the surprise of Castaños and Palafox, the advancing army was not under the command of either Moncey or Ney but Marshal Lannes. Ney was still making his way from Soria, where there is some evidence that he took a wrong turn; and Moncey had been replaced by Napoleon on 20 November; the latter commander being considered too cautious. Lannes despatched Wathier's light cavalry in advance down the Pamplona road and they reported that the Spanish had not completed their deployment, prompting Lannes to hasten his advance. Morlot's Division led with Mathieu's behind, while Lagrange's Division and the other two cavalry brigades took a more westerly route, emerging from the hills towards the village of Murchante and Cascante. Morlot engaged Roca's Division while Mathieu swung right and onto the plains below. Indeed, such was the speed of the French advance that Mathieu's skirmish line was already on the Cabeza Malla before O'Neille had reached his defensive positions there. As the troops from the Army of Aragon arrived they dislodged the French tirailleurs and, somewhat exhausted from their exploits, took their positions. La Peña, who had one and a half thousand cavalry, inexplicably made no effort to close the gap until Castaños personally delivered a rebuke that prompted La Peña to despatch two battalions only as far as the village of Urzante but his cavalry remained stationary.[19] He did, however, send word to Grimarest and Villariezo at Tarazona, with instructions to close-in with all haste.

Morlot, with Musnier in support, continued to engage Roca; the position was strong and the Spanish fought well but a French battalion found an unguarded approach and the defensive position was soon overrun, forcing the Spanish to flee to the confines of the city. Meanwhile in the centre, Lannes took full advantage of the Spanish disorder and their lack of reorganization and without waiting for his three (remaining) infantry and three cavalry formations to arrive on the main field and shake-out, he launched the attack on the two Spanish divisions of Saint March and O'Neille. Maurice Mathieu deployed his twelve battalions in front of both Saint March and O'Neille, and Wathier moved from the heights above Tudela to position himself between Mathieu's two brigades, while Colbert, who had marginalized the threat from La Peña, moved his brigade up to Mathieu's left wing. Supported by Grandjean, Mathieu began his advance, Wathier exposed the gap between the two Spanish divisions and Colbert moved around the southern flank, both were in behind the Spanish within minutes. The infantry advance broke the Spanish resolve and the lines gave way flooding back onto the Zaragoza road. At Cascante, Grimarest and Villariezo had joined La Peña but by the time the 4th Division advanced against Lagrange it was already too late. As light faded, the fate of the two Spanish armies had already been decided. It was a shattering blow to the Spanish cause; resulting in four thousand casualties and the loss of 26 guns. Tudela was a significant French victory and, together with Espinosa de los Monteros to the northwest, brought the two encircling manoeuvres to a satisfactory, if not entirely successful conclusion.

---

17   Oman, *History of the Peninsular War*, vol. I, p.431.

18   The brother of Joseph Palafox.

---

19   This removed Castaños from the main battle at a critical moment: Oliver & Partridge concludes, quite rightly, that this demonstrated poor judgement on the part of the Spanish Commander-in-Chief as he should have sent a more junior commander or aide.

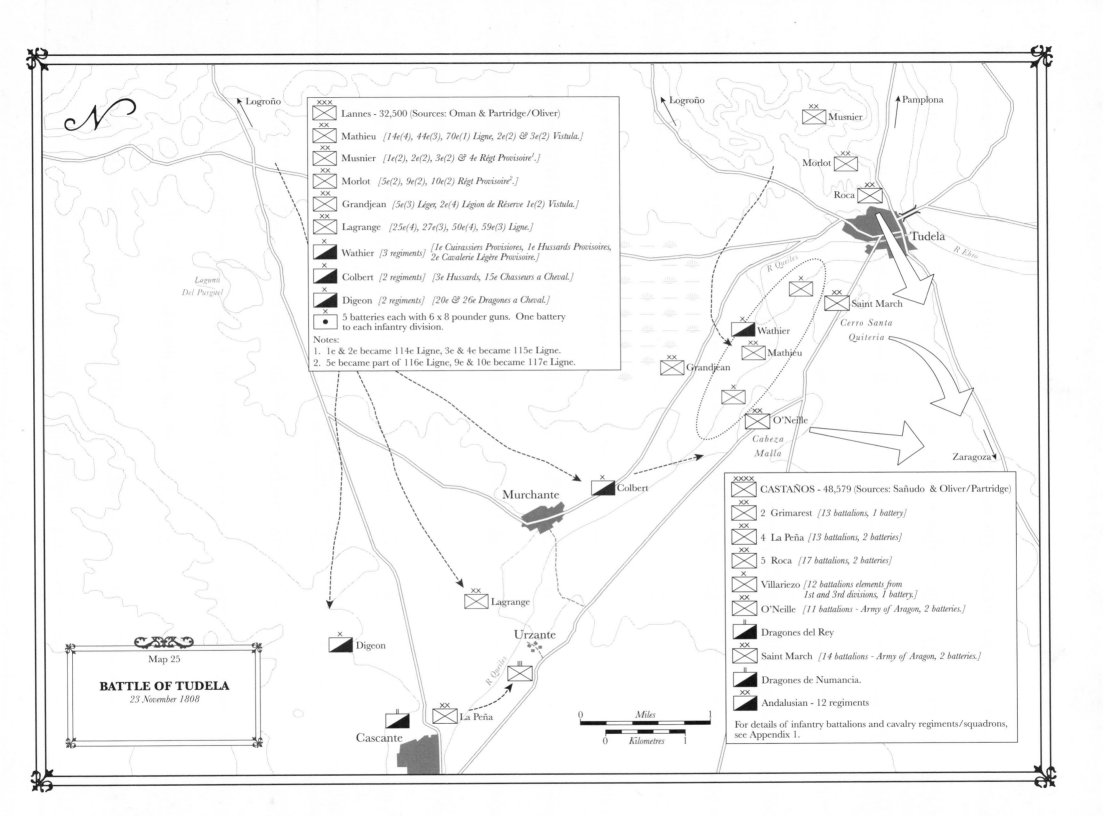

N

Logroño

Logroño

Pamplona

Musnier

Morlot

Roca

Tudela

R Ebro

Lannes - 32,500 (Sources: Oman & Partridge/Oliver)

Mathieu *[14e(4), 44e(3), 70e(1) Ligne, 2e(2) & 3e(2) Vistula.]*

Musnier *[1e(2), 2e(2), 3e(2) & 4e Régt Provisoire[1].]*

Morlot *[5e(2), 9e(2), 10e(2) Régt Provisoire[2].]*

Grandjean *[5e(3) Léger, 2e(4) Légion de Réserve 1e(2) Vistula.]*

Lagrange *[25e(4), 27e(3), 50e(4), 59e(3) Ligne.]*

Wathier *[3 regiments]* *[1e Cuirassiers Provisoires, 1e Hussards Provisoires, 2e Cavalerie Légère Provisoire.]*

Colbert *[2 regiments]* *[3e Hussards, 15e Chasseurs a Cheval.]*

Digeon *[2 regiments]* *[20e & 26e Dragones a Cheval.]*

5 batteries each with 6 x 8 pounder guns. One battery to each infantry division.

Notes:
1. 1e & 2e became 114e Ligne, 3e & 4e became 115e Ligne.
2. 5e became part of 116e Ligne, 9e & 10e became 117e Ligne.

Laguna Del Purguel

R Queiles

Saint March

Cerro Santa Quiteria

Wathier

Mathieu

Grandjean

O'Neille

Cabeza Malla

Zaragoza

Murchante

Colbert

CASTAÑOS - 48,579 (Sources: Sañudo & Oliver/Partridge)

2 Grimarest *[13 battalions, 1 battery]*

4 La Peña *[13 battalions, 2 batteries]*

5 Roca *[17 battalions, 2 batteries]*

Villariezo *[12 battalions elements from 1st and 3rd divisions, 1 battery.]*

O'Neille *[11 battalions - Army of Aragon, 2 batteries.]*

Dragones del Rey

Saint March *[14 battalions - Army of Aragon, 2 batteries.]*

Dragones de Numancia.

Andalusian - 12 regiments

For details of infantry battalions and cavalry regiments/squadrons, see Appendix 1.

Lagrange

Urzante

Digeon

R Queiles

Map 25

BATTLE OF TUDELA

23 November 1808

0   *Miles*   1

0   *Kilometres*   1

La Peña

Cascante

Chapter 11

NAPOLEON ENTERS MADRID AND MOORE ENTERS SPAIN

Castaños and Palafox expected to run into Ney as they withdrew from the shambles at Tudela. In fact Ney was still some 80km away, having only received orders to commence his turning movement on 18 November. He was also informed that Lannes would engage with the Spanish on or around 22 November and, despite pushing his men hard over the demanding terrain to come in support of his colleague, his force inevitably took longer than four days to cover a distance of nearly 200km. They arrived at Borja on 26 November and caught up with the tail end of Maurice Mathieu's Division, who were in hot pursuit of Castaños. However, despite their best efforts the Spanish army escaped, with many making off into the mountains of Cuenca. Ney's failure to encircle and annihilate the armies of the Centre and Left received characteristic Napoleonic disparagement, but in fact Bonaparte's time appreciation had been flawed. Both turning movements had, in effect, failed in their objectives and all three Spanish armies, despite being blooded and bruised, were temporarily ineffective but far from destroyed.

Napoleon, recognizing that the encircling movements had failed, now turned his attention to the final part of his plan. He left Joseph and his household troops at Burgos and launched his considerable force of 130,000 men towards Madrid. Ironically, Castaños had received a communiqué from the Central Junta on 25 November authorising the re-subordination of O'Neille and St March's divisions under his command. It was dated 21 November and, had it been received on that day, would have avoided all the wrangling. It was the least of Castaños's worries; a few days later a subsequent communiqué relieved him of command. 'Meanwhile the Supreme Junta was anxiously trying to devise some way of defending their exposed capital. The decision – extremely ill-timed – to remove generals Blake, Belvedere and Castaños from their commands left the arbiters of Spain's destiny with a difficult leadership problem to solve… They turned to General Benito San Juan's 12,000 soldiers, supported by the 8,000 survivors of the Army of Estremadura. Both these forces were eventually brought under the nominal command of a certain General Eguia, supposedly commander of the Reserve Army. This worthy lost no time in ordering his pitifully small command to march north from Madrid, San Juan and his 12,000 men towards the pass of Somosierra, Heredia and his 9,000 to the defiles through the Guadarramas further west.'[1] Other troops that could have been called up by the Supreme Junta were overlooked in the misguided belief that Napoleon's force was only around half its actual size and in the overconfident belief that

the passes could be held with relatively few men. Rather impulsively, San Juan deployed one-third of this meagre force forward at Sepulveda.[2] Napoleon's advance was swift and led by a strong cavalry screen provided by the divisions of Lasalle[3] and Milhaud. Six days after leaving Burgos he was at the foot of the Guadarrama mountains. The ineffective force at Sepulveda was neutralized and withdrew, but they were not able to rejoin San Juan as the road between them was already in French hands. Instead they headed west and towards the troops at the passes at la Fuenfría and Navacerrada. Napoleon on the other hand, had decided to concentrate his entire effort at Somosierra, and on 30 November advanced rapidly up the winding road.

'Had their trenches been constructed with intelligence, they would have been impregnable, from the advantages of the ground; but of these the engineers had not known how to avail themselves.'[4] Notwithstanding this view of Sarrazin, the sheer weight of numbers would inevitably have taken its toll on the defenders, who had an impossible task. The defile was not sufficiently steep to prevent penetration either side and, with only 8,500 men, San Juan was hard-pressed to hold the pass and the heights on either flank. At dawn on 30 November, the 1st Division of the 1st Corps, that of Ruffin, was leading the line of march and entered the defile. After advancing about 25km, Ruffin came up against San Juan's position at the pass and deployed the 9e Léger to the right and the 24e Ligne to the left. The six battalions made slow but steady progress, pushing back the lines of Spanish skirmishers on both shoulders. The remaining four battalions of the 96e Ligne were following up along the road. At this point Napoleon rode up to the front and saw the massed Spanish guns across the road. He called up the battery from the Imperial Guard Cavalry, which unlimbered and ineffectively responded to the Spanish guns. Napoleon grew increasingly impatient. He wanted to inflict a decisive defeat and make a point to the Spanish and his own military commanders, but the infantry of Victor's Corps were taking too long, and a squadron of Polish light horse[5] were ordered to charge. 'A brilliant cavalry officer, General Montbrun advanced at the head of the Polish light horse, an elite troop recently formed by Napoleon in Warsaw, following his policy of having all nations and arms represented in the Imperial Guard. General Montbrun, at the head of these gallant young men, hurried to the gallop towards the 16 pieces of cannon of the Spanish, braving a horrible fire of musketry and grapeshot. The light horse was engulfed in a discharge that devastated their ranks, bringing 30 or 40 riders down. However, they soon rallied and passing over their wounded comrades, they resumed their charge and on arrival at the gun position, sabred the gunners, and captured the 16 guns.'[6] 'The epic and murderous charge lasted no longer than ten minutes, but of the 159 light cavalry who engaged, 83 were cut down in the action, a number which included all the officers from the 3rd Squadron. Captain Dziewanowski died of his wounds on 8 December 1808; lieutenants Nowicki, Rudowski,

---

2   Under the command of Colonel Sarden it consisted of five good battalions, three squadrons and a battery.

3   Lasalle had been released as the corps cavalry to Soult's Corps on 10 November and replaced by Franceschi.

4   Sarrazin, *History of the War in Spain and Portugal*, p.54.

5   The Poles are often reported as being equipped with lances: Chandler, Oman and Napier are firm in their assertion that this regiment was not equipped with lances until three months after the charge. Napoleon's correspondence No. 14,819 supports that assertion.

6   Thiers, *Histoire Du Consulat et De L'Empire*, vol. IX, pp.455–456.

---

1   Chandler, *The Campaigns of Napoleon*, p.640

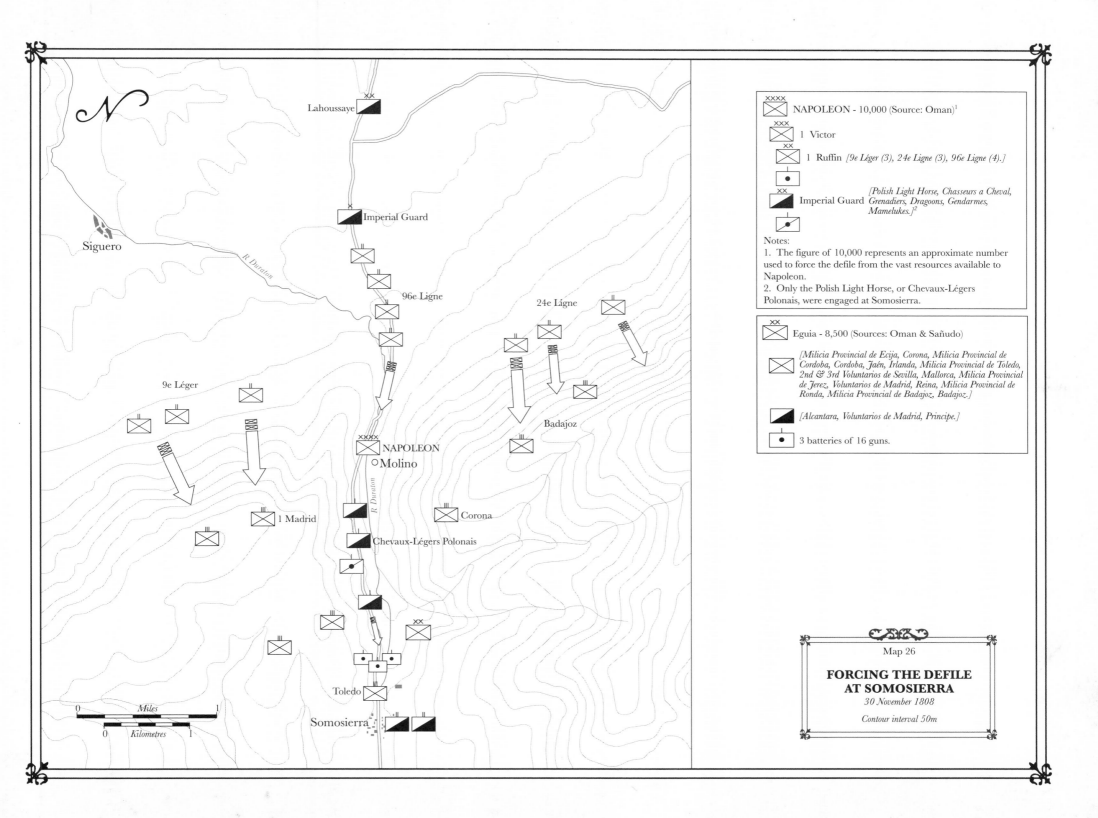

Lahoussaye

Siguero

R Duraton

Imperial Guard

96e Ligne

24e Ligne

9e Léger

Badajoz

NAPOLEON
Molino

1 Madrid

R Duraton

Corona

Chevaux-Légers Polonais

Toledo

Somosierra

Miles
0   1

Kilometres
0   1

Legend (top box):

NAPOLEON - 10,000 (Source: Oman)[1]

1 Victor

1 Ruffin *[9e Léger (3), 24e Ligne (3), 96e Ligne (4).]*

Imperial Guard *[Polish Light Horse, Chasseurs a Cheval, Grenadiers, Dragoons, Gendarmes, Mamelukes.]*[2]

Notes:
1. The figure of 10,000 represents an approximate number used to force the defile from the vast resources available to Napoleon.
2. Only the Polish Light Horse, or Chevaux-Légers Polonais, were engaged at Somosierra.

Legend (bottom box):

Eguia - 8,500 (Sources: Oman & Sañudo)

[Milicia Provincial de Ecija, Corona, Milicia Provincial de Cordoba, Cordoba, Jaén, Irlanda, Milicia Provincial de Toledo, 2nd & 3rd Voluntarios de Sevilla, Mallorca, Milicia Provincial de Jerez, Voluntarios de Madrid, Reina, Milicia Provincial de Ronda, Milicia Provincial de Badajoz, Badajoz.]

[Alcantara, Voluntarios de Madrid, Principe.]

3 batteries of 16 guns.

Map 26

**FORCING THE DEFILE
AT SOMOSIERRA**
30 November 1808
Contour interval 50m

and Kryanwski were killed instantly; Squadron Commander Kozietulski, Captain Krasinski Piotr, lieutenants Niegolewski and Sokolowski, along with aide-de-camp Ségur who also participated in the charge, were all injured.'[7]

Napoleon had made his statement and the pass was taken opening the road to Madrid. On the afternoon of 1 December the advance parties of Latour-Maubourg and Lasalle's cavalry reached the outskirts of the city. The next day, when the main body came within sight of the metropolis, 'the troops exploded with enthusiasm when they saw the capital, they remembered that this day, 2 December, was the second anniversary of the coronation and the battle of Austerlitz'.[8] By 4 December the capital was in French hands. 'So ended the great French counter-offensive. Madrid, Burgos, Santander and Bilbao had been reoccupied; Barcelona relieved; Roses taken; and important victories won at Gamonal, Espinosa, Tudela, Somosierra, Cardedeu and Molíns de Rei [see Chapter 12]. The Armies of the Left and Right had been routed, the Army of the Centre split into three, and the Army of the Reserve confined to Zaragoza. Meanwhile thousands of men were dead, wounded or missing; hundreds of guns and incalculable quantities of stores in the hands of the French; and the new government was a fugitive'.[9]

The day prior to Napoleon's entry into the Spanish capital, General Hope had at last united with General Moore at Salamanca. Moore had assumed command of the British army on 6 October; his portfolio differed from that given by the British government to the army that landed at Mondego in August. He was to link up with Baird's force, which was being moved by ship to La Coruña, and then prosecute operations in Spain in support of the Spanish armies.

Poor initial assessments by his staff and equally dismal local advice resulted in a plan that split Moore's advance (see map 27). The first three groups arrived at Salamanca between 13 and 23 November, but Hope's group, which contained all but one battery of the artillery and most of the cavalry and stores, did not arrive until 3 December. Baird fared little better. He had arrived off the Galician coast on October 13th but the local commanders knew nothing of agreements to land this force and, by the time clearance and clarification had been sought and provided, two weeks had elapsed. Having landed, Baird's troubles were far from over. There were few provisions and no means of transporting the little that existed. By the time Moore's army had united at Salamanca on 3 December, Baird was still 150km to the north.

Had Moore's force marched by a single route and had Baird's force been allowed to land on arrival at La Coruña, and properly supported, there is every reason to believe they could have united by mid November. As such they could have easily come to the aid of the Junta and the defence of Madrid, but this assumption was by no means certain. Moore had another clear directive; he was not to take unnecessary risks with Britain's only field army. 'To all intents and purposes, therefore, the French had little cause to concern themselves about the British until mid December. Even then, as we shall see, they had only the very vaguest idea on Moore's whereabouts and intentions. Nevertheless, despite the chronic inadequacies of the commissariat service and its allies, the British army was destined to play an important part in determining the final outcome of Napoleon's campaign of 1808, and the Emperor himself would, in due course, be moved to pay tribute to Moore's abilities'.[10]

---

7   Delaître, *Baron Charles Delaître, général d'Empire*, pp.177–181.

8   Hugo, *Histoire des Armées Françaises 1792–1833*, vol. IV p.106. To be clear, Napoleon had been crowned in 1804 and the battle at Austerlitz had been fought and won in 1805.

9   Esdaile, *The Peninsular War, A New History*, p.139.

10   Chandler, *The Campaigns of Napoleon*, p.628.

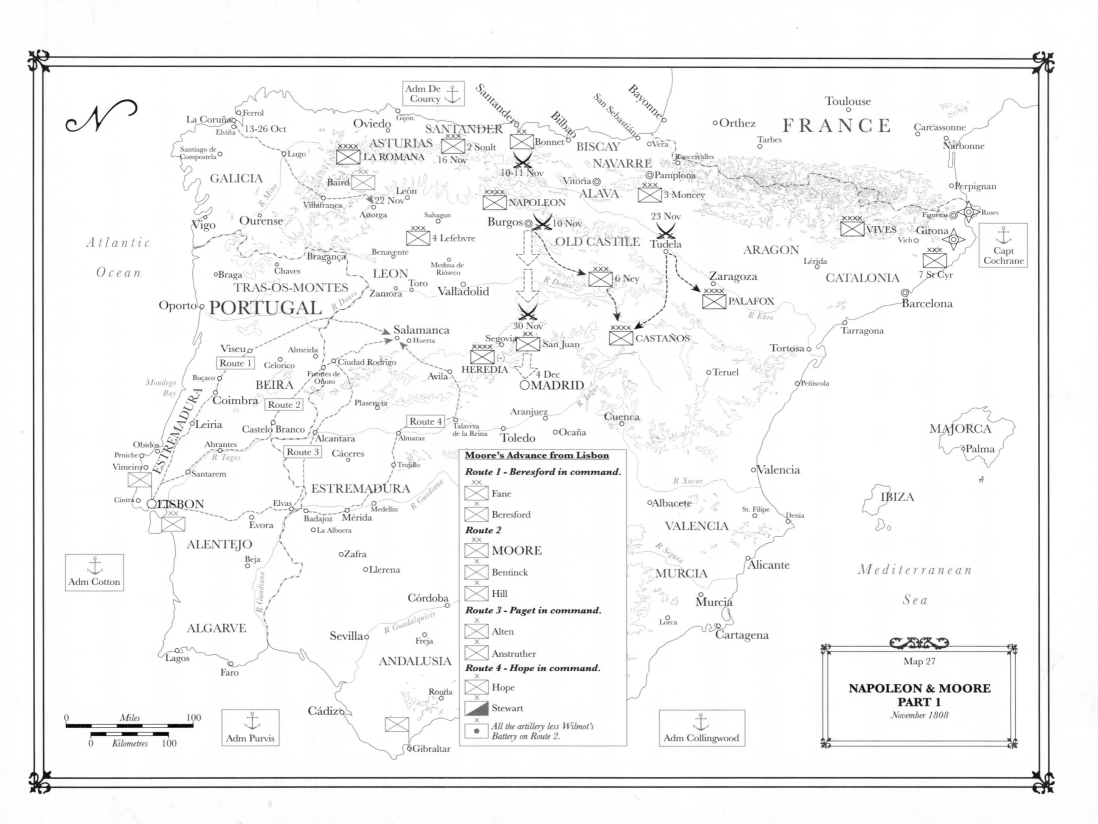

N

Atlantic
Ocean

Adm De
Courcy

Santander

Bayonne

Toulouse

FRANCE

La Coruña   Ferrol
13-26 Oct
Elviña

Oviedo   Gijón

Santiago de
Compostela

Lugo

GALICIA

SANTANDER
XXX

2 Soult
16 Nov

Bonnet

BISCAY

Bilbao

San Sebastián
Vera

Orthez
Tarbes

Carcassonne

Narbonne

ASTURIAS
XXXX   LA ROMANA

NAVARRE

Roncesvalles

Vitoria

Baird
XXX

León
22 Nov

10-11 Nov

ALAVA

Pamplona
3 Moncey

Perpignan

Vigo

Ourense

Villafranca
Astorga

Sahagún

NAPOLEON
XXXX

23 Nov

Figueras
Roses

Braga

Bragança

4 Lefebvre
XXX

Burgos

10 Nov

OLD CASTILE

Tudela

ARAGON

Lérida

VIVES
XXXX

Girona

Capt
Cochrane

Chaves

Benavente

Zaragoza

7 St Cyr
XXX

Oporto

PORTUGAL

TRAS-OS-MONTES

LEON

Zamora
Toro

Medina de
Ríoseco

Valladolid

R Douro

6 Ney
XXX

PALAFOX
XXXX

CATALONIA

Barcelona

Viseu

Route 1

Almeida

Celorico

Salamanca
Huerta

30 Nov

R Ebro

Tarragona

Tortosa

Mondego
Bay

Buçaco

BEIRA

Ciudad Rodrigo

Segovia
XXXX

San Juan

CASTAÑOS
XXXX

Teruel

Peñiscola

Coimbra

Route 2

Fuentes de
Oñoro

Ávila

HEREDIA
XXXX (-)

Leiria

Plasencia

Route 4

4 Dec

MADRID

Cuenca

MAJORCA

Palma

Obidos

Castelo Branco

Alcántara

Cáceres

Almaraz

Talavera
de la Reina

Aranjuez

Toledo

Ocaña

R Tagus

R Xucar

Valencia

IBIZA

Peniche
Vimeiro
XXX

Abrantes

Route 3

R Tagus

Trujillo

VALENCIA

Albacete

St. Filipe
Denia

Cintra

LISBON
XXX

Santarem

ESTREMADURA

R Guadiana

Moore's Advance from Lisbon

Route 1 - Beresford in command.

Fane
XX

Beresford
X

R Segura

Alicante

ALENTEJO

Evora

Medellín
Mérida
Badajoz
La Albuera

Elvas

Route 2

MOORE
XX

MURCIA

Murcia

Mediterranean

Sea

Adm Cotton

Beja

Zafra

Llerena

Bentinck
X

Hill
X

Lorca

Cartagena

ALGARVE

Córdoba

R Guadalquivir

Freja

Route 3 - Paget in command.

Alten
X

Anstruther
X

Route 4 - Hope in command.

Hope
X

Lagos

Faro

Sevilla

ANDALUSIA

Ronda

Stewart

All the artillery less Wilmot's
Battery on Route 2.

Map 27

NAPOLEON & MOORE
PART 1
November 1808

Cádiz

Gibraltar

Adm Collingwood

0   Miles   100

0   Kilometres   100

Adm Purvis

Chapter 12

THE CAMPAIGN IN CATALONIA: AUTUMN 1808

Following the failed siege of Girona in July and August 1808, Reille withdrew to Figueras while Duhesme retired to Barcelona, surrendering all his artillery en route (see Chapter 7). Both commanders had long abandoned entertaining any form of offensive until additional reserves had arrived. During September and early October the Conde de Caldagues, with an ad hoc force of about 2,000 and a battery of field guns, undertook an ineffective blockade of Barcelona. The new Captain-General, the Marquis Del Palacio, seemed unsure of whether to use the few thousand regulars at Girona and Roses to engage Reille. His indecisive nature eventually led to his dismissal and Vives, the Captain-General of the Balearic isles, was reappointed to the dual role in late October. His assumption coincided with the arrival of many new troops to the region; a total of 20,000 from Andalusia, Valencia, and Aragon as well as Caraffa's Division,[1] which was being sent by sea from Portugal.

Vives turned his attention and his new force against Duhesme but within days General Gouvion St Cyr had arrived at Perpignan ahead of 24,000 men, ordained as the nucleus of the new French 7th Corps. 'The seventh corps was composed, as one will see later, of troops of several nations and, largely, of new formations.'[2] St Cyr was determined to clear the Spanish garrison at Roses as it posed a constant threat to the main east coast line of communication with France and he was quite clear in his assessment that 'in order to ensure the possession of Figueras it would be necessary to take Roses'.[3] Furthermore, several British ships anchored there were part of a Royal Navy blockading force tasked to attack French shipping attempting to revitalize Barcelona.[4] The town's fortifications consisted of a main citadel, to the north-west of the small fishing village, and the Fort Trinity, located on the forward slope of the Puig Rom, constructed to provide protection to shipping in the bay.

On 6 November St Cyr marched towards Roses, detailing Souham to cover the Girona road and Chabot that to Figueras, while he continued east with his other two divisions, those of Reille and Pino, who were to conduct the siege. St Cyr himself stayed inland, passing the overall responsibility to Reille, as Reille had conducted operations in the area the previous August.

The Royal Navy's 74-gun ship *Excellent* and bomb vessel *Meteor* engaged Reille and Pino as they took up their positions to the north and east of the town. This was familiar territory to the French, they had held it, and much of Catalonia, as a possession from 1640 to 1659 and again from 1694 to 1697; indeed, only as recently as 1794 the French had bombarded the citadel, inflicting a large breach that the Spanish had repaired with 'bit and pieces' at the outbreak of the French invasion. Siege artillery would make short work of the repaired northern face, but Reille had none with him. It was en route from France and was not expected for another week.

The civil population of 1,500, well versed in conflict with their northern neighbour, largely abandoned the town by sea. Some absconded to the surrounding hills and joined the groups of *somatenes*, whose ranks grew daily in line with their daring and determination. 'At the request of O'Daly, the Spanish commander, Captain West of the *Excellent* bolstered the defence by landing all his marines as well as a naval officer and 50 seamen. These provided their worth the next day when West led a sortie to relieve a party of Spaniards who had sallied from the fortress and become surrounded, he had the somewhat novel experience for a naval officer of having a horse shot from under him during the sharp action that followed.'[5] While the French waited for the heavy artillery they set about digging the parallels around the citadel; it was impossible work, as the marsh soil was waterlogged and collapsed their trenches before they could be riveted. To make matters worse it rained continuously from 8 to 15 November and, 'General Souham was being constantly harassed on the Fluvia, and one had to fear that, at any moment, the enemy would direct on him a vigorous attack that would have undermined the operation at Roses'.[6] Reille, somewhat at a loss as to how best to proceed, elected to storm Fort Trinity, which he considered achievable without the need of a breach. The fort was held by 80 Spanish from the Irish Corps and bolstered by 25 British marines, landed from HMS *Excellent*; West nevertheless moved 30 more redcoats into the position by way of reinforcement.[7] The assault, on 15 November, was made by seven companies from the Italian 2e Léger, but failed with the loss of their battalion commander. Attention was diverted from this disappointment the following day with the arrival of the first siege guns from Perpignan, and Reille directed them eagerly to the heights of the Puig Rom (map 28, batteries 1 and 2)[8] and they soon opened fire on the structure.

Heavy guns were also moved into the battery constructed by the French on the shore-side of the town (map 26, point 3), from where they began to engage the town and citadel and, most significantly, the ships and bomb vessels that lay in the bay. This forced the Royal Navy further out to sea and *ipso facto* out of range, enabling the French sappers and gunners to make considerably better progress. On 26 November Pino's Italians delivered an attack on the town itself and, after some heavy fighting, succeeded in clearing the buildings. Two batteries were

---

1   This was one of the three Spanish divisions that had supported Junot in November 1807.

2   St Cyr, *Journal des Opérations de L'Armée De Catalogne en 1808 et 1809*, p.26.

3   Ibid, letter from St Cyr to Napoleon dated 17 November 1808.

4   For a good account of the Royal Navy role and contribution see Díaz Capmany, Pedlar and Reay, *El Setge de Roses de 1808*, The Royal Navy in the Bay of Roses 1808–09 by Justin Reay pp.240–284.

5   Hall, *Wellington's Navy*, p.51.

6   St Cyr, *Journal des Opérations de L'Armée De Catalogne en 1808 et 1809*, p. 50. Souham was holding the road to Girona and was concentrated around the river Fluvia.

7   Hall, *Wellington's Navy*, p.51.

8   These batteries had considerable difficulty engaging the fort, as their platforms were either too high or too low to achieve the desired angle. Indeed Battery 1 may not have been used at all.

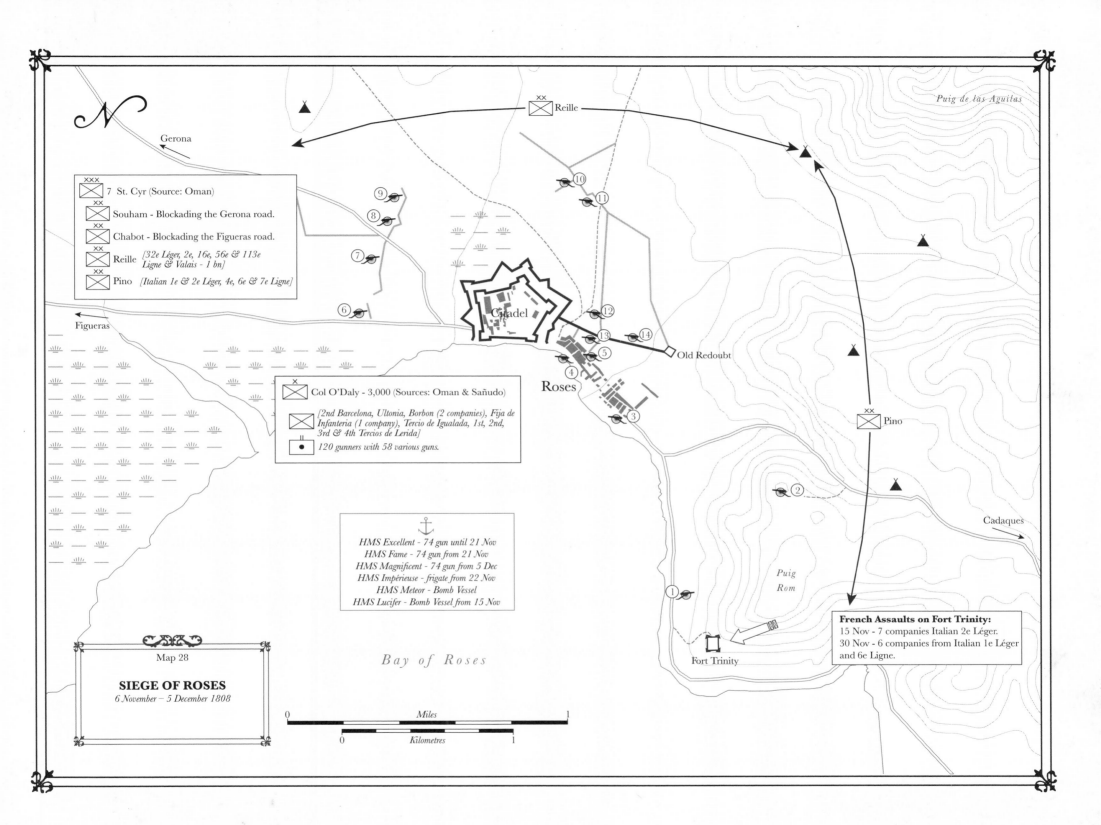

N

Gerona

Puig de las Aguilas

Reille

7 St. Cyr (Source: Oman)

Souham - Blockading the Gerona road.

Chabot - Blockading the Figueras road.

Reille *[32e Léger, 2e, 16e, 56e & 113e Ligne & Valais - 1 bn]*

Pino *[Italian 1e & 2e Léger, 4e, 6e & 7e Ligne]*

Figueras

Citadel

Roses

Old Redoubt

Pino

Col O'Daly - 3,000 (Sources: Oman & Sañudo)

[2nd Barcelona, Ultonia, Borbon (2 companies), Fija de Infanteria (1 company), Tercio de Igualada, 1st, 2nd, 3rd & 4th Tercios de Lerida]

• 120 gunners with 58 various guns.

Cadaques

HMS Excellent - 74 gun until 21 Nov
HMS Fame - 74 gun from 21 Nov
HMS Magnificent - 74 gun from 5 Dec
HMS Impérieuse - frigate from 22 Nov
HMS Meteor - Bomb Vessel
HMS Lucifer - Bomb Vessel from 15 Nov

Puig Rom

Bay of Roses

French Assaults on Fort Trinity:
15 Nov - 7 companies Italian 2e Léger.
30 Nov - 6 companies from Italian 1e Léger and 6e Ligne.

Fort Trinity

Map 28

SIEGE OF ROSES
6 November – 5 December 1808

0   Miles   1

0   Kilometres   1

immediately constructed in the ruins (map 28, batteries 4 and 5) and quickly made their mark on the weaker eastern walls of the citadel. Frustratingly, naval support to subdue these new batteries was limited; the weather had improved, drying out the ground and aiding the sappers in shoring-up the entrenchments and the parallels that were now approaching the citadel walls with considerable speed. Despite some relief to the defenders on 27 and 28 November, when the Royal Navy landed 200 men from the Borbon regiment, Colonel O'Daly's resolve was failing.

The enterprising Captain Cochrane had arrived with HMS *Impérieuse* on 22 November and decided that Fort Trinity provided numerous opportunities to thwart the French. 'On 24 November, a boatload of over a hundred men led by Cochrane himself landed to reinforce the defenders of Roses. And while the heavy guns of the *Impérieuse* and the bomb vessels began to silence the more exposed of the French batteries, Cochrane threw all his ingenuity into converting what was left of the castle into a vast mantrap… But Cochrane could only delay the inexorable French assault. A week later it came. Covered by precise gunfire, which even Cochrane had to admire, a thick column of enemy infantry curled its way steadily down the valley and hurled itself into the breach. The defences held out, and the attack was repelled with heavy loss.'[9] Reille was frustrated at this second failure and elected to leave the fort and concentrate on the citadel, which the French batteries were by now relentlessly bombarding from the east and west. O'Daly realized he had to act and, during the night of 3 December, he despatched 500 of his best men to destroy the batteries close to the citadel walls that were causing so much damage (batteries 4, 5, 12 and 13). While valiant, their attempt was futile. They were beaten back and the next day Reille pushed the parallels and guns forward to within a couple of hundred yards of the walls. O'Daly, realizing the situation was hopeless, sent out an officer to discuss terms. Reille was accepting nothing short of unconditional surrender, and the next day O'Daly obliged. Cochrane and the British marines escaped from Fort Trinity and blew the magazine with a slow burning fuse, but O'Daly and his 2,500 defenders were captured and sent to France. French losses were not light but in the greater scheme, St Cyr had been held up for over a month and prevented from accomplishing his main mission, namely the relief of Barcelona. Leaving Reille with about 5,500 men to garrison Figueras and Roses and to contain Girona, St Cyr headed south in haste with the balance of his force, about 16,500 men.[10]

Speed was now vital; there were two main roads from northern Catalonia to Barcelona but only one remained open. The *somatenes*, with help from the Royal Navy, had rendered the coast road impassable with large sections blown into the sea. St Cyr was more than aware that the interior road could be held at a number of places with a small force. If Vives had chosen to throw his entire 20,000 Catalans into preventing St Cyr's advance, the French cause would have been hopeless. On 9 December St Cyr sent back all his artillery and heavy baggage to Figueras and, with enough rations for six days, the French force set off.[11]

The Junta at Girona sent word to Vives that a French force had bypassed the city and were heading south, lightly equipped, via the interior route. The Catalan Captain-General immediately ordered Lazan to follow from Girona with his weak division, and sent out Reding to block the interior road and Milans[12] to cover the coast road. This latter group moved inland to San Celoni when they discovered the coast road clear and were engaged by St Cyr during the afternoon of 15 December. Meanwhile Vives, on receiving news of this combat, had a change of heart and elected to reinforce Reding with another brigade, which he personally escorted. Lazan was at this time still some way to the north. The rest of the Catalan forces, some 10,000 men, were left surrounding Barcelona. It was a serious miscalculation.

On the morning of 16 December St Cyr emerged from the narrow defiles into the valley of the Besos, which was much broader and surrounded by pine-clad hills. Vives had reached the area only a few hours prior and had hastily deployed his force in two lines covering the road. He reported, 'I marched with my division along the road from Granolers to Llinars … at sunrise I came close to the enemy, I deployed my line of battle, and my cannon started to fire upon an enemy column which was seen marching by my left.' With Lazan closing from the north and Milans from the east, rations almost depleted and ammunition running low, St Cyr realized his options were limited and (like Dupont at Bailén) chose to instigate a quick attack. He formed up his two strongest divisions, those of Souham and Pino, and gave orders accordingly. 'There must be no attempt to feel his position; not one battalion must be deployed. Though his position is strong we must go straight at it in column, and burst through the centre by striking at the one point with our whole force.'[13]

Pino led the assault but inexplicably[14] deployed elements of Fontane's Brigade (under Major Cometti) to the north of the road and the majority of Mazuchelli's Brigade to the south, thereby extending his attack on a wide frontage instead of at a single point. He quickly lost momentum, prompting Reding to hurl two squadrons of the Hussars of Granada into the fray while simultaneously ordering his division to advance. St Cyr rode up to witness the debacle, and furious at Pino's disobedience, threw in his last card. He immediately ordered Souham's entire division to swing south and into the Granada Division that was now regrouping, whilst at the same time ordered the balance of Pino's troops (under Fontane) forward to occupy the Spanish guns and infantry in the centre. The sheer weight of numbers at a single point decided the affair and Reding's right wing was quickly penetrated. 'While Souham's Division contained the disorder with one brigade, another brigade was at the same time threatening the Spanish left which was the weakest and widely spread, prepared General Pino, with the second brigade to attack in column and break our line.'[15] The Granada Division, led by Reding, formed a rearguard of sorts but St Cyr sent in the two Italian cavalry regiments to follow up and the

9   Vale, *The Audacious Admiral Cochrane*, pp.48–49.

10   St Cyr, *Journal des Opérations de L'Armée De Catalogne en 1808 et 1809*, p.64. The divisions of Souham, Pino and Chabot – 15,000 infantry in 26 battalions and 1,500 cavalry.

11   Ibid, p.67.

12   Commanding about 3,000 *miqueletes*.

13   St Cyr, *Journal des Opérations de L'Armée De Catalogne en 1808 et 1809*, p.78.

14   Although Vacani (an Italian officer of engineers) in his report concluded that Pino deployed left and right of the road, contrary to his orders, to distract the attention of the Spanish reserves.

15   Toreno, *Guerra de la Independencia, El 2 de mayo de 1808*, vol. II, p.254.

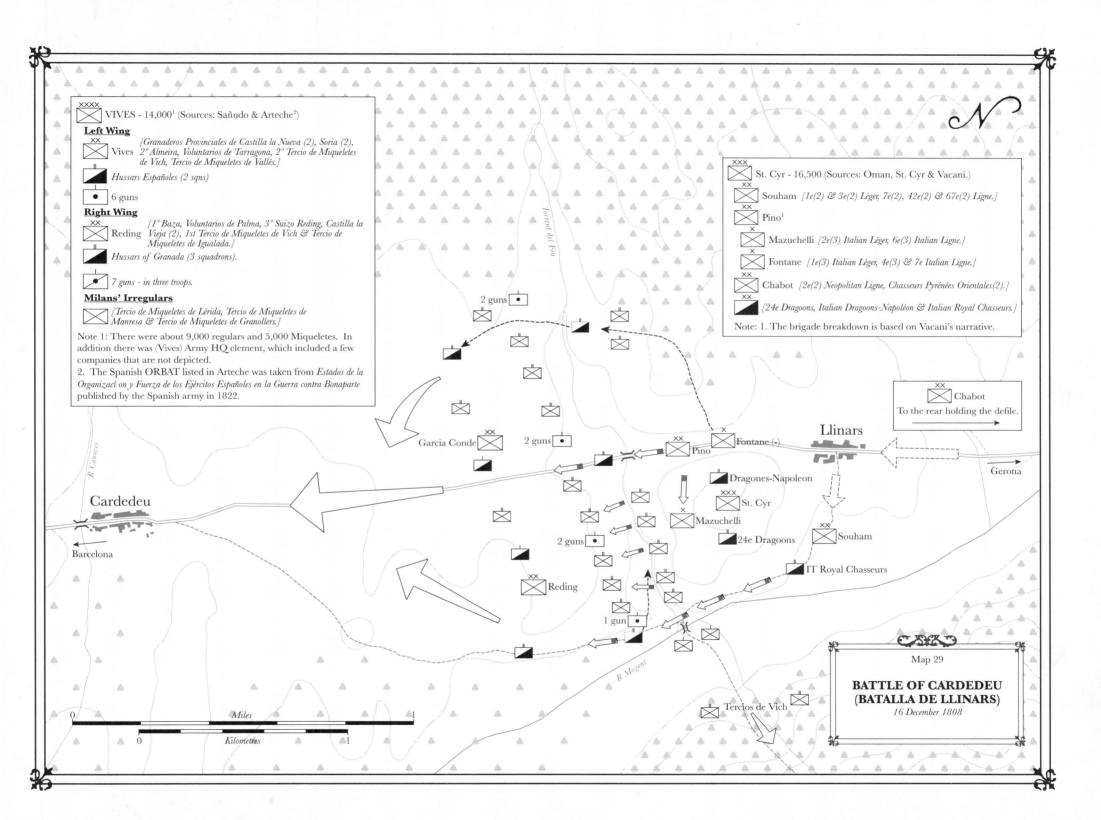

VIVES - 14,000[1] (Sources: Sañudo & Arteche[2])

Left Wing

Vives — *[Granaderos Provinciales de Castilla la Nueva (2), Soria (2), 2° Almeira, Voluntarios de Tarragona, 2° Tercio de Miqueletes de Vich, Tercio de Miqueletes de Vallés.]*

Hussars Españoles (2 sqns)

6 guns

Right Wing

Reding — *[1° Baza, Voluntarios de Palma, 3° Suizo Reding, Castilla la Vieja (2), 1st Tercio de Miqueletes de Vich & Tercio de Miqueletes de Igualada.]*

Hussars of Granada (3 squadrons).

7 guns - in three troops.

Milans' Irregulars

[Tercio de Miqueletes de Lérida, Tercio de Miqueletes de Manresa & Tercio de Miqueletes de Granollers.]

Note 1: There were about 9,000 regulars and 5,000 Miqueletes. In addition there was (Vives) Army HQ element, which included a few companies that are not depicted.

2. The Spanish ORBAT listed in Arteche was taken from *Estados de la Organizací on y Fuerza de los Ejércitos Españoles en la Guerra contra Bonaparte* published by the Spanish army in 1822.

St. Cyr - 16,500 (Sources: Oman, St. Cyr & Vacani.)

Souham *[1e(2) & 3e(2) Léger, 7e(2), 42e(2) & 67e(2) Ligne.]*

Pino[1]

Mazuchelli *[2e(3) Italian Léger, 6e(3) Italian Ligne.]*

Fontane *[1e(3) Italian Léger, 4e(3) & 7e Italian Ligne.]*

Chabot *[2e(2) Neopolitan Ligne, Chasseurs Pyrénées Orientales(2).]*

[24e Dragoons, Italian Dragoons-Napoléon & Italian Royal Chasseurs.]

Note: 1. The brigade breakdown is based on Vacani's narrative.

Chabot
To the rear holding the defile.

N

Torrent del Fou

2 guns

R Canoves

Garcia Conde

2 guns

Cardedeu

Barcelona

2 guns

Reding

R Mogent

1 gun

Tercios de Vich

Llinars

Fontane (-)

Pino

Gerona

Dragones-Napoleon

St. Cyr

Mazuchelli

24e Dragoons

Souham

IT Royal Chasseurs

Map 29

**BATTLE OF CARDEDEU
(BATALLA DE LLINARS)**
16 December 1808

Miles
0 1

Kilometres
0 1

withdrawal verged on a rout. Vives managed to escape but he had lost five of the seven guns, two colours and over 1,500 men were taken prisoner with 1,000 killed or wounded. Reding was able to rally some of his men at Monmalo to the south and they rejoined the forces around Barcelona.[16] Milans also reappeared from the mountains and joined Caldagues, but Lazan felt compelled to return to Girona.

Caldagues, who had been left in charge of the blockade at Barcelona, had succeeded in repulsing a sortie by Duhesme on the same day as the Battle at Cardedeu. However, on hearing news of Vives' defeat, he elected to pull back his force to the west of the river Llobregat and concentrate at Molins de Rei and San Boy. The road to Barcelona was thus open and St Cyr marched his somewhat exhausted and spent force elatedly into the city on 17 December. St Cyr had good reason to be swollen with pride; his operation to relieve Barcelona had been executed with precision and exactitude. His force was considerably more vulnerable than Dupont's at Bailén and his troops less capable. However, the Catalan army was still at large, Caldagues had been joined by Reding, their combined formations numbered about 15,000 and St Cyr wasted no time drawing up plans to destroy them. Reding had assumed command of the Catalan force in the absence of Vives, who was making his way back overland from Tarragona having been dropped off there by the frigate *Cambrian* following his escape from Cardedeu. Reding was in a quandary; although keen to defend his reputation amongst the Catalans, he was not convinced about the defendable qualities of the terrain on the Llobregat. He considered the defile at Ordal to be a far superior location, but that entailed a withdrawal and would leave the road to Zaragoza and Lérida unguarded. He requested direction from Vives, who was still en route to rejoin the Army; but his inconclusive reply was not the guidance he was seeking. Reding felt obliged to stay put and on the morning of 21 December, with Duhesme and a single division holding Barcelona, St Cyr advanced from the city with his original three divisions supported by that of Chabran.

His plan was simple; he was to concentrate his attack on the Spanish position at Molins de Rei by sending Chabran's Division directly to the bridge, ahead of the main body, by way of a deception. The balance would then cross the river further south and turn the Spanish right flank. The weather was terrible, with high winds and falling snow. The encamped Spanish had little reason for optimism; for the large part they were deployed on exposed hilltops overlooking the valley and river below. Chabran's 4,000-strong division, supported by the 14e Cuirassiers, advanced in the dark and arrived at 0500 hours, making considerable noise to attract the attention of the Spanish army on the far side of the river. St Cyr predicted Reding's reaction: the Spanish commander withdrew the defensive force to the south and then moved it north to counteract what he now perceived to be the main threat. Chabran continued his deception using the few French guns that were available to engage the Spanish guns on the far bank, some of which were of heavy calibre and well positioned.

At around 0600 hours, Souham's Division appeared from the south on the west bank of the river, having crossed the fords at Sant Juan Despi. He dwelt opposite the ford by Sant Feliu and covered the crossing of Pino's Division before pushing on north up the road to Sant Vicens. The 24e Dragoons led the advance and little tangible effort was made to thwart their progress. Pino split his attack with Mazuchelli's Brigade to the left of Souham's Division and Fontane's Brigade on the heights opposite Sant Feliu. Chabot's Division followed Pino's over the ford and then headed up the defile, and had soon manoeuvred three battalions, completely unseen, to a position that quickly threatened Reding's flank. The Spanish right wing was withdrawn, allowing Chabot to strengthen his position and continue to advance north threatening Reding's withdrawal route to Tarragona. At Molins de Rei, Chabran had orders to cross the bridge and attack Reding's left flank once the attacks from the south were well enough advanced. However, he missed his opportunity and by the time his forces crossed the Llobregat, Reding had already issued the order for a general withdrawal. To escape down the Tarragona road was now far too precarious, so the bulk of the Spanish forces took off into the hills to the north. One thousand two hundred prisoners were taken, including the Conde de Caldagues, and a magazine with over three million cartridges and many muskets, and most significantly, a number of the field guns that the French badly needed.

St Cyr pushed his four divisions out to cover the many defiles leading to Barcelona and Tarragona: Chabran went to Mantoril, Chabot to Sant Sadurni, Souham to Vendrell and Pino to Villanueva de Sitjas. With the pass at Ordal in French hands the way was now open to Tarragona, but St Cyr's initial aims were to reopen and maintain communication with his forces in northern Catalonia and with France. Additionally, there was still the aggravating itch of the fortress at Girona, and the lesser problem of the fort at Hostalrich. But the 7th Corps commander had justification to be content, and the Catalans conversely were in complete disorder. Vives, who had arrived at the tail end of the engagement at Molins de Rei resigned and was replaced by Reding as Captain-General who immediately set about rebuilding the shattered and demoralized army. It was not to be an easy task.

---

16 The battle at Cardedeu (or Llinars) is very confusing and not helped by the fact that the maps in St Cyr's first edition of his journal were incorrect. Nevertheless, it is worth reading the reports of Reding and Vives in conjunction with those of St Cyr and the report of the Italian engineer officer, Vacani.

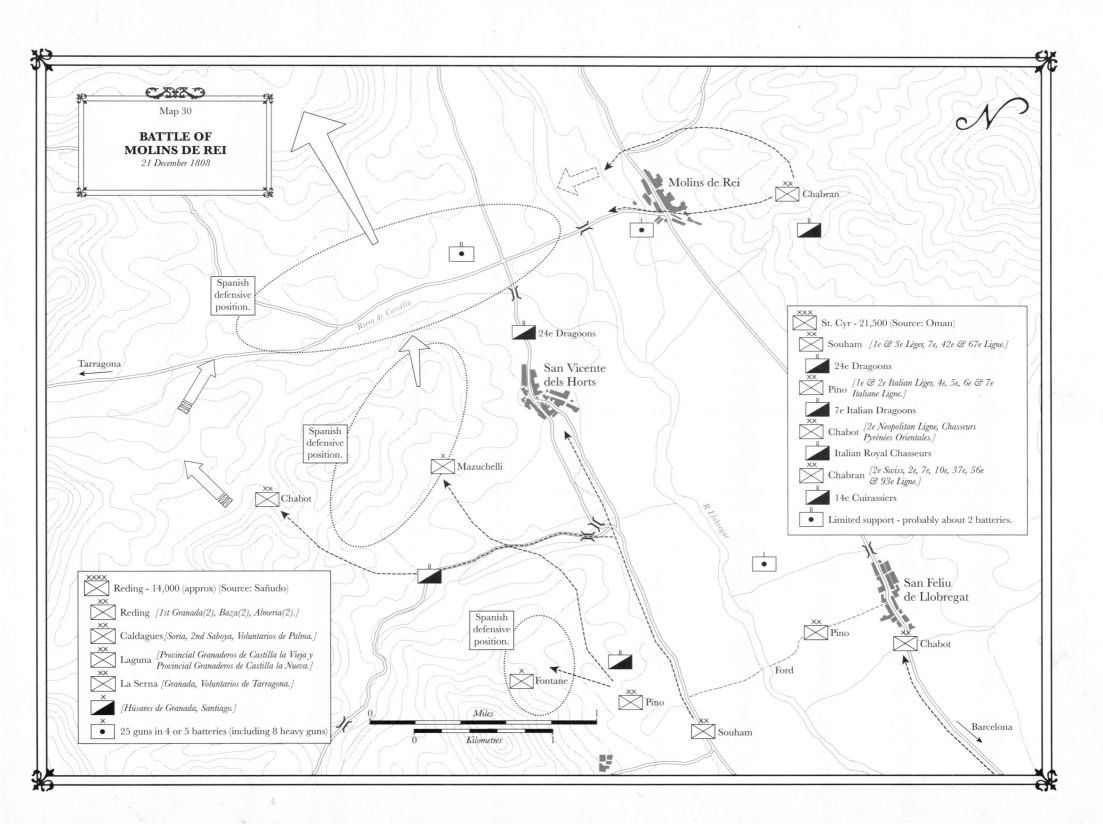

Map 30

BATTLE OF MOLINS DE REI

21 December 1808

Molins de Rei

Chabran

Spanish defensive position.

Riera de Cervelló

Tarragona

24e Dragoons

San Vicente dels Horts

Spanish defensive position.

Mazuchelli

Chabot

R Llobregat

St. Cyr - 21,500 (Source: Oman)

Souham *[1e & 3e Léger, 7e, 42e & 67e Ligne.]*

24e Dragoons

Pino *[1e & 2e Italian Léger, 4e, 5e, 6e & 7e Italiane Ligne.]*

7e Italian Dragoons

Chabot *[2e Neopolitan Ligne, Chasseurs Pyrénées Orientales.]*

Italian Royal Chasseurs

Chabran *[2e Swiss, 2e, 7e, 10e, 37e, 56e & 93e Ligne.]*

14e Cuirassiers

Limited support - probably about 2 batteries.

San Feliu de Llobregat

Reding - 14,000 (approx) (Source: Sañudo)

Reding *[1st Granada(2), Baza(2), Almeria(2).]*

Caldagues *[Soria, 2nd Saboya, Voluntarios de Palma.]*

Laguna *[Provincial Granaderos de Castilla la Vieja y Provincial Granaderos de Castilla la Nueva.]*

La Serna *[Granada, Voluntarios de Tarragona.]*

[Húsares de Granada, Santiago.]

25 guns in 4 or 5 batteries (including 8 heavy guns)

Spanish defensive position.

Fontane

Pino

Ford

Chabot

Barcelona

Souham

0 Miles 1

0 Kilometres 1

Chapter 13 ⊶

ISOLATION AND RETREAT: DECEMBER 1808 TO JANUARY 1809

In late November Moore faced a considerable dilemma. General Hope, leading the group with Moore's cavalry and guns, was still a few days march to the south, Baird's Division lay at Astorga, some 150km to the north, and the British army's cavalry, led by Lord Paget, lay even further back towards Lugo.[1] News of Spanish setbacks at Espinosa, Burgos and Tudela filtered through to Moore; there was now no Spanish force between his army and the French forces that grew larger and loomed closer. Milhaud's dragoons were at Valladolid and Lefebvre at Carrion to the north; Soult, although still in pursuit of La Romana's army[2] in the north, was not out of the equation and Victor's whereabouts was unclear. Equally unclear were Napoleon's intentions: would he continue south and tackle Madrid directly, or would he turn his attention west and 'drive the Britannic leopard from the soil of the Peninsula'?

Frustrated, downhearted and fearing the worst, Moore issued orders for a general retreat on 28 November. Baird complied, but Hope hurried to unite with Moore at Salamanca before returning to Portugal. At last, on 3 December, Hope brought not only Moore's guns and cavalry, but also news that the French were continuing south and, as such, posed little immediate threat to Moore's army. Within 48 hours, Moore issued a counter-order to Baird, instructing him to return to the plains of Leon. During the intervening days, Moore's decision to withdraw had drawn scorn from his own officers and men, deputations from the Junta at Madrid, bilateral offers from La Romana to the north and open hostility from Frere, the British Plenipotentiary in Madrid. In retrospect, with Napoleon unaware of his exact whereabouts, the consequent lack of danger at that time and the determination of the Spanish to defend their capital, his original decision had been flawed. On 10 December Moore attempted to make amends by moving against the French lines of communication, but at the same time he sent word to Viscount Castlereagh[3] requesting the movement of all available transport ships to La Coruña[4] if subsequently he was forced to fall back.

Both Moore and Baird were to converge; their combined force would number about 25,000 including 2,450 cavalry and 1,300 gunners with 66 field guns.[5] At about this time an intercepted dispatch reached Moore, its contents revealing French intentions and dispositions but more significantly, indicated that Napoleon was firmly under the impression that the British were heading back to Lisbon. Soult's Corps was still at Carrion but had orders (according to the dispatch) to move east and therefore into considerable danger. This intelligence prompted Moore to change his plans and his army's direction. By 23 December they were at Mayorga, and had linked up with Baird. With the army united, Moore curiously reorganized the formations and some of the units (see map 31); it is believed his aim was to mix the more experienced Army of Portugal with the newly arrived troops from Galicia. Much to Moore's disappointment Soult did not commence his eastward movement (as detailed in the captured dispatch), prompting Moore to order Paget and his cavalry, to 'stir the hornet's nest' by undertaking a surprise attack on Soult's cavalry brigade at Sahagún.

Debelle's light cavalry were completely unaware that the advance piquets of Moore's army lay just 15km from their position. Paget rode early on 21 December with the 10th and 15th Hussars and, on nearing the French, discovered they had no outposts. Sending General Slade with the 10th Hussars in a direct route to the village, he took the 15th Hussars and rode around the southern edge of Sahagún in an attempt to cut off the French retreat. In the early morning mist, Debelle hastily drew up his two regiments[6] in a field of vines, as Paget emerged on his left flank. There was no sign of Slade and with surprise lost Paget ordered a left wheel and an immediate attack, catching the French off-guard as they manoeuvred to meet the charge. The shock effect of this rapid cavalry action was quite brilliantly executed; the British hussars rode down the chasseurs and drove them back, with considerable force, against the dragoons. Both French regiments broke and fled. The chasseurs suffered extensive casualties (and were subsequently disbanded); the dragoons managed to break clean and rode, at great speed, to deliver the news to an incredulous Marshal Soult.

Moore had followed Paget, and the bulk of the army was in and around Sahagún that evening. He instructed his commanders to provide for a day's rest before moving to attack Soult. Orders were also sent to La Romana, who was to join the British force with his 8,000 men[7] and advance from Mansilla, south of Leon. Soult, meanwhile, had correctly concluded that Moore was within striking distance and called for immediate support. Junot was en route between Vitoria and Burgos but Lorge's dragoons and Delaborde's Division were closer and able to move to Palencia within hours. Franceschi's cavalry was also on the Palencia road having evacuated Valladolid, and they were also summoned. As planned, Moore began to move east during the afternoon of 23 December, by which time both Delaborde and Lorge were already at Palencia and Franceschi only hours away. La Romana sent word that his force was on the move but in a

---

1 It had not left La Coruña until 15 November.

2 La Romana had assumed command of the Army of Galicia from Blake in mid-November 1808.

3 The British Secretary for War.

4 Rear Admiral De Courcy had concerns about leaving his station in the Bay of Biscay due to increased French activity in the area so, in mid-December, the Admiralty tasked Rear Admiral Hook to take charge of the large transport fleet which lay off the coast at Lugo.

5 About 4,000 men were sick and returned to Portugal escorted by the 5/60th and the 3rd Foot.

6 The 8e Dragoons and the 1e Provisional Chasseurs.

7 La Romana had (in a commendably short time) reestablished the Galician army, which now numbered some 20,000; but the majority were rapidly trained and ill equipped. La Romana sensibly only offered to deploy the part of his army he considered ready for combat.

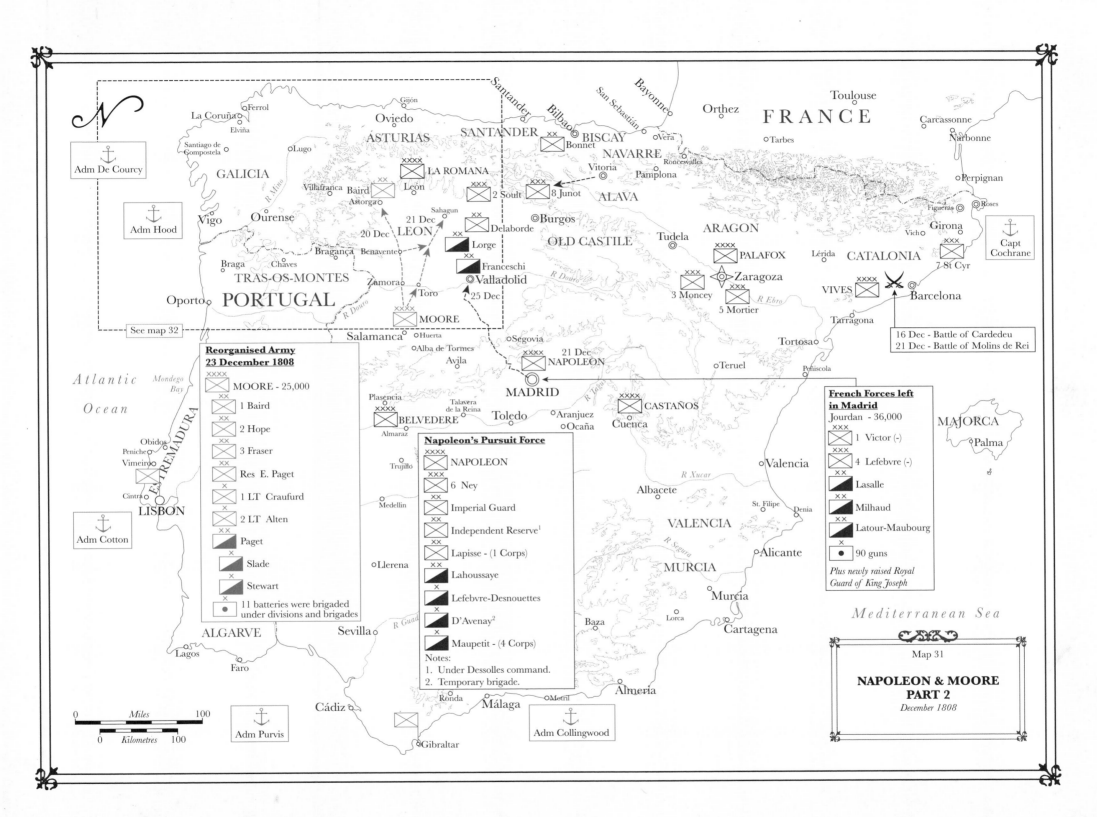

N

Adm De Courcy

Adm Hood

Adm Cotton

Adm Purvis

**Reorganised Army
23 December 1808**

MOORE – 25,000

1 Baird

2 Hope

3 Fraser

Res E. Paget

1 LT Craufurd

2 LT Alten

Paget

Slade

Stewart

11 batteries were brigaded
under divisions and brigades

Napoleon's Pursuit Force

NAPOLEON

6 Ney

Imperial Guard

Independent Reserve[1]

Lapisse - (1 Corps)

Lahoussaye

Lefebvre-Desnouettes

D'Avenay[2]

Maupetit - (4 Corps)

Notes:
1. Under Dessolles command.
2. Temporary brigade.

**French Forces left
in Madrid**

Jourdan – 36,000

1 Victor (-)

4 Lefebvre (-)

Lasalle

Milhaud

Latour-Maubourg

90 guns

*Plus newly raised Royal
Guard of King Joseph*

Adm Collingwood

Map 31

**NAPOLEON & MOORE
PART 2**

December 1808

16 Dec - Battle of Cardedeu
21 Dec - Battle of Molins de Rei

See map 32

Miles 100

Kilometres 100

subsequent communiqué, two hours later, Moore received the news he had feared for some time. The French forces were crossing the Guadarrama mountains, Napoleon had turned north, and his intended target required no elaboration.

Moore needed no reminder of the danger he was now facing. Within three hours of receiving the communiqué, he had ordered all the forces to withdraw. His instructions were simple. The retreat was to start at noon the following day: the main body would withdraw in two groups, Hope and Fraser by Mayorga and Castro Gonzalo, Baird by a more northerly route crossing the river Esla at Valencia de Don Juan. The Reserve Division and the two light brigades were to remain at Sahagún for 24 hours and provide the rearguard. All the cavalry under Paget were to move east, form a screen, and harass any of Soult's forces that ventured forth. The army was to regroup at Astorga where, it was hoped and anticipated, Moore would make his stand. La Romana was asked to hold the bridge at Mansilla for as long as possible and then retire north through León. However, 'La Romana did not advance with his army beyond Mansilla, being satisfied with sending a group of 5,000 men to Mayorga. He even recalled this group before they reached their destination because he was worried about intentions of the Englishmen, considering that he had been scarcely considered in the (Moore's) orders. He was alone.'[8]

Paget's cavalry screen operated unmolested for a couple of days until the vanguard of Napoleon's force appeared, stirring the British cavalry into action. Colbert's Brigade, the Guard Cavalry Brigade under Lefebvre-Desnouettes and Lahoussaye's Division of dragoons all arrived at much the same time on 26 December and began to close in on Paget's screen. By 28 December the screen had fallen back across the frontage with every regiment engaged somewhere along the line. Craufurd's Light Brigade was holding the bridge at Castro Gonzalo and, once Paget had crossed over, the light troops blew the structure as the French cavalry appeared. Paget deployed his regiments at all the crossing points along the Esla, buying time for the Reserve Division and the two light brigades to close up on the main body at Astorga. For over 24 hours this ploy held up the French advance until Lefebvre-Desnouettes ordered his troopers to find alternate crossing points, up or down stream. Once found, the Guard Cavalry crossed swiftly with about 600 cavalry and were equally hastily engaged by the British on the far bank. The French gained some early success in the engagement but were soon overwhelmed; a number of French cavalry were captured including General Lefebvre-Desnouettes. The French returned to the relative safety of the east bank and began probing for alternative crossings until Paget turned the Royal Horse Artillery guns of Downman's Troop on the massing cavalry, which sufficed to dampen their resolve and bring proceedings to an end for the time being.

It took Napoleon's sappers two days to repair the bridge at Castro Gonzalo, by which time the entire British army had united at Astorga. Against Moore's direction, La Romana had elected to join the British there, leaving his 2nd Division to cover the bridge at Mansilla.[9] Soult's forces closed in on this crossing point and on 30 December engaged the Spanish, quickly overwhelming the defenders before moving on to León, which was occupied on 31 December. Napoleon had

moved up from Benavente the same day, and both forces were a day's march from Moore's rearguard. La Romana urged Moore to make a stand at the two passes to the rear of Astorga on the Cordillera Cantábrica. There was no doubt that the features were highly defendable; Moore's army was raring for a fight and to the Allied rear lay Ponferrada and Villafranca, which housed considerable stores, ammunition and guns. Yet Moore rejected the idea. The tone of his dispatches indicate a resignation to extricate Britain's only field army, coupled with disenchantment for the Spanish authorities and a feeling that his mission had already been accomplished by distracting Napoleon from southern Spain. Moore's decision not to fight was met, over the coming weeks, with a combination of fury and disillusionment across Spain. The reaction, from within his own rank and file, was instant. Discipline had been sliding since the first announcement to withdraw in Salamanca and again in Sahagún. It now turned into open disobedience and outright depravity in some units. Moore's condemnation of this behaviour and of the failure of his officers (who were equally disillusioned) to deal with it did little to ease the situation. The British army, renowned for its tough discipline and moral fortitude, unravelled with alarming speed. It was clearly a failure of command. Those units where the officers and non-commissioned officers maintained routine and control did not suffer the same fate. Oman summed it up when he stated, 'Already several battalions were beginning to march with an advance guard of marauders and a rear guard of limping stragglers, the sure signs of impending trouble.'[10]

When word that Moore had pulled back from Astorga reached Napoleon he considered the pursuit over. 'The meeting of the French troops took place on 1 January in Astorga which Napoleon had entered without finding resistance. He was preparing to pursue the Englishmen with his habitual swiftness when he received despatches that informed him, without any doubt, the outlook of hostility by Austria; he was therefore forced to stop and to return to Valladolid.'[11] Napoleon handed the reins to Soult and settled down to complete some overdue paperwork in Benavente. Much later he was to comment that, had he known the British fleet were delayed in reaching La Coruña through contrary winds, he would have continued the pursuit personally. He wanted to inflict a decisive victory on the British and when he felt the opportunity slip, he was content to leave a sideshow to a subordinate. He broke up the pursuing force, sending many formations back to Madrid or into Leon and, at much the same time, disbanded Junot's 8th Corps and largely incorporated it into Soult's Corps, which now led the pursuit with about 25,000 men.[12] Ney's 6th Corps followed Soult, a day's march to their rear with an additional 16,000 exhausted men.

In order to keep his options open, Moore sent the two light brigades to Vigo[13] while the balance of his force withdrew to La Coruña. La Romana followed Craufurd and Alten as far as Orense and halted there for some days in an attempt to revitalize his depleted force.[14] The task

---

8   Le Noble, *Mémoires seur Les Opérations Militares Des Francais en Galicia, en Portugal, et dans la vallée du Tage, en 1809*, p.36.

9   La Romana refused to blow the bridge as he considered the river fordable at numerous places.

10   Oman, *History of the Peninsular War*, vol. I. p.558.

11   Le Noble, *Mémoires seur Les Opérations Militares Des Francais en Galicia, en Portugal, et dans la vallée du Tage, en 1809*, p.39.

12   In fact the 2nd Corps numbered some 33,000 by this time. However, Bonnet's Division was still at Santander and there were a number sick and wounded.

13   Vigo was the port where the British fleet had been originally directed to wait.

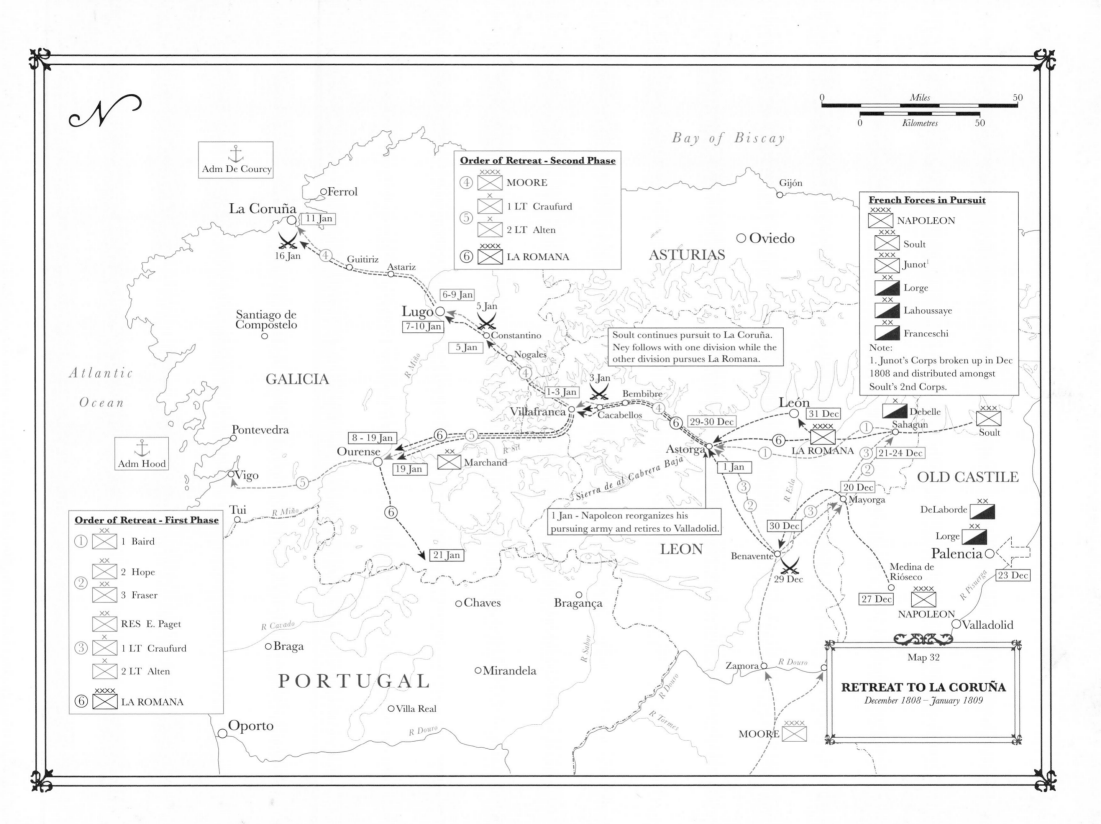

Order of Retreat - Second Phase

④ ⛝ MOORE
⑤ ⛝ 1 LT Craufurd
⛝ 2 LT Alten
⑥ ⛝ LA ROMANA

French Forces in Pursuit

⛝ NAPOLEON
⛝ Soult
⛝ Junot[1]
◼ Lorge
◼ Lahoussaye
◼ Franceschi

Note:
1. Junot's Corps broken up in Dec 1808 and distributed amongst Soult's 2nd Corps.

Adm De Courcy

Bay of Biscay

Gijón

Ferrol
La Coruña 11 Jan
16 Jan ④ Guitiriz
Astariz

○ Oviedo

ASTURIAS

6-9 Jan
Lugo 5 Jan
7-10 Jan ✕ 5 Jan
Constantino
5 Jan
Nogales
④

Santiago de Compostelo

Atlantic Ocean

GALICIA

Soult continues pursuit to La Coruña. Ney follows with one division while the other division pursues La Romana.

3 Jan
1-3 Jan ✕ Bembibre
Villafranca ④ Cacabellos
León 31 Dec
29-30 Dec ⑥
Astorga ① LA ROMANA ① 21-24 Dec
Sahagun Soult
Debelle

Adm Hood

Pontevedra

Ourense ⑥ ⑤
8 - 19 Jan
19 Jan ⛝ Marchand
R Sil
1 Jan
③ ②
20 Dec
Mayorga

OLD CASTILE

Vigo ⑤
⑥
21 Jan
Tui R Miño
30 Dec
Benavente

LEON

1 Jan - Napoleon reorganizes his pursuing army and retires to Valladolid.

DeLaborde
Lorge
Palencia ○
R Pisuerga

Order of Retreat - First Phase

① ⛝ 1 Baird
② ⛝ 2 Hope
⛝ 3 Fraser
⛝ RES E. Paget
③ ⛝ 1 LT Craufurd
⛝ 2 LT Alten
⑥ ⛝ LA ROMANA

Chaves ○ Bragança ○

R Cavado

Braga ○

○ Mirandela

PORTUGAL

○ Villa Real

R Sabor

29 Dec

Medina de Ríoseco
27 Dec ⛝ NAPOLEON

23 Dec

Map 32

RETREAT TO LA CORUÑA
December 1808 – January 1809

Zamora ○ R Douro
○ Valladolid

R Douro
R Tormes

MOORE ⛝

Oporto ○

of forming the rearguard to Moore's main body now fell to Edward Paget and the Reserve Division, supported by the 15th Hussars; the balance of Henry Paget's cavalry was now leading the retreat.[15] It was a ghastly affair, morale had all but collapsed and discipline in some units was completely spent; only those units with good commanders completed the retreat with few losses and reasonable order.[16] It 'was a dreadful march over an immense snow mountain with ruts cut in the snow, ice two-feet deep, and large holes, so that the horses could scarce move. The road strew'd and block'd up with ordnance, carriages and others of every description, number of dead horses. Men, women and children frozen to death.'[17] Soult recorded, 'The English troops, on leaving Astorga, took the route to Bembibre and Valladolid. They marched in great disorder and the soldiers committed many excesses.'[18]

As the main body departed Villafranca on 3 January, Paget was fighting a rearguard action 10km back at Cacabellos with his reserve division. Colbert, with the 15e Chasseurs and the 3e Hussars, was leading the French vanguard and, in an act of desperation for personal distinction, led a hasty charge to try and take the bridge. Colbert was shot during the action and Paget's Division succeeded in holding up the French for a full day before withdrawing under cover of darkness. Paget's troops were called on again two days later to slow up the French progress at Constantino, where the sappers had failed to blow the central arch of the bridge, which was subsequently assailed by Merle's infantry. Once again, the French were held back sufficiently long enough to enable the gunners and infantry to withdraw as night fell.

The main body had begun arriving at Lugo late on 5 January 1809. The men were utterly worn out, especially those in Fraser's Division who had marched an extra 50km due to a mix-up in the passage of orders. Moore realized he needed to buy more time for his shattered army; the Lugo position was strong, and the large depot that had been established there was affording badly needed supplies. Late on 6 January Soult's pursuing force arrived in front of the position and, equally exhausted, waited until the following day before undertaking a series of probing attacks on the British line. Having offered battle, Moore fully expected the French attack to take place during 8 January, but to his disappointment and frustration Soult still considered his force too weak and he clearly had no intention of taking up the offer of battle until Ney had come up from Villafranca. Moore could not afford to wait for Ney to tip the balance in Soult's favour and that night he gave new orders for his force to move west and complete the last leg of the retreat to the coast.

On the night of 11 January Hope, Baird and Fraser's divisions reached the outskirts of La Coruña. Paget formed up at El Burgo, just outside the town and established a defence around the bridge, which the engineers blew. Paget's Division was once again called upon to buy more time as the British fleet was beating north from Vigo against unfavourable winds and was not expected until 14 January. Paget's gallant division held up the French advance for another 24 hours, although in fairness Soult was merely probing Paget's lines while the French main body were closing up and the cavalry were looking for alternate routes to La Coruña. When Moore ordered Paget to pull back the French sappers pounced on the broken bridge and reconstructed it within a few hours. On 13 January the infantry crossed, but the French sappers had to strengthen the structure to enable the massed cavalry and the guns to follow. During this lull, the British were busy loading the sick and wounded onto the first vessels in the harbour and distributing new muskets and clothing from the ample stores left in the city. Moore also had all the ammunition, powder and musket cartridges distributed to the army and ordered the rest destroyed.[19] The resulting explosion in the two magazines caused structural damage and, according to Napier, 'killed many persons who had remained too near the spot'.[20]

Moore also deployed his infantry and three troops of guns in a defensive line on the nearest heights surrounding the approaches to the town. The balance of the artillery (except for one troop with Paget's reserve) and the cavalry were embarking in the transports although many of the horses were in such an appalling state they had to be shot, as there was insufficient space and many would not have survived the passage.[21] The heights of Peñasquedo offered a better defensive position than the Monte Mero, but required a greater force to exploit the advantage than was available to the British commander. Moore had little choice but to establish his line on the lower hills; his position to the right afforded no high ground, with the flat plains running up to the walls of La Coruña itself. Fraser's Division was positioned to cover this open ground but they were too far away to be used as a rapid reserve for the main force. Accordingly, Paget's Reserve Division was placed to the rear between the two defensive positions to be able to deploy and react to circumstances at either end.

Late in the afternoon of 15 January, Soult's three divisions were complete on the west of the river Mero and he pushed them all forward to the Peñasquedo heights where they quickly took their positions and established two batteries (ten guns) on the western end from where they could comfortably engage Bentinck's Brigade. Delaborde and Merle were ordered to establish positions on the east and centre of the heights of Peñasquedo and they wasted little time in driving the British piquets out of Palavea, forcing Hope to pull his men back to the Monte Mero. As light

---

14   He only had 6,000 men left from the 22,000 he had listed with the army at León on 25 December 1808. He remained at Orense until 19 January 1809 when Marchand came up before him forcing him to retreat south to the Portuguese border.

15   These two officers were brothers. Henry, 2nd Earl of Uxbridge (later Marquis of Anglesey) was Wellington's cavalry commander for part of the Peninsular War and Waterloo, where he lost a leg. Edward commanded the reserve division during this part of the war, lost an arm four months later at Wellington's crossing of the Douro and returned to command the 1st Division in 1812 but was captured within days of arriving back in the Peninsula.

16   Oman lists these as the two battalions of the Guards, the 1/43rd, 4th, 42nd, 71st, 79th, 92nd, 2/95th and the cavalry. Oman, *History of the Peninsular War*, vol. I, p.565.

17   Extract from Captain Evelegh's Coruña diary: MD 1254, James Clavell Library, Woolwich, p.14.

18   Soult, *Mémoires de Maréchal Soult*, p.62.

19   Oman and Napier state the 13th, but Colonel John Harding, Commander Royal Artillery in his report *The Services of the Royal Regiment of Artillery in the Peninsular War 1808 to 1814*, Major Leslie in the Royal Artillery Journal 1908, and Captain Adam Wall's *Diary of Operations in Spain under Sir John Moore*, p.14, (MS James Clavell Library, Woolwich), all state that 14 January is when the magazines were blown. As the gunners were responsible for the destruction of the surplus powder it would be fair to assume the date of the 14th to be more accurate.

20   Napier, *History of the War in the Peninsula*, vol. I, p.325.

21   Oman quotes that 2,000 horses and draught cattle were shot or stabbed and flung into the sea amidst scenes of great distress.

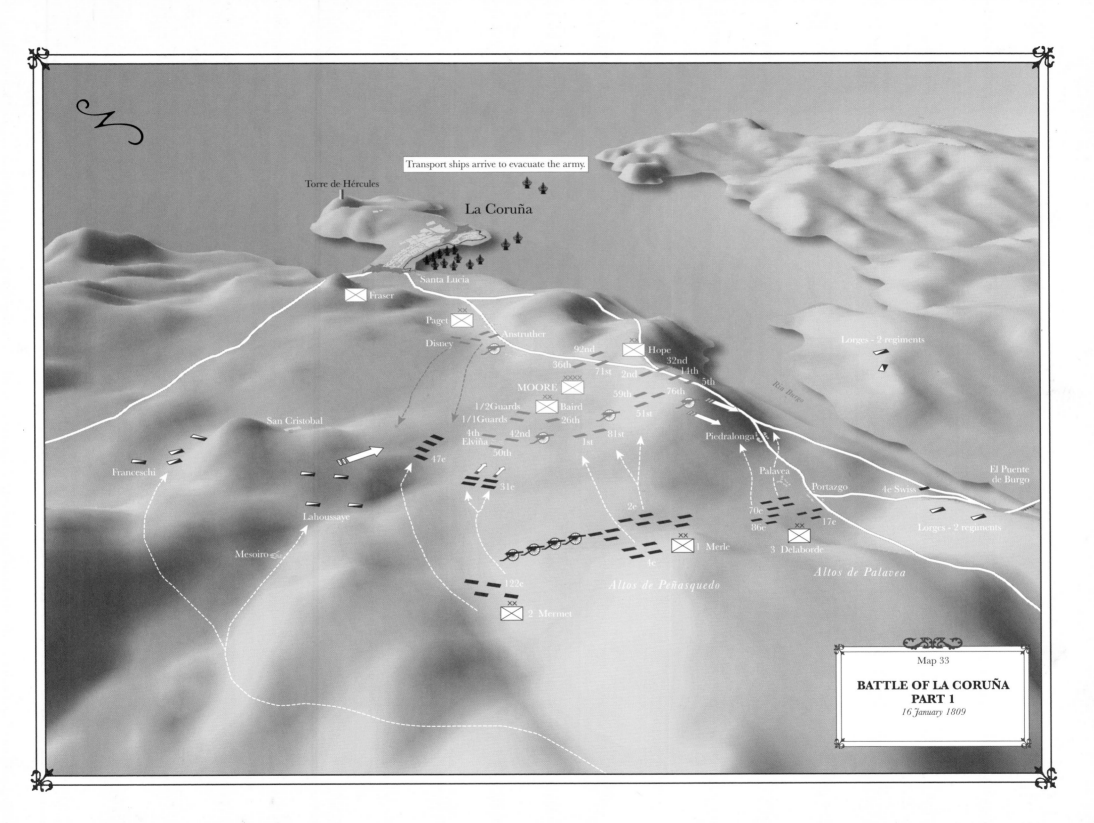

Transport ships arrive to evacuate the army.

Torre de Hércules

La Coruña

Santa Lucia

Fraser

Paget

Disney

Anstruther

92nd

Hope

36th

71st   2nd

MOORE

59th

5th

32nd

14th

76th

San Cristobal

1/2 Guards   Baird

26th

51st

1/1 Guards

4th   42nd

Elviña

81st

1st

Piedralonga

Franceschi

47e

50th

Palavea

Portazgo

4e Swiss

51e

2e

70e

17e

86e

Lahoussaye

122e

2e

4e

2 Mermet

1 Merle

3 Delaborde

Mesoiro

Altos de Peñasquedo

Altos de Palavea

Ría Burgo

Lorges - 2 regiments

El Puente de Burgo

Lorges - 2 regiments

Map 33

BATTLE OF LA CORUÑA
PART 1
16 January 1809

faded an attack early on 16 January seemed imminent, yet Soult appeared to be in no hurry and the demands of the terrain slowed things considerably. Mermet deployed to the west, where the hills were less pronounced, and was tasked with engaging the troops in and around Elviña and to get a brigade around the British right wing. This was to be Soult's main effort and accordingly, Franceschi[22] and Lahoussaye's cavalry divisions were sent even further to the west to assist and exploit any success gained by Mermet's infantry. The rest of the French guns were to deploy at intervals between the French formations along the heights, however, as there was no lateral track, manoeuvring them into place took considerable time. By midday, the French attack had still not materialized and Moore concluded that Soult had no intention of instigating an attack that day. He gave orders to Edward Paget to return to the harbour immediately, the other brigades were to follow at dusk and the entire force was to embark that night.

At about 1345 hours, Moore was in a melancholy mood. Despite the fact that the embarkation would likely be complete that night and with favourable winds the fleet would be clear of the harbour by daybreak, he had hoped for an opportunity to fight. Psychologically it was important, as the men both craved and needed the opportunity for action, and Moore too considered it important to redress some of the unfortunate decisions and subsequent depravations of recent weeks – and, perhaps most significantly, to silence his critics. His downhearted demeanour was suddenly transformed when the two batteries of guns overlooking Bentinck's position at Elviña opened, and ten minutes later Hope rode up with news that the French were attacking across the front. Moore reached Bentinck's position just as the head of General Gaulois's Brigade which, preceded by hundreds of voltigeurs, had begun to push the skirmishers of the 50th out of the village. Moore also noted the movement of another of Mermet's brigades to the far right, manoeuvring to outflank the British position with a large number of dragoons in support. Moore set off to ascertain the situation further east, and sent orders to Fraser to redeploy from in front of La Coruña and be prepared to link up with Paget and engage the forces moving west. The attacks by Merle and Delaborde were less immediate and, having ascertained that the French main effort was in front of Baird, Moore rode back to the far right flank. He instructed the 4th to throw back their right wing to cover the flanking movement by the 47e and then returned to the small hillock above the village of Elviña. On arrival, he was informed that Bentinck had been wounded[23] and he therefore stayed to direct operations, ordering the 42nd to retake the village from the 31e Léger with the rallying cry, 'My brave Highlanders! Remember Egypt! Think of Scotland!' He also ordered the 4th to hold their position on the right, and meet the flanking movement of Lefebvre's Brigade. The 50th supported the 42nd as they began fierce hand-to-hand fighting in the narrow streets of the small village[24] but both battalions met with limited success

and fell back. The veteran French troops were fighting with considerable tenacity and Moore felt compelled to call up Warde's Brigade of Guards which was in reserve. It was during the deployment of the Guards that Moore received his mortal wound, being struck in the left shoulder by a cannon ball from the guns on the heights of Peñasquedo. He gave orders for the 42nd to join the Guards and sent a message to Hope to assume command and was then carried to the rear in a blanket. The time was about 1500 hours.[25]

Meanwhile, Paget's infantry had advanced to prevent the French getting in behind the right wing of Baird's Division. Anstruther's Brigade[26] led with the 95th in line followed by the 52nd. Lahoussaye's dragoons ineffectively engaged them en route but they continued a steady advance towards elements of the 47e Ligne who were deployed in front of the 4th Foot. Lahoussaye made a couple of attempts to charge the advancing skirmish line but the ground was entirely unsuited to mounted operations and these charges did not even cause the 95th to form square.[27] Lahoussaye then dismounted his dragoons and they engaged the British infantry with their carbines, but they were no match for the Baker rifles and Brown Bess muskets. With this left flanking manoeuvre seemingly unsuccessful, Mermet instigated another attempt to retake Elviña, which was by now back in British hands. Merle's left-hand brigade, that of Reynaud, was allocated in support. Manningham responded by altering the arcs of fire of his two right-hand battalions, the 3/1st and 2/81st, to enable them to engage the advancing French infantry in the flank. This renewed engagement was as furious as the first and continued for some hours until ammunition on both sides was almost spent. As dusk fell the village remained in British hands.

In front of Hope's Division, Delaborde had done little more than hold his attention. Foy had been tasked with taking the village of Piedralonga, which he succeeded in doing early in the afternoon by driving out the advanced piquets of the 2/14th Regiment positioned there. Hope responded by sending the battalion back, supported by two companies of the 92nd, who together succeeded in retaking the village and continued to hold it for the rest of the day, despite a subsequent and sustained French counter-attack which secured part of the southern end. On the far left the French cavalry divisions, having failed in their attempts to turn the British right and engaged throughout the afternoon by both Paget and Fraser, withdrew to the area around the village of Mesoiro to the rear left of Soult's main body, where they took no further part in proceedings.

As dusk fell, fighting petered out across the front. Moore survived long enough to be informed that the army had prevailed and had bought enough time to secure a safe departure. He died soon after and was buried at early dawn on the ramparts of La Coruña. Beresford's Brigade was left to cover the withdrawal and by 2100 hours, Baird and Hope's divisions followed Paget's weary troops down to the harbour and onto the waiting vessels. As dawn broke on 17 January

---

22　There is disagreement as to whether Franceschi was actually present at La Coruña. Oman and Napier indicate he was, Fortescue, citing Balagny, states he was not. French sources are inconclusive.

23　Like Moore, somewhat later in the battle, Bentinck was wounded in the arm when he was struck by a cannon ball. This highlights the domination of the French artillery on this defensive position from their massed battery position on the Peñasquedo Heights.

24　There is confusion as to whether Charles Napier (brother of the great historian) was actually ordered by Moore to advance or whether he rather took it upon himself to follow the Highlanders. Napier was wounded and captured during the attack.

25　The exact time of Moore's fatal wounding is unclear but this author supports Zbigniew Guscin's assessment, *Moore 1761–1809*, pp.147–148, that it had to be earlier than the 1650 hours (David Chandler's suggested time) based on eyewitness accounts.

26　Anstruther was not in command, having died of dysentery (Oman), or exhaustion (Butler, *Wellington's Operations in the Peninsular*, vol. I, p.121) during the retreat.

27　The ground around La Coruña was entirely unsuitable for cavalry operations, being composed of so many hedges, low walls and ditches that forming up and charging was almost impossible.

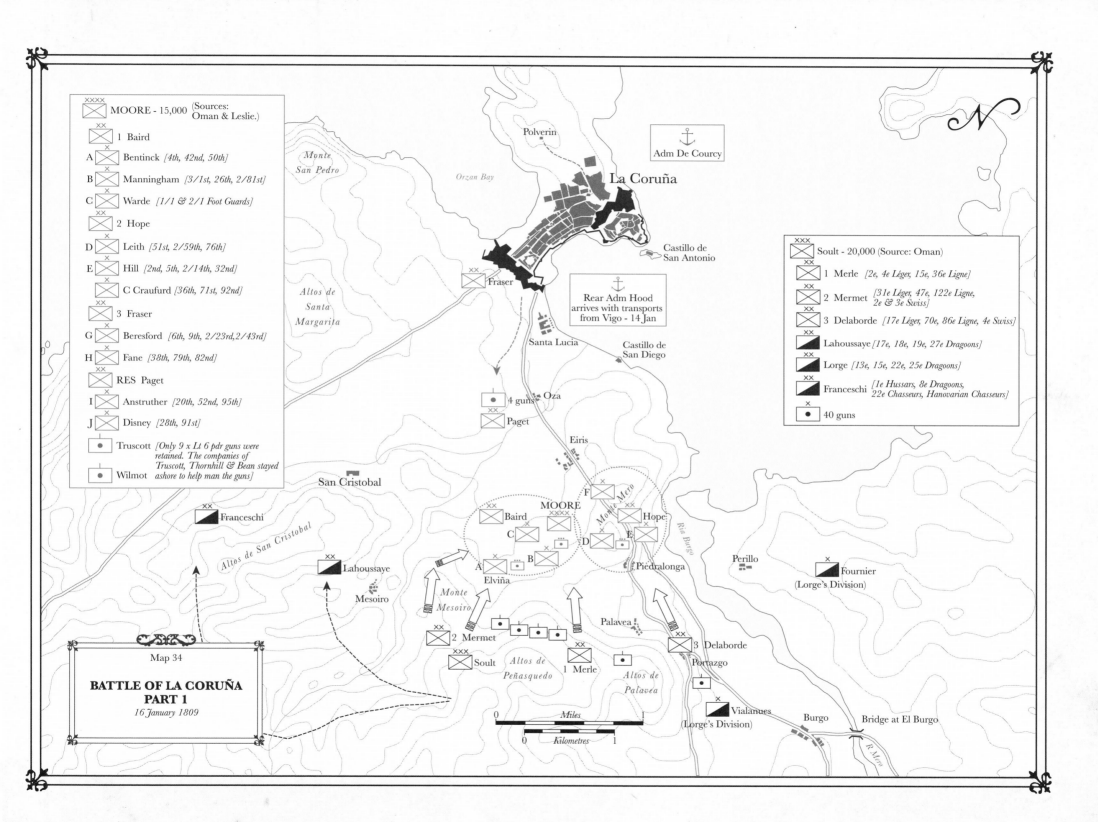

MOORE - 15,000 (Sources: Oman & Leslie.)

1 Baird
A Bentinck [4th, 42nd, 50th]
B Manningham [3/1st, 26th, 2/81st]
C Warde [1/1 & 2/1 Foot Guards]
2 Hope
D Leith [51st, 2/59th, 76th]
E Hill [2nd, 5th, 2/14th, 32nd]
C Craufurd [36th, 71st, 92nd]
3 Fraser
G Beresford [6th, 9th, 2/23rd, 2/43rd]
H Fane [38th, 79th, 82nd]
RES Paget
I Anstruther [20th, 52nd, 95th]
J Disney [28th, 91st]
Truscott [Only 9 x Lt 6 pdr guns were
retained. The companies of
Truscott, Thornhill & Bean stayed
Wilmot ashore to help man the guns]

Soult - 20,000 (Source: Oman)
1 Merle [2e, 4e Léger, 15e, 36e Ligne]
2 Mermet [31e Léger, 47e, 122e Ligne, 2e & 3e Swiss]
3 Delaborde [17e Léger, 70e, 86e Ligne, 4e Swiss]
Lahoussaye [17e, 18e, 19e, 27e Dragoons]
Lorge [13e, 15e, 22e, 25e Dragoons]
Franceschi [1e Hussars, 8e Dragoons, 22e Chasseurs, Hanovarian Chasseurs]
40 guns

Polverin
Adm De Courcy
Orzan Bay
La Coruña
Monte San Pedro
Castillo de San Antonio
Fraser
Rear Adm Hood arrives with transports from Vigo - 14 Jan
Altos de Santa Margarita
Santa Lucia
Castillo de San Diego
4 guns Oza
Paget
Eiris
San Cristobal
F
Monte Mero
Baird MOORE Hope
Franceschi C D E
Altos de San Cristobal B Piedralonga
Lahoussaye A Elviña Perillo Fournier (Lorge's Division)
Mesoiro Monte Mesoiro Palavea Río Burgo
2 Mermet Palavea
Soult 1 Merle Altos de Peñasquedo Portazgo
Altos de Palavea
Vialanues (Lorge's Division)
Burgo Bridge at El Burgo
R. Mero

0 Miles 1
0 Kilometres 1

Map 34

**BATTLE OF LA CORUÑA
PART 1**
16 January 1809

the French had already accepted that darkness had provided the cover for Moore's army to embark and escape. Soult moved a battery of guns to the heights above Fort San Diego and opened fire on the shipping at anchor below, causing some alarm but little else. Beresford withdrew on 18 January from a safe point to the north-east of the citadel. The fleet carried home about 26,000 men and the army had been saved, but the troops that disembarked in Britain five days later were an appalling sight. 'It is sufficient for me to observe, that not all the consciousness of victory, cheering and gratifying as that is, was capable of alleviating, in the slightest degree, the grief of the army for the loss of its chief. Perhaps the British army has produced some abler men than Sir John Moore; it has certainly produced many who, in point of military talent, were and are quite his equals; but it cannot, and perhaps never could, boast of one more beloved, not by his own personal friends alone, but by every individual that served under him.'[28]

The retreat to the Atlantic coast and the engagement on the outskirts of the Galician port had a profound effect on British public opinion; indeed, they seem destined to bring the curtain down on further British involvement in Iberia. Soult and his men had every right to consider the battle a French victory.[29] 'Moore ordered the reserve that were deployed on the outskirts of La Coruña and covered by the town of Eirís, to advance. This reinforcement reestablished the combat. Their action even threatened the French [main] battery position, but its efforts were vain. The town of Elviña, taken and recaptured twice, remained in our power. The night put an end to the battle, intensely disputed by both parts.'[30] Moore had distracted the French from their mission and, by so doing, saved the nation, a point acknowledged some while later by Wellington when he said, 'we'd not have won, I think, without him'; and even Napoleon conceded that, 'It was only Moore's action which stopped me taking Spain and Portugal.' Aside from the arguments of who actually won the battle of La Coruña, the fact remained that Napoleon had succeeded in driving the leopard into the sea, but at a cost.

---

28 Vane, *Narrative of the Peninsular War*, vol. I, pp.287–288.

29 It is one of the many victories etched on the Arc de Triomphe, along with the names of the many distinguished generals who commanded troops during Napoleon's regime.

30 Soult, *Mémoires de Maréchal Soult*, p.69.

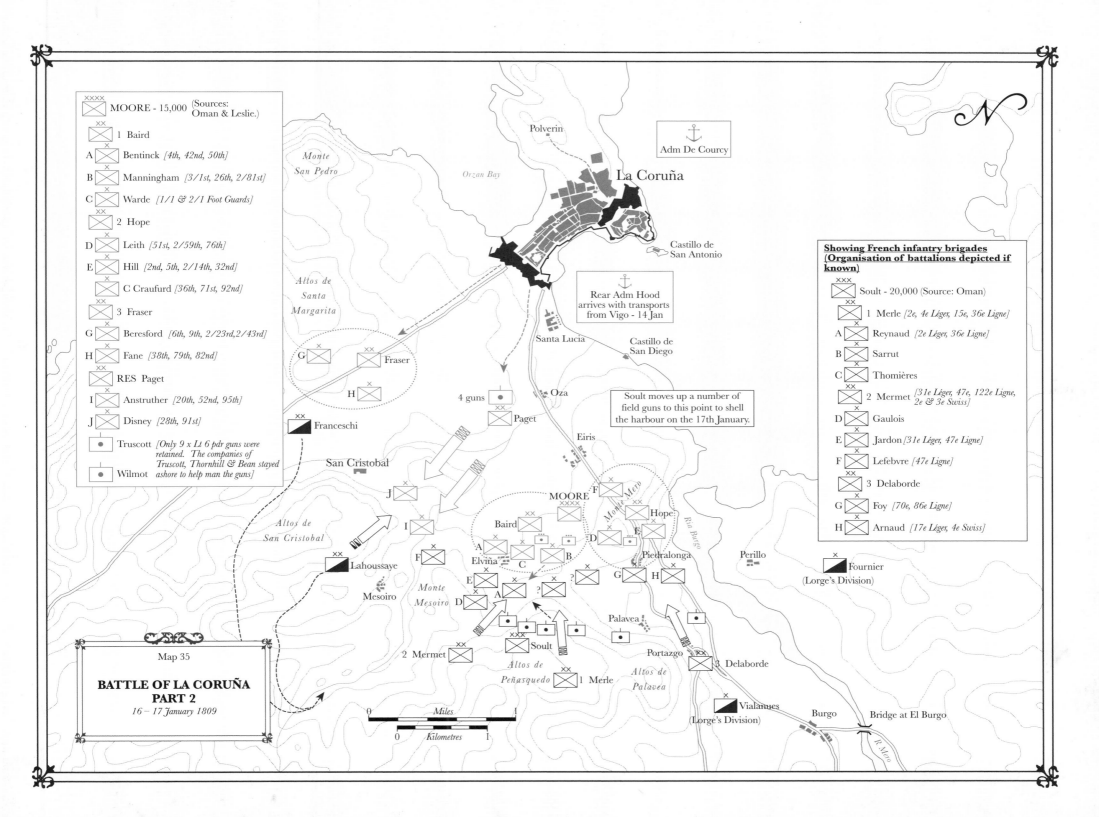

MOORE - 15,000 (Sources: Oman & Leslie.)

1 Baird

A Bentinck [4th, 42nd, 50th]

B Manningham [3/1st, 26th, 2/81st]

C Warde [1/1 & 2/1 Foot Guards]

2 Hope

D Leith [51st, 2/59th, 76th]

E Hill [2nd, 5th, 2/14th, 32nd]

C Craufurd [36th, 71st, 92nd]

3 Fraser

G Beresford [6th, 9th, 2/23rd, 2/43rd]

H Fane [38th, 79th, 82nd]

RES Paget

I Anstruther [20th, 52nd, 95th]

J Disney [28th, 91st]

Truscott [Only 9 x Lt 6 pdr guns were retained. The companies of Truscott, Thornhill & Bean stayed ashore to help man the guns]

Wilmot

Showing French infantry brigades (Organisation of battalions depicted if known)

Soult - 20,000 (Source: Oman)

1 Merle [2e, 4e Léger, 15e, 36e Ligne]

A Reynaud [2e Léger, 36e Ligne]

B Sarrut

C Thomières

2 Mermet [31e Léger, 47e, 122e Ligne, 2e & 3e Swiss]

D Gaulois

E Jardon [31e Léger, 47e Ligne]

F Lefebvre [47e Ligne]

3 Delaborde

G Foy [70e, 86e Ligne]

H Arnaud [17e Léger, 4e Swiss]

Adm De Courcy

Polverin

Monte San Pedro

Orzan Bay

La Coruña

Castillo de San Antonio

Altos de Santa Margarita

Rear Adm Hood arrives with transports from Vigo - 14 Jan

Santa Lucia

Castillo de San Diego

4 guns

Oza

Eiris

Soult moves up a number of field guns to this point to shell the harbour on the 17th January.

Paget

Franceschi

San Cristobal

J

Altos de San Cristobal

I

Lahoussaye

F

Mesoiro

Monte Mesoiro

Elviña

A

C

B

MOORE

Baird

F

Monte Mero

Hope

D

E

Ria Burgo

Piedralonga

Perillo

Fournier
(Lorge's Division)

E

D

A

G

H

?

?

?

Palavea

Portazgo

2 Mermet

Soult

1 Merle

Altos de Peñasquedo

Altos de Palavea

3 Delaborde

Vialannes
(Lorge's Division)

Burgo

Bridge at El Burgo

R. Mero

0   Miles   1

0   Kilometres   1

Map 35

**BATTLE OF LA CORUÑA
PART 2**

16 – 17 January 1809

Chapter 14 ⊶╼━

NAPOLEON DEPARTS FOR FRANCE: THE SITUATION IN EARLY 1809

Napoleon's plan for the recapture of Madrid and the annihilation of the Spanish armies had been simplistic enough, but while it succeeded in securing the former, it certainly failed in the latter. His plans to use his reorganized French army to continue the motion into southern Spain and Portugal were completely disrupted by the discovery of Moore. Napoleon's decision to take chase brought to a halt any further advances south and ultimately derailed his plans for national subjugation. The only Spanish army caught up in the pursuit of the British was that of La Romana. He had joined Moore at Astorga and then followed Craufurd and Alten's brigades when they branched south to Vigo. Reaching Orense on 8 January, he intended to remain there and revitalize his severely depleted force, which by now only numbered 6,000. Ten days later his plans were hurriedly transformed when Marchand's Division (from the 6th Corps) arrived on the outskirts of the town. La Romana headed south to the relative safety of the mountains on the northern Portuguese border. Fortunately for the Spanish commander, Marchand did not follow and the Spanish were able to undertake some form of rest and recuperation. By 13 February La Romana reported 9,000 men under arms, including many veterans.

In Catalonia, despite the decisive defeats of Vives at Cardedeu and Reding at Molins de Rei, St Cyr was compelled to delay further offensive action in order to revitalize and reorganize his somewhat convoluted command. Vives' resignation prompted the Junta to replace him with Reding who, although not a Catalan, had hitherto proved himself sufficiently courageous. He was to need all that courage in the early days of his new command as many provincial towns in the region were in a state of virtual anarchy. He quickly dealt with this and then set about reorganising the Catalan army, which included the second brigade of his old Division of Granada[1] and the balance of the reserves from Majorca. By early February, with many of the dispersed *miqueletes* and *somatenes* having returned to their colours, Reding's army exceeded 30,000 men.

Following the battle at Tudela, Lannes handed back command of the 3rd Corps to Moncey[2] who was joined by Ney two days later. By 30 November the two marshals were in front of Zaragoza; however, before any form of siege could commence, Ney was to receive new orders from Napoleon to instigate the immediate pursuit of Castaños. Moncey considered the 3rd Corps alone inadequate for the task, and withdrew a safe distance from the city walls and Palafox's Army of Aragon to await reinforcement. It proved a lengthy wait, for Mortier did not arrive with the 5th Corps for another three weeks. This delay provided Palafox and the citizens of Zaragoza an additional month to prepare for the inevitable second siege and not for the first time, they used their opportunity wisely. By 20 December, when the siege commenced, Palafox's army numbered some 34,000 regulars (of varying quality) and a number of armed citizens.

As Napoleon departed the capital to give chase to Moore, he ordered Lefebvre's 4th Corps[3] and Lasalle's Cavalry Division to destroy the remnants of the Estremaduran Army[4] who were regrouping under their new commander Galluzzo between Almaraz and Alcantara. By the end of December this mission had only been partially achieved; Galluzzo's army was no longer an effective field formation but it was far from destroyed, having largely dispersed to the relative safety of the Sierra de Guadalupe.[5] Lefebvre then completely ignored Napoleon's orders to return to Talavera and remain there; instead he inexplicably turned north and, by 5 January, was positioned at Avila. This insubordination was to cost him his command.[6] The remainder of the old Army of the Centre had evaded Bessières (who assumed command of the pursuit from Ney) and had reached Cuenca in mid-December; command had already passed from Castaños to the Duke of Infantado. No longer under an immediate threat from Bessières, or from King Joseph's forces in Madrid, Infantado allowed his exhausted and ill-equipped force two weeks of badly needed rest. He sent the balance of Roca's Division back to the Army of Valencia, which had almost ceased to exist (it numbered less than 1,500) although half its original 8,000-strong force were in Zaragoza, seconded to Palafox's army for the defence of the city. The district of Cuenca was not blessed with great resources; the majority of food and new clothing had to be brought up from Valencia. However, when the supplies and equipment arrived, the Duke of Infantado instigated the reorganization of the four original divisions of the Army of Andalusia into two new divisions, a vanguard and a reserve.

On 25 December General Venegas, in command of the Vanguard Division, was sent by Infantado to surprise Perreimond's Brigade of dragoons (from Latour-Maubourg's Division) at Tarancon and General Senra was sent with another column (of about 4,000 men) to eject the French from Aranjuez. Venegas was successful but Senra wisely called off his attack when he realized the strength of the French force at his objective. Joseph deduced that this limited Spanish offensive was clearly the precursor to something more substantial and immediately sent a request to his brother for immediate support. In fact, Joseph's concern was partially justified; Lefebvre had just commenced his insubordinate movement north and the rest of his force was widely spread, however Napoleon responded to his brother in the most contemptuous tones, but he did consent to hasten the return of Dessolles and to re-route the 4th Corps back to the area from Avila.

---

1   This had been in Valencia waiting to be called forward.

2   Lannes had suffered a bad fall near Pamplona and his wounds were far from healed.

3   This corps was complete with the exception of three battalions from Level's Division.

4   Originally under Belvedere and San Juan, now totalling about 6,000–7,000.

5   The Central Junta handed over command of Galluzzo's remnants to Cuesta.

6   Sebastiani, Lefebvre's senior divisional commander, took over in mid-January.

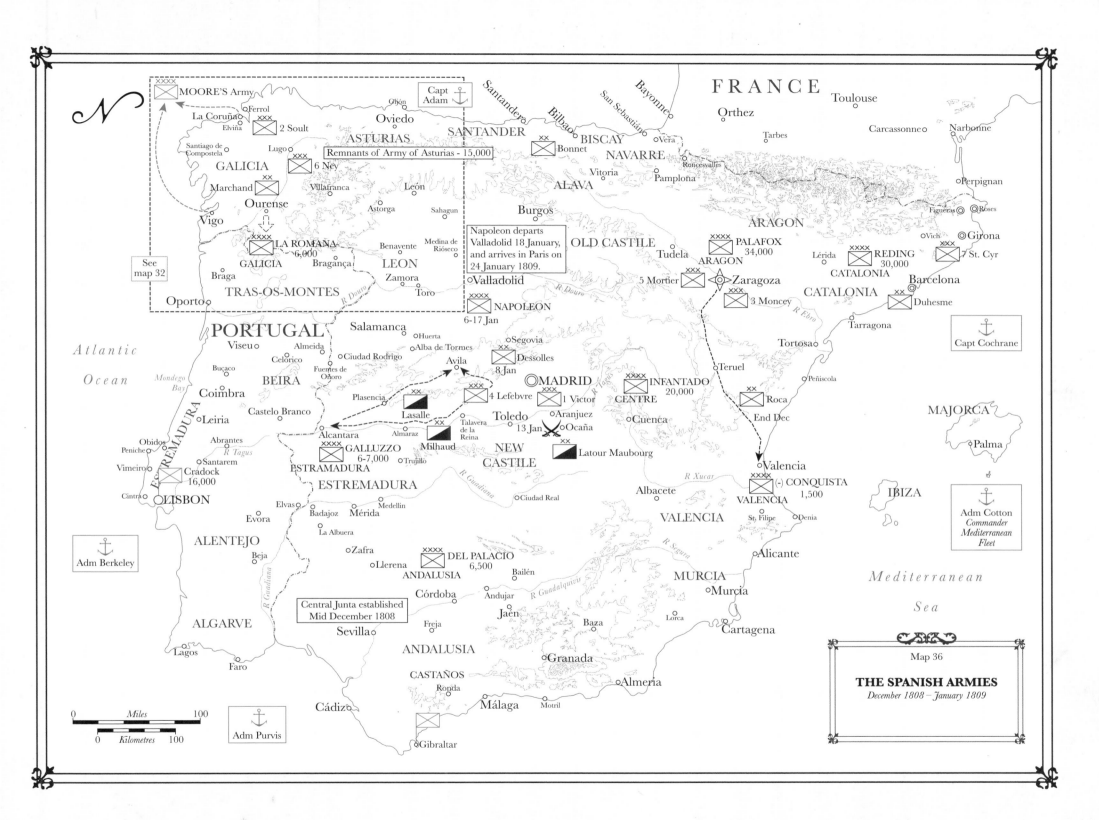

MOORE'S Army

Capt Adam ⚓

Ferrol
La Coruña
Elviña
2 Soult
Santiago de Compostela
GALICIA
Lugo
6 Ney
Marchand
Ourense
Villafranca
Vigo
Astorga
LA ROMANA 6,000
GALICIA
Benavente
Braga
Bragança
Zamora
Toro
TRAS-OS-MONTES
Oporto

Gijón
Oviedo
ASTURIAS
SANTANDER
Santander
Bilbao
Remnants of Army of Asturias - 15,000
León
Sahagun
Burgos
Medina de Ríoseco
LEON
Valladolid

NAPOLEON 6-17 Jan

Napoleon departs Valladolid 18 January, and arrives in Paris on 24 January 1809.

FRANCE
Bayonne
San Sebastián
Orthez
Toulouse
Tarbes
Carcassonne
Narbonne
BISCAY
NAVARRE
Vera
Roncesvalles
Vitoria
Pamplona
Perpignan
ALAVA
ALAGON
ARAGON
OLD CASTILE
Figueras
Roses
Vich
Girona
Bonnet
PALAFOX 34,000
ARAGON
Tudela
Lérida
REDING 30,000
7 St. Cyr
CATALONIA
5 Mortier
Zaragoza
Barcelona
3 Moncey
CATALONIA
Duhesme

See map 32

Santander

R. Douro

R. Douro

R. Ebro

Tortosa
Tarragona

Capt Cochrane ⚓

Salamanca
Huerta
Segovia
Viseu
Alba de Tormes
Avila
Dessolles 8 Jan
MADRID
INFANTADO 20,000
CENTRE
Teruel
Peñiscola

Almeida
Celorico
Ciudad Rodrigo
Fuentes de Oñoro
Plasencia
4 Lefebvre
1 Victor
Cuenca
Roca End Dec

Atlantic Ocean
Mondego Bay
BEIRA
Lasalle
Toledo 13 Jan
Aranjuez
Ocaña
Valencia

MAJORCA

Coimbra
Buçaco
Castelo Branco
Alcantara
Almaraz
Talavera de la Reina
Palma

Leiria
Milhaud
NEW CASTILE
Latour Maubourg

Obidos
Peniche
Abrantes
Santarem
GALLUZZO 6-7,000
Trujillo
R. Xucar

Vimeiro
Cradock 16,000
ESTRAMADURA
R. Tagus
R. Guadiana
VALENCIA
(-) CONQUISTA 1,500

IBIZA

Cintra
LISBON
Elvas
Medellin
Ciudad Real
Albacete
VALENCIA
St. Filipe
Denia

Adm Cotton Commander Mediterranean Fleet ⚓

ALENTEJO
Evora
Badajoz
Mérida
La Albuera
Zafra
DEL PALACIO 6,500
ANDALUSIA
Bailén
R. Segura
Alicante

Adm Berkeley ⚓

Beja
Llerena
Andujar
R. Guadalquivir
MURCIA
Murcia

ALGARVE
Córdoba
Jaén
Baza
Lorca

Central Junta established Mid December 1808

Freja
Sevilla
ANDALUSIA
CASTAÑOS
Ronda
Granada
Cartagena
Almeria

Mediterranean Sea

Lagos
Faro
Cádiz

Málaga
Motril

Miles 100
Kilometres 100

Adm Purvis ⚓

Gibraltar

Map 36

THE SPANISH ARMIES
December 1808 – January 1809

Having provided forewarning of his intention to move against the capital (with the operations of Venegas and Senra), Infantado failed to follow up and the opportunity passed. In fact, he had been trying to cajole the Central Junta into providing additional troops for a far larger coordinated attack, not just on Madrid but also on French lines of communication and on the besieging forces at Zaragoza. Such an ambitious scheme was too premature and, having revised his aims and with only the support of Del Palacio's Army of Reserve of Andalusia, Infantado finally began to move towards the capital on 11 January. Three days previously, Dessolles had arrived back in Madrid and the 4th Corps (now under Sebastiani) was at the city perimeter. Joseph established his lines of defence and organized a force under Victor to engage the Spanish threat that, much to his surprise, had still not materialized. Victor's force began to move on 12 January towards Tarancon where Venegas had remained since evicting the French dragoons there on Christmas Day. His force, which numbered about 15,000, included a large amount of cavalry but only two of his three divisions. They arrived late in the day and discovered the area clear of Spanish troops. Venegas, having received advance warning of the massing French forces to the west, had recalled Senra's Brigade from the outskirts of Aranjuez and had fallen back to Uclés, where he had waited for further direction from his army commander. Infantado however, sent forward a few more battalions and informed Venegas that he was en route with the reserves from Cuenca, but gave no timescale. Venegas was in a predicament, his orders were ambiguous, yet his force numbered over 11,000 and the position at Uclés had some distinct defensive possibilities. He felt compelled to make a stand and wait for the arrival of the rest of Infantado's army.

Venegas drew up his force in a long line along the north–south ridge, either side of the town, which was situated in the centre of the feature.[7] The long line of infantry preceded by two lines of brigaded cavalry in front of the town left him almost no reserve. Every battalion and squadron was well under strength, they were in dire need of proper clothing and footwear, they had little food and even less ammunition. With more guns,[8] Venegas could have utilized the two hills to the rear of the town, deployed in depth and made the position more difficult to turn. As it was, the long line of Spanish battalions invited a flanking manoeuvre and Victor, a most capable and experienced field commander, was well aware of the low morale of the defenders and wasted no time in appreciating and exploiting this weakness. His cavalry reconnaissance had already pushed well forward (on 12 January) and had reported back on both the lie of the land and the Spanish deployment. Victor's

experience from campaigning in Italy and Prussia provided him the confidence to split his force and so, early on 13 January, he sent Ruffin's entire division well to the north in a wide arc, while he advanced with the balance of his force directly towards the Spanish position.

As the French approached the Spanish outposts under General Arellano at Tribaldos, the defenders fell back on Uclés as planned. Villatte followed and pushed right up to the outskirts of Uclés supported by Latour-Maubourg, who moved some of his cavalry north of the road facing the Spanish right wing. Victor, on arrival, called up a battery of field guns, which unlimbered and began a harassing fire on the two lines of Spanish cavalry in front of the town. However, these actions were just a distraction. With Ruffin well advanced to the north, he despatched Puthod's Brigade, supported by some cavalry, on a right flanking manoeuvre. This force climbed the southern edge of the Cerro de Uclés and, once on top, deployed into column and advanced, rolling up one Spanish battalion after another. Pacthod's Brigade was sent in support to attack the Cerro just south of the town. The speed of these actions and their rapid success caught Venegas off guard. He tried in vain to move troops from the northern feature to reinforce the left, but these reinforcements were still clambering through the town as the first French troops began firing down into the houses and gardens from the top of the southern hill. Venegas, who had established his headquarters in the monastery, was forced to abandon his position and with news that Latour-Maubourg was pressing the by now weakened Spanish right wing, the Spanish commander knew the game was up.

He ordered a withdrawal to be covered by a small rearguard under General de Brigade Giron but no sooner had this got under way, than Ruffin's division appeared to their front. It was not exactly Victor's plan[9] but it served the French purpose admirably. Latour-Maubourg's cavalry had been released and were now driving the unfortunate Spaniards directly into the trap. Of Venegas's original force about 1,000 were killed but nearly 6,000 were captured, along with the four guns and most of the infantry colours.[10] Infantado, who was at this stage only a few kilometres to the east, withdrew via Cuenca to Chinchilla. Victor gave up the chase and turned his attention south and to the small force under Del Palacio. The victory at Uclés met with considerable Napoleonic approval and resulted in a corresponding sanction to Joseph to re-enter his capital in triumph. This he did, to much contrived pomp, on 22 January. Napoleon himself did not stay to witness the 'great' event; five days earlier, bored with the whole Iberian affair, he had set off for France and would never return.

---

7   Uclés is a confusing battle; the best account is in Researching & Dragona, vol. VI, No. 13, Marzo de 2001, pp.28–47, Sañudo Bayón, Guerrero Acosta & Sorando Muzás.

8   He only had three guns and one howitzer. One was placed with the cavalry in front of Uclés, another to the left supporting Senra and the last two were with Venegas in the monastery.

9   Hugo, *Histoire des Armées Françaises 1792–1833*, vol IV, p.111, suggests it was Victor's plan.

10   There is some disagreement as to exactly how many were captured.

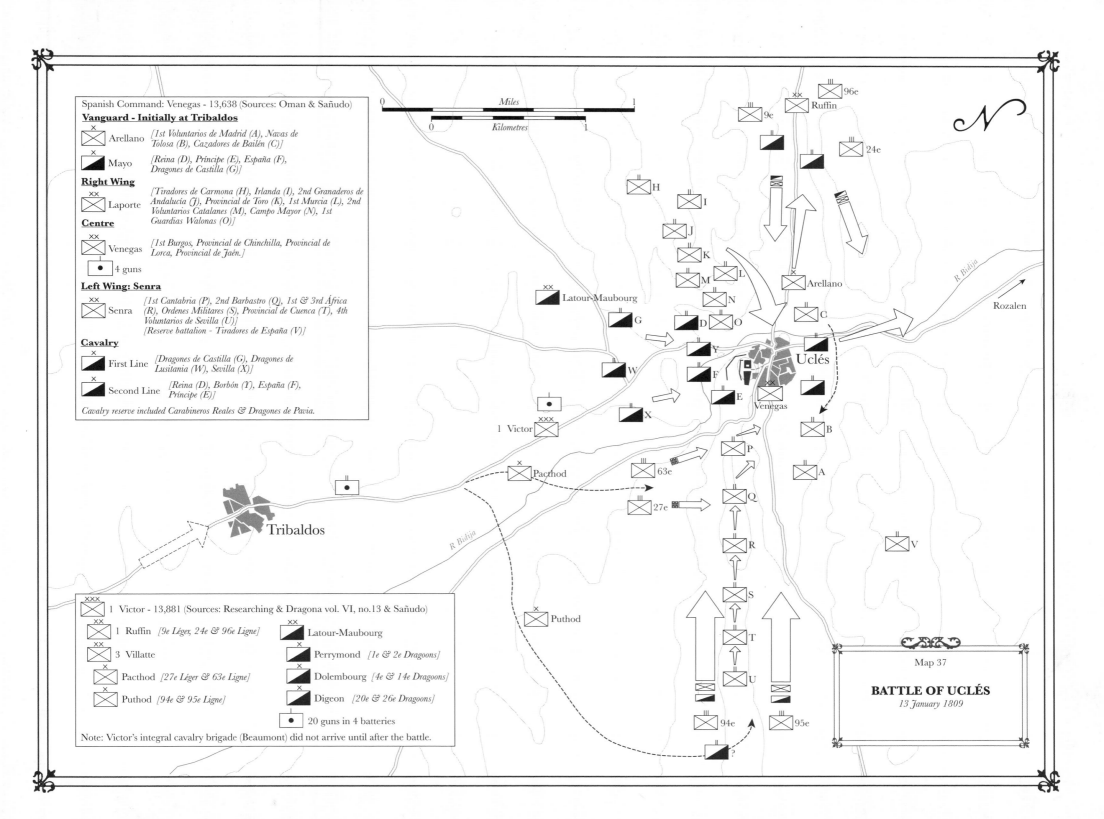

Spanish Command: Venegas - 13,638 (Sources: Oman & Sañudo)

Vanguard - Initially at Tribaldos

Arellano *[1st Voluntarios de Madrid (A), Navas de Tolosa (B), Cazadores de Bailén (C)]*

Mayo *[Reina (D), Príncipe (E), España (F), Dragones de Castilla (G)]*

Right Wing

Laporte *[Tiradores de Carmona (H), Irlanda (I), 2nd Granaderos de Andalucía (J), Provincial de Toro (K), 1st Murcia (L), 2nd Voluntarios Catalanes (M), Campo Mayor (N), 1st Guardias Walonas (O)]*

Centre

Venegas *[1st Burgos, Provincial de Chinchilla, Provincial de Lorca, Provincial de Jaén.]*

● 4 guns

Left Wing: Senra

Senra *[1st Cantabria (P), 2nd Barbastro (Q), 1st & 3rd África (R), Ordenes Militares (S), Provincial de Cuenca (T), 4th Voluntarios de Sevilla (U)]*
[Reserve battalion - Tiradores de España (V)]

Cavalry

First Line *[Dragones de Castilla (G), Dragones de Lusitania (W), Sevilla (X)]*

Second Line *[Reina (D), Borbón (Y), España (F), Príncipe (E)]*

Cavalry reserve included Carabineros Reales & Dragones de Pavia.

---

1 Victor - 13,881 (Sources: Researching & Dragona vol. VI, no.13 & Sañudo)

1 Ruffin *[9e Léger, 24e & 96e Ligne]*

3 Villatte

Pacthod *[27e Léger & 63e Ligne]*

Puthod *[94e & 95e Ligne]*

Latour-Maubourg

Perrymond *[1e & 2e Dragoons]*

Dolembourg *[4e & 14e Dragoons]*

Digeon *[20e & 26e Dragoons]*

● 20 guns in 4 batteries

Note: Victor's integral cavalry brigade (Beaumont) did not arrive until after the battle.

Map 37

BATTLE OF UCLÉS
13 January 1809

Chapter 15 ❦

CONTINUED FRENCH SUCCESS: FEBRUARY AND MARCH 1809

Prior to his departure Napoleon sent a number of dispatches to his brother. Two were significant. One, on 16 January, reinforced the need for Joseph to deal with Spanish non-compliance in the strictest of terms and, as if to make the point, Napoleon spent much of his final few days at Valladolid berating and threatening the Spanish deputations brought before him. This was a good example of how much Napoleon misunderstood the nature and tenacity of the Spanish; hanging and executions were only repaid by assassinations and reprisals. The second dispatch provided the strategic and operational plan for the next campaign, which was to be conducted on three fronts.[1]

Soult was to recapture Portugal from the north, rolling up Oporto before moving on to Lisbon. Victor, supported by much of the cavalry, was to advance into Estremadura and once it was subjugated, was to link up with Soult for the assault on the Portuguese capital. Their subsequent objective was Sevilla, which they were to undertake with support from Madrid, and ultimately they were to subdue the whole of Andalusia. The final front was to the north-east. Zaragoza was predicted to fall in February, thereby releasing the 3rd and 5th corps, which would then move on Valencia, by which time St Cyr (with the 7th Corps) was to have marched south and with the linking up of these three corps, the entire Peninsula would then be under French domination. Napoleon's plan, unlike the one he fashioned soon after his arrival in November 1808, was quite impractical and reinforces criticism that he misunderstood the characteristics and misconstrued the dynamics of the entire campaign. His time appreciation was flawed; his continued reliance on sustaining the force from the land was impractical and his failure to appoint a single commander-in-chief ultimately disastrous. However, his conviction that the nation would submit once their capital was taken and their armies beaten was perhaps his greatest failing.

The Central Junta established itself at Sevilla in mid-December, but their president died shortly after from bronchitis following the harrowing and exhausting retreat over the Sierra Morena from Madrid. With the arrival of considerable revenue from their South American colonies in January 1809, the government was again able to exert national influence over the local Juntas and rally, reform and rebuild the Spanish armies (see Appendix 2). La Romana's Army of Galicia was in a sorry state on the Portuguese northern border where they had escaped both Soult and Ney and were biding their time before linking back up with the

remnants of Acevedo's Division in the Asturias. Between northern Portugal and Estremadura there were no Spanish forces save for the small militia unit at Ciudad Rodrigo. In Estremadura, Cuesta had been given another chance and assumed the reins from Galluzzo, but his new command was small[2] and significantly demoralized. In Andalusia, the Army of the Reserve[3] was all that was left between the Central Junta and Joseph's forces in Madrid. This formation was really a weak division, consisting of only 6,500 men; their command was allocated to Del Palacio who had been recalled from Catalonia and had now established himself at La Carolina. By the end of January this force had been absorbed into the new Army of the Centre under General Cartaojal[4] and had been given the task of strengthening the defences on the approaches to Andalusia. In the east, the Conde de Conquista, in his capacity as Captain-General of the Army of Valencia, had built on the old divisions of Llamas and Roca[5] and by February had established a force of some ten thousand men. Meanwhile in Zaragoza, Palafox's entire Army of Aragon was holding out against two French corps, but was in desperate need of succour. The most likely provider was the Army of Catalonia; it was the strongest of all the Spanish armies at 40,000 men, but their attention was firmly rooted in their own regional struggle and they were now facing St Cyr, a far more capable commander and tactician than his predecessor.

Although these Spanish armies totalled 135,000, they faced a combined French force of nearly 290,000,[6] more than twice their size. Furthermore, it appeared that Spain had lost its principal ally. Anglo-Spanish relations had been dealt an almost terminal blow following Moore's retreat and embarkation. La Romana openly accused Moore of betrayal and bad faith, and the behaviour of the retreating British soldiers had done little to placate the situation. 'Needless to say, the issue cut both ways. British veterans of the campaign felt they had advanced into Spain in good faith only to find a country with neither enthusiasm for the struggle, nor competent leadership, nor adequate armies, and a country, moreover, in which, rather than being welcomed and assisted, they had from the start been lied to, deceived and treated as interlopers.'[7] Most of the Whig opposition felt the same way and used the recent setback to undermine, at every turn, the government's Spanish policy and the war in general. However the Portland ministry were determined not to abandon their Iberian strategy and in January 1809, Lord Liverpool summed up the government's determination. 'It was difficult to conceive the situation which would better warrant hopes of ultimate success, than that of Spain at this day. The people were unanimous in their resistance to the invader; and it was the only instance since the French revolution in which a whole people had taken up arms in their

---

1   Napoleon, *The Confidential Correspondence of Napoleon Bonaparte*, vol. II, pp.33–40.

2   No more than 10,500 infantry and about 2,500 cavalry.

3   Created when Reding marched north to Catalonia and the balance of other forces in the region had been mobilized under Castaños's Army of the Centre.

4   Cartaojal had assumed command of the force from Infantado who was judged, with some justification, to have sacrificed Venegas at Uclés.

5   Both had served with Castaños at Tudela.

6   Although only about two-thirds of this number was effective (see Appendix 2).

7   Esdaile, *The Peninsular War, A New History*, p.156.

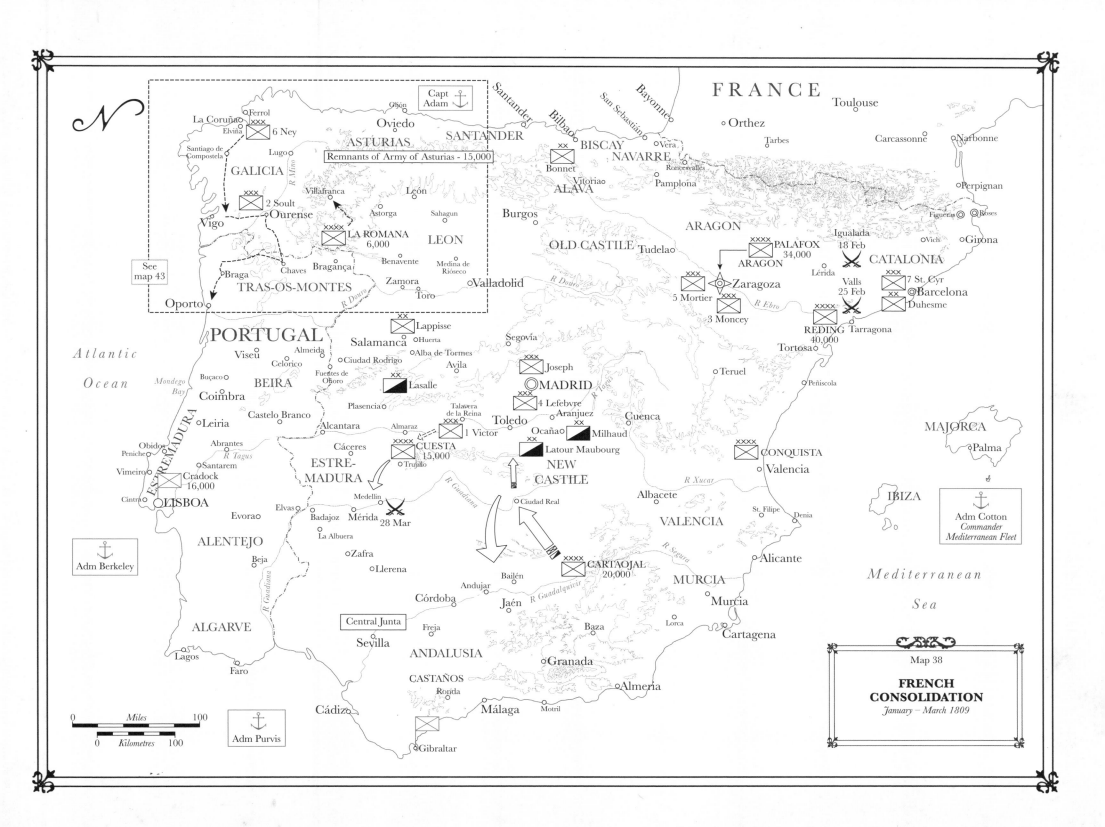

N

FRANCE

Toulouse

Capt Adam

La Coruña Ferrol 6 Ney
Elviña
Santiago de Compostela
GALICIA Lugo
Vigo 2 Soult Ourense
Villafranca
LA ROMANA 6,000
Braga Chaves Bragança
Oporto TRAS-OS-MONTES
Zamora Toro

Gijón Santander
Oviedo SANTANDER
ASTURIAS
Remnants of Army of Asturias – 15,000
León Astorga
Sahagun
Benavente Medina de Rióseco
Valladolid
LEON

Bilbao BISCAY San Sebastián Bayonne Orthez Tarbes Carcassonne Narbonne
Bonnet NAVARRE Vera Roncesvalles Pamplona
ALAVA Vitoriao
Burgos OLD CASTILE Tudela
PALAFOX 34,000 Igualada 18 Feb CATALONIA Perpignan
ARAGON Zaragoza Lérida Vich Girona
5 Mortier Valls 25 Feb 7 St. Cyr
3 Moncey R Ebro Barcelona
REDING Tarragona Duhesme
40,000
Tortosa Peñiscola

See map 43

Atlantic Ocean

Mondego Bay

PORTUGAL
Viseu Almeida
BEIRA Celorico
Coimbra Castelo Branco
Buçaco Ciudad Rodrigo
Leiria Fuentes de Oñoro
Abrantes Alcantara
Obidos Cáceres
Peniche Santarem
Vimeiro Cradock 16,000
Cintra LISBOA
Evora
ALENTEJO
Beja Zafra
Llerena

Salamanca Lappisse
Huerta
Alba de Tormes
Avila Segovia
Plasencia Joseph
Lasalle MADRID
Talavera de la Reina 4 Lefebvre
Almaraz Toledo Aranjuez Cuenca
1 Victor Ocaña Milhaud
CUESTA 15,000 Latour Maubourg
Trujillo NEW CASTILE
Medellín Teruel
Elvas Ciudad Real
Badajoz Mérida 28 Mar
La Albuera

CONQUISTA Valencia
VALENCIA
R Xucar
Albacete St. Filipe Denia
MAJORCA Palma
IBIZA Adm Cotton Commander Mediterranean Fleet

Mediterranean Sea

Adm Berkeley

ESTRE-MADURA

R Tagus
R Guadiana

Córdoba
Central Junta Freja
Sevilla
ANDALUSIA
CASTAÑOS Ronda
Cádiz Málaga Motril

Andújar Bailén Jaén
CARTAOJAL 20,000
R Segura
Baza Lorca
Murcia MURCIA
Alicante
Cartagena

Granada Almería

Miles 0 100
Kilometres 0 100

Adm Purvis

Gibraltar

Map 38

FRENCH CONSOLIDATION
January – March 1809

own defence.'[8] Within months the British were to reappear on the scene, but in the interim both the Spanish and Portuguese armies and people were subjected to the initial stages of Napoleon's plan of national subjugation.

The capture of Zaragoza was unfinished business from an earlier campaign and had been delayed considerably; it was not until 20 December that the combined corps of Mortier and Moncey began the second siege. In the interim, Palafox and the Zaragozanos had been busy; the Army of Aragon amounted to about 36,000[9] and approximately 10,000 armed civilians, but it was their efforts to improve the city's defences that was most notable. They had collected three months' provisions and considerable military stores, equipment, powder and ammunition. 'Of artillery there were some 160 pieces in the place, but too many of them were of small calibre: only about 60 were 16-pounders or heavier.'[10] However, despite these considerable preparations, their plans to construct defences on the Monte Torrero were not completed in time and the French were quick to exploit this weakness. Furthermore, Palafox decided to retain his entire army within the city confines and saw no advantage in leaving an external force to harass the French attackers and disrupt their lines of communication. In retrospect this was an error.

Moncey's corps was composed largely of the provisional regiments created by Napoleon for the conquest of Spain. They had suffered badly from sickness in the autumn and despite having four divisions Moncey could only put 20,000 men in the field at the commencement of the siege. Nevertheless, this force had not been idle in the lull; engineer stores had been collected, siege equipment constructed, and the gunners had taken receipt of 60 siege guns and considerable quantities of ammunition from the vast arsenal at Pamplona. Napoleon even assigned one of his aides-de-camp, General Lacoste, to coordinate the engineer operations. The second siege commenced on 20 December and was characterized by three distinct phases. The first phase lasted until 15 January 1809 and concentrated on capturing the outworks and in securing two bridgeheads at Pillar and San José (points 1 and 2, map 39). After a detailed reconnaissance Moncey commenced operations against the Spanish position on the Monte Torrero held by St March's Division. Regrettably for the defenders they were all too quickly dislodged in a combined attack by Morlot and Grandjean on 21 December and withdrew in haste into the confines of the city; losing seven guns and the colours of the 5th Murcia.[11] On the other side of the Ebro the French attack had not progressed quite so smoothly. Gazan had been tasked to carry the suburb of San Lazaro and his veteran troops were keen to impress in their first Iberian action. The attack started well, as Guérin's Brigade made short work of the Swiss battalion

holding the Torre de Arzobispo, but as they pressed home the assault, they were engaged by effective enfilade fire from a battery that had not hitherto been exposed. The French troops lost their momentum and swung left, towards the Convent of Jesús, where some of the defenders began to lose heart and pull back, but Palafox came up from the city with a reserve force and reoccupied the defensive positions driving the French back into the open ground. Gazan elected to withdraw, rather than commit his only reserve, pulling back east over the river Gallego, from where he reconsidered his options.

The next morning Moncey appealed to Palafox to surrender the municipality, declaring that Madrid had fallen and that the city had little hope against two French corps. It was an optimistic gesture that received an appropriately curt response, prompting Moncey to issue orders for the siege work to commence with all haste. His plan was to attack the south of the city on two fronts, and to establish two bridgeheads for subsequent operations in chorus with two diversionary attacks: one to the north blockading San Lazaro and the second on the castle of Aljafería (map 39, points 3 and 4). Moncey, having penned his plan, was not to witness its commencement as he was recalled to Madrid and replaced by Junot.[12] The former 8th Corps commander, although junior to Mortier, appears to have taken the lead during subsequent operations.[13] The first parallel was complete by first light on 30 December and the following day Palafox sent out 3,000 men to attack the lines at Aljafería and in front of Monte Torrero. They had limited success and were repelled by the French infantry who were quickly on the scene. On New Year's Day the French commenced work on the second parallels and the initial siege batteries were in place by 9 January, opening the following day with concentrated fire on the fortifications at San José and Pillar. The walls of the San José convent quickly crumbled, bringing the roof timbers and tiles crashing down on the defenders and rendering the entire structure unsafe and unsuitable for further efficient defence. The following day seven voltigeur companies from the 14e and 44e Ligne fell upon the crumbling defences and captured the convent. Twenty-four hours later the fort facing the second bridgehead was assaulted by the Poles of the 1st Vistula and similarly captured. The French now dominated the ground south of the city and were able to commence work on the last phase of the trenches and parallels.

Lacoste wasted no time in completing the third parallels despite heavy, close-range artillery and small arms fire from the city walls. From 12 to 17 January the French gunners populated these new batteries with guns and mortars, and the second phase of the siege commenced. It lasted ten days and concentrated on the walls and fortifications of the city itself. Five of the French batteries opened against Santa Engracia and another four on the area by the Palafox Battery (map 40, points 1 and 2). Their effect was immediate, as the repair of these walls had been substandard and Palafox hastened the construction of barricades and began preparing the civil population for the inevitable street fighting that would ensue. 'From the twentieth to

---

8   British Parliamentary Dispatch, XII, p. 22 from Liverpool's speech of 19 January 1809. Hall, *British Strategy in the Napoleonic War, 1803–15*, p.174.

9   Which included the remnants of Roca, O'Neill and St March's divisions which had fought at Tudela; the 10,000–12,000 men from battalions of the reserve, which had hitherto not been utilized; and a number of battalions from Murcia and Valencia – namely, the 1st & 2nd Battalion de Tiradores de Murcia, the Tiradores de Florida Blanca, the 3rd and 5th Voluntarios de Murcia and the Voluntarios de Valencia (source: Arteche).

10 Oman, *History of the Peninsular War*, vol. II, p.100.

11 The Zaragozanos were furious with the Valencians for abandoning this key feature so lightly and Palafox had great difficulty in protecting St March against the citizens.

12 Napoleon had been unhappy with Moncey's performance prior to the siege and had decided to replace him with the (by now) redundant 8th Corps commander. In fact the mission given to Moncey was to reopen communications between Zaragoza and Madrid and he took Suchet's Division with him to complete this task.

13 Sarrazin, *History of the War in Spain and Portugal*, p.71, states that Junot was indeed in command. Moncey '…was superseded in his command before Saragossa by General Junot – a thunderbolt of war'.

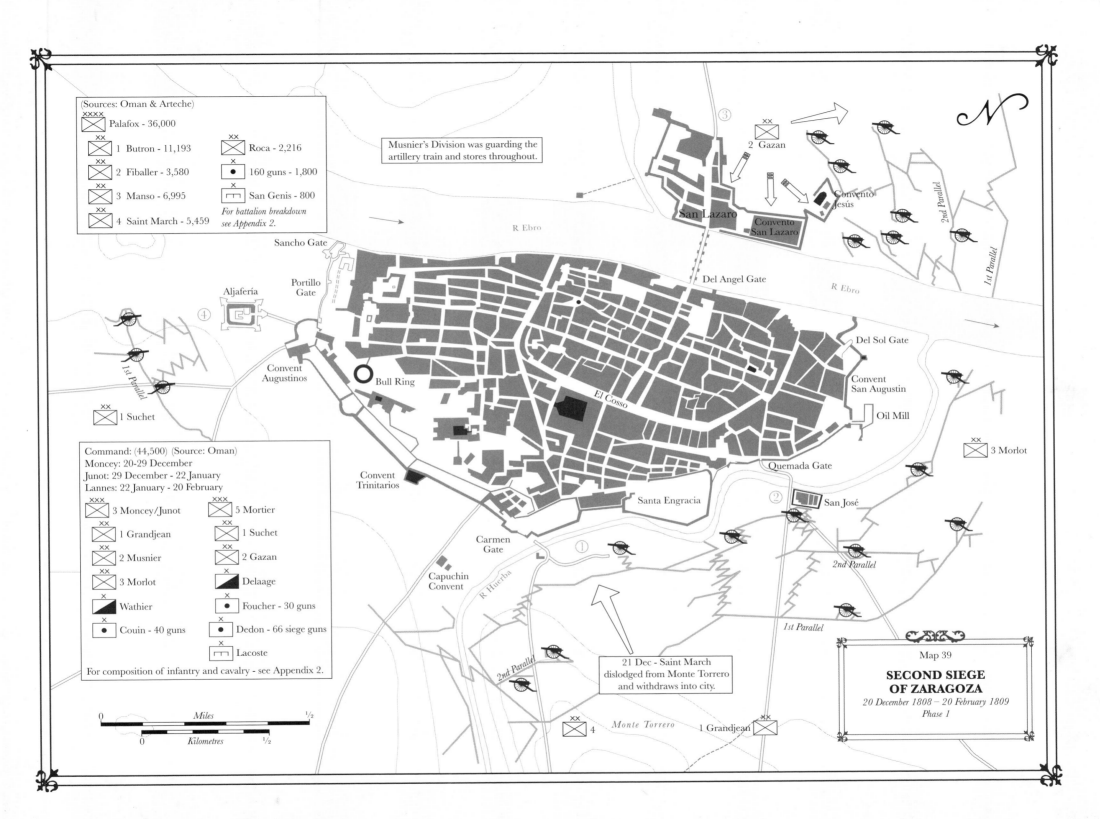

(Sources: Oman & Arteche)

Palafox - 36,000

1 Butron - 11,193   Roca - 2,216

2 Fiballer - 3,580   160 guns - 1,800

3 Manso - 6,995   San Genis - 800

4 Saint March - 5,459   *For battalion breakdown see Appendix 2.*

Musnier's Division was guarding the artillery train and stores throughout.

③

2 Gazan

Convento Jesús

San Lazaro

Convento San Lazaro

R Ebro

Del Angel Gate

R Ebro

1st Parallel

2nd Parallel

Sancho Gate

Portillo Gate

Aljafería

④

Del Sol Gate

Convent Augustinos

Bull Ring

El Cosso

Convent San Augustin

Oil Mill

3 Morlot

1st Parallel

1 Suchet

Quemada Gate

Command: (44,500) (Source: Oman)
Moncey: 20-29 December
Junot: 29 December - 22 January
Lannes: 22 January - 20 February

3 Moncey/Junot   5 Mortier

1 Grandjean   1 Suchet

2 Musnier   2 Gazan

3 Morlot   Delaage

Wathier   Foucher - 30 guns

Couin - 40 guns   Dedon - 66 siege guns

Lacoste

For composition of infantry and cavalry - see Appendix 2.

Convent Trinitarios

Santa Engracia

San José

②

Carmen Gate

①

2nd Parallel

Capuchin Convent

R Huerba

Delaage

2nd Parallel

1st Parallel

21 Dec - Saint March dislodged from Monte Torrero and withdraws into city.

| 0 | Miles | ½ |

| 0 | Kilometres | ½ |

4   Monte Torrero   1 Grandjean

Map 39

SECOND SIEGE OF ZARAGOZA

20 December 1808 – 20 February 1809

Phase 1

the twenty-sixth of January the Spaniards showed themselves, at several points, for the purpose of harassing the army employed in the siege. They were every where repulsed with loss, after having fought with bravery.'[14] The bombardment of the city forced the civil population into the cellars where the fever, which had taken a hold, now spread with alarming speed. A quarter of the regular forces were reported sick and the burden on the hospitals became intolerable. Palafox, his military commanders and civil leaders were doing their best to keep spirits up and had succeeded in despatching three boats down the Ebro, which had effectively run the gauntlet of the French infantry and gunners, delivering appeals to the Catalans and Valencians to come to their aid. One of these envoys was Palafox's younger brother, who succeeded in organizing and equipping a force at Alcañiz. Another force under Colonel Perena had been organized to the north.

On 22 January, Lannes reappeared from his convalescence and reassumed command from Junot. He had clear instructions to conclude the siege as quickly as possible and consequently turned his full attention to storming the city walls. He was acutely conscious of the growing external threat from Catalonia and resolved to pull back Mortier with Suchet's Division to counter this hazard. In so doing he closed the hitherto insufficient cordon but at the expense, for the time being, of maintaining open communications with the capital. Mortier was immediately directed north to screen Perena's force and Wathier was despatched south, with two battalions and two regiments of his cavalry, to neutralize Francisco Palafox. With these forces in place and news of three workable breaches, Lannes was keen to make a start. He allocated the first two breaches, at the foot of the Palafox Battery, to the light companies of Grandjean's Division and the third at Santa Engracia, to Musnier's 1st Vistula. At each location considerable reserves were positioned in the trenches immediately behind the approaches crossing the Huerba stream. On 27 January the assaults were delivered with speed and considerable courage, succeeding in both locations. The assault on Palafox Battery also secured the oil mill and the following day the third and final phase commenced, fighting street-by-street and house-by-house.

Lannes had learned a great deal about Verdier's street-fighting losses during the first siege. He elected not to hurl large units at the barricades but rather to utilize small groups to capture a block of houses, which would then be fortified and held for the next group to progress. It was to be a slow process and lasted 24 days. The French targeted, in particular, the churches (of which there were 53) and other fortified structures by sap and mine and then secured the adjacent housing. The Spanish in response retook the housing by removing the roof tiles, entering the buildings and then clearing them floor-by-floor. Losses on both sides were considerable; Lannes's losses were greater than he could afford and there was no sign that the defence was slacking. The determination of the Zaragozanos was, however, being undermined not by the attackers but by typhoid, which was consuming the inhabitants at a far greater rate than French bullet, bayonet and bombardment. Even Palafox had been struck down and was by now issuing delirious orders from his bed. The bulk of the population was huddled in the northern suburbs, out of reach of French artillery. Aware of this and with time against him, Lannes ordered Gazan to recommence

his activity against the suburb of San Lazaro, which, once taken, would provide the base from which to bombard the northern side of the city. On 8 February, following a sustained bombardment by the siege artillery in the northern battery positions, Gazan attacked and captured the Convent of Jesús and immediately commenced work on a third parallel in the area. By 18 February 52 siege guns were relentlessly bombarding the suburb and Gazan attacked through three breaches and captured the smoking ruins along with General Manso and 1,500 of his men. He now turned his heavy guns onto the northern suburbs.

Within the city the epidemic was raging, and both Grandjean and Musnier's men were making steady progress. It was evident that the tide had turned and Spanish resolve appeared to be wavering. On 19 February Palafox handed over command to St March and sent his aide-de-camp to Lannes to ask for terms. Lannes was in no mood to bargain and insisted on the unconditional surrender of the garrison, to which, after a brief resumption of hostilities, the Junta reluctantly consented. The next day the garrison marched out and the French took command of a city that was indescribable. 54,000 had died within the confines, only 6,000 by the sword. French losses were approximately 10,000. 'The example of Saragossa was invaluable to the nation and Europe. The knowledge of it did much to sicken the French soldiery of the whole war, and to make every officer and man who entered Spain march, not with the light heart that he felt in Germany or Italy, but with gloom and disgust and want of confidence. They never failed to do their duty, but they fought without the enthusiasm which helped them so much in all the earlier wars of the Empire'[15].

In Catalonia, since the battles of Cardedeu and Molins de Rei in December 1808, St Cyr had prosecuted no large-scale operations, permitting Reding time to reinforce, reorganize and reequip the Army of Catalonia.[16] In early February Reding, eager to redress the failures of the previous year, took the offensive. He was well aware of the situation at Zaragoza but resolved to come to their aid once he had neutralized the threat posed by St Cyr; and while his appreciation was sound his execution was demonstrably flawed. Reding sent General Castro north-west from Tarragona to Igualada, a four-day march that virtually ruled out any form of rapid concentration and relied on the *miqueletes* to keep open the 100km lines of communication. Reding's plan was to distract Duhesme at Barcelona with a demonstration by Alvarez's troops from Girona which, once in motion, would be the signal for a simultaneous attack by both wings; Castro heading east and Reding north. However, St Cyr was well aware of Castro's presence and had already set off with Pino, Chabot and Chabran to deal with the Catalan left wing. Fortunately for the Spanish, the French columns did not coordinate their advance, resulting in Chabot being caught somewhat exposed on 17 February. The next day, the tables were turned when an Italian brigade succeeded in getting in behind Castro's force, which then beat a hasty retreat, surrendering a considerable amount of badly needed provisions to the delight of French, whose rations were running worryingly low.

---

14 Sarrazin, *History of the War in Spain and Portugal*, p.72.

15 Oman, *History of the Peninsular War*, vol II, p.142.

16 He had amassed a total of about 5,600 men from Sante Fé, Antequera, Betschart's 4th Swiss and the Voluntarios de Palma.

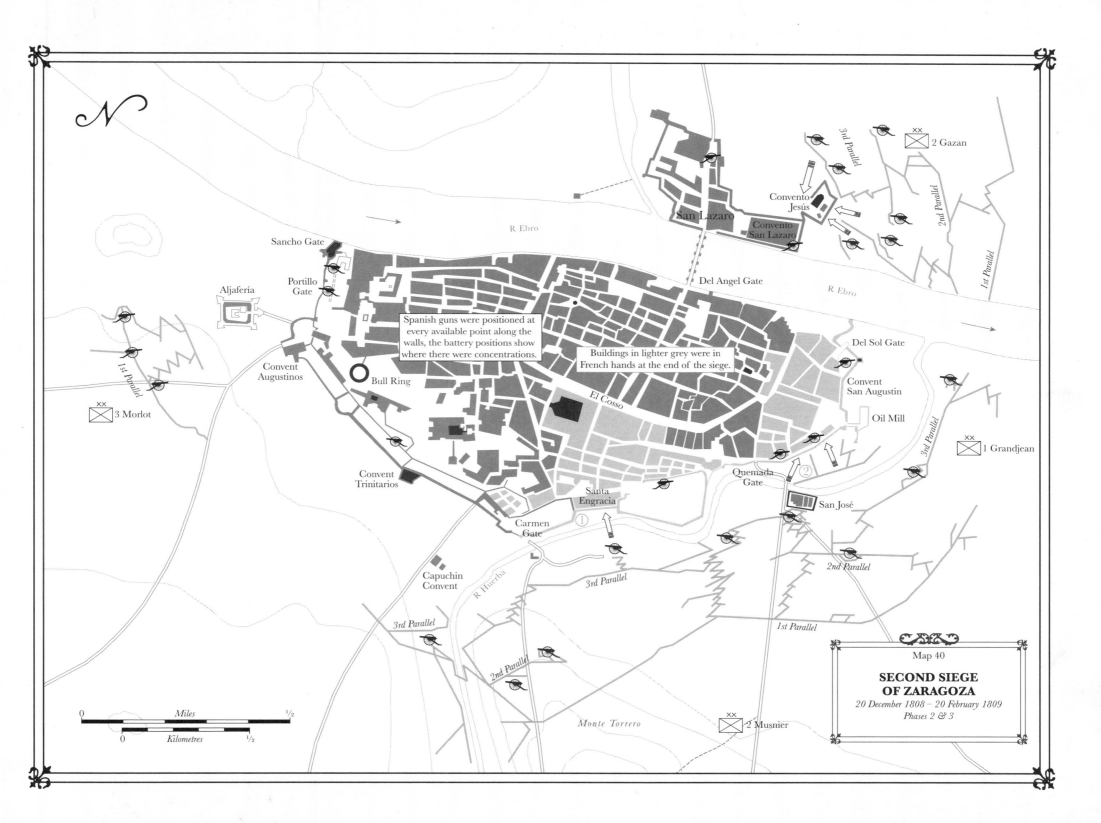

N

Sancho Gate

Portillo Gate

Aljafería

Convent Augustinos

Bull Ring

3 Morlot

1st Parallel

Convent Trinitarios

Capuchin Convent

R Huerba

3rd Parallel

3rd Parallel

2nd Parallel

Monte Torrero

2 Musnier

R Ebro

San Lazaro

Convento Jesús

Convento San Lazaro

3rd Parallel

2 Gazan

2nd Parallel

1st Parallel

Del Angel Gate

R Ebro

Del Sol Gate

Convent San Augustin

Oil Mill

1 Grandjean

3rd Parallel

Quemada Gate

San José

2nd Parallel

1st Parallel

Spanish guns were positioned at every available point along the walls, the battery positions show where there were concentrations.

Buildings in lighter grey were in French hands at the end of the siege.

El Cosso

Santa Engracia

Carmen Gate

Miles

0   ½

Kilometres

0   ½

Map 40

SECOND SIEGE OF ZARAGOZA

20 December 1808 – 20 February 1809

Phases 2 & 3

Leaving Chabot and Chabran in Igualada, St Cyr set off south with Pino to link up with Souham. These two groups joined at Villarodoña on 21 February; the same day Reding united with the rallied troops of Castro. Their combined force of 20,000 looked set to fall on the two French divisions left at Igualada, but Reding now realized that the city of Tarragona lay exposed to St Cyr's other force which was only two days march from its walls. He elected to return, leaving Castro with a quarter of the force to observe the French, and started out on one of the main roads, for reasons of speed, even though he knew the French were holding the approaches to the city. In fact St Cyr had no intentions towards Tarragona and had turned north on hearing of Reding's union with Castro, but altered his plan when he discovered that Reding was again heading south and elected to intercept him.

At about 0600 hours on the morning of 25 February, after marching through the night, Reding's exhausted Spanish troops reached the Bridge of Goy where they disturbed Souham's vedettes. Souham deployed his entire division in haste from Valls and drew up his two brigades to block the Spanish advance. Reding had already crossed the bridge and established his advance guard, and part of his main body to the west of the town, by the time Souham had reached the field. As the French deployed, more Spanish troops crossed the river and reinforced the Spanish lines that were now pushing the French back. At around 1200 hours, the Spanish had succeeded in forcing Souham back into Valls and, by so doing, had opened the road to Tarragona. Reding lost no time in bringing his baggage over the river Francoli and then gave orders for it to commence the move south. As this was taking place, St Cyr arrived from El Pla de Santa Maria with the Italian cavalry; the balance of Pino's Division was en route. St Cyr rode to the front of the French line displaying the Italian cavalry with great ceremony. Reding was completely taken with this bluff and, believing St Cyr to have arrived with large numbers of reinforcements, immediately recalled the baggage and sent it back across the Francoli, to be swiftly followed by the balance of his entire force. He then elected to fight a defensive battle, utilizing the heights to the west of the river.

The time it took Reding to redeploy his troops was exactly what St Cyr required. Fontane's Brigade arrived at about 1445 hours but Mazzuchelli took another 90 minutes, by which time Reding had long realized he had been duped. In haste, he despatched Marti across country to Tarragona, with orders to deploy elements of the garrison to cover a night withdrawal. St Cyr was well aware that this was Reding's intention and hastened the Italians to the front as soon as they arrived, commencing a four-pronged attack by brigades supported by the cavalry on the flanks and centre. The mass of French columns crossed the easily fordable river Francoli and then advanced towards the Spanish lines. At 100m the French received a coordinated discharge from along the Spanish frontage but, as the smoke cleared, the sight of the French columns still largely intact and maintaining their composure and forward momentum was enough to tip the balance. The Spanish front line broke and fell on the rear, which also gave way. Reding tried to rally his army and charged at the head of the cavalry Regiment of Granada towards the Bridge of Goy, where he was met by the 24e Dragoons. In the ensuing skirmish he received a number of sabre wounds, which were to prove fatal. The failing light and undulating countryside saved Reding's army. About 1,500 had been killed

or injured and a similar number captured along with the eight guns, several standards and the entire baggage train. The remainder of the army limped into Tarragona the following day; Reding died some weeks later of his wounds and St Cyr satisfied himself with blockading the city. The scale of his task in Catalonia was now all the more apparent, and he wasted no time in sending a dispatch to Paris requesting reinforcements.

Following his victory over Venegas at Uclés in mid-January, Victor had tried in vain to engage Del Palacio's small force to the south. He gave up when he received Napoleon's new plan and his new orders at the end of January, and moved directly to Talavera from where he could deploy, as directed, in support of Soult's invasion of Portugal. At much the same time, Del Palacio's force joined that of Cartaojal at La Carolina, where they remained for some time in an attempt to reconstitute the Army of the Centre. The new commander expected to be attacked by Victor at any time and was surprised to discover he had moved west, apparently leaving only a cavalry screen to his front. The Spanish were unaware however, that two divisions from Sebastiani's Corps had been moved to Toledo and Aranjuez and were now covering the approaches to Madrid. Cartaojal, uninformed of this fact, sent the Duke del Alburquerque forward with half his force in an attempt to capitalize on this perceptible opportunity. The existence of Sebastiani's troops came as a rude shock and Cartaojal pulled back and waited at Ciudad Real for another opportunity. By mid-March, frustrated at the lack of movement to his front, he attempted a quick attack on a regiment of Polish lancers at Yébenes. While the attack was successful it prompted a more robust counter from Sebastiani, who caught the Spanish commander off-guard at Ciudad Real and forced him to withdraw south in haste. In the process, Cartaojal lost 2,000 men, five guns and three standards but he also lost his command; the Supreme Junta deciding to replace him with Venegas at the end of March.

Meanwhile, Cuesta was enjoying a period of calm around Badajoz and Medellin and was busy knocking the Army of Estremadura into shape. He established his force of 15,000 into three divisions under Henestrosa, Trias and the Duke Del Parque. At the end of January, he pushed this force west towards Almaraz, forcing back the French cavalry screen. He then broke the central span of the bridge and deployed his divisions to cover the approaches to the Tagus from the east. At the end of February Joseph despatched Leval's German/Dutch Division[17] and Lasalle's cavalry to push back Cuesta, but the main offensive was not undertaken until a month later. Victor arrived at Talavera with his two divisions[18] and the entire cavalry division of Latour-Maubourg, which now linked up with the other formations already operating in the area, providing him a total force of about 22,000. On 14 March Victor commenced operations by crossing the river Tagus (well to the east) over the bridges at Talavera and Arzobispo. His aim was to secure the only suitable road for artillery and baggage, which ran through Almaraz, by sending all his infantry and Lasalle's cavalry over the river to drive back the Spanish and establish a bridgehead. Cuesta threw back his right wing under the Duke Del Parque to meet the threat

17   The third division from Sebastiani's Corps.

18   His 3rd Division (Lapisse's) was still at Salamanca and Victor complained that he wanted this division back to prosecute operations in Estremadura, questioning the suitability of Leval's Division as a replacement.

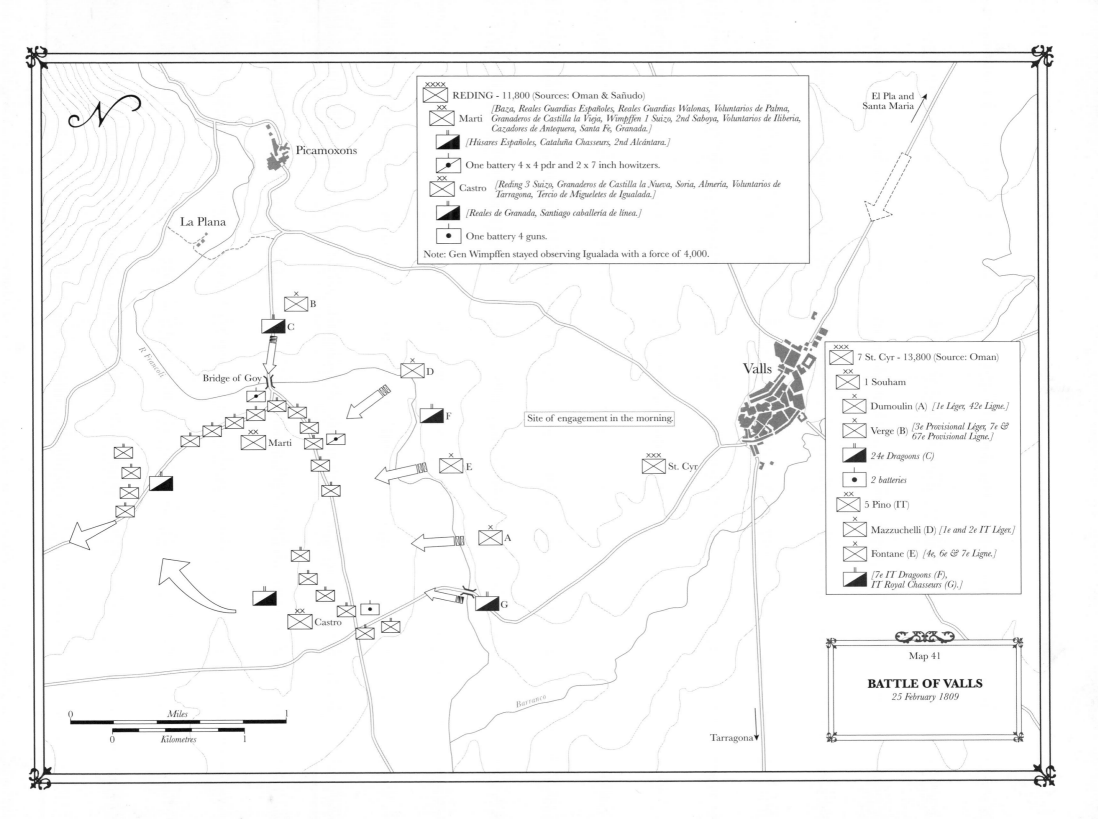

N

Picamoxons

La Plana

REDING - 11,800 (Sources: Oman & Sañudo)

Marti [Baza, Reales Guardias Españoles, Reales Guardias Walonas, Voluntarios de Palma, Granaderos de Castilla la Vieja, Wimpffen 1 Suizo, 2nd Saboya, Voluntarios de Iliberia, Cazadores de Antequera, Santa Fe, Granada.]

[Húsares Españoles, Cataluña Chasseurs, 2nd Alcántara.]

One battery 4 x 4 pdr and 2 x 7 inch howitzers.

Castro [Reding 3 Suizo, Granaderos de Castilla la Nueva, Soria, Almería, Voluntarios de Tarragona, Tercio de Migueletes de Igualada.]

[Reales de Granada, Santiago caballería de línea.]

One battery 4 guns.

Note: Gen Wimpffen stayed observing Igualada with a force of 4,000.

El Pla and Santa Maria

B

C

Bridge of Goy

D

F

Marti

Site of engagement in the morning.

E

St. Cyr

A

Valls

7 St. Cyr - 13,800 (Source: Oman)

1 Souham

Dumoulin (A) [1e Léger, 42e Ligne.]

Verge (B) [3e Provisional Léger, 7e & 67e Provisional Ligne.]

24e Dragoons (C)

2 batteries

5 Pino (IT)

Mazzuchelli (D) [1e and 2e IT Léger.]

Fontane (E) [4e, 6e & 7e Ligne.]

[7e IT Dragoons (F), IT Royal Chasseurs (G).]

Castro

G

R Francoli

Barranco

0 Miles 1

0 Kilometres 1

Map 41

BATTLE OF VALLS
25 February 1809

Tarragona

but the Spanish division was driven back, forcing Cuesta to withdraw south to Deleytosa where he concentrated his forces and awaited the arrival of reinforcements.[19] To speed the union, Cuesta moved further south, leaving Henestrosa's Division to provide the rearguard, which inflicted a commendable drubbing on the 10e Chasseurs who had slightly overextended their forward reconnaissance.

By 27 March Cuesta's army was complete and he returned north in order to engage the French force to his front. In the early morning of 29 March the two armies were lined up in two arcs facing each other between the towns of Medellin and Don Benito. Victor retained a substantial reserve of infantry and a cavalry regiment but the Spanish commander saw no need for a reserve and deployed his entire force. With Cuesta's extremities covered by the two rivers, Victor concluded that a flanking manoeuvre by the French cavalry was not possible[20] and consequently he gave clear instructions to his cavalry commanders on both French flanks to advance with the infantry, and only exploit head-on attacks under favourable circumstances. The French advance commenced at 1100 hours and, as the armies drew together, Latour-Maubourg sensed just such an opportunity and ordered the 2nd and 4th Dragoons to charge the centre of Del Parque's position. They headed straight for the Spanish battery, which stood its ground and

caused considerable carnage among the French cavalry, who quickly lost momentum and withdrew, exposing the flank of the 1st and 2nd Baden battalions, which, in turn, prompted the Spanish infantry to rush forward and engage them. Victor ordered his right wing to fall back and the centre and left fell back in unison, hard-pressed by the Spanish skirmishers. Victor halted the withdrawal on slightly higher ground but the Spanish troops continued their advance and the divisions of Henestrosa and Del Parque were soon at the front ranks of Latour-Maubourg's force and attacking the battery. The French dragoons were ordered to charge and Cuesta immediately responded by ordering a counter-charge by the three cavalry regiments to the right of the Spanish line.[21] This was a critical moment in the battle, but predictably the Spanish cavalry failed miserably to rise to the occasion; they panicked, withdrew and left the Spanish infantry exposed. Lasalle, who had been pulling back in the face of Alburquerque, witnessed events to the south and simultaneously released his cavalry to engage the three cavalry regiments of Alburquerque. 'After two hours of retrograde movement, General Lasalle's rearguard took the offensive, and charged a squadron of Spanish lancers that held the head of the hostile column. Afraid of this unexpected movement, the Spanish turned bridle and toppled the squadrons that were behind them.'[22] He drove them back and got in behind the Spanish infantry allowing the infantry to begin rolling up the line of Spanish lines. Nearly 8,000 men were slain and a further 2,000 taken prisoner, nine colours and 26 of the 30 guns were also lost.

---

19   Having been ordered by the Supreme Junta, the Duke of Alburquerque was en route with 4,500 men from the Army of the Centre, and the Marquis de Portago was also making his way from Badajoz with the nucleus (three battalions) of the new Estremaduran 4th Division.

20   A visit to the battlefield highlights the questionable nature of this assessment as the southernmost river, the Hortiga, is but a mere stream and easily fordable, almost along its length.

21   Infante, Almansa and Imperiales de Toledo – the first two were formerly part of La Romana's army.

22   Hugo, *Histoire des Armées Françaises, 1792–1833*, vol. IV, p.118.

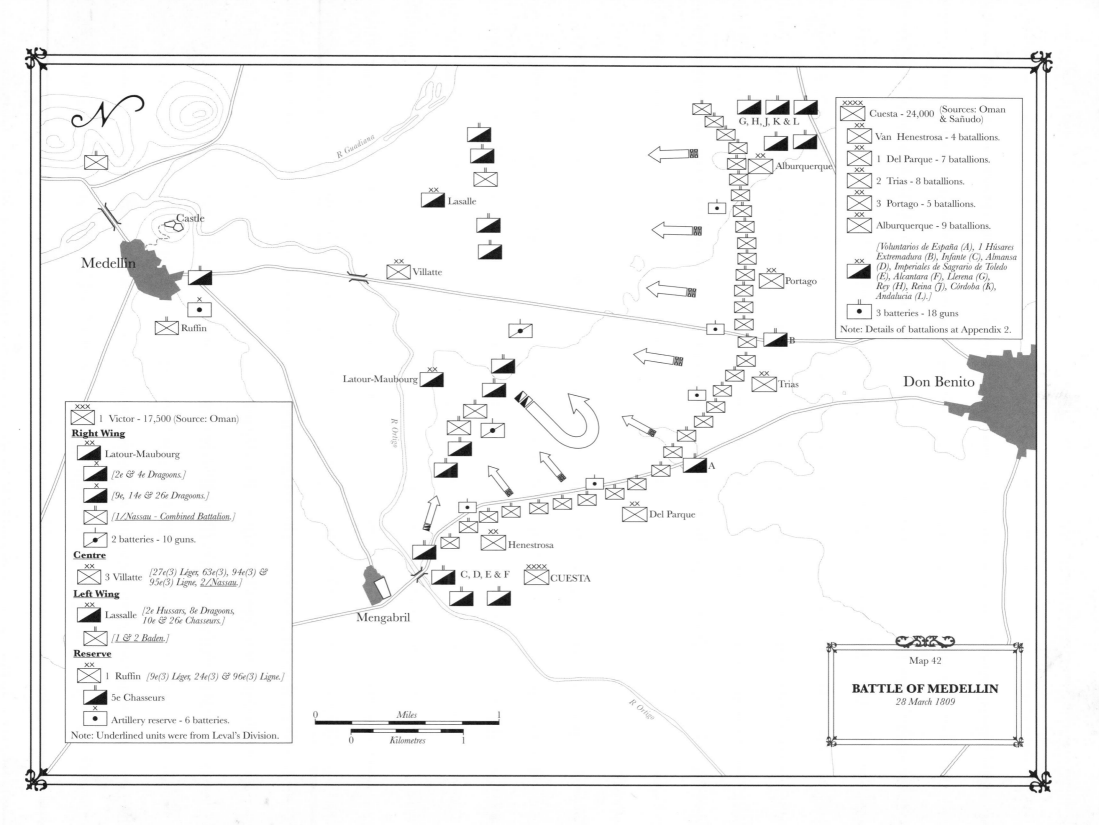

N

R Guadiana

G, H, J, K & L

Alburquerque

Lasalle

Villatte

Castle

Medellin

Portago

Don Benito

Ruffin

B

Latour-Maubourg

Trias

A

Del Parque

Henestrosa

C, D, E & F   CUESTA

Mengabril

R Ortigo

R Ortigo

Key box (top right):

▨ Cuesta - 24,000	(Sources: Oman & Sañudo)
▨ Van Henestrosa - 4 batallions.	
▨ 1 Del Parque - 7 batallions.	
▨ 2 Trias - 8 batallions.	
▨ 3 Portago - 5 batallions.	
▨ Alburquerque - 9 batallions.	

[*Voluntarios de España (A), 1 Húsares Extremadura (B), Infante (C), Almansa (D), Imperiales de Sagrario de Toledo (E), Alcantara (F), Llerena (G), Rey (H), Reina (J), Córdoba (K), Andalucia (L).*]

▨ 3 batteries - 18 guns

Note: Details of batallions at Appendix 2.

Key box (bottom left):

XXX

▨ 1 Victor - 17,500 (Source: Oman)

Right Wing

▨ Latour-Maubourg

▨ [*2e & 4e Dragoons.*]

▨ [*9e, 14e & 26e Dragoons.*]

▨ [*1/Nassau - Combined Battalion.*]

▨ 2 batteries - 10 guns.

Centre

▨ 3 Villatte [*27e(3) Léger, 63e(3), 94e(3) & 95e(3) Ligne, 2/Nassau.*]

Left Wing

▨ Lassalle [*2e Hussars, 8e Dragoons, 10e & 26e Chasseurs.*]

▨ [*1 & 2 Baden.*]

Reserve

▨ 1 Ruffin [*9e(3) Léger, 24e(3) & 96e(3) Ligne.*]

▨ 5e Chasseurs

▨ Artillery reserve - 6 batteries.

Note: Underlined units were from Leval's Division.

0 Miles 1

0 Kilometres 1

Map 42

BATTLE OF MEDELLIN
28 March 1809

Chapter 16

THE SECOND FRENCH INVASION OF PORTUGAL: JANUARY TO MARCH 1809

Before the final elements of Moore's army had completed evacuation from the harbour at La Coruña, Soult already knew his next assignment. He was to invade Portugal, take Oporto, move south and link up with Victor and their combined corps were then to retake Lisbon by 10 February. Victor had already secured a notable victory over Cuesta's forces at Medellin (Chapter 15) and opened the route to Portugal from the east, but as instructed, he waited for word from Soult before proceeding. Leaving aside the flawed time appreciation, there were three problems with the French plan. Firstly, suitable roads in Galicia and northern Portugal were virtually non-existent; secondly, combined operations of this nature, which relied on good communications between participants many miles apart, were unsound in this theatre of operations at this time.[1] Finally, Soult's corps had been reduced to about 23,000 men from the nominal rolls of 43,000 a few weeks previously. Many of his men had been detached and an even greater number were sick following the demanding pursuit of Moore's army over challenging terrain in severe weather. His cavalry was particularly affected, with many mounts having perished and the dismounted troopers unable to keep up with the hardened infantry.[2]

While Soult waited for the stragglers to regroup he set off to invest and capture the rich harbour of Ferrol, the second most important naval anchorage in Spain. He departed La Coruña on 23 January and by 26 January had control of the place as the governor, Melgarejo, was determined not to fight.[3] The next day, Soult received Napoleon's final communiqué from Valladolid, which reiterated his mission to invade Portugal, and graciously extended his timelines for the capture of Oporto and Lisbon to 5 and 16 February respectively. Soult returned to La Coruña where he made preparations to hand over command of Galicia to Ney and prepare his forces for the task ahead. Franceschi and Lahoussaye set off on 30 January to undertake a reconnaissance of the routes and to probe for any resistance. Soult was aware that the remnants of La Romana's Galician Army were in the area but rightly assumed they would do their utmost to avoid confrontation.[4] The unknown quantities were the Galician insurgents and the Portuguese military forces. Soult set off from Santiago on 8 February with the balance of his divisions following on the 9th and 10th once relieved by Ney's formations. On 16 February he made an abortive attempt to cross the river Minho between Tui and the coast. The heavy rains had swollen the river and the chosen crossing point was at the confluence of the river and the Atlantic swell; the conflict of currents rendered passage impossible. Soult nevertheless persevered with a handful of fishing boats and those soldiers who were not lost to the waters were taken prisoner by Colonel Champalimaud's Portuguese forces on the far bank. Such an inauspicious start demanded drastic action and so the entire Corps were redirected east to Orense, from where they would cross the first available bridge and pick up the poor mountain track to Chaves. The burden of his mission soon became apparent; the track was treacherous and brought him face-to-face with the Galician insurgents and into direct confrontation with La Romana.

Thirty kilometres shy of Orense, Soult finally accepted that the heavy baggage and guns were impeding progress considerably and resolved to send the wagons and 36 of the heavier guns[5] back to Tui under the protection of Merle, who was ordered to rejoin the main body on completion of the escorting duty. Soult arrived at Orense on 21 February, seized the undefended bridge and established a temporary headquarters that he would use until 4 March, allowing him to gather his thoughts and his force. Despite the best efforts of the insurgents, the latter was easier than the former, as Soult had received bad news from Ney who spelt out the level of uprising in Galicia and questioned the wisdom of Soult departing until the Spanish province was under control. Nevertheless, Soult did not dwell overly long on the predicament of his ambitious colleague and departed Orense on 4 March, at the same time that the first elements of his force were approaching La Romana's position at Monterey. The Spanish commander had already resolved to withdraw to León having failed to agree terms for combined operations with the local Portuguese army commander, General Silveira.[6] La Romana's withdrawal left Silveira somewhat exposed. His force numbered only about 12,000 men, more than half of which were *ordenança*, armed civilians equipped only with pikes and farm implements rather than firearms.[7] Silveira was forced to withdraw behind Chaves, as the terrain to the north was not defendable, but many of the *ordenança* refused to abandon the town to the French and elected to stay and defend it. The local 12th Chaves Regiment supported them in their plight. Chaves was a fortified town and it boasted 50 cannon, but both walls and guns were old and dilapidated and any hopes of a prolonged struggle were soon extinguished. Soult surrounded the town on 10 March, but

---

1 The same error was again made in 1810, when Masséna invaded Portugal for the third time, and was to have been supported by both Soult and Drouet.

2 Oman shows the following figures for 30 January: 3,059 present under arms. 3,008 absent and 572 sick.

3 See Noble, *Mémoires sur Les Opérations Militaires Des Francais en Galice, en Portugal et dans la vallée du Tage en 1809*, p.53 and Santiago Ganzález-Llanos Galvache, *La Guerra de la Independencia en Ferrol*, pp. 59–62 for details of the capitulation.

4 La Romana had moved out of Orense on 19 January and sought refuge at Monterey where he was slowly rebuilding his force, which numbered about 9,000 at this time.

5 Three batteries of four-pounder guns were all that remained with the invading army.

6 The organization and strengths of the reorganized Portuguese Army, now under the command of the British General Beresford, can be seen at Appendix 2.

7 The actions of this group were, in effect, classic guerrilla operations, but they are seldom recognized as such.

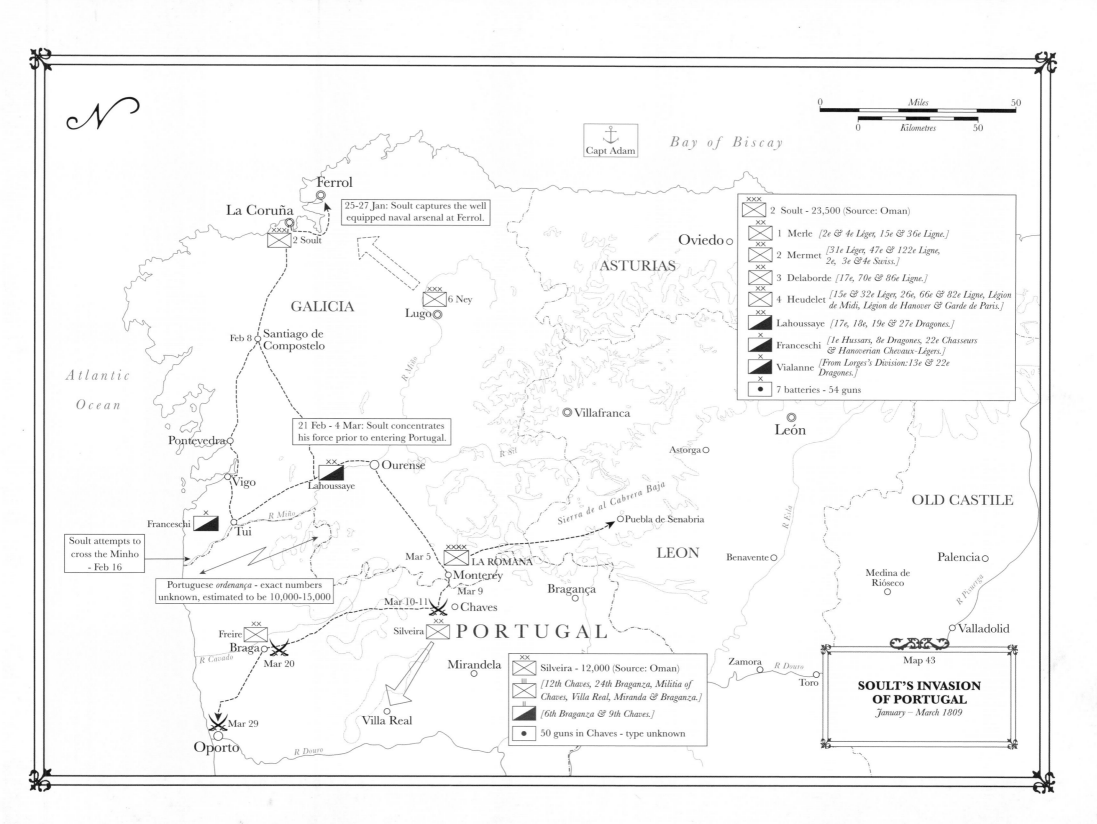

Bay of Biscay

Capt Adam

Ferrol

La Coruña

25-27 Jan: Soult captures the well equipped naval arsenal at Ferrol.

×××
2 Soult

6 Ney

GALICIA

Lugo

Oviedo

ASTURIAS

Feb 8 Santiago de Compostelo

Atlantic Ocean

R Miño

Villafranca

21 Feb - 4 Mar: Soult concentrates his force prior to entering Portugal.

León

R Sil

Pontevedra

Astorga

OLD CASTILE

Ourense

××
Lahoussaye

Vigo

R Miño

×
Franceschi

Tui

Soult attempts to cross the Minho - Feb 16

Portuguese *ordenança* - exact numbers unknown, estimated to be 10,000-15,000

Sierra de al Cabrera Baja

Puebla de Senabria

LEON

R Esla

Palencia

Medina de Ríoseco

R Pisuerga

Mar 5

××××
LA ROMANA

Benavente

Monterey

Mar 9

Bragança

Freire ××

Braga

R Cavado

Mar 20

Mar 10-11 Chaves

Silveira ××

PORTUGAL

Valladolid

Mirandela

Zamora R Douro

Toro

Map 43

SOULT'S INVASION OF PORTUGAL

January – March 1809

Mar 29

Oporto

R Douro

Villa Real

×××
2 Soult - 23,500 (Source: Oman)

××
1 Merle [2e & 4e Léger, 15e & 36e Ligne.]

××
2 Mermet [31e Léger, 47e & 122e Ligne, 2e, 3e & 4e Swiss.]

××
3 Delaborde [17e, 70e & 86e Ligne.]

××
4 Heudelet [15e & 32e Léger, 26e, 66e & 82e Ligne, Légion de Midi, Légion de Hanover & Garde de Paris.]

××
Lahoussaye [17e, 18e, 19e & 27e Dragones.]

×
Franceschi [1e Hussars, 8e Dragones, 22e Chasseurs & Hanoverian Chevaux-Légers.]

×
Vialanne [From Lorges's Division: 13e & 22e Dragones.]

●
7 batteries - 54 guns

××
Silveira - 12,000 (Source: Oman)

|||
[12th Chaves, 24th Braganza, Militia of Chaves, Villa Real, Miranda & Braganza.]

[6th Braganza & 9th Chaves.]

●
50 guns in Chaves - type unknown

lacking any heavy artillery and not wishing to lose more men in a frontal assault on the weaker parts of the municipality, he sent in a summons for surrender. It was rejected. Soult then calculated, quite rightly, that the garrison would lose heart if Silveira's force were driven from the surrounding hills. Delaborde and Lahoussaye speedily and eagerly complied and Silveira withdrew south towards Villa Real with his 6,000 men. Soult's prognosis was accurate; the town's defensive spirit promptly evaporated and they agreed to terms on 11 March. The next day, Soult marched into the town, rested and replenished his force and established a logistics base there for subsequent operations into central Portugal.

Soult had time to ponder his next move and, following reconnaissance reports that the defiles were only lightly defended on the Braga road, elected for this route rather than the road due south via Villa Real. He departed Chaves on 14 March with Franceschi and Delaborde forming the vanguard and Mermet and Lahoussaye following the next day. Heudelet escorted the baggage the day after that and finally, on 17 March, Merle departed bringing up the rear. Vialanne, with his cavalry brigade, had been detached and sent on the Villa Real road to occupy Silveira and buy time for the French force to be clear of the Portuguese region of Tras-os-Montes. In this respect, he was not entirely successful. Franceschi and Delaborde pushed on against sustained but ineffective resistance from the masses of *ordenança* and, on 17 March, reached the village of Carvalho D'Este, where a large gathering of regular and irregular troops held the high ground to their front. This ad hoc group, under the command of General Freire, consisted of only 2,000 regular troops supported by 23,000 *ordenança*, the vast majority with no firearms. Freire was understandably reluctant to pit this group of enthusiastic amateurs against the invincible *Grande Armée* and toyed with the idea of retreating to Oporto. Once his intentions were known he was accused of treachery, and, amidst constant threats to his life, he tried to escape but was spotted, imprisoned and later murdered by an enraged mob. Baron Eben, the commander of the 2nd Lusitanian Legion, assumed command and immediately set about reinforcing the Portuguese position on the Monte Adaufé and the high ground to the south of the road.

As Franceschi and Delaborde arrived they saw the forces arrayed on the high ground to their front but were reluctant to get embroiled, deciding instead to wait for the arrival of Soult. By 20 March, with the exception of Merle's Division which was acting as rearguard, Soult's Corps was complete. He undertook a rapid reconnaissance and issued his orders for a three-pronged, frontal attack. Mermet and Franceschi were to advance on the left; Delaborde remained in the centre, supported by the division of dragoons, and Heudelet split his division into two brigades, committing Graindorge to the north of Monte Adaufé, while keeping Maransin's Brigade and Vialanne's dragoons in reserve. The inexperienced Portuguese troops held their ground and delivered a furious if ineffective fire on Delaborde's infantry as they climbed the slopes. When the French reached the plateau, the Portuguese lines began to waver. 'Eben, in his report, says that at the moment of the French assault one of his guns in the battery commanding the high road burst, and killed many of those standing about, and that the rout

commenced with the stampede caused by this explosion.'[8] With the Portuguese in full flight, Soult released the cavalry with inevitable consequences. Lahoussaye's dragoons showed little mercy as they 'made a great butchery' of the fleeing Portuguese and captured their baggage and guns.

The Portuguese to the north of Monte Adaufé fared considerably better, as Graindorge had no immediate cavalry in support with which to follow up his success, and many of the *ordenança* withdrew intact and were able to inflict a sharp check on the troops of the Hanoverian Legion who began to overextend themselves. To the south, the troops of Mermet and cavalry of Franceschi took considerably longer to get into position, via a track running through the wooded hillside of the re-entrant. The result, however, was more of the same with Franceschi's troopers pursuing the fleeing Portuguese over the hills for many kilometres. Those they captured were shown no quarter; the French cavalry were rampant and vented their fury after weeks of being on the receiving end of the guerrilla attacks. 'The column of the left found an unfortunate marksman, mutilated in the most atrocious way by the Portuguese, who had captured him the previous day. These barbarians had pulled out his eyes, cut his hands; the ears, the nose and other parts, and they had forced them between his teeth. Abandoned in this state, the unfortunate soul requested the death like favour.'[9] The cavalry did not cease their pursuit until well past Braga, by which time 4,000 Portuguese were estimated killed and only 400 taken captive.

After three days in Braga, Soult recommenced his advance to Oporto, optimistic that he had crushed resistance in northern Portugal. The early reports from his reconnaissance forces quickly dispelled that hypothesis and, to make matters worse, he discovered that contact with his logistics base at Chaves was already severed. The reaction of the Portuguese intrigued rather than troubled the French commander who decided to hasten his advance to Oporto, ever conscious that he was already well behind Napoleon's expected schedule. Heudelet's Division was left at Braga to look after the sick and wounded, maintain communication forward to Oporto and to try and reopen communication with Chaves while Soult, with the balance of his force, advanced on all three available routes and encountered little or no opposition, other than the Portuguese defence on the river Avé, which was quickly overcome.

The French force arrived on the heights above Oporto on the afternoon of 27 March and the sight that met them hurriedly dispelled any hopes of a rapid conclusion to the first phase. A force of about 30,000 regular soldiers, militia and *ordenança*, supported by 197 guns, were established in a fortified line of redoubts, joined by abattis and palisades, which stretched from the Atlantic to the river Douro. The overall commander of the Portuguese force was the Bishop of Oporto, who had also assumed charge of the local Junta after the rioting in the city following the news of the disaster at Braga. In reality, the bishop exercised little control over the mob and demonstrated fairly questionable leadership over the defending forces; for no sooner had he delivered his orders, and a sober benediction, then he withdrew south of the river to the relative safety of the Serra Convento leaving three Portuguese brigadier generals to conduct operations. Lima Barreto was allocated the western section to the Atlantic and the

---

8   Oman, *History of the Peninsular War*, vol. II, p.235.

9   Noble, *Mémoires sur Les Opérations Militaires Des Francais en Galice, en Portugal et dans la vallée du Tage en 1809*, p.123.

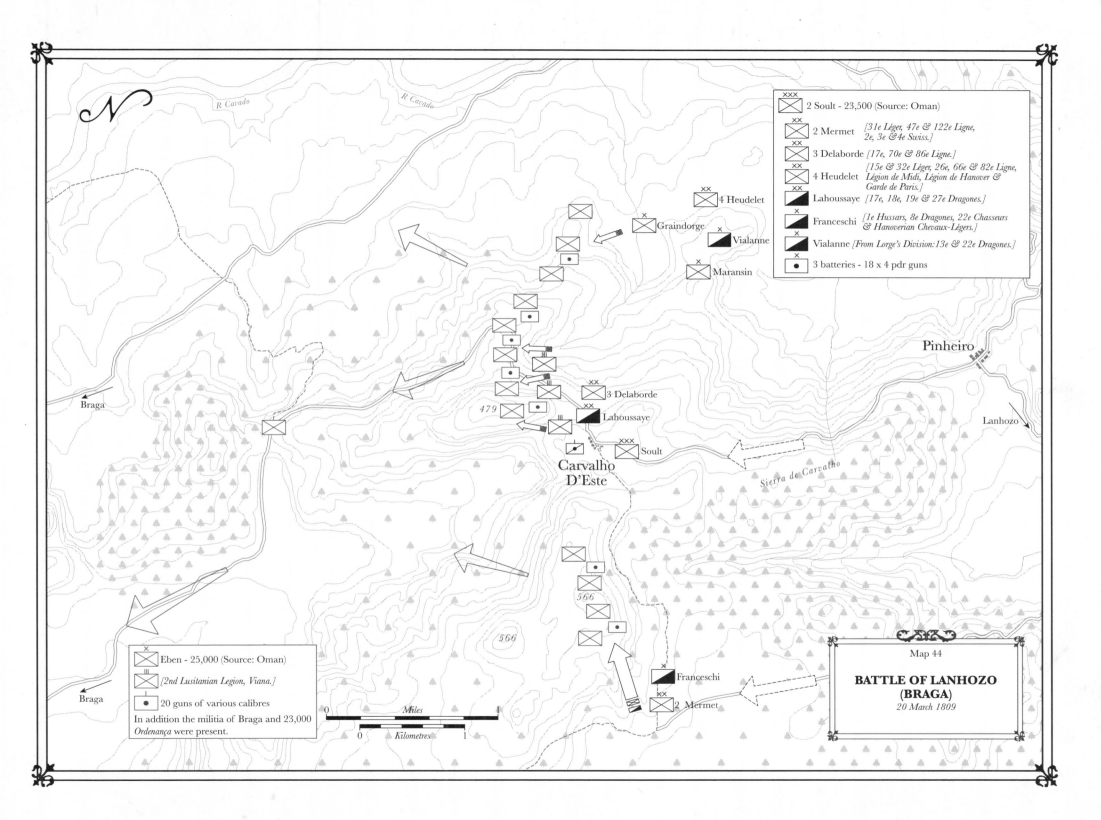

R. Cavado

R. Cavado

N

XX
4 Heudelet

Graindorge

× Vialanne

× Maransin

Pinheiro

Braga

479

3 Delaborde
XX
Lahoussaye

XXX
Soult

Lanhozo

Carvalho
D'Este

Sierra de Carvalho

566

566

Braga

Franceschi

2 Mermet

0   *Miles*   1

0   *Kilometres*   1

Map 44

**BATTLE OF LANHOZO
(BRAGA)**
20 March 1809

town of São João da Foz; Parreiras received the section north of the city and Vittoria the line and defences to the north-east and east.[10] Each commander was allocated a portion of the regular, militia, *ordenança* and trained gunners.

Soult spent what remained of the daylight on 27 March determining the scale, capabilities and weaknesses of the defence to his front. The following day, with little hope of success, he sent an offer of capitulation to the bishop; which solicited a predictable if somewhat irreligious response. During the confusion, often associated with the overt tensions and covert expectations of parley prior to possible conflict, General Foy had ridden into one of the redoubts, believing their intentions favourable to terms, only to discover his mistake by being taken prisoner. One of his battalion commanders who had accompanied him was not so lucky and was bayoneted as he drew his sword in an attempt to fight his way out. Soult needed no further authorization and finalized preparations for an attack the next morning. He was confident but justifiably cautious, given that the defenders outnumbered his force by nearly two to one. In textbook fashion, he executed Napoleon's theory of 'central position' to achieve local superiority against the numerically superior defenders by breaking them into constituent parts, isolating the stronger and attacking the weaker. Delaborde and Franceschi were to attack the Portuguese right, simultaneously Merle and one brigade of Lahoussaye's dragoons were to attack the left. Mermet and the other brigade of dragoons were to wait for these first two attacks to develop, while Vialanne's dragoons were to provide the reserve and to cover the French rear from roaming *ordenança*. The initial assaults were to commence before dawn but a heavy thunderstorm delayed proceedings until first light at 0700 hours.

Both Merle and Delaborde's attacks made good progress. Merle's infantry gained lodgement in the houses immediately under the redoubts and began to deliver a heavy and accurate fire upon the defenders forcing them to pull back and yield many of the outlying defences. From his vantage point, Soult could see both attacks unfolding and witnessed the movement of defenders from the centre to reinforce the Portuguese left at which point he ordered Merle to slow the rate of his advance and bade Delaborde to increase the effort on the Portuguese right. Delaborde obliged and had soon captured many outlying redoubts and gained a lodgement in the north-east corner of the city. General Parreiras then ordered more troops from the central defence to reinforce the right – it was exactly what Soult had anticipated. With the centre now considerably weakened he launched Mermet at the largest redoubt, supported by the dragoons. It was decisive; the redoubt was quickly overrun and with the adjoining abattis removed the dragoons poured through the gaps and mercilessly pursued the Portuguese into the city. The two wings quickly disintegrated and the thousands of defenders, with all semblance of order lost, tried to escape as best they could.

Some managed to skirt around the French flanks but the majority headed back into the city and, once there, mingled with the civil population which was trying to escape over the single pontoon bridge over the Douro. The sheer weight of numbers was too much for the structure to bear and one of the rafts sank, creating a gap into which countless unfortunate individuals were forced by the pressure of those pushing from behind. Hundreds, many women and children, were drowned or drowning, but their cries and the pleas to those on bridge to pull back were masked by the sound of French musketry and the Portuguese guns firing from the battery position by the Serra Convento. While many French came to the aid of the stricken crowd, many others were already well advanced in sacking the city and subjecting the inhabitants who had not attempted escape to the traditional atrocities. In some quarters the defenders had barricaded themselves into houses and fortified buildings and fierce street fighting erupted but it was quickly quelled and by late afternoon the city in its entirety was in French hands. Soult had delivered the first part of his plan but, 'after having wisely calculated all the chances of his position, Soult resolved not to march on Lisbon, before he was informed that Victor was advancing to second his operations: he waited for this intelligence the whole month of April'.[11] In reality Soult had taken Oporto and established garrisons in Braga and Chaves but he controlled nothing other than these immediate locations in northern Portugal.

---

10 Eben was denied a higher command following his questionable performance at Lanhozo and had to satisfy himself with commanding the 2nd Lusitanian Legion.

11 Sarrazin, *History of the War in Spain and Portugal*, p.78.

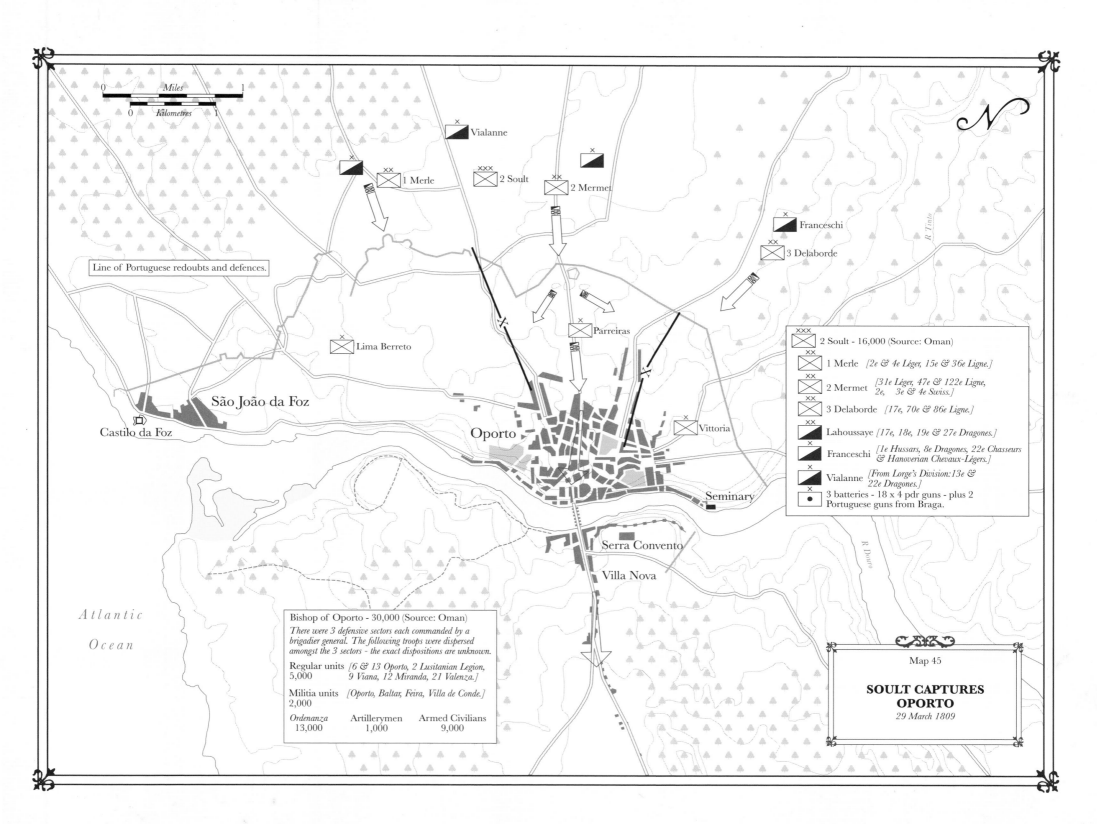

N

0 Miles 1
0 Kilometres 1

Vialanne

1 Merle   2 Soult   2 Mermet

Franceschi

3 Delaborde

Line of Portuguese redoubts and defences.

Lima Berreto

Parreiras

São João da Foz

Vittoria

Castilo da Foz

Oporto

Seminary

Serra Convento

Villa Nova

Atlantic

Ocean

R Tinto

R Douro

2 Soult - 16,000 (Source: Oman)

1 Merle   *[2e & 4e Léger, 15e & 36e Ligne.]*

2 Mermet   *[31e Léger, 47e & 122e Ligne, 2e,   3e & 4e Swiss.]*

3 Delaborde *[17e, 70e & 86e Ligne.]*

Lahoussaye *[17e, 18e, 19e & 27e Dragones.]*

Franceschi *[1e Hussars, 8e Dragones, 22e Chasseurs & Hanoverian Chevaux-Légers.]*

Vialanne *[From Lorge's Division:13e & 22e Dragones.]*

3 batteries - 18 x 4 pdr guns - plus 2 Portuguese guns from Braga.

Bishop of Oporto - 30,000 (Source: Oman)

There were 3 defensive sectors each commanded by a brigadier general. The following troops were dispersed amongst the 3 sectors - the exact dispositions are unknown.

Regular units *[6 & 13 Oporto, 2 Lusitanian Legion,*
5,000   *9 Viana, 12 Miranda, 21 Valenza.]*

Militia units *[Oporto, Baltar, Feira, Villa de Conde.]*
2,000

Ordenanza   Artillerymen   Armed Civilians
13,000   1,000   9,000

Map 45

SOULT CAPTURES OPORTO
29 March 1809

Chapter 17

WELLESLEY RETURNS

Soult took little solace from the capture of Oporto; he was facing a dilemma as to whether to continue to Lisbon, as previously ordered, or stay in central Portugal. His force was diminishing and morale was ebbing, he had not heard from Napoleon for two months and had no communication with Ney, Lapisse or Victor. Napoleon had assured him that he could count on support from Lapisse in northern Portugal and Victor for his assault on the capital. Despite the fact that the task given to Lapisse and his force of 9,000 was ambitious, he seemed content to sit out the winter months in Salamanca, largely as a result of having been completely deceived by the strength of Sir Robert Wilson's force[1] which was operating forward of the Portuguese border from a base at Almeida. Victor had requested that Lapisse be released to rejoin his corps[2] but this had been rejected by King Joseph and, despite Victor's relatively easy defeat on Cuesta's forces at Medellin, the French considered his force too weak to independently prosecute operations inside Portugal and elected to dwell at Mérida. Soult remained frustratingly unaware of all this French inactivity and of Ney's intentions and whereabouts, but he had received sporadic reports[3] that his garrisons at Tui and Vigo were under continuous siege by Galician insurgents. His position was most unenviable. He felt vulnerable, with his flank to the sea and his back to the mountains, and he quickly set about readjusting his force. Mermet, supported by Franceschi, were sent to cover the southern approaches from Coimbra; Foy's Brigade and one brigade of Lahoussaye's dragoons were sent to Tras-os-Montes to try and establish contact with Lapisse;[4] finally, Heudelet was to bring in all the sick and the stores from Braga and then set off north to succour Tui and Vigo and reestablish contact with Ney in Galicia. The balance remained in Oporto with the cavalry forming a screen to the north of the city.

Heudelet set out from Oporto on 6 April and reached General Lamartinière at Tui a few days later, but the news from Vigo was not good. On 27 March the Galician insurgents, supported by arms, ammunition and, most significantly, two heavy naval guns from the two Royal Navy frigates *Lively* and *Venus*, had forced the French commander to surrender. Heudelet elected to evacuate Tui, but on 12 April, as he was preparing to leave, Maucune arrived with a brigade from Ney's Corps. The French commanders exchanged rather depressing summaries of their individual predicaments and then Maucune set off north to Santiago, harassed all the way by the increasingly confident Galician irregulars. The news from the 6th Corps highlighted the ubiquity of the *Gallegos* and the resurgence of La Romana, but with communications beyond the province all but severed, no further information as to the situation in the rest of the country was forthcoming. Based on this available information Soult ordered Heudelet to pull back with Lamartinière to a line from Viana to Braga.

Loison's expedition to gather information from Lapisse stalled before he had reached the province of Tras-os-Montes. Silveira had retaken Chaves a few days after Soult had left the town garrisoned with a small force under Commandant Messenger. The Portuguese force then moved south to intercept Loison but erred by offering combat in front of Amarante, and pulled back into the town having suffered great loss. Importantly, in the process of their withdrawal, they managed to hold the bridge entering the town and established a reserve demolition upon it. Loison stormed the structure the following day but failed to secure a lodgement and conscious that the Portuguese could blow the bridge at any moment fell back and requested reserves from Oporto. Sarrut's Brigade, and a brigade of Lahoussaye's dragoons, arrived on 24 April but it still took them until 2 May to finally secure the crossing.[5]

Long before this, on 22 April, Sir Arthur Wellesley had landed back at Lisbon and was delighted to discover that the union of Victor and Soult had miscarried.[6] He decided to put into practice the time-honoured tactic that the best defence is a vigorous offence, and with 25,000 British and 16,000 Portuguese troops at his disposal (see Appendix 2) he devised a three-tier plan. A containing force under Brigadier General Mackenzie was despatched with haste to Abrantes with the sole purpose of preventing Victor from advancing into Portugal. He organized another force under Beresford, who was sent to link up with Silveira and cut off Soult's line of retreat, and finally the balance of his Anglo-Portuguese army was mobilized to move north and make the all-important assault on Oporto.

Beresford set off from Coimbra on 6 May, collected elements of Wilson's Brigade from Vizeu on the 8th and joined forces with Silveira at Lamego on 10 May. Wellesley's main force advanced on two routes; Hill and Cameron's brigades moved on the coastal route and were to cross the estuary of the Vouga in boats assembled by the townspeople of Aveiro and disembark at Ovar and then get in behind Franceschi's force.[7] The second group moved directly up the road towards Franceschi's piquets led by the cavalry under Stapleton Cotton; the lead cavalry reconnaissance found Franceschi's force but decided to wait for the arrival of the infantry before pressing the screen. However, the infantry had been delayed by the difficult night move, and by the time the Anglo-Portuguese force had crossed the river the day was spent and Franceschi withdrew under cover of darkness. Hill's force on the coast fared little better. It had taken considerable time to ferry the two brigades in the small boats, and consequently they too were unable to get in behind

---

1   This consisted of his own Lusitanian Legion, the nucleus of the 11rd and 23rd regiments, two militia regiments (Guarda and Trancoso) a handful of 200 or so cavalry and latterly about 1,500 newly raised Spanish forces from Leon: a total of about 3,000 infantry and 400 horse.

2   Lapisse's Division was the 2nd Division in Victor's Corps.

3   Received from Portuguese letters seized in the post offices at Oporto and Braga.

4   This group was placed under Loison's command.

5   The story of how this was achieved is fascinating and demonstrates a resilience of mind attributable to combat engineering of the highest excellence. See Oman, *A History of the Peninsular War*, vol II, pp.270–271.

6   Castlereagh had taken Wellesley's advice, which was entirely contrary to that of Moore, that Portugal could be defended with a force of 30,000, even if the French overran Spain.

7   Franceschi's force was not strong, consisting of four weak cavalry regiments of only 1,200 sabres, an infantry regiment and a battery of light guns.

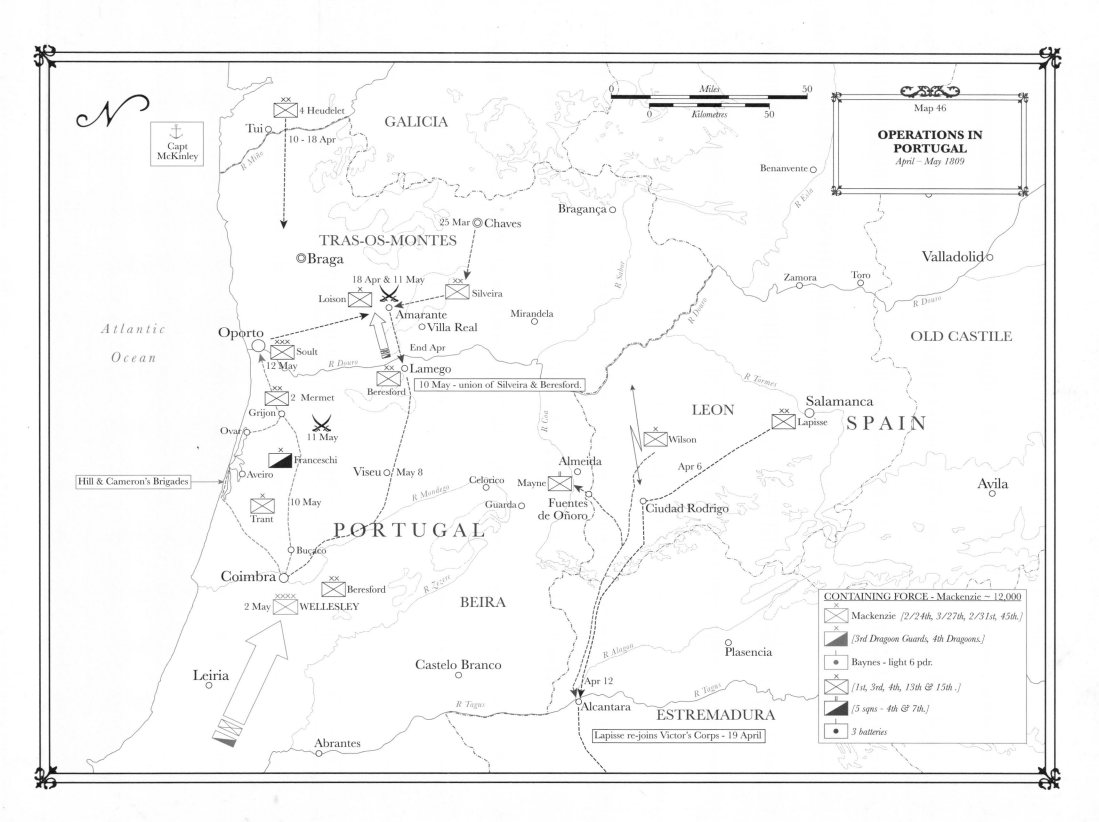

N

Capt McKinley

GALICIA

Tui

R Miño

4 Heudelet

10 - 18 Apr

Benanvente

R Esla

Map 46

OPERATIONS IN PORTUGAL

April – May 1809

TRAS-OS-MONTES

25 Mar Chaves

Bragança

Valladolid

Braga

Zamora

Toro

R Sabor

18 Apr & 11 May

Loison

Silveira

Amarante

Villa Real

Mirandela

R Douro

R Douro

OLD CASTILE

Oporto

Soult

R Douro

End Apr

12 May

Lamego

Beresford

10 May - union of Silveira & Beresford.

R Coa

R Tormes

LEON

Salamanca

Lapisse

SPAIN

2 Mermet

Grijon

Wilson

Ovar

11 May

Apr 6

Avila

Franceschi

Viseu · May 8

Celorico

Almeida

Atlantic Ocean

Hill & Cameron's Brigades

Aveiro

R Mondego

Guarda

Mayne

Fuentes de Oñoro

Ciudad Rodrigo

10 May

Trant

PORTUGAL

Buçaco

R Zezere

BEIRA

Coimbra

Beresford

2 May WELLESLEY

R Tagus

Castelo Branco

Plasencia

R Alagon

CONTAINING FORCE - Mackenzie ~ 12,000

Mackenzie *[2/24th, 3/27th, 2/31st, 45th.]*

[3rd Dragoon Guards, 4th Dragoons.]

Baynes - light 6 pdr.

[1st, 3rd, 4th, 13th & 15th.]

[5 sqns - 4th & 7th.]

3 batteries

Leiria

Apr 12

Alcantara

ESTREMADURA

R Tagus

Abrantes

Lapisse re-joins Victor's Corps - 19 April

Franceschi before he withdrew. The first phase of the plan had misfired; by late morning on 11 May, the two groups were reunited and they continued to move north to Gijón, where Franceschi had joined forces with Mermet's Division. After a probing action by Stewart's Brigade, Wellesley realized the French were not about to give up the position without a fight. Without delay he deployed two flanking groups that settled the dispute; the French withdrew, pursued by an over-zealous cavalry. By nightfall the French covering force was back north of the Douro and Soult had ordered the destruction of the pontoon bridge.

Soult also recalled all his forces to the immediate environs of Oporto and now began to make unhurried preparations for a retreat, confident that with the bridge destroyed and all available boats on the northern bank, Wellesley's rapid advance would grind to an abrupt halt. Mermet's Division was detailed to break camp and escort the convalescents and the baggage train east towards Amarante, the balance of forces were deployed along the northern bank but were concentrated in the city and to the west along the shores of the Douro to the sea. The lower reaches of the Douro were allocated a mere battalion to cover the length, despite there being many concealed approaches to the riverbed. Many of Soult's staff shared their commander's view that Wellesley would not attempt to cross the river in haste and certainly not in broad daylight. Meanwhile, south of the river Wellesley's entire force was concentrated, out of sight, behind the buildings at Villa Nova. Wellesley moved to the Serra Convento to reconnoitre the ground and observed Mermet's Division heading off into the distance, but he also noted the apparent lack of French activity to the east of the city. His intelligence officers returned with news that they had discovered a ferry along the southern shore that had been inadequately scuttled and was already in the process of being repaired by local villagers. At much the same time a local barber, who had just come from the northern bank in a small craft, brought news of four large wine barges that lay unguarded. Within an hour these were on the southern bank and coupled with the additional intelligence that the large Seminary building on the north bank appeared unoccupied, Wellesley seized the opportunity.

'Sir Arthur then ordered some guns to be brought up to the convent where we were which would command the landing place of our troops on the opposite side and would protect their formation; these guns were ordered to remain concealed until wanted.'[8] Wellesley despatched Murray (with a brigade-sized grouping[9]) to move well to the east and, making use of the ferry at Avintas, was to establish a bridgehead on the far side and create a diversion if necessary. As Murray set off, the barges[10] crossed the short expanse of water below the Seminary, dashing to and fro as fast as they could. After about an hour, General Paget and 400 men of the 3rd Foot were established on the northern bank and preparing the Seminary for defence when finally, at about 1030 hours, they were discovered. Foy, who had responsibility for this area,

immediately prepared his brigade to attack but it took another hour before the nearest regiment, the 17e Léger, moved forward. Wellesley watched anxiously with his staff from the south bank and gave the order to the artillery to respond, which they did with incredible accuracy: a shrapnel shell from Lane's 5.5in howitzer burst directly over the leading French gun, killing every member of the crew. Each successive attack was beaten back by the accurate fire of the British and German gunners firing shrapnel to great effect.[11] By the time Delaborde arrived with three additional battalions, Hill's entire brigade was firm on the north bank and reinforcing their defences in and around the Seminary buildings. Delaborde made a concerted effort to dislodge the red-coated infantry, but under the hail of accurate musketry from the Seminary roof, and artillery canister from the southern bank, this attack was also beaten back. Soult was increasingly worried, especially by this unexpected development, and responded by withdrawing Reynaud from the quayside to join the attack. The local population quickly exploited the void created by this readjustment and rushed to the shore despatching every available boat to the southern bank. These boats were then loaded with elements of H. Campbell and Stewart's brigades, who quickly deployed their troops in the southern area of the city and, once established, began to attack the French in the rear.

The effect was immediate and decisive; Soult realized that the city was lost and ordered an urgent retreat along the Valongo road. It was a disorderly affair that might have been catastrophic had Murray taken the initiative and blocked or engaged the retreating French. 'It was an opportunity that would have tempted a blind man to strike; the neglect of it argued want of military talent and of military hardihood; and how would it have appeared if Loison had not abandoned Amarante.'[12] This latter news reached Soult at 0100 hours, as he was resting his exhausted and demoralized force. Beresford had linked up with Silveira, concentrating about 11,000 men and, after an indecisive engagement on 11 May, Loison elected to withdraw north the following morning on the road to Braga. Soult was now in a most precarious position; his only road east out of Portugal was now blocked. Had his subordinate informed him earlier, he could have taken one of the roads north out of Oporto.[13] At dawn, Soult informed his men that their only hope was to abandon the baggage, spike the guns, distribute the contents of the military chest[14] and make off into the hills to the north. As they set off it began to rain, within hours it was pouring, and it was set to continue that way for three days. To the demoralized French force it appeared that things could not get worse, but in fact the rain was a blessing. It succeeded in reducing attacks from armed locals and, by 14 May, Soult had joined forces with Loison at Guimaraens. Wellesley, unaware that the bridge at Amarante was in Allied hands,

11   Despite this example, Wellesley remained sceptical as to the utility of shrapnel. Furthermore, he failed to give the gunners a mention in his subsequent despatches.

12   Napier, *History of the War in the Peninsula*, vol. II. Oman is equally scathing of this officer. Murray demonstrated similar qualities when he assumed command of the east coast expeditionary force in 1813.

13   Soult was justifiably incensed by Loison's failure to keep him informed, indeed this report was the first received since 8 May.

14   The chest was reputed to have contained £50,000 in Portuguese silver, few soldiers took advantage of the offer to help themselves, what was left was blown up with the surplus powder.

8   Dickson, *The Dickson Manuscripts*, vol I, p.20.

9   1st & 2nd Line KGL, company of the 5/60th, 2 squadrons of the 14th Light Dragoons and 2 guns from one of the KGL batteries.

10   Oman states these carried 30 men but Dickson believes the figure to be around 100, which was probably the total of the 4 barges.

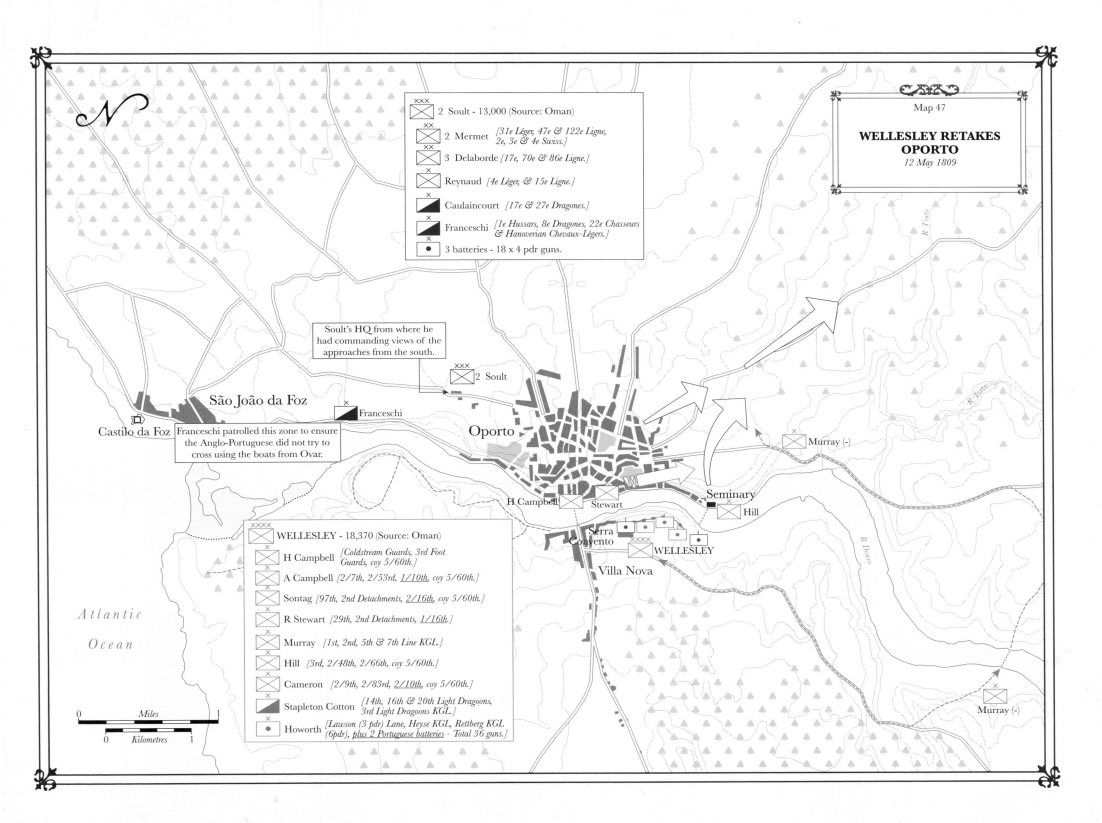

N

Map 47

WELLESLEY RETAKES OPORTO
12 May 1809

2 Soult - 13,000 (Source: Oman)

2 Mermet *[31e Léger, 47e & 122e Ligne, 2e, 3e & 4e Swiss.]*

3 Delaborde *[17e, 70e & 86e Ligne.]*

Reynaud *[4e Léger, & 15e Ligne.]*

Caulaincourt *[17e & 27e Dragones.]*

Franceschi *[1e Hussars, 8e Dragones, 22e Chasseurs & Hanoverian Chevaux-Légers.]*

3 batteries - 18 x 4 pdr guns.

Soult's HQ from where he had commanding views of the approaches from the south.

2 Soult

São João da Foz

Castilo da Foz

Franceschi

Franceschi patrolled this zone to ensure the Anglo-Portuguese did not try to cross using the boats from Ovar.

R. Tinto

Oporto

Murray (-)

Seminary

H Campbell   Stewart

Hill

Serra Convento   WELLESLEY

Villa Nova

R. Douro

WELLESLEY - 18,370 (Source: Oman)

H Campbell *[Coldstream Guards, 3rd Foot Guards, coy 5/60th.]*

A Campbell *[2/7th, 2/53rd, 1/10th, coy 5/60th.]*

Sontag *[97th, 2nd Detachments, 2/16th, coy 5/60th.]*

R Stewart *[29th, 2nd Detachments, 1/16th.]*

Murray *[1st, 2nd, 5th & 7th Line KGL.]*

Hill *[3rd, 2/48th, 2/66th, coy 5/60th.]*

Cameron *[2/9th, 2/83rd, 2/10th, coy 5/60th.]*

Stapleton Cotton *[14th, 16th & 20th Light Dragoons, 3rd Light Dragoons KGL.]*

Howorth *[Lawson (3 pdr) Lane, Heyse KGL, Rettberg KGL (6pdr), plus 2 Portuguese batteries - Total 36 guns.]*

Atlantic Ocean

Miles
0   1

Kilometres
0   1

Murray (-)

chose to rest his exhausted force at Oporto and only sent forward a small force under Murray to hassle the French rearguard. It never made contact. Beresford meanwhile had departed north to Chaves in an attempt to cut off Soult's line of retreat. He deployed Silveira's force at the halfway point to block the defiles of Ruivaens and Salamonde.

Once properly apprised of Soult's predicament, Wellesley departed Oporto on 14 May with his entire force (less Murray's group), and headed north to Braga in an attempt to catch his adversary. By last light on 15 May, after two hard days of marching, the Anglo-Portuguese army reached Braga. Soult had anticipated the move and had cut cross-country but now came face-to-face with Silveira's force holding the bridge at Ponte Nova, near Salamonde. Like Dupont the year prior at Bailén, Soult was now trapped and facing certain surrender, but a most daring night operation during which the bridge was stormed and taken by Major Dulong and 100 volunteers reopened an escape route. The sappers worked through the night to repair the structure and at first light Soult's forces escaped over it, leaving a brigade and two cavalry regiments[15] to slow down the Allied advance. Soult anticipated that the main road through Chaves would also be blocked and elected to head north via the more rugged and difficult route towards Montelegre and the Spanish border. When his force came up against another bridge held by the *ordenança* the celebrated Major Dulong was asked for a repeat performance. He duly obliged, being injured in the process, but Soult's Corps was now relatively safe and on 19 May, his force arrived exhausted – devoid of all their heavy equipment and guns but otherwise comparatively intact, having completed an incredible withdrawal, most of which was in contact.[16]

While Soult had been running for his life in Portugal, Ney had been trying to contain the growing Galician insurrection and tie down the resurgent armies of the Asturias and Galicia. Since the battle at Espinosa, the Army of the Asturias had been quietly reinforcing and reorganising. Other than a minor raid into Galicia against the garrison at Mondonedo in early April, this army had been inactive and were, despite repeated requests, reluctant to join forces with La Romana. La Romana went ahead regardless, resuming the offensive as the spring arrived and on 17 March his force recaptured Villafranca, driving out the French garrison based there. Ney was by now finding himself increasingly isolated and in early April, with news of Soult's difficulties in Portugal, he repeated his request to Madrid for support to reestablish communications with Soult and tie down the growing problems within Galicia. General Kellermann was finally allocated the task. His force of between 7,000 and 8,000 men left Astorga on 27 April and marched via Villafranca to Lugo, where he joined forces with Maurice Mathieu's Division. The French commanders devised a plan of attack into the Asturias on three routes. Ney would concentrate at Lugo and attack from the west, Kellermann would retrace his steps to Astorga and attack from the south and Bonnet would attack from the east.

Ney reached Oviedo on 19 May, having driven aside the division of Mahy and elements of the Army of the Asturias en route, but La Romana and the key members of the Junta of the

Asturias escaped by fishing boat the same day. Kellermann, who was delayed, joined forces with elements of Ney's force at the passes of Pajares, but the Asturian troops had long since dispersed into the mountains; as had Ballesteros, who had withdrawn west to support the provincial troops at Oviedo only to discover he was too late, and with Bonnet on his flank he headed south. Ney's Asturian expedition was therefore a complete failure, and to make matters worse, worrying reports were filtering through regarding the activities of both Mahy and the insurgents of southern Galicia. Leaving Kellermann in charge and ordering Bonnet to return to Santander (which he had to fight to retake on his return) Ney set off to return to Galicia via the coast road. He reached Castropol on 27 May, where he had hoped to deal with Worster, but the Spaniard had taken refuge in the surrounding hills and mountains. Instead Ney received news that Lugo was in great peril and had only been saved by the arrival of Soult and his 2nd Corps. Ney then received similar despatches concerning Santiago and hastened with his force to La Coruña, where Maucune received him having fallen back on the place following combat at Campo de Esrella, outside Santiago on 22 May.[17] It was a thoroughly depressing series of events for both Ney and Soult, who met on 30 May at Lugo to discuss a joint plan of future operations. Like the previous four months of the war, this meeting did not go well. Napoleon's vision for national subjugation had clearly failed and reports from the rest of the Peninsula yielded no room for complacency. Following Victor's victory over Cuesta at Medellin, the French were unable to exploit their success, despite the Army of Estremadura being virtually wiped out. Victor considered his force too weak to continue into Portugal alone and implored Joseph to send him more troops for the task. However, by the time he had received his old 2nd Division under Lapisse, he had received additional reports of a containing force under British command to his front. With no word from Soult he was therefore reluctant to advance into the unknown. Furthermore, unable to establish the exact size and composition of this new force to his front, he was convinced that any expedition south into Andalusia would be potentially suicidal. Instead, Victor positioned his three divisions between Mérida and Cáceres and waited for reinforcement, or guidance, from Madrid.

To the east, Blake had been made combined commander of the remnants of the Army of Aragon, the Army of Valencia (which had remained largely inactive) and the Army of Catalonia; following Reding's death from wounds received at the battle of Valls in February. After his victory at Valls, St Cyr had moved three divisions to Vich; Reille remained near the French border at Figueras, and Duhesme at Barcelona, which continued to be the 7th Corps' base for operations. However, from Vich, St Cyr was able to recommence the siege against Girona and to cover his southern flank against possible attack by Blake. St Cyr reopened communications with Reille by sending Lecchi's Italian Division north on a perilous journey that felt the full weight of the *somatenes*. At much the same time, Napoleon was preparing to depart for the Austrian War but before he embarked he sent instructions that both St Cyr and Reille were to be replaced. He was both unsatisfied with the progress in Catalonia and annoyed at the constant string of communiqués, which requested more men, money and stores and which were clearly light on achievement.

---

15   The brigade was from Merle's Division and the two cavalry units from Franceschi.

16   Oman makes an interesting comparison of Soult's withdrawal to that of Moore. See Oman, *History of the Peninsular War*, vol. II, pp.361–363.

---

17   Against el División del Miño, a force organized at the request of La Romana and the Central Junta.

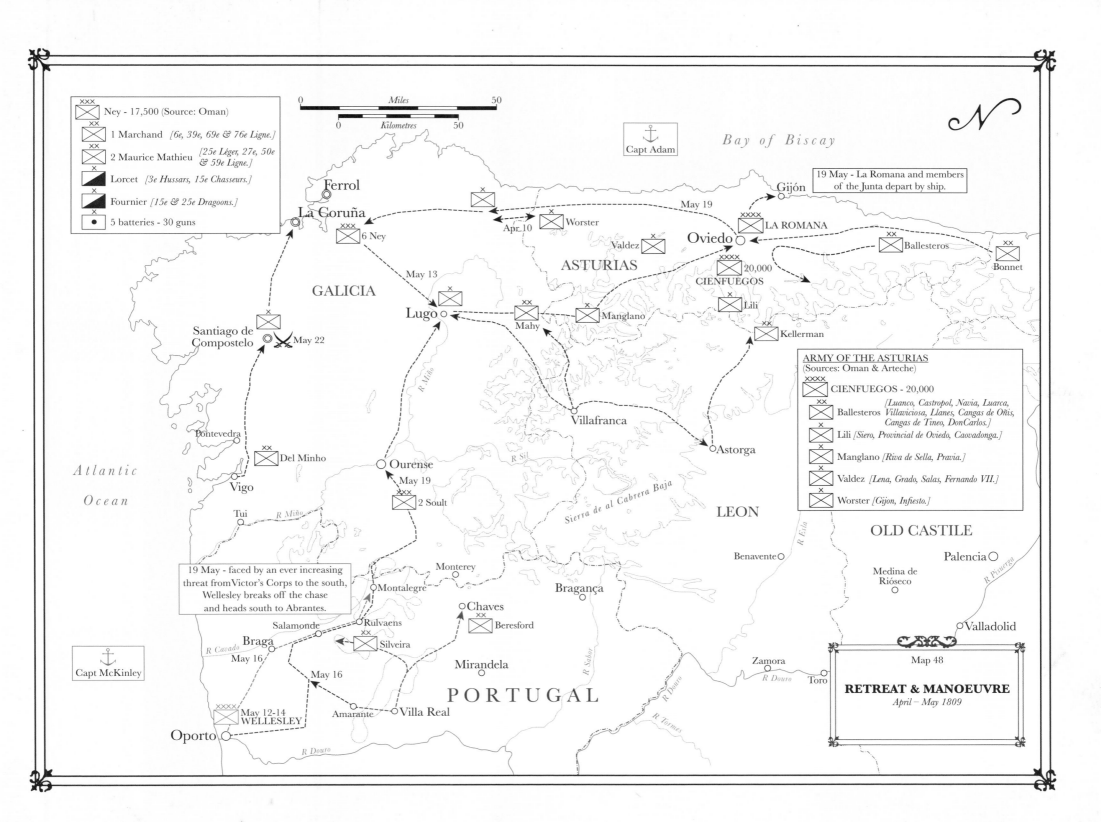

Legend (top left):

- ☒ Ney - 17,500 (Source: Oman)
- ☒ 1 Marchand *[6e, 39e, 69e & 76e Ligne.]*
- ☒ 2 Maurice Mathieu *[25e Léger, 27e, 50e & 59e Ligne.]*
- ◣ Lorcet *[3e Hussars, 15e Chasseurs.]*
- ◣ Fournier *[15e & 25e Dragoons.]*
- • 5 batteries - 30 guns

⚓ Capt Adam

Bay of Biscay

19 May - La Romana and members of the Junta depart by ship.

Gijón

☒ May 19 — Worster
Apr. 10
☒☒☒☒ LA ROMANA
☒ Valdez
Oviedo

Ferrol
La Coruña
☒ 6 Ney
May 19

ASTURIAS

☒☒ Ballesteros
☒☒ Bonnet

☒☒☒☒ 20,000
CIENFUEGOS

May 13
☒

GALICIA

☒ Lili

Santiago de Compostelo ⚔ May 22

☒ Lugo
☒☒ Mahy
☒ Manglano
☒☒ Kellerman

R. Miño

Pontevedra

☒☒ Del Miño

Vigo
Ourense
May 19
R. Sil

Villafranca

Sierra de al Cabrera Baja

Astorga

LEON

ARMY OF THE ASTURIAS
(Sources: Oman & Arteche)

- ☒☒☒☒ CIENFUEGOS - 20,000
- ☒☒ Ballesteros *[Luanco, Castropol, Navia, Luarca, Villaviciosa, Llanes, Cangas de Oñis, Cangas de Tineo, DonCarlos.]*
- ☒ Lili *[Siero, Provincial de Oviedo, Caovadonga.]*
- ☒ Manglano *[Riva de Sella, Pravia.]*
- ☒ Valdez *[Lena, Grado, Salas, Fernando VII.]*
- ☒ Worster *[Gijón, Infiesto.]*

OLD CASTILE

Tui
R. Miño

☒☒☒ 2 Soult

Benavente
R. Esla

Palencia

Medina de Ríoseco

19 May - faced by an ever increasing threat from Victor's Corps to the south, Wellesley breaks off the chase and heads south to Abrantes.

⚓ Capt McKinley

Monterey

Montalegre

Bragança

Valladolid

Salamonde
Rulvaens
☒☒ Silveira

Chaves
☒☒ Beresford

Mirandela

Zamora
R. Douro
Toro

Map 48

Braga
May 16
May 16
R. Cavado

PORTUGAL

Atlantic Ocean

May 16

☒☒☒☒ May 12-14
WELLESLEY

Amarante
Villa Real

R. Sabor

R. Tormes

RETREAT & MANOEUVRE
April – May 1809

Oporto
R. Douro

Verdier[18] replaced Reille almost immediately but St Cyr's replacement, Marshal Augereau, was stricken with a bout of gout en route and did not arrive for a few more weeks. Verdier recommenced the siege against Girona on 24 May, once St Cyr was content that Blake's intended area of operations was Aragon and not Catalonia.

Following the capitulation of Zaragoza, Mortier operated to the north of the Ebro, while Junot remained to the south. Mortier had pushed up to the Pyrenees and taken the fortress at Jaca which yielded another route to France. During the same sortie, Mortier tried to reopen communications with the 7th Corps; the column under Colonel Briche reached Chabot at Montblanch, but when they tried to return the strength of the *somatenes* was such that the unfortunate colonel and his men had to beat a hasty retreat back to Chabot's location and never made it back to the 5th Corps. Junot, meanwhile, had sent Musnier south-west to Daroca and Molina, and Grandjean south-east to Caspe and Alcañiz. The former mission had little success; Grandjean took a key stronghold on the Tortosa to Zaragoza road at Morella, but when on 25 March Blake commenced his advance with Roca's Valencian Division, the French fell back to Alcañiz and ceded their prize. At this juncture, Mortier and Junot decided that a union of their corps would be the best way to proceed, but orders from Paris, dated 5 April, resulted in a change in plan. Napoleon calculated that he might need Mortier's Corps for his Austrian War and sent orders for him to prepare to concentrate his divisions at Tudela. Joseph too was considering using Mortier, but in support of Ney, and when these two contradictory sets of orders arrived from both Paris and Madrid, Mortier was in a quandary. He decided to march to Burgos from where he could still satisfy both directives. It was the right decision, for a few days later Napoleon accepted Joseph's appeals to utilize the corps in the north-west of the country, and Mortier duly set off to Valladolid from where he was to control Old Castile and keep open the lines of communication with Ney and, as it turned out, Soult.

Coupled with the orders for Mortier on 5 April were instructions that command of the 3rd Corps was to pass from Junot to Suchet, one of Mortier's divisional commanders.[19] 'Order General Suchet to repair Saragossa and to take command of the 3rd Corps. The Duc of Abrantès is to return as soon as he is replaced by General Suchet.'[20] However, this communiqué was not promulgated in a timely manner and by the time it was propagated, Suchet was already heading west with Mortier's Corps. It was to be another six weeks before this capable officer retraced his steps and finally assumed command.

---

18   He had conducted the first siege of Zaragoza in 1808.

19   Joseph had sent numerous complaints to Napoleon as to Junot's conduct during and after Zaragoza. General Lejeune, an engineer officer who served with Junot at Zaragoza, considered him mentally unstable, having witnessed him explode with rage after having been persuaded to cancel a suicidal mission which was aimed at gaining him personal glory.

20   Napoleon, *The Confidential Correspondence of Napoleon Bonaparte*, vol. II, p.62.

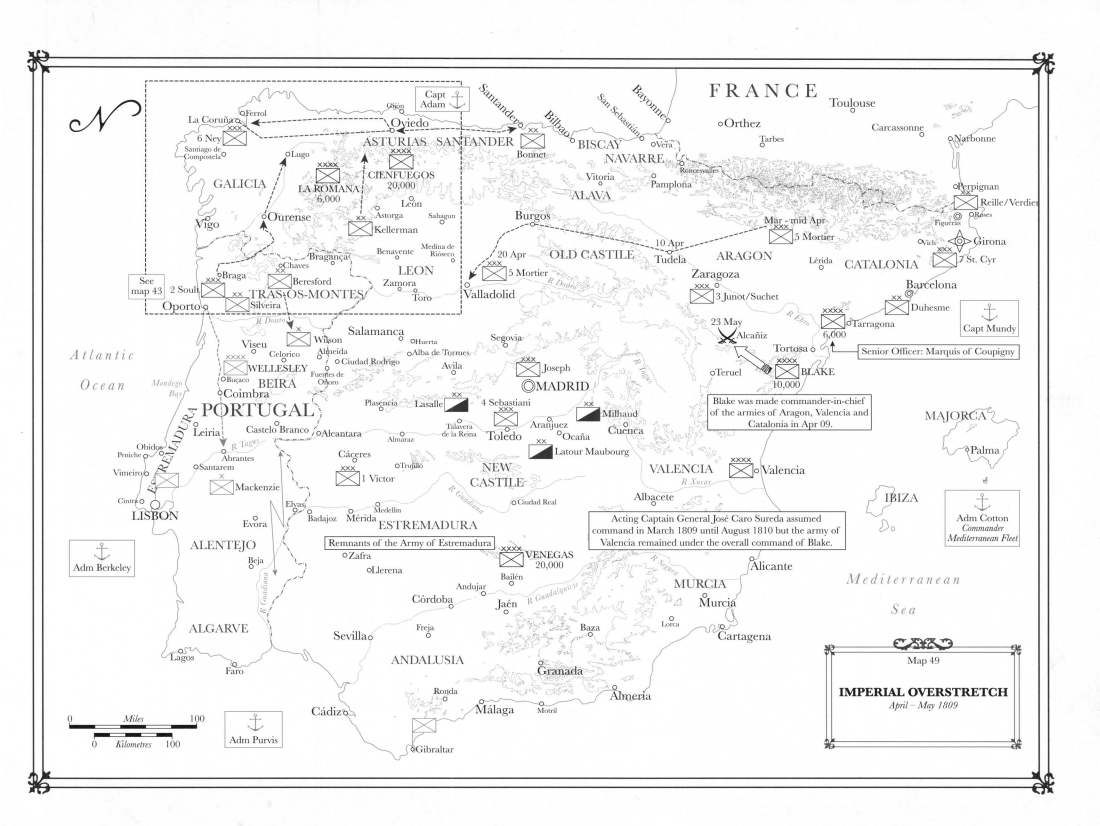

N

FRANCE

Capt Adam

La Coruña Ferrol Gijón Oviedo Santander Bilbao Bayonne Toulouse

6 Ney Orthez Tarbes Carcassonne Narbonne

Santiago de Compostela Lugo ASTURIAS SANTANDER San Sebastián Vera

GALICIA Bonnet BISCAY NAVARRE Roncesvalles Perpignan

LA ROMANA 6,000 CIENFUEGOS 20,000 Vitoria Reille/Verdier

Vigo Ourense León Pamplona ALAVA Roses Figueras

Astorga Sahagun Burgos Mar - mid Apr 5 Mortier Girona

Braganza Kellerman Benavente Medina de Ríoseco 10 Apr ARAGON Lérida CATALONIA 7 St. Cyr

See map 43 Braga Chaves LEON 20 Apr OLD CASTILE Tudela Zaragoza Barcelona

2 Soult Beresford Zamora 5 Mortier R Douro 3 Junot/Suchet Duhesme

TRAS-OS-MONTES Silveira Toro Valladolid 23 May Alcañiz Tarragona 6,000

Oporto Wilson Salamanca Segovia Tortosa Senior Officer: Marquis of Coupigny

Viseu Huerta Teruel BLAKE 10,000

WELLESLEY Celorico Almeida Alba de Tormes Avila Joseph

Buçaco BEIRA Ciudad Rodrigo Blake was made commander-in-chief of the armies of Aragon, Valencia and Catalonia in Apr 09.

Coimbra Fuentes de Oñoro MADRID

PORTUGAL Plasencia Lasalle 4 Sebastiani Aranjuez Milhaud MAJORCA

Leiria Castelo Branco Alcantara Talavera de la Reina Ocaña Cuenca Palma

Obidos Abrantes Almaraz Toledo Latour Maubourg VALENCIA R Xucar

Peniche Santarem Cáceres Latour Maubourg

Vimeiro Trujillo NEW CASTILE Valencia IBIZA

Cintra Mackenzie Elvas Medellin R Guadiana Ciudad Real Albacete

LISBON Evora Badajoz Mérida ESTREMADURA Acting Captain General José Caro Sureda assumed command in March 1809 until August 1810 but the army of Valencia remained under the overall command of Blake.

Adm Berkeley ALENTEJO Beja Remnants of the Army of Estremadura Zafra VENEGAS 20,000 Alicante Mediterranean

ALGARVE Llerena Andujar Bailén MURCIA Sea

Lagos Faro Córdoba Jaén Murcia Lorca

Freja Baza

Sevilla ANDALUSIA Cartagena

Ronda Granada Almeria

Cádiz Málaga Motril

Gibraltar

Atlantic Ocean Mondego Bay R Tagus R Tagus R Guadalquivir R Segura

Capt Mundy

Adm Cotton Commander Mediterranean Fleet

Adm Purvis

0 Miles 100
0 Kilometres 100

Map 49

IMPERIAL OVERSTRETCH
April – May 1809

Chapter 18

SUCHET: AN INAUSPICIOUS START

'This general [Suchet] has, in the French army, a great reputation for boldness and good fortune. An uncommonly good education has given him the advantages of a mind well stored with knowledge. He is extremely active, and appears to have been a favourite with Napoleon, because he always was as dextrous in pleasing his superiors, as he is severe towards those under his command.'[1] Quite simply, he was the right man for the job, for when he finally assumed command of his new Corps on 19 May he found both it and the situation in Aragon, in disarray.

With the movement of the 5th Corps from the area four weeks previously, the 3rd Corps was insufficient to hold down the key cities and towns as well as the large and inhospitable landmass inbetween. Grandjean's two brigades had both experienced setbacks: Habert at Monzon and Leval at Alcañiz. The latter was merely forced to pull back, but the former lost a 1,000-man vanguard when, following a flash storm, the river rose and cut them off. Suchet, on assuming command, realized that his new command was both demoralized in mind and deficient in number.[2] Both Grandjean and Musnier's divisions were undersized and the 3rd Division was absent, with one brigade seconded to Kellermann and employed in the Asturias, and the second split up and scattered around Navarre. Pay was in arrears; food scarce and the rigours of the siege of Zaragoza had not had time to heal. Recognition and plaudits following the siege had been largely bestowed upon the 5th Corps. Finally, the rising levels of insurgent attacks were taking their toll. Suchet, like Wellesley a month earlier, decided that the best form of defence was therefore a vigorous offence, and two days after assuming command, he marched from Zaragoza to join Leval at Hijar.

Meanwhile Blake, who had assumed command of the armies of Aragon, Catalonia and Valencia in April, was trying to corral these forces and make amends for his defeats at Zornoza and Espinosa. However, from Catalonia there were no troops to be had; the remnants from the battle of Valls were still recovering inside the walls at Tarragona. Blake marched to join the sole surviving division from Aragon, under the Marquis of Lazan, that was concentrated at Tortosa; he took with him all he could muster from Valencia.[3] Initially this was only Roca's Division from the old Army of the Centre but by mid-June another 12,000 were trained, equipped and en

route to join Blake. For now Blake's army numbered about 10,000 and it was this force that fell on Leval's Division on 19 May at Alcañiz, forcing him to withdraw. Four days later, Suchet presented himself in front of Blake at the same position; he had about 8,000 men and three batteries of guns. Suchet had some difficulty determining the Spanish dispositions and could not initially see the town of Alcañiz, which lay behind the hills to the west. Blake, having been in the area for some days, had established a strong defensive position west of the river; its significant vulnerability was that the bridge over the river Guadalope provided the only means of withdrawal. 'On a close examination of the position, it was hoped that by seizing upon the hill of Las Horcas, which from its situation before the defile of the bridge and the outlets of the town, covered the enemy's line, it would require no effort to silence the wings, by which means we should take a great number of prisoners.'[4] Suchet crafted his attack accordingly. His plan was to keep the two wings, under Areizaga and Roca, occupied with 'two movements' and then deliver the main effort onto the Spanish centre, which once captured would dominate the bridge and defile to the town.

Leval's Division was tasked with attacking Areizaga's Division on the Spanish right, supported by a diversionary attack on the Spanish left. However, the French attacks were not coordinated and Leval's first attempt was easily beaten back. Exposed, he felt compelled to re-engage despite the fact that the two battalions earmarked for the southern attack were still not in position. This second attempt was also repulsed, but during the controlled withdrawal the Spanish cavalry were badly assailed when they tried to charge the retreating infantry in the flank, only to receive the full weight of Wathier's one-and-a-half regiments who were up providing support. The other attacks had still not commenced but Blake concluded that the French main effort was against his right wing and moved the entire cavalry and two battalions from Roca's Division to bolster the right. As these troops were moving north, Musnier's Division undertook the main attack in the centre, at much the same time that the diversionary movement began on the French right. The three battalions of the 114e Ligne and two of the 1e Vistula formed into columns of battalions and marched, under the command of Brigadier General Fabre, steadily across the flat ground in front of the hill and then began to scale the feature. The diversionary attack on the Spanish left was not pressed and, in consequence, many of Roca's right-hand units were able to bring enfilade fire down on the advancing infantry attacking Lanzan's position. Fabre's men then walked into a hail of grape and canister from the massed Spanish guns to their front; the effect was decisive and instant. The advance ceased, the momentum was broken and the French lines briefly wavered and then broke. Suchet rallied his demoralized infantry but now recognized – beyond doubt – that these men did not posses the *esprit de corps* demonstrated by the veterans of his previous command[5] and wisely decided against renewing the offensive. As night fell he pulled back along the Zaragoza road, the confidence of the commander, and the morale of the officers and soldiers of the 3rd Corps severely shaken. A false alarm during this retreat had Leval's troops scattering in all directions and order was not fully restored until the following morning.

1   Sarrazin, *History of the War in Spain and Portugal*, pp.88–89.

2   There were only half the 20,000 accounted for in the muster rolls.

3   The Junta at Valencia was doing its best to provide both funds and troops for the greater Spanish cause.

4   Suchet, *Memoirs of the War with Spain*, vol. I, pp.19–20.

5   His old division had given an excellent account of themselves at Ulm, Austerlitz and Jena.

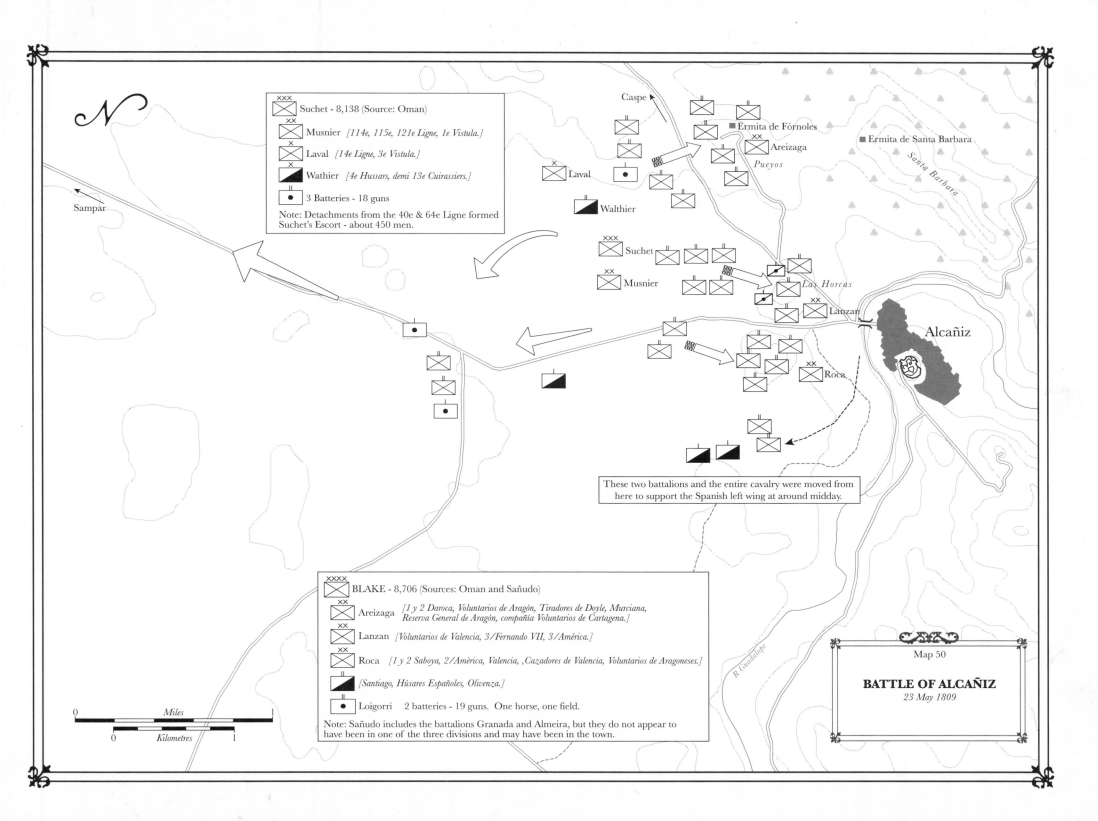

N

Sampar

Suchet - 8,138 (Source: Oman)

Musnier [114e, 115e, 121e Ligne, 1e Vistula.]

Laval [14e Ligne, 3e Vistula.]

Wathier [4e Hussars, demi 13e Cuirassiers.]

3 Batteries - 18 guns

Note: Detachments from the 40e & 64e Ligne formed Suchet's Escort - about 450 men.

Caspe

Ermita de Fórnoles

Ermita de Santa Barbara

Areizaga

Pueyos

Santa Barbara

Laval

Walthier

Suchet

Musnier

Las Horcas

Lanzan

Alcañiz

Roca

These two battalions and the entire cavalry were moved from here to support the Spanish left wing at around midday.

BLAKE - 8,706 (Sources: Oman and Sañudo)

Areizaga [1 y 2 Daroca, Voluntarios de Aragón, Tiradores de Doyle, Murciana, Reserva General de Aragón, compañía Voluntarios de Cartagena.]

Lanzan [Voluntarios de Valencia, 3/Fernando VII, 3/América.]

Roca [1 y 2 Saboya, 2/Amèrica, Valencia, ,Cazadores de Valencia, Voluntarios de Aragoneses.]

[Santiago, Húsares Españoles, Olivenza.]

Loigorri 2 batteries - 19 guns. One horse, one field.

Note: Sañudo includes the battalions Granada and Almeira, but they do not appear to have been in one of the three divisions and may have been in the town.

R Guadalope

Miles
0   1

Kilometres
0   1

Map 50

BATTLE OF ALCAÑIZ
23 May 1809

Suchet now appreciated the complexity and burden of his mission. Zaragoza itself was now threatened, forcing him to withdraw to the city and plead for reinforcement from Madrid. He recalled all his outlying posts, surrendered the open country and waited for the inevitable attack. It was not forthcoming. As it turned out, Blake was not in pursuit of the 3rd Corps; well aware that their forces were equally balanced, he decided to wait for the long-anticipated reinforcements from Valencia before taking up the offensive. 'Blake was satisfied to revive his troops after the attained victory, and was content to limit activity to military exercises and the movement of cantonments.'[6] Within three weeks Blake had amassed an army of 25,000 men and now felt confident to commence operations against Suchet. As he approached Zaragoza, news of Napoleon's crushing defeat at Essling raised Spanish morale and expectations considerably, but not to the point of convincing Blake to risk an all-out assault on the city itself. Instead he opted to cut the French lines of communication to Tudela and Logroño in an attempt to coerce the French to leave the city. This was an optimistic aspiration given the price of capturing the place only months earlier. With his lines threatened, but very much against his wishes, Suchet acknowledged that he would have to venture from the city confines and engage the Spaniards; a humiliating withdrawal was not an option.

Joseph had agreed to the return of Robert's Brigade[7] from Kellermann's forces, which were still operating in the Asturias, but their arrival was going to take time. In the interim, Suchet deployed General Fabre with 1,200 men down the valley of the river Huerva, to provide timely warning of any Spanish approach. He had left Leval with 2,000 men and a battery of guns to cover the city of Zaragoza, from the commanding heights of Monte Torrero, and to counter any possible flanking manoeuvre by the Spanish. Blake split his advancing force; on 13 June he advanced Areizaga's Division to Botorita, while the same day he moved with the main body from Cariñena to Longarès and Muel. Just short of Botorita, Areizaga crossed the Huerva and effectively cut off Fabre who was located in the village, on the left bank, forcing Suchet to react in support of his subordinate. He advanced with his entire force, less one battalion,[8] brushing aside Creagh's small vanguard and was preparing to advance upon the Spanish position at Botorita when Musnier's troops came up against Blake's main body, which by now had advanced, from Longarès and Muel. Blake hoped that Suchet's demoralized force would withdraw back to Zaragoza but Suchet had no such intentions. He established his headquarters in the Abbey of Sante-Fé and worked out his battle plans for the following day. He also sent officers back up the Tudela road to collect Fabre's Brigade (which had extracted itself over the mountains) and to hasten the forces of Robert who were, by now, a few kilometres from Zaragoza.

With the exception of Musnier's Division, the balance of Suchet's forces was positioned across the valley floor, while those of Musnier were pushed out on to the heights on the French right facing the two lines of Spanish infantry. Suchet was in no great hurry; Robert had not yet arrived on the field, and most of the next morning was spent in bickering fire between outposts. Blake was frustrated by this relative inactivity and, at around midday, resolved to take the offensive.[9] As the Spanish began to move, Suchet also ordered his forces to attack. 'The movement commenced along the whole line, at the very instant when the Spanish army put itself in motion, and extended its left as if with the intention to outflank us. General Suchet proceeded at once to the extreme right, for the purpose of preventing this manoeuvre; he detached the lancers and 200 skirmishers to the flank, whilst a battalion of the 114e marched direct upon the enemy in column of attack.'[10] At the same time the balance of Musnier's Division fell upon that of Roca and for some while the fighting was inconclusive. In the centre, Roca's troops succeeded in pushing back the 155e Ligne prompting Suchet to deploy the battalion of the 64e Ligne and the 2e Vistula but neither were used as Harispe managed to restore the line.

At this moment, a violent thunderstorm broke, lasting many minutes and reducing visibility to a few metres. When the downpour abated Suchet immediately ordered Wathier to charge the Spanish cavalry to their front and to support Habert's Brigade in their attempt to get in behind the troops of Roca and Lazan. O'Donojú's cavalry were quickly overcome and their commander killed; Wathier's light cavalry pursued the retreating Spanish down the road to Maria where they captured the two battalions and a troop of guns left to hold the place. Habert's infantry had followed up in the wake of the cavalry charge and when they were past the line of Spanish infantry on the hill they swung right off the road and into the rear of Roca's division. Blake immediately ordered Lazan to pivot at an oblique angle to the road and establish a hasty defensive line, through which Roca's troops withdrew in an orderly fashion. It was a well-executed manoeuvre, which enabled Blake's entire force to withdraw and break contact. He rejoined Areizaga at Botorita but after a quick counsel decided to withdraw to Belchite that evening. He arrived on 16 June and turned to face Suchet, who was hot on his heels with a strengthened force of 13,000 men; Blake conversely had lost many men during the retreat and only had nine guns remaining, as the others had been lost the previous day. Blake realized that a battle would be suicidal for his depleted force and therefore ordered his army to withdraw and disperse. Suchet now had the breathing space he so badly required.

---

6   Toreno, *Guerra de la Independencia, El 2 de Mayo de 1808*, vol. III, p.92.

7   This brigade included the 116e and 117e Ligne – a total of six battalions, 3,000 men.

8   The 121e Ligne, who were left at Zaragoza under the command of Colonel Hazo.

9   It was at this point that, arguably, he could have called up Areizaga's Division, which would have been with him within two hours. The division had already achieved its aim by forcing Suchet to split his force.

10   Suchet, *Memoirs of the War with Spain*, vol. I, p.31.

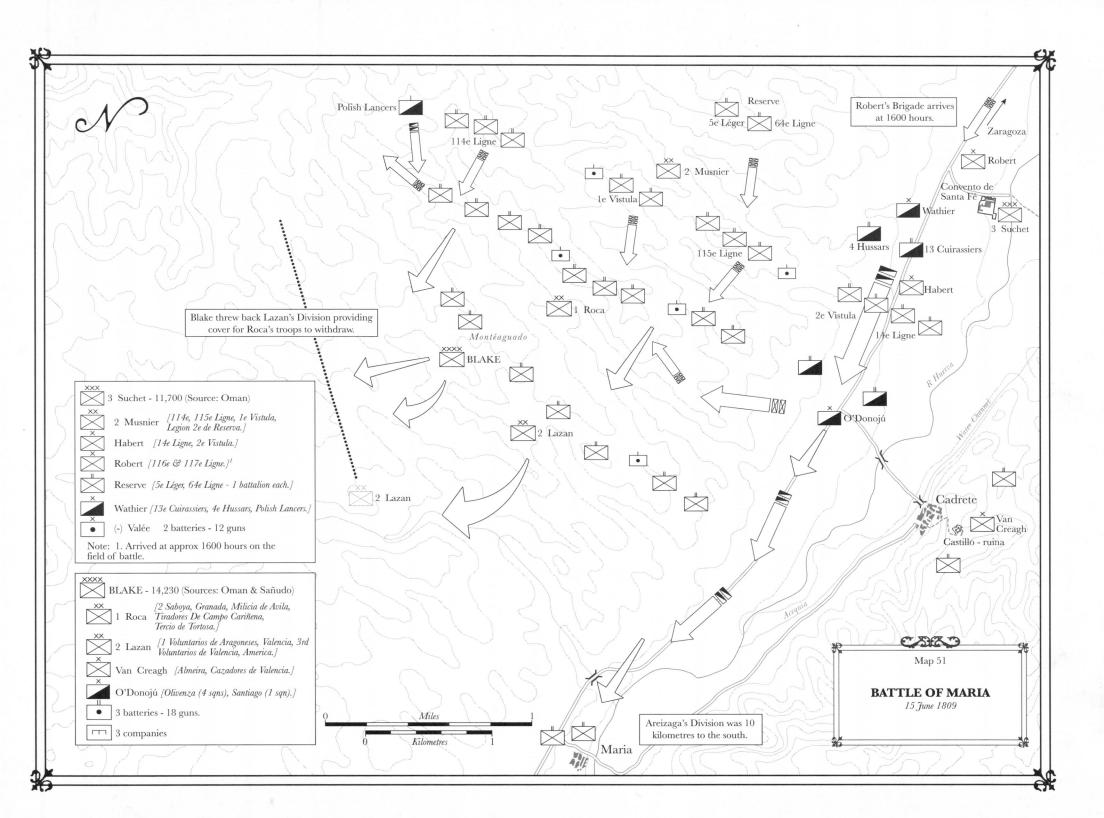

N

Polish Lancers

Reserve
5e Léger 64e Ligne

Robert's Brigade arrives
at 1600 hours.

Zaragoza

Robert

114e Ligne

2 Musnier

Convento de
Santa Fé

Wathier

3 Suchet

1e Vistula

4 Hussars 13 Cuirassiers

115e Ligne

Habert

2e Vistula

Blake threw back Lazan's Division providing
cover for Roca's troops to withdraw.

14e Ligne

R Huerva

1 Roca

Montéaguado

BLAKE

O'Donojú

2 Lazan

Water Channel

2 Lazan

Cadrete

Van
Creagh

Castillo - ruina

3 Suchet - 11,700 (Source: Oman)

2 Musnier [114e, 115e Ligne, 1e Vistula,
Legion 2e de Reserva.]

Habert [14e Ligne, 2e Vistula.]

Robert [116e & 117e Ligne.]¹

Reserve [5e Léger, 64e Ligne - 1 battalion each.]

Wathier [13e Cuirassiers, 4e Hussars, Polish Lancers.]

(-) Valée   2 batteries - 12 guns

Note: 1. Arrived at approx 1600 hours on the
field of battle.

BLAKE - 14,230 (Sources: Oman & Sañudo)

1 Roca [2 Saboya, Granada, Milicia de Avila,
Tiradores De Campo Cariñena,
Tercio de Tortosa.]

2 Lazan [1 Voluntarios de Aragoneses, Valencia, 3rd
Voluntarios de Valencia, America.]

Van Creagh [Almeira, Cazadores de Valencia.]

O'Donojú [Olivenza (4 sqns), Santiago (1 sqn).]

3 batteries - 18 guns.

3 companies

Areizaga's Division was 10
kilometres to the south.

Map 51

BATTLE OF MARIA
15 June 1809

0   Miles   1

0   Kilometres   1

Maria

Chapter 19 ❧

THE TALAVERA CAMPAIGN: MAY TO JULY 1809

Having freed Oporto, deprived Soult of his artillery and driven him from Portugal, Wellesley now turned his attention to his next priority; that of Victor's 1st Corps in Estremadura. Leaving Silveira to watch the northern corridor, and detaching all the Portuguese who had accompanied him during the previous operation to watch the approaches from Leon, Wellesley sent his army south amidst reports from Mackenzie that Victor was beginning to stir. However, before committing to a plan of campaign, Wellesley wrote to Cuesta and asked for his views on how – and whether – to prosecute future operations collectively.

Victor, strengthened by the return of Lapisse's Division on 19 April, still considered himself too weak to move against either Cuesta to the south or the Portuguese to the west. He elected to wait for word from Madrid, or from Soult, before executing his part of Napoleon's plan. While he waited, he received reports that a Portuguese force[1] had taken the Roman bridge at Alcantara. It was a provocation he could not ignore and he swiftly despatched Lapisse and a brigade of dragoons to remove them. A skirmish on 14 May resulted in Mayne's eviction, during which the Lusitanian Legion unsuccessfully tried to blow the bridge. It was of little consequence, and a few days later Victor withdrew his men and Mayne returned to reoccupy the town and the crossing. Victor was well aware that just lingering indefinitely in Estremadura would not meet with Napoleonic approval and with a lack of provisions and his force demonstrating levels of sickness at unprecedented rates; he decided to submit a cogent case to Madrid requesting reinforcement or repositioning. He was granted the latter, and between 14 to 19 June he withdrew to the north bank of the Tagus and established his corps between Almaraz and Talavera, confident that the river and his defensive position would be sufficient to hold any attack by Cuesta's Army of Estremadura.

Meanwhile, Wellesley and Cuesta discussed various proposals for combined operations: these were all predicated on Victor's advanced position and subsequent plans had to be readjusted in light of Victor's redeployment. Wellesley was in a melancholy mood. Since evicting Soult little money had been received, his army was two months in arrears, he could not pay what he owed to the Portuguese, rations were in short supply, replacement equipment was held up for want of transport and pay for the mule trains and the long-awaited reinforcements[2] were taking forever to reach him from Lisbon. Furthermore, his correspondence with Cuesta

had not gone well. He wrote to the British Plenipotentiary, Frere, on 13 June, outlining his frustration, 'I can only say that the obstinacy of this old gentleman is throwing out of our hands the finest game that any armies ever had'.[3]

With the arrival of a sum of money and the basis of a plan, but still devoid of various reinforcements, Wellesley crossed into Spain on 3 July. The French, having withdrawn the reconnaissance patrols from the border, had no idea of the whereabouts of the British force. Even as late as 8 July when Wellesley reached Plasencia, Joseph appeared ignorant of this significant threat, just four days' march from the capital. To be fair, his attention had been drawn south when, on 20 June, Venegas had descended from the Sierra Morena and proceeded to push back Sebastiani's outposts at Madridejos. Although Sebastiani estimated the Spanish force to be 40,000, in fact it was only 13,000 infantry and 2,000 cavalry, but Sebastiani's protestations to Madrid prompted Joseph to order Victor to return the divisions of Leval and Merlin to their rightful corps. He himself came down with every available man from the central reserve at Madrid. Sebastiani had refused to fight until these reinforcements arrived; as they approached Venegas he headed back to the safety of the Sierra. Joseph pursued him, but news of Cuesta's advance further west called an early halt to this recklessness.

The Spanish had repaired the bridge at Almaraz and had begun to cross the river Tagus. Joseph left Sebastiani on the line of the river Guadiana, to watch Venegas, and then returned north to support Victor, who had fallen back eastwards towards Madrid, on receipt of the news of the Cuesta's movement. Cuesta's force posed a significant threat; recruiting and training had been undertaken at a commendable rate and the army now stood at over 40,000 men. On 8 July Wellesley reached Plasencia and made arrangements to link up with Cuesta who was now (across the Tagus) positioned around Almaraz. The two commanders met on 10 July and, after four hours of strained discussion and debate, not helped by the fact that Wellesley did not speak much Spanish and Cuesta spoke no French or English, they agreed a plan that was issued the following day. With Venegas tasked to occupy Sebastiani, the two commanders expected to confront a combined force of Victor's Corps and King Joseph's Reserves, numbering about 35,000, at or around Talavera. It is clear that both Allied commanders were ignorant of events to the north; where Soult was now massing 50,000 men, poised to march south if required.[4] Furthermore, the very subject of the strength and composition of the Allied northern screening force created considerable tension between the Allied commanders. In the end a mere 600 men under the Marquis de Reino were despatched to join forces with Sir Robert Wilson's small Portuguese brigade and cover the passes at Perales and Puerto de Baños. It was a serious miscalculation.

---

1   This was Mayne with the 1st Battalion of the Loyal Lusitanian Legion supported by a regiment of militia, and a squadron of the Legion's cavalry and a battery of their guns.

2   Including the new Light Division under General Robert Craufurd, consisting of the 43rd, 52nd and 95th, as well as Ross and Bull's troops of the Royal Horse Artillery and the 48th and 61st of Foot and 23rd Light Dragoons. However, he had to relinquish the 2/29th and the 2/30th, who returned to Gibraltar, and two squadrons of the 20th Light Dragoons and one squadron of the 3rd Hussars KGL, who went to Sicily.

3   The relationship between Cuesta and Wellesley was strained: Cuesta did not trust him as a foreigner, but most significantly he believed Wellesley was trying to gain the post of *generalissimo* of all the Spanish armies behind his back. This proposal was initially floated by Frere and supported by some in the Central Junta in Sevilla. With this in mind, it is hardly surprising that Cuesta's attitude to Wellesley was tinged with resentment and suspicion.

4   Napoleon, *The Confidential Correspondence of Napoleon Bonaparte*, vol. II, p.66.

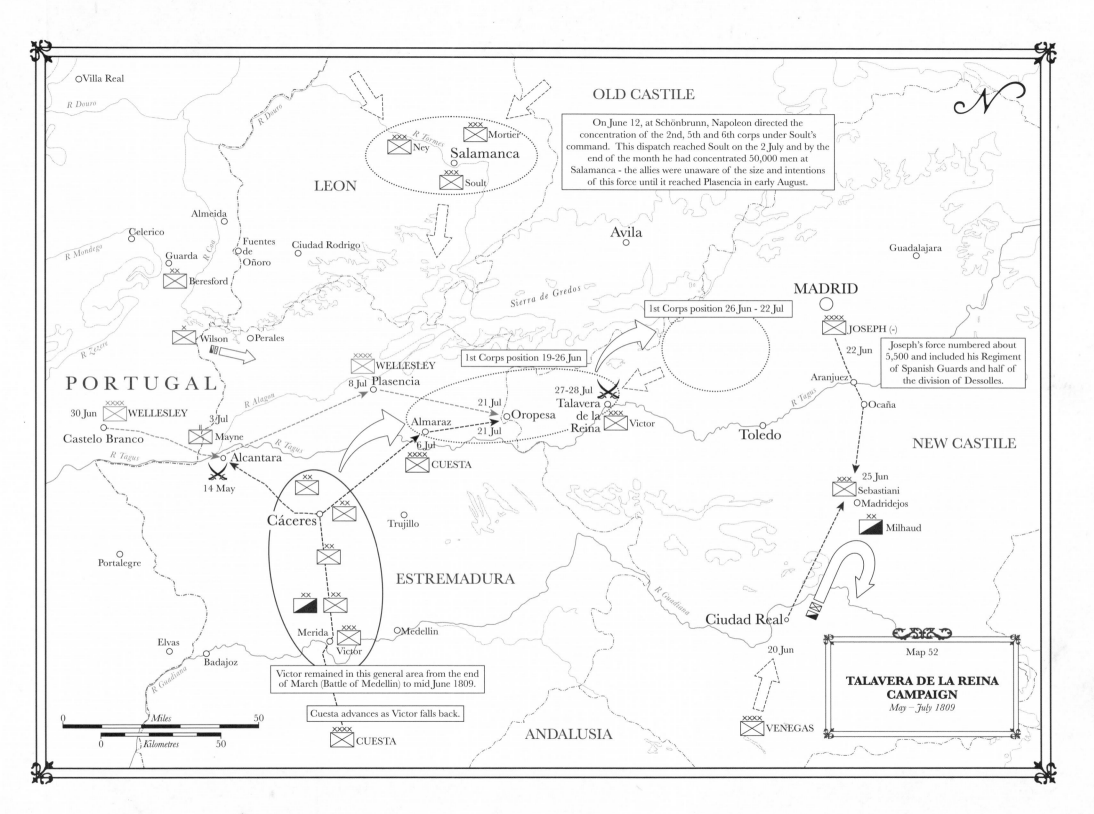

OLD CASTILE

On June 12, at Schönbrunn, Napoleon directed the concentration of the 2nd, 5th and 6th corps under Soult's command. This dispatch reached Soult on the 2 July and by the end of the month he had concentrated 50,000 men at Salamanca - the allies were unaware of the size and intentions of this force until it reached Plasencia in early August.

Villa Real

R Douro

R Douro

R Tormes Ney   Mortier

Salamanca

Soult

LEON

Avila

Guadalajara

MADRID

Almeida

Celerico

R Mondego

R Coa

Guarda   Beresford

Fuentes de Oñoro

Ciudad Rodrigo

Sierra de Gredos

Do

1st Corps position 26 Jun - 22 Jul

JOSEPH (-)

22 Jun

R Zezere

Wilson   Perales

PORTUGAL

WELLESLEY

8 Jul Plasencia

1st Corps position 19-26 Jun

Aranjuez

Joseph's force numbered about 5,500 and included his Regiment of Spanish Guards and half of the division of Dessolles.

30 Jun   WELLESLEY

R Alagon

3 Jul

21 Jul

27-28 Jul

Talavera de la Reina

Ocaña

R Tagus

Castelo Branco

Mayne

R Tagus

Almaraz

Oropesa

Victor

Toledo

NEW CASTILE

R Tagus

Alcantara

6 Jul

21 Jul

14 May

CUESTA

25 Jun
Sebastiani

Cáceres

Trujillo

Madridejos

Milhaud

Portalegre

ESTREMADURA

R Guadiana

Ciudad Real

Elvas

Merida   Medellin

Badajoz

Victor

Map 52

R Guadiana

Victor remained in this general area from the end of March (Battle of Medellin) to mid June 1809.

TALAVERA DE LA REINA CAMPAIGN

May – July 1809

Cuesta advances as Victor falls back.

20 Jun

ANDALUSIA

CUESTA

VENEGAS

Miles

0   50

Kilometres

0   50

Of more immediate concern however, were events on the Allied right flank. Venegas had been sent orders, and a timetable, to ensure that his force of 23,000 occupied Sebastiani long enough to prevent him breaking clean and joining the French at Talavera. Both Wellesley and Cuesta had delayed their advance until 18 July to allow enough time for Venegas to receive and act on his part of the plan. Cuesta's forces joined Wellesley's at Oropesa on 21 July and the following morning began to engage Latour-Maubourg's cavalry screen. The French cavalry pulled back but Joseph now had confirmation that the British and Spanish had joined forces and immediately recalled Sebastiani who, along with his reserves, were to march to support Victor who had established a good defensive position at Talavera. At the same time, he sent word to Soult to abandon plans for the invasion of northern Portugal or to besiege Ciudad Rodrigo and to move south and engage the Allies in the rear.

The Allied plan vis-à-vis threat assessment was now out of kilter. To make matters worse, Venegas had not closed sufficiently with Sebastiani's force, enabling the 4th Corps to extract itself and move to Toledo. The 4th Corps fell back, crossing the Alberche, and joined the balance of Victor's Corps that was in a strong defensive position of the eastern bank, with the left flank against the Tagus and the right against a steep wooded feature. The Allies pressed to the line of the Alberche, despite the presence of the two French corps, and with the river fordable in numerous places Wellesley elected for a dawn attack the next day. What followed remains subject to disagreement. Cuesta was reluctant to assent to Wellesley's plan, but British reports claim that later that night he agreed to operations the following morning. Accordingly, the British force began moving into position at 0300 hours, but there was no sign of the Spanish. Wellesley rode to Cuesta's camp and a heated exchange between the commanders failed to resolve the impasse. The attack was delayed by 24 hours to allow Cuesta to conduct a more thorough reconnaissance.[5] The delay provided Victor time to gather better intelligence on the force to his front; the substantial British presence was a surprise. Joseph too had received similar confirmation of the size and composition of the Allied force and later in the day ordered Victor and Sebastiani to fall back that night and concentrate at Toledo. The Allied attack, planned for 24 July, thereby discovered vacated French positions; the second part of the Allied plan had failed.

Relations between the Allied commanders were now strained to breaking point and when Cuesta announced his intention to pursue Victor, Wellesley refused to follow. Cuesta, keen to dispel growing animosity towards him within the Central Junta, set off on his own later in the day. The following evening he came across elements of Victor's force a few kilometres from Toledo, but was astonished to discover that there were nearly 50,000 Frenchmen behind them. The French were equally astonished to discover that only the Spanish were to their front. Cuesta beat a hasty retreat with the French hot on his heels; Zayas's Division supported by two cavalry regiments bought enough time for Cuesta to rejoin the British and take up a position in front of Talavera.[6]

At about midday on 27 July, when the last remnants of Cuesta's army were passing over the Alberche, French cavalry appeared and the British divisions of Sherbrooke and Mackenzie, who had deployed forward to cover the Spanish, also withdrew to the west bank. During the withdrawal Mackenzie's Division was taken in the flank by Lapisse's Division, which had crossed the Alberche further to the north and then advanced south, unobserved, through the trees and the smoke of burning huts.[7] The speed and ferocity of the French attack broke the 2/31st, 2/87th and 88th battalions, but the 45th and the company of the 5/60th held firm and Wellesley was able to rally the battalions on these pivots while Anson's light horse covered their flanks. Lapisse continued to press, supported by two batteries of horse artillery, but the line held and the red-coated infantry fell back in reasonable order and assumed their places within the defensive line. At the same time, a number of French batteries[8] deployed onto the front of the Cerro de Cascajal and opened up on the lines nearest to them. At about 1900 hours, the infantry of both Victor and Sebastiani followed, the latter preceded by Merlin's light cavalry who used the cover of the olive trees to push up to reconnoitre the Spanish lines. As the chasseurs came in sight, the front battalions of both Manglano and Portago's divisions opened fire, and then followed the most extraordinary scenes as four of the forward battalions broke and ran to the rear for no apparent reason.[9] The battalions on both sides and those to the rear held firm and at no time was there a gap that could have been exploited. To the north however, in the British defensive line, just such an exploitable opportunity was presented to Victor. Hill's two brigades had not deployed to their destined positions but were situated some 500–700m to the rear, either side of the slopes of the Cerro de Medellin. Victor had quickly grasped that the Medellin was the vital ground and with the Sierra de Segurilla devoid of troops he elected to risk a night attack to seize the feature and turn the Allied flank.

At about 2100 hours, Ruffin's three regiments moved forward in battalion columns, with the 9e Léger in the centre to deliver a frontal attack while the 24e Ligne and 96e Ligne were to undertake flanking attacks on the right and left respectively. The 9e Léger came upon Löwe's Brigade and completely surprised the Germans who, along with the rest of the Allied line, had not anticipated commencement of battle until the following dawn. 'In retreating, the skirmishers [of the 9e] received the fire of the seventh line battalion, which regiment and part of the fifth being thrown into confusion by the suddenness of the attack, were charged by the French column, and gave way; they were, however, rallied by Major Berger and Adjutant Delius, the latter of whom received a severe wound in the arm.'[10] The 9e Léger continued up the Medellin

5   Toreno, *Guerra de la Independencia, El 2 de Mayo 1808*, vol. III, p.108, offers no support to Cuesta's reasons for delay but dismisses suggestions that Cuesta did not attack because the 23rd was a Sunday, and that a Spanish staff officer talked directly with the French, one supposes, warning them of their predicament.

6   Even this episode created friction between the commanders as Cuesta refused to withdraw to the west of the Alberche until 27 July, but he did agree that Wellesley's defensive line was sound and he immediately fell in line with his plans.

7   Oman, *History of the Peninsular War*, vol II, p.504. These huts had been constructed by Victor's soldiers a few days prior on the Cazalegas Heights and had been set alight by the British as they withdrew.

8   Initially this was the two horse artillery batteries of the 1st Corps and was followed by the three field batteries from the three divisions of the same corps.

9   This incident has been inaccurately reported in some British sources, even suggesting that the entire Spanish line and all their artillery gave way. The four battalions in question; the 1st and 2nd Badajoz, Leales de Fernando VII and Toledo (Toreno incorrectly lists Trujillo) were hunted down by Cuesta's cavalry and after a court martial the following day 25-30 were executed. The number would have been higher had Wellesley not intervened. However, it has to be added that there were British stragglers amongst the throng which fled west, spreading alarm and despondency ~ Napier, *Autobiography of*, p.108.

10   Beamish, *History of the King's German Legion*, vol I, pp.208–9.

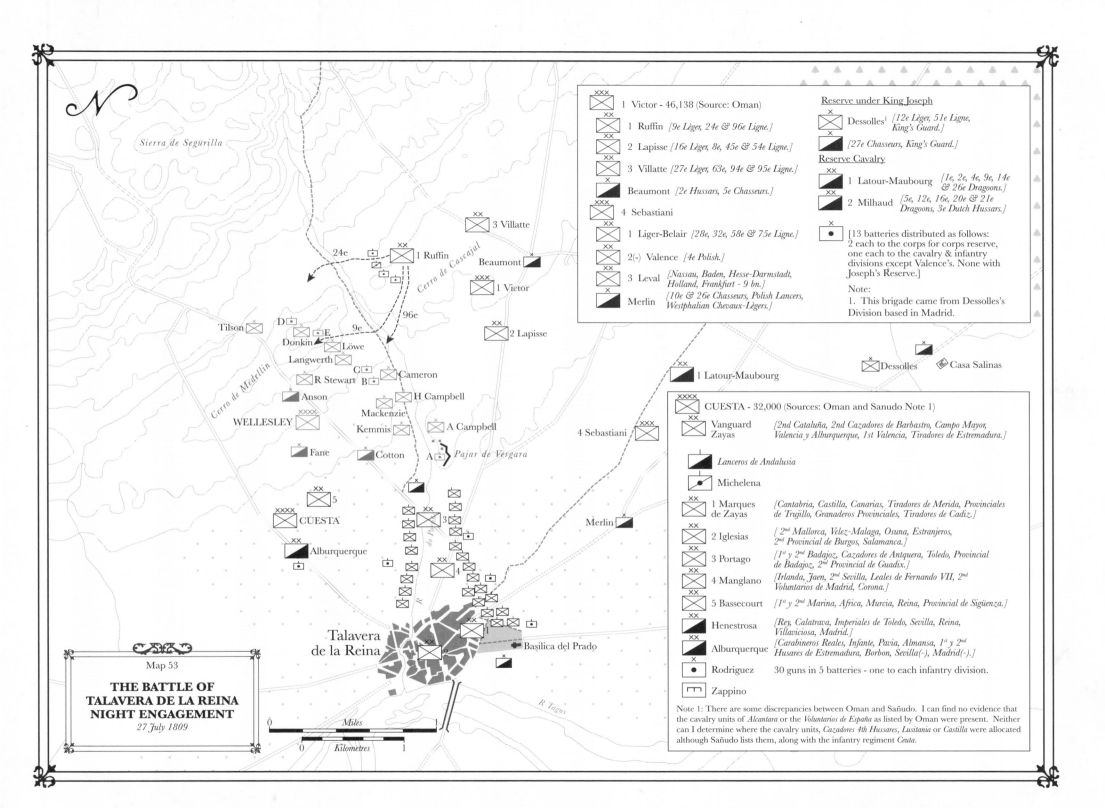

N

Sierra de Segurilla

3 Villatte

24e

1 Ruffin   *Cerro de Cascajal*   Beaumont

Beaumont

1 Victor

96e

Tilson   D   9e   E   Donkin   Löwe   Langwerth   C   R Stewart   B   Cameron

2 Lapisse

Anson   H Campbell

Mackenzie

WELLESLEY   Kemmis   A Campbell

Fane   *Pajar de Vergara*   A

Cotton

4 Sebastiani

5

CUESTA   3

Merlin

Alburquerque   4

Talavera
de la Reina   Basílica del Prado

R Tagus

Map 53

**THE BATTLE OF
TALAVERA DE LA REINA
NIGHT ENGAGEMENT**
27 July 1809

0   *Miles*   1

0   *Kilometres*   1

1 Victor - 46,138 (Source: Oman)

1 Ruffin *[9e Lèger, 24e & 96e Ligne.]*

2 Lapisse *[16e Lèger, 8e, 45e & 54e Ligne.]*

3 Villatte *[27e Lèger, 63e, 94e & 95e Ligne.]*

Beaumont *[2e Hussars, 5e Chasseurs.]*

4 Sebastiani

1 Liger-Belair *[28e, 32e, 58e & 75e Ligne.]*

2(-) Valence *[4e Polish.]*

3 Leval *[Nassau, Baden, Hesse-Darmstadt, Holland, Frankfurt - 9 bn.]*

Merlin *[10e & 26e Chasseurs, Polish Lancers, Westphalian Chevaux-Lègers.]*

Reserve under King Joseph

Dessolles[1] *[12e Lèger, 51e Ligne, King's Guard.]*

[27e Chasseurs, King's Guard.]

Reserve Cavalry

1 Latour-Maubourg *[1e, 2e, 4e, 9e, 14e & 26e Dragoons.]*

2 Milhaud *[5e, 12e, 16e, 20e & 21e Dragoons, 3e Dutch Hussars.]*

[13 batteries distributed as follows: 2 each to the corps for corps reserve, one each to the cavalry & infantry divisions except Valence's. None with Joseph's Reserve.]

Note:
1. This brigade came from Dessolles's Division based in Madrid.

1 Latour-Maubourg   Dessolles   Casa Salinas

CUESTA - 32,000 (Sources: Oman and Sanudo Note 1)

Vanguard Zayas *[2nd Cataluña, 2nd Cazadores de Barbastro, Campo Mayor, Valencia y Alburquerque, 1st Valencia, Tiradores de Estremadura.]*

Lanceros de Andalusia

Michelena

1 Marques de Zayas *[Cantabria, Castilla, Canarias, Tiradores de Merida, Provinciales de Trujillo, Granaderos Provinciales, Tiradores de Cadiz.]*

2 Iglesias *[2nd Mallorca, Velez-Malaga, Osuna, Estranjeros, 2nd Provincial de Burgos, Salamanca.]*

3 Portago *[1st y 2nd Badajoz, Cazadores de Antquera, Toledo, Provincial de Badajoz, 2nd Provincial de Guadix.]*

4 Manglano *[Irlanda, Jaen, 2nd Sevilla, Leales de Fernando VII, 2nd Voluntarios de Madrid, Corona.]*

5 Bassecourt *[1st y 2nd Marina, Africa, Murcia, Reina, Provincial de Sigüenza.]*

Henestrosa *[Rey, Calatrava, Imperiales de Toledo, Sevilla, Reina, Villaviciosa, Madrid.]*

Alburquerque *[Carabineros Reales, Infante, Pavia, Almansa, 1st y 2nd Husares de Estremadura, Borbon, Sevilla(-), Madrid(-).]*

Rodriguez 30 guns in 5 batteries - one to each infantry division.

Zappino

Note 1: There are some discrepancies between Oman and Sañudo. I can find no evidence that the cavalry units of *Alcantara* or the *Voluntarios de España* as listed by Oman were present. Neither can I determine where the cavalry units, *Cazadores 4th Hussares, Lusitania* or *Castilla* were allocated although Sañudo lists them, along with the infantry regiment *Ceuta*.

and were approaching the crest when they were engaged by the three battalions of Stewart's Brigade who, on hearing the musketry, were hastened forward by General Hill, who had just returned from dinner in Talavera to deploy his two brigades.[11] The two forces collided and came to a standstill, at which point Hill led a charge with the 29th that broke the French resolve. With the 9e Léger pulling back in the centre, the two flanking regiments fell back at much the same moment and the British set about reorganizing their defences and posting piquets at the river's edge. An uneasy night followed with sporadic firing and the sound of artillery guns and caissons manoeuvring into position for the inevitable battle the next day.

As the sun rose early in the summer sky, 40,000 French soldiers were arrayed in columns, facing the Allied lines, supported by all thirteen batteries. 'No great while elapsed, however, after the dawn appeared, ere the enemy once more put themselves in motion. The height upon our left was still the grand object of their desire; and they prepared to storm with all the force which they found it practicable to bring against it.'[12] At first light, nine of the French batteries opened up on the British part of the field and their fire was so accurate that Wellesley, who was on the Medellin behind Hill's troops, ordered Stewart and Tilson's Brigades to retire from the skyline and lie down. In addition, he requested that Cuesta move Uclés's heavier calibre battery to join Lawson in the Pajar de Vergara.[13] Ruffin's Brigade were given another chance to take the Cerro de Medellin and after a few minutes began their advance. The damp morning air mixed with the thick white smoke from the guns obscured their advance and Hill was only aware of approaching French infantry as his light companies withdrew. Crucially, Victor had instructed Villatte and Lapisse only to commence their advance once Ruffin was in control of the Medellin and Joseph, who was commanding the French left, held back the 4th Corps until the balance of the 1st Corps had moved forward. As a result, the commitment of the majority of the French army was predicated on the success of Ruffin's attack on the Medellin. Ruffin advanced up the slope, with the 96e on the left, the 24e in the centre and the 9e Léger on the right, and when they came within a hundred metres of the skyline, Hill ordered his men up and forward. As they came over the crest the French were well within effective range and the entire line fired upon the columns, bringing them to a standstill. 'The brigades of General Tilson and R. Stewart were here; they permitted the enemy, again and again, to arrive within a few paces of the ridge, and they drove them back in admirable style with the bayonet, till, disheartened by so many repulses, they at last retreated altogether, leaving the ground covered with their dead.'[14] Sherbrooke also directed his left-hand battalion, the 2nd KGL, to assail the unfortunate 96e in their flank.

Ruffin's Division had been badly mauled and losses from the two attacks now amounted to about a third of their original muster. Victor ordered the artillery to cease firing and pondered

his next move with a mounting realization that his opponents were made of sterner stuff than he had hitherto acknowledged. An informal truce of sorts evolved, with men from both sides filtering down to the river Portiña to drink and fill canteens and for breakfast to be consumed. For more than two hours stretcher-bearers recovered their wounded. Victor reported this second failure to Joseph who insisted on seeing the Allied dispositions personally before committing to any further attacks. The reconnaissance and subsequent council took place at the heights of the Cerro de Cascajal; Jourdan considered the opportunity spent and advised a defensive posture, which was supported by Sebastiani and Joseph. They could see Wellesley moving reinforcements to the rear of the Cerro de Medellin and the valley and hills to the north; any attempt to turn the Allied left would require considerable forces, weaken the French left and leave them vulnerable to a counter-attack by the Spanish into their flank and dangerously expose their line of retreat along the road to Madrid. Victor remained firm in his conviction that another attack was feasible and requested that the 4th Corps assail the Allied centre while he dealt with the right, and went further by announcing that 'if the attack did not succeed it would be necessary to give up making war' – a claim he was to regret. During this hour-long council, two pieces of news arrived which settled the dispute: Venegas had reappeared, his advance guard was skirmishing with the French force at Toledo and secondly, and more decisively, a dispatch from Soult confirmed that he was still a week away from closing on the Allied rear. A defensive posture was no longer an option.

Milhaud's Division of dragoons were tasked with screening the Spanish to the south, Sebastiani's 4th Corps was to attack the Allied right and centre, while Victor would take the Cerro de Medellin and turn the Allied left flank. Behind this mass of infantry were 12 cavalry regiments and far to the rear of them were Joseph's Guards, who formed the reserve. As the French manoeuvred into position, Wellesley was able to witness their progress and counter-move. Anson and Fane's cavalry brigades were moved into the valley behind and below the Medellin; Bassecourt's Infantry Division were sent on to the forward slopes of the Sierra de Segurilla; Alburquerque's Cavalry Division moved (slightly later) to a position behind the British cavalry, supported by its horse artillery battery; Rettburg's KGL Battery was split into troops and the second troop fell back to a position of the far left of the British line and finally another Spanish 12-pounder battery was split, with four guns to the Pajar de Vergara in support of Lawson's lighter three-pounder battery, and the other two guns to the left of Rettburg's left-hand troop.[15]

At 1400 hours Joseph gave orders for the gunners to commence proceedings and about 60 guns, in forward positions, opened up. Only 36 Allied guns could respond and the closeness of the French batteries to the lines of Allied infantry had an instant effect. Fifteen minutes later the advance commenced; firstly on the French left, then in the centre about 45 minutes later and finally on the right at about 1530 hours. Leval had instructions not to close with the infantry to his front for fear that he would expose the French left flank. However, the vines and olive trees obscured his view and his officers lost control of the eager German troops, who suddenly found themselves embroiled with Campbell's men and the ten guns in the redoubt.

11 Oman attributes the error of Hill's two brigades not being in their correct position to Hill, which seems reasonable.

12 Vane, *Narrative of the Peninsular War*, vol. I, p.406.

13 Toreno, *Guerra de la Independencia, El 2 de Mayo 1808*, vol. 3, p.112.

14 Vane, *Narrative of the Peninsular War*, vol. I, p.407.

15 Cuesta was very cooperative towards Wellesley's requests for support and reinforcement.

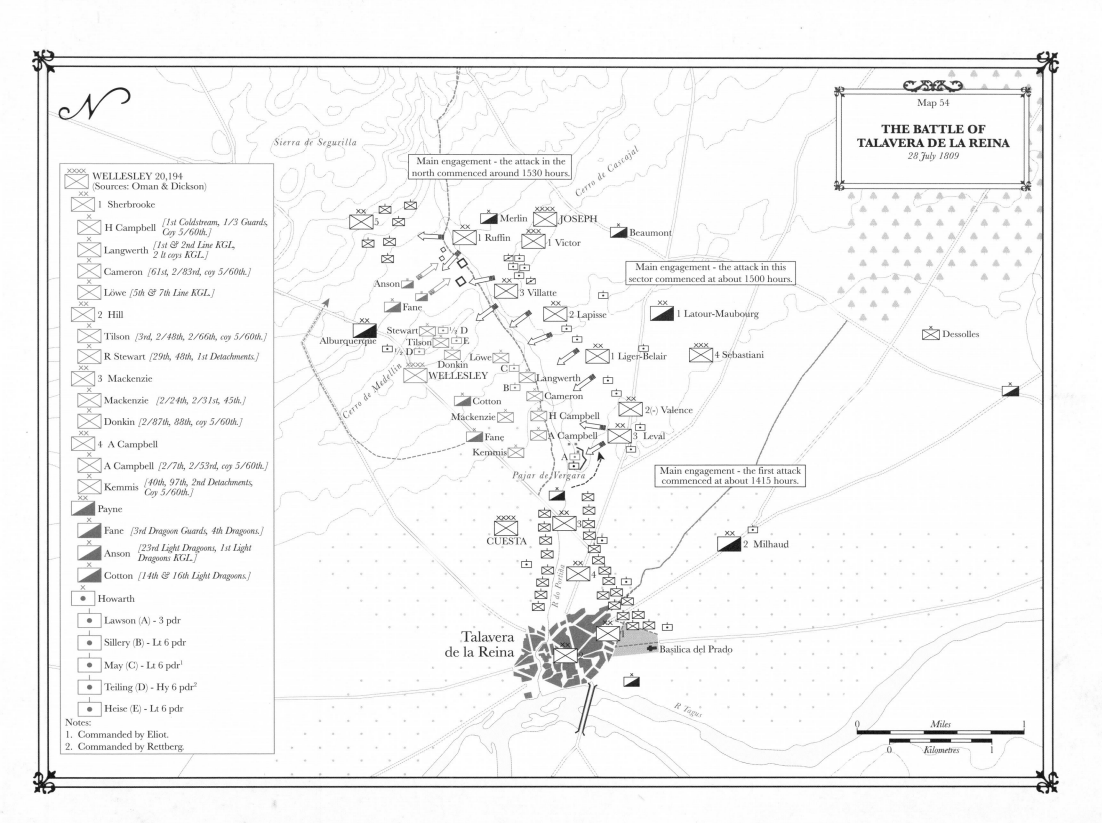

N

WELLESLEY 20,194
(Sources: Oman & Dickson)

1 Sherbrooke
H Campbell [1st Coldstream, 1/3 Guards, Coy 5/60th.]
Langwerth [1st & 2nd Line KGL, 2 lt coys KGL.]
Cameron [61st, 2/83rd, coy 5/60th.]
Löwe [5th & 7th Line KGL.]
2 Hill
Tilson [3rd, 2/48th, 2/66th, coy 5/60th.]
R Stewart [29th, 48th, 1st Detachments.]
3 Mackenzie
Mackenzie [2/24th, 2/31st, 45th.]
Donkin [2/87th, 88th, coy 5/60th.]
4 A Campbell
A Campbell [2/7th, 2/53rd, coy 5/60th.]
Kemmis [40th, 97th, 2nd Detachments, Coy 5/60th.]
Payne
Fane [3rd Dragoon Guards, 4th Dragoons.]
Anson [23rd Light Dragoons, 1st Light Dragoons KGL.]
Cotton [14th & 16th Light Dragoons.]
Howarth
Lawson (A) - 3 pdr
Sillery (B) - Lt 6 pdr
May (C) - Lt 6 pdr[1]
Teiling (D) - Hy 6 pdr[2]
Heise (E) - Lt 6 pdr

Notes:
1. Commanded by Eliot.
2. Commanded by Rettberg.

Map 54

**THE BATTLE OF
TALAVERA DE LA REINA**
28 July 1809

Main engagement - the attack in the
north commenced around 1530 hours.

Main engagement - the attack in this
sector commenced at about 1500 hours.

Main engagement - the first attack
commenced at about 1415 hours.

Sierra de Segurilla

Cerro de Cascajal

5
Merlin JOSEPH
1 Ruffin Beaumont
1 Victor

Anson
3 Villatte
Fane
2 Lapisse 1 Latour-Maubourg
Stewart ½ D
Tilson E
½ D Löwe 1 Liger-Belair 4 Sebastiani Dessolles
Alburquerque Donkin C
Cerro de Medellín WELLESLEY B Langwerth
Cameron 2(-) Valence
Cotton
Mackenzie H Campbell
Fane A Campbell 3 Leval
Kemmis A
Pajar de Vergara

3
CUESTA 4
2 Milhaud

Talavera
de la Reina Basilica del Prado

R do Portiña

R Tagus

0 Miles 1

0 Kilometres 1

They lost their momentum and Campbell ordered a charge, which drove back the Germans back[16] before returning and reforming their lines alongside the Pajar de Vergara. Leval rallied his men upon Valance's two Polish battalions and at about 1600 hours he delivered a second attack, which was also repulsed, and at a critical point, a squadron of Henestrosa's cavalry[17] charged into the German flank forcing them to form square and they withdrew in this formation through the groves.[18]

In the centre, both Liger-Belair and Lapisse had drawn up their divisions in two lines, the front, in column of division and the second, in column of battalion. They crossed the Portiña and advanced towards Sherbrook's four brigades on the forward right face of the Medellin. The British general had briefed his men to let the French advance to within 50m and this they did with incredible fortitude, all eight battalions firing as one when the lines were within effective musket range. 'The leading ranks of Lapisse's and Sebastiani's front went down in swathes – one French witness says the infantry of the regiments of the 4th Corps lost a third of their numbers in ten minutes.'[19] However, the follow-up charge against the French, as they fled back across the river, was not executed with the same military precision. The two KGL battalions and the guards to the south overextended their pursuit and the initial success could have been easily turned into disaster had Mackenzie not brought forward his brigade[20] and anchored it next to Campbell, providing a line behind which the guards and Germans could rally. Wellesley, sensing the danger, also sent down the 48th (Stewart's Brigade) to hold the line as the battalions moved back to their original positions. Both Mackenzie and the commanding officer of the 48th, Lieutenant Colonel Donnelan, were killed in the execution of providing this critical support.

---

16 They captured some French guns in the process, which they spiked before retiring.

17 El Regimiento del Rey.

18 Leval lost a total of 17 guns during his two attacks.

19 Oman, *History of the Peninsular War*, vol II, p.539. Oman does not credit Liger-Belair with the command of Sebastiani's Division, which he vacated when he assumed command of the 4th Corps.

20 The significance of this action was not recognized by Wellesley.

To the north, no concerted attempt had been made on the Medellin itself as Villatte's second brigade had been instructed to wait for some success to their right or left before committing to the attack. As a consequence, the massed French guns on the Cascajal had continued to ply their trade with deadly consequences, prompting Wellesley to order the infantry to retire behind the skyline and lie low. In the valley between the Medellin and Sierra de Segurilla the French advance commenced when the battle across the Portiña (in the centre) was at its height. Ruffin's depleted regiments were on the right and Cassagne's Brigade (27e Léger and 63e Ligne) were on their left on the valley floor, supported by Merlin's light cavalry to the rear. Wellesley, content that the attack in the centre was under control, turned his full attention to this area of the field and ordered Anson to charge the advancing infantry with Fane in support. The four French regiments on the valley floor formed squares by regiment, each with three battalions, providing fruitful targets for the Allied guns on the north side of the Medellin. Anson's Brigade thundered down the valley with the German dragoons to the left and the light dragoons to the right. There is considerable confusion as to what happened next, and many contradictory eyewitness accounts, but in essence the terrain broke up the charge and the cavalry regiments, somewhat depleted and blown, were unable to break the squares. Those that had made it thus far now continued up the valley directly into Merlin's four regiments with inevitable consequences. This disaster could have tipped the balance but Ruffin and Villatte (who had accompanied his brigade commander) could see Fane's heavy cavalry to their front and Alburquerque behind them. They elected to retire and the battle came to a standstill.

Victor, despite this third disappointment, was eager to continue, but Joseph and Jourdan did not share his fervour and orders were sent along the French lines to fall back to the positions of 27 July. Sebastiani's Corps withdrew as the light began to fade[21] but Victor, furious at being denied another chance, hung on to the heights of Cascajal until 0300 hours the following morning. As dawn broke on 29 July the hills and plains in front of the Allied positions were deserted.

---

21 During this time a fire broke out on the lower slopes of the Medellin and the long grass quickly ignited, killing and further wounding many of the injured that lay at this part of the field.

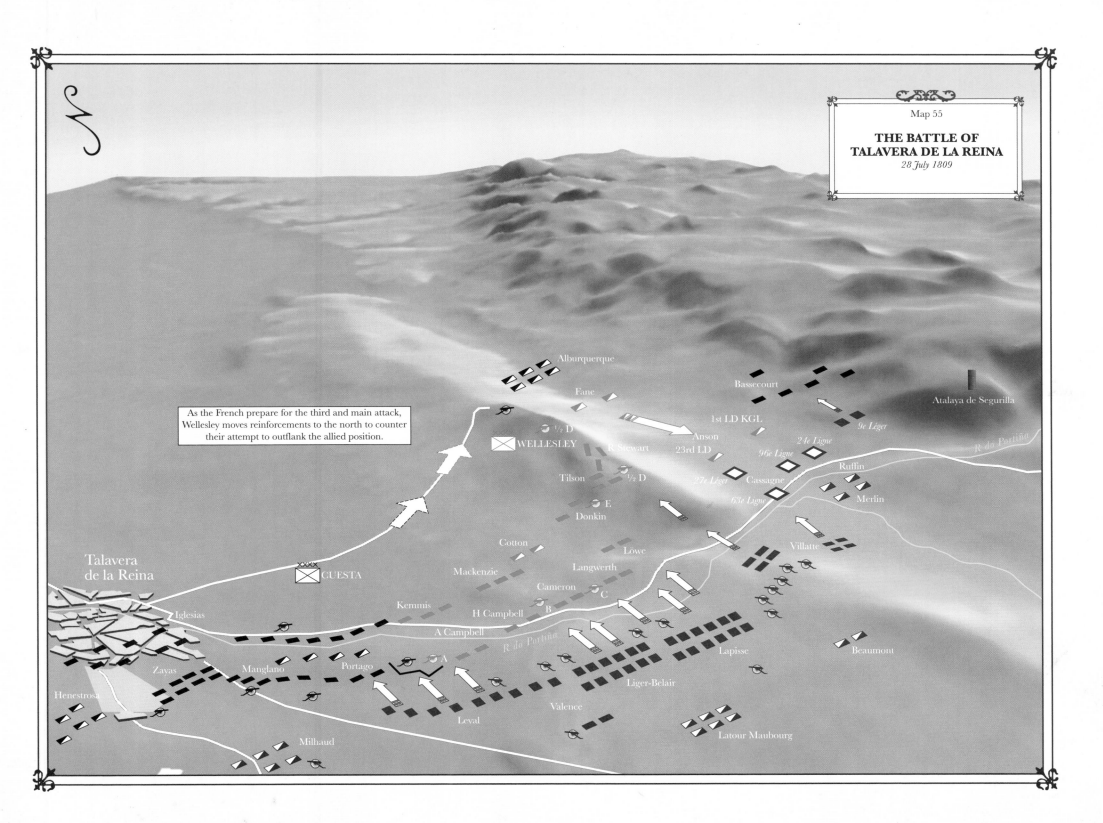

Map 55

**THE BATTLE OF
TALAVERA DE LA REINA**
28 July 1809

As the French prepare for the third and main attack,
Wellesley moves reinforcements to the north to counter
their attempt to outflank the allied position.

Alburquerque

Bassecourt

Atalaya de Segurilla

Fane

1st LD KGL

9e Léger

½ D

Anson

24e Ligne

WELLESLEY

R. Stewart

23rd LD

96e Ligne

Tilson

½ D

27e Léger

Cassagne

Ruffin

63e Ligne

Merlin

E

Donkin

Cotton

Löwe

Villatte

Talavera
de la Reina

Langwerth

CUESTA

Mackenzie

Cameron

Kemmis

C

H Campbell

B

Iglesias

A Campbell

R. do Portiña

Lapisse

Beaumont

Zayas

Mauglano

A

Portago

Henestrosa

Leval

Liger-Belair

Valence

Milhaud

Latour Maubourg

Chapter 20

THE END OF THE TALAVERA CAMPAIGN: AUGUST 1809

'I cannot understand the affairs of Spain, nor what has taken place there. Where was the French army on the 29th and 30th? And where was the English army during these two days? The King says that for the last month he has been manoeuvring with 40,000 men against 100,000. Tell him that it was his own fault, and that it is the very thing of which I complain.'[1] Any intention to follow up the victory at Talavera was out of the question. Casualties on both sides were high and, even with the arrival that morning of the first elements of Craufurd's Light Brigade from Lisbon, the truth was the Allies were exhausted. Allied command was aware of Soult's presence to the north but had no idea that this force numbered more than 50,000 and was preparing to move in their direction. Oblivious to the threat, Cuesta and Wellesley rested their armies for three days and pondered their next moves. Wellesley wasted little time in reiterating his suggestion to Cuesta to send a division to the passes in order to cover the northern flank.

Joseph, meanwhile, had fallen back to a position behind the Alberche, where on 30 July he deployed in anticipation of receiving an attack. As the morning wore on, it became apparent that the Anglo-Spanish army had not pursued his force and he therefore turned his attention south towards Venegas. Venegas, it will be recalled, had erroneously allowed Sebastiani to break contact on 24 July and, despite clear indication that a solitary brigade was guarding the capital, this Spanish force had not made best use of this opportunity (see Chapter 19). Lacy was sent to Toledo,[2] while Venegas went, with the balance of his army, to Aranjuez and remained inactive there for eight days despite the road to the capital being undefended. When Joseph realized that Wellesley and Cuesta had gone firm at Talavera he reinforced Toledo, but was not clear as to Venegas's whereabouts until 1 August. At this point he moved the 4th Corps east to cover the road to Madrid and, for the Spanish the opportunity passed. The 1st Corps were, in the intervening time, occupied by Wilson's advance with his small Portuguese and Spanish force that had moved on the Allied northern flank and was now only about 60km from Madrid. Victor moved to intercept this force, which he had been led to believe, was much larger, prompting Wilson to vanish into the mountains, satisfied that his force had drawn Victor away from the main effort.

During this manoeuvring Wellesley and Cuesta remained at Talavera and spent much of the time in dispute over future operations. Cuesta wanted Wellesley to provide half his force to march north to cover the passes along with the division of Bassecourt. The British commander was clear that he would not split his force but offered to move intact, which met with Cuesta's approval. From the content of the dispatches penned over these few days, it is apparent that both Allied commanders were still unclear as the size of the French forces moving south to meet them. Soult had concentrated the 2nd, 5th and 6th corps at Salamanca and began the advance with Mortier's Corps on 27 July; Soult followed three days later and Ney followed up on 1 August. Soult was conscious of Beresford and Del Parque's forces on or around the Portuguese border but calculated that they would quickly withdraw once Wellesley and Cuesta were defeated or pulled back. Mortier came across the Spanish covering force on 30 July and swiftly swept them aside, entering Plasencia on 1 August. The 2nd Corps arrived the next day and Soult pushed Mortier southeast towards Almaraz and Talavera: a move anticipated by Cuesta, who now withdrew to Oropesa and then south over the Tagus at the bridge at Arzobispo[3] after a brief encounter with Mortier's vanguard. The day before both Wellesley and Cuesta had at last received confirmation of the size of the French force bearing down upon them and Wellesley had already directed his force to move with haste westwards along the southern bank.

By the morning of 7 August, Cuesta was firm at Arzobispo while Wellesley's force was positioned between Mesa de Ibor and the re-broken bridge at Almaraz; the latter being held by Craufurd's Light Brigade. Soult and Mortier were to the north of the Army of Estremadura, probing for suitable crossing points, and Ney was en route to Almaraz in an attempt to secure passage at this location. Soult was the first to strike; he advanced to the water's edge along a considerable expanse of the river, and Lahoussaye's dragoons crossed at a shallow point causing considerable havoc in the Spanish defences, at which point the 1/40e Ligne were let loose with the explicit task of capturing the bridge. The Spanish had been caught unawares; Soult had cleverly timed the attack to coincide with siesta and, despite repeated attempts to counter-attack, the Spanish were finally overwhelmed by the sheer numbers of French cavalry and infantry who were, by now, pouring over the narrow bridge and at various crossing points along the river. Spanish losses were considerable, especially in artillery. They lost not only their integral 16 guns but also 14 of the 17 guns captured from the French at Talavera. Cuesta withdrew west towards Wellesley's rearguard at Mesa de Ibor, and to his considerable relief, was not pursued by Soult. The road to Mesa de Ibor was virtually impassable for artillery and Ney had reported that passage to the west was equally impractical. Instead, Soult decided to move with alacrity along the northern bank of the Tagus in an attempt to capture Castelo Branco and secure central Portugal before Wellesley could manoeuvre north in support of Beresford. If successful, the British would find themselves with their backs to the Portuguese capital. It was a sound plan but it had a principal weakness. Instead of obliging Soult by moving north-west, Wellesley could

---

1   Napoleon, *The Confidential Correspondence of Napoleon Bonaparte*, vol. II, p.69. Napoleon to Clark, 15 August 1809.

2   It was his half-hearted attempt to take the place that resulted in the message from its governor, General Valence that arrived on the field of battle on the 28th and served to influence Joseph's ultimate decision.

3   Oman redresses some of the fierce criticism by British historians of Cuesta's actions, which were fuelled by the fact that he abandoned the British hospitals in Talavera to the French. See Oman, *History of the Peninsular War*, vol. II, pp.579–582.

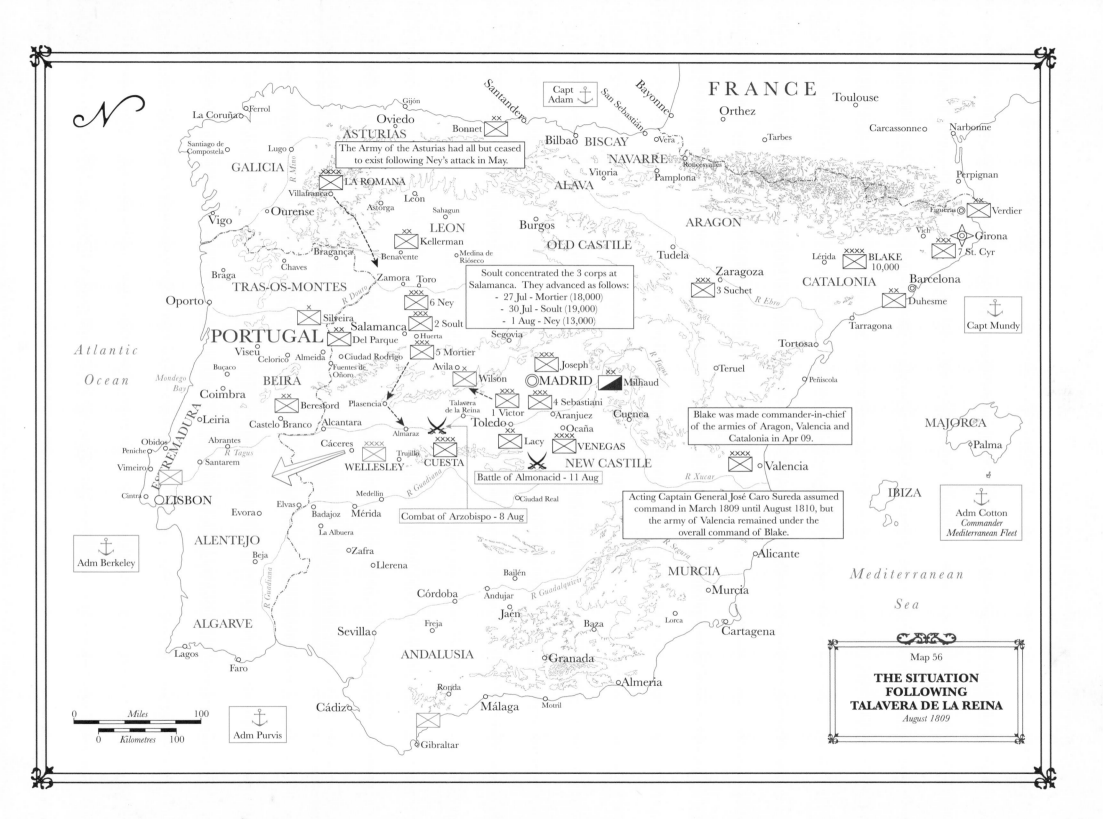

N

FRANCE

Toulouse

Orthez

Carcassonne

Narbonne

Perpignan

BISCAY

Santander

Bayonne

San Sebastián

Vera

Bilbao

NAVARRE

Vitoria

Pamplona

ALAVA

Roncesvalles

ARAGON

Tudela

Zaragoza

R Ebro

3 Suchet

CATALONIA

Lérida

BLAKE 10,000

Verdier

Figueras

Girona

7 St. Cyr

Vich

Barcelona

Duhesme

Tarragona

Tortosa

Teruel

Peñiscola

La Coruña

Ferrol

Gijón

Oviedo

Bonnet

ASTURIAS

The Army of the Asturias had all but ceased to exist following Ney's attack in May.

Santiago de Compostela

Lugo

GALICIA

Vigo

Ourense

LA ROMANA

Villafranca

León

Astorga

Sahagun

LEON

Kellerman

Medina de Ríoseco

Burgos

OLD CASTILE

Braga

Chaves

Bragança

Benavente

TRAS-OS-MONTES

Zamora

Toro

R Douro

6 Ney

2 Soult

Silveira

Salamanca

Del Parque

Huerta

5 Mortier

Segovia

Soult concentrated the 3 corps at Salamanca. They advanced as follows:
- 27 Jul - Mortier (18,000)
- 30 Jul - Soult (19,000)
- 1 Aug - Ney (13,000)

Oporto

PORTUGAL

Viseu

Celorico

Almeida

Ciudad Rodrigo

Fuentes de Oñoro

Avila

Wilson

Joseph

MADRID

Milhaud

R Tagus

Atlantic Ocean

Mondego Bay

Coimbra

BEIRA

Beresford

Plasencia

Talavera de la Reina

1 Victor

4 Sebastiani

Toledo

Aranjuez

Cuenca

Blake was made commander-in-chief of the armies of Aragon, Valencia and Catalonia in Apr 09.

MAJORCA

Palma

Leiria

Castelo Branco

Alcantara

Almaraz

Ocaña

VENEGAS

Lacy

NEW CASTILE

R Xucar

Valencia

Acting Captain General José Caro Sureda assumed command in March 1809 until August 1810, but the army of Valencia remained under the overall command of Blake.

IBIZA

Obidos

Peniche

Vimeiro

Cintra

LISBON

EXTREMADURA

Cáceres

WELLESLEY

CUESTA

R Guadiana

Battle of Almonacid - 11 Aug

Combat of Arzobispo - 8 Aug

Abrantes

Trujillo

Santarem

Evora

Elvas

Medellin

Badajoz

Mérida

R Guadiana

Ciudad Real

ALENTEJO

Beja

Zafra

La Albuera

Llerena

Bailén

Andujar

R Guadalquivir

MURCIA

Murcia

Alicante

Mediterranean

Sea

Lagos

Faro

Córdoba

Jaén

Freja

Baza

Lorca

Cartagena

ALGARVE

Sevilla

ANDALUSIA

Ronda

Granada

Almeria

Motril

Cádiz

Málaga

Gibraltar

Capt Adam

Capt Mundy

Adm Cotton
Commander
Mediterranean Fleet

Adm Berkeley

Adm Purvis

Miles 100

Kilometres 100

Map 56

THE SITUATION FOLLOWING TALAVERA DE LA REINA

August 1809

turn back east, combine forces with Cuesta and Venegas and attack Madrid with as many as 70,000 men against Joseph's depleted force of less than 50,000. Joseph, having been forced to retire from 'his' capital once, was acutely aware of the likelihood and danger of just such an eventuality and accordingly deprived Soult of the authority to commence his plan. Furthermore, in order to reinforce the point, he ordered Ney back north to link up with Kellermann, who had just reported that La Romana was once again stirring from Galicia. The ever-ambitious Ney needed no persuasion to break from the yoke of Soult's command, and headed north on 10 August with considerable zeal. Joseph, conscious that Venegas was still at large, recalled Victor to cover the southern flank of the capital and replaced his divisions with those of Mortier.

With Victor en route, Joseph considered the capital secure and ventured forth with Sebastiani's Corps, Milhaud's Division and the central reserve in an attempt to tackle Venegas and eliminate the threat from the Army of La Mancha once and for all. On 5 August the French force came up against the bulk of the Spanish army at Aranjuez, but the crossing points were limited and a hasty attack by Sebastiani was beaten back with strength, forcing Joseph to reconsider his options. He decided to move his force west and, by 8 August, he had crossed the lightly held bridge at Toledo. However, Venegas had second-guessed Joseph's intentions and mirrored his westward movement, and by 10 August, both forces were concentrated at Almonacid. They were balanced numerically[4] and both were prepared to fight.

Following a council of war, Venegas fired up his subordinates and issued orders for an attack the following morning. Sebastiani preempted the Spanish offensive and attacked them early on 11 August, before the Spanish lines had been fully established and before Joseph had arrived with the royal reserve. Venegas's deployment bore many similarities to that at Uclés, in that it was linear although he had a slightly stronger reserve. The position was not bad, but the open plains to the north and south made it easy to turn. Sebastiani wasted little time in appreciating that the large hill to the south, Los Cerrojones, which formed the Spanish left, was the vital ground. This was held with a single brigade from Giron's Division; the other brigade formed the reserve and was located on the hill south of the town, amongst the ruins of the old castle. At about 0530 hours, Sebastiani's Division began the offensive by occupying the Spanish centre; Merlin's light cavalry engaged the Spanish right while Valence's Poles attacked the hill of Los Cerrojones directly. With these three attacks ongoing, Leval's Division moved to turn the southern flank.

Giron's lone Spanish brigade on Los Cerrojones, assisted by the cavalry, put up an excellent fight and forced Leval's troops to form square. However, the sheer weight of numbers finally took its toll on the defenders, but not without considerable losses to the Polish regiment. The Spanish fell back and rallied on their second brigade, located south of the town on the Cerro Santo. Sebastiani now pushed home the attacks on Lacy and Zerain's Divisions, who were forced to give ground. Sebastiani's troops entered the town (compelling Castejon to fall back beyond the dwellings) and captured a half battery of guns in the process. Venegas now tried to reform his defence on the Cerro Santo, and he made an excellent effort to reorganize in contact, but at that very moment Dessolles's Division arrived and immediately engaged itself in the fight. 'General Leval, at the head of the Polish and German divisions, moved behind the Spanish left flank; General Rey, with the regiments of the 28e and 32e supported by two battalions of the 58e and one of the 12e Léger under the conduct of General Godinot, attacked and climbed the mountain under a rain of grapeshot; General Liger-Belair with the 75e, two battalions of the 12e Léger and one of 58e, forced the enemy's right; in few of instants, all heights and the castle were occupied by the French army.'[5] Venegas ordered a retreat and threw Vigodet's Division across the road to cover their withdrawal. This division had not been involved in the fighting and was virtually intact, numbering about 4,000 men. The French attacked the rearguard with both infantry and cavalry, but Vigodet's men managed to hold off these assaults long enough to enable the Spanish main body to escape. They promptly joined them when they considered their task complete, and were pursued, somewhat ineffectively, for a considerable distance by Milhaud's dragoons.

The Army of La Mancha lost many regimental colours and 21 of its guns but it remained a force to be reckoned with, and as such, continued to pose a threat to the capital. Venegas's disobedience to Cuesta's orders prior to Talavera and his failure to capitalize on the opportunity to enter Madrid led to his dismissal. Areizaga replaced him. Following Almonacid, Joseph pushed Victor south to cover the passes and left Sebastiani covering the immediate south of the capital. At which point Soult reiterated his desire to invade Portugal and requested the return of Ney from Salamanca. His request was flatly denied; Ney was more than preoccupied with the union of La Romana and Del Parque to his front but the Talavera Campaign was at an end. The results had been inconclusive, neither side being able to deliver the decisive blow.

---

4 However, the French enjoyed their traditional (early-stage) numerical superiority in cavalry.

5 Hugo, *Histoire des Armées Françaises, 1792-1833*, vol. IV, p.134.

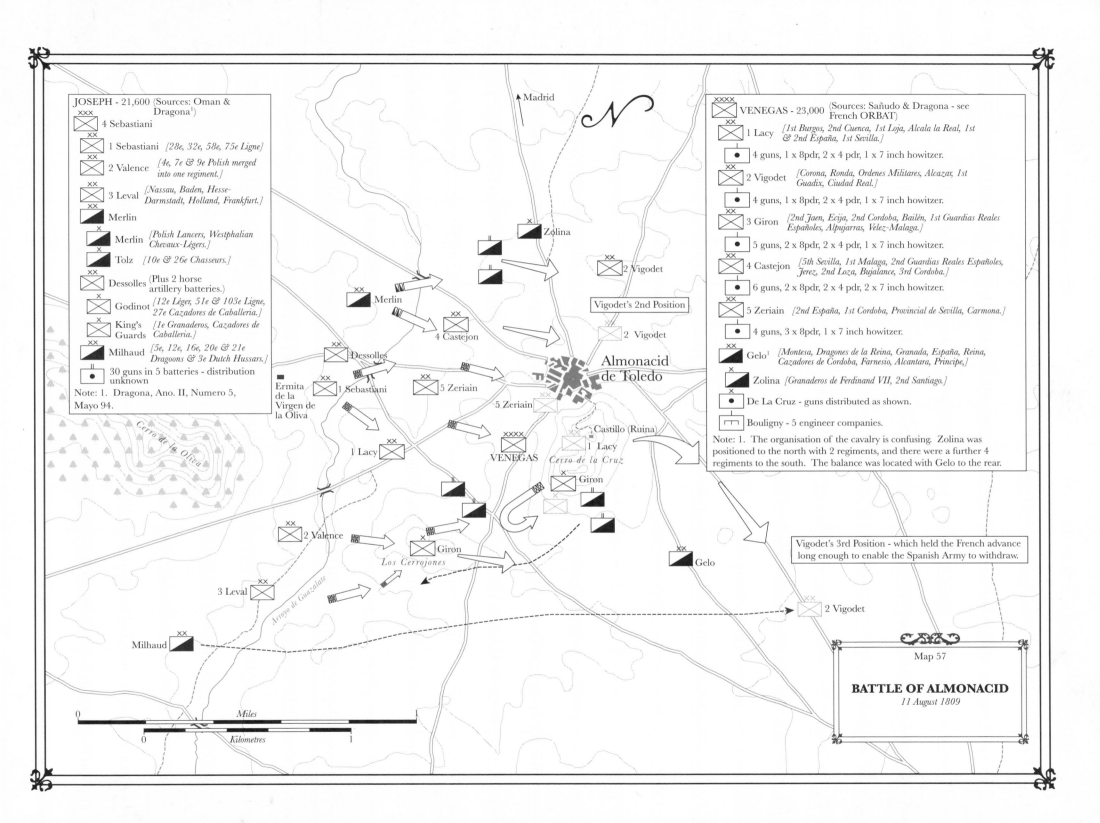

↑ Madrid

N

JOSEPH - 21,600 (Sources: Oman & Dragona[1])

☒☒☒ 4 Sebastiani

☒☒ 1 Sebastiani *[28e, 32e, 58e, 75e Ligne]*

☒☒ 2 Valence *[4e, 7e & 9e Polish merged into one regiment.]*

☒☒ 3 Leval *[Nassau, Baden, Hesse-Darmstadt, Holland, Frankfurt.]*

◼ Merlin

◼ Merlin *[Polish Lancers, Westphalian Chevaux-Légers.]*

◼ Tolz *[10e & 26e Chasseurs.]*

☒☒ Dessolles (Plus 2 horse artillery batteries.)

☒ Godinot *[12e Léger, 51e & 103e Ligne, 27e Cazadores de Caballeria.]*

☒ King's Guards *[1e Granaderos, Cazadores de Caballeria.]*

◼ Milhaud *[5e, 12e, 16e, 20e & 21e Dragoons & 3e Dutch Hussars.]*

▮● 30 guns in 5 batteries - distribution unknown

Note: 1. Dragona, Ano. II, Numero 5, Mayo 94.

VENEGAS - 23,000 (Sources: Sañudo & Dragona - see French ORBAT)

☒☒ 1 Lacy *[1st Burgos, 2nd Cuenca, 1st Loja, Alcala la Real, 1st & 2nd España, 1st Sevilla.]*

▮● 4 guns, 1 x 8pdr, 2 x 4 pdr, 1 x 7 inch howitzer.

☒☒ 2 Vigodet *[Corona, Ronda, Ordenes Militares, Alcazar, 1st Guadix, Ciudad Real.]*

▮● 4 guns, 1 x 8pdr, 2 x 4 pdr, 1 x 7 inch howitzer.

☒☒ 3 Giron *[2nd Jaen, Ecija, 2nd Cordoba, Bailén, 1st Guardias Reales Españoles, Alpujarras, Velez-Malaga.]*

▮● 5 guns, 2 x 8pdr, 2 x 4 pdr, 1 x 7 inch howitzer.

☒☒ 4 Castejon *[5th Sevilla, 1st Malaga, 2nd Guardias Reales Españoles, Jerez, 2nd Loza, Bujalance, 3rd Cordoba.]*

▮● 6 guns, 2 x 8pdr, 2 x 4 pdr, 2 x 7 inch howitzer.

☒☒ 5 Zeriain *[2nd España, 1st Cordoba, Provincial de Sevilla, Carmona.]*

▮● 4 guns, 3 x 8pdr, 1 x 7 inch howitzer.

◼ Gelo[1] *[Montesa, Dragones de la Reina, Granada, España, Reina, Cazadores de Cordoba, Farnesio, Alcantara, Principe,]*

◼ Zolina *[Granaderos de Ferdinand VII, 2nd Santiago.]*

▮● De La Cruz - guns distributed as shown.

⊞ Bouligny - 5 engineer companies.

Note: 1. The organisation of the cavalry is confusing. Zolina was positioned to the north with 2 regiments, and there were a further 4 regiments to the south. The balance was located with Gelo to the rear.

Cerro de la Oliva

Ermita de la Virgen de la Oliva

Merlin

Dessolles

4 Castejon

Zolina

2 Vigodet

Vigodet's 2nd Position

2 Vigodet

Almonacid de Toledo

1 Sebastiani

5 Zeriain

5 Zeriain

Castillo (Ruina)

1 Lacy

Cerro de la Cruz

VENEGAS

1 Lacy

Giron

Los Cerrojones

2 Valence

Giron

Gelo

Vigodet's 3rd Position - which held the French advance long enough to enable the Spanish Army to withdraw.

3 Leval

Arroyo de Guazalate

Milhaud

2 Vigodet

0 Miles 1

0 Kilometres 1

Map 57

BATTLE OF ALMONACID
11 August 1809

Chapter 21

THE DISASTROUS AUTUMN CAMPAIGN: 1809

Throughout September Viscount Wellington[1] received repeated requests from the Central Junta at Sevilla to combine forces and resume an offensive. Wellington persistently refused, highlighting French numerical superiority on the one hand and a chronic lack of supplies for his own forces on the other. Undeterred, the Junta continued with their plans. The remnants of the Army of La Mancha were to unite, with three divisions of infantry and 13 regiments of cavalry from the Army of Estremadura, to create a force in excess of 50,000 men under the overall command of General Areizaga. Once united, they were to move on the Spanish capital. The balance of the Army of Estremadura was placed under the Duke del Alburquerque and tasked to support Areizaga by way of a distraction to Soult and Victor at Almaraz and Talavera respectively. To the west, La Romana had been summoned to Sevilla to act as the military representative to the Junta and replaced in the field by the Duke del Parque. He assumed command of the old Army of Galicia, his native force, which in the interim he had been recruiting and training in Leon. To this army, the local government in the Asturias reluctantly seconded the Division of Ballesteros; these two formations became collectively known as the new Army of the Left.

Joseph did not expect the Spanish to take the offensive and had no intention of doing so himself. Reinforcements had been promised from Germany and the possibility that they would be led by Napoleon himself had not been ruled out. Victor remained covering the passes in La Mancha with Sebastiani to his rear; Soult and Mortier lingered in the Tagus valley and Ney stayed in Salamanca: although he personally had taken leave in France and Marchand was in temporary command. Joseph was ensconced in Madrid but was about to lose his chief of staff, as Jourdan's health was failing.[2] However, as it transpired, events ignited in Leon before La Mancha. By 25 September Del Parque had concentrated about 25,000 infantry and 1,500 cavalry and was awaiting the arrival of Ballesteros. Facing him were the 6th Corps, centred on Salamanca and numbering just over 14,000, and the division of Kellermann, which added another 5,000.[3] By 5 October Del Parque had advanced from Ciudad Rodrigo to Tamames; as soon as news of this Spanish advance reached Marchand he resolved to attack. On 17 October Marchand departed Salamanca with his entire corps, except for two battalions of the 50e Ligne

who were left to hold the city, and arrived north of Tamames the following day where he was delighted to see the Spanish deployed to his front, ready to give battle.

Having deduced that the Spanish left was their weakest point, from where he could easily turn the division to his immediate front, he attacked at once. Maucune was despatched to this flank along with the light cavalry and a squadron of dragoons. When they were in position, Marcognet's Brigade attacked the troops along the slopes to their front and a regiment from the reserve brigade was detached to contain the Spanish right. As the French approached the Spanish left, Del Parque pulled in La Carrera's line and readied his considerable reserve. The French skirmish line came into contact with the forward battalions and immediately Maucune unleashed the light cavalry, which caught the Spanish off-guard and quickly and skilfully penetrated the line and captured one of the Spanish batteries. Del Parque responded by deploying Anglona's Cavalry Brigade, which formed up to the south and charged into the flank of the advancing French. The 69e Ligne were on the French right; they noticed the danger early and formed square in sufficient time to repel the charge and keep the French flank intact. The French continued their advance and Del Parque responded by moving forward most of the battalions of Belvedere's reserve. Their arrival strengthened the line and broke the impetus of the attacking infantry. It was much of the same on the other flank where, despite repeated attempts to take the position, Losada's *Gallegos* held firm, generously supported by the two Spanish batteries posted there. The French began to pull back but were given no time to rally as Losada's men fell upon the retreating French, together with elements of La Carrera's troops who sallied from the village itself to join the rout. Maucune witnessed the collapse of the French left and immediately called off the attack in his area and pulled back.[4] Marchand was able to rally Marcognet's Brigade on the remnants of La Basse's Brigade and the whole made off under a cavalry screen.

Given the quality of the troops in the 6th Corps, this was a significant victory; Del Parque had deployed his troops well, maintained a significant reserve and made good use of the ground. He followed up his success and entered Salamanca on 25 October, which Marchand had abandoned when he realized that Kellermann would not reach him in time. Del Parque, sensing an opportunity, requested the support of Beresford's Division positioned just across the border, but the Regency at Lisbon (very much on Wellington's advice) refused to comply and Del Parque went firm, content that he had successfully completed his part of the Junta's plan. His hold on the city was only to last two weeks, for he was forced to retire when Kellermann advanced towards the city at the head of 23,000 men.[5] However, in order for Kellermann to assemble this force he had to strip out most of the troops forming the many garrisons in Leon and, in so doing, opened the way for *guerrillero* chiefs, like Julian Sanchez, to raise large groups of men and commence extensive guerrilla operations in the province.

---

1   Following Talavera, the British government elevated Wellesley to the peerage with the title of Viscount Wellington of Talavera. He signed his first dispatch 'Wellington' on 16 September. He was not made a duke until after the final victory in France, and abdication of Napoleon, in April 1814.

2   Jourdan was delighted to hand the baton of responsibility to Soult and head back to Paris.

3   This included his own division of dragoons which constituted the bulk at 3,000 horse and 2,000 infantry – a battalion from each of the 2e, 3e and 4e Swiss regiments; a battalion of the Garde de Paris; and a battalion each from the 12e Léger, 32e and 122e Ligne.

4   He only withdrew with one of the Spanish guns, which he had taken to replace one of the French pieces that had become unserviceable. The remaining five guns were retaken by the Spanish.

5   He had taken temporary command of the 6th Corps from Marchand.

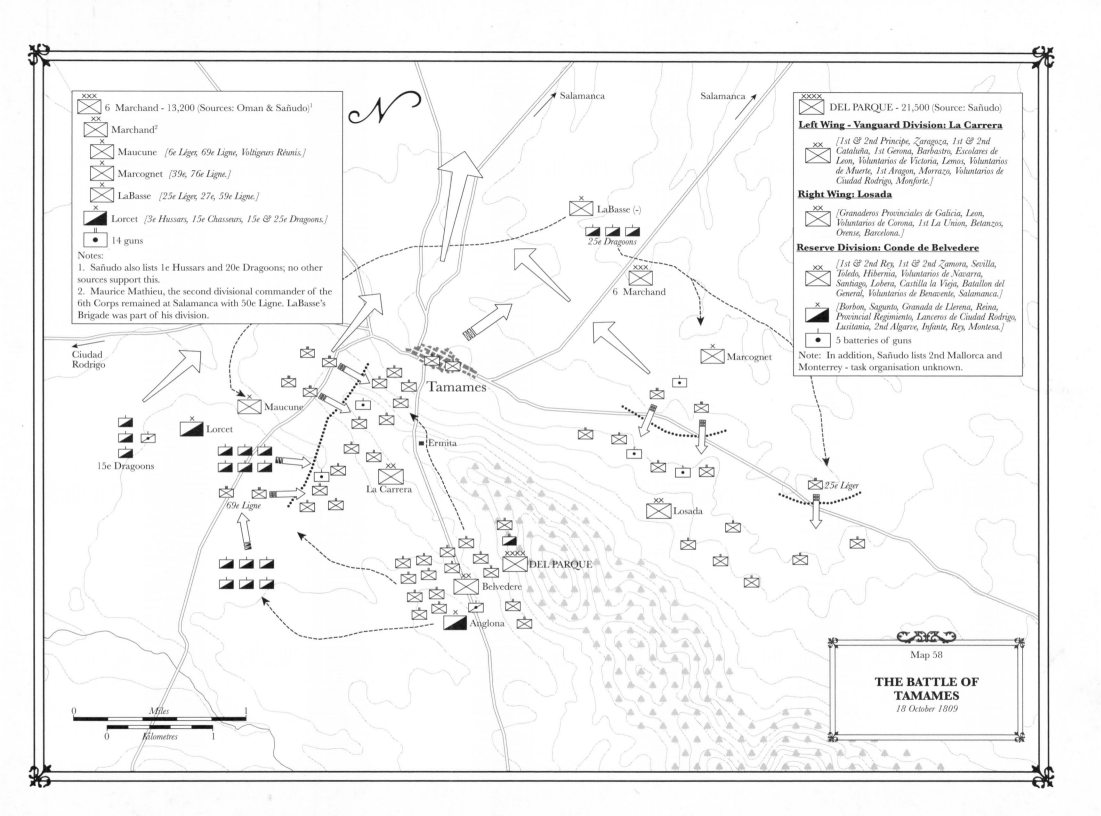

6 Marchand - 13,200 (Sources: Oman & Sañudo)[1]

Marchand[2]

Maucune *[6e Léger, 69e Ligne, Voltigeurs Réunis.]*

Marcognet *[39e, 76e Ligne.]*

LaBasse *[25e Léger, 27e, 59e Ligne.]*

Lorcet *[3e Hussars, 15e Chasseurs, 15e & 25e Dragoons.]*

14 guns

Notes:
1. Sañudo also lists 1e Hussars and 20e Dragoons; no other sources support this.
2. Maurice Mathieu, the second divisional commander of the 6th Corps remained at Salamanca with 50e Ligne. LaBasse's Brigade was part of his division.

DEL PARQUE - 21,500 (Source: Sañudo)

Left Wing - Vanguard Division: La Carrera

[1st & 2nd Principe, Zaragoza, 1st & 2nd Cataluña, 1st Gerona, Barbastro, Escolares de Leon, Voluntarios de Victoria, Lemos, Voluntarios de Muerte, 1st Aragon, Morrazo, Voluntarios de Ciudad Rodrigo, Monforte.]

Right Wing: Losada

[Granaderos Provinciales de Galicia, Leon, Voluntarios de Corona, 1st La Union, Betanzos, Orense, Barcelona.]

Reserve Division: Conde de Belvedere

[1st & 2nd Rey, 1st & 2nd Zamora, Sevilla, Toledo, Hibernia, Voluntarios de Navarra, Santiago, Lobera, Castilla la Vieja, Batallon del General, Voluntarios de Benavente, Salamanca.]

[Borbon, Sagunto, Granada de Llerena, Reina, Provincial Regimiento, Lanceros de Ciudad Rodrigo, Lusitania, 2nd Algarve, Infante, Rey, Montesa.]

5 batteries of guns

Note: In addition, Sañudo lists 2nd Mallorca and Monterrey - task organisation unknown.

Salamanca

Salamanca

LaBasse (-)

25e Dragoons

6 Marchand

Marcognet

Ciudad Rodrigo

Maucune

Lorcet

15e Dragoons

69e Ligne

La Carrera

Tamames

Ermita

Losada

25e Léger

DEL PARQUE

Belvedere

Anglona

Map 58

THE BATTLE OF TAMAMES

18 October 1809

0 Miles 1

0 Kilometres 1

Before Del Parque had been forced to retire from Salamanca, the next phase of the Junta's offensive had already begun. In early November, Alburquerque had opened with a deception operation against the French along the Tagus, driving in Soult's outposts from Almaraz to Mesa de Ibor; but the French command was not taken by the ruse as their intelligence had picked up that the British and Portuguese had remained in their positions near Badajoz and Campo Mayor and Heudelet's 2nd Corps[6] was left in place to monitor and contain Alburquerque. Meanwhile, on 3 November, Areizaga had commenced his move north with an army of nearly 60,000 men and 60 guns; the largest fielded by the Spanish since Tudela. However, morale was low and many senior officers questioned the wisdom of taking the fight to the French. Areizaga was not among the doubters, considering a bold and rapid strike as the best plan of action. The rapidity of his northerly advance took the French completely by surprise but momentum was lost when the Spanish commander received intelligence that Victor was closing with similar speed. Areizaga then halted for three days at La Guardia in an attempt to gain a better operational picture. It was an error that allowed Joseph and Soult to collect their thoughts and concentrate their forces in front of Madrid.

From 11 to 19 November both sides executed a series of moves and counter-moves.[7] On 18 November, during this manoeuvring, the largest cavalry-on-cavalry engagement of the war took place near Ocaña when Milhaud's Division and Paris's Brigade[8] combined to pitch 3,000 cavalry against the 4,000 of the combined Spanish cavalry divisions. The following morning the scene was set for the inevitable clash of arms. Areizaga's force was in excess of 50,000 men, those of the French about 33,500, leaving Joseph and Soult the dilemma of deciding whether or not to wait for Victor to balance the numerical inferiority. Considering the position at Ocaña to offer little by way of defensive attributes, the French command elected for an immediate attack. Ignoring the Spanish left, which was protected by a ravine, they concentrated on the long line of Spanish infantry in open ground east of the town, which was flanked on the far right by the majority of Freire's cavalry.

Soult drew up a simple plan: Leval and Werlé's Divisions were to attack the Spanish centre and right, supported by Girard and a regiment from Gazan's Division. To their left, the entire French cavalry (less for one squadron on the far right) were massed, ready to engage the Spanish cavalry to their front at the moment that the Poles and Germans closed with the ranks of Spanish infantry. Their task was to push back the inferior Spanish horse and turn the Spanish line. To the right of the Germans, the balance of Gazan's Division and a brigade from Dessolles' Division were poised to keep the Spanish centre busy while, on the far right, the King's Reserve were positioned to screen any movement by Zayas and to act as general reserve. In front of Dessolles, Soult had positioned five of the eight French batteries, in battery lines but at a slight angle that enabled them to enfilade the Spanish infantry.

The plan quickly ran into trouble as both Lacy and Castejon's infantry counter-charged the Poles and Germans as they advanced, throwing them into confusion and no little disorder. However, the Spanish were unable to hold the upper hand for long as the mass of French cavalry had been ordered forward and they moved (apparently) undetected through the sparse cover afforded by the olive groves before launching themselves at the ranks of Spanish cavalry. 'The enemy's forces in the action were very considerable, and according to the news that I have acquired later on, they possessed upwards of 9,000 cavalry: their operation was to attack our right wing with most of these forces, and so defeat it, for which they made a great changes early in their left wing to achieve this.'[9] This uneven contest was concluded with predictable results; four French regiments were assigned to continue chase while the balance of the French cavalry swung right and into the back of the Spanish lines. Lacy and Castejon now found themselves dangerously exposed and were forced to pull back. Such was the surprise and speed of the French cavalry attack that many of the Spanish infantry formations had insufficient time to form square. The cavalry cut their way through the lines of infantry, destroying or capturing battalion after battalion. Many ran forward directly into the sights of Girard's Division but found their escape barred. Jacomé's Division was virtually annihilated and, as the Spanish centre and right disintegrated, Dessolles and the King's Guard crossed into Ocaña and attacked Vigodet and Copons. It was all over, and Areizaga, having issued orders to Zayas to cover the Spanish retreat, climbed on his horse and departed the scene.

The Spanish losses were catastrophic: about 4,000 killed or wounded and 14,000 taken prisoner; 30 colours and 50 guns were captured. It is difficult not to find considerable fault at Areizaga's combat appreciation and leadership and yet Ocaña provides but another example of the superiority of French cavalry, which ultimately turned the battle. 'Ocaña caused a deep impression. Andalusia was by now open. Jose would have ordered the invasion if the British would not have been in Badajoz together with the Army of Alburquerque. So it was prudent to destroy part of those troops and wait for new reinforcements from the north, which would arrive once the peace agreement with Austria had been signed.'[10]

'This disaster took place on 17 of November; it was succeeded by another hardly less ruinous, which occurred in a different part of the country, on the 28th of the same month.'[11] Del Parque, ebullient with success from Tamames, disregarded a directive from the Central Junta to join forces with Alburquerque and prosecute operations in the Tagus valley; he was keen to inflict a second defeat on Marchand and the 6th Corps lay tantalisingly to his front.[12] Outnumbered by three to one, Marchand withdrew in the face of Del Parque's advance, initially from Alba de Tormes and subsequently Salamanca. As he pulled back he sent repeated requests for assistance to both Kellermann and Soult. On 21 November Del Parque then began to manoeuvre his army in between the forces of Marchand, those of Kellermann and the capital. This was a bold move

6   Soult had handed over command of the corps to Heudelet in October when he assumed the role of Joseph's chief of staff.

7   See the map in Ontalba y Ruiz, *La Batalla de Ocaña*, p.101.

8   Paris had assumed command of the 4th Corps cavalry from Merlin, and was to die during the engagement.

9   Giron, *Interrogatorio al Marqués de las Amarillas*, p.66. The figure of 9,000 French cavalry is a gross exaggeration.

10 Toreno, *Guerra de la Independencia, El 2 de Mayo de 1808*, vol. III, p.185.

11 Vane, *Narrative of the Peninsular War*, vol. I, p.439.

12 Soult had detached a brigade from the Corps and Ney, its commander, was still absent on leave.

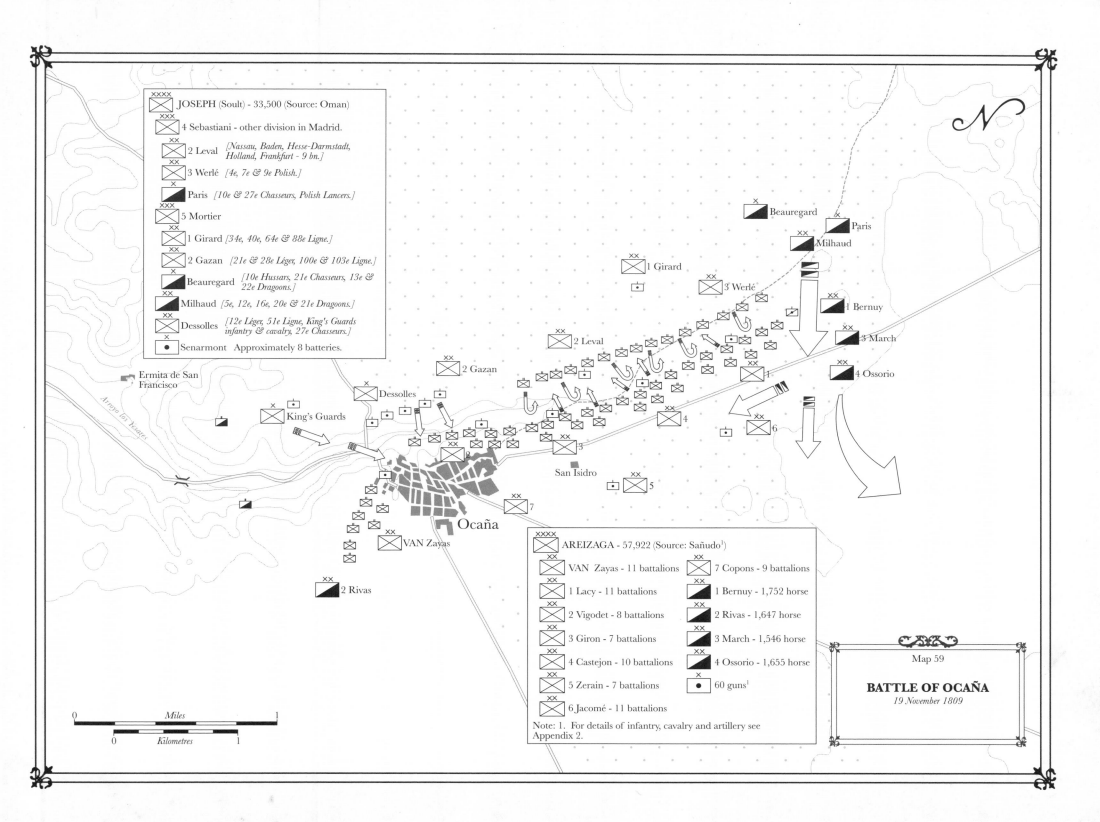

JOSEPH (Soult) - 33,500 (Source: Oman)

4 Sebastiani - other division in Madrid.

2 Leval   *[Nassau, Baden, Hesse-Darmstadt, Holland, Frankfurt - 9 bn.]*

3 Werlé   *[4e, 7e & 9e Polish.]*

Paris   *[10e & 27e Chasseurs, Polish Lancers.]*

5 Mortier

1 Girard   *[34e, 40e, 64e & 88e Ligne.]*

2 Gazan   *[21e & 28e Léger, 100e & 103e Ligne.]*

Beauregard   *[10e Hussars, 21e Chasseurs, 13e & 22e Dragoons.]*

Milhaud   *[5e, 12e, 16e, 20e & 21e Dragoons.]*

Dessolles   *[12e Léger, 51e Ligne, King's Guards infantry & cavalry, 27e Chasseurs.]*

Senarmont   Approximately 8 batteries.

Ermita de San Francisco

Arroyo los Veates

King's Guards

Dessolles

San Isidro

Ocaña

VAN Zayas

2 Rivas

1 Girard

2 Leval

2 Gazan

3 Werlé

Beauregard

Paris

Milhaud

1 Bernuy

3 March

4 Ossorio

AREIZAGA - 57,922 (Source: Sañudo[1])

VAN Zayas - 11 battalions	7 Copons - 9 battalions
1 Lacy - 11 battalions	1 Bernuy - 1,752 horse
2 Vigodet - 8 battalions	2 Rivas - 1,647 horse
3 Giron - 7 battalions	3 March - 1,546 horse
4 Castejon - 10 battalions	4 Ossorio - 1,655 horse
5 Zerain - 7 battalions	60 guns[1]
6 Jacomé - 11 battalions	

Note: 1. For details of infantry, cavalry and artillery see Appendix 2.

Miles
0   1

Kilometres
0   1

Map 59

BATTLE OF OCAÑA
19 November 1809

which may have succeeded in cutting the Valladolid to Madrid line, had it not been for the disaster at Ocaña two days previously. Reinforcements hitherto destined to support the French main effort in and around the capital were now en route to the area. By 24 November the whole of the 6th Corps (once again intact), Kellermann's Division and some infantry released from garrison duties were concentrated at Puente de Duero. They numbered only about 16,000, half the Spanish numbers to their front, but they were prepared to make a stand. To their surprise Del Parque began to withdraw; he had just received news of the disaster at Ocaña, and now realized that additional French forces would be in the area within days.

Del Parque stole a day's march on the French, and confident he had shaken off their pursuit, rested his force at Alba de Tormes, deploying his divisions on both sides of the river. While he rested, Kellermann moved with commendable speed and wrong-footed the overconfident Spanish commander. Arriving on the north bank with his 3,000 cavalry he wasted little time: Lorcet's Brigade of hussars and chasseurs led the charge with three successive waves of dragoons. It was a bold decision as the French infantry were still two hours' march to the north, but the strength and discipline of the French cavalry combined with the element of surprise caused chaos in the Spanish lines. Losada's Division was their first target and, once broken, they turned their attention to La Carrera and Belvedere, who formed brigade squares and succeeded in maintaining formation but any form of retreat would have been precarious. Their lines were cut and the bridge over the Tormes jammed with troops, baggage and artillery vying in a desperate bid to escape. In time, the French infantry and artillery began to arrive and La Carrera, realising it would be suicidal to delay any longer, ordered his men to retreat as best they could. Most made it across as dusk fell and Del Parque used the hours of darkness to break clean and count his losses, which amounted to 3,000 men, five colours and nine guns.

Thus ended the Central Junta's autumn offensive. It was an undisputed failure, which was to bring the executive to its knees. 'Heartened by the fact that the French initially showed no signs of advancing, the Junta frantically tried to mend its fences. Orders were issued for the election of deputies to the new *Cortes*, which it was announced would open on 1 March 1810. A levy of a further 100,000 men was announced and all remaining exemptions from military service abolished. Fresh edicts appeared against desertion. Church plate, table silver, personal jewellery, horses and draught animals were all made the subject of fresh requisitioning. An "extraordinary contribution" that amounted to a graduated income tax was decreed. A start was made on the fortification of the passes that spanned the Sierra Morena. And, finally, Palafox and Montijo were imprisoned,[13] and La Romana appointed to the Captain-Generalcy of Valencia in an attempt to get him out of the way.'[14] Even before Ocaña, Wellington had decided to withdraw inside Portugal, a decision that was predictably badly received by the Spanish. The relationship between the Allies was at an all-time low but Wellington was content to secure Portugal and wait in the hope that the new Spanish administrative body would, like a new broom, sweep clean.

To the east, following the battle at Maria (see Chapter 18), Suchet had used the breathing space acquired through this victory to establish his force in Zaragoza and from Jaca in the Pyrenees to Molina at the base of the Sierra de Albarracin in the south. He had his hands full trying to subdue the guerrilla warfare that now raged in Aragon. 'In the end of August a column of 3,000 men stormed the convent of San Juan de la Peña, close to Jaca, which Sarasa and Renovales[15] were wont to make their headquarters. It was an ancient building containing the tombs of the early kings of Aragon, who reigned in the mountains before Saragossa had been recovered from the Moor; it had never seen an enemy for 800 years, and was reputed holy and impregnable. Hence its capture dealt a severe blow to the insurgents.'[16] By the end of 1809, Suchet could fairly claim to have established control in Aragon but his lines of communication with the 7th Corps in Catalonia were still blocked by Blake.

St Cyr, following his clear victory at Valls in February, (see Chapter 15) returned to Barcelona after a couple of half-hearted attempts to take Tarragona. The British naval blockade and the continued low intensity operations by the *miqueletes*, to the north and west, had reduced supplies to critical levels. The route from France was still blocked by the fortress at Girona and St Cyr now turned his full attention to capturing the structure and reopening this critical line of communication. However, the capture of Girona was to take many more months of bitter and bloody struggle.

---

13 For planning a *coup d'état*.

14 Esdaile, *The Peninsular War, A New History*, p. 218-219.

15 Two local guerrilla chiefs; Renovales had been a colonel in the regular army at the siege of Zaragoza.

16 Oman, *History of the Peninsular War*, vol. 3, p. 12.

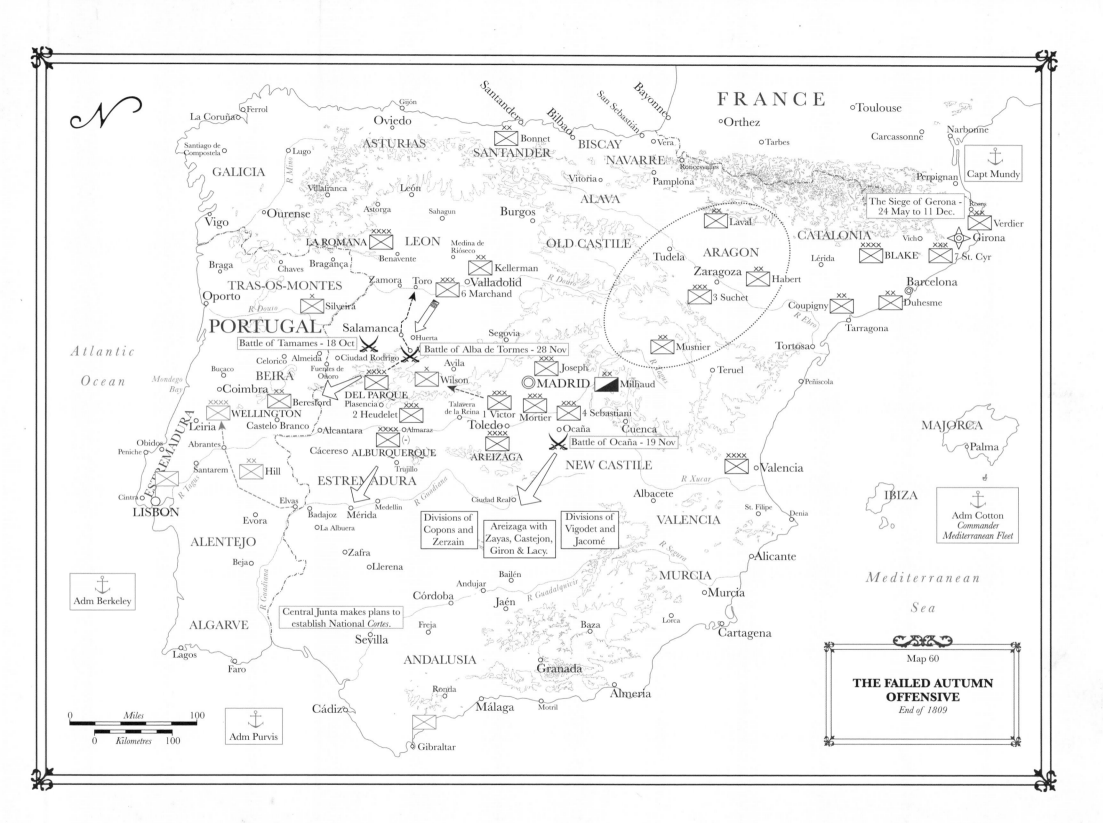

N

FRANCE

Toulouse
Orthez
Carcassonne
Narbonne
Perpignan

Capt Mundy

The Siege of Gerona -
24 May to 11 Dec.

Rhosas
XX Verdier
Girona
CATALONIA
Vich
XXXX BLAKE
XXX 7 St. Cyr
Lérida
Barcelona
Coupigny
XX Duhesme
Tarragona
Tortosa

La Coruña
Ferrol
Gijón
Oviedo
ASTURIAS
SANTANDER
Santander
Bilbao
BISCAY
San Sebastián
Bayonne
Vera
XX Bonnet
NAVARRE
Vitoria
ALAVA
Pamplona
Roncesvalles
Tarbes

Santiago de
Compostela
Lugo
León
Burgos
OLD CASTILE
ARAGON
Tudela
XX Laval
Zaragoza
XX Habert
GALICIA
Villafranca
Astorga
Sahagun
Medina de
Ríoseco
XXXX LA ROMANA
LEON
XX Kellerman
Valladolid
R Douro
XXX 3 Suchet
Vigo
Ourense
Zamora
Toro
XXX 6 Marchand
XX Musnier
R Tagus
Teruel
Peñiscola

Braga
Chaves
Bragança
Benavente
TRAS-OS-MONTES
Oporto
R Douro
Silveira
PORTUGAL
Salamanca
Battle of Tamames - 18 Oct
Huerta
Segovia
Battle of Alba de Tormes - 28 Nov
Avila
XX Joseph
MADRID
XX Milhaud

Celorico
Almeida
Ciudad Rodrigo
Wilson
Atlantic
Ocean
Mondego
Bay
Buçaco
BEIRA
Fuentes de
Oñoro
XXXX DEL PARQUE
Plasencia
2 Heudelet
Talavera de
la Reina
1 Victor
Mortier
XXX 4 Sebastiani
Coimbra
Beresford
Castelo Branco
Alcantara
Almaraz
Toledo
Ocaña
Cuenca
MAJORCA
Palma
Leiria
WELLINGTON
XXXX AREIZAGA
Battle of Ocaña - 19 Nov
NEW CASTILE
IBIZA
Obidos
Peniche
Abrantes
Santarem
XX Hill
Cáceres
ALBURQUERQUE
Trujillo
ESTREMADURA
Ciudad Real
Valencia
Adm Cotton
Commander
Mediterranean Fleet

Cintra
LISBON
Elvas
Badajoz
Mérida
Medellin
R Guadiana
Albacete
St. Filipe
Denia
VALENCIA
Evora
La Albuera
R Xucar
ALENTEJO
Beja
Zafra
Llerena
R Guadiana
Divisions of
Copons and
Zerzain
Areizaga with
Zayas, Castejon,
Giron & Lacy.
Divisions of
Vigodet and
Jacomé
R Segura
Alicante
Mediterranean

Adm Berkeley
Bailén
Andujar
Córdoba
Jaén
R Guadalquivir
Baza
MURCIA
Murcia
Lorca
Sea

Central Junta makes plans to
establish National Cortes.
Freja
Cartagena

Miles 100
Kilometres 100
Adm Purvis
ALGARVE
Lagos
Faro
ALENTEJO
Sevilla
Córdoba
ANDALUSIA
Ronda
Granada
Almeria
Map 60

THE FAILED AUTUMN
OFFENSIVE
End of 1809

Cádiz
Málaga
Motril
Gibraltar

Chapter 22

THE CAPTURE OF GIRONA: MAY TO DECEMBER 1809

Although the war in Catalonia was, at this time, secondary to the main effort, Napoleon had appreciated that the 7th Corps required considerable reinforcement in order to implement its assigned tasks. Consequently, in the spring of 1809, an additional 13 battalions were sent to the region[1] along with numerous siege guns, gunners, sappers and cordon and campaign accoutrements. Leaving Duhesme at Barcelona, St Cyr with the divisions of Souham, Pino, Lecchi and Chabot moved north from the plains of Tarragona to Vich. From there he hoped to reopen communications with Reille, monitor and screen Blake and finally recommence siege operations at Girona. At the end of April, and during early May, preparations had began at Girona but before the operations started in earnest a communiqué arrived from Paris relieving both St Cyr and Reille of their respective commands. Napoleon had tired of the relative inactivity in Catalonia and despised St Cyr's constant requests for more men, money and materiel. Marshal Augereau was nominated as his successor and Verdier as Reille's. The latter was in the area, but the former would not arrive for some time and St Cyr was therefore in the unenviable position of having to commence the siege against the backdrop of disappointment and loss in credibility.

With the arrival of Lecchi's 4,000 men from Vich, Verdier opened the siege on 24 May. The Spanish garrison was commanded by Alvarez and numbered some 5,700 regulars supported by 1,000 armed locals; they had a mass of guns but an inadequate number of trained gunners. In contrast to Zaragoza, the regulars managed and conducted the siege, but for some months they were to receive little by way of reinforcement as Blake was conducting operations against Suchet, and Coupigny was absorbed in a conspiracy to bring down Duhesme at Barcelona. It was not until both schemes failed that the Catalan Junta turned its full attention to Girona. 'Nevertheless, the governor don Mariano Alvarez, was an active and sensible officer who never wasted an opportunity to trouble the enemy and to slow their works and his instructions to subordinate officers tasked with executing sallies would be that, in event of their returning, they would be welcomed; *to the cemetery*.'[2] Despite being their second attempt, the French commanders and engineers were at a loss as to how to tackle the siege: attack from the east, take the main citadel, cross the river, reduce the town and then engage the forts on the Monjuich and Capuchin heights, or vice versa. In the end they elected for the heights and associated forts as their first target, and finally on 6 June they commenced the construction of the trenches, parallels and gun pits on the plateau of Monjuich. Two 24-pounder batteries (map 61, points 2 and 3) were constructed opposite the towers and redoubts of San Luis, San Narciso and San Daniel and a further mortar battery on the Green Mound was established to fire into the town itself in an attempt to break the morale of the defenders (map 61, point 1). More batteries were established in mid-June when the first objectives were carried by assault; the first two batteries were moved forward and two additional 16-pounder batteries were also opened (map 61, points 4 and 5). By the end of the month, a large 20-gun battery was established only 400m from the walls (map 61, point 6) and within days a functional breach had been fashioned in the north-eastern bastion. Following an abortive attempt on 4 and 5 July, a more concerted effort was made on the 7th; but this was also to fail with considerable losses to the French. The morale of the besiegers plummeted and Verdier[3] elected to bombard the structure and the defenders, unremittingly, for the next four weeks. Preparations then commenced to mine the glacis in no fewer than 23 places, but on 10 August, before Verdier could deliver the attack, the defenders spiked the guns, blew the structure and evacuated the crumbling remains.

During July the *somatenes* had increased the intensity of operations against St Cyr's cordon and the French convoys destined to resupply Verdier. With Blake's forces effectively out of the game, following their rout at Belchite on 18 June, Coupigny had been ordered north as he possessed the only intact force in the province. It was not until 17 August that Alvarez received his first reinforcements numbering only 800 men; he had to wait another two weeks for more substantial numbers to arrive. With the loss of the Monjuich, the fortified convent of San Daniel and the tower of San Juan had also been vacated, leaving nothing between the besiegers and the old, inadequate city walls. Only in the areas where the defenders had strengthened and widened the *enceinte* could heavier guns be placed, along the rest of the walls only very light pieces could be positioned. In their favour, the defenders could rely on the elevated flanking fire from the forts on the Capuchin heights and the nearer redoubts; furthermore, attacks on the bastion of Santa Maria could be enfiladed from the area of Gironella. Conversely, for the French the hillside leading down from the Monjuich was solid rock and would necessitate the building up, rather than digging down, of parallels. Unsurprisingly, the French sappers elected to commence operations from the ruins of the suburb of Pedret and selected four points of attack for the second phase of the operation (map 62, points A to D). New batteries were established in the ruins of the Monjuich, and further forward as parallels were constructed (map 62, points 7 and 8). The existing batteries were retained, if they were still considered effective, and mortars were established on the heights; these combined with the mortars on the Green Mound to ceaselessly bombard the town, forcing the population to take to the cellars. Sickness began to ravage both the defenders and besiegers: 'By malaria, dysentery and sunstroke Verdier had lost 5,000 men, in addition to the casualties in the siege.'[4] The sick were transported to the hospitals at Figueras and Perpignan; the *somatenes* allowed them unhindered passage out but not back.

---

1   These were all the German units from Berg, Würzburg and Westphalia.

2   Toreno, *Guerra de la Independencia, El 2 de Mayo de 1808*, vol. III, p.143.

3   St Cyr had handed over full responsibility for the siege to Verdier and had established himself at San Feliu de Guixols, placing the remaining French troops in a semi-circle covering all the approaches to the town.

4   Oman, *History of the Peninsular War*, vol. III, p.39.

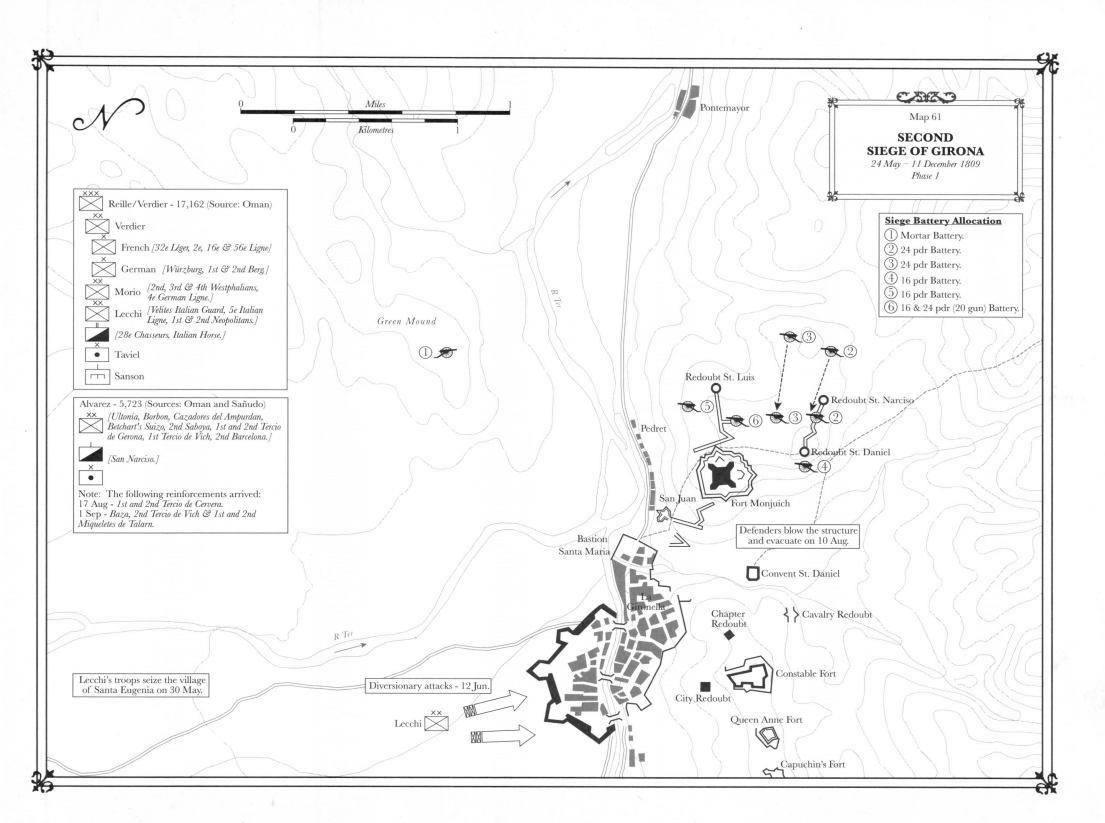

N

0   Miles   1

0   Kilometres   1

Pontemayor

Map 61

SECOND SIEGE OF GIRONA
24 May – 11 December 1809
Phase 1

Reille/Verdier - 17,162 (Source: Oman)

Verdier

French [32e Léger, 2e, 16e & 56e Ligne]

German [Würzburg, 1st & 2nd Berg.]

Morio [2nd, 3rd & 4th Westphalians, 4e German Ligne.]

Lecchi [Velites Italian Guard, 5e Italian Ligne, 1st & 2nd Neopolitans.]

[28e Chasseurs, Italian Horse.]

Taviel

Sanson

Alvarez - 5,723 (Sources: Oman and Sañudo)

[Ultonia, Borbon, Cazadores del Ampurdan, Betchart's Suizo, 2nd Saboya, 1st and 2nd Tercio de Gerona, 1st Tercio de Vich, 2nd Barcelona.]

[San Narciso.]

Note: The following reinforcements arrived:
17 Aug - 1st and 2nd Tercio de Cervera.
1 Sep - Baza, 2nd Tercio de Vich & 1st and 2nd Miqueletes de Talarn.

Siege Battery Allocation
① Mortar Battery.
② 24 pdr Battery.
③ 24 pdr Battery.
④ 16 pdr Battery.
⑤ 16 pdr Battery.
⑥ 16 & 24 pdr (20 gun) Battery.

R Ter

Green Mound

①

③

②

Redoubt St. Luis

⑤

⑥ ③ ②

Redoubt St. Narciso

Redoubt St. Daniel

④

Pedret

San Juan

Fort Monjuich

Defenders blow the structure and evacuate on 10 Aug.

Bastion Santa Maria

Convent St. Daniel

La Gironella

Chapter Redoubt

Cavalry Redoubt

Constable Fort

City Redoubt

R Ter

Lecchi's troops seize the village of Santa Eugenia on 30 May.

Diversionary attacks - 12 Jun.

Lecchi

Queen Anne Fort

Capuchin's Fort

By 30 August four substantial breaches had been created, but the supporting approaches were still a long way short and Verdier's force had dwindled to 10,000. Worse still Blake, who had returned to Tarragona in July, had received orders and funding to enable him to come to the aid of the force at Girona. His battalions were still under-strength but his army mustered some 14,000 men; however, the memories of Belchite were still fresh in his mind and he was reluctant to engage in another pitched battle. He marched north and on 1 September came face-to-face with the French screening force. St Cyr's force numbered slightly less than that of Blake, but the hapless French commander was keen to depart the Peninsula with a victory and was enthusiastic at the prospect of a pitched battle with Blake. Verdier had been ordered to leave Morio and Lecchi at Girona and march with his own division of 4,000 to join St Cyr. As a result, St Cyr's force now outnumbered the Spanish, but they were about to be outwitted. Blake had detached the division of Garcia Conde (also about 4,000 strong) along with provisions and cattle, and this now moved around the flank of St Cyr and presented itself in front of an astonished Polish officer commanding Lecchi's Division in his absence. The Spanish crashed through the centre of the demoralized Italians, routed them and then entered Girona to victorious acclaim. Before word of this disaster could be passed to St Cyr, the Spanish ventured forth in strength and destroyed many of the parallels and forward trenches on the forward slopes of the Monjuich. St Cyr was furious at being outwitted by Blake and immediately despatched Verdier, with Pino's six Italian battalions, to return to Girona and reestablish the cordon and recommence the siege. Blake and St Cyr now faced each other with balanced forces of about 10,000, but the Spanish commander once again refused to fight and when St Cyr advanced, Blake withdrew to Hostalrich and dispersed his army into the mountains in small groups.

On 11 September Verdier's siege batteries reopened and the workforce repaired all the broken trenches and parallels only to have them destroyed again four days later when a subsequent attack by the defenders caught the French off-guard. By 19 September Verdier judged an assault possible but requested more troops from St Cyr to execute the task. This was refused[5] but he offered to provide Pino's Division to hold the Monjuich and to make a separate diversion against the town from the west. Verdier had little choice but to accept. He reorganized the remainder of his original siege force into three columns; each of about 1,000 men and a fourth group of about 150 to act as a feint. This last group attacked the breach at San Cristobal; the Italians stormed Santa Lucia; the French the Redoubt of the Germans; and the Germans, San Pedro. Alvarez and

his men watched as Pino's men took up their posts, releasing the siege infantry, and preparing for the inevitable assault. On 19 September, at 1600 hours, the diversionary attack against the fortifications on the Capuchin heights commenced and simultaneously the four columns moved forward to their respective breaches. The diversion was quickly dispelled and the guns in the forts on the heights were able to engage the attackers unhindered. The assaults were delivered with more success but they failed to penetrate the inner barricades. The Italians succeeded in scaling the breach but found a 4m drop on the far side and, despite holding the *enceinte* for some time, were eventually beaten back by the weight of fire from the rooftops and loop-holed buildings. The attack collapsed along with the morale of the assailants. Verdier and St Cyr dispatched spiteful communiqués to Paris, each criticising the other. Verdier took himself off to convalesce at Perpignan having accused his force of cowardice, which countered by reporting sick in droves.

St Cyr now decided to starve the town and withdrew the immediate cordon. On 11 October Augereau finally appeared, 'like all new commanders, had wished to distinguish himself, that he might be able to acquaint Bonaparte at once with his arrival, and with a victory which would induce his master to applaud himself for having chosen one of his most famous lieutenants'.[6] Alas, it was not to be. He recommenced the bombardment and occasionally harassed the walls, but it was through starvation that the townsfolk were losing heart, and when Blake made his third and final attempt to succour the town on 18 October[7] Augereau decided to deal with the troublesome Spaniard and attack him and his depot at Hostalrich. By early November this had been achieved. The news was a hammer blow to the Gironese; morale plummeted and for the first time differences of opinion emerged between Alvarez and some of the military commanders. A conspiracy to overthrow Alvarez was uncovered and before the culprits could be dealt with, they escaped to the French lines and apprised the commander of the dire situation within the walls. Augereau immediately ordered the siege operations to recommence and, on 2 December, Pino's Italians gained a lodgement in the town, four days later they captured the city redoubt. A failed attempt to recapture the structure was Alvarez's last throw of the dice. Early on 11 December the starved survivors of the garrison marched out and surrendered; two-thirds of the original defenders had perished and one-third of those who had arrived in September had also died. French losses were equally devastating with 14,000 men estimated lost or incapacitated. The capture of Girona provided a significant prize but, like Zaragoza, the price had been high.

---

5   Relations between the two officers were not good. St Cyr resented Verdier's appointment and the fact that the new commander had communicated directly to Paris soon after assuming command.

6   Sarrazin, *History of the War in Spain and Portugal from 1807 to 1814*, p.105.

7   He had made a second attempt at the end of September.

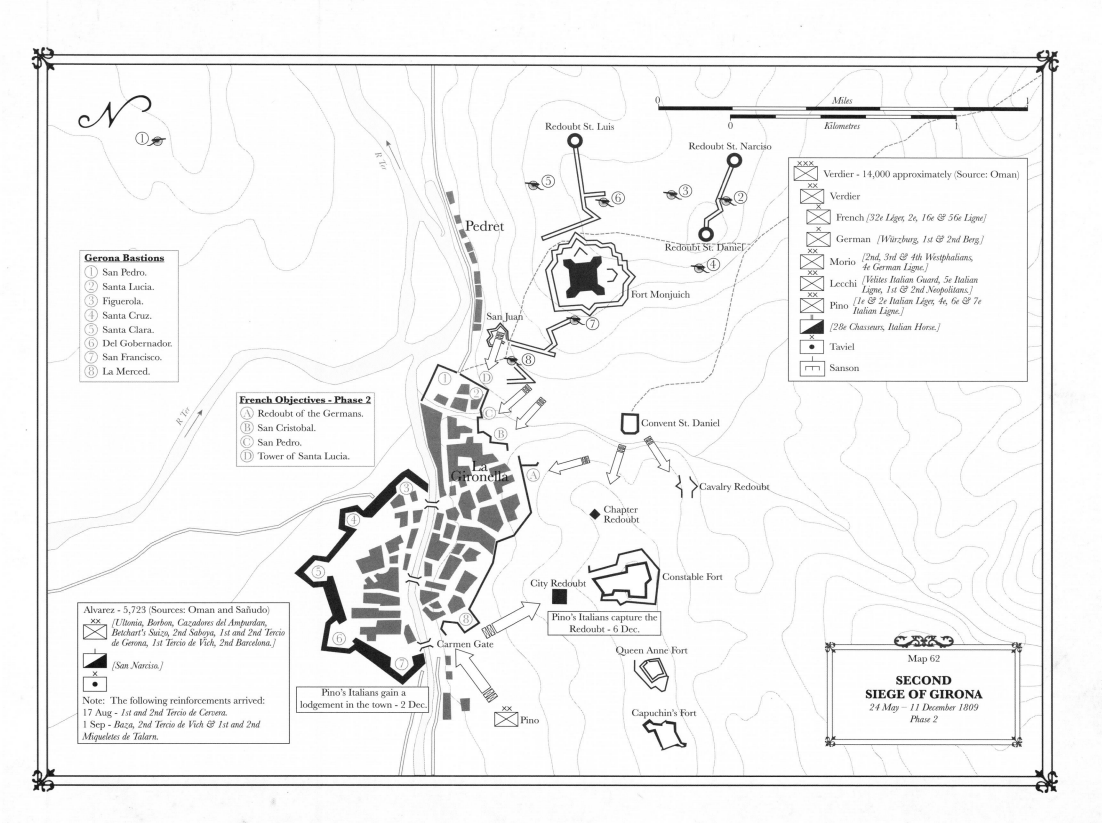

N

Redoubt St. Luis

Redoubt St. Narciso

Redoubt St. Daniel

Pedret

R Ter

Fort Monjuich

San Juan

Gerona Bastions
1. San Pedro.
2. Santa Lucia.
3. Figuerola.
4. Santa Cruz.
5. Santa Clara.
6. Del Gobernador.
7. San Francisco.
8. La Merced.

French Objectives - Phase 2
Ⓐ Redoubt of the Germans.
Ⓑ San Cristobal.
Ⓒ San Pedro.
Ⓓ Tower of Santa Lucia.

R Ter

La Gironella

Convent St. Daniel

Cavalry Redoubt

Chapter Redoubt

City Redoubt

Constable Fort

Pino's Italians capture the Redoubt - 6 Dec.

Queen Anne Fort

Carmen Gate

Capuchin's Fort

Alvarez - 5,723 (Sources: Oman and Sañudo)

[Ultonia, Borbon, Cazadores del Ampurdan, Betchart's Suizo, 2nd Saboya, 1st and 2nd Tercio de Gerona, 1st Tercio de Vich, 2nd Barcelona.]

[San Narciso.]

Note: The following reinforcements arrived:
17 Aug - *1st and 2nd Tercio de Cervera.*
1 Sep - *Baza, 2nd Tercio de Vich & 1st and 2nd Miqueletes de Talarn.*

Pino's Italians gain a lodgement in the town - 2 Dec.

Pino

Miles

Kilometres

Verdier - 14,000 approximately (Source: Oman)

Verdier

French *[32e Léger, 2e, 16e & 56e Ligne]*

German *[Würzburg, 1st & 2nd Berg.]*

Morio *[2nd, 3rd & 4th Westphalians, 4e German Ligne.]*

Lecchi *[Velites Italian Guard, 5e Italian Ligne, 1st & 2nd Neopolitans.]*

Pino *[1e & 2e Italian Léger, 4e, 6e & 7e Italian Ligne.]*

[28e Chasseurs, Italian Horse.]

• Taviel

Sanson

Map 62

SECOND SIEGE OF GIRONA
24 May – 11 December 1809
Phase 2

Chapter 23

Subjugation of Andalusia: January to February 1810

Despite the comprehensive victory at Uclés, Joseph and Soult waited until events in Leon had stabilized and the whereabouts and intentions of the British were apparent before reassuming the offensive. Victory at the battle of Alba de Tormes, which drove Wellington deep into Portugal, coupled with substantial reinforcements inward bound from Germany in December 1809,[1] enabled the French command to consider the conquest of Andalusia a realistic proposition. Two plans were drawn up, the first was time-consuming and cautious, the second rapid and ambitious; the latter was adopted. The conquest of the last bastion of Spain would enable Joseph to ultimately control his kingdom and he was impatient for swift and decisive results. A series of additional distractions were planned; Suchet was ordered to attack the province of Valencia; Ney's objective was Ciudad Rodrigo while Heudelet was left at Talavera, watching both Alburquerque and the Portuguese border.

The conquest of Andalusia commenced on 7 January 1810, but an early meeting with Victor at Ciudad Real provided the opportunity to gather better intelligence about the passes over the Sierra Morena, which in turn served to alter the original plans. Victor was sent via Almaden to make a very wide right flanking manoeuvre, while the balance of the force[2] were to strike south over the passes at and adjacent to Despeña-Perros. The two groups would then link up at Córdoba. Joseph attacked the passes in four places, and with the exception of Sebastiani's assault on the far left, all were taken with ease. Areizaga with his three divisions[3] fell back as the four groups of French troops regrouped south of the passes. Spurred on by the rapidity of their success they pursued the demoralized Spaniards, who by now had abandoned any hope of holding the road to Sevilla, electing instead to head south to Jaén. Victor too was enjoying similar success and by the night of 22 January, the two forces had linked up southwest of Andujar and two days later they entered Córdoba.

The following day, Joseph and Soult instigated the next part of their plan. Dessolles was to remain at Córdoba, Sebastiani was sent to take Granada and the balance was to move on Sevilla. Joseph was clearly unaware of Alburquerque's small army, which had moved east in an attempt to support Zerain but then fell back on Sevilla when he realized he was too late. Zerain joined Alburquerque a few days later and then stayed in Sevilla while Alburquerque and Copons, with

about 10,000 men including 1,000 cavalry and 20 guns, advanced to Carmona to make a stand. The order for Alburquerque to execute this defensive manoeuvre was the last the Central Junta was to issue; on 23 January the assembly dispersed and the members fled. The city collapsed into anarchy and a new revolutionary government was installed. Alburquerque had no intention of placing his force in the hands of a mob, and on hearing of the strength of the French force now advancing from Córdoba he wasted no time in deciding to withdraw to Cádiz. His plan was to establish a defensive position; an action that was without doubt to save southern Spain.

Joseph left Córdoba on 25 January and reached the outskirts of Sevilla on the night of the 29th. Palafox, having been freed from prison by the mob,[4] was desperately trying to organize some form of defence. Their cause was hopeless and Palafox and his supporters absconded on the night of 28 January, making their way to Cádiz. The city, effectively undefended, surrendered on 31 January and Joseph entered in triumph the following day. Meanwhile, Sebastiani had taken Jaén on 23 January, and then marched on Granada, which he entered on the 28th, and having detained the garrison with the confines of the Alhambra, set off for Málaga. By 10 February he had captured Málaga, Velez, Motril and Almunecar.

After so many disappointments, Joseph could not hide his delight at the speed and success of capturing Sevilla and made a histrionically triumphant entrance to the temporary capital of Spain. Where, once established, he set about issuing a series of elegant but quixotic proclamations. Meanwhile, Soult sent Victor south to capture Cádiz and complete the conquest. The loss of Sevilla was a monumental blow to the Spanish cause as it had housed the main arsenal in Spain, and all its foundries were in pristine condition and well stocked. Had the French been able to move these commodities by sea and trade them on the open market their worth would have significantly assisted the national war effort. The euphoria of the rapid and seemingly lucrative conquest of Andalusia was, however, about to change.

Alburquerque had arrived at Cádiz on 3 February and, incorporating the recruits he had collected en route, now had a force of 12,000 men. He broke the only bridge leading to the Cádiz peninsula and conferred with Venegas, the military governor, to ensure that all boats, large or small, had been destroyed or brought over to the home banks. Batteries had been placed at all the key points but most significantly, the Spanish gunboats had free rein within the inner and outer harbours and were supported by 12 Spanish and four British battle ships. Victor arrived during the early evening of 5 February, having covered the march from Sevilla in only four days, and was astonished to see the large Allied naval presence and the abundance of troops on the Isla de Leon and the Cádiz peninsula. Nevertheless, he called upon the town to surrender and received a curt reply from the defenders prompting him to take a closer look at the defences and lie of the land. He rapidly concluded that the situation was far from promising; further noting that without heavy artillery and naval support the likelihood of capturing the city was remote. He conveyed this disappointing news back to Joseph at Sevilla, who was mortified to discover that his personal and significant triumph was to be denied at the last hurdle. He immediately

---

1   Two strong divisions under Loison and Reynier numbering about 20,000, another 90,000 were expected within months.

2   Joseph's Guard, the division of Dessolles, the 5th Corps complete, Werlé's Division from the 4th Corps, and the cavalry divisions of Latour-Maubourg and Milhaud.

3   Castejon, originally with Areizaga, had been sent to assist Vigodet to the east.

4   La Romana was also freed and was given Del Parque's command but chose instead to present himself to the Castilian Army whereupon he was promptly made their new chief.

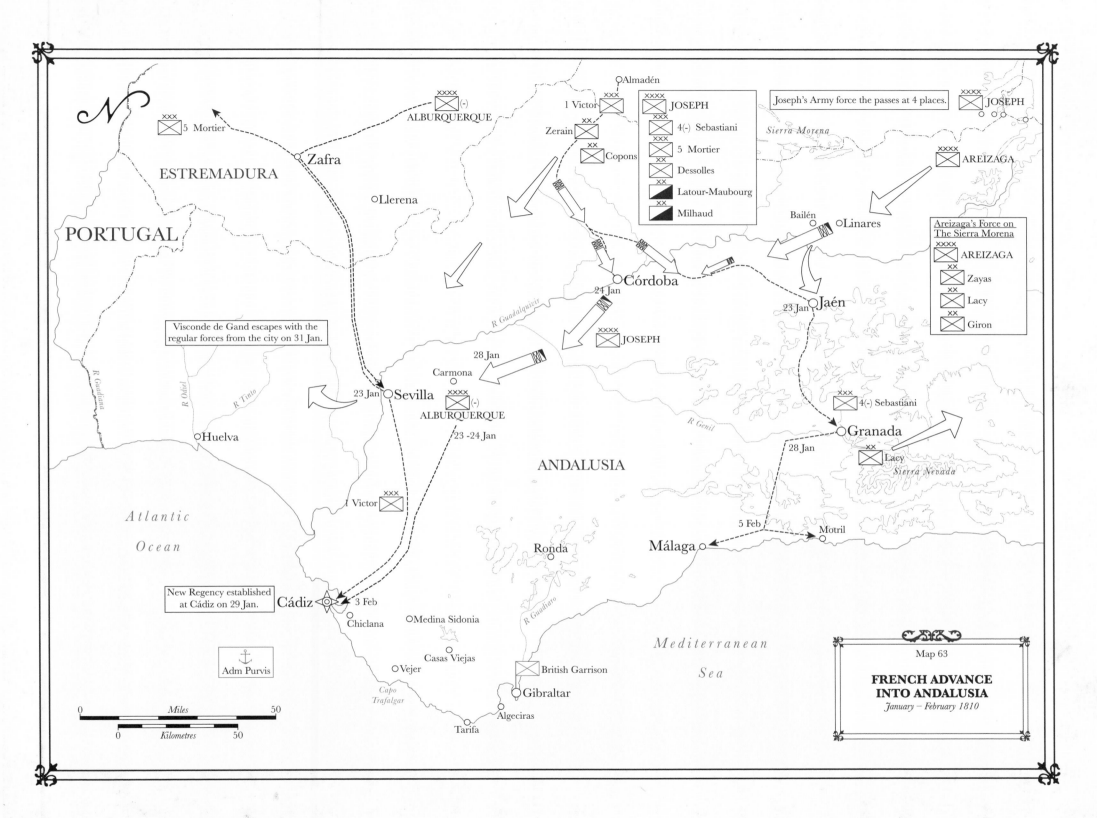

N

Almadén

1 Victor

Zerain

Copons

ALBURQUERQUE

5 Mortier

Zafra

ESTREMADURA

Llerena

PORTUGAL

R Guadiana

R Odiel

R Tinto

Huelva

Visconde de Gand escapes with the
regular forces from the city on 31 Jan.

Carmona

23 Jan Sevilla

ALBURQUERQUE

23 -24 Jan

28 Jan

24 Jan Córdoba

R Guadalquivir

JOSEPH

R Genit

ANDALUSIA

Ronda

R Guadiaro

JOSEPH

Joseph's Army force the passes at 4 places.

JOSEPH
4(-) Sebastiani
5 Mortier
Dessolles
Latour-Maubourg
Milhaud

Sierra Morena

JOSEPH

AREIZAGA

Bailén

Linares

23 Jan Jaén

Areizaga's Force on
The Sierra Morena

AREIZAGA
Zayas
Lacy
Giron

4(-) Sebastiani

28 Jan Granada

Lacy

Sierra Nevada

5 Feb Motril

Málaga

1 Victor

New Regency established
at Cádiz on 29 Jan.

Adm Purvis

0   Miles   50
0   Kilometres   50

Cádiz 3 Feb

Chiclana

Medina Sidonia

Casas Viejas

Vejer

Capo
Trafalgar

British Garrison

Gibraltar

Algeciras

Tarifa

Atlantic
Ocean

Mediterranean
Sea

Map 63

**FRENCH ADVANCE
INTO ANDALUSIA**
January – February 1810

departed Sevilla to judge the situation for himself. Faced with the reality, Joseph felt compelled to write to Napoleon asking for the release of the French fleet at Toulon, the only such fleet in the Mediterranean. However, with the British Mediterranean fleet still stationed around the Balearic isles, any movement of French ships in support of operations against Cádiz was out of the question. His request was ignored and, to make matters worse, it had also become apparent that the French heavy artillery had limited utility, as it lacked sufficient range to engage anything other than the suburb of San José. Blockade was the only option remaining, but with sustainment of the city from the sea a relatively straightforward affair, the likelihood of success was slim. Within the city the new Regency set about establishing itself, issuing proclamations and creating an air of normality.

Within days Spanish reinforcements began to arrive by sea. The first to appear were the regulars from Sevilla[5] who had evaded capture by Mortier's Corps and embarked at Ayamonte. Many others were to follow including British and Portuguese troops[6] from Lisbon under General Stewart. This seemingly harmonious situation belied considerable undercurrents between Alburquerque and Venegas and the local Junta for defence,[7] as well as the fledgling Regency. Eventually the Regency was able to remove Venegas by offering him the post of Viceroy to Mexico, replacing him with Alburquerque; although this general's appointment was only to last until the immediate crisis had abated.

'His (Soult's) troops occupied San Lucar de Barrameda, at the mouth of the Guadalquivir, Rota, Puerto de Santa Maria, Puerto Real and Chiclana. He placed a strong garrison in Medina Sidonia. He sent Marshal Mortier into Estremadura, for the purpose of subduing the province, gaining possession of Badajoz, and opening a communication with the second corps, of which General Reynier had taken the command.'[8] A large contingent from Sebastiani was also tasked to venture into Murcia, leaving Victor as the mainstay of the besieging force. Soult's command was thus stretched to the limit maintaining the siege, trying to hold existing conquests, secure other key positions and subdue the ceaseless activity of the guerrilleros. Joseph meanwhile toured the province visiting Rota, Málaga, Granada and Jaén and offering assurances of protection and support to the nobility, 'but he was soon gone, and the native officials whom he appointed were powerless against Sebastiani, the church plunderer, and Soult, the judicious collector of works of art'.[9]

Victor tried to push forward onto the Isla de Leon and north to the forts of San José and Matagorda (map 64, points 1 & 2) but the numerous waterways and extensive fenland hindered every attempt. Some time later the French secured the Trocadero and established a number of batteries upon it. A fight prevailed for the Fort Matagorda, which the Spanish had destroyed in early February, but which they had recaptured on 22 February[10] and hastily repaired. Victor was determined to secure the place, as it was clear that it held the key to controlling shipping within the harbour. He moved 40 heavy guns on to the Trocadero and a long and angry artillery duel ensued. By early March the structure was in French hands and, although Victor was now able to exercise greater control over the harbour, the structure itself offered little by way of advantage in the advancement of the siege of Cádiz.

---

5   Comprising mainly of Zerain's Division, who had stayed when Alburquerque departed for Cádiz

6   79th, 2/87th & 94th along with two battalions from the 20th Portuguese Line Regiment.

7   Which had been established by the city with Venegas as its President.

8   Sarrazin, *History of the War in Spain and Portugal From 1807 to 1814*, p.122.

9   Oman, *History of the Peninsular War*, vol III, p.152.

10 In fact a company of the 94th and some British artillerymen had secured the ruins.

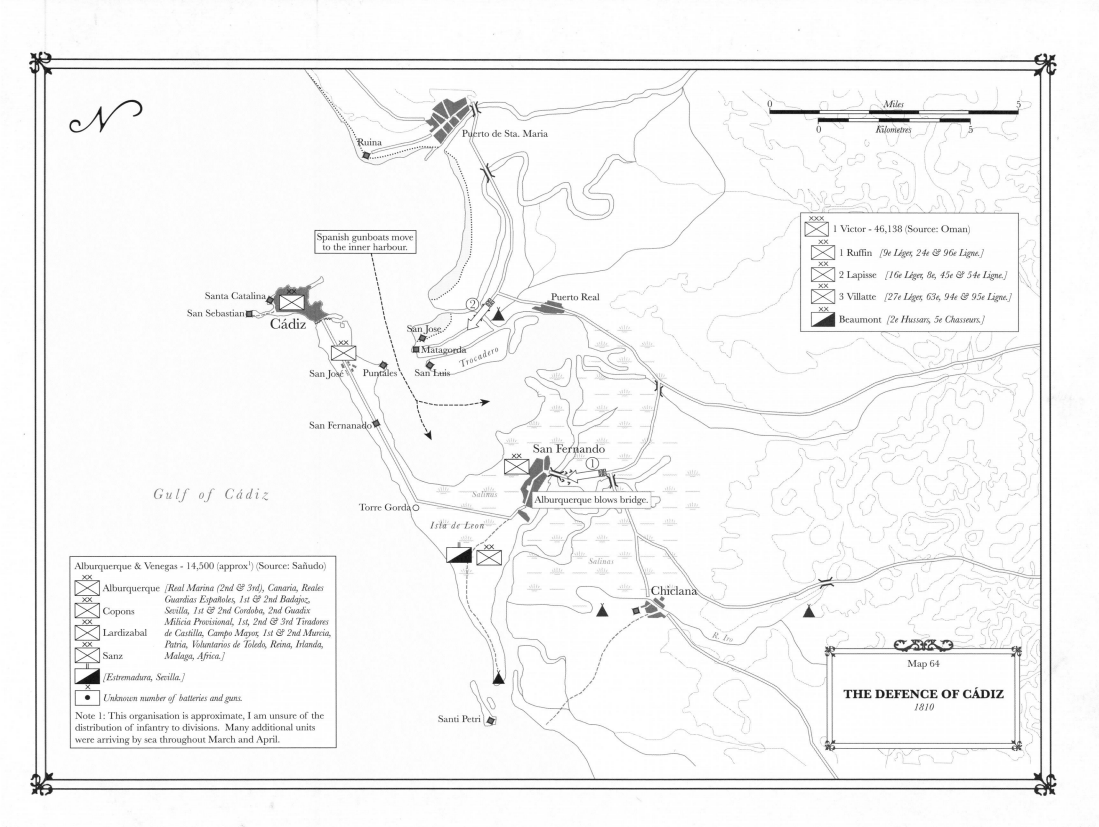

N

Ruina

Puerto de Sta. Maria

Spanish gunboats move
to the inner harbour.

Santa Catalina
San Sebastian
Cádiz

Puerto Real

San Jose
Matagorda
San José   Puntales   San Luis   *Trocadero*

San Fernanado

Gulf of Cádiz

San Fernando

Alburquerque blows bridge.

Salinas

Torre Gorda

Isla de Leon

Salinas

Chiclana

R. Iro

Santi Petri

✕✕✕	1 Victor - 46,138 (Source: Oman)	
✕✕	1 Ruffin	*[9e Léger, 24e & 96e Ligne.]*
✕✕	2 Lapisse	*[16e Léger, 8e, 45e & 54e Ligne.]*
✕✕	3 Villatte	*[27e Léger, 63e, 94e & 95e Ligne.]*
✕✕	Beaumont	*[2e Hussars, 5e Chasseurs.]*

Alburquerque & Venegas - 14,500 (approx[1]) (Source: Sañudo)

✕✕	Alburquerque	*[Real Marina (2nd & 3rd), Canaria, Reales Guardias Españoles, 1st & 2nd Badajoz, Sevilla, 1st & 2nd Cordoba, 2nd Guadix Milicia Provisional, 1st, 2nd & 3rd Tiradores de Castilla, Campo Mayor, 1st & 2nd Murcia, Patria, Voluntarios de Toledo, Reina, Irlanda, Malaga, Africa.]*
✕✕	Copons	
✕✕	Lardizabal	
✕✕	Sanz	
		[Estremadura, Sevilla.]
✕ •		*Unknown number of batteries and guns.*

Note 1: This organisation is approximate, I am unsure of the
distribution of infantry to divisions. Many additional units
were arriving by sea throughout March and April.

Map 64

THE DEFENCE OF CÁDIZ
1810

Chapter 24

Aragon and the East Coast: January to May 1810

While Soult was finalising plans for the Andalusian campaign, Suchet had been ordered to make a dash for Valencia. Since assuming command of the demoralized 3rd Corps in May, Suchet had secured the breathing space he required to rebuild his charge following his victory at Maria in June 1809. He had achieved a great deal in the intervening months and, by the close of the year, had no Spanish army in his area of operations and had effectively dispersed the hitherto considerable guerrilla threat in Aragon. Furthermore, the arrival of the Corps de Réserve de l'Armée d'Allemagne, following the termination of the war in Austria, provided the first of the masses of reinforcements destined for the Peninsula. They arrived at Burgos on New Year's Day and were redesignated the 8th Corps, under Junot's command, which in turn were to form part of the new Army of Portugal (see Chapter 25). One of Junot's divisions under Lagrange was pushed to the east of Pamplona, releasing Leval for other operational tasking.

Suchet did not concur with Soult's assessment that the Valencians would capitulate at the first sight of the *Grande Armée;* after all they had not done so eighteen months earlier when Moncey sought to capture the place. Suchet was to be proved right. Advancing, as ordered, on two routes he left Musnier with a single brigade in Zaragoza. The two forces joined up at Murviedro and then marched on Valencia. General Caro, the local Spanish commander, had wisely elected to withdraw his force within the fortifications of the city. Suchet arrived on 10 March and quickly appreciated, as Moncey had done two years prior, that without siege artillery his task was hopeless. Four days later, amidst reports that the guerrilla factions had renewed their efforts in Aragon, Suchet withdrew. For the 3rd Corps, the first three months of the year had been all but wasted.[1]

In Catalonia during this time, Augereau had been busy consolidating his position following the prolonged and costly siege of Girona. Verdier's battered division was left to recover in cantonments between Figueras and Girona, while Augereau moved south, taking Souham and Pino, with the aim of reopening the road between France and Barcelona. Pino went via Hostalrich, which he attempted to besiege, but soon lost heart and continued south, leaving Mazzuchelli's Brigade to continue the blockade. Souham advanced via Vich and entered the town on 11 January, a few hours after the Army of Catalonia had vacated it.[2] Souham pursued O'Donnell's weakened and demoralized force into the mountains but on 12 January suffered a setback when the Spanish turned on their hunters and thrust the vanguard back with loss. The pursuit continued, but Souham soon lost interest and then shifted his force across the mountains to rejoin the road to Barcelona. In the meantime, Augereau and Pino had entered Barcelona and his first task was to relieve Duhesme of his command and send him back to France; the two generals were old adversaries. Having opened the road Augereau now considered the option of besieging Tarragona but was quickly apprised by the residing quartermaster that the city stores and magazines were empty. He had no choice but to postpone further offensive operations and ordered instead the two divisions to retrace their steps and collect the mass of stores that were being stockpiled at Perpignan, Figueras and Girona.

Pino returned on the Hostalrich road and on arrival at Girona collected the massive supply train and concurrently joined forces with a further 8,000 reinforcements sent from France to strengthen the French Army of Catalonia.[3] Souham was less fortunate. He returned via Vich, where O'Donnell fell upon the smaller French force and very nearly secured victory over it. Souham's two cavalry squadrons turned the contest and Souham himself was badly wounded, invalided to France and replaced by Augereau's brother. By 13 March, over 1,000 wagons were ready to move from Girona and Augereau decided to escort the convoy personally. Taking the eastern road he passed Hostalrich, which was still under siege from Mazzuchelli's Brigade, and on to Barcelona, arriving a few days later with his three divisions and a mass of stores and munitions.

Towards the end of March, Augereau sent two divisions, those of his brother and Severoli, to Reus, from where they were to establish a base for offensive operations against Tarragona. To cover their flank, a brigade was despatched under Schwartz to Manresa. On 29 March, Augereau and Severoli arrived on the outskirts of Tarragona and demanded the city's surrender. The French were unaware that O'Donnell had arrived days earlier and established 6,000 men inside the walls. To add to their woe, a small force under General Caro had been deployed to attack the troops holding open the French lines of communication with Barcelona. During an early skirmish, Caro was wounded and forced to hand over command to Campo Verde. This Spanish officer achieved a considerable victory by driving Schwartz out of Manresa and inflicting considerable loss on the French force. In frustration, Augereau recalled the two divisions and by 9 April the entire French army was once again camped in and around the walls of Barcelona. Two days later Severoli was sent north to assume command of the siege operation at Hostalrich and was followed a few days later by Augereau's entire force which fell back as far as Girona. This inexplicable retrograde movement, coupled with the failure to support the 3rd Corps in their siege of Lérida, was too much for Napoleon and on 24 April he dismissed his third army

---

1   In fact on return Suchet was to receive a Napoleonic rebuke for undertaking the operation because on 1 March he had been instructed that the province of Aragon had been made an independent military command, answerable to Paris and not Madrid. However, Suchet's move to Valencia was already well advanced when he received the communiqué. To return at that stage would have left Habert on his own and dangerously exposed on the eastern route; he therefore elected to continue.

2   Now under command of Major General Henry O'Donnell and numbering about 7,000. Blake had resigned in late December and been temporarily succeeded by the Marquis of Portago and subsequently General Garcia Conde.

3   A division from the Confederation of the Rhine under General Rouyer and a Neapolitan Brigade.

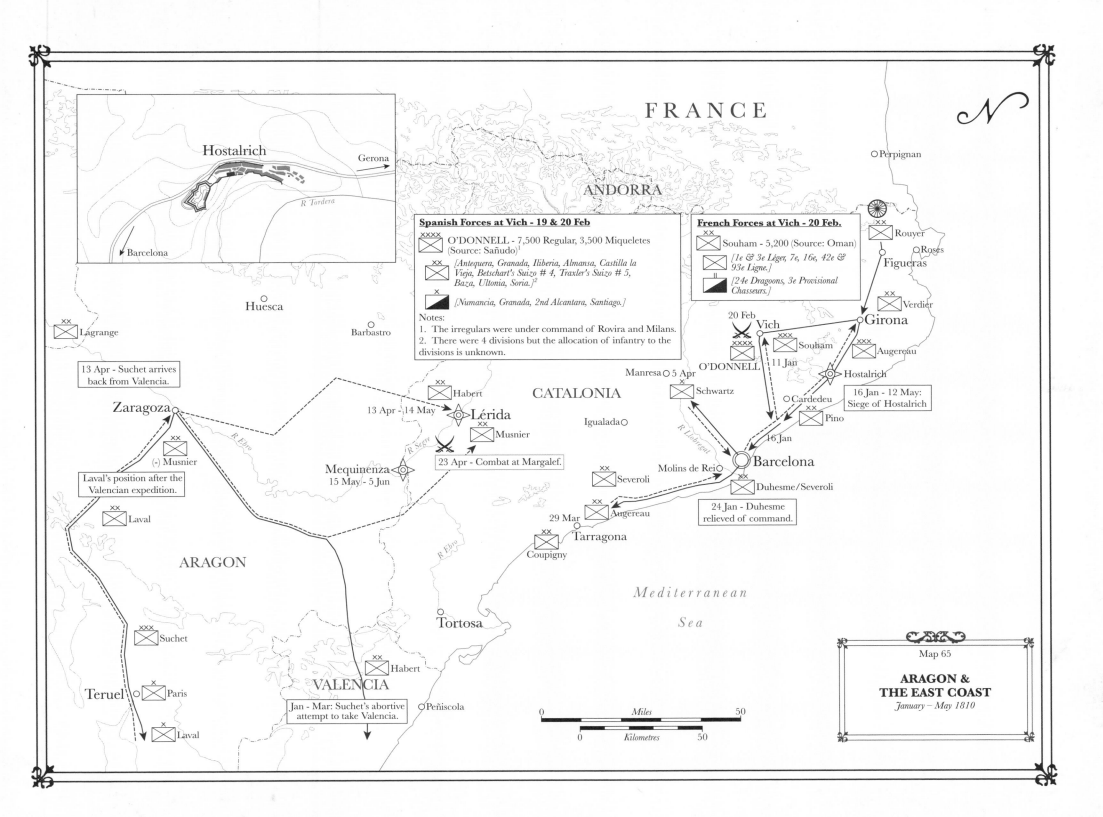

commander in Catalonia. The replacement, Marshal Macdonald, was currently in Italy and not able to arrive for another month, during which time the Army of Catalonia enjoyed some infrequent success. At Hostalrich on 12 May, with all rations expended, Estrada, the governor, decided to rush the lines and make for the mountains. Although many defenders were successful, Estrada and a few officers and about 300 men were captured.

Suchet had arrived back at Zaragoza on 13 April to discover the orders from Paris detailing him to commence the siege of Lérida without delay. He instructed Leval to cover the area south of the city towards Daroca in the valley of Jiloca; the other two divisions were then sent to Lérida, Habert by a northerly route and Musnier on a road south of the Ebro. By 13 April Suchet's force of 13,000 was positioned around the city and poised to commence the siege. Following discussions with the French engineers, Suchet established the artillery park to the north-east and turned his attention to the eastern walls, which were deemed to be the most vulnerable.[4] A flying bridge was positioned south of the park and over the next few days the guns were moved forward and work commenced on the parallels.

While these preparations were ongoing, the balance of Suchet's forces established a cordon amidst rumours of an approaching Spanish force. In fact the rumours were untrue (at this time) but the vacuum created by the movement of a French force to cover the southern approaches prompted Garcia Conde,[5] the commander of the defending force within Lérida, to send word to O'Donnell specifying the weakness of the French force south of the river. O'Donnell decided to strike and commenced his move with a force of about 9,000 men[6] and by 23 April he was a mere 20km south of the city. Following a brief engagement between O'Donnell's leading division (commanded by Ybarrola) and a small French guard force, the Spaniards withdrew in considerable haste at the appearance of Musnier and a substantial body of infantry, supported by cavalry. The French pursued the Spanish a few kilometres to Margalef, where the Spanish felt compelled to make a stand despite the position lacking defensive qualities and providing no real protection from the French cavalry. 'The action fought at Margalef was, like all cavalry engagements, as sudden as it was quickly decided; the credit of it was chiefly due to the 13th Regiment of Cuirassiers, which happening to occupy a favourable position, resolutely took

advantage of it.'[7] O'Donnell rushed forward with the second division, but he arrived in time to see Ybarrola in the terminal stages of a rout. O'Donnell covered the Spanish withdrawal and Suchet turned his attentions back to Lérida.

Suchet chose to parade large numbers of Spanish prisoners (from Ybarrola's force) in front of the city and summoned Garcia Conde to surrender. He declined, but the indisputable failure of O'Donnell's force in the field had certainly shaken the morale of the defenders. The same day, as if to reinforce the point, Suchet ordered a battalion from the regiments of 114e and 121e Ligne to attack the two redoubts west of Fort Garden. The 114e succeeded in taking El Pilar but the 121e were unsuccessful and without both strong points the French were forced to withdraw. On 29 April, work recommenced on the parallels but was hindered by the heavy seasonal rains; nevertheless, by 7 May the first batteries were in place. 'Although so closely exposed to the enemy's fire, without any other protection than the darkness of the night, and the silence which they maintained, they exerted themselves with the greatest alacrity to get the work in a sufficient state of forwardness to afford them complete shelter by day break.'[8]

The engineers declared two practicable breaches on 13 May (map 66, points 1 and 2) and they were both stormed and carried that evening. House-to-house fighting ensued, and the outcome was inevitable; it was just a question of how much time and how many casualties. The civilian inhabitants and the military garrison fell back to the confines of the castle, at which point Suchet ordered every gun and mortar in range to bombard the place. At noon on 14 May, Garcia Conde could stand the slaughter no longer and surrendered. 'The loss of Lérida was of considerable consequence as it opened, for the invaders, communications between Aragón and Cataluña.'[9] However, news had reached Suchet of Augereau's withdrawal to Girona and his replacement by Macdonald. Until that officer should arrive and assume command Suchet elected not to link up with the 7th Corps. Instead he turned his attention to the fort at Mequinenza. A brigade had been sent to invest the structure on 15 May, but the engineers needed to build a road to enable the siege park to get sufficiently close. By 1 June, the road was complete and the fort was taken four days later. Suchet now controlled all the key points within Aragon, but the concentration of his forces to achieve this advantageous position had enabled the guerrilleros to regroup and recommence operations. Suchet was thereby forced to turn his attention back to dealing with this resurgent threat.

---

4   The Fort Garden and the two redoubts, well equipped with men and artillery, covered the western approach and the northern approach was deemed too steep.

5   He had distinguished himself by getting a large convoy of provisions into Girona in September 1809.

6   7,000 infantry, 400 cavalry, a battery of guns and 1,500 *miqueletes*.

7   Suchet, *Memoirs of the War with Spain*, vol I, p.131.

8   Ibid, p.137.

9   Toreno, *Guerra de la Independencia El 2 de Mayo de 1808*, vol III, p.244.

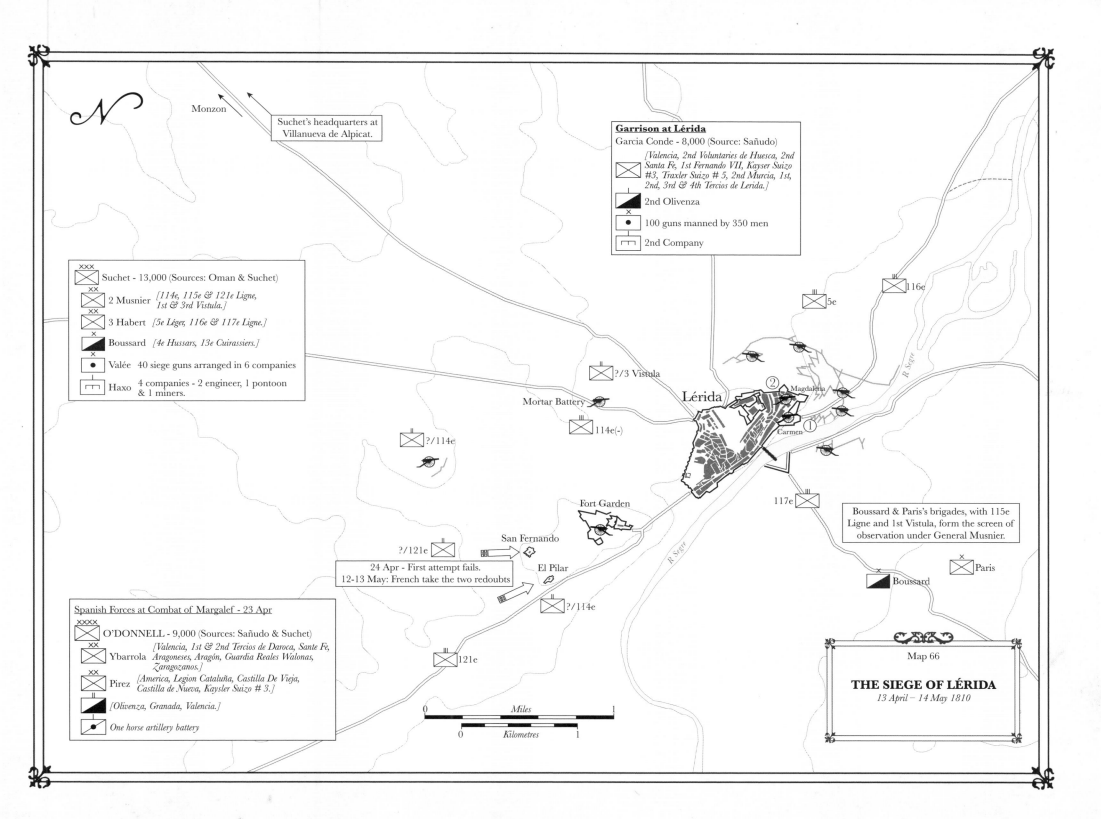

Monzon

Suchet's headquarters at Villanueva de Alpicat.

Garrison at Lérida

Garcia Conde - 8,000 (Source: Sañudo)

[Valencia, 2nd Voluntaries de Huesca, 2nd Santa Fe, 1st Fernando VII, Kayser Suizo #3, Traxler Suizo # 5, 2nd Murcia, 1st, 2nd, 3rd & 4th Tercios de Lérida.]

2nd Olivenza

100 guns manned by 350 men

2nd Company

Suchet - 13,000 (Sources: Oman & Suchet)

2 Musnier *[114e, 115e & 121e Ligne, 1st & 3rd Vistula.]*

3 Habert *[5e Léger, 116e & 117e Ligne.]*

Boussard *[4e Hussars, 13e Cuirassiers.]*

Valée 40 siege guns arranged in 6 companies

Haxo 4 companies - 2 engineer, 1 pontoon & 1 miners.

116e

5e

?/3 Vistula

Lérida

② Magdalena

Mortar Battery

114e(-)

① Carmen

?/114e

Fort Garden

117e

San Fernando

?/121e

Boussard & Paris's brigades, with 115e Ligne and 1st Vistula, form the screen of observation under General Musnier.

El Pilar

24 Apr - First attempt fails.
12-13 May: French take the two redoubts

Paris

?/114e

Boussard

Spanish Forces at Combat of Margalef - 23 Apr

O'DONNELL - 9,000 (Sources: Sañudo & Suchet)

Ybarrola *[Valencia, 1st & 2nd Tercios de Daroca, Sante Fe, Aragoneses, Aragón, Guardia Reales Walonas, Zaragozanos.]*

Pirez *[America, Legion Cataluña, Castilla De Vieja, Castilla de Nueva, Kaysler Suizo # 3.]*

[Olivenza, Granada, Valencia.]

One horse artillery battery

121e

R Segre

Miles

0   1

0   1
Kilometres

Map 66

THE SIEGE OF LÉRIDA
13 April – 14 May 1810

Chapter 25

1810: The Year of Sieges

The failures of the Talavera Campaign and the Walcheren Expedition[1] coupled with the change in the British administration – with Portland being replaced by Perceval as Prime Minister in October 1809 – left Wellington exposed to the growing Whig opposition to war in general and his plans to defend Portugal in particular. In his favour, Earl Liverpool and Earl Bathurst respectively replaced Canning and Viscount Castlereagh as Foreign Secretary and Secretary for War; both newcomers were prepared to accept Wellington's proposals, but they were at pains to point out that his contingency planning must take full account of the requirement to embark the British force if the third French invasion of Portugal proved too powerful. Wellington's preparations to negate this eventuality were threefold. The Portuguese army, both regular and militia, was being completely reorganized; secondly he ordered the construction of a series of defences across the Lisbon peninsula known as the Lines of Torres Vedras; and finally he made preparations for the vacation and devastation of the countryside in front of these lines.

The French preparations were equally impressive. With Britain's failed Walcheren Expedition and victory over Austria at Wagram, Napoleon set about releasing large numbers of men to reinvigorate the Peninsular Campaign. In excess of 100,000 men were destined for Iberia and Napoleon clearly intended to command them personally until French offers of an Austrian marriage were unexpectedly accepted, compelling him to remain in France to supervise both his divorce and his impending wedding. This decision was to continue to deprive the French Peninsular armies of a single commander-in-chief. Worse still Napoleon authorized autonomous power to the 3rd and 7th corps commanders and established military governments[2] in Navarre, the Basque Provinces, Burgos, Valladolid, Palencia and Toro. Between December 1809 and September 1810, a total of 138,000 reinforcements arrived in Spain. These can be broken down into five categories. Firstly, the Corps de Réserve de l'Armée d'Allemagne arrived complete and became the 8th Corps under General Junot. This corps, along with the 2nd and the 6th corps and Kellermann and Bonnet's divisions, formed the new French Army of Portugal. The second group were the Young Guard divisions, consisting of 19 battalions and three provisional regiments of cavalry. These elite troops were considered Napoleon's personal guard and when he elected not to appear, their employment was curtailed to the area just south of the Pyrenees. Thirdly, Napoleon had created fourth battalions for virtually every regiment serving in Spain. These battalions were to form the 9th Corps, which began forming up at Bayonne at the beginning of the year and which crossed into Spain that summer. The fourth group were a 4,000-strong gendarmerie, hand-picked men who had the unenviable task of keeping open the lines of communication between the French border and Spanish capital. Finally there were about 8,500 new artillery and cavalry units and sub-units and 27,000 general draft replacements.

In April 1810, Marshal Masséna was appointed to command the new French Army of Portugal; he arrived to assume his new command a month later. At 52 years of age, he was second only to Jourdan in seniority. 'Masséna arrived at his headquarters with few immediate accoutrements, welcomed his lieutenants with friendly simplicity but quickly followed, like a complaining courtesan, about his fatigue, which did little to captivate their attention or their respect.'[3] His exertions in the late Austrian war, coupled with the rigours of the journey to Spain, had certainly taken their toll on the old warrior, but his appointment was inevitably going to cause friction with Ney who had a history of insubordination with everyone except the Emperor. Junot's behaviour to his new commander was less acceptable as, 'he had neither the merit nor the rank of maréchal Ney, whose pride was therefore less excusable and given his junior position, having been placed under the orders of maréchal Masséna should have been accustomed to obey to him'.[4] It was not an auspicious start.

Troop movements in early 1810 were numerous and quite confusing. Mortier had failed to catch the Viscount de Gand, following his rapid departure from Sevilla, and instead set off to invest Badajoz. He arrived on 12 February only to discover that La Romana, who had taken over command from Del Parque, was heading in his direction with a numerically superior force. Mortier asked for reinforcement and was informed that the 2nd Corps was on its way, but the two forces did not link up in time and Mortier was forced to withdraw to Sevilla, while Heudelet retired to Mérida. However, La Romana's southerly movement had opened the way for Ney to begin probing the Portuguese border with a view to investing the Ciudad Rodrigo. This French manoeuvring attracted the attention of the Anglo-Portuguese army within Portugal, and Wellington now divided his force to respond. 'Wellington's front, facing the French, was formed by Hill's Corps in the Alentejo, Lecor's Portuguese brigade in the Castelo Branco district, and Craufurd's force on the Agueda. Neither Hill nor Lecor was in actual contact with the enemy, and La Romana's army, spread out from the Pass of Perales to Zafra and Aracena in a thin line, lay between them and Reynier and Mortier's outposts. It was otherwise with Craufurd, who was placed north of La Romana's left division, that of Martin Carrera; he was in close touch with Ney's corps all along the line of the Agueda, as far as the Douro.'[5]

Masséna's first action was to send Junot forward with his by now complete 8th Corps to Toro. Meanwhile Kellermann and Bonnet were warned off for operations in Leon and the Asturias respectively. In the latter province, General Acre had 4,000 men at his disposal, the balance having been stripped out by Del Parque prior to Tamames. Bonnet, following the arrival of his reinforcements in January, had 7,000 men and was now in a position to make advances into the

---

1 The attempt by the British Government to create a major distraction in northern Europe by sending 40,000 men under Lord Chatham to make a landing in part of the Zeeland in Holland.

2 These governments had complete civil and military autonomy answerable to Paris alone.

3 Thiers, *Histoire du Consulate et de L'Empire*, vol XII, pp.305–306.

4 Ibid, vol XII, pp.306–307.

5 Oman, *History of the Peninsular War*, vol III, pp.231–232.

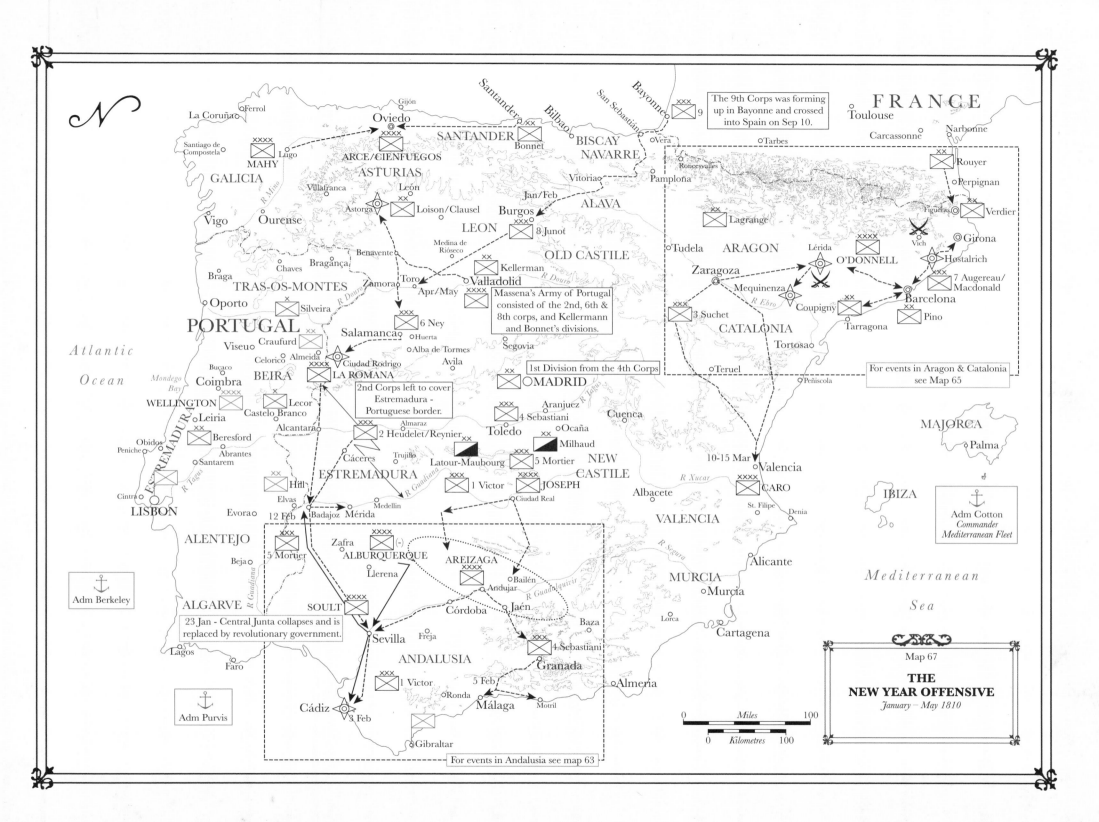

N

La Coruña Ferrol Gijón SANTANDER Bilbao BISCAY Bayonne FRANCE Toulouse
Santiago de Compostela Oviedo ARCE/CIENFUEGOS Santander NAVARRE San Sebastián Vera Carcassonne Narbonne
MAHY Lugo ASTURIAS León Vitoria ALAVA Pamplona Roncesvalles Tarbes Rouyer Perpignan
GALICIA Villafranca Astorga Loison/Clausel Jan/Feb Burgos Lagrange Figueras Verdier
Vigo Ourense LEON 8 Junot ARAGON Lérida O'DONNELL Vich Girona
TRAS-OS-MONTES Benavente Medina de Ríoseco OLD CASTILE Tudela Zaragoza Hostalrich
Braga Bragança Zamora Toro Valladolid Kellerman Mequinenza R Ebro Barcelona
PORTUGAL Oporto Silveira Apr/May R Douro 6 Ney Coupigny 7 Augereau/Macdonald
Viseu Craufurd Salamanca Huerta Segovia CATALONIA Pino
Coimbra Celorico Almeida Ciudad Rodrigo Alba de Tormes Avila Tarragona Tortosa
BEIRA LA ROMANA MADRID Teruel Peñiscola
WELLINGTON Leiria Castelo Branco Lecor Alcantara Almaraz Toledo 4 Sebastiani Aranjuez Cuenca 10-15 Mar Valencia MAJORCA Palma
Obidos Beresford Abrantes Cáceres Trujillo 2 Heudelet/Reynier Ocaña NEW CASTILE R Xucar IBIZA
Peniche Santarem ESTREMADURA Latour-Maubourg 5 Mortier Milhaud Albacete St. Filipe Denia
Hill Elvas Medellin 1 Victor JOSEPH VALENCIA Alicante
LISBON Evora Badajoz Mérida Ciudad Real MURCIA Murcia
ALENTEJO Zafra ALBURQUERQUE AREIZAGA Bailén R Segura Mediterranean Sea
Beja Llerena Andujar R Guadalquivir Baza Lorca
ALGARVE SOULT Córdoba Jaén Cartagena
Lagos Sevilla Freja 4 Sebastiani
Faro ANDALUSIA Granada Almería
1 Victor 5 Feb
Cádiz Ronda Málaga Motril
Gibraltar

The 9th Corps was forming up in Bayonne and crossed into Spain on Sep 10.

Massena's Army of Portugal consisted of the 2nd, 6th & 8th corps, and Kellermann and Bonnet's divisions.

1st Division from the 4th Corps

2nd Corps left to cover Estremadura - Portuguese border.

For events in Aragon & Catalonia see Map 65

23 Jan - Central Junta collapses and is replaced by revolutionary government.

For events in Andalusia see map 63

Adm Berkeley

Adm Purvis

Adm Cotton
Commander Mediterranean Fleet

Miles 0 100
Kilometres 0 100

Map 67

THE NEW YEAR OFFENSIVE
January – May 1810

Asturias. By 31 January, he had captured the capital, having swept Acre's forces aside with relative ease but Porlier, a local and active guerrilla commander, cut off Bonnet's lines of communication with Santander, forcing the French to abandon their acquisition. Two weeks later he returned to reclaim the Asturian capital, but reinforcements from Mahy's Galician force enabled Cienfuegos[6] to once again recapture the city on 19 March. Ten days later, it was once again in French hands; Bonnet had also gathered reinforcements and this time he secured the prize by driving the remnants of the Army of the Asturias deep into Galicia. During this period of rapidly changing fortunes, Loison[7] had been sent from Valladolid to establish a headquarters at either Astorga or Benavente, from where he was to act in unison with Bonnet and threaten Galicia.

Loison arrived in front of Astorga on 11 February, and discovered a much larger garrison than expected and the walls and outlying defences considerably strengthened. Despite a suitable siege train, Loison made an attempt to get the governor, José Santocildes, to surrender; it failed and so did Loison's equally half-hearted endeavour to link up with Bonnet at Oviedo. Two weeks later, with more of Junot's Corps arriving in the region, the task of taking Astorga was allocated to Clausel but the need for a proper siege train was now apparent. A large and powerful train had been allocated to the Army of Portugal but this was still way to the rear, being held up through a lack of draught animals. Junot was anxious to get on with the job and when he discovered that a limited train was available from Burgos and Segovia, he despatched his own integral corps' resources to collect it. While waiting for the siege train and reinforcements Clausel commenced the investment on 21 March and was supported by Solignac's Division and Junot's cavalry brigade, commanded by St Croix, which provided flank protection from Mahy's forces in southern Galicia. Clausel and Valazé, Junot's chief engineer, decided upon a diversionary attack on the defences in front of the suburb of La Reteibia, with the main effort being directed on the older walls of the north-west corner adjacent to the church. Work commenced on the parallels and supporting trenches and was met with stiff resistance from the 14 Spanish guns and numerous sorties from the garrison of 2,500 men under Santocildes. Fierce fighting took place in the two suburbs of Puerto del Rey and St André, but both areas were soon captured and occupied by the French. To raise the spirits of the defenders, Mahy began manoeuvring to attack the French force and sent words of encouragement to Santocildes to that effect, but his small force of only 5,000 men were easily countered and Echevarria, en route to bolster the Spanish force, was surprised by St Croix's dragoons and suffered considerably.

On 15 April, the siege train finally arrived and once the artillery was manhandled into position the effect was immediate. By 21 April, the walls at the north-western corner had collapsed and, as there was no ditch, the breach was broad and accessible (map 68, point 1). Junot sent in a summons for surrender but Santocildes considered his position far from hopeless as the large church opposite the breach still provided strong defensive possibilities. Junot, frustrated at Santocildes's arrogance and eager to conclude the business as soon as possible, sent

in 700 men[8] at 1900 hours that evening. They penetrated the breach but could not advance against the weight of fire from the church and the suburb of La Reteibia. The assailants remained in the rubble and began to strengthen and advance their trenches and prepared for a lengthy standoff, but as dawn broke, Santocildes surrendered. He had received word of Mahy's inability to break the French cordon and with the walls breached and ammunition running low, he realized his position was unpromising.

Junot left the 22e Ligne with the task of providing two of its battalions to garrison the town, while the other two were marched north and made contact with Bonnet. Junot marched back to Valladolid and Toro with the balance of his corps and then made contact with Ney who was poised to commence siege operations against the considerably more formidable structure of Ciudad Rodrigo. The fortress was a medieval structure and its proactive governor, General Andrès Herrasti, had extended the earthworks to incorporate the large suburb of San Francisco and had levelled other outer buildings, which would have provided cover to an attacker. However, despite all these physical preparations the fortress was comfortably overlooked by two hills known as the Cabéco Alto and Bajo,[9] placing the walls of the fort well within artillery range. Herrasti had insufficient forces to hold the Cabéco Alto and Bajo; the garrison numbered 5,500 men, half that number alone would have been required to hold the hills.

Elements of Ney's Corps arrived on the outskirts of the fort as early as 26 April, but it was not until 30 May, when Ney arrived in person with an additional four infantry brigades and the reserve cavalry, that the cordon was fully activated and the siege commenced.[10] If Wellington had chosen to move against Ney, Junot would have been able to bring up 8,000 men in a day and another 7,000 a day later. In all, the French could concentrate about 50,000 men, far outnumbering Wellington who had 18,000 British and 15,000 Portuguese to hand.[11] He was in no position to take risks and quickly rejected any suggestion of attacking Ney or providing succour to the town. Masséna arrived in early June and approved Ney's plan to attack the town from the two heights to the north-west. On 1 and 5 June, Ney had constructed flying bridges across the Agueda above and below the town and Marchand's Division, half of Mermet's Division and Lamotte's Corps's cavalry brigade had all crossed to the northern bank. The siege train followed between 8 and 15 June, until a total of 50 guns had arrived, which were moved to the artillery and engineer parks north of the Cabéco Alto. Substantial engineer stores had been prepared by Maucune and Ferey's brigades the month prior and, as a result, progress on the first parallels and six battery emplacements was remarkably prompt despite furious counter-fire from the Spanish guns massed on the *enceinte* facing the French works. Julian Sanchez became increasingly concerned at the pace of French progress and requested permission from Herrasti to escape the

---

6   The Asturian Junta replaced Acre with the new captain general, Cienfuegos.

7   Loison had recently arrived back in Spain at the head of a number of new conscript battalions; his force was ultimately to join Ney's 6th Corps.

8   Comprising the voltigeur and grenadier companies of the 47e Ligne and the Régiment de Irlandais, from Solignac's Division.

9   British accounts name the features the Greater and Lesser Teson.

10   The reason for the delay was the enduring problem of a lack of provisions and it took a characteristic act of insubordination by Ney who requisitioned rations from Avila, outside his area of operations/responsibility, ruffling Joseph's feathers in the process.

11   Excluding Hill's Division, which numbered 12,000 and was located at Portalegre to the south.

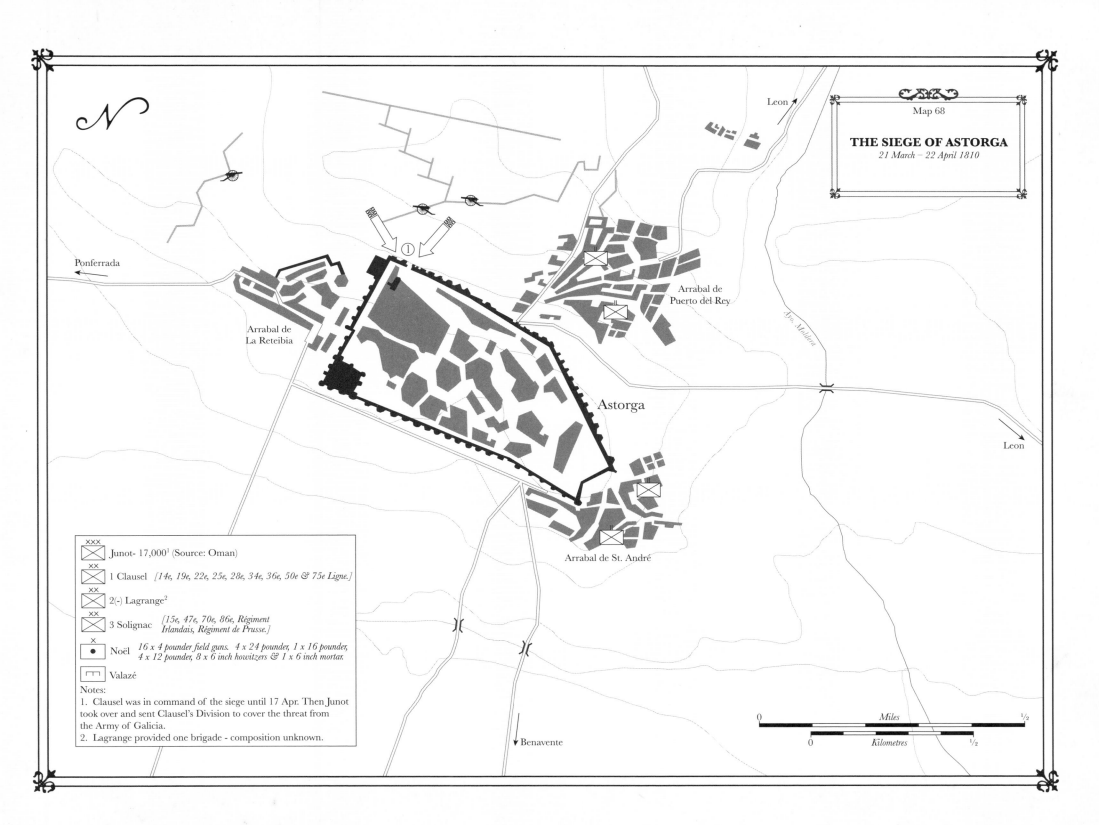

N

Map 68

THE SIEGE OF ASTORGA
21 March – 22 April 1810

Leon

Ponferrada

Arrabal de
Puerto del Rey

Arrabal de
La Reteibia

Astorga

Leon

Arrabal de St. André

Benavente

Junot- 17,000[1] (Source: Oman)

1 Clausel   *[14e, 19e, 22e, 25e, 28e, 34e, 36e, 50e & 75e Ligne.]*

2(-) Lagrange[2]

3 Solignac   *[15e, 47e, 70e, 86e, Régiment*
            Irlandais, Régiment de Prusse.]

Noël   *16 x 4 pounder field guns. 4 x 24 pounder, 1 x 16 pounder,*
       4 x 12 pounder, 8 x 6 inch howitzers & 1 x 6 inch mortar.

Valazé

Notes:
1. Clausel was in command of the siege until 17 Apr. Then Junot
took over and sent Clausel's Division to cover the threat from
the Army of Galicia.
2. Lagrange provided one brigade - composition unknown.

0   *Miles*   ¹/₂

0   *Kilometres*   ¹/₂

cordon with his cavalry, which he was well aware could not survive the inevitable bombardment. His 200 lancers crossed the bridge during the night of 21/22 June, surprising the lacklustre cordon provided by Marchand's Division, and made off into the night, arriving at Craufurd's camp the following morning where they were able to give a complete report on the situation.

Accurate and sustained fire from the small Spanish force inside the Convent of Santa Cruz was hindering the start of work on the second parallel and Ney decided to capture the structure. On the night of the 23/24 June, 300 hand-picked grenadiers and a handful of engineers tried to storm the convent. Captain François led the infantry and Captain Maltzen the engineers: both were killed in the abortive operation[12] and Ney decided to call off the attack and elected instead to bombard the place before making a second attempt. On 25 June 46 guns, arranged in six battery emplacements (map 69, points 1 to 6), opened up on the north-western walls and began to cause considerable havoc. Many fires broke out inside the town and the suburb of Santa Cruz was almost completely destroyed. That night, when the French attacked the ruins for a second time, Herrasti withdrew the Spanish troops positioned there but not before the Spanish guns had completely destroyed a French battery when a chance round ignited the powder magazine in the French trenches. However, after four days of continual bombardment, the *faussebraie* at the base of the projecting angle was crumbling and Ney considered this damage sufficient for an assault. Herrasti was in no mood for capitulation, replying to Ney's summons 'that after 49 years of service he knew the laws of war and his military duty'.[13] Ney was apathetic to this refusal but when he heard that Masséna, who had taken little active part thus far, had intervened and hastened General Éblé (the artillery commander) from Salamanca and tasked

him to reconsider Ney's plan of attack,[14] the French commander was enraged. He gathered his engineers and sappers and issued orders for an immediate resumption of the bombardment, which resumed on 28 June. During the night of 1/2 July work began on the second parallel, and the same night Ney attacked the suburb of San Francisco to prevent artillery and small-arms fire from this area hampering the construction. The attack was successful, insofar as the French secured a foothold in the old convent, from where they slowly expanded their position until the night of 3/4 July when Herrasti withdrew from the buildings. The French wasted little time in securing the area and establishing a mortar battery among the ruins.

Herrasti was by now becoming progressively more concerned and sent repeated appeals to Wellington for help, but received only words of encouragement and no promise of military support. With the forward French gun position completed a battery was manhandled into position (map 69, point 7) and two of the original six batteries were also advanced (map 69, positions, 8 and 9). On 4 July these batteries engaged the fortress to considerable effect and, by 8 July, they had blasted a breach 40m wide; an 800lb mine finished the arrangements. On 9 July Ney ordered the storming battalions to get ready, but as they were lining up, a white flag appeared on the ramparts. Herrasti agreed to capitulate and the 4,000 Spanish defenders walked out the following morning and were marched to Bayonne. The town had been devastated; in the northern sector not a house or church was intact, and it was clear that Herrasti had done all he could in defence of the place. Many members of the Regency at Cádiz were understandably perplexed – and some furious – at Wellington's inactivity, but he was saving himself for the next phase of the French operation – the third invasion of Portugal.

12   Thiers, *Histoire du Consulate et de L'Empire*, vol XII, p.334.

13   Oman, *History of the Peninsular War*, vol III, p.250.

14   Thiers, *Histoire du Consulate et de L'Empire*, vol XII, p.333. Éblé had remained in Salamanca to continue the preparation of the artillery stores and ammunition.

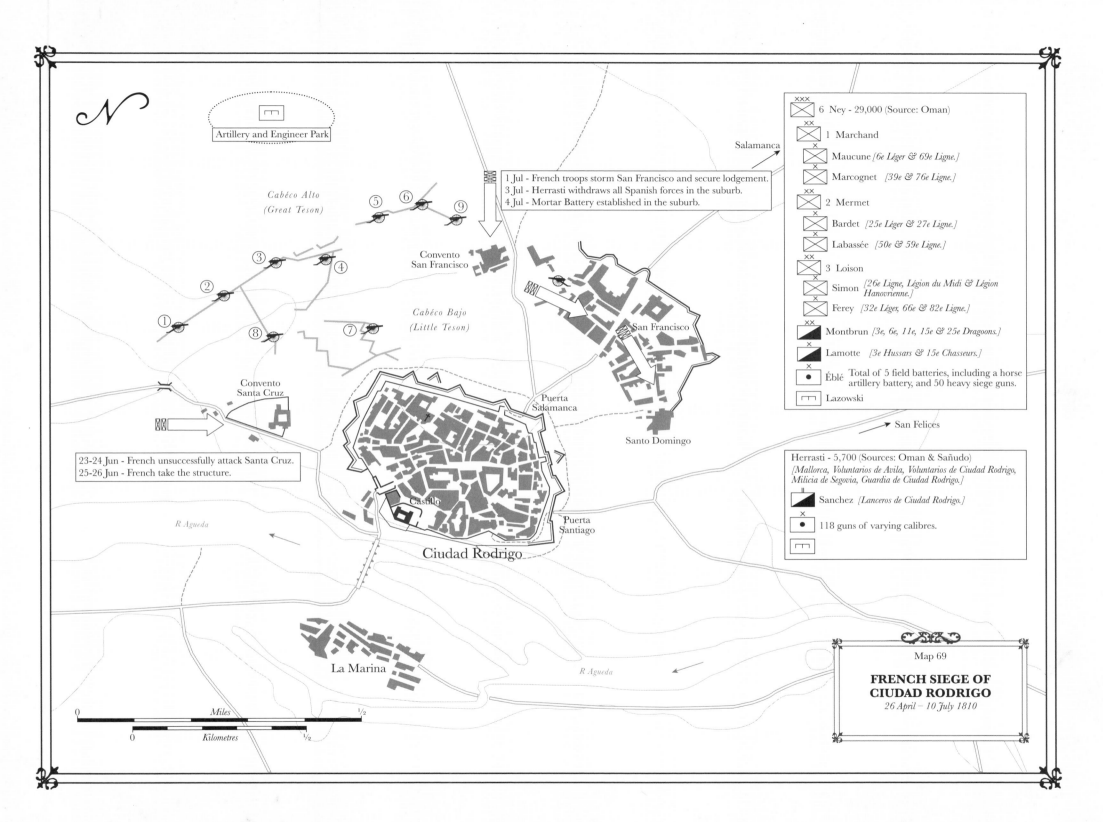

N

Artillery and Engineer Park

Salamanca

1 Jul - French troops storm San Francisco and secure lodgement.
3 Jul - Herrasti withdraws all Spanish forces in the suburb.
4 Jul - Mortar Battery established in the suburb.

Cabéco Alto
(Great Teson)

⑤ ⑥ ⑨

③ ④

②

① ⑧ ⑦

Convento
San Francisco

Cabéco Bajo
(Little Teson)

San Francisco

Convento
Santa Cruz

Puerta
Salamanca

Santo Domingo

San Felices

23-24 Jun - French unsuccessfully attack Santa Cruz.
25-26 Jun - French take the structure.

Castillo

Puerta
Santiago

Ciudad Rodrigo

R Agueda

La Marina

R Agueda

0   *Miles*   ½

0   *Kilometres*   ½

6   Ney - 29,000 (Source: Oman)

1   Marchand

Maucune   *[6e Léger & 69e Ligne.]*

Marcognet   *[39e & 76e Ligne.]*

2   Mermet

Bardet   *[25e Léger & 27e Ligne.]*

Labassée   *[50e & 59e Ligne.]*

3   Loison

Simon   *[26e Ligne, Légion du Midi & Légion Hanovrienne.]*

Ferey   *[32e Léger, 66e & 82e Ligne.]*

Montbrun   *[3e, 6e, 11e, 15e & 25e Dragoons.]*

Lamotte   *[3e Hussars & 15e Chasseurs.]*

Éblé   Total of 5 field batteries, including a horse artillery battery, and 50 heavy siege guns.

Lazowski

Herrasti - 5,700 (Sources: Oman & Sañudo)
[Mallorca, Voluntarios de Avila, Voluntarios de Ciudad Rodrigo, Milicia de Segovia, Guardia de Ciudad Rodrigo.]

Sanchez   *[Lanceros de Ciudad Rodrigo.]*

118 guns of varying calibres.

Map 69

**FRENCH SIEGE OF
CIUDAD RODRIGO**

26 April – 10 July 1810

Chapter 26 ⊶┼⊶

THE THIRD FRENCH INVASION OF PORTUGAL

Wellington's front facing the French in the spring of 1810 consisted of Hill's composite Anglo-Portuguese Corps at Portalegre, Lecor's Portuguese Brigade at Castelo Branco and Craufurd's Light Division around Almeida. Craufurd's right wing touched that of Martin Carrera, La Romana's left-hand division, and both these divisions were in contact with Ney's outposts. Craufurd was one of the few commanders in whose ability Wellington had huge confidence.[1] Promotion had been slow in coming, despite considerable operational service, much of which had been coupled with failure and missed opportunities. He had been military attaché during the Austrian Wars in 1794, participated in the failed Dutch expedition in 1799 and the unhappy Buenos Aires campaign in 1807, where he surrendered his brigade but was cleared of blame at the subsequent court martial. He did not participate at the battle of La Coruña (as Moore had sent his brigade to Vigo) and had missed Talavera by a matter of hours.

With the arrival of the first of the French reinforcements at Salamanca, Craufurd's position became dangerously exposed. Wellington had written to Craufurd on 8 March, outlining his intentions. 'I am desirous of being able to assemble the army upon the Coa, if it should be necessary; at the same time I am perfectly aware that if the enemy should collect in any large numbers in Estremadura, we should be too forward for our communications with General Hill… But till they will collect in Estremadura… I am adverse to withdrawing from a position so favourable as the Coa affords … I intend that the Divisions of General Cole and General Picton should support you … without waiting for orders from me, if it should be necessary, and they will be directed accordingly.'[2] Craufurd's first test came on the night of 19 March, when Ferey (commanding a brigade from Loison's Division) assembled his six voltigeur companies and attacked the pass at Barba del Puerco. The attempt was repulsed but Craufurd placed his men on full alert in anticipation that the action was a precursor to a general attack by Ney. As it transpired, this was not the case and a full month elapsed before the next major move by the French.

By 10 July Ciudad Rodrigo had fallen (see Chapter 25) and Masséna now turned his attention to Portugal. Almeida was his first objective, but he had to wait for replacement ammunition for his siege guns to arrive from Salamanca before he could sanction the advance. The distance from Ciudad Rodrigo to Almeida is only 30km and between the two fortresses stood Fort Concepción, an isolated but structurally sound 18th-century stronghold. However, it required a considerable force to garrison effectively – certainly more troops than Craufurd could spare – and he was under clear orders to vacate and demolish the structure if the French instigated a westerly movement. On 21 July, in the face of Ney's advance by Loison's infantry and Treillard's cavalry, Craufurd reluctantly obeyed these orders. The French vanguard skirmished with the 14th Light Dragoons and the King's German Legion cavalry before halting at Val de Mula, 6km from Almeida and just inside Portugal. The third French invasion of Portugal had begun.

Wellington was well aware that a single bridge spanned the river Coa in the area of Craufurd's screen and the commander-in-chief's detailed orders made it clear that Craufurd was not to delay overly long or to engage the French east of the river. In retrospect Craufurd would have been wise to move early from the immediate environs of Almeida and establish a defensive line west of the river. 'For two days the Light Division remained thus in the face of an entire French corps; but Craufurd, in the teeth of Wellington's orders, made no attempt to cross the Coa, and on the third day Ney resolved to chastise him for his temerity.'[3] At dawn on 24 July he formed his force in one broad and deep column, with Lamotte and Gardanne's cavalry brigades leading, and hurled them at the British cavalry piquets in front of the pueblo of Val de Mula. The piquets scattered and fell back, alerting Craufurd's line to stand-to. There would have been enough time to withdraw over the Coa if Craufurd had chosen to do so, but he was determined to administer the attacking French a short sharp rebuke before withdrawing. It was the act of a man desperate for recognition, and it nearly cost him and his division dearly.

It took another hour before the two leading French infantry and cavalry brigades fell upon Craufurd's thin line. Twelve battalions marched west with considerable determination against the Anglo-Portuguese force deployed south of Almeida, with their backs to the river. The numerous guns on the battlements of Almeida provided limited support and made almost no impression on Lamotte's cavalry as they rushed to exploit the gap between the walls and the 43rd. Craufurd, clearly shaken by the strength of the attack and suddenly aware of the precariousness of his position, ordered the cavalry and guns to gallop for the bridge; the caçadores were to follow and then the balance of infantry. However, extracting the force under heavy and sustained fire and over demanding terrain was to prove patently difficult. An artillery caisson overturned at the bend of the road leading to the bridge, delaying the movement of the Portuguese infantry. When the guns and caçadores were safely across the ravine they deployed on the far bank (map 70, point 1) and began to provide badly needed fire support to the British infantry.[4] Most of the 95th were on the east bank knoll above the bridge when Craufurd gave the order for the 43rd to withdraw. Part of the battalion was already on the home bank when Major McLeod of the 43rd saw the 52nd making best speed toward the bridge, but in clear danger of being intercepted and cut off. McLeod rallied his men and charged back uphill to retake the hill (map 70, point 2) they had just

---

1   Although Urban's book, *Rifles*, provides a refreshingly different view of 'Black Bob' Craufurd's questionable leadership and lack of popularity amongst the Light Division officers and rank and file.

2   Rev A. H. Craufurd, *General Craufurd and his Light Division*, pp.87–88.

3   Oman is sympathetic to Craufurd's potentially costly insubordination but Fortescue, taking Napier's lead, is not: Fortescue, *History of the British Army*, vol XIII, ch. XXXVII, p.476.

4   The cavalry were sent upstream to watch the fords at Alveirenos.

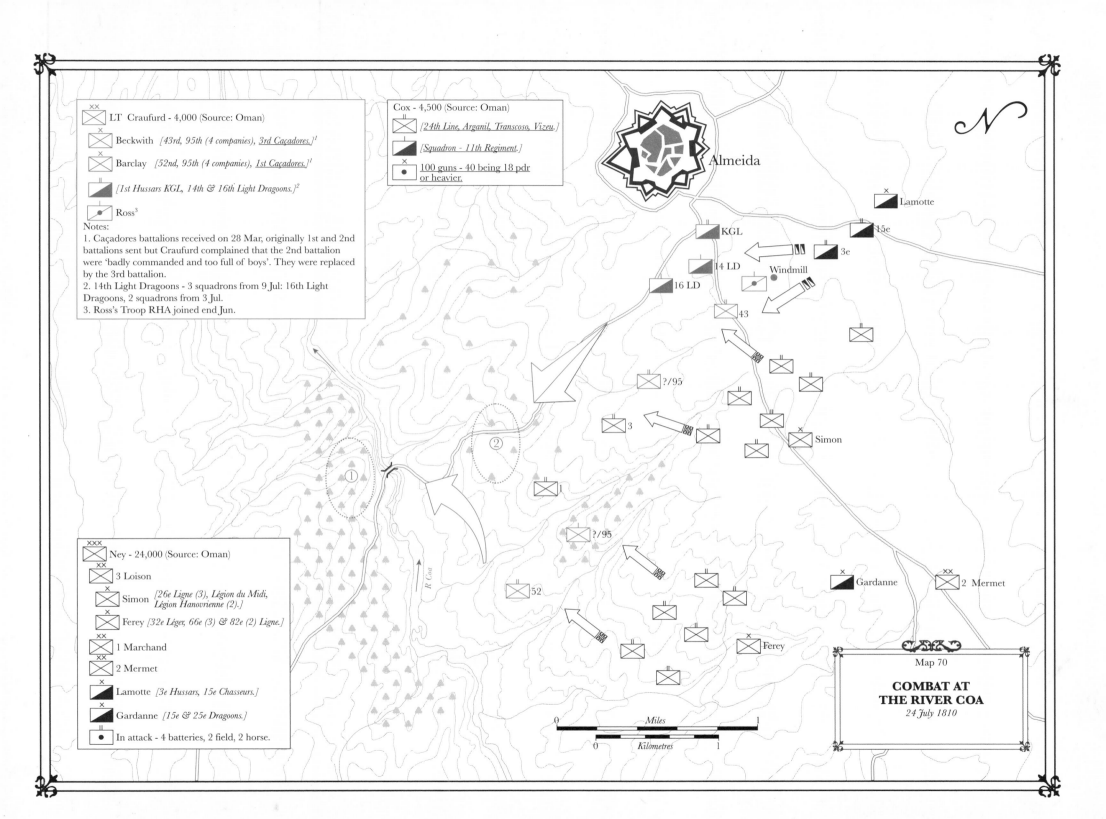

LT Craufurd - 4,000 (Source: Oman)

Beckwith [43rd, 95th (4 companies), 3rd Caçadores.][1]

Barclay [52nd, 95th (4 companies), 1st Caçadores.][1]

[1st Hussars KGL, 14th & 16th Light Dragoons.][2]

Ross[3]

Notes:
1. Caçadores battalions received on 28 Mar, originally 1st and 2nd battalions sent but Craufurd complained that the 2nd battalion were 'badly commanded and too full of boys'. They were replaced by the 3rd battalion.
2. 14th Light Dragoons - 3 squadrons from 9 Jul: 16th Light Dragoons, 2 squadrons from 3 Jul.
3. Ross's Troop RHA joined end Jun.

Cox - 4,500 (Source: Oman)

[24th Line, Arganil, Transcoso, Vizeu.]

[Squadron - 11th Regiment.]

100 guns - 40 being 18 pdr or heavier.

Ney - 24,000 (Source: Oman)

3 Loison

Simon [26e Ligne (3), Légion du Midi, Légion Hanovrienne (2).]

Ferey [32e Léger, 66e (3) & 82e (2) Ligne.]

1 Marchand

2 Mermet

Lamotte [3e Hussars, 15e Chasseurs.]

Gardanne [15e & 25e Dragoons.]

In attack - 4 batteries, 2 field, 2 horse.

Almeida

Lamotte

KGL

15e

3e

14 LD

Windmill

16 LD

43

?/95

3

Simon

1

?/95

52

Gardanne

2 Mermet

Ferey

R Coa

Miles

0   1

Kilometres

0   1

Map 70

COMBAT AT THE RIVER COA

24 July 1810

vacated. This courageous and rapid action bought sufficient time for the 52nd to break clean and with the battalion on the west bank, the 43rd then followed. 'The French skirmishers, swarming on the right bank, opened a biting fire, which was returned as bitterly; the artillery on both sides played across the ravine, the sounds were repeated by numberless echoes, and the smoke rising slowly, resolved itself into an immense arch, spanning the whole chasm, and sparkling with the whirling fuzes of the flying shells.'[5] Ney came up at this point and immediately ordered the 66e to storm the bridge, but they were cut to pieces by the sustained and concentrated musket and rifle fire from the Anglo-Portuguese infantry on the elevated hillsides. Ney, in frustration, then ordered the Bataillon d'Élite to repeat the performance; they suffered the same fate. When the 66e had been sent back and repulsed for a second time, Ney accepted the futility of forcing the crossing and fighting petered out. Craufurd held his position on the west bank until midnight and then withdrew under cover of darkness to Pinhel.[6]

Over the next couple of days, Masséna's cavalry confirmed that the Allies had retreated a considerable distance west of the Coa and, once satisfied of this fact, the commander of the French Army of Portugal settled down to invest Almeida. The fort was well constructed, in good condition, well provisioned and under the command of Brigadier General William Cox, a British officer in Portuguese service. Wellington had calculated that the structure would hold out for two to three months, delaying the French advance until the onset of the autumn rains. Ney was tasked with the venture and he wasted no time in calling forward the guns from Ciudad Rodrigo. The rocky subsoil complicated the construction of the trenches and parallels and it was not until 24 August that the first 11 batteries were in place and ready to open fire. Fifty guns bombarded the city but the counter-battery and harassing fire from the Portuguese gunners prevented the French constructing the second set of parallels and closing to the city walls. Despite fires in several parts of the town the governor was unperturbed, but at 1900 hours on 26 August, the situation changed spectacularly. A French round ignited a powder trail in the castle courtyard, which in turn ignited the main magazine. The resulting explosion was simply cataclysmic. The medieval castle and nearby cathedral vanished completely and many parts of the south and west walls were irreparably damaged. Sprünglin, a French staff officer, recalled that, 'the earth trembled and we saw an immense whirlwind of fire and smoke… Great blocks of stone were hurled into the trenches where they killed some of our men… When the smoke cleared, a great part of Almeida had disappeared, and the rest was a heap of debris.' The following evening Cox surrendered.

During the siege Wellington had been trying to second-guess Masséna's intentions once Almeida was in French hands. With Ney busy at Almeida, Junot was advanced to the Portuguese border to be able to support Ney at a moment's notice; however, it was Reynier's movements that caused greater uncertainty. A column from the 2nd Corps appeared at the Pass of Perales and continued to Navasfrias, a few kilometres from the Portuguese border (map 71, point 1), leading Wellington to conclude that Masséna might be intending to mask Almeida and then pour into

Portugal with all three corps. In response, he ordered Hill north but Reynier's men were not acting under orders; they were operating on their own initiative in an attempt to gain provisions and make rudimentary reconnaissance. These independent movements, prompting the relocation of Hill, were in fact completely counterproductive to Masséna's overall scheme and he was quick to issue further orders to Reynier telling him to move his force south to Zarza la Mayor (map 71, point 2). Wellington duly returned Hill to Sarzedas and Castelo Branco. A secondary movement by General Serras also confused the Allies. Serras had been left to hold the plains of Leon during the siege of Ciudad Rodrigo but, on Masséna's orders, he was tasked with moving to threaten northern Portugal. He advanced to Puebla de Sanabria, where he drove out the weak Spanish division under General Taboada[7] and, leaving the 2nd Swiss to garrison the town, he returned to Zamora. In response, Silveira gathered all available Portuguese militia in Bragança, headed north and linked up with the remnants of Taboada's formation, and together they recaptured the town. Serras rushed back to the area on hearing the news, but arrived too late to alter the outcome.

Despite capturing Almeida on 27 August it was still some days before Masséna's advance into Portugal began in earnest. The losses to the 6th and 8th corps following the sieges, and the need to leave additional garrison troops at Ciudad Rodrigo and Almeida, had depleted Massena's original force to the point where he required reinforcement before being able to commence the invasion.[8] He requested a division from the newly forming 9th Corps in Salamanca but received no response and was forced to order Reynier to move north in support of the next phase. In so doing he was acutely aware that he was leaving no force to maintain his lines of communication to the south and rear, but any further delay would have invited interference from the torrential autumn rains. Recalling Reynier was, therefore, the lesser of the two evils. Reynier left Zarza on 10 September and by the 15th he was nearing Guarda. On that day Ney and Junot broke camp and moved west, followed by Montbrun's Cavalry Division, the army guns and the baggage. Reynier, with the exception of Heudelet's Division (left at Guarda) joined Ney at Celorico and proceeded west along the Mondego valley. Junot was allocated a more northerly route, which turned out to be an extreme challenge, but by 17 September it was clear that all three corps were converging on Viseu.

'The 2e and the 6e corps arrived on the 19th at Viseu, whose entire population was in flight, with the exception of some disabled, men and women, who had been unable to go by themselves. Although the English had destroyed the ovens, the windmills, the grain stores, and set fire to the grain mills, yet one collected a lot of vegetables, even enough livestock and the soldiers who thought they would find nothing more than that carried on their backs, seemed satisfied and confident.'[9] This good fortune was, however, tempered by the news that Colonel Trant had fallen on the park of reserve artillery as it followed the 8th Corps on the more exposed northerly route. Masséna lost

5   Napier, *History of the War in the Peninsula*, vol III, p.292.

6   During the engagement Picton had come forward to the Coa bridge from the west, but refused to march his 3rd Division in support. The two generals parted after acrimonious words.

7   This was Echevarria's old brigade.

8   This point highlights poor staff work prior to the invasion. French losses were, in fact, light under the circumstances and the need to garrison the towns would have been known in advance. The fact that the invasion was held up, and plans altered, on this premise is quite revealing.

9   Thiers, *Histoire du Consulat et du L'Empire*, vol XII, p.359.

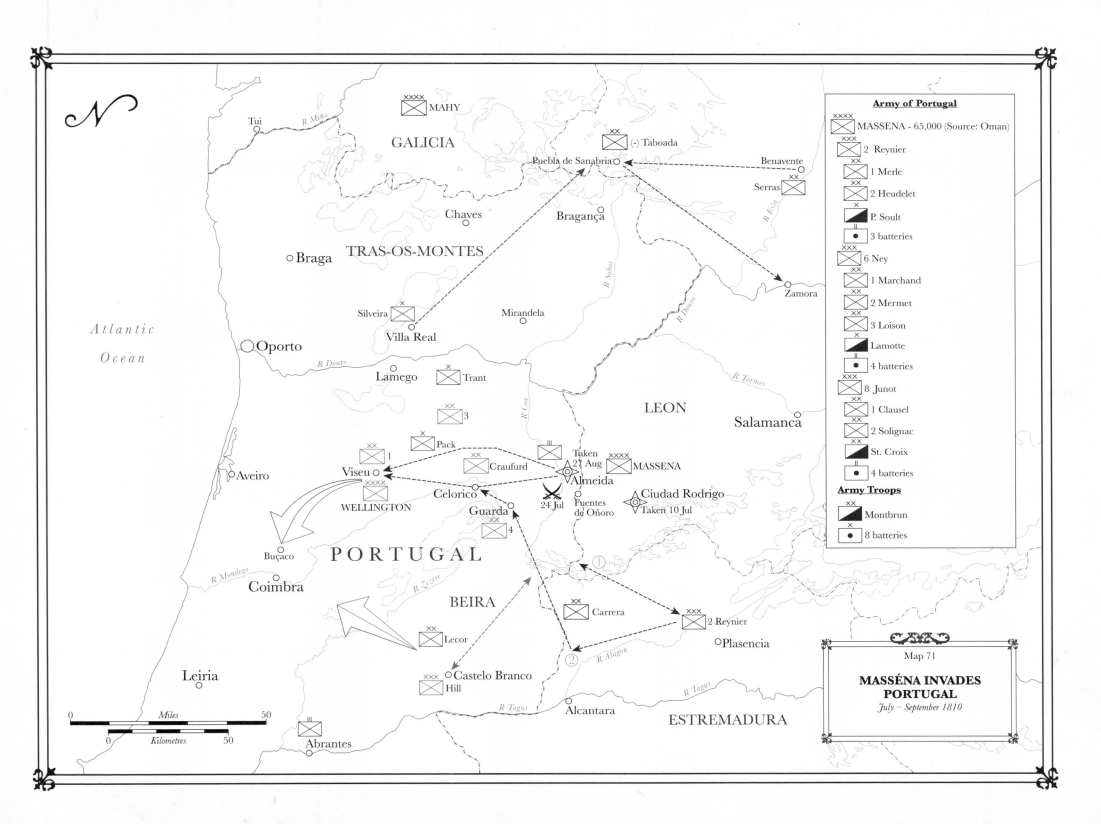

N

GALICIA

Tui

R. Miño

XXXX MAHY

XX (-) Taboada

Puebla de Sanabria

Benavente

XX Serras

R. Esla

Chaves

Bragança

TRAS-OS-MONTES

Braga

R. Sabor

Mirandela

R. Douro

Zamora

Silveira X

Villa Real

Atlantic Ocean

Oporto

R. Douro

Lamego

Trant XX

R. Tormes

3 XX

LEON

Salamanca

Pack X

R. Coa

Taken
27 Aug

XXXX MASSENA

Aveiro

1 XX Viseu

Craufurd XX

III

Almeida

Celorico

24 Jul

Ciudad Rodrigo

Taken 10 Jul

Fuentes
de Oñoro

XXXX WELLINGTON

Guarda

Buçaco

4 XX

①

R. Mondego

PORTUGAL

Coimbra

BEIRA

R. Zezere

XX Carrera

XXX 2 Reynier

Plasencia

② *R. Alagon*

Leiria

Lecor XX

R. Tagus

XXX Hill

Castelo Branco

Alcantara

R. Tagus

ESTREMADURA

III Abrantes

| 0 | *Miles* | 50 |

| 0 | *Kilometres* | 50 |

Army of Portugal

XXXX MASSENA – 65,000 (Source: Oman)

XX 2 Reynier

XX 1 Merle

XX 2 Heudelet

X P. Soult

● 3 batteries

XXX 6 Ney

XX 1 Marchand

XX 2 Mermet

XX 3 Loison

X Lamotte

● 4 batteries

XXX 8 Junot

XX 1 Clausel

XX 2 Solignac

X St. Croix

● 4 batteries

Army Troops

XX Montbrun

● 8 batteries

Map 71

**MASSÉNA INVADES
PORTUGAL**

July – September 1810

another couple of days as Montbrun reorganized the protection of the guns and caissons before moving on. In his frustration, he wrote to Berthier on 22 September. 'The grand park and the baggage are still in the rear, and will only get up tomorrow. It is impossible to find worse roads than these; they bristle with rocks; the guns and train have suffered severely, and I must wait for them. I must leave them two days at Viseu when they come in, to rest themselves, while I resume my march to Coimbra where I am informed I shall find the Anglo-Portuguese concentrated.'

Ney's advance guard began moving again on 20 September, but it was not until the 24th that Masséna finally pressed on from Viseu, having made a number of organizational changes to the 2nd and 8th corps.[10] The same day the first skirmish took place between elements of Reynier's Corps and Craufurd's Light Division and Pack's Portuguese Brigade at Mortagoa on the Viseu to Buçaco road. The Allies were ordered to withdraw by Wellington and, as the advance guards of both the 2nd and 6th corps skirmished with the 95th and 43rd, the balance of Allied troops were manoeuvring into position to the rear of the Buçaco heights. Hill had arrived on 22 September and by early morning on the 25th Wellington's forces were in place. He had chosen the Serra do Buçaco that runs at a right angle to the Viseu to Coimbra road. The ridge is a watershed about 15km long and rises about two hundred metres from the valley floor. Wellington anchored his right wing on the river Mondego, where the ridge commences, and allocated this important sector to Hill's Division. Leith was to Hill's left, then Picton, Spencer, and Craufurd's Light Division, which was covering the road with Pack's Brigade in support. To the rear and left of Craufurd were the other two independent Portuguese Brigades (A. Campbell and Coleman) and Löwe's King's German Legion Brigade, who were the reserve. Finally, to the north-west, at the end of the ridge was Cole's Division covering the steep slope.

Reynier, leading the French advance, had pushed back the Allied skirmishers to the ridge during the afternoon of 25 September. Ney arrived that evening and Reynier then moved to his left and established his main body just behind the hamlet of San Antonio de Cantaro. The following morning, Wellington's six divisions were complete and in place, but Ney and Reynier could only identify a small force to their front and they concluded that this was merely a rearguard. They could clearly see the Light Division on the spur covering the Portuguese light troops to the north, but they were unaware of the four Allied divisions running down the spine of the ridge, who were deployed rear of the slope. 'When on the Serra, the troops are to be kept a little behind the ridge, so that they may not be seen by the enemy until it becomes necessary to move them up on the ridge to repel an attack.'[11] Masséna rode up to the front at about 1400 hours on 26 September and, following a more detailed reconnaissance, correctly concluded that Wellington was offering battle and that evening drew up his orders for a two-pronged attack. Ney was to assault up the road while Reynier was to attack the ridge to his front. Reynier was to attack first and then, once on the crest, was to reform his men and swing right, cutting the Coimbra road behind the Serra. Ney was to move once Reynier was firm on the heights and Junot was to form the reserve on the

road behind Moura, ready to support either attack as necessary. Many of Masséna's subordinates voiced concern at the prospect of tackling Wellington head-on in a defensive position of his choosing but the French commander, dismissive of their caution, wrote his orders and then retired to Mortaga for a few hours' sleep.[12]

Wellington had forbidden campfires for fear of revealing positions and strengths. For many of the British and Portuguese soldiers, this was to be their first battle and the mood was sombre. In contrast, down in the plains below, hundreds of campfires burned as the many French veterans prepared for the approaching encounter, confident of victory and keen to make their mark. Dawn was slow to emerge as a habitual mist permeated the hills, but as soon as the light was strong enough Reynier commenced his attack. Merle's two brigades (Sarrut left and Graindorge right) advanced up the hill in battalion columns, with the tirailleurs driving back the skirmishers from the 45th, 74th and 88th battalions of Mackinnon's Brigade. The gaps in the Allied line were exploitable and in the fog Picton acted on his instincts, sending half the 45th and two battalions of the 8th Portuguese;[13] if he had known that 11 battalions were now converging on this point he would have sent more, but he was distracted by the movement of the 31e Léger to his front, who were now advancing. In much the same way the tirailleurs pushed back the Portuguese skirmishers, and as they closed on the 74th and 21st, Arentschildt's two Portuguese batteries[14] opened with grape and ball, ploughing long lines through the mass of French infantry. The advance was brought to a complete halt when the converging Allied infantry fired from both sides of the hills overlooking the road. The 31e tried to deploy, but the sheer weight of fire broke up their momentum and, as time progressed, their cohesion and self-confidence. Picton, satisfied that the impetus of this attack was spent, handed over command to Mackinnon and rushed to his left, where the massed columns of Merle's infantry were now visible.

Wallace, commanding the 88th, moved to the brow of the hill just as the first of Merle's troops reached the top of the rise, and he quickly appreciated that an immediate counter-attack was the best option; to allow the exhausted infantry time to recover from their exertions could have proved disastrous. At this moment the 45th and 8th Line began to arrive from the right and Wallace ordered the companies of the 45th to form on the right of the 88th. He then charged diagonally across the plateau with these two battalions, while the 8th Line provided fire support from the hill to their right. During this manoeuvre Wellington appeared with two guns of Thomson's Battery that were quick into action, firing into the flank of the 36e Ligne. Picton arrived at much the same time and began to rally the disorganized Allied skirmishers who had fallen back in the face of the French advance. It was enough to stem the French tide. The 36e Ligne had been thrust sideways into the flanks of the 2e and 4e Léger, who had now lost their

10 Following the changes, the 2nd Corps was slightly stronger at 17,024 and 8 Corps slightly weaker at 15,904.

11 Fortescue, *A History of the British Army*, vol. VII, ch. XXXVIII, p.511. Written instructions from the Quartermaster General to Hill, 25 September 1810.

12 This caused considerable ill-feeling as many took it for read that he would stay and visit the men on the eve of battle.

13 The 8th Line (two battalions) was task-organized with Baron Eben and the Lusitanian Legion in Leith's 5th Division under Colonel Douglas. In official Portuguese lists (Soriano da Luz) Eben is listed as commanding the 8th only and the Legion was under Colonel Grant. Exactly how Picton was able to task the 8th to move so early in the battle is unclear.

14 Each battery consisted of one six-pounder and five three-pounder guns. Captains Jacinto P. M. de Freire and Joao Porfirio de Silva commanded them.

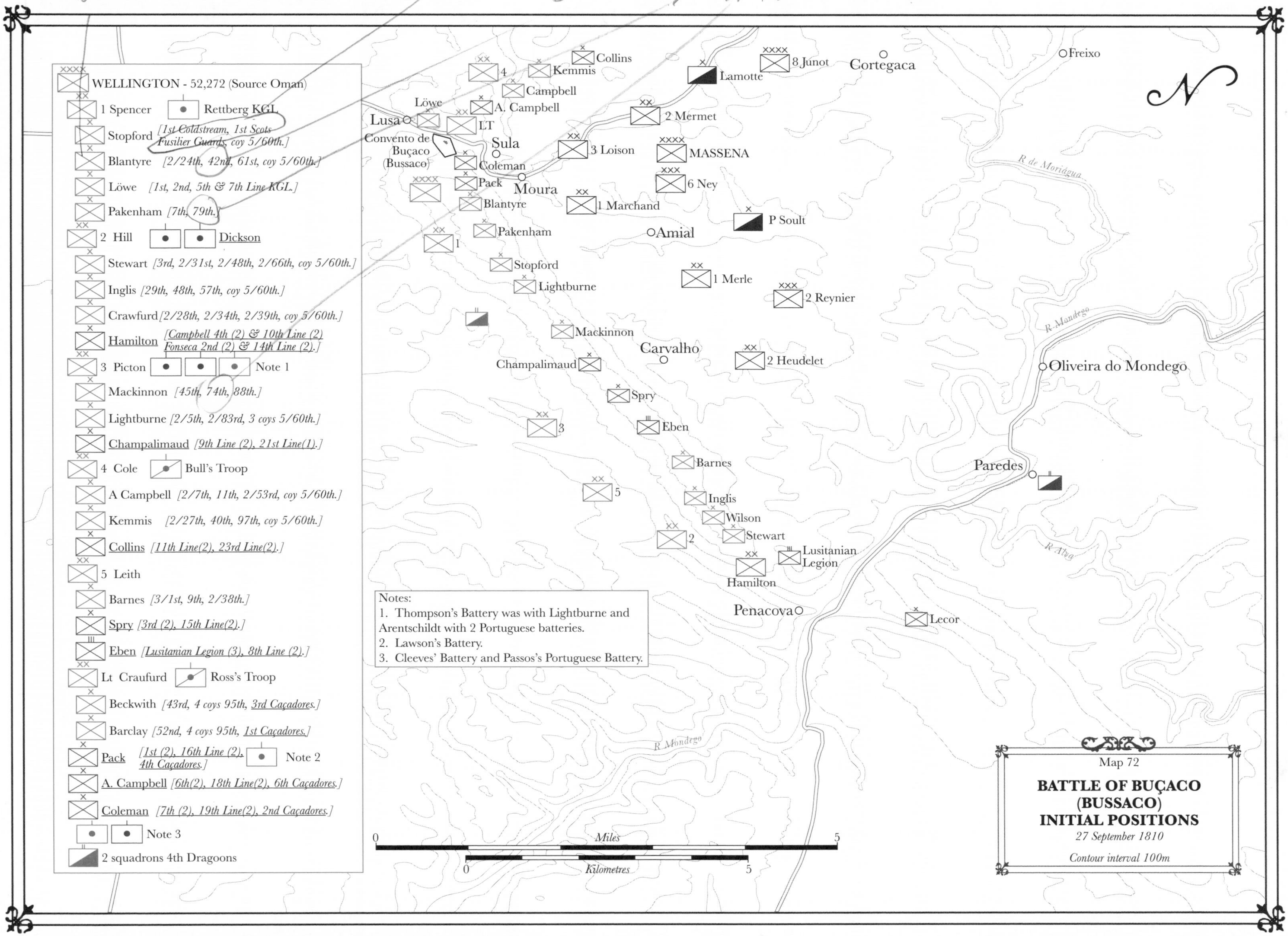

60 Yenhow   SG   42nd BW   29 Ferguson's Hldrs   → 74th (later AHP 1787 (Campbell's Hldrs)

N

WELLINGTON – 52,272 (Source Oman)

1 Spencer — Rettberg KGL

Stopford [1st Coldstream, 1st Scots Fusilier Guards, coy 5/60th.]

Blantyre [2/24th, 42nd, 61st, coy 5/60th.]

Löwe [1st, 2nd, 5th & 7th Line KGL.]

Pakenham [7th, 79th.]

2 Hill — Dickson

Stewart [3rd, 2/31st, 2/48th, 2/66th, coy 5/60th.]

Inglis [29th, 48th, 57th, coy 5/60th.]

Crawfurd [2/28th, 2/34th, 2/39th, coy 5/60th.]

Hamilton [Campbell 4th (2) & 10th Line (2) / Fonseca 2nd (2) & 14th Line (2).]

3 Picton — Note 1

Mackinnon [45th, 74th, 88th.]

Lightburne [2/5th, 2/83rd, 3 coys 5/60th.]

Champalimaud [9th Line (2), 21st Line (1).]

4 Cole — Bull's Troop

A Campbell [2/7th, 11th, 2/53rd, coy 5/60th.]

Kemmis [2/27th, 40th, 97th, coy 5/60th.]

Collins [11th Line(2), 23rd Line(2).]

5 Leith

Barnes [3/1st, 9th, 2/38th.]

Spry [3rd (2), 15th Line(2).]

Eben [Lusitanian Legion (3), 8th Line (2).]

Lt Craufurd — Ross's Troop

Beckwith [43rd, 4 coys 95th, 3rd Caçadores.]

Barclay [52nd, 4 coys 95th, 1st Caçadores.]

Pack [1st (2), 16th Line (2), 4th Caçadores.] — Note 2

A. Campbell [6th(2), 18th Line(2), 6th Caçadores.]

Coleman [7th (2), 19th Line(2), 2nd Caçadores.]

— Note 3

2 squadrons 4th Dragoons

Notes:
1. Thompson's Battery was with Lightburne and Arentschildt with 2 Portuguese batteries.
2. Lawson's Battery.
3. Cleeves' Battery and Passos's Portuguese Battery.

Freixo

Cortegaca

Collins

4   Kemmis

Campbell

A. Campbell

8 Junot

Lamotte

Lusa   Löwe

Convento de Buçaco (Bussaco)

LT

Sula

Coleman

Pack

Moura

Blantyre

Pakenham

Stopford

Lightburne

Mackinnon

Champalimaud

Spry

Eben

3

5

2

2 Mermet

3 Loison

MASSENA

6 Ney

1 Marchand

P Soult

1 Merle

2 Reynier

Carvalho

2 Heudelet

Oliveira do Mondego

Amial

Barnes

Inglis

Wilson

Stewart

Lusitanian Legion

Hamilton

Penacova

Paredes

Lecor

R de Moriágua

R. Mondego

R. Alva

R. Mondego

0   Miles   5

0   Kilometres   5

Map 72

BATTLE OF BUÇACO (BUSSACO) INITIAL POSITIONS

27 September 1810

Contour interval 100m

structure and any semblance of direction. They broke and were chased down the hill by a jubilant Allied infantry who did not stop their pursuit until Reynier's guns engaged them[15] as they neared the bottom of the rise. 'Our soldiers, as intelligent as brave, far from letting themselves hurl down from the top to the bottom of the position, stopped at the start of the escarpment, and at every available point that they can occupy, poured a murderous fire upon the enemy.'[16] Notwithstanding these noble sentiments, the achievement of the Connaught Rangers and the companies of the 45th (under Major Gwynne) demonstrated courage and quick thinking of the highest order.

Reynier, witnessing the failure of his right flank, immediately despatched Foy's Brigade to follow up in support of the 31e Léger.[17] Foy placed himself at the head of the 17e Léger and headed for the space between the first two engagements. This area was lightly held by the left wing of the 74th, the other half of the 45th and some elements of the 8th Portuguese, who had earlier moved north in support of the 88th. Champalimaud moved the two battalions of the 9th Portuguese; however with the engagement against the 31e Léger still ongoing to their right, this Allied force would be unlikely to hold Foy's seven battalions very long. Leith's entire division was now moving north along the ridge with one of Dickson's batteries that he had collected from the 2nd Division.[18] The additional Portuguese battery was dropped off with Arentschildt, and the 18 guns now began to provide direct and crucial support to the defensive actions. Leith continued along the ridge to join Picton with Barnes's Brigade and the Lusitanian Legion. His arrival was timely, as the 8th Portuguese were under severe pressure and beginning to fall back, but Leith deployed the 9th and 2/38th to provide immediate support and then, at the head of the three battalions, charged the leading elements of Foy's troops who were already on the summit. Foy recollected: 'The head of my column fell back on its right, despite my efforts; I could not get them to deploy, disorder set in, and the 17th and 70th raced downhill in headlong flight.'[19] This reversal marked the end of the French offensive actions at this part of the ridge.

'Masséna had taken his place in the centre of the line, on an elevated hillock, although exposed to all the hostile artillery, he could hardly discern the two points of attack, so much of the country, that was for the English of a perfect clarity, was for us unclear and difficult.'[20] Reynier was later to claim that he was beaten by three times his number, but in fact it was the superiority of the Allied position that caused his three attacks to fail. Masséna's difficulty in finding a suitable position to monitor Reynier (and subsequently Ney) highlights the Allied advantage. Ney moved as ordered when he noted, through the mist, Merle's column at the plateau. He advanced with two divisions up and one in reserve; Loison was to the right of the road and Marchand to the left. Loison started his advance before Marchand, with his two brigades side by side, in contrast to the 1st Division that led with Maucune's Brigade. Simon's Brigade was to the right with the 26e Ligne leading and Ferey to his left with the 66e Ligne in front. Both brigade commanders led with strong groups of tirailleurs and they soon clashed with the equally strong line of Allied skirmishers deployed on the lower slopes and in the village of Sula.[21] Craufurd had the balance of his division lying down to be out of the sight of the advancing French, who had to fight hard uphill to gain ground against the Allied skirmishers. Loison was forced to use some of his battalions to assist the tirailleurs in their task. Somewhat exhausted, Simon sought brief refuge in the few dwellings in Sula, but Ross's guns were firing shrapnel in quick succession and Cleeves's Battery (map 74, point 1) was hitting both brigades in the flank. Loison ordered his generals to push on and capture Ross's guns as a matter of urgency. Both French brigades advanced in column of double companies, but they still had to deal with accurate and sustained sniper fire from the Allied skirmishers who had been reinforced by the 1st Caçadores.

'Still the French pressed on undauntingly. The British sharp-shooters came running in over the lip of the assent to the main body; Ross drew back his guns; and the head of the French column could be heard, though still unseen, not many yards away. Then Craufurd, who was watching on the top of a boulder, in a shrill voice gave his word to the British battalions (43rd and 52nd) to charge; and nearly 1,800 bayonets plunged with a mighty shout over the edge of the slope. Four companies only, the two on the extreme left of the 43rd and on the extreme right of the 52nd, found any but skirmishers before them, and these four dashed headlong into the mass of the French. The head of the column stood for a moment, and the front ranks fired a volley which knocked down a few of the British; but the nearest companies of the 43rd and the 52nd wheeled up upon the flanks of the enemy, and gave them in quick succession three volleys so terrible that the whole turned and ran; the four British companies plying the bayonet with fearful slaughter in the thick of them, and overthrowing, apparently, even more than they killed or wounded.'[22]

The semi-circle of fire surrounding the heads of the two brigade columns was intense and as they tried to retire many men lost their footing and fell back on those behind. Simon's entire brigade and most of Ferey's were now spent. A solitary battalion, the 2/32e Léger, had broken left during the climb and now found itself in the ground below Cleeves's King's German Legion Battery, but before it could close on the guns, Coleman's left-hand battalion, the 1/19th, had

15 This was a good indication that the French guns were of limited use at Buçaco, for even at maximum elevation the guns could not engage the Allied positions.

16 Thiers, *Histoire du Consulat et du L'Empire*, vol XII, pp.367–368.

17 In fact Reynier was incensed that Foy had not started earlier: 'you could get the troops forward if you chose, but you don't chose'. Foy had misunderstood his commander's intent, and was waiting for the 31e Léger to gain a foothold before advancing in support.

18 Leith had orders to close in on Picton if he was sure there were no French to his front.

19 Oman, *A History of the Peninsular War*, vol III, p.377. Extract from Foy's Diary, pp.103–104.

20 Thiers, *Histoire du Consulat et du L'Empire*, vol XII, p.368. In fact Masséna was not in the centre of the two attacks; he was with Ney in the north and unable to get a clear picture of Reynier's progress to the south. This was largely the problem.

21 Craufurd had deployed the entire battalions of the 95th and 3rd Caçadores and Pack had done the same with the 4th Caçadores.

22 Fortescue, *A History of the British Army*, vol VII, ch. XXXVIII, pp.523–525. I have reproduced this entire passage as it contradicts Oman, who stated that the British rose and fired and then charged. However, both Napier (George Napier was commanding a company in the 43rd) and Booth (Levinge's *Historical Record of the Forty-third*) state there was a charge, followed by subsequent volleys.

Robert Walter Stewart, Lord Brackyr 11th Baron
Ross 17th Lt Dragoons — to Lt Col Cmd 2/42 in Peninsular from June 1809

N

Convento de Buçaco
(Bussaco)

Löwe 4

LT Sula

Coleman

3 Loison

Pack

Moura

Blantyre

WELLINGTON

1

Pakenham

Stopford

Cerquêdo

Lightburne

½ 45

8

Santo António
de Cântaro

17e

3 74

½ 45

Mackinnon

9

Champatimaud

Cacemes

Palheiros

8. Junot

Lamotte

2 Mermet

MASSENA

6 Ney

1 Marchand

Cerdeirinha

Amial

1 Merle

36e
2e
4e

Pendurada

88

2 Reynier

47e

P. Soult Soalhal

70e
31e

2 Heudelet

21

Ouraça

Lourinhal

Spry

Carvalho

Aveledo

Eben

5

Barnes

×××	2 Reynier
××	1 Merle
×	Sarrut [1/2e, 2/2e, 3/2e, 4/2e Léger, 1/36e, 2/36e, 3/36e, 4/36e Léger.]
×	Graindorge [1/4e, 2/4e, 3/4e, 4/4e Léger.]
××	2 Heudelet
×	Foy [1/17e, 2/17e, 3/17e Léger, 1/70e, 2/70e, 3/70e, 4/70e Ligne.]
×	Arnaud [1/31e, 2/31e, 3/31e, 4/31e Léger.]

Reserve

×××	[1/47e, 2/47e, 3/47e, 4/47e Ligne.]
	P. Soult [1e Hussars, 22e Chasseurs, 8e Dragoons, Hanoverian Chasseurs.]
●	3 batteries

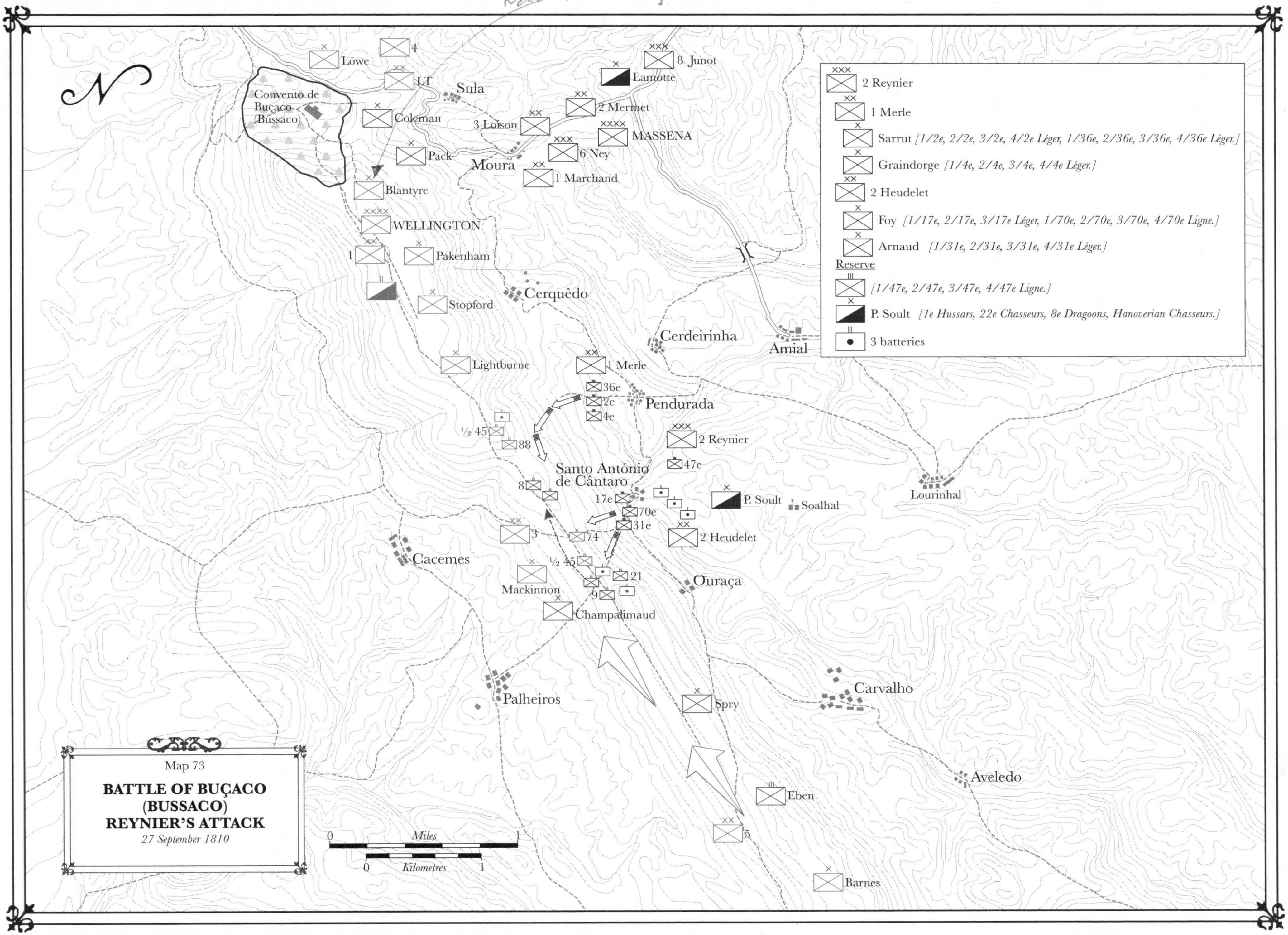

Map 73

**BATTLE OF BUÇACO
(BUSSACO)
REYNIER'S ATTACK**

27 September 1810

Miles
0 — 1

Kilometres
0 — 1

charged and dispatched them back to the low ground to join the rest of the retreating French. Maucune's Brigade had fared little better. The three Allied batteries of Cleeves, Parros and Lawson (map 74, points 1, 2 and 3 respectively) had battered the brigade as it moved towards the foot of the hill. After a prolonged battle with Pack's skirmishers in the wood at the bottom of the slope they emerged at the far end, but had lost their cohesion and, despite a number of attempts to storm the hill, they were beaten back by Pack's four battalions and Lawson's guns firing canister. Marcognet had followed Maucune, but his brigade had stopped when it came under heavy fire from Cleeves, Parros and Ross's guns. They were taking heavy losses and after a time Ney withdrew them out of range of the Allied guns. Ney had seen Maucune's attack flounder and Loison's men retreating. Later in the day Ney pushed forward lines of tirailleurs; those to the south bickered with the skirmishers of the 1st Division and to the north with the light companies of Löwe's German Legion Brigade and Campbell's 6th Caçadores, whom Craufurd had called forward to replace his exhausted men.

The genius of Wellington's deployment and the need for caution, so pressingly urged by his subordinates, was now abundantly apparent to Masséna and he resisted the temptation to throw Junot's infantry into the fight. French losses had been considerable; Graindorge had been killed, Maucune, Foy and Merle wounded, and Simon wounded and captured. Allied losses were light by comparison. Captain Kincaid of the 95th summed up the French frustration: 'On the day of the battle, the 27th, the French General Simon, who led the attack upon our Division, was wounded and taken prisoner; and as they were bringing him in, he raved furiously for General Craufurd, daring him to single combat; but as he was already a prisoner, there would have been but little wit in indulging him in his humour.' Buçaco had been fought and won. Many have criticized Wellington for fighting a battle that appeared to achieve little. The French were able to bypass the position a few days later. However, this simplistic view misses the point. The failure at Buçaco was a significant blow to Masséna and was to intrude on his consciousness during events that were to follow.

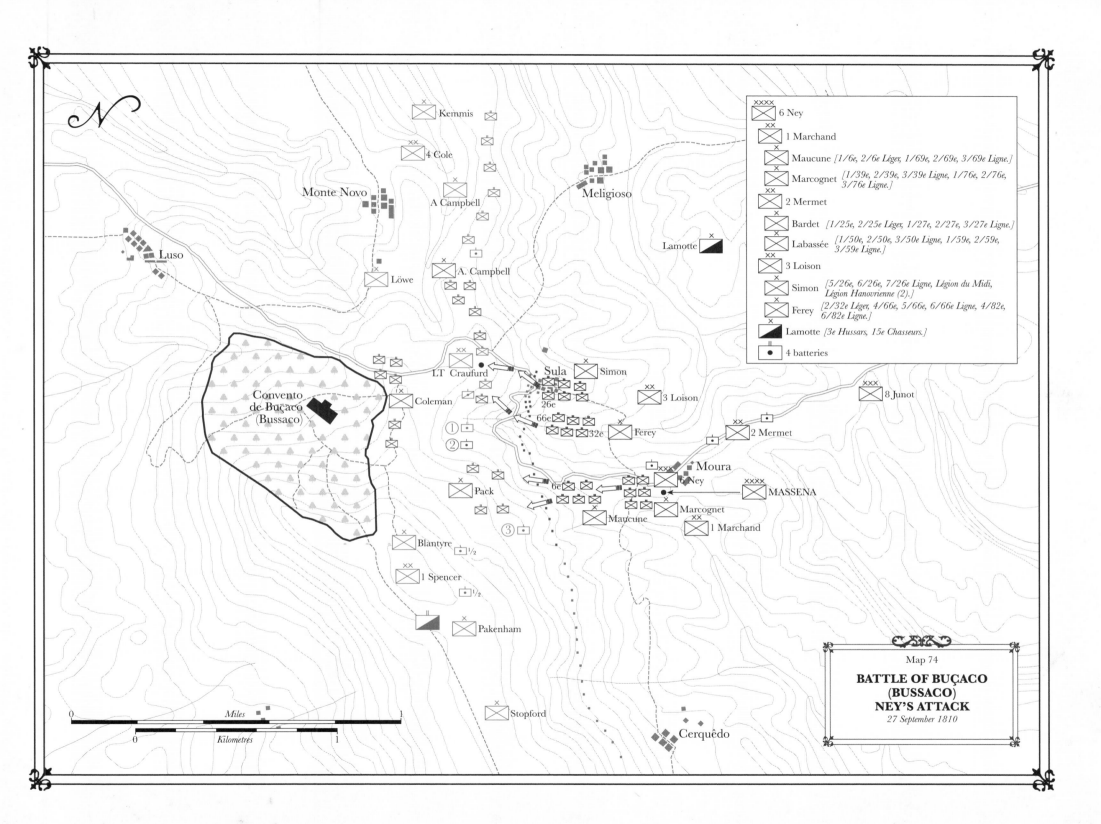

N

Kemmis

4 Cole

Monte Novo

A Campbell

Meligioso

Lamotte

Luso

A. Campbell

Löwe

Convento
de Buçaco
(Bussaco)

LT Craufurd

Sula

Simon

Coleman

26e

3 Loison

8 Junot

66e

32e   Ferey

2 Mermet

①

②

Moura

6 Ney

Pack

6e

MASSENA

Maucune

Marcognet

Blantyre

½

③

1 Marchand

1 Spencer

½

Pakenham

Stopford

Cerquêdo

Legend

6 Ney

1 Marchand

Maucune *[1/6e, 2/6e Léger, 1/69e, 2/69e, 3/69e Ligne.]*

Marcognet *[1/39e, 2/39e, 3/39e Ligne, 1/76e, 2/76e, 3/76e Ligne.]*

2 Mermet

Bardet *[1/25e, 2/25e Léger, 1/27e, 2/27e, 3/27e Ligne.]*

Labassée *[1/50e, 2/50e, 3/50e Ligne, 1/59e, 2/59e, 3/59e Ligne.]*

3 Loison

Simon *[5/26e, 6/26e, 7/26e Ligne, Légion du Midi, Légion Hanovrienne (2).]*

Ferey *[2/32e Léger, 4/66e, 5/66e, 6/66e Ligne, 4/82e, 6/82e Ligne.]*

Lamotte *[3e Hussars, 15e Chasseurs.]*

4 batteries

Map 74

**BATTLE OF BUÇACO
(BUSSACO)
NEY'S ATTACK**

27 September 1810

Miles   0   1

Kilometres   0   1

Chapter 27

THE LINES OF TORRES VEDRAS

Following Buçaco, Masséna contemplated three options. Withdrawal to Almeida to recoup, march north to capture Oporto or outflank the Allied position at Buçaco and pursue his original mission to capture Lisbon. Masséna did not dwell overly long in discarding the first two, despite advice to the contrary from his close council and regardless of an apparent lack of suitable routes. Early on 28 September, he despatched part of the cavalry to reconnoitre both flanks; an action he arguably should have undertaken prior to fighting the battle. Soult's light cavalry reported that the southern flank offered no real possibilities but St Croix's reconnaissance reports from the north and east were more promising. The marshal issued immediate orders for the withdrawal to Mortagoa, and from that village to head north on a mule track to Boialvo and then to the village of Agueda. He organized a series of deception actions in front of the ridge at Buçaco commencing at about 1200 hours, but these minor actions did not deceive the Allies for a moment. Ney and Reynier's infantry were seen preparing defensive trenches either side of the main road, preparations that were clearly designed to enable the French rearguard to hold any Allied counter-attack and buy time for the withdrawal.

That evening Wellington, having watched the retreating French columns from the heights, retired to the convent and wrote orders for the withdrawal of the Allied army to Coimbra and Lisbon.[1] By 30 September, the Allies were clear of Coimbra; lines of local inhabitants fleeing the city ahead of the French, who arrived the next day, closely followed them. 'Lord Wellington, being allowed a perfectly free hand by the government, used it to compel all the people to leave their homes, destroy all their provisions and mills, and retire with their cattle to Lisbon.'[2] The Portuguese government had consented to Wellington's scorched-earth policy, but had not pursued its instigation with much zeal. The sacrifice made by the inhabitants living immediately north of the Lines was considerable; to the inhabitants of Coimbra it was particularly acute. 'It could not occur to us, that, though the devastating system must inevitably bear hard upon the French, the most serious evils would, in all probability, arise out of it, both to ourselves and our allies, from the famine and general distress which it threatened to bring upon a crowd so dense, shut up within the walls of a single city. There can be no question now, that this very measure, more perhaps than any other, preserved Portugal from subjugation, and

England from defeat; but, at that moment, there were few amongst us, who seemed not disposed to view it with reprobation.'[3]

Other than a brief skirmish with Trant's force at Sardão,[4] the French move on Coimbra was unhindered and, after a brief encounter with the British cavalry north of the city, Masséna's force occupied the deserted dwellings. The lure of plunder reduced the French to a rabble and bought Wellington, and the citizens of Coimbra, two valuable days. On 4 October Masséna headed south, having left the 3,500 sick and wounded with only a single company to guard them.[5] Anson's light cavalry brigade[6] who had been left to monitor French movement, were pursued with vigour by the French vanguard under Montbrun[7] and during one such encounter, captured British troops spoke of their destination – the Lines of Torres Vedras. Masséna was delighted to hear that Wellington had every intention of offering him an opportunity to avenge Buçaco; he had been convinced that he (like Moore) was beating a retreat to waiting Royal Navy vessels in the Tagus estuary.

By 7 October the entire French force was concentrated at Leiria and, late in the day, Masséna received the disheartening news that the Portuguese force under Trant, who had shadowed the French advance and now severed his lines of communication, had retaken Coimbra. Wilson and Miller arrived soon after with their brigades and Trant handed the city over to them and escorted the French prisoners to Oporto. Rumours of the reverse and of reprisals against their captured colleagues did little to endear the French to their commander, who they felt had left the men to an inevitable fate. Masséna continued his advance on 8 and 9 October, confident that victory over the Anglo-Portuguese would restore their loyalty. The French vanguard encountered some opposition, resulting in some quite heavy cavalry-on-cavalry skirmishing, but by nightfall on 10 October the last elements of Wellington's army had withdrawn behind the Lines. They were to be joined two weeks later by La Romana and two divisions from his Army of Estremadura that had marched from Andalusia.

Wellington's plans for the defence of Portugal rested on a series of defensive fortifications in lines to protect the capital and, should these outer defences fail, another set to cover the point of embarkation. Wellesley had made an initial reconnaissance of the area with a Portuguese engineer officer, Major Neves Costa, in 1808 but it was after Talavera that Wellington had undertaken a detailed reconnaissance with Murray, his Quartermaster General, and Fletcher, his Chief Engineer. The lines were not continuous; rather they were a series of fortified camps and closed earthworks, heavily armed and positioned with interlocking and overlapping arcs of fire. Anything that provided cover to the front was removed and the wood used for *abattis*. The original plan had been for a series of forts from Alhandra to the mouth of the Rio São Lourenço; but

---

1 Wellington has received considerable criticism for not attacking the French rearguard and punishing Masséna's flank march across his front. Some French writers have attributed his failure to 'timidity'. However, Wellington had achieved his aims at Buçaco and with the Lines of Torres Vedras to his rear, such accusations are inappropriate and miss the point as to why Wellington fought the battle.

2 Marbot, *Memoirs*, vol. II, p.108.

3 Vane, *Narrative of the Peninsular War From 1808 to 1813*, vol. II, p.13.

4 Sardão and Agueda was really one village separated by a bridge, the former lying north of the river.

5 This company was from the 44e Équipage de la Marine; they had an impossible task and were left, along with the convalescents, to certain capture.

6 Consisting of the 16th Light Dragoons and the 1st Hussars of the King's German Legion.

7 Consisting of the cavalry brigades of Soult, St Croix, Lamotte and Ornano (from Montbrun's division) and Taupin's Infantry Brigade from the 8th Corps.

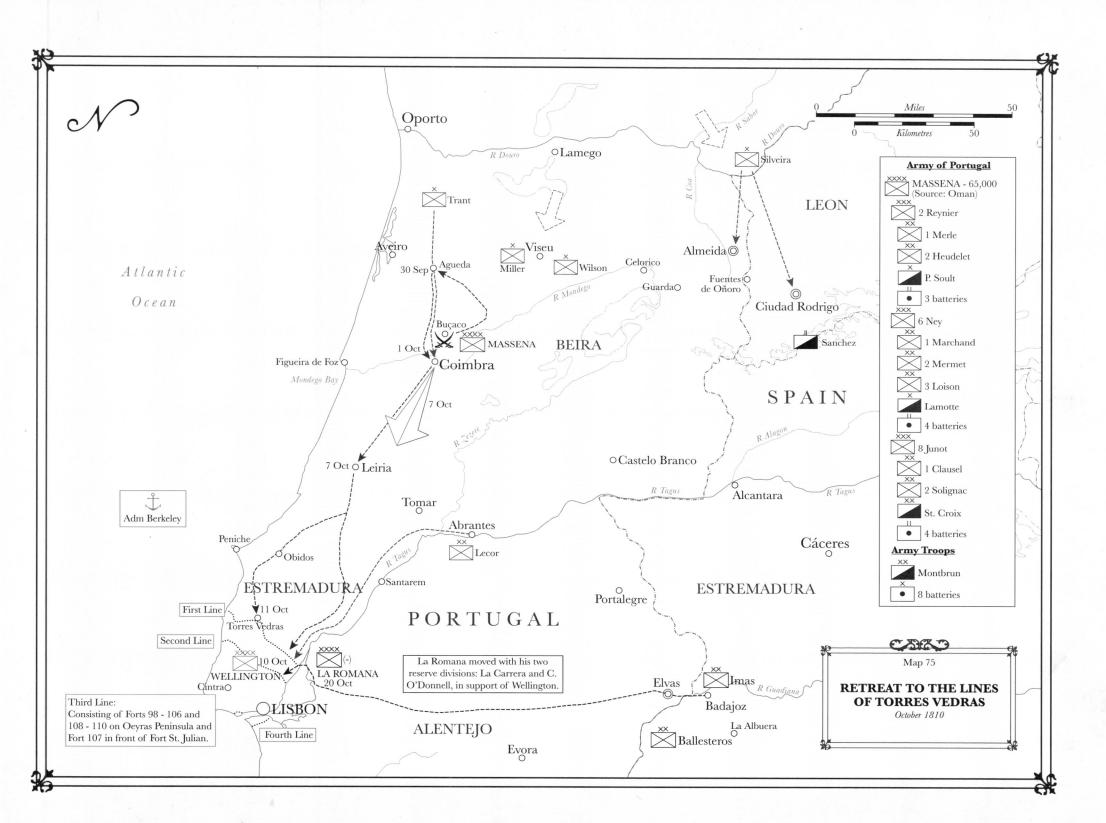

N

Oporto

Lamego

R Douro

LEON

Silveira

Trant

Aveiro

Viseu

Miller

Wilson

Celorico

Almeida

Fuentes
de Oñoro

30 Sep · Agueda

R Mondego

Guarda

Ciudad Rodrigo

Atlantic

Ocean

Buçaco

1 Oct

BEIRA

MASSENA

Sanchez

SPAIN

Figueira de Foz

Coimbra

Mondego Bay

7 Oct

R Zezre

R Alagon

Adm Berkeley

7 Oct · Leiria

Castelo Branco

R Tagus

Alcantara

R Tagus

Tomar

Cáceres

Abrantes

Lecor

Peniche

Obidos

R Tagus

Santarem

ESTREMADURA

Portalegre

ESTREMADURA

PORTUGAL

First Line

11 Oct

Torres Vedras

Second Line

10 Oct

LA ROMANA
20 Oct

La Romana moved with his two
reserve divisions: La Carrera and C.
O'Donnell, in support of Wellington.

Elvas

Imas

R Guadiana

WELLINGTON

Cintra

Badajoz

Third Line:
Consisting of Forts 98 - 106 and
108 - 110 on Oeyras Peninsula and
Fort 107 in front of Fort St. Julian.

LISBON

Fourth Line

ALENTEJO

La Albuera

Ballesteros

Evora

Army of Portugal

MASSENA – 65,000
(Source: Oman)

2 Reynier

1 Merle

2 Heudelet

P. Soult

3 batteries

6 Ney

1 Marchand

2 Mermet

3 Loison

Lamotte

4 batteries

8 Junot

1 Clausel

2 Solignac

St. Croix

4 batteries

Army Troops

Montbrun

8 batteries

Miles 0 ▬▬▬ 50

Kilometres 0 ▬▬▬ 50

Map 75

**RETREAT TO THE LINES
OF TORRES VEDRAS**
October 1810

Masséna's delay in invading Portugal had provided Wellington more time to expand and elaborate on this original strategy. 'The length of retrenchment completed at the period the army occupied the lines, including the periphery of 126 enclosed works, when calculated on the data before mentioned, required 29,751 men for its defence, and there were mounted on it 427 pieces of artillery, independently of the works to cover an embarkation at St Julian's, which were calculated for 5,350 men, and contained 94 pieces of artillery.'[8] To man these fortifications Wellington had not used any of his British and Portuguese regulars, other than the troops of the artillery and engineers. The Royal Navy helped man some of the fortifications in the third line, but the majority of defenders came from the Portuguese militia and *ordenança* at his disposal. His main force (34,000 British, 24,500 Portuguese and 8,000 Spanish) was concentrated in areas behind the lines, able to reinforce any point at short notice. To aid this rapid redeployment five signal stations were established along the length of the first line;[9] manned by naval personnel and using a mixture of naval semaphore and Portuguese signalling. They boasted that a message could be sent the length of the line in a mere seven minutes. 'Indeed one of the most amazing features of the project was the secrecy in which it was carried out. The Lines were a year in building; they cut across the four principal highways from Lisbon to the north; and they were built entirely by locally recruited Portuguese labour. Yet, not only was Masséna ignorant of their existence until four days before they were sighted by his advance guard, but the British Ministry in London and all but a few staff officers in the British army were equally unaware of their construction. Even the British minister in Lisbon, little more than 20 miles away, appears to have had no knowledge of them.'[10]

On the morning of 11 October Montbrun's vanguard came up against the Lines at Alhandra and Sobral and drove back the piquets in front of both locations. He could see the fortifications but was unsure what lay behind them, and with only one brigade of infantry he was reluctant to try anything ambitious. He paused and sent word back to Masséna. Wellington used the time to prepare and move his forces in anticipation of a possible French reaction. Early on 12 October, Montbrun moved Taupin's Brigade west in front of Hamilton and Hill's divisions and Wellington assumed this was to be the point. However, Junot's Corps was en route to fill the gap vacated by Taupin in front of Sobral and later in the day the outposts from Erskine and Löwe's brigades were ejected from the village. On the same day, the 2nd Corps moved to Carregado, north of Villa Franca and the 6th Corps closed up to the rear of the 2nd and 8th corps. Wellington had revised his original assessment and now believed the greater threat to be in front of Sobral, and once again he counter-moved his army accordingly. Junot wisely elected to wait for the arrival of Masséna, who appeared the following morning in time to witness the 19e Ligne dislodging the 71st Foot from their barricades to the south of the village of Sobral. Masséna was astounded at what lay before him and, with the memory of Buçaco fresh in his mind, quickly appreciated the difficulty in breaking the Lines by assault. Eager to determine the extent of the defences,

he rode east to reconnoitre the Lines out to the Tagus; at the eastern end he approached too close and received a warning shot from the guns in redoubt 120. He doffed his headdress, saluting the battery, and rode solemnly to his headquarters at Alemquer where he called for a council. The Lines were 'not therefore a simple line of entrenchments of which one could rush the attack with the audacity, they were a continuation of natural obstacles, whose design had curiously increased the difficulty by linking closed fortifications dominating the entrances, removing in one moment the impetus and just as difficult achieving surprise because, while that of the English, thanks to the roads that they had established, could carry themselves in a couple of hours from one side to the other and unite with all their strength on the point of attack, the French met an accident of land that forbade them all manoeuvre of any kind'.[11]

Junot urged an attack while Ney and Reynier proposed caution. The lesson from Buçaco had not been lost and Masséna reluctantly concurred with the majority of his council, but he stubbornly refused to withdraw. Instead he opted to remain in front of the Lines, establish a blockade and wait for reinforcement from Mortier or Drouet. Such a plan was deeply flawed; his army was struggling to find sufficient rations, all forms of communication with Spain were severed and the terrain in front of the Lines offered scant protection to his men. The degeneration of the French force was rapid; so rapid in fact that Wellington even considered taking the offensive. At the end of October, Masséna was becoming anxious and dispatched General Foy with a battalion escort (4/47e Ligne) to make for Spain, and ultimately Paris, to seek support. On 10 November, with his army starving and deserting at an alarming rate, Masséna gave the orders to pull back and by 14 November the infantry broke contact under cover of a dense fog.

The next morning Wellington was informed that the French were gone. The 1st, 2nd and Light divisions were directed to march out and determine the whereabouts and intentions of Masséna's force. The appalling state of the areas vacated by the French, the dead bodies, the animal carcasses and the filth highlighted the sorry state of Masséna's demoralized army. On 16 November Wellington moved more formations out of the Lines, leaving only the 3rd, 4th and 5th divisions and the new 6th Division[12] within. On the 17th, Craufurd came up against Masséna's rearguard in front of Santarem and was preparing to attack when Wellington arrived on the scene, and bade him wait the arrival of Hill and Spencer. Reynier's position was strong and the decision not to attack was the right one, but the redeployment of Hill and Hamilton to Abrantes, based on false intelligence from Fane, now deprived Wellington of any further offensive capability. He called forward Leith and Cole's divisions, but they were two days' march to the rear. In the meantime Fane had reached Abrantes and reported, contrary to his original assessment, that the French were not in the town or making any movement north towards it. Wellington realized that he must therefore have Masséna's entire force to his front and, given the strength of the French force, the deterioration in the weather and the possibility that French reinforcements might appear from Estremadura or Leon, he decided to refrain from offensive action and retired to the Lines leaving only Spencer, Craufurd and Pack to monitor Santarem.

8   Jones, *Journal of Sieges*, vol. III, pp.91–92.

9   There was a similar system on the second and third lines.

10 Norris and Bremner, *The Lines of Torres Vedras*, The British Historical Society of Portugal 1986, p.12.

11 Thiers, *Histoire du Consulat et du L'Empire*, vol. XII, pp.396–397.

12 The new 6th Division consisted of Alex Campbell's Portuguese Brigade only.

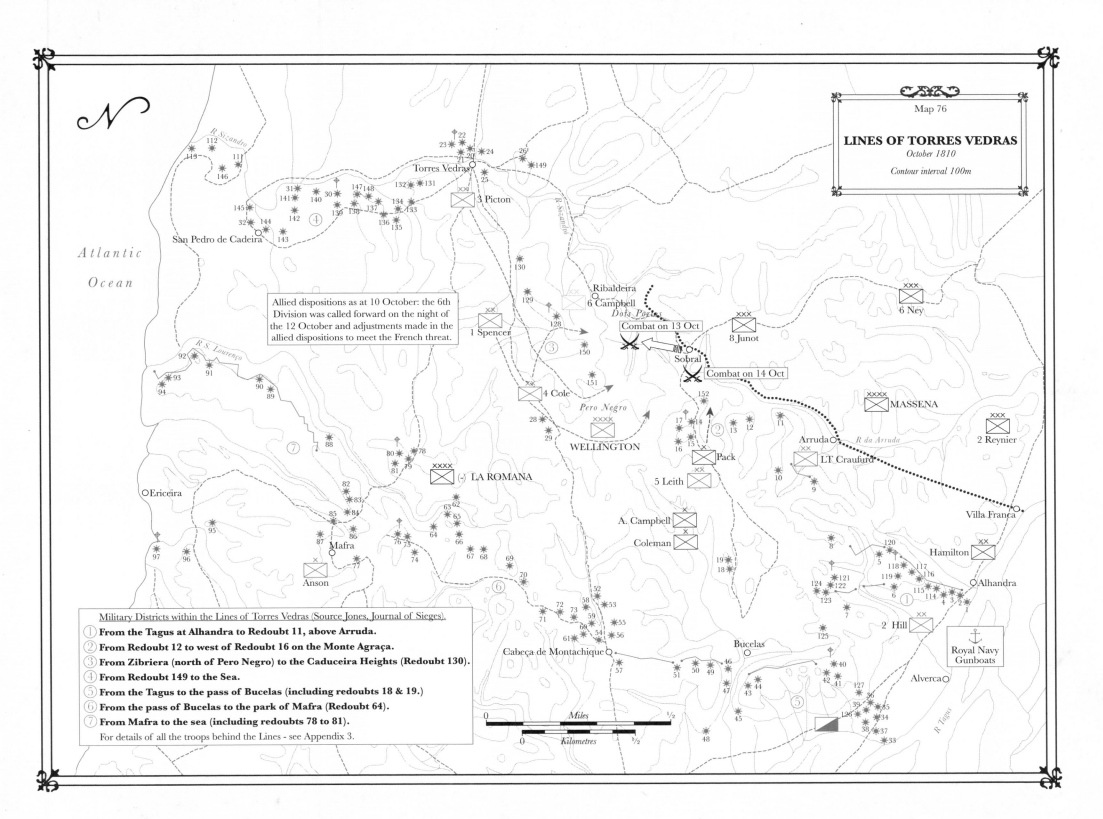

N

Atlantic Ocean

Map 76

LINES OF TORRES VEDRAS

October 1810

Contour interval 100m

Allied dispositions as at 10 October: the 6th Division was called forward on the night of the 12 October and adjustments made in the allied dispositions to meet the French threat.

Torres Vedras

San Pedro de Cadeira

3 Picton

Ribaldeira
6 Campbell

Dois Portos

Combat on 13 Oct

8 Junot

6 Ney

1 Spencer

Sobral

Combat on 14 Oct

4 Cole

Pero Negro

WELLINGTON

MASSENA

Pack

Arruda

R da Arruda

2 Reynier

LT Craufurd

5 Leith

Villa Franca

(-) LA ROMANA

A. Campbell

Coleman

Hamilton

Ericeira

Alhandra

Mafra

2 Hill

Anson

Royal Navy Gunboats

Bucelas

Alverca

Cabeça de Montachique

R Tagus

Military Districts within the Lines of Torres Vedras (Source Jones, *Journal of Sieges*).

1. **From the Tagus at Alhandra to Redoubt 11, above Arruda.**
2. **From Redoubt 12 to west of Redoubt 16 on the Monte Agraça.**
3. **From Zibriera (north of Pero Negro) to the Caduceira Heights (Redoubt 130).**
4. **From Redoubt 149 to the Sea.**
5. **From the Tagus to the pass of Bucelas (including redoubts 18 & 19.)**
6. **From the pass of Bucelas to the park of Mafra (Redoubt 64).**
7. **From Mafra to the sea (including redoubts 78 to 81).**

For details of all the troops behind the Lines - see Appendix 3.

0   *Miles*   ½

0   *Kilometres*   ½

Masséna's army was in desperate need of rations and he was at a loss as to why General Gardanne, the commander at Ciudad Rodrigo, had not materialized with this assistance as he had repeatedly requested. Foy, en route to Paris, had left his battalion to form the nucleus of Gardanne's force, to which was added all the spare men from Ciudad Rodrigo and all the convalescents from the Army of Portugal, who had been left in the region many months before.[13] In fact Gardanne had departed Ciudad Rodrigo on 20 November with 5,000 men, but his heavy convoy and ad hoc formation made slow progress over the appalling roads, made worse by the abysmal weather. On 27 November, he reached the river Codes, which he considered was running too fast, and was too deep to ford. He turned back, unaware that he was only 20km from Loison's position, leaving Masséna's half-starved troops to make do with the meagre provisions that Santarem and the immediate countryside could offer.

In southern Spain little of consequence had occurred throughout the year. Soult remained most of the time at Sevilla in a viceregal capacity of his own making. The independently minded Victor was still besieging Cádiz; Sebastiani was sent into Murcia and Mortier into Estremadura. Soult ignored recurring requests from Joseph in Madrid for revenue, and created countless excuses deferring any attempt by Joseph to visit Andalusia and finally tried to reinforce his independence by raising a small force of Spanish auxiliaries. However, the longer Cádiz held out, the greater the confidence of the Regency grew; by May there were 18,000 Spanish and 8,000 British and Portuguese troops within the lines of defence. Blake had been made commander-in-chief of the army in April, replacing Alburquerque, whose quarrelsome nature had become ever more frustrating to the authorities. Blake was also left in command of the Army of Murcia and he now combined the two forces, creating three divisions in each.[14] He also set about instigating a combined plan of operations in both provinces, with La Romana executing raids in Estremadura while Blake taunted Sebastiani in Murcia. The former commander was the more adept at tying up increasing numbers of Frenchmen, and by October had withdrawn to Badajoz and the Portuguese border and subsequently joined Wellington at Torres Vedras with two divisions. Blake's operations in Murcia started well, then stagnated under Freire's temporary command, but were to turn to disaster in the autumn when Blake returned. During an offensive on 3 November, he was wrong-footed at Baza by Milhaud, who arrived unexpectedly and caught the Spanish in line of march. The defeat was not significant, but it brought to an end any further attempts to relieve Granada.

In the north of Spain, the French had more than 70,000 men[15] being held down by no more than the 25,000 combined regulars of Silveira, Mahy and Cienfuegos. The Anglo-Spanish squadron established at La Coruña began to cause havoc in the Asturias against Bonnet's garrisons, until it was to fall prey to the unforgiving seas in the Bay of Biscay. In Old Castile, Navarre and the upper Ebro, the massed French forces were kept occupied by the numerous guerrilla bands (numbering less than 20,000) that were operating and intensifying in the region. Mina emerged as a ruthlessly effective commander and became, with incredible rapidity, the man with the greatest prize upon his head. Sanchez was also operating with relative impunity around Ciudad Rodrigo, and other names achieved notoriety: Merino or 'El Cura', Tapia, Abril, Louga, Tenderin, Saornil and Principe. Their exploits are legendary – if occasionally embellished – and they were often at odds with the local populace, but their existence and operations contributed to distract, disrupt and demoralize the French forces in north and north-western Spain. To the north-east, as the year came to a close, little of significance took place. Suchet had conquered Lérida and Mequinenza by June, and then received imperial orders to take Valencia with an implicit task of capturing Tarragona and Tortosa in the process.

---

13   An attempt to get men from Almeida was thwarted by Silveira.

14   The old Army of Estremadura had the vanguard, the 2nd and the 4th divisions and the old Army of Murcia had the 1st, 3rd and 5th divisions. In addition, in Cádiz there was a cavalry division and there were two small cavalry divisions in Murcia.

---

15   Kellermann, 3,000; Serras, 9,000; Bonnet, 8,000; Young Guard, 11,500; Biscay, 8,000; Navarre, 8,500; Santander, 3,500; 9th Corps, 18,500; and various garrisons, 2,500. Source: Oman, *A History of the Peninsular War*, vol. III, p.484.

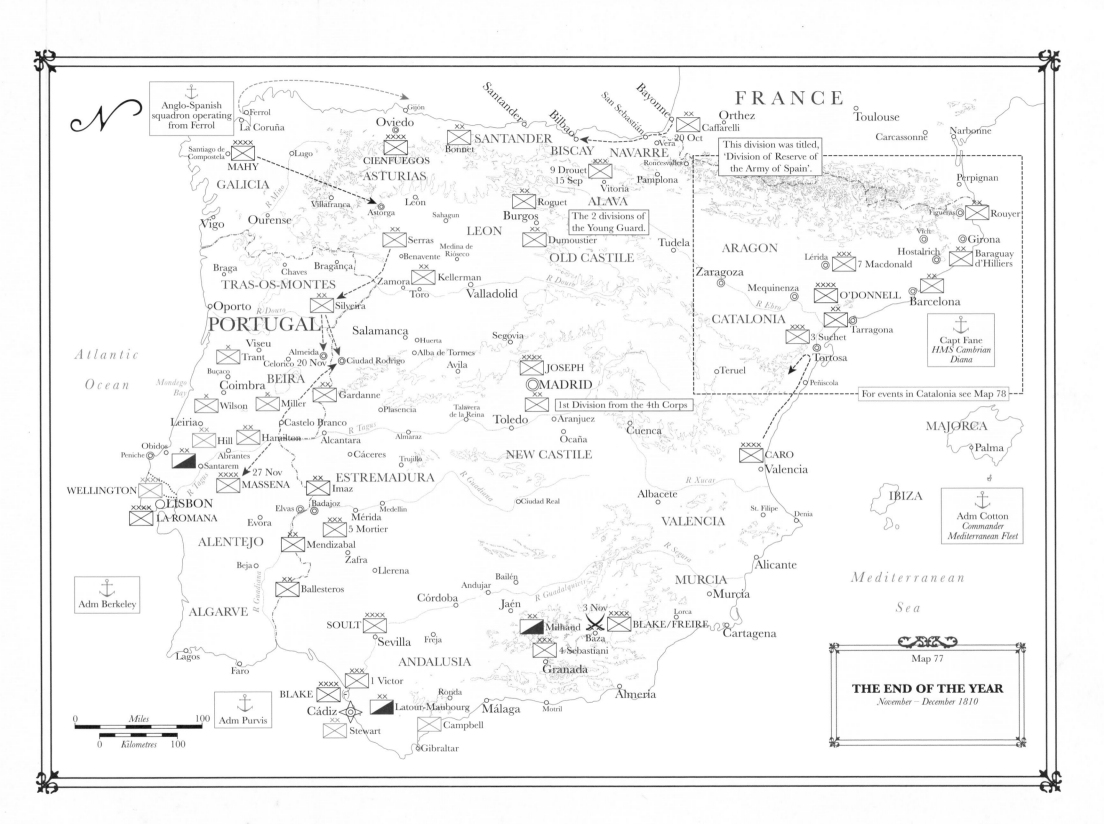

N

Anglo-Spanish squadron operating from Ferrol

FRANCE

Ferrol
La Coruña
Santiago de Compostela
MAHY
GALICIA
Vigo
Ourense
Lugo
Villafranca
Astorga
León
Sahagun
Oviedo
CIENFUEGOS
ASTURIAS
Bonnet
SANTANDER
Gijón
Santander
Bilbao
San Sebastián
Bayonne
Orthez
Caffarelli
20 Oct
Vera
Roncesvalles
BISCAY
NAVARRE
Pamplona
Vitoria
ALAVA
Roguet
Burgos
Dumoustier
OLD CASTILE
Tudela
Toulouse
Carcassonne
Narbonne
Perpignan

This division was titled, 'Division of Reserve of the Army of Spain'.

9 Drouet
15 Sep

The 2 divisions of the Young Guard.

ARAGON
Zaragoza
Mequinenza
Lérida
7 Macdonald
O'DONNELL
CATALONIA
3 Suchet
Teruel
Tortosa
Peñiscola
Figueras
Rouyer
Vich
Girona
Hostalrich
Baraguay d'Hilliers
Barcelona
Tarragona

Capt Fane
HMS Cambrian
Diana

For events in Catalonia see Map 78

Braga
Chaves
Bragança
TRAS-OS-MONTES
Serras
Benavente
Medina de Ríoseco
Zamora
Toro
Kellerman
Valladolid
R Douro

Oporto
R Douro
Silveira
PORTUGAL
Salamanca
Segovia
Huerta
Alba de Tormes
Avila

Viseu
Trant
Almeida 20 Nov
Celorico
Ciudad Rodrigo
BEIRA
Buçaco
Coimbra
Wilson
Miller
Gardanne
Plasencia

JOSEPH
MADRID
1st Division from the 4th Corps

Atlantic Ocean
Mondego Bay
Leiria
Obidos
Peniche

Hill
Hamilton
Abrantes
Santarem
MASSENA
27 Nov
Imaz
ESTREMADURA
Castelo Branco
Alcantara
Cáceres
Trujillo
Almaraz
Talavera de la Reina
Toledo
Aranjuez
Ocaña
Cuenca
NEW CASTILE
Ciudad Real

WELLINGTON
LISBON
LA ROMANA
Elvas
Badajoz
Mérida
Medellin
Mendizabal
5 Mortier
Zafra
Llerena

ALENTEJO
Evora
Beja
Ballesteros

CARO
Valencia
MAJORCA
Palma
IBIZA
Adm Cotton
Commander
Mediterranean Fleet
VALENCIA
Albacete
St. Filipe
Denia
R Xucar
R Segura
MURCIA
Murcia
Alicante

Mediterranean Sea

Adm Berkeley

Córdoba
Andujar
Bailén
Jaén
3 Nov
Milhaud
Baza
BLAKE/FREIRE
Lorca
Cartagena

SOULT
Sevilla
Freja
4 Sebastiani
Granada
ANDALUSIA
Almería

ALGARVE
Lagos
Faro
BLAKE
1 Victor
Cádiz
Latour-Maubourg
Stewart
Campbell
Gibraltar
Ronda
Málaga
Motril

Adm Purvis

0 Miles 100
0 Kilometres 100

Map 77

THE END OF THE YEAR
November – December 1810

Chapter 28 ⇥

OFFENSIVE ON THE EAST COAST: TORTOSA

In June 1810 General Suchet received instructions from Napoleon outlining his Valencian objectives. He was to be assisted in his task by Macdonald, but it was the 7th Corps commander's preoccupation with the replenishment of Barcelona that allowed the Spanish Army of Valencia, under General Caro, to put Suchet's advance guard in great danger during the execution of the first phase of the operation. A month after the capture of Mequinenza (see Chapter 24) Suchet despatched 12,000 men to the very gates of Tortosa, and en route this small force captured the ferry at Amposta thereby cutting the main road from Tarragona to Valencia. A division under the command of Bassecourt was sent from the south to confront this force but it was prevented from outflanking Suchet's force by one of Leval's brigades at Morella. However, Suchet was less successful in preventing Henry O'Donnell from descending from the north – having destroyed many of the French outposts on the way – and entering Tortosa, thereby bolstering the town's defences. 'On the 3rd of August, having drawn up in Tortosa some columns of picked men, to who he [O'Donnell] addressed, in the presence of the people of the town a speech, in order to stir up their enthusiasm, he sallied out by the *tête-du-pont* at four o'clock in the afternoon and marched straight forward on our intrenchments without firing a musket. Our advanced posts were drawn in by this brisk attack, but they soon recovered from their surprise … the Spaniards fell back, and were pushed with great vigour.'[1]

By the end of July Caro had joined forces with Bassecourt, providing an army of 10,000 men which were to have joined O'Donnell for this latter attack, but they arrived too late. Suchet, no longer concerned with O'Donnell, now turned his attention towards the Valencians who were lingering in the area. He could only spare 6,000 men, but Suchet had scant regard for Spanish military prowess and was aware that Caro's force was partially manned by guerrillas and unregimented peasants. As it transpired, they were not put to the test as Caro withdrew in haste in the face of Suchet's advance; such questionable leadership and dubious resolve led to the Spaniard's dismissal. On 20 August Suchet finally received confirmation that Macdonald and three of his divisions[2] were finally en route to join him.

The two French commanders met at Lérida on 29 August and agreed that a simultaneous attack on the fortresses at Tortosa and Tarragona was too ambitious given the threat and forces available. They agreed that Suchet would tackle Tortosa first while containing the Valencians,

and Macdonald would occupy the Catalans by positioning his three brigades in the north, poised to fall on O'Donnell's flank at a moment's notice should he make a move to succour Tortosa or disrupt Suchet's operations. O'Donnell, having regrouped his forces, was clear that with depleted numbers and questionable morale, instigating an offensive against either the 3rd or 7th corps was unwise. He elected instead to strike north and make a series of lower-level attacks in the French rear. Leaving the divisions of Eroles and Obispo in front of the 7th Corps, he went with his 3rd Division (commanded by Campoverde) on a covert march north, while simultaneously despatching 500 men from Tarragona aboard transports and escorted by two frigates – one British, one Spanish. The land approach was perilous, passing close to the garrisons at Barcelona, Hostalrich and Girona, but by 13 September, O'Donnell had concentrated 6,000 infantry and 400 cavalry at Vidreras. Just off the coast at Palamos, the transports waited to disembark the additional 500 men.

On the morning of 14 September, O'Donnell's main force fell upon General Schwartz's small force[3] at La Bispal, while another attacked San Feliu, a third Calonje, and the amphibious landing force stormed the port at Palamos. The attacks were an overwhelming success, capturing over 1,000 officers and men and 17 guns. With surprise spent, the Spanish dispersed;[4] Campoverde headed off into the Pyrenees, captured Puigcerda, beat up some smaller French outposts and then in mid-October appeared to the north of Macdonald's force, establishing himself at Cardona and Calaf. Macdonald had not been drawn north by O'Donnell's raid as hoped, but the 7th Corps commander was increasingly concerned for the safety of his small garrisons to the north, and greatly alarmed at reports that convoys had been blocked or captured. Consequently, when Campoverde unexpectedly appeared immediately north of his position, he elected to attack, but the Spaniard's position at Cardona was strong and after a ham-fisted attack by Eugenio, which was repulsed with considerable loss, Macdonald pulled back. At much the same time disturbing news arrived from Baraguay d'Hilliers that the situation had deteriorated further, that supplies in Barcelona were all but exhausted, and that convoys continued to be attacked by the *somatenes* under the effective coordination of the Baron de Eroles. On 4 November Macdonald considered that he could delay his return no longer and headed north to Catalonia; arriving at Girona six days later, he immediately set about restoring some order in the region. Convoys were provided force protection, ensuring that badly needed supplies began to get through, and there followed a number of successful raids on guerrilla camps and bases.

To the south, the siege of Tortosa had not yet begun. The withdrawal by Macdonald had left Suchet's north flank exposed to rising levels of attacks by insurgents from Catalonia and Aragon, but he was also suffering from the unseasonably dry autumn. The siege train had been collected at Mequinenza in the weeks preceding the arrival of Suchet's forces at Tortosa in August.

---

1   Suchet, *Suchet's Memoirs of the War with Spain*, vol. I, pp.198–99.

2   Commanded by Frére (vice Souham wounded at Vich), Severoli & Pignatelli.

3   There were only 700 men; the rest of his brigade was widely dispersed to meet the threat of sea raids, mainly by British Royal Marines.

4   O'Donnell had been wounded in the foot and returned to Tarragona by sea. His wound turned gangrenous and he was forced to hand over command to Miguel Iranzo.

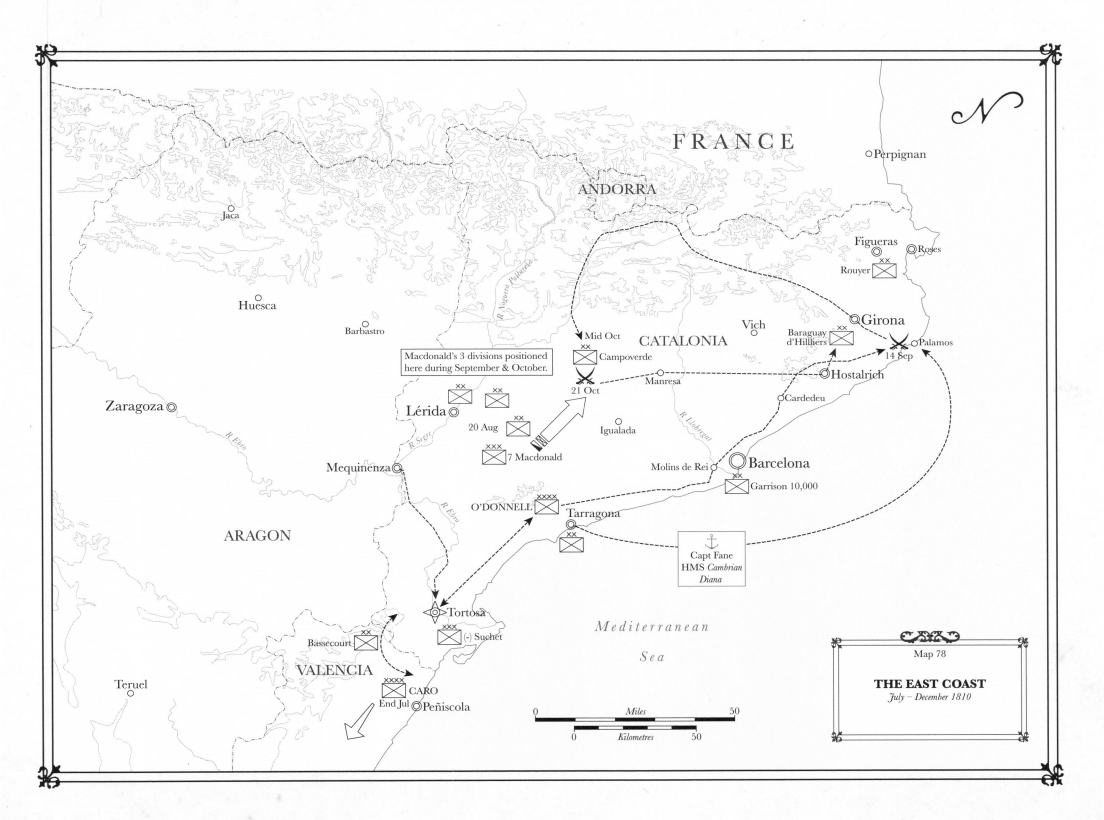

N

FRANCE

○ Perpignan

ANDORRA

○ Jaca

Figueras
○ Roses
Rouyer

Huesca ○

Barbastro ○

CATALONIA

Vich ○

Baraguay d'Hilliers

◎ Girona
○ Palamos
14 Sep

Mid Oct

Campoverde

Macdonald's 3 divisions positioned
here during September & October.

21 Oct

Manresa ○

◎ Hostalrich

Cardedeu ○

Zaragoza ◎

Lérida ◎

R Segre

20 Aug

Igualada ○

R Llobregat

7 Macdonald

Mequinenza ◎

Molins de Rei ○

◎ Barcelona

Garrison 10,000

ARAGON

R Ebro

O'DONNELL

Tarragona ○

Capt Fane
HMS *Cambrian*
Diana

✦◎ Tortosa

Mediterranean

(-) Suchet

Sea

Bassecourt

VALENCIA

Teruel ○

CARO

End Jul ◎ Peñiscola

Miles
0   50

Kilometres
0   50

Map 78

THE EAST COAST
July – December 1810

Transport of the train by road was virtually impossible and in consequence the decision was taken to move the heavy ordnance by river, but the low level of the Ebro complicated and delayed progress. Twenty-six guns were finally transported in early September following some early rains, but successful insurgent attacks on a number of other convoys as they sailed painfully slowly downstream thwarted other attempts to move more guns. To make matters worse, Leval, one of Suchet's trusted lieutenants, died after a short illness on 16 September and was replaced by Harispe. Eventually Suchet was forced to move additional guns and ammunition overland; movement was slow but by the beginning of December, 52 siege guns were accumulated in the park, along with 30,000 rounds of ammunition and considerable quantities of powder. Furthermore, Macdonald, having stabilized the situation in northern Catalonia and resupplied Barcelona, had returned south and was once again providing flank protection, enabling Suchet to move his army forward and arrive in front of the city on 16 December. Since the last siege on the place (during the Wars of the Spanish Succession) a number of outer works had been constructed and many of the inner walls and fortifications had been strengthened, making the town a formidable obstacle. The Spanish garrison consisted of 7,200 men, including 600 gunners, and a weak battalion of urban guards.[5]

On the night of 15/16 December, three flying bridges were established across the Ebro to the north and south of the town. For the next three days the investing troops moved into place, dislodging the few Spanish troops on the Sierra de Alba, and established a cordon. Generals Haxo and Valée concluded that the southern end of the town provided the best approach; not only were the defences there not mutually supporting but the ground was also easier to dig. On 19 December the heights in front of Fort Orleans were captured and work began immediately on the first parallel. This work was in reality a distraction for the main effort in the plains below, which commenced the following night. 2,300 men toiled through the night, masked by 'a violent wind and hazy weather,' and by morning they had dug 500m of trenches and approached to within 160m of the San Pedro bastion. The next morning, when the trenches became visible to the astonished defenders, they trained all their firepower on the structures to little effect. The next night, the trenches encroached to within 80 yards of the walls and just over 100 yards from the Temple demilune. General Valée had marked out seven battery positions (map 79, points 1–7)

as well as three battery positions on the west of the river to enfilade the San Pedro and the boat bridge leading to the *tête-du-pont* (map 79, points 8–10).

Brigadier General Yriarte, the governor's second-in-command, realized that an effort had to be made to delay the French siege operations as they were progressing with alarming speed. On the night of 27/28 December two attacks were executed by 3,000 men; one from the El Rastro portal towards the trenches in front of Fort Orleans, and the second from the San Pedro gate to the trenches within yards of the walls. The first attack was a complete failure, but the second inflicted considerable damage to the second parallel and it was not until Abbé arrived with four battalions that the Spanish were evicted. It took the French 36 hours to repair the damage, but by the time they had done so, all ten French batteries were in place. On 29 December, they opened simultaneously. 'The demi-bastion of San Pedro, was in a few hours, reduced to silence. The fort, and advanced batteries of Orleans, still retained a few serviceable pieces, and the bastion of San Juan possessed one, and one only, in its flank; but the embrasures of the demi-bastion were destroyed, and there was an open breach in the curtain.'[6] In addition, the boat bridge was rendered all but unserviceable and the Spanish withdrew from the *tête-du-pont* the following day.

During 30 December fire continued, and that night work began on the third parallel, with the aim of mining the scarp and filling the ditch from the resulting debris. The Spanish were well aware of French intentions and increased their rate of fire, driving out the French sappers, but the following night the French returned and by daybreak they had succeeded in constructing a small third parallel and established a battery of 24-pounder guns within it (map 79, point 12). At 1000 hours on 1 January 1811, as ammunition was being moved up to enable it to open, a white flag appeared on the ramparts of San Pedro. The terms requested by Alacha were, under the circumstances, quite unacceptable and when the 12th battery opened on 2 January, creating a breach of 15m wide, Alacha once again hoisted the flag of surrender. Suchet was suspicious of Alacha's motives; he continued to batter the breach and gather his assaulting troops, and sent demands for an unconditional surrender. The hesitant replies from the governor encouraged Suchet to march boldly to the gates at San Pedro and demand to see Alacha, who appeared, and having been bullied into capitulating on the spot, duly did so.

---

5 Oman, *History of the Peninsular War*, vol. IV, p.230. These are the Spanish figures, supported by Arteche: Suchet states in his *Memoirs* that he captured 9,461 prisoners.

6 Suchet, *Suchet's Memoirs of the War with Spain*, vol. I, pp.251–252.

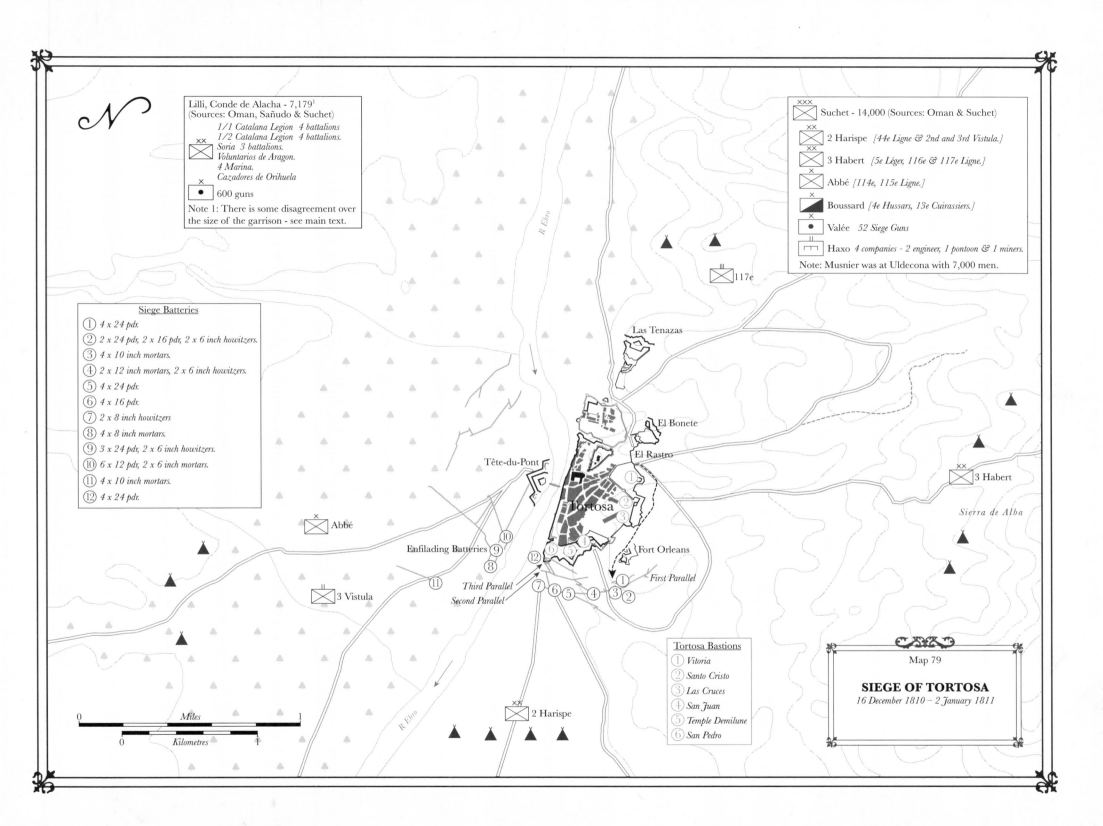

N

Lilli, Conde de Alacha - 7,179[1]
(Sources: Oman, Sañudo & Suchet)

1/1 Catalana Legion 4 battalions
1/2 Catalana Legion 4 battalions.
Soria 3 battalions.
Voluntarios de Aragon.
4 Marina.
Cazadores de Orihuela

● 600 guns

Note 1: There is some disagreement over
the size of the garrison - see main text.

Suchet - 14,000 (Sources: Oman & Suchet)

2 Harispe *[44e Ligne & 2nd and 3rd Vistula.]*

3 Habert *[5e Léger, 116e & 117e Ligne.]*

Abbé *[114e, 115e Ligne.]*

Boussard *[4e Hussars, 13e Cuirassiers.]*

● Valée *52 Siege Guns*

Haxo *4 companies - 2 engineer, 1 pontoon & 1 miners.*

Note: Musnier was at Uldecona with 7,000 men.

Siege Batteries
① *4 x 24 pdr.*
② *2 x 24 pdr, 2 x 16 pdr, 2 x 6 inch howitzers.*
③ *4 x 10 inch mortars.*
④ *2 x 12 inch mortars, 2 x 6 inch howitzers.*
⑤ *4 x 24 pdr.*
⑥ *4 x 16 pdr.*
⑦ *2 x 8 inch howitzers*
⑧ *4 x 8 inch mortars.*
⑨ *3 x 24 pdr, 2 x 6 inch howitzers.*
⑩ *6 x 12 pdr, 2 x 6 inch mortars.*
⑪ *4 x 10 inch mortars.*
⑫ *4 x 24 pdr.*

R Ebro

117e

Las Tenazas

El Bonete

El Rastro

3 Habert

Tête-du-Pont

Sierra de Alba

Abbé

Tortosa

Fort Orleans

Enfilading Batteries ⑩ ⑨
⑧

⑫ ⑥ ⑤ ④

① *First Parallel*

⑪

Third Parallel
Second Parallel

⑦ ⑥ ⑤ ④ ③ ②

3 Vistula

Tortosa Bastions
① *Vitoria*
② *Santo Cristo*
③ *Las Cruces*
④ *San Juan*
⑤ *Temple Demilune*
⑥ *San Pedro*

R Ebro

2 Harispe

0 ————— Miles ————— 1
0 ————— Kilometres ————— 1

Map 79

SIEGE OF TORTOSA
16 December 1810 – 2 January 1811

Chapter 29

Soult's Invasion of Estremadura: January to March 1811

Napoleon's plans for the invasion of Portugal, which he had drawn up in the spring of 1810, judged Masséna's Army of Portugal, supported by the new 9th Corps, to be sufficient for the task. When rumours emerged to the contrary, embellished by articles in English newspapers that La Romana had joined Wellington behind the Lines of Torres Vedras, Napoleon was quick to apportion blame on Soult. Soult had been plainly instructed in September to ensure that Mortier kept in touch with the Army of Estremadura; had he done so, the Spanish general would not have been able to break clean from his position on the Portuguese border and march west unmolested. This criticism would have been valid had La Romana not marched with a third of his force; leaving two intact divisions[1] (numbering 12,000 men) with another 6,000 garrisoning Badajoz, Olivenza and Alburquerque. In addition, a Portuguese force of about 8,500 lay between Mortier and the Tagus.[2] In an act of conciliation, a chastened Soult offered to conquer Estremadura, but he knew this posed a dilemma. He was prepared to supplement Mortier's Corps of 13,000 with another 7,000 from his Andalusian Army, but he was not ready to give up the balance of 20,000 men preserving his viceroyalty.

Soult took some time organizing the invasion force. It was to consist of numerous cavalry formations and plentiful siege artillery to tackle the numerous fortresses along the border. Half of Victor's cavalry and one regiment from Sebastiani[3] were called to Sevilla, along with the 63e Ligne from the 1st Corps. By early January 1811 the force was ready and it advanced on two axes. Latour-Maubourg advanced on the right with most of the cavalry, while Soult took the left route with the balance of forces and the siege artillery. The two groups were to meet up in the plains of Estremadura and then to advance to Badajoz, but this plan was to founder. The siege train consisted of 34 guns, with 6,000kg of powder, and was drawn by 2,500 oxen. This unwieldy train, hindered by heavy rains, was soon in trouble; many of the beasts perished, prompting the Spanish drivers to desert en masse. On 6 January Soult, accompanied by Briche's

light cavalry,[4] joined Latour-Maubourg at Zafra but Gazan's 2nd Division, protecting the siege train, were stuck at the pass of Monasterio. To make matters worse French cavalry patrols had received rumours of a large body of infantry to the west; rigorous probing confirmed it was the division of Ballesteros, which had been ordered to move south at much the same time that Soult had begun the invasion. Soult realized that the siege train provided an easy target for Ballesteros and he ordered Mortier (with Gazan's Division) to undertake the task of eradicating the danger. Following a minor skirmish west of Fregenal, Ballesteros withdrew west, drawing Gazan into a pursuit that was to last nearly three weeks before, on 24 January, the two divisions clashed at Villanueva de los Castillejos. Ballesteros fought a sound defensive battle[5] and then withdrew over the Portuguese border, at which point Gazan broke off the chase. Ballesteros's deeds, although not decisive, succeeded in removing half of Soult's force for a considerable period of time and certainly delayed French ambitions at Badajoz. Nevertheless, Soult used the respite to move his siege train north and, on 7 January, he despatched Briche's Brigade to Mérida and Latour-Maubourg to Albuera to monitor Badajoz.

With the remainder of his dwindling force Soult marched to Olivenza. He arrived there on 11 January to find the fortress in a sorry state, having been persistently neglected since it was ceded to Spain by Portugal in 1801. Notwithstanding the indefensible nature of the structure, Mendizabal had ordered one of his brigades to occupy the fortification, but with only a single battery of guns there was not much the ailing Swiss Governor, General Manuel Herck, could do to delay the inevitable. Soult seized the lunette south of the fort (map 80, point 1) and placed four field pieces into the structure, which opened the next day. It did not take Soult's engineers long to decide the best point of attack. The bastion of San Pedro still bore the scars of hasty repairs from the 1801 siege, and it was opposite here that two more batteries were marked out. Despite heavy rains the work on the parallels continued unopposed, with Herck making no attempt to disrupt the digging by sortie. The first elements of the siege train began to arrive on 19 January and two days later the first parallel was complete. Two batteries of 12-pounder guns were moved into place and opened the following morning (map 80, points 2 and 3). The north-west side of the San Pedro crumbled immediately, revealing the old breach, and Mortier wasted no time in making arrangements for the storming parties. 'Watching the columns assemble for the assault; the population who had up to now watched with fervour became disturbed. The garrison and its chief didn't look to strengthen it [the breach], and 23 January opened its doors, delivered us some stores, a small amount of artillery and 4,000 prisoners.'[6]

Soult now faced a further dilemma. By the time he had earmarked two battalions to escort the prisoners he was left with only 5,500 infantry. He had received no word of Gazan, but instructions from Paris charged him to join Masséna on the Tagus without delay. Not wishing to

---

1   The divisions of Mendizabal and Ballesteros.

2   A cavalry brigade under Madden near Badajoz, an infantry brigade near Elvas and four militia regiments.

3   The 4e, 14e and 26e Dragoons and the 2e Hussars from Victor and the 27e Chasseurs from Sebastiani.

4   21e Chasseurs and 10e Hussars.

5   Losses have been exaggerated on both sides. Gazan alleged 1,500 Spanish were lost, conversely Toreno claims the action to have been 'quite glorious... which caused the enemy considerable losses'. Oman, *History of the Peninsular War*, vol. IV. p.34. Toreno, *Guerra de la Independencia – La Derrota de Napoleon*, vol. I. p.164.

6   Thiers, *Histoire du Consulat et de L'Empire*, vol. XII, p.557.

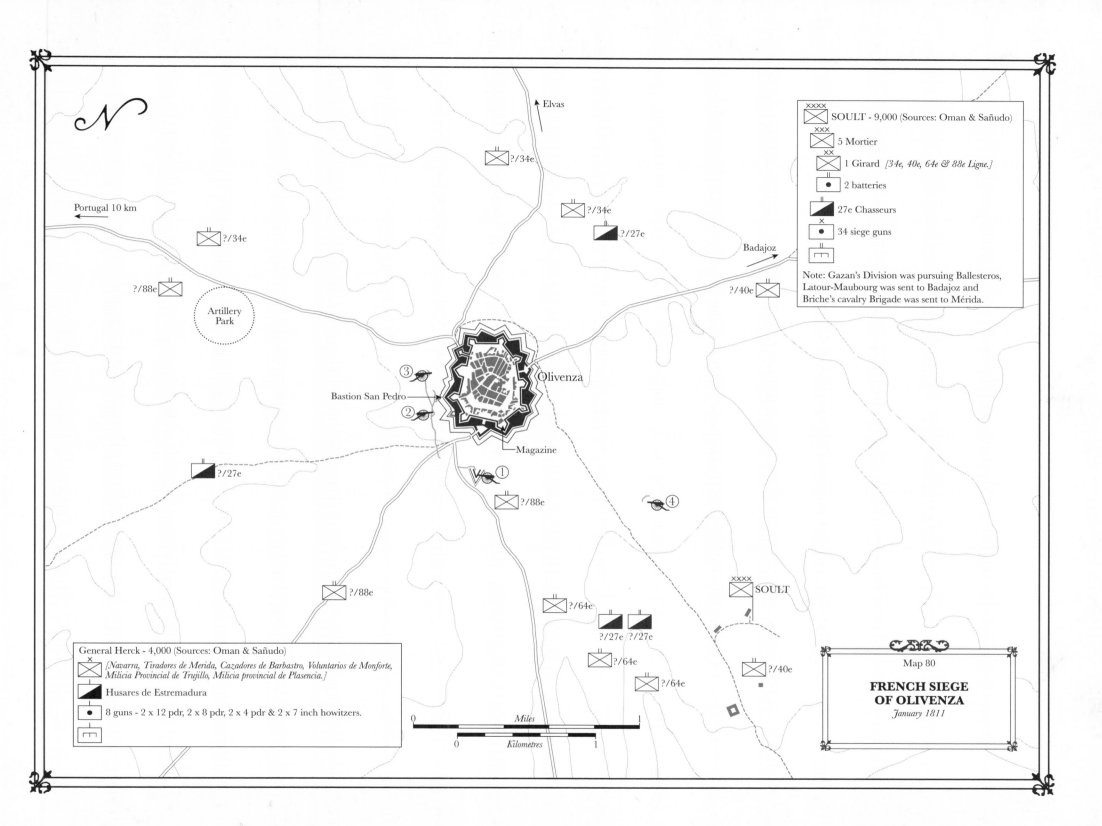

N

Elvas

?/34e

Portugal 10 km

?/34e

?/34e

?/27e

?/34e

Badajoz

?/88e

Artillery
Park

?/40e

3

Olivenza

Bastion San Pedro

2

Magazine

?/27e

1

?/88e

4

?/88e

?/64e

SOULT

?/27e ?/27e

?/64e

?/40e

?/64e

SOULT - 9,000 (Sources: Oman & Sañudo)

5 Mortier

1 Girard *[34e, 40e, 64e & 88e Ligne.]*

2 batteries

27e Chasseurs

34 siege guns

Note: Gazan's Division was pursuing Ballesteros, Latour-Maubourg was sent to Badajoz and Briche's cavalry Brigade was sent to Mérida.

General Herck - 4,000 (Sources: Oman & Sañudo)

[Navarra, Tiradores de Merida, Cazadores de Barbastro, Voluntarios de Monforte, Milicia Provincial de Trujillo, Milicia provincial de Plasencia.]

Husares de Estremadura

8 guns - 2 x 12 pdr, 2 x 8 pdr, 2 x 4 pdr & 2 x 7 inch howitzers.

0   Miles   1

0   Kilometres   1

Map 80

FRENCH SIEGE OF OLIVENZA

January 1811

aggravate the Emperor's discontent, but much against his judgement, he felt compelled to go ahead with the plans against Badajoz. It was a risky decision, but he considered that by so doing La Romana would be forced to quit Lisbon and therefore he would relieve the pressure on his colleague. Consequently, three days after taking the surrender at Olivenza, Soult marched the 20km to Badajoz. Latour-Maubourg crossed the river Guadiana and cut off the access and egress from the north. Badajoz itself could not be compared to Olivenza. The governor, General Rafael Menacho,[7] was a far more capable and honourable man than Herck, and he commanded a far more competent garrison of some 5,000 men and about 150 relatively modern guns. The north and east sides of the fortified town were difficult to attack due to the dominating Fort San Cristobal, the river and the stream. The most obvious area was between the Pardaleras Fort and the riverbank, but the paucity of French investing troops rendered this option vulnerable to Spanish artillery fire from the north bank. Therefore, Soult and Mortier agreed on an initial attack from the south, with the mission to capture the Pardaleras in the first phase.

Work commenced during the night of 28/29 January, but it was not until the 30th that the work became visible to the defenders, who responded by executing a vigorous attack on the siege works the following day. Soult lost his chief engineer and a number of other sappers in the attack but the Spanish also suffered the loss of Colonel Bassecourt, the commander of the 1st batallion of the Sevilla Regiment who had led the sortie. Bad weather then delayed proceedings for three days, during which time all the existing works were flooded. On 3 February, as the weather lifted, Gazan's Division arrived a few kilometres to the south; their appearance could not have been better timed. Within hours they were in action, ejecting a second Spanish force that had gained access to the trenches. On 4 February, while the damage was being repaired, Soult brought up two batteries and bombarded the town, but the range was too great for the shot to have a significant effect. The following day the entire situation changed.

On hearing of Soult's invasion into Estremadura, Wellington and La Romana had made arrangements to reinforce Mendizabal's force. The two divisions[8] of the Army of Estremadura encamped behind the Lines of Torres Vedras were marched east; Carlos de España's Brigade of nearly 2,000 men was ordered to march from Abrantes, and was joined by Butron's Cavalry Division and Madden's Portuguese Cavalry Brigade. La Romana had intended to command the whole but he was taken ill and on 23 January he succumbed to his illness. Command should have fallen to Carlos O'Donnell, but he had been sent at short notice to the east coast; Mendizabal was the next in line. He was provided with fairly clear guidance as to how to use his army of 14,000 men, but he nevertheless chose to execute a plan of his own design. He inserted the bulk of his infantry and Madden's cavalry into Badajoz via the bridge from the northern bank. The only French troops on this side were Latour-Maubourg's dragoons who attacked and pursued Butron's cavalry beyond the river Gévora and to the foot of the heights of San Cristobal, but failed to cut them off. With this large force inside the town, Mendizabal felt more confident and almost immediately executed an attack on Soult's lines. On 7 February, at 1500 hours,

5,000 men emerged from the Trinidad gate and the bulk, under Carlos de España's command, fell on Phillipon's Brigade at the Cerro de San Miguel. They destroyed all three batteries and held the trenches and parallels against repeated counter-attacks by the 34e and 40e. The smaller Spanish force to the south was a mere demonstration, and when Mortier realized this he released four battalions[9] to assist in counter-attacking de España's more determined attack. This French infantry attacked de España's flank with vigour, threatening their lines of retreat, which prompted the Spanish to fall back into the town in an act of self-preservation. The next day Mendizabal withdrew his two divisions from the town and encamped on the heights of San Cristobal. It was a good defensive position but Mendizabal, contrary to Menacho's proposal, made no effort to strengthen the location with trenches.

Soult turned his attention back to the siege and on 11 February made a determined effort to capture the Pardaleras Fort by escalade. Against all odds it succeeded and Menacho turned all available guns onto the structure, forcing the attackers to dig a communication trench to join the nearest parallel. Bad weather again delayed proceedings and prevented Soult from sending a force north of the river to deal with Mendizabal. However, early on 18 February the water level had dropped sufficiently to enable Mortier to cross with a prepared force, which advanced under the cover of an early morning fog and surprised the piquets at the bridge. The Spanish infantry raced from their camps and hastily tried to establish their defensive lines, but the rapidly advancing French were upon them within minutes. The 100e attacked the gap to the south[10] while the 34e and 88e attacked the centre, supported by the cavalry to the north. When Briche's Brigade had reached the summit he wheeled left and the cavalry began to sweep down on the ill-prepared infantry who did not know whether to form square and meet this threat or deploy in line to face the infantry climbing the hill to the east. To make matters considerably worse, Latour-Maubourg had arrived undetected behind the hill and had fallen upon the Spanish and Portuguese horse that were unaccountably grouped at the base of the hill. The combined cavalry broke and ran even though they outnumbered the advancing French dragoons.[11] Latour-Maubourg's dragoons showed considerable presence of mind and allowed the fleeing cavalry to escape, while they wheeled left and turned their attention to the rear flank of Mendizabal's collapsing infantry.

The only part of the Spanish line that was holding its own was to the south against the attack by the 100e Ligne; Mendizabal tried desperately to form large squares to meet the cavalry threat, but this form of defence could not contain the combination of infantry and cavalry and two of the squares collapsed. Some of the army (mainly in the centre) were able to extricate themselves by shuffling back off the hill and making their way back into Badajoz, but over half of Mendizabal's force was captured, including six colours and all their artillery.

---

7   He had served through the French War of 1792–95 and had commanded a regiment at Bailén.

8   La Carrera and Carlos O'Donnell's.

9   From the 28e Léger and the 64e, 88e and 100e Ligne

10   Which had been created when Soult turned the guns in batteries 1 and 2 (map 81) onto the south end of the hill, forcing Mendizabal to withdraw the battalions further north along the hill.

11   Oman states that both Butron and Madden's behaviour was disgraceful: Oman, *History of the Peninsular War*, vol. IV. p.53. However, Toreno, *Guerra de la Independencia – La Derrota de Napoleon*, vol. I, p.171, places the blame on Madden whom he accuses of breaking in the first instance.

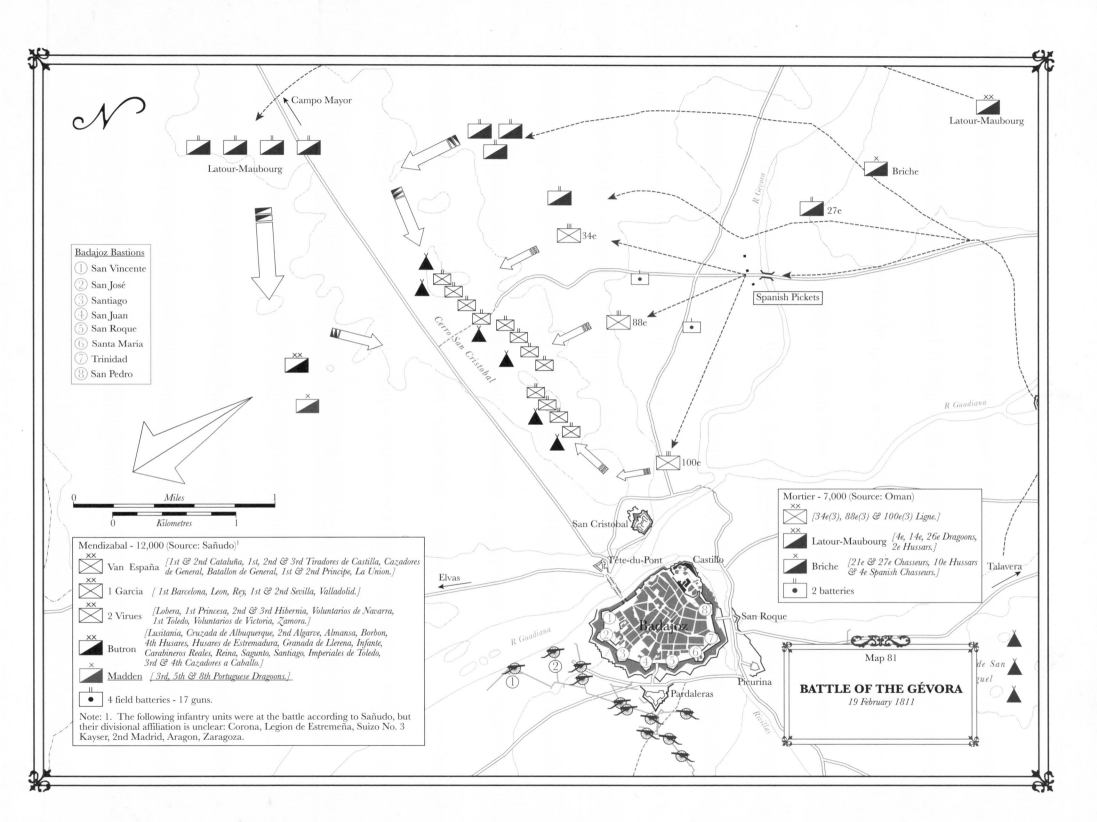

Campo Mayor

Latour-Maubourg

Latour-Maubourg

Briche

27e

34e

Badajoz Bastions
① San Vincente
② San José
③ Santiago
④ San Juan
⑤ San Roque
⑥ Santa Maria
⑦ Trinidad
⑧ San Pedro

88e

Spanish Pickets

100e

R Gevora

R Guadiana

0   *Miles*   1

0   *Kilometres*   1

San Cristobal

Téte-du-Pont

Castillo

Elvas

Talavera

San Roque

R Guadiana

Badajoz

Picurina

Pardaleras

R Rivillas

de San ...guel

Mendizabal - 12,000 (Source: Sañudo)[1]

Van España   *[1st & 2nd Cataluña, 1st, 2nd & 3rd Tiradores de Castilla, Cazadores de General, Batallon de General, 1st & 2nd Principe, La Union.]*

1 Garcia   *[1st Barcelona, Leon, Rey, 1st & 2nd Sevilla, Valladolid.]*

2 Virues   *[Lobera, 1st Princesa, 2nd & 3rd Hibernia, Voluntarios de Navarra, 1st Toledo, Voluntarios de Victoria, Zamora.]*

Butron   *[Lusitania, Cruzada de Albuquerque, 2nd Algarve, Almansa, Borbon, 4th Husares, Husares de Estremadura, Granada de Llerena, Infante, Carabineros Reales, Reina, Sagunto, Santiago, Imperiales de Toledo, 3rd & 4th Cazadores a Caballo.]*

Madden   *[3rd, 5th & 8th Portuguese Dragoons.]*

● 4 field batteries - 17 guns.

Note: 1. The following infantry units were at the battle according to Sañudo, but their divisional affiliation is unclear: Corona, Legion de Estremeña, Suizo No. 3 Kayser, 2nd Madrid, Aragon, Zaragoza.

Mortier - 7,000 (Source: Oman)

[34e(3), 88e(3) & 100e(3) Ligne.]

Latour-Maubourg   *[4e, 14e, 26e Dragoons, 2e Hussars.]*

Briche   *[21e & 27e Chasseurs, 10e Hussars & 4e Spanish Chasseurs.]*

● 2 batteries

Map 81

BATTLE OF THE GÉVORA
19 February 1811

For the Allies the defeat was a disaster. The Army of Estremadura had been ruined at negligible cost to the French, and Soult could now tackle Badajoz from both sides of the river at will. Despite this, French progress was slow. Menacho continued to employ his artillery adroitly, the accurate fire costing the French many more lives, and it was not until the night of 24/25 February that Soult finally managed to establish two batteries (map 82, batteries 1 and 2), which were able to counter the fire of the defending guns. By 2 March the French had reached the edge of the ditch in front of the San Juan bastion where they found the palisades intact and the counterscarp undamaged. A mining operation was immediately commenced, but the work was stopped by another vigorous sortie on 3 March; it was to be the last executed by Menacho, for a chance musket ball killed him as he watched its progress from the ramparts. José Imaz, who replaced him, possessed none of the proactive nature or innovative skills of his predecessor, and from this moment on, the French were quick to note that the defence lacked the vibrancy of the preceding days.

From 4 March, work began on a battery position that would house the guns to engage the selected point for the breach. Four days later the counterscarp was mined and the battery of six heavy 24-pounder guns began to pummel the curtain between Santiago and San Juan (map 82, points 3 and 4) from a distance of only 60m. Two days later the breach was pronounced practicable and Soult sent a letter offering the most honourable terms. The subsequent council of war was a farce; Imaz, despite being aware of Beresford's progress towards the place, accepted the majority vote to capitulate despite making a personal demonstration to the contrary. Imaz surrendered that afternoon and the outlying fort of San Cristobal and the *tête-du-pont* were occupied that evening. On 11 March nearly 8,000 men marched out by the Trinidad gate[12] leaving a further 1,000 sick in the hospitals. The town was found to contain, '170 pieces of ordnance, mortars, or howitzers, 80,000 quintals of gunpowder, a large quantity of cartridges for the infantry; and what was still more precious to the conquerors, two complete bridge equipages, in excellent condition'.[13] The Regency at Cádiz ordered that Imaz should face trial for his shameful conduct but the subsequent hearing dragged on and, indeed had not been concluded by the end of the war.

Soult was immensely relieved that the whole affair had been relatively painlessly concluded for, a few days previously he had received three pieces of news. Firstly, Masséna had finally given orders to evacuate Santarem and retreat north (see Chapter 31); releasing Soult from his Napoleonic task to march in support of his colleague and attack Wellington, (conversely, it meant that Wellington was now free to employ troops in the direction of Estremadura and Andalusia). Secondly, he had received the most disturbing news from Victor who reported from the lines in front of Cádiz that a large British expeditionary force had landed at Algeciras and Tarifa on 25 and 26 February and was about to move towards and attack the rear of the lines (see Chapter 30). Finally, the force he had left at Sevilla under Daricau reported that the threat from Ballesteros had re-materialized; Remond had been defeated at river Tinto on 2 March and was now marching toward the provincial capital. Following the capitulation, Soult wasted little time in assembling a force[14] to return south with all haste.

He left behind a small force of some 11,000 men under Mortier with the dual task of garrisoning Badajoz and continuing the offensive within Estremadura. It was a tall order for such a small group, particularly as Masséna's withdrawal freed up elements of the Allied armies who were now able to manoeuvre south. An attack on the considerable fortress at Elvas was out of the question, but the forts at Campo Mayor and Alburquerque, which were poorly maintained and lightly manned, were prospective objectives. Mortier was aware of an Allied relieving force destined for Badajoz, but was unaware at this time as to whether this force had been re-tasked in light of the capitulation by Imaz. In fact it had not, and by 22 March the 4th Division, Hamilton's Portuguese Division and the remnants of the Army of Estremadura under Castaños had joined the 2nd Division and a brigade of heavy cavalry at Portalegre, only 60km from the border fortress. Mortier, lacking any definite intelligence as to the whereabouts and intentions of this Allied relieving force, elected to continue offensive operations. On the day that Soult marched south, he ordered an infantry battalion to garrison Olivenza, left six others to garrison and repair Badajoz under General Phillipon[15] and struck north-east with the balance of infantry, a brigade of cavalry and an ad hoc siege train to capture the old-fashioned fortress at Campo Mayor.

The governor at Campo Mayor, Major José Joaquim Talaya, possessed an inadequate protection force, consisting of half a battalion of militia, about 300 *ordenança* and a company of artillery. He was aware of Mortier's advance and of the Allied force that was also closing in and was determined to hold out until they arrived. Campo Mayor is only one day's march from Badajoz; Mortier arrived in the early afternoon of 14 March and that night his force of 7,000 seized the outlying fort of São João. The works were 200m from the bastion of de Concelho and the French engineers marked out trenches either side of the structure. The following morning two of the battery positions were ready to receive the guns that had been brought up during the night. They were quickly in action against the walls and the de Concelho bastion. Talaya had 50 guns at his disposal but many were virtually useless; he moved what guns he could to counter the threat and held out for a day or so. Mortier countered by opening another battery to the north east of the town on the open and slightly raised ground. By 19 March the bastion of de Concelho was breached but Talaya refused the summons and that night succeeded in repelling the subsequent attack, however the next day the entire bastion collapsed rendering continued resistance futile.

While Mortier was marching for Campo Mayor, Latour-Maubourg had ridden to Alburquerque with his two remaining cavalry regiments.[16] He reached the dilapidated fort on 15 March and summoned the governor to surrender with the threat that the infantry and guns were on their way.[17] Major General José Cagigal's command consisted of two regular battalions of Fernando VII, 17 brass guns and a handful of trained gunners. Arguably, he was better equipped than Talaya, but

---

12   There is some disagreement as to whether they left by the gate or via the breach.

13   Sarrazin, *History of the War in Spain and Portugal From 1807 to 1814*, pp. 164–65.

14   Comprising 21e and 28e Léger, 103e Ligne under Gazan, and the 4e and 14e Dragoons from Latour-Maubourg's Division.

15   These were the six battalions of the 34e and 40e Ligne which were part of Phillipon's Brigade.

16   The 26e Dragoons and the 2e Hussars.

17   In fact, Mortier had sent some of the guns and two infantry battalions.

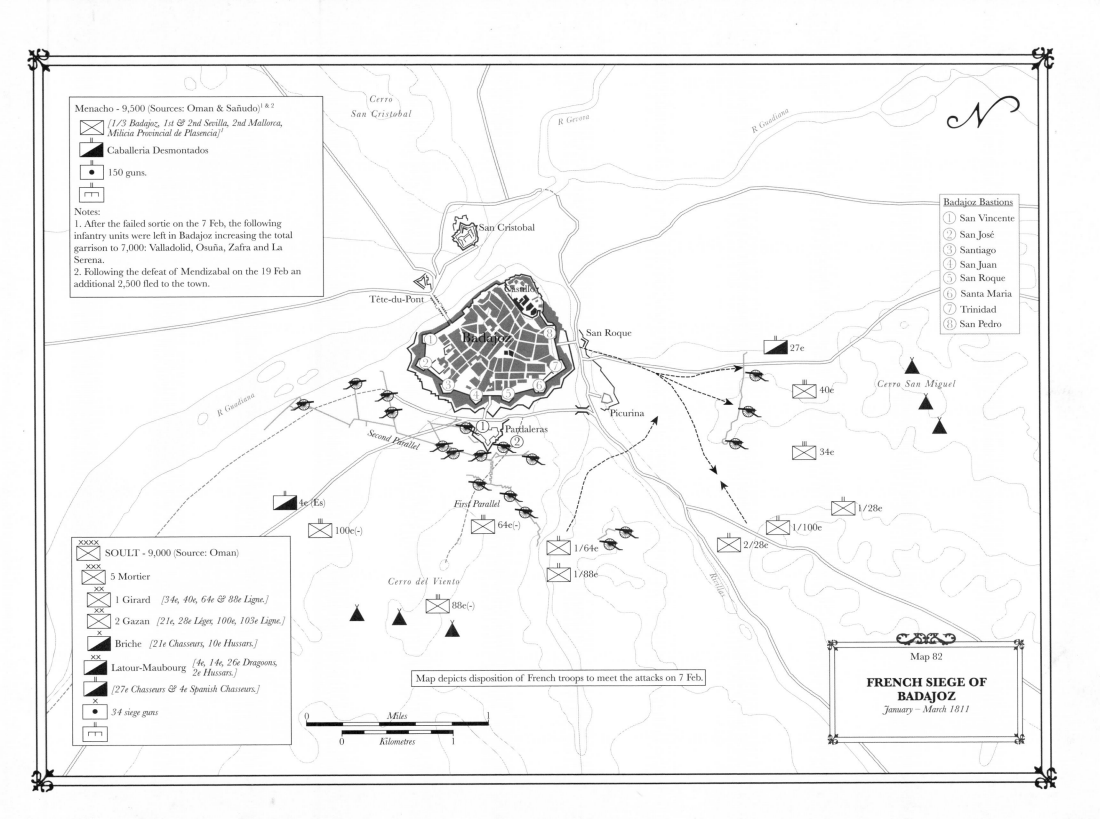

Menacho - 9,500 (Sources: Oman & Sañudo)[1 & 2]

[1/3 Badajoz, 1st & 2nd Sevilla, 2nd Mallorca, Milicia Provincial de Plasencia][1]

Caballeria Desmontados

150 guns.

Notes:
1. After the failed sortie on the 7 Feb, the following infantry units were left in Badajoz increasing the total garrison to 7,000: Valladolid, Osuña, Zafra and La Serena.
2. Following the defeat of Mendizabal on the 19 Feb an additional 2,500 fled to the town.

Badajoz Bastions

① San Vincente
② San José
③ Santiago
④ San Juan
⑤ San Roque
⑥ Santa Maria
⑦ Trinidad
⑧ San Pedro

Cerro San Cristobal

R Gevora

R Guadiana

San Cristobal

Tête-du-Pont

Castillo

Badajoz

San Roque

Cerro San Miguel

27e

40e

34e

Picurina

1/28e

1/100e

2/28e

Pardaleras

Second Parallel

R Guadiana

First Parallel

64e(-)

1/64e

1/88e

4e (Es)

100e(-)

Cerro del Viento

88e(-)

Rivillas

SOULT - 9,000 (Source: Oman)

5 Mortier

1 Girard   [34e, 40e, 64e & 88e Ligne.]

2 Gazan   [21e, 28e Léger, 100e, 103e Ligne.]

Briche   [21e Chasseurs, 10e Hussars.]

Latour-Maubourg   [4e, 14e, 26e Dragoons, 2e Hussars.]

[27e Chasseurs & 4e Spanish Chasseurs.]

34 siege guns

Map depicts disposition of French troops to meet the attacks on 7 Feb.

Map 82

FRENCH SIEGE OF BADAJOZ

January – March 1811

0   Miles   1

0   Kilometres   1

he and his men were demoralized and he unpardonably surrendered the following morning, long before the make-believe guns and bayonets had arrived. Latour-Maubourg had no instructions or intentions of holding the place and destroyed what he could, and after sending the 26e Dragoons to the fortified town of Valencia de Alcantara he returned to Campo Mayor. The dragoons arrived at Valencia de Alcantara the next day and on discovering it had been abandoned, they blew up the gates and burst the few guns and then returned south.

Meanwhile at Campo Mayor, Mortier was completely unaware of the 18,000 Allied troops who were now only four days' march from the fort. On 21 March he returned to Badajoz with the bulk of the force, leaving Latour-Maubourg with about 2,400 men[18] to dismantle and demolish Campo Mayor. On 25 March, in the early morning, Beresford's force was finally spotted advancing in three columns towards the town. By chance Latour-Maubourg was at the outposts, three miles to the north, when the Allied force was observed. He gave orders for the outposts to delay the Allied advance and rode back with all speed to the town, where he ordered the force to abandon all baggage and march south as quickly as possible. A column of guns and drivers had already left earlier that day. Despite Wellington's direction that the limited cavalry was to be used with caution, Beresford nevertheless pushed his cavalry forward in an attempt to delay the French withdrawal sufficiently long for the infantry and guns to close. What then followed provoked acrimonious debate in the immediate aftermath of the combat and for many years after the war. General Robert Long, commanding the cavalry, on orders despatched them on a wide left flanking ride and when they emerged from the ravine the force was split, with the

heavy cavalry some way to the rear. At this point the 26e Dragoons formed up to charge and in response Long directed Lieutenant Colonel Head, the commanding officer of the 13th Light Dragoons, to attack. The two cavalry formations smashed into each other with considerable energy and Latour-Maubourg seized the opportunity to extract the balance of his force. Long remained with the Portuguese cavalry in reserve and as the French dragoons began to break he began to move them forward in support of the Light Dragoons. By now the disorganized 26e Dragoons, who had lost all cohesion, began firing their carbines at the advancing Portuguese, which caused them to break formation and bolt. Long found himself somewhat isolated and unable to control the continued pursuit of the French by Head and his Light Dragoons. He sent orders for the heavy brigade to close unaware that Beresford had prevented this movement in the belief that the 13th Light Dragoons had been captured. In fact, Head and his men had by now caught up with the guns that had left Campo Mayor earlier in the day.

There is little doubt that if Beresford had followed up the success of the cavalry with determination, he would have captured a large part of Latour-Maubourg's force. Wellington was to comment that the conduct of the 13th Light Dragoons and the 1st Portuguese Cavalry 'was that of a rabble'. It was a stinging rebuke, particularly as de Grey's Heavy Brigade received praise for having done nothing but look on. Notwithstanding this rather extraordinary episode, Beresford captured Campo Mayor virtually intact, within days the breach was repaired, and it was re-garrisoned by the Faro Regiment. Beresford now turned his attention to his principal mission – the recapture of Badajoz.

---

18   This included the 100e Ligne, the 2e and 10e Hussars, the 26e Dragoons and a number of sappers, gunners and a large detachment from the military train.

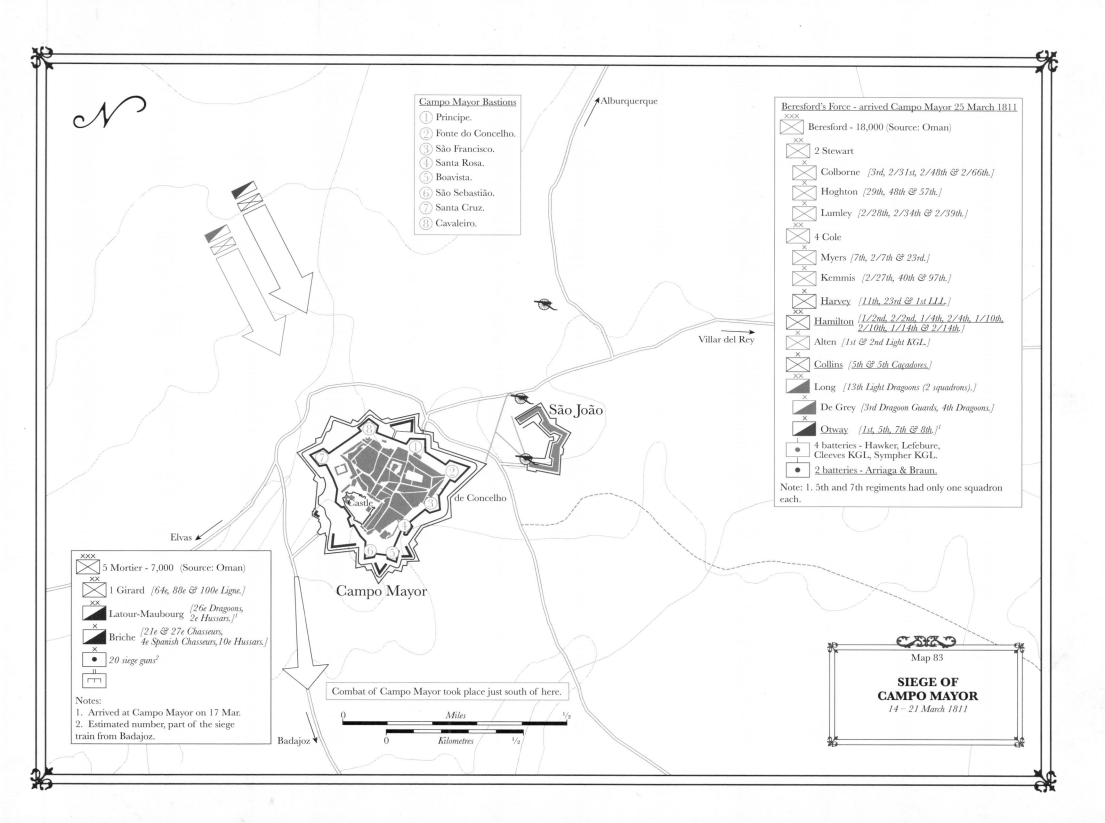

N

Campo Mayor Bastions
1. Principe.
2. Fonte do Concelho.
3. São Francisco.
4. Santa Rosa.
5. Boavista.
6. São Sebastião.
7. Santa Cruz.
8. Cavaleiro.

→ Alburquerque

Villar del Rey →

São João

Castle

de Concelho

Elvas ←

Campo Mayor

Combat of Campo Mayor took place just south of here.

Badajoz ↓

0   Miles   ½

0   Kilometres   ½

Beresford's Force - arrived Campo Mayor 25 March 1811

Beresford - 18,000 (Source: Oman)

2 Stewart

Colborne *[3rd, 2/31st, 2/48th & 2/66th.]*

Hoghton *[29th, 48th & 57th.]*

Lumley *[2/28th, 2/34th & 2/39th.]*

4 Cole

Myers *[7th, 2/7th & 23rd.]*

Kemmis *[2/27th, 40th & 97th.]*

Harvey *[11th, 23rd & 1st LLL.]*

Hamilton *[1/2nd, 2/2nd, 1/4th, 2/4th, 1/10th, 2/10th, 1/14th & 2/14th.]*

Alten *[1st & 2nd Light KGL.]*

Collins *[5th & 5th Caçadores.]*

Long *[13th Light Dragoons (2 squadrons).]*

De Grey *[3rd Dragoon Guards, 4th Dragoons.]*

Otway *[1st, 5th, 7th & 8th.]¹*

4 batteries - Hawker, Lefebure, Cleeves KGL, Sympher KGL.

2 batteries - Arriaga & Braun.

Note: 1. 5th and 7th regiments had only one squadron each.

5 Mortier - 7,000 (Source: Oman)

1 Girard *[64e, 88e & 100e Ligne.]*

Latour-Maubourg *[26e Dragoons, 2e Hussars.]¹*

Briche *[21e & 27e Chasseurs, 4e Spanish Chasseurs,10e Hussars.]*

20 siege guns²

Notes:
1. Arrived at Campo Mayor on 17 Mar.
2. Estimated number, part of the siege train from Badajoz.

Map 83

SIEGE OF CAMPO MAYOR
14 – 21 March 1811

Chapter 30

THE SOUTH OF SPAIN: JANUARY TO MARCH 1811

As he departed on his adventure into Estremadura, Soult took a huge gamble by not nominating either Victor or Sebastiani as the overall commander in his absence. Ironically, Napoleon was to criticise Soult for this recklessness, suggesting that jealousy of Victor was the overriding reason. Conversely, had the Spanish themselves possessed a single commander-in-chief, and had the combined Spanish armies chosen to attack Andalusia while Soult was absent, the outcome could have been disastrous for the French. As it was, Victor was lucky to escape complete destruction when in late February an attack was made on his rear. Having seconded half his cavalry, one infantry regiment[1] and some artillery, Victor's force besieging Cádiz now only numbered 19,000. The withdrawal of Copons in late January left the Spanish with a small advantage in numbers, but the addition of the Anglo-Portuguese division[2] of about 5,000, under the command of Lieutenant General Graham, provided the Allies a marked superiority. The Regency was quick to appreciate this numerical advantage and proposed an option to Graham for a combined attack. He readily agreed and subsequent planning concluded that an attack on Victor's rear would have a greater impact than a mere sortie from the Isla de Leon. By way of simultaneous diversion, the guerrilleros in and around Granada were to preoccupy Sebastiani[3] and hinder any opportunity of reinforcement from the east. La Peña, the senior Spanish officer in Cádiz was given command of the 8,000 Spanish earmarked for the operation. Another 1,600 were collected en route from an irregular force operating in the Ronda Mountains to the east. Graham curiously elected to leave behind most of the Portuguese and German infantry and the 2/47th within the confines of Cádiz, but replaced these forces with an equal number from Gibraltar.

Elements of the British force sailed from Cádiz on 21 February, but were unable to enter the harbour at Tarifa, as the frequent severe winds forced the transports beyond their target destination. Instead most were landed at Algeciras on 23 February, and some of the troops from Gibraltar joined the British force at this juncture. La Peña set sail with the larger force on 24 February and despite experiencing equally disagreeable weather, was able to land at Tarifa.

The entire force was ashore by the 27th. Notwithstanding orders from London that Graham was 'to refuse to act in any joint expedition of which he was not given command,' he accepted that the Spanish force contribution was twice that of his Anglo-Portuguese division and, on that basis, consented to overall Spanish command.

La Peña's first decision was to march via the interior road in preference to the coast road. Lardizabal's vanguard led the force on the night move and, after a hazardous march across flooded terrain, they reached Casa Viejas on 2 March where they promptly chased off the small French piquet. Captured French soldiers revealed the existence of a much larger force at Medina Sidonia,[4] prompting La Peña to change course and head south to Vejar but, following appeals from Graham, the Spaniard agreed to move by day. It was sound council, for no sooner had the expeditionary force set off than they discovered that much of the route was under water. After a march lasting 16 hours the exhausted men finally reached Vejar at midnight. During this time, Zayas had been busy executing his part of the plan from within Cádiz (see inset map, map 84). He threw out a pontoon bridge across the mouth of the Santi Petri and established a battalion of Ordenes Militares on the far side. They quickly constructed a makeshift tête-du-pont under the protection of the heavy guns in the castle of Santi Petri and the battery of guns on the near bank (see map 64).

Victor at this time was receiving conflicting reports from his commanders. Cassagne had reported that the main force still lay on the Medina Sidonia road, but the French dragoons (ousted from Vejar) were adamant that the main force was to their front. At much the same time Victor received reports of Zayas's sortie to his rear, but he kept his nerve. Cassagne was told to stand firm and Victor resolved to attack and destroy the tête-du-pont at the headland of Santi Pertri on the night of 3 March. Six picked companies of voltigeurs made short work of the Spanish battalion, who could not be supported by the artillery during the hours of darkness. However, the defenders had the presence of mind to sink two of the pontoons and float the bridge back to the Isla de Leon. Victor was now clear that the intention of the Allied force was to attack his rear and link up with the defenders at Cádiz. Villatte was ordered to block the coast road to Santi Petri and the Isla de Leon, while Ruffin and Leval were to move to Chiclana and wait for the Allies to come up against Villatte's block and then fall on their flank.

At about 0900 hours on 5 March Lardizabal's force came up against and attacked Villatte. The initial assault was repulsed, but a second was made with support from the leading brigade of Anglona's Division and at the same time Zayas refloated the pontoon bridge and began to advance from the rear. Villatte vacated his position and moved north as instructed, and La Peña sensibly restrained Lardizabal from pursuing him. The conflict had been short but quite intense and losses were between 300 and 400 on each side, but La Peña had every reason to be content as he had reestablished communication with Cádiz. Graham at this time was about ten miles south along the coast on the Cerro de Puerco,[5] observing Villatte's forced withdrawal, but his mood was soon to change when he received orders to vacate the hill and close in on La Peña's

---

1   The 63e Ligne from Villatte's Division.

2   Comprising of two composite battalions of the Guards, the 2/47th, 2/67th, 2/87th, a half battalion of the 2/95th, two battalions of the 20th Portuguese and a battalion of German deserters. In addition, there were two squadrons of the 2nd Hussars KGL and two field batteries.

3   Sebastiani, when he received word of the amphibious force, was convinced that his corps was their intended target.

4   Cassagne's force consisted of five battalions, a cavalry regiment and a battery of guns, totalling about 3,000 men.

5   Literally 'Boar Hill', but known in many British histories as Barrosa Hill.

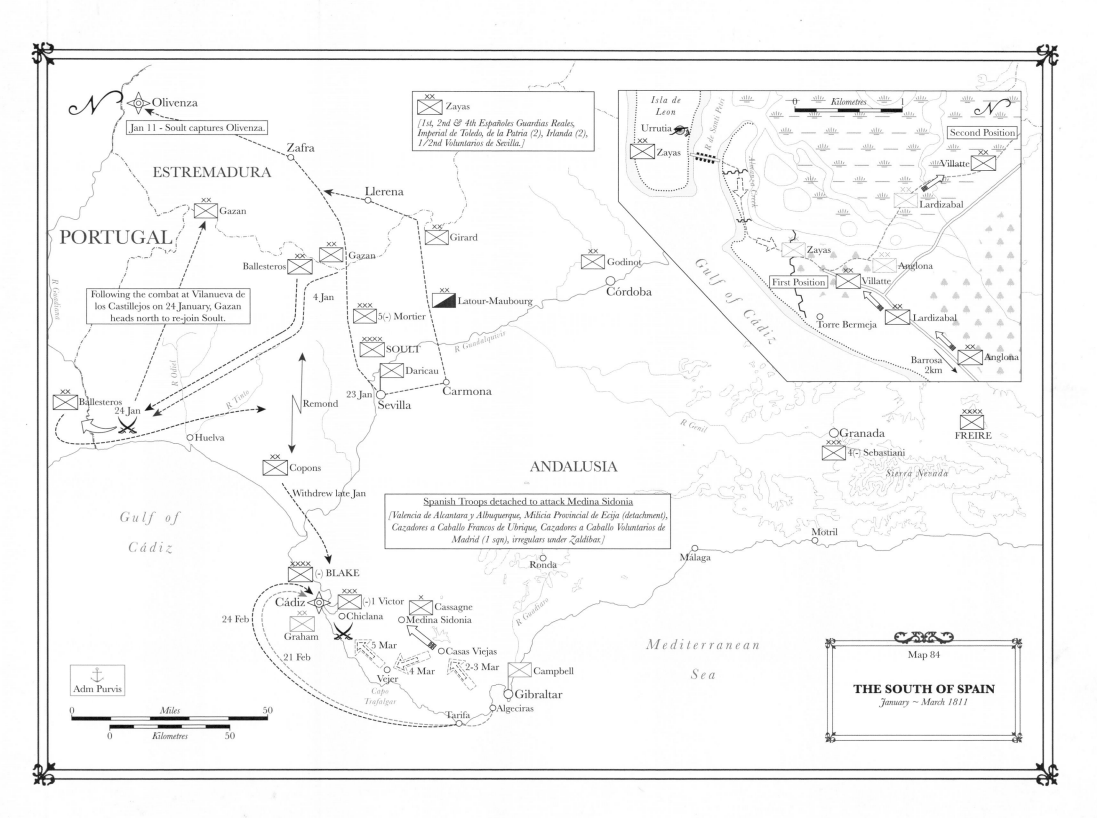

N Olivenza

Jan 11 - Soult captures Olivenza.

Zafra

ESTREMADURA

PORTUGAL

Llerena

xx Gazan

xx Girard

Ballesteros xx xx Gazan

4 Jan

Following the combat at Vilanueva de
los Castillejos on 24 January, Gazan
heads north to re-join Soult.

xx Godinot

xx Latour-Maubourg

Córdoba

xxx 5(-) Mortier

xxxx SOULT

R Guadalquivir

xx Ballesteros
24 Jan

Remond

xx Daricau

23 Jan

Sevilla

Carmona

Huelva

xx Copons

ANDALUSIA

Withdrew late Jan

Gulf of
Cádiz

Spanish Troops detached to attack Medina Sidonia
[Valencia de Alcantara y Albuquerque, Milicia Provincial de Ecija (detachment),
Cazadores a Caballo Francos de Ubrique, Cazadores a Caballo Voluntarios de
Madrid (1 sqn), irregulars under Zaldíbar.]

R Genil

Granada

xxx 4(-) Sebastiani

xxxx FREIRE

Sierra Nevada

Motril

Ronda

Málaga

R Guadiaro

xxxx (-) BLAKE

Cádiz xxx (-)1 Victor

24 Feb xx Chiclana

Graham

21 Feb

5 Mar

4 Mar 2-3 Mar

Vejer

Capo
Trafalgar

x Cassagne

Medina Sidonia

Casas Viejas

xx Campbell

Mediterranean

Sea

Gibraltar

Tarifa Algeciras

Adm Purvis

Miles 50

Kilometres 50

Zayas

[1st, 2nd & 4th Españoles Guardias Reales,
Imperial de Toledo, de la Patria (2), Irlanda (2),
1/2nd Voluntarios de Sevilla.]

Isla de
Leon

Kilometres

Urrutia

xx Zayas

R de Santi Petri

Himbeza Creek

Second Position

xx Villatte

xx Lardizabal

xx Zayas

xx Anglona

First Position xx Villatte

Gulf of Cádiz

Torre Bermeja

xx Lardizabal

Barrosa
2km

xx Anglona

Map 84

THE SOUTH OF SPAIN
January ~ March 1811

forces at Bermeja. Graham considered the hill vital ground and was loath to comply, but the assurance that some of Anglona's forces (under General Beguines's command) would replace the British, along with the cavalry under Whittingham, served to reassure him. Leaving one battalion on the hill under Colonel Browne, Graham withdrew his force through the pine woods northwest towards Bermeja. Victor received reports that the British force was abandoning the Cerro at about the same time he was informed that Cassagne's departure from Medina Sidonia had been delayed and that the additional brigade could not be expected for another two to three hours. Perplexed as to the reasons for the British withdrawal and unable to see the few battalions who remained,[6] he decided to seize the hill and then strike at the Allied flank. At about half past midday, when Graham's force had travelled about 1.5km into the thick woods, Victor emerged from the trees, further to the east on the Chiclana road, with the 7,000 men from Ruffin and Leval's divisions and three squadrons of dragoons. The French advanced at a rapid pace and closed with the small force on the Cerro, prompting the Spanish infantry and cavalry to withdraw; Browne initially refused to join them but after a few minutes realized his solitary defence was useless and he set off in haste in search of Graham.

Graham, on receiving word of the French manoeuvre and Spanish withdrawal, turned his column around and headed back south with all speed. In the dense pinewoods he had been unable to gauge the situation, but as he emerged he quickly appreciated that his best option was a surprise attack on the French before they had linked up and established themselves on the hill. Wheatley's leading brigade was ordered to engage Leval's men as they pushed down the road and up the lower slopes, and Barnard's four rifle companies and the 20th Portuguese were quickly deployed into a skirmishing screen to buy sufficient time for the brigade to deploy.[7] The British emerged unexpectedly from the edge of the wood, with Leval's battalions advancing in column across their front at a range of about 400m. The advancing skirmish line caught them completely unprepared and they frantically manoeuvred to engage this unexpected threat; Duncan's ten guns were into action with remarkable speed and began to fire devastating volleys of canister.

To their right, Browne's battalion was turned by Graham and returned to attack the five battalions of Ruffin's Division, who were now firmly established on the hill with their divisional battery to their left. Against such unfavourable odds the result was inevitable and after two attempts to reform the rapidly depleted lines, Browne's men stayed down and scattered, finding individual firing positions. However, this loss (about half of Browne's troops) had bought time for Dilke's Brigade to form up and begin the main assault. They positioned themselves to the right of Browne, where there was some cover and dead ground and were assisted by the convex slope, which hindered the effectiveness of the French guns. The entire brigade reached the summit almost intact, but as it neared the top, the French charged. The two battalions of the 24e Ligne were unable to break or penetrate the red line and Victor, who was at the top of the Cerro, hastily ordered the two battalions of Grenadiers to assist. They too were unable to make an impression and their momentum soon began to falter under the sustained and heavy musketry fire of the British infantry in line. By now four French battalions were faced off against the three British and began exchanging murderous fire at very short range; the encounter lasted many minutes before the entire French line began to waver. Victor tried to throw the 96e Ligne into the fray but they were engaged by the remnants of Browne's battalion and made little headway. After a while, the French lines gave way and, in no little disorder, the battalions retreated back over the hill.

To their right Leval's Division was faring little better. Duncan's battery had neutralized the French guns and was continuing to pour devastating volleys of canister into the French ranks. The French perceived they were up against superior numbers and with the exception of the 2/54e Ligne, seemed paralysed into inactivity. Major Gough led the 2/87th forward and during the fierce fight with the 8e Ligne Sergeant Masterson captured the first eagle of the campaign. Leval was by now aware that he was losing the fight, and in a last desperate attempt he ordered the two battalions of the 54e Ligne forward. Once again the British lines held the advance and after a short while the commanding officer of the 28th, Lieutenant Colonel Belson, gave orders for the battalion to fire by platoon. The order was quickly taken up along the line and the effect was instantaneous, both sides sensing it was the turning point; the French were beaten and the British charged. The French held the first two charges but their resolve broke at the third attempt and they were only saved by the intervention of the dragoons. Throughout this encounter La Peña had failed to march in support of his colleague. Graham was understandably furious at La Peña's behaviour and refused to cooperate further with the Spaniard. On 7 March, with the Allied commanders unable to agree on future operations, they marched back to the Isla de Leon and the following day Victor reoccupied the French lines in front of the city – the fruits of the battle of Barrosa (or Chiclana) had been lost.

---

6   The troops were exhausted after many long marches and lay down in the long grass.

7   In their haste to deploy, the brigade structures became slightly altered. Duncan asked Dilkes to supply some infantry to support the guns, he instructed the Coldstream Guards to fall out and oblige, but two companies of the 2/47th had already been earmarked by Graham and when the Coldstream realized they were not needed they joined Wheatley's Brigade.

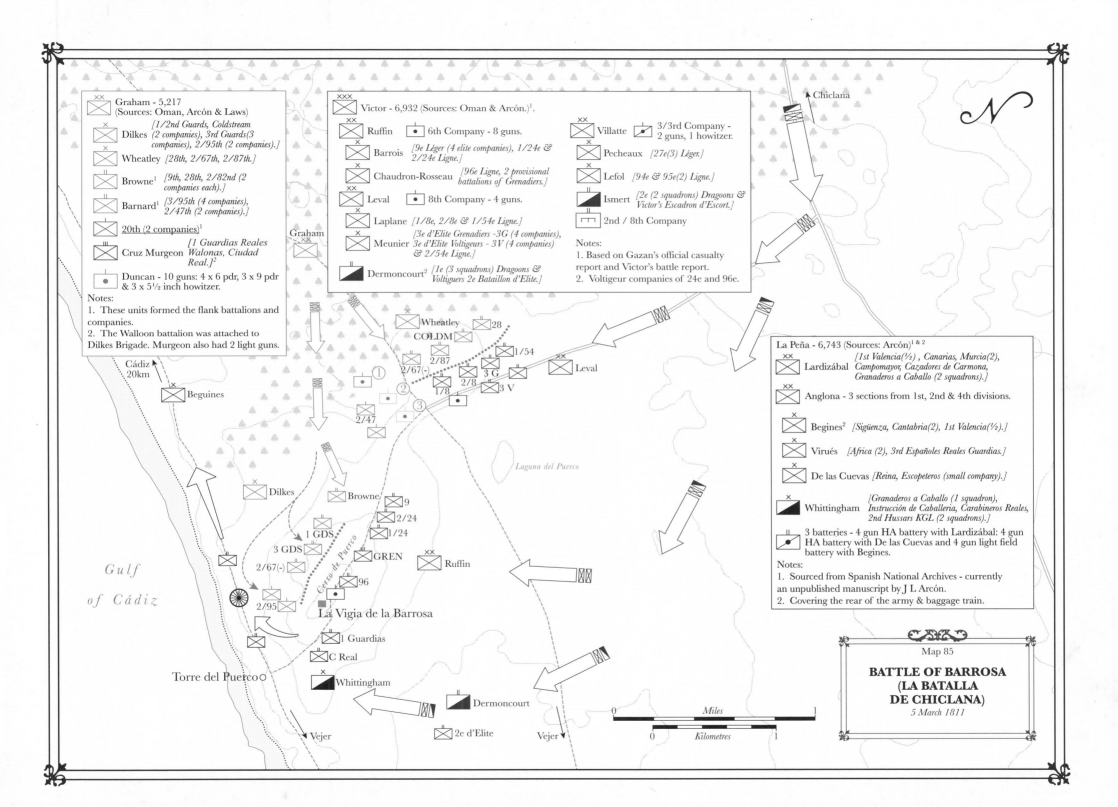

Graham - 5,217
(Sources: Oman, Arcón & Laws)

[1/2nd Guards, Coldstream
Dilkes (2 companies), 3rd Guards(3 companies), 2/95th (2 companies).]

Wheatley [28th, 2/67th, 2/87th.]

Browne[1] [9th, 28th, 2/82nd (2 companies each).]

Barnard[1] [3/95th (4 companies), 2/47th (2 companies).]

20th (2 companies)[1]

Cruz Murgeon [1 Guardias Reales Walonas, Ciudad Real.][2]

Duncan - 10 guns: 4 x 6 pdr, 3 x 9 pdr & 3 x 5½ inch howitzer.

Notes:
1. These units formed the flank battalions and companies.
2. The Walloon battalion was attached to Dilkes Brigade. Murgeon also had 2 light guns.

Cádiz 20km

Beguines

Graham

Victor - 6,932 (Sources: Oman & Arcón.)[1].

Ruffin 6th Company - 8 guns.

Barrois [9e Léger (4 elite companies), 1/24e & 2/24e Ligne.]

Chaudron-Rosseau [96e Ligne, 2 provisional battalions of Grenadiers.]

Leval 8th Company - 4 guns.

Laplane [1/8e, 2/8e & 1/54e Ligne.]

Meunier [3e d'Elite Grenadiers -3G (4 companies), 3e d'Elite Voltigeurs - 3V (4 companies) & 2/54e Ligne.]

Dermoncourt[2] [1e (3 squadrons) Dragoons & Voltiguers 2e Bataillon d'Elite.]

Villatte 3/3rd Company - 2 guns, 1 howitzer.

Pecheaux [27e(3) Léger.]

Lefol [94e & 95e(2) Ligne.]

Ismert [2e (2 squadrons) Dragoons & Victor's Escadron d'Escort.]

2nd / 8th Company

Notes:
1. Based on Gazan's official casualty report and Victor's battle report.
2. Voltigeur companies of 24e and 96e.

Chiclana

Wheatley 28
COLDM
2/87 1/54
2/67(-) 3 G
1/8 2/8 3 V Leval

Laguna del Puerco

2/47

La Peña - 6,743 (Sources: Arcón)[1 & 2]

Lardizábal [1st Valencia(½), Canarias, Murcia(2), Campomayor, Cazadores de Carmona, Granaderos a Caballo (2 squadrons).]

Anglona - 3 sections from 1st, 2nd & 4th divisions.

Begines[2] [Sigüenza, Cantabria(2), 1st Valencia(½).]

Virués [Africa (2), 3rd Españoles Reales Guardias.]

De las Cuevas [Reina, Escopeteros (small company).]

Whittingham [Granaderos a Caballo (1 squadron), Instrucción de Caballeria, Carabineros Reales, 2nd Hussars KGL (2 squadrons).]

3 batteries - 4 gun HA battery with Lardizábal: 4 gun HA battery with De las Cuevas and 4 gun light field battery with Begines.

Notes:
1. Sourced from Spanish National Archives - currently an unpublished manuscript by J L Arcón.
2. Covering the rear of the army & baggage train.

Dilkes

Browne 9
2/24
1/24
1 GDS
3 GDS GREN
2/67(-) 96
2/95 Ruffin

La Vigia de la Barrosa

1 Guardias
C Real
Whittingham

Torre del Puerco

Dermoncourt
2e d'Elite

Vejer

Vejer

Gulf of Cádiz

Cerro de Puerco

Miles
0 1
Kilometres
0 1

Map 85
**BATTLE OF BARROSA
(LA BATALLA
DE CHICLANA)**
5 March 1811

Chapter 31

MASSÉNA: RETREAT AND DEMISE, MARCH TO MAY 1811

By 18 November 1810 Masséna had completed the withdrawal of his army from the Lines of Torres Vedras and was concentrated in a column from Santarem to Tomar. He had elected not to turn on Oporto where he could have revitalized his force and resumed the offensive in the spring. More critically he also rejected the idea of crossing the Tagus and occupying the east bank as far south as the mouth of the Tagus estuary; thereby controlling the shipping with artillery and extending east into southern Portugal, to potentially link up with Soult's army from Andalusia. In fact this option was covered by Wellington on 19 November when he sent Hill[1] and Hamilton across the Tagus and the two divisions moved north on the east bank to a point where they could observe Ney's troops at Golegão. Following Buçaco, the humiliation of withdrawal from the Lines was almost too much to bear and Masséna arrayed his forces in the hope that Wellington would venture north and offer battle. It was not to be. Wellington deployed south and west of the French (see map 86) in a concentrated blocking movement designed to contain the unlikely possibility of a French offensive. It was the penultimate phase in Wellington's strategy to thwart Masséna's invasion by starving his army into submission.

Masséna continued to wait for support and supplies from Ciudad Rodrigo and reinforcements from Drouet or Soult, or both. General Gardanne's attempt to link up in late November had failed despite coming tantalisingly close. Frustratingly, days turned to weeks and no word or corroboration was received; supplies ran out and disease attacked the ranks. By the end of the year, Masséna's army, which had started the invasion with 65,000 men, was down to 45,000. By mid-December, Drouet had finally concentrated the 9th Corps around Almeida, having incorporated the remnants of Gardanne's by now depleted force. On 14 December he decided to throw caution to the wind and depart the fort with his entire force, crossing the Coa in two columns. Claparéde was dispatched north to Transcosa, forcing Silveira to withdraw as he approached, while Drouet (with the divisions of Conroux and Gardanne) headed west down the Mondego valley. By the end of December Drouet had made contact with Masséna, but Wilson, who returned to attack Conroux's rearguard at Espinhal, immediately cut his lines of communication. Meanwhile, Claparéde was clearly enjoying the relative freedom of his command and twice attacked Silveira.

The second attack on 11 January 1811 forced the Portuguese brigade back as far as Lamego, prompting Baccelar to withdraw Trant, Miller[2] and Wilson to fall back and cover Oporto. This combined force concentrated a few kilometres south of Lamego, forcing Claparéde to withdraw back to Transcosa. Later he moved to between Celorico and Guarda but he still remained cut off from Masséna and Drouet.

Drouet's arrival had done little to assist Masséna's predicament; the 8,000 additional men were insufficient to tip the balance in favour of an offensive and in reality the additional mouths were an extra burden on the already inadequate provisions. To make matters worse, the weather deteriorated and there was still no word from Paris, Madrid or Sevilla. Things were little better for Wellington. He began to have doubts that his scheme of starvation was actually working. Furthermore, news from home did little to inspire confidence; in October 1810, George III had been declared permanently insane and arrangements were in progress to invest the Prince of Wales as Regent. It was widely considered that the Prince would dissolve the Tory administration and replace it with an anti-war Whig government. All Wellington and Perceval's work and achievements in Iberia seemed doomed to be undone. However, the Prince was to surprise all in February 1811, by announcing that he had no intention of dismissing the government; Wellington's Peninsular policy was for now secure. Despite this reprieve, Wellington remained troubled; on the one hand relations with the Portuguese government and authorities were increasingly strained, and on the other he suspected Masséna of planning a new offensive for the spring. Wellington's correspondence at the time betrayed his apprehension. There was no such anxiety in Napoleon's communiqué that accompanied Foy and reached Masséna on 5 February. It was upbeat, instructing the 'Old Fox' to hold his position and wait for support from the French armies of the south and centre. Like so many of Napoleon's over-the-horizon directives, it was profoundly out of touch with reality, but it did succeed in lifting Masséna's spirits and he responded by pushing reconnaissance parties well to the east in the hope of making contact with Soult.

Masséna's optimism was short-lived and when these reconnaissance parties returned empty-handed he convened a council of war at Golegão, on 19 February, at which he proposed two options: withdrawal, or an offensive east of the Tagus. He clearly favoured the former. Ney suggested a move south and east to link up with Soult; Junot strongly dismissed the withdrawal from Portugal and suggested that the army split either side of the Tagus and wait for Mortier's Corps while Reynier's suggestion was along similar lines to that proposed by Junot. Masséna had, however, made up his mind and the meeting concluded acrimoniously, the commanders returning with orders to make preparations for a withdrawal. On 3 March Masséna finally issued orders for an immediate retreat, but extracting the force from in front of the Lines would be a perilous affair. On 5 May only three divisions were firm on the ground;[3] the balance was concentrating prior to commencing the retreat. The speed of the French movement clearly

---

1   On 29 November, Hill was taken ill and replaced temporarily by William Stewart until 30 December when Beresford was despatched to assume command of the semi-independent 2nd Division. Hill returned in 1811 and reassumed command from Beresford in June.

2   Miller was no longer in command having died early in the New Year.

3   Heudelet at Santarem, Clausel on the Rio Mayor and Loison at Punhente – Oman, *A History of the Peninsular War*, vol. IV, p.83.

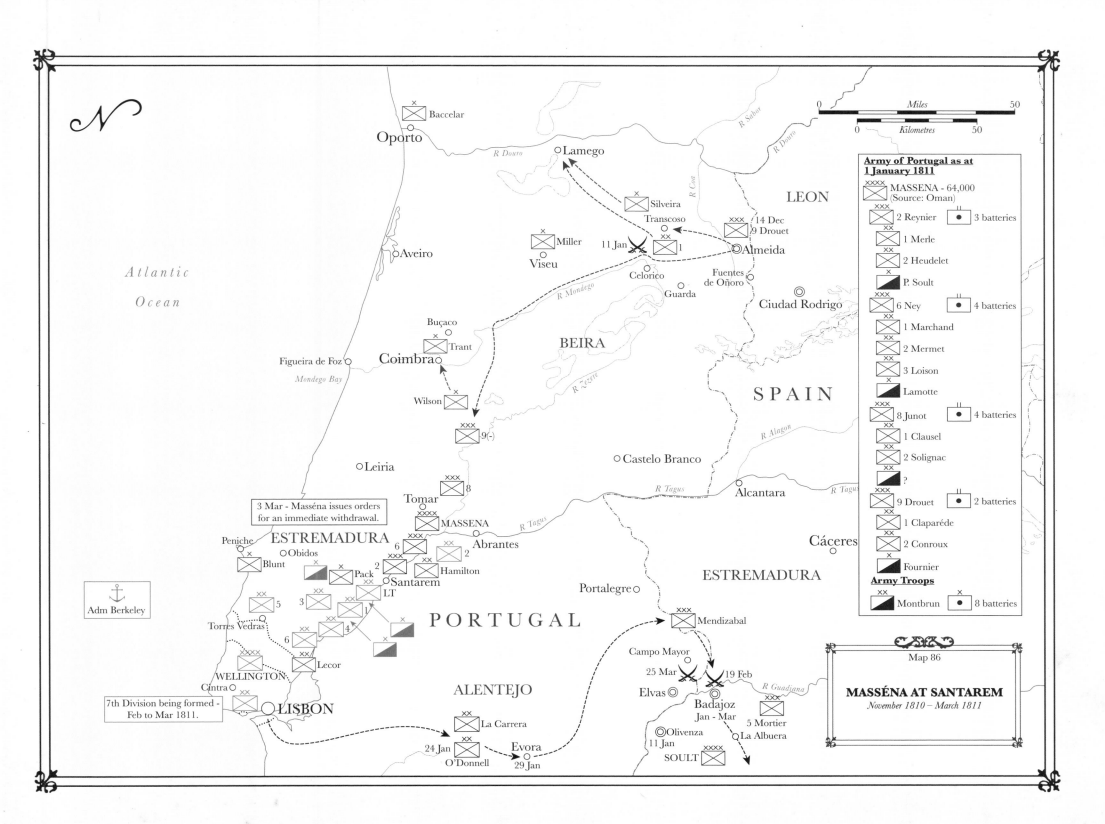

N

Baccelar

Oporto

R Douro

Lamego

LEON

Silveira

Transcoso

14 Dec
9 Drouet

Miller

11 Jan   1

Almeida

Viseu

Aveiro

Atlantic

Ocean

Celorico

Fuentes
de Oñoro

Guarda

Ciudad Rodrigo

R Mondego

BEIRA

SPAIN

Buçaco

Figueira de Foz

Trant

Coimbra

Mondego Bay

Wilson

R Zezere

9(-)

Leiria

Castelo Branco

8

R Tagus

Alcantara

R Tagus

Tomar

3 Mar - Masséna issues orders
for an immediate withdrawal.

MASSENA

R Tagus

ESTREMADURA

6

2

Abrantes

Cáceres

Peniche

Obidos

Pack   2

Hamilton

Blunt

Santarem

LT

ESTREMADURA

⚓
Adm Berkeley

5

3

4

PORTUGAL

Portalegre

Mendizabal

Torres Vedras

6

Lecor

Campo Mayor

WELLINGTON

Cintra

ALENTEJO

25 Mar

19 Feb

R Guadiana

Elvas

7th Division being formed -
Feb to Mar 1811.

LISBON

La Carrera

Badajoz
Jan - Mar

5 Mortier

24 Jan

Evora

La Albuera

O'Donnell

29 Jan

Olivenza
11 Jan

SOULT

Army of Portugal as at
1 January 1811

MASSENA - 64,000
(Source: Oman)

2 Reynier   ● 3 batteries

1 Merle

2 Heudelet

P. Soult

6 Ney   ● 4 batteries

1 Marchand

2 Mermet

3 Loison

Lamotte

8 Junot   ● 4 batteries

1 Clausel

2 Solignac

?

9 Drouet   ● 2 batteries

1 Claparéde

2 Conroux

Fournier

Army Troops

Montbrun   ● 8 batteries

Map 86

MASSÉNA AT SANTAREM
November 1810 – March 1811

surprised Wellington who, with the imminent arrival of the 7th Division, was himself planning a series of offensive operations.[4] By the following morning French intentions were clear but it was too late; the rearguard divisions had withdrawn, blowing the bridges at Alviella and Pernes. Wellington immediately ordered that Santarem was to be occupied and sent Erskine[5] and Pack in pursuit of Junot. Ney (minus Loison) and Drouet formed the covering force for the balance of the Army of Portugal and on 7 May the two formations had gone firm at Leiria; the 2nd and 8th corps were moving rapidly to get in behind them on two separate routes to the east. When intelligence came through of this French concentration at Leiria, Wellington halted all but Nightingale's Brigade on the Tomar road and redirected the main effort on the Leiria to Coimbra road to support the Light Division and Pack's Portuguese who were already well advanced in that direction.

On 8 March, Wellington reached Torres Novas and received reports from his cavalry scouts that the French were withdrawing across the frontage and displaying no desire to fight. At the same moment, reports arrived from Badajoz of Menacho's fate and that of French progress. Wellington gave orders for Beresford to break off the chase and march directly to the Spanish fortress to provide relief (see Chapter 29). His division was to be supported by Cole's 4th Division and de Grey's heavy dragoons who were to join him once released from the pursuit of 16 March. This left Wellington with about 46,000 men against Masséna's 49,000 (although the 7th Division, when they arrived would bolster the Allied numbers by 5,000). Ney and Drouet continued to hold Leiria and Junot joined them to the north on the Coimbra road at Pombal, while Reynier had also arrived and gone firm at Espinhal 30km to the east. Loison, who had remained north of Tomar until Junot and Reynier had extracted their formations, had withdrawn on a track inbetween Junot and Reynier and emerged on 12 March at Condeixa. By this time, Wellington had concentrated his force on the Coimbra road, leaving only Nightingale to follow Reynier. When the Allied vanguard reached Leiria the French withdrew, committing all manner of atrocities as they went. 'Even the towns which had given shelter to the head-quarters of the French generals were not spared. Torres-Novas, Thomar, and Pernes, were all of them sacked on the evening previous to their evacuation; the convent of Alcobaça was burned to the ground; the Bishop's palace, and the whole town of Leiria, shared the same fate – in a word, it seemed as if these men had resolved to make a desert of the country which they had failed to conquer; and that the war … had been turned against its peaceable inhabitants.'[6]

Ney formed the rearguard, buying time for Drouet and Junot to pull back to Coimbra. The first of the skirmishes took place at Pombal on 11 March. It was a trifling affair, well handled by Ney but less so by Erskine. The following morning, Ney was once again firm, this time at Redhina; Junot was 8km further north at Condeixa and Drouet was skirting south of Coimbra on the Celorico

road, tasked with escorting the sick and wounded and the reserve artillery. Montbrun had made an attempt on Coimbra but, aided by the swollen river and Trant's forward artillery on the north bank, his assault was easily repulsed. To the south Ney was now embroiled in a more serious contest at Redhina; he had withdrawn from Pombal under cover of darkness with Mermet's Division forming the first line in the rearguard. The Light Division continued to lead the Allied advance and came upon the French early on 12 March but Wellington was unsure of the exact strength of the force to his front, or the identity of a formation to his right[7] and he needed a better assessment of Junot's whereabouts to determine how quickly he could respond. He decided to wait for the arrival of the 4th Division, which took a few hours: at 1400 hours, the Light Division on the right and the 3rd Division to the left executed an encircling movement. Mermet pulled back to the second position held by Marchand and the Allies were forced into a repeat performance before Ney pulled back to Condeixa. As this was unfolding, the 6th Division had been despatched on a wide left flanking manoeuvre to threaten the French right and provide some support to Trant at Coimbra. As it transpired their support was not required, for Masséna had elected to break clean, with all speed, using the southern bank of the Mondego. The 2nd Corps was to fall back and join the 9th and 8th corps who had already joined the route, while Ney was to make a stand at Condeixa to buy time. Unlike the previous actions, Ney was forced to move east following his delaying tactics and the appearance of Picton's 3rd Division in the throes of a right flanking movement, which threatened to cut off the French line of retreat, brought a swift end to events at Condeixa. Ney had been expected to hold up the Allied advance for at least a day and his failure to do so almost resulted in the capture of Masséna himself, as well as endangering Loison and Montbrun[8] who were out to the flanks.

As dawn broke on 14 March, a dense fog hung in the air and Erskine took the opportunity to close in on Ney. In the process he ran into Marchand, who was holding the village of Casal Novo; the layout favoured the defenders; positioned on rising ground and encircled by stone walls. Erskine rather rashly concentrated his battalions behind the three companies of the 52nd that were sent forward to clear the piquets. As the fog lifted the five battalions suddenly realized they were dangerously exposed, bunched together, overlooked and in range of both French infantry and artillery. In the time it took Picton to come to their aid, the Light Division had needlessly lost many men. Marchand fell back to establish a third defensive position on the heights of Chão de Lamas, behind that of Mermet at Casal de Azan and Villa Seca. Mermet was quickly turned and the Allies advanced to Marchand's position where they were forced to execute another holding and flanking manoeuvre before Ney finally pulled back to Miranda de Corvo where he linked up with Junot and Montbrun. Reynier had also pulled back earlier in the day and the entire French army, less Drouet, was now concentrated with their backs to the mountains and their flank to the Mondego.

---

4   Some elements landed on the 1st and 6th March but the bulk did not arrive until 21 March.

5   Erskine was commanding the Light Division in Craufurd's absence while on leave. Wellington had begrudgingly consented to the application for leave: in a letter responding to the application he wrote that, "Adverting to the number of General officers senior to you in the army, it has not been an easy task to keep you in command". A. H. Craufurd, *General Craufurd and his Light Division*, p.169.

6   Vane, *Narrative of the Peninsular War*, vol. II, pp.82–83.

7   This was in fact Loison's Division at Rabaçal.

8   Montbrun had been held up by a Portuguese sergeant in the militia (José Correia Leal) who did not conceal that Trant had withdrawn from the city all but one battalion and two guns. He fabricated a story of needing to confer with his commander, thereby buying sufficient time to witness the French forces being called off with great urgency.

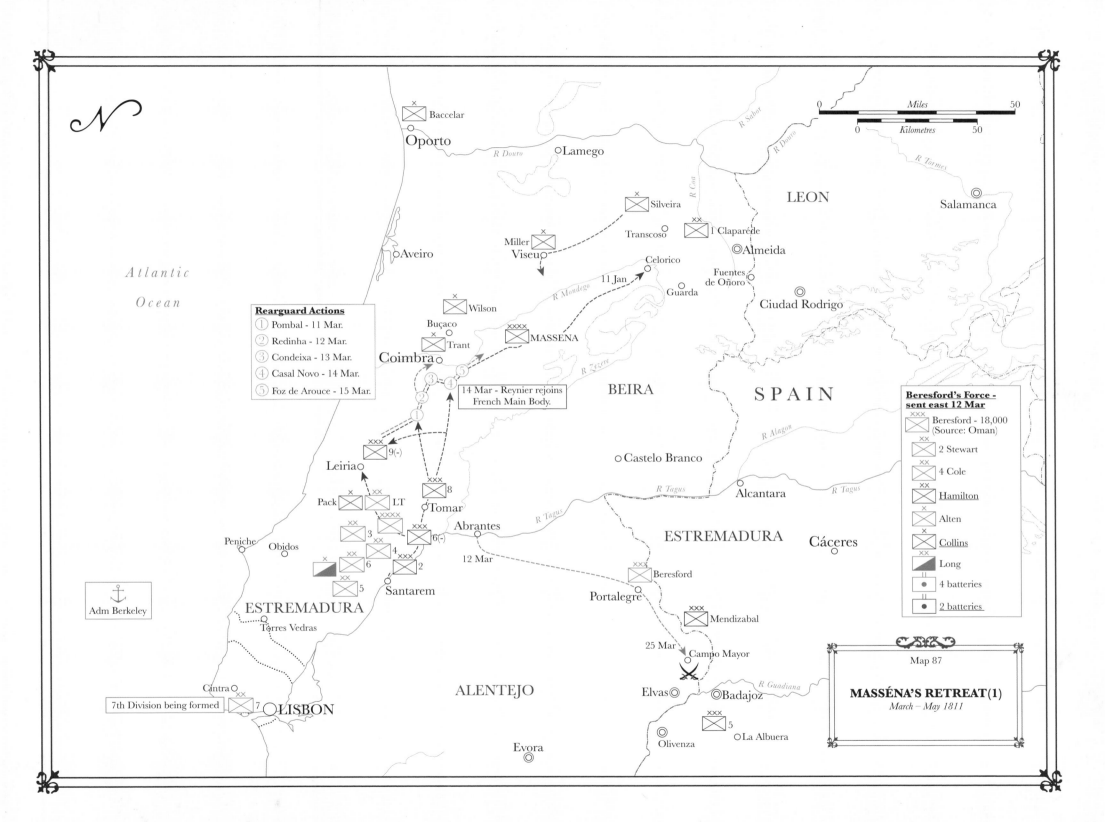

N

Atlantic
Ocean

Baccelar
Oporto

R Douro   Lamego

LEON

R Sabor   *R Douro*

R Tormes

Salamanca

Silveira

Transcoso

1 Claparéde

Almeida

Miller
Viseu

R Mondego   Celorico

11 Jan

Guarda

Fuentes
de Oñoro

Ciudad Rodrigo

Aveiro

Wilson

Buçaco
Trant

MASSÉNA

Coimbra

R Zezere

5

3 4

14 Mar - Reynier rejoins
French Main Body.

BEIRA

SPAIN

Rearguard Actions
① Pombal - 11 Mar.
② Redinha - 12 Mar.
③ Condeixa - 13 Mar.
④ Casal Novo - 14 Mar.
⑤ Foz de Arouce - 15 Mar.

2

1

9(-)

Leiria

Pack   LT

8
Tomar

Abrantes

R Tagus

Castelo Branco

R Alagon

Alcantara

R Tagus

ESTREMADURA

Cáceres

**Beresford's Force -
sent east 12 Mar**

Beresford - 18,000
(Source: Oman)

2 Stewart

4 Cole

Hamilton

Alten

Collins

Long

4 batteries

2 batteries

Peniche   Obidos

3

6   4
5   2

6(-)

12 Mar

Santarem

Beresford

Portalegre

Mendizabal

Adm Berkeley

Torres Vedras

ESTREMADURA

25 Mar   Campo Mayor

ALENTEJO

Elvas   Badajoz

R Guadiana

Cintra

7th Division being formed   7

LISBON

Evora

Olivenza

5

La Albuera

Map 87

MASSÉNA'S RETREAT (1)
March – May 1811

The French commander was now well aware of the precariousness of his position and determined to put some space between his army and that of the Allies; he ordered all the wagons to be stripped of their non-essential stores and reloaded with the wounded. They started off that night with Reynier leading, Junot following and Ney once again forming the rearguard. The following morning, a low-lying mist denied Wellington early confirmation of a French withdrawal. When the Allies finally set off in pursuit they passed through the burning town of Miranda de Corvo, strewn with discarded baggage and the distressing sight of 500 live but hamstrung horses, mules and donkeys in the most dreadful state. The Light and 3rd divisions finally caught sight of Ney's men at about 1600 hours that afternoon near the village of Foz de Arouce. Ney had disobeyed Masséna's order to cross the stream and destroy the bridge; instead he had sent back three of his brigades to the east bank and retained three on the exposed western hills to delay the Allied advance. Wellington, riding well advanced, was able to see the extent of the French defence and ordered an immediate attack. Elements of the 95th arrived almost unopposed at the bridge, having moved down a ravine. The sound of musket fire by the bridge then caused instant panic amongst the French troops deployed at the front of the position as they supposed their line of retreat had been severed. Ney realising the danger responded by ordering the 3/69e Ligne[9] to counter-attack; they secured the bridge and Ney's troops filtered back in some disarray to the eastern bank.[10]

Masséna made full use of the night to continue his easterly movement with the main body. The following morning the hills overlooking the river Ceira were devoid of French, but Wellington was relatively sanguine; he had succeeded in preventing Masséna from moving north, taking Coimbra and threatening Oporto. He decided to wait a day for the army's supplies to catch up, which provided time for him to readjust his force and send the 4th Division and de Grey's Heavy Dragoons south to link up with Beresford. Further orders were sent back dismissing the Lisbon militia and ordenança from their duties on the Lines, and additional orders sent north to Trant and Wilson to close in on the river Mondego to discourage any French intentions to the north.

By 21 March the first elements of Masséna's force reached Celorico, where they joined up with Drouet, and the next day Reynier's Corps reached Guarda where they linked up with Claparéde (commanding Drouet's 1st Division). Drouet had continued his eastward movement and opened communication with Ciudad Rodrigo and Almeida – the crisis, for now, was over. The pursuing Allies were 30km distant and out of contact with Ney's gallant and exhausted divisions who had fought a series of brilliant rearguard actions, buying time for the French main body to extract themselves largely intact. Although the Allies had been out-marched, Wellington had cause to be entirely satisfied with the turn of events. 'If in the course of history of war a battle had taken place in which one side lost 30,000 men and the other a matter of a few hundreds, it would have been echoed down the pages of history as the greatest victory ever won.

But that, in fact, is the measure of the decisive nature of Masséna's defeat at the Lines of Torres Vedras.'[11] Masséna, conversely, was far from content. L'enfant chéri de la victoire had failed to justify the high hopes invested in him, victory had eluded his army, his pride was dented and his reputation in the balance. He decided upon a bold and uncertain change of plan.

Instead of continuing east to Almeida and Ciudad Rodrigo he issued orders to head south towards Guarda and Sabugal, from where he intended to re-invade Portugal. This was all too much for Ney, whose relationship with Masséna had deteriorated from dismal to dire over the previous months. The resulting insubordinate correspondence left Masséna no choice; Ney was removed of his command[12] and ordered to move to Valladolid and await instructions from Napoleon. On 23 March the 6th Corps arrived at Celorico and was immediately set on the road (with the 8th Corps) to Guarda where they were to link up with Reynier. Drouet was en route to Almeida and his long-absent 1st Division was to join him there. By 26 March Reynier had passed through Sabugal and had swung west to instigate the first part of Masséna's re-invasion plan. However, it soon became abundantly clear that there were no rations to be had in this uninhabited and largely infertile land that formed the watershed between the rivers Coa and Zezere. Reynier's plea to Masséna arrived at army headquarters at much the same time as that from Junot, and another from Drouet outlining the most uncertain situations at Almeida and Ciudad Rodrigo – both from a lack of food. The communiqués served their purpose; Masséna gave up his quest, now possessing the necessary documents to both validate and exonerate his decision and on 29 March he gave orders for the army to march to Plasencia.

Reynier came down to Sabugal, where he was to establish a defensive line and wait for Junot to pass through and beyond the line. Meanwhile the 6th Corps was to go firm at Guarda, waiting for word that the 8th Corps and the army headquarters had extracted themselves. Masséna was remarkably fortunate that Wellington's forces had held themselves back in order to facilitate the procurement and distribution of supplies prior to resuming the offensive. On 24 March, Slade's Cavalry Brigade entered Celorico amid reports that some troops had departed south, but this was not confirmed until 27 March, when elements of Slade's reconnaissance force picked up evidence that the majority of the French army was indeed south of Guarda. Wellington was confused as to Masséna's motives but realized that he could not advance too far without waiting for the Allied main body to come to the front. They began to arrive two days later, with the Light Division and two cavalry brigades closing in on Guarda while the 3rd and 6th divisions closed on separate axes from the west. Less than a week in command, Loison[13] was caught by surprise and made off at speed, making no attempt to hold his ground. Slade followed but by all accounts displayed excessive caution allowing Loison sufficient time and space to extract his entire force east of the

9   There is some disagreement in French sources as whether it was the 3/69e or the 27e Ligne.

10   Oman draws an interesting comparison to this combat and that on the Coa in July 1810. At that engagement, ironically the defenders were the Light Division and Ney led the assault.

11   The 8th Duke of Wellington, Foreword, p.5 of The Lines of Torres Vedras, The British Historical Society of Portugal, by A. H. Norris and R. W. Bremner.

12   He had commanded the 6th Corps since 1804 and his dismissal was not well received by the officers and men. Napoleon however approved of Masséna's actions and vowed to remove corps altogether and have divisions report directly to the army commander. Ney continued to be employed in key positions, forming an integral part of Napoleon's army for the invasion of Russia the following year.

13   He has assumed command of the 6th Division vice Ney.

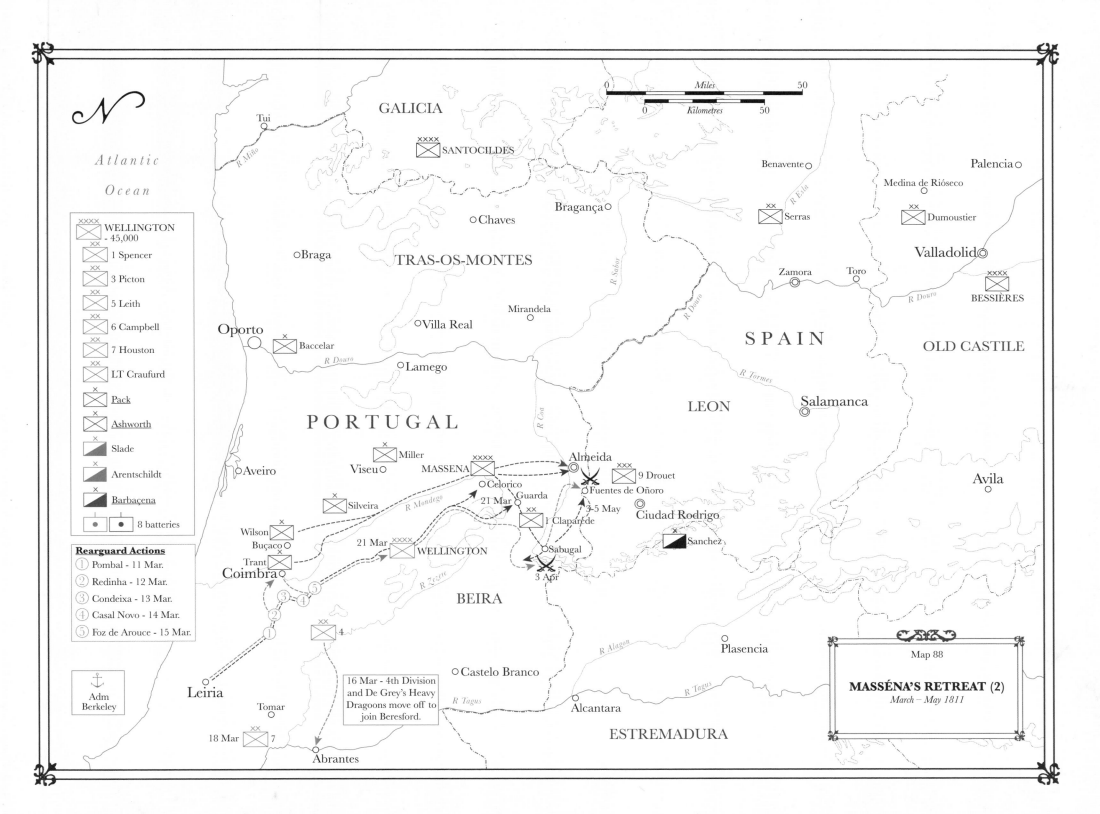

N

Atlantic

Ocean

GALICIA

Tui

XXXX
SANTOCILDES

Benavente○   Palencia○

Medina de Ríoseco○

Legend:

XXXX	WELLINGTON – 45,000
XX	1 Spencer
XX	3 Picton
XX	5 Leith
XX	6 Campbell
XX	7 Houston
XX	LT Craufurd
X	Pack
X	Ashworth
	Slade
X	Arentschildt
X	Barbaçena
● ●	8 batteries

Rearguard Actions
① Pombal - 11 Mar.
② Redinha - 12 Mar.
③ Condeixa - 13 Mar.
④ Casal Novo - 14 Mar.
⑤ Foz de Arouce - 15 Mar.

Adm
Berkeley

Chaves○   Bragança○

TRAS-OS-MONTES

○Braga

Mirandela○

○Villa Real

XX Serras

○Oporto

X Baccelar

R Douro

○Lamego

Zamora◎   Toro○

Valladolid◎

R Douro

XXXX
BESSIÈRES

SPAIN

OLD CASTILE

LEON

Salamanca◎

R Tormes

PORTUGAL

XX Miller   ○Viseu

XX MASSENA ○Celorico
Silveira   21 Mar Guarda
XX
Wilson   *R Mondego*
Buçaco○   XXXX
Trant   21 Mar WELLINGTON
Coimbra

BEIRA

XX
Arentschildt

XXXX   Almeida◎
MASSENA   ⚔
          Fuentes de Oñoro
        XXX
        9 Drouet

Avila○

3-5 May

XX
1 Claparede

Sabugal○   ⚔
3 Apr

Ciudad Rodrigo◎

X Sanchez

R Coa

R Zezere

XX 4

R Alagon

○Castelo Branco

Plasencia○

16 Mar - 4th Division
and De Grey's Heavy
Dragoons move off to
join Beresford.

R Tagus

Leiria○

Tomar○

Dumoustier

R Esla

ESTREMADURA

Alcantara○

R Tagus

Aveiro○

18 Mar XX 7

○Abrantes

Map 88

MASSÉNA'S RETREAT (2)
March – May 1811

Coa by nightfall. By 31 March Junot had reached Sabugal and passed through Reynier's defensive line, going firm a few kilometres to the east. Wellington's reconnaissance forces and overall intelligence picture confirmed that the bulk of Masséna's army was still entrenched on the Coa and he was determined to dislodge it from Portugal.

Wellington waited until his entire force, including the long-awaited 7th Division,[14] was concentrated before executing his plan. He opted for a south flanking manoeuvre in the hope of isolating and destroying the French 2nd Corps.[15] The 6th Division were left at Rapoulla de Coa to occupy the French 6th Corps, leaving the other five divisions and two cavalry brigades to execute the entrapment and destruction of Reynier's Corps. The Light Division and the two cavalry brigades[16] constituted the flanking force which aimed to cross the Coa well to the south and get in behind Reynier's defensive lines, which were to be simultaneously engaged by the 3rd and 5th divisions to their front, who in turn were to be supported by the 1st and 7th divisions. The attack was to commence early on 3 April but the dense fog prevented the troops from seeing their objectives and Picton and Dunlop sent word to Wellington asking for clarification that the operation was still to commence. Unfortunately, Erskine had already set off with the cavalry and light infantry and in the confusion Beckwith missed his chosen crossing point and crossed the Coa too early in the scheme of manoeuvre.[17] Drummond followed, placing both the brigades far too close to the line of Reynier's defences and not to their rear as planned. French piquets engaged the wading infantrymen as they struggled against the deeper-than-anticipated crossing and fast-flowing current. They established themselves on the far bank but were now dangerously exposed and continued their advance north, unaware that they were about to come up against the left flank of the entire French corps.

Merle had responsibility for the French left and had positioned the 4e Léger at the extreme south of the French line. Alerted by the fire of the piquets, Merle was quick to realise the danger and hurriedly reformed the regiment to face the threat. He advanced in column of division to meet the light troops who were characteristically strung out in strong skirmish lines. The massed French columns succeeded in pushing back the advancing Allies but at considerable cost, as their dense formation provided an easy target for the 95th armed with Baker rifles. The retreating 95th and companies of skirmishing caçadores formed on the 43rd and the balance of the 3rd Caçadores, and this determined line now succeeded in pushing back the 4e Léger until they reached the line of the 2e Léger and 36e Ligne (from Sarrut's Brigade). Beckwith's men sought refuge behind stone walls and, assisted by a heavy rainstorm, held their position despite repeated attacks by Merle's infantry and latterly by Pierre Soult's cavalry. Once across the river, Drummond had taken a more easterly route but turned left at the sound of gunfire and now came to the

assistance of Beckwith's beleaguered force. The renewed attack succeeded in pushing Merle's Division back off the heights, but before the exhausted light infantrymen had time to reorganize, Godard's Brigade, which Reynier had sent to assist Merle, engaged them in the flank. At this juncture, the Allies were outnumbered by two to one.

During the early stages of this engagement the fog lifted rapidly and both Wellington and Reynier were able to assess their respective predicaments. Wellington's concern for his Light Division was surpassed by Reynier's concern for the survival of his entire corps. Having stripped out his centre to support his left wing, he had disrupted the balance of his defence and now to his front he could clearly see the two Allied divisions to the west of the Coa, making best speed for the fords. Reynier ordered an immediate retreat; Merle was to extract himself under cover of Godard's two regiments, while the balance of the Corps was to strike east to Alfayates. The 5th Division crossed into Sabugal unopposed but did not pursue Arnaud's men. Meanwhile, the 17e Léger and 70e Ligne were embroiled in a fierce contest with the 3rd Division, holding their ground long enough to enable Merle to extract his force. The French were in grave danger but at this juncture Wellington ordered his Army to halt; intelligence (false, as it transpired) had been received indicating that the 8th Corps was on the move south in support of their beleaguered colleagues. Reynier was able to extract his corps; but the action at Sabugal prompted Wellington to observe that it 'was one of the most glorious that British troops were ever engaged in'. Beckwith's leadership during the fighting receiving the highest praise from the Allied command, and more significantly, from his rank and file.

The following afternoon Masséna abandoned plans to hold the line of the Coa and withdrew Loison's Corps to join Junot and Reynier in and around Alfayates. On 4 April the Army of Portugal moved east, with the 2nd Corps marching to Fuentes de Oñoro, the 6th Corps and the 8th Corps moving to the area surrounding Ciudad Rodrigo from where they reopened communications with Drouet at Val de Mula. The Allied army followed, but Wellington had no intention of pursuing Masséna deep into Spain. His forces were exhausted and the numbers of sick at alarming levels. Instead he turned his attention to removing the last French bastion on Portuguese soil at Almeida. Trant was tasked to commence the process with his characteristically audacious methods and was promised the support of Slade's cavalry brigade and Bull's horse artillery troop a few days later. The French covering force withdrew into or beyond Almeida and Wellington surrounded and blockaded the fortified town, but he still lacked sufficient heavy guns and materials to conduct a proper siege. Some days later Masséna withdrew his army deeper into Spain and by mid-April the 2nd, 6th and 8th corps were at Ledesma, Salamanca and Toro respectively while the 9th Corps held the line of observation at San Muñoz.

Wellington capitalized on the respite to rest and recuperate his force. The Light Division supported by the 14th Light Dragoons and the 1st Hussars KGL were sent forward to make contact and monitor Drouet. The 5th Division was in support behind them; the 1st, 3rd and 7th divisions and the balance of the Portuguese were established in cantonments in or around the border while the 6th Division supported by Pack's Brigade were blockading Almeida. With the troops in place under Spencer's command, Wellington set off for Estremadura (see Chapter 32), having assessed that Masséna would sit tight. His assessment was wrong: Masséna

---

14 Nicknamed the 'Mongrels' as the division included, *inter alia*, the Light Brigade of the King's German Legion, the *Chasseurs Britanniques* and the Brunswick Oels light infantry.

15 Oman, rightly questions the south flanking option stating that a north-flanking manoeuvre would have driven a wedge between the 9th Corps and the balance of Masséna's depleted Army.

16 This entire grouping was under Erskine's command but Beckwith was commanding the Light Division.

17 Maps depicting the movements are contradictory and confusing and not in line with historical or eyewitness accounts of the action. I have largely used Fortescue's map, which while it is the clearest, it is incorrect in some aspects.

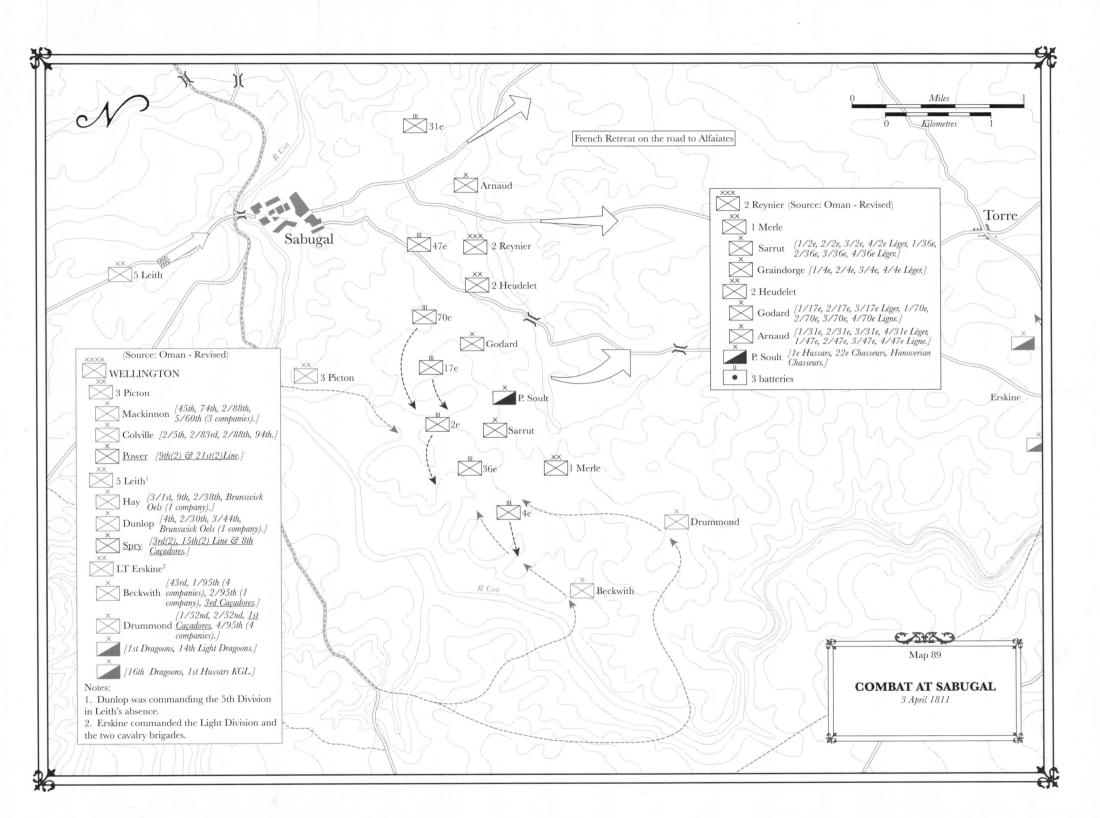

N

31e

French Retreat on the road to Alfaiates

Arnaud

Torre

Sabugal

47e

2 Reynier

5 Leith

2 Heudelet

70e

Godard

3 Picton

17e

P. Soult

2e

Sarrut

36e

1 Merle

4e

Drummond

Erskine

R Côa

Beckwith

2 Reynier (Source: Oman - Revised)

1 Merle

Sarrut *[1/2e, 2/2e, 3/2e, 4/2e Léger, 1/36e, 2/36e, 3/36e, 4/36e Léger.]*

Graindorge *[1/4e, 2/4e, 3/4e, 4/4e Léger.]*

2 Heudelet

Godard *[1/17e, 2/17e, 3/17e Léger, 1/70e, 2/70e, 3/70e, 4/70e Ligne.]*

Arnaud *[1/31e, 2/31e, 3/31e, 4/31e Léger, 1/47e, 2/47e, 3/47e, 4/47e Ligne.]*

P. Soult *[1e Hussars, 22e Chasseurs, Hanoverian Chasseurs.]*

3 batteries

(Source: Oman - Revised)

WELLINGTON

3 Picton

Mackinnon *[45th, 74th, 2/88th, 5/60th (3 companies).]*

Colville *[2/5th, 2/83rd, 2/88th, 94th.]*

Power *[9th(2) & 21st(2)Line.]*

5 Leith[1]

Hay *[3/1st, 9th, 2/38th, Brunswick Oels (1 company).]*

Dunlop *[4th, 2/30th, 3/44th, Brunswick Oels (1 company).]*

Spry *[3rd(2), 15th(2) Line & 8th Caçadores.]*

LT Erskine[2]

Beckwith *[43rd, 1/95th (4 companies), 2/95th (1 company), 3rd Caçadores.]*

Drummond *[1/52nd, 2/52nd, 1st Caçadores, 4/95th (4 companies).]*

[1st Dragoons, 14th Light Dragoons.]

[16th Dragoons, 1st Hussars KGL.]

Notes:
1. Dunlop was commanding the 5th Division in Leith's absence.
2. Erskine commanded the Light Division and the two cavalry brigades.

Map 89

COMBAT AT SABUGAL
3 April 1811

was determined to restore his reputation and justify himself to the Emperor, his peers and his subordinates. He commenced planning for a renewed offensive oblivious to the fact that Napoleon had already decided to replace him,[18] but until Marshal Marmont arrived on 12 May there was still time for Masséna's plans and reputation to be put to the final test. Masséna's chosen cantonments in Spain were sufficiently well supplied and rich in reinforcements; consequently, within a couple of weeks his army was returned to a respectable strength, paid, replenished, clothed and re-shod. Replacement mounts were however, impossible to procure and so the army remained weak in numbers of cavalry[19] and devoid of nearly all its artillery. On 20 April, Masséna wrote to Bessières requesting support, which arrived in the form of two cavalry brigades, providing an additional 1,700 sabres, a horse artillery battery and, most significantly, 30 teams of gun horses.[20] This latter provision enabled Masséna to put five complete batteries of guns and caissons into an army park, which would be distributed as he saw fit. By 1 May the combined army was established at Ciudad Rodrigo and the next morning, divided into two columns, they crossed the Agueda and headed west.

On 25 April Wellington had fortuitously received a report from Spencer that *inter alia* included intelligence from Dr Curtis, the head of the Irish College at Salamanca, outlining considerable French activity in the region. He immediately headed north and by 29 April was back with his Allied army, and he began to reconnoitre suitable ground for the inevitable encounter. He chose the area between Fort Concepción and Fuentes de Oñoro along the stream Dos Casas and between the River Turones, which runs parallel about three kilometres to the west. The Light Division[21] and the cavalry fell back in face of the French advance and by the afternoon of 3 May almost the entire French army was in view, advancing in two columns. The southern column, the stronger of the two, was heading directly for the village of Fuentes de Oñoro. The light companies of Nightingale, Howard, Löwe, Mackinnon, Colville and Power's brigades[22] were deployed in the dwellings. The significance of Fuentes de Oñoro was quickly realized by Masséna who had noted the defensive nature of the ground further north, and therefore elected to break through to the south where the ground provided less defendable qualities and greater opportunities for the offence. He was, however, unable to determine the exact Allied dispositions as Wellington had, true to form, deployed the majority of his force out of sight but Masséna, also true to form, spent little time in reconnaissance and immediately ordered Ferey to take the village while Reynier was tasked to distract the 5th Division to the north.

The importance of the position at Fuentes de Oñoro was quickly apparent and both commanders demonstrated a clear determination to hold the village. The tight streets and numerous blind alleys surrounded by waist-high stone walls provided excellent cover to the infantry.[23] 'Toward one hour in the afternoon, General Ferrey, preceding the light cavalry of the Gen Fournier, advanced by the main road on Fuentes d'Oñoro. General Fournier, with the 7e, 3e and 20e de chasseurs, charged the cavalry of the English as well as their light infantry, and rejected them suddenly one and the other on the village of Fuentes d'Oñoro.'[24] Ferey closed with considerable speed on the village and despite the heavy fire of the Allied skirmish line, charged across the Dos Casas and forced the Allied infantry out of some of the dwellings on either bank. These were quickly counter-attacked by Williams and regained. Ferey wasted no time in responding. His second brigade followed the first and swiftly gained the upper hand; within minutes the Allied infantry were again being forced back but they rallied at the church and were able to retain a foothold in the western edge. It was Wellington's turn to demonstrate his resolve and he responded by sending three battalions from Spencer's Division to regain the losses. The 2/24th, 71st and 79th entered the village from the west and, with support from Williams's[25] 28 companies, began to push back the French but at considerable cost. Eventually French steadfastness began to dissolve and Ferey's infantry fled back out of the village, pursued up the eastern bank by the Allied infantry. Masséna responded by tasking four battalions from Marchand's Division,[26] which deployed initially to enable the retreating troops to rally and then supported them (along with a battery) in a second counter-attack. They succeeded in driving the Allies back a second time and regained possession of the dwellings on the east bank, but failed in their repeated attempts to secure a foothold. As the light faded, the serious fighting ended and was replaced by sporadic musketry along the line.[27]

Masséna realized that another frontal assault on the village would only succeed if supported by a secondary manoeuvre. He had already discounted a serious attempt on the right, as the terrain provided a series of obstacles at right angles to the line of attack. Instead he ordered Montbrun to reconnoitre the ground to the south. His reports arrived at Masséna's headquarters in the early afternoon of 4 May and from these, the French commander penned his new plan. Seventeen thousand infantry and 3,500 cavalry were to undertake a left flanking manoeuvre, while another 14,000 were to assail the village of Fuentes de Oñoro, and finally, Reynier was to keep Erskine and Campbell's divisions occupied to the north. The south flanking force was to comprise of all the cavalry except that attached to the 2nd and 6th corps, Marchand and Mermet's divisions of the 6th Corps and Junot's only division, that of Solignac. In the centre, Ferey remained in place and was supported by Conroux and Claparéde. The redistribution of

---

18 He made this decision on 15 April.

19 Masséna only possessed 3,000 cavalry, compared to the 10,000 he had the year previously.

20 Bessières's questionable contribution solicited a Napoleonic rebuke some weeks later when he was criticized for not bringing a larger force of up to 10,000 men to assist Masséna in his operations.

21 Craufurd had returned to resume command (from Beckwith) on 4 May.

22 A total of 28 companies who were supported by the 2/83rd and the whole group were under command of Lieutenant Colonel Williams of the 5/60th.

23 However, the casitas were also constructed of stone and this made loop-holing almost impossible and added to the carnage as many infantry were caught inside dwellings with no means of escape.

24 Thiers, *Histoire du Consulat et de L'Empire*, vol. XII, pp.664–65.

25 Williams was seriously wounded during the first attack.

26 The exact battalions appear to be unrecorded. Thiers mentions it was a regiment, but all of Marchand's regiments had three battalions.

27 Oman makes an interesting observation from Marbot, *The Memories of Baron de Marbot*, vol. II, p.459; that the second attack may have succeeded if the 66e Ligne had not fired on the backs of the Légion Hanoverienne, whom they mistook for British as they wore red coats.

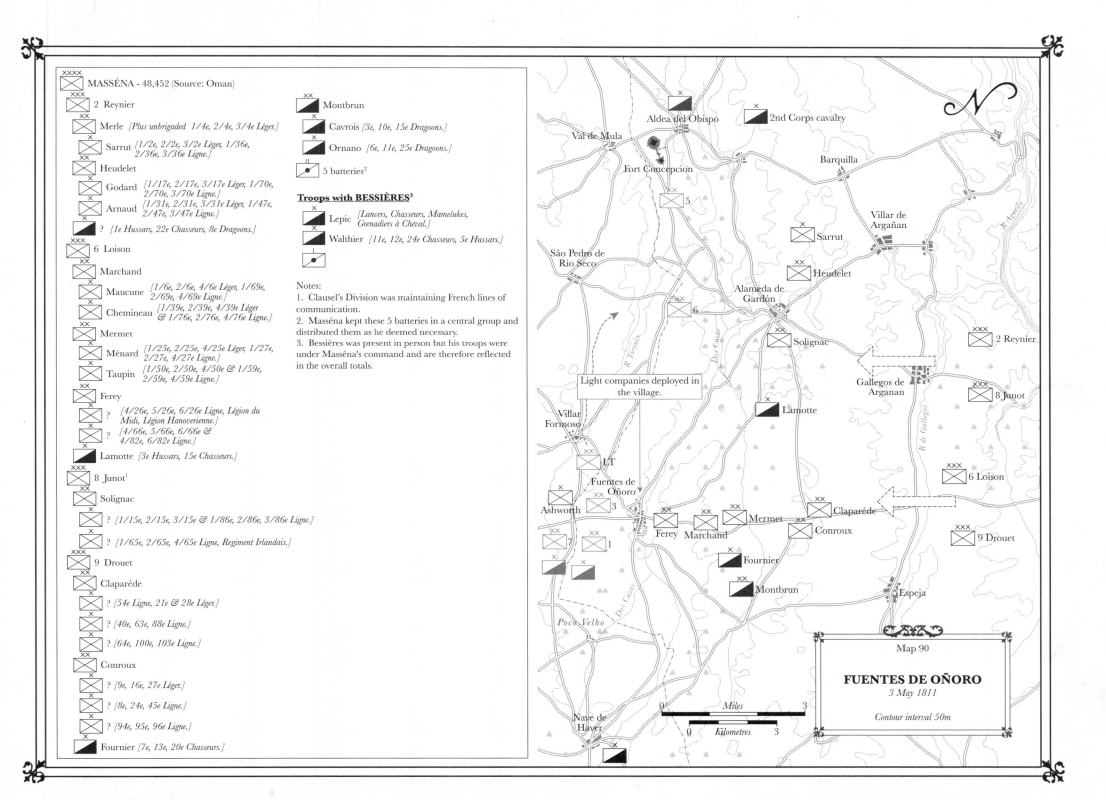

MASSÉNA - 48,452 (Source: Oman)

2 Reynier

Merle *[Plus unbrigaded 1/4e, 2/4e, 3/4e Léger.]*

Sarrut *[1/2e, 2/2e, 3/2e Léger, 1/36e, 2/36e, 3/36e Ligne.]*

Heudelet

Godard *[1/17e, 2/17e, 3/17e Léger, 1/70e, 2/70e, 3/70e Ligne.]*

Arnaud *[1/31e, 2/31e, 3/31e Léger, 1/47e, 2/47e, 3/47e Ligne.]*

? *[1e Hussars, 22e Chasseurs, 8e Dragoons.]*

6 Loison

Marchand

Maucune *[1/6e, 2/6e, 4/6e Léger, 1/69e, 2/69e, 4/69e Ligne.]*

Chemineau *[1/39e, 2/39e, 4/39e Léger & 1/76e, 2/76e, 4/76e Ligne.]*

Mermet

Ménard *[1/25e, 2/25e, 4/25e Léger, 1/27e, 2/27e, 4/27e Ligne.]*

Taupin *[1/50e, 2/50e, 4/50e & 1/59e, 2/59e, 4/59e Ligne.]*

Ferey

? *[4/26e, 5/26e, 6/26e Ligne, Légion du Midi, Légion Hanoverienne.]*

? *[4/66e, 5/66e, 6/66e & 4/82e, 6/82e Ligne.]*

Lamotte *[3e Hussars, 15e Chasseurs.]*

8 Junot[1]

Solignac

? *[1/15e, 2/15e, 3/15e & 1/86e, 2/86e, 3/86e Ligne.]*

? *[1/65e, 2/65e, 4/65e Ligne, Regiment Irlandais.]*

9 Drouet

Claparéde

? *[54e Ligne, 21e & 28e Léger.]*

? *[40e, 63e, 88e Ligne.]*

? *[64e, 100e, 103e Ligne.]*

Conroux

? *[9e, 16e, 27e Léger.]*

? *[8e, 24e, 45e Ligne.]*

? *[94e, 95e, 96e Ligne.]*

Fournier *[7e, 13e, 20e Chasseurs.]*

Montbrun

Cavrois *[3e, 10e, 15e Dragoons.]*

Ornano *[6e, 11e, 25e Dragoons.]*

5 batteries[2]

Troops with BESSIÈRES[3]

Lepic *[Lancers, Chasseurs, Mamelukes, Grenadiers à Cheval.]*

Walthier *[11e, 12e, 24e Chasseurs, 5e Hussars.]*

Notes:
1. Clausel's Division was maintaining French lines of communication.
2. Masséna kept these 5 batteries in a central group and distributed them as he deemed necessary.
3. Bessières was present in person but his troops were under Masséna's command and are therefore reflected in the overall totals.

Map 90

FUENTES DE OÑORO

3 May 1811

Contour interval 50m

forces began after dusk, with the sappers leading to repair some of the crossing points in advance of Montbrun's massed cavalry. Wellington was well aware that during the cessation in hostilities his right flank was under observation and he instigated readjustments to accommodate this danger. The four cavalry regiments were pushed south and spread thinly to cover the ground between Poco Velho and Nave de Haver and were supported by the 7th Division, who deployed two battalions into Poco Velho[28] and the balance on the hill to the west of the village.[29] The Light Division was recalled to its original position behind Fuentes de Oñoro and in the village, the light companies were returned to their battalions and replaced by the 71st and 79th with the 2/24th in support.

As dawn broke on 5 May, two regiments of Montbrun's dragoons (on the extreme south) advanced upon Nave de Haver, where Julian Sanchez and two squadrons of the 14th Light Dragoons were positioned. In the face of such a superior force Sanchez made off to Freneda, leaving the Light Dragoons to contest the ground as they pulled back by bounds to Poco Velho. As the 14th rode into Nave de Haver, the balance of Montbrun's force began to descend on the town. Arentschildt's two regiments tried in vain to halt the advance, their broken squadrons falling back to the environs of the Poco Velho. As they reformed, the masses of columns of French infantry came into view, driving the two battalions out of the town and leaving them at the mercy of Montbrun's cavalry; they were saved from annihilation by a gallant charge of two squadrons of German hussars. The 7th Division was now in a most dangerous position as the French, who were now turning north to support the attack on Fuentes de Oñoro from the east, were outflanking them on both sides. Wellington was completely taken by the strength and speed of the southerly movement and realized he had to act with great haste to save the 7th Division. The Light Division was ordered south to make contact with the 7th and assist them in their withdrawal; at the same time the 1st and 3rd divisions and Ashworth's Portuguese Brigade were to form a new defensive line facing south.

For some considerable time there were two separate but simultaneous engagements, one to the south, involving the extraction of the 7th Division, and the other to the east of the village of Fuentes de Oñoro. It was not until the troops to the south had withdrawn that the battle became one. Arentschildt and Slade's cavalry brigades, against overwhelming odds, bought enough time for the 7th Division to rally and form squares just in time to meet the gallant charges by the French cavalry. Montbrun made a series of resolute attempts to break the Allied squares, but having failed withdrew to wait for infantry support. At this moment, Craufurd appeared to Houston's rear and went firm, providing the cover and support the 7th Division required to commence a controlled withdrawal. They fell back as ordered to a position providing left flanking protection, with Sontag's Brigade to the right of Spencer on the west bank of the River Turones, and Doyle's Brigade to their immediate left at Freneda. The Light Division now took up the fight and in battalion squares began to leapfrog back, supported by the cavalry and Bull's horse

artillery troop. Montbrun, Fournier and Wathier's combined cavalry made repeated attempts to break the Allied ranks, supported by 15 guns in two horse artillery batteries. The French artillery was in turn harassed by the Allied cavalry and Bull's Troop; the latter was operating in three two-gun troops and riding forward between squares, unlimbering and firing off a few rounds before racing off to the rear, only to repeat the sequence at another location. It was during one of these daring engagements that Captain Norman Ramsey found himself cut off by a group of chasseurs. Supported by a squadron from the 1st Dragoons and 14th Light Dragoons, who had returned to provide assistance, Ramsey and his troop galloped at the encircling chasseurs and succeeded in cutting their way out, subsequently seeking refuge behind the 1st Division lines a short distance to the north. The Light Division and balance of the cavalry followed, leaving Montbrun to continue his attacks against the formed Allied line with some success on the extreme right against the 3rd Guards.

The attack upon Fuentes de Oñoro with the divisions of Ferey, Claparéde and Conroux was to coincide with an attack from the south by Marchand, Mermet and Solignac. It required the first elements of the south flanking force to be well advanced before executing the attack with Ferey and Drouet's divisions. The attack from the east was to precede that from the south. Ferey and Drouet's divisions were to have taken the village and established themselves on the hilltop on the western side before Loison's divisions and Solignac were to advance and engage the Allied line. The six divisions would then engage the front and flanks of the Allied formations, rolling them up piecemeal. It was a good plan, and notwithstanding a lack of artillery to counter the six Allied batteries, it stood every chance of success.

Two hours after Montbrun's cavalry had commenced operations to the south, Ferey's Division began to advance back across the river and into the village, driving the 71st and 79th from the houses on the far bank. The French continued the advance, forcing the Highlanders to the back of the village where they rallied and were reinforced by the reserve battalion, the 2/24th. They then reassumed the offensive, evicting Ferey's exhausted men back to the lower part of the village and Drouet immediately responded, despatching his elite troops in an attempt to regain the initiative. Three *bataillons d'élite*[30] resplendent in their bearskins (which caused them to be mistaken for Imperial Guard) engaged the defenders with élan and considerable courage. It was a fierce and bloody contest, resulting in many casualties to both sides. The French grenadiers succeeded in pushing back the Allies to the top of the village but their attacks lacked sufficient momentum to capture the entire village and carry the heights behind. The battle hung in the balance and Wellington, sensing the gravity of the situation, began to trickle additional light troops into the dwellings to assist in the defence and regain the initiative. Drouet conversely sensed victory and ordered Conroux and Claparéde to reinforce the three elite battalions with another 12 battalions; for the first time the village was in French hands. Mackinnon then requested Wellington's permission to charge and retake the village; the commander-in-chief was only paces away, and judging the attacks by Montbrun to have stalled and those of Loison to be delayed, gave his enthusiastic consent. The Connaught Rangers led

---

28   The 85th and the 2nd Caçadores.

29   This action demonstrated that Wellington has underestimated the strength of Masséna's southerly movement for the 7th Division were newly arrived, untried and comprised of a mixture of units and nationalities.

---

30   Composed of the 18 grenadier companies from his two divisions.

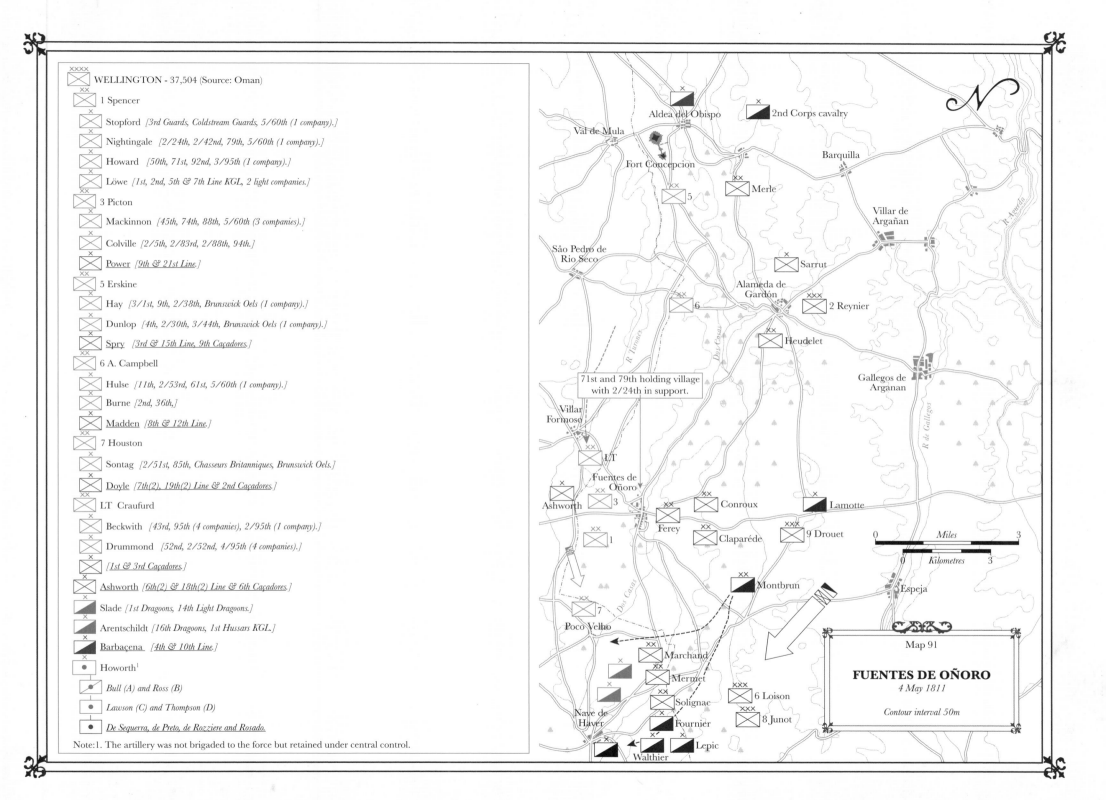

WELLINGTON - 37,504 (Source: Oman)

1 Spencer

Stopford [3rd Guards, Coldstream Guards, 5/60th (1 company).]

Nightingale [2/24th, 2/42nd, 79th, 5/60th (1 company).]

Howard [50th, 71st, 92nd, 3/95th (1 company).]

Löwe [1st, 2nd, 5th & 7th Line KGL, 2 light companies.]

3 Picton

Mackinnon [45th, 74th, 88th, 5/60th (3 companies).]

Colville [2/5th, 2/83rd, 2/88th, 94th.]

Power [9th & 21st Line.]

5 Erskine

Hay [3/1st, 9th, 2/38th, Brunswick Oels (1 company).]

Dunlop [4th, 2/30th, 3/44th, Brunswick Oels (1 company).]

Spry [3rd & 15th Line, 9th Caçadores.]

6 A. Campbell

Hulse [11th, 2/53rd, 61st, 5/60th (1 company).]

Burne [2nd, 36th,]

Madden [8th & 12th Line.]

7 Houston

Sontag [2/51st, 85th, Chasseurs Britanniques, Brunswick Oels.]

Doyle [7th(2), 19th(2) Line & 2nd Caçadores.]

LT Craufurd

Beckwith [43rd, 95th (4 companies), 2/95th (1 company).]

Drummond [52nd, 2/52nd, 4/95th (4 companies).]

[1st & 3rd Caçadores.]

Ashworth [6th(2) & 18th(2) Line & 6th Caçadores.]

Slade [1st Dragoons, 14th Light Dragoons.]

Arentschildt [16th Dragoons, 1st Hussars KGL.]

Barbaçena [4th & 10th Line.]

Howorth[1]

Bull (A) and Ross (B)

Lawson (C) and Thompson (D)

De Sequerra, de Preto, de Rozziere and Rosado.

Note:1. The artillery was not brigaded to the force but retained under central control.

71st and 79th holding village with 2/24th in support.

Map 91

FUENTES DE OÑORO

4 May 1811

Contour interval 50m

the counter-attack and clashed with the 9e Léger with unimaginable ferocity, throwing back the equally determined French infantry. At the same time the 74th charged down another lane into the village and the sight of their kinfolk rallied the Highlanders of the 71st and 79th, who along with the light companies joined in the advance, forcing back the French at every point. Within minutes the village was back in Allied hands; it was, as Wellington was to state, 'a close run thing'. The jubilant Allied infantry pursued the retreating French down to the river but were soon forced back from the casitas by the river's edge through the action of Drouet's divisional eight-pounder battery, which fired repeated volleys of canister into the front edge of the hamlet.

Drouet called up his reserve to extract his beaten force and by about 1400 hours the fighting was over. With the village back in Allied hands, the French attack from the south stalled; the four French batteries were brought to the front and cannonaded the Allied line. The reply by the six Allied batteries in range[31] quickly neutralized their fire and after a sharp cannonade the French batteries withdrew. For Masséna, the frustration was unbearable. His aide-de-camp summed it up when he stated that 'the day slipped by in vain attacks'. The failure of the main attack rendered the flank attack hopeless. Two days later at Ciudad Rodrigo, Masséna was delivered two letters from Berthier; the first contained reprimands for his conduct during the campaign from the Emperor, the second details of his dismissal and replacement. For Masséna, the war in Iberia was over.

---

31 All batteries except those of Ross and de Rozzier.

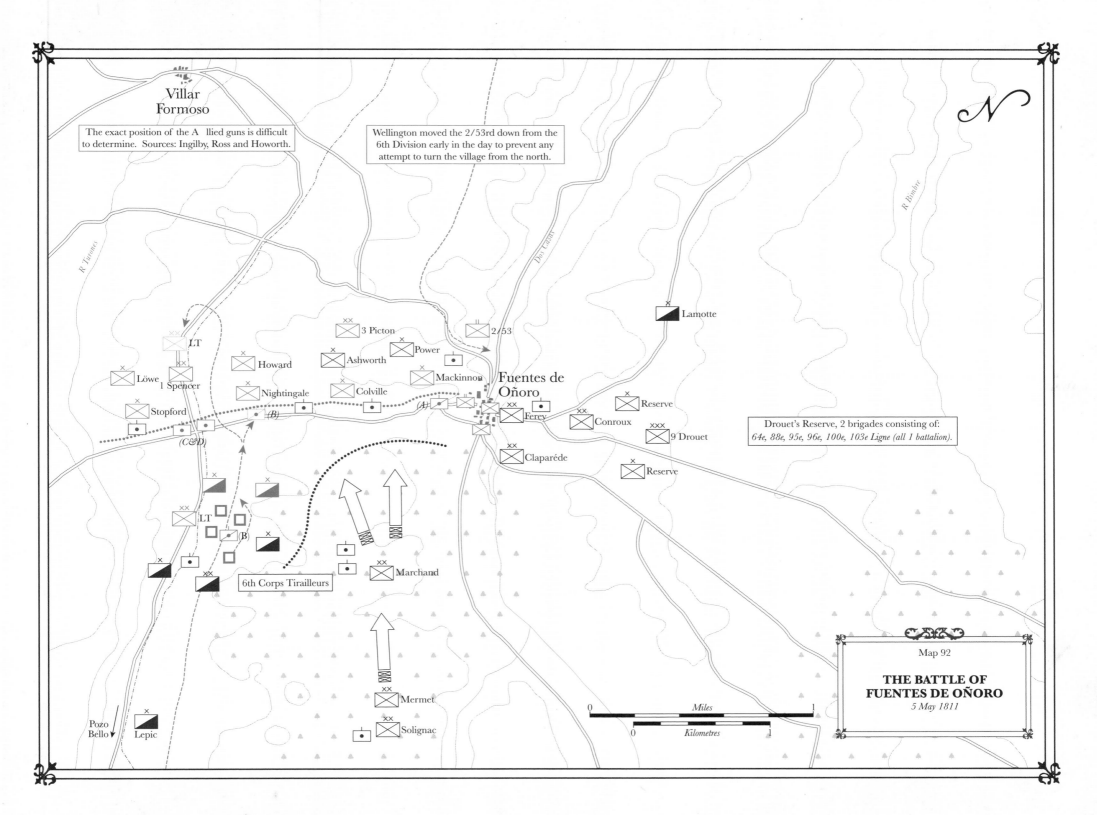

Villar Formoso

The exact position of the A llied guns is difficult to determine. Sources: Ingilby, Ross and Howorth.

Wellington moved the 2/53rd down from the 6th Division early in the day to prevent any attempt to turn the village from the north.

N

R Turones

R Bimbre

Dos Casas

Lamotte

LT

3 Picton

2/53

Löwe

1 Spencer

Howard

Ashworth

Power

Mackinnon

Fuentes de Oñoro

Stopford

Nightingale

Colville

(A)

Ferey

Reserve

(B)

Conroux

(C&D)

9 Drouet

Drouet's Reserve, 2 brigades consisting of:
64e, 88e, 95e, 96e, 100e, 103e Ligne (all 1 battalion).

Claparéde

Reserve

LT

(B)

6th Corps Tirailleurs

Marchand

Mermet

Pozo
Bello

Lepic

Solignac

0 Miles 1

0 *Kilometres* 1

Map 92

**THE BATTLE OF
FUENTES DE OÑORO**
5 May 1811

Chapter 32

THE ALLIED CAMPAIGN IN ESTREMADURA: MARCH TO AUGUST 1811

Wellington's orders to Beresford were to cross the Guadiana with the expeditionary force at Juromenha by building a bridge to open communication from Elvas into Estremadura. Speed was all-important, for as every day passed the French engineers repaired the breaches and strengthened the defences at Badajoz. Despite arriving at Elvas on 27 March it was not until 3 and 4 April[1] that the forward elements of the expeditionary force crossed unopposed and undetected into Spain. However, that night seasonal rains washed away the bridging piers, leaving the three battalions isolated and in a dangerously exposed condition on the far bank, where they remained for the next two days until repairs were conducted and the bulk of the force was able to join them. Allied intelligence confirmed that Mortier had withdrawn the majority of his force south of the Guadiana, leaving a small group on the north bank within the confines of Fort San Cristobal. Intelligence officers also gleaned the existence of a French garrison at Olivenza, just 10km from the bridge-crossing site. However, Allied luck ran out the following night when Girard sent out French cavalry reconnaissance, supported by infantry, which surprised a poorly deployed cavalry piquet. Fifty men and two officers of the 13th Light Dragoons were captured, and even more significantly the French cavalry discovered the existence of the large Allied army south of the Guadiana. Armed with this information Latour-Maubourg[2] realized he could no longer remain in his camps close to (but outside the immediate confines of) Badajoz, and having established General Phillipon and 3,000 men in the city itself, he began to move his force south to La Albuera and Santa Marta, having chosen to sacrifice a further battalion to buy time.[3]

'On the 9th the army advanced in two columns on Olivenza, which we expected the enemy would evacuate, as it was known they had a very small garrison in a large place, with very little artillery or stores, but on our approach we found it the contrary, as they fired from the place with artillery at our cavalry that patrolled to the front.'[4] Beresford summoned Colonel Neboyer, the governor, and received a determined response, which in turn prompted Beresford to despatch Major Dickson[5] to Elvas to procure the necessary siege guns and equipment. 'On the 10th I fitted out six heavy brass 24-pounders. With 300 rounds a gun. On the 11th they marched by way of Juromenha and reached our camp at Olivenza on the 13th.'[6] Dickson and Captain Squire selected the recently repaired lunette to the south of the town as the first battery position (map 93, point 1) and on the night of 14 April four of these heavy guns were, with some difficulty, moved into the lunette. 'On the morning of the 15th I begun to batter a curtain close to a flank, and in four hours the breach was nearly practicable, and the French garrison so much alarmed that they surrendered at discretion being about 460 in number.'[7]

On 30 March, Beresford had met up with Castaños and made arrangements for the remnants of the Army of Estremadura[8] to join the Anglo-Portuguese force in the expulsion of the French from Estremadura and the recapture of Badajoz. Castaños had eagerly accepted the suggestion and commenced operations by seizing the bridge at Mérida on 10 April, over which he sent Penne Villemur's cavalry to join in the pursuit of the French. Beresford could not therefore allow the siege at Olivenza to slow down combined operations and, after delivering orders for the capture of the place, he left Cole and his 4th Division to conduct the siege[9] while he took his other two divisions and set off in pursuit of Latour-Maubourg. By 11 April they had reached La Albuera, cutting the Badajoz to Sevilla road, but still there was no sign of the French force. The same day Penne Villemur reached Almendralejo. By 19 April the French had crossed the Sierra Morena and evacuated Estremadura; at which point Beresford left the British cavalry at Zafra and the Spanish at Llerena and then withdrew the infantry to Badajoz.

Ballesteros had continued to undertake hit-and-run operations on the French base at Sevilla, from the relative safety of the Condado de Niebla; these were low-level in intensity, but nevertheless posed a tolerable nuisance to Soult. However, the news that Zayas was en route to join Ballesteros prompted Soult to despatch Maransin with a force of about 5,000 infantry and cavalry to prevent their union. The link-up of Spanish forces was thus thwarted and Ballesteros retreated to the hills, but Maransin decided (without clear orders) to pursue the Spanish force and on 12 April defeated them at Fregenal. Ballesteros still managed to extricate his force relatively intact and those that had fled to the hills returned within days to their colours, providing 3,500 additional troops to assist the Allied cause in the region in due course. Another Spanish force was also to appear in Estremadura at the end of the first week in May. The Regency at

---

1   There were two reasons for this; firstly, Captain Squire, the bridging engineer, needed time to construct piers on either side of the river, which were then connected by the only five pontoons available. Secondly, rations were in short supply and had to be requested along with replacement footwear for the 4th Division.

2   Mortier had been recalled to Paris and had handed over command to Latour-Maubourg on 26 March.

3   This policy was strongly criticized by Napoleon and in the end only bought five days of respite.

4   Dickson, *The Dickson Manuscripts*, vol. III, 1811, p.382.

5   Dickson was a British captain in the Portuguese service and the senior gunner officer present. The siege at Olivenza and the subsequent sieges of Badajoz were to bring the officer to Wellington's attention. By the end of the war he was, despite still being a captain, commanding the entire Allied artillery as a brevet lieutenant colonel.

6   Dickson, *The Dickson Manuscripts*, vol. III, 1811, p.383.

7   Ibid. There were about 365 active and about 100 sick.

8   About 3,000 infantry and 1,000 cavalry.

9   Once concluded, the Portuguese militia garrisoned Olivenza, and Cole's Division rejoined the army having received new footwear on 16 April.

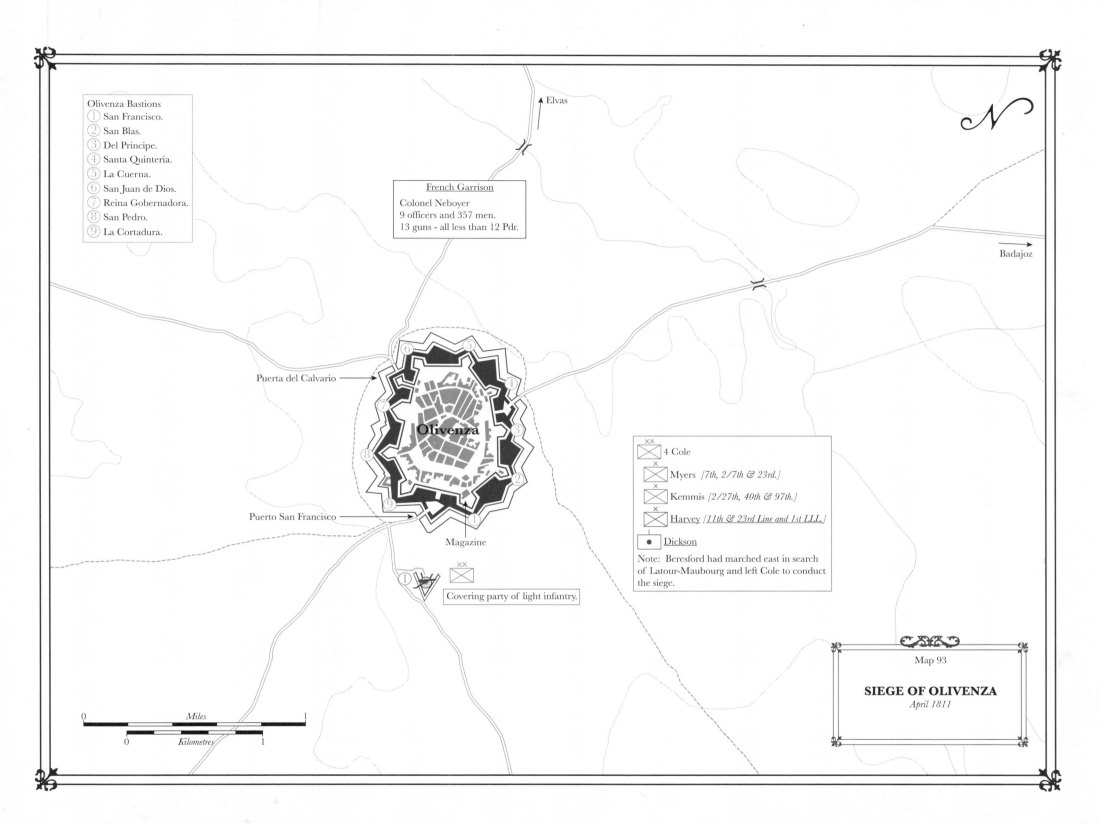

Olivenza Bastions
1. San Francisco.
2. San Blas.
3. Del Principe.
4. Santa Quinteria.
5. La Cuerna.
6. San Juan de Dios.
7. Reina Gobernadora.
8. San Pedro.
9. La Cortadura.

↑ Elvas

French Garrison

Colonel Neboyer
9 officers and 357 men.
13 guns - all less than 12 Pdr.

→ Badajoz

Puerta del Calvario →

Olivenza

Puerto San Francisco →

Magazine

4 Cole

Myers *[7th, 2/7th & 23rd.]*

Kemmis *[2/27th, 40th & 97th.]*

Harvey *[11th & 23rd Line and 1st LLL.]*

● Dickson

Note: Beresford had marched east in search of Latour-Maubourg and left Cole to conduct the siege.

Covering party of light infantry.

Map 93

SIEGE OF OLIVENZA
April 1811

0 Miles 1

0 Kilometres 1

Cádiz had resolved to send Blake and the divisions of Zayas and Lardizabal to further strengthen the Allied armies and they joined Ballesteros on 7 May adding 10,000 infantry, 800 cavalry and some field artillery.

Long before this union the siege of Badajoz had commenced. Wellington's unexpected arrival on 21 April (see Chapter 31) at Elvas had induced Beresford to relinquish the pursuit of Latour-Maubourg and return, with the infantry, to the environs of Badajoz. This withdrawal of all the forces did not meet with the endorsement of Beresford's Chief of Staff, who wrote: 'This one rather regrets. Cole's Division with Alten – the Loyal Lusitanian Legion at Olivenza and the Militia would be sufficient for the Siege – and with the Cavalry and other two Divisions then occupying Llerena, we keep all Estremadura, and maintain a most imposing attitude towards Andalusia.'[10] Wellington conducted a full reconnaissance of Badajoz on the 22nd, gave his orders on the 23rd and returned north on the 25th. His orders were characteristically detailed and dictated the scheme of manoeuvre for the next few weeks. The investment of Badajoz was to commence the moment Dickson arrived with the necessary ordnance and engineer stores from Elvas, Campo Mayor and Olivenza. Wellington was quite specific in the scheme of attack: the outlying forts and defences were to be taken prior to the commencement of operations against the city. Soult would inevitably attempt to relieve the defenders and attack the besieging force. The strength of his force was difficult to predict but would certainly include every available man in Andalusia. If that force turned out to be far greater than one corps, should Soult chose to lift the siege of Cádiz or postpone operations in Granada, then Beresford was to retire behind the Guadiana. However, if that force was numerically equitable, Beresford was empowered to decide whether to fight or retire, if he was to desire the former, Wellington had selected the ground around La Albuera as the most suitable. In all of this, the cooperation of the Spanish was crucial and Wellington laid out a series of requirements for the forces of Castaños, Ballesteros and Blake. Command and control was a more prickly issue and on this point Wellington, with the experiences of Talavera still at the forefront of his mind, was adamant; there was to be a single commander-in-chief. However, as Castaños was senior to Blake and as the former had already consented (when they met on 30 March) to being under Beresford's command, the issue was averted and Wellington's concerns allayed.

Wellington's decision to tackle the outlying Fort San Cristobal and the defences of Picurina and Pardaleras were based on advice from his chief engineer Colonel Fletcher. It was to be a costly mistake, which was to be repeated during the second Allied siege some months later. The investment was delayed due to persistent rain that raised the river Guadiana by as much as 3m, destroying the makeshift bridge at Juromenha and rendering the flying bridges inoperable. To all intents and purposes Beresford's lines of communication and withdrawal were severed. It raised sufficient concern for him to despatch the 4th Division to undertake a reconnaissance of an alternative route via Mérida and to link up with Morillo, the Spanish commander at that location. On 5 May the weather had improved, the bridges were reestablished and Fletcher and Dickson reported that their respective stores and ordnance were at hand. 'Major General Stewart

reports that he completed the investment of Badajoz, by 9 o'clock in the morning of yesterday the 5th without loss with the brigades of Lumley, Alten and the Portuguese Brigade of Algarve [this should read Fonseca]. Colonel Kemmis's Brigade from Montijo to Bivouac tomorrow between El Tesorio on the left bank of the Gévora. The rest of the Army to Bivouac in the nearest part of the Oak-wood on the Valverde side of Badajoz, and the duty to be taken by Brigades.'[11] The digging of the first parallels was started on 8 May at three points approximately 400m from the San Cristobal, the Picurina and the Pardaleras. On the north side the ground was unforgiving, and after a few centimetres the working parties encountered impenetrable rock and were forced to build up to provide any form of cover. The French guns bombarded the work from the main fort and the San Cristobal killing or wounding three of the nine engineer officers in Fletcher's troop.

On 10 May Phillipon despatched a reserve battalion from the main fort, which crossed the river and executed a sortie on the meagre works. They were driven back but the Allies over extended the pursuit and ran upon a wall of canister from the French guns on the ramparts, killing or wounding many as they scrambled to get back out of range. The battery was considered ready to receive guns the following day and five 24-pounder guns were moved into place. However, the slightly over zealous Portuguese artillery officer began to open with the guns before the battery position was complete. The ensuing counter battery fire from the ramparts quickly destroyed four of the five Allied guns. Work at the other two sites progressed more successfully, and the parallel and battery position in front of the Picurina was ready to receive guns on 11 May; they opened on the defences with some success. More guns were despatched to the north bank from Dickson's park and the sappers were tasked to establish a second battery further down the hill (map 94, battery 4), from where Dickson hoped to neutralize the French guns in the main fortress that were able to enfilade the first battery from the bastion of San Vincente. These new guns, and replacements for the original battery, opened on 12 May and were quickly under accurate and sustained counter-battery fire. However, the attackers did not have overly long to ponder their dilemma for within hours news arrived of a French force, estimated at 23,000, approaching from the south. Beresford, having resolved to fight, called off the siege and issued orders for his force to assemble near La Albuera. The approaching French force was far smaller than it could (and perhaps should) have been, for just as he had in January, Soult had refused to abandon Andalusia and had left both Victor and Sebastiani's forces largely untouched. Had he brought an additional 10,000 men, Beresford would most likely have refused battle. The Allies had set off on 13 May from Badajoz and, when it became clear that Soult was committed to the direct route via Santa Marta and La Albuera, Beresford ordered his entire force, less the 4th Division,[12] to move south to La Albuera. La España's Brigade was with Cole, and Blake's army had moved further north to Almendral following a meeting with Beresford during the afternoon of 13 May. At the meeting

10   D'Urban, *The Peninsular Journal, 1808–1817*, pp.203–04.

11   Ibid, p.211.

12   Kemmis's Brigade was on the north bank at Badajoz with orders to cross over the flying bridge at Caya. On the night of the 15/16 May the waters rose and the brigade was forced to march via the next bridge at Juromenha. In consequence, save three companies, they did not reach the field of battle in time.

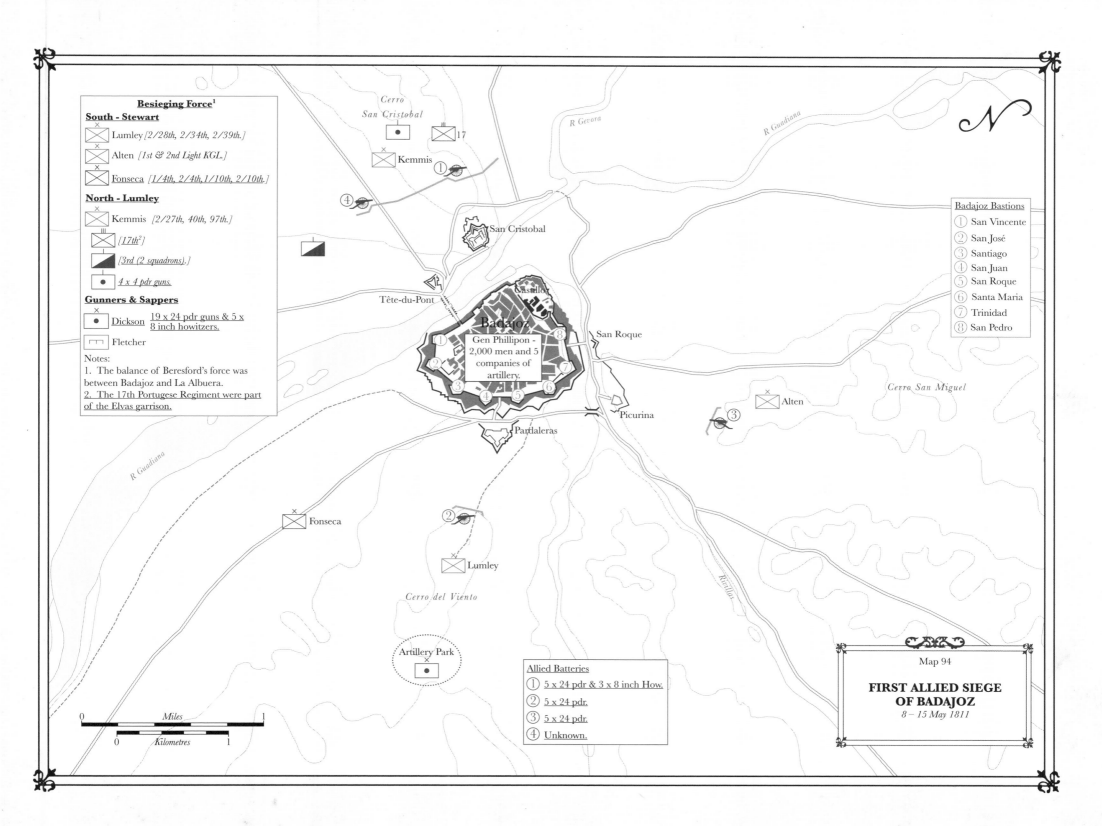

Besieging Force[1]

South - Stewart

⊠ Lumley *[2/28th, 2/34th, 2/39th.]*

⊠ Alten *[1st & 2nd Light KGL.]*

⊠ Fonseca *[1/4th, 2/4th, 1/10th, 2/10th.]*

North - Lumley

⊠ Kemmis *[2/27th, 40th, 97th.]*

⊠ *[17th[2]]*

◣ *[3rd (2 squadrons).]*

● *4 x 4 pdr guns.*

Gunners & Sappers

● Dickson — *19 x 24 pdr guns & 5 x 8 inch howitzers.*

⊡ Fletcher

Notes:
1. The balance of Beresford's force was between Badajoz and La Albuera.
2. The 17th Portugese Regiment were part of the Elvas garrison.

Badajoz Bastions
① San Vincente
② San José
③ Santiago
④ San Juan
⑤ San Roque
⑥ Santa Maria
⑦ Trinidad
⑧ San Pedro

Cerro San Cristobal

R Gevora

R Guadiana

17

Kemmis ①

④

San Cristobal

Tête-du-Pont

Castillo

Badajoz

Gen Phillipon - 2,000 men and 5 companies of artillery.

① ⑧ San Roque

② ⑦

③ ④ ⑤ ⑥ Picurina

Cerro San Miguel

Alten ③

Pardaleras

R Guadiana

Fonseca

② Lumley

Riuillas

Cerro del Viento

Artillery Park

Allied Batteries
① 5 x 24 pdr & 3 x 8 inch How.
② 5 x 24 pdr.
③ 5 x 24 pdr.
④ Unknown.

Map 94

FIRST ALLIED SIEGE OF BADAJOZ
8 – 15 May 1811

N

0 — *Miles* — 1

0 — *Kilometres* — 1

Beresford's overall command was confirmed and Castaños consented to pass his solitary brigade to Blake. The latter commander also made it clear that he intended fighting the French, irrespective of Beresford's intentions, for he anticipated mass desertion if orders were issued for a retreat into Portugal. By midday on 15 May the Allied force began to take up their positions; the brigade of the King's German Legion occupied the town, Stewart's Division formed up to the north-west, Hamilton's Division formed up to his left with Collin's Brigade to his rear and Long's cavalry to Stewart's right. Blake was expected that evening and was to move into position to the right of Long and form the Allied right wing. Cole and de España were to move from Badajoz that night and were expected early on 16 May.

From 13 May the Allied cavalry was in touch with Soult's vanguard at Villafranca and Los Santos. General Long was in charge of the Allied horse; his relationship with Beresford had not improved since his headstrong cavalry engagement south of Campo Mayor two months previously (see Chapter 29). Long chose to withdraw in the face of the French advance which infuriated Beresford, who considered Long's actions to have yielded ground of importance far too easily. Beresford had some justification as Long's force heavily outnumbered the French cavalry and his withdrawal had surrendered all the ground to the east of La Albuera to Soult's light cavalry reconnaissance, allocated to Briché. The French cavalry had arrived in the afternoon on 15 May and were able to see the troops in the town and some of those to the north-west,[13] but Stewart's Division was out of sight, although some of Long's cavalry were visible and it was likely that troops were positioned between these two groups. During the day, Soult rode forward from Santa Marta to undertake his own reconnaissance,[14] and concurred that the Spanish were not yet in line, which encouraged him to attack early the following morning.

Indeed, Blake was inexplicably late in arriving as he only had 8km to march. The troops began arriving at just before midnight and were not complete until 0300 hours. In the confusion, Blake's army took up positions too far to the left and in full view of the east bank and, as dawn broke, the error was vividly apparent and much frenzied adjustment ensued in an attempt to rectify the error with speed to provide adequate cover to the Allied right flank. At much the same time Cole and de España arrived from Badajoz, and the Spanish brigade moved through the Allied lines and took up their position to the front of Blake's reorganising force. The Spanish cavalry were on the far right and Miranda's battery of guns to the rear of the infantry.

Soult's main body had camped at Santa Marta and commenced their forward movement soon after midnight; his army took between five and six hours to cover the 20km distance. Werlé formed the reserve, and his brigade was the last to arrive at around 0730 hours. Soult had resolved to undertake a left flanking manoeuvre and not to attack the town from the east as Beresford's deployment had expected. His intelligence had estimated that Blake was still a day's march from union with Beresford and his flanking manoeuvre was designed to get in behind Beresford and cut off his line of retreat, whilst at the same time cutting Blake's line of advance. Despite the exposed redeployment of Blake's force in the early morning, it appears that Soult

remained unaware that the Spanish had arrived when he commenced his plan.[15] The approaches for the flanking formations were in dead ground and wooded; grey overcast skies and limited visibility complemented to maximise surprise. By way of deception, Soult resolved to feint a frontal attack against the town from the east, which commenced at around 0800 hours[16] with an advance by elements of Latour-Maubourg and Bron de Bailly's cavalry probing across the river just south of the main bridge, supported by two horse artillery batteries. The counter-battery fire and charges by the Allied cavalry[17] finally forced this group to retreat, but not before they had bought time for Godinot to move his brigade into position and begin attacking the bridge and the line of German skirmishers on the far bank. To the north, Briche's light cavalry were making demonstrations against Otway's cavalry on the far bank and protecting Godinot's right flank. Godinot soon captured the bridge but his infantrymen were coming under sustained fire from Arriaga's Battery of nine-pounders, which had been well sited by Dickson. Nevertheless, from the French perspective, the feint appeared to be working; Beresford's attention was firmly fixed in this direction and he began to move Campbell and Colborne's brigades closer to the town. However, Colborne soon found himself in range of the French guns and Dickson moved Braun's guns to join those of Arriaga, while Hartmann sent forward Hawker and Lefebure to assist in the countering the French artillery.

Fortunately for the Allies, not all eyes were trained east; Colonel von Schepeler, a Brunswick-Oel officer attached to Zayas's headquarters, suspected deception and the unmistakable glint of French bayonets heading through the woods to the south was enough to convince the German of Soult's real intentions. Girard, in overall command of this flanking manoeuvre, had his own and Gazan's infantry divisions and was supported by Latour-Maubourg and the rest of the cavalry (except Briche's Brigade), while Werlé formed the reserve. Once informed, Beresford immediately grasped Soult's intent and, without delay, he set about realigning his force to meet this new threat. He sought Blake and tasked him to pivot on his current position and face south; in turn Stewart was to vacate his position and move south to support the Spanish, and finally Hamilton was to move down and occupy the positions vacated by Stewart's brigades. Cole was to remain in place holding open the line of retreat, should this be required.

Soult had accompanied the flanking force and, although he could see the Spanish to his front, he was not concerned. His recent experiences at the battle of Gévora generated an optimism of his being able to sweep them up in much the same manner. There was ample time for the Allies to reorganize to meet this unexpected change but Blake hesitated, unconvinced that the frontal attack to the east of the town was not the main effort.[18] He ordered Zayas to

---

13 Most likely only Otway's cavalry, as Hamilton's troops were in dead ground.

14 Dempsey, *Albuera 1811*, p.86 from Lapène, *Conquête*, p.150.

15 Ibid, p.95.

16 Although, Latour-Maubourg records the fighting as having commenced with this cavalry action at 0700.

17 Long had disregarded a direct order by D'Urban to stand the cavalry down when Blake's forces were in place. D'Urban had led the 4th Dragoons to the rear but Long had held the 3rd Dragoon Guards near Arriaga's Battery and posted the 13th Light Dragoons to the right of the Spanish line. His actions were prudent given the opening French moves but his insubordination was the final straw for Beresford, who removed him and handed command of the cavalry to Lumley.

18 He could still see Werlé in support of Godinot and three French batteries as well as Bron's dragoons.

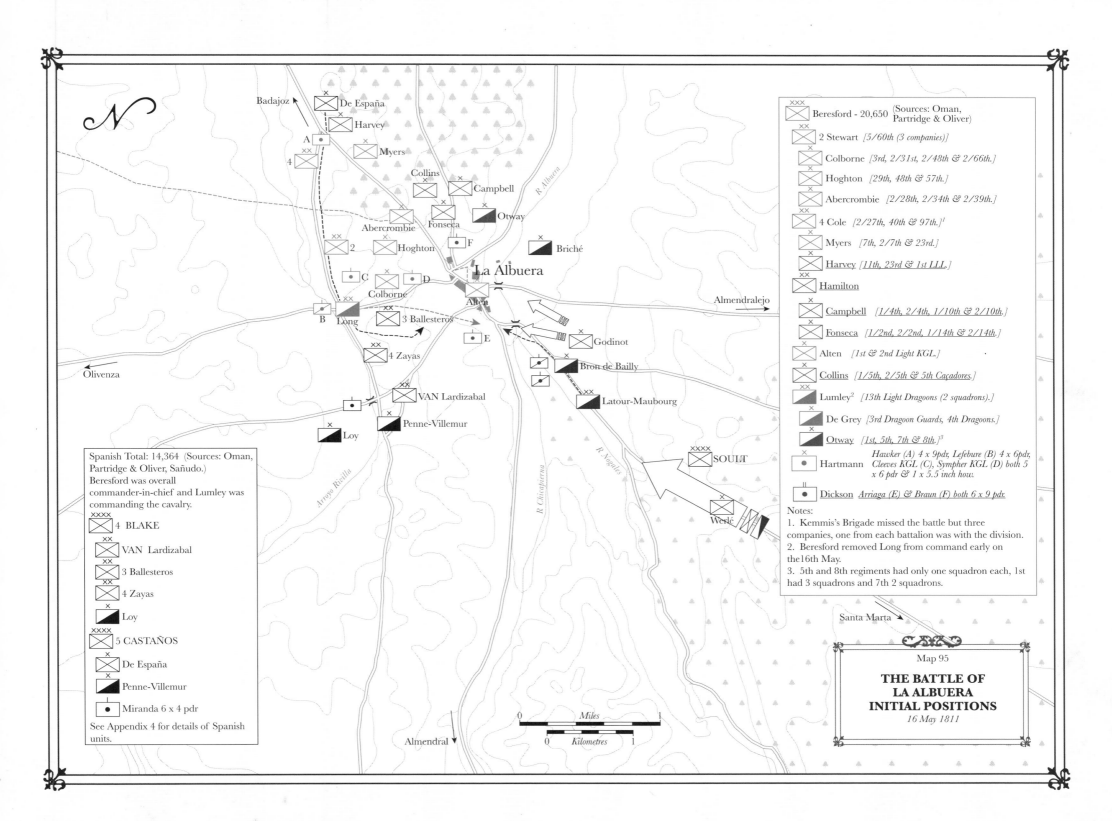

N

Badajoz

De España
Harvey
A
4
Myers
Collins
Campbell
Abercrombie
Fonseca
Otway
Hoghton
F
Briché
2
La Albuera
C
D
Colborne
Alten
B Long
3 Ballesteros
Almendralejo
E
4 Zayas
Godinot
Olivenza
Bron de Bailly
VAN Lardizabal
Latour-Maubourg
Penne-Villemur
SOULT
Loy

R. Albuera

R. Nogales

R. Chicapierna

Arroyo Rivilla

Santa Marta

Almendral

Werlé

Spanish Total: 14,364 (Sources: Oman, Partridge & Oliver, Sañudo.) Beresford was overall commander-in-chief and Lumley was commanding the cavalry.

4 BLAKE	
VAN Lardizabal	
3 Ballesteros	
4 Zayas	
Loy	
5 CASTAÑOS	
De España	
Penne-Villemur	
Miranda 6 x 4 pdr	

See Appendix 4 for details of Spanish units.

Beresford - 20,650 (Sources: Oman, Partridge & Oliver)

2 Stewart [5/60th (3 companies)]
Colborne [3rd, 2/31st, 2/48th & 2/66th.]
Hoghton [29th, 48th & 57th.]
Abercrombie [2/28th, 2/34th & 2/39th.]
4 Cole [2/27th, 40th & 97th.][1]
Myers [7th, 2/7th & 23rd.]
Harvey [11th, 23rd & 1st LLL.]
Hamilton
Campbell [1/4th, 2/4th, 1/10th & 2/10th.]
Fonseca [1/2nd, 2/2nd, 1/14th & 2/14th.]
Alten [1st & 2nd Light KGL.]
Collins [1/5th, 2/5th & 5th Caçadores.]
Lumley[2] [13th Light Dragoons (2 squadrons).]
De Grey [3rd Dragoon Guards, 4th Dragoons.]
Otway [1st, 5th, 7th & 8th.][3]
Hartmann Hawker (A) 4 x 9pdr, Lefebure (B) 4 x 6pdr, Cleeves KGL (C), Sympher KGL (D) both 5 x 6 pdr & 1 x 5.5 inch how.
Dickson Arriaga (E) & Braun (F) both 6 x 9 pdr.

Notes:
1. Kemmis's Brigade missed the battle but three companies, one from each battalion was with the division.
2. Beresford removed Long from command early on the 16th May.
3. 5th and 8th regiments had only one squadron each, 1st had 3 squadrons and 7th 2 squadrons.

Map 95

THE BATTLE OF LA ALBUERA INITIAL POSITIONS
16 May 1811

pivot one brigade only and sent an aide-de-camp to seek clarification from Beresford.[19] Meanwhile, Beresford had arrived back on the Spanish position and was angered that his orders had not been carried out. Failing to find Blake, he set about reorganizing the Spanish force as the first French infantry began to appear 2km to the south. Beresford stayed long enough to satisfy himself that the Spanish would reform in time and then turned his mount north to hurry Stewart's reinforcements. Girard's Division led the attack in *ordre mixte* with a battalion column on either flank, with a further battalion in line leading to a central column of four battalions in column of divisions (or double companies – see map 96). The strong French skirmish line advanced and they were surprised to see the Spanish respond by deploying a skirmish line of their own. The Spanish remained steady and traded fire with their French counterparts, who were unnerved by this unexpected response and were then thrown back as Ballesteros executed controlled bayonet charges. Soon afterwards the 5th Corps artillery (three field batteries) arrived and began to open heavy and accurate fire on the Spanish line; Miranda's battery did their best to respond while they waited for Hartmann's reorganization of the Allied artillery to bring them badly needed support. Suddenly the French line of tirailleurs dramatically parted and Girard's main body, attacking *ordre mixte*, passed through the gap with every confidence that Spanish resolve would now evaporate. The distance closed and, at 50m, the Spanish fired as one along their line, bringing the French advance to an instant halt. Both sides were soon taking heavy casualties.

Cleeves's Battery was the first of the artillery support to arrive, and it deployed on Zayas's right flank as the infantry of Colborne's Brigade followed closely behind. The 3rd Foot were the first infantry battalion up and they deployed to right of the regiment of Irlanda. This additional weight of musket and canister fire on the flank of the French broke the French left wing. The Buffs then advanced towards the retreating French, unaware that Latour-Maubourg had ordered the Polish Lancers to charge the British in the flank and rear. The Poles caught the Buffs completely by surprise; in no-man's land, in haphazard fashion and, unable to form square in defence against the 'merciless' Poles,[20] the battalion was destroyed in minutes. The rampant lancers then continued through Cleeves's Battery and on to the other two battalions.[21] Lumley ordered the 4th Dragoons, supported by two Spanish squadrons, to counter the lancers and they succeeded in driving off the Poles, but had to retreat when they themselves were counter-attacked by the 2e Hussars, who were up in support. Towards the tail end of this bloody encounter a heavy spring shower lashed the combatants and, as it passed, Hoghton arrived to the rear of Zayas and soldiers of the 29th and 57th began to fire at the milling lancers who were circling the remnants of Colborne's Brigade. Unfortunately, some of their shots hit the backs of the Spaniards still facing their front

and engaging the French infantry.[22] The lancers rode off through the rear lines of Zayas, brushing aside the Spanish general and his aides, before coming face-to-face with Beresford and his staff who had to make a fight of it before the Poles rode off.

Subsequent to this withdrawal and the arrival of Stewart's other two brigades, the battle slackened. Girard's front line was badly mauled following Colborne's flank attack, but the French general was of the opinion that the Allied readjustment heralded the start of the Allied collapse and he called forward Gazan's battalions in columns to resume the offensive. However, this took an inordinate amount of time, as the French columns had great difficulty getting into position through the field festooned with dead and dying, and the Allies took full opportunity of this respite to reorganize their own defences. The Spanish infantry, who had fought so valiantly and suffered numerous casualties, now pulled back to allow the fresh troops to take up the line.[23] In the process of this passage of lines, the French skirmishers temporarily took the higher ground as it was evacuated, but they withdrew again as Abercrombie and Hoghton's brigades marched forward into position. At the same time the French completed their own readjustment and with Gazan's men now to the front, the signal was given for the advance and they closed on the British lines. 'In a few minutes nearly all officers were killed or wounded. It had been necessary to spread out to answer his two by two fires [deployment and fire by line], but the two French divisions were too close together and it was impossible to manoeuvre, and they were obliged to withdraw for to remain taking the destructive fire of the fusillades was useless.'[24]

Hoghton advanced down the rise to within 20m of the French lines and occasionally a battalion attempted to charge, but the French were unable to move, so dense were their formations. Hoghton was also well aware of the massed French cavalry to his flank and could not afford to overextend his Brigade. The result was an exchange of fire, at murderously close range, which went on for many minutes.[25] Stewart was injured, Hoghton killed and his place taken by Inglis of the 57th who instructed his battalion to 'Die hard, 57th, die hard!' before succumbing to the effects of French canister. 'The Die Hards' had lost their commanding officer and the other two-battalion commanders were wounded. The French, if anything, were suffering worse: Pepin had been killed and Maransin and Sylvester-Brayer wounded, along with another 115 officers in both divisions. With the battle in stalemate both commanders had little choice but to deploy their reserves, both realizing this was the last throw of their dice. Beresford's dilemma was that he did not want to use Cole; he appeared to have lost sight of Hamilton's Division and had no contact with Blake. In an attempt to move some Spanish battalions back to assist Hoghton's battalions he clumsily tried to do so himself instead of

---

19 Napier has accused Blake of insubordination but Dempsey, *Albuera 1811*, p.107, offers a logical explanation in that Blake was genuinely unsure and, given the delay in the French flanking movement and the fact that they were in dead ground after crossing the ford, he wanted to wait to be sure.

20 Who have been accused of giving no quarter; a sentiment the British declared would therefore apply to the Poles in future engagements.

21 The 2/48th and 2/66th: the 2/31st was still en route.

22 Realizing the error, both the commanding officer of the 57th, Lieutenant Colonel Inglis and one of Beresford's aides-de-camp, Major Arbuthnot, rode at great risk in front of the 57th and 29th respectively, shouting at the troops to cease their fire.

23 Some of the Spanish officers made it quite clear to the British as they passed that they were only falling back because they were ordered to – Napier, unfortunately, despite not being at La Albuera, writes that 'the Spanish line fell back in disorder,' *History of the War in the Peninsula*, vol. III, p.561.

24 Thiers, *Histoire du Consulat et du Empire*, vol. XII, pp.689–690.

25 It is estimated that this standoff lasted about an hour.

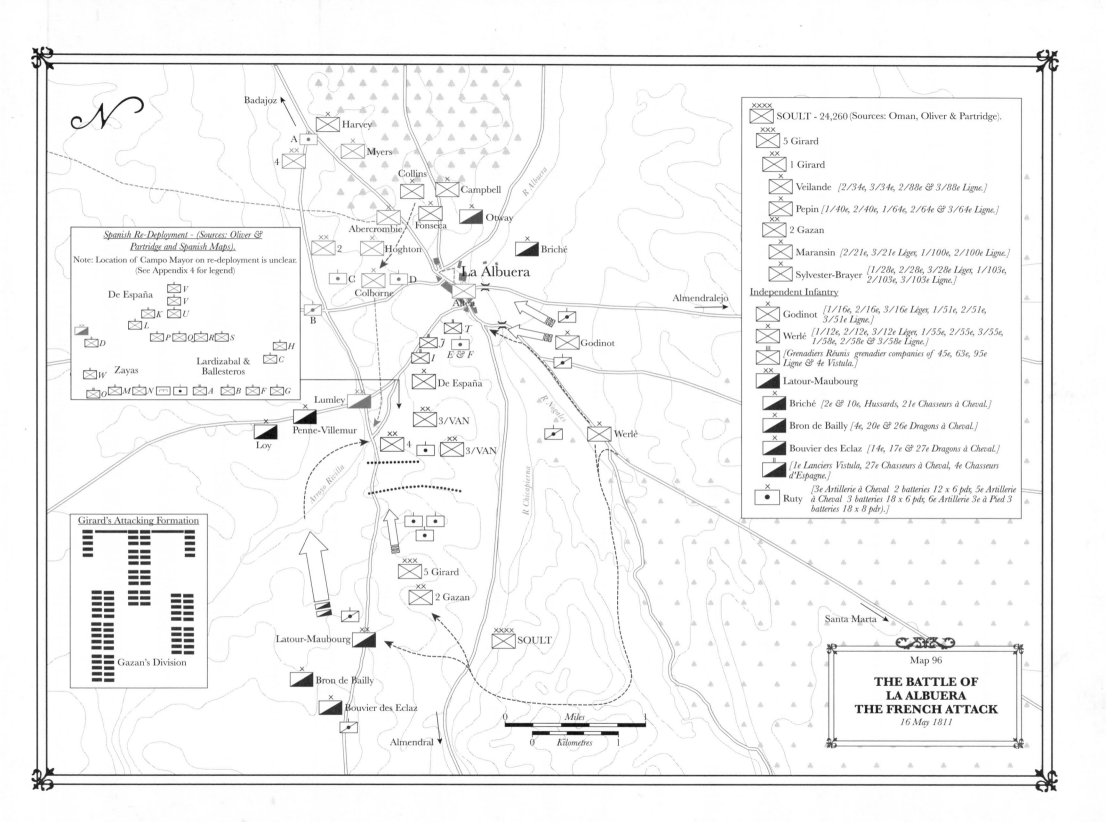

N

Badajoz ↑

Harvey

A •

4

Myers

Collins

Campbell

Abercrombie

Fonseca

Otway

R. Albuera

Briché

Spanish Re-Deployment - (Sources: Oliver &
Partridge and Spanish Maps).

Note: Location of Campo Mayor on re-deployment is unclear.
(See Appendix 4 for legend)

De España — V
— V

K U
L

P Q R S

D

Lardizabal &
Ballesteros

H
C

Zayas

W

O M N • A B F G

2

Hoghton

C D

Colborne

B

La Albuera

Aljea

T

J

E & F

I

Almendralejo →

Godinot

De España

Lumley

Penne-Villemur

Loy

3/VAN

4

3/VAN

R. Nogales

Werlé

R. Chicapierna

Girard's Attacking Formation

Gazan's Division

5 Girard

2 Gazan

Latour-Maubourg

Bron de Bailly

Bouvier des Eclaz

Almendral ↓

Santa Marta →

SOULT

0   Miles   1

0   Kilometres   1

SOULT - 24,260 (Sources: Oman, Oliver & Partridge).

5 Girard

1 Girard

Veilande *[2/34e, 3/34e, 2/88e & 3/88e Ligne.]*

Pepin *[1/40e, 2/40e, 1/64e, 2/64e & 3/64e Ligne.]*

2 Gazan

Maransin *[2/21e, 3/21e Léger, 1/100e, 2/100e Ligne.]*

Sylvester-Brayer *[1/28e, 2/28e, 3/28e Léger, 1/103e,*
2/103e, 3/103e Ligne.]

Independent Infantry

Godinot *[1/16e, 2/16e, 3/16e Léger, 1/51e, 2/51e,*
3/51e Ligne.]

Werlé *[1/12e, 2/12e, 3/12e Léger, 1/55e, 2/55e, 3/55e,*
1/58e, 2/58e & 3/58e Ligne.]

[Grenadiers Réunis grenadier companies of 45e, 63e, 95e
Ligne & 4e Vistula.]

Latour-Maubourg

Briché *[2e & 10e, Hussards, 21e Chasseurs à Cheval.]*

Bron de Bailly *[4e, 20e & 26e Dragons à Cheval.]*

Bouvier des Eclaz *[14e, 17e & 27e Dragons à Cheval.]*

[1e Lanciers Vistula, 27e Chasseurs à Cheval, 4e Chasseurs
d'Espagne.]

Ruty *[3e Artillerie à Cheval 2 batteries 12 x 6 pdr, 5e Artillerie*
à Cheval 3 batteries 18 x 6 pdr, 6e Artillerie 3e à Pied 3
batteries 18 x 8 pdr).]

Map 96

THE BATTLE OF
LA ALBUERA
THE FRENCH ATTACK
16 May 1811

seeking one of their general officers. When this failed, he rode off in search of Hamilton[26] and found him near the village of Albuera where he had moved to extend support to the KGL. With the Allied command in confusion, the opportunity seemed ripe for a final French attack with Werlé's Brigade supported by the numerically superior cavalry, but Soult was about to make a different deduction. He wrote in his dispatch, 'When I ascended the heights … I was surprised to see such large numbers of troops. Shortly thereafter, I was to learn from a Spanish prisoner that Blake had already joined Beresford … and I resolved to give up my original plan and hold the ground already won.' This seems strange, as he had spent many hours fighting a large Spanish force, which can only have been that of Blake. Furthermore, his decision to cling to the small depression in which his two divisions were jammed, overlooked by two occupied hills, in the belief that this was ground worth holding is extraordinary for a man of Soult's calibre. From this point on the French were to fight a defensive not an offensive battle.

Notwithstanding this decision, Gazan's men were slowly gaining the upper hand, supported by sustained fire from Ruty's three field batteries to the rear right. Colonel Hardinge[27] grew increasingly alarmed at the situation and in the absence of Beresford decided that something had to be done to resolve the situation, and consequently he rode to Cole to seek his support. Cole faced a dilemma; he could see the battle from his position and he could ascertain that the 2nd Division were losing the fight, but nevertheless he had clear orders from Beresford to keep open the line of withdrawal. He rode to Lumley and discussed a plan to advance together, then returned to issue orders for the 4th Division to advance. Beresford, who was still searching for Hamilton,[28] now witnessed the 4th Division marching south contrary to his orders. Beresford, fearing for his line of withdrawal, now ordered Alten to fall back out of the village, Collins to take Cole's place and for Dickson to pull back his two batteries north on the Badajoz road. Soult also witnessed the advance of the Allied 4th Division and realized that he too would have to commit his reserve in conjunction with his cavalry to prevent losing the advantage.

He ordered Werlé to advance and for Latour-Maubourg to attack Cole's lines. Loy, who was in front of Cole's advance, gave way but the French cavalry were unable to make inroads into the Allied lines. Werlé's Brigade arrived and replaced the French cavalry, deploying in regimental columns of divisions;[29] the brigade advanced and another musketry duel commenced at short range. However, at this point the Spanish, who had time to recover, now advanced and Abercrombie's Brigade was able to move slightly around the French left flank[30] and Hamilton

sent Fonseca's Brigade in support. At much the same time Alten was sent back into the village. The pendulum was swinging back in favour of the Allies. Myers's Brigade continued to advance and eventually Werlé's formation gave way. The sight of their comrades falling back and of the continued reinforcement of the Allied lines was too much for Gazan and Girard's exhausted infantry, and they too followed their colleagues. Soult looked on incredulously; he had been on the verge of victory with the Allies beaten, but they just did not seem to realize it and now his army was fleeing from the field. He now had to stabilize the situation. The artillery and cavalry, along with the grenadiers, were ordered to hold the line and prevent any attempt to turn the withdrawal into a rout. The bloodiest battle of the war had been fought with losses that neither side could afford. Numbers are irrelevant; the gallant French 5th Corps was in ruins, the courageous brigades of Colborne, Hoghton and Myers were decimated and Zayas's glorious Spaniards rendered inoperable. Criticism of Beresford is equally inappropriate; he won the battle. He was more aware than any historian that the price was high, too high. He was to write to Wellington following the battle in a clear state of depression; he more than anyone else realized the human cost of the Allied victory on the hills south of La Albuera that day.

Soult remained on 17 May purely to arrange transport for the wounded and before dawn on 18 May he began his withdrawal over the Sierra Morena. Beresford sent the cavalry to pursue the French, more by way of maintaining visibility on their movements than in any offensive manner, while at the same time despatching Hamilton and Madden back to Badajoz to re-invest the fortification. To the north, following victory at Fuentes de Oñoro in early May and the escape of the French garrison at Almeida early in the morning of 11 May, Wellington decided to march south once again, this time taking the 3rd and 7th divisions with their integral artillery, to resolve matters in Estremadura.[31] He arrived at Elvas on 19 May and, though devastated at the losses at La Albuera, he was nevertheless relatively sanguine with the situation as he found it. The battle had been won, Soult was heading south and Badajoz was encircled. However, the depth of feeling regarding Beresford was such that Wellington could not ignore it. An opportunistic solution was at hand; Hill had returned from sick leave and was expected at the front within days, and reports from Lisbon of administrative difficulties with the Portuguese authorities required careful but firm handling, a task with which Beresford could be trusted. Hill arrived on 27 May and the change of command was swift: Beresford left for Lisbon the following day. In the interim Wellington had been keen to increase the pressure on Soult who had extracted his army with consummate ease and no little skill. The French were, however, forced to leave behind many sick and wounded both at La Albuera and en route. Beresford had sent a message to Phillipon at Badajoz requesting his assistance; the response was a harsh reminder of the nature of the man governing the southern gate to Spain; 'We can't, and thus they must perish.'

Leaving the 2nd and 4th divisions to recuperate as best they could, Wellington assumed responsibility for the siege; the 3rd and 7th divisions joined Hamilton's Portuguese Division,[32] the former taking responsibility for the north bank and the Fort San Cristobal and the latter two

---

26   He had sent one of his aides-de-camp, Colonel Arbuthnot, to give instructions to Hamilton to come forward, but he could not find him in his original position.

27   Colonel Sir Henry Hardinge, the Deputy Quartermaster General of the Portuguese army. He had served on Sir John Moore's staff in the campaign at the end of 1808. His action that day was controversial but, as ever, fortune favoured the bold.

28   It seems extraordinary on a relatively flat and featureless area that he was unable to locate Hamilton or any of his command group.

29   Providing three columns, each with a two-company frontage and a depth of nine companies.

30   This was due to the fact that Latour-Maubourg withdrew Bron de Bailly's cavalry from the French right, providing Abercrombie greater freedom of movement.

31   Spencer was left in command in the north with strict instructions to maintain a defensive posture.

32   Houston's Division arrived on 25 May and Picton's Division two days later.

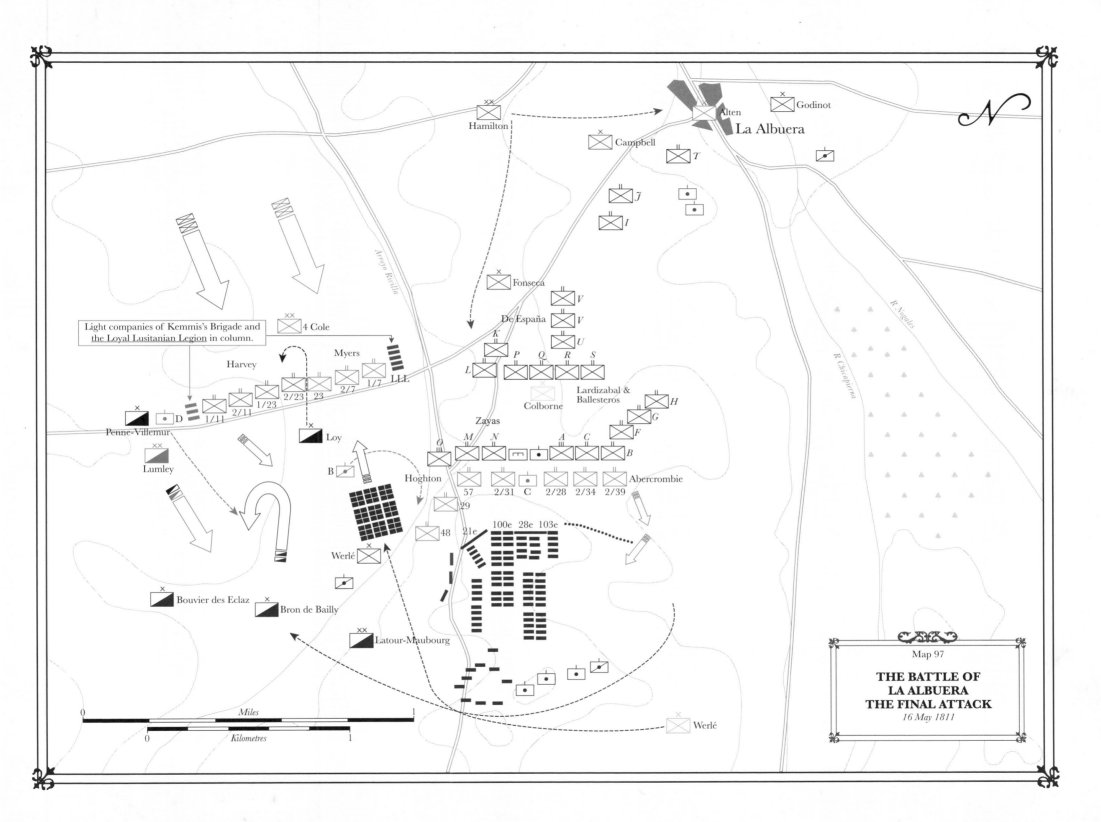

Light companies of Kemmis's Brigade and the Loyal Lusitanian Legion in column.

Harvey

Myers

4 Cole

LLL

Penne-Villemur

D

1/11   2/11   1/23   2/23   23   2/7   1/7

Loy

Lumley

B

Hoghton

Werlé

Bouvier des Eclaz

Bron de Bailly

Latour-Maubourg

Hamilton

Campbell

La Albuera

Alten

Godinot

T

J

I

Fonseca

De España

V

V

U

Colborne

Lardizabal & Ballesteros

H

G

F

Zayas

K

L   P   Q   R   S

O   M   N   A   C   B

57   2/31   C   2/28   2/34   2/39   Abercrombie

29

48   21e   100e   28e   103e

Werlé

Map 97

**THE BATTLE OF
LA ALBUERA
THE FINAL ATTACK**
16 May 1811

Miles

0   1

Kilometres

0   1

Arroyo Rivilla

R. Nogales

R. Chicapierna

formations, the south bank and the main fortress. Fletcher was once again the chief engineer and Dickson the artillery commander. The engineer plan remained ostensibly the same as that adopted earlier in the month, with the exception that the attacks on the south side would not be a ruse, but a serious attempt to breach the main fort; they would concentrate on the castle itself. The ground to the north, on the Cerro San Cristobal, was worse than before as Phillipon had removed the small amount of topsoil that existed, leaving only exposed rock. 'The sites of batteries 1, 2 and 3 were so rocky, that their terreplein could not be sunken except by the miners: every exertion had been used throughout the night to bring soil for their parapets from the rear, but it being 10 p.m. before the parties were fully at work, and day beginning to dawn at half-past 3 a.m., the interval of obscurity did not suffice to raise the solid mass of those batteries more than two feet.'[33] While the unhappy soldiers of the 7th Division tried to build up rather than dig down, Dickson had been busy establishing a large siege train from Elvas consisting of 46 guns.[34]

The French guns opened the next morning, knocking down the gabions and exposing the workforce behind who were then picked off by musket fire. Wellington resolved this by ordering wool-packs to be placed to absorb the round shot, but this merely resulted in the French using mortars to lob the shells, which they did with considerable accuracy. However, by the morning of 3 June batteries were ready to open at both locations. It took the gunners some time to compensate for the intricacies and irregularities of the 17th-century ordnance and in time they began having an effect on both the castle walls and the fort, but they were suffering badly from the accurate counter-battery fire. On the second day they fared little better and the end of the daylight left only 13 of the 20 guns serviceable. 'The failure of the old brass pieces was becoming so alarming that an interval of seven to eight minutes was ordered between each round, to give the metal time to cool.'[35]

By the afternoon on 6 June the breach on the north wall of the Fort San Cristobal was considered serviceable and the assault was delivered at midnight. It failed, as the ditch behind the counterscarp was far deeper than envisaged and, after an hour of trying, the assault was called off. Fletcher decided to batter the walls for a few days more and when six iron 24-pounder guns arrived from Lisbon, these were placed in Battery 7 in an attempt to make some headway on the castle walls, which were proving very resistant. Three days later the engineers conceded that an assault on the castle walls was still some way off, but they considered the fort to be worthy of a renewed attempt. That night the 7th Division delivered its second assault, but it was to suffer the same fate as the earlier attempt. The next day, with news of Marmont's southerly movement and no prospect of a rapid improvement, Wellington called off the siege and made preparations to move his force to defensive positions east of the Guadiana.

---

33   Jones, *Journal of Sieges*, vol. I, pp.38–39.

34   Most of these pieces were 17th-century brass guns that were to prove inadequate for the task ahead.

---

35   Jones, *Journal of Sieges*, vol. I, p.46.

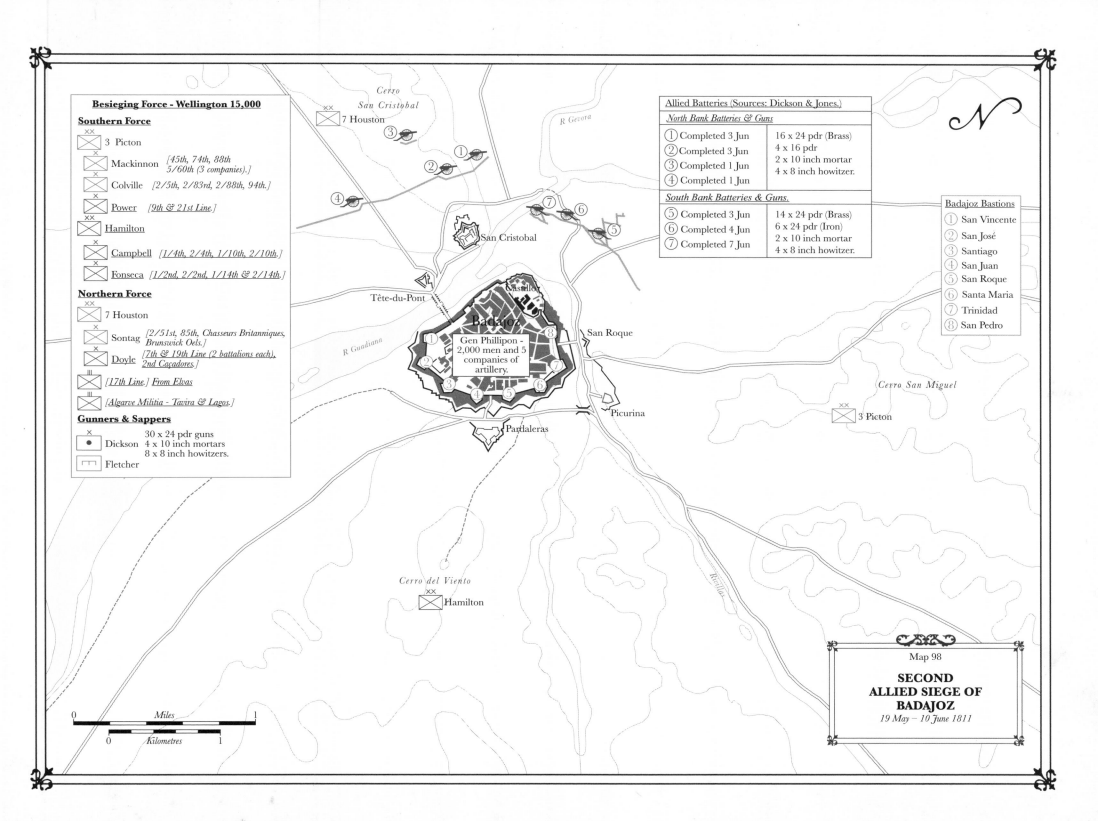

Besieging Force - Wellington 15,000

Southern Force

⊠⊠ 3 Picton

⊠ Mackinnon *[45th, 74th, 88th 5/60th (3 companies).]*

⊠ Colville *[2/5th, 2/83rd, 2/88th, 94th.]*

⊠ Power *[9th & 21st Line.]*

⊠⊠ Hamilton

⊠ Campbell *[1/4th, 2/4th, 1/10th, 2/10th.]*

⊠ Fonseca *[1/2nd, 2/2nd, 1/14th & 2/14th.]*

Northern Force

⊠⊠ 7 Houston

⊠ Sontag *[2/51st, 85th, Chasseurs Britanniques, Brunswick Oels.]*

⊠ Doyle *[7th & 19th Line (2 battalions each), 2nd Caçadores.]*

⊠ *[17th Line.] From Elvas*

⊠ *[Algarve Militia - Tavira & Lagos.]*

Gunners & Sappers

⊠ Dickson — 30 x 24 pdr guns / 4 x 10 inch mortars / 8 x 8 inch howitzers.

⊡ Fletcher

Allied Batteries (Sources: Dickson & Jones.)

North Bank Batteries & Guns

① Completed 3 Jun	16 x 24 pdr (Brass)
② Completed 3 Jun	4 x 16 pdr
③ Completed 1 Jun	2 x 10 inch mortar
④ Completed 1 Jun	4 x 8 inch howitzer.

South Bank Batteries & Guns.

⑤ Completed 3 Jun	14 x 24 pdr (Brass)
⑥ Completed 4 Jun	6 x 24 pdr (Iron)
⑦ Completed 7 Jun	2 x 10 inch mortar
	4 x 8 inch howitzer.

Badajoz Bastions

① San Vincente
② San José
③ Santiago
④ San Juan
⑤ San Roque
⑥ Santa Maria
⑦ Trinidad
⑧ San Pedro

Cerro San Cristobal

7 Houston

R Gevora

San Cristobal

Tête-du-Pont

Castillo

Badajoz

Gen Phillipon - 2,000 men and 5 companies of artillery.

R Guadiana

San Roque

Cerro San Miguel

3 Picton

Picurina

Pardaleras

Rivillas

Cerro del Viento

Hamilton

Map 98

SECOND ALLIED SIEGE OF BADAJOZ

19 May – 10 June 1811

Miles 0 — 1

Kilometres 0 — 1

Chapter 33 ⊶╪⊶

THE WATERSHED: MID-1811

At 2200 hours on 7 May, three bursts of artillery fire at five-minute intervals were heard from the ramparts of Almeida. Wellington and his men had no idea that this was Brennier's signal to Masséna confirming receipt of his orders to escape. Masséna had steadily moved back his force since his distressing defeat at Fuentes de Oñoro, and he now received the confirmation he required to complete the task. With the defeated Army of Portugal in retreat, Wellington laid plans to invest Almeida, but Brennier had other intentions. On the night of 10 May his garrison, which numbered about 1,300 men, rushed out of the northern gate in two columns and stormed the Allied lines, manned at this point by the 1st Portuguese of Pack's Brigade. They pierced the line with ease and made good their escape. Five minutes later massive explosions rocked the structure as the mines on time fuses erupted, and although some on the south side failed to detonate it was of little consequence; the fort was wrecked and Wellington could barely contain his fury. He labelled the debacle as the 'most disgraceful military event' involving the British army in the Peninsula.

Masséna's satisfaction at extracting Brennier was short-lived, for within days the considerably younger Marshal Marmont had arrived to replace him. Armed with Napoleonic directives to reorganize the structure of the Army of Portugal he wasted little time in dismantling the corps structure and sending home the two surplus commanders (Junot and Loison) who took many of their divisional generals with them. He stripped out Drouet's 9th Corps and, as instructed, sent this general with the remainder south to support Soult. Six infantry divisions were created and new commanders were appointed, supported by a cavalry division and three brigades (see Appendix 4). By 25 May the army already numbered nearly 30,000 men, although the familiar shortages of suitable mounts severely restricted the effectiveness of both the cavalry and artillery. The news of the defeat at La Albuera convinced Marmont to march south with his entire force in support of his colleague, in a display of solidarity typically lacking in Napoleon's Peninsular lieutenants. By early June Marmont was moving with some speed to thrust back the weak holding force under General Spencer while the balance of his force headed south. Spencer was caught off-guard and pulled back to Alfayates, and at this point Marmont marched off to rejoin his main body, crossing the Tagus at Almaraz, while Spencer headed south on Wellington's instructions to concentrate the Anglo-Portuguese army as the southern force withdrew from Badajoz to Elvas.

Drouet's small corps arrived at Sevilla on 13 June and the infantry were quickly redistributed to the 1st and 5th corps,[1] and the cavalry was likewise formed as the 3rd and 4th squadrons of dragoon regiments in the cavalry division and the brigades of the Army of the South. Soult now had 28,000 men under arms and within a week he would have a combined force of more than twice that number. Soult and Marmont met at Mérida on 18 June and the two commanders made plans to march west. By the evening of 19 June it was clear that the Allies had retreated over the Guadiana, and Marmont entered Badajoz in triumph. News that Spencer had joined Wellington dissolved French intentions of attacking the Anglo-Portuguese force. This defensive stance marked the watershed in the war. In the words of Oman, 'The offensive, though it was hardly realized as yet, had passed to Wellington'[2] and the French were to remain on a defensive footing from now until Toulouse in April 1814.

During this manoeuvring, Wellington had convinced Blake to double back and approach Sevilla, which was inadequately protected, by the back door. Blake had 12,000 men but elected to invest the fruitless French garrison in the castle of Niebla and wasted the opportunity. Three days after entering Badajoz, Soult received news of another dangerous development in Andalusia; Freire's Army of Murcia had moved against the 4th Corps. Leaving a small force under Drouet,[3] Soult headed back south, while Marmont stayed to monitor Wellington. But within days rations were running short and Marmont pulled back, leaving a division at Trujillo, while the balance of the army headed back north. Marmont's move south had vacated Leon and Bessières had reluctantly agreed to fill the void, but his force would not be up to full strength until September.

The Army of the North had been created in January 1811 with the aim of pacifying the north of Spain, which included the suppression of organized crime, subjugation of the guerrillas, neutralization of the Spanish armies in Galicia and the Asturias and supporting the Army of Portugal. It was all too much for Bessières, who grew increasingly angry about the ever-growing demands made upon him from Paris, which signified a clear misapprehension of his tasks vis-à-vis his available force and the geographical demands of his area of responsibility. Wellington realized the opportunity and convinced Castaños to urge General Santocildes to capitalize on the situation. His early advances caused Bessières all sorts of problems, but, by the end of July General Abadia had replaced Santocildes and the initiative soon lost momentum. At much the same time, Bessières was recalled to Paris and replaced by General Dorsenne, who immediately set about instigating plans for the invasion of Galicia and the Asturias.

---

1 Most of the units were the 4th battalions from the regiments in these corps.

2 Oman, *History of the Peninsular War*, vol. IV, p.453.

3 The reorganized 5th Corps.

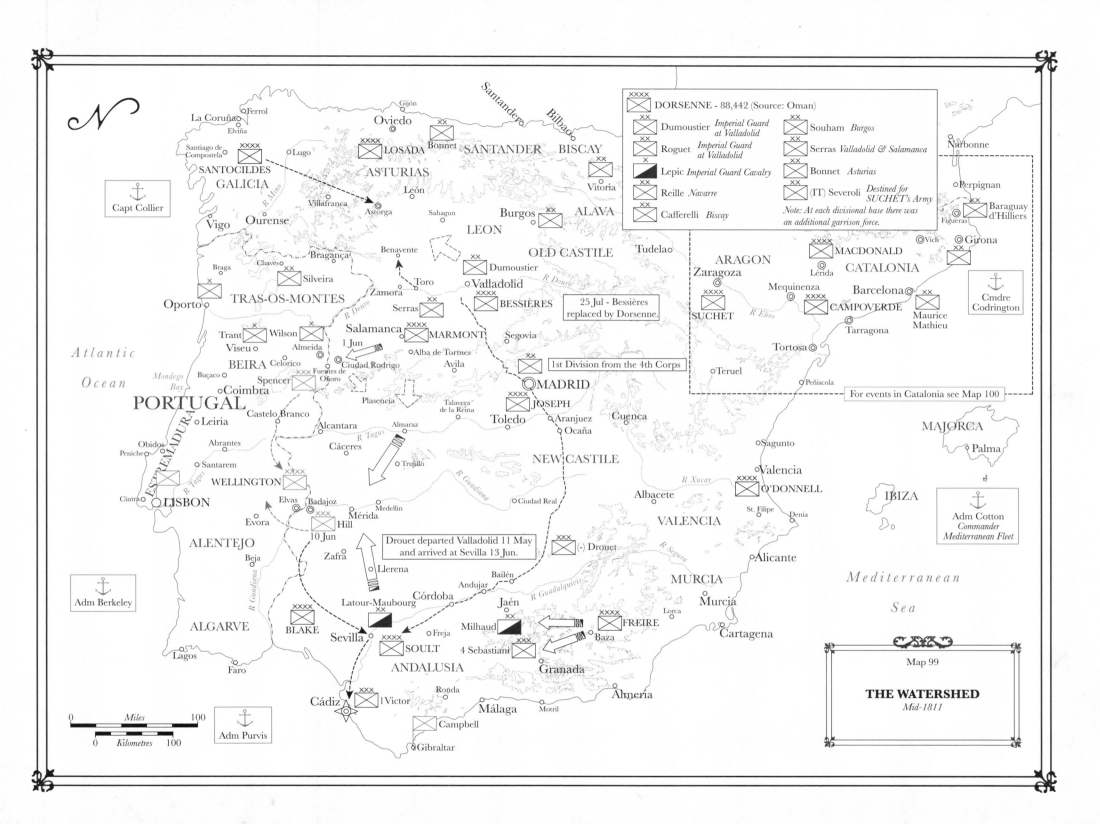

N

Capt Collier

La Coruña   Ferrol
Elviña
Santiago de   Lugo
Compostela
SANTOCILDES
GALICIA
Vigo
Ourense

Gijón
Oviedo
ASTURIAS   LOSADA   Bonnet   SANTANDER   BISCAY
León
Santander   Bilbao
Vitoria
ALAVA
Sahagun   Burgos
LEON   OLD CASTILE   Tudela

DORSENNE - 88,442 (Source: Oman)

Dumoustier   *Imperial Guard at Valladolid*   Souham *Burgos*

Roguet   *Imperial Guard at Valladolid*   Serras *Valladolid & Salamanca*

Lepic *Imperial Guard Cavalry*   Bonnet *Asturias*

Reille *Navarre*   (IT) Severoli   *Destined for SUCHET's Army*

Cafferelli *Biscay*   *Note: At each divisional base there was an additional garrison force.*

Narbonne
Perpignan
Baraguay d'Hilliers
Figueras
Vich   Girona
MACDONALD
CATALONIA
Zaragoza
ARAGON   Lérida
SUCHET   Mequinenza
CAMPOVERDE
Barcelona
Maurice Mathieu
Tarragona
Tortosa
Peñiscola

Cmdre Codrington

Braga   Chaves
Bragança
Silveira
TRAS-OS-MONTES
Oporto
Villafranca
Astorga
Benavente
Toro
Zamora
Serras
Salamanca
MARMONT
1 Jun
Ciudad Rodrigo

Dumoustier
Valladolid   R Douro
BESSIÈRES
Segovia

25 Jul - Bessières replaced by Dorsenne.

1st Division from the 4th Corps

For events in Catalonia see Map 100

Trant   Wilson
Viseu
Almeida
BEIRA   Celorico
Spencer   Fuentes de Oñoro
Buçaco
Coimbra
Alba de Tormes
Avila
MADRID
JOSEPH
Toledo
Aranjuez
Ocaña
Cuenca
NEW CASTILE

Atlantic Ocean

Mondego Bay

PORTUGAL
Leiria
Castelo Branco
Alcantara
Cáceres
Plasencia
Talavera de la Reina

Obidos   Abrantes
Peniche   Santarem
WELLINGTON
Cintra   LISBON
Elvas   Badajoz
Evora   Hill   Mérida   Medellin
10 Jun
Zafra
ALENTEJO
Beja

Almaraz
Trujillo
R Tagus
R Guadiana
Ciudad Real

MAJORCA
Palma

Sagunto
Valencia
O'DONNELL
Albacete
VALENCIA
St. Filipe   Denia
IBIZA

Adm Cotton
Commander Mediterranean Fleet

Drouet departed Valladolid 11 May and arrived at Sevilla 13 Jun.

Drouet (-)
R Xucar
Alicante
MURCIA
Murcia

Adm Berkeley

ALGARVE
Lagos
Faro

Llerena
Córdoba
Latour-Maubourg
BLAKE
Sevilla
SOULT
ANDALUSIA
Freja

Bailén
Andujar
Jaén
Milhaud
4 Sebastiani
Granada

R Guadalquivir
FREIRE
Baza
Lorca
Cartagena

Mediterranean Sea

Cádiz   1 Victor
Ronda
Málaga   Motril
Campbell
Gibraltar
Almería

0   Miles   100
0   Kilometres   100

Adm Purvis

Map 99

THE WATERSHED
Mid-1811

Chapter 34

FIGUERAS AND TARRAGONA: THE EAST COAST, APRIL TO AUGUST 1811

On the east coast, four days after the fall of Tortosa, the Army of Catalonia had a new captain-general following Henry O'Donnell's retirement on medical grounds. The Marquis of Campoverde's appointment had been characterized by Catalan hostility and the opening foray in January at Pla under General Sarsfield was a positive start, but his subsequent attempt to take Monjuich by a *coup de main* operation was a complete failure. The attacks by the *somatenes* on French convoys passing Girona and Hostalrich were far more effective, but even these were not sufficiently serious to prevent Suchet and Macdonald aborting plans for a combined operation against Tarragona. However, this combined planning was brought to an abrupt halt when Napoleon sent a communiqué on 10 March transferring the three provinces of Lérida, Tarragona and Tortosa, and that of Barcelona east of the Llobregat, to Suchet's command. Macdonald's performance had, like so many of his predecessors, failed to impress the Emperor and his area of responsibility was now restricted to the province of Catalonia (see map 100). Suchet was also to receive the three divisions of the old 7th Corps that were stationed in these areas, namely Frère's French Division, Pino's Italian Division and Compère's Neapolitan Division, raising Suchet's army to about 44,000 men. Even if he had wanted to, Macdonald would no longer be able to provide flank protection to Suchet's operations; instead he was to concentrate on dismantling the *somatenes'* bases at Cardona, Berga and Urgel and rendering them inoperable as a force.

Suchet now made preparations for the defence of Aragon against Mina to the north-west and Villa Campa to the south before marching on Tarragona. Musnier was left at Zaragoza to coordinate the defence with a total of 18 battalions, leaving Suchet a total of 29 battalions[1] for the expeditionary force. Frère and Harispe's divisions commenced from Lérida, while Habert moved from Tortosa with the siege guns and ammunition. It was a calculated risk, for Campoverde was well established in and around Tarragona and had he decided to attack Habert's Division, which had only six battalions, he may well have succeeded in destroying the siege train and delaying any subsequent siege operations against the town for many months.

However, before the movement had commenced, the Spanish had succeeded in retaking the 18th-century fortress of San Fernando, at Figueras, on 9 and 10 April. The operation to recapture the key fortress and vital French staging base was daring in the extreme and a vivid example of the tenacity and courage of the Catalan fighters. Rovira, a *miquelete* chief, contacted three young Catalans who were employed within the confines of the fortress and who passed off as *Afrancesados*; they made copies of the keys to one of the gates. Campoverde was acquainted with the plan and gave it his full backing, offering support should it succeed. On 7 April Rovira collected about 2,000 men east of Figueras at Olot; they marched under cover of night to the walls, where they were met by their compatriots and surprised the garrison of 700 men as they slept. The governor, Brigadier General Guillot, was captured along with 16,000 muskets, around 200 serviceable guns, rations, clothing and a military chest containing 400,000 francs. By dawn the place was entirely in Catalan hands and General Peyri, who was in the town below with his Italian battalion, had no choice but to withdraw.

Macdonald wrote to Suchet, imploring him to return the troops, which had been regrouped under his command. 'My dear general, in the name of public welfare, the service of the emperor requires imperatively and without delay, the most speedy succour, otherwise upper Catalonia is lost.'[2] Suchet was not so sure; the information regarding Figueras had taken 12 days to reach him and it would take the same amount of time again to gather the dispersed 7th Corps units and return them. Already the numbers of defenders within the fort had increased to 3,000 and on 16 April some regulars arrived from Eroles's Division, which was operating to the west. Baraguay d'Hilliers had come with all the men he could spare from Girona, but he was bound to leave behind considerable numbers to counter the increased activity of the *somatenes* at Hostalrich and Girona and the presence of the Royal Navy offshore at Roses. A larger group from Quesnel's Division[3] also joined him, and by 17 April he had collected a force of about 6,500 infantry and 500 cavalry, but he waited for news from Suchet at Lérida before taking the offensive. A further 14,000 men[4] were also on the way from France, sent when Napoleon received news of the disaster at Figueras.

Meanwhile Campoverde had established Courten's Division within Tarragona and departed north on 12 April with Sarsfield's Division and elements of the division of Baron Eroles.[5] On 3 May they encountered the French cordon some kilometres from Figueras, but their attempts to revitalize the defenders were mixed in fortune. They succeeded in getting some badly needed gunner expertise within the walls, but the supplies were lost when d'Hilliers fell upon the flank of the Spanish who had massed their forces to break through the thin line. D'Hilliers had anticipated the move and counter-concentrated his main body and used the cover afforded by the olive groves. Suchet had made up his mind not to march in support of d'Hilliers, but instead decided to make full use of the distraction of Figueras and move forthwith to Tarragona. He left

---

1   Nineteen were French, eight Italian and two Polish.

2   Suchet, *Memoirs of the War with Spain*, vol. II, p.13.

3   This was based at Perpignan and had responsibility for keeping open the border.

4   A division under Plauzonne that included the 3e and 16e Léger, the 11e, 79e and four battalions of the 67e Ligne.

5   The total force included about 6,000 infantry and nearly 1,000 cavalry.

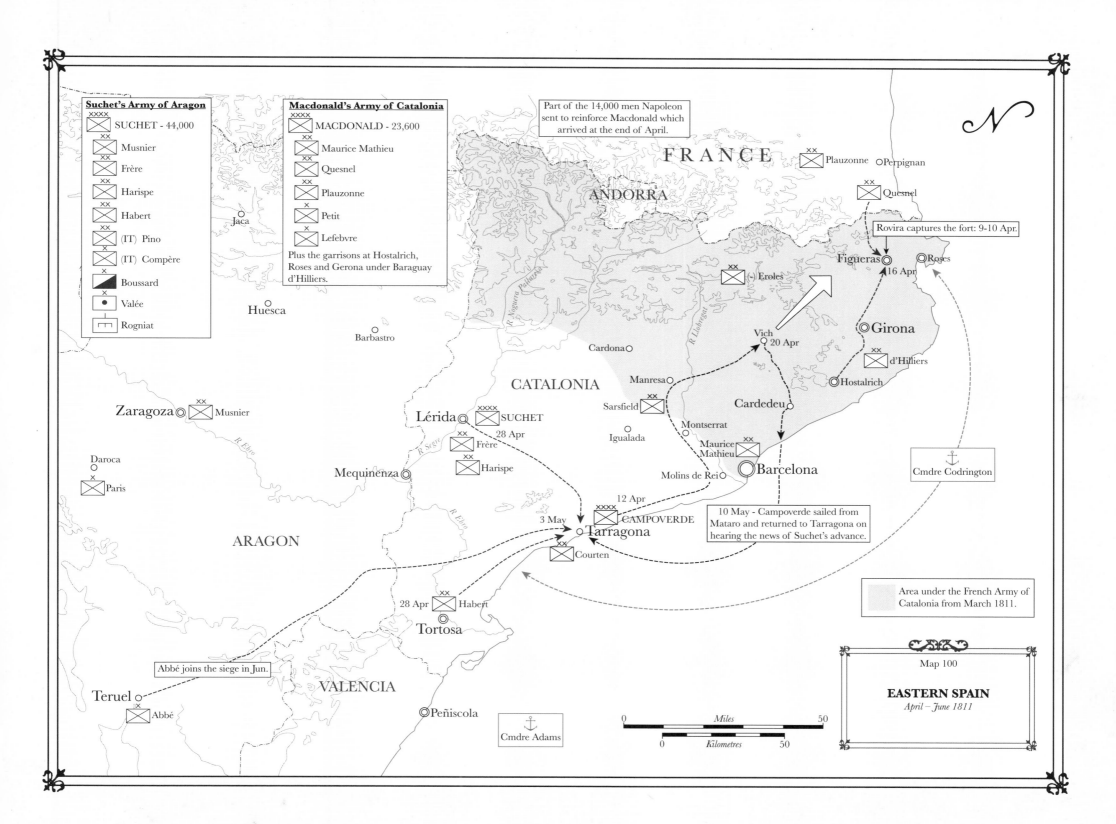

Suchet's Army of Aragon

- SUCHET – 44,000
- Musnier
- Frère
- Harispe
- Habert
- (IT) Pino
- (IT) Compère
- Boussard
- Valée
- Rogniat

Macdonald's Army of Catalonia

- MACDONALD – 23,600
- Maurice Mathieu
- Quesnel
- Plauzonne
- Petit
- Lefebvre

Plus the garrisons at Hostalrich, Roses and Gerona under Baraguay d'Hilliers.

Part of the 14,000 men Napoleon sent to reinforce Macdonald which arrived at the end of April.

Rovira captures the fort: 9-10 Apr.

10 May - Campoverde sailed from Mataro and returned to Tarragona on hearing the news of Suchet's advance.

Abbé joins the siege in Jun.

Cmdre Codrington

Cmdre Adams

Area under the French Army of Catalonia from March 1811.

FRANCE

ANDORRA

CATALONIA

ARAGON

VALENCIA

Plauzonne — Perpignan

Quesnel

Figueras — 16 Apr — Roses

Girona

(-) Eroles

d'Hilliers

Hostalrich

Vich — 20 Apr

Cardedeu

Manresa

Sarsfield

Cardona

Montserrat

Igualada

Maurice Mathieu

Molins de Rei — Barcelona

Jaca

Huesca

Barbastro

Zaragoza — Musnier

Daroca

Paris

Lérida — SUCHET

28 Apr

Frère

Harispe

Mequinenza

12 Apr

CAMPOVERDE

3 May — Tarragona

Courten

28 Apr — Habert

Tortosa

Teruel

Abbé

Peñiscola

N

0   Miles   50

0   Kilometres   50

Map 100

EASTERN SPAIN

April – June 1811

Lérida on 28 April and arrived on the outskirts of the old Roman port on 3 May. Habert had departed Tortosa but was taking longer to arrive than anticipated, harassed by Commodore Codrington's frigates all the way. As soon as Campoverde received word of Suchet's intentions and his southerly movement, he withdrew 4,000 men and embarked from Mataro on 10 May, arriving at Tarragona that evening, while Sarsfield was sent inland to threaten Suchet's interior lines of communication. At Tarragona, Courten had withdrawn his entire division (4,500 men) inside the fortified town to support the garrison (2,500 men) but it was not until 10 May, when Campoverde arrived with his additional 4,000 men, that the extensive walls and outlying fortifications were adequately defended.

While Suchet waited for Habert to arrive, Valée and Rogniat (the artillery and engineer commanders) conducted their reconnaissance and Suchet allocated his infantry to the plethora of tasks to tackle the requirements of the siege, the geography and the threat. His engineer and gunner advisors agreed that an attack from the north was virtually impossible and that one from the east was too problematic, leaving the western approach the most viable. They both agreed that preliminary operations would be required to take Fort Olivo and to drive off the Anglo-Spanish squadron[6] that was operating unhindered in the harbour. Habert was positioned on the right and was to provide protection to the trenching parties, gunners and sappers, while Harispe took the left, leaving Frère in the centre; he was to keep the majority of his division and a squadron of cavalry to act as a mobile reserve to deal with the omnipresent *miquelete* threat.

The naval threat had to be neutralized before the trenching and parallels could commence, so the initial task was to establish a redoubt within which the 24-pounder guns could be placed to drive the shipping out to sea and therefore out of effective range. This was not achieved until 13 May and the first parallel was not started until three days later. With the arrival of Campoverde's reinforcements, the defenders now had sufficient forces to man the walls and carry out sorties, which they conducted with considerable vigour. While the slow process of digging and reinforcing the first parallel continued, Suchet used the time to approach Fort Olivo by digging a series of trenches and gun pits in anticipation of the assault. The northern edge of the fort had a deep ditch etched out of the rock but on the south side of the structure there were two entry and exit points. The depth of the ditch on the northern side made it difficult to generate sufficient rubble to fill sufficiently, consequently Suchet elected to attack the fort by distracting the north wall and sending large numbers of infantry round the structure in an attempt to gain entry on the south side. On 29 May the attack was delivered and, as the assaulting troops made their way south, quite by chance they came upon the Spanish battalion who were transiting from the town to relieve the guard in Fort Olivo. The two groups of infantry were locked in chaotic hand-to-hand fighting and, in the darkness, some of the attackers gained entry to the fort with this relief force as they tried to extract themselves. This group were able to destroy a wall to allow the balance of the French infantry to enter and by morning, despite a determined counter-attack by the Spanish, the fort was in French hands. Campoverde ordered

all the guns on the north side of Tarragona to bombard the place, but the French burrowed down and held on; they only needed to deny the fort to the defenders.

Campoverde then convened a council of war, informing the garrison that the only way to defeat Suchet was to attack his lines of communication and to fall upon his rear. Following his gallant rendition, he then promptly departed by sea in an attempt to galvanize the *somatenes* of central Catalonia and gather the remnants of Eroles and Sarsfield's divisions to act as the nucleus for this force. With the original governor, General Caro, already deployed south in a similar mission to solicit support from the Army of Valencia, command fell to General Juan Senen Contreras. On 1 June the French batteries opened on the Fort Francoli and the San Carlos and Orleans bastions, and by the night of 7 June Contreras ordered the Spanish defenders in the fort to withdraw and abandon the structure. It was a mistake to give up this fort without a fight, for with this structure in their hands, the French began work unhindered on the second parallel and by 16 June the new batteries in this forward trench line were ready to open. Despite two sorties on the nights of 11 and 14 June the attackers were making steady progress and on the night of 16 June the Prince's Lunette was taken by assault. The defenders' position was now increasingly ominous and Contreras sent pleas for help to Campoverde who had been absent for three weeks, having promised that he only needed seven days to raise reinforcement. There was a glimmer of hope on 16 June when Miranda's Division came up from Valencia providing an additional 11,000 men, but the Spanish divisional commander merely cut the French lines of communication soliciting no response from Suchet.

At 1900 hours on 21 June the lower town was stormed by five columns of massed grenadier and voltigeur companies through the breaches in the San Carlos and Orleans bastions. Both these attacks were successful and by the morning the French had control of the lower town and the harbour. Work began immediately on a third parallel within this newly acquired zone. Campoverde meanwhile had resolved to attack, but the outlying French cavalry piquets provided early warning of their advance and the attack was beaten off with ease. News of a British expeditionary force[7] prompted Campoverde to request their help and Colonel Skerrett and Commodore Codrington landed on 26 June to assess the situation. Skerrett had clear orders from General Graham, the Governor of Gibraltar, not to land his troops if he considered the town a lost cause. Both Skerrett and Codrington had reservations as to their chances and these were confirmed when Campoverde allocated Skerrett's force the mission of keeping open the lines of retreat north of the city. They chose not to land the British infantry, causing deep resentment and a corresponding worsening of morale among the defenders. It was of little consequence; on 27 June, 22 breaching guns opened fire at dawn and at 1700 that evening the assault was made. Following a night of street fighting and atrocities the town was in French hands. 'We took nearly ten thousand men and twenty pair of colours; including the guns in the Olivo and the lower town, we were in possession of three hundred and thirty-seven pieces of ordnance, fifteen thousand muskets, one hundred and fifty thousand weight of powder, forty thousand cannon-balls and bombs and four millions of cartridges.'[8]

---

6   This was Commodore Codrington's group, consisting of two 74-gun line-of-battle ships, two frigates and several Spanish gunboats.

7   The force, under Colonel Skerrett, had come from Gibraltar to assist the defenders at the request of the Regency and consisted of 1,200 men: the 2/47th, a detachment of the 3/95th and some light companies.

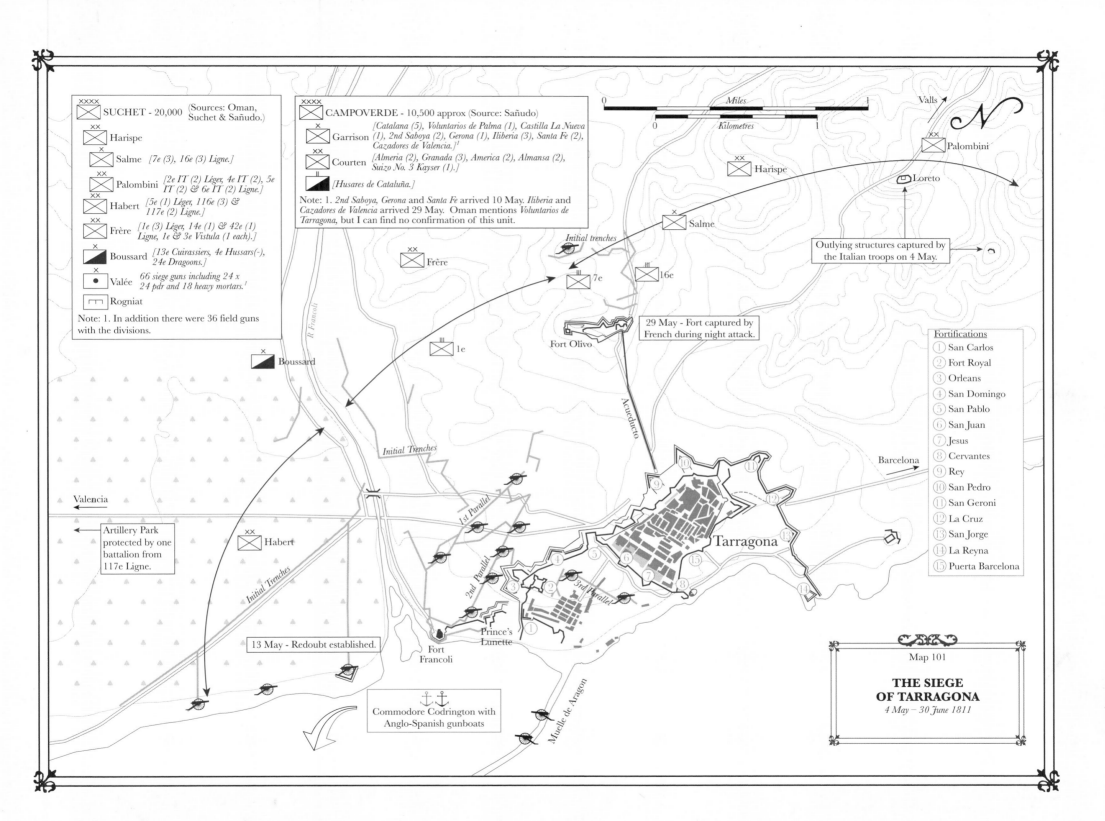

SUCHET - 20,000 (Sources: Oman, Suchet & Sañudo.)

Harispe

Salme *[7e (3), 16e (3) Ligne.]*

Palombini *[2e IT (2) Léger, 4e IT (2), 5e IT (2) & 6e IT (2) Ligne.]*

Habert *[5e (1) Léger, 116e (3) & 117e (2) Ligne.]*

Frère *[1e (3) Léger, 14e (1) & 42e (1) Ligne, 1e & 3e Vistula (1 each).]*

Boussard *[13e Cuirassiers, 4e Hussars(-), 24e Dragoons.]*

Valée *66 siege guns including 24 x 24 pdr and 18 heavy mortars.[1]*

Rogniat

Note: 1. In addition there were 36 field guns with the divisions.

CAMPOVERDE - 10,500 approx (Source: Sañudo)

Garrison *[Catalana (5), Voluntarios de Palma (1), Castilla La Nueva (1), 2nd Saboya (2), Gerona (1), Iliberia (3), Santa Fe (2), Cazadores de Valencia.][1]*

Courten *[Almeria (2), Granada (3), America (2), Almansa (2), Suizo No. 3 Kayser (1).]*

[Husares de Cataluña.]

Note: 1. *2nd Saboya, Gerona* and *Santa Fe* arrived 10 May. *Iliberia* and *Cazadores de Valencia* arrived 29 May. Oman mentions *Voluntarios de Tarragona*, but I can find no confirmation of this unit.

Palombini

Harispe

Loreto

Salme

Frère

7e

16e

Outlying structures captured by the Italian troops on 4 May.

Initial trenches

1e

Fort Olivo

29 May - Fort captured by French during night attack.

Acueducto

R Francoli

Boussard

Initial Trenches

Valencia

Artillery Park protected by one battalion from 117e Ligne.

Habert

Initial Trenches

Initial Trenches

13 May - Redoubt established.

Fort Francoli

Prince's Lunette

1st Parallel

2nd Parallel

3rd Parallel

San Carlos

Tarragona

Barcelona

Commodore Codrington with Anglo-Spanish gunboats

Muelle de Aragon

Valls

Fortifications

1. San Carlos
2. Fort Royal
3. Orleans
4. San Domingo
5. San Pablo
6. San Juan
7. Jesus
8. Cervantes
9. Rey
10. San Pedro
11. San Geroni
12. La Cruz
13. San Jorge
14. La Reyna
15. Puerta Barcelona

Map 101

THE SIEGE OF TARRAGONA

4 May – 30 June 1811

Campoverde's reputation crumbled along with the walls of Tarragona; he held a council of war on 1 July and elected to abandon Catalonia altogether. Sarsfield was furious and Codrington refused to sanction the findings of the council or transport the Catalan forces; he consented only to repatriate Miranda to Valencia. Suchet, meanwhile, was repairing his latest conquest, the capture of which was to earn him his marshal's baton, and he made contact with Maurice Mathieu at Barcelona and established a plan to reopen communications with Macdonald, who had remained motionless on the outskirts of Figueras. Suchet realized he would have to help his colleague and headed north at the head of Harispe and Frère's divisions, which arrived at Vich on 15 July. He immediately despatched flying columns to determine the whereabouts of the French and Spanish forces in the area. When Macdonald was located he was found to be clearly in control of the situation and would be able to reestablish control in northern Catalonia once Figueras capitulated. Accordingly, Suchet headed back south to open lines of communication between Barcelona and Lérida, and in so doing was required to capture the precipitous Montserrat hillock which housed Our Lady of Montserrat, a Renaissance church and large monastery. There were no fortifications on top of the steep rocky feature, but two batteries covered the main approach road and the buildings and walls had been loop-holed. On 25 July, Abbé's Brigade made the assault with five battalions and met stiff resistance from the Spanish gunners, who stood by their colours to the last. With the guns finally silenced, Abbé was preparing his men for the final assault when the defenders started streaming from the complex; the skirmishers sent to the rear of the hill had found access, collected 300 men, and delivered a surprise attack from that direction. Our Lady of Montserrat had fallen and with it the invincibility of this holy edifice. Suchet was now able to spend the next few months securing his gains in Catalonia and strengthening those areas under his responsibility before embarking on his Valencian expedition.

Macdonald, meanwhile, was continuing the blockade of Figueras, which by mid-July was entering its third month. The experiences and track record of the 7th Corps in prosecuting siege operations were not good and it is therefore of little surprise that, despite having the necessary equipment, Macdonald elected to starve the defenders into submission rather than conduct a regular siege. By mid-July he was regretting that decision, as many of the soldiers who had newly arrived from France fell ill from the unsanitary conditions which they found within the confines of the cordon. Conversely, within the walls Martinez, the city's governor and military commander, had about 3,000 men still able to assist the defence and was feeling confident. 'They had the enemy closely positioned to the walls of the castle in a double line of circumvallation. Marshal Macdonald had tried in vain to summon the surrender with the governor Juan Antonio Martinez, who played down their misfortunes.'[9] However, within weeks the mood was to change; news from Tarragona followed confirmation that the Spanish Army of Catalonia had, to all intents and purposes, ceased to exist. Furthermore, Rovira[10] returned in early August from Cádiz where he had unsuccessfully tried to convince the Regency to come to the aid of the Catalan cause. It was the last straw for Martinez, who nevertheless vowed to make a fight of it and, on the night of 16 August, he gathered every man who could still walk and tried to break through the cordon to the north-east of the town. They cleared the piquets and outposts, but then came up against two *abattis* that were covered by flanking fire from two batteries. After trying to clear the obstacle for some time and having taken considerable casualties, they pulled back. The next morning a summons was sent for surrender and Martinez, having run out of options and with his rations all but exhausted, approved the terms of the summons two days later.

For the first time in the war the French finally had a reasonable semblance of control over the province. On 9 July General Luis Lacy arrived to assume command from Campoverde; the army was in tatters and his first order was that of a levy on all able-bodied men between 18 and 40. Within days of assuming command, more for propaganda than effect, he undertook a raid over the Pyrenees into southern France. It succeeded in outraging Napoleon if little else, who vented his anger in a dispatch to Suchet. By mid-September, Lacy had the basis of an army with three weak divisions under Sarsfield, Eroles and Milans, and with the help of the Royal Navy they once again made their presence felt.

---

8   Suchet, *Memoirs of the War with Spain*, vol. II, p.103.

9   Toreno, *Guerra de la Independencia, La Derrota de Napoleon*, vol. I, p.269.

10   The *miquelete* chief who had led the capture of the fort in April.

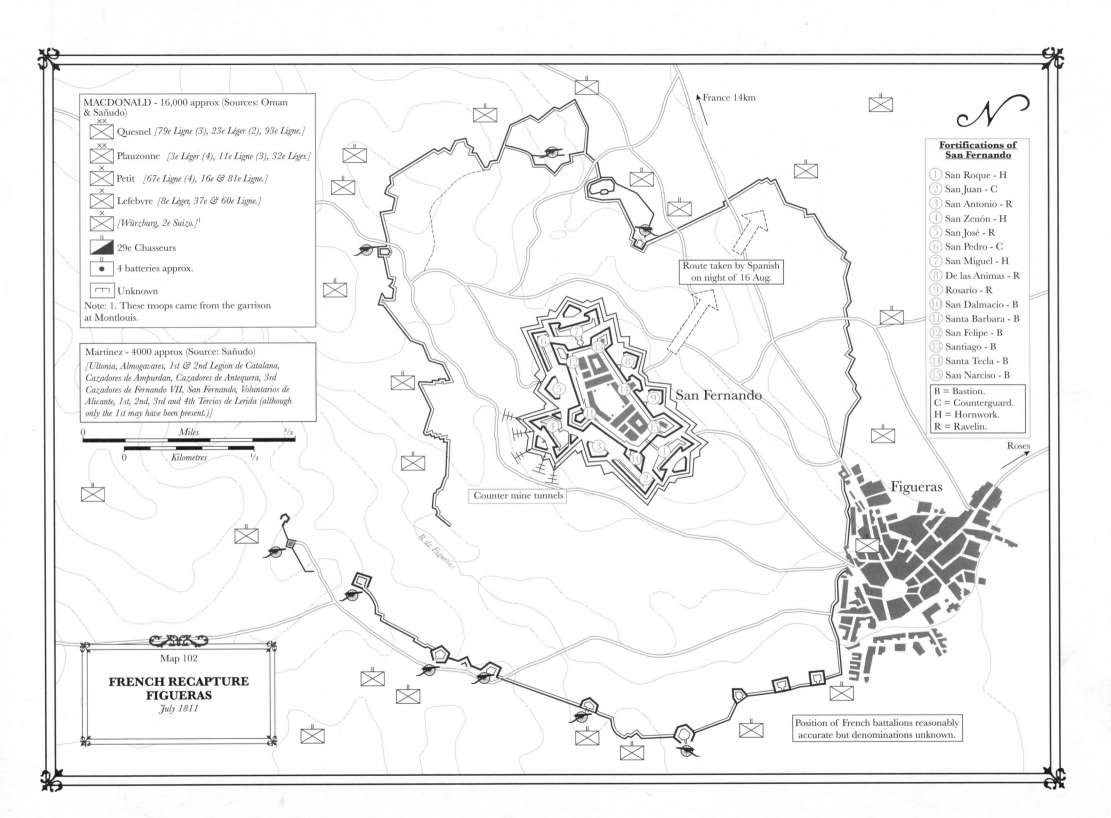

MACDONALD - 16,000 approx (Sources: Oman & Sañudo)

XX Quesnel *[79e Ligne (3), 23e Léger (2), 93e Ligne.]*

XX Plauzonne *[3e Léger (4), 11e Ligne (3), 32e Léger.]*

X Petit *[67e Ligne (4), 16e & 81e Ligne.]*

X Lefebvre *[8e Léger, 37e & 60e Ligne.]*

X *[Würzburg, 2e Suizo.]*[1]

29e Chasseurs

4 batteries approx.

Unknown

Note: 1. These troops came from the garrison at Montlouis.

Martinez - 4000 approx (Source: Sañudo)

[Ultonia, Almogavares, 1st & 2nd Legion de Catalana, Cazadores de Ampurdan, Cazadores de Antequera, 3rd Cazadores de Fernando VII, San Fernando, Voluntarios de Alicante, 1st, 2nd, 3rd and 4th Tercios de Lerida (although only the 1st may have been present.)]

0 ————— *Miles* ————— ½

0 ————— *Kilometres* ————— ½

Map 102

FRENCH RECAPTURE FIGUERAS

July 1811

France 14km

Route taken by Spanish on night of 16 Aug.

Fortifications of San Fernando

① San Roque - H
② San Juan - C
③ San Antonio - R
④ San Zenón - H
⑤ San José - R
⑥ San Pedro - C
⑦ San Miguel - H
⑧ De las Animas - R
⑨ Rosario - R
⑩ San Dalmacio - B
⑪ Santa Barbara - B
⑫ San Felipe - B
⑬ Santiago - B
⑭ Santa Tecla - B
⑮ San Narciso - B

B = Bastion.
C = Counterguard.
H = Hornwork.
R = Ravelin.

San Fernando

Roses

Figueras

Counter mine tunnels

R. de Figueras

Position of French battalions reasonably accurate but denominations unknown.

Chapter 35

NATIONWIDE STRUGGLE: JUNE TO SEPTEMBER 1811

D uring the last week in June, Wellington was convinced that the union of Soult and Marmont would inevitably result in an attack on the Allied defensive positions along the Portuguese border and he made preparations accordingly. In fact Soult and Marmont had no such intentions. On 27 June the first indication that there was to be no general engagement manifested itself when Godinot's Division vacated Olivenza, blew the walls, and marched south on the main road back to Andalusia. Conroux's Division followed within hours. 'The enemy, instead of following us up, as had been anticipated, confined their operations entirely to the southern side of Guadiana, never venturing upon anything on our bank of the river, except an occasional recognisance; and these recognisances, being conducted generally by cavalry, were generally successful, as far as success was desired.'[1] Soult was entirely preoccupied, not just with Blake's diversion but predominantly with news of Freire's movements against Sebastiani. At Marmont's insistence, he was forced to leave Drouet[2] and Latour-Maubourg on the Guadiana to assist Marmont against any possible offensive by Wellington and the Allies. They remained until mid-July, when provisions began to dwindle, at which point Marmont pulled back as far as the Tagus.[3] Wellington responded within days and the bulk of the Anglo-Portuguese army moved north leaving only Hill, with the 2nd and Hamilton's Portuguese divisions, around Elvas.[4]

Blake, lacking suitable artillery, had failed to capture the medieval castle at Niebla and was caught napping by Soult's unexpected return south. Both Conroux and Godinot were let loose against the Spanish force, while Soult continued south to Sevilla with a minimal escort. The two divisions came up against Blake on 2 July, prompting him to beat a hasty retreat south while Ballesteros took off into the hills to the north. Blake embarked from Ayamonte on 8 July and, after a brief stay at Cádiz, was sent by the Regency to assume command of the Army of Murcia.[5]

---

1 Vane, *Narrative of the Peninsular War,* vol. II, p.174.

2 Now commanding the 5th Corps.

3 Leaving one division at Trujillo.

4 Wellington received substantial cavalry reinforcements over the next few months. See Appendix 4 for reorganization of the Anglo-Portuguese army.

5 He arrived on 31 July with the divisions of Zayas (now under J. O'Dónnell's command) and Lardizabal. The Regency also made him captain-general of the Army of Valencia and he moved to the city in September.

Freire's advance westwards had shaken the 4th Corps; Leval, who had assumed command from Sebastiani in May, was unable to make a stand and, inevitably, withdrew from the provinces of Granada and Jaén to inside the city of Granada. It was with no little difficulty that he maintained communications with his Polish division at Málaga. Blake's reinforcements (Blake himself had continued to Valencia) arrived on 3 August, the same day that Soult despatched Latour-Maubourg and the bulk of Conroux's infantry, who arrived at Granada four days later having marched at a remarkable speed. Thus reinforced, Leval was able to thwart Spanish intentions and then divide the Murcian army and push them back into the hills. Blake returned from a flying visit to Valencia to discover his 'other' army in disarray and weaker by some 4,000 men. They spent the next few months operating in small groups from their mountain camps but the threat to the east of Andalusia had been extinguished.

In the north Santocildes's initiatives against Astorga had persuaded Bessières of the need to withdraw Bonnet south. Santocildes had countered the move, but as time passed the initiative passed back to the French with the arrival of three new divisions[6] to bolster the Army of the North. In addition, Dorsenne had arrived to assume command from Bessières and Abadia had been sent by Castaños to replace Santocildes. By early August Dorsenne was able to put his offensive into action and advanced with his two divisions of the Young Guard north-westwards towards Abadia. Roguet was to get in behind the Galician army and cut off its retreat while Dumoustier was to link up with Bonnet and capture the beleaguered force. Abadia had been warned of this very eventuality, and when intelligence reached him on 9 August of Dorsenne's advance from Valladolid he wasted little time in ordering a general withdrawal. Dorsenne's force was lightly equipped for speed, but they were unable to catch the Spanish and were forced to turn back due to a lack of provisions. Having strengthened the garrison at Astorga, he then returned with haste amid news that Porlier had nearly taken Santander. In addition, Wellington had moved his headquarters north to the outskirts of Almeida and Dorsenne was always mindful of the need to support Ciudad Rodrigo in the absence of Marmont.

Six days after the surrender of Figueras, Berthier had written from Paris ordering Suchet to commence operations against Valencia. Napoleon's time appreciation was characteristically optimistic: 'I must inform you that, in every case, it is the imperative order of the Emperor that your head-quarters are to be on Valencian territory on or about 15 September and as far forwards towards the city as possible.' Suchet, content that all was now in order in both Catalonia and Aragon, commenced his Valencia operation, reinforced by Severoli's Italian Division and part of Reille's Division from the Army of the North.[7] His command was now 70,000 men and expectations were high.

---

6 Souham, Reille and Caffarelli – see map 99.

7 Suchet had requested this additional division on the basis that it was merely engaged with Mina's irregulars.

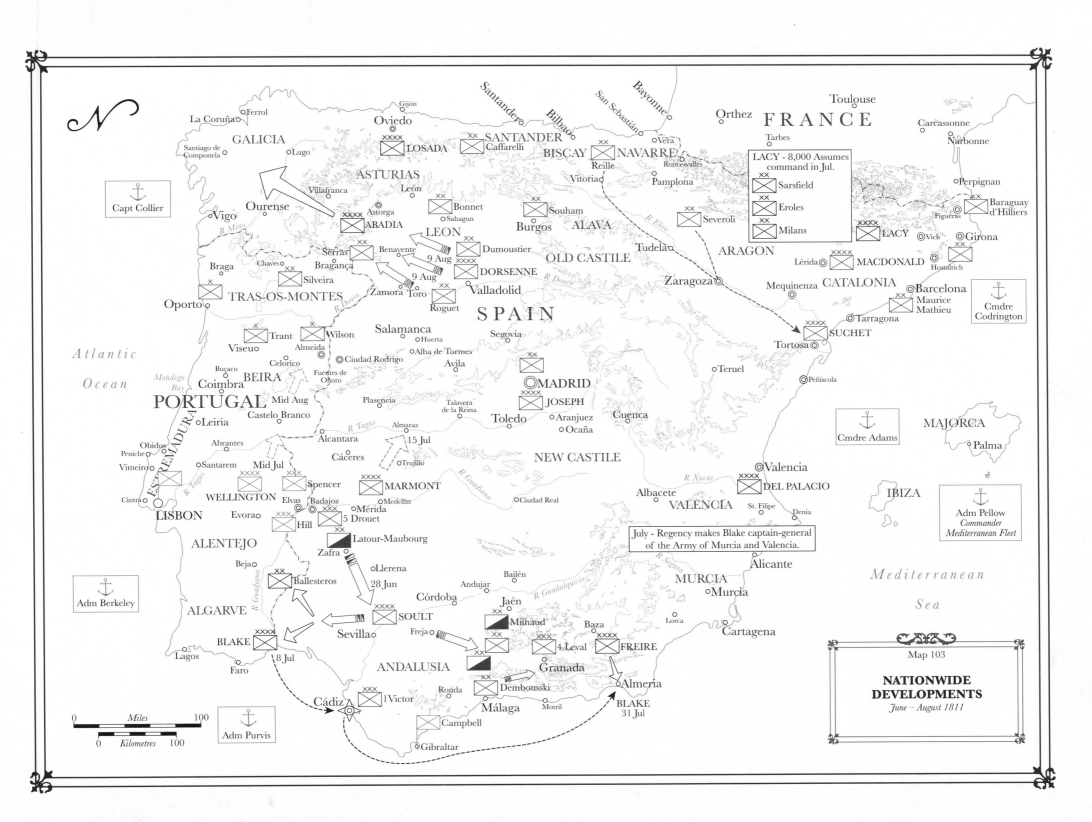

Map 103

NATIONWIDE DEVELOPMENTS
June – August 1811

LACY – 8,000 Assumes command in Jul.
Sarsfield
Eroles
Milans

July – Regency makes Blake captain-general of the Army of Murcia and Valencia.

Chapter 36

THE CONQUEST OF VALENCIA: SEPTEMBER 1811 TO JANUARY 1812

As autumn approached, Suchet's tasks and responsibilities in Aragon and Catalonia remained extensive. In addition to providing support to General Macdonald[1] in the north against a resurgent Army of Catalonia under Lacy, he also had to garrison Zaragoza, Tortosa, Lérida and now Tarragona. From his large army he hand-picked a mere 25,000 for the offensive into Valencia and began his advance on 15 September. He moved south on three routes: the main body concentrated at Tortosa and moved on the coast road with the siege artillery; the second went on the mountain route through Alcañiz and Morella and then linked up with the coast road at Castellon; and the final group went via Teruel, having departed from upper Aragon and Zaragoza.

This last group, only 5,000 strong, was taking a fearful risk, for had Blake come north in strength and challenged them the consequences would have been unavoidable. However, Blake had other plans. 'He accelerated the completion of the immense works which the Valencians were throwing up in defence of their capital, and availed himself of the uninterrupted intercourse by sea, to procure arms, provisions, money, and every kind of assistance of which he stood in need. Taking advantage of the spirit of the inhabitants, he exited them to resist the advance of the French, and called out all the male population, between the ages of 15 and 50, for militia duty.'[2] Blake had decided to make his first line of defence on the ancient, but recently renovated[3] fort of Saguntum at Murviedro, about 30km north of the regional capital. In addition he placed two outposts at Peñiscola and Oropesa. However, the main defences were on the north bank of the Guadalaviar, just in front of the city of Valencia where he planned to fight the main defensive battle.

'We had no choice but to resort to the road from Tortosa which runs along the seashore, since the train could not proceed by any other; but the forts of Peñiscola and Oropesa presented two obstacles in the way: the former was, fortunately for us, at some distance from the road, and it was possible to mask it, and thereby to neutralize its influence. But the fort of Oropesa had full command of the road.'[4] However, Suchet found a way around the fort and by 23 September his advance guard, led by Harispe, had taken control of Murviedro, driving the isolated pockets of defenders back into the fortress. Palombini's Italian Division covered the right flank and took control of Petrés and Gilet, while Habert's Division crossed the river on the French left flank. Cavalry reconnaissance was sent further south and advanced to within 10km of the city, meeting no resistance, for Lardizabal and San Juan (commanding the Spanish cavalry) had withdrawn in the face of the French advance to their respective positions on the Guadalaviar. Suchet decided to capture the fort of Saguntum before moving south to engage Blake on his chosen ground. The irregularity of the structure enticed him to attempt an assault without waiting for his siege artillery. Armed with small arms and ladders, the first attack was delivered during the night of 27/28 September; however, the main assaulting columns were discovered by a Spanish patrol some time before the prescribed hour of attack and were forced to initiate proceedings prematurely, losing both surprise and the distraction of the two diversionary attacks (see map 105). The defenders displayed gallant and determined resistance and, despite bringing up the French reserve, the assault was a complete failure. Suchet accepted the inevitable and ordered the siege train to make best speed once it had completed the task of battering Oropesa.

The arrival of the train was to take another two weeks during which time Suchet's force was motionless. Blake now faced a dilemma, with the invading French army at a standstill before him, he felt compelled to do something. He had two options: attack the force in an attempt to lift the siege, or penetrate Aragon and cut off Suchet's lines of communication. Having tried and failed to get British naval support to land a small expeditionary force on the Levante coast,[5] and given the poor morale and operational effectiveness of elements of his force,[6] Blake was more inclined to the latter option. Ultimately, his plans were relatively timid and designed more to incite guerrilla support in Aragon than to pose a serious threat in Suchet's rear. Nevertheless, the attack by the combined forces of Martin and Duran, which fell on the garrison at Calatayud,[7] and the surprise attack by El Empecinado on a relief column from Zaragoza, at El Frasno, prompted renewed calls by Suchet for the exclusive use of Reille and Severoli. In the meantime, Obispo was despatched to Segorbe and O'Donnell, with Villacampa's infantry and San Juan's cavalry, was tasked to move to Benaguacil; equidistant between Segorbe and Blake's main force. Against the troublesome demonstrations Suchet despatched Palombini's Division and Robert's Brigade to evict Obispo from Segorbe and, when they returned, Harispe was again despatched (with Robert) to Benaguacil.

---

1   He was recalled to Paris at the end of October 1811 and replaced by General Decaen. The 7th Corps at this stage numbered about 23,000 men – see Appendix 4.

2   Suchet, *Memoirs of the War with Spain*, vol. II, pp.143–144.

3   The fortress had been completely rebuilt on the orders of Blake when he had last commanded in Valencia, before joining the Regency at Cádiz as military advisor. A year's work had transformed the citadel into a tenable fortress even if the design was asymmetrical and somewhat unscientific, although it was by no means completed at the commencement of the siege.

4   Suchet, *Memoirs of the War with Spain*, vol. II, p.149.

5   Arcón, *Sagunto La Batalla por Valencia*, vol. II, p.32.

6   Mahy had written to Blake on 12 September informing him that the morale and effectiveness of the Murcian element was extremely questionable.

7   Martin's 5th Division (of the Army of Valencia) and the Division Volante de Soria, under Duran, mustered 6,000 men, which attacked the 1,000-man garrison on 26 September.

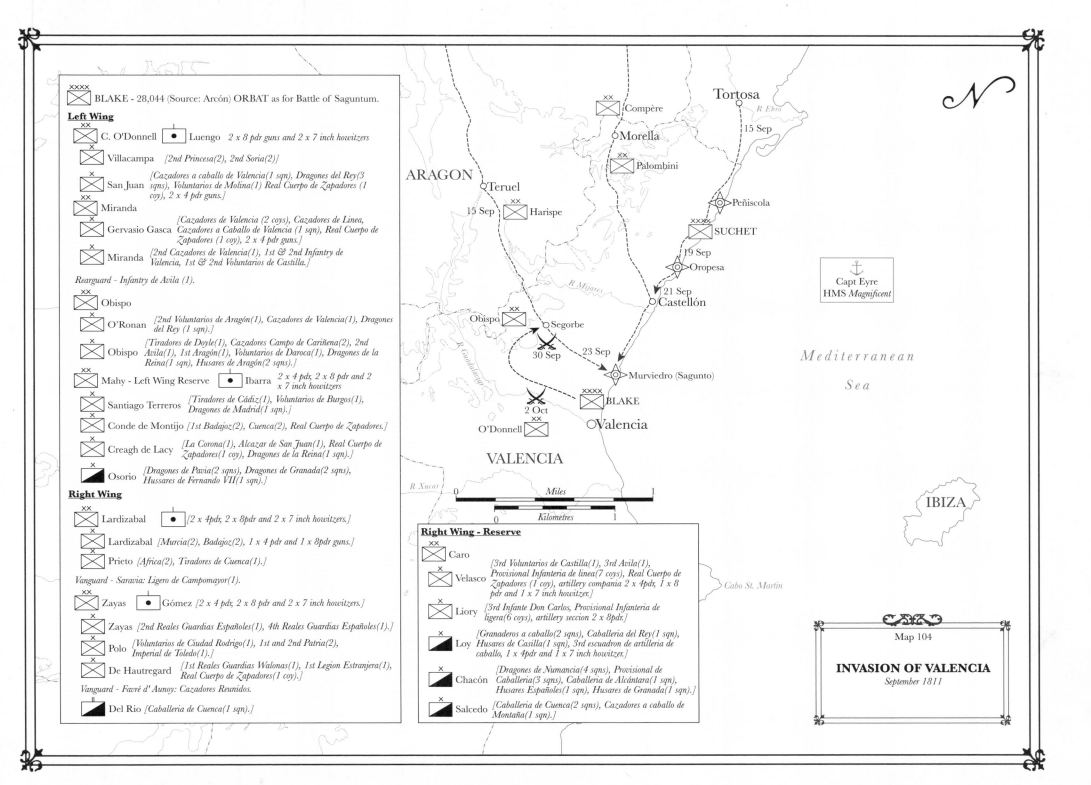

BLAKE - 28,044 (Source: Arcón) ORBAT as for Battle of Saguntum.

Left Wing

C. O'Donnell · Luengo *2 x 8 pdr guns and 2 x 7 inch howitzers*

Villacampa *[2nd Princesa(2), 2nd Soria(2)]*

San Juan *[Cazadores a caballo de Valencia(1 sqn), Dragones del Rey(3 sqns), Voluntarios de Molina(1) Real Cuerpo de Zapadores (1 coy), 2 x 4 pdr guns.]*

Miranda

Gervasio Gasca *[Cazadores de Valencia (2 coys), Cazadores de Linea, Cazadores a Caballo de Valencia (1 sqn), Real Cuerpo de Zapadores (1 coy), 2 x 4 pdr guns.]*

Miranda *[2nd Cazadores de Valencia(1), 1st & 2nd Infantry de Valencia, 1st & 2nd Voluntarios de Castilla.]*

Rearguard - Infantry de Avila (1).

Obispo

O'Ronan *[2nd Voluntarios de Aragón(1), Cazadores de Valencia(1), Dragones del Rey (1 sqn).]*

Obispo *[Tiradores de Doyle(1), Cazadores Campo de Cariñena(2), 2nd Avila(1), 1st Aragón(1), Voluntarios de Daroca(1), Dragones de la Reina(1 sqn), Husares de Aragón(2 sqns).]*

Mahy - Left Wing Reserve · Ibarra *2 x 4 pdr, 2 x 8 pdr and 2 x 7 inch howitzers*

Santiago Terreros *[Tiradores de Cádiz(1), Voluntarios de Burgos(1), Dragones de Madrid(1 sqn).]*

Conde de Montijo *[1st Badajoz(2), Cuenca(2), Real Cuerpo de Zapadores.]*

Creagh de Lacy *[La Corona(1), Alcazar de San Juan(1), Real Cuerpo de Zapadores(1 coy), Dragones de la Reina(1 sqn).]*

Osorio *[Dragones de Pavia(2 sqns), Dragones de Granada(2 sqns), Hussares de Fernando VII(1 sqn).]*

Right Wing

Lardizabal · *[2 x 4pdr, 2 x 8pdr and 2 x 7 inch howitzers.]*

Lardizabal *[Murcia(2), Badajoz(2), 1 x 4 pdr and 1 x 8pdr guns.]*

Prieto *[Africa(2), Tiradores de Cuenca(1).]*

Vanguard - Saravia: Ligero de Campomayor(1).

Zayas · Gómez *[2 x 4 pdr, 2 x 8 pdr and 2 x 7 inch howitzers.]*

Zayas *[2nd Reales Guardias Españoles(1), 4th Reales Guardias Españoles(1).]*

Polo *[Voluntarios de Ciudad Rodrigo(1), 1st and 2nd Patria(2), Imperial de Toledo(1).]*

De Hautregard *[1st Reales Guardias Walonas(1), 1st Legion Estranjera(1), Real Cuerpo de Zapadores(1 coy).]*

Vanguard - Favré d' Aunoy: Cazadores Reunidos.

Del Rio *[Caballeria de Cuenca(1 sqn).]*

Right Wing - Reserve

Caro

Velasco *[3rd Voluntarios de Castilla(1), 3rd Avila(1), Provisional Infanteria de linea(7 coys), Real Cuerpo de Zapadores (1 coy), artillery compania 2 x 4pdr, 1 x 8 pdr and 1 x 7 inch howitzer.]*

Liory *[3rd Infante Don Carlos, Provisional Infanteria de ligera(6 coys), artillery seccion 2 x 8pdr.]*

Loy *[Granaderos a caballo(2 sqns), Caballeria del Rey(1 sqn), Husares de Casilla(1 sqn), 3rd escuadron de artilleria de caballo, 1 x 4pdr and 1 x 7 inch howitzer.]*

Chacón *[Dragones de Numancia(4 sqns), Provisional de Caballeria(3 sqns), Caballeria de Alcántara(1 sqn), Husares Españoles(1 sqn), Husares de Granada(1 sqn).]*

Salcedo *[Caballeria de Cuenca(2 sqns), Cazadores a caballo de Montaña(1 sqn).]*

Map on right side:

Tortosa

R Ebro

15 Sep

Compère

Morella

Palombini

Teruel

ARAGON

15 Sep   Harispe

Peñiscola

SUCHET

19 Sep

Oropesa

R Mijares

21 Sep

Castellón

Obispo

Segorbe

Obispo

30 Sep

23 Sep

Mediterranean

Sea

Murviedro (Sagunto)

2 Oct

BLAKE

O'Donnell

Valencia

VALENCIA

R Guadalaviar

R Xucar

Capt Eyre
HMS *Magnificent*

Cabo St. Martin

IBIZA

0 ___ Miles ___ 1

0 ___ Kilometres ___ 1

Map 104

INVASION OF VALENCIA
September 1811

With his flank now free of Blake's potentially troublesome demonstrations, Suchet turned his attention back to the fort at Saguntum, but he still had another ten days to wait until the siege train arrived. Valée and Rogniat arrived on 11 October, a day ahead of the train, and they scrutinized the plans of their subordinates, making several adjustments in order to provide greater' protection to the men digging, riveting and arming the battery positions. They also decided to use the steepness of the hill to their advantage by marking the battery positions well forward, shortening the distance to the walls, but also making it difficult for the defenders to use their guns as a defence against this work as they would have to fire at an elevation less than horizontal.[8] The French made full use of this advantage, although they too were forced to utilize a number of mortars and howitzers to overcome the problems presented by the elevation of the fort. On the night of 16 October a number of battery positions (1 to 4) were ready, and a total of ten guns, howitzers and mortars were moved into place.[9]

'On the 16th the enemy placed in the batteries, twelve pieces of 24 [-pounder guns], eight [-inch] mortars and howitzers and this day they brought up the ammunition. The morning of the 17th at the break of dawn, the enemy greeted us with a terrible discharge of cannon, mortar and howitzer which was extensive and began to cause casualties to various individuals, I received the first, a strong bruise in the right leg from a stone that had already injured the artillery commander.'[10] The bombardment continued all day. Although quickly dislodging the repaired works, they made little impression on the old stone erected by the Moors. 'The breach was not much enlarged on the first day, though each of our cannon fired a hundred and fifty balls; we had to renew the fire the following day.'[11] The governor, Colonel Andriani placed seven companies under his second-in-command, Colonel Cisneros, in the ciudadela and they played a constant fire on the heads of the saps from the Dos de Mayo battery and the tower of San Pedro. As the assault trenches came closer to the walls and therefore inside the effective range of the musket, the French began to suffer appreciable casualties.

The fire 'was kept up more vigorously on the 18th; and with a more satisfactory result. In the afternoon, the generals commanding the artillery and engineers reconnoitred the breach; and, in conformity with their advice, the marshal determined to order the assault for the hour of five the same evening.'[12] The breach was still narrow and the debris in large stones and sections, presenting a considerable challenge to the assaulting infantry; it was a brave call by Valée and Rogniat. One hundred hand-picked men from the 5e Léger, the 114e and 117e Ligne collected in the late afternoon under Colonel Mathis, and a reserve, of 400 men from the Italian Division,

were placed under Major Olini. The Spanish suspected an assault and began to rebuild the ramparts with sandbags, answering every French shot with a volley of musket fire and taunting their besiegers to 'come to close quarters with them'. Rogniat recalled, that 'the enemy were presented on the summit with a lot of resolution, neither our rifle bullets nor our cannon could dislodge them or impede them in their incessant reestablishment of the walls with sandbags'.[13]

The assault went in at 1700 hours and was quickly bogged down; the many officers leading the assaulting parties left the cover of the trenches to cross the remaining 70m up to the base of the wall and breach. 'The most active cleared two-thirds of the slope which was contracted at the summit into a re-entrant angle scarcely accessible to two men abreast, and terminated in a vertical escarpment; but as there was no solid footing and on so inclined a plane, the earth and stones sunk under the trampling of the besiegers, and they were overwhelmed with musket-shot, grenades, stones, and earth bags.'[14] Habert, an experienced commander,[15] wasted no time in determining that the attack would not succeed once the momentum was spent and, as soon as he judged this to be the case, he ordered the assaulting parties back to the trenches. Suchet pondered his next move; he could not afford to squander soldiers from his minimal invasion force and the two failed attempts had done little for French morale. Nevertheless, the trenches were extended and more batteries established, but Suchet was clear that there would not be another assault until the whole curtain of the Dos de Mayo battery had been properly breached. This was to take time.

This delay unexpectedly played into Suchet's hands, for Blake was under increasing pressure from the Valencians[16] to undertake a preemptive strike on Suchet's forces at arm's length from the city. Blake was utterly convinced that this was not the best way to proceed, but nevertheless penned plans for Obispo to link up with Mahy, and act as his advance guard for an attack down the Segorbe road into the rear of the French while he attacked them simultaneously from the south. The plan misfired when Suchet despatched Palombini to return in support of the beleaguered town of Teruel: operations against Suchet's lines of communication reached a climax on 17 October, at Ayerbe in the Upper Aragon, where Espoz's Navarrese Division inflicted serious losses on Severoli's Division. Musnier was as a result holding Zaragoza with a mere 2,000 men, and news of the movement into the region by generals Duran and Martin, coupled with the intelligence of Obispo's northerly movement, predicated Suchet's decision to detach Palombini and deprived him of 5,000 men at a critical moment. Blake realized the opportunity and changed his plans; Obispo was to move via Sancti-Espiritu by way of a diversion and the Army of Valencia was then to execute a general advance upon the vastly smaller French force south of Saguntum. It was a reasonable plan and may have succeeded had Palombini not

---

8   This was a common problem facing defenders. In 1783, during the siege of Gibraltar, Lieutenant Köhler RA designed a wooden carriage that enabled the gun barrel to be depressed to elevations below zero (i.e. negative elevations) to overcome this dilemma.

9   Battery No. 8, with the two six-inch mortars, was also complete but the other batteries were not completed until after the assault on 18 October. Source: Report by Le Colonel de Génie, chef d'attaque, Henri, dated 27 October 1811.

10 This is from the extensive report detailed by the second-in-command of the defence, Colonel Sanchez Cisneros. Arcón, *Sagunto La Batalla por Valencia*, vol. II, p.61.

11 Suchet, *Memoirs of the War with Spain*, vol. II, p.170.

12 Ibid, p.170.

13 Arcón, *Sagunto La Batalla por Valencia*, vol. II, p.65.

14 Suchet, *Memoirs of the War with Spain*, vol. II, p.172.

15 He had fought in the expeditions to Ireland and Egypt and at Jena and Eylau.

16 Blake's appointment as Captain-General of the Valencian army was not popular with the Valencians who questioned his motives and courage from the outset. It did not help that the brother of the previous Captain-General, Del Palacio, was the publisher/editor of a local paper, *El Amigo de la Verdad*, in which criticism of Blake was frequent, shaping the views of the populace.

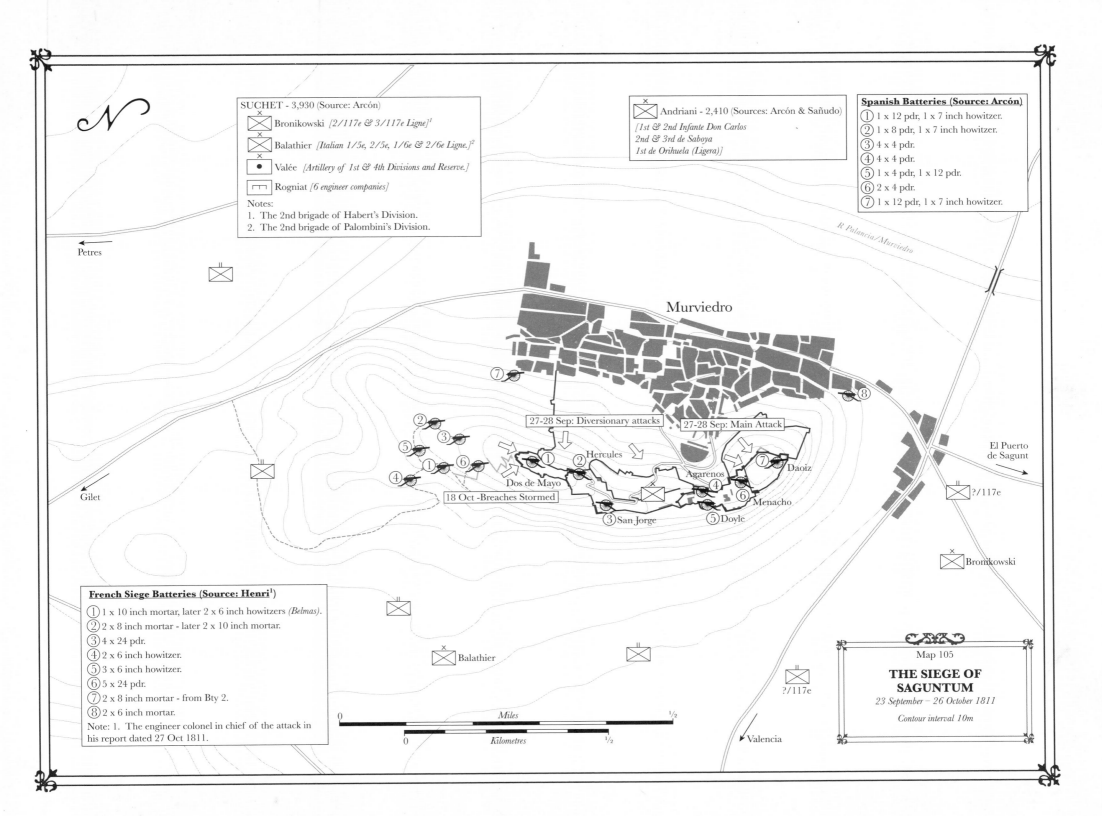

N

SUCHET - 3,930 (Source: Arcón)

☒ Bronikowski *[2/117e & 3/117e Ligne]*[1]

☒ Balathier *[Italian 1/5e, 2/5e, 1/6e & 2/6e Ligne.]*[2]

● Valée *[Artillery of 1st & 4th Divisions and Reserve.]*

⊓ Rogniat *[6 engineer companies]*

Notes:
1. The 2nd brigade of Habert's Division.
2. The 2nd brigade of Palombini's Division.

☒ Andriani - 2,410 (Sources: Arcón & Sañudo)

*[1st & 2nd Infante Don Carlos
2nd & 3rd de Saboya
1st de Orihuela (Ligera)]*

Spanish Batteries (Source: Arcón)

① 1 x 12 pdr, 1 x 7 inch howitzer.
② 1 x 8 pdr, 1 x 7 inch howitzer.
③ 4 x 4 pdr.
④ 4 x 4 pdr.
⑤ 1 x 4 pdr, 1 x 12 pdr.
⑥ 2 x 4 pdr.
⑦ 1 x 12 pdr, 1 x 7 inch howitzer.

Petres

Gilet

R. Palancia/Murviedro

Murviedro

27-28 Sep: Diversionary attacks

27-28 Sep: Main Attack

⑦

① Hercules

②

Agarenos

⑦ Daoiz

Dos de Mayo

18 Oct -Breaches Stormed

④

⑥ Menacho

③ San Jorge

⑤ Doyle

El Puerto de Sagunt

?/117e

Bronikowski

French Siege Batteries (Source: Henri[1])

① 1 x 10 inch mortar, later 2 x 6 inch howitzers *(Belmas)*.
② 2 x 8 inch mortar - later 2 x 10 inch mortar.
③ 4 x 24 pdr.
④ 2 x 6 inch howitzer.
⑤ 3 x 6 inch howitzer.
⑥ 5 x 24 pdr.
⑦ 2 x 8 inch mortar - from Bty 2.
⑧ 2 x 6 inch mortar.

Note: 1. The engineer colonel in chief of the attack in his report dated 27 Oct 1811.

Balathier

?/117e

Valencia

Miles

Kilometres

Map 105

THE SIEGE OF SAGUNTUM

23 September – 26 October 1811

Contour interval 10m

suddenly reappeared the night prior to the Valencian attack. Both Suchet and Blake were unaware of Musnier's bold move to send Mazzuchelli from Zaragoza to Teruel by way of relief and this fact, coupled with Duran and Martin's uncertainty of how best to proceed, enabled Palombini to retrace his steps and provided Suchet the opportunity to strengthen his main line and to despatch an additional brigade (that of Robert) to support Chlopicki at Sancti-Espiritu, on the eve of battle.

Blake found himself under increasing pressure and eventually felt compelled to action.[17] At 1400 hours on 24 October 1811, a three-cannon salvo was fired from the walls of the city of Valencia, acting as a signal for the Spanish forces to advance to their initial positions. General Blake left his headquarters in the city and took the Camino Real road to El Puig, where, on arrival at 2200 hours, he established his new headquarters in the Castillo. A makeshift hospital was set up in Rafelbuñol and preparations made for a number of carts to transport the wounded to hospitals in Valencia and Bétera. By nightfall all the Spanish forces were in place except Obispo, who was still heading south from his original mission. Supporting the force along the Playa del Puig coastline was HMS *Minstrel*, an 18-gun corvette, and six Spanish vessels.[18] 'Marshal Suchet found himself placed in the alternative of either abandoning his artillery and raising the siege in order to seek a more favourable field of battle, or to fight, between two fortresses, against superior numbers and with scarcely a chance of being able to effect a retreat. But, in spite of the serious disadvantages of his position, he did not hesitate to accept battle on a spot in advance of Saguntum.'[19] Suchet left Bronikowski in charge at Saguntum, with nearly 4,000 men to maintain the blockade and continue siege preparations, ordered Robert to support his right wing and line of retreat, and then moved to the Val de Jesús with the balance of his force.

At around 0630 hours on 25 October, Blake came down from the Castillo at El Puig and went to the Cartuja de Ara Christi where he delivered the orders for the advance.[20] During the night he had been apprised of Obispo's failure to appear and had ordered two battalions[21] from O'Donnell's command to deploy and cover the Gilet road. The main advance was to commence on the left with San Juan's all-arms vanguard at 0730 hours, followed by the main body of the left wing at 0800. O'Donnell was to advance using the Camino Liria as his axis with Miranda to his right. The Spanish right wing, which had less distance to travel, was allocated start times of 0830 and 0900 hours for Zayas's and Lardizabal's divisions respectively. Caro's cavalry preceded Lardizabal at around 0845 hours, using the Camino Real as its axis. Lardizabal was to take his reinforced battery forward (this almost certainly included the guns from Zayas's battery) and establish a battery position from which to engage the French main body. In view of Obispo's failure to show, O'Ronan was ordered to move at around 0800 hours and probe the defile of Sancti-Espiritu, while Creagh's Division (from Mahy's reserve) was tasked to replace them on the Cabezbort.

The screen of French tirailleurs and a squadron of the 4e Hussars were already engaged in bickering fire with the Spanish skirmishers and elements of San Juan's vanguard for about two hours (about 0700 to 0900 hours). However, Suchet remained confused as to Spanish intentions, and at about 0830 hours decided to move south up the Camino Real to a position just short of the first hostels at 'Hostalets' to try and get a better feel for the Spanish dispositions. The area was covered with a combination of olive and carob trees and visibility on the flat plains was limited, but Suchet spotted the small hillock of El Hostalet between the Camino Liria road and the hills of the Montenegro. The Spanish were in possession of the hillock (as Vizcaino's troops had taken El Hostalet at around 0800 from elements of the 4e Hussars) but Suchet quickly appreciated the tactical value of any rise, however modest, on the featureless plains and immediately ordered Harispe to retake the mound at about 0900 hours. Since occupying the hill Villacampa had deployed additional skirmishers to screen those of the French who were coming down the slopes of the Montenegro. San Juan had also deployed additional skirmishers to the front of the hill and two companies of Molina on it; the Dragones del Rey with two four-pounder guns to the right, and the balance of the Molina behind the hill in reserve.[22] Critically however, Miranda was having considerable difficulty negotiating the terrain, which contained several ditches and walls, and was unable to advance at the same pace as Villacampa. Within minutes Miranda's advance ground to a halt completely when one of his two guns became stuck and he decided to extract it rather than push on, with the result that a large gap grew between the two divisions and mutual support was lost.

On the Spanish left, O'Ronan began to move up the defile between the El Caballo and Coll de la Calderona. His force was taken by surprise by the 44e Ligne who had camped there the night before but who were now drawn up in formation, ready to receive the advancing Spaniards. It was about 0930 hours and, after a short exchange of fire, O'Ronan elected to withdraw back the way he had come. Chlopicki sent Robert after him and took the remainder of his brigade, plus the three squadrons of Dragoons de Napoleon, and headed further down the track to a better vantage point from where he could survey the plains below. While this insignificant action had been taking place, both Zayas and Lardizabal (on the Spanish right) had advanced to the areas of Puzol and Hostalets respectively. Suchet, once he had given orders to Harispe to take the El Hostalet hillock, had withdrawn back north up the Camino Real. He was conscious that Zayas was trying, with the aid of the naval gunfire, to get around the French right flank and approach the town of Murviedro. He resolved to split the Spanish left and right with Palombini's Division, who were now called forward.

As Chlopicki arrived at his vantage point he could now see that the French had retaken the El Hostalet hillock. O'Donnell reacted by sending Villacampa's four battalions and four additional guns forward while the Dragones del Rey advanced to prevent elements of the

17 This version of events differs from the hitherto accepted accounts of the battle – see Preface.

18 Originally, a flotilla of 12 Royal Navy ships was despatched by the Admiralty from Malta to support Blake's operations against Suchet. En route the flotilla was hit by a fierce storm and broken up. The six Spanish ships were the *Picudo*, *Santo Christo de Grao*, *Valeroso*, *Santa Faz*, *San Antonio* and *Obusera No. 9*.

19 Suchet, *Memoirs of the War with Spain*, vol. II, p.180.

20 Blake had changed his orders, which is why he needed to reissue plans on the morning of battle.

21 This was O'Ronan's Brigade and they deployed late on the 24th to a position just west of the Cabezbort.

22 It was these forces that Harispe engaged so hotly at around 0900 when he was first ordered to capture the El Hostalet, not those of Lardizabal as traditionally reported.

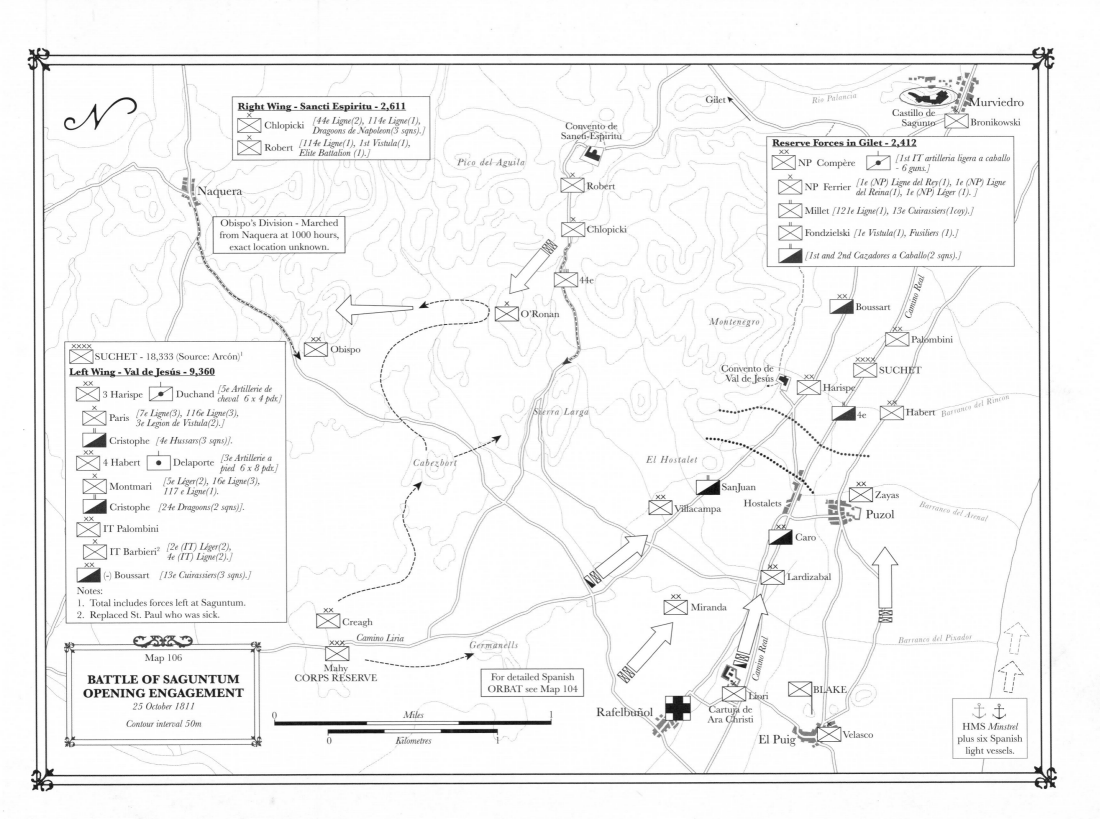

N

Right Wing - Sancti Espiritu - 2,611

Chlopicki *[44e Ligne(2), 114e Ligne(1), Dragoons de Napoleon(3 sqns).]*

Robert *[114e Ligne(1), 1st Vistula(1), Elite Battalion (1).]*

Reserve Forces in Gilet - 2,412

NP Compère — *[1st IT artilleria ligera a caballo - 6 guns.]*

NP Ferrier *[1e (NP) Ligne del Rey(1), 1e (NP) Ligne del Reina(1), 1e (NP) Léger (1).]*

Millet *[121e Ligne(1), 13e Cuirassiers(1coy).]*

Fondzielski *[1e Vistula(1), Fusiliers (1).]*

[1st and 2nd Cazadores a Caballo(2 sqns).]

Gilet

Rio Palancia

Castillo de Sagunto — Murviedro

Bronikowski

Convento de Sancti-Espiritu

Pico del Aguila

Robert

Chlopicki

44e

O'Ronan

Boussart

Palombini

SUCHET

Harispe

Montenegro

Convento de Val de Jesús

Naquera

Obispo's Division - Marched from Naquera at 1000 hours, exact location unknown.

Obispo

4e

Habert

Barranco del Rincon

Sierra Larga

Cabezbort

El Hostalet

SUCHET - 18,333 (Source: Arcón)[1]

Left Wing - Val de Jesús - 9,360

3 Harispe — Duchand *[5e Artillerie de cheval 6 x 4 pdr.]*

Paris *[7e Ligne(3), 116e Ligne(3), 3e Legion de Vistula(2).]*

Cristophe *[4e Hussars(3 sqns).]*

4 Habert — Delaporte *[3e Artillerie a pied 6 x 8 pdr.]*

Montmari *[5e Léger(2), 16e Ligne(3), 117 e Ligne(1).]*

Cristophe *[24e Dragoons(2 sqns).]*

IT Palombini

IT Barbieri[2] *[2e (IT) Léger(2), 4e (IT) Ligne(2).]*

(-) Boussart *[13e Cuirassiers(3 sqns).]*

Notes:
1. Total includes forces left at Saguntum.
2. Replaced St. Paul who was sick.

SanJuan

Villacampa

Hostalets

Zayas

Puzol

Barranco del Arenal

Caro

Creagh

Camino Liria

Germanells

Mahy
CORPS RESERVE

Miranda

Lardizabal

Barranco del Pixador

Map 106

BATTLE OF SAGUNTUM OPENING ENGAGEMENT

25 October 1811

Contour interval 50m

For detailed Spanish ORBAT see Map 104

0 — Miles — 1

0 — Kilometres — 1

Rafelbuñol

Cartuja de Ara Christi

Liori

BLAKE

El Puig

Velasco

HMS *Minstrel* plus six Spanish light vessels.

116e Ligne from supporting the 7e Ligne on the hill itself. Colonel Lanzarote, commanding the Dragones del Rey, stated in his report that the ground was completely unsuitable for cavalry and that the 116e repulsed the Spanish dragoons with ease. Lanzarote, while trying to rally and regroup for a second attempt, was suddenly and unexpectedly charged by the 4e Hussars and then peppered by canister. The Dragones fled: this seemingly insignificant episode ignited the series of events that led to the collapse of the Spanish left and ultimately the battle. With San Juan's Dragones in a desperate situation, the Hussars began to pursue the fleeing cavalry and O'Donnell, considering his entire wing in jeopardy, ordered a retreat upon Mahy's advance guard (Miyares's Brigade) at the Barranco del Pixador.[23]

The hussars made better speed than the infantry, but soon realized that Villacampa's men had rallied behind Mahy's vanguard and that Loy and Caro's cavalry had taken the bold decision to charge and were heading back toward the El Hostalet with the intention of capturing it. Harispe ordered Chef d'Esquadron Duchand, commanding the horse artillery, to deploy forward and once again engage at close quarters with canister and grape. They had some initial success but were too far advanced and, when the 4e Hussars charge was driven back by the mass of almost 1,000 cavalry, they lost three of their guns to the advancing Spanish. It was about 1100 hours and at this moment the battle hung in the balance. Harispe's infantry, intimately supported by Palombini's Italians, held their nerve and their ground; the latter defeating the cavalry charge with well-sustained fire. Suchet had returned to this part of the field to witness the Spanish recovery and rallied Boussart's cuirassiers, during which he was hit in the shoulder by a musket ball.[24] Once released, the cuirassiers thundered into the Spanish. 'At first I feared that my men would be discouraged by the rout of the 4e Hussars and our first squadron; but I was speedily reassured, and experienced the most intoxicating sensation that it is possible to feel on the field of battle.'[25] The follow-up to the charge by Harispe's infantry and hussars recovered the three lost guns, captured five of the Spanish guns, four standards and continued until the banks of the Pixador. General Caro was wounded and taken prisoner and O'Donnell's left wing was broken. The initiative had now passed to the French.

Events on the far left were also about to have a significant impact. Obispo had finally emerged from Naquera, just in time to see O'Ronan's force withdrawing at speed from Robert's Brigade, which had emerged from the defile of Sancti-Espiritu. Obispo deployed in an attempt to engage Robert, but the French commander kept Obispo in check and repeatedly defeated any attempt by the Spaniard to advance. At the Pixador ravine, about half of O'Donnell and Miranda's forces rallied behind Mahy's advance guard and brought Harispe to an abrupt halt, providing the opportunity for Caro's cavalry to overrun Harispe's left flank and take his artillery. However, this brief advantage was soon to undone by Mahy who, fearing that Robert would outflank the feature as he pursued O'Ronan, ordered Creagh to abandon Cabezbort. This, in turn, opened the door for Chlopicki who, until this point, had been content to watch Villacampa and Mahy, but with Roberts in action to his right and Harispe's success to his front he was, despite his orders to the contrary, keen for some of the action. He states in his report that at about noon he advanced upon an impressive array of Spanish troops deployed at the foot of Los Germanells[26] intent on attacking the Spaniards. Much to his surprise the Spanish did not wait for him; Mahy quickly abandoned the feature, and with it any hope of holding the Spanish left. While O'Ronan, Obispo and Creagh made good their escape into the mountains to the west, Harispe quickly combined forces with Chlopicki and together they pursued the already routed forces of O'Donnell who fled behind Mahy's reserve. About 100 French hussars and dragoons took nearly 2,000 Spanish prisoners until they were stopped by the skirmishers of the line regiment of Cuenca and Voluntarios de Molina who deployed across the Bétera road.

Blake was watching the battle from the heights at El Puig and could clearly see his left in full flight, and accordingly issued orders for the right wing to withdraw. General Montmarie finally took possession of Puzol after a fierce fight during which the Spanish yielded 800 prisoners. Zayas's Division had to withdraw in contact and was assisted in this by the Walloon Guards,[27] who had been brought up by Blake and established some distance behind the village of Puzol. Lardizabal's left flank was now dangerously exposed by the collapse of the Spanish left wing, and he began an orderly withdrawal in the face of ruthless harassment by the 24e Dragoons who, fortuitously for the Spanish, were constrained by the dense vegetation on either side of the Camino Real. Lardizabal redeployed at the Cartuja with Liori's Brigade, and together they thwarted further French advances; meanwhile Zayas had gone firm at El Puig with Velasco. However, there was to be no rearguard action; Blake, acutely aware of the danger of an exposed left flank, had already ordered a general retreat to Valencia.

On the morning of 26 October, a day after the battle, Suchet sent in a summons to Colonel Andriani and, after a short discussion about terms, the garrison surrendered. The morale of the defenders had been severely shaken by the failure of their countrymen the day before, and by the effect that the French siege artillery was now having on the makeshift walls of the fortress.[28] Following the battle of Saguntum and the capitulation of the stronghold, Blake still had 22,000 men under arms, but their morale was incontestably dubious. An immediate attempt on Valencia was a tempting proposition to Suchet, but when he had counted up his losses, deducted men to garrison Saguntum and detach a brigade to escort the prisoners to Tortosa, he was left with only 15,000 combatants. He was reluctant, even at this stage, to call up Ficatier's Brigade from Segorbe and Oropesa as he was determined to keep open his lines of communication. He decided to consolidate his gains and summoned both Severoli and Reille's divisions from Aragon in anticipation of the next phase of his offensive; however he required Napoleonic

---

23 O'Donnell blames San Juan, who in turn directs his accusations towards Miranda and the latter blames Lardizabal on the extraordinary pretext that he had not kept in touch with his right flank.

24 Suchet wrote this in his memoirs but the account of a Private Graindor in the 2/166e, and Suchet's own chief of staff, state that he was hit (by a spent ball) during a reconnaissance in the early morning.

25 De Gonneville, *Recollections of Colonel De Gonneville*, vol II, p.98

26 This contradicts Oman who accorded considerable praise on Chlopicki's early attacks on O'Donnell's flank as significant contributory factors in the subsequent collapse and rout of the Spanish left wing.

27 The battalion of Reales Guardias Walonas were part of Zayas's reserve.

28 However, Andriani's decision to capitulate was based on the fact that the French had already breached the walls. This was not the case; the breach (at the Dos de Mayo) was in the outer defences only, the inner defensive walls were still intact.

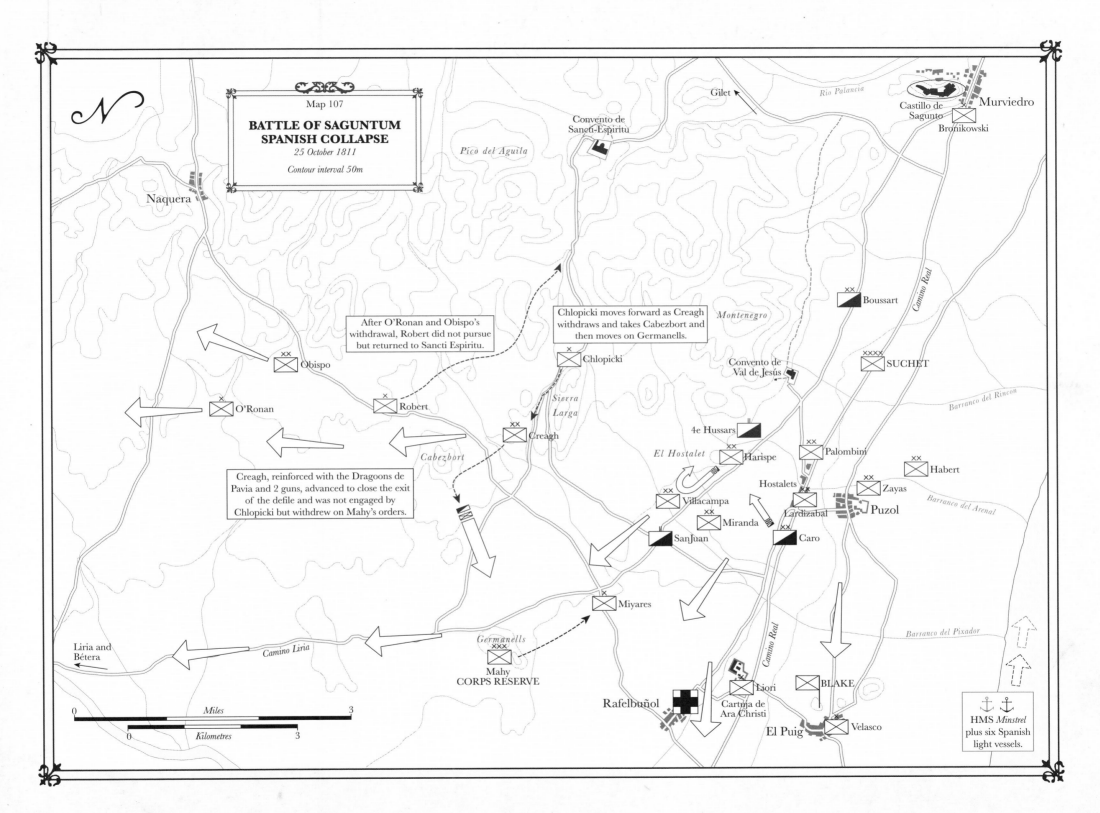

N

Map 107

BATTLE OF SAGUNTUM
SPANISH COLLAPSE

25 October 1811

Contour interval 50m

Naquera

Rio Palancia

Castillo de
Saguntum

Murviedro

Bronikowski

Gilet

Convento de
Sancti-Espiritu

Pico del Aguila

Boussart

Montenegro

After O'Ronan and Obispo's
withdrawal, Robert did not pursue
but returned to Sancti Espiritu.

Chlopicki moves forward as Creagh
withdraws and takes Cabezbort and
then moves on Germanells.

Obispo

Chlopicki

Convento de
Val de Jesús

SUCHET

O'Ronan

Robert

*Sierra
Larga*

Barranco del Rincon

Cabezbort

Creagh

4e Hussars

El Hostalet

Palombini

Habert

Harispe

Hostalets

Zayas

Creagh, reinforced with the Dragoons de
Pavia and 2 guns, advanced to close the exit
of the defile and was not engaged by
Chlopicki but withdrew on Mahy's orders.

Villacampa

Miranda

Lardizabal

Puzol

Barranco del Arenal

SanJuan

Caro

Miyares

Germanells

Mahy
CORPS RESERVE

Liria and
Bétera

Camino Liria

Barranco del Pixador

HMS *Minstrel*
plus six Spanish
light vessels.

Liori

BLAKE

Rafelbuñol

Cartuja de
Ara Christi

El Puig

Velasco

0 — Miles — 3

0 — Kilometres — 3

approval before he could move them, and this was to take time. This delay enabled Blake to take stock of his position and strengthen the defensive lines in and around Valencia.

The divisions of Severoli and Reille arrived in the region on 24 December, increasing Suchet's force to 33,000, about 10,000 more than Blake. On Christmas Day, all Suchet's divisions advanced south towards the Spanish lines. His plan of attack was ambitious, with the aim of forcing passage across the river Guadalaviar (now called the Turia) and trapping Blake's entire army. In essence, it was encirclement, with one column forcing the crossing to the east between Valencia and the sea and a second to the west. Both columns would join up south of the city completing the encirclement.

By first light on 26 December French engineers had constructed both light and heavy bridges across the Guadalaviar at Riba-Roja and half the French force[29] had crossed. Blake's vedettes had been driven in early during the operation, depriving him of intelligence on French intentions and strengths. As the day unfolded, it became clear that forces under Harispe were moving south to Torrent to cut off the road to Murcia, and one brigade from Musnier's Division and the cavalry were preparing to follow. The second of Musnier's brigades, that of General Robert, was holding the bridge waiting for Reille's Division to cross. This intelligence was fairly conclusive but Blake failed to react upon it, being entirely preoccupied with events on the Spanish right, where Habert's column had already crossed the estuary of the river Guadalaviar and was beginning to swing west. Blake considered Habert the real danger and, by the time he realized his mistake, the French main force was poised to join Habert and close the ring.

About this time that the Spanish divisions of Villacampa and Obispo realized they were about to be surrounded and abandoned their positions, racing south to escape the trap. About half this Spanish force managed to escape but the rest was cut off. Meanwhile, Palombini was attempting to break through the Spanish lines at Mislata. His first attack stalled, but Palombini rallied his men and delivered a second attack against Zayas, whose division had been left exposed by the withdrawal of Villacampa and Obispo. Blake tried to readjust his defence but realized the situation was hopeless and recalled both Zayas and Lardizabal to within the confines of Valencia. Blake was now trapped and surrounded; he had 17,000 men (the divisions of Miranda, Zayas, Lardizabal and what was left of the reserve battalions) but his defensive task was extensive and Valencia's walls would not hold out for long. By 1 January most of the siege guns had arrived from Saguntum and Suchet opened trenches against the fort of Monte Oliveto and the southern point of the suburb of San Vincente. By the 4th January seven batteries had been established; Blake did not wait for these guns to open on the inadequate outer defences, instead he withdrew his defensive force into the narrow confines of the city itself.

Suchet lost no time in building fresh batteries in the newly captured ground and, on 6 January, over 1,000 shells were dropped into the city. Suchet then sent a group to invite Blake to capitulate; he refused and the relentless bombardment continued for another two days. It was enough to convince Blake of the futility of further defiance and on 9 January the citadel and the city were handed over the French. Blake himself was escorted straight to France and did not remain to take part in the formal surrender. Over 16,000 regular troops were made prisoner and transported to France, marching in two columns under the escort of Pannetier's Brigade. No less than 374 cannon (mainly heavy guns from the city itself) and 21 colours were taken. After only 14 days, Suchet had captured the vitally important city that had hitherto proved elusive, opening up the possibility of operations further south towards Alicante to sever a vital supply line to the Spanish cause. However, this French tactical success both concluded and provoked French operational reorganizations that were to have far-reaching strategic consequences. If Valencia had fallen two months earlier, this eventuality may not have transpired.

---

29   The divisions of Harispe, Musnier, Reille and all the French cavalry.

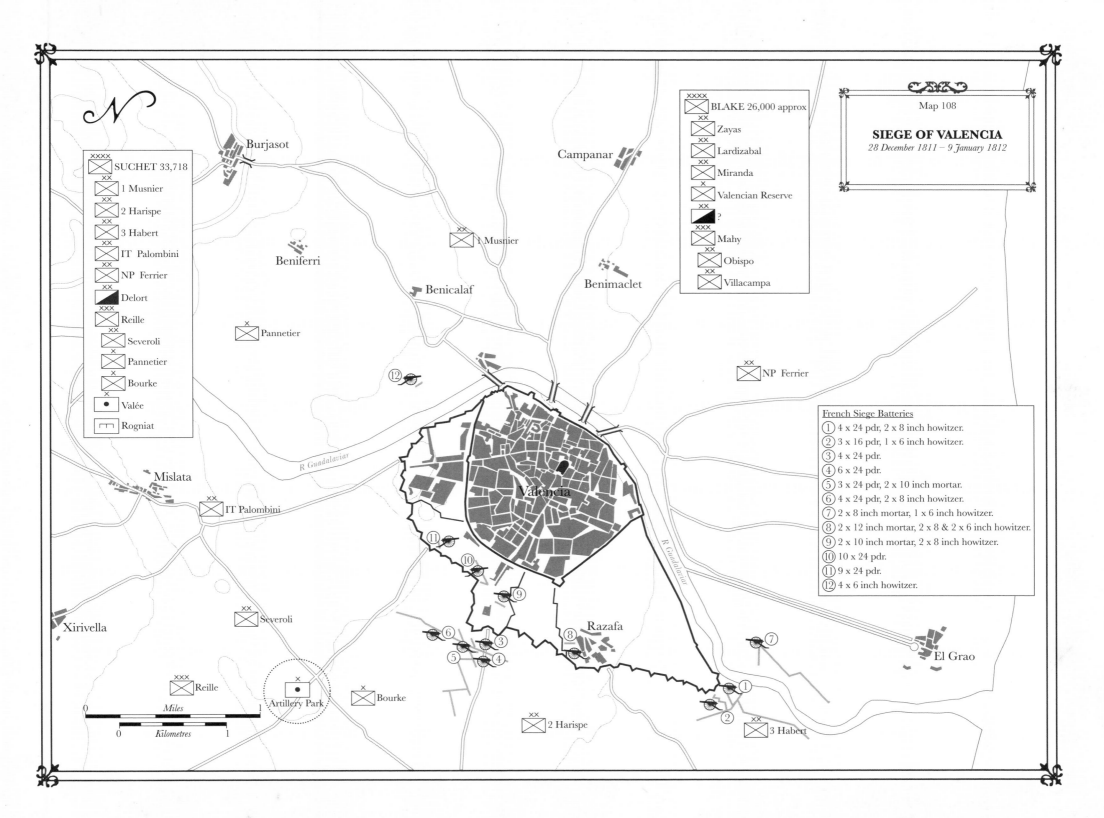

N

SUCHET 33,718
1 Musnier
2 Harispe
3 Habert
IT Palombini
NP Ferrier
Delort
Reille
Severoli
Pannetier
Bourke
Valée
Rogniat

BLAKE 26,000 approx
Zayas
Lardizabal
Miranda
Valencian Reserve
?
Mahy
Obispo
Villacampa

Map 108

SIEGE OF VALENCIA
28 December 1811 – 9 January 1812

French Siege Batteries
① 4 x 24 pdr, 2 x 8 inch howitzer.
② 3 x 16 pdr, 1 x 6 inch howitzer.
③ 4 x 24 pdr.
④ 6 x 24 pdr.
⑤ 3 x 24 pdr, 2 x 10 inch mortar.
⑥ 4 x 24 pdr, 2 x 8 inch howitzer.
⑦ 2 x 8 inch mortar, 1 x 6 inch howitzer.
⑧ 2 x 12 inch mortar, 2 x 8 & 2 x 6 inch howitzer.
⑨ 2 x 10 inch mortar, 2 x 8 inch howitzer.
⑩ 10 x 24 pdr.
⑪ 9 x 24 pdr.
⑫ 4 x 6 inch howitzer.

Burjasot

Campanar

Beniferri

1 Musnier

Benicalaf

Benimaclet

Pannetier

NP Ferrier

R Guadalaviar

Mislata

IT Palombini

Valencia

Severoli

R Guadalaviar

Xirivella

Razafa

El Grao

Reille

Artillery Park

Bourke

2 Harispe

3 Habert

Miles
0   1

Kilometres
0   1

Chapter 37

THE CULMINATION OF A YEAR OF MIXED FORTUNES: DECEMBER 1811

Napoleon was encouraged by Suchet's success on the east coast and, with the battle of Saguntum fought and won, he not only concurred with Suchet's request for Severoli and Reille but also ordered Joseph to detach a force from the Army of the Centre to attack Blake in the rear. However, the strength of the Army of the Centre at this time was only about 15,000 infantry and cavalry, and many of these were needed to garrison the capital and maintain the existing lines of communication. Consequently, Napoleon turned to the Army of Portugal and, in his dispatch of 20 November, Marmont was ordered to provide 6,000 men[1] to join those from the Army of the Centre under D'Armagnac. In addition to this force, another 3,000 to 4,000 men would also have to be detached to assume the duties of those contributed by Joseph and to keep open communications with this entire group as it moved east. Marmont ordered the divisions of Foy, Sarrut and Montbrun to march east and link up with D'Armagnac. Having left Clausel observing Wellington near the border he then moved his headquarters, as ordered, to Valladolid.

Montbrun was placed in overall command of Marmont's three divisions but they never succeeded in joining D'Armagnac, as the terrain and diminishing weather forced them to take a more southerly route, and by the time they passed Albacete Suchet had already brought events in Valencia to a swift conclusion. Blake, responding to this new threat to his rear and left, had ordered Freire[2] to march north and join Bassecourt's two divisions who were providing some degree of limited flank protection. This distraction worked and D'Armagnac elected to pull back and wait for Montbrun to join him before continuing.

In Catalonia, Marshal Macdonald had been recalled to Paris in late October and replaced by Decaen, who found himself facing a resurgent force under Lacy.[3] The new commander's options were limited given his tasks and available force and Eroles, who executed a series of raids

in early November across the Pyrenees into southern France, did not help his lot. Napoleon's characteristic rage at this violation of French soil did little to assist Decaen, but the event did result in the deployment of more national frontier guards to the region. The garrison at Barcelona remained out of communication until December, when Decaen finally managed to get a large convoy into the place.

With Marmont's army now split between containing Wellington and assisting Suchet, his force was stretched. To assist, Napoleon allocated Bonnet's Division (from the Asturias) and Souham's Division (located at Benavente/Zamora) from Dorsenne's Army of the North. In addition, Dorsenne was ordered to move the balance of his force eastwards and to return personally to France at the head of the two divisions of the Imperial Guard, who were needed for the Russian campaign. (For the full details of the divisional movement of the armies of the North and Portugal over this period see Appendix 5.) Marmont's huge area of responsibility was further complicated by the need to replace the large garrisons at León, Benavente, Salamanca and Valladolid. Subsequent directives then prevented him withdrawing Bonnet from the Asturias and instructed him to leave at least one division in the Tagus valley, further curtailing his freedom of manoeuvre. Despite this, Marmont remained confident that he could concentrate and respond sufficiently rapidly should Wellington move on Ciudad Rodrigo.

To the south, the raid by the combined forces of both Hill's Anglo-Portuguese and Castaños's Army of Estremadura against Girard's Division had been a resounding success, which ultimately led to the French commander's dismissal,[4] the virtual annihilation of his formation and the need for Soult to reinforce Drouet. At much the same time, Soult received notification of a recall of troops for the impending Russian campaign.[5] Leval's Corps had done little since restoring the territory lost during Freire's attacks in the middle of the year. Victor remained locked in the struggle to take Cádiz but was making little headway. Soult's frustrations at not being able to mass sufficient strength to subdue Andalusia led him to try to raise Spanish forces locally to assume garrison duties[6]; but these reluctant sentinels were to fade away at the earliest opportunity. In July, after a brief stay at Cádiz, Ballesteros had moved by ship to Algeciras where he joined forces with the guerrilla forces on the Sierra de Ronda. Their combined groups were so troublesome to the French that Soult was compelled to eradicate this threat before pursuing further offensives in eastern Murcia. His frustration hinged on the ability of these groups to take refuge in Cádiz, Gibraltar or Tarifa and to move unconstrained by sea to execute harassing operations at another locality. The first two bases were considered impregnable, but that of Tarifa was thought feasible. On 21 November Barrois moved with his division to Los Barrios and San Roque; Pécheux with his brigade to the passes that led into the plains of Gibraltar; and Leval (with a composite division) closed in on Málaga. Ballesteros received early notification of these movements and,

---

1   In fact Marmont had to find 9,000 men, as the Army of the Centre could only spare 3,000.

2   Freire, with the remnants of the Army of Murcia, had been busy recruiting and training new troops once Mahy had departed north in October to support Blake at Saguntum.

3   Lacy's command had grown to about 14,000 men but he was a strict disciplinarian and not a Catalan, which led to numerous disagreements with the Junta and the irregulars.

4   He was replaced by General Barrois. The remnants of Girard's Division, the 34e and 40e Ligne, were sent back to France but they never made it as they were detailed by Dorsenne when they reached Burgos.

5   This included Dembouski's Polish Division and the Polish Lancers.

6   There were, at their height, about 5,000 of these *Juramentados*. They were largely formed of deserters who volunteered rather than be sent to France.

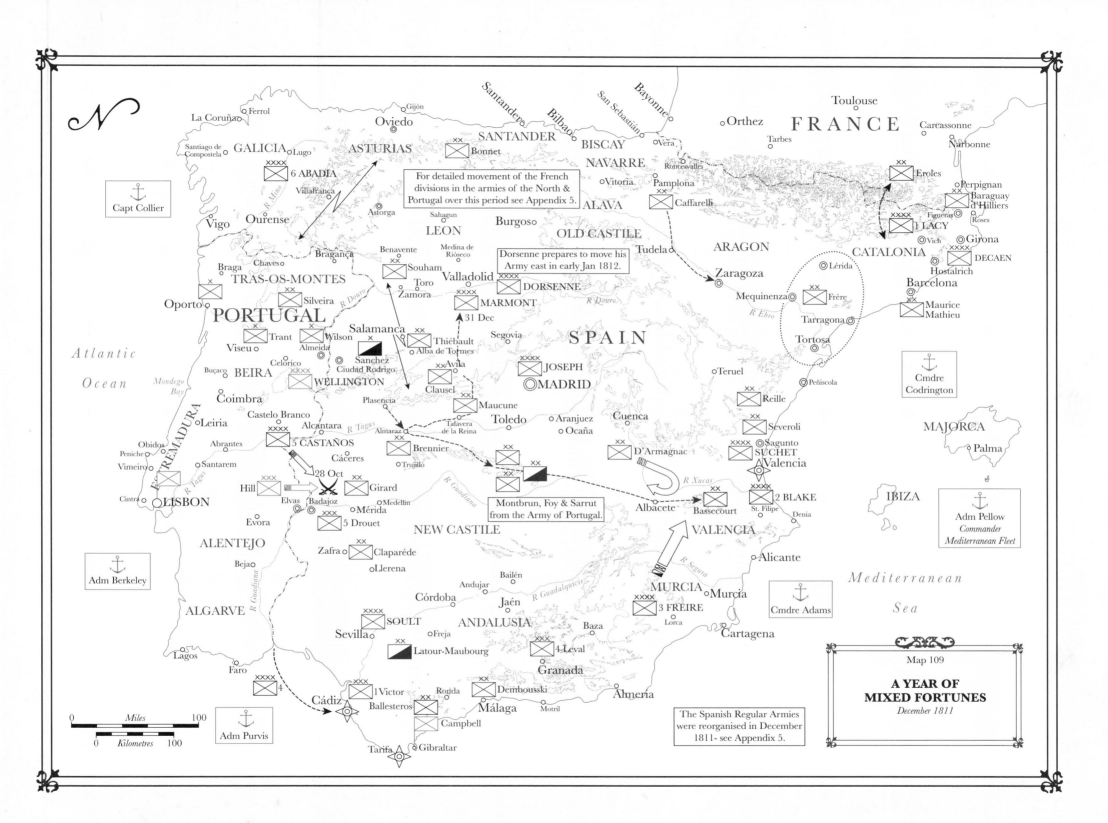

N

La Coruña ○ ○ Ferrol
Santiago de ○
Compostela ○ Lugo
GALICIA

Gijón ○
Oviedo ○
ASTURIAS

Santander ○ Bilbao
Bayonne ○
SANTANDER
☒☒ Bonnet
BISCAY
San Sebastián ○
Vera ○

Toulouse
FRANCE
Orthez ○
Carcassonne ○
Tarbes ○

Narbonne ○

Capt Collier

☒☒☒☒ 6 ABADIA
Villafranca ○

For detailed movement of the French
divisions in the armies of the North &
Portugal over this period see Appendix 5.

NAVARRE
Roncesvalles ○
Vitoria ○
Pamplona ○

ALAVA
☒☒ Caffarelli

ARAGON

☒☒ Eroles
Perpignan ○
Baraguay
d'Hilliers ☒☒
Figueras ◎
Roses ○
☒☒☒☒ LACY
Vich ○ Girona ◎

Ourense ○
Vigo ○
Braga ○ Chaves ○
TRAS-OS-MONTES
Bragança ○
LEON
Astorga ○
Sahagun ○
Medina de
Ríoseco ○
Burgos ○
OLD CASTILE
Tudela ○
Zaragoza ◎
Mequinenza ◎
Lérida ○
☒☒ Frère
Tarragona ◎
Tortosa ◎

Barcelona ○
Maurice
Mathieu ☒☒
Hostalrich ◎
DECAEN ☒☒

Oporto ○
PORTUGAL
☒ Silveira
Benavente ○
☒☒ Souham
Toro ○
Zamora ○
Valladolid ○
☒☒☒☒ DORSENNE
☒☒ MARMONT
31 Dec

Dorsenne prepares to move his
Army east in early Jan 1812.

R Douro
SPAIN

Cmdre
Codrington

Viseu ○ ☒ Trant ☒ Wilson
Almeida ◎
Salamanca ○
☒☒ Thiébault
Alba de Tormes ○
Segovia ○
Teruel ○
Peñiscola ◎
MAJORCA
Palma ○

Atlantic
Ocean
Mondego
Bay
BEIRA
Buçaco ○ Celorico ○
Coimbra ○
Castelo Branco ○
Leiria ○
Abrantes ○
☒☒☒☒ WELLINGTON
■ Sanchez
Ciudad Rodrigo ◎
☒☒ Avila
☒ Clausel
Plasencia ○
Maucune ☒☒
☒☒☒☒ JOSEPH
MADRID ◎
Toledo ○
Aranjuez ○
Ocaña ○
Cuenca ○
☒ D'Armagnac
☒☒ Severoli
Sagunto ◎
☒☒☒☒ SUCHET
Valencia ◎
☒☒ Reille
IBIZA

Obidos ○
Peniche ○
EXTREMADURA
Santarem ○
Alcantara ○
R Tagus
☒☒☒☒ 5 CASTAÑOS
Cáceres ○
28 Oct
Almaraz ○
Talavera de
la Reina ○
Montbrun, Foy & Sarrut
from the Army of Portugal.
Albacete ○
☒☒ Bassecourt
St. Filipe ○
Denia ○
VALENCIA
Alicante ○
☒☒☒☒ 2 BLAKE

Vimeiro ○
Cintra ○
LISBON ○
Hill ☒☒☒
Elvas ◎
Badajoz ◎
☒☒ Girard
Medellin ○
Trujillo ○
Mérida ○
Evora ○
☒☒ 5 Drouet
NEW CASTILE
R Guadiana
R Xucar
R Segura
Mediterranean
Sea

Adm Pellow
Commander
Mediterranean Fleet

ALENTEJO
Zafra ○
Beja ○
Llerena ○
☒☒ Claparéde
Andujar ○
Bailén ○
Córdoba ○
Jaén ○
R Guadalquivir
MURCIA
Murcia ○
Lorca ○
Baza ○
☒☒☒☒ 3 FREIRE
Alicante ○
Cmdre Adams

Adm Berkeley

ALGARVE
Lagos ○
Faro ○
☒☒☒☒ 4
Cádiz ✦
☒☒☒☒ 1 Victor
Ballesteros ☒☒
Sevilla ○
☒☒☒☒ SOULT
Freja ○
ANDALUSIA
■ Latour-Maubourg
☒☒ 4 Leval
Granada
Ronda ○
☒☒ Dembousski
Málaga ○
Motril ○
Cartagena ○
Almería ○

Miles 100
Kilometres 100

Adm Purvis

Campbell ☒☒
Tarifa ✦
Gibraltar ○

The Spanish Regular Armies
were reorganised in December
1811- see Appendix 5.

Map 109
A YEAR OF
MIXED FORTUNES
December 1811

with some difficulty, extracted himself to Gibraltar. Soult also issued orders for a small force of 12,000 men and a siege train of 16 guns to assemble outside Cádiz. Victor was placed in charge of the operation and while the siege train and supplies were being assembled he moved to Vejar (approximately halfway between Cádiz and Tarifa) to clear and reconnoitre the route. Of the two routes only the coastal road would suffice to carry the train, and this had been destroyed in many places and was covered by fire from the many British warships that patrolled this area of coastline. Garbé, the chief engineer, resolved to repair the only viable route and by the time the train arrived on 8 December the road was serviceable, although torrential rains and harassing fire from the British ships had impeded their progress considerably. To make matters worse, on 17 and 18 December, Ballesteros had emerged from Gibraltar and fallen on the rear of this vulnerable column.

In October General Campbell, the Governor of Gibraltar, had placed an additional brigade at Tarifa under Colonel Skerrett to bolster the handful of British companies who had been there since 1810. Three days later the Spanish sent another brigade from Cádiz, under General Copons, providing a total force in excess of 3,000 bayonets. However, Tarifa itself was not a contemporary fortress, possessing no more than 2.5m-thick medieval walls for protection. The hill to the north-east of the town provided the perfect platform for modern siege guns and it possessed no outer works to deny it to an attacker. 'The *tarifeños* were brave and provided an additional 300 sailors. The governor was Colonel Don Manuel Davan and the commanders of the engineers and artillery, Don Eugenio Iraurgui and Don Pablo Sánchez. There were also English ships of war. The defence, however, was largely conducted by Don Francisco Copons y Navia and assisted by the advice of the English Colonel Skerret[t].'[7] The main problem was that the *enceinte* was too narrow to accommodate guns; Sánchez had a total of 26 pieces but only 12 were positioned inside the town. Two of the heavier guns were mounted in the towers, to the north-east, where the *enceinte* was wider and six nine-pounder field guns and four field mortars were positioned at various intervals along the walls. The balance of 14 guns were in the three batteries on the island and in the redoubt of Santa Catalina which protected the causeway to what was arguably the most defendable aspect of Tarifa. Copons and Skerrett had distributed their forces equally, each keeping two battalions in the town and one on the island.[8]

Ballesteros had fallen back when attacked by Barrois and was content to cut the French lines of communication with Cádiz. At much the same time, Skerrett had debouched from the fort with the intention of engaging the French vanguard. He had advanced about 5km from Tarifa but when he realized the strength of the approaching French force he withdrew. On the morning of 20 December the force advanced towards the town in two columns and, after a lengthy

skirmish, pushed back all the Allied piquets. Early on 23 December, the French engineers conducted a reconnaissance and unsurprisingly elected to establish the siege batteries on the hills to the north-east, commencing the first parallel the same evening. The going was relatively easy and they faced limited counter-fire from the guns in the town as a ravine and a large hedge masked the trenches. The heavier 24-pounder guns on the island, and those of the British and Spanish gunboats, could reach the French working parties but observers in the towers were directing their fire to negligible effect. The appalling weather continued causing problems for both sides but by the night of 28 December two battery positions were ready. The next morning the 12 guns and howitzers opened and the vulnerability of the fortress was immediately evident. One of the first shots went clean through the wall and within hours the Spanish guns on the facing wall had been silenced and a breach had been fashioned. Skerrett proposed to evacuate the town but Colonel Gough of the 87th, Major King, and Captain Smith[9] urged that the town could and should be defended. Skerrett's track record at Tarragona (see Chapter 34) was widely known and King sent word back to General Campbell at Gibraltar of Skerrett's intentions and Copons' determination to hold on to the town. Campbell's furious reply and the withdrawal of the naval transports thwarted Skerrett's plans.

The next morning Leval considered the breach serviceable and sent in a summons that was promptly rejected; however, the assault planned for that night had to be delayed due to another torrential downpour. At 0900 hours the following morning the grenadier companies stormed the breach, while the voltigeur companies attempted to force entry at the Portcullis, supported by the brigades of Cassagne and Pécheux who executed simultaneous demonstrations. The assailants attacked against the fire of muskets alone from the Irlanda, Cantabria, 47th and 87th. The grenadiers hesitated at the foot of the breach and began firing back instead of pushing on; with their momentum lost, the group swung right and towards the voltigeurs who were attempting to gain entry at the Portcullis. The hastily prepared defences were able to hold and the mass of French soldiers now found themselves under very heavy fire from the curtain. Many French officers tried to kick-start the attack, but their efforts were in vain and after a short while the French resolve broke and the attackers fled from the walls. The morale of the French force was now in terminal decline; the foul weather, lack of food and a humiliating failure gave them little or no cause for celebration on New Year's evening. Victor was furious, and was not about to compromise his honour by abandoning his mission. When the torrential rains again abated on 2 January he ordered the batteries to be repaired and re-manned, but when another tempest arose the following day even he had to concede defeat. The men and animals were so weak and the ground so sodden that only one gun and two howitzers could be extracted. The miserable retreat provided an apposite finale to a wretched operation. Soult's aspirations to expand operations in eastern Murcia and support Suchet in Valencia were in ruins.

---

7   Toreno, *La Derrota de Napoleon*, vol. II, p.100.

8   The 47th and 87th were in the town; the Battalion of Flank Companies on the island, while the Convent of
    San Francisco was held by a company of the 82nd and the redoubt of Santa Catalina by a company of the 11th.
    The Spanish dispositions are unknown.

9   King was commanding the Battalion of Flank Companies and Smith was the senior Sapper.

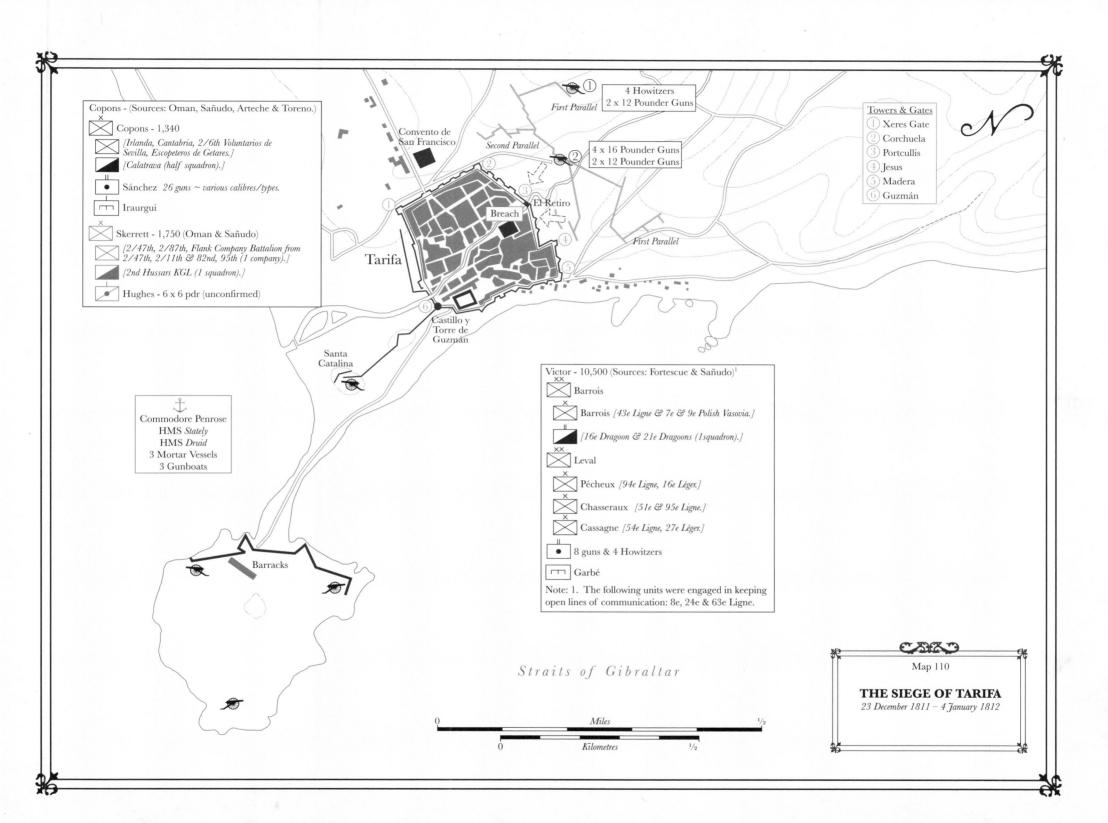

Copons - (Sources: Oman, Sañudo, Arteche & Toreno.)

Copons - 1,340

[Irlanda, Cantabria, 2/6th Voluntarios de Sevilla, Escopeteros de Getares.]

[Calatrava (half squadron).]

Sánchez 26 guns ~ various calibres/types.

Iraurgui

Skerrett - 1,750 (Oman & Sañudo)

[2/47th, 2/87th, Flank Company Battalion from 2/47th, 2/11th & 82nd, 95th (1 company).]

[2nd Hussars KGL (1 squadron).]

Hughes - 6 x 6 pdr (unconfirmed)

Towers & Gates

① Xeres Gate
② Corchuela
③ Portcullis
④ Jesus
⑤ Madera
⑥ Guzmán

N

Convento de San Francisco

First Parallel

4 Howitzers
2 x 12 Pounder Guns

Second Parallel

4 x 16 Pounder Guns
2 x 12 Pounder Guns

El Retiro

Breach

First Parallel

Tarifa

Castillo y Torre de Guzmán

Santa Catalina

Commodore Penrose
HMS *Stately*
HMS *Druid*
3 Mortar Vessels
3 Gunboats

Victor - 10,500 (Sources: Fortescue & Sañudo)[1]

Barrois

Barrois [43e Ligne & 7e & 9e Polish Vasovia.]

[16e Dragoon & 21e Dragoons (1 squadron).]

Leval

Pécheux [94e Ligne, 16e Léger.]

Chasseraux [51e & 95e Ligne.]

Cassagne [54e Ligne, 27e Léger.]

8 guns & 4 Howitzers

Garbé

Note: 1. The following units were engaged in keeping open lines of communication: 8e, 24e & 63e Ligne.

Barracks

Straits of Gibraltar

Map 110

THE SIEGE OF TARIFA
23 December 1811 – 4 January 1812

0 Miles ½

0 Kilometres ½

Chapter 38

CAPTURING THE 'KEYS TO SPAIN': JANUARY TO APRIL 1812

In late 1811 Wellington faced a dilemma. His most commendable option seemed to be the concentration of his force to the south, thereby capitalizing on Hill's successful raids into Estremadura, driving Drouet from the region and then commencing the siege of Badajoz. However, as Wellington was to write to Lord Liverpool, 'It would not answer to remove the army to the frontiers of Estremadura (where a chance of effecting some important object might have been offered), as in that case General Abadia would have been left to himself, and would have fallen an easy sacrifice to the Army of the North.'[1] Wellington deduced that Soult was out of the game and Drouet adequately contained by Hill; he calculated that Marmont and Dorsenne would soon move into winter quarters and disperse their forces, and for this he planned and waited. As early as July 1811 Alexander Dickson had been dispatched to Oporto to collect and transport the siege guns that had arrived from England.[2] In addition, he had been tasked to arrange all the requisite powder and shot, while Fletcher had been similarly tasked with regard to engineer stores. By late November, 25 of the heavy guns were already in place at Almeida along with 80,000 shot and considerable quantities of powder. Reports of a general easterly movement by Marmont's army began to emerge in mid-December, but it was to be another ten days before the Allies realized the extent of this French strategic readjustment (see Chapter 37). In early January Wellington despatched orders for the divisions to break cantonment and move up to the line of the Agueda. On 6 January they crossed the river in appalling conditions and two days later they closed in his chosen target, the northern key to Spain, Ciudad Rodrigo.

Wellington, despite threatening to be his own engineer following the last attempt at Badajoz, had consulted Fletcher and together they decided to follow Ney's example from his siege in 1810. Since then the walls had been substantially repaired and an additional redoubt had been constructed on the forward slopes of the Cabéco Alto. Lieutenant Colonel Colborne and a composite force of 450 men stormed and captured this structure on the first night.[3] The following day, as the French gunners in the city and the convent of San Francisco pounded the structure, Colborne withdrew and the Allies made full use of the cover the structure provided to assist in the construction of the first parallel. The men welcomed the work as it served to counter the freezing wind; those on sentry duty (mainly the Portuguese soldiers) were chilled to the bone and some were found dead at their posts. With his four available divisions Wellington established a rotational system, each working one night in four. As early as the night of 10 January the first three batteries were ready to receive guns and, as dawn broke on the 11th, they commenced a sustained fire at the areas of the walls selected for the breach. These three batteries attracted fierce counter-fire from the French guns, which hindered progress on the second parallel but Wellington, ever conscious of news of the approaching French relieving force,[4] decided to try and blast serviceable breaches from the first three batteries in the first parallel. Work continued on the second parallel as it provided a task for the men and a fallback should his initial intentions fail.

On the night of 11 January the French moved a howitzer up into the suburbs of San Francisco, which enfiladed the first battery, and slowed progress in sapping forward to the line for the second parallel. Two nights later Wellington resolved to capture the convent and with it the troublesome howitzer; the 40th stormed the building and succeeded in driving out the defenders, convincing Barrié to withdraw the balance of French forces from the suburbs. With this flanking threat removed and with all the French attention now focused on preventing the construction of the second parallel, Wellington ordered the construction of what became the fourth battery, from where he elected to batter a second breach. The heavy guns in the first three batteries continued to batter the walls, but with no fire allocated to counter-battery missions the attempt to sap forward from the second parallel had to be abandoned as continuous storms of grape began to take an unacceptable toll on the workforce.

On 18 January the seven guns in the fourth battery opened with rapid results. By nightfall the wall at the site of the second breach had collapsed, taking with it the very gun that had flanked and therefore enfiladed the main breach. Wellington elected to assault the two breaches the following night. The 3rd Division was tasked with carrying the main breach with Mackinnon's Brigade attacking directly from the edge of the second parallel, while Campbell's Brigade was given three tasks; the 2/83rd[5] were detached to provide covering fire, the 77th were placed in reserve while the 94th and 2/5th attacked the walls from the convent of Santa Cruz to act as a diversion before joining the assault at the main breach. To their right Colonel O'Toole attacked across the bridge with the objective of capturing the two French guns that enfiladed the approach of the 2/5th. To the north, the Light Division attacked the lesser breach with Vandeleur's Brigade, which detached three companies of the 95th to provide covering fire, while Barnard's Brigade remained in reserve. Finally, Pack's Brigade executed a false attack on the Santiago gate to the east of the town.

The defenders had not anticipated attacks from all directions and early success by the 2/5th in gaining a lodgement on the western walls caught the defenders cold. By the time the three separate groups reached the main breach they became mixed and scrambled to the summit of

1   Oman, *History of the Peninsular War*, vol. V. p.158.

2   Dickson, *The Dickson Manuscripts*, vol. 3 p.419: in a letter from Dickson to Beresford, 19 July 1811.

3   This group consisted of 2 companies from each battalion and 1 company from the 1st and 3rd Caçadores.

4   In fact he need not have worried for Marmont and Dorsenne did not know that the siege had commenced until 15 January. Barrié had sent 3 messages on the nights of 9 and 10th January but these had been intercepted by de España and Sanchez's patrols. Fortescue, *A History of the British Army*, vol. VIII, p.355.

5   Except for the light company which accompanied O'Toole's 2nd Caçadores.

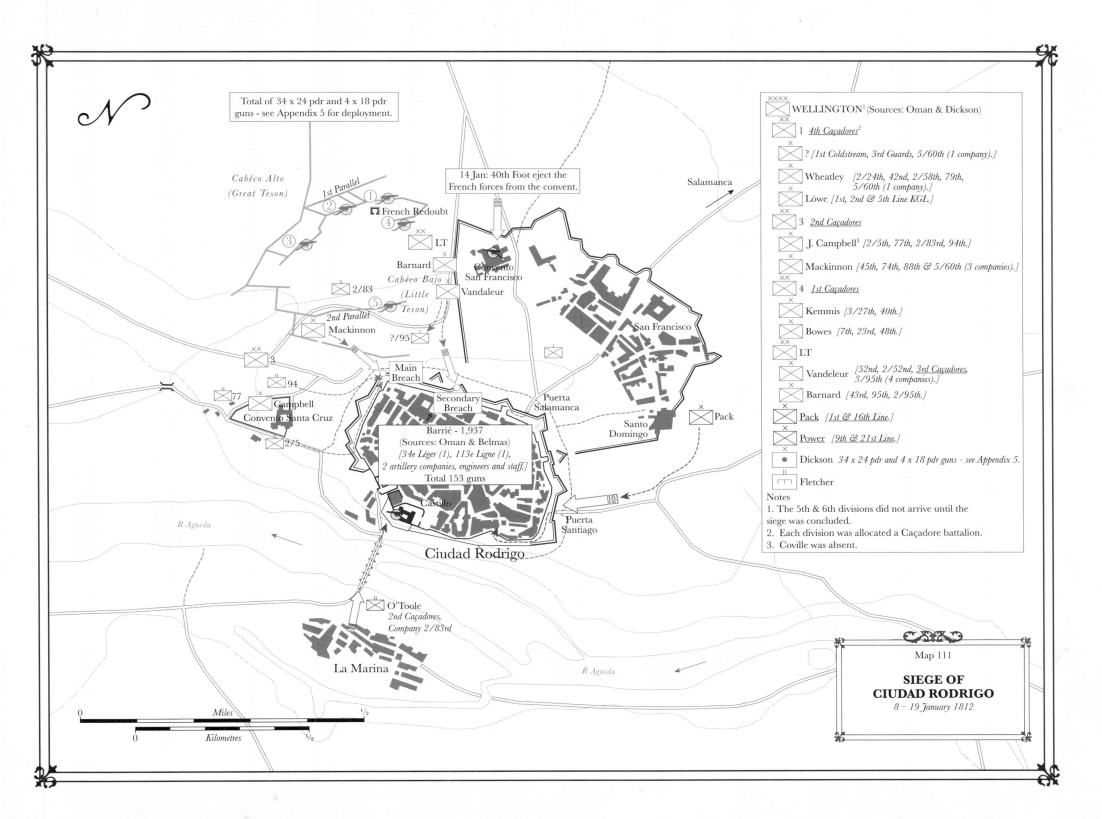

N

Total of 34 x 24 pdr and 4 x 18 pdr guns - see Appendix 5 for deployment.

14 Jan: 40th Foot eject the French forces from the convent.

Salamanca

Cabéco Alto (Great Teson)

1st Parallel

① ② ④ ③

☐ French Redoubt

LT

Barnard

Convento San Francisco

Cabéco Bajo (Little Teson)

Vandaleur

San Francisco

2/83

2nd Parallel

Mackinnon

?/95

3

Main Breach

Secondary Breach

Puerta Salamanca

94

Campbell

77

Convento Santa Cruz

2/5

Barrié - 1,937
(Sources: Oman & Belmas)
[34e Léger (1), 113e Ligne (1),
2 artillery companies, engineers and staff.]
Total 153 guns

Santo Domingo

Pack

Castillo

Puerta Santiago

Ciudad Rodrigo

R Agueda

O'Toole
2nd Caçadores,
Company 2/83rd

R Agueda

La Marina

0   *Miles*   ½

0   *Kilometres*   ½

WELLINGTON[1] (Sources: Oman & Dickson)

1   *4th Caçadores*[2]

? *[1st Coldstream, 3rd Guards, 5/60th (1 company).]*

Wheatley *[2/24th, 42nd, 2/58th, 79th, 5/60th (1 company).]*

Löwe *[1st, 2nd & 5th Line KGL.]*

3   *2nd Caçadores*

J. Campbell[3] *[2/5th, 77th, 2/83rd, 94th.]*

Mackinnon *[45th, 74th, 88th & 5/60th (3 companies).]*

4   *1st Caçadores*

Kemmis *[3/27th, 40th.]*

Bowes *[7th, 23rd, 48th.]*

LT

Vandeleur *[52nd, 2/52nd, 3rd Caçadores, 3/95th (4 companies).]*

Barnard *[43rd, 95th, 2/95th.]*

Pack   *[1st & 16th Line.]*

Power   *[9th & 21st Line.]*

● Dickson   *34 x 24 pdr and 4 x 18 pdr guns - see Appendix 5.*

⊓ Fletcher

Notes
1. The 5th & 6th divisions did not arrive until the siege was concluded.
2. Each division was allocated a Caçadore battalion.
3. Coville was absent.

Map 111

SIEGE OF CIUDAD RODRIGO

8 – 19 January 1812

the debris to be met with a hail of grape from two well-sited guns. The infantry discarded their muskets and scrambled, bayonets between their teeth, along the planks to reach and slay the gunners delivering such a deadly fire. Meanwhile Vandeleur had already forced the lesser breach and the two assaults by the Portuguese had also succeeded. The city was lost. It was an incredible achievement, but what followed was a disgraceful display of murder, debauchment and ill-discipline that was merely a precursor to the capture of subsequent Peninsular towns taken by assault. Allied losses were not significant, given the scale of the objective and speed of capture, but among the nine dead officers lay Craufurd and Mackinnon. 'Poor Craufurd! – whilst the memory of the brave and skilful shall continue to be cherished by British soldiers, thou wilt not be forgotten; and the hand which scrawls humble tribute to thy worth must be cold as thine own, ere the mind which dictates it shall cease to think of thee with affection and regret.'[6]

Wellington turned his attention south and despatched Dickson with the siege train to Elvas but retained his army in the north to maintain the deception. The French commanders were in no little disarray as they reorganized their forces, adjusted their areas of responsibility and considered their new tasks in light of Napoleon's dispatch which only reached them at the end of December (see Chapter 37). Marmont and Dorsenne met at Valladolid on 12 January to discuss options but they had no definitive intelligence as to Wellington's whereabouts and intentions. The dispersion of their forces and the seasonally bad weather delayed concentration which, when achieved, was too late to save Ciudad Rodrigo. With the arrival (in Paris) of news of the fall of the border fortress, another communiqué was soon to follow and, apart from heavy criticism of Marmont's handling of the situation thus far, Napoleon made his intentions clear. Marmont was to remain in Salamanca and conduct offensive operations from there, whilst at the same time he was to reoccupy the Asturias. Napoleon and his staff had concluded that Wellington would not move south, as this would open the way for Marmont to invade Portugal. It was a serious miscalculation.

By the time this communiqué had arrived from Paris, Dickson was already well south and the first of the Anglo-Portuguese divisions close behind. By 26 February all but one of the divisions was on the move; the 5th Division and cavalry units from the Portuguese, Spanish and King's German Legion remained to keep up the deception. To the north the Army of Galicia[7] stood poised to come south in aid of this force and Castaños, with the majority of de España's Division from the Army of Estremadura, was now ensconced in Ciudad Rodrigo. Julian Sanchez's cavalry brigade had now grown to about 1,200 sabres and was an extremely efficient formation, which by this time was a regular force, titled the 1st and 2nd Lanceros de Castilla. By 16 March the infantry had concentrated near Elvas,[8] where Dickson was also positioned with the large siege train and associated engineer stores.

Soult, like Marmont, had been convinced all along that Wellington's next move would be against Badajoz and, as he was not constrained by Napoleonic decree, began to move north

between 20 and 30 March to provide relief to General Phillipon and the Badajoz garrison. He took with him the infantry brigades of Barrois and Vichery and six regiments of dragoons from his extensive cavalry resources. He planned to link up with the two divisions from Drouet's Corps, which remained in Estremadura, providing a force of about 25,000. Before departing Soult had conferred with Marmont and reached agreement that the latter would secure his left flank and join forces against Wellington if the situation required. Marmont moved the divisions of Brennier, Foy and Sarrut to Talavera, Monbeltran and Almaraz respectively with Montbrun's cavalry in support.[9] Soult left Sevilla on 30 March, confident that Wellington's superior force (of about 55,000) could therefore be contained and, if necessary, engaged by the combined forces from the armies of the South and Portugal.

On 16 March, with the Allied armies concentrated and the siege train ready, Wellington began his advance in two columns tasked to drive in the remnants of Drouet's Corps and to subsequently establish the covering force. The first column under Graham consisted of the 1st, 6th and 7th divisions and Slade and Marchant's cavalry, and advanced on the southerly route; while the second under Hill, consisting of elements of Spanish troops from the Army of Estremadura, the 2nd Division, Hamilton's Portuguese Division and Long and Campbell's cavalry, took the northerly route. The balance of the Anglo-Portuguese force was to act a reserve and escort the siege train, while the balance of the Army of Estremadura (less de España's Division, and those troops task-organized with Hill's Corps) and the divisions of Penne Villemur and Morillo, were to cross the border, head south and attack Sevilla should the opportunity present itself. Drouet withdrew in the face of Graham's advance and although the Allies followed up, they were soon recalled when Wellington received intelligence of Soult's northerly movement. Marmont had by now started his advance into northern Portugal and withdrawn Brennier, Sarrut and Montbrun (see map 115). Drouet had withdrawn Daricau's Division and the sole remaining division of the Army of Portugal, that of Foy, still lay at Talavera, by now in hazardous isolation.

As the covering forces deployed, the engineers and gunners made their preliminary reconnaissance of Badajoz. Phillipon and his garrison had been characteristically industrious in improving the town's defences. 'In the castle they had formed an interior retrenchment, and had mounted many guns on the ramparts. They had also well secured the rear of the Fort Christoval [sic], raised its glacis and counterscarp before the flank breached, thrown up a formidable redoubt on the site of the breaching battery, and had brought into a state of great forwardness a covered communication from the *tête-du-pont* to the fort.'[10] With two failed attempts on the San Cristobal and the main castle, it was not surprising that Fletcher elected to tackle the fort from a different angle. 'They had well enclosed the gorge of the Pardaleras outwork, and had connected it with the place by intermediate works; and had erected very powerful batteries looking into the rear of it.'[11] Intelligence from a French sapper deserter also revealed that the south-western wall was heavily mined, 'and would necessitate three or four lodgements being

6   Vane, *Narrative of the Peninsular War*, vol. II, p.268.

7   Consisting of 4 divisions, all under strength, with a total of about 15,000 men.

8   The 5th Division, having departed Ciudad Rodrigo on 9 March, did not join the force until 20 March.

9   Foy, Sarrut and Montbrun had just returned from their operations against the Valencian Army.

10   Jones, *Journal of Sieges*, vol. I, p.149. The redoubt was called the Lunette Verlé.

11   Ibid, p.149.

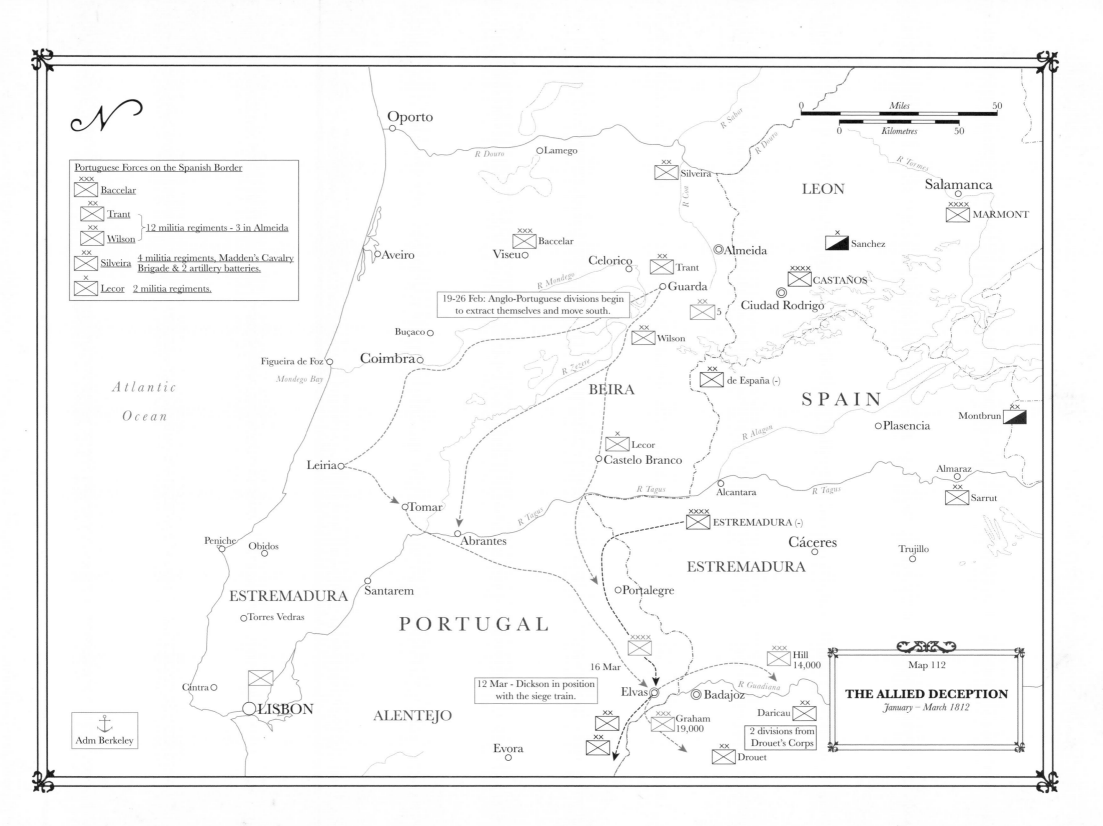

N

Oporto

R Douro

Lamego

Silveira

LEON

Salamanca

R Sabor

R Douro

R Tormes

MARMONT

Portuguese Forces on the Spanish Border

Baccelar

Trant

Wilson — 12 militia regiments - 3 in Almeida

Silveira — 4 militia regiments, Madden's Cavalry Brigade & 2 artillery batteries.

Lecor — 2 militia regiments.

Viseu

Baccelar

Celorico

Trant

Almeida

Sanchez

CASTAÑOS

Ciudad Rodrigo

19-26 Feb: Anglo-Portuguese divisions begin to extract themselves and move south.

Aveiro

R Mondego

Guarda

5

Buçaco

Wilson

Coimbra

BEIRA

de España (-)

SPAIN

Figueira de Foz

R Zezere

Montbrun

Mondego Bay

Plasencia

R Alagon

Lecor

Atlantic

Ocean

Castelo Branco

R Tagus

R Tagus

Almaraz

Leiria

Alcantara

Sarrut

Tomar

R Tagus

ESTREMADURA (-)

Peniche

Obidos

Abrantes

Cáceres

Trujillo

Santarem

ESTREMADURA

Portalegre

ESTREMADURA

PORTUGAL

Torres Vedras

Hill 14,000

Map 112

16 Mar

THE ALLIED DECEPTION

January – March 1812

12 Mar - Dickson in position with the siege train.

Elvas

R Guadiana

Badajoz

Daricau

Cintra

LISBON

ALENTEJO

Graham 19,000

2 divisions from Drouet's Corps

Evora

Drouet

Adm Berkeley

formed, [and] could not be recommended'.[12] By process of elimination therefore, the bastions of Santa Maria and La Trinidad were selected which, in turn, dictated the need for a preliminary operation to capture the Picurina.

The investment was complete by the early morning on 17 March and that night Fletcher took advantage of the foul weather to mark out a long parallel only about 200m from the Picurina structure. A workforce of nearly 2,000 men immediately set to work and by dawn the 600m-long parallel, and an equally long communication trench to the engineer park, was well advanced. The French had not fired a shot as they had been focused on the San Cristobal, expecting a third attempt from this direction. As dawn broke and the weather cleared, Phillipon realized his mistake and immediately responded with a heavy and sustained fire on the trenches and set about reorganizing his own defensive plans. The continuing bad weather was a mixed blessing; the visibility was down to a few hundred metres, frustrating French counter-fire, but the ground became increasingly unworkable and the trenches began to fill with water. Nevertheless, the first two batteries were traced out the following night and Phillipon, somewhat alarmed at the speed of the besiegers' progress, decided to execute a sortie in broad daylight. 'A sortie, executed with vigour, moved away the English of their trenches, permitted to fill a part of it, but was followed by an offensive return of the enemy and our soldiers, instead of retiring without false pride, since their goal was reached, persisted to dispute the ground, and had 20 killed and 160 wounded.'[13] Losses to the attackers were smaller but included the chief engineer, Fletcher, who was unable to participate in the rest of the siege.[14]

With repairs completed, work commenced on extending the trenches north, opposite the bastion of San Pedro, from where the batteries were to be constructed to engage the Trinidad bastion. The weather did not abate and by 22 March the outlook was bleak. 'At four p.m. fell one of the heaviest showers imaginable, which again filled the trenches with water. The pontoon bridge across the Guadiana was carried away by the rise of the river; eleven of the pontoons sunk at their anchors, and the current became so rapid that the flying bridges could with difficulty work. It therefore became a question if it would be possible to supply the army with provisions, and bring over the guns and ammunition for the attack; and serious apprehensions were entertained that it would be necessary to withdraw before the place.'[15] However, later that night the first two batteries were armed (see Appendix 5) and, on 24 March, the weather cleared and that night Batteries 3 to 6 were also armed; the following morning 28 guns and howitzers opened against the Picurina and the eastern walls. The first two batteries concentrated on the Picurina, but by nightfall they had made little impact. Nevertheless Wellington, ever conscious of the need to conclude the siege before the union of Soult and Marmont, ordered the outwork be stormed that evening.

General Kempt, supported by 500 men from the 3rd and Light divisions attacked at 2200 hours. 'The three columns having thrown themselves in the pit (because the English persisted in their system of not progressing the attack until all the troops were inside the ditch) one [group] moved until the reverse of the work, and tried to pull apart the palisades to enter the structure, but moved back under the vivacity of the fusillade; the second having wanted to penetrate by the breach, was also toppled; but the third applying the ladders on the face arrived until the parapet, at the same moment that the second column resumed their attack up the salient. The small garrison having to cope with two invasions at the same time, was insufficient, and was in short time obliged to put down their tired weapons.'[16] Captain Oates of the 88th had led the third column and Captain Powys of the 2/83rd the second; their leadership was inspirational, and against the odds and with considerable losses the Picurina was taken. Phillipon attempted a rapid counter-attack but this was beaten back. The engineers now began the task of establishing the main breaching batteries within the lodgement. It was to be an exigent task, as the exposed back of the captured structure had to be shielded from the fire of the three bastions that covered the approach. From 26 to 30 March the work parties toiled ceaselessly, sustaining considerable losses, to carve out the three battery positions and many more lives were lost in the process of manhandling the guns into place. One battery opened on 30 March and the other two breaching batteries followed the next day; it was a significant development and one that caused considerable concern to the defenders.

At first, the breaching batteries made slow progress against the Trinidad and Santa Maria bastions but, after three days, the heavy Russian naval guns began to make an impression and thoughts now turned to draining the flooded area that lay directly in the path of the assault. As darkness fell on 2 April Lieutenant Stanway of the Royal Engineers, his assistant W. Barney, and 20 sappers moved to the dislodge the clay wall which had been jammed against the *bàtardeau* by the defenders. But as this structure was below the water line the subsequent explosion failed to the obstruction. An attempt was made to sap down to the *bàtardeau*, but this was abandoned the next day after considerable loss of life. The attackers accepted that the assaulting infantry would have to attack the breaches from the west bank.

Phillipon was by now growing increasingly concerned. Work parties sallied by night to clear the debris from the ditch at the foot of the counterscarp in what was a virtually suicidal mission as the enfilade batteries (Numbers 4, 5, 6, 10 and 11) all poured grape into the brave workforce. Furthermore, the furious fire from the defenders' guns had severely depleted their stocks of ammunition and powder; by 3 April half the round shot had been fired, there was no common shell and very little grape remaining. On the morning of 5 April Fletcher, who that very morning had been able to get up for the first time from his bed, judged the breaches practicable. However, Wellington could clearly see the extent of the defensive preparations being made at both breaches to receive the assault and, with memories of Ciudad Rodrigo fresh in his mind, coupled with intelligence that the wall between the two breaches had been poorly constructed (which proved the case), he decided to batter a third breach on the curtain between the Santa Maria and Trinidad bastions.

12 Ibid, pp.152–3.

13 Thiers, *Histoire du Consulat et du L'Empire*, vol. XIII, p. 366. Oman states that the French lost 304 men in this foray.

14 Fletcher was hit in the groin by a musket ball but it struck a coin, which cushioned the impact and almost certainly saved his life; but the coin was forced nearly 2cm into the leg, confining him to bed. Wellington was adamant that Fletcher was to remain in charge of the engineer works for the attack and he would go to his tent every morning at 0800 hours to discuss the plan for the day.

15 Jones, *Journal of Sieges*, vol. I, pp.168–69.

16 Thiers, *Histoire du Consulat et du L'Empire*, vol. XIII, p.367.

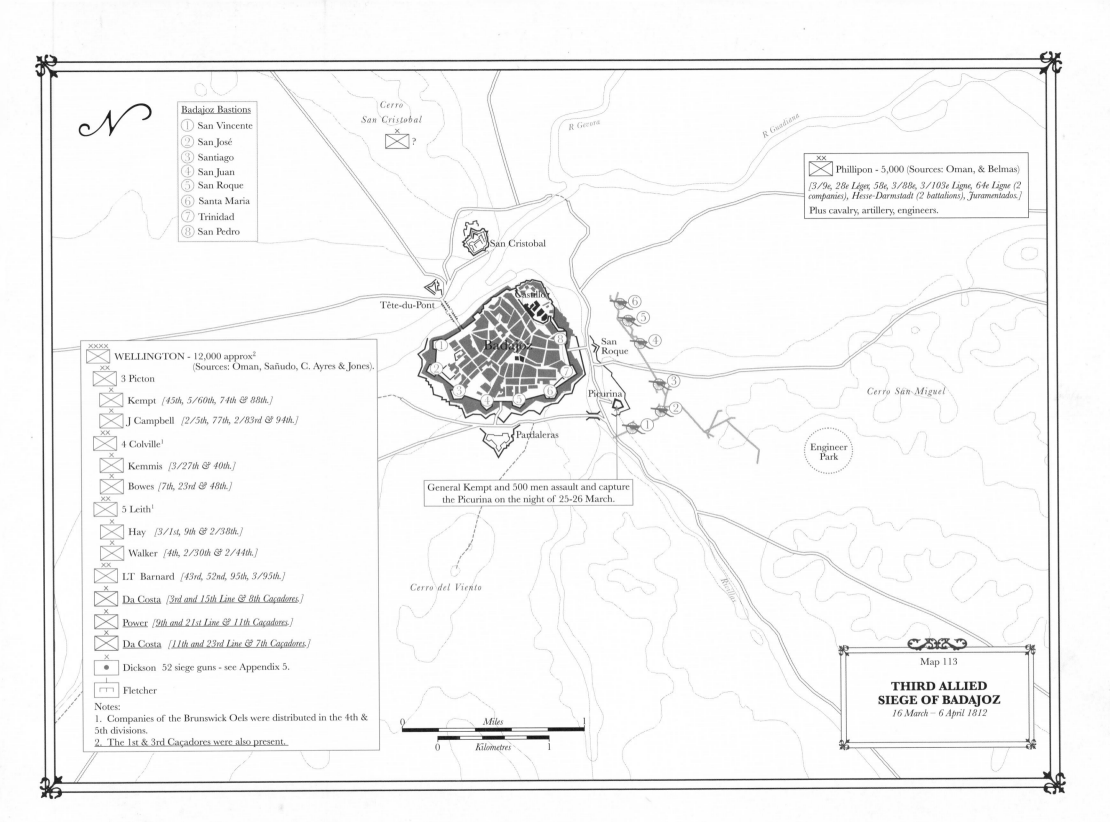

Badajoz Bastions
1. San Vincente
2. San José
3. Santiago
4. San Juan
5. San Roque
6. Santa Maria
7. Trinidad
8. San Pedro

Phillipon - 5,000 (Sources: Oman, & Belmas)
[3/9e, 28e Léger, 58e, 3/88e, 3/103e Ligne, 64e Ligne (2 companies), Hesse-Darmstadt (2 battalions), Juramentados.]
Plus cavalry, artillery, engineers.

WELLINGTON - 12,000 approx[2]
(Sources: Oman, Sañudo, C. Ayres & Jones).

3 Picton

Kempt *[45th, 5/60th, 74th & 88th.]*

J Campbell *[2/5th, 77th, 2/83rd & 94th.]*

4 Colville[1]

Kemmis *[3/27th & 40th.]*

Bowes *[7th, 23rd & 48th.]*

5 Leith[1]

Hay *[3/1st, 9th & 2/38th.]*

Walker *[4th, 2/30th & 2/44th.]*

LT Barnard *[43rd, 52nd, 95th, 3/95th.]*

Da Costa *[3rd and 15th Line & 8th Caçadores.]*

Power *[9th and 21st Line & 11th Caçadores.]*

Da Costa *[11th and 23rd Line & 7th Caçadores.]*

Dickson 52 siege guns - see Appendix 5.

Fletcher

Notes:
1. Companies of the Brunswick Oels were distributed in the 4th & 5th divisions.
2. The 1st & 3rd Caçadores were also present.

General Kempt and 500 men assault and capture the Picurina on the night of 25-26 March.

Cerro San Cristobal

R Gevora

R Guadiana

San Cristobal

Tête-du-Pont

Castillo

Badajoz

San Roque

Cerro San Miguel

Picurina

Pardaleras

Engineer Park

Cerro del Viento

Rivillas

0   Miles   1

0   Kilometres   1

Map 113

THIRD ALLIED SIEGE OF BADAJOZ
16 March – 6 April 1812

The assault was scheduled for 1930 hours on 6 April, immediately following the cessation of battering fire to deny the defenders time to prepare all manner of horrors on the far side of this new entry point. The Light and 4th divisions were tasked with tackling the breaches; the Light to tackle the Santa Maria and Colville's 4th Division the other two. Three subsidiary and two false attacks were to be executed simultaneously. The false attacks were to be performed by the Portuguese brigades; Power's against the *tête-du-pont* and the Portuguese brigade from the 5th Division against the Pardaleras redoubt. The subsidiary attacks were to be conducted by the light companies from Leith's Division on the San Vincente bastion, by Picton's 3rd Division on the castle by escalade, and finally by the trench guards furnished by the 4th Division on the San Roque lunette, where they were to distract their fire and destroy the dam. Frustratingly for Wellington, preparations to commence the attack at 1930 were delayed, and a new time of 2200 hours was set. Picton had preempted this new timing by ordering his men forward at 2145 hours when they had been discovered in their forming-up area, were exposed and taking fire. Conversely, on the far side of the town the officer in charge of the ladder party lost his way, delaying this attack until 2300. The attack of the 4th and Light divisions did however go in on time, and they had reached the edge of the glacis before being discovered. Under heavy fire many did not wait for the ladders before jumping into the ditch, which they discovered to their horror was full of water (from the blocked *bàtardeau*) and far deeper than expected, and under the weight of their impedimenta many were drowned. To their left the forlorn hope of the Light Division were making their way down into the ditch 'when a bright light of flame shooting upwards displayed all the terrors of the scene. The ramparts crowded with dark figures and glittering arms, were seen on the one side, and on the other, the red columns of the British, deep and broad, were coming on like streams of burning lava; it was the touch of the magician's wand, for a crash of thunder followed, and with incredible violence the storming parties were dashed to pieces by the explosion of hundreds of shells and powder barrels.'[17] The 500 volunteers forming the forlorn hope of each column were practically wiped out; momentum was completely lost and the two divisions became inextricably mixed as those in the right column swerved left to avoid the flooded ditch. 'Again the assailants rushed up to the breaches, and again the sword-blades, immovable and impassable, stopped their charge, and the hissing shells and thundering powder-barrels exploded unceasingly. Hundreds of men had fallen, and hundreds more were dropping, but still the heroic officers called aloud for new trials…'[18] Just after midnight Wellington recalled the two divisions; they retreated reluctantly but their sacrifice had not been in vain. The concentration of French forces at the breaches had weakened their strength and attention elsewhere. Both Picton and Leith had capitalized on this distraction and the 3rd and 5th divisions had gained lodgments. The garrison of the castle was not large and by the time of the third attempt by Campbell's Brigade they had overwhelmed the defenders. To the west, Leith's men struck lucky, discovering a small section of wall only 5.5m high, and they were up and over in sufficient numbers to establish themselves. When a few hundred were formed General Walker took the adjacent bastion of San José, at which point the defenders from the next two bastions grouped together and drove the attackers back. However, more and more British infantry were pouring into the castle and before long the French resistance broke and the British poured into the streets. Soon after midnight Badajoz had fallen. Phillipon escaped into the San Cristobal but surrendered at dawn.

Wellington was to write: 'The capture of Badajoz affords as strong an instance of the gallantry of our troops as has ever been displayed. But I greatly hope that I shall never again be the instrument of putting them to such a test as they were put to last night.'[19] It was an emotional victory for Wellington; the keys to Spain were in his hands, but before dawn, and long before Phillipon had surrendered to Fitzroy Somerset, his fine army had disgraced themselves. 'Unfortunate Badajoz, met with the usual fate of places taken at the point of a bayonet.'

---

17   Napier, *History of the War in the Peninsula*, vol. IV, p.422.

18   Ibid, p.424.

19   Wellington to Lord Liverpool – Oman, *A History of the Peninsular War*, vol. V, p.255.

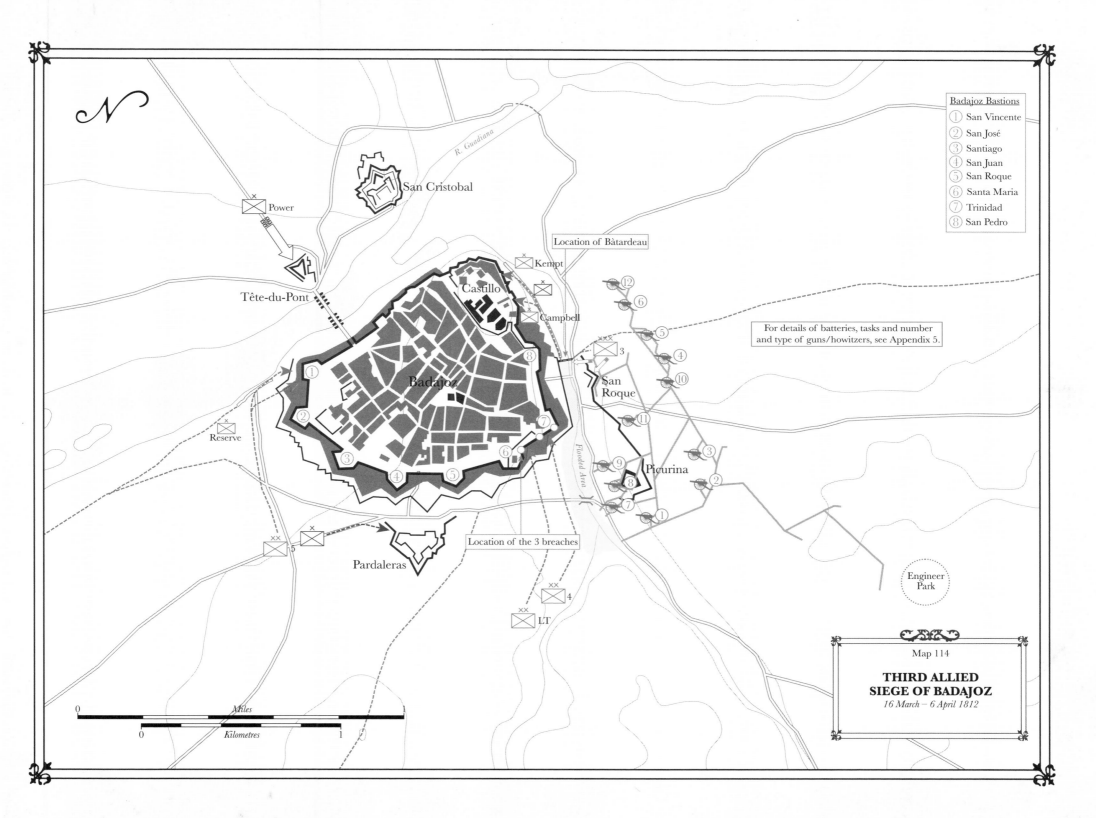

N

R. Guadiana

San Cristobal

Power

Tête-du-Pont

Kempt

Castillo

Location of Bàtardeau

Campbell

Badajoz

San Vincente
① San Vincente
② San José
③ Santiago
④ San Juan
⑤ San Roque
⑥ Santa Maria
⑦ Trinidad
⑧ San Pedro

Badajoz Bastions

For details of batteries, tasks and number and type of guns/howitzers, see Appendix 5.

San Roque

Flooded Area

Picurina

Reserve

Pardaleras

Location of the 3 breaches

Engineer Park

5

4

LT

0 ___ Miles ___ 1

0 ___ Kilometres ___ 1

Map 114

THIRD ALLIED SIEGE OF BADAJOZ

16 March – 6 April 1812

Chapter 39

THE SALAMANCA CAMPAIGN: OPENING MOVES, JUNE AND JULY 1812

Soult's fury at Marmont's failure to link up and prevent the Allied capture of Badajoz was understandable but misguided, for Marmont's hands were tied by Napoleonic orders which forbade any such union and instead ordered him to capitalize on any Allied southerly movement by invading northern Portugal. Soult now had other problems on his hands and, leaving Drouet and Daricau's divisions to screen the Allied army, he rushed back with the balance of his force to save Sevilla. The Spanish divisions of Penne Villemur and Morillo reached the walls of the city on 7 April, causing considerable alarm to the governor, General Rignoux, who sent desperate appeals to Soult. Ballesteros was also on his way from Gibraltar, but he withdrew on the 6th amidst false reports that Conroux was marching to intercept him from the lines at Cádiz. With Soult now closing at speed any hope of a success was dashed and the two Spanish divisions pulled back to the safety of the Sierra de Aracena.

Soult had hoped that Drouet would be able to push northwards and establish a link with Foy and the Army of Portugal, while maintaining a screen against the Allies around Badajoz. However, Stapleton Cotton,[1] acting largely on his own initiative, had pushed Drouet back and an engagement at Villagarcia, initially against Drouet's cavalry[2] and subsequently his infantry, resulted in the 5th Corps having to withdraw south and abandon their position in Estremadura completely. Hill meanwhile remained with his corps of about 14,000 men[3] in an observation role, awaiting instructions to support Wellington's main body which had once again moved north.

Marmont completed preparations for the invasion of northern Portugal. His available force was smaller than he would have liked. Bonnet remained, in line with Napoleon's instructions, in the Asturias; Foy was south at Almaraz; Souham was along the river Esla screening Santocildes's Army of Galicia; and Ferey's Division was broken up to garrison Valladolid, Salamanca, Zamora, Toro, Avila, Benavente and a number of other towns (see Appendix 5). With his remaining four infantry divisions[4] and a brigade of light cavalry he moved towards the border, arriving in front of Ciudad Rodrigo on 30 March. De España had left 3,000 men under General

Vives within the city before withdrawing west. Marmont, lacking siege artillery, had no intentions against Ciudad Rodrigo but despatched Clausel with two divisions to move rapidly to Almeida in the hope of securing the place by a *coup de main*. Clausel returned two days later with the news that the governor, Le Mesurier, combined with Trant's Portuguese militia, was well established and organized; any hope of an opportunistic success was implausible. With this news Marmont elected to move south and evicted Lecor from Castelo Branco, then surprised Trant at Guarda, and was preparing to push further west when news of Wellington's northerly advance brought a halt to events. He remained at Sabugal for about a week and then, on 22 April, pulled back to Fuente Guinaldo just as 40,000 Anglo-Portuguese troops bore down upon his force of half that number. The next day Wellington's troops occupied the town and Marmont was east of the Agueda, in the firm realization of just how close he had been to disaster.

On the east coast, Suchet's plans to capitalize on the capture of Valencia were severely curtailed through the withdrawal – by Napoleon – of troops to support his Russian war. He lost all his six Polish battalions and Reille and Palombini's divisions and now had less than 15,000 men with which to prosecute offensive operations. Nevertheless, Harispe and Habert were sent south to engage the remnants of the Spanish 2nd and 3rd armies and Severoli was sent north to tackle Peñiscola. Harispe seized Denia on 20 January and Severoli was gifted Peñiscola by its treacherous governor Navarro, who decided that the national cause was all but lost and joined the French.[5] Soon after this Suchet fell ill and Joseph O'Donnell (the newly appointed commander of the 2nd and 3rd armies) used the respite to rebuild the armies of Valencia and Murcia in and around Alicante.

Reille had been withdrawn to establish the new Army of the Ebro along with Palombini and was joined in February by Severoli. Plans for a fourth division were not realized but Reille now had more than 20,000 men and, in conjunction with Decaen's Army, Napoleon felt confident that Catalan resistance would be finally broken. In anticipation, he issued orders that the region be united into the French empire. Mina and other guerrilla chiefs had other ideas: they not only thwarted Napoleon's intentions for subjugation but also continued to harass the French forces, disrupt lines of communication, capture vital communiqués, release Spanish prisoners being escorted north, liberate large amounts of funding heading south and disrupt the movement of troops out of the Iberian theatre in support of the Russian war. Decaen and Maurice Mathieu remained on the defensive and Reille found himself with enough to occupy his force in province of Aragon.

In Murcia, Freire, with the remnants of the Army of Murcia, had moved south causing renewed alarm in Andalusia; supported by the Royal Navy, they cleared all the ports from Almeria to Almunecar of French troops. The British warships then made a raid on Málaga, seizing and destroying the harbour facilities. Soult did nothing in defence of these trifling attacks.

---

1   With the three cavalry brigades: Le Marchant and Slade's heavy brigades and Ponsonby's light brigade.

2   Consisting of Lallemand's dragoons and Perrymond's hussars.

3   This was the same force that he had been entrusted with in 1811 (see map 87) plus Slade's cavalry brigade.

4   Those of Clausel, Maucune, Sarrut and Brennier. He left behind Montbrun's cavalry division to assist in keeping open his lines of communication and so his attacking force numbered 25,000.

5   In fact Navarro had been taken prisoner at Falset in 1811, only to escape custody having given his word. He consequently feared for his life if he were to be recaptured.

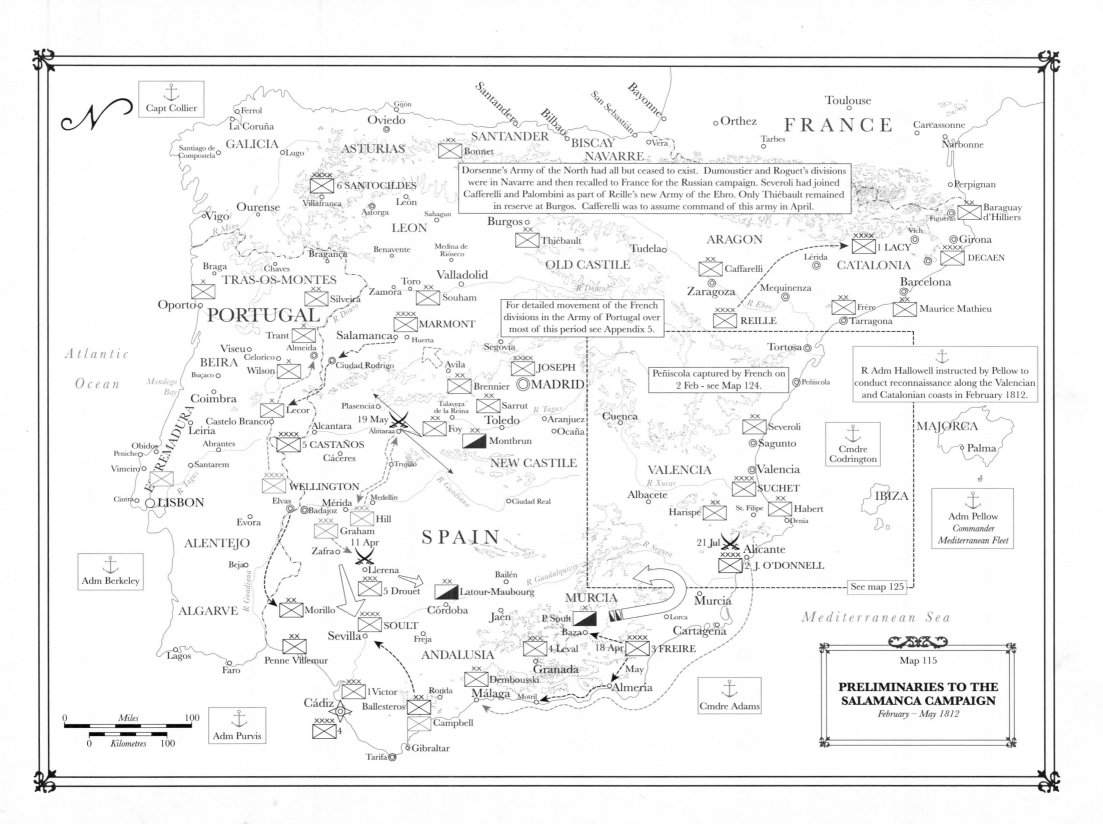

Capt Collier

Dorsenne's Army of the North had all but ceased to exist. Dumoustier and Roguet's divisions were in Navarre and then recalled to France for the Russian campaign. Severoli had joined Cafferelli and Palombini as part of Reille's new Army of the Ebro. Only Thiébault remained in reserve at Burgos. Cafferelli was to assume command of this army in April.

For detailed movement of the French divisions in the Army of Portugal over most of this period see Appendix 5.

Peñiscola captured by French on 2 Feb - see Map 124.

R Adm Hallowell instructed by Pellow to conduct reconnaissance along the Valencian and Catalonian coasts in February 1812.

Cmdre Codrington

Adm Pellow
*Commander
Mediterranean Fleet*

Adm Berkeley

Adm Purvis

Cmdre Adams

Map 115

**PRELIMINARIES TO THE
SALAMANCA CAMPAIGN**
February – May 1812

as he was completely preoccupied by the movements of the Spanish within Andalusia, by Hill in Estremadura and amidst reports that Wellington was once again heading south to liberate the region. Furthermore, following the latest Napoleonic decree, he now found himself subject to (long overdue) command from Madrid. Before departing east, Napoleon had instructed Berthier to empower Joseph with command of all the armies[6] in Spain and had sent Marshal Jourdan as his chief of staff. Joseph thus authorized took on a new lease of life, and with Jourdan began to pen the *Mémoire of May 1812* in which he laid down a number of observations designed to unite the efforts of the whole and dispense with individual aims and aspirations. He concluded that the Imperial army could not hold down the entire country and achieve simultaneous concentration to counter Allied operations. He proposed a reserve of 20,000 to be held centrally. Soult had reason for concern, for such a reserve could not be expected from France and the abandonment of Andalusia in order to create the force was recommended. Soult countered these proposals with ideas of his own and, when these were ignored, he wrote privately to Paris outlining the inadequacies of both Joseph and Jourdan and their questionable strategy. The letter was intercepted en route[7] and passed to the King of Spain who now possessed the evidence to accuse Soult of treason.

In the interim, Joseph had further orders which he proceeded to issue to Marmont and Soult, instructing them to move elements of their respective forces south and north to enable the two armies to unite and react to defeat Wellington's next move. Soult simply ignored the order, while Marmont at least backed up his refusal with good reason. Wellington was in front of him with five divisions; to disperse his force at this juncture was inadvisable and the threat to Andalusia was negligible. Consequently Wellington's next move, when it came, exploited the circumstances masterfully. For some days following Marmont's withdrawal from Fuente Guinaldo, Wellington had mulled over the two options at his disposal. In the end he chose to focus his offensive against Marmont simply because an attack on Soult would realize more by way of reinforcement from the north than vice versa. Whilst he considered his next course of action, he issued instructions for the force to be sustained and fully resupplied; awaiting every piece of intelligence as to Marmont's and Soult's movements and plans with eager anticipation. Intercepted dispatches and a captured payroll indicated future French intentions; Bonnet was to join Marmont from the Asturias, but more significantly Jourdan had outlined the importance of the bridge-forts and magazines at Almaraz. This was the vital link between Soult and Marmont and it provided just the target Wellington had been seeking.

Having received his orders on 7 May Hill left 11,000 men under Sir William Erskine to contain Drouet and departed with 7,000 to execute a *coup de main* on the forts and crossing at Almaraz. British engineers repaired the bridge at Mérida and, by 15 May, Hill entered Trujillo

where he established his logistics base before setting off to complete a thorough reconnaissance. 'The fortifications constructed by Marmont for defence of the bridge of boats [8] at Almaraz were formidable.'[9] Fort Napoleon on the south bank and Fort Ragusa on the north bank crowned the two hills on either side of the Tagus. Between Fort Napoleon and the bridge of boats was a *tête-du-pont* and on the north bank a fleche supported the Fort Ragusa, in which the magazines were housed.[10] The road to Almaraz from the south crosses over a mountain range, impassable to wheeled vehicles and artillery, which is obseved from an old castle and a number of fortified houses. Hill's reconnaissance on 17 May revealed the difficulty of the terrain and the relatively formidable nature of the pass at Miravete. He elected to execute a deception against the Castillo and fortified houses while sending a lightly equipped group, under his own command, to attack the forts directly by escalade. As the sun rose on 18 May, General Chowne commenced the deception attack, warning the French at Almaraz of the approaching force, 'and Major Aubert, who was in command, had strengthened the garrison of the fort and taken up two of the centre boats of the bridge'.[11] With the guns on the south face of the fort pounding the exposed troops to their front, Hill decided to execute an attack without waiting for his entire force to come up. With the 50th complete, and half the 71st, Hill ordered them forward to escalade at three points. The assailants were under a very heavy fire as they arrived at the structure, and then when they jumped into the ditch they discovered their ladders were too short. 'Under a shower of missiles of every description they spliced two ladders together; scrambled up the first step of the scarp, which by chance was unduly broad, pulled up their ladders after them, ran up to the rampart and closed hand to hand with the garrison.'[12] At the critical moment the grenadiers of the 39e Ligne gave way and within minutes all three groups of British infantry had establish a foothold. Aubert led a counter-attack but it failed, and the garrison surrendered or fled to the *tête-du-pont* at about the same time that the balance of the troops arrived to the flank of the structure. The battalion of Étrangers, who were largely formed by Prussian prisoners,[13] demonstrated questionable resistance and took flight across the bridge.

The British gunners, who had accompanied the assault group, now turned the guns in the Fort Napoleon to reply to the fire from the Ragusa. With panic now rife amongst the French ranks this group also fled and, within 40 minutes, all the forts were in Allied hands. Two men of the 92nd swam the river to recover boats from the far bank and with these Hill was able to repair the pontoon bridge and occupy the Ragusa. The 4th Étranger lost their colours; 18 guns were captured (and spiked) along with a huge amount of powder and cartridge from the magazine. The powder was used to blow the structures and most importantly the bridge, and with it

---

6   Initially, he only placed Soult, Marmont and Suchet under his brother's command but a subsequent decree included Decaen and Caffarelli as the new commander of the Army of the North.

7   Interestingly, this letter was sent in duplicate and a second copy was captured by irregulars and reached Wellington's headquarters where it was deciphered by Scovell, giving Wellington a colourful insight into the disunity in the French higher command. Urban, *The Man Who Broke Napoleon's Codes*, pp.224–225. It was to result in the Duke of Dalmatia's recall to Paris sometime later.

8   The stone bridge had been destroyed earlier in the campaign.

9   Fortescue, *History of the British Army*, vol. VIII, p.425.

10   Oman states that the magazines and storehouses were in a small village, called Lugar Nuevo, on the south bank between the bridgehead and the road to the old stone bridge to Almaraz. However, no other account supports this and neither does Dickson's map from his manuscripts.

11   Fortescue, *History of the British Army*, vol. VIII, p.427.

12   Ibid, p.428.

13   Arteche, *Guerra de la Independencia*, vol. XII, p.24, footnote.

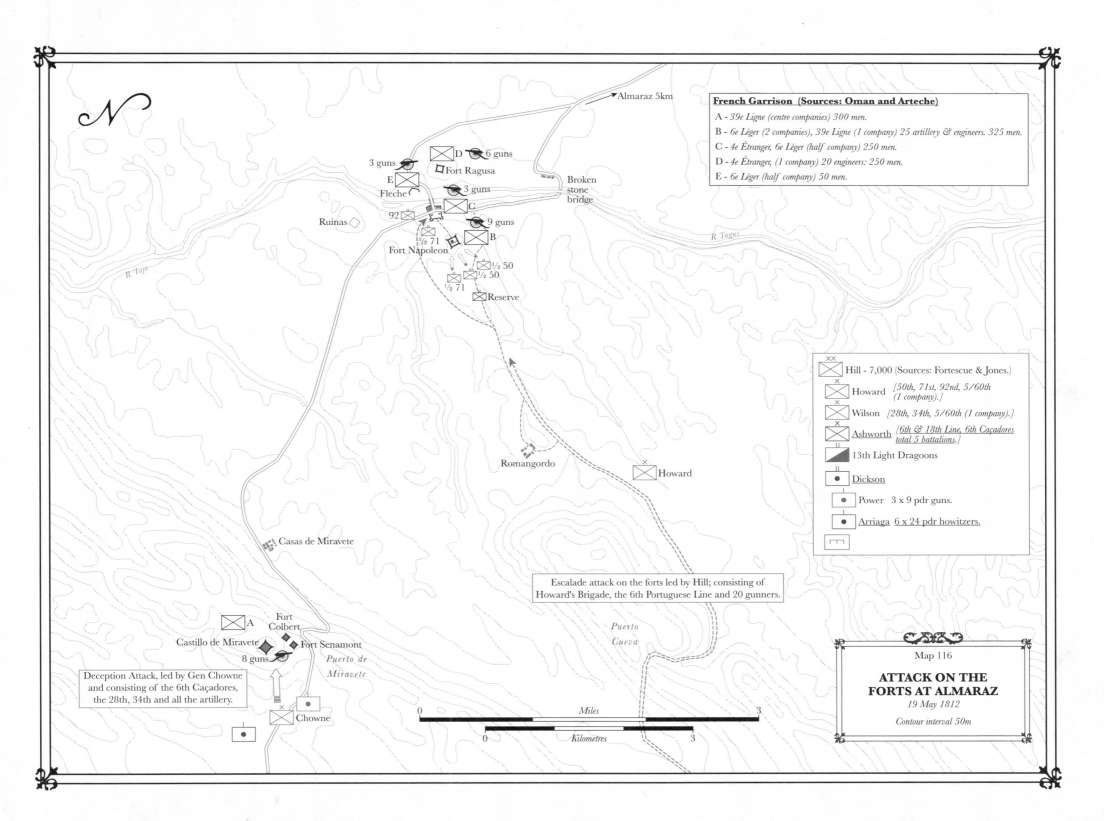

N

Almaraz 5km

D ⚓ 6 guns

3 guns ⚓

E ▫ Fort Ragusa

Fleche

Broken
stone
bridge

R Tagus

⚓ 3 guns

92   C

Ruinas ◇

Fort Napoleon   ⚓ 9 guns   B

½ 71

½ 50

½ 50

½ 71

Reserve

R Tajo

Hill - 7,000 (Sources: Fortescue & Jones.)

Howard   *[50th, 71st, 92nd, 5/60th (1 company).]*

Wilson   *[28th, 34th, 5/60th (1 company).]*

Ashworth   *[6th & 18th Line, 6th Caçadores total 5 battalions.]*

13th Light Dragoons

Dickson

Power   3 x 9 pdr guns.

Arriaga   6 x 24 pdr howitzers.

Romangordo

Howard

Casas de Miravete

Escalade attack on the forts led by Hill; consisting of
Howard's Brigade, the 6th Portuguese Line and 20 gunners.

Puerto
Cueva

A

Fort
Colbert

Castillo de Miravete   ◆   ◆ Fort Senamont

⚓ 8 guns

*Puerto de
Miravete*

Map 116

**ATTACK ON THE
FORTS AT ALMARAZ**

19 May 1812

Contour interval 50m

Deception Attack, led by Gen Chowne
and consisting of the 6th Caçadores,
the 28th, 34th and all the artillery.

Chowne

Miles

0   3

Kilométres

0   3

communication between the armies of the South and Portugal. On 20 May Hill pulled back to Miravete where he decided to reduce the Castillo at Miravete using Dickson's guns. However, during the day he received false information from Erskine, who feared he was in danger of being attacked, and Hill withdrew in haste to Trujillo, justifiably satisfied with the success of the mission.

French north–south communications were now severely disrupted and, to make matters worse, Major Sturgeon of the Royal Staff Corps[14] had managed to repair the bridge at Alcantara. Wellington now had an enormous advantage; he possessed the very thing he had just denied his opponent. All was now ready for the commencement of the Salamanca Campaign; it was the first large-scale coordinated advance since the Talavera Campaign of 1809, and was timed to coincide with numerous diversions. Hill,[15] following his success at Almaraz, was to contain Drouet and prevent any reinforcement of Marmont by the Army of the South. He was to be aided in his task by Ballesteros, who had 8,000 infantry and 500 cavalry[16] at his disposal, and was poised to occupy Soult's forces at Sevilla in the unlikely event that he should move north in support of his colleague. The Army of Galicia was tasked with threatening Marmont's flank, by laying siege to the substantial French garrison at Astorga, in an attempt to draw Marmont north-west. This, in turn, was intended to subvert Bonnet's operations in the Asturias and to assist Porlier's Cantabrian irregulars who were occupying Bonnet across the province. Silveira's four militia regiments were to march east and blockade Zamora; they were to be supported by D'Urban's Portuguese cavalry brigade.[17] To the north a new Spanish 7th Army under Mendizabal had been established by combining and controlling the operations of the two semi-regular formations of Porlier and Longa and a number of smaller irregular groups under, among others, Merino, Salazar and Saornil. This new army, supported by a Royal Navy task force[18] led by Sir Home Popham, was to keep Caffarelli's Army of the North fully preoccupied. Finally, an elaborate plan had been put in place with Lord William Bentinck, the commander of the British forces on Sicily, to land an expeditionary force in Catalonia or Valencia to 'harass Suchet'. The scheme was highly popular with the Regency, who offered to put Whittingham's Division in Majorca and Roche's Division at Alicante at Bentinck's disposal. Although this latter diversion did not occur within the predetermined timeframe, rumour of its impending arrival was enough to preoccupy Suchet up and down the east coast.

With all these diversions more or less in place, Wellington began his advance in three columns on 13 June. The Anglo-Portuguese force was about 47,000-strong and was to be joined a few days later by Carlos de España's Division, adding another 3,000 bayonets. Marmont had about 10,000 fewer troops, but significantly he also had inferiority in cavalry. On receiving news of the Allied advance, he had issued orders for the concentration of his force near Salamanca. Foy had withdrawn to Avila, following the loss of the crossing at Almaraz, and now made his way north; Clausel moved from Peñaranda, Ferey from Valladolid, Sarrut from Toro, and Thomières from Zamora, all converging on Salamanca where Maucune and Brennier were already positioned. Bonnet had also been summoned but he was not expected until the end of the month. Marmont was willing to give battle but was waiting for the arrival of Bonnet's strong division and reinforcement from the Army of the North before committing his force. He had sought and received assurance from Caffarelli that a force of about 8,000 would be made available, including crucially about 1,000 cavalry. The responses from Madrid were less forthcoming, with Jourdan echoing Soult's assertions that the threat was most likely to manifest in the south, and refused any promises of support until the Allied main effort was incontestably apparent.

Soult continued his haughty allegations well into June, playing perfectly into the hands of the Allied plan. He had sent some minor reinforcement to Drouet, but nothing to cause alarm to Hill and there had been two minor engagements; one at Bornos on 1 June where Ballesteros was defeated, and a second at Maguilla when Slade had ventured too close to Lallemand and received a severe check. The combined deception operations in the north had thus far been very successful in delaying any form of reinforcement from Caffarelli. However, the arrival of Bentinck's expeditionary force, the advance of the Galician army and that of the Portuguese militia under Silveira were both delayed; the British force due to indecision, the Spanish 6th Army due to a change in command[19] and the Portuguese militia who required time to mobilize. Wellington's main concern at this juncture was the possibility that Joseph may leave a minimal force in Madrid and march north in support of Marmont.

When Wellington arrived at the outskirts of Salamanca he did not pursue the withdrawing French. Instead he sent two columns north and south of the city, which joined on the far side and deployed in a defensive posture. Wellington then turned his attention to the three forts[20] that Marmont had left garrisoned within the city. The British commander wanted to entice Marmont to attack him on ground of his own choosing and preferably prior to any French reinforcement. He was very confident, in the light of losses at Ciudad Rodrigo and Badajoz, that the French commander would not allow the three forts to fall unopposed, and was also aware of the importance placed on the city by Napoleon following the loss of Ciudad Rodrigo.[21] Earlier reports that the French had been busy fortifying parts of the city in an attempt to protect their vast stores of food and ammunition located there reinforced this belief. Wellington established his headquarters within the city on the night of 17 June, and the 6th Division were tasked with investing the forts. Closer examination revealed the extent of the French works; a huge part of the city in front of the convents of San Vincente, San Cayetano and La Merced had been flattened and the debris used to double the thickness of the walls and block up all the accesses.

---

14   The Royal Staff Corps were Wellington's engineers, under control of Horse Guards, as distinct from the Royal Engineers who belonged to the Master General of the Ordnance. See Fortescue, *History of the British Army*, vol. VIII, p.431.

15   His force was now 18,000 strong, including the cavalry brigades of Long, Slade and Campbell.

16   Arteche, *Guerra de la Independencia*, vol. XII, p.410, Appendix E.

17   D'Urban temporarily gave up his post as Beresford's chief of staff.

18   This was a large force, consisting of Home Popham's flagship, HMS *Venerable*, five frigates, several smaller vessels and two battalions of marines and a battery of artillery.

19   Castaños had moved up from Santiago in June and assumed command of the 6th Army as well as that of Estremadura. The Galician army that was put in the field was placed under the command of Santocildes.

20   In fact they were not built as forts but were fortified convents.

21   Jones, *Journal of Sieges*, vol. I, pp.243–244. See footnote and extracts from the letter of Prince Berthier to Marshal Marmont dated 18 February.

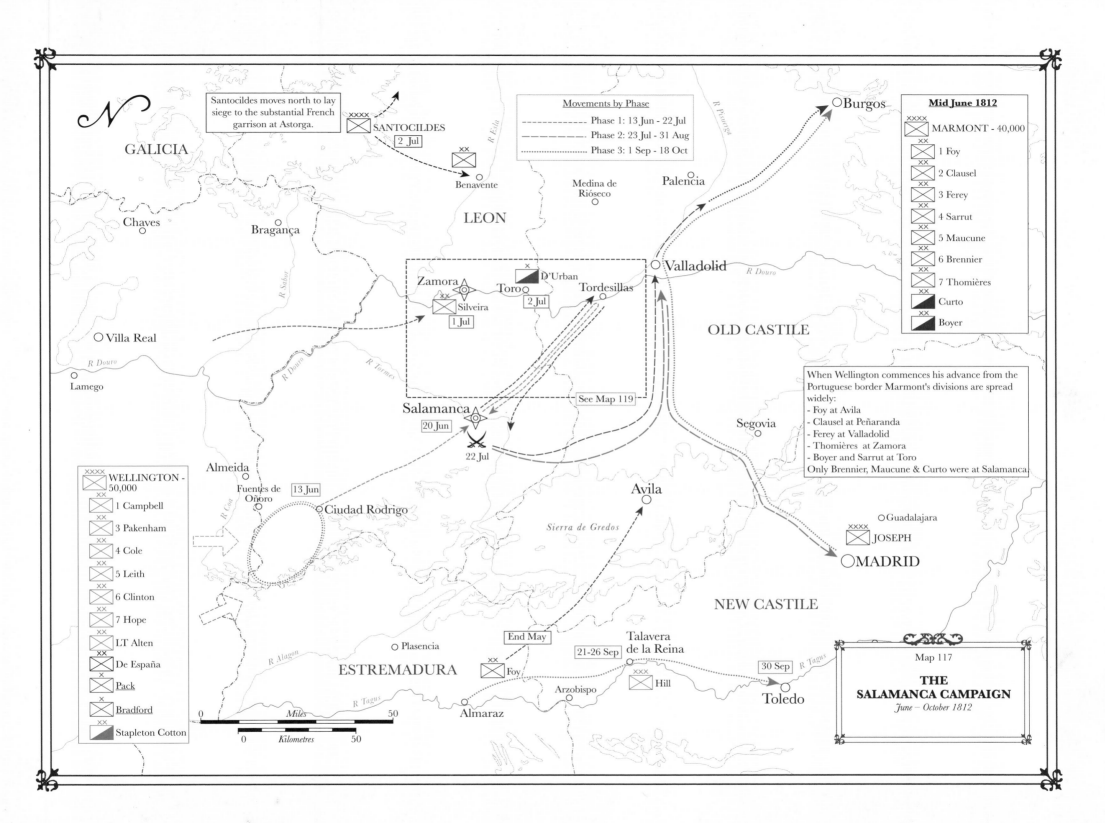

N

GALICIA

Chaves

Bragança

Villa Real

Lamego

R Douro

Santocildes moves north to lay
siege to the substantial French
garrison at Astorga.

XXXX SANTOCILDES

2 Jul

R Esla

Benavente

LEON

Medina de
Ríoseco

Palencia

Movements by Phase

———— Phase 1: 13 Jun - 22 Jul
– – – – Phase 2: 23 Jul - 31 Aug
·········· Phase 3: 1 Sep - 18 Oct

R Pisuerga

○ Burgos

Mid June 1812

XXXX MARMONT - 40,000

XX 1 Foy
XX 2 Clausel
XX 3 Ferey
XX 4 Sarrut
XX 5 Maucune
XX 6 Brennier
XX 7 Thomières
XX Curto
XX Boyer

Zamora
XX Silveira
1 Jul

Toro ○
D'Urban
2 Jul

Tordesillas

Valladolid

R Douro

OLD CASTILE

See Map 119

Salamanca
20 Jun

22 Jul

Segovia

When Wellington commences his advance from the
Portuguese border Marmont's divisions are spread
widely:
- Foy at Avila
- Clausel at Peñaranda
- Ferey at Valladolid
- Thomières at Zamora
- Boyer and Sarrut at Toro
Only Brennier, Maucune & Curto were at Salamanca.

XXXX WELLINGTON -
50,000
XX 1 Campbell
XX 3 Pakenham
XX 4 Cole
XX 5 Leith
XX 6 Clinton
XX 7 Hope
XX LT Alten
XX De España
X Pack
XX Bradford
X Stapleton Cotton

Almeida ○

Fuentes de
Oñoro ○

13 Jun

○ Ciudad Rodrigo

R Coa

Avila

Sierra de Gredos

○ Guadalajara

XXXX JOSEPH

○ MADRID

NEW CASTILE

○ Plasencia

R Alagon

ESTREMADURA

R Tagus

End May

XX Foy

Miles

0   50

0   50
Kilometres

Talavera
de la Reina

21-26 Sep

XXX Hill

Arzobispo ○

Almaraz ○

30 Sep *R Tagus*

Toledo ○

Map 117

**THE
SALAMANCA CAMPAIGN**
June – October 1812

'The walls of those buildings, by removing the roofs, were made in parts to form the scarp and counterscarp, so that by preserving some walls and building up others, with much ingenuity, two redoubts, full of bomb-proofs, with well covered perpendicular scarps, deep ditches, and casemated counterscarps, had been obtained.'[22] Wellington's accompanying siege train was clearly insufficient for the task.

As early as 31 May Dickson had been tasked to move with six heavy howitzers from Elvas to Ciudad Rodrigo, but they were not expected for another five days. Even these howitzers were not the ideal weapons of choice; heavy guns were needed to batter the considerable walls. Engineer stores were also in short supply, with only sufficient digging tools for 400 men. Lieutenant Colonel May RA and Lieutenant Colonel Burgoyne RE were the unfortunate officers designated to make the best of this unenviable predicament. On the night of 17 June work began immediately on a battery position in front of the north wall of the San Vincente. This was completed and armed the following night, and all seven pieces opened fire on 19 June. They quickly made an impression on the walls but at considerable expense to the gunners and sappers facing the counter-battery fire from the 30 well-sited French guns. Two smaller batteries had also been commenced on the night of 18 June and, when Dickson arrived with the six howitzers on 20 June, a redistribution of ordnance was made. However, before this could be brought to bear more ammunition needed to be brought up from Almeida, which was not to arrive for another six days. In the interim Marmont had returned.

The commander of the Army of Portugal had concentrated his entire army (except Bonnet) and advanced on 20 June, driving in the cavalry vedettes and pushing up to less than 1km from the Allied force. Wellington deployed five divisions and two Portuguese brigades[23] in response, with Alten's cavalry on the right flank, Ponsonby's to the left, and the balance of Bock and Le Marchant in reserve along with the 5th and Carlos de España's divisions and Hulse's Brigade from the 6th Division. The Allied force numbered about 43,500 men and to their front were arrayed less than half that number.[24] Initially, it looked as though Marmont was going to oblige Wellington by attacking in three columns. There was a small skirmish in the village of Castellanos de Moriscos during which the 68th enjoyed their Peninsular baptism of fire by beating off three French attacks. At dusk, the battalion was withdrawn from the village, and Wellington's force prepared for the expected attack at dawn. During the night Foy and Thomières joined Marmont but no attack was delivered; Marmont remained undecided and at dusk had called a council of war. Clausel and Foy suggested caution, and the chance of losing 6,000 men to save 800 and risking the honour of the army was enough to deter Marmont from taking the offensive. All through 22 June the two armies faced each other and, despite repeated attempts to stimulate a French attack, Wellington was unsuccessful. The next morning the French army had disappeared. 'If in some occasion Lord Wellington can be accused of extreme caution, this is,

without dispute, the case; however, friends and supporters have not been able to recognize it this way.'[25] One such friend was Napier who wrote that, 'Lord Wellington saw clearly enough the false position of the enemy, but he argued, that if Marmont came up to fight, it was better to defend a very strong position, than to descend and combat in the plain'.[26] Wellington had without doubt missed an opportunity to engage and potentially destroy the Army of Portugal; the next time they would meet, Marmont's forces would be much enhanced.

Attention returned to the forts, but the paucity of ammunition solicited a change in plan. The San Vincente was to be left alone and the new battery (Number 3) was to be allocated the howitzers and all the remaining shot and shell, and tasked to concentrate on the San Cayetano. That evening, with all the ammunition expended, Wellington ordered an attempt to storm the barely practical breach. The light companies of Bowes and Hulse's brigades furnished the assault group; their attempt was to be a costly failure. The siege was now placed on hold. By midday on 26 June the ammunition arrived from Almeida and, at about 1500 hours, the battering recommenced with fire concentrated once again on the San Cayetano, while the howitzers moved to Battery 2 and began to fire heated shot onto the roof of the San Vincente. The flames soon began to take hold, despite the best efforts of the defenders to extinguish them; the hastily constructed defensive enhancements had large amounts of timber, which now undermined the very walls. The next day, the incessant battering on the San Cayetano had produced a good breach and a second attack was ordered. As the assault group formed up and began to move along the trenches, dug during the previous two nights, the captain commanding the San Cayetano displayed the white flag. The San Vincente, engulfed in smoke, soon followed and by last light the forts and the city were entirely in Allied hands.

Since withdrawing from the east of Salamanca, Marmont had been eagerly awaiting the arrival of Caffarelli's reinforcements, but a communiqué on 26 June from the commander of the Army of the North confirmed his worse fears. Caffarelli was totally preoccupied with the resurgent guerrilla activity and the concurrent threat of Home Popham's Royal Navy force and could only spare a brigade of light cavalry and some field guns. It was a crushing blow as Marmont was counting on the additional 10,000 men to take the offensive and relieve the forts. Early on 27 June, when Duchemin signalled that he could only hold out another 72 hours, Marmont felt compelled to act. However, before the end of the day the forts had fallen and prudence dictated a withdrawal to the north bank of Douro,[27] from where he hoped to link up with Bonnet and the meagre reinforcements from Caffarelli. To the south, Soult had reinforced Drouet but did not pose a threat to Hill's blocking force. More significantly he continued to refuse orders from Madrid to move north in support of the greater cause. Wellington was unaware at this time of Soult's insubordination and the overall intelligence picture was unclear, complicated by some contradictory signals from Madrid; Wellington decided to spend the first days of July waiting.

22 Jones, *Journal of Sieges*, vol. I, p.248. See also footnotes pp.264–267.

23 From right to left: the 1st, 7th, 4th, Light, 3rd, Pack and Bradford.

24 Marmont had about 18,000 infantry and 2,000 horse at this stage, as Foy and Thomières's divisions were not yet up. They added another 10,000 men the next day.

25 Arteche, *Guerra de la Independencia*, vol. XII, pp.38–39.

26 Napier, *History of the War in the Peninsula*, vol. V, p.129.

27 Joseph considered this northerly withdrawal a betrayal as he lost communications with Madrid and left the way open for the Allied army.

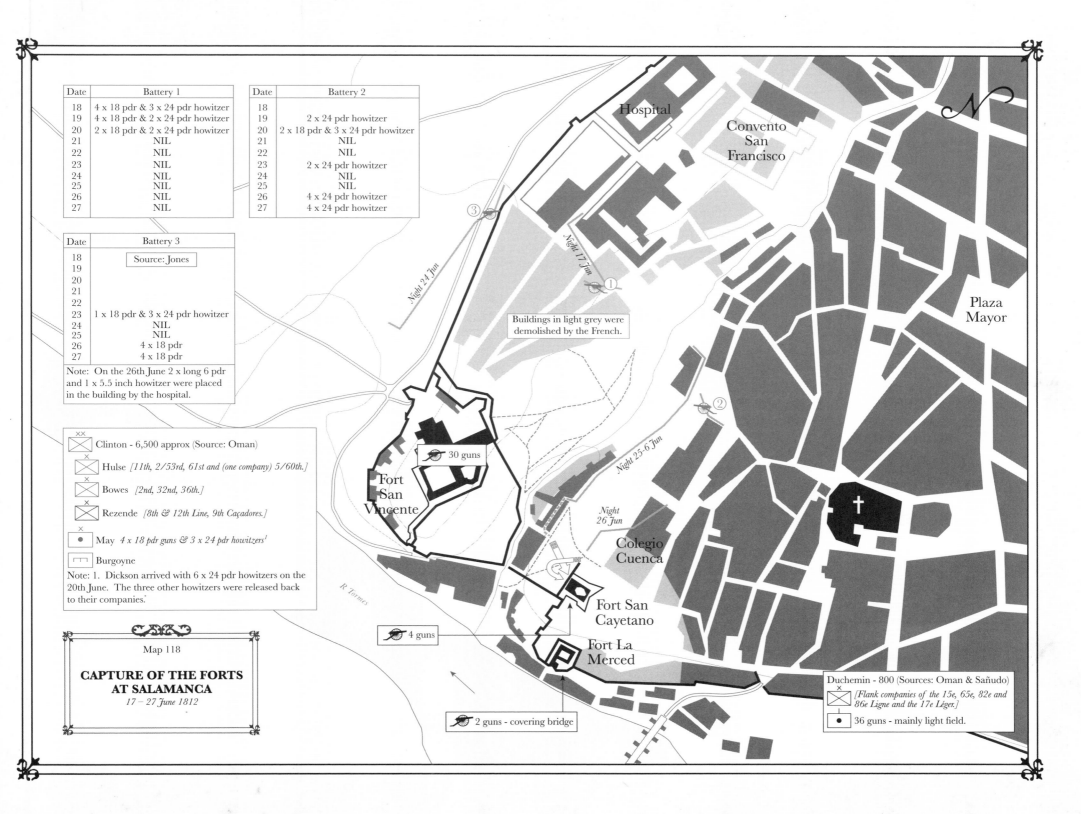

Date	Battery 1
18	4 x 18 pdr & 3 x 24 pdr howitzer
19	4 x 18 pdr & 2 x 24 pdr howitzer
20	2 x 18 pdr & 2 x 24 pdr howitzer
21	NIL
22	NIL
23	NIL
24	NIL
25	NIL
26	NIL
27	NIL

Date	Battery 2
18	
19	2 x 24 pdr howitzer
20	2 x 18 pdr & 3 x 24 pdr howitzer
21	NIL
22	NIL
23	2 x 24 pdr howitzer
24	NIL
25	NIL
26	4 x 24 pdr howitzer
27	4 x 24 pdr howitzer

Date	Battery 3
18	Source: Jones
19	
20	
21	
22	
23	1 x 18 pdr & 3 x 24 pdr howitzer
24	NIL
25	NIL
26	4 x 18 pdr
27	4 x 18 pdr

Note: On the 26th June 2 x long 6 pdr
and 1 x 5.5 inch howitzer were placed
in the building by the hospital.

Clinton - 6,500 approx (Source: Oman)

Hulse [11th, 2/53rd, 61st and (one company) 5/60th.]

Bowes [2nd, 32nd, 36th.]

Rezende [8th & 12th Line, 9th Caçadores.]

May 4 x 18 pdr guns & 3 x 24 pdr howitzers[1]

Burgoyne

Note: 1. Dickson arrived with 6 x 24 pdr howitzers on the
20th June. The three other howitzers were released back
to their companies.

Map 118

**CAPTURE OF THE FORTS
AT SALAMANCA**

17 – 27 June 1812

Hospital

Convento
San
Francisco

Plaza
Mayor

Night 17 Jun

Night 24 Jun

Buildings in light grey were
demolished by the French.

30 guns

Fort
San
Vincente

R Tormes

Night 25-6 Jun

Night
26 Jun

Colegio
Cuenca

Fort San
Cayetano

4 guns

Fort La
Merced

2 guns - covering bridge

Duchemin - 800 (Sources: Oman & Sañudo)

[Flank companies of the 15e, 65e, 82e and
86e Ligne and the 17e Léger.]

36 guns - mainly light field.

Finally, on 7 July, Bonnet[28] linked up with Marmont's army and five days later the last communiqué arrived from Madrid. Jourdan outlined the need to keep the Army of the Centre in Madrid to protect the capital and to head off Hill should he choose to come north in support of Wellington. Furthermore, it advocated that Marmont should take the offensive and two days later, with the bridge at Toro repaired, two divisions crossed the Douro and drove back the Allied cavalry piquets. Wellington concluded that Marmont was trying to turn the Allied left flank, march on Salamanca and cut the lines of communication. He responded accordingly, and sent orders to reposition his forces to cover the Toro to Salamanca road. By 17 July they were in place, but then intelligence arrived confirming that the two French divisions (of Foy and Bonnet) had re-crossed to the north side of the Douro and blown the bridge. That night Marmont counter-marched his army to Tordesillas and early on 17 July, Clausel and Maucune's divisions had crossed the bridge and occupied the positions vacated by the Anglo-Portuguese only hours earlier. These two divisions provided protection for the balance of the army which followed and later that night they were complete on the south bank. Wellington had been completely taken by the feint and now reacted with speed to readjust his force and in the process became embroiled in the cavalry-on-cavalry combat at Castrejon. Wellington had deployed the rearguard, consisting of the 4th and Light divisions and most of the cavalry; the 5th Division were despatched to Torrecilla de la Orden to provide flank protection, while the balance were positioned on the heights above the river Guarena. Marmont's entire army came into view advancing on two routes and the rearguard had to fight hard to retain the line as they fell back the 12km until they regrouped with the main body. At Castrillo, Clausel tried to outflank the 4th Division by deploying his own division and that of Brennier, but was thwarted by the prompt and gallant actions of Alten's cavalry brigade.

With the entire Anglo-Portuguese army now arrayed in a defensive posture to his front, Marmont called a halt to the advance. The next morning the two armies faced each other across the Guarena; Marmont had sent his cavalry in search of a weak point while Wellington willed his adversary to attack. Later in the day, Marmont issued orders for the army to march by column towards Cantalapiedra and Wellington responded by making a corresponding movement. The parallel march had begun. The next day, Marmont continued south in an attempt to outflank the Allied right wing with an eye to launching an immediate attack should the Allied line become too strung out. Wellington shadowed the French movement on the north bank of the Guarena, and when Marmont's force crossed the river it seemed inevitable that the two columns would collide. The Duke of Ragusa says in his memoirs: 'The armies, well formed and in united lines moved in two parallel columns, the left in the lead remaining in platoon formation the entire distance; from which they could be formed into line of battle instantly on receiving the order. The Duke of Wellington informed me after the event that the army had moved as a single regiment. Indeed, the troops presented a most imposing sight. The enemy followed a parallel plateau to mine, offering a position everywhere in the case in that I had wanted to attack him. The two armies went this way at a short distance one of another with the same speed, order and the conservation of their formations.'[29] Late in the afternoon the armies drifted apart. Wellington camped north of Salamanca on the Cabeza Vellosa while Marmont headed south and established camps around the fords over the river Tormes at Huerta. The next day Marmont crossed the Tormes and Wellington followed suit, establishing positions on the heights to the south of the river. The operation lasted the entire day and by nightfall the entire French army, and all but the 3rd Division and D'Urban's cavalry brigade, were west of the river and poised for the next move.

---

28 He brought with him, 6,500 infantry, a light battery and 100 chasseurs, which raised Marmont's Army to 43,000 and 78 guns. Oman, *A History of the Peninsular War*, vol. V, p.391.

29 Arteche, *Guerra de la Independencia*, vol. XII, p.51.

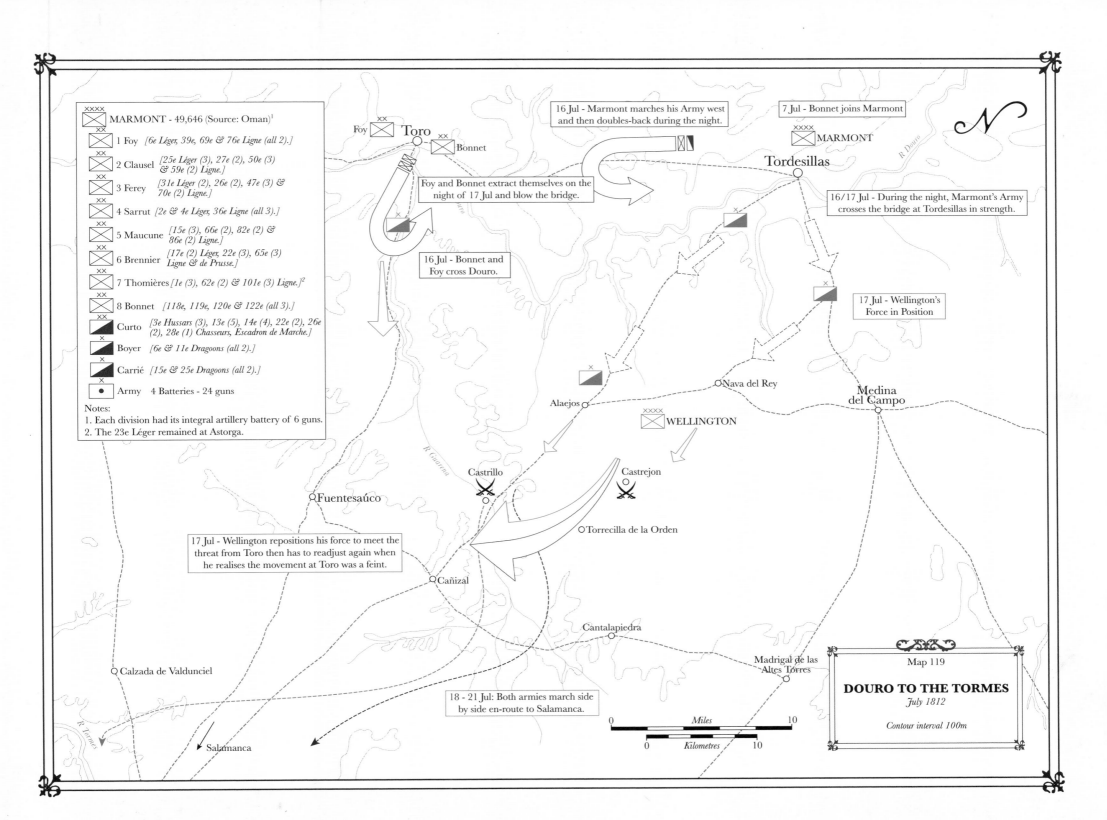

MARMONT - 49,646 (Source: Oman)[1]

1 Foy *[6e Léger, 39e, 69e & 76e Ligne (all 2).]*

2 Clausel *[25e Léger (3), 27e (2), 50e (3) & 59e (2) Ligne.]*

3 Ferey *[31e Léger (2), 26e (2), 47e (3) & 70e (2) Ligne.]*

4 Sarrut *[2e & 4e Léger, 36e Ligne (all 3).]*

5 Maucune *[15e (3), 66e (2), 82e (2) & 86e (2) Ligne.]*

6 Brennier *[17e (2) Léger, 22e (3), 65e (3) Ligne & de Prusse.]*

7 Thomières *[1e (3), 62e (2) & 101e (3) Ligne.]*[2]

8 Bonnet *[118e, 119e, 120e & 122e (all 3).]*

Curto *[3e Hussars (3), 13e (5), 14e (4), 22e (2), 26e (2), 28e (1) Chasseurs, Escadron de Marche.]*

Boyer *[6e & 11e Dragoons (all 2).]*

Carrié *[15e & 25e Dragoons (all 2).]*

Army   4 Batteries - 24 guns

Notes:
1. Each division had its integral artillery battery of 6 guns.
2. The 23e Léger remained at Astorga.

Foy

Toro

Bonnet

7 Jul - Bonnet joins Marmont

MARMONT

Tordesillas

16 Jul - Marmont marches his Army west and then doubles-back during the night.

Foy and Bonnet extract themselves on the night of 17 Jul and blow the bridge.

16/17 Jul - During the night, Marmont's Army crosses the bridge at Tordesillas in strength.

16 Jul - Bonnet and Foy cross Douro.

17 Jul - Wellington's Force in Position

R Douro

R Guareña

Nava del Rey

Medina del Campo

Alaejos

WELLINGTON

Castrillo

Castrejon

Fuentesaúco

Torrecilla de la Orden

17 Jul - Wellington repositions his force to meet the threat from Toro then has to readjust again when he realises the movement at Toro was a feint.

Cañizal

Cantalapiedra

Calzada de Valdunciel

Madrigal de las Altes Torres

R Tormes

Salamanca

18 - 21 Jul: Both armies march side by side en-route to Salamanca.

Map 119

DOURO TO THE TORMES

July 1812

Contour interval 100m

Miles

0   10

Kilometres

0   10

Chapter 40

THE BATTLE OF SALAMANCA (LOS ARAPILES): 22 JULY 1812

It was a filthy night with driving rain and high winds, which spooked the horses, many of which broke free from their tethers and bolted in all directions trampling anything in their path. The next morning the sun rose early in a cloudless sky and its immediate warmth provided welcome relief to both armies. Marmont was keen to get on and force Wellington's hand. He was convinced that Salamanca would be abandoned and that the Allies would make best speed towards Ciudad Rodrigo; his aim was to prevent this escape and to engage the Allied rearguard with vigour. Marmont's assessment was completely accurate except for one point; should Marmont present an opportunity, Wellington was prepared to strike and strike decisively.

Wellington did not, however, expect Marmont to err; he had twice demonstrated an insightful tactical ability, firstly in his crossing of the Douro, and secondly by advancing south-west in an attempt to outflank the Allies. At dawn, fully anticipating the requirement to retreat, Wellington had sent D'Urban escorting the entire baggage train on the road to Ciudad Rodrigo. Marmont and Foy caught sight of this train as it moved off into the distance; this sighting was to play a pivotal part in shaping the events that followed. Marmont and Foy could see little else from their vantage point at the small chapel of Nuestra Señora de la Peña (map 120, point 1) except the 7th Division who were on the ridgeline to their front. Wellington was on that very ridge at much the same time and could see Foy's Division clearly. He ordered Hope to deploy piquets[1] into the foreground to prevent the French probing too far and discovering the 5th, 6th and 7th divisions in dead ground behind the feature. The Allied skirmishers advanced too near the French lines and Foy was subsequently ordered to drive them back with a corresponding number of French skirmishers who set out from the heights.

Marmont began to move his main body to the south and west in an attempt to cut off Wellington's retreat, which prompted the Allied commander to shift position to the Lesser Arapile held by Anson's Brigade. He arrived in time to witness French skirmishers manoeuvring at speed from the wood line and making for the Greater Arapile. Wellington had not appreciated the tactical value of the ground in the half-light of the previous evening; he now realized that the feature was within cannon range of the Lesser Arapile and disturbingly close. He responded by tasking the 7th Caçadores to make a similar dash to secure the key ground but the Portuguese light infantry lost the race, despite making good speed. The French skirmishers held on to the

feature until about 0900 hours when Bonnet moved his division onto the prominence; 'it was a sort of perfectly strong pivot, around which one could turn to operate the projected manoeuvre'.[2] Five French divisions followed[3] and established themselves in the wooded hills to the rear of the Great Arapile from where they prepared to move west to sever the Allied line of retreat. Foy remained at Calvarisa with Ferey and Boyer in support.

At about 1100 hours, Marmont rode to the top of the Greater Arapile to get a better view of the Allied positions. He was able to see all of Cole's Division with Pack's Brigade in support holding the ground on and around the Lesser Arapile, and the majority of the 7th Division deployed opposite Foy but he also made out troop movement to their rear. Wellington, having seen Marmont's attempts to outflank the Allied right, had already issued orders for the movement of his main body out of their concentration area to the ground behind the 4th and 7th divisions. Marmont concluded that the Allies were about to attack Bonnet and possibly Foy and Ferey. This assessment was partially correct, as Wellington had indeed ordered the 1st and Light divisions forward to take the Greater Arapile but then subsequently cancelled the order, and re-tasked the divisions to positions to the north of the 4th Division. Wellington doubted the wisdom of committing troops to the attack and in fact issued contingency orders for a withdrawal. The fact that no attack materialized and that no other troops were visible from this considerable vantage point were also to have an effect on Marmont's next moves.

'It was noon; and all day would have passed in similar manoeuvres, without losses on one side or the other, and certainly towards the night Lord Wellington would have beaten a retreat to regain Ciudad Rodrigo, returning us Salamanca without fight, when marshal Marmont by a fatal impatience not to fight but of manoeuvre, wanted to cut off the Allied rearguard, that he believed ready to clear out.'[4] Just before 1400 hours troops began to emerge from the wood line and move west along the plateau that overlooked the Allied positions in and around the village of Arapiles. What happened next is subject to considerable incongruity, with Marmont's recollection of events at variance to that of his divisional commanders. Maucune's Division emerged first and according to Marmont's orders was to place himself to the left of the Grande Arapile; Thomières was to move in support of Maucune and Clausel in support of Thomières. Brennier was to remain on the high ground to the rear where a number of batteries were to deploy and the heavy and light cavalry were to fall in on the left and right flanks respectively. What actually transpired was at odds to Marmont's orders and as it all evolved under his gaze,[5] apparently to his satisfaction, it is puzzling. The movements seem to confirm Marmont's intentions to cut off the Allied retreat and engage the force to his front.

Maucune positioned his division above the village and deployed his light companies into the open ground on the slope to his front. His divisional artillery then deployed and began to

---

[1] The 68th and 2nd Caçadores complete were deployed across this frontage.

[2] Thiers, *Histoire du Consulat et de L'Empire*, vol. XV, p.92.

[3] Thomières, Clausel, Maucune, Brennier and the cavalry division of Curto.

[4] Thiers, *Histoire du Consulat et de L'Empire*, vol. XV, p.94.

[5] There is considerable debate as to exactly when Marmont was wounded and whether he was still in command when the full extent of the left flanking manoeuvre was known. See Muir, *Triunfo de Wellington: Salamanca 1812*, pp.123–124.

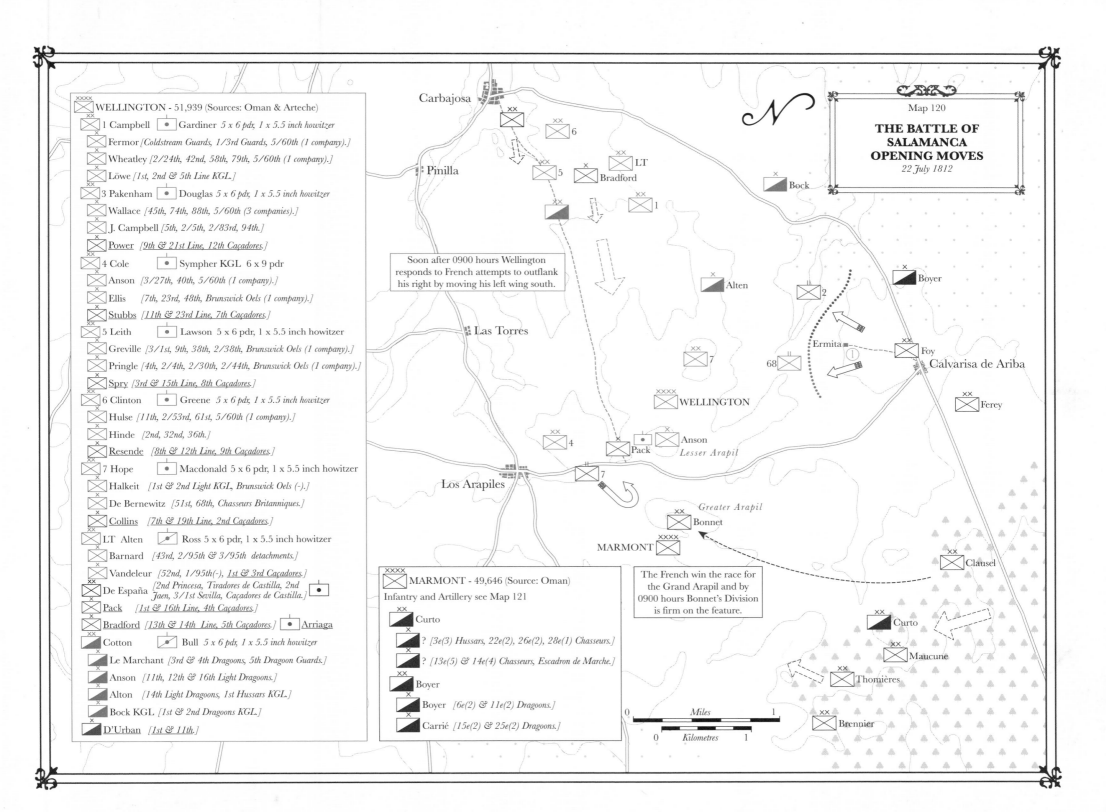

THE BATTLE OF SALAMANCA OPENING MOVES 22 July 1812

Map 120

WELLINGTON - 51,939 (Sources: Oman & Arteche)

1 Campbell — Gardiner *5 x 6 pdr, 1 x 5.5 inch howitzer*
Fermor *[Coldstream Guards, 1/3rd Guards, 5/60th (1 company).]*
Wheatley *[2/24th, 42nd, 58th, 79th, 5/60th (1 company).]*
Löwe *[1st, 2nd & 5th Line KGL.]*
3 Pakenham — Douglas *5 x 6 pdr, 1 x 5.5 inch howitzer*
Wallace *[45th, 74th, 88th, 5/60th (3 companies).]*
J. Campbell *[5th, 2/5th, 2/83rd, 94th.]*
Power *[9th & 21st Line, 12th Caçadores.]*
4 Cole — Sympher KGL *6 x 9 pdr*
Anson *[3/27th, 40th, 5/60th (1 company).]*
Ellis *[7th, 23rd, 48th, Brunswick Oels (1 company).]*
Stubbs *[11th & 23rd Line, 7th Caçadores.]*
5 Leith — Lawson *5 x 6 pdr, 1 x 5.5 inch howitzer*
Greville *[3/1st, 9th, 38th, 2/38th, Brunswick Oels (1 company).]*
Pringle *[4th, 2/4th, 2/30th, 2/44th, Brunswick Oels (1 company).]*
Spry *[3rd & 15th Line, 8th Caçadores.]*
6 Clinton — Greene *5 x 6 pdr, 1 x 5.5 inch howitzer*
Hulse *[11th, 2/53rd, 61st, 5/60th (1 company).]*
Hinde *[2nd, 32nd, 36th.]*
Resende *[8th & 12th Line, 9th Caçadores.]*
7 Hope — Macdonald *5 x 6 pdr, 1 x 5.5 inch howitzer*
Halkeit *[1st & 2nd Light KGL, Brunswick Oels (-).]*
De Bernewitz *[51st, 68th, Chasseurs Britanniques.]*
Collins *[7th & 19th Line, 2nd Caçadores.]*
LT Alten — Ross *5 x 6 pdr, 1 x 5.5 inch howitzer*
Barnard *[43rd, 2/95th & 3/95th detachments.]*
Vandeleur *[52nd, 1/95th(-), 1st & 3rd Caçadores.]*
De España *[2nd Princesa, Tiradores de Castilla, 2nd Jaen, 3/1st Sevilla, Caçadores de Castilla.]*
Pack *[1st & 16th Line, 4th Caçadores.]*
Bradford *[13th & 14th Line, 5th Caçadores.]* — Arriaga
Cotton — Bull *5 x 6 pdr, 1 x 5.5 inch howitzer*
Le Marchant *[3rd & 4th Dragoons, 5th Dragoon Guards.]*
Anson *[11th, 12th & 16th Light Dragoons.]*
Alton *[14th Light Dragoons, 1st Hussars KGL.]*
Bock KGL *[1st & 2nd Dragoons KGL.]*
D'Urban *[1st & 11th.]*

MARMONT - 49,646 (Source: Oman)
Infantry and Artillery see Map 121

Curto
? *[3e(3) Hussars, 22e(2), 26e(2), 28e(1) Chasseurs.]*
? *[13e(5) & 14e(4) Chasseurs, Escadron de Marche.]*
Boyer
Boyer *[6e(2) & 11e(2) Dragoons.]*
Carrié *[15e(2) & 25e(2) Dragoons.]*

Carbajosa
Pinilla
Las Torres
Los Arapiles

Ermita
Calvarisa de Ariba

LT
Bradford
Bock
Boyer
Alten
Foy
Ferey
WELLINGTON
Anson
Lesser Arapil
Pack
Bonnet
MARMONT
Greater Arapil
Clausel
Curto
Maucune
Thomières
Brennier

Soon after 0900 hours Wellington responds to French attempts to outflank his right by moving his left wing south.

The French win the race for the Grand Arapil and by 0900 hours Bonnet's Division is firm on the feature.

Miles
0 — 1
Kilometres
0 — 1

shell the village and was followed by two further batteries that deployed to Maucune's right and also opened on the troops sheltering in the village below.[6] At much the same time, Bonnet's divisional battery had been hauled to the top of the Greater Arapile and a considerable artillery bombardment commenced across the front. Sympher's battery behind the village was reinforced by Lawson's battery and their reply began to have some effect. Macdonald's horse artillery battery was also brought up to provide support to the 4th Division[7] on and around the Lesser Arapile, but the two guns hauled to the summit were forced to withdraw under heavy and accurate fire from Bonnet's divisional battery to their front, and the soldiers of the 3/27th on the brow of the hillock were also forced to take cover as best they could. The French artillery superiority began to take its toll and Wellington had few options to redress the balance.

Maucune's skirmishers came to the base of the hill and began to engage the troops in the village, twice taking some of the houses on the southern side before being driven back by counter-attacks. Wellington was convinced this action preceded a main attack and he began to readjust his force accordingly. The 5th Division was moved to the front right and relieved the brigade of the 4th Division that returned to strengthen the division's hold (with Pack's Portuguese) around the Lesser Arapile; the 6th Division was brought up to their rear as a reserve in depth. The 7th Division was similarly tasked to move behind the 5th Division and the 1st and Light divisions now replaced them, holding the Allied left facing Foy. The balance of infantry and cavalry were held, for the time being, in reserve at Las Torres. Pakenham's 3rd Division and D'Urban's Portuguese Cavalry Brigade had remained on the north side of the Tormes, until Wellington was convinced that no threat lay in this direction, and some time earlier he had ordered them to cross the Tormes and take up a new position near Aldea Tejada.

While these moves were taking place, more French columns emerged from the woods and moved west. Thomières emerged first, followed by Clausel, and Wellington fully expected these divisions to swing north in support of Maucune and Bonnet in a full-scale frontal attack. 'But the battalions in support of them did not come forward, nor did Bonnet attack on the right of them, nor Thomières on their left. The former remained stationary, on and about the Grande Arapile: the latter continued to march westward along the plateau: a perceptible gap began to appear between him and Maucune.'[8] It was about 1530 hours and Wellington was taking a light lunch in a farm courtyard near Las Torres, observing the movements of the French along the plateau through his telescope. According to Greville's *Memoirs* Wellington suddenly cried 'By God! That will do!' and then sprang on his horse and rode off with his staff in hot pursuit. Wellington noted firstly that the gap created by Thomières had effectively extended the French line a distance of 7km, secondly that the line was not arrayed for battle, and most significantly that it lacked depth. In an instant Wellington appreciated the precariousness of Marmont's position and elected to instigate a quick attack. Leaving the 1st and Light divisions to cover the left flank,

the 4th and 5th divisions and Pack's Portuguese were ordered to attack Bonnet, Clausel and Maucune, with the 6th and 7th divisions in support; while the Spanish and Stapleton Cotton's cavalry were to hold the right flank. However, it was Wellington's insight to incorporate the 3rd Division in the scheme of attack that was to provide the catalyst for French destruction.

Wellington was determined to pass the orders to Pakenham personally as that part of his plan was the most challenging. He rode with great speed towards the 3rd Division and gave quick perfunctory orders to D'Urban, whom he met en route; he was to assist the 3rd Division in their task and to provide protection to their right flank. Moments later, Wellington briefed Pakenham: 'Edward move on with your 3rd Division, take those heights in your front – and drive everything before you.'[9] He then rode back to the 5th Division, with his staff strung out and having great difficulty in keeping up, and shouted verbal orders that Arentschildt was to move west in support of Pakenham's turning movement. Once back with the main body he gave immediate orders for Leith to commence the advance as soon as Bradford had moved up and secured his right flank. Only 30 minutes had elapsed since Wellington had taken the decision to attack.

During this time, at about 1545 hours, Marmont sustained a wound from a bursting shell fired from one of Macdonald's two horse artillery guns (under the command of Lieutenant Dyneley) on the Lesser Arapile. Once again there is disagreement in French accounts; Marmont claimed that he was descending the heights to take command of the French left personally, but Foy and many others considered that the foundations for the disaster that followed had already been laid. Command switched to Bonnet and within minutes it was clear that the French left was in dire trouble. Pakenham and D'Urban had advanced from Aldea Tejada in dead ground and arrayed in four columns. D'Urban and Arentschildt's cavalry were covering the right flank, and then came the brigades of Power, Campbell and Wallace with the two gun batteries on the far left.[10] Thomières was advancing west along the spine of the plateau with Curto slackly deployed to his left; his regiments were marching one behind the other and their battalions likewise.[11] It was clear from this formation that the last thing Thomières expected to encounter was a frontal attack and was clearly shocked to see Wallace's Brigade and the Allied cavalry bearing down upon him from a distance of about 800m. He hurriedly formed his battalions and his divisional battery was in action with great speed and began to deliver a devastating deluge of canister and grape on the advancing infantry. In response Douglas, commanding the 3rd Division direct support artillery, deployed on a ridge to the west and began to neutralize the French battery and pour enfilade fire into the flanks of the French masses. When the British and Portuguese infantry closed with the line of French tirailleurs, Thomières ordered his columns to charge downhill in support. Any chance of retaining cohesion was lost; the French momentum was insufficient to make a deep impression and the haphazard lines began to waver. At this point some of Curto's light horse finally arrived and inflicted some Allied casualties before being driven off by

---

6   At this stage they consisted of the light companies of the Guards Brigade of the 1st Division and the Fusilier Brigade of the 4th Division.

7   The 4th Division's integral battery was that of Sympher.

8   Oman, *History of the Peninsular War*, vol. V, p.434.

9   Gratton, *With the Connaught Rangers*, pp.241–242.

10   See Muir, *Triunfo de Wellington: Salamanca 1812*, p.133. This seems a more likely formation than that listed in Oman and would have simplified the movement into line for the subsequent attack.

11   The order of march was 110e Ligne, 62e Ligne and then 1e Ligne.

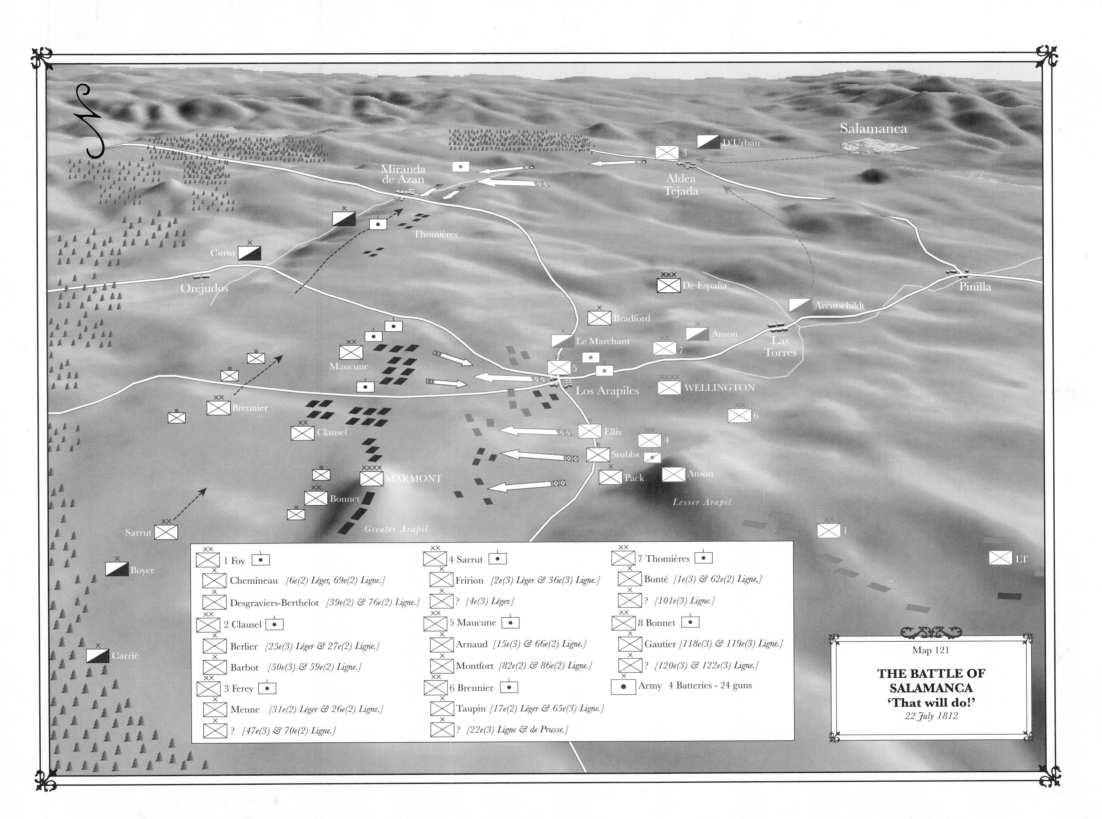

Salamanca

D'Urban

Miranda
de Azan

Aldea
Tejada

Thomières

De España

Curto

Arentschildt

Bradford

Orejudos

Anson

Le Marchant

Las
Torres

Pinilla

Maucune

7

Los Arapiles

WELLINGTON

Brennier

6

Clausel

Ellis

4

Stubbs

Anson

MARMONT

Bonnet

Pack

Sarrut

Lesser Arapil

Boyer

Greater Arapil

1

Carriè

LT

1 Foy			**4 Sarrut**			**7 Thomières**	
Chemineau	*[6e(2) Léger, 69e(2) Ligne.]*		Fririon	*[2e(3) Léger & 36e(3) Ligne.]*		Bonté	*[1e(3) & 62e(2) Ligne,]*
Desgraviers-Berthelot	*[39e(2) & 76e(2) Ligne.]*		?	*[4e(3) Léger.]*		?	*[101e(3) Ligne.]*
2 Clausel			**5 Maucune**			**8 Bonnet**	
Berlier	*[25e(3) Léger & 27e(2) Ligne.]*		Arnaud	*[15e(3) & 66e(2) Ligne.]*		Gautier	*[118e(3) & 119e(3) Ligne.]*
Barbot	*[50e(3) & 59e(2) Ligne.]*		Montfort	*[82e(2) & 86e(2) Ligne.]*		?	*[120e(3) & 122e(3) Ligne.]*
3 Ferey			**6 Brennier**			Army 4 Batteries - 24 guns	
Menne	*[31e(2) Léger & 26e(2) Ligne.]*		Taupin	*[17e(2) Léger & 65e(3) Ligne.]*			
?	*[47e(3) & 70e(2) Ligne.]*		?	*[22e(3) Ligne & de Prusse.]*			

Map 121

**THE BATTLE OF
SALAMANCA**
'That will do!'
22 July 1812

Arentschildt. Pakenham sensed the moment and released the infantry, and within minutes the French division was inoperative; half of the 4,500 men had been killed or taken, Thomières was dead and his battery captured.

The engagement at Miranda de Azán had commenced at around 1630 hours and lasted only a matter of minutes. By the time it was over the battle in the centre was well under way, having commenced at around 1640 hours.[12] Leith was the first to advance with Greville's strengthened brigade leading with Pringle and Spry's brigades in the second line. Cole had started slightly later and was deployed in a single line of seven battalions. Anson (Cole's third brigade) remained on task on the Lesser Arapile and so Pack was ordered to cover Cole's left flank and occupy Bonnet. To the rear of the attacking divisions the 7th and 6th moved up to provide depth. At around this time Bonnet was also injured and command now passed to Clausel. 'Thus in less than half an hour, and before an order of battle had been formed by the French, their commander-in-chief and two other generals had fallen, and the left of their army was turned, thrown into confusion and enveloped.'[13] Clausel was doing his best to remedy the situation by hastening Brennier forward in support of Maucune, Sarrut to behind his own division, while Ferey was making best speed from the French right.

Leith's infantry closed in on Maucune's tirailleurs, taking many casualties from the three batteries deployed between the forward lines and main body of French troops. Leith urged on his light troops, which cleared the tirailleurs and then forced the French gunners to retreat, opening the ground to Maucune's formations that were curiously deployed in squares.[14] Leith gave the order to fire and charge; almost immediately the squares were penetrated, the French lost order and began to fall back, and at this very instant Le Marchant charged through the smoke and decimated the 66e Ligne. The second regiment (the 15e Ligne) had time to prepare and fared better, but the sheer weight of 1,000 British dragoons broke their cohesion and they too fell back. Le Marchant's three regiments had lost their formation but they gave chase and soon came up on the 22e Ligne, the first of Brennier's regiments, who put up a gallant defence but were soon fleeing and with them the balance of Brennier's men. Le Marchant's charge had effectively destroyed the French left centre.

To Leith's left, Cole and Pack were having less success. Their advance appears to have started much later than the 5th Division;[15] Cole had pushed out a strong skirmish line consisting of the entire battalion of 7th Caçadores and four light companies. Pack had deployed to Cole's left and had orders to assail the Greater Arapile if he considered this a viable option. Stubbs's Brigade was the first in action against the 122e Ligne who were deployed between the Arapile and Clausel's Division, which was Cole's target. The Portuguese succeeded in pushing back the 122e and, with the 7th Caçadores left to contain them, the two brigades turned their full attention

to the division to their front. It was a desperate struggle and by the time Cole's troops had made the summit they were exhausted. To their left Pack had decided to assail the Arapile, unaware of the massed reinforcements to the rear. The Portuguese troops were clambering up the front of the hill when the 120e Ligne rose, fired and charged, forcing them back in disorder to the foot of the Lesser Arapile where Anson's Brigade covered them. At much the same moment Clausel's Division, heartened by the sight of Pack's troops in flight, charged at Cole's wavering infantry and pushed them back to the foot of the Lesser Arapile.

Clausel was aware of the state of affairs on the French left but nevertheless decided to press home the advantage in this part of the field. Leaving Sarrut to provide an anchor for the three broken divisions moving east, he advanced through the gap (created by the withdrawal of Cole and Pack) with his own division and that of Bonnet and the heavy cavalry. Ferey, who was by now on the field, was ordered to hold the Greater Arapile and act as reserve. It was a bold plan, and it began to make an impression until Wellington deployed his ample reserves. Leaving the Light Division to screen Foy, he still had the 1st, 6th, 7th and de España's divisions as available options. As it transpired, the 6th Division were sufficient to repulse the attack, and within minutes the two French divisions and dragoons were trying to extract themselves from the attentions of the 6th Division, the remnants of the 4th Division and the German Legion Brigade of the 1st Division. While this was ongoing, the 3rd and 5th divisions and D'Urban's cavalry were driving back the remnants of Thomières, Maucune and Brennier's divisions and, in the latter stages, were assisted by the 7th Division, Bradford's Brigade and Anson's cavalry. Every time the French rallied and stood, a left or right flanking manoeuvre was required to keep them moving rearward. These broken but far from demoralized formations 'fought with a fury' and were assisted by Sarrut's intact battalions. The mass fell back to the woods and sought refuge behind Ferey's division, which was holding the hill to the front of the wood line. Ferey was clear that he had to hold the line at all costs, for to fail would have resulted in the certain loss of the entire army. He deployed his nine battalions in a single line; those on the ends deployed in squares.

Clinton's Division was the first to engage, eager to enjoy their share of the action before night fell; they did not wait for the 3rd and 5th divisions to reform on their right before advancing against Ferey's lines. The British were about to receive some of their own medicine as the French, deployed in line, poured fire into the advancing infantry, supported by artillery fire on both flanks discharging murderously accurate grape and canister. For many minutes the two lines poured fire into each other's ranks until finally Ferey gave the order to pull back to the edge of the wood. Half his division did not return, lying where they fell, but their heroic actions had bought an hour's respite for the Army of Portugal. British losses in Clinton's Division were equally horrific; Rezende's Brigade was all that was left to continue to press, they advanced to the wood line supported by Ellis's Brigade, the 5th Division and Anson's cavalry. Hopelessly outnumbered, the French fought on until the darkness fell and then withdrew through the woods.

Clausel had already ordered Foy to pull back and he had extracted himself skilfully from contact with the Light Division, although he magnanimously admitted, 'Night alone saved my division.' The retreating army poured over the bridge at Alba de Tormes[16] and the fords at Huerta, and by daybreak they were on the far bank but far from safe. Clausel was being treated in hospital at Alba,

---

12 Bradford had taken longer than expected to get into position to cover the Allied right flank.

13 Napier, *History of the war in the Peninsula*, vol. V, p.171.

14 It is assumed Maucune had seen the Allied cavalry massing on the west of the village of Arapiles and given the order to form square to meet the threat.

15 Oman quotes Ludwig von Wachholz of the Brunswick Oels who states it started at 1545 hours.

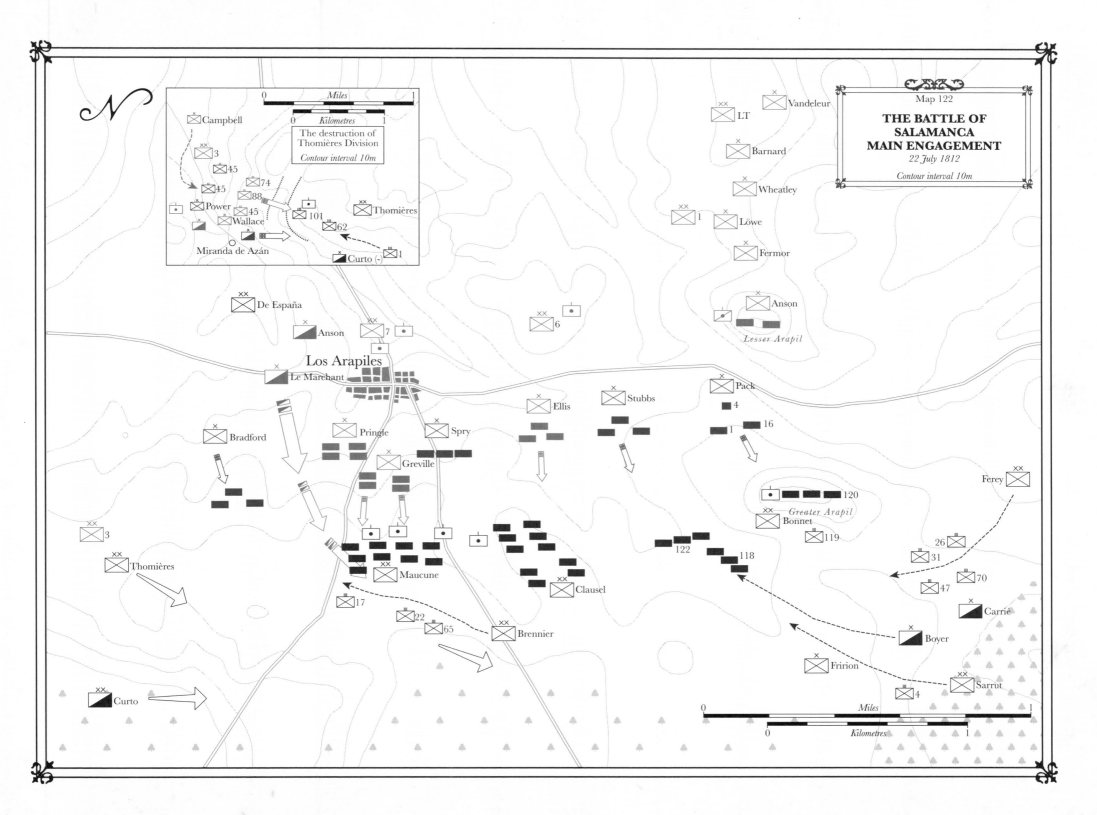

N

Campbell

The destruction of Thomières Division

Miles

0   1

Kilometres

0   1

Contour interval 10m

3

45

74

88

45

45

Power

Wallace

101

Thomières

62

Miranda de Azán

Curto (-) 1

De España

Anson

7

Los Arapiles

Le Marchant

Bradford

Pringle

Spry

Greville

Ellis

Stubbs

Pack

4

1   16

Maucune

17

22

65

Brennier

Thomières

3

Curto

6

120

Greater Arapil

Bonnet

119

122

118

Clausel

Ferey

26

31

70

47

Carrié

Boyer

Fririon

Sarrut

4

Vandeleur

LT

Barnard

Wheatley

1

Löwe

Fermor

Anson

Lesser Arapil

Map 122

THE BATTLE OF SALAMANCA MAIN ENGAGEMENT

22 July 1812

Contour interval 10m

0   *Miles*   1

0   *Kilometres*   1

having been shot in the foot, and the remnants of the Army of Portugal were in a precarious state. 'We had five or six thousand men out of fight, and the English had lost about the same. We had, it is true, abandoned nine pieces of cannon that descended onto the heights in the plain, and having lost their horses could not be brought back.'[17] In fact the Allies' losses were far fewer and the number of guns captured numbered 20, and to this tally were added two eagles and six colours. It was an astounding victory and is best summed up by Foy: 'The battle of Salamanca is the most masterly in its management, the most considerable in the number of troops engaged, and the most important in results of all the victories that the English have gained in these latter days. It raises Lord Wellington almost to the level of Marlborough.'[18] Foy was particularly critical of Marmont's handling of the early stages and is supported by other French sources: 'Clausel could but partially repair the Marshal's errors. He succeeded in rallying the left and the centre on his right. This manoeuvre, performed in the presence of a victorious army, does great honour to General Clausel, who, by his coolness and presence of mind, saved the French from complete destruction.'[19]

The French retreat continued through the night and into the following morning. Foy had been left behind to cover the bridge at Alba de Tormes, and he pulled back once the main body had received a generous head start. Wellington ordered Anson to cross the bridge and Bock to cross the ford at La Encina, while he rode at the head of Anson's light dragoons.[20] As the

village of Garcihernández came into view, elements of Foy's rearguard could be seen filling water bottles from the wells. They hastily recommenced their retreat, one brigade of infantry beating up the road and one brigade heading across the hills, while the French cavalry deployed across the road on the far bank. Wellington did not wait for the German cavalry to come up before ordering Anson to attack but, as the light dragoons crossed the stream and began to form up, the French cavalry broke and headed off up the road, overtaking the retreating infantry. The leading squadron of the 1 KGL was doing its utmost to cover the ground and join the fray when they were fired upon from their left flank. Chemineau's Brigade of the 6e Léger and 76e Ligne had been cut off by the rapid retreat and had formed square. Captain von der Decken, commanding the 3rd Squadron, ordered his squadron to attack the nearest square. 'The two front ranks, kneeling, presented a double row of deadly steel, while in rear of these, the steady musquets of four standing ranks were levelled at the devoted horsemen. At this critical moment, when the sword was about to be matched against the firelock, and the chivalrous horsemen against the firm foot soldier – when victory hung in the scales – an accidental shot from the kneeling ranks, which killing a horse, caused it and the rider to fall upon the bayonets – gave triumph to the dragoons.'[21] Against all odds a battalion of the 76e was penetrated and most of the first battalion was captured; the 6e Léger, having witnessed what happened to their comrades, made off with the 2 KGL hot on their heels, inflicting further casualties.

With the infantry some way behind, Wellington called off the pursuit; he had every reason to be pleased. Marmont conversely, hitherto firmly of the opinion of Wellington's impotence for the offensive, had paid dearly.

---

16 Wellington thought a Spanish garrison was still holding the bridge, but De España had withdrawn the Spanish troops a few days prior and had not informed the Allied commander.

17 Thiers, *Histoire du Consulat et de L'Empire*, vol. XV, p.100.

18 Foy wrote this in his diary 6 days after the battle. Oman, *History of the Peninsular War*, vol. V, p.472.

19 Sarrazin, *History of the War in Spain and Portugal*, p.280.

20 There were only two squadrons each of the 11th and 16th Light Dragoons under command, the balance were escorting prisoners.

---

21 Beamish, *History of the King's German Legion*, vol. II, p.83.

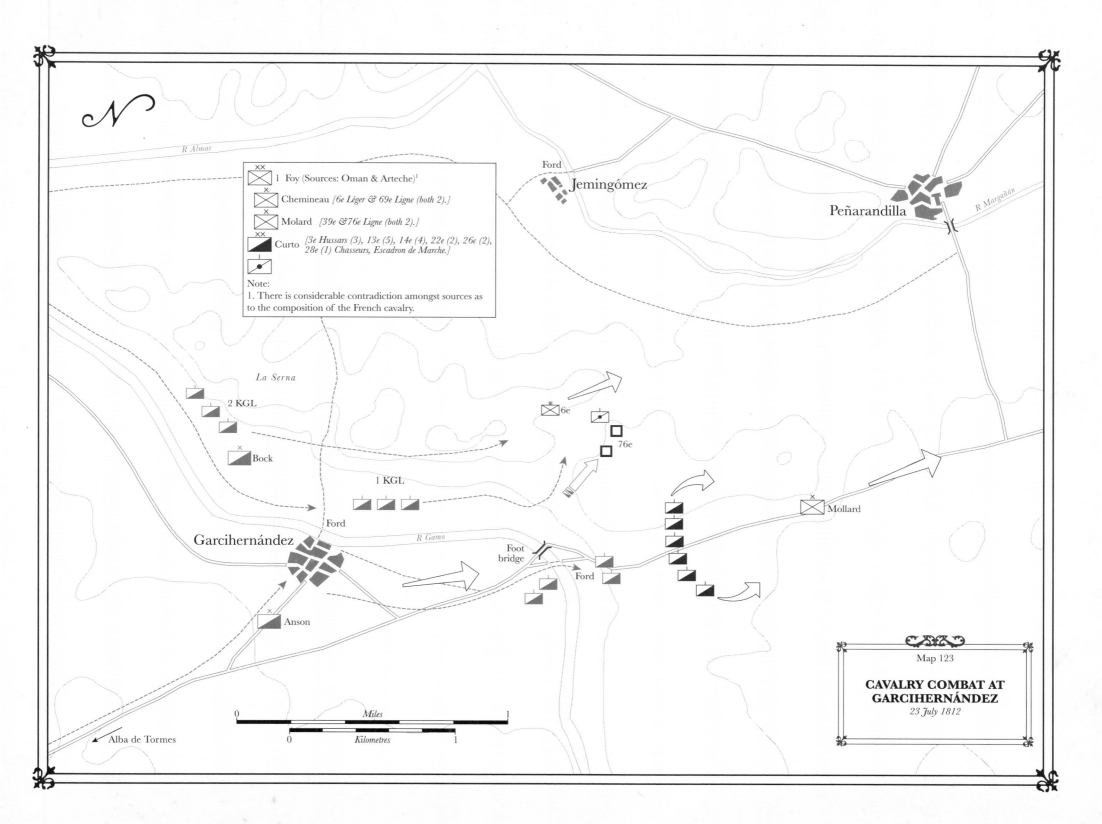

N

Legend:

XX
1 Foy (Sources: Oman & Arteche)[1]

X
Chemineau [6e Léger & 69e Ligne (both 2).]

X
Molard [39e & 76e Ligne (both 2).]

XX
Curto [3e Hussars (3), 13e (5), 14e (4), 22e (2), 26e (2), 28e (1) Chasseurs, Escadron de Marche.]

Note:
1. There is considerable contradiction amongst sources as to the composition of the French cavalry.

R Álmar

R Margañàn

Ford
Jemingómez

Peñarandilla

La Serna

2 KGL

6e

76e

Bock

1 KGL

Garcihernández

R Gamo

Mollard

Foot bridge

Ford

Ford

Anson

Alba de Tormes

0   Miles   1

0   Kilometres   1

Map 123

CAVALRY COMBAT AT GARCIHERNÁNDEZ
23 July 1812

Chapter 41

SUCHET'S CONSOLIDATION ON THE EAST COAST: JANUARY TO JULY 1812

The rapid capitulation of Valencia (see Chapter 36) did not save its inhabitants from the customary horrors of the post-siege licentiousness. Suchet saw the capitulation differently, noting that 'A few agents of the disturbance, spies and agitators, were arrested and sent to France, as well as friars, who were treated as prisoners of war, in consequence of instructions sent from Paris to that effect… the clergy was protected, and public worship treated with the respect it deserved.'[1] In reality, up to 1,500 friars were gathered up and seven of the purported ringleaders were executed; the balance was transported to France along with the other 'agents of the disturbance'. 'Similar luck fell to those 200 prisoners who fell behind on the road from Segorbe to Teruel.'[2]

With Valencia in French hands, Suchet informed Montbrun that the services of his force[3] (from the Army of Portugal) were no longer required. The Duke of Albufera considered himself strong enough to tackle Mahy and Freire, who were at this point in time concentrating around Alicante. However, Montbrun chose to ignore this rebuff and, in a display of personal ambition, marched on Alicante; driving back Freire[4] from Elche, he came up against the walls of the seaport on 15 January. The structure had been much improved in the preceding year and four divisions and 6,000 regular troops[5] now lay within. Montbrun quickly realized the futility of trying to capture the town and the danger of outstaying his welcome and he withdrew, taking out his frustration on the local towns and villages as he went. This pointless foray delayed the return of this considerable group of troops to the Tagus, with extensive consequences; furthermore, Montbrun's cavalier and destructive behaviour had incensed Suchet.

Notwithstanding the rapid fall of Valencia, and Suchet's confidence at prosecuting the capture of Peñiscola, Alicante and Cartagena, the fact remained that his force had been severely depleted by Napoleon's redistribution of forces in advance of his Russian campaign. The loss of the six Polish battalions was a blow, but the need to reunite Reille with Caffarelli to create a new Army of the Ebro (see Chapter 39), and with growing insurrection in southern Aragon which deprived Suchet of Palombini, left a mere 9,000 men at his disposal. He pushed Harispe (supported by Delort's Brigade) to Xativa with orders to watch Freire's 3rd Army, in and around Alicante; with the clear qualification not to advance too far south as there were many reports of yellow fever in Murcia. Habert was sent to Gandia, from where he took the small port and castle at Denia,[6] and was instructed to remain in touch with Harispe and support him if necessary. Musnier was directed north, initially to Peñiscola, but subsequently to maintain communications with Frère at Tortosa. The job of probing Peñiscola therefore fell to Severoli and his force, consisting of five battalions and part of the large siege train from Saguntum.

'The fortress of Peñiscola is seated on a rock, rising out of the sea about one hundred and twenty toises from the coast, with which it communicates only by a neck of land about thirty toises in breadth. The town, which occupies nearly the whole surface of the rock, is closed on all sides by good works, and commanded by a strong castle…. This little Gibraltar, as our soldiers called it, might be considered in some measure, unassailable by the ordinary processes.'[7] The garrison consisted of over 1,000 men and was commanded by General Garcia Navarro, who had lost considerable hope following the fall of Valencia. Severoli distributed his force along the coast and on the hills overlooking the fortress; the Poles were detailed to cover the siege park. Severoli decided to bombard the place and then issue a summons in the hope of an early success, although he considered the likelihood of success to be slim. The first battery of 12 heavy mortars was prepared and, on 28 January, it began a slow and relatively ineffectual fire upon the fortifications. On the night of 31 January Lieutenant Colonel Plagnoil began work on a long parallel, which ran north to south and culminated on the beach area in front of the isthmus. Work was rapid as the soil was sandy and the structure was made entirely of fascines and gabions; the gunners were quick to establish two batteries in it and another two on the heights.

The Royal Navy continued to resupply the garrison and provide advice to Navarro who, in turn, expressed his concerns to Freire in a series of letters. One such communiqué was captured by the French, in a small boat off the coast at Denia; the contents revealed Navarro's state of mind. Suchet, once apprised, immediately ordered Severoli to despatch a forceful summons to the garrison; this was received on 3 February and immediately accepted by Navarro, who expressed his wish to see Spain 'united under the protecting authority capable of terminating and repairing her calamities'.[8] The following day, the fort was in French hands and Suchet began to plan the next phase of his conquest of the east coast, but he fell ill before this new offensive could begin. By the time he emerged from his sickbed at the end of April, the situation in the Peninsula had swung back in favour of the Allies.

---

1   Suchet, *Memoirs of the War with Spain,* vol. II, p.238.

2   Toreno, *Guerra de la Independencia – La Derrota de Napoleon,* vol. II, p.93.

3   This group consisted of Montbrun's cavalry division, the infantry divisions of Foy and Sarrut and five gun batteries – about 10,000 men in all. See Chapter 37.

4   He had his own troops from Murcia, Villacampa's Division and all the (remaining) cavalry from the armies of Valencia and Murcia.

5   The divisions of Creagh, Obispo and Bassecourt.

6   He captured 40 small ships and 66 guns in the process due to Mahy's carelessness.

7   Suchet, *Memoirs of the War with Spain,* vol. II, p.244.

8   Ibid, p.248.

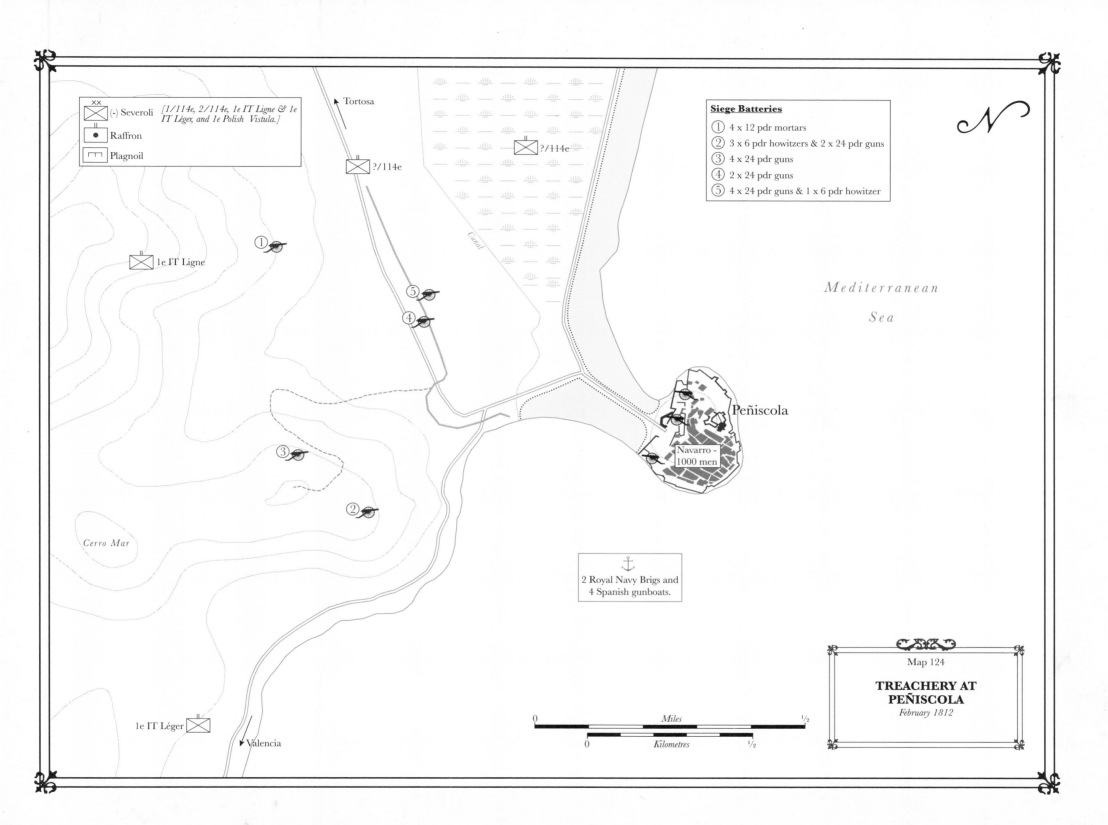

Key / Legend:

⊠ (-) Severoli *[1/114e, 2/114e, 1e IT Ligne & 1e IT Léger, and 1e Polish Vistula.]*

● Raffron

⊓ Plagnoil

Siege Batteries

① 4 x 12 pdr mortars
② 3 x 6 pdr howitzers & 2 x 24 pdr guns
③ 4 x 24 pdr guns
④ 2 x 24 pdr guns
⑤ 4 x 24 pdr guns & 1 x 6 pdr howitzer

→ Tortosa

⊠ ?/114e

⊠ ?/114e

Canal

①

⊠ 1e IT Ligne

⑤

④

Mediterranean

Sea

Peñiscola

Navarro - 1000 men

③

②

Cerro Mar

⚓

2 Royal Navy Brigs and
4 Spanish gunboats.

⊠ 1e IT Léger

↓ Valencia

N

Map 124

TREACHERY AT PEÑISCOLA

February 1812

0 ———— *Miles* ———— ½
0 ———— *Kilometres* ———— ½

Following his return to health, Suchet's immediate concern was one of an administrative rather than a military nature. Napoleon had ordered Suchet to extract 200 million reals in war contributions from the kingdom of Valencia and he now had to spend considerable time in organizational and clerical work within the territory to pay this debt. He was also embroiled in a constant struggle with Madrid to avoid having to provide additional forces from his army to stem the tide of Allied success in the west. He was quick to point out his special relationship with Paris and the fact that large numbers of reinforcements could only be realistically obtained from Soult's Army of Andalusia. Joseph O'Donnell[9] had been given command of the combined armies of Murcia and Valencia and had taken advantage of the lull in hostilities to raise and train a force of about 20,000 men. Freire, O'Donnell's second-in-command, had executed a series of raids; firstly on Baza in April, and then, aided by the Royal Navy, on the south coast villages and ports as far west as Almunecar.

Suchet, having successfully fought off Joseph's stipulations from Madrid, still lacked sufficient strength to prosecute operations south of the line held by Harispe and Habert, and given the rumours that were circulating of an approaching British expeditionary force, any attempt to take the initiative would most likely end in disaster. The long-awaited Anglo-Sicilian diversion was finally gathering pace and O'Donnell had been warned off to provide Roche's Division in support of this force. He had also been warned by Wellington to content himself with containing Suchet's force to his front, and not to try anything that might upset the status quo within the region. Unfortunately, in mid-July, O'Donnell considered an opportunity to his front simply too good to pass up. Faced with a number of possible disembarkation sites for the Anglo-Sicilian expeditionary force, Suchet was compelled to retain a large force north of Valencia that could react, either in support of Decaen, or within his own area of operations as required. In consequence, the balance of his force was spread thinly across the frontage from Denia (through Alcoy) to Villena and this tempted O'Donnell to make productive use of Roche's Division while it was still under his command.

O'Donnell's plan was ambitious; he intended to surround the French forces at Ibi and Castalla and destroy them before the reserve could be deployed from Alcoy. From his hideout in the northern hills, Bassecourt was to fall on the town and distract the reserve at the vital moment.

By way of a further distraction, all available sea transport ships were to deploy to Denia, create a diversion and keep Habert occupied. The Spanish approached on three routes, marching through the night of 20 July; O'Donnell's group[10] arrived in front of the French early the following morning somewhat blown from their efforts and unaware of the whereabouts of Roche and Santesteban's columns. As the Spanish appeared, Delort evacuated Castalla and took up a more suitable defensive posture on a hillside further north, and sent word to Mesclop (at Ibi) to send reinforcements, and to the two cavalry detachments at Biar and Onil to do likewise. O'Donnell witnessed Delort's withdrawal and now found himself in a predicament; if he waited for the arrival of the other two Spanish columns he knew that the French force would also have received reinforcement. He therefore decided to attack and began by engaging the French cavalry, but the attacks were not undertaken in a coordinated manner and made little impression on Delort's men. A short time later, the first of the French reinforcements began arriving on the scene. The 24e Dragoons thundered into Mijare's force on the Spanish left with considerable impact and, having disrupted this part of the Spanish line, the French dragoons reformed and then attacked O'Donnell's centre. The two guns up with O'Donnell were ridden down, having discharged only a single round apiece. The Spanish were frantically trying to reform when Mesclop's infantry arrived and engaged Montijo's Brigade on the Spanish right and drove it from the field. The entire mass of Spanish infantry retired in confusion, and from the original force of 6,000 men, more than half were killed or captured. Santesteban arrived after the fight was over and beat a hasty retreat.

To the east, Roche had exploited Mesclop's move in support of Delort and quickly overwhelmed the token French force left in the town of Ibi. They overran the dwellings but could not take the fort; devoid of siege artillery or heavy guns and with news of Mesclop on his way back to support this beleaguered group, Roche withdrew. O'Donnell's plan was undone; one brigade had been decimated and the other two achieved little or nothing. O'Donnell tried to heap blame on Santesteban, claiming the Spanish cavalry commander had stood idly by as the French cavalry moved from Biar through the pass, but in reality his time-appreciation was flawed and his plan too fragmented. On hearing the news, Wellington was furious, O'Donnell's army was to be out of action for many months and Suchet was able to consolidate his position in southern Valencia.

---

9   Not to be confused with his brothers, Carlos O'Donnell who commanded at Sagunto and Valencia, or Henry O'Donnell who was undoubtedly the most capable of the three siblings.

10   With three brigade-sized formations under Brigadier General Luis Michelena, Brigadier General Montijo and Colonel Fernando Mijares.

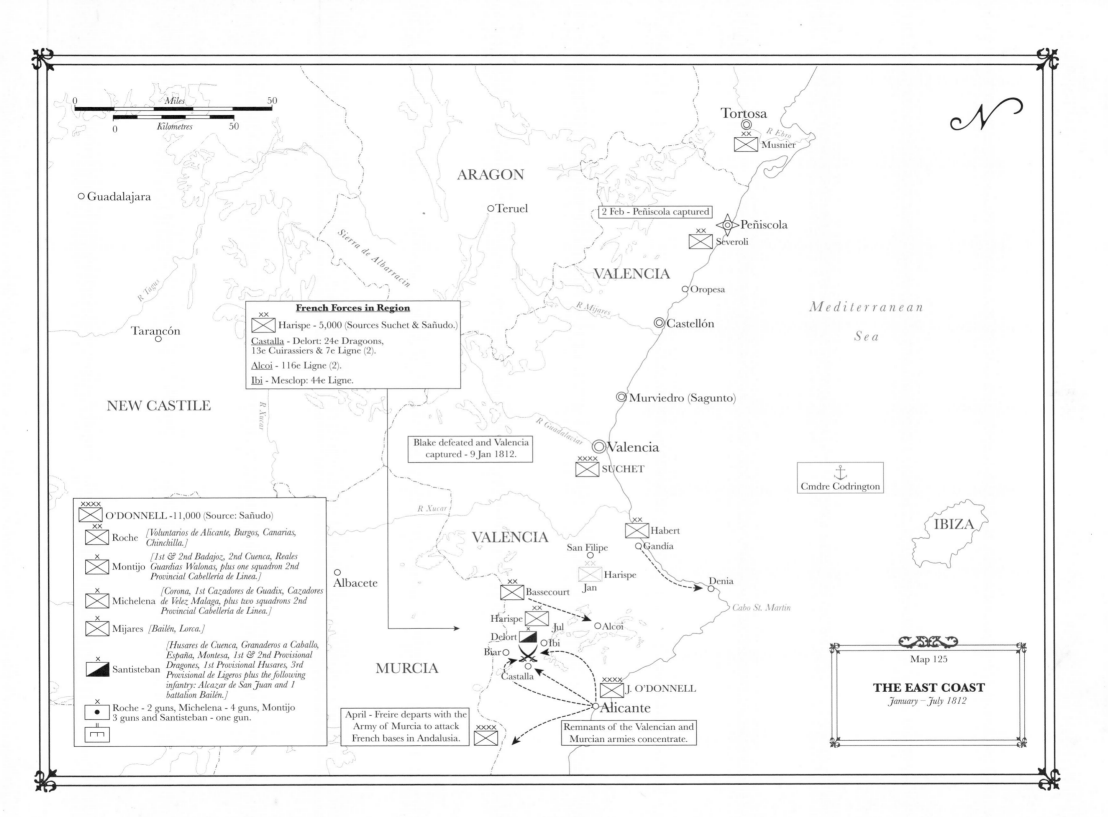

Tortosa

R Ebro

Musnier

ARAGON

Teruel

2 Feb - Peñiscola captured

Peñiscola

Severoli

VALENCIA

Oropesa

Mediterranean
Sea

Guadalajara

Sierra de Albarracin

R Tagus

R Mijares

Castellón

French Forces in Region

Harispe - 5,000 (Sources Suchet & Sañudo.)

Castalla - Delort: 24e Dragoons,
13e Cuirassiers & 7e Ligne (2).

Alcoi - 116e Ligne (2).

Ibi - Mesclop: 44e Ligne.

Tarancón

Murviedro (Sagunto)

NEW CASTILE

R Xucar

R Guadalaviar

Blake defeated and Valencia
captured - 9 Jan 1812.

Valencia

SUCHET

Cmdre Codrington

O'DONNELL -11,000 (Source: Sañudo)

Roche   [Voluntarios de Alicante, Burgos, Canarias,
Chinchilla.]

Montijo   [1st & 2nd Badajoz, 2nd Cuenca, Reales
Guardias Walonas, plus one squadron 2nd
Provincial Caballería de Linea.]

Michelena   [Corona, 1st Cazadores de Guadix, Cazadores
de Velez Malaga, plus two squadrons 2nd
Provincial Caballería de Linea.]

Mijares   [Bailén, Lorca.]

Santisteban   [Husares de Cuenca, Granaderos a Caballo,
España, Montesa, 1st & 2nd Provisional
Dragones, 1st Provisional Husares, 3rd
Provisional de Ligeros plus the following
infantry: Alcazar de San Juan and 1
battalion Bailén.]

Roche - 2 guns, Michelena - 4 guns, Montijo
3 guns and Santisteban - one gun.

IBIZA

VALENCIA

Habert

San Filipe

Gandía

Albacete

Harispe
Jan

Denia

Cabo St. Martin

Bassecourt

Harispe

Alcoi

Jul

Delort

Ibi

Biar

Castalla

MURCIA

J. O'DONNELL

April - Freire departs with the
Army of Murcia to attack
French bases in Andalusia.

Alicante

Remnants of the Valencian and
Murcian armies concentrate.

Map 125

THE EAST COAST
January – July 1812

Chapter 42 ⊶⊷

AFTER SALAMANCA: JULY TO AUGUST 1812

By 25 July, with his 'forces much fatigued by the battle and their previous and subsequent marches,' Wellington gave up his pursuit of Marmont. On the same day, he received news that Joseph had abandoned his capital and was heading north, presumably to link up with the remnants of the Army of Portugal. Joseph was frustrated and annoyed; his repeated orders for the redeployment of Soult's army from Andalusia had been ignored or countermanded. Following the fall of Badajoz, D'Erlon had remained in Estremadura, along with Daricau's infantry and Perreymond's cavalry division. Other than a brief advance north across the Tagus beyond Medellin, during Hill's successful raids on the forts at Almaraz, the French force was once again complete south of the river.

In early June Ballesteros had ventured from Gibraltar, this time to harass the besieging forces at Cádiz, and surprised Victor's cordon causing considerable damage to the cantonment areas before being beaten off by Conroux. Soult decided to remove the troublesome Ballesteros, but before he had assigned and released a force, his attention was diverted northwards by Hill's rapid advance. Slade was leading the advance and, like Long at Campo Mayor, had overextended his pursuit once contact had been made with Lallemand's Brigade; the subsequent action at Maguilla resulted in over 100 officers, men and mounts being taken prisoner. Slade's consequent report infuriated Wellington and prompted him to pen the following words in his despatch to Hill: 'I have never been more annoyed than by Slade's affair, and I entirely concur with you the necessity of inquiring into it. It is occasioned by the trick our officers of cavalry have acquired of galloping at everything – and then galloping back as fast as they galloped on the enemy.'[1] Soult was convinced that Hill's actions were the precursor to a main effort in his area and, as a result, felt completely vindicated in his refusal to move in support of Marmont. Drouet pulled back both Daricau and D'Erlon's divisions in the face of Hill's advance and Soult instructed his subordinate to go firm. Soult estimated that Hill's force numbered 15,000[2] supported by 5,000 Spanish regular troops, and accordingly ordered Barrois's infantry and Soult's cavalry to march north in support of the planned containment operation against this Allied concentration. The French forces had linked up by 19 June but Hill was well aware that this combined French force now outnumbered his own by three to one, and he immediately pulled back in the face of the French advance.

Hill established a position at La Albuera and called out the garrison regiments from Elvas and Badajoz to provide him numerical equality. The Allied cavalry was sent south to form a screen to his front and he awaited the inevitable attack. It never materialized, for two principal reasons. Firstly Drouet overestimated Hill's strength, but more significantly Soult, ever mindful of the need to keep a tight grip on affairs in Andalusia, was reluctant to move north. By accepting the fight he might succeed in pushing Hill back but in so doing he would have lost the rationale for retaining this buffer force and with it the ability to hold Andalusia. Drouet was accordingly ordered to contain Hill and no more. The standoff lasted until 2 July when, with Wellington's consent, Hill advanced on Drouet's position in an attempt to bring on a general action. Drouet withdrew and proceeded to do the same the next day – and, indeed, for five subsequent days, until on 7 July the two forces were in much the same positions they had occupied the previous month.

To the south, Ballesteros had recovered sufficiently to strike east at Málaga; setting out from Gibraltar he fell on the town on 14 July, and succeeded in capturing the port and many supplies, although the garrison escaped into the citadel. Devoid of other, more pressing distractions, Soult now turned his full attention to eradicating this troublesome Spanish force. He despatched Villatte east and Leval west in order to trap and destroy Ballesteros, but the Spaniard evaded his pursuers and, by 1 August, he was once again safe within the confines of Gibraltar, his force intact. However, news of Ballesteros's evasion was tempered by reports of a much more devastating nature – Marmont's defeat at Salamanca. The news was confirmed on 8 August and even though the significance of the catastrophe must have been plain to Soult, he still made overtures to Joseph to come south, join forces and attack Hill in an attempt to draw Wellington away from Madrid. Right to the last, Soult's egotism outweighed his patriotism; an insensitivity that symbolized his contribution to *la grande stratégie* since his arrival in Andalusia two and a half years previously.

Soult did not wait for Joseph's reply before issuing orders for the phased evacuation of Andalusia. It commenced from the west and by 30 August the entire army was concentrated in and around Granada. General Cruz Murgeon and Colonel Skerrett[3] secured Sevilla the day after Soult's departure and, by 29 August, publicly announced the Cádiz (1812) Constitution amidst scenes of joy and relief. Soult gathered his forces and his thoughts at Granada for a few days, thankful that he was not being pursued. Having destroyed the fortifications at the Alhambra, he set off in mid-September to link up with Suchet. Ballesteros did not follow and the Army of Murcia gave the force a wide berth, affording Soult unhindered movement, and by the end of September the two armies were united.

In mid-June Rear Admiral Sir Home Popham sailed from La Coruña with a small fleet[4] and by the end of the month, in conjunction with the irregular forces in the north of Spain, began to

---

1   Wellington to Hill, Salamanca 18 June 1812. However, for a more balanced assessment of the affair at Maguilla it is worth consulting Fletcher, *Galloping at Everything*, ch. VI.

2   In fact he had 8,000.

3   Murgeon's Division was 4,000 strong while Skerrett's ad hoc grouping was about 1,600.

4   Consisting of two line-of-battle ships – *Venerable* and *Magnificent* – five frigates – *Medusa*, *Isis*, *Diadem*, *Surveillante* and *Rhin* – and two sloops – *Sparrow* and *Lyra*. Popham's appointment to this command and task was quite contentious; see Hall, *Wellington's Navy*, pp.200–201.

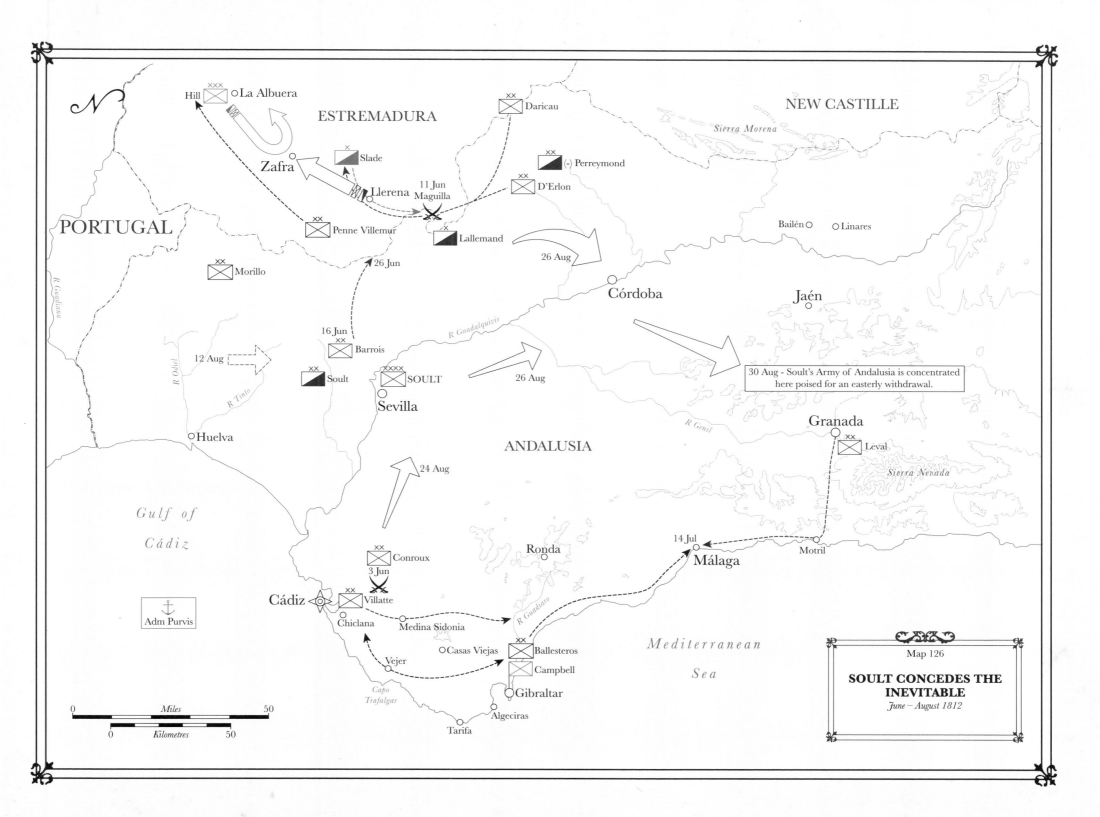

N

La Albuera
Hill
ESTREMADURA
NEW CASTILLE

Sierra Morena

Daricau

Slade
Zafra
(-) Perreymond

Llerena
11 Jun
Maguilla
D'Erlon

Penne Villemur
Bailén
Linares

Lallemand
26 Aug

Morillo
26 Jun

R Guadalquivir

Córdoba
Jaén

16 Jun

12 Aug
Barrois

Soult
SOULT
26 Aug

Sevilla
30 Aug - Soult's Army of Andalusia is concentrated here poised for an easterly withdrawal.

R Guadiana
Huelva
ANDALUSIA
Granada

R Odiel
Leval

R Tinto
R Genil
Sierra Nevada

Gulf of
Cádiz

24 Aug

14 Jul
Motril
Málaga

Ronda

Conroux
3 Jun

Adm Purvis

R Guadiaro

Cádiz
Villatte
Mediterranean
Chiclana
Medina Sidonia
Sea

Vejer
Casas Viejas
Ballesteros
Map 126

Capo
Trafalgar
Campbell
SOULT CONCEDES THE INEVITABLE
June – August 1812

Gibraltar

0   Miles   50
Algeciras

0   Kilometres   50
Tarifa

attack the large number of depleted French garrisons along the Biscay coastline. The irregulars, who were technically under the command of Mendizabal, had lacked a siege train with which to conduct operations, but both guns and men were provided by Popham's force and the combined operations began to have an instant impact. The task force was able to move to threaten an objective, wait for French reinforcements to come overland, and then lift anchor and sail off to another objective. Caffarelli was deeply concerned by this new threat; he had thinned down most of these outlying garrisons to strengthen the force available to support the Army of Portugal and he now found himself having to reconsider, readjust his defences and delay any southerly movement. After capturing a number of small ports in late June and July, Popham and Mendizabal had their greatest success on 2 August when they captured Santander, providing the ad hoc Spanish 7th Army a badly needed base that was both secure and supportable from the sea. Ten days later they followed up this success by taking Bilbao, which was abandoned by the French commander when he realized he was surrounded. However, by the end of the month Caffarelli had recaptured the place and strengthened the garrison.

To the east, the long-awaited expeditionary force[5] had finally arrived off the Catalan coast at the end of July. Baron de Eroles wasted no time in rowing out to the waiting ships and encouraging Maitland to disembark without delay. However, when Sarsfield and Lacy appeared later, their versions of events within the region and their assessments of Decaen's force strengths were considerably less fanciful and encouraging. Furthermore, instructions that the Anglo-Sicilian force would have to be self-sufficient convinced Maitland to try his luck further south. He arrived at Alicante on 7 August and linked up with the divisions of Whittingham and Roche establishing a force of 14,000 men, over and above the Spanish 2nd Army and remnants of the 3rd. Suchet responded by withdrawing Habert and Harispe to hold the line of the river Xucar, south of Valencia. When Maitland finally advanced, with some difficulty into the Spanish interior, he discovered all the towns and villages devoid of French troops.

On 25 July, Wellington had received news of Joseph's northerly movement from the capital. Joseph had left Madrid on 22 July, the day after Palombini's Division had arrived to reinforce the Army of the Centre, and marched north with great speed. On hearing news that Marmont was poised for a general engagement with Wellington around Salamanca, he swung his force west in the hope of providing reinforcement. However, by nightfall on the 24th, rumours of the lost battle were filtering back and Joseph wasted little time in returning to defend his capital. Wellington followed Clausel, who was now commanding the Army of Portugal, only as far as the river Douro and then pushed forward a strong cavalry screen to test the French resolve. Clausel

withdrew, vacating Valladolid, and Wellington now had to decide whether to follow the retreating Army of Portugal or turn his attention to the Army of the Centre and the Spanish capital. He chose the latter and, leaving a small containing force under Clinton[6] and having ordered Santocildes[7] to come to the east of Valladolid, he swung south towards Madrid. By 7 August the vanguard of this force had reached Segovia and, as they progressed over the pass at Guadarrama they were surprised to discover the approaches devoid of French troops. The first contact was made at Galapagar, but this token force soon withdrew in the face of the Allied advance and Wellington ordered D'Urban's Portuguese and the dragoons of the KGL[8] to retain contact with the retreating French.

Joseph meanwhile had resigned himself to the inevitability of having to vacate his capital; he had strengthened the *enceinte* on the Retiro heights and placed 2,000 men within the structure under command of Lafon Blaniac, in the hope that they could hold out long enough to enable Soult's army to join forces with his own and for the combined force to recapture the city. By 11 August D'Urban had reached Majalahonda, just 10km from Madrid, and had continued to push back the small French screen to his front. Before departing Joseph needed confirmation that this Allied force, advancing towards the capital, was of some strength and with the requisite determination to fight. Accordingly, Treillard was ordered to take his 2,000-strong cavalry force, supported by Palombini, and drive straight at the Allies to determine their strength and resolve. It was a fierce fight, the Portuguese and Germans fought bravely and Dyneley's troop of guns was temporarily lost, but Treillard's moment of victory was thwarted when Ponsonby's cavalry appeared in front of the leading elements of the 7th Division. Joseph had the confirmation he was seeking.

The next day Wellington entered Madrid unopposed to cries of 'Long Live Wellington, Long Live the English'. 'August 12, with effect, Lord Wellington entered Madrid; and he certainly could be satisfied with the gratitude and enthusiasm lavished upon him the inhabitants who were liberated of the servitude they had endured since 1808.'[9] The Retiro was stormed on the night of 13 August and surrendered the following day. With great dignity the Constitution was proclaimed and Carlos de España was made governor; a considerable number of *Afrancesados* were rounded up and for the first time in four years a mood of optimism permeated.

---

5   See Appendix 5.

6   The 6th Division had been badly mauled at Salamanca and this provided an opportunity for the formation to convalesce and reorganize. Many of the newly arrived replacements had been at Walcheren and were still riddled with sickness and unable to march and needed time to acclimatize and recover.

7   Santocildes sent two divisions, the balance of the Army of Galicia were still embroiled in the siege of Astorga.

8   They were supported by Macdonald's battery RHA and the 1st Light KGL.

9   Arteche, *Guerra de la Independencia*, vol. XII, p.105.

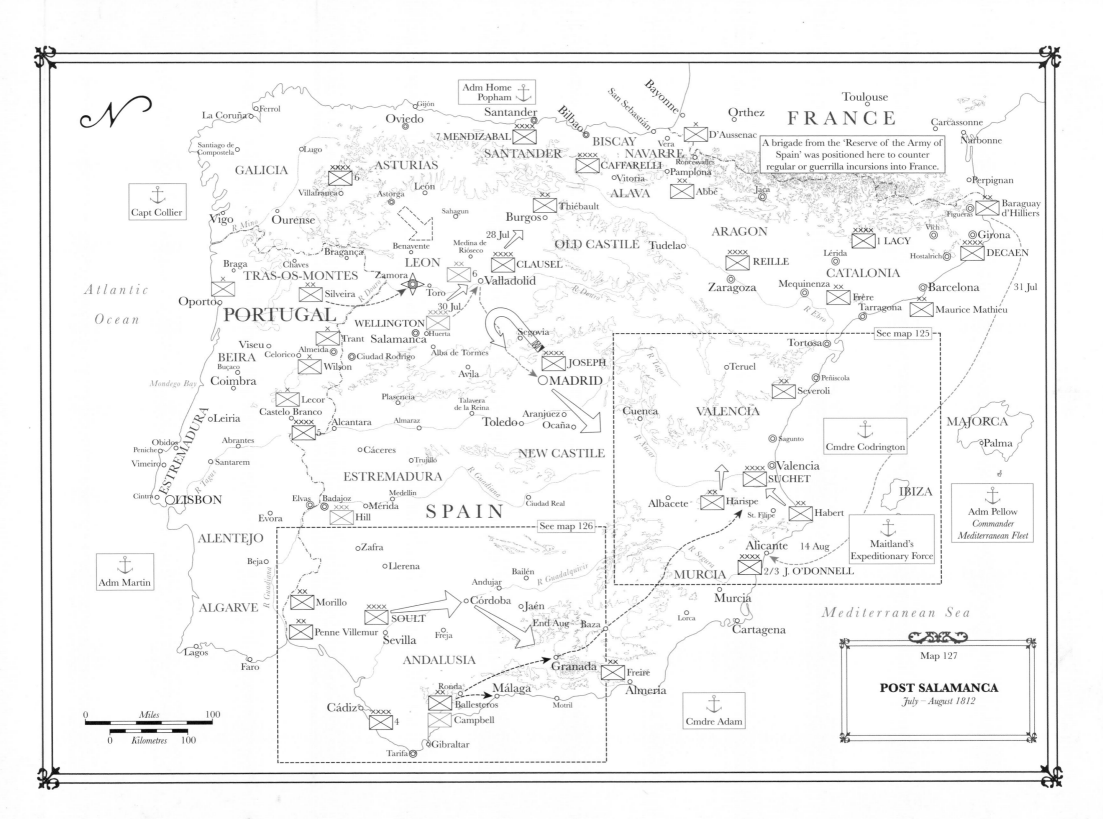

N

Adm Home Popham ⚓

A brigade from the 'Reserve of the Army of Spain' was positioned here to counter regular or guerrilla incursions into France.

FRANCE

Bayonne
Toulouse
Orthez
Carcassonne
Narbonne
San Sebastián
Vera
D'Aussenac
Perpignan
Santander
Bilbao
BISCAY
NAVARRE
Roncesvalles
Pamplona
Jaca
Figueras
Baraguay d'Hilliers
7 MENDIZABAL
SANTANDER
CAFFARELLI
Vitoria
ALAVA
Abbé
Vich
Girona
DECAEN
Hostalrich
Burgos
Thiébault
ARAGON
Lérida
Barcelona
31 Jul
28 Jul
OLD CASTILE
Tudela
REILLE
CATALONIA
CLAUSEL
Zaragoza
Mequinenza
1 LACY
Medina de Ríoseco
Valladolid
Frère
Maurice Mathieu
Tarragona

La Coruña
Ferrol
Gijón
Oviedo
Santiago de Compostela
Lugo
León
Astorga
Sahagun
GALICIA
ASTURIAS
6
Villafranca
Benavente
Vigo
Ourense
R. Miño
Braga
Chaves
Zamora
LEON
6
Toro
Segovia
Bragança
Silveira
R. Douro
R. Douro
R. Ebro
TRAS-OS-MONTES
Oporto
30 Jul
PORTUGAL
WELLINGTON
Salamanca
Huerta
JOSEPH
MADRID
See map 125
Trant
Viseu
Celorico
Almeida
Ciudad Rodrigo
Alba de Tormes
Avila
Tortosa
Teruel
Peñiscola
Severoli
BEIRA
Buçaco
Wilson
Coimbra
Plasencia
Talavera de la Reina
Cuenca
VALENCIA
Sagunto
Mondego Bay
Lecor
Castelo Branco
Alcantara
Almaraz
Toledo
Aranjuez
Ocaña
NEW CASTILE
MAJORCA
Leiria
5
Palma
Capt Collier ⚓
Cáceres
Trujillo
Cmdre Codrington ⚓
Obidos
Peniche
Vimeiro
Abrantes
Santarem
R. Tagus
ESTREMADURA
Ciudad Real
Valencia
SUCHET
IBIZA
Cintra
LISBON
Elvas
Badajoz
Medellin
Mérida
SPAIN
R. Guadiana
Albacete
Harispe
St. Filipe
Habert
ALENTEJO
Evora
Hill
Zafra
Llerena
Bailén
R. Guadalquivir
Alicante
14 Aug
Adm Pellow
Commander Mediterranean Fleet
Beja
See map 126
Adm Martin ⚓
Andujar
2/3 J. O'DONNELL
Maitland's Expeditionary Force ⚓
ALGARVE
R. Guadiana
Morillo
SOULT
Córdoba
Jaén
End Aug
Baza
R. Segura
MURCIA
Murcia
Mediterranean Sea
Penne Villemur
Sevilla
Freja
ANDALUSIA
Granada
Lorca
Cartagena
Lagos
Faro
Ronda
Málaga
Freire
Almeria
Cádiz
Ballesteros
Motril
4
Campbell
Cmdre Adam ⚓
Tarifa
Gibraltar

Atlantic Ocean

0 Miles 100
0 Kilometres 100

Map 127

POST SALAMANCA
July – August 1812

Chapter 43 ⚔

FAILURE, HUMILIATION AND RETREAT: SEPTEMBER TO NOVEMBER 1812

Wellington remained in Madrid for the rest of August waiting for confirmation of Soult's next move. Hill's dispatch of 17 August, which reached Madrid a week later, was the first corroboration that Soult was finally evacuating Andalusia. Wellington instructed Hill to move north to Madrid once he was sure the threat to his front had abated. Hill crossed the river Guadiana on 1 September and did not reach the environs of the capital until the end of the month. On 31 August, with no definite intelligence as to Soult's exact future intentions but satisfied that Hill was finally on the move, Wellington felt compelled to commence his autumn campaign by advancing north to re-engage the Army of Portugal who had grown in confidence and had evicted the Galician division from Valladolid. His intention was not to stray too far from the capital as he considered an attack upon it – by a combined force of Joseph, Suchet and Soult – the most likely French course of action. He left half his force in an around Madrid (under the command of Alten) and advanced with just over 30,000 men.

Clausel halted at Burgos and reorganized and replenished his army, and by 15 August had retraced his steps and captured Valladolid. Foy and Taupin were immediately despatched to Toro and progressed, in the most daring fashion, to march to the assistance of the garrisons at Astorga and Zamora. The former had surrendered 36 hours prior to their arrival but the Gallegos had abandoned the place; they had greater success at Zamora, evacuating the garrison and destroying the structure. On hearing of Wellington's advance, Clausel recalled Foy to Valladolid but the French had no intention of making a stand. When Wellington's force appeared in front of the city on 4 September, Clausel had already made preparations for the heavy baggage to be moved to Burgos and he vacated the place on 6 September, having left a small rearguard to cover their withdrawal. The pursuit was not conducted with any great vigour, Wellington, it should be recalled, did not want to stray too far from Madrid and he was waiting for Castaños's[1] 11,000 *Gallegos* to join forces with the Anglo-Portuguese. By 19 September the measured pursuit brought Wellington's army to the gates of the highly fortified structure at Burgos.

The responsibility for Burgos lay with the Army of the North. Caffarelli had only recently visited the place, and strengthened the garrison to 2,000 men under General Dubreton. On the

---

[1]   He was at this time commanding the 6th Army (of Galicia).

night of 19 September the 5th and 7th divisions and the cavalry formed the outer cordon; the 6th Division took the southern bank of the river Arlanzón while the 1st Division, supported by the two Portuguese brigades, closed in on the north bank. Wellington, after consulting his artillery and engineer commanders, wasted little time in selecting the unfinished hornwork of San Miguel as their first objective. The structure was taken at considerable cost; the false attack by Major Cocks on the rear of the hornwork was a demonstration of raw courage and impulsive leadership that led to the triumph. However, the Napoleon Battery dominated the captured ground, forcing the assailants to dig deeply for every centimetre of encroachment. Work commenced immediately on the first battery location, which was completed on the night of 23 September and armed with two 18-pounder guns and three 5.5in howitzers. However, before any of these pieces had opened, or work had commenced on the second battery, Wellington decided to chance his luck and storm the north-western wall with 400 volunteers, supported by a diversionary attack from the south. It failed miserably, and for Wellington to gamble with his men in such an uncharacteristically speculative manner was perhaps a clear indication of his frustration at having such an inadequate siege train up with his force.

Two days later the guns in the first battery opened, but the 18-pounder guns were found to be ineffective and were soon replaced by two 24-pounder howitzers. However, howitzers were not going to batter the walls successfully, so Wellington's engineers opted to blow breaches by the use of mines; the first was ready for detonation on 29 September (map 128, point 3). In the estimation of the engineers the resulting breach was serviceable, but the forlorn hope found the task impossible and withdrew with some loss and a few choice words of advice for their engineer colleagues. Frustration simmered with the commander and his staff but, with the available siege artillery, Wellington had no choice but to try another mine. The second attempt was to be supported by the erection of two new batteries nearer the point of assault on the castle walls. Battery 3 was completed by 1 October and the three heavy 18-pounder guns were moved into the pit, but before they even had time to open fire the French had brought down heavy counter-battery fire, which disabled two of the pieces within minutes. The same fate was to befall Battery 4 the following day.

The gunners were able to repair one of the heavy guns and therefore moved the two pieces back to Battery 1, from where they could batter the wall area brought down by the first mine. By 4 October, both the guns and the second mine were ready. At 1700 hours it was fired (map 128, point 4) and its effect was sufficient to open the wall into which the 2/42nd poured and secured the outer *enceinte*. Immediate preparations were made to sap forward to the next line of defences, but this work was severely hindered on 5 and 8 October when Dubreton, concerned at the proximity of this work, ordered the lines to be attacked. By 18 October Wellington gave orders for what was to be the last assault; the detachments of the German Brigade of the 1st Division were to storm the new breach (map 128, point 5), the detachments of the Guard's Brigade of the 1st Division were to storm the area by the captured outer *enceinte* (map 128, points 3 and 4), and finally a third mine was to be detonated by the church of San Roman (map 128, point 6) and this was to be stormed by the 9th Caçadores and the Spanish regiment, the 1st Asturias. Marksmen from all the other works were placed along the line to support the assaults, which in the view of

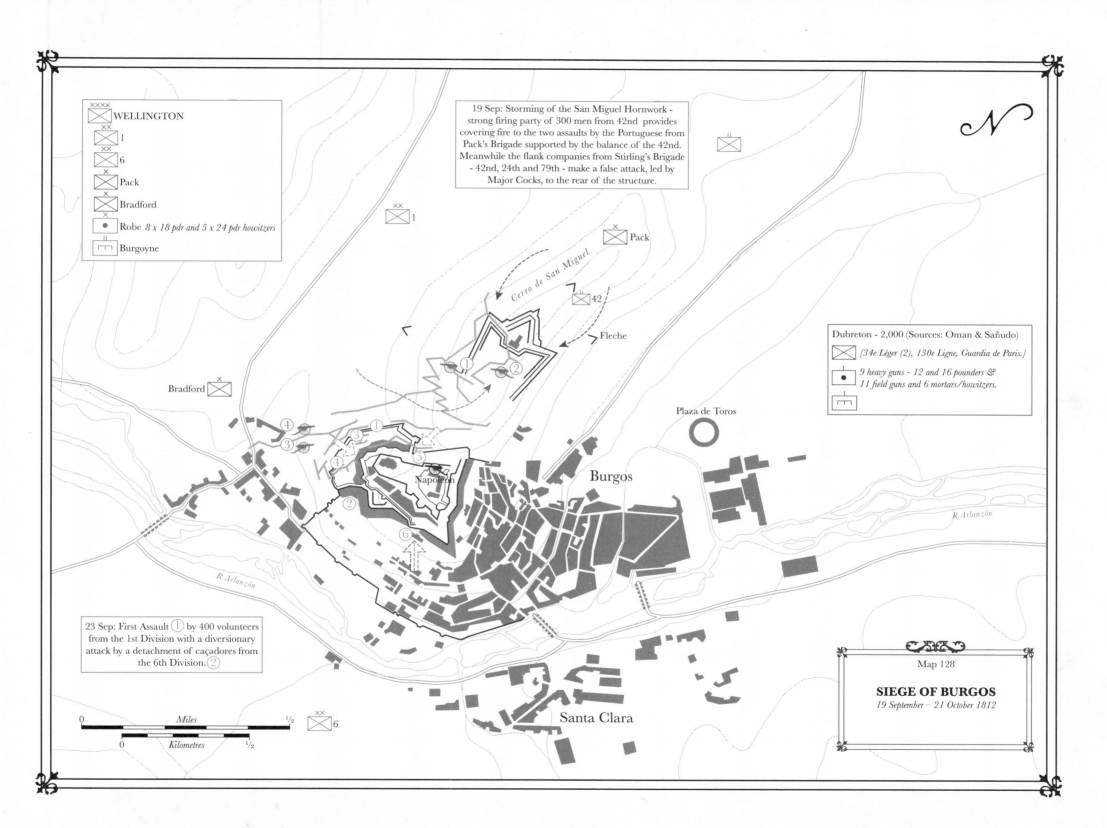

WELLINGTON

1

6

Pack

Bradford

Robe *8 x 18 pdr and 5 x 24 pdr howitzers*

Burgoyne

19 Sep: Storming of the San Miguel Hornwork - strong firing party of 300 men from 42nd provides covering fire to the two assaults by the Portuguese from Pack's Brigade supported by the balance of the 42nd. Meanwhile the flank companies from Stirling's Brigade - 42nd, 24th and 79th - make a false attack, led by Major Cocks, to the rear of the structure.

Dubreton - 2,000 (Sources: Oman & Sañudo)

[34e Léger (2), 130e Ligne, Guardia de Paris.]

9 heavy guns - 12 and 16 pounders & 11 field guns and 6 mortars/howitzers.

Cerro de San Miguel

42

Fleche

Pack

1

Bradford

Plaza de Toros

Burgos

Napoleon

R Arlanzón

R Arlanzón

23 Sep: First Assault ① by 400 volunteers from the 1st Division with a diversionary attack by a detachment of caçadores from the 6th Division. ②

Santa Clara

0   Miles   ½

0   Kilometres   ½

6

Map 128

SIEGE OF BURGOS
19 September – 21 October 1812

Major Burgoyne, the chief engineer, were being undertaken with inadequate troops; his arguments were dismissed by Wellington. The attack started at 1630 hours and both the Germans and Guards secured lodgements: 'both detachments conducted themselves with the utmost order and gallantry, and failed merely from the inferiority of their numbers… The mine under the church of St Roman made a large breach in the terrace in front, but did little injury to the church itself. On its explosion, however, and the advance of the Portuguese and Spaniards, the garrison abandoned it, and exploded their own mines, which destroyed [a] great part of the church, and the besiegers lodged themselves in the ruins.'[2] The next day, with news of the Army of Portugal stirring to their flank, Wellington realized that his time in front of the walls at Burgos was up; the siege had been a resounding and expensive failure.

In September Souham assumed command of the Army of Portugal from Clausel and, with reinforcement from the greater part of the Army of the North, he was now moving to attack the Allied force. On 21 October Wellington gave the order for the retreat, and the following morning the advance guard of the Souham's army entered Burgos, much to the relief of the gallant Dubreton and his exhausted garrison. Souham's combined French force numbered about 53,000[3] and Wellington, with only 24,000 Anglo-Portuguese and about 11,000 Spanish (from the Galician 6th Army) found himself completely unable to counter such a large threat. Furthermore, contrary to previous intentions, Wellington had strayed a considerable distance from the capital and although Hill had just over 30,000 Anglo-Portuguese in Madrid and Castile and about another 12,000 Spanish troops[4] within striking distance, even these numbers would have been inadequate against the combined 60,000 of the armies of the South and Centre who were concentrated on the east coast.

Wellington's intentions not to stray too far from Madrid had, by his own actions, been undone and he had clearly delayed too long at Burgos; he owed much gratitude to the Cantabrian *guerrilleros* who had occupied huge numbers of the Army of the North, and to Soult, whose tardy withdrawal from Andalusia had delayed any coordinated attempt on the capital in his absence. To be fair, however, in early October Wellington had put in motion two plans designed to delay any strategy Joseph and Soult may have had in making a move on the capital. The first was to use the British expeditionary force under Mackenzie (Maitland had fallen ill) to create a diversion in the region of Valencia, and the second was to move Ballesteros with part of the 4th Army to Alcaraz, where he was to link up with the remnants of the 3rd Army and threaten the flank of any advance from Valencia. Unfortunately, for the Allies, the former plan had not taken into account Suchet's army, which was more than capable of holding its own in Valencia (even if its offensive capability was constrained by limited numbers), and the latter plan was undone by the most bizarre of intrigues. Following Salamanca and his triumphant entrance into Madrid, the Cortes had, somewhat

contentiously, decided to appoint Wellington as *generalissimo* of the Spanish armies. Ballesteros was furious and 'on 24 October he dispatched an open letter to the Minister of War, Carvajal, in which he made a great show of his patriotic services, claimed that Spain did not need foreign aid, denounced Wellington's appointment as a national humiliation, accused Britain of attempting to subvert Spain's independence, and threatened to resign unless the offending decree was immediately rescinded.'[5] Ballesteros had seriously miscalculated his standing and support and was promptly arrested, but the debacle had cost precious time and by the time the 4th Army was ready to move north it was already too late.

Fortuitously for the Allies, throughout the first two weeks of October, Joseph and Soult had been locked in a series of acrimonious exchanges[6] but by the middle of the month both armies were finally moving west on separate routes but with a single objective. By 25 October the French cavalry vanguard and the Allied cavalry screen clashed in a brief skirmish in front of Ocaña, forcing Hill to withdraw to a defensive position on the north of the Tagus, which he subsequently discarded in favour of a position closer to the capital. On 30 October Joseph and Soult executed a combined advance, unaware that Hill had (by Wellington's order) already vacated this second line of defence. Wellington had doubts about his own ability to hold Souham on the Douro and was eager to keep the Allied options open by pulling Hill's force back to the Sierra de Guadarrama, from where he could link up with Wellington's retreating force or move west along the Tagus valley.[7] Wellington also gave orders that the troops from the Spanish 3rd and 4th armies, who were up with Hill, were to return by a circuitous route to the south, link up with Del Parque's force and await further instructions.

Wellington's withdrawal from Burgos was made on two routes; the 7th Division along with the cavalry of Bock, Anson and Sanchez formed the rearguard. On 23 October they had to fight their first action against Curto's cavalry division and Maucune's infantry at Venta Del Pozo. During the early stages of this encounter the Allies were holding their own, but when Boyer's dragoons and three additional cavalry units from the Army of the North arrived the Allies had to fall back under immense pressure, and had to fight another sharp action at Villadrigo before darkness saved them. Wellington issued orders for all the bridges on the rivers Carrion and Pisuerga to be blown, but the bridge at Tariego was overlooked, enabling Maucune to secure a foothold on the west bank (see map 130). Foy also secured a crossing at Palencia, driving back Cabrera's Galician Division and the attached cavalry. With these two bridges in French hands and the two French forces in danger of linking up, Wellington launched the 5th Division at Maucune's troops at Villa Muriel just in time to stem the flow and thwart the union. However the respite was short, as French reinforcements continued arriving at an alarming rate and for the first time Wellington realized the strength of the forces at his heels. Even with the crossing

---

2   Jones, *Journal of Sieges in Spain 1811 to 1814*, vol. I, p.327.

3   The Army of Portugal was recruited to 38,000 and reinforced by Aussenac's Brigade of 3,500 from Bayonne and Caffarelli had concentrated another 12,000, having left 20,000 to garrison the towns and to fend off Mendizabal's ad hoc 7th Army and the troublesome Home Popham.

4   This included De España's 4,000, the 3,500 of Penne Villemur and Murillo from Andalusia and the 5,000 from the old 3rd Army of Murcia under Freire and Elio.

5   Esdaile, *The Peninsular War, A New History*, p.415.

6   Largely predicated on the discovery of a despatch written by Soult to the Minister of War hinting that Joseph was in secret negotiation with the Cortes in contradiction and virtual treachery of the French cause.

7   Given the superiority of French cavalry and the flat ground to the Tagus valley Hill considered the withdrawal north the only viable option.

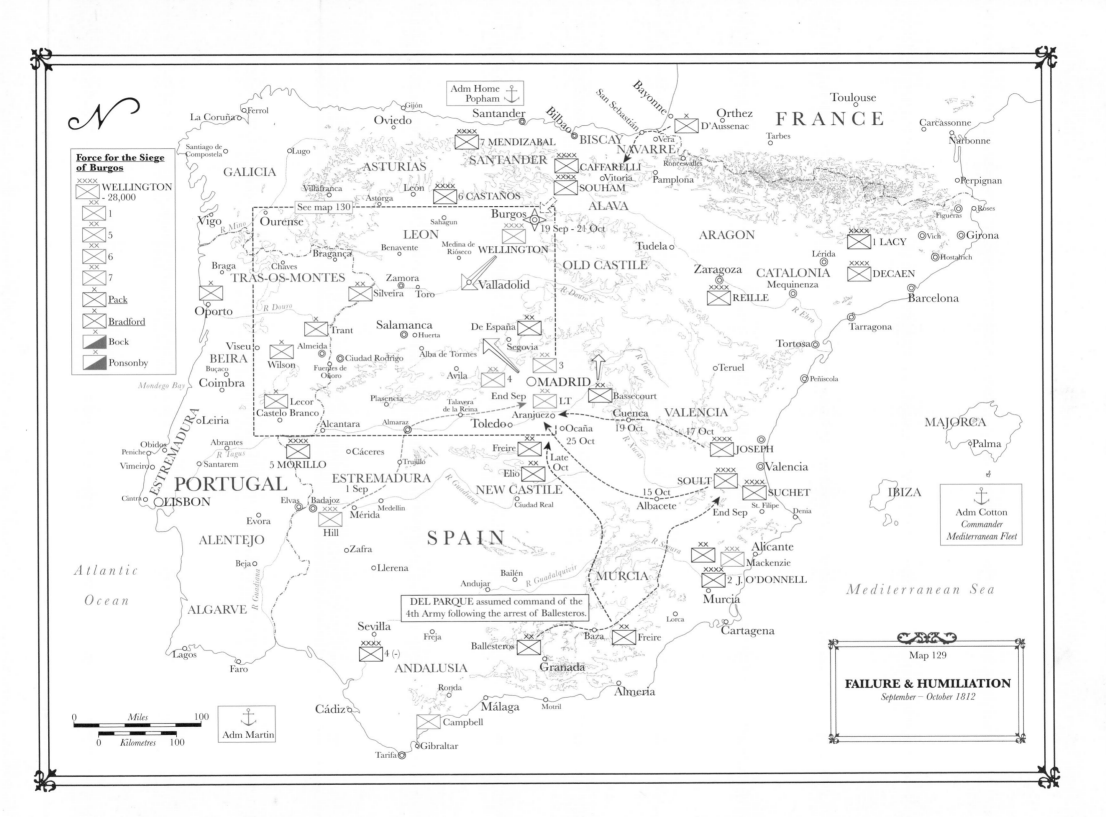

Force for the Siege of Burgos

- WELLINGTON – 28,000
- 1
- 5
- 6
- 7
- Pack
- Bradford
- Bock
- Ponsonby

Adm Home Popham

Adm Cotton
Commander Mediterranean Fleet

Adm Martin

Adm Cotton

DEL PARQUE assumed command of the 4th Army following the arrest of Ballesteros.

See map 130

FRANCE
Toulouse
Bayonne
Carcassonne
Narbonne
Perpignan
Orthez D'Aussenac
Tarbes
San Sebastián
Vera
Roncesvalles
Pamplona
Roses
Figueras
Vich
Girona
Hostalrich
1 LACY
DECAEN
Barcelona
Tarragona
Tortosa

BISCAY
Santander
Gijón
Oviedo
Bilbao
7 MENDIZABAL
SANTANDER
CAFFARELLI
NAVARRE
Vitoria
SOUHAM
ALAVA
ARAGON
CATALONIA
Mequinenza
REILLE
Zaragoza
Lérida
Teruel
Peñiscola

La Coruña
Ferrol
Santiago de Compostela
Lugo
GALICIA
ASTURIAS
Villafranca
León
Astorga
6 CASTAÑOS
Burgos
19 Sep – 24 Oct
OLD CASTILE
Tudela
R. Ebro

Vigo
Ourense
LEON
Sahagún
WELLINGTON
Benavente
Medina de Ríoseco

R. Miño
Braga
Bragança
Chaves
TRAS-OS-MONTES
Zamora
Silveira
Toro
Valladolid
R. Douro

Oporto
R. Douro
Trant
Salamanca
Huerta
De España
Segovia

Viseu
Almeida
Wilson
Fuentes de Oñoro
Ciudad Rodrigo
Alba de Tormes
Avila
3
Teruel

BEIRA
Buçaco
Coimbra
Leiria

Mondego Bay
Lecor
Castelo Branco
Plasencia
Talavera de la Reina
4
MADRID
LT
End Sep
Bassecourt
Cuenca
VALENCIA
MAJORCA
Palma

ESTREMADURA
Alcantara
Almaraz
Toledo
Aranjuez
Ocaña
25 Oct
19 Oct
R. Tagus
R. Júcar

5 MORILLO
Cáceres
Trujillo
Freire
Elio
Late Oct
17 Oct
JOSEPH
Valencia
SOULT
SUCHET
St. Filipe
Denia
IBIZA

Abrantes
R. Tagus
Santarém
NEW CASTILE
1 Sep
15 Oct
Albacete
End Sep

PORTUGAL
Obidos
Peniche
Vimeiro
Cintra
LISBON
Elvas
Badajoz
Mérida
Medellin
Hill
Ciudad Real
SPAIN
R. Segura
Alicante
Mackenzie

ALENTEJO
Evora
Zafra
Llerena
Andújar
Bailén
MURCIA
2 J. O'DONNELL
Murcia
Lorca
Cartagena

Atlantic Ocean
ALGARVE
Beja
R. Guadiana
R. Guadalquivir
Baza
Freire

Lagos
Faro
Sevilla
Freja
Ballesteros
Granada
Almería
Mediterranean Sea

4 (-)
ANDALUSIA
Ronda
Málaga
Motril

Cádiz
Campbell
Tarifa
Gibraltar

Miles 0 — 100
Kilometres 0 — 100

Map 129

FAILURE & HUMILIATION
September – October 1812

at Villa Muriel contained Souham could pour large numbers through the crossing at Palencia, and Wellington was now forced to deploy the 5th Division facing east and north to cover both threats. At dawn on 26 October the anticipated attack had not materialized, and Wellington chose to withdraw the 5th Division with orders for it to close up with the Allied main body, which had cunningly re-crossed to the east bank of Pisuerga, forcing Souham to follow suit. Crossing the Pisuerga once again at Valladolid, Wellington had the bridge blown and felt content for the first time in many hours that he had thwarted the French pursuit. His relief was premature, for Foy had advanced to Tordesillas and through a daring operation had secured the far bank and repaired the bridge, providing a crossing over the Douro and into Wellington's rear. Any chance of respite evaporated and hasty orders were issued for an immediate withdrawal; Wellington's plan to hold the line of the Pisuerga and Douro and wait for Hill's reinforcement was in ruin.

The Allied withdrawal south and east of the confluence of the Pisuerga and Douro provided a convenient point for Caffarelli to announce his part of the bargain as paid, and his intention to return north. This decision forced Souham to delay six days at Valladolid, whilst he reorganized his force (of 40,000) and sought word from Soult and Joseph before progressing. Wellington was unaware of these developments and on 29 October sent word to Hill, who by this time had withdrawn north of Madrid, outlining the precariousness of his position and reiterating that a retreat via the Tagus valley might be the most prudent option. However for Hill, changing course at this juncture would have placed his left flank at right angles to the advance of Soult and Joseph, and he continued to harbour reservations about the Tagus option. Keen to close with Wellington and combine forces, he elected to continue north at all speed and by 30 October his entire force was clear of the Guadarrama mountains. With Wellington only two marches to the north, and with no sign of Soult or Joseph, Hill decided to rest his force. The French advance from the east had been held up while Joseph pondered the fate of his capital; if both the armies of the South and Centre continued their pursuit, the combined forces of Elio and Freire, who had been joined by Empecinado, would certainly reoccupy the city. Reluctantly, Joseph accepted the inevitable and on 6 November the King's Army began to march north to link back up with Soult's forces that were, by now, astride the Guadarrama.

In the first few days of November Wellington had remained with his headquarters at Rueda and now resolved to unite his army and retreat on Salamanca. It was a difficult decision, for by so doing, the three French armies were free to fuse, generating a force of over 100,000[8] against his Allied army of 70,000. By 8 November the Allies were grouped around Salamanca but Wellington had to wait two more days for the three French armies to unite and reveal their intentions. Howard's Brigade, holding the Alba de Tormes, was the first to come under fire as Soult began to bombard the town and push forward to the crossing in an attempt to determine if the Allies intended to hold the position. Once confirmed, the French command now argued over the best way to proceed. Memories of French miscalculation over this very terrain were still fresh in the French minds and, in the middle of the heated debate Joseph unexpectedly relieved Souham of command, under the pretext that his performance in the preceding weeks had been tardy. Soult's plan was eventually chosen and, as this proposed a crossing of the Tormes well to the south, the 12th and 13th were taken up with the readjustment of the French armies. At dawn on 14 November Pierre Soult's cavalry crossed the fords at Galisancho and Lucinos and by nightfall the entire Army of the South was across the Tormes. Wellington began to move Hill south to thwart this crossing but the speed of the French manoeuvre caught the Allies off-guard. Hill was ordered to fall back to the position at the Arapiles, where the balance of the force was to join up with them and on 15 November he resolved to offer battle.

Soult was not, however, about to throw away his tactical advantage or repeat the mistakes of Marmont, instead he headed directly west, in an attempt to cut off the Allied line of retreat to Ciudad Rodrigo. Soon after midday, Wellington realized Soult's intention and ordered a general retreat. The heavy rains hindered the French pursuit but in fact there was considerable discontent in the French ranks and amongst many of its generals, for they considered that scant use had been made of their numerical advantage and the low morale of the Allies – something tangible should have come of the affair, and what better place to have extracted revenge? Soult's forces alone continued the pursuit with little vigour and from 18 November onwards the Allied army was unmolested, but a serious lack of food, exhaustion and hypothermia took a heavy toll. 'Under these circumstances, many irregularities and excesses were committed by the men in the course of their march, many of whom took to marauding for the purpose of obtaining food, whilst others from exhaustion or indifference lagged behind and fell into the hands of the enemy. Lord Wellington on his arrival at headquarters wrote a letter, severely censuring the commanders of the different brigades and regiments, which produced a powerful effect… On 18 November, the head-quarters of Lord Wellington were at Ciudad Rodrigo, and on the two following days, we crossed the Agueda, and were distributed into cantonments, where we were suffered to enjoy the repose necessary to prepare us for the toils of the succeeding campaign.'[9] In the meantime, it was to be a long, hard winter.

---

8   The October returns show the Army of the South with 47,000, of Portugal 45,000 and of the Centre with 15,000.

9   Hamilton, *Hamilton's Campaign with Moore and Wellington*, pp.135–136.

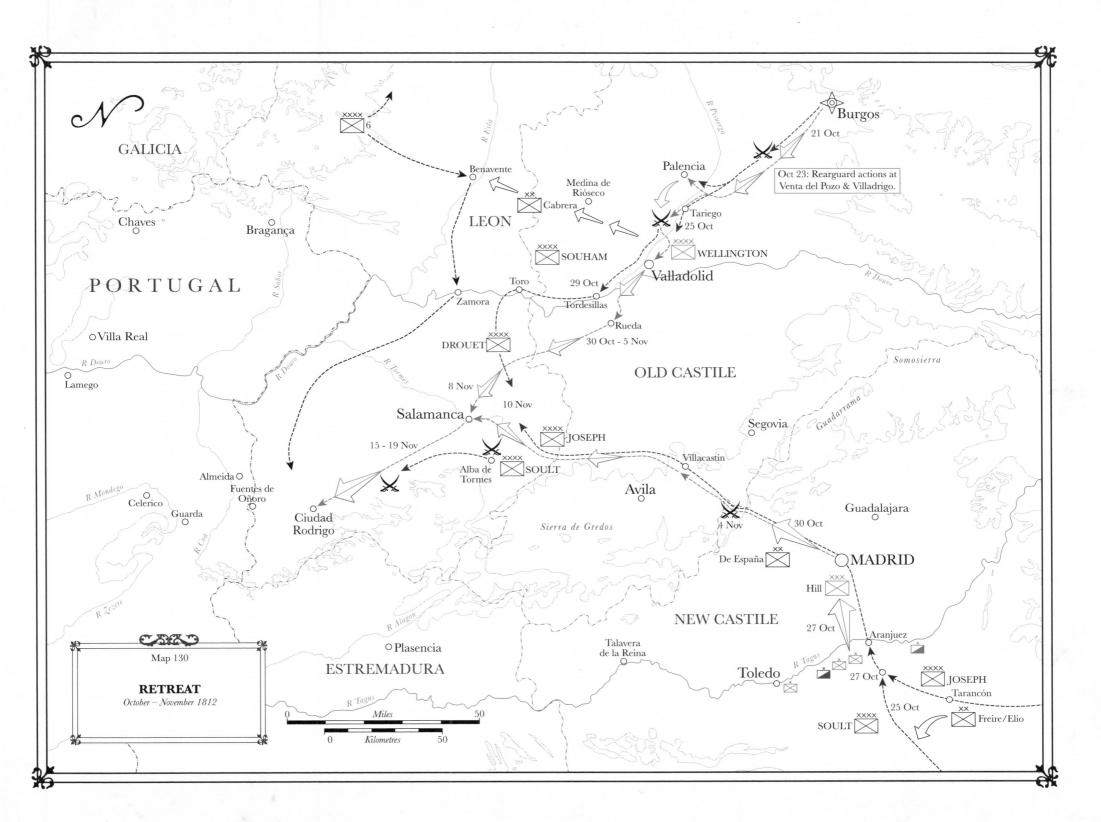

GALICIA

PORTUGAL

Chaves

Bragança

Villa Real

R Douro

Lamego

R Mondego

Almeida

Celerico

Fuentes de
Oñoro

Guarda

R Coa

R Zêzere

Plasencia

ESTREMADURA

R Tagus

LEON

Benavente

Medina de
Ríoseco

×× Cabrera

×××× SOUHAM

Zamora

Toro

Tordesillas

Rueda

29 Oct

×××× DROUET

8 Nov

10 Nov

Salamanca

15 - 19 Nov

Alba de
Tormes

×××× SOULT

Ciudad
Rodrigo

Sierra de Gredos

R Tormes

R Douro

OLD CASTILE

30 Oct - 5 Nov

Avila

Segovia

Guadarrama

Villacastin

30 Oct

4 Nov

De España ××

Somosierra

R Douro

Burgos

21 Oct

Oct 23: Rearguard actions at
Venta del Pozo & Villadrigo.

Palencia

R Pisuerga

Tariego
25 Oct

×××× WELLINGTON

Valladolid

×××× JOSEPH

Guadalajara

MADRID

Hill ×××

27 Oct

Aranjuez

×

27 Oct

×× ×

NEW CASTILE

Talavera
de la Reina

Toledo

R Tagus

R Alagon

SOULT ××××

25 Oct

×××× JOSEPH

Tarancón

×× Freire/Elio

N

Map 130

RETREAT

October – November 1812

Miles

0   50

Kilometres

0   50

Chapter 44

PROLOGUE TO VITORIA: JANUARY TO MAY 1813

The Anglo-Portuguese army reoccupied almost the same cantonments they had inhabited the year previously.[1] There was much to lament; the failed opportunities following Salamanca, the mismanagement at Burgos, the humiliating retreat and the strained relationships between allies had replaced the political and military optimism of the *Grande Armée* being driven from Spanish soil by the turn of the New Year. Wellington's elevation to *generalissimo*, following his triumphant entry to Madrid, was fraught with tension from the outset and the chronic financial situation in Portugal inevitably diluted Portuguese resolve, but the fact remained that much had changed in the preceding 12 months. Andalusia, Estremadura and the Asturias were free of French control; over 20,000 French soldiers had been taken prisoner and shipped to England; Cádiz, Sevilla, Granada, Astorga, Ciudad Rodrigo and Badajoz had been liberated and the great arsenals and stores in Madrid, Salamanca and Valladolid had been captured or destroyed. True, the retreat from Burgos had been a harrowing affair; indeed, soldiers who had the misfortune to experience the retreat of 1812 and that of Moore to La Coruña and Vigo in 1808–1809 were quick to confirm the latter under Wellington to have been the more harrowing. (Neither, of course, could compare to the ongoing retreat from Moscow of the most formidable army ever collected by Bonaparte.) But in précis, the French system in Spain was defunct, Joseph's legitimacy was over, the French hierarchy were locked in dispute and the invincibility of the *Grande Armée* in Iberia was at an end.

The reception the British soldiers received on their return to Portugal was also a great cause for concern for the Allied hierarchy. Provoked at the lack of civility by the Portuguese populace, discipline began to slide and much time was taken up in hearing and resolving disputes and bringing offenders (Portuguese civilians or British servicemen) to trial or court martial. 'In this village, though Portugal has been free from the enemy nearly two years, though the British Government has gave £100,000 to the poor in addition to the large subscription raised by the British officers of this army, and though they have seen us drive the French from their doors, yet when I entered my billet I had no mark of civility or welcome shown me and the people, though apparently good in circumstances, would give me nothing but a straw mattress on the dirty floor. All other officers have met with the same reception here this evening. I frightened these ungrateful wretches a little I believe by assuring them that in less than two months they will have their old friends the French with them to teach them good manners.'[2] This situation, lamentable as it was,

paled into insignificance compared to the financial difficulties facing the Portuguese central government: the war had bled the coffers dry and the system of taxes was in great need of revision.

Yet the difficulties within Spain were even more acute. Wellington, in his capacity as *generalissimo*, wanted to transform the Spanish regular army into a force capable of equitable contribution in future operations. It was an ambitious aim. 'With desertion rife and conscription barely functioning, many units were badly under-strength; large numbers of the 130,000 men theoretically serving under the colours were sick; there was insufficient cavalry and artillery, the little that there was also being dispersed amongst the different divisions in penny packets; the troops were at best ill-supplied and at worst on the brink of actual starvation; footwear and transport were lacking; indiscipline of all sorts was rife; and far too many officers still served no other role than to add a military air to the streets of Cádiz, La Coruña or Alicante.'[3] The Cortes in Cádiz were reluctant to grant Wellington a *carte blanche* with regard to his terms and reforms, and a change in the Regency in March 1813 virtually rendered his appointment untenable. Wellington did succeed in reorganizing the structure to four Spanish armies (see Appendix 6) but he was able to take less than 25,000 men with him into the field at the start of the 1813 campaign.

Amidst the most extraordinarily depressing rumours from Eastern Europe, Joseph, and Jourdan were not without their problems. The first was to decide whether to give up Madrid and concentrate the armies in the north-east of the country, making Valladolid the political and military centre of operations. They did not do so for two reasons. Firstly, this would have sounded the death knell for the Franco-Spanish monarchy, and secondly and more significantly, Wellington's dispositions left open offensive options through either New or Old Castile and the former would have dangerously exposed Suchet's right flank. It therefore took some weeks for the three armies to readjust their positions (see Appendix 6) and throughout this movement the *guerrilleros* increased the intensity and sophistication of their attacks.

In the early part of 1813, Joseph began to receive fresh communiqués from Paris along with outline reports following the abortive Russian campaign. The scale of the disaster was apparent, delivering a considerable blow to Napoleonic invincibility and French prestige. The latest directives ordered Joseph to move his headquarters to Valladolid (despite his appreciation to the contrary), to continue to hold Madrid as the southernmost point of his area of responsibility, and to concentrate operations against the insurgents in Biscay and Navarre. Soult was recalled to Paris, Gazan appointed to assume his command and, perhaps worst of all, an order for wholesale drafts of soldiers to provide for the new Army of Germany, whilst maintaining all six of the existing French armies in Spain.[4] Gazan's first order was to pull back the Army of the South into Madrid, releasing the Army of the Centre to move north and to take over responsibility for the province of Avila, which in turn, freed up some of Drouet's forces to reinforce Clausel who had assumed command of the Army of the North.[5]

---

1   See Appendix 6 for details of the cantonments by division.

2   Webber, *With the Guns in the Peninsula*, pp.126–127.

3   Esdaile, *The Peninsular War, A New History*, p.431.

4   In fact the demands on the French armies was relatively small – 15,000 men were withdrawn, leaving almost 200,000 in Iberia.

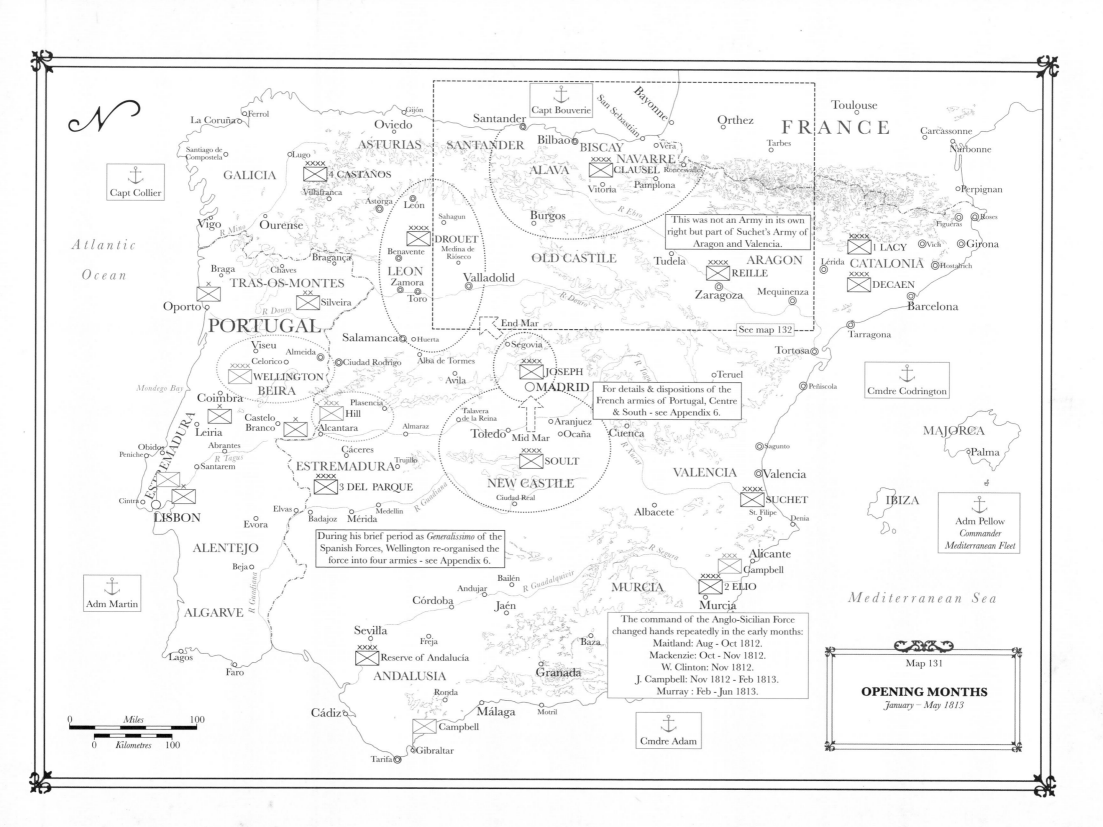

N

Atlantic

Ocean

Capt Collier

Mediterranean Sea

FRANCE

Capt Bouverie

This was not an Army in its own right but part of Suchet's Army of Aragon and Valencia.

See map 132

XXXX 4 CASTAÑOS

XXXX DROUET

XXXX CLAUSEL

XXXX 1 LACY

XXXX REILLE

XXXX DECAEN

GALICIA

ASTURIAS

SANTANDER

BISCAY

NAVARRE

ALAVA

OLD CASTILE

ARAGON

CATALONIA

La Coruña   Ferrol
Gijón   Oviedo   Santander   Bayonne   Orthez   Toulouse
Santiago de Compostela   Lugo   San Sebastián   Vera   Tarbes   Carcassonne
   Villafranca   Bilbao   Narbonne
Vigo   Ourense   Astorga   León   Sahagún   Vitoria   Roncesvalles   Perpignan
   Braga   Chaves   Bragança   Benavente   Medina de Ríoseco   Burgos   Pamplona   R Ebro   Figueras   Roses
   Oporto   R Douro   Silveira   Zamora   Valladolid   Tudela   Vich   Girona
PORTUGAL   Toro   R Duero   Zaragoza   Lérida   Hostalrich
TRAS-OS-MONTES   Salamanca   Huerta   Mequinenza   Tarragona
   Viseu   Almeida   Ciudad Rodrigo   Alba de Tormes   Barcelona
   Celorico   Segovia   R Tagus   Tortosa

XXXX WELLINGTON

XXXX JOSEPH

XXXX HILL

XXXX SOULT

XXXX 3 DEL PARQUE

XXXX SUCHET

XXX Campbell

XXXX 2 ELIO

XXXX Reserve of Andalucía

BEIRA
Coimbra
Castelo Branco   Plasencia   Alcántara   Cáceres
Leiria   Avila
ESTREMADURA
Abrantes   R Tagus
Obidos   Santarem
Peniche
Cintra
LISBON   Évora   Badajoz   Mérida   Medellin   R Guadiana
   Elvas   Trujillo
ALENTEJO
ESTREMADURA
Beja   R Guadiana
ALGARVE
Lagos   Faro

For details & dispositions of the French armies of Portugal, Centre & South - see Appendix 6.

NEW CASTILE
Toledo   Mid Mar   Aranjuez   Ocaña   Cuenca   VALENCIA   Valencia
End Mar
Ciudad Real   Teruel   Peñiscola   Sagunto   St. Filipe   Denia
Talavera de la Reina
Madrid
Segovia
Avila

MAJORCA   Palma

IBIZA

Cmdre Codrington

Adm Pellow
Commander Mediterranean Fleet

During his brief period as *Generalissimo* of the Spanish Forces, Wellington re-organised the force into four armies - see Appendix 6.

MURCIA
Andújar   Bailén   R Guadalquivir   Albacete   Alicante   Campbell   Murcia   R Segura
Córdoba   Jaén   Baza

Adm Martin

The command of the Anglo-Sicilian Force changed hands repeatedly in the early months:
Maitland: Aug - Oct 1812.
Mackenzie: Oct - Nov 1812.
W. Clinton: Nov 1812.
J. Campbell: Nov 1812 - Feb 1813.
Murray : Feb - Jun 1813.

ANDALUSIA
Sevilla   Freja   Granada   Ronda
Cádiz   Málaga   Motril
Campbell
Gibraltar
Tarifa

Cmdre Adam

Map 131

OPENING MONTHS
January – May 1813

Miles   0   100
Kilometres   0   100

'The Insurgents in Guipuzcoa, Navarre, and Aragon have had six months to organize and train themselves: their progress has been prodigious: they have formed many formidable corps, which no longer fear to face our troops when numbers are equal. They have called in the English, and receive every day arms, munitions, and even cannon on the coast. They have actually begun to conduct regular sieges.'[6] Joseph's bleak assessment was partly self-inflicted, emanating from orders requesting Caffarelli to move south for the Burgos campaign. The news of victory at Salamanca and the subsequent thinning of garrisons gave the people hope and that hope was transmitted into armed action. However, no longer was that struggle to be delivered by poorly armed bands with questionable intentions, but by a whole locality in arms. Authorities reestablished themselves in towns that had been vacated and they began to levy and collect taxes, with which they created and trained new regiments. These groups formed part of the Spanish 7th Army, which was commanded in name by Mendizabal but in reality by Longa. Longa was a gunsmith from Rioja who had taken to the hills early in the campaign but had now been gazetted as a colonel in the regular army. In addition, other chiefs began to place their irregulars on a more regular footing: Porlier in the eastern Asturias, (El Pastor) Jauregui in Biscay, Mina from Navarre, and Durán south of the Ebro.

Napoleon had very firm views on the importance of the region and how to conduct operations there. Clausel had been selected, as he was considered the most proactive officer in Iberia at that time, and Napoleon was clear as to how to succeed. 'By a continual taking of the offensive it ought to be possible to reach a prompt and happy result.' Inactivity and reaction had left the initiative with the insurgents and the French on the back foot. Offensive operations were to be undertaken against all insurgent groups in all localities simultaneously to prevent even the remotest refuge. Finally, a series of fortified structures or blockhouses were to be built at intervals along the *Great Chaussée* to ensure that communications with France were maintained at all times. Notwithstanding Napoleon's hapless state of mind following his retreat from Moscow, this set of directives continues to demonstrate a fundamental misreading of the situation, a misconstruction of the terrain and a misunderstanding of the people. A less willing subordinate than Clausel may have deviated sufficiently from the Napoleonic directives and achieved success. Clausel tried to follow them to the letter with predictable results.

In January Palombini's Division marched north from Old Castile to join the Army of the North and arrived at Burgos on the 28th, having driven off Merino and his group who had been blocking the road from Valladolid. He then escorted a convoy of drafts and convalescents destined for France, but on reaching Vitoria received intelligence that Longa had cut the road to his rear. He backtracked as far as Poza de la Sal but found nothing, and decided to establish his headquarters in the village and disperse his force to forage for food. Longa waited until his battalions were some way off and fell on their Italian headquarters; Palombini was able to hold on until dawn when the battalions began to return at the sound of musket fire and assist him. Fortunate at this escape, and perhaps more aware of the nature of the threat he was facing, Palombini struck east and relieved a beleaguered garrison at Santo Domingo de la Calzada before heading north to Bilbao, where he relieved Dumoustier's Brigade of Imperial Guards. Clausel joined him there and preparations began for the siege of Castro-Urdiales, but before they could march the few kilometres to the sea fort Mendizabal arrived with a large force that effectively blockaded the French siege train. Clausel, desperate for an early success, despatched Palombini's Division to Castro-Urdiales with the order to take the place by escalade. Mendizabal barred his route with more than 3,000 men and heavy fighting took place on 24 March with heavy losses on both sides. Once Clausel finally reached Castro-Urdiales he realized that without heavy artillery his task was futile and, by way of a substitute, ordered the Italians further up the coast to take Santoña. Meanwhile at Tafalla, Mina with two heavy guns had blockaded the French garrison there, forcing General Abbé, the Governor of Navarre, to march to their aid with 3,000 men. Mina had deployed his men[7] astride the pass at Tiebas, which they preceded to hold despite repeated attacks and eventually Abbé was forced to retreat, somewhat dejected, to Pamplona.

Barbot's Division, which was the first of those from the Army of Portugal in the region, was directed to assist Abbé in clearing the area between Pamplona and the Ebro. Two battalions were ambushed at Lerin and soundly beaten. This victory, however, marked the watershed; the divisions of Taupin and Foy had also arrived, and they were tasked with tracking down and destroying Mina and his force. Palombini, having succeeded at Santoña was despatched to the east and in April he began to have some success and was later joined by Foy. Clausel had joined Abbé and Barbot in the hunt for Mina and despite leaving Taupin to cover western Navarre, the *Chaussée* was continually being cut and two additional divisions were requested from the Army of Portugal to reopen the critical line. Sarrut's Division remained seconded to Clausel and joined Foy in late April at Bilbao. By mid-May, Castro-Urdiales had fallen to the French but at a cost. The *guerrilleros* were largely still intact, open lines of communication with France remained sporadic, and for some months the Army of the North and all but two divisions of the Army of Portugal had been employed in this corner of Spain while the Allies manoeuvred for the next great offensive. The insurrection in Northern Spain had achieved its aim.

---

5   In fact this change had been made in January 1813, when Caffarelli had been ordered back to Paris.

6   *Correspondence de Roi Joseph*, vol. IX, p.206.

---

7   Four infantry battalions and one regiment of cavalry.

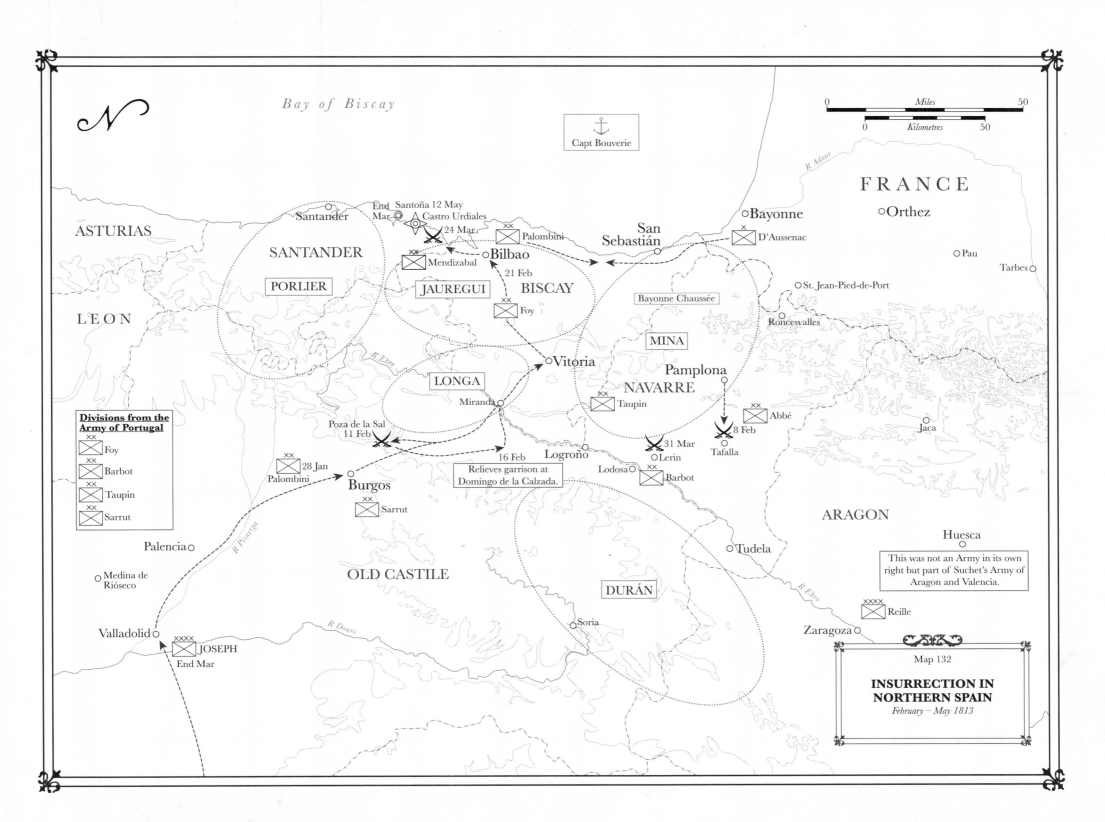

N

Bay of Biscay

Capt Bouverie

FRANCE

0 Miles 50
0 Kilometres 50

ASTURIAS

Santander

SANTANDER

PORLIER

LEON

End Santoña 12 May
Mar Castro Urdiales
24 Mar

Palombini

Bayonne Orthez

San Sebastián D'Aussenac

Pau

Tarbes

Mendizabal

JAUREGUI

Bilbao

BISCAY

21 Feb

Foy

St. Jean-Pied-de-Port

Bayonne Chaussée

Roncesvalles

MINA

Vitoria

LONGA

Miranda

Pamplona

NAVARRE

Taupin

Abbé

8 Feb

Jaca

Divisions from the
Army of Portugal

Foy

Barbot

Taupin

Sarrut

Poza de la Sal
11 Feb

28 Jan
Palombini

Burgos

16 Feb
Relieves garrison at
Domingo de la Calzada.

Logroño

Lodosa

31 Mar
Lerin
Tafalla

Barbot

ARAGON

Huesca

Sarrut

Palencia

Medina de
Ríoseco

OLD CASTILE

R Pisuerga

Tudela

DURÁN

This was not an Army in its own
right but part of Suchet's Army of
Aragon and Valencia.

R Ebro

Soria

Reille

Zaragoza

Valladolid

R Douro

JOSEPH
End Mar

Map 132

INSURRECTION IN
NORTHERN SPAIN
February – May 1813

Chapter 45

OPERATIONS ON THE EAST COAST: LATE 1812 TO APRIL 1813

By October 1812, with the westerly movement of Soult and Joseph to New Castile and Madrid, the threat to the Allied forces on the east coast diminished. 'The 2nd Spanish Army was formed on 4 December 1812 [from the old second and third armies] and consisted of six divisions commanded by generals, Miyares, Villacampa, Sarsfield, Roche, el Empecinado and Durán; a recollection of the operations that they had executed until that point and the situation within the regions that they moved, dictated that they would have to operate in large formations, the opportunities for tactical level operations were virtually non-existent and, accordingly, they remained concentrated. If that army consisted, as stated, of 20,000 men of all arms, General Elio, the commander-in-chief, spent most of March and April in his headquarters and only really had at his disposal the divisions of Mijares and Roche, Villacampa and Sarsfield were deployed in Aragon, and el Empecinado and Durán in the high lands where the Tagus and Douro are born.'[1] The other Spanish division in the area was that of General Whittingham,[2] which consisted of six infantry battalions and two weak cavalry regiments. This formation was incorporated into the Anglo-Sicilian force, which had landed under Maitland in August 1812 (see Chapter 42). Although Roche's Division was technically under Elio's new command, it too received funding through a British subsidy and, as such, Wellington task-organized it more with the expeditionary force than with the 2nd Spanish Army.

Until Sir John Murray arrived on 25 February, command of this expeditionary group had changed a number of times. Murray's Peninsular record was not impressive; he had commanded a brigade at Oporto, following which he received considerable criticism for his failure to cut off Soult's line of retreat (see Chapter 17). It was surprising, therefore, that Wellington agreed to the appointment. The all-up strength of this Allied force was 21,000 and, when combined with the 15,000 available to Elio, the Allies could field a force larger than that available to Suchet in the region.[3] With the departure of the armies of the Centre and South from the area, Suchet grew increasingly concerned at this numerical imbalance; regular contact with his forward formations was lost and his right flank was dangerously exposed.

Soon after assuming command, Murray decided to blood the force with a strike on the exposed French brigade at Alcoi. His intentions to encircle the town and trap the brigade were straightforward enough, but his execution demonstrated that little had been learned since O'Donnell's ill-fated attack the year previously at Castalla. Murray's force advanced on four axes which failed to link up, allowing the brigade to slip away with relative ease. Murray sat motionless for a few days pondering his next move, before sending Whittingham forward to probe the road heading north out of the town and Donkin to make a simultaneous demonstration against the French right. The French forces withdrew and closed up to provide an element of flank and mutual support and waited for the Allied attack. The attack did not materialize; Murray decided to hold his current line and instead put in motion the next part of his plan. He intended an assault on Valencia from the sea and asked for support from Elio, who duly obliged by providing a division that marched to Yecla. Roche's division was earmarked for the amphibious assault but, before this formation was at sea, a political crisis had broken out in Sicily and Lord Bentinck requested that some forces be returned under his banner. This minor readjustment seems to have paralysed Murray into further inactivity, which mystified Suchet. For a full month the division of Mijares lay temptingly secluded in front of the French line, and eventually Suchet could no longer contain himself. 'The occasion seemed to present itself spontaneously in the first days of April. A Spanish division of Elio's corps came and posted itself at Yecla, within reach of Fuente la Higuera which we occupied in advance guard, and at a considerable distance from the advance guard of the enemy established at Villena. The marshal hoped to be able to cut off this division. He assembled the *élite* of his forces in the night of the 10th at Fuente la Higuera; thence he marched direct upon Villena with Habert's division, the cavalry and the reserve, while general Harispe moved upon Yecla in the night, by rapid march which was totally unperceived by the enemy.'[4]

Harispe surprised Mijares who, outnumbered, withdrew to the hills in the direction of Jumilla; his first two battalions made good their escape, but the French cavalry caught the second pair. They formed square and beat off two attacks, but were broken on the third and annihilated. As the second French column, led by Suchet and consisting of Habert's Division, closed on Villena, Elio threw a battalion into the castle and then dispersed his force. The French column arrived at Villena on 11 April, and on discovering the castle occupied, blew the gates, inducing the unfortunate Spanish battalion ensconced there to capitulate before Suchet stormed the place. Murray manoeuvred to counter this French offensive; he concentrated his force at Castalla and placed Adam's Light Brigade to cover the pass from Biar. Suchet wasted little time before moving south and, on discovering the Allied light troops holding the village and pass east of Biar, ordered that both be cleared. The task was to prove more difficult that he anticipated. 'The combat of Biar, which filled the midday hours of April 12th, was one of the most creditable rearguard actions fought during the whole Peninsular War.'[5] Adam had deployed the Calabrians in the village, supported by the light companies of the 2/27th and the 3rd KGL; the balance of the brigade was on the shoulders of the pass overlooking the town. The 1e Léger and 14e Ligne were

---

1   Arteche, *Guerra de la Independencia*, vol. XIII, pp.37–38.

2   This was a Mallorcan division, which had been raised and trained in the Balearic isles by Whittingham, and was funded by a British subsidy.

3   Despite having 75,000 under his overall command, he only had a force of about 15,000 in Valencia.

4   Suchet, *Memoirs of the War with Spain*, vol. II, p.303.

5   Oman, *A History of the Peninsular War*, vol. VI, p.288.

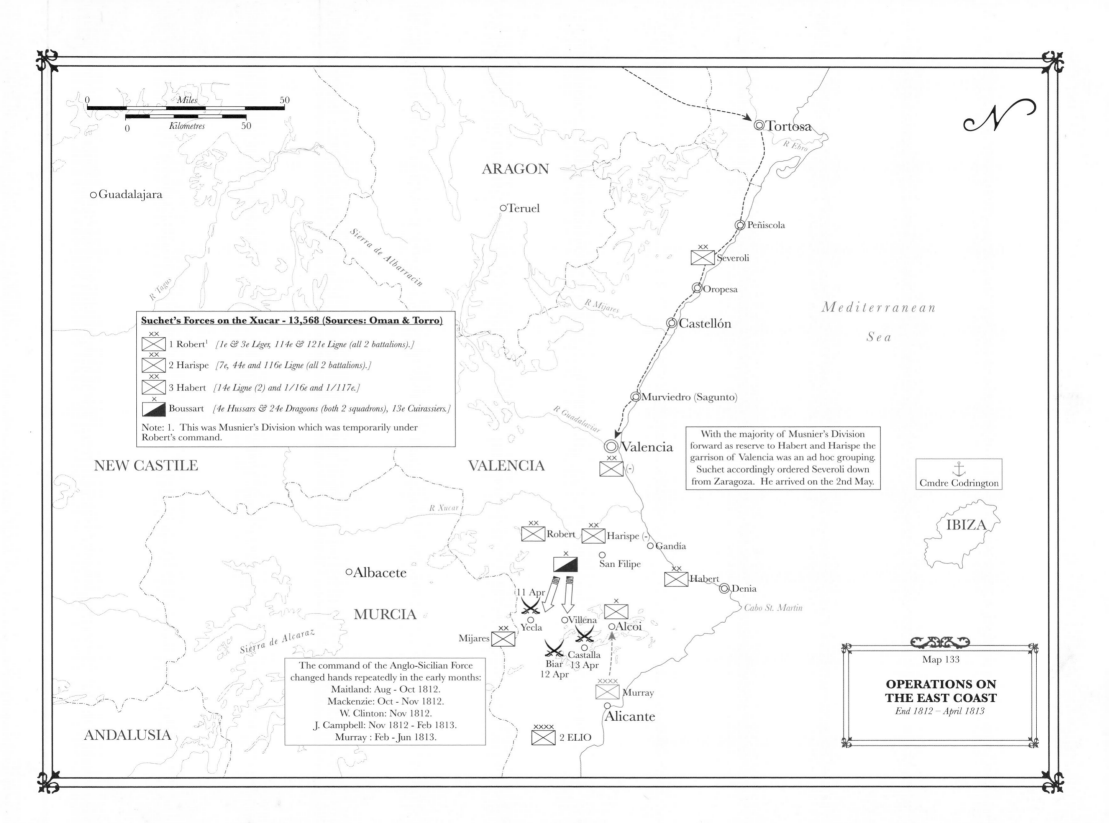

N

0 _____ Miles _____ 50
0 _____ Kilometres _____ 50

ARAGON

○Guadalajara

○Teruel

◎Tortosa

R Ebro

◎Peñiscola

XX Severoli

◎Oropesa

R Mijares

◎◎Castellón

Mediterranean Sea

Suchet's Forces on the Xucar - 13,568 (Sources: Oman & Torro)

XX 1 Robert[1] *[1e & 3e Léger, 114e & 121e Ligne (all 2 battalions).]*

XX 2 Harispe *[7e, 44e and 116e Ligne (all 2 battalions).]*

XX 3 Habert *[14e Ligne (2) and 1/16e and 1/117e.]*

X Boussart *[4e Hussars & 24e Dragoons (both 2 squadrons), 13e Cuirassiers.]*

Note: 1. This was Musnier's Division which was temporarily under Robert's command.

NEW CASTILE

◎Murviedro (Sagunto)

R Guadalaviar

◎Valencia
XX (-)

VALENCIA

With the majority of Musnier's Division forward as reserve to Habert and Harispe the garrison of Valencia was an ad hoc grouping. Suchet accordingly ordered Severoli down from Zaragoza. He arrived on the 2nd May.

⚓ Cmdre Codrington

IBIZA

R Xucar

○Albacete

XX Robert   XX Harispe (-)   ○Gandía

X   ○San Filipe

XX Habert   ○Denia

Cabo St. Martin

MURCIA

11 Apr

Sierra de Alcaraz

XX Mijares   ⚔ Yecla   ○Villena   X   ○Alcoi

⚔ Castalla 13 Apr
Biar 12 Apr

XXXX Murray

The command of the Anglo-Sicilian Force changed hands repeatedly in the early months:
Maitland: Aug - Oct 1812.
Mackenzie: Oct - Nov 1812.
W. Clinton: Nov 1812.
J. Campbell: Nov 1812 - Feb 1813.
Murray : Feb - Jun 1813.

○Alicante

XXXX 2 ELIO

Map 133

OPERATIONS ON THE EAST COAST
End 1812 – April 1813

ANDALUSIA

tasked to clear the dwellings but withdrew after taking heavy losses, at which point Suchet decided to encircle the defensive position. It took some time, but once the wings of this movement were well advanced, the defenders withdrew to the higher ground further up the pass. From these new positions the Allied lines poured fire on the 121e and 114e Ligne, who were forming up for the second attack; the four mountain guns of Williamson's Company were particularly effective in raking the unfortunate French infantry. Suchet became increasingly agitated at the delay and at the losses that he could ill afford; he hastily summoned nine battalions that deployed in depth to force the defile. Adams watched the French battalions arrive and shake out into formation and then withdrew in perfect order[6] to take up his position in the main defensive line in front of Castalla.

Suchet emerged from the pass in the late afternoon and saw the Allied force deployed in some strength to his front. Forcing the defile had taken much longer than he had hoped, but in fact Harispe was still some way to the rear and so the French commander decided to suspend further operations until the following day. As dusk fell, Suchet continued to reconnoitre the Allied positions, and the more he looked the more uncomfortable he became. Many of his subordinates encouraged him, claiming that the majority of foreign troops would not stand, but Suchet harboured doubts. The next morning Suchet's concerns remained, but despite this at about noon the French advance began, led by the entire French cavalry on the left flank. Boussart drew up the squadrons to the north of the castle and sent two squadrons further east to gauge the strength and dispositions to the east of the town. Their subsequent report was not encouraging. Some while later the infantry deployed, with Habert's Division marching down the road, and with Robert's Division to their right. Harispe remained in the rear to act as reserve and to safeguard the road (and withdrawal route) through the pass. Suchet's orders were for Castalla to be screened and Mackenzie's forces to be contained by Habert while the main effort was to be an outflanking manoeuvre on the right by Robert.

Valée had deployed the majority of the artillery with Habert and these guns quickly opened against Mackenzie's position to the left of Castalla, but despite being supported by a strong line of voltigeurs, it was quickly apparent that this was not going to develop into a serious attack. On the French right, Robert had deployed five companies of light infantry in skirmish order to move through the scrub and surprise the Allied line by providing diversionary (and supporting) fire at the exact time that three French regiments were to be launched at Whittingham's centre from the base of the hill. Whittingham had received a similar order[7] to try and outflank the

French right. Consequently, when the French attacks began to materialize to their front, three of Whittingham's regiments were desperately trying to get back to their original positions to reestablish the line on the Allied left. The fighting was fierce across a 2km frontage and at several points the French infantry reached the crest, but were counter-attacked by the Spanish and driven down. 'The Spaniards of Whittingham, and with them the 27th English that we have already said was part of the vanguard of Adam, alone they repulsed with their fire the French when deploying and when they were already on the summit, but then they rushed at them with bayonets drenched [in blood] and killed or made prisoners of many.'[8]

Robert's infantry tried to hold their ground, and in some places attempted to deploy into line, but they were not able to make the movement under such heavy fire; their momentum waned and a series of bayonet charges finally broke their resolve. 'The marshal regretting an action which he had no wish to turn into a general engagement, did not attempt to form the two columns anew, and to return to the charge; he rallied them, and called in his cavalry.'[9] Suchet was well aware that to break off in contact, in broad daylight and over open terrain was extremely precarious. His decision to leave an entire division in reserve is perhaps testament to his apprehension in executing an attack in the first instance. This act, and the tardiness with which Murray reorganized his force and disseminated orders to capitalize on the situation, reduced the danger. Boussart's cavalry rallied on the French right to provide flank protection while Robert's dispirited troops – many with injuries – moved back, covered by Harispe's Division until they reached the mouth of the defile. From here they deployed along with Habert's Division in a second line of defence. Valée brought the guns back and deployed them across the road leading to the pass. Some of Mackenzie's men had followed the retreating French but they merely bickered with the rearguard and Suchet made use of the night to break clean.

Suchet makes light of this short campaign in his memoirs, but his first significant failure in open battle had a noteworthy effect. 'After these three days' fighting, our success in which was counterbalanced by the fruitless attack of Castalla, the movements of the Anglo-Spanish army led marshal Suchet to conjecture that an operation was combined to compel him to evacuate Valencia.'[10] With his left flank seriously exposed, and expecting to be attacked at any moment, he withdrew to the line of the river Xucar, and called Pannetier's Brigade down from Aragon to strengthen his defence. Elio had regrouped the division of Mijares and brought forward Villacampa, but Murray dithered and it was to be some weeks before the next part of the Allied offensive was put into action.

---

6   Although two of the guns, which had been disabled, were left behind.

7   Murray maintained after the fight that he had given no such order, but it was delivered by Colonel Cantanelli, a Sicilian officer on Murray's staff, and remains a mystery! See Oman, *A History of the Peninsular War*, vol. VI, p.295.

8   Arteche, *Guerra de la Independencia*, vol. XIII, p.49.

9   Suchet, *Memoirs of the War with Spain*, vol. II, p.307.

10   Ibid, p.308.

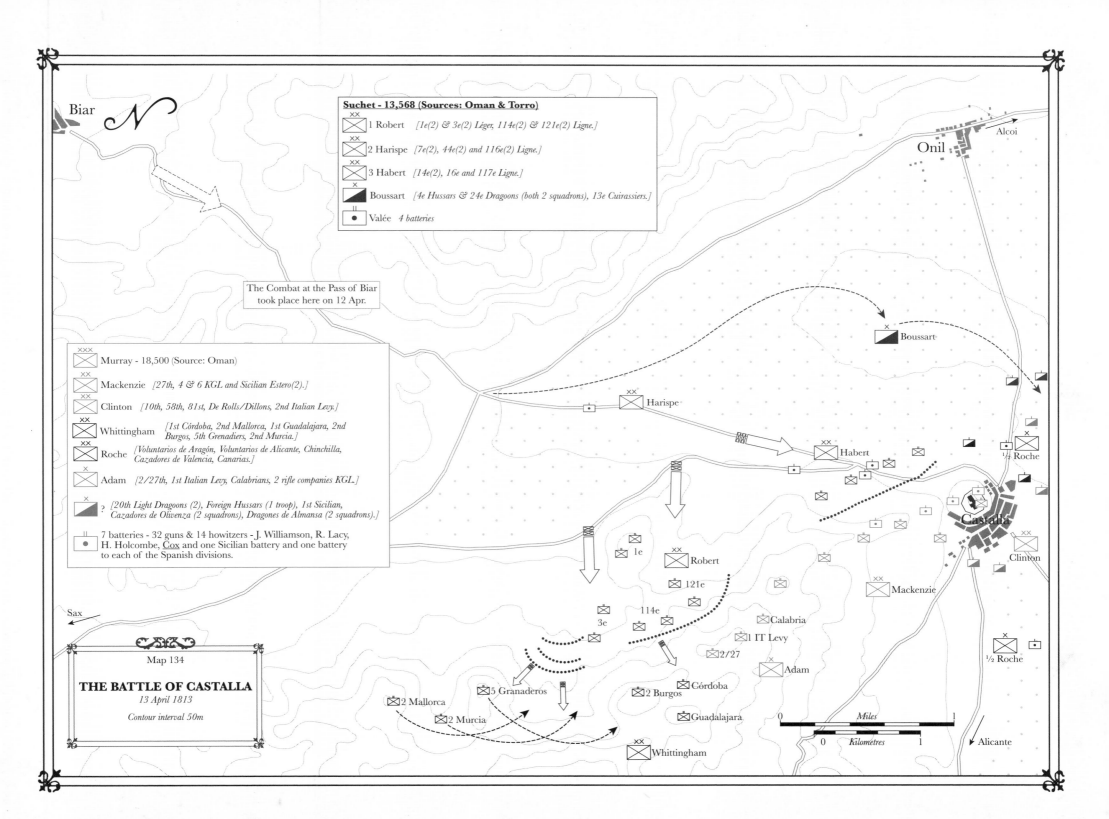

Biar

N

Onil

Alcoi

Suchet - 13,568 (Sources: Oman & Torro)

1 Robert   *[1e(2) & 3e(2) Léger, 114e(2) & 121e(2) Ligne.]*

2 Harispe   *[7e(2), 44e(2) and 116e(2) Ligne.]*

3 Habert   *[14e(2), 16e and 117e Ligne.]*

Boussart   *[4e Hussars & 24e Dragoons (both 2 squadrons), 13e Cuirassiers.]*

Valée   *4 batteries*

The Combat at the Pass of Biar
took place here on 12 Apr.

Boussart

Harispe

Habert

½ Roche

Murray - 18,500 (Source: Oman)

Mackenzie   *[27th, 4 & 6 KGL and Sicilian Estero(2).]*

Clinton   *[10th, 58th, 81st, De Rolls/Dillons, 2nd Italian Levy.]*

Whittingham   *[1st Córdoba, 2nd Mallorca, 1st Guadalajara, 2nd
Burgos, 5th Grenadiers, 2nd Murcia.]*

Roche   *(Voluntarios de Aragón, Voluntarios de Alicante, Chinchilla,
Cazadores de Valencia, Canarias.]*

Adam   *[2/27th, 1st Italian Levy, Calabrians, 2 rifle companies KGL.]*

?   *[20th Light Dragoons (2), Foreign Hussars (1 troop), 1st Sicilian,
Cazadores de Olivenza (2 squadrons), Dragones de Almansa (2 squadrons).]*

7 batteries - 32 guns & 14 howitzers - J. Williamson, R. Lacy,
H. Holcombe, Cox and one Sicilian battery and one battery
to each of the Spanish divisions.

Castalla

Clinton

Sax

1e

Robert

121e

Mackenzie

Calabria

114e

3e

1 IT Levy

2/27

Adam

5 Granaderos

Córdoba

½ Roche

2 Mallorca

2 Burgos

2 Murcia

Guadalajara

0   *Miles*   1

0   *Kilométres*   1

Whittingham

Alicante

Map 134

THE BATTLE OF CASTALLA

13 April 1813

Contour interval 50m

Chapter 46

VICTORY OVER KING JOSEPH: THE VITORIA CAMPAIGN, MAY TO JUNE 1813

With the failure of the Salamanca Campaign at the forefront of his mind, Wellington was determined not to repeat his mistakes[1] as he planned for the offensive of 1813. His preparations were conducted in great secrecy and against the backdrop of Napoleon's catastrophic Russian failure. From correspondence as early as February, it was clear that Wellington's aims were ambitious, and it was not until early May that all the constituent parts were in place to commence operations. The Anglo-Portuguese army had spent the winter months recovering, reorganizing and retraining and by early May numbered about 81,000. It included 56 British and 53 Portuguese infantry battalions; 18 British and four Portuguese cavalry regiments; and 102 field and siege guns organized into 17 batteries. To this force he added the 'new' Spanish 4th Army, which consisted of the divisions of Castile, Galicia and Estremadura. This Army consisted of 18,000 infantry and 3,000 cavalry, and was placed under the command of General Giron, the nephew of Castaños.

The concentration of the southern force was perhaps the most problematic, as the cantonments were more widely spread, forcing Wellington to draw in the formations on two main routes and concentrate south of Salamanca. When Alten and Fane's cavalry pushed forward on 25 May Villatte withdrew, and Wellington, leaving Hill established at Salamanca, rode north to orchestrate the next phase. Timing was critical, for to dwell overly long may have resulted in a French response in strength at Salamanca; however, when the northern columns made their presence known by commencing their advance on 26 May, a French offensive was improbable. Graham, who was commanding the northern columns, advanced on a narrow front preceded by a heavy cavalry screen. The three columns converged to cross the river Esla over the pontoon bridge, which Wellington ordered laid when the elements of Grant, Bock and D'Urban's cavalry (supported by infantry) had secured a footing on the far bank, exploiting an inadequate screen fashioned by Digeon's dragoons. With the Allies firm on the east bank, Zamora was evacuated and Wellington wasted little time in capitalizing on this advantage the next day; Toro was taken and Digeon's

rearguard caught at Morales. At much the same time Hill had begun his move north and, by 3 June, most of the Anglo-Portuguese army was concentrated in or around Toro. Giron was a few kilometres to the north; De España had been left to garrison Salamanca, and Sanchez was sent south of the Douro to cover the southern flank.

The French high command was in disarray; as early as March Joseph had been ordered to provide a large number of soldiers for the new Army of Germany. His three armies were spread over a vast distance, making any form of concentration both slow and hazardous, and he still felt compelled to clear orders through Paris[2] before dissemination, resulting in untimely reaction and a lack of flexibility. The original plan to defend the line of the Douro had been thwarted by the speed of the Allied advances, and the order was given to evacuate Madrid while Jourdan considered holding the line on the Pisuerga and retaining Valladolid. However, the river was not a formidable obstacle and Joseph still lacked sufficient numbers to make a concerted defence. Orders were issued to fall back to Burgos. On receiving this intelligence, Wellington reorganized his force to advance on four separate routes and began to make preparations for the move of the British base from Lisbon to Santander. Giron[3] was despatched on a wide flanking march aimed to destabilize the French defensive position at Burgos and cut off their line of retreat on the main road to France.

By 10 June the French were firm at Burgos. Jourdan considered the position strong, but it soon became apparent that the Allied columns were advancing further north than expected. Foy, Clausel and Sarrut, who were yet to join the concentration, were in danger of being intercepted. Despite the inherent defensive qualities of Burgos, Joseph realized he had to continue to fall back to the Ebro. The French rearguard left Burgos[4] on 13 June and three days later was established on the line of the Ebro. Sarrut and Lamartinière had joined the concentration (leaving only Clausel and Foy absent), raising the French numbers to 50,000 infantry and 10,000 cavalry. Gazan remained on the south bank with three brigades; his task was to act as a screen or rearguard if pressed, or as a vanguard should the opportunity present. In fact, the French position on the Ebro was untenable even before it had been fully occupied; the Allied advance to the north was so rapid that the French line had been turned. The Allies had crossed the Ebro at three places; the Spanish 4th Army continued on their northerly route while Wellington concentrated the balance, except for the 6th Division,[5] and struck east.

Wellington issued orders on 17 June splitting the final advance into three columns, resulting in skirmishes at Osma and San Millan the following day. The French continued to fall back and by 19 June the three armies were complete east of the river Zadorra, and although Clausel and

---

1 According to Oman, Wellington admitted to four errors: the first that he had tried to take Burgos by irregular means with an inadequate train; that he underestimated the strength of the united French armies; that he kept his army split overly long; and the fourth that he had allocated a critical part of his plan to Ballesteros, who had no formal authority to operate independently.

2 Napoleon was at the German front, having fought the battle at Lützen on 2 May.

3 Giron had informed Wellington in early June that his men only had 60 rounds in their pouches and no reserve of ammunition, forcing Wellington to use the 4th Army for tasks other than direct fighting.

4 General d'Aboville was responsible for the destruction of the defences at Burgos prior to evacuation; his botched operation killed many French troops and Spanish civilians but failed to bring down the outer wall.

5 The 6th Division were left at Medina de Pomar to provide rear security and to cover the (possible) advance of Foy from Bilbao, but at the same instant Longa's Division joined Wellington's main body and he wasted no time in deploying them as a covering force for Graham's column.

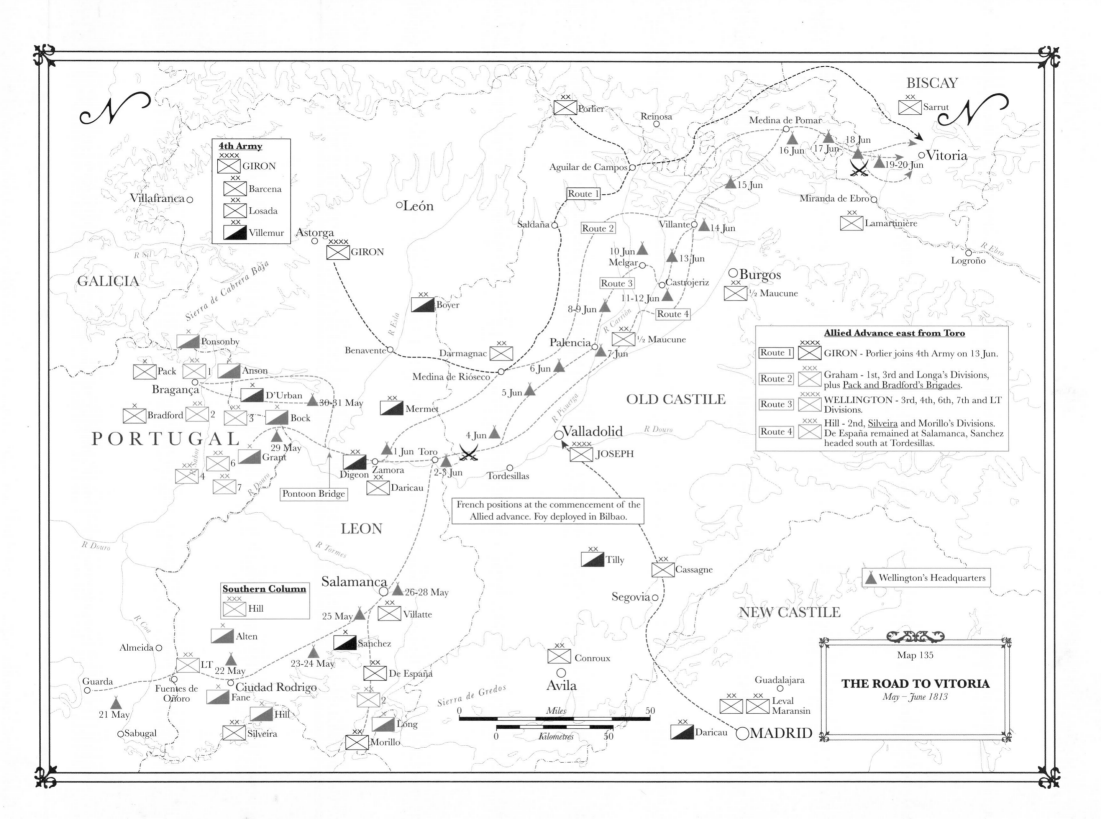

BISCAY

N

N

4th Army
GIRON
Barcena
Losada
Villemur

Villafranca

León

Porlier

Reinosa

Medina de Pomar

16 Jun 17 Jun 18 Jun

Sarrut

19-20 Jun Vitoria

Aguilar de Campos

Route 1

Saldaña

15 Jun

Miranda de Ebro

GALICIA

Astorga

GIRON

GIRON

Route 2

Villante 14 Jun

Logroño

Lamartinière

R Ebro

R Sil

Sierra de Cabrera Baja

10 Jun

13 Jun

Melgar

Boyer

R Esla

Route 3

Castrojeriz

Burgos

½ Maucune

Ponsonby

11-12 Jun

Route 4

Pack 1 Anson

Benavente

Darmagnac

Palencia

8-9 Jun

R Carrión

Allied Advance east from Toro

Bragança

D'Urban 30-31 May

Medina de Ríoseco

6 Jun

½ Maucune

7 Jun

Route 1 GIRON - Porlier joins 4th Army on 13 Jun.

Bradford 2 3 Bock

Mermet

5 Jun

R Pisuerga

OLD CASTILE

Route 2 Graham - 1st, 3rd and Longa's Divisions, plus Pack and Bradford's Brigades.

PORTUGAL

29 May Grant

4 Jun

Valladolid

R Douro

Route 3 WELLINGTON - 3rd, 4th, 6th, 7th and LT Divisions.

6

4 7

Digeon 1 Jun Toro

Zamora

2-3 Jun

Tordesillas

JOSEPH

Route 4 Hill - 2nd, Silveira and Morillo's Divisions. De España remained at Salamanca, Sanchez headed south at Tordesillas.

R Douro

Daricau

Pontoon Bridge

French positions at the commencement of the Allied advance. Foy deployed in Bilbao.

LEON

R Douro

Tilly

Cassagne

Wellington's Headquarters

R Coa

R Tormes

Salamanca

26-28 May

Segovia

Southern Column
Hill

25 May Villatte

NEW CASTILE

Almeida

Alten

Sanchez

Avila

Map 135

Guadalajara

21 May

LT 22 May

23-24 May

De España

Conroux

Guarda

Fuentes de Oñoro

Ciudad Rodrigo Fane

2

Sierra de Gredos

Miles

0   50

THE ROAD TO VITORIA
May – June 1813

Sabugal

Silveira

Hill

Long

Morillo

Kilometres

0   50

Leval Maransin

Daricau MADRID

Foy were not yet up with this concentration, Joseph and Jourdan decided to make a stand. The massive baggage train, swollen with every sort of plunder, was sent off immediately on the *Grande Chaussée*, but as it had to negotiate the bottleneck at Vitoria and then wind its way out of the valley floor, progress was predictably slow. The first convoy set off on 20 June, under the protection of the former Vitoria garrison, but the second commenced at dawn on the 21st under the escort of Maucune's entire division – a decision that deprived Joseph of this capable formation for the approaching battle. There is much debate as to whether Vitoria was the right place for the French to make a stand; the dominating ground is to the west on the Allied approaches, the river Zadorra bends and twists through the undulating terrain and to try and cover the entire length of the obstacle with the available French force was impossible. Be that as it may, more should have been done by the defenders to enhance the obstacle itself; unobserved bridges were not destroyed,[6] the numerous fords were not all covered and the artillery was not placed forward to cover potential crossing points.

Gazan's army, as it was the largest, was deployed forward; in terms of a frontage the length was about 5km, but when the twists and turns of the Zadorra were factored in the length more than doubled. Consequently, a brigade only lightly held the heights of Puebla and from their rearward position they were unable to observe the defile and road from Madrid. A single light company was holding the bridge at Villodas and a single cavalry regiment and a troop of horse artillery were observing the crossing at Mendoza. Behind Gazan, the Army of the Centre was established under D'Erlon's command and the Spanish Division under Casapalacio was detached to cover the *Chaussée* and the bridge at Durana. Reille initially took post as a third line established in front of Vitoria, but with evidence of Longa on the Murguia road and rumour of Wellington on the Bilbao road, Sarrut placed a brigade and then later his entire division, supported by half of Mermet's cavalry under Curto, north of the Zadorra. The majority of the cavalry was held back in reserve, poised to react as circumstances evolved. 'The day following 20, instead of going out on horseback to reconnoitre the land, Jourdan and Joseph didn't leave Vitoria. Marshal Jourdan was racked with a violent fever, resulting age, fatigue and stress. Joseph, whom had other eyes than those of the marshal, postponed until the following day 21 the reconnaissance of the positions. He flattered himself, and Marshal Jourdan also, that the English, with their circumspect outlook, would look for a place to outflank through the mountains, but would not hurry to attack us frontally.'[7]

During the reconnaissance on 21 June, Jourdan grasped the importance of the ground around Zuazo which had been vacated by Reille the day prior; he contemplated readjusting the forces to provide more defence in depth and ease command and control, but as he and Joseph surveyed the terrain and discussed options, reports of considerable Allied movement began to arrive. Wellington's battle plan presented considerable time and space challenges if the arrival of the four separate columns at their chosen points was to be simultaneous. On 20 June Wellington had

conducted a thorough reconnaissance of the French positions; he was puzzled by Joseph's lack of defence along the river, and it was not until late in the day that he was convinced of French intentions to receive battle. The balance of the day was taken up with the dissemination of orders, battle preparation and the organizing and preliminary movement of the columns.

The attack commenced at 0800 hours the following morning. 'Indeed, one of the brigades of the Morillo's Division, had the honour of commencing this most important and glorious of battles as operations opened to win the mountains.'[8] Hill's column crossed the Zadorra south of the Puebla de Arganzon and began to move north through the defile. Advanced French piquets were observed on the heights and Hill despatched Morillo's two brigades to take the skyline. The heights were lightly held and Morillo quickly took the first summit and then began to move east along the heights, at which point Hill despatched Cadogan with the 71st and all the light companies from Cadogan and Byng's brigades. At much the same time, Gazan had ordered Maransin's Brigade to support the voltigeurs[9] and they arrived at the summit and began to push back the Spanish as Cadogan arrived. 'The struggle now became keen. Morillo was wounded, but refused to quit the field; and Colonel Cadogan of the 71st was almost immediately stricken to the death, but insisted upon being carried to the highest point of the ridge from which he could watch the progress of the battle.'[10]

The French contested every inch of ground; Rey's Brigade from Conroux's Division was sent to join the fight while St Pol's Brigade, the reserve brigade from Daricau's Division, filled the area around Subijana de Alava vacated by Maransin. The Allied advance along the heights continued and the French command began to grow increasingly anxious at this ingress on their left flank. Villatte was ordered south to establish a position further east along the elevation to halt the Allied advance (see map 137). Simultaneously, and at Gazan's insistence, Conroux's Division, supported by the brigades of Maransin (who by this stage had withdrawn off the Puebla heights), and St Pol were ordered to evict O'Callaghan from the village of Subijana. These movements severely weakened the French centre and, as Jourdan observed the troops deploying, doubts began to surface in his mind as to the exactitude of Gazan's claim that movements on the French right were merely feints. It was around 1100 hours and a number of French advanced posts had already reported increased activity along the line of the Zadorra. Wellington was on the high ground north of the village of Nanclares from where he could survey the entire French deployment and Joseph and his staff near the village of Ariñez. The 4th and Light divisions were ready to attempt to cross the river to Wellington's front but they were to wait for the two flanking movements to be in place before advancing. The objective of Graham's column was far to the east and required a lengthy flank march before he could swing south; when he did so he came up against Sarrut's entire division supported by light cavalry. Graham halted and, as ordered, resisted the temptation to get embroiled in a fight and glanced to his right to determine the progress of Picton and Dalhousie's divisions. They were nowhere in sight. He deployed

6   Oman, *A History of the Peninsular War*, vol. VI, p.391, states that 'none of the eleven bridges between Durana to the north and Nanclares to the south was blown up'.

7   Thiers, *Histoire du Consulat et de L'Empire*, vol. 16, p.120.

8   Arteche, *Guerra de la Independencia*, vol. XIII, p.109.

9   Joseph's orders were that Maransin should have been supported by an entire division from the outset.

10   Fortescue, *A History of the British Army*, vol. IX, p.171.

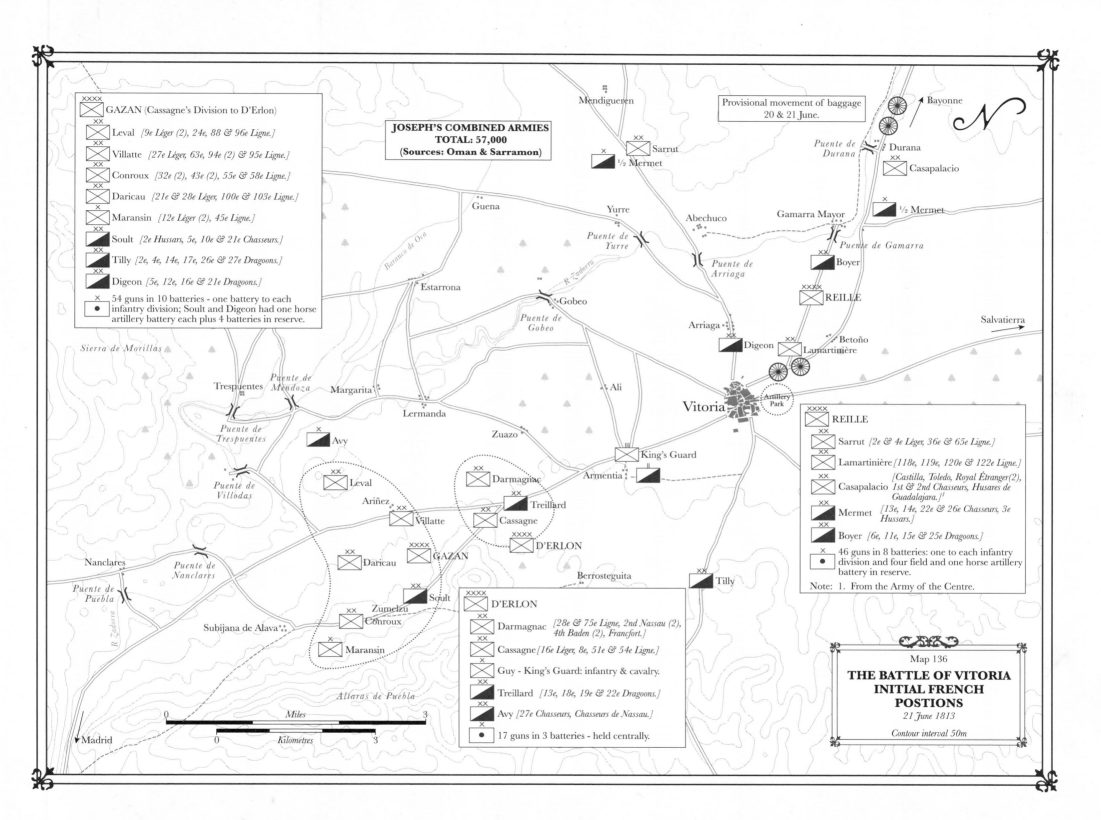

JOSEPH'S COMBINED ARMIES
TOTAL: 57,000
(Sources: Oman & Sarramon)

GAZAN (Cassagne's Division to D'Erlon)

Leval *[9e Léger (2), 24e, 88 & 96e Ligne.]*

Villatte *[27e Léger, 63e, 94e (2) & 95e Ligne.]*

Conroux *[32e (2), 43e (2), 55e & 58e Ligne.]*

Daricau *[21e & 28e Léger, 100e & 103e Ligne.]*

Maransin *[12e Léger (2), 45e Ligne.]*

Soult *[2e Hussars, 5e, 10e & 21e Chasseurs.]*

Tilly *[2e, 4e, 14e, 17e, 26e & 27e Dragoons.]*

Digeon *[5e, 12e, 16e & 21e Dragoons.]*

× 54 guns in 10 batteries - one battery to each
• infantry division; Soult and Digeon had one horse
artillery battery each plus 4 batteries in reserve.

REILLE

Sarrut *[2e & 4e Léger, 36e & 65e Ligne.]*

Lamartinière *[118e, 119e, 120e & 122e Ligne.]*

Casapalacio *[Castilla, Toledo, Royal Étranger(2), 1st & 2nd Chasseurs, Husares de Guadalajara.]*[1]

Mermet *[13e, 14e, 22e & 26e Chasseurs, 3e Hussars.]*

Boyer *[6e, 11e, 15e & 25e Dragoons.]*

× 46 guns in 8 batteries: one to each infantry
• division and four field and one horse artillery
battery in reserve.

Note: 1. From the Army of the Centre.

D'ERLON

Darmagnac *[28e & 75e Ligne, 2nd Nassau (2), 4th Baden (2), Francfort.]*

Cassagne *[16e Léger, 8e, 51e & 54e Ligne.]*

Guy - King's Guard: infantry & cavalry.

Treillard *[13e, 18e, 19e & 22e Dragoons.]*

Avy *[27e Chasseurs, Chasseurs de Nassau.]*

• 17 guns in 3 batteries - held centrally.

Provisional movement of baggage
20 & 21 June.

Map 136

THE BATTLE OF VITORIA
INITIAL FRENCH
POSTIONS
21 June 1813

Contour interval 50m

Longa, Pack and Anson in a line across the roads and brought forward the 5th Division to their rear while despatching Bradford west to confirm the whereabouts of the central column. Reille was present in person with his forward division and he became increasingly concerned as more and more Allied troops came into sight. He issued immediate orders for Sarrut and Curto to fall back to the line of the Zadorra, where he established defensive positions on the north bank covering the bridges at Abechuco, Gamarra Mayor and Durana.

Graham advanced to within a mile of the river, from where he could see the French hastily preparing defences on the north bank, while their guns were deployed on the home bank to provide sweeping fire support. Graham elected to clear these defences by formal attack. The 1st Division, supported by the two Portuguese brigades, closed in on Abechuco; the 5th Division and a section of guns from Lawson's Company were tasked to take Gamarra Mayor, while Longa's force quickly overran the 3e Ligne in Gamarra Menor before moving on towards Durana. 'The Spaniards and Portuguese, with noble emulation and a value that their allies rewarded with a general applause, rolled-up the enemy that retired for steps with their characteristic energy from position to position successively offered by the irregular land and the rivulets to the Zadorra; Longa's distinguished troops had already taken possession of a small hamlet of Gamarra Menor right at the riverbank of the river, at the same time that other troops went by the bridge of Durana, settling down in the town of its same name.'[11] At Durana, Longa came face to face with the Franco-Spanish Division of Casapalacio; the two sides satisfied themselves with exchanges of skirmishing fire, but as Longa's infantry were in range of the *Grande Chaussée* they effectively covered movement and achieved Wellington's aim of controlling, if not actually cutting, the main line of communication.

Meanwhile the 5th Division had secured the village of Gamarra Mayor from the 118e and 119e Ligne;[12] Robinson's Brigade had led the charge, the 4th Foot led by Lieutenant Colonel Brooke, gained the initial foothold through which the 2/47th and 2/59th passed. Attempts to push on and take the bridge were thwarted for some time as the French artillery swept the approaches. With these two attacks well advanced and progressing satisfactorily, Graham was content to hold the 1st Division and two Portuguese brigades in front of Abechuco and wait for developments to commence on his right. It was now past 1400 hours and there was still no sign of Lord Dalhousie. The sounds of battle from Graham's direction had long been heard and Wellington had already ordered the Light Division to close up to the river, but at around noon he was to receive intelligence from a Spanish peasant that the bridge at Tres Puentes was unguarded. He decided to exploit the opportunity with haste and requested the peasant to guide Kempt's Brigade along the circuitous path to the narrow bridge. The brigade, led by the 1/95th, ran the distance with rifles primed and ready, they crossed the unguarded bridge only to find the area overlooked from the knoll by a large French force.[13] As the French artillery opened, the light infantry sought refuge behind a large convex bank; the French gunners only had time to fire

two shots (one of which killed the unfortunate Spanish guide) before the curve of the hill hindered any further effective fire. Kempt sent back for the 15th Hussars who also crossed the bridge and sought similar refuge in the shadow of the hill. Captain Cooke of the 43rd wrote 'that we could see three bridges within a quarter of a mile of each other, in the elbow of the enemy's position. We had crossed the centre one while the other two, right and left, were still covered by French artillery.' Many minutes passed and Kempt's men lay expecting to be attacked at any moment, when suddenly the 3rd Division[14] was across the river and engaging D'Armagnac's troops on the knoll with great ferocity. Brisbane's Brigade fell on the bridge at Mendoza while Colville attacked the ford about 300m upstream. Avy's depleted cavalry brigade was watching this section of the river, but it and a troop of horse artillery withdrew in haste when they found themselves assailed from the north and west. The French chasseurs rode in circles, seemingly at a loss as to how to respond, and within minutes both brigades were established south of the river. Power's Portuguese and Grant's Brigade, the first from the 7th Division, were not far behind. At the bridge at Puente de Villodas, the small French voltigeur company withdrew with alacrity when the realized they were about to be cut off. The Light, 3rd, 4th and 7th divisions were across the obstacle and moving east with purpose. It was about 1500 hours.

Leval was now in the most unstable position; outnumbered three to one and with the reserve deployed elsewhere,[15] he had to redeploy with speed or face certain annihilation. Joseph and Jourdan, watching from the hillock at Ariñez, gave immediate orders for Leval to withdraw along with Maransin, Daricau and Conroux to a line currently held by D'Armagnac and Cassagne, who in turn, were to move north and complete the line from the right-hand division to the river and block the 3rd and 7th divisions. Recalling Villatte was more problematic as his counter-attack against the 71st and Morillo's infantry had driven the Allies back along the ridge and their success was only halted with the arrival of the balance of Cadogan's Brigade, the 50th and the 92nd. While Villatte was manoeuvring his third regiment to renew the offensive, he received word of the general withdrawal.

At the other end of the line, D'Armagnac's battalions won the race for the village of Margarita, as Colville was delayed crossing the ford in single file. Colville's advance was blocked, but to his right the first of Picton's men were heavily engaged with the right-hand brigade of Leval and, as they began to gain the upper hand, D'Armagnac's flank became exposed. He withdrew Chassé's Brigade and established it 1km to the rear, anchored on his second brigade[16] around the village of Lermanda. Grant's Brigade now pushed through the exhausted and depleted troops of Colville, with Vandeleur's light infantry following hot on their heels, but they were both soon checked by the

---

11 Arteche, *Guerra de la Independencia*, vol. XIII, p.121.

12 Gauthier's Brigade from Lamartinière's Division.

13 This was D'Armagnac's Division, which had been moved from Ariñez: Joseph was with this group as he had pushed forward to try and determine the strengths and intentions of the Allies in this sector of the field.

14 Dalhousie, the senior lieutenant general, was in command of this column and through his interpretation of Wellington's orders refused to advance further than the edge of the hills, electing instead to wait for developments to his right before progressing. Picton was further forward (Dalhousie having been delayed by the progress of two of his batteries) and could see Hill's progress to the south and was growing increasingly impatient when one of Wellington's ADCs rode up with orders for Dalhousie to move in support of the 4th and Light divisions. It was good enough for Picton who chose to attack immediately, offering the suggestion to the startled ADC that 'the 4th and Light may support him if they so wished'.

15 The regiment from Daricau's Division and the Army reserve of Villatte had been deployed to the Puebla Heights.

16 That of Nueunstein consisting of the regiments of 2nd Nassau, the 4th Baden and the Frankfurt.

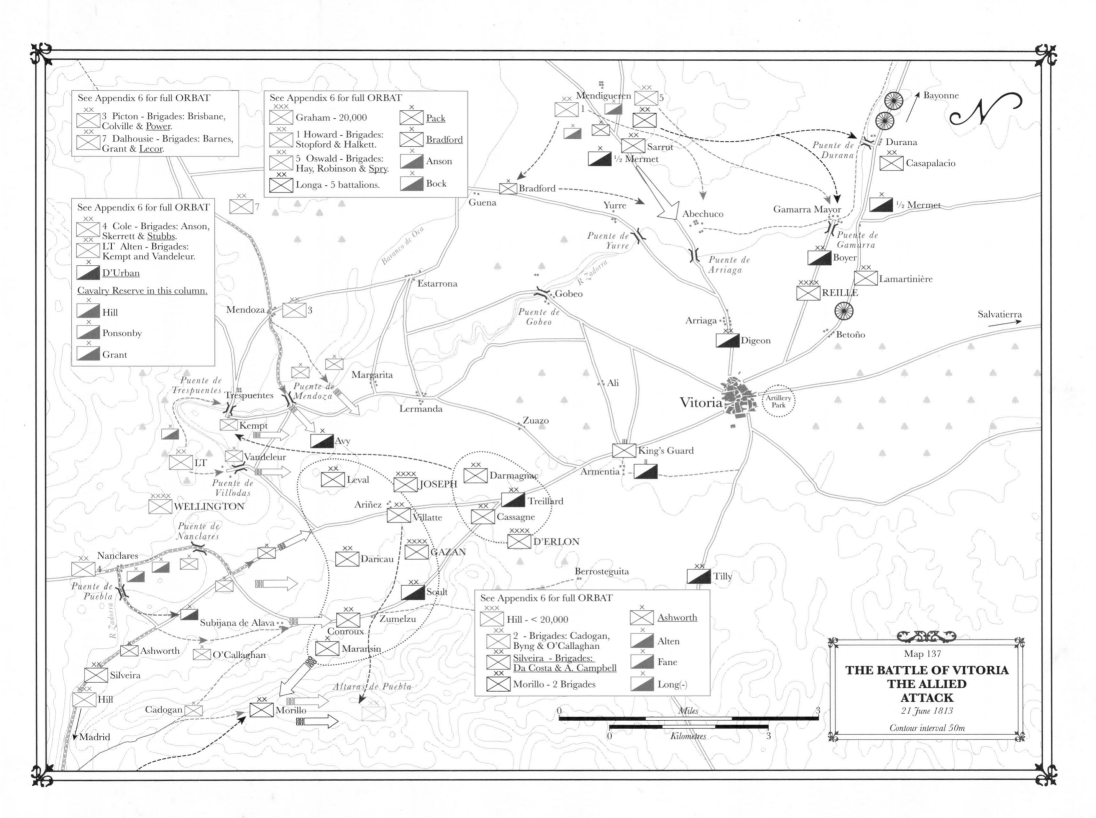

See Appendix 6 for full ORBAT

3 Picton - Brigades: Brisbane, Colville & Power.
7 Dalhousie - Brigades: Barnes, Grant & Lecor.

See Appendix 6 for full ORBAT

Graham - 20,000
1 Howard - Brigades: Stopford & Halkett.
5 Oswald - Brigades: Hay, Robinson & Spry.
Longa - 5 battalions.

Pack
Bradford
Anson
Bock

See Appendix 6 for full ORBAT

4 Cole - Brigades: Anson, Skerrett & Stubbs.
LT Alten - Brigades: Kempt and Vandeleur.
D'Urban
Cavalry Reserve in this column.

Hill
Ponsonby
Grant

See Appendix 6 for full ORBAT

Hill - < 20,000
2 - Brigades: Cadogan, Byng & O'Callaghan
Silveira - Brigades: Da Costa & A. Campbell
Morillo - 2 Brigades

Ashworth
Alten
Fane
Long(-)

Mendigueren
5
1
Sarrut
½ Mermet
Bradford
Guena
Yurre
Abechuco
Gamarra Mayor
½ Mermet
Puente de Durana
Durana
Casapalacio
Bayonne
Boyer
Puente de Gamarra
Lamartinière
REILLE
Salvatierra
Digeon
Betoño
Arriaga
Puente de Arriaga
Puente de Yurre
Gobeo
Puente de Gobeo
Estarrona
Baranco de Oca
R Zadorra
Mendoza
3
7
Margarita
Ali
Lermanda
Zuazo
Vitoria
Artillery Park
King's Guard
Armentia
Puente de Trespuentes
Trespuentes
Puente de Mendoza
Kempt
Avy
Leval
JOSEPH
Darmagnac
Treillard
LT
Vandeleur
Puente de Villodas
WELLINGTON
Ariñez
Villatte
Cassagne
D'ERLON
Puente de Nanclares
Nanclares
4
Daricau
GAZAN
Berrosteguita
Tilly
Puente de Puebla
R Zadorra
Subijana de Alava
Conroux
Zumelzu
Soult
Ashworth
O'Callaghan
Silveira
Hill
Cadogan
Maransin
Altaras de Puebla
Morillo
Madrid

N

Map 137

THE BATTLE OF VITORIA
THE ALLIED
ATTACK
21 June 1813

Contour interval 50m

0   Miles   3

0   Kilometres   3

combined divisions of D'Armagnac and Cassagne. To their right Picton had captured the vacated heights above the village of Ariñez and was now engaging the French infantry in the village itself. Monquery was holding the village with Leval's second brigade, that of Morgan, lying to their rear. Following a heavy artillery bombardment, Picton ordered his infantry to advance with Power left, Brisbane right and Kempt in reserve. Elements of the 95th were skirmishing in front and initially penetrated the village, but were repulsed by the 103e Ligne. Any French optimism was short-lived as the 74th and 88th attacked the village simultaneously and quickly cast out the defenders, while Brisbane's third battalion (the 45th) swung into the flank of Remond's Brigade. To Brisbane's left, Power's Portuguese had equally successfully engaged Morgan's Brigade and both brigades now began streaming to the rear, leaving a large gap between Cassagne and Conroux.

Jourdan had to reconfigure his force with haste, and orders were issued for D'Armagnac to pull back behind Cassagne (on the French left) and for Conroux, Maransin and Daricau's two brigades to pull back and form a third defensive line just in front of Vitoria. While both the French and Allied forces were regrouping in the centre, the attack in the north stalled. The accurate fire from two well-sited French batteries had taken the momentum from Grant's Brigade, which was now sheltering in a ditch some 200m from the French line. While Dalhousie pondered, Vandeleur ordered the light brigade to attack; they swept Grant's infantry along with infectious enthusiasm and the village was soon in Allied hands. On Wellington's orders, Dickson had begun to move up the reserve artillery and the guns were now deploying just off the central road, along with a number of divisional batteries that had also been forced along the same path. Opposite them, also forced through the lack of suitable roads, a number of French batteries were lined up and there commenced the largest artillery duel of the entire war, with 75 Allied guns plying their trade against 76 French guns.[17] 'The nature of the country, and want of roads, was the means of throwing a large proportion of our Artillery together, away from their divisions, which I availed myself of, and by employing them in masses it had a famous effect.'[18] The Allied infantry began to advance toward the third French defensive line with, from left to right: Colville, Grant, Power, Brisbane, Stubbs, Byng and O'Callaghan. Behind them, in support, were Vandeleur, Kempt, Anson, Skerrett and Ashworth, with Silveira's two brigades acting as reserve. It was a splendid spectacle, but less so for the infantry in the lead ranks who found themselves advancing into the massed muzzles of the French cannon. Casualties were heavy, but as the Allies closed, it was plain that the fight had gone from the French; they had already fallen back twice and rumours that the road to Bayonne was severed did little to sustain their morale.

The rumours were accurate, but events on the Allied far left were not progressing as well as expected. Longa was the only commander to have succeeded in crossing the river and cutting the *Chaussée*; he had pushed back the Franco-Spanish force under Casapalacio and had gained a lodgement on the far bank, but a lack of guns and the unconcealed presence of Mermet's cavalry prevented further ingress. Longa had achieved the main aim and cut the road; he sat tight, waiting for Oswald to cross (at Gamarra Mayor) and enable the two forces to link up before pressing on. Alas, Oswald was locked in a fearsome struggle. Robinson's Brigade had succeeded in taking the village and had for a brief time held the bridge before Reille turned a second battery upon them and Lamartinière rallied his man, who then counter-attacked and drove the Allies back into the village. 'In any case, it is certain that there was very severe fighting at this point, for a French officer has recorded that the contending parties charged and counter-charged each other seven times.'[19] Graham, who had the bulk of the force, cleared the village of Abechuco but then made no concerted attempt to take the bridge of Arriaga, despite outnumbering the defenders two to one. The presence of 20 French guns and numerous cavalry formations clearly visible on the far bank, and an overestimation of the strength of the defending force, no doubt led Graham to refrain from executing a serious assault.

In the centre, large numbers of Allied light troops had penetrated between the armies of Gazan and D'Erlon. Indeed Gazan was in grave danger of being turned on his right, by Morillo and Cadogan who were advancing along the spine of the Altaras de Puebla, and he wasted little time in electing to retire. His withdrawal left a large gap and rendered D'Erlon's defence untenable. Jourdan considered making an attempt to force the *Chaussée* but decided against the idea, and issued orders for a general retreat on the road to Salvatierra; the balance of the train and baggage was to lead, followed by the armies of South and Centre, while the Army of Portugal was to hold their line and cover the withdrawal. The orders were received too late. With three armies converging on a single road, preceded by huge amounts of baggage and stores, and the assortment being pursued with vigour, the result was pandemonium. 'A dozen blocks and upsets had occurred before the first ten minutes were over, and chaos supervened. Many carriages and wagons never got off on a road at all... Dozens of carriages broke down – whereupon light-fingered fugitives began to help themselves to all that was split.'[20]

Grant's Hussars were the first on the scene but it was the sounds of musket and gunfire that accompanied their arrival which had a significant effect on the battle. The Army of Portugal, hearing this engagement to their rear, realized that they were in considerable danger of being surrounded, with no means of withdrawal. Reille ordered an immediate retreat, all the guns were abandoned and the cavalry were tasked with holding back the advancing infantry to buy time. However, Anson's light dragoons skirted Digeon's screen and now charged at Fririon's Brigade; hundreds of French stragglers were captured, but the units and formations withdrew intact. In the centre the 2nd Division pressed the pursuit with vigour but the cavalry did not support them and the opportunity to sweep up large numbers of fleeing French passed.[21] However, the materiel captured was simply colossal[22] and even the subsequent night of looting could not diminish the glory of the victory and the culmination of a brilliant campaign.

17   Oman lists the French having 46 guns from the Army of the South, 12 from the Army of the Centre and 18 from the Army of Portugal and the Allies as having 54 British, 18 Portuguese and 3 Spanish guns.

18   Dickson, *Dickson Manuscripts*, vol. V, p.916.

19   Fortescue, *A History of the British Army*, vol. IX, p.181.

20   Oman, *A History of the Peninsular War*, vol. VI, p.435.

21   Oman points out that 'Wellington's thunderings in previous years against reckless cavalry action' no doubt echoed in the ears of the cavalry commanders.

22   The number of captured guns, 151 plus 415 caissons, compares with Leipzig and Waterloo.

Longa
Casapalacio
Oswald
Lamartinière
Mermet
Vitoria
Soult
Tilly
Maransin
Dos Pelos
Sanchez
Digeon
Howard
St. Pol
Villatte
Darmagnac
Cassagne
Colville
JOSEPH
Leval
Dalhousie(-)
Remond
Conroux
Morillo
Grant
Vandeleur
Power
Alten
Brisbane
Kempt
Picton
Stubbs
Anson
WELLINGTON
Skerrett
O'Callaghan
Grant (-)
Byng
Cole
Ashworth
Hill
Campbell
Da Costa
D'Urban
Ponsonby
Long
Hill
Fane

Map 138

**THE BATTLE OF VITORIA
THE FRENCH DEFEAT**

21 June 1813

The next day the pursuit did not commence until 1000 hours. Giron and Longa were tasked to follow Maucune along the *Grande Chaussée* into Biscay while the balance of the Allied army marched in pursuit of Joseph. With reports of Clausel's Army of Aragon approaching from the south, Wellington felt compelled to leave the 5th Division and Hill's cavalry brigade to guard the city; they anticipated relief by the 6th Division, who were expected at any moment. As the main army approached Salvatierra, George Murray[23] suggested that a detachment sent north through the mountains to Villafranca might be able to cut off Maucune and trap the convoy with the advancing Spanish force. Wellington approved the idea and Graham was duly despatched. However, the passage of orders was confused, resulting in a counter-march by the bulk of Graham's force and the arrest of Captain Norman Ramsey for alleged flagrant disobedience of Wellington's order.[24] By the time Graham reached Villafranca, in the afternoon on 24 June, the majority of French had already passed through the town and were established at Tolosa.

The balance of Wellington's force continued to pursue the main French force on the Salvatierra to Pamplona road. Cassagne formed the rearguard but they were rarely pressed and Joseph concluded that the main Allied effort had been concentrated on the *Chaussée* and accordingly sent Reille north to join Foy and to establish a defensive line along the Bidassoa. At much the same time, Wellington received news that Clausel, unaware of the defeat of Joseph, was closing in on Vitoria. His arrival at Trevino alarmed Pakenham (the 6th Division commander) in the city and he immediately sent word to Oswald and Giron who turned in response to his plea. However, Clausel had no intention of attacking Vitoria, and instead he moved east in an attempt to link up with Joseph. With Mina on one flank and (false) news of an Allied force heading south from Salvatierra, Clausel abandoned any idea of taking a shortened route, but a second attempt to outmanoeuvre also failed. He reluctantly gave up any immediate plans of a rendezvous with Joseph, electing instead to head back to Aragon and link up with Suchet. However, his delay in reaching this decision had placed his force in grave peril as Wellington, on arrival at Pamplona, realising that Joseph was already well on the way to France and on receiving intelligence from Mina as to Clausel's whereabouts, decided to swing south in an attempt to intercept and destroy him.

Grant was sent ahead of the Light and 4th divisions (two additional divisions were to follow when relieved of their task to invest Pamplona), but Clausel, as if sensing the danger, made considerable distance on 27 June, spending only a few hours at Tudela before pressing on to Zaragoza. Sanchez had joined Mina in the chase, but they were also unable to cut off Clausel's retreat. At 0500 hours on 28 June Wellington issued fresh orders to this left flank, instructing them to cut the road to Jaca and with it Clausel's route to France. Two days later he countermanded the order; there was no guarantee Clausel would head north and the gap between his left and right wings was by now unacceptably large. However, Wellington's hunch proved to be correct, for on 2 July Clausel headed for Jaca where he halted for two days. Mina and Durán fell on Paris's garrison at Zaragoza and, with the option of returning to his base extinguished, Clausel crossed into France and linked up with the armies of the South and Centre at St Jean-Pied-de-Port.

---

23 Wellington's Quartermaster General – about the only member of his staff who could proffer gratuitous advice.

24 This episode caused considerable animosity amongst the artillery officers (and indeed many officers across the force) his hitherto impeccable Peninsular record was irreparably damaged costing him promotion. He died at Waterloo. See Duncan, *History of the Royal Artillery*, vol. II, pp.357–360.

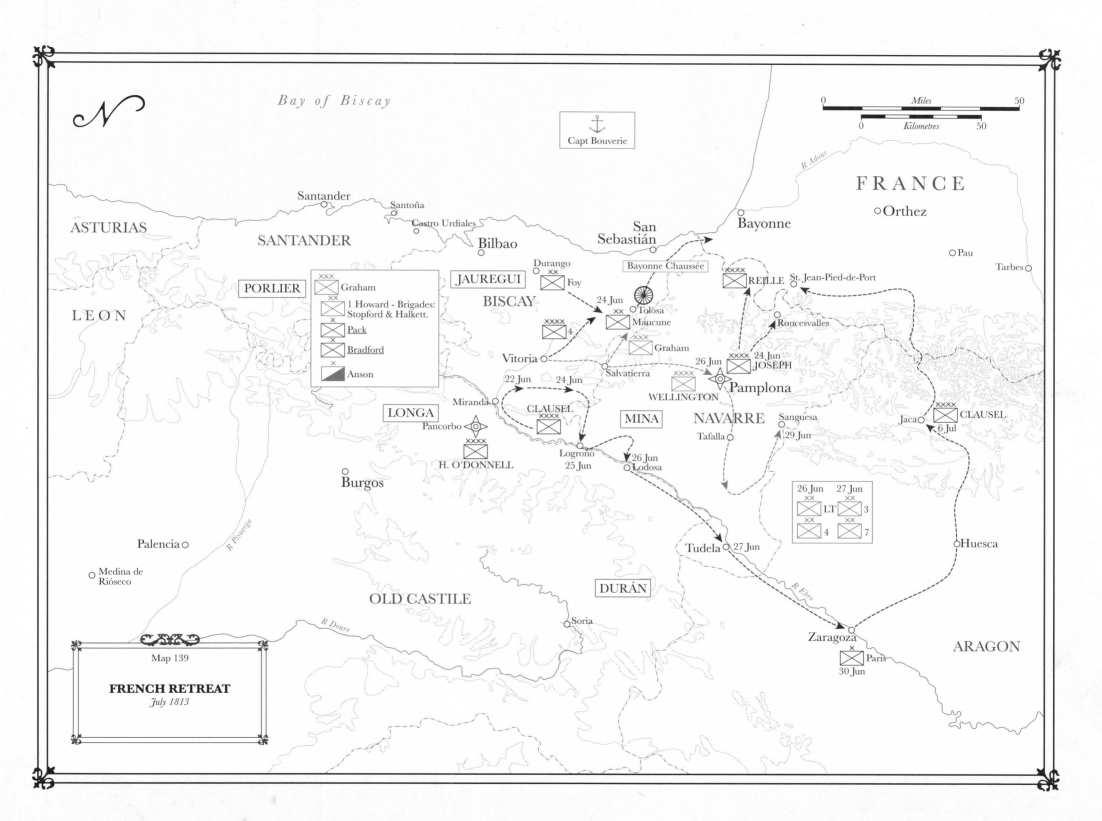

Bay of Biscay

⚓ Capt Bouverie

N

FRANCE

○ Orthez

○ Pau

Tarbes ○

Bayonne

San Sebastián

Bayonne Chaussée

REILLE ⊠XX

St.-Jean-Pied-de-Port ○

Santander ○

Santoña ○

Castro Urdiales ○

Bilbao

Durango ○
⊠XX Foy

JAUREGUI

BISCAY

24 Jun Tolosa ○

⊠XX Maucune

Roncesvalles ○

ASTURIAS

SANTANDER

PORLIER

⊠XXX	Graham
⊠XX	1 Howard - Brigades: Stopford & Halkett.
⊠XX	Pack
⊠XX	Bradford
◣	Anson

LEON

⊠XXXX 4

Vitoria ○

Salvatierra ○

⊠XX Graham

26 Jun ⊠XXXX **JOSEPH** 24 Jun

22 Jun   24 Jun

Miranda ○

⊠XXXX **WELLINGTON**

Pamplona ✦

LONGA

Pancorbo ○ ✦

⊠XXXX **CLAUSEL**

MINA

NAVARRE

Sanguesa ○

Jaca ○ ⊠XXXX **CLAUSEL**
6 Jul

H. O'DONNELL ⊠XXXX

Logroño ○
25 Jun

26 Jun
Lodosa ○

Tafalla ○

29 Jun

Burgos ○

26 Jun	27 Jun
⊠XX LT	⊠XX 3
⊠XX 4	⊠XX 7

Huesca ○

Palencia ○

DURÁN

Tudela ○ 27 Jun

R Pisuerga

Medina de Ríoseco ○

OLD CASTILE

Soria ○

R Douro

R Ebro

Zaragoza ○

ARAGON

⊠X Paris
30 Jun

Map 139

FRENCH RETREAT
July 1813

R Adour

Chapter 47

WHILE WELLINGTON WAITS, SOULT TAKES THE INITIATIVE: JULY 1813

During the Allied advance to Vitoria, Giron's demonstration on the Valmaceda road had persuaded Foy that the Galician army's target was Bilbao, and he chose to remain dispersed in the area covering the main approaches to the town. At Bergara on 21 June, Foy met Maucune, who had departed Vitoria that morning escorting the baggage train along the *Chaussée* to France. They discussed options, but it was not until the following morning that news of the disaster began to emerge. Maucune set off for the border in haste, while Foy prepared to buy time for his colleague. By chance, Clausel's appearance south of Vitoria had drawn Giron temporarily back south and Foy's first encounter was therefore against Longa's smaller force, which had continued to pursue the convoy. The engagements were of a bickering nature but it soon became apparent that Giron was closing on Longa's Division and additional intelligence indicated the presence of an Anglo-Portuguese force also closing from the south. Foy recalled Maucune and the two divisions fought a series of rearguard combats at Villareal, Villafranca and Tolosa and, by 27 June, with confirmation that the convoy had safely reached the French border, the divisions withdrew. After six days in contact, Graham and Giron were unable to continue their pursuit of the French as their troops were in chronic need of rest and resupply.

As Foy pulled back he paid a flying visit to the garrison at San Sebastián and provided the governor, General Rey, badly needed reinforcements in the form of 2,000 infantry[1] and as many gunners as he could spare. On 29 June Reille, who had arrived at Vera on 27 June, ordered Foy to fall back to the Bidassoa. Within hours of evacuating the area in front of the fortress an irregular force of some 3,000 men blockaded the stronghold and cut the *Chaussée*. By 30 June Reille had organized his army, the divisions of Foy and Maucune, and the Bayonne Reserve into a defensive line from Vera to the coast, and when Longa's Cantabrians approached, the French covering force at San Marcial withdrew north across the Bidassoa and by 1 July the French in this sector had evacuated Spain.

The same day, Wellington began to move north from Pamplona, having regrouped his force following the fruitless pursuit of Clausel. The Army of Reserve of Andalusia, under command of Henry O'Donnell, had successfully taken the forts of Pancorbo (see map 139) and was called forward to take charge of the blockade of Pamplona. However, until his arrival on 13 July, Wellington was forced to leave part of his main force on task. The 3rd, 4th and 6th divisions along with the majority of Allied cavalry remained at Pamplona while the Light, 2nd, 7th and Silveira's Portuguese Division marched north to make contact with Graham on the Bidassoa. Hill detached Byng's Brigade to join Morillo's Division in order to cover any attempt by the French to succour Pamplona via the pass at Roncesvalles, and with the balance of three brigades, led the march towards Maya.

Gazan had reached St Jean-Pied-de-Port on 27 June but there were insufficient provisions to feed his force and, leaving Conroux there, he set off on the road to Bayonne with the balance of his army. They had reached Cambo les Bains in early July and received some supplies, artillery guns and ammunition from the great arsenal at Bayonne; the commander also received new orders tasking him to relieve D'Erlon's badly depleted force in the defence of the key central passes of the Bastan. Despite having twice D'Erlon's numbers, Gazan's Army had not enjoyed the respite that the Army of the Centre had been afforded since 26 June. The Army of the South therefore assumed their new task with indifference and it was during this relief in place that Cameron's Brigade, forming Hill's vanguard, came up against a few companies of the 16e Léger (Braun's Brigade, part of Cassagne's Division) who were waiting to be relieved by soldiers from Gazan's Army. Maransin's Brigade was soon on the scene and bickering fire opened along the frontage. Within hours Gazan had arrived with Villatte's Division and Hill was badly outnumbered; the 7th Division were still a two-day march south and the Light Division static at Pamplona. Hill held his ground and waited for Wellington to arrive the following day.

When Wellington arrived he wasted little time in ordering the French positions to his front to be 'pressed', conscious that French morale was low and that the full strength of the Allied force would be difficult to determine in the hilly terrain. Gazan pulled back, sending word to Joseph that he intended making a stand at Maya. The French reached Maya on 6 July and Wellington closed on the defensive line and waited for the 7th Division to move up and for the Light Division to have advanced to within a day's march of their position. Wellington kept Gazan busy, unaware that the French higher command was in the process of readjusting the balance of their defensive line. Conroux had convinced Joseph and Jourdan that the forces advancing through Roncesvalles to St Jean-Pied-de-Port were far greater than they were in reality; once convinced, they began to send large numbers of reinforcements to the area.[2] As a consequence, when Wellington delivered his attack at Maya on 7 July it was against Gazan's three divisions only; the attack itself was to misfire, but Gazan considered his position somewhat exposed and lacking depth, and later, on 8 July, he withdrew into France. Hill occupied the pass and the 7th and Light divisions established themselves in cantonments at Elizondo and Sanestéban respectively, while Ashworth and Da Costa's Portuguese brigades guarded the passes towards Sumbilla. To the east, Byng and Morillo maintained their position at Roncesvalles and were

---

1   General Deconchy's brigade of four battalions.

2   Including, Leval, Cassagne, D'Armagnac and Thouvenot's provisional division from the Army of the North – Foy had collected this latter formation together from the garrisons in Biscay.

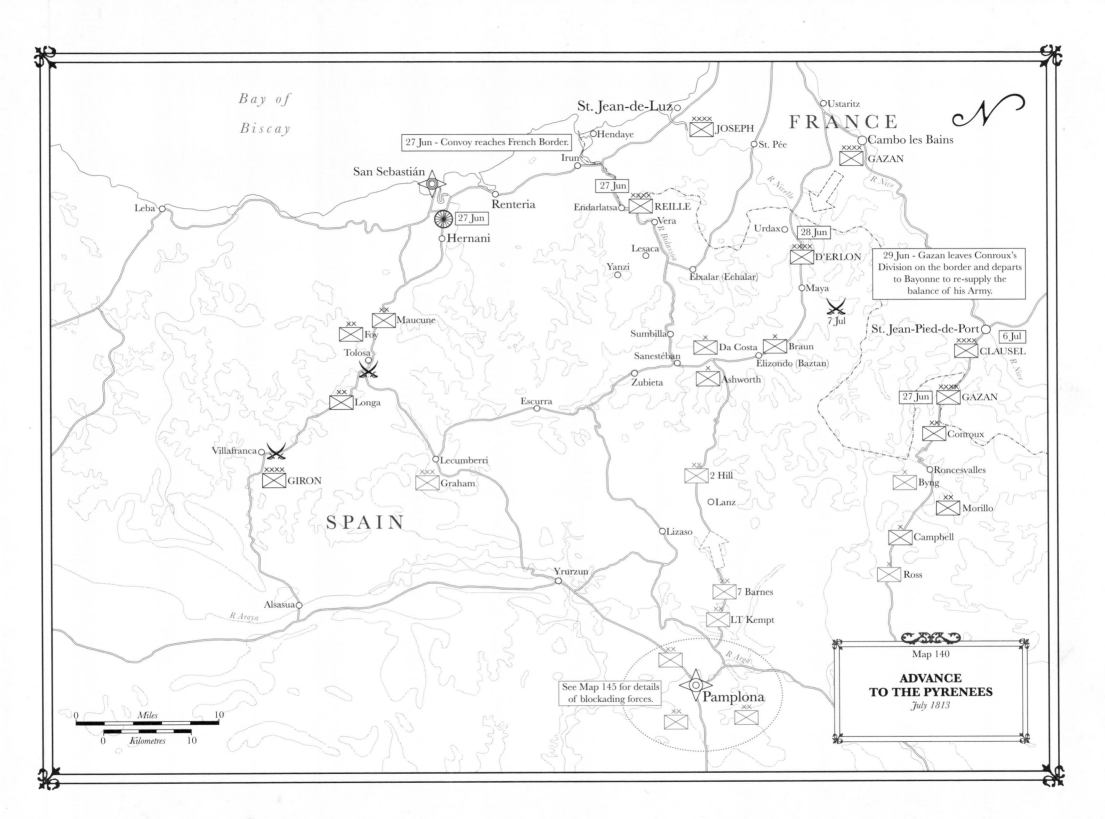

Bay of
Biscay

FRANCE

Ustaritz

St. Jean-de-Luz

JOSEPH

Hendaye

Cambo les Bains

St. Pée

GAZAN

27 Jun - Convoy reaches French Border.

Irun

San Sebastián

27 Jun

Renteria

Endarlatsa

REILLE

Vera

Urdax

28 Jun

27 Jun

D'ERLON

Hernani

Leba

Lesaca

Yanzi

Elxalar (Echalar)

Maya

7 Jul

29 Jun - Gazan leaves Conroux's
Division on the border and departs
to Bayonne to re-supply the
balance of his Army.

St. Jean-Pied-de-Port

6 Jul

Maucune

Foy

Sumbilla

Da Costa

Braun

CLAUSEL

Tolosa

Sanestéban

Elizondo (Baztan)

27 Jun

GAZAN

Longa

Zubieta

Ashworth

Conroux

Escurra

Roncesvalles

Villafranca

Lecumberri

Byng

GIRON

Graham

2 Hill

Morillo

SPAIN

Lanz

Campbell

Lizaso

Ross

Alsasua

R Araya

Yrurzun

7 Barnes

LT Kempt

See Map 145 for details
of blockading forces.

R Arga

Pamplona

Miles

Kilometres

Map 140

**ADVANCE
TO THE PYRENEES**
July 1813

now supported by Ross and Campbell's brigades. On 15 July, as O'Donnell's forces arrived to assume responsibility for the cordon at Pamplona, Wellington then readjusted these forward lines of defence by moving the Light Division to Vera and the 7th Division to Echalar. He then turned his full attention to the capture of San Sebastián.

As early as 4 July, 'The Marquis of Wellington, having his head-quarters at Lanz, sent instructions to the commanding engineer [Fletcher] and commanding officer of artillery [Dickson], to prepare for commencing the siege of San Sebastián; and, with that view, desired them to order transports with the battering train and siege stores from Bilbao to Passages, and the heavy brigade of 18-pounders to move forward from Vitoria.'[3] On 12 July, Wellington conducted a reconnaissance with Graham, Dickson and Major Charles Smith (the senior engineer, Fletcher being still at Pamplona); they agreed upon a plan. 'To open trenches in the Chofre sand hills to the north of the Uremea and to construct batteries to batter the exposed town wall facing that river, and as a preliminary to drive the enemy from the Convent and redoubt of San Bartolomé, where they had established a strong post about 800 yards in front of the town, which being effected, to raise batteries in that situation to aid the main attack, and to oblige the enemy to withdraw from the circular work on the causeway.'[4] The same day, as the siege guns began to arrive, work commenced on opening the trenches. Batteries 1 and 2 were the first to be completed and equipped with guns on the night of 13 July; they opened the following day against the walls of San Bartolomé.[5] Wellington stayed long enough to witness this initial bombardment and then rode back towards the Pyrenees, leaving Graham in command.

By the evening of 15 July the guns and howitzers in batteries 1 and 2 had sufficiently damaged the walls of the convent to convince Oswald that an assault was worth trying. The 8th Caçadores were sent forward to storm the ruins, but were swiftly beaten back with considerable loss. 'At that moment the battalion commander Thomas who defended the convent with 400 men, made a sortie to his front with the grenadiers and voltigeurs of the 34e Ligne, and pursued the Englishmen at the tip of the bayonet all the way to his batteries.'[6] The two batteries recommenced fire the following day, assisted by a field battery[7] from across the river that had the task of engaging the reserves in the ruins of San Martin and the redoubt. By 17 July Oswald opted for a second attack and 'At 10 o'clock a.m. the Convent and Redoubt were assaulted by the 9th Regiment, three companies of the Royal Scots, and strong detachments of the Portuguese, and carried after considerable resistance.'[8] With the ruins in Allied hands, work began immediately on two new batteries (numbers 3 and 4, map 141) to engage the main redoubt. Guns were also moved to Battery 11 on the Monte Olia to counter the fire of the Miradór Battery that was hampering works on the Chofre sand hills (batteries 12 to 14).

By 20 July six siege batteries opened (see Appendix 6) and by the end of the day the parapet of the sea wall had begun to collapse, but at a cost. The French had concentrated their counter-battery fire against the largest battery on the Chofre and, by nightfall, five of the 11 guns had been damaged or prevented from firing. Following a night of foul weather, Graham sent in a summons to Rey, which was promptly refused, and firing then recommenced until 24 July to good effect. By the 23rd the breach at point 'A' was considered 'perfectly practicable', 'but Sir Richard Fletcher having communicated to Colonel Dickson, that, according to information he had received, the wall was much thinner and weaker at 'B', and that Sir Thomas Graham wished the battery to be directed against that point.'[9] While work commenced on this second breach, the working party on the left bank discovered a drainage channel that ran to the walls and into the city, although it had been blocked up beneath the counterscarp. The engineers decided to place a mine at this point and incorporate the explosion into the overall plans for the assault that were now being drawn up.

The plan necessitated that daybreak and low tide coincide but, as luck would have it, this was not the case; low tide occurred about half an hour prior to first light. Graham delayed the action for 24 hours as the area adjacent to the main breach (point 'A') was ablaze and he considered this would hinder the assault. The attack was therefore set for 25 July; Graham had elected to go early, at 0500 hours, 20 minutes before dawn to capitalize on the low tide, but it was a decision that was to contrive failure. The mine was markedly more successful that the sappers had anticipated, bringing down the entire counterscarp and the western part of the hornwork, but Oswald's allocation of troops to this sector was woefully inadequate to capitalize on this success.[10] Meanwhile, the main attack had lost momentum in the dark with the attackers unable to see or avoid the many ingenious traps installed by the defenders. The French waited until the first elements of the main attack, led by the Royal Scots, were at the lip of the breach before bringing down the most furious fire, pinning down the attackers and bringing their momentum to an abrupt halt. As dawn began to break, the gunners on the sand hills were standing by their colours ready to provide supporting fire, but from the spectacle that confronted them as the sun rose, it was soon clear that the attack had already failed.

Following this rather unexpected turn of events there were the inevitable recriminations, primarily against Oswald, but Major Gomm of the 9th vented his anger towards the scientific services. 'Our soldiers have on all occasions stood fire so well that our artillery have become as summary in their process as our engineers. Provided that they have made a hole in the wall, by which we can claw up, they care not about destroying the defences.'[11] Wellington was appraised of the failure at 1100 hours and immediately rode back to San Sebastián to take stock of the

---

3   Jones, *Journal of Sieges*, vol. II, p.13.

4   Dickson, *The Dickson Manuscripts*, vol. V, p.960. The main attack was therefore to be conducted against the same point undertaken by the Duke of Berwick in 1719.

5   For details of the guns within the batteries and the sequence of events see Appendix 6.

6   Belmas, *Journaux des Sieges*, vol. IV, p. 608. It is curious that Belmas records this attack as being made by the English and not the Portuguese.

7   Consisting of 5 x 9 pdr and 2 heavy 5½-inch howitzers.

8   Dickson, *The Dickson Manuscripts*, vol. V, p.962. The redoubt was adjoining the convent and not the one to the north of the suburb of San Martin.

9   Jones, *Journal of Sieges*, vol. II, p.36.

10   A few companies of the 8th Caçadores – Oman and Dickson.

11   Oman, *A History of the Peninsular War*, vol. VI, p.583. However, the discussion, from the Gunner point of view, is laid out in May, *A Few Observations on the Mode of Attack and Employment of Heavy Artillery at Ciudad Rodrigo and Badajoz in 1812 and St. Sebastian in 1813*. It was published in 1819.

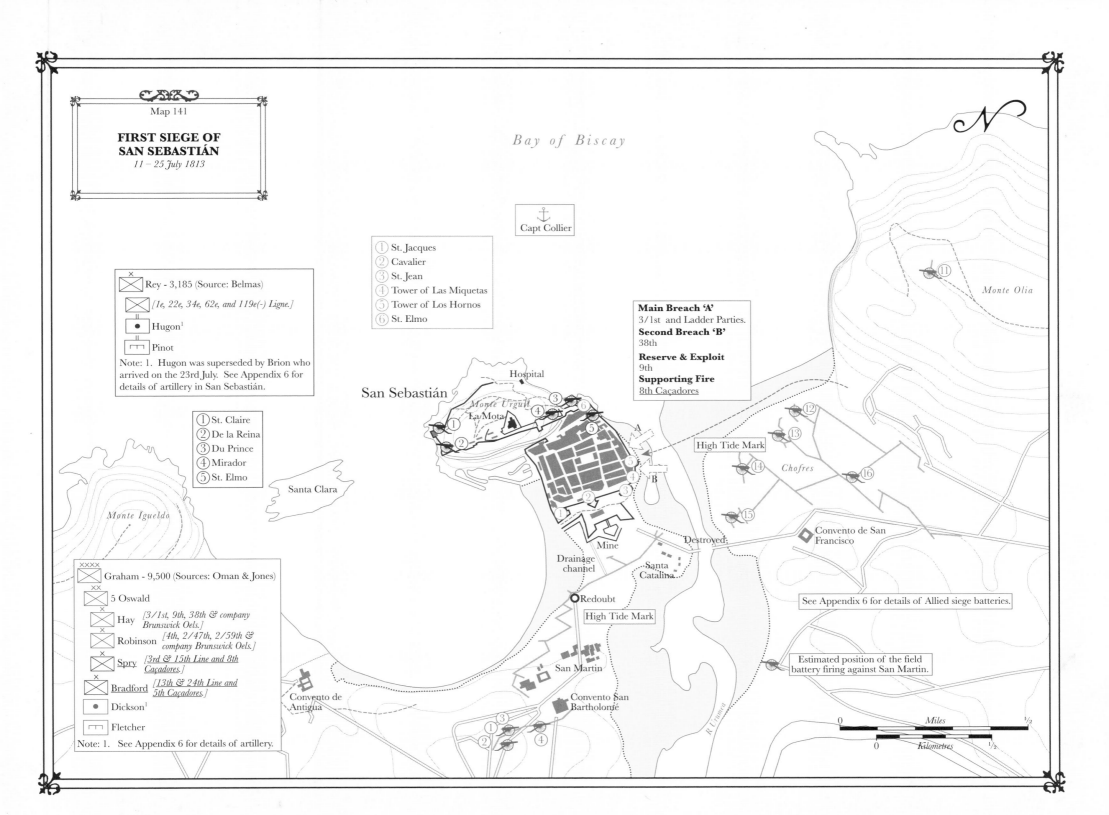

Map 141

FIRST SIEGE OF SAN SEBASTIÁN

11 – 25 July 1813

Bay of Biscay

N

⚓ Capt Collier

① St. Jacques
② Cavalier
③ St. Jean
④ Tower of Las Miquetas
⑤ Tower of Los Hornos
⑥ St. Elmo

Rey - 3,185 (Source: Belmas)

[1e, 22e, 34e, 62e, and 119e(-) Ligne.]

● Hugon[1]

Pinot

Note: 1. Hugon was superseded by Brion who arrived on the 23rd July. See Appendix 6 for details of artillery in San Sebastián.

① St. Claire
② De la Reina
③ Du Prince
④ Mirador
⑤ St. Elmo

Main Breach 'A'
3/1st and Ladder Parties.
Second Breach 'B'
38th
Reserve & Exploit
9th
Supporting Fire
8th Caçadores

Monte Olia

⑪

Monte Igueldo

Santa Clara

Hospital

San Sebastián

Monte Urgull
La Mota

① ② ③ ④ ⑤ ⑥

A

High Tide Mark

⑫
⑬
⑭ *Chofres*
⑯
⑮

B

Convento de San Francisco

Mine

Destroyed

Drainage channel

Santa Catalina

See Appendix 6 for details of Allied siege batteries.

○ Redoubt

High Tide Mark

Graham - 9,500 (Sources: Oman & Jones)

5 Oswald

Hay *[3/1st, 9th, 38th & company Brunswick Oels.]*

Robinson *[4th, 2/47th, 2/59th & company Brunswick Oels.]*

Spry *[3rd & 15th Line and 8th Caçadores.]*

Bradford *[13th & 24th Line and 5th Caçadores.]*

● Dickson[1]

Fletcher

Note: 1. See Appendix 6 for details of artillery.

Convento de Antigua

San Martin

Convento San Bartholomé

Estimated position of the field battery firing against San Martin.

R. Urumea

① ② ③ ④

0 ___ Miles ___ ½
0 ___ Kilometres ___ ½

situation and to hear reports at first hand. 'In consequence, his Lordship decided to suspend all proceedings till the arrival of additional ordnance and ammunition from England, and directed that the guns should be withdrawn from the batteries and dragged to Passages.'[12] Having delivered these orders, Wellington set off on the road back to his headquarters at Lesaca and was met on the road and informed that Hill's divisions at the pass at Maya were under sustained attack.

Wellington had long maintained the need to capture both San Sebastián and Pamplona before commencing the final push into France. Furthermore, the political situation in northern Europe was fragile; following Napoleon's spectacular victories at Lützen and Bautzen (over Russia and Prussia) the Armistice of Plaswitz had given rise to considerable uncertainty. Until the intentions of Austria[13] were known Wellington had wisely elected to remain on the Spanish side of the Pyrenees. Both Lord Liverpool, the Prime Minister and Lord Bathurst, the Secretary for War had suggested he hold the line of the Pyrenees in much the same way as he had done with the Lines of Torres Vedras;[14] he brusquely dismissed the idea, but was more guarded in his criticism of their joint proposal to move with the majority of his army to Germany. 'In regard to my going to Germany, I am the Prince Regent's servant; but nobody would enjoy the same advantage here, and I should be no better than any other in Germany. If a British army should be left in the Peninsula, therefore, it is best I should remain with it.'[15] Adding to his woes, he received notification from the Spanish Ministry of War that Castaños and Giron were to be removed from their posts, and the news of Sir John Murray's bungled attempt to capture Tarragona brought no solace from the east coast. Furthermore, relations with the Admiralty were strained to breaking point following his continued protestations to Bathurst: 'Your Lordship will have seen that the blockade of the coast is merely nominal. The enemy have reinforced *by sea* the only two posts they have on the north coast of Spain.' He added that 'were the naval forces off San Sebastián more substantial he could contemplate a simultaneous assault on the fortress from both its seaward and landward sides'.[16] The Admiralty rejected indifference on their part but 'acknowledged that San Sebastián was not being completely blockaded and that French coastal traffic in the area was not being interdicted, but, quoting Collier, they doubted if supplies beyond "a few eggs and fowls" were being taken in'.[17]

Joseph's attempts to hide the scope of the French disaster at Vitoria were quickly undone and Napoleon's fury was swift and calculated. 'Command of both the battered survivors of the Vitoria campaign and the large reserve forces stationed at Bayonne had been placed in the hands of Marshal Soult. In part, this was undoubtedly meant as one last snub for Joseph, who had, as we have seen, suffered much from Soult's presumption and insubordination, but there was, too, a measure of harsh reality: greedy and untrustworthy though he may have been, "King Nicholas" was one of the very few subordinate commanders to whom Napoleon could give a command that numbered almost 85,000 fighting troops – and, what is more, one on whom rested perhaps the only chance of persuading Austria, which was teetering on the brink of joining the Allies, to remain neutral.'[18] Soult had long desired just such an opportunity and on arrival at Bayonne on 11 July, he wasted no time in reorganizing his forces and taking the fight to Wellington. The former armies would cease to exist and they would reform under a new 'Army of Spain'[19] which was to be divided in three 'Lieutenancies' of the Right, Centre and Left under the commands of Reille, D'Erlon and Clausel respectively. Each corps[20] comprised three divisions, while Villatte assumed command of the mass of Reserves (see Appendix 6 and map 142).

Soult's offensive plan was essentially the same as the one penned by Jourdan; he would join Reille and Clausel and attack through the pass at Roncesvalles while D'Erlon would advance through the pass at Maya and the whole would then converge on Pamplona. Both D'Erlon and Clausel's forces were cantoned in and around their starting points and were therefore ready to commence operations long before Reille's troops who had moved from their positions on the coast in front of Graham. To maintain surprise, Villatte's reserve forces had replaced Reille's forces, releasing them to begin their easterly movement on 20 July. The lateral communication and heavy rains slowed their progress, but they were in place by last light on 24 July. At dawn on 25 July, Soult's Army of Spain attacked across the frontage.

12   Jones, *Journal of Sieges*, vol. II, p.46.

13   Austria had reluctantly supported Napoleon during the Russian Campaign in 1812.

14   Liverpool to Wellington, *Supplementary Dispatches*, vol. VIII, pp.64–65.

15   Wellington to Bathurst, 12 July from Hernani, *Dispatches*, vol. X, p.524.

16   Hall, *Wellington's Navy*, pp.214–215 – from *Dispatches*, vol. X, pp.561–562 and vol. XI, pp.17–19. The problem stemmed from the Admiralty reorganization of the naval contribution to war in light of the outbreak of hostilities with the United States the previous summer.

17   Hall, *Wellington's Navy*, p.216.

18   Esdaile, *The Peninsular War, A New History*, p.460.

19   Suchet's Army on the East Coast remained independent.

20   Napoleon had forbid the use of the term.

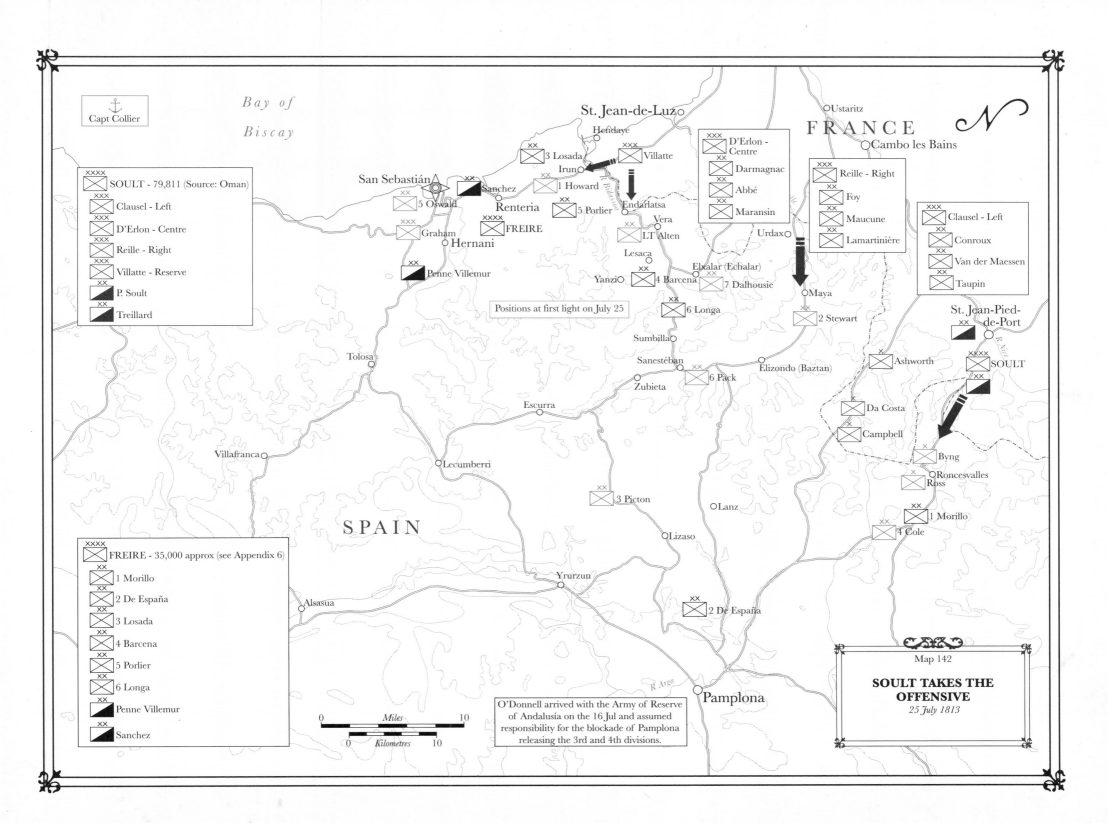

Bay of Biscay

Capt Collier

SOULT - 79,811 (Source: Oman)
Clausel - Left
D'Erlon - Centre
Reille - Right
Villatte - Reserve
P. Soult
Treillard

FRANCE

Ustaritz

St. Jean-de-Luz
Hendaye
3 Losada
Villatte
Irun
1 Howard
Sanchez
San Sebastián
5 Oswald
Renteria
FREIRE
Graham
Hernani
Penne Villemur

Cambo les Bains

D'Erlon - Centre
Darmagnac
Abbé
Maransin

Reille - Right
Foy
Maucune
Lamartinière

Clausel - Left
Conroux
Van der Maessen
Taupin

5 Porlier
Endarlatsa
Vera
LT Alten
Lesaca
Yanzi
4 Barcena
7 Dalhousie
Elxalar (Echalar)
Urdax
Maya

Positions at first light on July 25

2 Stewart

St. Jean-Pied-de-Port

6 Longa
Sumbilla
Sanestéban
6 Pack
Elizondo (Baztan)
Zubieta
Escurra

Ashworth
Da Costa
Campbell
Byng
Roncesvalles
Ross

SOULT

Tolosa

Villafranca
Lecumberri
Lanz
3 Picton
1 Morillo
4 Cole

SPAIN

Lizaso

FREIRE - 35,000 approx (see Appendix 6)
1 Morillo
2 De España
3 Losada
4 Barcena
5 Porlier
6 Longa
Penne Villemur
Sanchez

Yrurzun
2 De España
Alsasua

0   Miles   10
0   Kilometres   10

O'Donnell arrived with the Army of Reserve of Andalusía on the 16 Jul and assumed responsibility for the blockade of Pamplona releasing the 3rd and 4th divisions.

R Arga
Pamplona

Map 142

SOULT TAKES THE OFFENSIVE
25 July 1813

Chapter 48

The Battle of the Pyrenees: 25 July to 1 August 1813

The main attack against the pass at Roncesvalles advanced on two routes; Clausel on the main track to the east and Reille on the secondary path further west. Soult was aware that he would achieve no surprise in Clausel's sector, for the terrain was open and there had already been some skirmishing fire between the forward elements of this force and the Allied light companies on the night of 14 July. However, he hoped that Reille's column would catch the Allies off guard. Van der Maessen led Clausel's column, followed by Taupin and Conroux and then the cavalry, guns and all the transport for both corps, which in the hilly terrain along narrow tracks, resulted in a line that stretched for many kilometres. To the west Foy led Reille's advance, followed by Maucune and Lamartinière and two batteries of mountain guns. This column, although smaller, had the most deplorable of routes; impossible at night, during the day the troops could only move in file.

Wellington was not entirely taken in by this French advance because, as early as 23 July, he had despatched Cole to the area amidst reports of considerable French movement towards St Jean-Pied-de-Port. 'In a letter to Sir Lowry Cole, the Quartermaster General, on July 23, had sent him Wellington's instructions that he was to support Byng's troops as effectually as possible, and in the event of being compelled to give up the passes he was to make arrangements further back for stopping the enemy's progress towards Pamplona.'[1] The next day Murray was to write again that 'Lord Wellington has desired I should express still more strongly how essential he considers it that the passes in front of Roncesvalles should be maintained to the utmost and every arrangement made for repelling effectually every direct attack that the enemy may make in that quarter'.[2] This latter directive reached Cole after the fighting had already started.

Soult's attack commenced before dawn with two demonstrations; the one in the west was designed to hold the attention of Campbell's Portuguese Brigade but had little success; however, that in the east was staged by the 59e Ligne and some local National Guards who came up against the Regiment of León at the foundry at Orbaiceta. The Spanish battalion fought well and held their ground but the distinct sounds of battle to the east unnerved the Allies at the pass who feared that their flank was being turned. At about 0600 hours the first main attack was delivered against the pass and the Spanish battalion (and attached light companies) by two battalions of Barbot's Brigade, the 1e Ligne and the 25e Léger. It failed completely and the attackers sought refuge amongst the stones and gorse and resorted to bickering fire that continued for many hours before Clausel's aide-de-camp rode up to Barbot and informed him that he would be 'cashiered unless he delivered a resolute attack'. A second and third attempts also failed and it was not until a battery of guns was brought into action, and Van der Maessen led the 27e and 130e Ligne on a flanking manoeuvre, that the position was finally forced; Byng giving the order for the troops to fall back to the main position at Altobiscar.

Cole had, by a stroke of good fortune, moved Ross's Brigade to the Lindus during the night of 24 July and ordered his other two brigades to close in on Roncesvalles from the south. At around 1100 hours, the outlying piquets from the Brunswick Oels detected movement to the north, and within minutes the elite companies of the 6e Léger clashed with the German piquet and then with the leading company of the 20th. Following a spirited bayonet charge by both sides, the 20th fell back and, supported by the other two battalions of the brigade, were able to hold the French despite repeated attempts to force the defile. By the time Maucune's Brigade was up and thoughts turned to a flanking manoeuvre, evening was fast approaching and the fog had already begun to descend. The same fog was to bring an end to the fighting at Altobiscar where Clausel had decided against another frontal attack and was preparing to move Conroux's Division in a wide flanking manoeuvre to the south-east.

At Maya events had progressed more favourably for Soult. 'On 25 July, the enemy attacked and carried the pass of Maya with an overwhelming force. It was a day of brave confusion.'[3] Confused it certainly was, not helped by the fact that both Hill and Stewart had ridden off to visit Campbell in the early morning and were absent when the attack commenced. D'Erlon attacked on two routes, Maransin on the track to Urdax, and D'Armagnac and Abbé on the *Chemin des Anglais*. D'Armagnac made short work of the forward piquet, manned by 80 men[4] from the light companies, and the 50th were sent forward to try and stabilize the situation. The 92nd were later sent to reinforce the 50th and, when they too were seen in retreat, half the 71st were despatched to cover their withdrawal. All cohesion was lost, along with four Portuguese light guns,[5] and Stewart tried to rally his troops at a second position around the (still standing) tented camps of the 71st and 92nd, but Maransin's Division with Abbé in support were quick to close. However the temptation to loot from the camp equally quickly diminished French momentum, much to the fury of their officers. Stewart fell back to a third line and, having received reinforcement from the 82nd, met the third attack with a counter, but after an hour and a half, the French had regained the upper hand. They were about to press in numbers when General Barnes arrived to the rear with the reserve brigade of the 7th Division[6] which he launched, unseen and at a diagonal angle, into the leading French infantry, causing Maransin's leading brigade to recoil. D'Erlon thought the entire 7th Division had arrived and immediately went on the defensive.

1 Beatson, *With Wellington in the Pyrenees*, p.90, Murray to Cole, Lesaca, 23 July 1813.

2 Ibid, Murray to Cole, Lesaca, 24 July 1813.

3 Sherer, *Recollections of the Peninsula*, p.256.

4 Commanded by Captain Moyle Sherer.

5 From Da Cuna's Company. This loss infuriated Wellington who laid the blame firmly on Stewart's shoulders.

6 Consisting of the 6th Foot and the Brunswick Oels, the 82nd was also from this brigade; only the 3rd Provisional Battalion was missing.

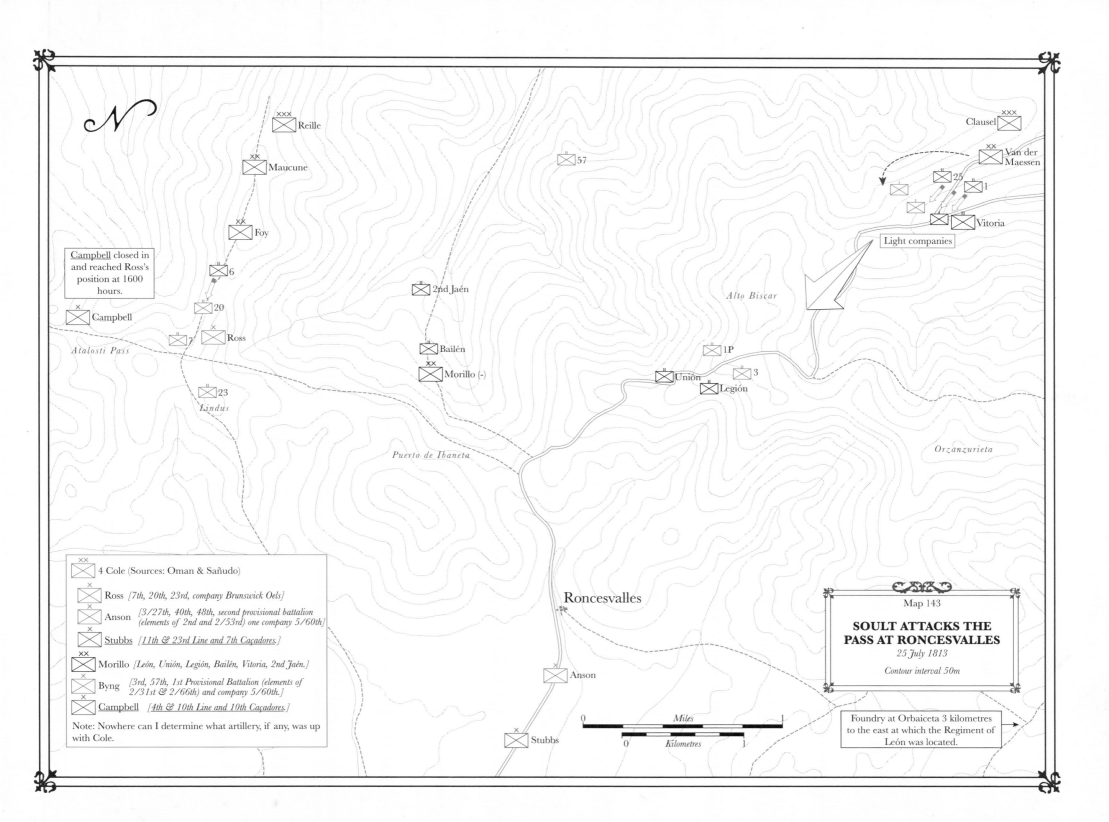

N

Reille

Maucune

Foy

Campbell closed in
and reached Ross's
position at 1600
hours.

6

Campbell

20

Atalosti Pass

7 Ross

23

Lindus

57

2nd Jaén

Alto Biscar

Bailén

Morillo (-)

1P

Union 3

Legión

Puerto de Ibaneta

Orzanzurieta

Clausel

Van der
Maessen

25

1

Vitoria

Light companies

4 Cole (Sources: Oman & Sañudo)

Ross *[7th, 20th, 23rd, company Brunswick Oels]*

Anson *[3/27th, 40th, 48th, second provisional battalion
(elements of 2nd and 2/53rd) one company 5/60th]*

Stubbs *[11th & 23rd Line and 7th Caçadores.]*

Morillo *[León, Unión, Legión, Bailén, Vitoria, 2nd Jaén.]*

Byng *[3rd, 57th, 1st Provisional Battalion (elements of
2/31st & 2/66th) and company 5/60th.]*

Campbell *[4th & 10th Line and 10th Caçadores.]*

Note: Nowhere can I determine what artillery, if any, was up
with Cole.

Roncesvalles

Anson

Stubbs

Map 143

**SOULT ATTACKS THE
PASS AT RONCESVALLES**

25 July 1813

Contour interval 50m

Foundry at Orbaiceta 3 kilometres
to the east at which the Regiment of
León was located.

0	Miles	1

0	Kilometres	1

Soult was most frustrated at his progress, but frustration gave way to satisfaction the following morning when he discovered that the Allies had withdrawn during the night from both passes. Wellington had been briefed on the debacle at Maya and the loss of the pass but remained in the dark as to events at Roncesvalles. He rode with all speed the following morning, but it was not until late afternoon that he received the news that Cole had surrendered the vital second pass and that he was retreating towards Zubiri, where he understood he was to link up with Picton and hand over command to him. It was a disaster: all of Wellington's orders were designed to hold the line from an ingress at Maya, and the loss of Roncesvalles had altered the situation completely. He sent immediate orders to Picton to detain the enemy at all costs, but as he was penning the instructions the Allies were already abandoning Zubiri and pulling back to Pamplona. Uncharacteristically, Picton considered the position at Zubiri too easily turned and agreed with Cole to fall back, seemingly oblivious to Wellington's original instructions to the contrary.

Soult's follow-up on the morning of 27 July was again delayed by sending Reille into the mountains on inadequate tracks with questionable guides. Clausel arrived at Zabaldica, in front of the defensive position established by Picton and Cole, at about 1000 hours and, leaving Conroux's Division opposite the Spanish, he pushed his other two divisions onto the high ground to the west. Soult, who was up with Clausel, surveyed the dispositions of the forces arrayed to his front, and having done so, refused Clausel's request to attack and elected to wait for the arrival of Reille. As he rode onto the feature, opposite Anson and Campbell's brigades, he witnessed the Allied ranks erupt in loud cheers, which rolled along the lines. Although he did not know it at that time, Wellington had just arrived on the position, having ridden from Almándoz that morning. Soult's decision to wait for Reille and D'Erlon had bought Wellington the time he required; orders had been issued to the 2nd, 6th and 7th divisions to join the Allied main body with all speed. Little of significance happened for the rest of the day, other than an attempt by a regiment of Conroux's Division to evict the Spanish from 'Spanish Hill'. 'The position was strong, but not as high as those adjacent to it; the regiment of Pravia which had the regiment of Príncipe in reserve, defended it bravely, engaging the attackers so vigorously as to abandon any ideas of repeating the attack.'[7]

That evening, following a council of war, Soult issued orders for an attack the following morning. However, with rumours of considerable Allied reinforcements en route, the French attack would await the arrival of D'Erlon (who had the furthest distance to cover). On the other side of the valley, Wellington had made few changes to the Allied dispositions but concentrated on plans for the integration of Pack, Hill and Dalhousie into the defensive lines. 'On the morning of July 28 a splendid sunrise succeeded the storm of the previous evening. The Allies were under arms, but the French showed no signs of attacking beyond some movements of troops from their left to their right, they retained for several hours their positions of the evening before.'[8] 'I have in my front Soult, with from thirty to thirty five thousand men, but he does not appear inclined

to attack us.'[9] In fact, Soult had set 1300 hours as the time for a coordinated attack, but at noon, as the first of the troops from the 6th Division began to arrive on the field and extend the Allied left wing, (precisely at the point Clausel intended to turn the Allied first line) he ordered Conroux to attack immediately and his other two divisions to do likewise. This counter-order caused considerable confusion, as the other two divisions were not ready. Schwitter and Rey's brigades advanced side-by-side up the road beyond the village of Sorauren; they soon found themselves under fire from three sides and the attack began to falter. Meanwhile the main attack was now underway across the front; the determined French infantry fought with considerable bravery and tenacity. The 31e Léger and 70e Ligne (from Lecamus's Brigade) were the first to reach the summit before being charged by Ross and driven back. To their left, Van der Maessen's brigades both penetrated Campbell's lines and were making headway for the summit before being counter-attacked by Stubbs's Brigade, which Cole had moved forward to strengthen the line. Stubbs held the line for a while but when the 10th Caçadores broke on the left they exposed Ross's flank and, at much the same time, the 47e Ligne (from Taupin's Brigade) also penetrated the lines and took control of the chapel of San Salvador before also moving up the slope to link up with Van der Maessen's men. To their left Maucune had succeeded in getting the 17e Léger on the summit and Clausel considered that 'despite all the difficulties of the enterprise, [there was] some hope of success'.

It was not to be. The men were exhausted and the attacks had begun losing momentum; after a lull of several minutes the defenders began to regain the heights. Maucune's troops were the first to be driven off the feature, at which point Wellington ordered two battalions from Anson's Brigade to fall on Van der Maessen's flank, and Byng was ordered left to support Ross. The attack in the flank by the 3/27th and the 48th settled the dispute in the centre. Gauthier's attempts to take the Spanish Hill had been repulsed on three occasions, with some spirited defence by the Spanish battalions situated there. Foy's presence at Alzuza was merely a distraction to keep Picton occupied, and on the far (Allied) right the cavalry faced off but, as ordered, neither took the offensive. The fight on the far left, between Pack and Conroux, continued inconclusively for some time until Pack tried to storm the village and was forced back with loss. Sporadic firing continued across the front for over an hour and the French officers tried repeatedly to rally their men, but at about 1600 hours it was clear the attacks had all failed and Soult ordered all the units to return to their original positions.

For General Cassan and the French defenders of Pamplona, the drop off in distant musketry and the lack of Allied activity in his area meant only one thing – relief would not be immediately forthcoming. To the north the Light, 2nd and 7th divisions were withdrawing, as ordered, but foul weather and treacherous tracks were slowing progress and disrupting timely arrival. 'On our retreat we were pushed so hard by the enemy, and in one of the darkest nights possible, that Sir Rowland Hill ordered me to get rid of, and destroy, every incumbrance. We left [destroyed] the forage cart and 3 cars of the 9 Pr. Brigade, and the ground on the edge of the precipice of some 300 feet gave way and a 9 Pr. Gun went down, and of course was lost. The shaft animals

7   Arteche, *Guerra de la Independencia*, vol. III, p.184. There is debate as to whether the battalion from the 4th Portuguese Line Regiment (Campbell's Brigade) were on the feature at this time or indeed at any time.

8   Beatson, *With Wellington in the Pyrenees*, p.167.

9   Wellington to Graham, in a letter written in the field at 1030 hours.

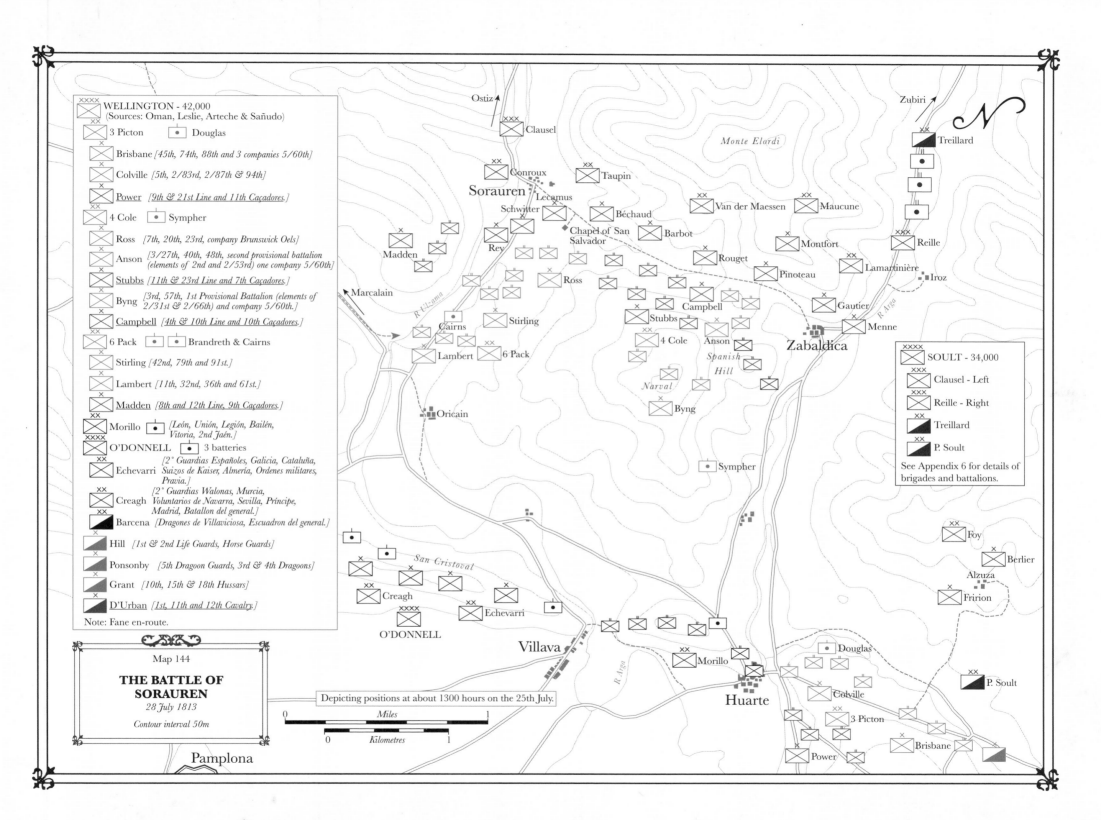

WELLINGTON - 42,000
(Sources: Oman, Leslie, Arteche & Sañudo)

3 Picton — Douglas

Brisbane *[45th, 74th, 88th and 3 companies 5/60th]*

Colville *[5th, 2/83rd, 2/87th & 94th]*

Power *[9th & 21st Line and 11th Caçadores.]*

4 Cole — Sympher

Ross *[7th, 20th, 23rd, company Brunswick Oels]*

Anson *[3/27th, 40th, 48th, second provisional battalion (elements of 2nd and 2/53rd) one company 5/60th]*

Stubbs *[11th & 23rd Line and 7th Caçadores.]*

Byng *[3rd, 57th, 1st Provisional Battalion (elements of 2/31st & 2/66th) and company 5/60th.]*

Campbell *[4th & 10th Line and 10th Caçadores.]*

6 Pack — — Brandreth & Cairns

Stirling *[42nd, 79th and 91st.]*

Lambert *[11th, 32nd, 36th and 61st.]*

Madden *[8th and 12th Line, 9th Caçadores.]*

Morillo — *[León, Unión, Legión, Bailén, Vitoria, 2nd Jaén.]*

O'DONNELL — 3 batteries

Echevarri *[2° Guardias Españoles, Galicia, Cataluña, Suizos de Kaiser, Almería, Ordenes militares, Pravia.]*

Creagh *[2° Guardias Walonas, Murcia, Voluntarios de Navarra, Sevilla, Príncipe, Madrid, Batallon del general.]*

Barcena *[Dragones de Villaviciosa, Escuadron del general.]*

Hill *[1st & 2nd Life Guards, Horse Guards]*

Ponsonby *[5th Dragoon Guards, 3rd & 4th Dragoons]*

Grant *[10th, 15th & 18th Hussars]*

D'Urban *[1st, 11th and 12th Cavalry.]*

Note: Fane en-route.

SOULT - 34,000

Clausel - Left

Reille - Right

Treillard

P. Soult

See Appendix 6 for details of brigades and battalions.

Map 144

THE BATTLE OF SORAUREN

28 July 1813

Contour interval 50m

Depicting positions at about 1300 hours on the 25th July.

0 — Miles — 1

0 — Kilometres — 1

with it.'[10] The 7th Division made better progress and by early on 29 July they were in touch with Wellington's main force. D'Erlon had moved forward from Irurita in the wake of Hill's withdrawal[11] and by early on 29 July was at Lanz, and he made contact with Soult a few kilometres to the south. Soult was emboldened by the news that his third corps had finally joined forces, but any further attempt to relieve to Pamplona was out of the question as he was well aware that Wellington had recalled several of his divisions to the north-west.

His new plan thrust D'Erlon's forces from rearguard to vanguard and his objective from south to west, as he aimed to cut the Pamplona to Tolosa road and thereby split the forces of Wellington and Graham; forcing the latter to lift the siege at San Sebastián. D'Erlon, reinforced with Treillard's cavalry, were to move against Hill while the other two corps were to execute an intricate series of manoeuvres, designed to extricate by division at night, without revealing their intentions. The orders were both impractical and hazardous, for the chosen route of 'advance' was on the road to Ostiz and this necessitated the majority of the force crossing directly in front of Cole and Pakenham's[12] divisions to transit through Sorauren. At midnight Taupin and Van der Maessen moved off, but Maucune was unable to relieve Conroux's division as the former had great difficulty extracting his force and moving it through wooded slopes on small tracks. Conroux, impatient to get in behind the other two divisions on the line of march, had already removed one of his brigades. On the French left, Foy had withdrawn from Alzuza, but his movement was also troubled and he had not concentrated at Iroz until around 0500 hours; he set off immediately behind Lamartinière who was providing cover, but was quickly slowed by the tail end of Maucune's force which was still struggling to move to Sorauren. As dawn began to break, one of Conroux's brigades was still in Sorauren with Maucune to its left, followed by Foy and Lamartinière; they lay exposed and vulnerable to the Allied guns, which had been moved to the front the day prior.[13]

Wellington was up early on 30 July and viewed the scene from the heights opposite the French positions. The Allied guns had already opened prior to daybreak, but as the light improved the Allied commander saw, to his amazement, the three French divisions moving across the Allied frontage in column. The 6th Division attacked Conroux's remaining brigade at once and the 4th Division followed a while later into the flank of Foy's Division, while Picton began to close

up the road to Roncesvalles and attack into Lamartinière's left wing. Maucune and Foy's divisions were practically destroyed. Further up the valley, Taupin and Van der Maessen had halted to wait for Conroux to close up, at which point the 7th Division moved forward from their concealed position on the Allied left flank, and fell upon the unsuspecting troops. Clausel opted to withdraw northwards: 'it is doubtful whether Clausel had more than 8,000 men out of his original 17,000 in hand that evening. The survivors were not fit for further fighting.'[14] Meanwhile, two of Reille's divisions had escaped as best they could over the hills and rejoined Clausel at Olague, but Foy's Division became detached in the confusion and fled north via the Val de Baigorry and did not link up again with the main body until the end of the campaign.

Soult had not stayed to witness the destruction of his army. He had left before dawn and joined D'Erlon and Treillard already moving west to engage Hill, who had moved out of the town of Lizaso and into a more defendable position a few kilometres to the south. Ashworth's Portuguese held the road with Da Costa to his right and Cameron his left with Pringle[15] in reserve. D'Erlon had called forward Maransin and so his command was complete: D'Armagnac was to engage and occupy Ashworth, while Abbé was moved around the French right and engaged the 50th and 92nd frontally. The attack succeeded but a counter-attack by the 34th bought enough time for Hill's entire force to withdraw with minimal loss. Ashworth's Portuguese had fought off some determined attacks by D'Armagnac, and then Da Costa's men had shown equal determination and resolve providing the pivot on which the balance of the force extracted itself. They withdrew to Yguaras, pursued by D'Erlon, who began to reorganize his force for a second attack when he noted the arrival of O'Donnell's two divisions supported by Morillo and Campbell's Portuguese Brigade; their arrival brought to a halt any further offensive operations.

Soult retraced his steps to Olague where he received the ruinous briefing on the state of his other two corps; he realized at once that he must withdraw D'Erlon, concentrate his force and retreat. Soult then selected a withdrawal route over the Puerto de Arraiz to Sanestéban and tasked D'Erlon to remain in place until the demoralized remnants of Clausel and Reille's forces had passed the junction. For the second time these rather unexpected orders had wrong-footed Wellington, who had fully expected Soult to head directly north over the Puerto de Velate. Following events at Sorauren, Picton had been sent north on the Roncesvalles road and Pakenham was now sent east to join him; however, Foy, who was on this path, had a substantive headstart and neither force were to catch him. Only the 7th Division had been allocated the road to Sanestéban and far to their left were the Light Division, which Wellington had sent to cut the Pamplona to Tortosa road, and which was now ordered to retrace their steps to Zubieta.

Soult led the retreat, followed by the two cavalry divisions, then Reille, Clausel and D'Erlon as rearguard. It was a tortuous affair, with the horses and pack animals making slow progress and holding up the infantry. At the pass, Clausel moved his formations east onto secondary paths running parallel to the main track, while Reille did likewise to the west. Abbé's Division was the

10 Tulloh, *Letter to Dickson – Viscarret August 16, 1813, Dickson Manuscripts*, vol. V. p.1022. Oman also states (vol. VI. p.682) that Ross also lost a gun in similar circumstances but neither his *Memoir* (pp.43-44) nor the *Letters of Augustus Frazer*, who was commanding the Royal Horse Artillery, support this suggestion.

11 D'Erlon's tardy advance is the subject of much criticism; see Thiers, *Histoire du Consulat et de L'Empire*, vol. XVI, p.14 and Beatson, *With Wellington in the Pyrenees*, p.167. Although Oman, *History of the Peninsular War*, vol. VI, p.p. 684-686, offers some mitigation.

12 This was the 6th Division; he assumed command from Pack, who had been injured during the battle.

13 This included Sympher's Battery who was in direct support to Cole. However, it is clear that Cairn's Battery, which was the direct support fire unit for the 7th Division, had supported the 6th during the fight on the 28th and again on the 30th. Brandreth's Battery was the direct support to the 6th Division and Brandreth and his officers did receive the clasp for the actions in the Pyrenees, so they were certainly there, but it is unknown what contribution they made to the two battles. Wellington's dispatch of 1 August only mentions the loss of the four Portuguese guns at Maya, much to the justifiable annoyance of the Royal Artillery.

14 Oman, *History of the Peninsular War*, vol. VI, p.698.

15 O'Callaghan was commanding the brigade for Pringle, the senior brigadier, had taken over command of the 2nd Division as Stewart had been wounded at Maya.

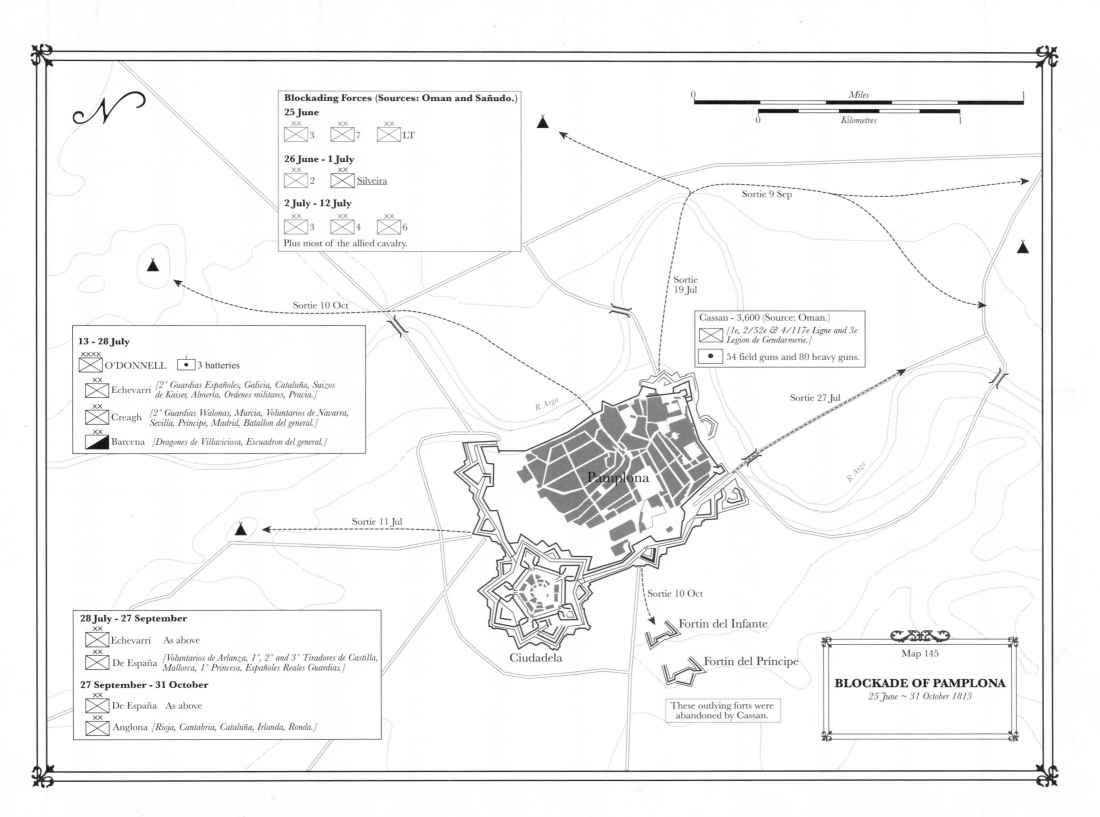

N

Blockading Forces (Sources: Oman and Sañudo.)

25 June

3   7   LT

26 June - 1 July

2   Silveira

2 July - 12 July

3   4   6

Plus most of the allied cavalry.

Sortie 9 Sep

Sortie 19 Jul

Sortie 10 Oct

Cassan - 3,600 (Source: Oman.)

[1e, 2/52e & 4/117e Ligne and 3e Legion de Gendarmerie.]

54 field guns and 80 heavy guns.

Sortie 27 Jul

R Arga

13 - 28 July

O'DONNELL   3 batteries

Echevarri   *[2° Guardias Españoles, Galicia, Cataluña, Suizos de Kaiser, Almería, Ordenes militares, Pravia.]*

Creagh   *[2° Guardias Walonas, Murcia, Voluntarios de Navarra, Sevilla, Príncipe, Madrid, Batallon del general.]*

Barcena   *[Dragones de Villaviciosa, Escuadron del general.]*

Pamplona

R Arga

Sortie 11 Jul

Sortie 10 Oct

Fortín del Infante

28 July - 27 September

Echevarri   As above

De España   *[Voluntarios de Arlanza, 1°, 2° and 3° Tiradores de Castilla, Mallorca, 1° Princesa, Españoles Reales Guardias.]*

27 September - 31 October

De España   As above

Anglona   *[Rioja, Cantabria, Cataluña, Irlanda, Ronda.]*

Ciudadela

Fortín del Príncipe

These outlying forts were abandoned by Cassan.

Map 145

BLOCKADE OF PAMPLONA

25 June ~ 31 October 1813

last to leave, and before they had done so Hill had engaged the defensive line, causing Abbé to pull back to the heights of Urroz, where he was forced to make a stand, for the divisions of Maransin and D'Armagnac had still not passed the junction. Hill was aware that Dalhousie would be with him within hours but he nevertheless ordered two attacks, which were unsuccessful, and it was not until the 7th Division arrived and executed the third attack that Abbé finally gave ground. D'Armagnac now found his division in the rear and assumed the role of rearguard. Hill followed Wellington's orders and continued to move east to Lanz and then north on the road to Maya; he was unaware that the balance of the French army had preceded D'Erlon on the road to Sanestéban and, on this road, only the 7th Division remained in pursuit.

That evening Wellington wanted confirmation that Soult had taken the Sanestéban road before issuing amendments to his original orders. Despite this short respite, Soult had the most uncomfortable night at Sanestéban as reports filtered in to his headquarters of an Allied presence at Elizondo (Cole and Byng), and more disturbingly, that the cavalry he had despatched to Vera had only encountered Spanish forces (Longa) and there was no sight of Villatte's reserve in the area. Nevertheless, this route was preferable to striking east and at 0230 hours on 1 August, the 118e Ligne[16] led the withdrawal followed by Treillard, Lamartinière, the baggage, Maucune, the three divisions of D'Erlon, and then finally Clausel's divisions acting as rearguard. Wellington was cautious in his pursuit, only sending the 4th Division (at Elizondo) to support the 7th Division who were advancing from the south; the Light Division had not reappeared from their lengthy return march and were given no new instructions. Giron's request to move on the position at Vera and strengthen the bridge crossing at Yanzi was denied; it was a decision Wellington was to regret. 'Graham realized the necessity of stopping the retreat of the French up the Bidassoa valley; but he was at this time anxious for his own front around Irun, for he thought it likely that Villatte might be reinforced from Soult's army and that he would be attacked … all that could be attempted to interrupt the enemy's retreat was to reinforce Longa, and to desire him to endeavour to hold the bridge at Yanci, with a greater force.'[17]

The length of the French column hindered their progress and forced inevitable contact with the rearguard as they bought time for the balance of the force. On 1 August the 4th Division started early, and was already attacking Clausel by 0700 hours in and around Sumbilla. Within minutes all three of Clausel's divisions were crowded back-to-back in the narrow valley and, after a lengthy engagement, Clausel ordered the force to take the track into the hills from where they formed a line of defence and withdrew gradually to Echalar. At the vanguard, events were no less chaotic. Longa's men had concealed themselves in the undergrowth overlooking the bridge at Yanzi and began to engage the French cavalry as they came in range. The French panicked and galloped back up the track, nearly running down Reille in the process. The 118e Ligne and 2e Léger were then brought up to clear the small Spanish force and the French advance had just resumed when more Spanish reinforcements arrived and drove off the French infantry. The French regained the hill following a second assault and held it long enough to extract their force.

The next morning the 4th and 7th divisions pushed up the road to Echalar, while the exhausted Light Division undertook a wide flanking march via Vera in an attempt to turn Soult's left wing. However, the subsequent Allied attack was ill-timed, as only the 7th Division were up in time (the 4th and Light divisions arrived later). But it mattered little, as the demoralized French forces gave way across the frontage. 'I deceived myself in the strangest way when I told your Excellency that the troops had their morale intact, and would do their duty… When tested, they started with one furious rush, but showed no power of resistance.'[18] It was an unfair criticism of a force that had fought with renewed determination and no little amount of courage until it was abundantly apparent that the campaign plan was flawed. Had Wellington pursued the broken French army he may have succeeded in its complete capture or surrender, but no such pursuit materialized; Wellington, ever mindful of the political situation in the north of Europe, did not judge the time right for the invasion of France. Instead he reestablished the defensive line along the Pyrenees and resumed the siege at San Sebastián.

---

16   Not the 120e Ligne as reported by Oman.

17   Graham to Wellington, Oyarzun, July 30th at 0700 hours.

18   Soult to Clark, 2 August.

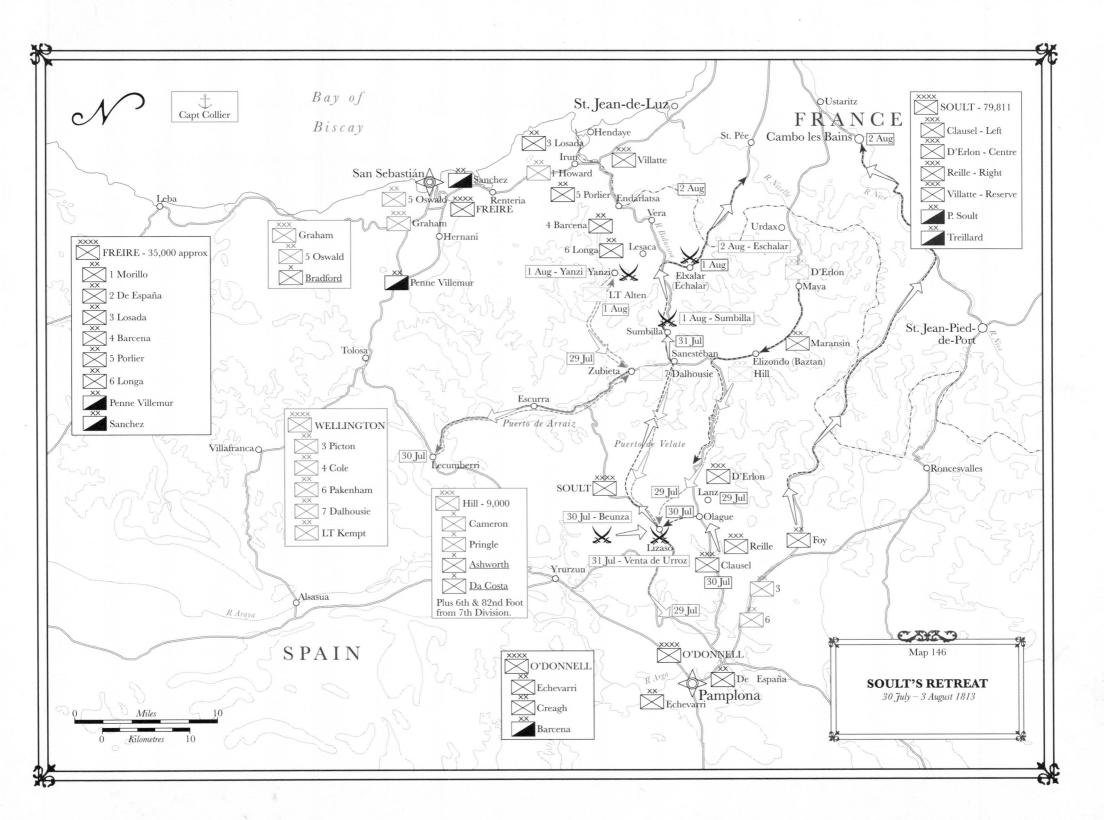

Bay of Biscay

Capt Collier

FRANCE

SPAIN

FREIRE - 35,000 approx
- 1 Morillo
- 2 De España
- 3 Losada
- 4 Barcena
- 5 Porlier
- 6 Longa
- Penne Villemur
- Sanchez

WELLINGTON
- 3 Picton
- 4 Cole
- 6 Pakenham
- 7 Dalhousie
- LT Kempt

- Graham
- 5 Oswald
- Bradford

Hill - 9,000
- Cameron
- Pringle
- Ashworth
- Da Costa

Plus 6th & 82nd Foot from 7th Division.

O'DONNELL
- Echevarri
- Creagh
- Barcena

SOULT - 79,811
- Clausel - Left
- D'Erlon - Centre
- Reille - Right
- Villatte - Reserve
- P. Soult
- Treillard

Leba

San Sebastián

3 Losada
Irun
Hendaye
Howard
Villatte
5 Porlier
Endarlatsa
4 Barcena
Vera
6 Longa
Lesaca

Sanchez
Renteria
FREIRE
5 Oswald
Graham
Hernani

St. Jean-de-Luz
St. Pée
Ustaritz
Cambo les Bains
2 Aug
Urdax
D'Erlon
Maya
St. Jean-Pied-de-Port

2 Aug
2 Aug - Eschalar
1 Aug
Elxalar (Echalar)
1 Aug - Yanzi Yanzi
LT Alten
1 Aug
1 Aug - Sumbilla
Sumbilla
31 Jul
Sanestéban
Maransin
Elizondo (Baztan)
Hill
29 Jul
Zubieta
7 Dalhousie
Roncesvalles

Penne Villemur

Tolosa

Villafranca

Escurra
Puerto de Arraiz
Puerto de Velate

30 Jul
Lecumberri

SOULT
29 Jul
Lanz
29 Jul
D'Erlon

30 Jul - Beunza
30 Jul
Olague
Lizaso
31 Jul - Venta de Urroz
Reille
Foy

Alsasua
R Araya

Yrurzun
Clausel
30 Jul
3
29 Jul
6

O'DONNELL
De España
Echevarri

Pamplona
R Arga

Map 146

SOULT'S RETREAT
30 July – 3 August 1813

Miles
0   10

Kilometres
0   10

Chapter 49

THE EAST COAST: MAY TO SEPTEMBER 1813

'The story of Murray's operations about Tarragona is not the story of an honest and excusable failure, but one which provokes bitter irritation over the doings of a British general who showed himself not only timid and incompetent, but shifty, mendacious, and treacherous to his allies.'[1]

Murray's diversion on the east coast was integral to Wellington's plans for the 1813 campaign (see Chapter 46). In outline, the intention of the commander-in-chief was for Murray to disembark with a minimum of 10,000 men from Alicante and join forces with Copons to take Tarragona. This act would, in Wellington's estimation, induce Suchet to march north to relieve the town, at which point the 2nd and 3rd Spanish armies under Elio and Del Parque respectively would then take the offensive and recapture Valencia.

Murray began to gather his expeditionary force towards the end of May, replacing the British outposts with Elio's men while Del Parque moved to the interior on Elio's left shoulder. Both Spanish armies were given orders to advance northwards once the French forces to their front were seen to be disengaging. With sufficient transports at Alicante harbour, Murray was able to embark in excess of 16,000 men, which sailed on 31 May. Two days later, with favourable winds, the fleet approached Tarragona, prompting Copons to come down from his headquarters at Reus to discuss tactics with Murray. The commander of the 1st Spanish Army had at his disposal about 16,000 men, but many were tied up watching French garrisons to the north; nevertheless he consented to provide 7,000 immediately, including two battalions which joined Col Prevost, and two Allied battalions[2] tasked to capture the small French fort of San Felipe de Balaguer and to subsequently close the defile at the Col De Balaguer, thereby frustrating French reinforcement from the south. Murray's fixation that Suchet was about to attack him from the south was only surpassed by his belief that Decaen was poised to fall on him with an even greater force from the north. This fatalistic view, and the fact that Wellington had stipulated that 'he would forgive everything excepting that the corps should be beaten or dispersed,' coloured Murray's perception and doomed the operation from the outset.

On the evening of 3 June Murray surveyed his target. It was woefully inadequately manned and equipped; General Bertoletti had a mere 1,500 men, consisting of two battalions, a company of *Juramentados*, two artillery companies and the motley crews from three vessels, which had assisted in blockading the port. No attempt had been made to repair the damage from the siege of 1811 to the outer *enceinte* and structures, other than at the San Carlos bastion and Fort Royal (map 147, points 1 and 2) and a single gun, manned by a company, had been placed at each point with the aim of denying the bay.[3] Murray then made the extraordinary decision to lay siege to these weakly defended outposts instead of capturing them by assault, and while the troops began to construct batteries, 'Hallowell, the senior naval officer present, [was] directing three bombs and two gunboats into Tarragona's roadstead during the hours of darkness to bombard the garrison and inhibit any attempts at disrupting the attacker's works. While these labours progressed Murray asked Pellew to demonstrate with the main body of the fleet off the northern part of the coast to try and prevent the French sending forces to succour the fortress.'[4] Under cover of Hallowell's fire, the first two batteries were completed by 6 June and opened with six of the heavy guns; defenders and attackers assumed this would precede a determined assault, but Murray had other ideas. A third breaching battery was ordered built, adjacent to the river Francoli and, when all three batteries engaged the Fort Royal on 7 June, the structure was all but destroyed. At this juncture Murray, following his engineer officer's assessment[5] that once captured the structure would be of limited use in any subsequent operation to gain the main fort, decided not to go ahead with the planned assault. Instead, two new batteries (map 147, 4 and 5) were to be built on the forward slopes of Monte Olivo, delaying the operation and frustrating Murray's commanders and staff to the point of distraction. While this new work was ongoing, Murray received news on 8 June that the fort at Balaguer had been taken[6] and that the road to the south had been effectively sealed. The two new batteries were operational by the evening of 10 June and yet still Murray dithered: 'The time thus lost in attacking was gained for the defence of the place, and Bertoletti, the governor, well knew that if he persevered he should be sure to be relived, before he was menaced in his last enclosure.'[7]

Suchet had observed the Allied fleet pass his headquarters, at Valencia on 31 May, and had reacted by sending Pannetier ahead with an ad hoc flying brigade that reached Tortosa on 8 June. At this point he linked up with Musnier's Division, but then received the news that the road to Tarragona was now cut. Suchet, having left Harispe, Habert and Severoli on the Xucar, was following but was some days behind with the balance of the Army. Unaware of Decaen's whereabouts, Pannetier was ordered to move through the interior and find alternative routes to the city, while to the north, Maurice Mathieu had finally left Barcelona with 6,000 infantry and 300 cavalry. Reports of the two French movements were enough to convince Murray to give up the game and, on 12 June, he ordered the force to re-embark. In panic, orders and counter-orders emanated from Murray's headquarters and, with the threat largely in the mind,

---

1   Oman, *History of the Peninsular War*, vol. VI, p.489.

2   2/67th and De Roll-Dillon's Swiss.

3   Suchet, *Memoirs of the War with Spain*, vol. II, p.311.

4   Hall, *Wellington's Navy*, pp.187–188.

5   The engineer officer was Major Thackeray. This exchange with Murray provided key evidence at the subsequent court martial.

6   On 7 June a mortar bomb struck the magazine, injuring a third of the French defenders. The commandant surrendered.

7   Suchet, *Memoirs of the War with Spain*, vol. II, p.312.

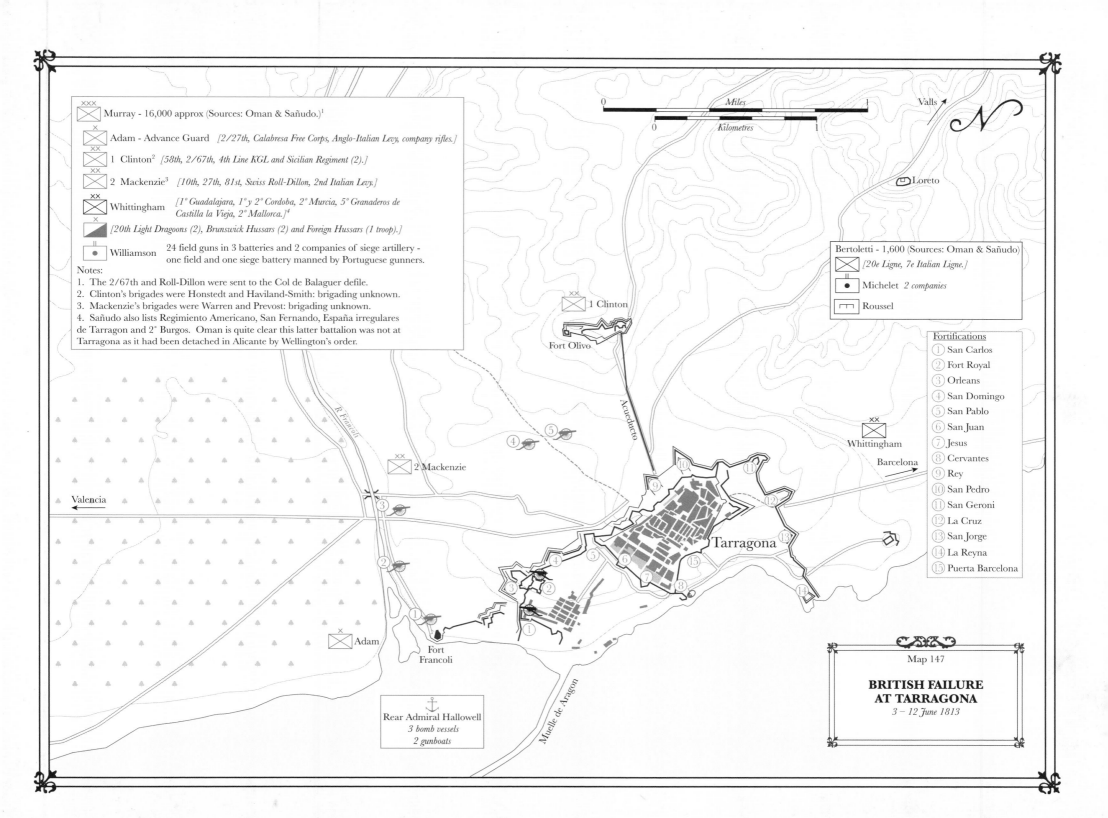

Murray - 16,000 approx (Sources: Oman & Sañudo.)[1]

Adam - Advance Guard *[2/27th, Calabresa Free Corps, Anglo-Italian Levy, company rifles.]*

1 Clinton[2] *[58th, 2/67th, 4th Line KGL and Sicilian Regiment (2).]*

2 Mackenzie[3] *[10th, 27th, 81st, Swiss Roll-Dillon, 2nd Italian Levy.]*

Whittingham *[1° Guadalajara, 1° y 2° Cordoba, 2° Murcia, 5° Granaderos de Castilla la Vieja, 2° Mallorca.][4]*

[20th Light Dragoons (2), Brunswick Hussars (2) and Foreign Hussars (1 troop).]

Williamson 24 field guns in 3 batteries and 2 companies of siege artillery - one field and one siege battery manned by Portuguese gunners.

Notes:
1. The 2/67th and Roll-Dillon were sent to the Col de Balaguer defile.
2. Clinton's brigades were Honstedt and Haviland-Smith: brigading unknown.
3. Mackenzie's brigades were Warren and Prevost: brigading unknown.
4. Sañudo also lists Regimiento Americano, San Fernando, España irregulares de Tarragon and 2° Burgos. Oman is quite clear this latter battalion was not at Tarragona as it had been detached in Alicante by Wellington's order.

Bertoletti - 1,600 (Sources: Oman & Sañudo)

[20e Ligne, 7e Italian Ligne.]

Michelet *2 companies*

Roussel

Fortifications
① San Carlos
② Fort Royal
③ Orleans
④ San Domingo
⑤ San Pablo
⑥ San Juan
⑦ Jesus
⑧ Cervantes
⑨ Rey
⑩ San Pedro
⑪ San Geroni
⑫ La Cruz
⑬ San Jorge
⑭ La Reyna
⑮ Puerta Barcelona

0 Miles 1
0 Kilometres 1

Valls

Loreto

1 Clinton

Fort Olivo

Acueducto

Whittingham

Barcelona

R. Francoli

Valencia

2 Mackenzie

Tarragona

Adam

Fort Francoli

Muelle de Aragon

Rear Admiral Hallowell
3 bomb vessels
2 gunboats

Map 147

**BRITISH FAILURE
AT TARRAGONA**

3 – 12 June 1813

of the Allied commander, stores, mounts and artillery guns were ordered to be abandoned. This was bad enough, but the day before, Murray had promised full support to Copons who was now in the process of deploying his army along the line of the river Gaya to meet the approach of Maurice Mathieu; the Spanish commander, abandoned to his fate, was fortunate to have been able to extract his force without loss. Once on board the transports, Murray made a series of rash proposals, it is assumed to try and cover for his extraordinary behaviour in front of Tarragona. Murray's commanders were furious at being associated with such a fiasco and Hallowell, when apprised of Murray's plan to make a fresh landing at the Col de Balaguer, commented that, 'knowing as I do, by experience, the indecisiveness of the General's character, I do not auger favourable result from his intended operation. We have already been disgraced more than any British Army ever was, and I fear every movement made by the present commander will add to the disaster.'[8] For six days the fleet moved up and down the Catalan coast until 18 June when Lord Bentinck arrived from Sicily to assume command; having heard the sorry testimony he ordered (as per Wellington's instructions) the fleet back to Alicante, where it arrived complete by 26 June.

When Suchet headed north he had left the majority of his army in Valencia under the command of Harispe, with orders to maintain a defensive posture. Facing him were two Spanish armies who, with about 32,000 men,[9] had more than twice the French numbers. The Spanish advance started late as Del Parque agreed to Elio's request to change places, the latter favouring the interior left flanking mission rather than the head-on encounter. Elio despatched Villacampa to dislodge the Italians on the extreme northern edge of the line while he advanced with Mijares and Sarsfield and seized the defile of the Cabrillas. Del Parque, however, was caught ill prepared during his advance, when Harispe moved forward from his defensive positions and engaged the Spanish, who were dispersed on a wide front on two roads with no mutual support. The French cavalry made short work of the unsuspecting infantry at Carcagente; Del Parque drew back and once again took up a defensive position at Castalla. Meanwhile Villacampa, who had managed to evade the Italians, had got in behind the force and was threatening to cut the Valencia to Catalonia road until he was withdrawn in haste on receiving news of Suchet's imminent return from Tortosa and the failure of Del Parque's mission.

Bentinck was determined to salvage something from the disastrous month of June and visited Del Parque at the end of the month at Castalla to discuss future operations. His encounter did little to raise hopes: he wrote to Wellington that he found the 3rd Army very demoralized following their repulse at Carcagente and seemed 'anxious not to commit their troops'. Nevertheless, Bentinck proposed a combined operation that necessitated a considerable detour through the interior on questionable roads, and through unfertile and barren land unable to sustain a force in excess of 30,000 men. As it transpired, the scheme was never executed; news of Vitoria changed the dynamics of the war and the campaign on the east coast. For Suchet the news was a hammer-blow, because 'at the moment when he least expected such an event, he received information of the battle fought at Vittoria on 21 June, in consequence of which the main army, commanded by king Joseph, had been forced to retreat to the Pyrenees, and to seek protection under the walls of Bayonne. The position of the marshal was so completely altered by that occurrence, as to make it imperative upon him to evacuate the kingdom of Valencia without delay.'[10] Suchet needed to discover whether Clausel, who had just fallen back on Zaragoza, would remain in the city, enabling joint plans for the defence of Aragon; or whether he would retire over the Pyrenees, in which case Suchet's only option lay in Catalonia. Orders were immediately sent to Suchet's field divisions and, by 4 July, most of his army was concentrated around Valencia. The next day the citadel was blown up and they departed, but instead of rolling up the garrisons as they passed, Suchet decided to leave small garrisons in each outpost (a company in Denia, a battalion in Peñiscola, two battalions in Saguntum and another company in Morella) and then even greater forces at Tortosa, Barcelona and Lérida. In all 10,000 men were penny-packeted in this way, reducing his eventual field army by a third. It was to be a huge mistake.

In Catalonia Decaen, having stripped out the garrisons, finally joined forces with Maurice Mathieu at Villafranca and, with their 8,000 men, now went in search of Copons who had fled back to the mountains following Murray's departure. Decaen's target was Vich, the only large town in Spanish hands in the region; however, as he closed in, word arrived of events at Vitoria. Decaen withdrew to ponder the situation and, in the process, Lamarque was trapped on the heights of La Salud and only saved from annihilation by the arrival of Beurmann. Lamarque had been tasked with command of the second axis of attack and on hearing gunfire from Vich had continued to forge ahead on the understanding that Decaen's column was already engaged; in fact the locals were merely firing a gun salute in celebration of news from Vitoria.[11] Lamarque's enthusiasm nearly lost him his brigade; but the questionable conduct of the entire French operation, and the tardiness displayed against Murray's unfortunate exploits, were enough for the Minister of War in Paris to pen orders for the replacement of Decaen. Catalonia had claimed yet another French commander's scalp.

By 9 July Suchet received a dispatch from Clausel informing him of his intention to strike north and rejoin Joseph's army. Any plans for holding Aragon were no longer viable and Suchet sent word to Paris ordering him to evacuate Zaragoza with all haste. However, the dispatch never reached his garrison commander and the French seemed equally oblivious to the 14,000 *guerrilleros* under Mina, Durán and Sanchez, who were now closing in on the city. Mina enticed the garrison to venture out from behind their defences and engage his force to the south; Duran then obliged to open hostilities from the north. Paris withdrew back into the confines of the city walls for 24 hours before accepting the precariousness of his predicament and he withdrew east towards Lérida. It was not long before Mina's cavalry had overtaken the column, which included a number of carriages carrying the accumulation of *Afrancesados* who had moved gradually north-east as the French retreated. By 11 July Paris realized that any hope of continuing east and linking up

---

8   Hall, *Wellington's Navy*, pp.188–189.

9   Elio had about 20,000 and Del Parque about 12,000: the two divisions of El Empecinado and Durán were not really under Elio's control and were already operating to the west in New Castile.

10   Suchet, *Memoirs of the War with Spain*, vol. II, pp.322–323.

11   See Arteche, *Guerra de la Independencia*, vol. XIII, pp.292–293.

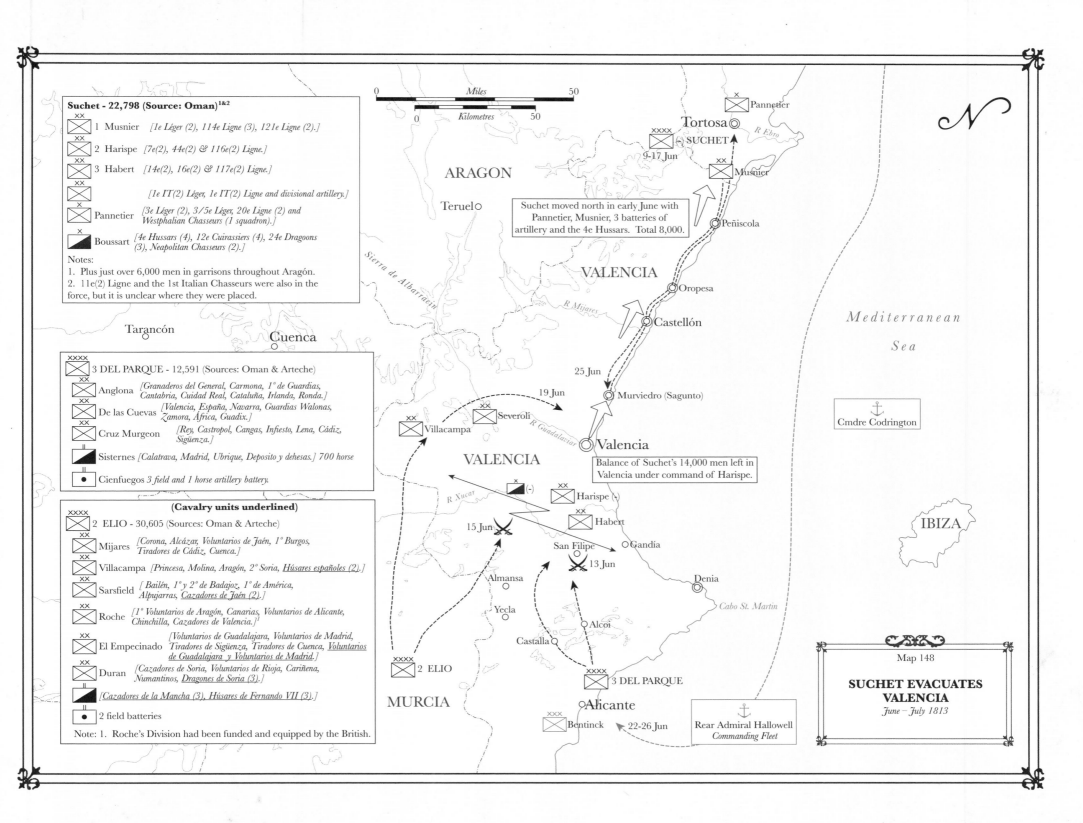

Suchet – 22,798 (Source: Oman)[1&2]

XX 1 Musnier *[1e Léger (2), 114e Ligne (3), 121e Ligne (2).]*

XX 2 Harispe *[7e(2), 44e(2) & 116e(2) Ligne.]*

XX 3 Habert *[14e(2), 16e(2) & 117e(2) Ligne.]*

XX *[1e IT(2) Léger, 1e IT(2) Ligne and divisional artillery.]*

X Pannetier *[3e Léger (2), 3/5e Léger, 20e Ligne (2) and Westphalian Chasseurs (1 squadron).]*

X Boussart *[4e Hussars (4), 12e Cuirassiers (4), 24e Dragoons (3), Neapolitan Chasseurs (2).]*

Notes:
1. Plus just over 6,000 men in garrisons throughout Aragón.
2. 11e(2) Ligne and the 1st Italian Chasseurs were also in the force, but it is unclear where they were placed.

3 DEL PARQUE – 12,591 (Sources: Oman & Arteche)

XX Anglona *[Granaderos del General, Carmona, 1º de Guardias, Cantabria, Cuidad Real, Cataluña, Irlanda, Ronda.]*

XX De las Cuevas *[Valencia, España, Navarra, Guardias Walonas, Zamora, Africa, Guadix.]*

XX Cruz Murgeon *[Rey, Castropol, Cangas, Infiesto, Lena, Cádiz, Sigüenza.]*

  Sisternes *[Calatrava, Madrid, Ubrique, Deposito y dehesas.]* 700 horse

● Cienfuegos *3 field and 1 horse artillery battery.*

(Cavalry units underlined)

2 ELIO – 30,605 (Sources: Oman & Arteche)

XX Mijares *[Corona, Alcázar, Voluntarios de Jaén, 1º Burgos, Tiradores de Cádiz, Cuenca.]*

XX Villacampa *[Princesa, Molina, Aragón, 2º Soria, Húsares españoles (2).]*

XX Sarsfield *[Bailén, 1º y 2º de Badajoz, 1º de América, Alpujarras, Cazadores de Jaén (2).]*

XX Roche *[1º Voluntarios de Aragón, Canarias, Voluntarios de Alicante, Chinchilla, Cazadores de Valencia.][1]*

XX El Empecinado *[Voluntarios de Guadalajara, Voluntarios de Madrid, Tiradores de Sigüenza, Tiradores de Cuenca, Voluntarios de Guadalajara y Voluntarios de Madrid.]*

XX Duran *[Cazadores de Soria, Voluntarios de Rioja, Cariñena, Numantinos, Dragones de Soria (3).]*

  [Cazadores de la Mancha (3), Húsares de Fernando VII (3).]

● 2 field batteries

Note: 1. Roche's Division had been funded and equipped by the British.

Suchet moved north in early June with Pannetier, Musnier, 3 batteries of artillery and the 4e Hussars. Total 8,000.

Balance of Suchet's 14,000 men left in Valencia under command of Harispe.

Cmdre Codrington

Map 148

SUCHET EVACUATES VALENCIA

June – July 1813

Rear Admiral Hallowell
Commanding Fleet

with Suchet was hopeless and he instead decided to head north into the relative safety of the Pyrenees. He arrived at Jaca on 12 July, to discover that Clausel had passed through the border fort the day before. Meanwhile Mina and Durán had commenced the siege of Zaragoza (against the 500 men left there in accordance with Suchet's orders) and by 5 August the city was once again in Spanish hands.

Suchet approached Tortosa on 12 July and remained there for five days while he took stock of the situation. During this time he received word that he was now in command of Decaen's force in addition to his own, and he issued a series of orders[12] and then prepared for the inevitable attack from the south. He moved to establish a defensive line near Tarragona, although he considered the structure of Tarragona itself too spoilt to provide effective resistance.[13] Bentinck's advance guard entered Valencia on 9 July and, having concentrated the 2nd and 3rd Spanish armies in the vicinity, the whole set off northwards on 16 July. Bentinck had incorrectly deduced that Suchet would abandon Catalonia if pressed and therefore selected a most ambitious plan of operations. Elio was left to besiege Valencia, while Bentinck would engage Suchet head-on, assisted by Copons from the north, leaving Del Parque to tackle Tortosa. Bentinck had received inaccurate reports that Suchet had abandoned Tarragona and accordingly despatched Clinton's Division by sea to capture the structure while he followed with the balance of the Allied force via the coast road. Clinton soon discovered that Tarragona was far from abandoned and furthermore, Suchet's entire army, supported by ever-increasing numbers from the Army of Catalonia, was less than a day's march to the north. He beat a hasty retreat and landed the force at Col de Balaguer where he joined Bentinck, who was equally surprised to discover that the French had every intention of holding ground and, given the opportunity, re-assuming the offensive.

Bentinck remained for two weeks at the narrow coastal pass during which time he was reinforced by the arrival of Del Parque's forces; the additional men merely added to his troubles as he could not sustain his own troops, even by sea. However, Suchet brought the issue to a head by advancing against Bentinck on 14 August and the Allies withdrew the following night. The pursuit could have been more advantageous to the French as the Allies struggled to ferry the force across the Ebro at Amposta and were engaged from the front, as well as in the flank, in a vigorous sally by the French governor General Robert from Tortosa. However, little of consequence occurred for the rest of the month. Del Parque and Whittingham were ordered to march to the Pyrenees (via Zaragoza) to join the main Allied army. Suchet used the time to reorganize and revitalize his force and to engage in prolonged and inconclusive correspondence with Soult over the latter's plans for the transference of Suchet's army to join him north of the Pyrenees. 'I feel as you do, and not without the most painful anxiety, how important it is to raise the fallen fortunes of the emperor in Spain, and especially to ward off any kind of danger from the frontiers of the empire.'[14] Suchet had absolutely no intention of subordinating himself to Soult; stalling at every opportunity, he finally requested that any plans be sent to the Emperor, fully aware that it would be many weeks before a reply was forthcoming, as Napoleon was embroiled in preparations for battle outside Leipzig. As it was no reply was ever sent.

Following two weeks of inactivity, Suchet had sent Decaen back to reopen roads in northern Catalonia, supported by Severoli's under-strength Italian Division. Bentinck misread the intentions of this northerly movement, believing it to be once again the precursor to a French evacuation of the province. On 27 August he marched north to Tarragona, where he was joined by the fleet and paid a visit by Copons, who agreed to bring south as many men as possible for combined operations. On 12 September, Adam ventured forth with the vanguard brigade and occupied the pass at Ordal; he was soon supported by other elements of Bentinck's force, but before the main body had arrived Suchet had attacked this small group in force and at night. The engagement continued throughout the day of 13 September until that night, when the beleaguered and severely depleted Allied force made good their retreat. Suchet's cavalry followed up the next day but were checked by Bentinck's main force, initially at Villafranca, and then at Venta de Monjos before breaking clean. Bentinck left Catalonia ten days later and then sailed for Palermo on 22 September, where he re-assumed command of the Anglo-Sicilian force. He handed over command of the east coast expeditionary force to Clinton, the senior divisional commander – who, Wellington was to later say, 'Did nothing in particular – and did it pretty well'.

---

12 See Suchet, *Memoirs of the War with Spain*, vol. II, pp.328–334.

13 A damning indictment of Murray.

14 Suchet to Soult, despatch dated Villafranca 16 of September.

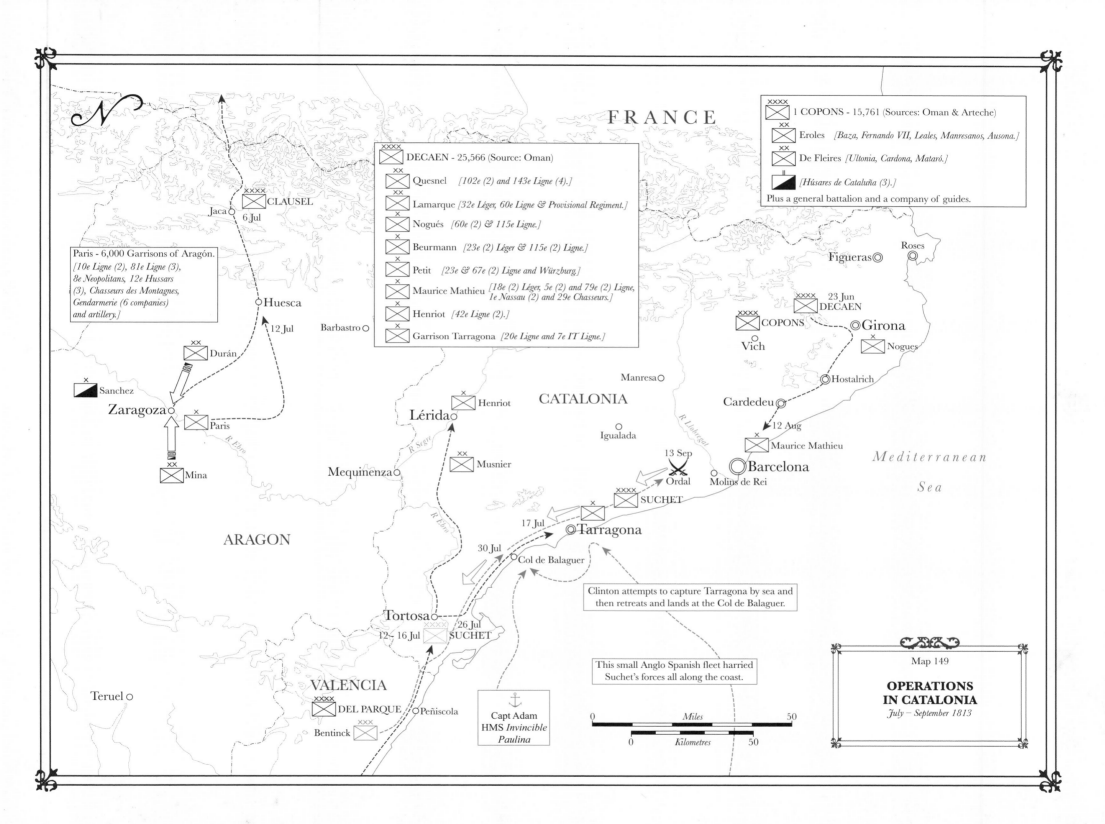

N

FRANCE

CATALONIA

ARAGON

VALENCIA

Mediterranean Sea

1 COPONS - 15,761 (Sources: Oman & Arteche)

Eroles   *[Baza, Fernando VII, Leales, Manresanos, Ausona.]*

De Fleires   *[Ultonia, Cardona, Mataró.]*

[Húsares de Cataluña (3).]

Plus a general battalion and a company of guides.

DECAEN - 25,566 (Source: Oman)

Quesnel   *[102e (2) and 143e Ligne (4).]*

Lamarque   *[32e Léger, 60e Ligne & Provisional Regiment.]*

Nogués   *[60e (2) & 115e Ligne.]*

Beurmann   *[23e (2) Léger & 115e (2) Ligne.]*

Petit   *[23e & 67e (2) Ligne and Würzburg.]*

Maurice Mathieu   *[18e (2) Léger, 5e (2) and 79e (2) Ligne, 1e Nassau (2) and 29e Chasseurs.]*

Henriot   *[42e Ligne (2).]*

Garrison Tarragona   *[20e Ligne and 7e IT Ligne.]*

Paris - 6,000 Garrisons of Aragón.
[10e Ligne (2), 81e Ligne (3), 8e Neopolitans, 12e Hussars (3), Chasseurs des Montagnes, Gendarmerie (6 companies) and artillery.]

CLAUSEL
Jaca   6 Jul

Huesca
12 Jul

Barbastro

Durán

Sanchez

Zaragoza
Paris

Mina

R Ebro

Mequinenza

Lérida

R Segre

Henriot

Musnier

Manresa

Igualada

R Llobregat

13 Sep
Ordal

SUCHET
17 Jul

Tarragona

30 Jul
Col de Balaguer

Tortosa
12 – 16 Jul   26 Jul
SUCHET

Roses

Figueras

23 Jun
DECAEN

COPONS
Vich

Girona

Nogues

Hostalrich

Cardedeu

12 Aug
Maurice Mathieu

Barcelona
Molins de Rei

Clinton attempts to capture Tarragona by sea and then retreats and lands at the Col de Balaguer.

This small Anglo Spanish fleet harried Suchet's forces all along the coast.

Teruel

DEL PARQUE
Peñiscola

Bentinck

Capt Adam
HMS *Invincible*
Paulina

0	Miles	50

0	Kilometres	50

Map 149

OPERATIONS IN CATALONIA
July – September 1813

Chapter 50 ⊶

THE FALL OF SAN SEBASTIÁN: AUGUST AND SEPTEMBER 1813

While Wellington waited for events in central Europe to conclude one way or the other, he turned his attention back to San Sebastián and Pamplona.[1] He considered the latter would fall without the need for a siege but San Sebastián was a different matter; the tenacity of its governor and the inadequate naval blockade required an active and measured response to bring General Rey and his charge to its knees.

Fletcher and Dickson agreed to repeat the mode of attack from the first siege, but to increase the number of guns in the breaching batteries. Wellington agreed to the proposal, despite strong objections from Lieutenant Colonel Burgoyne, the second engineer, who had a good case as Rey had erected a formidable second line of defences behind the old breaches and had also built new retrenchments in the hornwork and repaired the counterscarp damaged by the mine on 25 July. New barricades, covered walkways and new traverses complemented these other improvements and almost constant resupply by sea had replenished stores and ammunition. 'They still had sixty pieces in the batteries, four mortars and three howitzers: and their warehouses were quite well provided of provisions and supplies of all type.'[2] The sea also provided considerable replacement and augmentation to the besiegers, including the first company of sappers and miners who replaced the military artificers.[3]

With many new guns available a number of new batteries were opened (see Appendix 6) and the battering recommenced at 0900 hours on 26 August. Batteries 5 and 6 engaged the high curtain behind the hornwork, while batteries 13 and 14 continued against the area of the old breaches. In addition, two batteries equipped with howitzers and mortars also opened fire on the city; but the decision to use high-elevation projectiles into the city proved controversial as much of the town was set alight, causing considerable hardship to the civilian population. The battering progressed well, although that against the hornwork was less successful and Wellington suggested the construction of a battery closer to the walls. Battery 7 was complete on 28 August and opened the next morning; the effect was instant 'against the face of the demi-bastion and the high curtain, that the whole was made fully practicable, forming one great breach in conjunction with that effected by the batteries of the right attack'.[4] On the night of 26 August, the small rocky island of Santa Clara was captured and a gun and howitzer erected there a few days later (Battery 10).

By 29 August the French counter-battery fire had dwindled; Lieutenant Colonel Fraser (in Battery 5) noted that 'the enemy's fire is now comparatively trifling: it is hardly worth regarding'.[5] The next day, Wellington, Graham, Leith, Dickson and Fletcher came to the battery to reconnoitre the breach and to discuss the assault. Leith, who had returned to assume command of the 5th Division, was in a foul mood, Wellington had questioned the resolve of his men and had stated 'that (he) shall be obliged to disgrace the Fifth Division' by calling for 40 volunteers from each battalion of the 1st, 4th and Light divisions 'to show the Fifth Division how to mount a breach'.[6] When this ad hoc group assembled Leith refused to allow any of them to form the forlorn hope, and allocated only supporting roles. The attack was set for 1100 hours on 31 August, one hour before low tide. At 1055 hours, Lieutenant Maguire, with 20 men from the 4th Foot, emerged from the gap in the trenches and ran toward the gapping breach; Maguire was shot at the base of the opening but others 'reach the top of the breach. A mine springs, but behind them! All seems well. They reach the top and halt – if they are supported it will do.'[7] 'The artillery, from five days' continued firing, they knew the range precisely, and the practice against the high curtain was admirable; for although the shot passed immediately over the troops on the face and at the foot of the breach, and swept amongst the defenders of the curtain, it occasioned no casualties among the assailants.'[8] The defenders swarmed to their pre-prepared positions in great numbers, the breach was – once again – hard to climb and a 20ft drop greeted those who made it to the top. 'Graham continued to feed both attacks [map 150, points A and B] steadily from the trenches, sending first the reserve of Robinson's brigade, then Hay's brigade … and finally the volunteers… But for all their efforts these last could accomplish no more than their despised comrades; and, after over an hour of desperate endeavour and the fall of many hundreds of brave men, the capture of San Sebastián seemed to be as remote as ever.'[9]

'At a little after half past eleven, Bradford's Portuguese infantry were ordered forward on the right. The water was waist-deep and the guns of the Castle and St Elmo ploughed great gaps in the column as it advanced; but these brave men pressed on undismayed, and on reaching the shore parted right and left, the 13th to the northern breach and the 24th to the great breach between the towers.'[10] Reinforced, Robinson's men fought with renewed aggression, but as the tide was rising time was running out. Suddenly there was a huge explosion behind the main breach,

---

1 In fact Austria had ended the Armistice of Plässwitz on August 12th and declared war on France but the news did not reach London until 27 August and Wellington's headquarters until 3 September.

2 Belmas, *Journeaux des sieges*, vol. IV, p.630.

3 The new Sappers and Miners wore red jackets in place of the traditional blue.

4 Jones, *Journal of Sieges*, vol. II, p.71.

5 Fraser, *Letters of Colonel Sir Augustus Simon Fraser*, p.230.

6 Fortescue, *History of the British Army*, vol. IX, pp.353–354.

7 Fraser, *Letters of Colonel Sir Augustus Simon Fraser*, pp.234–235.

8 Jones, *Journal of Sieges*, vol. II, p.78. This is one of the first examples of close support artillery in what was later termed a 'creeping barrage'.

9 Fortescue, *History of the British Army*, vol. IX, p.355.

10 Ibid, p.356.

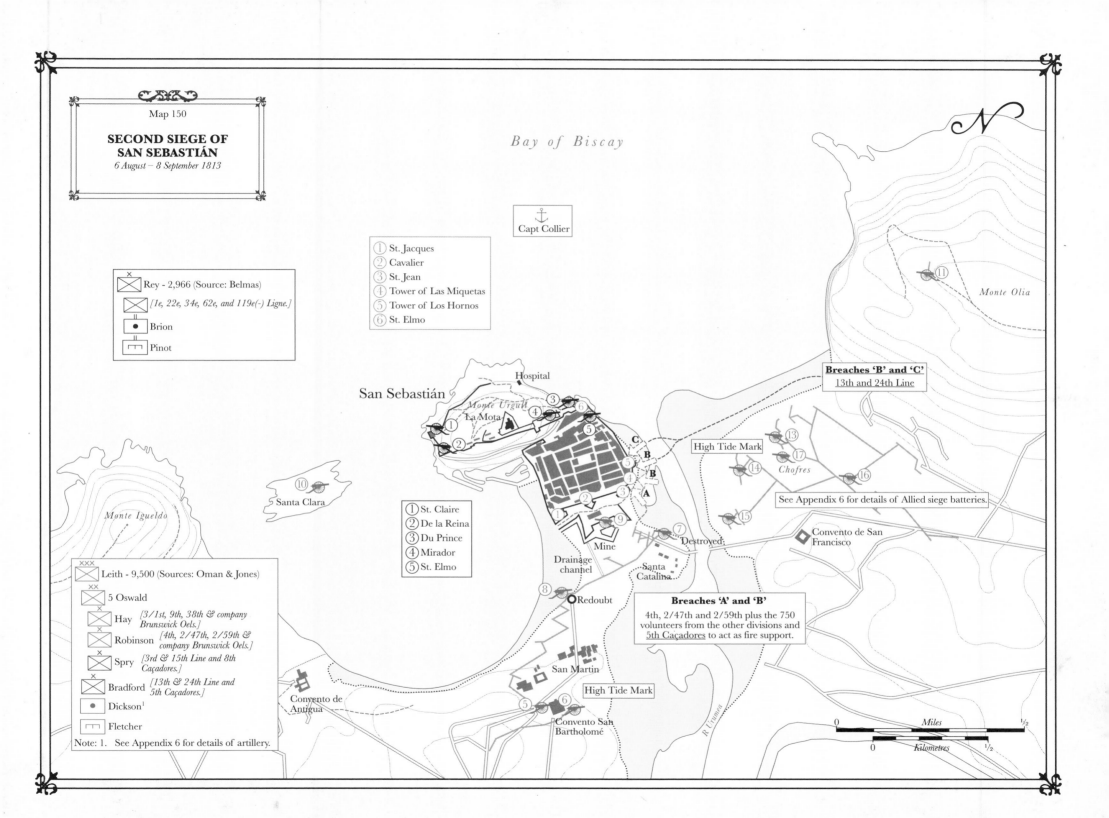

Map 150

**SECOND SIEGE OF
SAN SEBASTIÁN**

6 August – 8 September 1813

Bay of Biscay

⚓ Capt Collier

① St. Jacques
② Cavalier
③ St. Jean
④ Tower of Las Miquetas
⑤ Tower of Los Hornos
⑥ St. Elmo

✕ Rey - 2,966 (Source: Belmas)

[1e, 22e, 34e, 62e, and 119e(-) Ligne.]

● Brion

Pinot

Breaches 'B' and 'C'
13th and 24th Line

San Sebastián

Hospital

Monte Urgull
La Mota

High Tide Mark

⑪ *Monte Olia*

C
B
B
A

⑬
⑰
⑭ *Chofres*
⑯

See Appendix 6 for details of Allied siege batteries.

⑩ *Santa Clara*

Monte Igueldo

① St. Claire
② De la Reina
③ Du Prince
④ Mirador
⑤ St. Elmo

Mine

⑮

Convento de San Francisco

Destroyed

⑦

Drainage channel

Santa Catalina

Breaches 'A' and 'B'
4th, 2/47th and 2/59th plus the 750
volunteers from the other divisions and
5th Caçadores to act as fire support.

✕✕✕ Leith - 9,500 (Sources: Oman & Jones)

✕✕ 5 Oswald

✕ Hay [3/1st, 9th, 38th & company Brunswick Oels.]

✕ Robinson [4th, 2/47th, 2/59th & company Brunswick Oels.]

✕ Spry [3rd & 15th Line and 8th Caçadores.]

✕ Bradford [13th & 24th Line and 5th Caçadores.]

● Dickson[1]

Fletcher

Note: 1. See Appendix 6 for details of artillery.

⑧ Redoubt

San Martin

High Tide Mark

Convento de Antigua

⑤ ⑥ Convento San Bartholomé

R. Urumea

0   Miles   ½

0   Kilometres   ½

caused when a quantity of stockpiled powder ignited, and this misfortune for the defenders provided just the opportunity the Allies needed. It was about 1315 hours; the fight, which had been in the balance for some considerable time, now swung in the favour of the attackers, and by 1415 the artillery was ordered to cease fire and the battle was all but over. Rey escaped from the fortified town with about 1,000 men to the castle and its garrison, where they held out for many days before capitulating. The sack of the town which followed the initial success and the destruction caused by the fires provoked furious correspondence and accusation from Cádiz and the local Junta.[11] Allied losses were also considerable; Fletcher had been killed with a ball through the heart and Leith, Oswald and Robinson were all wounded.

At much the same time the forlorn hope had emerged from the trenches, the long-awaited attempt by Soult to succour San Sebastián was developing into three separate but significant engagements a few kilometres to the east. Aware of the progress the Allies were making, Soult had intended to commence his advance on 30 August, but he had not received all the equipment he required to bridge the Bidassoa. Frustration turned to good fortune the following morning when a heavy mist enabled the French to move up to and in some areas to cross the river without being detected. Lamartinière's Division were the first to cross and quickly establish a bridgehead; Maucune followed them and once across, the French sappers began to build the boat bridge to enable the guns, ammunition caissons and stores to follow. On the home bank Villatte[12] and Foy's brigades were in reserve, but as the mist lifted Soult grew impatient; even though he only had half his force across and a single field battery, he decided to press on and engage the Spanish position he could see to his front. Lamartinière was allocated the centre and Maucune the Spanish left; they began to climb the feature but the nature of the terrain prevented the French from holding a tight formation. Freire, conversely, was in complete control and waited until the French got near the Spanish lines before ordering a charge across the front. The startled French troops made little attempt to hold their ground; the impetus of the flight of the screen of tirailleurs was enough to break the resolve of the French columns into which they ran. Having driven the French back to the base of the hill, the Spanish troops then returned to their original posts.

This engagement had at least provided sufficient distraction to enable Villatte's Division to cross the fords near the broken bridge at Béhobie and by 1000 hours Soult elected to repeat the attack with all three divisions. The result was much of the same. 'So desperate, as Wellington says, was the attack on the centre and the right of the position of San Martial [sic] that the body of the French force arrived at the hermitage that crowns the height, it was evicted with great loss by the 1st brigade of our 5th Division that of Porlier's Division, helped at its head the

2nd Battalion Marina who was positioned on the Cerro de Porto where the 3rd Division had been positioned.'[13] The retreating French troops fell back to the river, many attempting to cross at the bridge of boats, which subsequently collapsed under the weight. Freire had requested the support of the 4th Division to assist his defence; it was refused, but Wellington sent word back to San Sebastián requesting Graham to release Bradford's Portuguese to move in support of Freire's army, unaware that a few moments earlier Bradford's men had begun their attack across the estuary of the Urumea and up to the battered walls of the sea port.

In the centre Clausel's attack was progressing with more conviction and he had three divisions across under cover of the morning mist; the fourth division, that of Maransin, he elected to keep on the home bank to maintain communications with D'Erlon to his left. As the mist lifted at about 0730 hours, Miller's Portuguese troops were engaged by both artillery and a line of tirailleurs from Taupin's Division, and he elected to pull back to join Inglis (who had been moved to support him) and establish a first defensive line (out of range of the French artillery) on the home bank. Taupin and D'Armagnac continued their advance and forced Miller and Inglis back to a second (higher) ridgeline, but by now Clausel was beginning to feel overextended. He could see Longa's Spaniards to his right, and there were signs of increasing activity on his left, as elements of the Light Division supported by a number of Echavarri's battalions began to tighten the noose. At much the same time he realized the presence of two hitherto unseen brigades (from the 4th Division) on his far right; a discovery which coincided with the arrival of a dispatch from Soult informing him that the San Marcial operation had failed and ordering him to pull back. At about 1500 hours, as the first French troops began to move back down the spurs, a torrential storm engulfed the area reducing visibility to a few feet, causing many soldiers to lose their footing and their way. Worse still, the river rose at alarming speed, rendering the fords inoperable, and with the bridge at Vera in Allied hands a series of desperate attacks were made to capture the crossing. In one such attempt General Van der Maessen was killed, but by the following dawn, the French had secured the bridge and escaped.[14]

D'Erlon's attack on the French left had misfired early in proceedings as the French commander found himself attacked by two Portuguese brigades and thought the force much larger than it was. He wrote to Soult asking for the return of Foy's Division, without which he couldn't answer for the safety of his army. In fact both Portuguese brigades forced Abbé's Division back from Urdax and became so embroiled in the contest that Dalhousie, when ordered by Wellington, was unable to extract his brigade and move it in support of Inglis. By the time D'Erlon realized his mistake, the battle for San Marcial had been lost.

11   See Toreno, *Guerra de la Independencia, La Derrota de Napoleon*, vol. III, pp.138–140, and Arteche, *Guerra de la Independencia*, vol. XIII, pp.251–258 for a Spanish perspective and Oman, *History of the Peninsular War*, vol. VII, pp.30–35 for some additional explanation and perhaps mitigation of sorts.

12   Villatte's Division also included a brigade with King Joseph's guards and the Rheinbund regiments.

13   Arteche, *Guerra de la Independencia*, vol. XIII, p.274.

14   Skerrett, who was commanding a brigade in the Light Division for the first time, did not realize the need to reinforce the small contingent holding the bridge and outhouses. Had he have done so he would have cut off up to three French divisions. See Oman, *History of the Peninsular War*, vol. VII, pp.54–56.

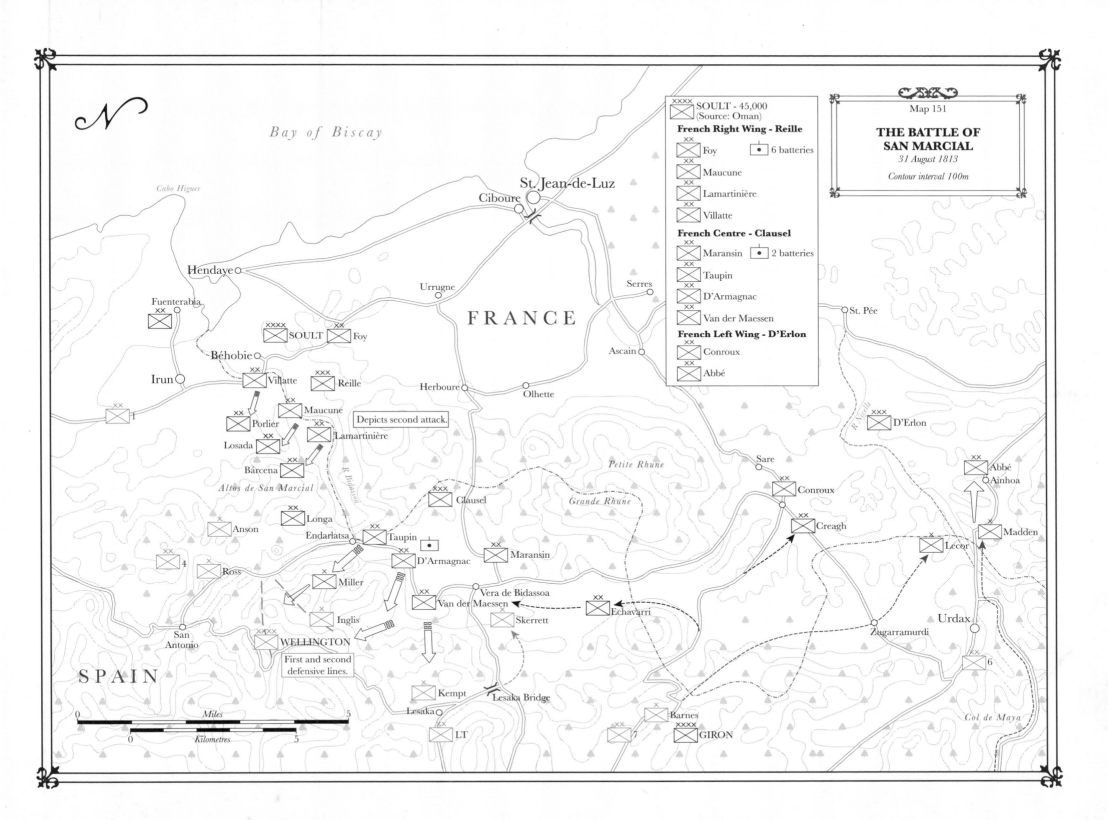

Bay of Biscay

Cabo Higuer

N

SOULT - 45,000
(Source: Oman)

French Right Wing - Reille
Foy • 6 batteries
Maucune
Lamartinière
Villatte

French Centre - Clausel
Maransin • 2 batteries
Taupin
D'Armagnac
Van der Maessen

French Left Wing - D'Erlon
Conroux
Abbé

Map 151

THE BATTLE OF SAN MARCIAL
31 August 1813

Contour interval 100m

St. Jean-de-Luz
Ciboure

Hendaye
Urrugne
Serres

FRANCE
St. Pée

Fuenterabia
SOULT Foy
Béhobie
Ascain
Irun
Villatte Reille
Herboure
Olhette
D'Erlon

Maucune
Porlier
Lamartinière
Depicts second attack.
Losada
Bárcena

Altos de San Marcial
Petite Rhune
Sare
Abbé
Ainhoa
Clausel
Grande Rhune
Conroux
Anson
Longa
Creagh
Endarlatsa Taupin
Maransin
Madden
4 Ross
Miller D'Armagnac
Lecor
San Antonio
Inglis
Vera de Bidassoa
Van der Maessen Echavarri
Urdax
WELLINGTON
Skerrett
Zugarramurdi
First and second defensive lines.
6

SPAIN
Kempt
Lesaka Bridge
Lesaka
Col de Maya
LT 7
Barnes
GIRON

Miles 0 ... 5
Kilometres 0 ... 5

Chapter 51 ⊷⟊⟶

THE ALLIES ENTER FRANCE: OCTOBER 1813

The battles fought at San Marcial and Vera were the last the *Grande Armée* was to fight in Spain. Soult withdrew in expectation of an Allied follow-up and, when this did not materialize, he set about establishing a defensive line from the sea to the upper Nive through a series of redoubts. He was greatly relieved to receive notification that Clausel's three divisions had escaped, but disconsolate to hear that General Rey had lost the first stage of the defence of San Sebastián and was deeply frustrated at being powerless to provide succour or an effective distraction. During the first few days of September the Allies continued to bombard Rey and the remnants of his force holed up in the Monte Urgall. On 8 September, 61 guns and mortars opened as the preliminary to an assault; after two hours the gallant French defenders raised the white flag, bringing to an end another bloody but courageous chapter in the history of siege warfare in the Peninsula.

News from central Europe was confusing; the Austrian declaration of war on France was received at Wellington's headquarters on 3 September, but within days reports arrived of the heavy defeat of the Austrian army at Dresden. A few days later new information was arriving outlining French setbacks at Katsbach and Kulm. Eventually Wellington bowed to public pressure and agreed to commence the invasion of France, amidst strong reports that the (northern) Allies were preparing another concentration against Napoleon. 'However, I shall put myself in a situation to menace a serious attack, and to make one immediately, if I should see a fair opportunity, or if I should hear that the allies [in central Europe] have been really successful, or when Pamplona should be in our possession.'[1] It was not an easy decision, and neither was the option he faced regarding the inclusion of the Spanish element of his force. Wellington was reluctant to take any Spanish troops with him, for although they had demonstrated ability and resolve at San Marcial, he knew they were poised to exact revenge on the civil population once across the border. The Spanish military chest was empty, their soldiers had not been paid for some months and lacked food and basic equipment, but numerically, Wellington simply could not afford to dispense with their services. Numerous other issues were also concerning him: the Allied army in general lacked sufficient military transport, support from the Admiralty was affected by the war with America, the siege at Pamplona still lay unresolved and news from the east coast was far from conclusive.

Soult had deployed his force from St Jean-Pied-de-Port to the coast. Foy and Paris were positioned as the left flanking guard at St Jean-Pied-de-Port itself, then moving west: D'Erlon with Abbé, D'Armagnac and Daricau (vice Van der Maessen), from Mondarrain to Ainhoe; followed by Clausel with Maransin, Conroux and Taupin from the river Nivelle to the Rhune (inclusive); and finally Reille, who was covering the estuary of the Bidassoa with Maucune and Boyer (vice Lamartinière). This latter division was to be kept behind that of Maucune and held centrally in reserve along with Villatte's Division. The dispositions of the French troops clearly indicated that Soult considered the central and eastern sectors to be the most likely routes of an Allied advance. Wellington's plan was to maximise both surprise and deception. Activity was organized at Roncesvalles to foster the illusion, but in fact Hill's divisions at Roncesvalles (2nd Division) and at Maya (6th Division), supported by Hamilton's Portuguese Division,[2] were to stand firm; the majority of the forces to their rear were to move west. Hill was to hold the attention of the forces to his front but to stop short of any large-scale engagement. The advance began in this sector at 0700 hours on 7 October with the 6th Division driving out the French piquet from the foundry at Urdax, and then engaging in vociferous skirmishes in front of D'Erlon's divisions.

In the central sector, Giron's two divisions plus the Light Division and Longa's Cantabrian Division began their attack soon after Hill. Giron deployed one brigade to cover their right flank from possible counter-attack, and Wellington provided considerable support to this area in the shape of the 4th, the 7th and the 3rd divisions. Giron advanced with a broad line of skirmishers which quickly met opposition from the 12e Léger and 32e Ligne of Conroux's Division, who were holding the ridge up to the Grande Rhune; the contest continued for many hours before the Spanish finally reached the crest. To their left, Kempt, who was commanding the right-hand brigade (95th, 43rd and 17th Portuguese) of the Light Division, was having similar success, and at about the same time as Giron's men scaled the feature, his right-hand battalion reached the top but found the way barred by the presence of two battalions of Clausel's reserve. The other brigade, from the Light Division, was under the command of Colborne (2/95th, 52nd and 1st and 3rd Caçadores) and had a more formidable task in assaulting the Bayonnette Ridge and the Fort St Benôit. Between these two brigades Longa's Spaniards formed the centre.

Kempt's Brigade reached their summit first but Colborne's men had the harder task, having to take the St Benôit redoubt before progressing. When they reached their respective summits each brigade was able to see the other, and they made moves to link up. The 9e Léger, who had been holding Longa's men, suddenly realized that if the two light brigades were able to join forces that they would be isolated and cut off. The French rushed through the remaining gap to their rear; many were captured, but in the confusion many of the other French troops in the area made good their escape. With this rearward movement, Taupin's Division had all but collapsed, enabling the Allies to establish a firm hold on the ridges leading to the Grande Rhune, but their attempts to capture the main feature were thwarted by Clausel who reorganized his force to counter the threat.

At the western end of the line a more significant action was ongoing. Maucune's solitary force was covering the area from Biriatou to the coast; it was the weakest division in Soult's army (at only 4,000 men) and its weaker brigade, belonging to Pinoteau, was the furthest west; although

---

1 Wellington, *Dispatches*, to Bathurst, 19 September 1813, Vol. XI, p.124.

2 Hamilton had just returned to take command of Silveira's two brigades – of Da Costa and A. Campbell. Silveira was on sick leave.

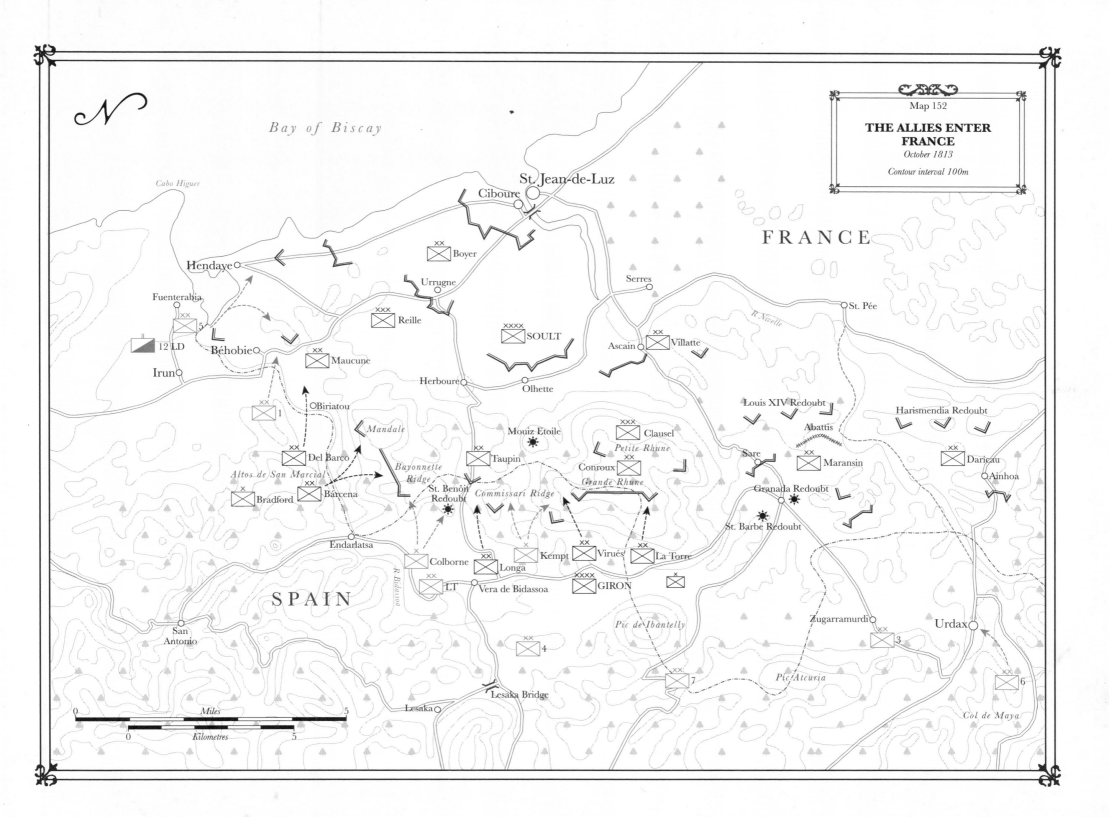

N

Bay of Biscay

FRANCE

St. Jean-de-Luz

Ciboure

Hendaye

Cabo Higuer

Fuenterabia

5

12 LD

Béhobie

Irun

Boyer

Urrugne

Serres

St. Pée

R. Nivelle

Reille

Ascain

Villatte

SOULT

Maucune

Herboure

Olhette

Biriatou

1

Mandale

Louis XIV Redoubt

Harismendia Redoubt

Mouiz Etoile

Clausel

Petite Rhune

Abattis

Del Barco

Bayonnette Ridge

Taupin

Conroux

Sare

Maransin

Daricau

Altos de San Marcial

Bárcena

St. Benôit Redoubt

Commissari Ridge

Grande Rhune

Granada Redoubt

Ainhoa

Bradford

Endarlatsa

Colborne

Longa

Kempt

Virués

La Torre

St. Barbe Redoubt

R. Bidassoa

LT

Vera de Bidassoa

GIRON

SPAIN

San Antonio

Pic de Ibantelly

Zugarramurdi

Urdax

3

4

7

Pic Atcuria

6

Lesaka Bridge

Lesaka

Col de Maya

0 — *Miles* — 5

0 — *Kilometres* — 5

Map 152

THE ALLIES ENTER FRANCE
October 1813

Contour interval 100m

it had been enhanced by two battalions from Boyer's Division stationed 8km to the rear near Urrugne. At daybreak, against Pinoteau's meagre force, Wellington launched 24,000 men. General Hay had assumed command of the 5th Division (vice Leith and Oswald both wounded at San Sebastián) and in the early hours of 7 October, under cover of a violent thunderstorm, he moved his three brigades down to the water's edge where they sought cover in the ditches and the dyke wall. To their right the 1st Division was moving down the road towards the village of Irun. 'The columns which moved by the direct road to Irun (and it was not possible to advance by another) completely filled it. The night was at first stormy; thunder and lightning, and some rain. It afterwards was so sultry as to be the subject of everyone's remark; the little wind there was was like the breath of an oven.'[3] They too sought cover behind a long, low ridge at the base of the heights of San Marcial. Further upstream, General Freire was slowly making his way down from the heights to the water's edge with two of his divisions; the 3rd and 4th commanded by Del Barco and Bárcena[4] and supported by the guns of Bull's Troop and Mitchell's Company.

The 5th Division were to move first, serving as the trigger for the 1st Division and then the Spanish. General Hay had been given a start time of 0715 hours and at the allotted time he surveyed the water; considering it still on the ebb, he decided to delay a few minutes. At 0725 hours the leading elements of the three brigades of the 5th Division began to cross the by now exposed sand and mud flats to their front, supported by the fire of the heavier batteries on the San Marcial. A few moments later the 1st Division made a dash across their (shorter) stretch of the estuary and to their right the Spanish poured down the hillsides towards their six allotted fords. In places the water was deeper than expected and one young officer watching from the home bank noted that many of the soldiers had to 'hold their firelocks and cartouche-boxes over the heads to keep them dry'.[5] Dawn was just breaking and, in the half-light, the sentries from the 3e Ligne, 15e Ligne and 10e Léger were stunned by this incredulous scene that began unveiling to their front. The light companies from the 5th Division reached the far bank before a shot was fired; the German Legion and Guards were less fortunate but the strength of the French piquets was woefully inadequate and within minutes the 1st Division was across in force having overwhelmed the defenders. The redoubt and two French battalions held up the Spanish left division initially but the passage to their right met less resistance, and once across, these troops quickly moved behind the French defenders, neutralizing their resistance and enabling the second division to cross.

The 5th Division pushed on to take the position at the Café Républicain, which was manned by a French battery and a battalion from the 17e Léger. They then closed on the main French position, at the Croix des Bouquets, which was already being attacked by elements of the 1st Division who had swung right after capturing the village of Béhobie. The second battalion of the 17e Léger, who had been stationed there, fled to the redoubt on the Louis XIV hill, but the 1st and Spanish divisions soon surrounded the position from the south. Sharp fighting continued at the Croix des Bouquets; Reille was up in person trying to rally his men in the hope that they could hold out until Boyer's Division arrived from Urrgane. His efforts were in vain, as at 0900 hours the position was taken. In just over one and a half hours the Allies were in control of the heights on the north of the Bidassoa. The fight to the east continued for some time, but with the Allies firmly established in the west in large numbers, the outcome was never in doubt.

On 8 October Freire pushed forward on an axis west of the Grande Rhune while the 6th and 7th divisions did likewise to the east. Clausel was well aware that his position was hopeless and he withdrew from the redoubts at Sare, and the two commanders within the redoubts on the Rhune followed suit. Soult was quick to apportion blame on everyone except himself for what was clearly an operational error of his own design. The crossing was over and the Allies were in France; their losses were small but the psychological advantage was beyond measure. However, some of that operational advantage was unquestionably lost when Wellington decided not to press on with the offensive – a decision that was greeted with surprise by the French and no little criticism from (less informed) Allied quarters. Wellington was right to delay; he was still awaiting news of the outcome of the impending and pivotal battle at Leipzig, and of the siege at Pamplona that was close to conclusion. Within Pamplona (see map 145) the situation had been growing steadily worse and, by the end of September, Cassan's troops were on half-rations; they soon began to slaughter the horses of the Legion of Gendarmerie and then, when they had been consumed, their attention turned to dogs, cats and rats. Scurvy broke out within the ranks and numbers of effective soldiers dwindled dramatically, which eventually forced Cassan to seek terms from Carlos de España. His initial requests were absurd and supported by Wellington; de España dismissed them out of hand, and on 1 November, after a series of heated exchanges, Cassan finally vacated the city.

---

3   Fraser, *Letters of Colonel Sir Augustus Simon Fraser*, pp.289–290.

4   Del Barco replaced Losada who had been injured during the battle of San Marcial.

5   Gleig, *The Subaltern*, p.51.

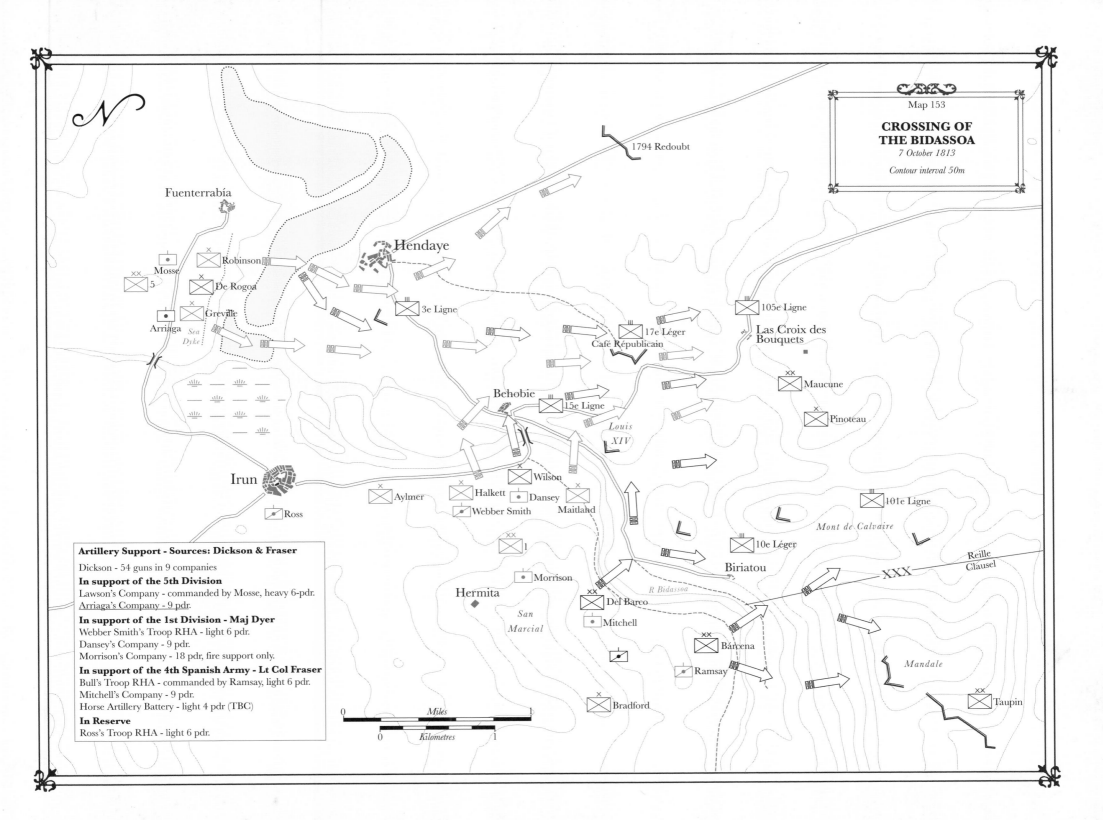

N

Map 153

CROSSING OF THE BIDASSOA

7 October 1813

Contour interval 50m

1794 Redoubt

Fuenterrabía

Robinson

Mosse

De Rogoa

Greville

Arriaga

Sea Dyke

Hendaye

3e Ligne

17e Léger

Café Républicain

105e Ligne

Las Croix des Bouquets

Maucune

Pinoteau

Behobie

15e Ligne

Louis XIV

Irun

Wilson

Aylmer   Halkett

Dansey

Webber Smith

Maitland

101e Ligne

1

10e Léger

Mont de Calvaire

Biriatou

Reille

Clausel

XXX

Morrison

Hermita

San Marcial

R Bidassoa

Del Barco

Mitchell

Bárcena

Ramsay

Mandale

Taupin

Bradford

Artillery Support - Sources: Dickson & Fraser

Dickson - 54 guns in 9 companies

In support of the 5th Division
Lawson's Company - commanded by Mosse, heavy 6-pdr.
Arriaga's Company - 9 pdr.

In support of the 1st Division - Maj Dyer
Webber Smith's Troop RHA - light 6 pdr.
Dansey's Company - 9 pdr.
Morrison's Company - 18 pdr, fire support only.

In support of the 4th Spanish Army - Lt Col Fraser
Bull's Troop RHA - commanded by Ramsay, light 6 pdr.
Mitchell's Company - 9 pdr.
Horse Artillery Battery - light 4 pdr (TBC)

In Reserve
Ross's Troop RHA - light 6 pdr.

0   *Miles*   1

0   *Kilometres*   1

Chapter 52 ❦

TO THE GATES OF BAYONNE:
OCTOBER TO DECEMBER 1813

Soult was determined to hold his second defensive line along the course of the Nivelle, and wasted little time in channelling all available effort into the enhancement of the natural defences and the construction of numerous redoubts and flanking fortifications. He also made plans for a third defensive line, along the Nive and in front of Bayonne, just in case. Determined not to be outwitted a second time on his seaward flank, he placed 11,000 men from the divisions of Boyer and Leval[1] in the works in front of Ciboure, known as the Bordagain lines. Clausel retained responsibility for the central sector and D'Erlon the French left, which included Foy's Division deployed at Bidarray to cover any Allied designs on their right flank. Soult had 62,000 men (excluding Foy) to execute his defensive plan. Facing him were 82,000 men: 38,000 British, 22,000 Spanish and the same number of Portuguese. Wellington organized his force into three columns: Hill had the interior, Beresford the centre and Lieutenant General Sir John Hope,[2] who had just arrived, assumed responsibility for the coastal column. A number of changes had also been made at divisional level; perhaps the most notable was that of Lecor (a Portuguese officer without a British commission) who was given command of the 7th Division vice Dalhousie who had gone back to England.

Following the surrender at Pamplona, de España was tasked to move with all haste to Roncesvalles where he was to release Hill's four divisions and then remain in support of Mina covering the pass. Thereafter Hill was to move with similar haste west and take up his position against D'Erlon; unfortunately the weather had closed in and this manoeuvring was to take longer than scheduled. 'I have the pleasure to inform you that Pamplona surrendered yesterday, the garrison being prisoners of war. Hill, however, being up to his knees in snow, it is absolutely necessary to defer our movement for a day or two; and I beg that every precaution be taken to prevent communication to the enemy.'[3] Hill was finally in place early on 9 November and the three columns commenced their respective attacks the following day.

The attack by Hope's column on the far left by the coast was to be a false attack designed to occupy the defenders without pressing home any serious assault. In the centre, the Light Division had to secure the redoubts on the Petite Rhune in the first phase. Having moved into position in the dark, Colborne's Brigade was to storm the Mouiz Etoile while Kempt tackled the series of redoubts on the Petite Rhune. The success of this initial operation was critical. 'The day broke with great splendour, and as the first ray of light played on the summit of the lofty Atchubia the signal guns were fired in rapid succession from its summit. The soldiers instantly leapt up, and the French beheld with astonishment several columns rushing forward from the flank of the Great Rhune.'[4] To their right four Allied divisions (the two Spanish, the 4th and 7th) were advancing against a mere two French brigades, which constituted the balance of Maransin's Division (the third brigade was that engaged by the Light Division). Heavily outnumbered, the French were quickly overwhelmed; the outlying redoubts of St Barbe and Granada were occupied and Clausel's first line collapsed, accelerated in its demise by the ingress of some of the 3rd Division troops on the French left flank. The 3rd Division were locked in a hard struggle against Conroux's Division; they had come up against the line of *abattis*, which took three attempts to breach, before elements of the division (94th) pressed on to Amotz and deployed on the ground west of the bridge. Conroux was completely immersed in this contest and unable to provide any reinforcement to Maransin. The Allies now prepared to attack Clausel's second line, held by Taupin's Division. The attack was delivered at 1000 hours and was supported some time later by elements of the Light Division who had completed their initial mission in some style. It was a fierce contest which relied on each French commander holding his nerve, for should one redoubt give way, defence of those on either flank would be untenable. Clausel was desperate for support from the army reserves, but alas there was no sign of Villatte's reserve. The St Ignace Redoubt was the first to fall and, despite orders to Taupin to recapture the structure, the collapse of Clausel's second line was now inevitable. By 1400 hours the Allies had driven the French north of the river across the central frontage.

The fight on the Allied right started much later, as Hill's forces had a much longer march to their start point. The 6th Division and Hamilton's Portuguese were tasked with capturing the bridge at Amotz, which necessitated crossing the Nivelle (to the south) and then capturing the Harismendia Redoubt by way of a preliminary operation. It was to be easier than anticipated, for when the divisions had forded the river and began their advance on the redoubts, the defenders, demoralized by the sight of the French collapse to their right, fell back and abandoned the works. Clinton and Hamilton's men rushed forward to secure the fortifications before reorganizing for the assault on the bridge. To their right, Stewart's Division had been embroiled in a hard fight for the redoubt in front of Ainhoa. For some time success looked doubtful but suddenly the defenders withdrew, on Abbé's order, when the divisional commander realized that his colleague had lost his nerve and yielded the forts and ground to the rear right, thereby rendering any long-term defence of the forward structures impossible. On the far right Morillo's Division was up providing flank protection, but fortunately for this Spanish force, Foy had chosen to ignore D'Erlon's orders to move one of his brigades to a position immediately behind Abbé and the Spanish were not engaged.[5] As news

---

1 Leval was commanding Maucune's old division. Maucune was recalled to Paris in disgrace following his performance in October.

2 Not to be confused with Major General John Hope who had commanded the 7th Division.

3 Wellington to Hope, Vera, 1 November 1813.

4 Napier, *History of the War in the Peninsula*, vol. VI, p.338. It is worth reading this passage in full as Napier was commanding the 43rd that day against the forts of the Petite Rhune.

5 Foy chose to ignore the order, electing instead to move against Andrade's Brigade from Mina's Division on the *Chemin des Anglais*. His insubordination was lucky to escape Soult's wrath and official justice.

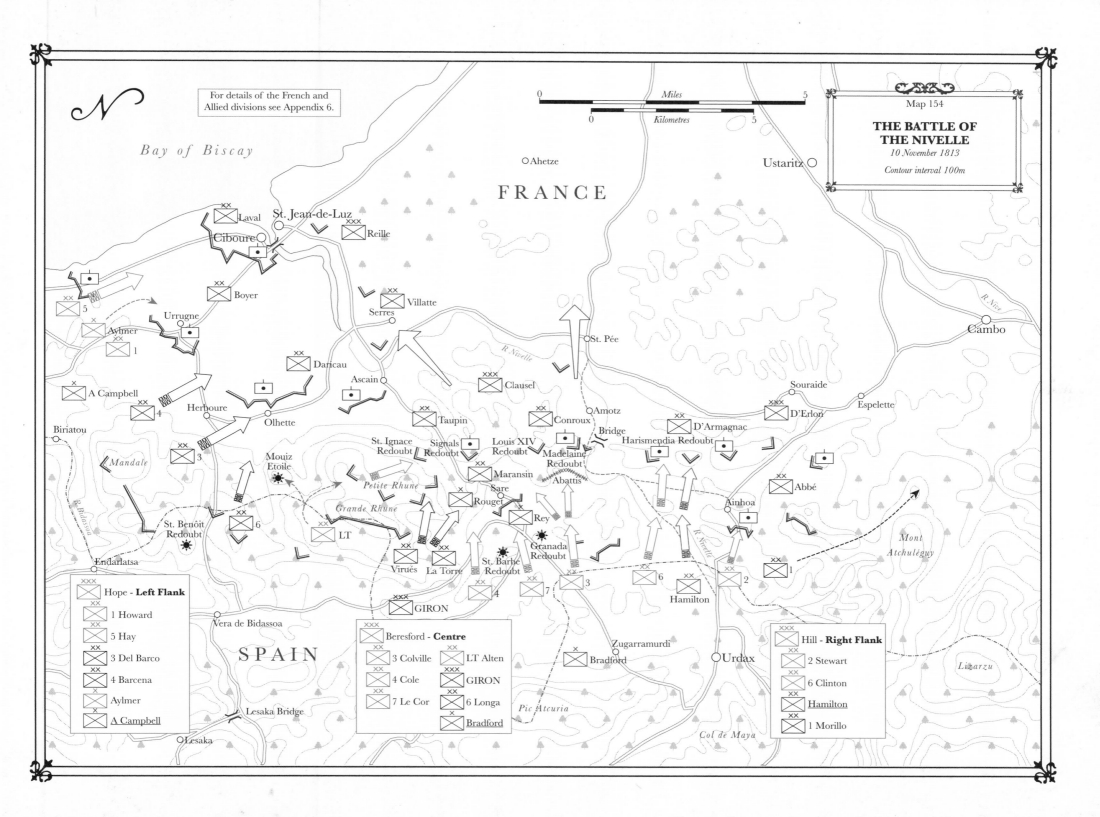

N

Bay of Biscay

For details of the French and
Allied divisions see Appendix 6.

0 — Miles — 5

0 — Kilometres — 5

Map 154

**THE BATTLE OF
THE NIVELLE**
10 November 1813

Contour interval 100m

FRANCE

Ahetze

Ustaritz

Laval
St. Jean-de-Luz
Reille

Ciboure

Boyer

R. Nive

Urrugne

Villatte

Serres

5

Aylmer

1

St. Pée

Cambo

A Campbell

4

Dancau

Souraide

Herboure

Ascain

Clausel

D'Armagnac

D'Erlon

Espelette

Olhette

Taupin

Conroux

Amotz

Bridge

Mouiz
Etoile

St. Ignace
Redoubt

Signals
Redoubt

Louis XIV
Redoubt

Madelaine
Redoubt

Harismendia Redoubt

Biriatou

Mandale

3

Petite Rhune

Maransin

Abattis

Abbé

St. Benôit
Redoubt

Grande Rhune

LT

6

Sare
Rouget

Rey

Ainhoa

Mont
Atchuléguy

R. Bidassoa

Endarlatsa

Virués

La Torre

St. Barbe
Redoubt

Granada
Redoubt

Hamilton

1

2

Vera de Bidassoa

4

7

3

6

SPAIN

GIRON

Lizarzu

Zugarramurdi

Bradford

Urdax

Lesaka Bridge

Pic Atcuria

Col de Maya

Lesaka

	Hope - **Left Flank**
	1 Howard
	5 Hay
	3 Del Barco
	4 Barcena
	Aylmer
	A Campbell

	Beresford - **Centre**	
	3 Colville	LT Alten
	4 Cole	GIRON
	7 Le Cor	6 Longa
		Bradford

	Hill - **Right Flank**
	2 Stewart
	6 Clinton
	Hamilton
	1 Morillo

emerged that the Allies had captured the bridge at Amotz (achieved by the 3rd Division) and that troops were already pouring across the structure, D'Erlon ordered a withdrawal from the Harismendia Redoubt and the battle for the Nivelle was all but over.

By dawn on 11 November, Soult's army was dispersed and demoralized; to make matters worse, news had also arrived of the disaster at Leipzig. Soult's army lay tantalisingly defenceless to the Allied front and yet Wellington, once again, practised caution. 'We have today been in expectation of an order to advance, but as yet it has not arrived. From what I can discover, it is not likely that we shall carry our advance much further into France; but opinion seems divided whether the Nive or the Ardour will be the line we shall take up, and I think there is no doubt that we can do which we please, for the spirit of the French army is too low to give us hope of its committing itself by risking a general action.'[6] Somewhat puzzled, but thankful for the respite, Soult pulled his entire army back to a third defensive line in front of Bayonne. Wellington had also received oddments of information regarding Leipzig but resolved to wait for more definitive news before continuing. While Wellington pondered his next move, he took the decision to send home 20,000 of the Spanish troops who were in a dreadful state, lacking supplies and equipment and, in some units displaying intolerable levels of indiscipline. Wellington had long voiced concern about the dangers of Spanish retribution on the French populace, and this was certainly a factor, but in truth relations between Spain and Britain were anyway strained to breaking point.[7] With scant advice from London, Wellington made this difficult military decision with a firm eye to the political future.

Wellington was in no hurry to commence large-scale operations but was clear in his mind of the need to improve the defensive disposition of his force in front of Bayonne. By now force levels were more or less equal, with Wellington having around 65,000 infantry and gunners against Soult's deployable force of about 57,000.[8] The reorganization of the Allied lines started on 9 December, with Hill crossing the three fords near Cambo with some difficulty; Foy's Division gave way instantly and Stewart and Lecor moved north behind Vivian's light cavalry and in Foy's wake. Morillo was pushed well out to the east to provide flank protection. At Ustaritz, the 6th Division had crossed the river and driven in D'Armagnac's piquets with similar ease. The 3rd Division followed them to the riverbank and then provided protection to the team earmarked to repair the broken bridge (first bridge, map 155). D'Armagnac and Daricau pulled back to Villafranque and were joined by Foy and Abbé, and the four divisions established an initial line of defence across the road behind Villafranque. Hill acknowledged the strength of the position and declined to attack, electing instead to clear the village of Villafranque, which was still being held by two of D'Armagnac's battalions. This was achieved

by nightfall. On the Allied left, Hope advanced on a wide frontage, with the 5th Division left and the 1st Division astride the road; to their right were the 4th and Light divisions, advancing at much the same pace in order to provide flank protection and to provide a contiguous line linking the Allied left and the other half of Beresford's force. The French forces gave way and after a brief skirmish at Anglet, they pulled back to the camp of Beyris.[9]

As ordered, Hope made no attempt to follow up, but that night he outlandishly withdrew his entire force, less the two Portuguese brigades, all the way back to their original cantonments near St Jean-de-Luz. Soult was bewildered by the Allied decision to gain ground then equally quickly give it up again. With only the Portuguese brigades left dangerously unsupported and not suspecting a ruse, he resolved to attack them and the Light Division the next morning. D'Erlon's four divisions were brought west of the Nive to support the attack against the Light Division in the position at Arcangues. Despite the Allied dispositions it was an ambitious plan, as D'Erlon's men had been fighting all day and were soaked to the skin, and to march them 10km and then throw them into a fight was asking a great deal. At Arcangues, Alten had held the Light Division at readiness along the ridge on either side of the road, but he was not expecting trouble and had just given the order to withdraw the forward piquet line soon after first light. Two of Clausel's divisions (Maransin and Taupin) led the attack in this quarter, making a half-hearted attempt to clear the ridge and when this failed, two artillery batteries were brought forward and an inconclusive standoff ensued. However, when elements of the 7th Division began to appear along the main road, Clausel felt compelled to withdraw Daricau's Division to support that of Abbé who was covering the road and the left flank; but by early afternoon, when Clausel caught sight of the 3rd and 6th divisions re-crossing the Nive to add their weight, he knew his position was untenable and withdrew. To their right, what had started as a subsidiary attack by Leval and Boyer was now transformed into the main effort. The initial French attacks had considerable success against the piquets from the two Portuguese brigades and drove them back against their main defensive positions around the village of Barrouillet; the Portuguese were quickly supported by one of the brigades from the 5th Division.[10] Boyer then tried to turn the position on the Allied right and the fighting spilled into the wooded area, creating much confusion. Foy's Division, which was en route to assist Clausel, was redirected by Soult to Reille and immediately thrown into the fray to support the right turning manoeuvre. The balance of the 5th Division arrived, but the additional two brigades were not enough to stem the tide and the battle hung in the balance for a considerable time. However, when the 1st Division began to appear, French resolve wavered; Lord Aylmer's Brigade drove in Foy's exposed southern flank and then pressed them back to the wood line, compelling Reille to deploy Villatte to enable his other three divisions to break clean and pull back. The Allied line was intact but it could so easily have been lost; Hope had displayed considerably more courage than common sense.

---

6   Ross, *Memoir*, letter dated 12 November 1813, in camp in front of St. Pée.

7   See Arteche, *Guerra de la Independencia*, vol. XIV, pp.61–63 and Toreno, *Guerra de la Independencia, La Derrota de Napoleon*, vol. III, pp.189–194.

8   Wellington's figures include about 36,000 British, 23,000 Portuguese and 4,500 Spanish for he had kept Morillo's Division. The figure does not include the cavalry. Soult's figure included his nine divisions (Taupin's Division had been disbanded but Villatte's Reserve is included) but did not include his cavalry at 8,000 or the large garrison in Bayonne, at nearly 9,000. See Appendix 6.

9   This was a series of fortifications, which the French had been constructing in front of Bayonne for some months (since Vitoria) in anticipation of an Allied attack on France.

10   Robinson's Brigade. The other two brigades were still some kilometres to the rear.

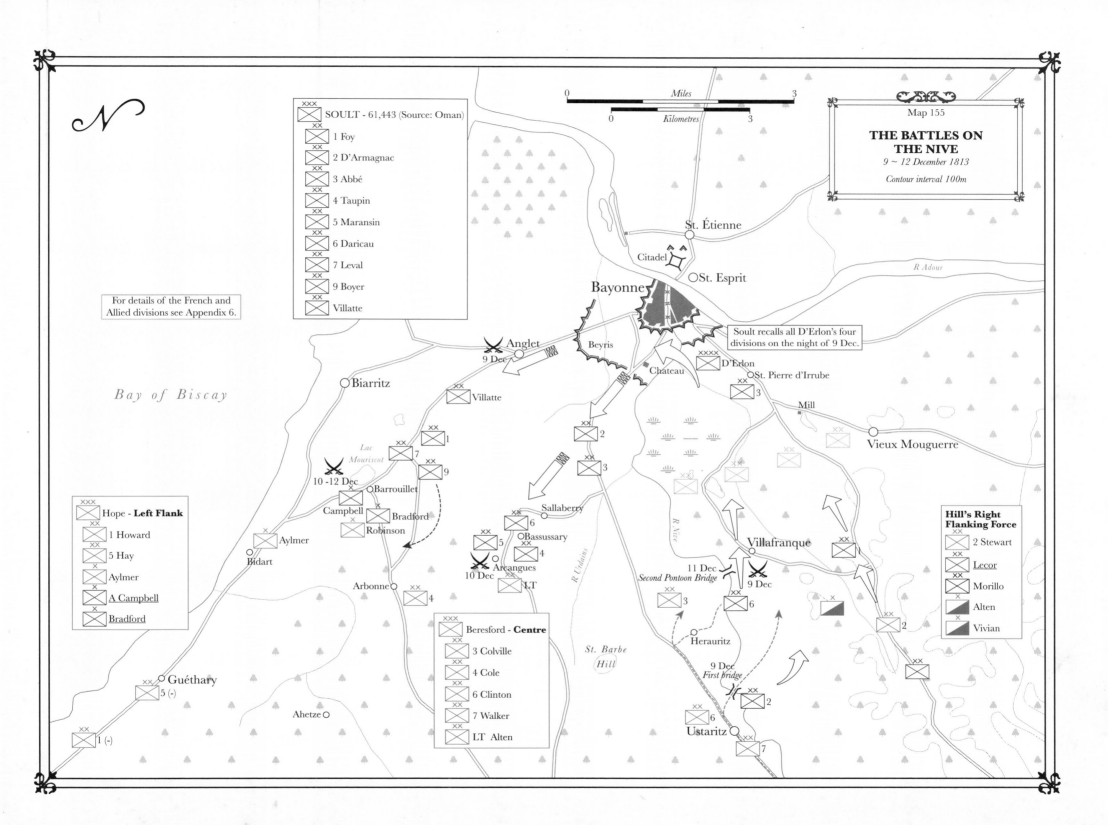

N

Map 155

**THE BATTLES ON
THE NIVE**

9 ~ 12 December 1813

Contour interval 100m

0   Miles   3

0   Kilometres   3

SOULT - 61,443 (Source: Oman)

1 Foy
2 D'Armagnac
3 Abbé
4 Taupin
5 Maransin
6 Daricau
7 Leval
9 Boyer
Villatte

For details of the French and
Allied divisions see Appendix 6.

St. Étienne

Citadel

St. Esprit

R Adour

Bayonne

Beyris

Anglet
9 Dec

Soult recalls all D'Erlon's four
divisions on the night of 9 Dec.

D'Erlon

Chateau

St. Pierre d'Irrube

3

Mill

Bay of Biscay

Biarritz

Villatte

2

Vieux Mouguerre

*Lac
Mouriscot*

1

7

3

10 -12 Dec

9

Barrouillet

Sallaberry

Campbell

Bradford

Robinson

6

Bassussary

5

4

R Nive

R Urdains

Villafranque

1

Hope - Left Flank

1 Howard
5 Hay
Aylmer
A Campbell
Bradford

Aylmer

Bidart

Arcangues
10 Dec

LT

4

Arbonne

11 Dec
Second Pontoon Bridge

9 Dec

**Hill's Right
Flanking Force**

2 Stewart
Lecor
Morillo
Alten
Vivian

3

6

2

Herauritz

*St. Barbe
Hill*

Beresford - Centre

3 Colville
4 Cole
6 Clinton
7 Walker
LT Alten

9 Dec
First bridge

2

Guéthary

5 (-)

Ahetze

6

2

Ustaritz

7

1 (-)

Over the next two days both commanders waited for the other to take the offensive. Hill was still unsupported on the east bank of the Nive and it was here that Wellington anticipated Soult would strike; accordingly he ordered Beresford to build a second bridge (see map 155) opposite Villefranque to facilitate rapid reinforcement, or evacuation, in either direction. The 6th and 7th divisions were warned off using this crossing by order. As it turned out Wellington guessed correctly, but in the intervening two days both sides continued low-level engagements around Barrouillet, which took their toll on the 5th Division, who had to be replaced by the 1st in the front line, and delayed Soult's plans for offensive operations on the east bank. Indeed, such was the intensity of some of the engagements that Wellington pondered the possibility that Soult would once again place his main effort on the west bank and he moved the 7th Division back across the river to be better positioned to counter such an eventuality.

On 12 December, as fighting dwindled at Barrouillet, Wellington was confident that he could provide timely reinforcement to the left bank, but that confidence was tested later in the day when he received reports that heavy rains in the Pyrenees had swollen the Nive and broken the second bridge. Strenuous attempts were made to repair the structure and contingency orders were disseminated for the force to cross at Ustaritz. Early the next day, reports from the Buffs' outposts confirmed that the French eastward movement had taken place during the night and that a large number were now back on the east bank and forming up for battle. Soult had some difficulty deploying his army on such a narrow front, but he was keen to commence hostilities as he knew only too well that time was of the essence. Hill had deployed four of his six brigades forward on the three pieces of high ground covering the two approaches; Lecor was in reserve, about 1km to the rear, with Da Costa and Buchan's Portuguese brigades. It was well past 0800 hours when the first attack was delivered; fortuitously for the Allies the two attacks were not undertaken simultaneously.

Abbé advanced down the main road from St Pierre d'Irrube and pushed Ashworth's Caçadores out of the farm dwellings at Hiriberry and then began to advance uphill towards the main Portuguese position. Stewart, who was positioned between Ashworth and Barnes and the Allied artillery, began to move British companies to reinforce the right, leaving the centre left dangerously undermanned. Within three hours, following some questionable leadership by the commanding officer of the 71st, it looked like the Allied centre was doomed. On the Allied right, the Buffs (reinforced by the three brigade light companies) had withdrawn in the face of Chassé's Brigade who preceded Foy down the track along the spine of the Mouguerre ridge. The speed

of the withdrawal again demonstrated some questionable leadership[11] and, on the Allied right, it took some considerable courage by Colonel Cameron leading a counter-attack (with elements of the 57th and the 1st Provisional battalion) to stabilize the situation. This small force was able to contain the three French brigades, but their attack had been delivered hastily and Foy began to prepare a more concerted response.

On the Allied left, Daricau was making a cautious attempt to dislodge Pringle's men from the heights at the Chateau of Larralde; one could be forgiven for assuming this action was merely a feint, but given Soult's condemnation of Daricau's efforts following the battle, it was clearly not. Daricau may have achieved little on the field of battle that day, but he did prevent Pringle providing badly needed reserves to the Allied centre where the arrival of a French horse artillery battery was making life very unpleasant for the defenders. Furthermore, the ten Allied guns manned by the gunners of Tulloh and Ross were now being picked off by French marksmen, who were beginning to infiltrate the flanks on either side of the main road. Hill had received news that the 6th Division, which had marched the long route via Ustaritz, was now about an hour distant, along with confirmation that the pontoon bridge had also been repaired and that support could also be expected from that quarter, but timings were vague. He decided to deploy his reserve, a brigade to both the Allied centre and right, in the hope of buying enough time. Da Costa provided support to the centre and Buchan to the right. The arrival of Da Costa's men coincided with a general counter-attack against Abbé's exhausted force that was still waiting, after four hours in combat, for some additional support. The French line gave way and at this juncture Soult ordered Gruardet's Brigade forward to hold the line, but they were unable to stem the rearward momentum. In the centre the fight was all but over.

On the right, Foy was still in possession of Vieux Mouguerre and Hill decided to drive his division back off the heights, using Byng and Buchan's brigades in a second counter-attack which met light resistance and forced Foy back along the ridge. Soult thought this might be an attempt to outflank his force and sent Maransin out to the French left to prevent this eventuality. At much the same time, the first elements of the 6th Division came onto the field, and decided the contest. The Allies strengthened their new positions and settled down into their winter quarters, while Soult deployed his demoralized force along the Adour, placing four divisions in Bayonne under Reille, and the balance from that city to Port de Lanne, firm in the knowledge that Wellington could concentrate and attempt to force the line at a point of his choosing. It was to be an uneasy winter.

---

11   Both Colonel Bunbury of the 3rd Foot and Colonel Sir Nathaniel Peacock of the 71st Foot were later cashiered.

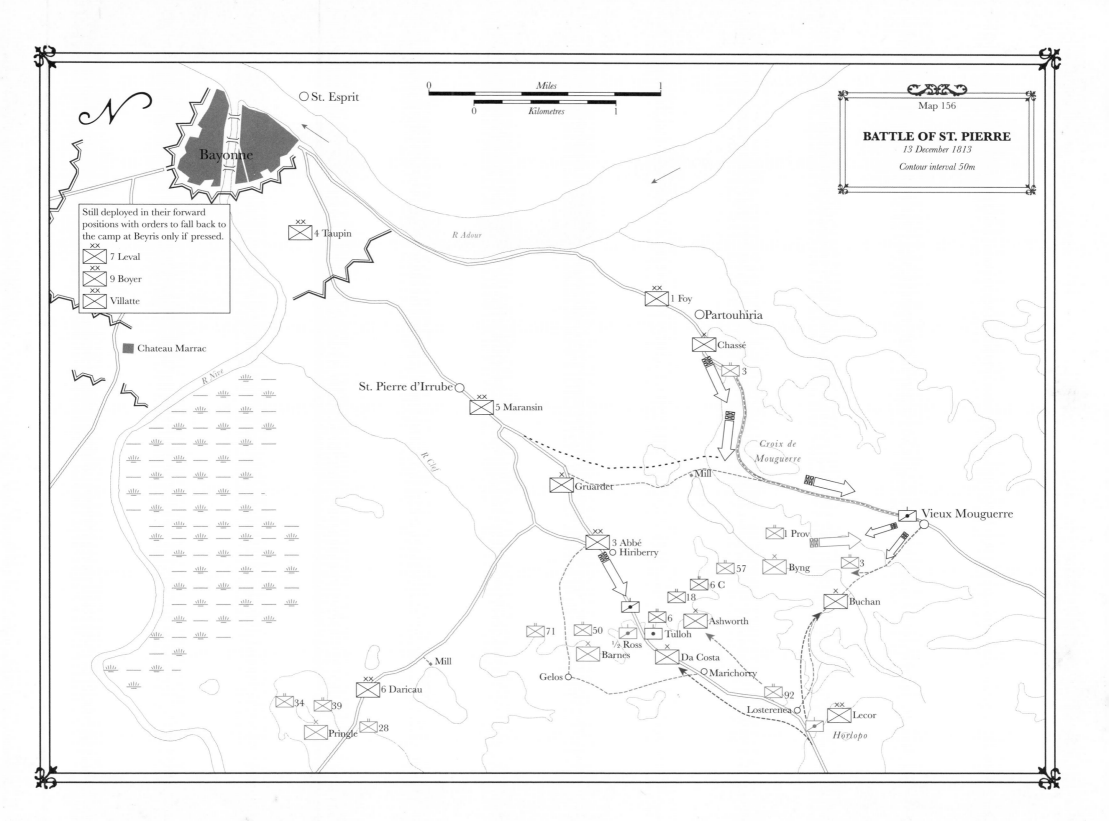

N

○ St. Esprit

Miles
0 — 1

Kilometres
0 — 1

Map 156

BATTLE OF ST. PIERRE
13 December 1813

Contour interval 50m

Bayonne

R Adour

⊠⊠ 4 Taupin

Still deployed in their forward
positions with orders to fall back to
the camp at Beyris only if pressed.

⊠⊠ 7 Leval

⊠⊠ 9 Boyer

⊠⊠ Villatte

■ Chateau Marrac

⊠⊠ 1 Foy

○ Partouhiria

⊠ Chassé

3

R Nive

R Chef

St. Pierre d'Irrube ○

⊠⊠ 5 Maransin

*Croix de
Mouguerre*

⊠ Gruardet

• Mill

⊠⊠ Vieux Mouguerre

⊠ 1 Prov

⊠⊠ 3 Abbé
○ Hiriberry

⊠ 57

⊠ Byng

⊠ 3

⊠ 6 C

⊠ Buchan

⊠ 18

⊠ Ashworth

⊠ 71

⊠ 50

⊠ 6

⊠ Tulloh

½ Ross

• Mill

⊠ Barnes

⊠ Da Costa

Gelos ○

○ Marichorry

⊠⊠ 6 Daricau

⊠ 92

⊠ 34

⊠ 39

Losterenea ○

⊠⊠ Lecor

⊠ Pringle

⊠ 28

Horlopo

Chapter 53

RESPITE PRECEDES THE STORM: DECEMBER 1813 TO FEBRUARY 1814

Yet again Soult had reason to be grateful for his adversary's caution following undisputed success. However, Wellington was determined not to overextend his advance into France until he was sure that the (northern) Allies would not negotiate with Napoleon, and until that time, he was content to strengthen the new line and wait for the weather to improve. Despite Wellington's strategic misgivings, the fact remained that the military chest was embarrassingly insolvent and this was despite huge efforts by the British government to find money to fund the war. Napoleon's plans to free up his veteran Peninsular armies, by fabricating a deal with Ferdinand at Valençay, had backfired and, by the end of the year, he was beginning to comprehend the desire for his removal, both at home and across Europe. 'France is invaded, all of Europe is in arms against France, and above all against me. You are no longer King of Spain. I do not want Spain either to keep or to give away. I will have nothing more to do with that country except to live in peace with it, and have the use of my army.'[1] But the hope that Britain, Spain and Portugal would fall out with each other was a pipe dream. 'Inter-Allied relations were not good, and it is possible that in time the French might have won a great deal. Yet in the event, the Alliance was not found wanting: though the British, Spaniards and Portuguese hated one another, in the end they hated Napoleon still more.'[2]

Soult was determined to hold the line of the Adour, for the river was his main line of communication with the rest of France and, having reinforced the garrison at Bayonne, he then distributed the remainder of his force east along the river from the city. Within days his numbers were thinned; firstly by Napoleon's scheme to create 40 new battalions branded as the 'Army of Reserve of the Pyrenees,' which necessitated Soult giving up many of his veterans to form the requisite cadres; and secondly, through Napoleon's continued optimism that a treaty with Spain was imminent, and his consequent orders to despatch north troops from both Soult and Suchet's armies in anticipation of this treaty. By the end of January 1814 Soult's available force had been depleted by 20,000 to just over 60,000 men, while that of Suchet was run down

by 10,000, constituting half his available field force for offensive operations.[3] Soult had lost Leval, Boyer and Treillard, placing him at a numerical disadvantage to the Allies, and when the Cortes, as anticipated by everyone except Napoleon, rejected the proposals from Valençay, Soult was forced to readjust his defences with the reassuringly inadequate guidance that he was to 'make the best of the situation'. When Napoleon's strategic plan did arrive, it was incongruous; ordering Soult to minimize the garrison in Bayonne and resume the offensive. 'Let him seize the opportunity boldly, and he should be able to gain the advantage over the English: he has talent enough to understand what I mean.'[4] By the time this extraordinary directive arrived, Wellington had already begun the final chapter.

Wellington's plan hinged on his numerical superiority, which enabled him to engage Soult's main body and simultaneously deploy a besieging force against the garrison at Bayonne. Soult had rearranged his seven divisions along the Adour, east from Bayonne; not for an instant did he consider that Wellington might attempt a crossing of the Adour to the west of the city, near the river's estuary. Wellington split his main body, under generals Hill and Beresford,[5] and despatched them towards Soult's left wing in order to divert French attention. Hill commenced his march on 14 February and Beresford two days later; both forces succeeded in driving the French divisions back eastwards and away from Bayonne and, on 18 February, when Wellington was satisfied that he had sufficient distance between Soult's field army and Bayonne, he rode back to St Jean-de-Luz to discuss preparations for the bridging operation across the Adour. For this venture, under the command of General Hope, Wellington allocated 34,000 men. Frustratingly, with everything in place the weather turned and any hope of commencing the bridging operation was dashed; Wellington returned to the east. Two days later, with an improvement in the weather, General Hope began to ferry his force across the Adour and, by way of a diversion, set Aylmer, de España and Campbell the task of demonstrating against the fortifications of Camp Beyris and Camp Marrac while simultaneously tasking the gunners to engage the few French gunboats and the solitary corvette which patrolled the estuary. Both tasks were achieved and, by 1700 hours on 23 February, a battalion had crossed and was immediately deployed (by General Stopford) among the sand dunes at Le Boucau. The weather continued to improve, but it was to be another 36 hours before the bridging operation could commence, and in the interim more troops were ferried across the water, supported by the Royal Naval flotilla that had just arrived. The bridge was complete on the afternoon of 26 February and de España's Division, the corps artillery and balance of cavalry joined the 1st Division and Campbell's Brigade on the north bank. The suburbs of St Étienne were stormed and taken the next day and the investment was complete.[6]

---

1   Napoleon, *The Confidential Correspondence of Napoleon Bonaparte*, vol. II, p.252, no. 776.

2   Esdaile, *The Peninsular War*, p.482.

3   Although on paper Suchet had another 30,000 men, they were tied to garrison duties and manning the numerous outposts in Valencia and Catalonia.

4   Napoleon, *Correspondence*, to Clark, Troyes, 25 February 1814.

5   Hill had the 2nd Division, Lecor's Division and Morillo's Division and Fane's cavalry; while Beresford had the 4th and 7th divisions and the cavalry of Vivian and Somerset but was bolstered (four days later) by the arrival of the Light Division and (five days later) by the 6th Division. The 3rd Division remained in reserve.

6   For an excellent account of the bridging operation see Jones, *Journal of Sieges*, vol. II, ch. 2, pp.106–131.

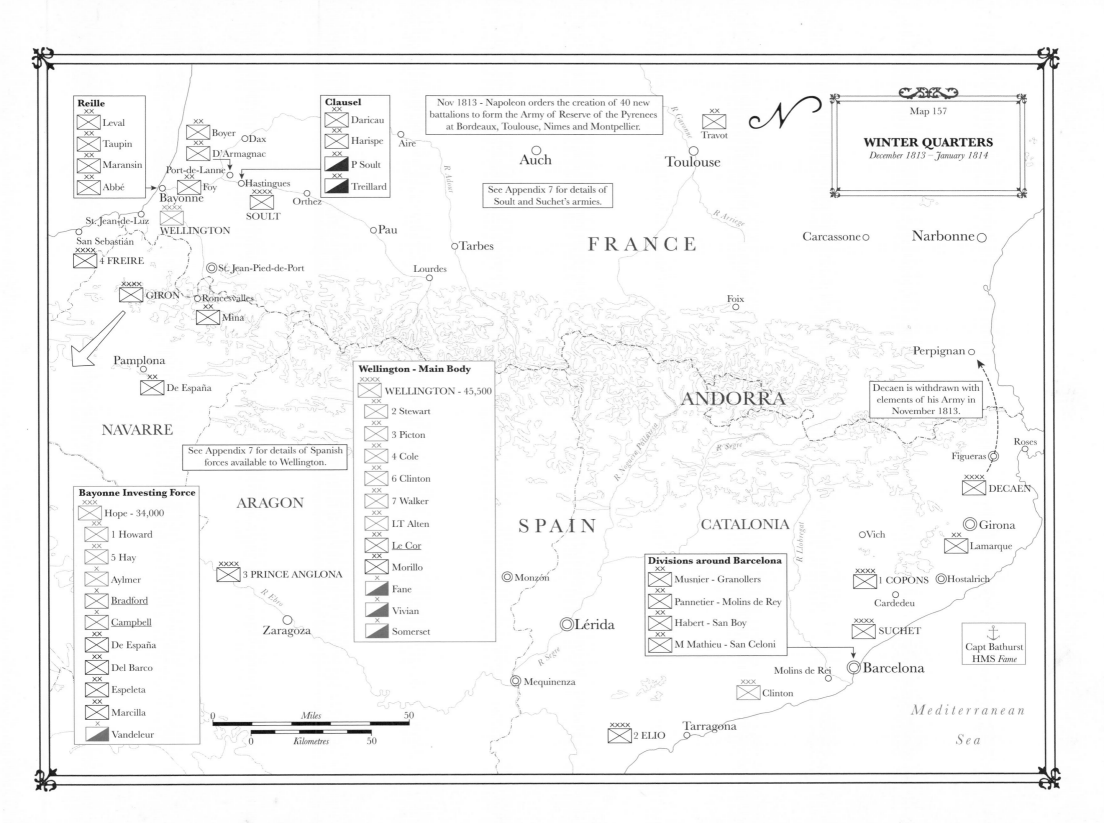

Reille

xx	Leval
xx	Taupin
xx	Maransin
xx	Abbé

Clausel

xx	Daricau
xx	Harispe
xx	P Soult
xx	Treillard

Nov 1813 - Napoleon orders the creation of 40 new battalions to form the Army of Reserve of the Pyrenees at Bordeaux, Toulouse, Nimes and Montpellier.

See Appendix 7 for details of Soult and Suchet's armies.

Map 157

WINTER QUARTERS
December 1813 – January 1814

Boyer

Dax

D'Armagnac

Port-de-Lanne

Foy

Hastingues

Bayonne

Orthez

SOULT

WELLINGTON

St. Jean-de-Luz

San Sebastián

xxxx 4 FREIRE

Aire

Auch

Travot

Toulouse

Carcassone

Narbonne

R. Garonne

R. Adour

R. Arriege

Pau

Tarbes

xxxx GIRON

St. Jean-Pied-de-Port

Roncesvalles

xx Mina

Lourdes

Foix

FRANCE

ANDORRA

Perpignan

Decaen is withdrawn with elements of his Army in November 1813.

Pamplona

xx De España

NAVARRE

See Appendix 7 for details of Spanish forces available to Wellington.

Wellington - Main Body

xxxx	WELLINGTON - 45,500
xx	2 Stewart
xx	3 Picton
xx	4 Cole
xx	6 Clinton
xx	7 Walker
xx	LT Alten
xx	Le Cor
xx	Morillo
x	Fane
x	Vivian
x	Somerset

R. Noguera Pallaresa

R. Segre

Figueras

Roses

xxxx DECAEN

SPAIN

CATALONIA

Vich

Girona

xx Lamarque

Bayonne Investing Force

xxx	Hope - 34,000
xx	1 Howard
xx	5 Hay
x	Aylmer
x	Bradford
x	Campbell
x	De España
xx	Del Barco
xx	Espeleta
xx	Marcilla
x	Vandeleur

ARAGON

xxxx 3 PRINCE ANGLONA

R. Ebro

Zaragoza

Monzón

Lérida

R. Segre

Mequinenza

Divisions around Barcelona

xx	Musnier - Granollers
xx	Pannetier - Molins de Rey
xx	Habert - San Boy
xx	M Mathieu - San Celoni

xxxx 1 COPONS

Hostalrich

Cardedeu

xxxx SUCHET

Capt Bathurst
HMS *Fame*

Molins de Rei

Barcelona

xxx Clinton

Tarragona

xxxx 2 ELIO

Mediterranean Sea

Miles 0 — 50

Kilometres 0 — 50

Late on 21 February Wellington had arrived back at Garris and received reports from his field commanders that enabled him to establish a good intelligence picture of Soult's dispositions, from which he penned a plan for his second extensive turning movement. Hill's force was reinforced by the Light and 6th divisions, as this group was to undertake the outflanking manoeuvre before turning and driving their quarry north towards Beresford's blocking force. The southerly manoeuvre commenced on 24 February, Hill split his force into two columns and by nightfall all 20,000 men had crossed the river Gave d'Oloron by a combination of fords and a pontoon bridge. Soult realized he had been outmanoeuvred and wasted little time giving orders for all his divisions to concentrate at Orthez. This they had achieved by the evening on 25 February. Wellington readjusted his force,[7] retaining two columns, and closed on the French concentration, confident that Soult would not stand for battle. Hill drove in Soult's outposts at the southern suburb of Départ and, much to Wellington's surprise, initial indications appeared to support a French desire for an engagement. Wellington now had to wait for the arrival of Beresford's force, which took another 36 hours, and then reorganize his army to deal with this unexpected turn of events. Paradoxically, this delay seems to have unnerved Soult who, following a council with Clausel, D'Erlon and four of his divisional commanders, decided to readjust his position on the night of 27 February in the hope that the sight of a strong French defensive position would 'impose upon the English'. Yet, despite being well aware of the Allied presence to the south, Soult decided to redeploy the majority of his force facing west, in what was unquestionably a good defensive position, but in so doing left the door ajar to the south.

Wellington's force outnumbered that of Soult by a mere 7,000, but the Allied commander knew that French resolve was shaky. Beresford was to attack the French right and immediately began the protracted march from Baigts towards St Boes, while Picton moved down the main road towards Orthez, screened by Somerset's cavalry. Halfway down the road to Orthez Picton was to left face and move towards the French centre, thereby providing a screen for the Light and 6th divisions in their crossing over the pontoon bridge at Benrex. Once across, the Light Division joined Beresford's force while the latter moved up the road and fell in behind the 3rd Division. Cole opened proceedings at about 0830 hours by attacking Taupin's piquets stationed in the village of St Boes. Ross's Brigade had the lead and achieved early success in driving Taupin's infantry back through the village and towards the road junction, but then came under effective fire from the well-sited French divisional battery and had to fall back to the safety afforded by the dwellings in the village. Attempts to reinforce the attack with Sympher's Battery and then Vasconcellos's Brigade gained no further advantage and the combined and accurate fire from both Taupin and Rouget's batteries disabled two of the guns of the King's German Legion and killed the battery

commander. Wellington, watching from a central position, ordered the 1st Caçadores to cover the flank of Vasconcellos's Brigade, which was by now under counter-attack. However, as they arrived both the 4th Division brigades gave ground, yielding the village to the French. Cole, now closely supported by Walker's Division, deployed defensively just out of range of the French infantry, their attempt to turn the French right having failed completely.

In the centre, the accurate and sustained musket fire of D'Armagnac and Foy's divisions had also thwarted Picton's attack. In fact, Wellington had only intended this attack to be a demonstration but when things began to reverse on the Allied left, he was looking to this part of the field to salvage the situation. At about 1100 hours Wellington changed the entire plan and decided to throw his full weight across the frontage. Brisbane's Brigade from the 3rd Division, supported by the 6th Division and some excellent gunnery from Turner's Battery, concentrated their efforts on Fririon's Brigade in Foy's defensive line. They penetrated it and then began to fan out along the ridgeline. When Turner's Battery arrived at the summit, Soult realized the danger this unexpected turn of events posed, and ordered Leclerc's squadron of the 21st Chasseurs to charge and silence the guns at all costs. The gallant horsemen suffered numerous losses and fell back; having failed in their mission, the British guns celebrated by pouring effective (enfilade) fire into the flanks of the French defensive lines. A short while later Foy was injured by a bursting shrapnel shell and carried to the rear, the resolve of his division went with him. To their left, the brigades of Keane and Power were engaged with D'Armagnac's regiments in a fierce contest that afforded no advantage to defender or attacker.

At the village of St Boes, renewed attacks by the 7th Division, supported by Anson's Brigade and the two divisional batteries, was beginning to make headway against Taupin's by now exhausted troops. The initial French defensive line was penetrated and the French fell back, but strangely they received no support from Rouget or Paris and when the 52nd fell on Taupin's left flank the contest was over. Taupin pulled back and Rouget and Paris followed; it was about 1430 hours. Some time earlier Foy's Division was already fragmenting. Once Foy's line collapsed, D'Armagnac's position was untenable and they too had to break contact and pull back. This, in turn, exposed Harispe in Orthez who also withdrew in contact, having just received a strong attack by Hill who had, by now, crossed the river Gave de Pau at the fords at Souars. Harispe joined Villatte and D'Armagnac and formed a second line of defence north of the village of Rontrun, but Hill, whose first attack broke Harispe's solitary brigade, quickly engaged the line. As the 6th, 7th and Light divisions moved east to support Hill's two divisions, Soult realized the danger and ordered an immediate retreat. The pursuit continued for a few miles until, exhausted, the Allies gave up the chase.

---

7   Morillo's Division had been left behind holding the garrison at the small fort at Navarrenx and did not rejoin the main army for the rest of the war.

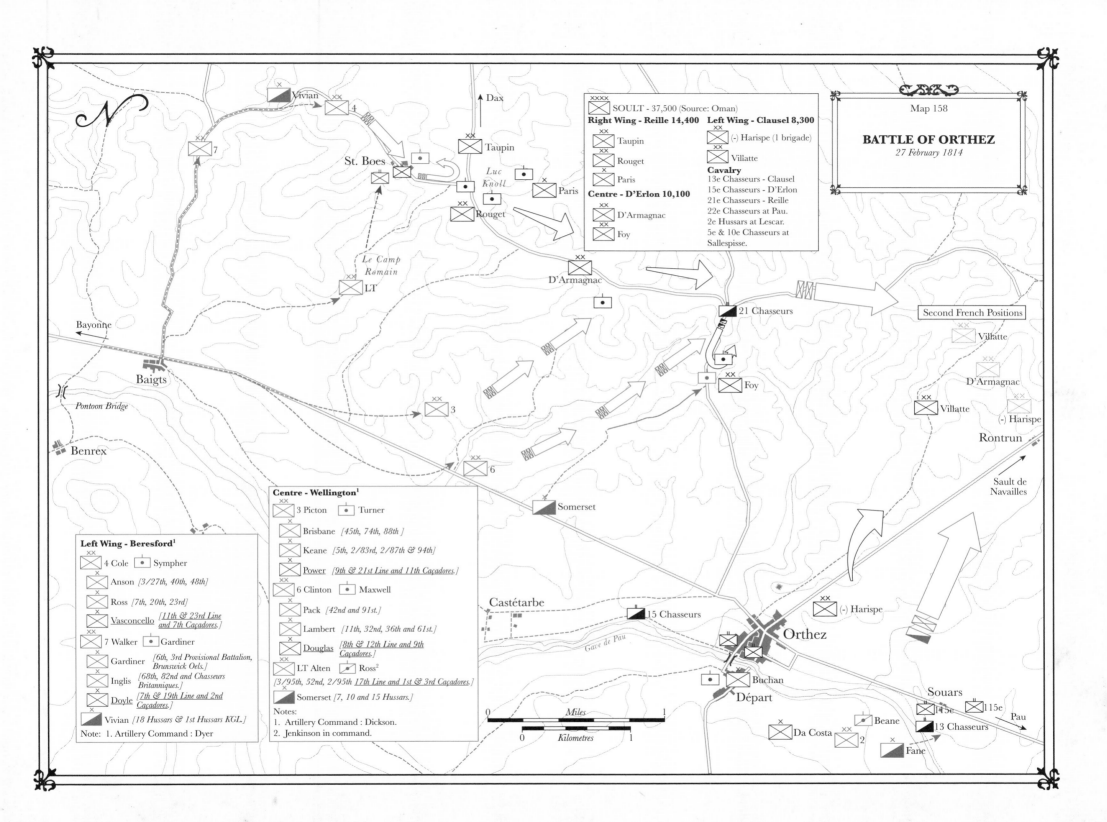

N

Vivian

4

Dax

Taupin

St. Boes

Luc
Knoll

Paris

7

Rouget

Le Camp
Romain

LT

D'Armagnac

Second French Positions

21 Chasseurs

Bayonne

Villatte

Baigts

D'Armagnac

Foy

Pontoon Bridge

3

Villatte

Benrex

(-) Harispe

Rontrun

6

Sault de
Navailles

Somerset

SOULT - 37,500 (Source: Oman)
Right Wing - Reille 14,400   **Left Wing - Clausel 8,300**
Taupin   (-) Harispe (1 brigade)
Rouget   Villatte
Paris   **Cavalry**
Centre - D'Erlon 10,100   13e Chasseurs - Clausel
D'Armagnac   15e Chasseurs - D'Erlon
Foy   21e Chasseurs - Reille
                                          22e Chasseurs at Pau.
                                          2e Hussars at Lescar.
                                          5e & 10e Chasseurs at
                                          Sallespisse.

Map 158

BATTLE OF ORTHEZ
27 February 1814

Centre - Wellington[1]
3 Picton   Turner
Brisbane   *[45th, 74th, 88th]*
Keane   *[5th, 2/83rd, 2/87th & 94th]*
Power   *[9th & 21st Line and 11th Caçadores.]*
6 Clinton   Maxwell
Pack   *[42nd and 91st.]*
Lambert   *[11th, 32nd, 36th and 61st.]*
Douglas   *[8th & 12th Line and 9th Caçadores.]*
LT Alten   Ross[2]
[3/95th, 52nd, 2/95th 17th Line and 1st & 3rd Caçadores.]
Somerset   *[7, 10 and 15 Hussars.]*
Notes:
1. Artillery Command : Dickson.
2. Jenkinson in command.

Castétarbe

15 Chasseurs

(-) Harispe

Orthez

Gave de Pau

Left Wing - Beresford[1]
4 Cole   Sympher
Anson   *[3/27th, 40th, 48th]*
Ross   *[7th, 20th, 23rd]*
Vasconcello   *[11th & 23rd Line and 7th Caçadores.]*
7 Walker   Gardiner
Gardiner   *[6th, 3rd Provisional Battalion, Brunswick Oels.]*
Inglis   *[68th, 82nd and Chasseurs Britanniques.]*
Doyle   *[7th & 19th Line and 2nd Caçadores.]*
Vivian   *[18 Hussars & 1st Hussars KGL.]*
Note: 1. Artillery Command : Dyer

Buchan

Départ

Souars

Beane

45e   115e

13 Chasseurs

Da Costa

2

Pau

Fane

0   Miles   1

0   Kilometres   1

Chapter 54

FINAL CONFRONTATION ~ MARCH AND APRIL 1814

The end of the war on the east coast was relatively uneventful. On 10 January 1814 Suchet received orders from Paris directing him to assemble his cavalry, some artillery and half his infantry on the Pyrenean frontier in anticipation of successful negotiation with Spain following Valençay. 'The preparatory measures were to be entered upon, even if the arrangements which had been negotiated with Spain should fail of the desired success.'[1] The balance of Suchet's force was to be similarly prepared to move north at a moment's notice. This necessitated the withdrawal of all of the outlying garrisons, but his request to abandon Barcelona was denied, so by the end of the month, he had 8,000 men left in that city and the balance of 10,000 in northern Catalonia centred on Girona. Clinton, who was commanding the Anglo-Sicilian force south of Barcelona, had miscalculated the speed of this French withdrawal from around the regional capital and his combined operation to capture the city (with Copons) on 16 January completely backfired, bringing to an end the exploits of this force on the east coast.[2] The following month an officer on Suchet's staff, who actually held a commission in the Spanish army, forged an ingenious scheme; Juan Van Halen had access to the cipher, signature and seal of Suchet's secret correspondence and used it to draw up the fictitious convention of Tarrasa, whereby the governors of Tortosa, Lérida, Mequinenza and Monzón were to be enticed into believing that Suchet had agreed with Copons to the evacuation of all outlying fortresses with full honours of war. The scheme failed at Tortosa, when Van Halen lost his nerve, but was successful at the other three fortresses and, by mid February, these were back in Spanish hands.[3]

Soult had lost 4,000 men at Orthez, killed wounded or captured, but more worryingly, half the amount again had deserted. At St Sever he faced a dilemma; withdraw north and cover Bordeaux or continue east to draw Wellington's army from both Bordeaux and the operation at Bayonne. He selected the latter and, by so doing, left the road open to France's third city, although at this stage Wellington had no great designs on Bordeaux. He was to change his stance on the issue on 4 March when he received a visit from agents of the mayor of Bordeaux, who promised to deliver the city in the name of Louis XVIII. Wellington however, had no intention of

proclaiming the old Borbón king on liberation of the city and warned many Frenchmen (with royalist sympathies) that the British government could take no responsibility in the matter. Nevertheless, having defeated Soult's forces at Aire two days prior to this timely visit by the Bordeaux delegation, he considered the opportunity to capture this key city too good to pass up, and accordingly sent Beresford with the 7th and 4th divisions, supported by Vivian's light cavalry, to capitalise on this unexpected turn of events. On 12 March Beresford arrived at the city gates at the head of the light cavalry and 7th division (the 4th had been left some way south) amidst a somewhat theatrical display. Royalist regalia and insignia adorned the city, and Beresford's protestations that his mission fell well short of liberation in the name of the French king, were almost an irrelevance.

With events at Bayonne and Bordeaux ongoing, Wellington now faced another predicament regarding future operations against Soult; for to thrust his army too far to the east was to encourage the possibility of union with Suchet's forces who, at this time, were flooding north from Catalonia. Suchet was, however, preoccupied with problems of his own and the arrival on the frontier of Ferdinand who, on Napoleon's instructions had been released in a last ditch attempt to exchange the Spanish king for the prisoners resulting from Van Halen's treachery. Ferdinand arrived at Perpignan on 21 March but any hope of a show of strength by Suchet had long since been dashed by the continual haemorrhaging of his army to support the heart of the Empire. Indeed any such demonstration would have changed nothing, for Ferdinand accepted the written pledge to release the prisoners from Lérida and Mequinenza, and allow free passage to the French garrisons at Saguntum, Tortosa and Barcelona, and then duly headed south with absolutely no intention of honouring it. He passed through the Catalonian towns in triumph, and then swung west to Zaragoza where overt displays of loyalty by serviles sent shock waves to the liberal majority in the Cortes at Madrid. Although concerned, the liberals could not have predicted their arrest by General Eguia at the head of 5,000 Valencian troops in early May, only days before Ferdinand returned to his capital in triumph. The Regency, the Cortes, the Liberal party and the Constitution had all been swept aside in a tide of royalist nationalism.

Wellington had remained at St Sever while Beresford had conducted the movement to Bordeaux but by mid March he was keen to resume the offensive. He had been reinforced by the arrival of a large enhancement of cavalry and, to replace Morillo's division that remained on-task providing a cordon at Navarrene,[4] two divisions from the Spanish 4th army were brought west and their place at Bayonne was taken by O'Donnell's Reserve Army of Andalusia. Furthermore, when news of Pannetier's movement north from Perpignan with 10,000 men from Suchet's army arrived at Wellington's headquarters, he assumed (incorrectly) that these troops were destined to reinforce Soult and, accordingly, recalled Beresford, with the 4th Division and the light cavalry, leaving Dalhousie with his division in a gloriously remote position at Bordeaux. On the French side, Soult had been surprised (once again) at the apparent timidity following the brief engagement at Aire; he had withdrawn south and established his force with Clausel concentrated at Vic en Bigorre, D'Erlon at Marciac and Reille at Maubourget. However, it was not long before

---

1 Suchet, *Memoirs*, vol. II, p.365.

2 On 10 March Clinton was ordered to break up the Anglo-Sicilian force and march with the British and German elements to the Adour.

3 For the full story see Oman, *History of the Peninsular War*, vol. VII, p.p. 415–421 and Suchet, *Memoirs*, vol. II, pp.373–377.

4 Although Wellington requested one brigade from this division be released and it rejoined Hill's Corps in mid March.

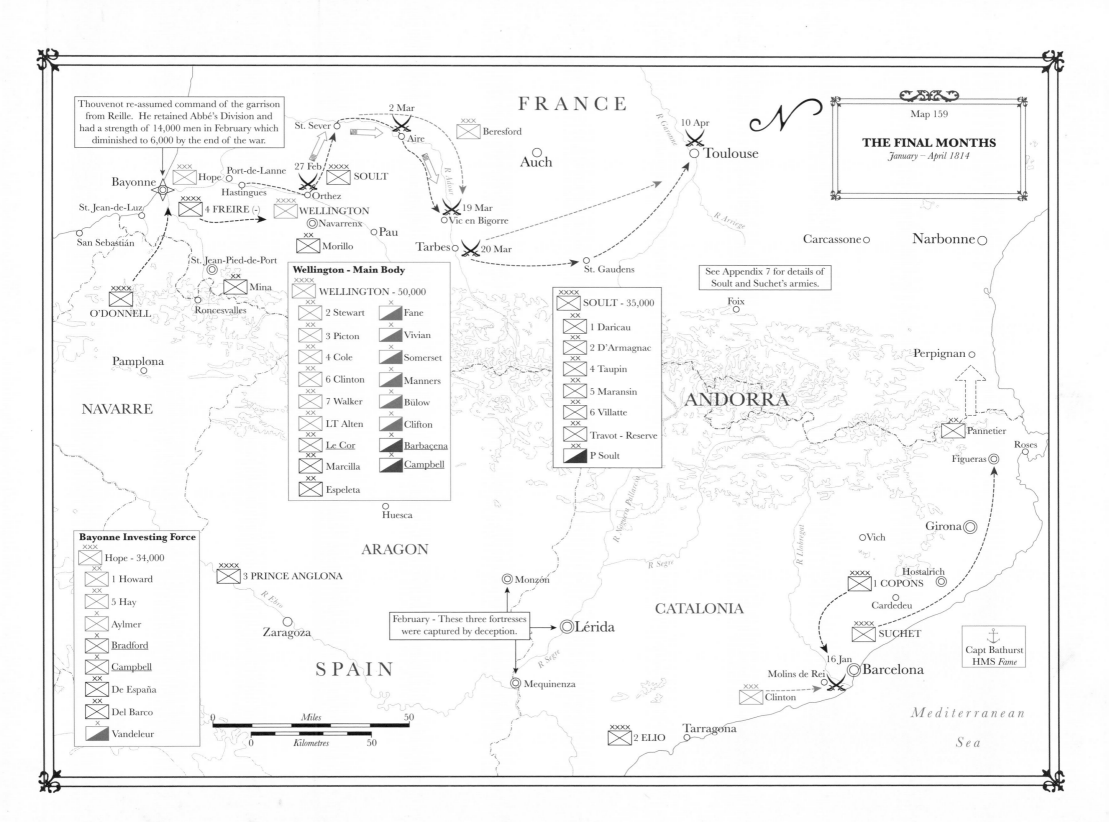

FRANCE

Map 159

THE FINAL MONTHS
January – April 1814

Thouvenot re-assumed command of the garrison from Reille. He retained Abbé's Division and had a strength of 14,000 men in February which diminished to 6,000 by the end of the war.

2 Mar

St. Sever

Aire

10 Apr

××× Beresford

Toulouse

Auch

27 Feb ×××× SOULT

Bayonne

××× Hope

Port-de-Lanne

Hastingues

×××× 4 FREIRE (-)

Orthez

×××× WELLINGTON

Navarrenx

19 Mar

Vic en Bigorre

Pau

Tarbes

20 Mar

R Arriege

Carcassone

Narbonne

St. Jean-de-Luz

San Sebastián

St. Jean-Pied-de-Port

×× Morillo

St. Gaudens

See Appendix 7 for details of Soult and Suchet's armies.

×××× O'DONNELL

Roncesvalles

×× Mina

Foix

Wellington – Main Body

×××× WELLINGTON – 50,000	
×× 2 Stewart	Fane
×× 3 Picton	Vivian
×× 4 Cole	Somerset
×× 6 Clinton	× Manners
×× 7 Walker	× Bülow
×× LT Alten	Clifton
×× Le Cor	× Barbaçena
×× Marcilla	× Campbell
×× Espeleta	

SOULT – 35,000

×××× SOULT – 35,000
×× 1 Daricau
×× 2 D'Armagnac
×× 4 Taupin
×× 5 Maransin
×× 6 Villatte
×× Travot – Reserve
P Soult

Perpignan

ANDORRA

Pamplona

NAVARRE

Huesca

ARAGON

Bayonne Investing Force

××× Hope – 34,000
×× 1 Howard
×× 5 Hay
× Aylmer
× Bradford
× Campbell
×× De España
×× Del Barco
× Vandeleur

Roses

Figueras

Girona

Pannetier

Hostalrich

Vich

R Segre

R Noguera Pallaresa

R Noguera Ribagorçana

CATALONIA

×××× 3 PRINCE ANGLONA

Zaragoza

R Ebro

Monzón

February – These three fortresses were captured by deception.

Lérida

Mequinenza

R Segre

SPAIN

×××× 1 COPONS

Cardedeu

×××× SUCHET

Capt Bathurst
HMS *Fame*

16 Jan

Molins de Rei

Barcelona

R Llobregat

××× Clinton

Tarragona

×××× 2 ELIO

Mediterranean Sea

| 0 | Miles | 50 |
| 0 | Kilometres | 50 |

he realised that this timidity in pursuit was connected with designs towards Bordeaux; an unwelcome development but nevertheless one which brought vital respite to his force (see map 158 and Appendix 7). Soult had also suffered a personal rebuke from Napoleon who, in a communiqué on 2 March, had accused the Duke of Dalmatia of being destitute of initiative and instructed him to resume the offensive. On 14 March suitably re-energized Soult began to attack Hill's outposts and pushed the Allied screen back as far as Aire where Wellington, somewhat surprised by Soult's offensive posturing, offered battle the following day. He concurrently despatched the Light Division north, to link up with the returning 4th Division, in order to execute a turning movement under Beresford's leadership. Soult's resolve thus tested proved fragile, and he withdrew only to be pursued with vigour, resulting in engagements at both Vic en Bigorre and Tarbes. It had been Wellington's aim to pin Soult against the Pyrenees and cut the French army's lines of retreat on Toulouse, but a hard rearguard fight at Tarbes on 20 March bought enough time and space for Soult to escape. Both armies were soon underway to Toulouse in a race for the fortified town.

As Wellington's army closed on the city reports that the inhabitants were keen to follow the example of Bordeaux provided a huge psychological boast to the Allied army who were feeling the strain of continuous campaigning. However, the capture of Toulouse was to be no easy task as the city, for the most part, sits on the far bank of the Garonne river; a wide fast flowing obstacle devoid of cover to the approaches. The bridging operation would be demanding in both time and resources, it would also be extremely vulnerable to French counter operations. On the night of 27 March the first attempt was made; Hill, in command of the 4th, 6th and Light divisions marched against the suburb of St Cyprien, and drove Daricau and D'Armagnac back within the outer works that the French were preparing to cover the suburb and bridge head. A few kilometres to the south an attempt was made to deploy the pontoon bridge at Portet, only to discover that the train lacked sufficient pontoons to span the gap and the attempt was called off.[5]

Wellington ordered a second attempt, which was executed on 30 March at a point five kilometres further south, where the river was narrower. It was successful, and Hill crossed with a force of 13,000 men, but quickly discovered that he was trapped between the Garonne and Ariège rivers, and with only the one pontoon bridge at the army's disposal there was nothing to do but recall him two nights later. Fortuitously for the Allies, Soult's reconnaissance during this period seems remarkably lacklustre; Hill had been on the near bank a full day before a cavalry patrol spotted the not insignificantly large Allied force. On 1 April Clausel was sent south to counter any attempt to cross the Ariège, but he withdrew north when Hill returned to the home bank. The following day Wellington decided to try his luck well to the north of the city at a small village named La Capellette. 'After dark we marched a few miles down the river side, and took up our night's lodging in a soft subtle field, while the rain poured for several hours. Next morning we marched down to the river, and crossed by pontoon bridge, which had been hastily constructed during the night. At the same time, small parties of the enemy appeared on the

opposite bank, and fired a few shots; but over we went with the band in front playing "British Grenadiers". We afterwards marched a few miles and were quartered in a church.'[6] By early evening on 4 April Beresford was across the river with the 3rd, 4th and 6th divisions, supported by their divisional artillery and the cavalry of Vivian, Manners and Somerset, but as the final cavalry units were crossing the heavy Spring rains recommenced and within hours the river had swollen to dangerous levels, breaking the bridge and dividing the Allied army. Beresford established his force in a defensive posture fully expecting a resolute counter attack by the French but it never materialised; for Soult had decided that the time proffered by this happenstance was better spent strengthening his defences in and around Toulouse.

By 7 April the rains had decreased and the river abated sufficiently for the pontoon bridge to be re-established, over which crossed the balance of the force, less for Hill's Corps and the Light Division. Hill remained opposite St Cyprien while the Light Division were ordered to provide protection to the sappers as they re-laid the bridge further south, in an attempt to close the distance between Hill and the balance of Wellington's army. While this was underway Wellington began his advance towards the city and notably, on 8 April, captured intact the bridge at Croix Daurade following an opportunistic charge by Vivian's hussars which was smartly followed-up by Ross's Brigade. 'The cavalry of general Soult, the marshal's brother, was witness of this happy accident… The marshal, disconcerted by this reverse, and seeing the safety in the strong defensive position of Toulouse, didn't dare to leave it and go looking for the English.'[7] On 9 April Soult anticipated an attack by Wellington from the north but the Allied commander was still waiting for the Light Division to join him. Later in the day they were close at hand and Wellington decided to attack the following day and issued the appropriate warning orders. The next morning, at 0800 hours, from his temporary headquarters at St Jory (ten kilometres north of the bridge at Croix Daurade) Wellington outlined his detailed battle plans.

The Light Division had crossed the pontoons at 0300 hours and was in position by dawn on the right of the 3rd Division whose own right flank was anchored on the Garonne. Their task was largely diversionary. To the left of Alten's Division were the two Galician Divisions who were to drive out St Pol's Brigade in La Pugade and then assault the Grande Redoute supported by Manner's dragoons. To their left were the 4th and 6th divisions under Beresford's overall command. Their task was to move along the western face of the Heights of Calvinet and then swing into the underbelly of the feature that had no additional defences, and was lightly held. Beresford was given sufficient latitude to determine the best place to turn and execute this attack.

Events opened on the west bank at 0500 hours with the attack of O'Callaghan's Brigade on the weaker defences of the outer suburbs of St Cyprien; the 28th and 34th secured a lodgement and subsequent entry behind the outer defences, without too much difficulty, and then began to fan out forcing Maransin to withdraw (as ordered) to within the inner defence line. Barnes's Brigade was sent to support that of O'Callaghan and these two brigades satisfied themselves with the containment of the French division within the inner defences. The gun batteries began to fire across the river in

---

5 Wellington's senior engineer, Lieutenant Colonel Elphinstone, had warned him two months earlier that the number of pontoons he could carry on the transport allocated to him would be insufficient to span a large river.

6 Spencer Cooper, *Rough Notes of Seven Campaigns*, p. 114.

7 Thiers, *Histoire du Consulat et de L'Empire*, vol. XVIII, p. 21.

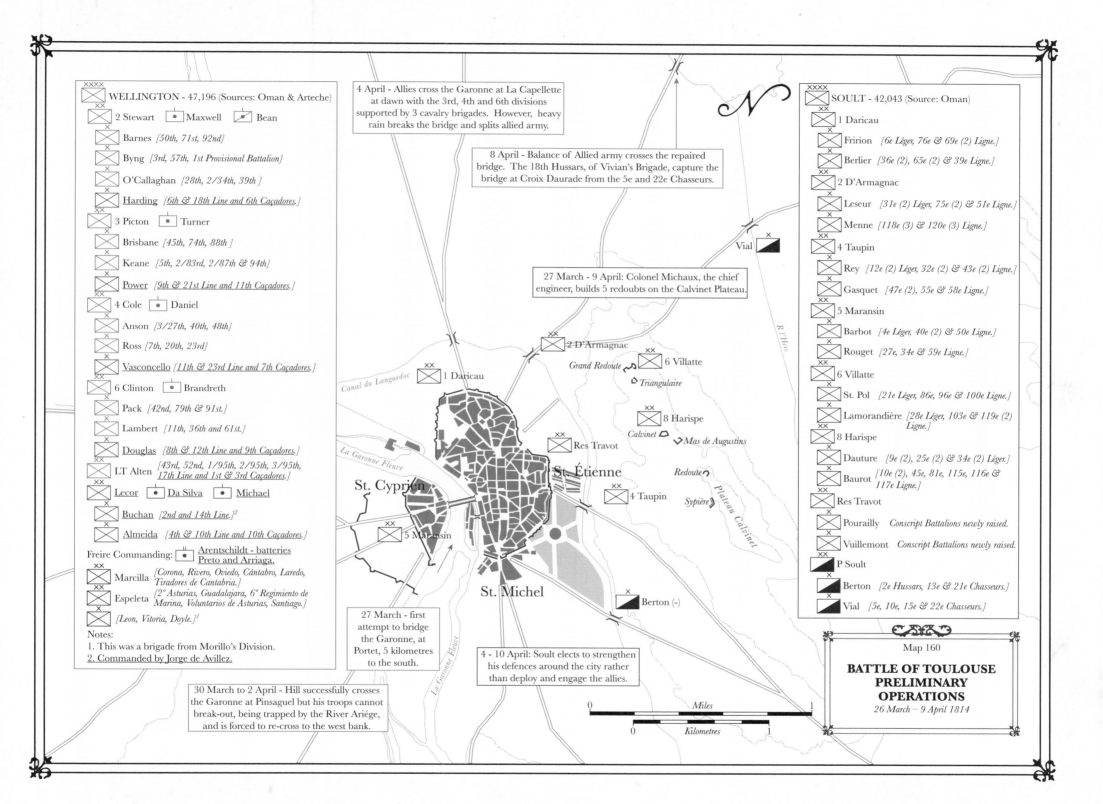

WELLINGTON - 47,196 (Sources: Oman & Arteche)

2 Stewart • Maxwell ⚑ Bean

Barnes [50th, 71st, 92nd]

Byng [3rd, 57th, 1st Provisional Battalion]

O'Callaghan [28th, 2/34th, 39th]

Harding [6th & 18th Line and 6th Caçadores.]

3 Picton • Turner

Brisbane [45th, 74th, 88th]

Keane [5th, 2/83rd, 2/87th & 94th]

Power [9th & 21st Line and 11th Caçadores.]

4 Cole • Daniel

Anson [3/27th, 40th, 48th]

Ross [7th, 20th, 23rd]

Vasconcello [11th & 23rd Line and 7th Caçadores.]

6 Clinton • Brandreth

Pack [42nd, 79th & 91st.]

Lambert [11th, 36th and 61st.]

Douglas [8th & 12th Line and 9th Caçadores.]

LT Alten [43rd, 52nd, 1/95th, 2/95th, 3/95th, 17th Line and 1st & 3rd Caçadores.]

Lecor • Da Silva • Michael

Buchan [2nd and 14th Line.]²

Almeida [4th & 10th Line and 10th Caçadores.]

Freire Commanding: • Arentschildt - batteries Preto and Arriaga.

Marcilla [Corona, Rivero, Oviedo, Cántabro, Laredo, Tiradores de Cantabria.]

Espeleta [2° Asturias, Guadalajara, 6° Regimiento de Marina, Voluntarios de Asturias, Santiago.]

[Leon, Vitoria, Doyle.]¹

Notes:
1. This was a brigade from Morillo's Division.
2. Commanded by Jorge de Avillez.

SOULT - 42,043 (Source: Oman)

1 Daricau

Fririon [6e Léger, 76e & 69e (2) Ligne.]

Berlier [36e (2), 65e (2) & 39e Ligne.]

2 D'Armagnac

Leseur [31e (2) Léger, 75e (2) & 51e Ligne.]

Menne [118e (3) & 120e (3) Ligne.]

4 Taupin

Rey [12e (2) Léger, 32e (2) & 43e (2) Ligne.]

Gasquet [47e (2), 55e & 58e Ligne.]

5 Maransin

Barbot [4e Léger, 40e (2) & 50e Ligne.]

Rouget [27e, 34e & 59e Ligne.]

6 Villatte

St. Pol [21e Léger, 86e, 96e & 100e Ligne.]

Lamorandière [28e Léger, 103e & 119e (2) Ligne.]

8 Harispe

Dauture [9e (2), 25e (2) & 34e (2) Léger.]

Baurot [10e (2), 45e, 81e, 115e, 116e & 117e Ligne.]

Res Travot

Pourailly   Conscript Battalions newly raised.

Vuillemont   Conscript Battalions newly raised.

P Soult

Berton [2e Hussars, 13e & 21e Chasseurs.]

Vial [5e, 10e, 15e & 22e Chasseurs.]

4 April - Allies cross the Garonne at La Capellette at dawn with the 3rd, 4th and 6th divisions supported by 3 cavalry brigades. However, heavy rain breaks the bridge and splits allied army.

8 April - Balance of Allied army crosses the repaired bridge. The 18th Hussars, of Vivian's Brigade, capture the bridge at Croix Daurade from the 5e and 22e Chasseurs.

27 March - 9 April: Colonel Michaux, the chief engineer, builds 5 redoubts on the Calvinet Plateau.

27 March - first attempt to bridge the Garonne, at Portet, 5 kilometres to the south.

4 - 10 April: Soult elects to strengthen his defences around the city rather than deploy and engage the allies.

30 March to 2 April - Hill successfully crosses the Garonne at Pinsaguel but his troops cannot break-out, being trapped by the River Ariége, and is forced to re-cross to the west bank.

Vial

2 D'Armagnac

Grand Redoute   6 Villatte

Triangulaire

1 Daricau

8 Harispe

Res Travot   Calvinet   Mas de Augustins

St. Étienne   Redoute

St. Cyprien   4 Taupin   Sypière   Plateau Calvinet

5 Maransin

St. Michel   Berton (-)

Canal du Languedoc

La Garonne Fleuve

R. l'Hers

N

Map 160

BATTLE OF TOULOUSE PRELIMINARY OPERATIONS

26 March – 9 April 1814

0 ___ Miles ___ 1

0 ___ Kilometres ___ 1

support of the 3rd Division; 'particularly Maxwell's Brigade, he had had ten or twelve men wounded and seven or eight horses, Bean three men and the like number of animals … we also fir'd [sic] seven rockets, these I think with some effect, cannot you send us a few more…'[8]

On the east bank, Picton had driven in the French piquets to a line behind the Languedoc Canal and Turner's Battery shelled the French defences at the two bridges. Things had progressed well in this part of the field, but then Picton's impatience and impetuosity finally got the better of him and, against orders, he tried to storm the bridge of Jumeaux. He was beaten back with some loss but this did not stop him having a second attempt later in the day, which ended in similar fashion. To Picton's left, Alten had stuck to his orders and driven back the French advance piquets to a line behind the canal and stood poised to support the Spanish attack to the left. Freire moved his two under strength divisions forward from the bridge crossing at Croix Daurade and advanced with purpose towards the village and knoll of Pujade where they came under fire from St Pol's Brigade, which had been placed there by Villatte. However, the French withdrew without offering stern opposition and fell back to Villatte's main defences at the line of redoubts and, as the Spanish took the village, Arentschildt moved his two Portuguese batteries onto the knoll to support the main attack.

Wellington's orders were clear, that the main attack was to be delivered simultaneously by the Spanish on to the north end of the Heights of Calvinet and by Beresford's two divisions from the south. The flanking movement of Beresford's group was led gallantly by Somerset's hussars and followed by the 4th and then 6th divisions. However, the terrain along the edge of the canal proved too muddy for the divisional batteries to follow so they were instructed to fall out and form up to provide additional fire support to the attack in the north. Unfortunately Freire was not informed of this intention and mistook the gun deployment for a precursor to Beresford's main attack and accordingly gave the signal for the Spanish divisions to advance. The Spanish pressed forward in excellent order, with two brigades up, one in support and one in reserve, but the attack had almost no chance of success. For one thing it had not been, as per Wellington's instructions, undertaken simultaneously with that of Beresford and it was against a defence with superior numbers in well-defended positions. It soon stalled as the attackers tried to negotiate the obstacle created by the cutting of the Peyriolle road just shy of the redoubt and it collapsed when the line of Spanish infantry seeking refuge in the cutting were enfiladed by D'Armagnac's defenders at the bridge of Matabiau.[9]

Meanwhile, Beresford continued his southerly movement but the defeat of the Spanish enabled Soult to move Taupin south to shadow and counter Beresford. Taupin rather hot headedly charged the two divisional groups that had swung right and were advancing in brigaded echelons with battalions in line; they charged in columns of battalions supported by flanking fire from Harispe's men in the Sypière redoubts and the cavalry of Vial and Berton on either flank. Somerset came up to counter the latter threat but Pack was compelled to deploy the 79th into square in anticipation of Vial's charge, which as it happened, stalled at the cutting of one of the many lateral roads that cross the feature. 'The troops that were the nearest to the French batteries now closed upon the masses that came pouring over the hill, and the struggle became tremendous; but as usual, the red jackets prevailed, and in a quarter of an hour we stood triumphant on the hill. Here we were ordered to lay down to avoid as much as possible a flanking fire that was kept up by the enemy.'[10]

Soult was exasperated by Taupin's impetuosity and immediately formed a second defensive line between the Mas de Augustins redoubt and suburb of St Étienne. A delay ensued, enabling Beresford to call up his artillery, which arrived after nearly two hours and joined Gardiner's Troop and Von Grüben's cavalry that had arrived in the interim. At about 1430 hours the three batteries opened and Beresford began his attack on this second French line, which was timed to coincide with a second attempt by the Spanish troops to the north. The Spanish attack was, once again, made with great determination and led by all their senior officers across the front, many of whom were killed or injured, but the position was simply too strong and this second gallant attempt was also to result in failure. However, to the south, Beresford's attack was delivered with precision; the 6th Division took the heights and swept all before them while the 4th Division and the cavalry provided flank protection and prevented any serious French counter attack. The two Highland regiments, the 42nd and the 79th stormed the redoubts and succeeded in driving the 4/116th and 7/117th battalions from the structures with relative ease before pushing on. They were countered in strength by Harispe's reserve of three battalions and driven back beyond the redoubts that the French then reoccupied. They were quickly recaptured but equally rapidly lost again to a second French counter-attack until the encounter was settled by the deployment of Lambert's Brigade who overwhelmed the defenders, established an immovable presence and broke French resolve. Villatte was ordered to retire from the Great Redoubt at around 1700 hours; his departure marked the end of the fighting and left the Heights of Calvinet in Allied hands.

The next morning the Allies readjusted their positions; Freire's Spanish divisions and those of the 4th and 6th had suffered many losses and needed early respite which was provided by the Light Division and troops from Hill's force on the west bank. Soult meanwhile made preparations to evacuate the city via the Carcassone road to the south and commenced the withdrawal after dark on 11 April. Early on 12 April Wellington entered the city to the popular acclaim of the Royalist majority amidst great rejoicing. At 1700 hours the same day, Colonel Ponsonby rode in from Bordeaux with reports that Napoleon had abdicated as early as 6 April; it was magnificent news but its arrival was tinged with the sadness, for those who had fallen during the battle for the city of Toulouse had done so in vain. Soult refused to believe the authenticity of the reports from Paris and sent back word to Wellington demanding an armistice until unequivocal evidence could

---

8   This is very curious as no rocket troop was in the Toulouse organisation for battle, but this report from Lieutenant Colonel Carncross, commanding the artillery with Hill, in a letter to Dickson (*Manuscripts*, vol. VII, p. 1355) is quite clear and is supported by other eye witness accounts (Spencer Cooper, *Rough Notes of Seven Campaigns*, p. 116) who mention that rockets were fired in support of Beresford's main attack later in the day. I conclude that some rockets were attached to the two horse artillery batteries on the field that day.

9   See Toreno, *Guerra de la Independencia La Derrota de Napoleon*, vol. III, p.p. 241-244 and Arteche, *Guerra de la Independencia*, vol. XIV, p.p.123-125.

10   Spencer Cooper, *Rough Notes of Seven Campaigns*, p. 117.

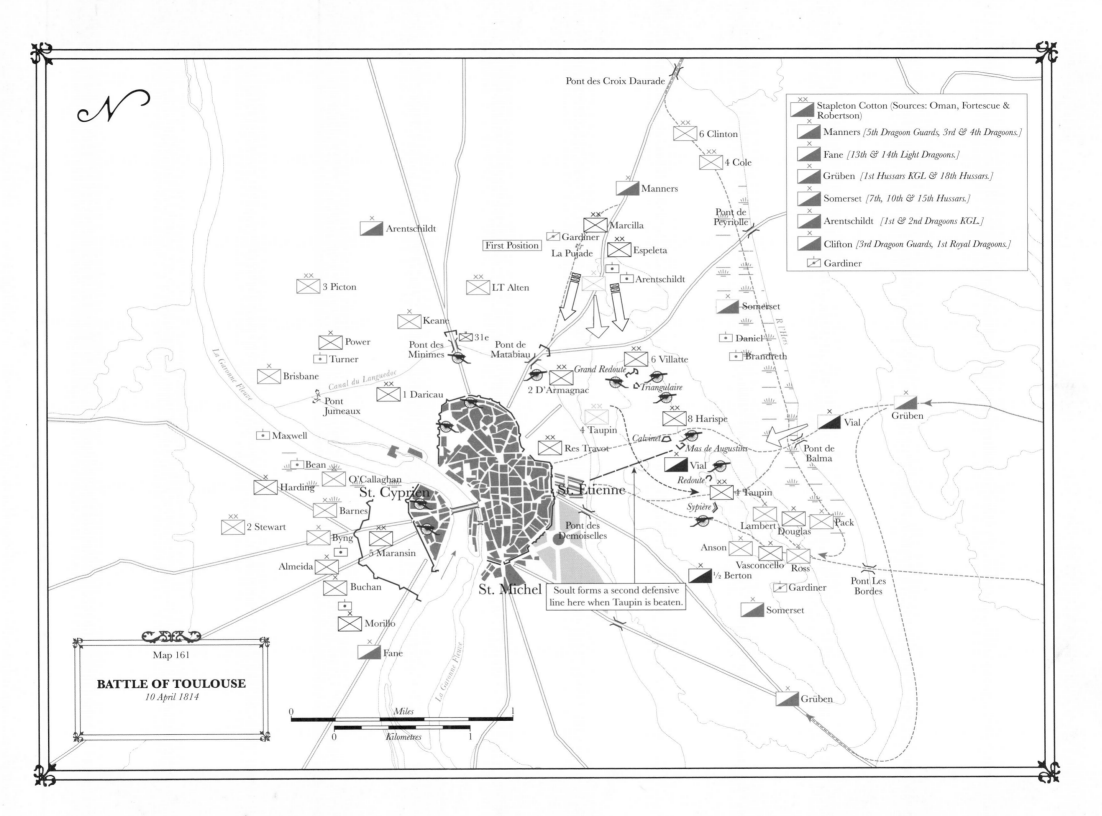

N

Pont des Croix Daurade

6 Clinton

4 Cole

Manners

Pont de Peyriolle

Marcilla

Gardiner
La Pujade

First Position

Espeleta

Arentschildt

Arentschildt

Somerset

3 Picton

LT Alten

Daniel

Keane

Brandreth

Power

31e

Pont de
Matabiau

Turner

Pont des
Minimes

6 Villatte

Grand Redoute

Brisbane

8 Harispe

Vial

Grüben

1 Daricau

2 D'Armagnac

Triangulaire

Canal du Languedoc

4 Taupin

Calvinet

Pont Jumeaux

Mas de Augustins

Maxwell

Res Travot

Vial

Pont de
Balma

La Garonne Fleuve

Redoute?

St. Cyprien

St. Étienne

4 Taupin

Pack

Bean

O'Callaghan

Sypière

Harding

Lambert

Douglas

Barnes

Anson

2 Stewart

Vasconcello

Ross

Byng

Gardiner

Pont Les
Bordes

5 Maransin

½ Berton

Almeida

Pont des
Demoiselles

Buchan

St. Michel

Soult forms a second defensive
line here when Taupin is beaten.

Morillo

Somerset

Map 161

BATTLE OF TOULOUSE
10 April 1814

Fane

0   Miles   1

0   Kilometres   1

Grüben

Legend:

⊠⊠ Stapleton Cotton (Sources: Oman, Fortescue &
Robertson)

Manners *[5th Dragoon Guards, 3rd & 4th Dragoons.]*

Fane *[13th & 14th Light Dragoons.]*

Grüben *[1st Hussars KGL & 18th Hussars.]*

Somerset *[7th, 10th & 15th Hussars.]*

Arentschildt *[1st & 2nd Dragoons KGL.]*

Clifton *[3rd Dragoon Guards, 1st Royal Dragoons.]*

Gardiner

be obtained. General Thouvenot, the governor of Bayonne, had similar misgivings and on 14 April executed a considerable sortie from the city against the Allied lines in the village of St Étienne, the scale and ferocity of which took the besiegers by surprise. 'The first brigade of the fifth division, which held it, had been driven back, as well as the picquets of the guards, and second light battalion of the legion, which were posted on the ground between the Bordeaux road and the Adour.'[11] Hay, who was officer of the day, was killed early and command and control further confused when Hope was wounded and captured along with his two aides-de-camp. 'General Hinüber, who had not failed to warn his brigade of the expected attack, and had assembled the several regiments on the alarm place[d], no sooner heard the firing on the other side of the river, than he led forward the first, second and fifth line battalions of the legion, in fine order, upon the village of Étienne … and before four o'clock, not only was St Étienne again in complete possession of the allies, but the whole of the ground from whence they had been driven … the French made many attempts to renew the attack on the British line, sending out swarms of tirailleurs and masses of men to renew the fight; but these were inevitably driven back; a field piece was now brought to bear on the retreating columns, and by six o'clock the firing had altogether ceased.'[12]

This sad tale was not the last of this epic conflict. On 16 April Habert, the governor of Barcelona, also executed a sortie from the city; an action with questionable military motive but one which personified French frustration at the loss of the war in Spain, the abdication of their champion, the loss of the Empire and the ultimate and impossible failure of the *Grande Armée*.

---

11 Beamish, *History of the King's German Legion*, vol. II, p. 302.

12 Ibid, p.p. 302-303.

Appendices

APPENDIX 1

STRENGTHS AND DISPOSITIONS 1808

First French Army of Spain: circa June 1808

1. Junot's Corps (The Army of Portugal)   24, 918
   a. 1st Division: General Delaborde (Brigades: Avril and Brennier)
   b. 2nd Division: General Loison (Brigades Charlot and Thomières)
   c. 3rd Division: General Travot (Brigades Graindorge and Fusier)
   d. Cavalry Division: General Kellermann (Brigades Margaron and Maurin)

2. Dupont's Corps (Observation of Gironde)   24,428
   a. 1st Division: General Barbou (Brigades Pannetier and Chabert)
   b. 2nd Division: General Vedel (Brigades Poinsot and Cassagne)
   c. 3rd Division: General Frère (Brigades Leval and Rostolland)[1]
   d. Cavalry Division: General Fresia (Brigades Rigaud and Dupré)
   e. Artillery Brigade: General Faultrier

3. Moncey's Corps (Observation of the Ocean Coast)   29,341
   a. 1st Division: General Musnier (Brigades Brun and Isemburg)
   b. 2nd Division: General Gobert (Brigades Lefranc and Dufour)
   c. 3rd Division: General Morlot (Brigades Bujet and Lefebvre)
   d. Cavalry Division: General Grouchy (Brigades Privé and Wathier)
   e. Artillery Brigade: General Couin

4. Bessières's Corps (Observation of the Pyrenees)   19,086
   a. 1st Division: General Merle (Brigades D'Armagnac and Gaulois)
   b. 2nd Division: General Verdier (Brigades Sabathier and Ducos)
   c. Cavalry Division: General Lasalle
   d. Garrison of Pamplona: General D'Agoult
   e. Garrison of San Sebastián: General Thouvenot

5. Duhesme's Corps (Observation of the Eastern Pyrenees)   12,714
   a. 1st Division: General Chabran (Brigades Goulas and Nicolas)
   b. 2nd Division: General Lecchi (Brigades Milosewitz and unknown)
   c. Cavalry Brigade: General Bessières
   d. Cavalry Brigade: General Schwartz

6. Imperial Guard: General Dorsenne   6,412

7. Additional troops that entered Spain, June to August: 48,204
   a. Division Mouton (Brigades Rey and Reynaud)
   b. Division Reille at Perpignan

   c. Division Chabot
   d. Brigade Bazancourt
   e. Brigade Chlopicki

Total of the First French Army of Spain   165,103

Notes:

1   General Mahler had commanded this division initially but had been killed during
    a training accident at Valladolid.

The French Army of Spain (under Napoleon) in November 1808[1]

1. 1st Corps: Marshal Victor   33,937
   a. 1st Division: General Ruffin
   b. 2nd Division: General Lapisse
   c. 3rd Division: General Villatte
   d. Cavalry Brigade: General Beaumont

2. 2nd Corps: Marshal Bessières (Soult after 9 November)   33,054
   a. 1st Division General Mouton (followed by General Merle)
   b. 2nd Division: General Merle (followed by General Mermet)
   c. 3rd Division: General Bonnet
   d. Cavalry Division: General Lasalle

3. 3rd Corps: Marshal Moncey   37,690
   a. 1st Division: General Maurice Mathieu (followed by General Grandjean)
   b. 2nd Division: General Musnier
   c. 3rd Division: General Morlot
   d. 4th Division: General Grandjean (later absorbed into the 3rd Division)
   e. Cavalry Brigade: General Wathier

4. 4th Corps: Marshal Lefebvre   22,895
   a. 1st Division: General Sebastiani
   b. 2nd Division: General Leval
   c. 3rd Division: General Valence
   d. Cavalry Brigade: General Maupetit

5. 5th Corps: Marshal Mortier   24,552
   a. 1st Division: General Suchet
   b. 2nd Division: General Gazan
   c. Cavalry Brigade: General Delaage

6. 6th Corps: Marshal Ney   38,033
   a. 1st Division: General Marchand
   b. 2nd Division: General Lagrange (followed by Maurice Mathieu)
   c. Cavalry Brigade: General Colbert

7. 7th Corps: General (Gouvion) St Cyr (from August 1808)   42,382
   a. 1st Division: General Chabran
   b. 2nd Division: General Lecchi

c. 3rd Division: General Reille

d. 4th Division: General Souham

e. 5th Division: General Pino

f. 6th Division: General Chabot

g. Cavalry Brigades: General Bessières, General Fontane and General Schwartz

8. 8th Corps: General Junot (dissolved in December 1808 – see Appendix 2)   25,730

   a. 1st Division: General Delaborde

   b. 2nd Division: General Loison

   c. 3rd Division: General Heudelet

   d. The Corps cavalry was composed of provisional regiments, which were dissolved

9. Reserves: 13,120

   a. Independent Reserve Division: General Dessolles

   b. Guards of the King of Spain: General Saligny

10. Reserve of Cavalry: 17,059

   a. Division of Dragoons: General Latour-Maubourg (3,695 sabres)

   b. Division of Dragoons: General Milhaud (2,940 sabres)

   c. Division of Dragoons: General Lahoussaye (2,020 sabres)

   d. Division of Dragoons: General Lorges (3,101 sabres)

   e. Division of Dragoons: General Millet (2,903 sabres)

   f. Division of Light Cavalry: General Franceschi (2,400 sabres)

11. Imperial Guard   12,100

Effective total of the French Army on 10 October 1808   244,125

Notes:

1   Plus an additional 5,200 troops en route from Germany and the French National Guards, located just inside the French border of 8,860: the gross total was 314,612. However, 32,643 were detached and 37,844 hospitalized or missing.

The Spanish Army: early 1808 (Source: Oman)

1. The Royal Guard: Cavalry 1,155; Infantry 6,029   7,184

2. Spanish Infantry of the Line   44,398

   (Each regiment had 3 battalions each of 4 companies and should have totalled 2,200 bayonets approximately.)

3. Light Infantry   13,655

   (Each regiment had only a single battalion of 6 companies numbering 1,200 bayonets approximately)

4. Foreign Infantry   12,981

   (The Swiss regiments had 2 battalions, the other nations, 2 battalions)

5. Militia   30,527

   (The 4 Grenadier regiments, 2 battalions each: 1,600 bayonets; the remainder 1 battalion, 600 bayonets)

6. Heavy Cavalry   7,232

   (Each regiment had 5 squadrons numbering about 700 sabres)

7. Light Cavalry   7,208

   (As above)

8. Field Artillery   4,410

   (Each regiment consisted of 10 batteries or companies. Six out of the 40 batteries were horse artillery. Four batteries were in Denmark with La Romana)

9. Garrison Artillery and their staff officers   2,269

10. Engineers   1,049

   (Consisting of an engineer battalion of 922, the balance being staff)

Total for Spanish army, in early 1808 (including 5,911 staff officers)   136,824

The Spanish armies: October to November 1808

Troops in the First Line

1. Blake's Army of Galicia   43,978

   a. Vanguard Brigade: General Mendizabal

   b. 1st Division: General Figueroa

   c. 2nd Division: General Martinengo

   d. 3rd Division: General Riquelme

   e. 4th Division: General Carbajal

   f. 5th Division: La Romana (recently arrived from Denmark)

   g. Asturian Division: General Acevedo

   h. Reserve Brigade: General Mahy

   (Blake's army formed the Army of the Left)

2. Galluzzo's Army of Estremadura   12,846

   a. 1st Division: Conde de Belvedere

   b. 2nd Division: General Henestrosa

   c. 3rd Division: General Trias

3. Castaños's Army of the Centre (largely the former Army of Andalusia)   51,000

   a. 1st Division: Conde de Villariezo

   b. 2nd Division: General Grimarest

   c. 3rd Division: General Rengel

   d. 4th Division: General La Peña

   e. 5th (Murcian-Valencian) Division: General Roca (vice General Llamas)

   f. Army of Castile: General Pignatelli (from 30 Oct General Cartaojal)

   (The armies of Galluzzo and Castaños formed the Army of the Centre)

4. Palafox's Army of Aragon   33,674

   a. 1st Division: General O'Neille

   b. 2nd Division: General St March

   c. 3rd Division: General Conde de Lazan

   d. Large Reserves at Zaragoza

5. Vives's Army of Catalonia   20,033
   a. Vanguard Division: Brigadier General Alvarez
   b. 1st Division: General Conde de Caldagues
   c. 2nd Division: General Laguna
   d. 3rd Division: General La Serna
   e. 4th Division: General Milans
   (The armies of Palafox and Vives formed the Army of the Right)

Total of Spanish First Line troops   161,531

Troops in the Second Line

6. Army of Granada (part of the Army of the Right)   15,000
7. Army of reserve of Madrid (part of Army of the Centre)   12,118
8. Galician reserves (part of Army of the Left)   3,610
9. Asturian reserves (part of the Army of the Left)   5,285
10. Estremaduran reserves (part of the Army of the Centre)   4,608
11. Andalusian reserves (part of the Army of the Centre)   13,371
12. Murcian and Valencian reserves (part of Army of the Centre)   5,774
13. Balearic isles (not attributed)   3,360

Total of Spanish Second Line troops   63,126

Spanish Army at the battle of Tudela: 23 November 1808 (Sources Sañudo and Partridge/Oliver)

1. 2nd Division: General Grimarest (13 batallones):
   a. Ceuta: 2 batallones
   b. Ordenes Militares: (three batallones)
   c. Milicia Provincial de Trujillo
   d. Milicia Provincial de Bujalance
   e. Milicia Provincial de Cuenca
   f. Milicia Provincial de Ciudad Real
   g. Cazadores de Cataluña
   h. Tiradores Voluntarios de España
   i. Cazadores de Carmona
   j. Tiradores de Cádiz (Not confirmed)

2. 4th Division: General La Peña (13 batallones)
   a. Africa (2 batallones)
   b. Burgos (2 batallones)
   c. Zaragoza
   d. Murcia (2 batallones)
   e. Granaderos Provinciales de Andalusia (2 batallones)
   f. Milicia Provincial de Siguenza
   g. Cazadores de las Navas de Tolosa
   h. Bailén
   i. Voluntarios de Sevilla

3. 5th Division: General Roca (17 batallones)
   a. Valencia (3 batallones)
   b. America (3 batallones)
   c. Milicia Provincial de Murcia
   d. Milicia Provincial de Avila
   e. 1st Cazadores de Valencia
   f. 2nd Cazadores de Valencia (3 batallones)
   g. 2nd Cazadores de Orihuela (3 batallones)
   h. Liria
   i. Peñas de San Pedro

4. Brigadier General Villariezo (12½ batallones from the 1st and 3rd Divisions)
   a. Guardias Walonas
   b. Reina
   c. Jaén
   d. Irlanda
   e. Barbastro (½ batallon)
   f. Campo Mayor
   g. Voluntarios de Valencia
   h. Milicia Provincial de Jaén
   i. Milicia Provincial de Burgos
   j. Milicia Provincial de Plasencia
   k. Milicia Provincial de Guadix
   l. Milicia Provincial de Sevilla
   m. Milicia Provincial de Lorca
   n. Milicia Provincial de Toro

5. O'Neille's Division (11 batallones)
   a. 3rd Real Guardia Español
   b. Estremadura
   c. 1st Ligera de Aragón
   d. 1st Ligera de Zaragoza
   e. 4th Tercio de Aragón
   f. 2nd Valencia
   g. 1st and 2nd Voluntarios de Murcia
   h. 1st Voluntarios de Huesca
   i. 3rd Cazadores de Fernando VII
   j. Suizos de Aragón

6. St March's Division (14 batallones)
   a. Voluntarios de Castilla
   b. Milicia Provincial de Soria
   c. Voluntarios de Turia (3 batallones)
   d. Voluntarios de Borbón
   e. Voluntarios de Alicante (3 batallones)
   f. Voluntarios de Chelva

g. 2nd Cazadores de Fernando VII

h. Cazadores de Segorbe

7. Army of Castilla (Cartajoal's Troops)[1]:

a. Cantabria (2 batallones)

b. Milicia Provincial de León

c. Granaderos del General del Ejército del Centro

d. Cazadores de Cuenca

8. Andalusian Cavalry Division (12 Regimientos)

a. Montesa

b. Farnesio

c. Borbón

d. España

e. Calatrava

f. Santiago

g. Principe

h. Alcántara

i. Dragones de Reina

j. Dragones de Sagunto

k. Dragones de Pavia

l. Cazadores de Olivenza

Notes:

1 These are units originally under Pignatelli's command, which was broken up following the failure by this formation to hold and then subsequently destroy the bridge at Logroño. There is much confusion as to the number and strength of the units who were redistributed and exactly where they were sent.

The Portuguese Army: December 1808 (Source: Chartrand)

24 First Line Infantry Regiments

a. 1st Lisboa

b. 2nd Abrantes

c. 3rd Estremoz

d. 4th Lisboa

e. 5th Elvas

f. 6th Porto, Lamego

g. 7th Setúbal

h. 8th Castello de Vide

i. 9th Tomar, Viana

j. 10th Lisboa

k. 11th Viseu

l. 12th Chaves, Vila Real

m. 13th Lisboa

n. 14th Tomar

o. 15th Vila Viçosa

p. 16th Lisboa

q. 17th Elvas

r. 18th Porto, Tomar

s. 19th Cascais

t. 20th Campo Mayor

u. 21st Valença, Guimarães

v. 22nd Elvas

w. 23rd Almeida

x. 24th Bragança

Six caçadores battalions: (Castelo Branco, Moura, Trancoso, Penamacor, Campo Maior, Vila Real): 2,419 men

Loyal Lusitanian Legion: 2,300 men

12 cavalry regiments (Lisbon (3), Beja, Évora, Chaves, Santarém, Almeida, Bragança): 3,641 men, 2,617 horses, 629 uniformes

The British Army under Sir John Moore: October 1808

1.	Cavalry (Lord Paget)	3,078
2.	1st Division: Lieutenant General Baird	7,424
	a. Warde's Brigade	
	b. Bentinck's Brigade	
	c. Manningham's Brigade	
3.	2nd Division: Lieutenant General Hope	7,512
	a. Leith's Brigade	
	b. Hill's Brigade	
	c. (Catlin) Craufurd's Brigade	
4.	3rd Division: Lieutenant General Fraser	5,677
	a. Beresford's Brigade	
	b. Fane's Brigade	
5.	Reserve Division: Major General E.Paget	3,938
	a. Anstruther's Brigade	
	b. Disney's Brigade	
6.	1st Flank Brigade: Colonel Craufurd	2,262
7.	2nd Flank Brigade: Brigadier General Alten	1,751
8.	Artillery (including drivers)	1,455
9.	Staff Corps	137
Total strength of the British army in October 1808		33,234

The British garrison at Lisbon on 14 December 1808: General Sir John Craddock

1. The following troops were left behind at Lisbon by Sir John Moore in October:

a. 2/9th, 29th, 40th, 45th, 82nd, 97th, and the 1st, 2nd, 5th and 7th line battalions of the KGL

b. Three squadrons of the 20th LD (the regiment was badly cut up at Vimeiro)

c. Five gun batteries, only one of which was horsed

2. The following battalions were sent back to Lisbon from Salamanca in late November 1808:
   a. 3rd and the 5/60th

3. The following troops arrived from England:
   a. 3/27th and 2/31st in November, and the 14th LD in December

Note:

This provided a force of about 12,000; although no more than 10,000 were effective. Consisting of 13 battalions of infantry, 7 squadrons of cavalry and 5 batteries of guns. However, this force was spread across Portugal and not based in Lisbon itself, until Craddock ordered them to fall back at the end of January 1809.

APPENDIX 2

STRENGTHS AND DISPOSITIONS 1809

The Spanish Army of the Centre: 11 January 1809

1.	Vanguard Division: Major General Duke of Alburquerque	3,929
2.	1st Division: Lieutenant General Marquis de Coupigny	5,121
3.	2nd Division: Major General Conde de Orgaz	5,288
4.	Reserve: Lieutenant General La Peña	4,295
5.	Cavalry (Estimate as returns incomplete)	2,814
6.	Artillery	386

(Comprising 20 guns in total – these were all lost to the French by 18 January; 5 guns at the battle of Uclés (only 4 were deployed as the 5th gun was broken) and the remaining 15 during the retreat of the Duke of Infantado with the balance of the Army of the Centre.)

7.	Engineers	383
	Total of the Spanish Army of the Centre	22,216

The French Army in Spain: 1 February 1809

1. 1st Corps: Marshal Victor (48 guns) 22,926
   a. 1st Division: General Ruffin
   b. 2nd Division: General Lapisse
   c. 3rd Division: General Villatte
   d. Cavalry Brigade: General Beaumont

2. 2nd Corps: Marshal Soult (54 guns)[1] 21,452
   a. 1st Division: General Merle
   b. 2nd Division: General Mermet[2]
   c. 3rd Division: General Delaborde[3]
   d. 4th Division: General Heudelet
   e. Cavalry Brigade: General Franceschi

3. 3rd Corps: General Junot (Suchet in April 1809) (40 guns) 16,071
   a. 1st Division: General Grandjean
   b. 2nd Division: General Musnier
   c. 3rd Division: General Morlot
   d. Cavalry Brigade: General Wathier

4. 4th Corps: General Sebastiani (30 guns) 15,399
   a. 1st Division: General Sebastiani
   b. 2nd Division: General Leval
   c. 3rd Division: General Valence
   d. Cavalry Brigade: General Maupetit

5. 5th Corps: Marshal Mortier (30 guns) 17,959
   a. 1st Division: General Suchet
   b. 2nd Division: General Gazan
   c. Cavalry Brigade: General Delaage

6. 6th Corps: Marshal Ney (30 guns) 16,176
   a. 1st Division: General Marchand
   b. 2nd Division: General Maurice Mathieu
   c. Cavalry Brigade: General Lorcet

7. 7th Corps: General Gouvion St Cyr (Augereau in June 1809)[4] 39,415
   a. 1st Division: General Souham
   b. 2nd Division: General Chabran
   c. 3rd Division: General Chabot
   d. 4th Division: General Reille
   e. 5th Division: General Pino
   f. 6th Division: General Lecchi
   g. German Division: General Morio
   h. Cavalry Brigades: General Bessières, General Fontane and General Schwartz

8. Reserve Cavalry[5] 10,892
   a. Division of Dragoons: General Latour-Maubourg (2,527 sabres)
   b. Division of Dragoons: General Milhaud (2,125 sabres)
   c. Division of Dragoons: General Lahoussaye, (1,335 sabres)
   d. Division of Dragoons: General Lorges, (1,228) sabres
   e. Division of Dragoons: General Millet, (1,470) sabres
   f. Division of Light Cavalry: General Lasalle (1,495) sabres

9.	Reserve at Madrid	11,207
10.	Northern Garrison: Marshal Bessières	19,902
11.	Grand Park of Artillery (Total 232 guns)	2,579
	Army total	193,978[6]

Notes:

1   Soult's Corps was particularly incapacitated; on paper they had 45,000, but after the gruelling advance to La Coruña they were left with half that number.

2   Mermet´s Brigade was broken up at the end of July, as the 2nd, 5th and 6th corps concentrated and moved south to engage the Anglo-Spanish army.

3   Many of these troops had come over from Junot's 8th Corps, which had been disbanded in December 1808, including the two divisional commanders, Delaborde and Heudelet.

4   Number of guns unknown but 2,700 gunners.

5   Number of guns unknown but 712 gunners.

6   However, if the 56,404 sick, 36,326 detached troops, and the 1,843 prisoners are added, the total of the French Army of Spain at this time is 288,551.

French and Spanish Forces at the second siege of Zaragoza – 20 December 1808 to 20 February 1809[1]

1.   3rd Corps: General Junot   16,071
     a. 1st Division: Grandjean (14e, 44e Ligne, 2e and 3e Vistula)   5,866
     b. 2nd Division: Musnier (114e and 115e Ligne, 1e Vistula, 2e Légion de Réserve)   3,544
     c. 3rd Division: Morlot (5e Léger, 116e, 117e and 121e Ligne)   2,637
     d. Corps Cavalry Brigade: Wathier (13e Cuirassiers, 4e Hussars, 1e Légion   1,652
        de Vistula, Régiment Provisoires)

2.   5th Corps: General Mortier   17,959
     a. 1st Division: Suchet (17e Léger, 34e, 40e, 64e, and 88e Ligne)   8,477
     b. 2nd Division: Gazan (21e, 28e, 110e and 103e Ligne)   7,110
     c. Corps Cavalry Brigade: Delaage (10e Hussars, 21e Chasseurs)   926

3.   Artillery Companies (exact distribution unknown but the numbers of artillery are included in the 3rd and 5th Corps totals)
     A pied:
     a. 1er Régiment: 5e and 20e companie
     b. 3e Régiment: 7e, 18e, 21e and 22e companie
     c. 5e Régiment: 1e, 2e, 7e, 15e and 20e companie
     d. 6e Régiment: 11e companie
     A cheval:
     a. 5e Régiment: 7e companie
     b. 6e Régiment: 3e companie

Notes:

1   The French forces were under Moncey from 20 to 29 December 1808; Junot from 29 December 1808 to 22 January 1809; and Lannes from 22 January to 20 February 1809.

Spanish Forces under Palafox

1.   1st Division: Brigadier General Butron (Guardias Walonas, Estremadura, Granaderos de Palafoz, Fusileros del Reyno, Don Carlos, Carmen, Portillo, Torreno, Calatayad, 1st and 2nd Ligero de Zaragoza, 1st Cazadores Catalanes and 2nd Voluntarios de Aragón)

2.   2nd Division: Brigadier General Firaller (Guardias Españoles, 2nd Valencia, 1st Voluntarios de Aragón, Aragónese, Cazadores de Fernando VII)

3.   3rd Division: Brigadier General Manso (Peñas de San Pedro, 1st Huesca, Florida Blanca, 1st Tiradores de Murcia, 1st, 2nd and 3rd Murcia, Suizos de Aragón)

4.   4th Division: General St March (Voluntarios de Borbon, Voluntarios de Castilla, Voluntarios de Chelva, Voluntarios de Turia, Cazadores de Fernando VII (Valencianos), Segorbe, Soria, 1st Alicante, 5th Murcia and 2nd Tiradores de Murcia)

5.   Roca's Division: (1st Savoia, Orihuela, 1st Cazadores de Valencia, Murcia, America, Avila)

6.   Artillery: 160 guns manned by 1,800 men

The Organization of the Portuguese Army in 1809

1.   Infantry of the Line[1]   27,076
     a. 1st Regiment: 1st of Lisboa or La Lippe
     b. 2nd Regiment: Laos or Algarve
     c. 3rd Regiment: 1st of Olivenza
     d. 4th Regiment: Freire
     e. 5th Regiment: 1st of Elvas
     f. 6th Regiment: 1st of Porto
     g. 7th Regiment: Setubal
     h. 8th Regiment: Evora
     i. 9th Regiment: Viana
     j. 10th Regiment: 2nd of Lisboa
     k. 11th Regiment: 1st of Almeida
     l. 12th Regiment: Chaves
     m. 13th Regiment: Peniche
     n. 14th Regiment: Tavira
     o. 15th Regiment: 2nd of Olivenza
     p. 16th Regiment: Vieira Telles
     q. 17th Regiment: 2nd Elvas
     r. 18th Regiment: 2nd of Porto
     s. 19th Regiment: Cascais
     t. 20th Regiment: Campo Mayor
     u. 21st Regiment: Valenza
     v. 22nd Regiment: Serpa
     w. 23rd Regiment: 2nd of Almeida
     x. 24th Regiment: Bragança

2.   Caçadores (light Infantry)[2]   3,152
     a. 1st Castello de Vide
     b. 2nd Moura
     c. 3rd Villa Real
     d. 4th Vizeu
     e. 5th Campomayor
     f. 6th Porto

3. Cavalry[3]   6,040
   a. 1st Alcanatar Dragones
   b. 2nd Moura
   c. 3rd Olivenza
   d. 4th Duke of Mecklenburg, Lisboa
   e. 5th Evora
   f. 6th Bragança
   g. 7th Lisboa
   h. 8th Elvas
   i. 9th Chaves
   j. 10th Santarem
   k. 11th Almeida
   l. 12th Miranda

4. Artillery   4,472
   (Four regiments with HQs at Lisbon, Faro, Estremoz and Oporto)

5. Engineers (no figures available)

6. The Lusitanian Legion   3,500 approx
   (Three battalions of infantry, each 10 companies of approximately
   1,000 men; 1 regiment of cavalry consisting of 3 squadrons and 1 battery
   of field artillery)

Total of the regular Portuguese army[4]   33,000 infantry
     6,300 cavalry
     5,000 artillery

Notes:

1   Each regiment consisted of 2 battalions with 7 companies.

2   Six single battalions with an effective strength of 770 per battalion. The 7th, 8th and 9th Caçadores were formed later out of the 3 battalions of the Lusitanian Legion. The 11th, 12th and 13th were raised in 1811.

3   Twelve regiments, numbered 1–12, each regiment with an approximate strength of 600 men in 4 squadrons.

4   After 1810 the Portuguese infantry was brigaded into pairs of regiments, many of which then joined British divisions. In 1809, the militia was going through considerable reorganization. It was to have 3 divisions, South, Centre and North.

The Reorganization of the Spanish Armies in early 1809

1. La Romana's (since November 1808) Army of Galicia   9,000
   (There were an additional 14–15,000 under arms in the Asturias, mainly the
   relics of Acevedo's Division following the Battle at Espinosa. Cienfuegos was
   Captain-General of the Army of the Asturias in early 1809 when their
   strength rose to about 20,000 men. La Romana returned to the Asturias and
   took command of this army (in addition to his own) in April 1809.

2. Cuesta's Army of Estremadura   13,000
   (Despite failings at Cabezon and Medina de Ríóseco the Junta decided to give this
   command to Cuesta, estimated at 10,500 infantry and 2,500 cavalry in January
   1809. The Army was all but wiped out following Medellin in March 1809 but was
   quickly rebuilt and joined Wellesley for the Talavera Campaign in mid-1809.)

3. Cartaojal's Army of the Centre   20,000 approx
   (This was the combined force of Del Palacio and the Infantado, but after
   his disastrous attempt on Toledo, General Venegas replaced him in April.)

4. Palafox's Army of Aragon[1]   32,000
   (The Army was destroyed during the second siege of Zaragoza, ending 20
   February, with only 8,000 remaining, which were largely taken prisoner and
   marched to France.)

5. Reding's Army of Catalonia[2]   32,000

6. Conde de Conquista's Army of Valencia[1 & 2]   10,000

Notes:

1   Blake assumed command of the armies of Aragon, Valencia and Catalonia in April 1809.

2   Acting Captain-General José Caro Sureda assumed command in March 1809 until August 1810 but the army of Valencia remained under the overall command of Blake.

(The Junta estimated the Spanish force at approximately 135,000 at the end of January 1809)

The Spanish battalions at the battle of Medellin (Sources: Oman and Sañudo)

1. Vanguard: Henestrosa: (four batallones)
   a. Granaderos Provinciales
   b. Voluntarios de Serena
   c. Granaderos de General
   d. Voluntarios de Antequera

2. 1st Division: Duke del Parque (7 batallones)
   a. 4/Reales Guardias Españoles
   b. Walonas Reales (2 batallones 2nd and 4th)
   c. Jaén (2 batallones)
   d. 2/Provinicial de Burgos
   e. 2/Osuna

3. 2nd Division: Trías: (8 batallones)
   a. 2/Mallorca
   b. 2/Voluntarios de Cataluña
   c. Provincial de Badajoz
   d. Mérida
   e. Irlanda (2 batallones, 2nd and 3rd)
   f. Provincial de Toledo
   g. Valencia de Alcantara y Alburquerque

4. 3rd Division: Portago: (5 batallones)
   a. Badajoz (dos batallones 1st and 2nd)
   b. 2/Voluntarios de Madrid
   c. Sevilla
   d. Provincial de Cádiz

5. Duke de Alburquerque: (9 batallones)
   a. Campo Mayor
   b. Provincial de Guadix
   c. Córdoba
   d. Tiradores de Cádiz
   e. Tiradores de Castilla (3 batallones)
   f. Tercios de Castilla
   g. 2/Marina

Note:

In addition, Plasencia and Salamanca were present (the latter regiment's colonel was killed) but their position in the ORBAT is unknown. Total, 35 batallones.

The British Army in Portugal by March 1809

See Army Strengths 1808: The British garrison at Lisbon, 14 December 1808 (Sources: Oman, Leslie and Dickson)

1. Mackenzie's Brigade (3/27th, 2/9th and the 29th) had been returned to Lisbon (on 12 March 1809) along with Tilson's Brigade (2/87th, 88th) and 2nd Coldstream Guards and 3rd Foot Guards, which had been sent directly there from England

2. In addition, 3 more batteries of artillery were sent to the Peninsula, which arrived on 4 March 1809, namely:
   a. Captain John May's Company
   b. Captain F. Glubb's Company
   c. Captain D. Sillery's Company

Along with half Lawson's Company (half strength but 6 pieces of ordnance) and Bredin's Company, there were now 8 batteries: 3 were RA and 3 were KGL. But there were still only sufficient horses for 2 batteries. Lieutenant Colonel Robe RA (commander of the artillery), reorganized the companies as follows by 23 March 1809:

a. Captain Sillery's Company: Light 6-pdr brigade (4x light 6-pdr and 2x 5½in howitzers) at Luminar

b. Captain Bredin's Company, duties at Lisbon and Fort Belem and reserve brigade of 6-pdrs for which there were no horses

c. Captain May's Company, 6-pdr brigade, (5x light 6-pdr and 1x 5½in howitzer) to be horsed and provide support to the Guards

d. Captain Glubb's Company, to occupy Cascais and provide men for transport duties and stores

e. Captain Lawson's Company: Light 3-pdr brigade (6x light 3-pdr) to support the cavalry

f. Captain Gesenius's Company (KGL), St Julian Forts and on receipt of horses would man a brigade in support of the KGL

g. Captain Teiling's Company (KGL) Brigade of artillery, to form the left wing of the army

h. Captain Heise's Company (KGL) Brigade of heavy guns (5x heavy 6-pdr and 1x 5½in howitzer)

This provided General Craddock with a total force (in Portugal) of 16,000

The Anglo-Portuguese Army in Portugal by 6 May 1809: Under Sir Arthur Wellesley at Coimbra (Sources: Oman, Leslie and Dickson)

1. Cavalry   3,454
   a. 1st Brigade: Stapleton-Cotton (14th, 16th and 20th Light Dragoons, 3rd Light Dragoons KGL)
   b. 2nd Brigade: Fane (3rd Dragoon Guards, 4th Dragoons)

2. Infantry[1]   21,787
   a. Brigade of Guards: H. Campbell (1st Coldstream, 3rd Foot Guards, company 5/60th)
   b. 1st Brigade: Hill (3rd, 2/48th, 2/66th, company 5/60th)
   c. 2nd Brigade: Mackenzie (3/27th, 2/31st, 45th)
   d. 3rd Brigade: Tilson (2/87th , 88th, 1st Lisbon, 5/60th [5 companies])
   e. 4th Brigade: Sontag (97th, 2nd Detachments, 2/16th Vieira Telles, company 5/60th)
   f. 5th Brigade: A. Campbell (2/7th, 53rd, 10th the 2nd Lisbon, company 5/60th)
   g. 6th Brigade: R. Stewart (29th, 1st Detachments, 1/16th Vieira Telles)
   h. 7th Brigade: Cameron (2/9th, 2/83rd, 2/10th the 2nd Lisbon, company 5/60th)
   i. King's German Legion: Murray (1st, 2nd, 5th, and 7th Line KGL)

3. Artillery[2]   1,845
   a. Baynes's Battery: Light 6-pdr
   b. Lane's Battery: Light 6-pdr
   c. Lawson's Battery: Light 3-pdr
   d. Rettberg's KGL Battery: Light 6-pdr
   e. Heise's KGL Battery: Long 6-pdr

4. Engineers   40

5. Wagon Train   105

Total[3]   27,231

Notes:

1   The following troops remained unattached in Lisbon: 2/24th, 2/30th, Independent light company KGL.

2   The arrival of 300 suitable mounts on the transports from Ireland enabled Lieutenant Colonel Robe to equip 5 brigades of artillery for the mission – as listed. The balance of 5 batteries (from the list of March 1809) remained at Lisbon.

3   General Beresford had been busy reorganizing the Portuguese army – see above. In addition to the regiments of 1st and 2nd of Lisbon and 16th Vieira Telles, the following infantry and cavalry units had been established by late April:

a.   3rd Regiment: 1st of Olivenza

b.   4th Regiment: Freire

c.   7th Regiment: Setubal

d.   13th Regiment: Peniche

e.   15th Regiment: 2nd of Olivenza

f.   19th Regiment: Cascais

g.   20th Regiment: Campo Mayor

h.   1st, 4th and 5th Caçadores

i.   1st Alcanatar Dragones

j.   4th Duke of Mecklenburg, Lisboa

k.   7th Lisboa

Areizaga's army at the battle of Ocaña: 19 November 1809 (Sources: Sañudo, Ontalba Juárez y Ruiz Jaén, La Batalla de Ocaña)[1]

1. Vanguard Division: José Zayas (11 battalions)
   a. Voluntarios de España (2 battalions)
   b. Granaderos Provinciales
   c. Cantabria (2 battalions)
   d. Voluntarios de Valencia
   e. 2nd Mallorca (2 battalions)
   f. Plasencia
   g. Provincial de Plasencia
   h. Maestranza de Ronda
   i. One battery: 4 guns, Gurierrez

2. 1st Division: Lacy (11 battalions)
   a. Milicia Provincial de Chinchilla
   b. 1st Córdoba
   c. Milicia Provincial de Córdoba
   d. Carmona
   e. 1st España
   f. 1st Burgos (2 battalions)
   g. Alcalá la Real
   h. Milicia Provincial de Cuenca
   i. Voluntarios de Sevilla
   j. 1st Loja
   k. One battery: 6 guns, Velarde

3. 2nd Division: Vigodet (8 battalions)
   a. Milicia Provincial de Ronda
   b. Milicia Provincial Alcázar de San Juan
   c. Milicia Provincial de Ciudad Real
   d. Voluntarios de Corona (2 battalions)
   e. Ordenes Militares (2 battalions)
   f. 1st Guadix
   g. One battery: 6 guns, De Molina

4. 3rd Division: Giron (7 battalions)
   a. 2nd Córdoba (2 battalions)
   b. Milicia Provincial de Toledo
   c. Reales Guardias Españoles (2 battalions)
   d. Milicia Provincial de Jaén
   e. Bailén
   f. One battery: 4 guns, Garvia

5. 4th Division: Castejon (10 battalions)
   a. De Línea Velez-Malaga (2 battalions)
   b. De LigeroVelez-Malaga
   c. Voluntarios de Sevilla
   d. Milicia Provincial de Jérez
   e. Milicia Provincial de Bujalance
   f. 2nd Loja
   g. 1st Málaga (2 battalions)
   h. 3rd Córdoba
   i. One battery: 6 guns, Castilla

6. 5th Division: Zerain (7 battalions)
   a. 2nd España
   b. Barbastro
   c. 2nd Milicia Provincial de Granada
   d. 2nd Milicia Provincial de Sevilla
   e. 3rd Reales Guardias Walonas
   f. 2nd Voluntarios de Madrid
   g. 2nd Voluntarios de Sevilla
   h. One battery: 4 guns, De Torres

7. 6th Division: Jacomé (9 battalions)
   a. Estremadura
   b. 1st and 2nd Badajoz (2 battalions)
   c. 4th Voluntarios de Sevilla
   d. Milicia Provincial de Málaga
   e. Milicia Provincial de Ecija
   f. Alpujarras
   g. Jaén
   h. 1st Marina
   i. One battery: 6 guns, Chamizo

8. 7th Division: Copons (9 battalions)
   a. Africa
   b. La Reina
   c. 2nd Marina (2 battalions)
   d. 2nd Murcia (2 battalions)
   e. 3rd Voluntarios de Sevilla
   f. Tiradores de Cádiz
   g. Milicia Provincial de Badajoz
   h. One battery: 6 guns, De Rio

9. 1st Cavalry Division: Bernuy (1,752 horses)

   a. Lanceros de Estremadura

   b. Almansa

   c. Rey

   d. Infante

   e. Madrid

   f. Carabineros Reales

   g. Reales Guardias de Corps (1 squadron)

10. 2nd Cavalry Division (1,647 horses):

   a. 1st and 2nd Husares de Estremadura

   b. Pavia

   c. Toledo

   d. La Reina - Dragones

   e. Alba de Tormes

   f. Lanceros de Jerez (1 squadron)

11. 3rd Cavalry Division: March (1,546 horses)

   a. Montaña de Córdoba

   b. La Reina: Línea

   c. 1st Alcantara

   d. Voluntarios de Sevilla

   e. Montesa

   f. 2nd Santiago

   g. Principe

12. 4th Cavalry Division: Ossorio (1,655 horses)

   a. España

   b. Farnesio

   c. Granaderos de Fernando VII

   d. 2nd Lusitania

   e. Granada

   f. Cazadores Francos de Castilla (2 squadrons)

   g. Lanceros de Utrera (1 squadron)

13. Artillery (other than shown)

   a. Cavalry: one horse artillery battery (number of guns unknown), Jiminez

   b. Reserve: 2 guns, De Haro

   c. Park 1: 8 guns, De Quesado

   d. Park 2: 8 guns, Correa

Note:

1   This ORBAT differs considerably from that outlined in Oman

APPENDIX 3

STRENGTHS AND DISPOSITIONS 1810

The French Army in Spain – 15 January 1810 (Source: Oman)

1.	1st Corps: Marshal Victor	28,180
	a. 1st Division: Ruffin	5,513
	b. 2nd Division: Darricau	8,110
	c. 3rd Division: Villatte	7,087
	d. Light Cavalry Brigade: Beaumont	1,127
	e. Division Dragoons: Latour-Maubourg	3,030
2.	2nd Corps: General Heudelet (Vice Soult)	18,830
	a. 1st Division: Merle	6,847
	b. 2nd Division: Heudelet	8,472
	c. Light Cavalry Division: P. Soult	1,093
	d. Division Dragoons: Lahoussaye	1,545
3.	3rd Corps: General Suchet	26,630
	a. 1st Division: Leval[1]	5,348
	b. 2nd Division: Musnier	8,465
	c. 3rd Division: Habert	4,757
	d. Cavalry Brigade: Boussard	2,172
4.	4th Corps: General Sebastiani[2]	13,360
	a. 1st Division: Left at Madrid	2,279
	b. 3rd (Polish) Division: Werlé	6,148
	c. Light Cavalry Brigade: Perreymond	1,939
	d. Division Dragoons: Milhaud	2,315
5.	5th Corps: Marshal Mortier	21,178
	a. 1st Division: Girard	8,951
	b. 2nd Division: Gazan	8,287
	c. Cavalry Division: Marisy	2,352
6.	6th Corps: Marshal Ney	39,572
	a. 1st Division: Marchand	7,177
	b. 2nd Division: Mermet	7,585
	c. 3rd Division: Loison	14,587
	d. Cavalry Division: Lorges	2,616
7.	7th Corps: Marshal Augereau[3]	51,472
	a. 1st Division: Souham	8,463
	b. 2nd Division: Pino	9,287
	c. 3rd Division: Verdier	14,318
	d. 4th Division: Duhesme	8,387

8. 8th Corps: General Junot   37,337
   a. 1st Division: Clausel   10,777
   b. 2nd Division: Lagrange   10,343
   c. 3rd Division: Solignac   8,074
   d. Cavalry Division: St Croix   5,479

Total strength of the French 8th Army Corps   236,559

Notes:

1   Not to be confused with the German Divisional Commander Leval – see note 2.

2   Leval's Division was escorting prisoners from Ocaña and never rejoined the 4th Corps for the duration of the war.

3   General Rouyer arrived on 1 February 1810, at Girona as the new 5th Division for the Corps, along with a Neapolitan Brigade – a total of 8,000 men.

French troops in Spain but not part of the eight Army Corps

1. Dessolles Division: en route for Andalusia   10,641
2. Government of Navarre: Dufour, Garrison Commander   9,676
3. Government of Biscay: Valentin, Garrison Commander   19,405
4. Kellermann's Dragoon Division (including 2, 3 and 4 Swiss)   5,313
5. Leval's Division (escorting prisoners – see Note 2 above)   9,739
6. 1st Division from 4th Corps – located in Madrid   13,917
7. Bonnet's Brigade at Santander   7,972
8. Imperial Guard   17,305
9. Others, in or around, Bayonne (future 9th Corps)   16,415
10. Miscellaneous   13,661

Total of French troops in campaign   360,603

Masséna's Army of Portugal – 15 September 1810 (Source: Oman) – Total 65,050

1. 2nd Corps: General Reynier   17,718
   a. 1st Division: General Merle
   b. 2nd Division: General Heudelet
   c. Cavalry Brigade: General P. Soult

2. 6th Corps: Marshal Ney   24,306
   a. 1st Division: General Marchand
   b. 2nd Division: General Mermet
   c. 3rd Division: General Loison
   d. Cavalry Brigade: General Lamotte

3. 8th Corps: General Junot   16,939
   a. 1st Division: General Clausel
   b. 2nd Division: General Solignac
   c. Cavalry Division: General St Croix

4. Reserve of Cavalry: General Montbrun   3,479
   a. Lorcet's Brigade
   b. Cavrois's Brigade
   c. Orano's Brigade

Note:

Kellermann and Bonnet's divisions were also attached to Masséna's Army, but were tied to their local duties: Kellermann in containing the plains of Valladolid, and Bonnet in holding Santander.

Wellington's Army within the Lines of Torres Vedras – 1 November 1810

1. Cavalry Division: General Stapleton Cotton   2,833
   a. De Grey's Brigade
   b. Slade's Brigade
   c. Anson's Brigade

2. 1st Division: General Spencer   6,948
   a. Stopford's Brigade
   b. Cameron's Brigade
   c. Erskine's Brigade
   d. Löwe's Brigade

3. 2nd Division: General Hill   5,251
   a. Colborne's Brigade
   b. Houghton's Brigade
   c. Lumley's Brigade

4. 3rd Division: General Picton   3,336
   a. Mackinnon's Brigade
   b. Colville's Brigade

5. 4th Division: General Cole   4,792
   a. Kemmis's Brigade
   b. Pakenham's Brigade

6. 5th Division: General Leith   3,229
   a. Hay's Brigade
   b. Dunlop's Brigade

7. 6th Division: Brigadier General Alex Campbell (own brigade only)   1,948

8. Light Division: Brigadier General Craufurd   2,765
   a. Beckwith's Brigade
   b. Barclay's Brigade

Total effective strength of British troops   34,059

Portuguese troops

1. Infantry of the Line:
   1st Brigade: Pack   2,267

2nd Brigade: Fonseca	2,414
3rd Brigade: Spry	2,163
4th Brigade: Archibald Campbell	2,407
5th Brigade: A. Campbell	2,442
6th Brigade: Coleman	2,196
7th Brigade: Baron Elben	2,083
8th Brigade: Sutton (vice Champalimaud)	1,961
9th Brigade: Collins (vice Harvey)	2,535
Total Portuguese infantry	22,645
2. Regular cavalry: General Fane's Division	1,193
3. Regular artillery: 9 batteries	701
Total Portuguese regular strength	24,539
4. Portuguese militia	11,092
5. Spanish troops within the Lines	8,000
Total of Allied troops within the Lines	66,598

APPENDIX 4

STRENGTHS AND DISPOSITIONS 1811

The (French) Army of Portugal – 1 January 1811

(Figures shown are soldiers under arms and fit for service[1])

In early 1811, Napoleon reorganized the French Army in Spain. His reasons were twofold; firstly, the independent commands had worked in isolation and therefore counter to strategic aims; and secondly, the corps system was creating more problems and less flexibility for some army commanders (notably the Army of Portugal).

1. 2nd Corps: Reynier (at Santarem)	12,581
a. 1st Division: Merle	4,368
b. 2nd Division: Heudelet	5,718
c. Cavalry Brigade: P. Soult	1,146
d. Artillery/Engineers (plus General Staff)	1,349
2. 6th Corps: Ney (at Tomar)	18,326
a. 1st Division: Marchand	4,987
b. 2nd Division: Mermet	6,252
c. 3rd Division: Loison	4,589
d. Cavalry Brigade: Lamotte	652
e. Artillery/Engineers (plus General Staff)	1,846

3. 8th Corps: Junot (at Torres Novas)	11,160
a. 1st Division: Clausel	4,007
b. 2nd Division: Solignac	4,997
c. Cavalry Brigade: ?	981
d. Artillery/Engineers (plus General Staff)	1,175
4. 9th Corps: Drouet (approaching Leiria)	17,889
a. 1st Division: Claparéde	7,863
b. 2nd Division: Conroux	7,592
c. Cavalry Brigade: Fournier	1,698
d. Artillery/Engineers (plus General Staff)	736
Reserve Cavalry: Montbrun	2,869
Reserve Artillery	1,588
Gendarmerie	197
General Staff	66
Total of the Army of Portugal	64,676[2]

Notes:

1 In addition, there were 39,252 sick.

2 This figure does not include the 17,299 who were detached from their respective corps.

The Spanish Armies at the battle of La Albuera – 16 May 1811 (Source: Oliver and Partridge with minor revision based on Sañudo's database)

1. 4th Army: Blake

   a. Vanguard Division: Lardizabal:

      i. Sección Brig Casinos (1st and 2nd Murcia (A), Fijo Milicia Provincial de Canarias (B))

      ii. Sección Brig Gouvea-Casinos (2/2nd de Leon (C), Campo Mayor (E), Cazadores Reunidos (D))

   b. 3rd Division: Ballesteros:

      i. Sección Brig Gouvea-Asensio (Provincial Compañias de Catalanes (F), 2nd Cazadores de Barbastro (G), Pravia (H))

      ii. Sección Brig Carvajal (Lena (I), Castropol (J), Cangas de Tineo c. (K), Infiesto (L))

   c. 4th Division: Zayas

      i. Sección Brig Cruz-Murgeon (2nd and 4th Reales Guardias de España (M and N), 2nd and 3rd Irlanda (O), Patria (P))

      ii. Sección Brig Polo (Imperiales de Toledo (Q), Legión de Estranjeros (R), Ciudad Rodrigo (S), 1st Reales Guardias Walonas (T))

   d. 4th Army Cavalry Brigade: Loy (Granaderos de Fernanado VII, Granaderos a Caballo, Escuadron Provincial de Instrucción, Provisional de Santiago, Husares de Castilla – all one squadron)

2. 5th Army: Castaños

    a. Sección de Carlos de España (Inmemorial de Rey (U), 1st and 2nd Zamora (V), Voluntarios de Navarra (W))

    b. 5th Army Cavalry Brigade: Penne-Villemur (Reales Carabineros de la Guardia, La Reina, Borbon, Lusitania, 2nd Algarve, Husares de Estremadura, Cazadores de Sevilla)

    c. Miranda's artillery battery : 6x 4-pdr guns[1]

Note:

1   Oman and Sañudo list the artillery battery from the 4th Army as being present, but Dickson, Duncan (probably based on Dickson) and Burriel (Sección de Historico Militar No 64) are quite adamant that the Spanish only had one battery at Albuera. It is possible the battery was in the Spanish artillery park, which is listed as having 24 pieces.

The Anglo-Portuguese Army – early June 1811

Wellington: the main body in Estremadura   *26,000*

1. 2nd Division: Major General Hill
    a. Colborne's Brigade
    b. Hoghton's Brigade
    c. Abercrombie's Brigade
    d. Howard's Brigade[1]

2. 3rd Division: Major General Picton
    a. Mackinnon's Brigade
    b. Colville's Brigade
    c. Power's Portuguese Brigade

3. 4th Division: Major General Cole
    a. Myers's Brigade
    b. Kemmis's Brigade
    c. Harvey's Portuguese Brigade

4. 7th Division: Major General Houston
    a. Sontag's Brigade
    b. Doyle's Portuguese Brigade
    Hamilton's Portuguese Division: General Hamilton
    Alten's German Brigade
    Ashworth's Portuguese Brigade
    Collins's Portuguese Brigade
    Lumley's Cavalry Division[2]
    Anson's Cavalry Brigade
    Otway's Portuguese Cavalry Brigade
    Madden's Portuguese Cavalry Brigade

General Stewart: The subsidiary army in and around Beira   *28,000*

1. 1st Division : General Spencer (less Howard's Brigade)
    a. Stopford's Brigade
    b. Nightingale's Brigade
    c. Löwe's Brigade

2. 5th Division : Major General Erskine
    a. Hay's Brigade
    b. Dunlop's Brigade
    c. Spry's Portuguese Brigade

3. 6th Division : Major General A.Campbell
    a. Hulse's Brigade
    b. Burne's Brigade
    c. Madden's Portuguese (infantry) Brigade[3]

4. Light Division: Brigadier General Craufurd
    a. Beckwith's Brigade
    b. Drummond's Brigade
    c. Pack's Portuguese Brigade
    d. Slade's Cavalry Brigade
    e. Barbaçena's Portuguese Cavalry Brigade

Notes:

1   This brigade from the 1st Division was added to the 2nd Division to make up for their terrible losses at Albuera. Four battalions from the division were sent home to recruit, namely: 2/28, 29, 2/48 and 2/39.

2   This included the new cavalry brigade consisting of the 11th and 13th Light Dragoons and the 2nd Hussars of the KGL.

3   Not to be confused with Madden's Portuguese Cavalry.

The French Army in Spain 15 July, 1811 (Source: Oman)

The Army of the South: Marshal Soult   60,487[1]

1. 1st Corps: Marshal Victor   27,201
    a. Conroux's Division   5,905
    b. Godinot's Division   8,133
    c. Villatte's Division   5,802
    d. Latour-Maubourg's Dragoon Division   2,905
    e. Perrymond's Light Cavalry Brigade   1,015
    f. Artillery, Engineers, Staff and Miscellaneous   3,441

2. 4th Corps: General Leval[2]   20,830
    a. Liger-Belair's Division   10,947
    b. Dembouski's Division   4,918
    c. Milhaud's Dragoon Division   2,484
    d. Ormancey's Light Cavalry Brigade   1,595
    e. Artillery and Engineers   886

3. 5th Corps: Count Drouet D'Erlon   12,456
    a. Girard's Division   4,253
    b. Claparéde's Division   4,183
    c. Briche's Light Cavalry Brigade   515
    d. Artillery and Engineers   618
    e. Forces garrisoning Badajoz   2,887

The Army of the Centre: King Joseph	23,139[3]
a. The King's French Guards	(approx) 2,500
b. Hugo's Spanish Division	5,060
c. Dessolles' Brigade	3,208
d. German Division	4,214
e. Lahoussaye's Dragoon Division	2,213
f. Treillard's Light Horse Brigade	663
g. Artillery, Engineers and Miscellaneous	5,281
The Army of Portugal ~ Marshal Marmont	38,633[4]
a. Foy's Division	5,541
b. Clausel's Division	6,501
c. Ferey's Division	5,072
d. Sarrut's Division	4,922
e. Maucune's Division	5,049
f. Brennier's Division	5,332
g. Montbrun's Dragoon Division	1,463
h. Lamotte's Light Cavalry Brigade	613
i. Fournier's Light Cavalry Brigade	701
j. Wathier's Light Cavalry Brigade	594
k. Artillery and Engineers	2,875
The Army of Aragon: Marshal Suchet	43,783[5]
a. Musnier's Division	7,689
b. Frère's Division	7,826
c. Harispe's Division	6,380
d. Habert's Division	4,433
e. Peyri's Italian Division	4,892
f. Compère's Neapolitan Brigade	1,808
g. Boussard's Cavalry Brigade	1,876
h. Artillery and Engineers	3,645
i. Garrisoned personnel	2,244
j. Draft soldiers on the march	2,990
The Army of the North: General Dorsenne (from 25 July)	88,442[6]
Central troops:	
a. Imperial Guard (Dumoustier and Roguet's Divisions)	15,166
b. Lepic's Guard Cavalry Brigade	1,189
c. Attached cavalry (Lancers of Berg)	835
d. Guard Artillery and Miscellaneous	878
Navarre troops:	
a. Reille's Division (Navarre)[7]	8,221
b. Navarre Miscellaneous	1,623
c. Caffarelli's Division (Biscay)[8]	7,543
d. Biscay Miscellaneous	4,340

e. Souham's Division (Burgos)[9]	7,971
f. Burgos Miscellaneous	8,714
g. Serras's Division (Valladolid and Salamanca)	5,063
h. Valladolid and Salamanca Miscellaneous	8,106
i. Bonnet's Division (Asturias)	7,962
j. Artillery, Engineers and other Miscellaneous[10]	2,367
k. Severoli's Italian Division (en route)	8,464
The Army of Catalonia: Marshal MacDonald	23,990[11]
a. Maurice Mathieu's Division	5,411
b. Quesnel's Division	3,890
c. Plauzonne's Division	4,389
d. Petit's Brigade	2,416
e. Lefebvre's Brigade	3,725
f. Garrison at Montlouis	1,429
g. Garrison at Roses	477
h. Garrison at Girona	1,429
i. Artillery, Engineers and Miscellaneous	824

Totals for the effective strength of the French Army in Spain on 15 July 1811

Army of the South: Marshal Soult	68,827
Army of the Centre: King Joseph	23,139
Army of Portugal: Marshal Marmont	38,633
Army of Aragon: Marshal Suchet	48,783
Army of the North: General Dorsenne	88,442
Army of Catalonia: Marshal MacDonald	23,590
Total effective strength (Notes 10 and 11)	291,414

Notes:

1   A further 8,340 were detached and active and 21,899 were sick. This astoundingly large figure was largely due to the high casualties at Albuera.

2   Leval assumed command from Sebastiani in May.

3   A further 2,398 were sick or detached.

4   A further 6,648 were detached and active and 12,668 were sick.

5   A further 7,305 were sick or detached.

6   A further 11,000 (approx) were sick or detached.

7   These divisions arrived in the area in September 1811.

8   Allocated in varying numbers to the five governments listed.

9   A further 6,669 were sick or detached.

10   The total figure including sick and detached equals 354,461.

11   These figures do not include General Monthion's 'Reserve of the Army of Spain' being held at Bayonne and numbering some 8,298 all ranks.

The Anglo-Portuguese Army – 15 September 1811

(The Anglo-Portuguese army underwent more reorganization during the summer months of 1811 than at any other time during the campaign.)

Forces under Wellington's command on the Beira Frontier — 46,731

1. 1st Division: Lieutenant General Sir Thomas Graham — 4,926
   a. H. Campbell's Brigade
   b. Stopford's Brigade
   c. Löwe's Brigade

2. 3rd Division: Major General Picton — 5,277
   a. Wallace's Brigade
   b. Colville's Brigade
   c. Palmeirim's Portuguese Brigade

3. 4th Division: Major General Cole — 6,483
   a. Pakenham's Brigade
   b. Kemmis's Brigade
   c. Collin's Portuguese Brigade

4. 5th Division: Brigadier General Dunlop — 5,005
   Hay's Brigade
   Dunlop's Brigade
   Spry's Portuguese Brigade

5. 6th Division: Major General A. Campbell — 5,687
   a. Hulse's Brigade
   b. Burne's Brigade
   c. Madden's Portuguese (infantry) Brigade

6. 7th Division: Major General Sontag — 5,102
   a. V. Alten's Brigade
   b. Sontag's Brigade
   c. Coleman's Portuguese Brigade

7. Light Division: Brigadier General Craufurd[1] — 4,200
   Barnard's Brigade
   2nd Brigade

8. Pack's Independent Portuguese Brigade — 2,206

9. McMahon's Independent Portuguese Brigade — 2,489

10. Cavalry Division: General Cotton[2] — 4,026
    a. Slade's Cavalry Brigade (1st Royal Dragoons and 12th Light Dragoons)
    b. Alten's Brigade (11th Light Dragoons and 1st Hussars KGL)
    c. Anson's Brigade (14th Light Dragoons and 16th Light Dragoons)
    d. De Grey's Brigade (3rd Dragoon Guards and 4th Dragoons)
    e. Madden's Portuguese Cavalry Brigade (1st, 3rd, 4th and 7th Regiments)

11. Artillery — 1,051
    a. Bull's Troop RHA
    b. Ross's Troop RHA
    c. Macdonald's Troop RHA
    d. Lawson's Battery RA
    e. Bredin's Battery RA
    f. Sympher's Battery KGL
    g. Portuguese 5 batteries designations unknown.

12. Engineers and Miscellaneous — 279

Forces under General Hill's command, September 1811 — 16,484

1. 2nd Division — 5,854
   a. Byng's Brigade
   b. Wilson's Brigade
   c. Howard's Brigade

2. Hamilton's Portuguese Division: Major General Hamilton — 5,082

3. Ashworth's Independent Portuguese Brigade — 2,419

4. Cavalry: Major General Sir William Erskine — 2,466
   a. Long's Cavalry Brigade (9th and 13th Light Dragoons and 2nd Hussars KGL)
   b. Le Marchant's Cavalry Brigade (3rd Dragoons and 4th Dragoon Guards)
   c. Portuguese Cavalry Brigade (5th and 8th Regiments)

5. Artillery — 570
   a. Lefebure's Troop RHA
   b. Hawker's Battery RA
   c. Meadow's Battery RA
   d. Arriaga's Portuguese Battery
   e. Braun's Portuguese Battery

6. Engineers and Miscellaneous — 93

Notes:

1 The Light Division included the 1st and 3rd Caçadores.

2 As many of the new arrivals were cavalry, the brigade breakdown has also been given.

APPENDIX 5

STRENGTHS AND DISPOSITIONS 1812

The Spanish Regular Armies in 1812 (Sources: Oman, Esdaile and Arteche)

The Spanish Regular Armies were reorganized in December 1811 as follows:

1. 1st Army (formerly the Army of Catalonia): Lacy. The Army of Catalonia had been reduced to an almost ineffective force of 8,000 by the end of 1811, following the Siege at Tarragona.

2. 2nd Army (formerly the Army of Valencia): Blake. The Army of Valencia was largely untested in large-scale combat until late 1811. Under Blake, it boasted 17,000 men but many of these were lost during the battle of Saguntum and the siege of Valencia.

3. 3rd Army (formerly the Army of Murcia): Freire. The Army of Murcia had never been a large force, mainly because the south-east corner of Spain had seen little large-scale action during the campaign. In January 1812 it numbered 5,500, rising to 8,000 later in the year.

4. 4th Army (formerly the Army of the Centre, which comprised the Army of Andalusia and La Mancha). Initially this army consisted of troops from the garrisons at Cádiz and Algeciras and numbered around 10,000. The Army of Reserve of Andalusia was a separate organisation again.

5. 5th Army (formerly the Army of Estremadura): Castaños.

6. 6th Army (formerly the Army of Galicia): Abadia.

7. 7th, 8th and 9th armies were largely groupings of irregular forces that were absorbed into other armies during the next reorganization in December 1812.

The (French) Army of the South – 1 March 1812 (Source: Oman)[1]

1. 1st Division: General Conroux (at Villamartin – Army Reserve)   5,445
   a. 1st Brigade: Meunier
   b. 2nd Brigade: Mocquery

2. 2nd Division: General Barrois (at Puerto Real, Cádiz – besieging force)   7,776
   a. 1st Brigade: Cassagne
   b. 2nd Brigade: Avril

3. 3rd Division: General Villatte (at Santa Maria, Cádiz – besieging force)   7,359
   a. 1st Brigade: Pécheux
   b. 2nd Brigade: Lefol

4. 4th Division: General Leval (at Granada – Murcian Covering Force)   9,404
   a. 1st Brigade: Rey
   b. 2nd Brigade: Vichery

5. 5th Division: General Drouet (at Zafra – Estremaduran Covering Force)   6,119
   a. 1st Brigade: Dombrowski
   b. 2nd Brigade: Reymond

6. 6th Division: Daricau (at Zalamea – Estremaduran Covering Force)   5,028
   a. 1st Brigade: Quoit
   b. 2nd Brigade: St Pol

7. 1st Cavalry Division: (at Ribera – Estremaduran Covering Force)   1,956
   a. 1st Brigade: General Perreymond
   b. 2nd Brigade: General Bonnemain

8. 2nd Cavalry Division – (at Córdoba ~ Army Reserve)   3,477
   a. 1st Brigade: General Digeon
   b. 2nd Brigade: General Lallemand

9. 3rd Cavalry Division: General P. Soult (at Granada – Murcian Covering Force)   2,338
   a. 1st Brigade: General Boille
   b. 2nd Brigade: General Ormancey

10. Spanish troops: Juramentados (infantry and cavalry)   5,471

11. Artillery (less for divisional artillery which is in divisional totals)   2,900

12. Engineers   920

13. Miscellaneous[2]   2,470

Total for the Army of the South[3]   60,663

Notes:

1   The 7th Polish Lancers are not included in this return and yet they stayed with the Army of the South until the end of 1812.

2   Three naval battalions, gendarmerie etc.

3   Not including the garrison at Badajoz (which numbered 3,526).

Divisional movements of the Army of Portugal and the Army of the North: December 1811 to March 1812

Army of Portugal

1. Foy:
   a. December, moved to Toledo.
   b. January, moved to Murcian border in support of Suchet's Valencian Operations.
   c. February, moved to the Tagus valley to support operations to contain Wellington.
   d. March established at Talavera but dispersed in Tagus valley later in the month.

2. Sarrut:
   a. December, moved to New Castile to link up with Foy and Montbrun's Divisions for Suchet's Valencian operations.
   b. January, moved to Murcian border.
   c. February, moved to the Tagus valley to support operations to contain Wellington.
   d. March, established at Almaraz until middle of the month then formed part of Marmont's strike force and moved to outskirts of Ciudad Rodrigo by the end of the month.

3. Clausel:
   a. December, at Avila.
   b. January, moved to Valladolid and then to the environs of Salamanca.
   c. February, returned to Avila.
   d. March, returned to the environs of Salamanca then formed part of Marmont's strike force and moved to outskirts of Ciudad Rodrigo by the end of the month.

4. Ferey:
   a. December, moved to La Mancha to keep open communications with Montbrun's column, which was en route for Valencia.
   b. January, moved to environs of Salamanca.
   c. February and early March, remained around Salamanca.
   d. Late March, split up to man the numerous garrisons of the Army of Portugal in Leon.

5. Maucune:

    a. December, at Talavera.

    b. January, moved to Valladolid and then to the environs of Salamanca.

    c. February, at Toro.

    d. March, returned to the environs of Salamanca then formed part of Marmont's strike force and moved to outskirts of Ciudad Rodrigo by the end of the month.

6. Brennier:

    a. December, at Almaraz.

    b. January, moved to Salamanca.

    c. February, returned to the Tagus valley to the mountain pass at Mombeltrán.

    d. March, remained at Mombeltrán then formed part of Marmont's strike force and moved to outskirts of Ciudad Rodrigo by the end of the month.

7. Bonnet: originally from the Army of the North.

    a. December, in Oviedo, under command of the Army of the North, transferred to the Army of Portugal by Berthier's dispatch of 13th December 1811.

    b. January, ordered to Salamanca but only reached Benavente.

    c. February, ordered (not directly) to return to the Army of the North with effect 7 February 1812 and began to move towards Burgos.

    d. March, returned under command of the Army of Portugal by virtue of Berthier's letter dated 21 February, which arrived on 2 March, stipulated that the division (once returned) was to remain in the Asturias.

8. Souham: originally from the Army of the North.

    a. December, in La Baneza, Benavente and Zamora under command of the Army of the North, transferred to the Army of Portugal by Berthier's dispatch of 13 December 1811.

    b. January, ordered to Salamanca.

    c. February, returned to Zamora.

    d. March, remained in Zamora and immediate area watching the Army of Galicia.

9. Montbrun (Cavalry Division):

    a. December, moved to New Castile to link up with Foy and take command of the column sent in support of Suchet's Valencian operations.

    b. January, moved to Murcian border.

    c. February, moved to the Tagus valley to support operations to contain Wellington.

    d. March, established with the divisions of Foy, Sarrut and Brennier in the Tagus valley. Then moved to León to maintain the lines of communication between the garrisons of the Army of Portugal.

Army of the North

1. Dumoustier: Young Guard (Called back to France for the Russian Campaign).

    a. December, in León.

    b. January, moved to Burgos.

    c. February, moved to Alva and eastern Navarre in preparation for move to France for the Russian Campaign.

2. Roguet: Young Guard (Called back to France for the Russian Campaign).

    a. December, in Valladolid.

    b. January, moved to Burgos, then called to support Marmont in Salamanca but moved to Navarre having reached Medina del Campo.

    c. February, moved to Alva and eastern Navarre in preparation for move to France for the Russian Campaign.

3. Severoli: (Transferred temporarily to the Army of Aragon and then to the Army of Ebro).

    a. December, en route to Valencia from Aragón.

    b. January, at Valencia and Peñiscola.

    c. February became part of the Army of Ebro under General Reille.

    d. March, moved to Lérida.

4. Reille: (Transferred temporarily to the Army of Aragon and then to the Army of Ebro).

    a. December, en route with Severoli to Valencia from Aragón.

    b. January, at Valencia and returned to the Ebro near Alcañiz.

    c. February, assumed command of the newly established Army of Ebro.

    d. March, operations against General Eroles in eastern Aragon and Catalonia.

5. Caffarelli: (Part of this division was temporarily assigned to the Army of Aragon).

    a. December, in Pamplona under the Army of the North, some battalions under the divisional commander were moved to Zaragoza.

    b. January, moved to Pamplona at the end of the month.

    c. February, in Pamplona.

    d. March, remained in Pamplona and undertook operations in the Pyrenees against Mina.

6. Thiébault:

    a. December, at Salamanca.

    b. January, at Salamanca.

    c. February, moved to Burgos.

The Anglo-Sicilian forces for the East Coast Expeditionary Force

1. Maitland's Force: Embarkation Return 25 June 1812 (Source Oman):

a. 20th Light Dragoons	167
b. Foreign Troop of Hussars	71
c. Royal Artillery	81
d. Marine Artillery	30
e. Royal Engineers	47
f. Staff	14
g. 10th Line	935

h. 58th Line		871
j. 81st Line		1,274
k. 4th Line KGL		989
l. 6th Line KGL		1,074
m. De Roll's		331
n. Dillon's		554
o. Calabrian Free Corps		352
Total		6,790

2. Campbell's Corps: Embarkation Return 14 November 1812:

a. 20th Light Dragoons	13
b. Guides	14
c. Royal Artillery	135
d. Grenadier Battalion	959
e. Light Infantry Battalion	603
f. 27th Line	853
g. 2nd Anglo-Italian Levy	1,217
h. Sicilian Artillery	155
j. Sicilian Grenadiers	605
Total	4,554

3. Embarked subsequently – 25 December 1812:

a. 20th Light Dragoons	231
b. Royal Artillery	60
c. 2nd Anglo-Italian Levy	178
d. Calabrian Free Corps	339
e. Sicilian cavalry	226
f. Sicilian Estero Regiment	1,262
Total	2296

The French Armies in Spain – 15 October 1812 (Source: Oman)

1. Army of the South: Marshal Soult[1]   47,528

a. 1st Division: Conroux	5,818
b. 2nd Division: Barrois (General Cassagne shortly after)	5,002
c. 3rd Division: Villatte	6,097
d. 4th Division: Leval	8,053
e. 5th Division: D'Erlon	5,218
f. 6th Division: Daricau	4,495
g. Cavalry Division: Perreymond	2,493
h. Cavalry Division: Digeon	3,104
i. Cavalry Division: P. Soult	1,833
j. Artillery	3,633
k. Engineers	868
l. Others	914

2. Army of the Centre: King Joseph[2]   15,231

a. The King's French Guards	2,500
b. Division D'Armagnac	5,238
c. Division Palombini	3,192
d. Division Casapalacios Españoles	1,430
e. Cavalry Division: Treillard	1,793
f. Artillery and Engineers	608
g. Others	470

3. Army of Portugal: Souham[3]   44,862

a. 1st Division: Foy	3,643
b. 2nd Division: Clausel	4,636
c. 3rd Division: Taupin	6,248
d. 4th Division: Sarrut	4,130
e. 5th Division: Maucune	5,262
f. 6th Division: Pinoteau (from Brennier)	2,817
g. 7th Division: Bonté (from Thomières)	2,534
h. 8th Division: Chauvel (from Bonnet)	4,617
i. Cavalry Division: Curto	2,163
j. Cavalry Division: Boyer	1,373
k. Artillery	1,859
l. Others	1,416
Attached troops	
a. Cavalry Brigade: Merlin	746
b. Infantry Brigade: Aussenac (from Bayonne Reserve)	3,418

4. Army of Aragon and Valencia: Suchet[4]   30,729

a. 1st Division: Musnier	5,583
b. 2nd Division: Harispe	4,115
c. 3rd Division: Habert	4,975
d. Cavalry Division: Boussard	1,922
e. Artillery	879
f. Others	957
Attached troops	
a. Division Reille	4,540
b. Division Severoli	3,909
c. Catalonian Brigade	3,849

5. Army of the North: Caffarelli[5]   37,689

a. Division Abbé	6,597
b. Division Van der Maessen	12,585
c. Brigade Dumoustier	4,076
d. Cavalry Brigade: Laferriére	1,662
e. Garrison Pamplona	1,689
f. Garrison Biscay	9,695
g. Garrison Santoña	1,385

6. Army of Catalonia: Decaen[6] — 29,699
   - a. Division Quesnel — 3,625
   - b. Division Lamarque — 3,628
   - c. Division Maurice Mathieu — 6,365
   - d. Brigade Petit — 1,619
   - e. Brigade Espert — 3,077
   - f. Garrison Figueras — 3,806
   - g. Garrison Tarragona — 1,514
   - h. Garrison Lérida — 1,709
   - i. Others — 4,356
7. Bayonne Reserve[7] — 7,244

Notes:

1 There were in addition, 6,353 sick and 1,968 detached personnel.

2 There were in addition, 1,914 sick and 687 detached personnel.

3 There were in addition, 11,166 sick and 4,724 detached personnel.

4 There were in addition 4,611 sick and 4,015 detached personnel.

5 There were in addition 5,217 sick.

6 There were in addition, 6,089 sick and 395 detached personnel.

7 There were in addition, 600 sick and 134 detached personnel.

Army	Effective strength	Sick	Detached
Army of the South	47,528	6,353	1,968
Army of the Centre	15,231	1,914	687
Army of Portugal	44,862	11,166	4,724
Army of Aragon and Valencia	30,729	4,611	4,015
Army of the North	37,689	5,217	–
Army of Catalonia	29,699	6,089	395
Bayonne Reserve	7,244	600	134
Totals	212,982	35,950	11,923

The Anglo-Portuguese Army – 23 Oct 1812 (Source: Oman) — 50,964

1. 1st Division: E. Paget — 3,970
2. 2nd Division: Hill — 7,915
3. 3rd Division: Pakenham — 4,229
4. 4th Division: Cole — 4,487
5. 5th Division: Pringle — 3,938
6. 6th Division: Clinton — 3,380
7. 7th Division: Bernewitz — 4,298
8. Light Division: Alten — 3,428
9. 1st Cavalry Division: Stapleton-Cotton — 2,827
10. 2nd Cavalry Division: Erskine — 1,947
11. Hamilton's Portuguese Division — 4,719
12. Pack's Portuguese Brigade — 1,681
13. Bradford's Portuguese Brigade — 1,645
14. Others — 2,500

Spanish troops operating with Wellington – October 1812 (Source: Oman) — *25,459*

1. 6th Army: Santocildes — 17,128
   - a. 1st Division: Barcena — 6,810
   - b. 2nd Division: Cabrera — 4,749
   - c. 3rd Division: Losada — 4,213
   - d. Cavalry Brigade: Figuelmonde — 1,356
2. 5th Army: under General Hill's Corps — 8,331
   - a. Division Morillo — 2,371
   - b. Division de España — 3,809
   - c. Cavalry: Villemur — 992
   - d. Cavalry: Sanchez — 1,159

Gun allocation to batteries – Ciudad Rodrigo 11–18 January 1812 (Source: Jones)

Major Dickson had the following guns: 34x 24-pdr guns (24G) and 4x 18-pdr guns (18G)

TABLE 1

	11 Jan	12 Jan	13 Jan	14 Jan	15 Jan	16 Jan	17 Jan	18 Jan
Battery 1	2 x 18G	2 x 18G	2 x 18G		3 x 24G	3 x 24G	3 x 24G	3 x 24G
Battery 2	2 x 18 G 7 x 24G	2 x 18 G 7 x 24G	2 x 18 G 7 x 24G	2 x 18 G 7 x 24G	2 x 18 G 9 x 24G	2 x 18 G 4 x 24G[1]	1 x 18 G 4 x 24G[2]	1 x 18 G 4 x 24G
Battery 3	16x 24G	16x 24G	16x 24G	16x 24G	16x 24G	16x 24G	15x 24G[3]	15x 24G[3]
Battery 4						7 x 24G	7 x 24G	7 x 24G
Battery 5								[4]

Notes for Table 1:

1 One gun destroyed, 4 immobilized.

2 Unknown damage.

3 Destroyed.

4 This battery was never manned, it was intended to house 1x 6-pdr and 1x 5½in howitzer.

Gun Allocation to Batteries – Badajoz – 23 March to 6 April 1812

(Source: Jones; Dickson's manuscripts, normally so detailed, have almost no information on the guns and ammunition allocation/expenditure during the siege)

Major Dickson had the following guns available for the siege; 16 x 24 pdr guns (24G), 20 x 18 pdr guns (18G)[1] and 16 x 24 pdr howitzers (24H)[2]

See Table 2

TABLE 2

Battery No	Battery Task	March 1812									April 1812					
		23	24	25	26	27	28	29	30	31	1	2	3	4	5	6
Battery 1	To enfilade left face of Picurina, howitzers to fire on interior	3x 18G 3x 24H	3x 18G 3x 24H	3x 18G 3x 24H	3x 18G 3x 24H³	3x 18G 3x 24H	3x 18G 3x 24H	3x 18G to 9 Bty 3x 24H	3x 24H³	3x 24H³	3x 24H³	3x 24H³	3x 24H³	3x 24H³	3x 24H³	3x 24H³
Battery 2	Direct fire on Picurina	4x 24G	4x 24G	4x 24G	4x 24G³	4x 24G³	4x 24G³	4x 24G³	1x 24G to 7 Bty 3x 24G to 8 Bty	-	-	-	-	-	-	-
Battery 3	Direct fire on San Roque lunette	-	4x 18G	4x 18G	3x 18G⁴	3x 18G	3x 18G	3x 18G	3x 18G	3x 18G	3x 18G to 11Bty	-	-	-	-	-
Battery 4	To enfilade the right face of Trinidad bastion	-	6x 24G 1x 24H	5x24G⁵	5x 24G	5x 24G	5x 24G	5x 24G	5x 24G to 7 Bty	-	-	-	-	-	-	-
Battery 5	To enfilade the right face of San Pedro bastion	-	4x 18G	4x 18G	3x 18G⁴	3x 18G	3x 18G	3x 18G	3x 18G	3x 18G	1x 18G 3x 24H⁶ 2x 18G to 11Bty	1x 18G 3x 24H	1x 18G 3x 24H	1x 18G 3x 24H	1x 18G 3x 24H	1x 18G 3x 24H
Battery 6	To enfilade the right face of San Roque lunette		3x 24H	3x 24H	3x 24H	3x 24H	3x 24H	3x 24H	3x 4H to 10 Bty	-	-	-	-	-	-	-
Battery 7	To breach right face of Trinidad								12x24G	12x24G	12x24G	12x24G	12x24G	12x24G	12x24G	12x24G
Battery 8	To enfilade Santa Maria bastion								3x 18G 3x 24G	3x 18G 3x 24G	3x 18G 3x 24G	3x 18G 3x 24G	3x 18G 3x 24G	3x 18G 3x 24G	3x 18G 3x 24G	3x 18G 3x 24G
Battery 9	To breach left flank of the Santa Maria bastion							8x 18G	8x 18G	8x 18G	8x 18G	8x 18G	8x 18G	8x 18G	8x 18G	8x 18G
Battery 10	To enfilade ditch in front of main breach								3x 24H	3x 24H	3x 24H	3x 24H	3x 24H	3x 24H	3x 24H	3x 24H
Battery 11	To neutralize the San Roque lunette										6x 18G	5x 18G⁴	5x 18G	5x 18G	5x 18G	5x 18G
Battery 12	To fire in direct support of the assault														14x 24H	14x 24H

Notes for Table 2:

1. These were Russian naval guns cast in the carronade style and collected by Dickson in Setubal port from Adm Berkley RN. There was much disagreement as to whether these guns should be used as the British and Portuguese ordnance differed in size.

2. There is considerable confusion over these guns as 24 pdr howitzers only existed for a short period in British service; furthermore, their bore was 5.68inches and was therefore often referred to as the 5.5inch Howitzer and often confused with the brass howitzer in common service. The advantage of using this gun was that the standard 5.5inch ammunition could be fired including spherical case, which was used to great effect at Badajoz.

3. The guns/howitzers in batteries 1 & 2 were not used from 26 March onwards.

4. One piece of ordnance disabled.

5. One 24 pdr gun and one 24 pdr howitzer disabled overnight.

6. Received from the Artillery Park.

APPENDIX 6

STRENGTHS AND DISPOSITIONS 1813

The Anglo-Portuguese Army during the winter of 1812–13 (Source: Oman)

1. 1st Division: General Howard at Guarda and Vizeu
2. 3rd Division: General Picton at Moimento de Beira
3. 4th Division: General Cole at San João de Pesquiera and along the Douro
4. 5th Division: General Pringle at Lamego
5. 6th Division: General Clinton at Cea and on the northern Serra Estrella
6. 7th Division: General Bernewitz at Moimento da Serra along the Serra Estrella
7. Light Division – General Alten (with V. Alten's cavalry brigade) at Fuentes de Oñoro and Alameida
8. 1st Cavalry Division – General Stapleton-Cotton at the confluence of the Mondego and Vouga Rivers
9. Pack's Portuguese Brigade – at Penafiel
10. Bradford's Portuguese Brigade – at Vila Real
11. D'Urban's Portuguese cavalry brigade to Bragança

Hill's Corps in the Tagus valley

12. 2nd Division: Hill at Coria, with his brigades covering the passes of the Sierra de Francia and de Gata
13. Hamilton's Portuguese Division – at Moraleja, Indanha and Penamacor
14. 2nd Cavalry Division – Erskine at Bronzas (When Erskine committed suicide, Wellington disbanded the 2nd Cavalry Division and Long's and Fane's brigades operated independently)

The French armies of the Centre, South and Portugal in Spain during the winter of 1812–13 (Source: Oman)

1. Army of the Centre:[1] commanded by Remand and then Semélé after Drouet moved to assume command of the Army of Portugal. HQ in Madrid, strength approximately 17,000
   a. Division D'Armagnac – Madrid
   b. King's French Guards – Madrid
   c. Division Cassagne – Arganda[2]
   d. Division Casapalacios Españoles – Segovia
   e. Cavalry Division ~ Treillard, dispersed around the city limits

2. Army of the South: Soult. HQ in Toledo, strength approximately 36,000.[2]
   a. 1st Division: Leval at Toledo[3]
   b. 3rd Division: Villatte at Talavera
   c. 4th Division: Conroux at Madridejos[3]
   d. 5th Division: Pécheux at Daymiel in La Mancha
   e. 6th Division: Daricau at San Clemente in the province of Cuenca
   f. Cavalry Division: Tilley at Toledo[4]
   g. Cavalry Division: P. Soult in La Mancha
   h. Cavalry Division: Digeon in La Mancha

3. Army of Portugal: Drouet. HQ in Valladolid, strength approximately 42,000[5]
   a. 1st Division: Foy at Avila and then later at Cuenca
   b. 2nd Division: Barbot at Valladolid
   c. 3rd Division: Taupin at Saldaña[6]
   d. 4th Division: Sarrut at León
   e. 5th Division: Maucune at Salamanca
   f. 8th Division: Chauvel at Salamanca[7]
   g. Cavalry Division: Curto at Medina de Ríoseco
   h. Cavalry Division: Boyer at Mayorga

Notes:

1. Palombini's Italian Division was en route to rejoin the Army of the North.
2. The former 2nd Division of the Army of the South had been taken by King Joseph and retained.
3. Conroux and Leval had switched their divisions since the last return in October 1812.
4. Tilley had replaced Perreymond.
5. The 6th and 7th divisions were well below strength and being reconstituted – by May 1813 they have been removed from the French order of battle – see below.
6. Oman states that Fririon was commanding the 4th Division. This must be an error as the 4th Division was Sarrut's; Fririon must have been temporarily commanding the 3rd Division for Taupin.
7. Chauvel had replaced Bonnet.

The French armies of the Centre, South and Portugal at the commencement of Wellington's advance (Source: Oman)

1. Army of the Centre: Drouet at Valladolid[1]
   a. King's French Guards: at Valladolid
   b. 1st Division D'Armagnac: at Medina de Ríoseco, actually under Reille's command
   c. 2nd Division Cassagne: at Segovia
   d. Division Casapalacios Españoles: at Segovia
   e. Cavalry Division: Treillard at Segovia

2. Army of the South: Gazan at Arevalo[2]
   a. 1st Division: Leval at Madrid
   b. 3rd Division: Villatte at Salamanca
   c. 4th Division: Conroux at Avila

d. 5th Division: Maransin's Brigade only at Toledo and some troops in Madrid

e. 6th Division: Daricau at Zamora and Toro

f. Cavalry Division: Tilley at Arevalo

g. Cavalry Division: P. Soult in Toledo and the environs of Madrid

h. Cavalry Division: Digeon at Zamora and Toro

3. Army of Portugal: Reille. HQ in Valladolid, strength approximately 42,000

a. 1st Division: Foy near Castro-Urdiales

b. 2nd Division: Barbot in Navarre

c. 3rd Division: Taupin in Navarre

d. 4th Division: Sarrut at Bilbao to Miranda

e. 5th Division: Maucune: Brigade at Palencia, Brigade at Burgos

f. 6th Division: Lamartinière at Burgos to Briviesca[3]

g. Cavalry Division: Mermet south of Benavente[4]

h. Cavalry Division: Boyer north of Benavente

Notes:

1   At some stage, presumably during the French reorganization in March 1813, Drouet re-assumed command of the Army of the Centre.

2   Gazan had assumed command of the Army of the South from Soult who was withdrawn to France in March 1813.

3   Lamartinière had assumed command from Chauvel and this division renumbered.

4   Mermet had assumed command from Curto who remained within the division.

The Spanish Regular Armies in 1813 (Sources: Esdaile, Chartrand and De la Cierva)

The Spanish regular armies were reorganized in December 1812, on Wellington's orders, as the new *Generalissimo* of the Spanish Forces, as follows:

1. 1st Army: unchanged. The former Army of Catalonia, this force increased to 16,000 men by mid-1813 under the command of General Copons (who assumed command from General Lacy in March 1813).

2. 2nd Army: was an amalgamation of the former 2nd (Valencian) and 3rd (Murcian) Armies, which numbered in excess of 30,000 men in mid-1813. The army was initially under the command of General Elio.

3. 3rd Army was the renamed 4th Army (of the Centre) and included elements of the former 5th (Estremaduran) Army. The army was initially under the command of General Del Parque.

4. 4th Army: swept up the remainder of the former 5th (Estremaduran) Army, and the 6th, 7th, 8th and 9th armies. Led initially by General Castaños, briefly by General Giron and then by General Freire, this formation numbered some 46,000 men by mid-1813. With the exception of Mina's force in Aragón and Eastern Navarre, (which numbered some 8,000) the balance served with Wellington's Anglo-Portuguese army until the end of the war. It had eight divisions.

Spanish troops under Wellington's command – July 1813 (Sources: Oman and Arteche)

Wellington's position as *generalissimo* was revoked by the new Regency in March 1813; consequently, the only Spanish forces under his command for the campaigns in 1813 were as follows:

1. 4th Army: General Freire[1]   35,000 approx

a. 1st Morillo's Division: León, Unión, Legión, Bailén, Vitoria, 2nd Jaén

b. 2nd De España's Division:1 3° Guardias Españoles, 1°Sevilla, Tiradores de Castilla, 1° de Mallorca, 1° de la Princesa

c. 3rd Losada's Galician Division: Toledo, Voluntarios de León, 1° Asturias, Monterey, Benavente, Rivero, Oviedo

d. 4th Barcena's Galician Division: 2° Asturias, Guadalajara, Constitución, Voluntarios de la Corona, Voluntarios de Asturias, Santiago

e. 5th Porlier's Asturian Division: 1° Cantabro, Laredo, Tiradores de Cantabria.

f. 6th Longa's Division: 1°, 2°, 3° and 4° Iberia, Guardias Nacionales, Húsares de Iberia, plus Salcedo's Guerrilla 'Corps' about 1,000 men

g. Penne Villemur's Cavalry Division: Algarve (4 squadrons), Husares de Extremadura (4 squadrons), Granaderos de Galicia, Granaderos de Cantabria, Cazadores de Galicia, Husares de Rioja, Husares de Castilla, 1° y 2° Lanceros de Castilla (4 squadrons)

h. Julian Sanchez's Cavalry (2 regiments)

i. Artillery

2. The Army of Reserve of Andalusia: Conde de Abispal (General H. O'Donnell)[2] 16,394

a. 1st Echevarri's Division: 2° Guardias Españoles, Galicia, Cataluña, Suizos de Kaiser, Almería, Ordenes Militares, Pravia

b. 2nd Creagh's Division: 2° Guardias Walonas, Murcia, Voluntarios de Navarra, Sevilla, Príncipe, Madrid, Batallon del general

c. Barcena's Cavalry Division: Dragones de Villaviciosa, Escuadron del general

d. Artillery: three companies

Notes:

1   Freire had replaced Giron who, like Castaños, had been withdrawn by the Cortes in June 1813 following the battle of Vitoria. Carlos De España's division (strength 3,342) came up and joined the 4th Army on 28 July 1813. This brought the total number of Spanish troops under Wellington's command to around 50,000.

2   General Giron assumed command of this army from August to December while O'Donnell was sent home to convalesce.

Anglo-Portuguese Army at the commencement of the Vitoria Campaign (Source: Oman)

Commander-in-Chief: Wellington   81,276[1]

1. 1st Division: General Howard   4,854
   a. Stopford's Brigade
   b. Halkett's Brigade

2. 2nd Division: General Sir Rowland Hill   10,834
   a. Cadogan's Brigade
   b. Byng's Brigade
   c. O'Callaghan's Brigade
   d. Ashworth's Portuguese Brigade

3. 3rd Division: General Sir Thomas Picton   7,437
   a. Brisbane's Brigade
   b. Colville's Brigade
   c. Power's Portuguese Brigade

4. 4th Division ~ General Sir Lowry Cole   7,816
   a. Anson's Brigade
   b. Skerrett's Brigade
   c. Stubbs's Portuguese Brigade

5. 5th Division: General Oswald (vice General Leith)   6,725
   a. Hay's Brigade
   b. Robinson's Brigade
   c. Spry's Portuguese Brigade

6. 6th Division: General Pakenham (vice Clinton)   7,347
   a. Stirling's Brigade
   b. Hinde's Brigade
   c. Madden's Portuguese Brigade

7. 7th Division: General Lord Dalhousie   7,287
   a. Barnes's Brigade
   b. Grant's Brigade
   c. Lecor's Portuguese Brigade

8. Light Division: General Alten   5,484
   a. Kempt's Brigade
   b. Vandeleur's Brigade

9. Silveira's Portuguese Division   5,287
   a. Da Costa's Brigade
   b. Campbell's Brigade

10. Independent Brigades   4,689
    a. Pack's Portuguese Brigade
    b. Bradford's Portuguese Brigade

11. Cavalry Brigades: 8,317
    a. R. Hill's Brigade
    b. Ponsonby's Brigade
    c. G. Anson's Brigade
    d. Long's Brigade
    e. V. Alten's Brigade
    f. Bock's Brigade KGL
    g. Fane's Brigade
    h. Grant's Brigade
    i. D'Urban's Portuguese Brigade
    j. Campbell's 6th Portuguese Cavalry

12. Horse Artillery Batteries   803
    a. Ross's Troop
    b. Bean's Troop
    c. Gardiner's Troop
    d. Webber-Smith's Troop
    e. Ramsey's Troop

13. Field Artillery Batteries[2]   3,504
    a. Arriaga's Portuguese Heavy Battery
    b. Brandreth's Battery
    c. Cairnes's Battery
    d. Da Cunha's Portuguese Battery
    e. Douglas's Battery
    f. Dubourdieu's Battery
    g. Lawson's Battery
    h. Maxwell's Battery
    i. Morrison's Battery
    j. Parker's Battery
    k. Sympher's Battery KGL
    l. Tulloh's Portuguese Battery

14. Engineers, Staff Corps and Miscellaneous   892

Notes:

1   With the 25,245 Spanish troops, available for the commencement of the campaign, Wellington had about 106,500 men.

2   Oman correctly states 17 batteries but misses Morrison's battery on his list. (See Dickson manuscripts vol. V, 1813, p.867).

The Allied army under Wellington at the battle of Vitoria – 21 June 1813 (Sources: Oman, Arteche, Sañudo, Sarramon and Dickson).

Wellington's Allied army total[1]   94,000

1. Spanish 4th Army on Northern Flank: Giron   18,000
   a. Barcena's Division: 2nd Asturias, Guadalajara, Constitución, Voluntarios de la Corona, Voluntarios de Asturias, Santiago.
   b. Losada's Division: Toledo, Voluntarios de León, 1st Asturias, Monterey, Benavente, Rivero, Oviedo.
   c. Porlier's Division: 1st Cántabro, Laredo, Tiradores de Cantabria.
   d. Villemur's Cavalry Division: Lanceros de Algarbe (4), Húsares de Estremadura

(4), Húsares de Galicia (2), Húsares de Cantabria (3), Húsares de la Rioja, Húsares de Castilla.[2]

   e. Unaffiliated troops: 5 battalions of engineers, Depósito de Instrucción, Cazadores Extranjeros, Tui, Colegio de Cadets en Olivenza, de Guias (one company), Legión Extremeña (2)

   f. Artillery: 10 batteries (approx)

2. Allied left column: Graham   21,000

   a. 1st Division: Howard: (Dubourdieu's Company – 9-pdr)

      Stopford's Brigade: 1st Coldstream, 1/3rd Guards, company 5/60th

      Halkett's Brigade: 1st, 2nd, 5th Line KGL and 1st and 2nd Light KGL

   b. 5th Division: Oswald: (Lawson's Company – 6-pdr)

      Hay's Brigade – 3/1st, 9th, 38th and company Brunswick Oels

      Robinson's Brigade – 4th, 2/47th, 2/59th and company Brunswick Oels

      Spry's Brigade – 3rd and 15th Line and 8th Caçadores

   c. Pack's Brigade: 1st and 16th Line and 4th Caçadores (Tulloh – unknown guns).

   d. Bradford's Brigade: 13th and 24th Line and 5th Caçadores (Tulloh – unknown guns)

   e. Longa's Division: 1st, 2nd, 3rd and 4th Iberia, Guradias Nacionales, Húsares de Iberia, plus Salcedo's Guerrilla 'Corps' about 1,000 men.[3]

   f. Anson's Cavalry Brigade: 12th and 16th Light Dragoons.

   g. Bock's Cavalry Brigade: 1st and 2nd Dragoons KGL (Ramsey's Horse Artillery Troop supported the 2 cavalry brigades)

3. Allied centre left column: Picton   15,000

   a. 3rd Division: Picton: (Douglas's Company – 9 pdr)

      Brisbane's Brigade: 45th, 74th, 88th and 3 companies 5/60th

      Colville's Brigade: 5th, 2/83rd, 2/87th and 94th

      Power's Brigade: 9th and 21st Line and 11th Caçadores

   b. 7th Division: Dalhousie: (Cairn's Company 9 pdr)

      Barnes's Brigade: 6th, 3rd Provisional battalion (elements of 2/24th and 2/58th) and 9 companies of Brunswick Oels

      Grant's Brigade: 51st, 68th, 82nd and Chasseurs Britanniques

      LeCor's Brigade: 7th and 19th Line and 2nd Caçadores

4. Allied centre right column: Cole   15,000

   a. 4th Division: Cole: (Sympher's Company 9-pdr)

      Anson's Brigade: 3/27th, 40th, 48th, second provisional battalion (elements of 2nd and 2/53rd), one company 5/60th

      Skerrett's Brigade: 7th, 20th, 23rd, company Brunswick Oels

      Stubb's Brigade: 11th and 23rd Line and 7th Caçadores

   b. Light Division: Alten: (Ross's Horse Artillery Troop 6 pdr)

      Kempt's Brigade: 43rd, 1/95th and 3/95th

      Vandaleur's Brigade: 52nd, 2/95th

      Portuguese Troops: 17th Line and 1st and 3rd Caçadores

   c. D'Urban's Cavalry Brigade: 1st, 11th and 12th Cavalry.

5. Allied right flank column: Hill   20,000

   a. 2nd Division: Hill: (Maxwell's Company 9-pdr)

      Cadogan's Brigade: 50th, 71st, 92nd company 5/60th

      O'Callaghan's Brigade: 28th, 2/34th, 39th and company 5/60th

      Byng's Brigade: 3rd, 57th, 1st Provisional Battalion (elements of 2/31st and 2/66th) and company 5/60th

      Ashworth's Brigade: 6th and 18th Line and 6th Caçadores

   b. Silveira's Division: (Cunas 6-pdr supporting Da Costa and Mitchell's 9pdr supporting A. Campbell)

      Da Costa's Brigade: 2nd and 14th Line

      Campbell's Brigade: 4th and 10th Line and 10th Caçadores

   c. Morillo's Division: León, Unión, Legión, Bailén, Vitoria, 2nd Jaén

   d. Alten's Cavalry Brigade: 14th Light Dragoons and 1st Hussars KGL

   e. Long's Cavalry Brigade (-): 13th Light Dragoons

   f. Fane's Cavalry Brigade: 3rd Dragoon Guards, 1st Dragoons (supported by Bean's Horse Artillery Troop 6-pdr)

6. Cavalry and Artillery Reserve: with Cole's Column   5,000

   a. Cavalry: (Gardiner's Horse Artillery Troop 6-pdr)

      Hill's Brigade: 1st and 2nd Life Guards, Horse Guards

      Ponsonby's Brigade: 5th Dragoon Guards, 3rd and 4th Dragoons

      Grant's Brigade: 10th, 15th and 18th Hussars

   b. Artillery: Dickson

      Smith's Horse Artillery Troop 9-pdr

      Parker's Company 9-pdr

      Arriaga's Portuguese 2 batteries 9-pdr

Notes:

1   Total strength 3,600 horse, only 2,000 at Vitoria.

2   Source: 'Francisco de Longa' by Pardo de Santallana.

3   6th Division en-route from Medina.

The French Army of Spain – July 1813 as reorganized by Marshal Soult[1]

Chief of Staff: General Gazan

   'Lieutenancies' of the Centre – D'Erlon, Right – Reille and Left – Clausel[2]

1. 1st Division: General Foy (Right)

   a. Brigade Fririon: 6e Léger, 69e (2) and 76e Ligne

   b. Brigade Berlier: 36e (2), 39e and 65e (2) Ligne

2. 2nd Division: General D'Armagnac (Centre)

   a. Brigade Chassé: 16e Léger, 8e and 28e (2) Ligne

   b. Brigade Gruardet: 51e, 54e and 75e (2) Ligne

3. 3rd Division: General Abbé (Centre)

   a. Brigade Rignoux: 27e Léger, 63e and 64e (2) Ligne

   b. Brigade Rémond: 5e (2) Léger, 94e (2) and 95e Ligne

4. 4th Division: General Conroux (Left)
    a. Brigade Rey: 12e (2) Léger, 32e (2) and 43e (2) Ligne
    b. Brigade Schwitter: 45e, 55e and 58e Ligne

5. 5th Division: General Van der Maessen (Left)
    a. Brigade Barbot: 25e Léger, 1e and 27e Ligne
    b. Brigade Rouget: 50e, 59e and 130e (2) Ligne

6. 6th Division: General Maransin (Centre)
    a. Brigade St. Pol: 21e Léger, 24e and 96e Ligne
    b. Brigade Mocquery: 28e Léger, 101e (2) and 103e Ligne

7. 7th Division: General Maucune (Right)
    a. Brigade Pinoteau: 17e Léger, 15e (2) and 66e Ligne
    b. Brigade Montfort: 34e Léger, 82e and 86e Ligne

8. 8th Division: General Taupin (Left)
    a. Brigade Béchaud: 9e (2) Léger, 26e and 47e (2) Ligne
    b. Brigade Lecamus: 31e Léger, 70e (2) and 88e Ligne

9. 9th Division: General Lamartinière (Right)
    a. Brigade Menne: 2e Léger, 118e (2) and 119e (2) Ligne
    b. Brigade Gauthier: 120e (3) and 122e (2) Ligne

10. Reserve: General Villatte[3]
    Brigadier Thouvenot and Brigadier Boivin: 4e Léger, 10e (2) Léger, 31e Léger, 3e Ligne, 34e Ligne, 40e (2) Ligne, 101e Ligne, 105e (2) Ligne, 114e Ligne, 115e (2) Ligne, 116e Ligne, 117e Ligne, 118e Ligne, and 119e Ligne: total 17 battalions.

11. Foreign troops[4]
    a. Neuenstein's German Brigade
    b. St Paul's Italian Brigade
    c. Casapalacios' Spanish Brigade
    d. King Joseph's Guard (under General Guy)

12. Army Cavalry: 13e, 15e and 22e Chasseurs.[5]

13. P. Soult's Cavalry Division.

14. Treillard's Cavalry Division.

Notes:

1   The total of the Army of Spain was 72,664 infantry, 7,147 cavalry plus 42,556 artillery, engineers, garrison troops, conscripts, sick, detached etc. All up 122, 367. This figure did not include Suchet's Army of Aragon and Valencia, or Decaen's Army of Catalonia.

2   Soult was emphatic that these lieutenancies were not army corps: D'Erlon had just under 21,000 infantry; Reille had 17,235 infantry and Clausel, 17,218 infantry. Each lieutenancy had a light cavalry regiment – see note 5. Each infantry division was to have a field battery; each cavalry division a horse artillery battery and the artillery reserve was to consist of two horse artillery batteries and two field batteries and in addition there were three mountain batteries equipped with 2- or 3-pdr guns carried on mules.

3   These troops were not brigaded and actually made up to five brigades. They were not allocated to one of the lieutenancies.

4   These troops were not allocated to one of the lieutenancies.

5   These three regiments were allocated, one to each lieutenancy. Sufficient for scouting purposes only.

Spanish troops under Wellington's command – October/November 1813

1.	4th Army: General Freire[1]	35,995
	1st Division: Morillo's	5,021
	2nd Division: C. De España	4,580
	3rd Division: Del Barco[2]	5,866
	4th Galician Division: Barcena	4,149
	5th Asturian Division: Porlier[3]	4,544
	6th Division: Longa	2,507
	7th Division: Mendizabal (in Spain)	nil
	8th Division: Mina[3]	8,472
	Penne Villemur's Cavalry (in Spain)	nil
	Julian Sanchez's Cavalry (in Spain)	nil
	Artillery and Engineers	856
2.	The Army of Reserve of Andalusia: General Giron	7,843
	a. Virues's Division	4,123
	b. La Torre's Division	3,720
	c. Barcena's Cavalry (in Spain)	nil

Notes:

1   Mina's irregulars had been included in Freire's army in an attempt to coordinate their efforts.

2   Vice Losada.

3   Porlier's Division, originally one brigade, had received a second by November 1813.

French artillery at the sieges of San Sebastián (Source: Belmas)

Bronze ordnance:
Guns: 1x 2-pdr, 9x 16-pdr, 5x 12-pdr, 8x 8-pdr, 6x 6-pdr, 12x 4-pdr and 3x 2-pdr
Culverins: 1x 8-pdr, 3x 3-pdr and 2x 2-pdr
Howitzers: 1x 8in, 1x 5½in
Mortars: 7x 12in and 2x 14in

Iron ordnance:
Guns: 11x 24-pdr, 4x 18-pdr, 2x 12-pdr, 10x 8-pdr and 2x 2-pdr
Mortars: 2x 12in

Total: 92 pieces

Wellington's Forces at the Battle of San Marcial/Defence of the Pyrenees (Sources: Oman and Arteche)

1. 1st Division: General Howard
    a. Stopford's Brigade: 1st Coldstream, 1/3rd Guards, Company 5/60th
    b. Halkett's Brigade: 1st, 2nd, 5th Line KGL and 1st and 2nd Light KGL
    c. Maitland's Brigade: 1/1st Guards and 3/1st Guards
    d. Aylmer's Brigade:[1] 76th, 2/84th and 85th

2. 4th Division: General Cole

    a. Anson's Brigade: 3/27th, 40th, 48th, second provisional battalion

    b. (Elements of 2nd and 2/53rd) one company 5/60th

    c. Ross's Brigade: 7th, 20th, 23rd, company Brunswick Oels

    d. Miller's Brigade: 11th and 23rd Line and 7th Caçadores

3. 6th Division: General Colville

    a. Stirling's Brigade: 42nd, 79th and 91st

    b. Lambert's Brigade: 11th, 32nd, 36th and 61st

    c. Madden's Portuguese Brigade: 8th and 12th Line and 9th Caçadores

4. 7th Division: General Dalhousie

    a. Barnes's Brigade: 6th, 3rd Provisional battalion (elements of 2/24th and 2/58th) and 9 companies of Brunswick Oels

    b. Inglis's Brigade: 51st, 68th, 82nd and Chasseurs Britanniques

    c. LeCor's Brigade: 7th and 19th Line and 2nd Caçadores

5. Light Division: Kempt

    a. Kempt's Brigade: 43rd, 1/95th and 3/95th

    b. Skerrett's Brigade: 52nd, 2/95th

    c. Portuguese troops: 17th Line and 1st and 3rd Caçadores

Spanish troops[2]

Freire's 4th Spanish Army

6. Losada's 3rd Division: Toledo, Voluntarios de León, 1st Asturias, Monterey, Masrina, Benavente, Rivero, Oviedo

7. Bárcena's 4th Division: 2nd Asturias, Guadalajara, Constitución, Corona, Voluntarios de Asturias, Santiago

8. Longa's 4th Division: 1st, 2nd, 3rd and 4th Iberia, Guardias Nacionales, Húsares de Iberia, plus Salcedo's Guerrilla 'Corps'

9. Porlier's 5th Division: 1st Cántabro, Laredo, Tiradores de Cantabria

10. Ugartemendías 7th Division: 1st, 2nd and 3rd de Guipuzcoa

    Giron's Army of Reserve of Andalusia

11. Echavarri's 1st Division: 2nd Batallon de Guardias Españolas, Galicia, Cataluña, Suizos de Kaiser, Almería, Ordened Militares, Pravia

12. Creagh's 2nd Division: 2nd Batallon de Guardias Walonas, Murcia, Voluntarios de Navarra, Sevilla, Príncipe, Madrid, Batallon del general

13. Barcena's Cavalry Division: Dragones de Villaviciosa, and one escuadron del general

Notes:

1   Aylmer's Brigade arrived from Gibraltar on 18 August 1813 and was allotted to Graham's grouping; although never formally attached to the 1st Division, it always acted with it.

2   One gun battery to each army.

Wellington's Allied army at the battle of the Nivelle – 10 November 1813 (Sources: Oman, Arteche, Dickson and Fraser)

1. 1st Division: General Howard

    a. Stopford's Brigade: 1st Coldstream, 1/3rd Guards, company 5/60th

    b. Hinüber's Brigade: 1st, 2nd, 5th Line KGL and 1st and 2nd Light KGL

    c. Maitland's Brigade: 1/1st Guards and 3/1st Guards

    d. Aylmer's Brigade:[1] 76th, 2/84th and 85th

2. 2nd Division: General Stewart

    a. Walker's Brigade: 50th, 71st, 92nd company 5/60th

    b. Pringle's Brigade: 28th, 2/34th, 39th and company 5/60th

    c. Byng's Brigade: 3rd, 57th, 1st Provisional Battalion (elements of 2/31st and 2/66th) and company 5/60th

    d. Ashworth's Brigade: 6th and 18th Line and 6th Caçadores

3. 3rd Division: General Colville

    a. Brisbane's Brigade: 45th, 74th, 88th and 3 companies 5/60th

    b. Keane's Brigade: 5th, 2/83rd, 2/87th and 94th

    c. Power's Brigade: 9th and 21st Line and 11th Caçadores

4. 4th Division: General Cole

    a. Anson's Brigade: 3/27th, 40th, 48th, 2nd Provisional Battalion

    b. (Elements of 2nd and 2/53rd) one company 5/60th.

    c. Ross's Brigade: 7th, 20th, 23rd.

    d. Vasconcellos's Brigade: 11th and 23rd Line and 7th Caçadores.

5. 5th Division: General Hay

    a. Greville's Brigade: 3/1st, 9th, 38th

    b. Robinson's Brigade: 4th, 2/47th, 2/59th

    c. De Regoa's Brigade: 3rd and 15th Line and 8th Caçadores

6. 6th Division: General Clinton

    a. Pack's Brigade: 42nd, 79th and 91st

    b. Lambert's Brigade: 11th, 32nd, 36th and 61st

    c. Douglas's Brigade: 8th and 12th Line and 9th Caçadores

7. 7th Division: General Le Cor

    a. Barnes's Brigade: 6th, 3rd Provisional Battalion (elements of 2/24th and 2/58th) and 9 companies of Brunswick Oels.

    b. Inglis's Brigade: 51st, 68th, 82nd and Chasseurs Britanniques.

    c. Doyle's Brigade: 7th and 19th Line and 2nd Caçadores.

8. Light Division: General Alten

    a. Kempt's Brigade: 43rd, 1/95th and 3/95th

    b. Colborne's Brigade: 52nd, 2/95th

    c. Portuguese troops: 17th Line and 1st and 3rd Caçadores

9. Hamilton's Portuguese Division
   a. Buchan's Brigade: 2nd and 14th Line
   b. Da Costa's Brigade: 4th and 10th Line and 10th Caçadores

10. Portuguese troops
    a. Wilson's Brigade: 1st and 16th Line and 4th Caçadores
    b. Bradford's Brigade: 13th and 24th Line and 5th Caçadores

11. Giron's Army of Reserve of Andalusia
    a. Virues's Division: 2º Guardias Españoles, Princípe, Navarra, Almería, Právia, 2º de Sevilla.
    b. La Torre's Division: Galicia, 2º de Cataluña, Madrid, Ordenes Militares, 1º de Murcia, batallon de general.

12. Four divisions from Freire's 4th Spanish Army
    a. Morillo's 1st Division: León, Union, Legion, Doile, Vitoria, 2º de Jaén, 4º de Navarra
    b. Del Barco's 3rd Division: Toledo, Voluntarios de León, 1st Asturias, Monterey, Masrina, Benavente, Rivero, Oviedo
    c. Bárcena's 4th Division: 2nd Asturias, Guadalajara, Constitución, Corona, Voluntarios de Asturias, Santiago
    d. Longa's 6th Division: 1º, 2º, 3º and 4º Iberia, 2º de Alaba, Batallon de Granaderos nacionale

13. Artillery:[2]

Allied left flank (60 guns)
   a. Mosse's Company: Heavy 6 pdr (with 5th Division)
   b. Ramsey's Troop RHA: Light 6-pdr
   c. Carmichael's Company: 9-pdr
   d. Webber Smith's Troop RHA: Light 6-pdr
   e. Michell's Company: 9-pdr (4 guns)
   f. Morrison's Company: 18-pdr
   g. Greene's Company: 9-pdr
   h. Cairn's Company: 9-pdr
   i. Arriaga's (Portuguese) Battery: 9-pdr
   j. Spanish battery 6-guns

Allied centre (24 guns)
   a. Ross's Troop RHA: Light 6-pdr
   b. Sympher's Company: 9-pdr
   c. Douglas's Company: 9-pdr
   d. Plus 2 troops of three guns: 3-pdr (mountain guns), one attached to the Light Division
   e. Two Spanish batteries: unknown calibre

Allied right flank (8 guns):
   a. Cunha Preto and Judice's Batteries: 6 x 9 pdr and 2 x 6 pdr.

Notes:
1 Aylmer's Brigade was not formally attached to the 1st Division.
2 Spanish artillery consisted of 20 guns in both field and horse artillery batteries spread across the four divisions of the 4th Army. Giron had no guns.

Soult's Army at the battle of the Nivelle – 10 November 1813 (Source: Oman)

1. 1st Division: General Foy
   a. Brigade Fririon: 6e Léger, 69e (2) and 76e Ligne
   b. Brigade Berlier: 36e (2), 39e and 65e (2) Ligne

2. 2nd Division: General D'Armagnac
   a. Brigade Chassé: 16e Léger, 8e and 28e (2) Ligne
   b. Brigade Gruardet: 51e, 54e and 75e (2) Ligne

3. 3rd Division: General Abbé
   a. Brigade Boivin: 27e Léger, 63e and 64e (2) Ligne
   b. Brigade Maucomble: 5e (2) Léger, 94e (2) and 95e Ligne

4. 4th Division: General Conroux
   a. Brigade Rey: 12e (2) Léger, 32e (2) and 43e (2) Ligne
   b. Brigade Baurot: 45e, 55e and 58e Ligne

5. 5th Division: General Maransin
   a. Brigade Barbot: 4e Léger, 34e, 40e (2) and 50e Ligne
   b. Brigade Rouget: 27e, 59e and 130e (2) Ligne

6. 6th Division: General Daricau
   a. Brigade St. Pol: 21e Léger, 24e and 96e Ligne
   b. Brigade Mocquery: 28e Léger, 100e (2) and 103e Ligne

7. 7th Division: General Leval
   Brigade Pinoteau: 17e Léger, 3e and 15e Ligne
   Brigade Montfort: 16e (2) Léger, 101e and 105e Ligne

8. 8th Division: General Taupin
   Brigade Béchaud: 9e (2) Léger, 26e and 47e (2) Ligne
   Brigade Dein: 31e (3) Léger, 70e and 88e Ligne

9. 9th Division: General Boyer
   Brigade Boyer: 2e (2) Léger, 32e (2) and 43e (2) Ligne
   Brigade Gauthier: 120e (3) and 122e (2) Ligne

10. Reserve: General Villatte
    Brigade Jamin: 34e (2) Léger, 66e, 82e 115e (2) Ligne. Plus a Spanish Brigade with 4 battalions, an Italian Brigade with 3 battalions and a German Brigade with 4 battalions

Artillery: 97 guns

Soult's Army at the battle of the Nive – Changes from battle of the Nivelle (Source: Oman)

1. 1st Division: General Foy – No change
2. 2nd Division: General D'Armagnac – received 31e (2) Léger

3. 3rd Division: General Abbé – General Baurot replaced Boivin

4. 4th Division: General Taupin vice Conroux (who was killed at Nivelle)

5. 5th Division: General Maransin – No change

6. 6th Division: General Daricau – lost 24e Ligne and received 119e Ligne

7. 7th Division: General Leval – No change

8. 8th Division: Dissolved

9. 9th Division: General Boyer – received 24e Ligne and 118e (3) Ligne but lost 32e and 43e Ligne

10. Reserve: General Villatte – lost the Italian Brigade and 115e Ligne but received 9e Léger

11. Paris's Brigade: 10e (2), 81e (2), 114e, 115e (2) and 117e Ligne

Ordnance Allocation to Batteries: First Siege of San Sebastián, 13 to 26 July 1813

Lt Col Dickson had the following guns for the siege; 14 x 24 pdr (24G), 5 x 24 pdr short (24GS), 6 x 18 pdr (18G), 6 x 8 Inch How (8H), 4 x 68 Pdr Carronades (68C), 4 x 10 inch Mor (10M).[1]

See Table 3

TABLE 3

Battery No	Battery Task	July 1813													
		13	14	15	16	17	18	19	20	21	22	23	24	25	26
Battery 1	Engage San Bartolomé	4x 18G	4x 18G	4x 18G	4x 18G	4x 18G	4x 18G								
Battery 2	Engage San Bartolomé	2x 8H	2x 8H	2x 8H	2x 8H	2x 8H	2x 8H								
Battery 3	Enfilade fire on eastern wall								6x 18G	6x 18G	6x 18G	6x 18G	6x 18G	6x 18G	
Battery 4	Enfilade fire on eastern wall								2x 8H	2x 8H	2x 8H	2x 8H	2x 8H	2x 8H	
Battery 11	Counter Mirandór Battery and fire against the castle					2x 24GS 2x 8H	2x 24GS 4x 8H	2x 24GS 4x 8H	2x 24GS 4x 8H	2x 24GS 4x 8H	2x 24GS 4x 8H	2x 24GS 4x 8H	2x 24GS 4x 8H	2x 24GS 4x 8H	
Battery 12	Against the town defences							2x 24G	2x 24G	2x 24G					
Battery 13	To create a breach							4x 24G	4x 24G	4x 24G	4x 24G	4x 24G	4x 24G	4x 24G	
Battery 14	To create a breach							8x 24G 3x 24GS	8x 24G 3x 24GS	7x 24G 3x 24GS (Note 2)	9x 24G 3x 24GS	9x 24G 3x 24GS	9x 24G 3x 24GS	9x 24G 3x 24GS	
Battery 15	Direct fire against breach and harassing fire										4x 68C	4x 68C	4x 68C	4x 68C	
Battery 16	To engage the town and castle											4x 10M	4x 10M	4x 10M	

Notes for Table 3:

1. It appears that only five of the short 24 pdr were landed from HMS Surveillante.

2. One 24G was knocked out and one had a blocked vent, which was not repaired until later on the 21 July. In addition, the 3 x 24 GS were mounted on land carriages.

Ordnance Allocation to Batteries: Second Siege of San Sebastián, 22 Aug to 8 Sep 1813 (Source: Jones)

Lt Col Dickson had the following guns for the siege; 56 x 24-pdr (24G), 14 x 18-pdr (18G), 18 x 8 Inch How (8H), 12 x 68-Pdr Carronades (68C), 16 x 10 inch Mor (10M), 1 x 12 inch Mor (12M).[1]

See Tables 4 & 5

Notes for Tables 4 & 5:

1 It is assumed that the five short-barrelled 24-pdrs were returned to HMS Surveillante in August. The one 12in mortar was a Spanish piece. Despite such a large train, Wellington gave orders that the siege artillery destined for Cuxhaven was not to be used: this included 15x 24-pdr guns, 8x 18-pdr guns and 4x 10in mortars. Note one additional 10in mortar was lost in the harbour during unloading.

2 These guns and howitzers were left in place from the previous siege.

3 Four guns were moved from Battery 6, only three were in place on the night of 27 August and one gun was destroyed on 28 August, replaced the same night by the remaining 24-pdr.

4 It was the original intention to have 5x 24-pdr guns and an 8in howitzer in this battery.

5 The 15x 24-pdr guns were brought across the riverbed of the Urumea over the next couple of days and placed in the Hornwork.

6 A further 24-pdr gun was mounted in Battery 10 on the island; yet another gun was lost during unloading.

7 The third 24-pdr gun was sent to Battery 10.

TABLE 4

Battery No.	Battery Task	August 1813									
		22	23	24	25	26	27	28	29	30	31
Battery 5	To breach the face of the left demi-bastion and the curtain above it		6x 18G	6x 18G	6x 18G	6x 18G	6x 18G	6x 18G	6x 18G	6x 18G	6x 18G
Battery 6	Guns – to breach the face of the left demi-bastion and the curtain above it Howitzers – general purposes of annoyance	7x 24G	7x 24G	7x 24G 2x 8H	7x 24G 2x 8H	7x 24G 2x 8H	3x 24G 2x 8H	3x 24G 2x 8H	3x 24G 2x 8H	3x 24G 2x 8H	3x 24G 2x 8H
Battery 7	To breach the face of the main bastion and the high curtain of the Hornwork							3x 24G[3]	3x 24G[3]	3x 24G	3x 24G
Battery 10	To enfilade the rear of the castle (Note 4)									1x 24G 1x 8H	1x 24G 1x 8H
Battery 11	Counter Mirandór Battery and fire against the castle	2x 8H[2]	2x 8H	2x 8H	2x 8H	2x 8H	2x 8H	2x 8H	2x 8H	2x 8H	2x 8H
Battery 13	Fire behind the breach and against the town defences and castle				1x 12M 5x 10M	1x 12M 5x 10M	1x 12M 5x 10M	1x 12M 5x 10M	1x 12M 5x 10M	1x 12M 5x 10M	1x 12M 5x 10M
Battery 14	Guns – fire at the breaches A to C Carronades and howitzers – to enfilade the curtain and land front between A and C	2x 24G[2] 4x 8H	2x 24G 4x 8H 4x 68C	6x 24G 5x 8H 4x 68C	6x 24G 5x 8H 4x 68C	6x 24G 5x 8H 4x 68C	6x 24G 5x 8H 4x 68C	6x 24G 5x 8H 4x 68C	6x 24G 5x 8H 4x 68C	6x 24 G 5x 8H 4x 68C	6x 24G 5x 8H 4x 68C
Battery 15	Fire at the breaches A to C	4x 24G	8x 24G	15x 24G	15x 24G	15x 24G	15x 24G	15x 24G	15x 24G	15x 24G	15x 24G
Battery 16	To engage the land front and castle				4x 10M	4x 10M	4x 10M	4x 10M	4x 10M	4x 10M	4x 10M
Battery 17	To engage the town, land front and castle								6x 10M	6x 10M	6x 10M

TABLE 5

Battery No.	Battery Task	September 1813									
		1	2	3	4	5	6	7	8	9	10
Battery 5	To engage the castle	6x 18G	6x 18G	6x 18G	6x 18G	6x 18G	3x 18G	3x 18G	3x 18G		
Battery 6	This battery was not used beyond 6 September	3x 24G 2x 8H	3x 24G 2x 8H	3x 24G 2x 8H	3x 24G 2x 8H	3x 24G 2x 8H[7]	2x 8H	2x 8H	2x 8H		
Battery 7	To breach the Mirandór Battery	3x 24G	3x 24G	3x 24G	3x 24G	3x 24G	3x 24G	3x 24G	3x 24G		
Battery 8	To neutralize/destroy the Reyna Battery						3x 18G	3x 18G	3x 18G		
Battery 9	To neutralize and destroy the Reyna and Mirandór batteries						17x 24G	17x 24G	17x 24G		
Battery 10	To enfilade the rear of the castle and its lower defences	1x 24G 1x 8H	1x 24G 1x 8H	1x 24G 1x 8H	1x 24G 1x 8H	1x 24G 1x 8H	2x 24G 1x 8H[6]	2x 24G 1x 8H	2x 24G 1x 8H		
Battery 11	Counter Mirandór Battery	2x 8H	2x 8H	2x 8H	2x 8H	2x 8H	2x 8H	2x 8H	2x 8H		
Battery 13	Fire behind the castle	1x 12M 5x 10M	1x 12M 5x 10M	1x 12M 5x 10M	1x 12M 5x 10M	1x 12M 5x 10M	1x 12M 5x 10M	1x 12M 5x 10M	1x 12M 5x 10M		
Battery 14	Guns – to counter the Mirandór Battery Carronades and howitzers – to engage the castle	6x 24G 5x 8H 4x 68C	6x 24G 5x 8H 4x 68C	6x 24G 5x 8H 4x 68C	6x 24G 5x 8H 4x 68C	6x 24G 5x 8H 4x 68C	6x 24G 5x 8H 4x 68C	6x 24G 5x 8H 4x 68C	6x 24G 5x 8H 4x 68C		
Battery 15	This battery was not used beyond 3 September	15x 24G	15x 24G	15x 24G	[5]						
Battery 16	At the castle and behind	4x 10M	4x 10M	4x 10M	4x 10M	4x 10M	4x 10M	4x 10M	4x 10M		
Battery 17	At the castle and behind	6x 10M	6x 10M	6x 10M	6x 10M	6x 10M	6x 10M	6x 10M	6x 10M		

APPENDIX 7

STRENGTHS AND DISPOSITIONS 1814

THE FRENCH ARMIES IN SOUTHERN FRANCE AND CATALONIA – 1814

The French Army of the Pyrenees: Marshal Soult – 20 January 1814[1]

1. 1st Division: General Foy   4,600
   a. Brigade Fririon
   b. Brigade Berlier

2. 2nd Division: General D'Armagnac   5,500
   a. Brigade Menne[2]
   b. Brigade Leseur

3. 3rd Division: General Abbé   5,300
   a. Brigade Baurot.
   b. Brigade Maucomble.

4. 4th Division: General Taupin   5,600
   a. Brigade Rey
   b. Brigade Schwitter

5. 5th Division: General Maransin   5,000[3]
   a. Brigade Barbot
   b. Brigade Rouget

6. 6th Division: General Daricau   5,200[4]
   a. Brigade St Pol
   b. Brigade Mocquery

7. 8th Division: General Harispe   6,600
   Brigade Paris
   Brigade Dauture

8. P. Soult's Cavalry Division   3,800[5]

Notes:

1   Total of Soult's army came to 60,100 including the garrison at Bayonne (8,800), the garrison of St Jean-Pied-de-Port (2,400) and artillery, sappers etc. (7,300). Between this period and the end of the war in April 1814, the commanders of the divisions changed – see table below.

2   Boyer took Chassé's Brigade and left Menne's Brigade (118e and 120e Ligne).

3   Rouget assumed command of this division once Maransin had been sent to Tarbes to organize the National Guard.

4   Villatte assumed command of this division once Daricau had been sent to Landes to organize the National Guard.

5   One brigade of this division had gone north along with Leval's 7th Division, Boyer's 9th Division, and Treillard's Cavalry Division.

The French Army of the Pyrenees: Infantry Divisional Commanders – 20 January to 10 April 1814

Formation/Battle	20 Jan 1814	27 Feb 1814	mid-March 1814	10 Apr 1814
1st Division	Foy	Foy	Fririon then Paris	Daricau
2nd Division	D'Armagnac	D'Armagnac	D'Armagnac	D'Armagnac
3rd Division	Abbé	Abbé	Abbé	Abbé
4th Division	Taupin	Taupin	Taupin	Taupin
5th Division	Maransin	Rouget	Rouget	Maransin
6th Division	Daricau	Villatte	Villatte	Villatte
8th Division	Harispe	Harispe	Harispe	Harispe

The French Army of the East Coast (Catalonia): Marshal Suchet – December 1813[1]

1. 1st Division: General Musnier – 3,561 at Granollers

2. 2nd Division: General Harispe[2] – 3,073 at Molins de Rei

3. 3rd Division: General Habert – 3,975 at San Boy

4. 4th Division: General M. Mathieu – 2,373 at San Celoni

5. 5th Division: Gen Lamarque – 4,205 at Girona

6. Cavalry, 5 regiments – 2,501 (3 at Barcelona and 2 in northern Catalonia)

Notes:

1   The total of the field army, including artillery and engineers, came to 22,688. In addition, there were 23,602 in garrisons in Valencia and Catalonia. Totalling 46,290.

2   General Pannetier assumed command of this division when Harispe joined Soult's army.

Spanish forces at Wellington's disposal – January 1814 (Source: Oman)

1. 3rd Army: Prince of Anglona[1] – 15,000–16,000. Positioned along the Ebro.

2. 4th Army: General Freire[2]   30,750
   a. 1st Morillo's Division: approx 4,000. In France with Wellington
   b. 2nd de España's Division: approx 4,000. In France with Wellington
   c. 3rd Del Barco's Division: approx 5,000. In France with Wellington
   d. 4th Espeleta and 5th Marcilla's Divisions. Total of 13,000 with more than 6,500 sick. Located with General Freire near San Sebastián
   e. 6th Longa's Division – approx 3,000. At Medina Pomar, Castile
   f. 7th Mendizabal's Division – approx 3,000. Blockading the French garrison at Santoña
   g. 8th Mina's (Navarrese) Division – approx 8,600. Blockading St Jean-Pied-de-Port.

3. The Army of Reserve of Andalusia: General Giron/General H. O'Donnell[3]   9,294
   a. Virues's Division
   b. La Torre's Division

Notes:

1   This army was almost destitute of artillery, cavalry and transport. Wellington did not intend to use it.

2   Mendizabal's Division was too far away to be considered available.

3   General Henry O'Donnell reassumed command of this army in January, having returned from convalescence.

GLOSSARY

Abatis (Abattis)	Trees cut and arranged to leave the branches facing outwards to form a barrier
Afrancesado	Spaniard loyal to Joseph Bonaparte – literally 'Frenchified one'
Alarmas	Galician Home Guard
Aragonese	Native of Aragón
Bastion	A construction with two front faces protruding into the ditch from the curtain to facilitate flanking fire from both sides along the ditch
Bátardeau	A wall built across the ditch of a fortification, with a sluice gate to regulate the height of water in the ditch on both sides of the wall
Carronade	Short, large-calibered ship's gun, which looks and operates similar to a howitzer
Casemate	A vaulted chamber for artillery guns
Caçadores	Portuguese light infantry (note Cazadores in Spanish)
Chevaux de Frise	Portable barrier embellished with swords and spikes
Cortes	Parliament
Counterscarp	The outer wall of the ditch
Cunette	A narrow trench dug in the bottom of a defensive ditch and flooded where possible
Demi-Lune	A triangular outwork built to protect the curtain wall and to provide cover to the flanks of a bastion (fr. see also Ravelin)
Embrasure	The gap in the parapet through which the gun was fired
Enceinte	The main perimeter of the fortified location
Enfilade	Sweeping fire from a flank
Faussebraie	An earth rampart built to protect the base of the curtain wall
Fernandinos	Supporters of Ferdinand VII
Fléche	Fieldwork made of earth in a 'V' shape, with the salient angle facing out from the defence. (Also known as a Redan)
Gallego	Native of Galicia
Glacis	Sloping ground immediately in front of the ditch
Halberd	Combined spear- and battle-axe
Halberdier	Man armed with a halberd
Juramentado	A Spaniard in the sworn service of Joseph Bonaparte
Loop-hole	Narrow vertical slit in a wall for shooting or looking through
Lugger	Small tug or transport craft
Madrileño	Native of Madrid
Miqueletes	Regular Catalan soldiers but not part of the Spanish Royal units, following a regional tradition from the Wars of the Spanish Succession
Ordenança	Portuguese Home Guard
Ordre Mixte	Formation in which column is mixed with line to combine momentum with firepower
Palisade	Strong wooden stake, about 3m long, driven into the ground short of the parapet of the glacis
Parallel	Deep trenches, parallel to the target, which provide cover from fire to the besiegers as they prepared battery positions
Parapet	Wall or bank in front of the trench or rampart that afforded protection to those behind it. Made of earth, masonry or wood
Ravelin	A triangular outwork built to protect the curtain wall and to provide cover to the flanks of a bastion. (See also Demi-Lune)
Revêtment	A strong exterior restraining wall supporting the front of the rampart and extending down to the ditch
Sap	Trenches that come forward of a parallel in order to construct batteries or new/additional parallels
Serviles	Opponents of the 1812 Constitution
Somatenes	Catalan Home Guard: so called because they reputedly turned out when the alarm bell (*somanten*) was rung
Tarifeños	Native of Tarifa
Terreplein/Terre-Pleine	Surface of the rampart behind the parapet, where guns are mounted
Tête-du-pont	Bridgehead
Tirailleurs	French term for skirmishing troops who were positioned in front of the main body of forces
Toise	A measurement of distance just over 6ft or nearly 2m
Trincadours	Small, fast gunboats, capable of being propelled by oar or sail
Vedette	Mounted sentry placed in advance of an outpost
Voltigeur	French light skirmishers from the 2nd elite company in the battalion
Zaragozanos	Native of Zaragoza

BIBLIOGRAPHY

MANUSCRIPT SOURCES

British Library, London

MSS 57320-57330 Papers, Sir John Moore.

Map: Wyld, James 1812–1887, Map showing the principal movements, battles and sieges in which the British army was engaged during the war from 1808 to 1814. (London 1840)

Centro Geografico del Ejército, Madrid

Archivo Cartográfico

James Clavell Library, Woolwich

MD 228. Battle of Albuera, 1811. Account of the battle by Lt W. Unger KGL

MD 228. Battle of Bussaco. Map by Lt W. Unger KGL

MD 914. Papers of Colonel Sir William Robe 1793–1818.

MD 2566. Diaries of Lt Gen G. Cookson 1768–1809

MD 81. Col Sir A. Dickson Papers

MD 340. Maj W. N. Ramsay Papers 1782–1815.

Service historique de la Défense, Paris

9870-9874, Balagny Papers

72858-72869, Gouvion Saint-Cyr Journal

Servicio Históico Militar, Madrid

Archivo de la Guerra de la Independencia

University of Southampton

Wellington Papers

Miscellaneous

British Military Map-Making in the Peninsular War – A Paper by P. K. Clark and Y. Jones (Madrid, 1974)

De Pato, J., La Invasión Francesa en Ferrol (Almanaque de Ferrol, Octubre de 1909)

McGuffie, T. H., 'Recruiting the ranks of the regular British army during the French Wars: recruiting, recruits and methods of enlistment', (*Journal of the Society of Army Historical Research*, June 1956, vol: XXXIV, No. 138)

Napier, G. W., The Lines of Torres Vedras, An Impregnable Citadel (Royal Engineers Journal, December 2008, vol. 122, No. 3)

PRINTED PRIMARY SOURCES

Anon, Cartas Desde Portugal y Espana, *Letters written by British troops during the retreat to La Coruña* (Graficas Arias Montano, 2008)

Batty, R., *Campaign of the Left Wing of the Allied Army in the Western Pyrenees and the South of France* (London, 1823)

Belmas, J., *Defensa de San Sebastián por las Tropas Francesas en 1813* (SIMTAC, 2006)

Belmas, J., *Journaux des Sièges Faits ou soutenus par Les Français dans la Péninsule 1807–1814* (Didot Freres, 1837). Four volumes

Boutflower, C., *The Journal of an Army Surgeon During the Peninsular War* (Spellmount, 1997)

Clausewitz, C. von, *Vom Krieg* (Dummlers Verlag, 1973)

Cooper, J.S., *Rough Notes of Seven Campaigns, 1809–1815* (Reprint of 1869 original, Spellmount, 1996)

Daniel, F., *Journal of an Officer in the Commissariat 1811–15* (London, 1820)

De Gonneville, *Recollections of Colonel De Gonneville* (London, 1875). Two volumes

Dickson, Maj Gen Sir A., *The Dickson Manuscripts*, (RAI, 1905 – Republished Trotman, 1987). Five volumes

D'Urban, Sir B., *The Peninsular Journal, 1808–1817* (Greenhill Books, 1988)

Esdaile, C. (ed), *Peninsular Eyewitnesses: the Human Experience of War in Spain and Portugal, 1808–1814* (Barnsley, 2008)

Fletcher, I. (ed), *Voices from the Peninsula* (Greenhill, 2001)

Foy, Gen, M., *History of the War in the Peninsula under Napoleon* (Worley Publications, 1989 – Originally published 1829). Two volumes and Atlas

Foy, M., *Junot's Invasion of Portugal* (Worley Publications, 2000)

Frazer, A, S., *Letters of Colonel Sir Augustus Simon Frazer, K.C.B.* (Longman, 1895, reprinted Naval & Military Press, 2001))

Giron, Gen P. A., *Interrogatorio Sobre las Batallas de Ocaña y Sierra Morena, 1809* (Foro, 2006)

Gleig, G.R., *The Subaltern, A Chronicle of the Peninsular War* (Pen & Sword, 2001)

Hamilton, Sgt A., *Hamilton's Campaign with Moore and Wellington during the Peninsular War* (Troy, 1847)

Harris, B., *The Recollections of Benjamin Harris* (A Dorset Rifleman), (Shinglepicker, 1995)

Henegan, Sir R., *Seven Years Campaigning in the Peninsula and the Netherlands 1808–1815* (Nonsuch Publishing, 2005). Two volumes

Hough, Henry, *Diary of 2Lt H Hough, Royal Artillery 1812–1813* (Ken Trotman, 2008)

Hugo, A., Militaire, *Histoire Des Armées Françaises de Terre et de Mer de 1792–1833* (Rignoux & Co., Paris, 1837). Twenty volumes

Ingilby, Lt, *Diary of Lieutenant Ingilby R.A., in the Peninsular War* (RAI Proceedings, Vol XX, pp.241–262)

Jones, Sir J., *Journal of Sieges Carried on by the Army under The Duke of Wellington in Spain 1811–14* (Naval & Military Press, Reprint of original 1846). Three volumes

Kincaid, Capt J., *Random Shots from a Rifleman* (Reprint of 1835 original, Spellmount, 1998)

Le Marchant, D., *Memoirs of the Late Maj Gen Le Marchant 1766–1812* (Reprint of 1841 original, Spellmount, 1997)

Le Noble, P., *Memorias de las Operaciones Militares de los Franceses en Galicia, Portugal y el Valle del Tajo en 1809* (Arenas, 2005, Reprint of the original Paris, 1821)

Light, 2nd Capt, H., *The Expedition to Walcheren 1809* (Trotman, 2005)

Ludlow Beamish, N. (ed), *History of the King's German Legion* (Naval & Military Press, 1997, Reprint of 1832–37 edition). Two volumes

May, Sir J., *A Few Observations, Mode of Attack, Employment of Heavy Artillery at Ciudad Rodrigo, Badajoz in 1812 and St. Sebastian in 1813* (Egerton, 1819)

Mercer, C., *Journal of the Waterloo Campaign* (W. Blackwood, 1870). Two volumes

Millar, B., *The Adventures of Sergeant Benjamin Miller* (Facsimile Copy, Naval & Military Press, Undated)

Napier, W.F.P., *History of the War in the Peninsula and in the South of France, 1807–1814* (Constable, London 1992, Original Print 1835). Seven volumes

Napoleon, *The Confidential Correspondence of Napoleon Bonaparte with his brother Joseph* (Appleton, 1856). Two volumes

Rathbone, J. (ed), *Wellington's War, His peninsular dispatches* (Book Club, 1984)

Ross, Sir H., *Memoir of* (Trotman, 2008; see also MD917, James Clavell Library, Woolwich)

Saint-Cyr, Gen, G., *Journal Des Operations De L'Armée De Catalogne en 1808 et 1809* (Paris, 1865)

Sarrazin, Gen, *History of the war in Spain and Portugal* (Colburn, 1815, Reprinted Trotman, 1999)

Schaumann, A.L.F., *On the Road with Wellington* (London, 1924)

Sherer, M., *Recollections of the Peninsula* (Reprint of 1824 original, Spellmount, 1996)

Soult, N., *Las Memorias Del Mariscal Soult, Las Tropas Napoleonicas en Galicia 1808–1809* (Arenas, 1999)

Southey, R., *History of the Peninsular War 1807–1811* (Murray, London, 1827). Four volumes

Suchet, Marechal, L.G., *Suchet's Memoirs of the War with Spain* (Translated version, London 1829). Two volumes

Swabey, Lt, W., *Diary of the Campaigns in the Peninsula for the years 1811, 12 and 13* (Ken Trotman, 1984)

Toreno, Conde de, *Guerre de la Independencia, El 2 de Mayo de 1808* (Ferni, Geneve 1974). Three volumes

Toreno, Conde de, *Guerre de la Independencia, La Derrota de Napoleon* (Ferni, Geneve, 1974). Three volumes

Vane, C.W, Marquis of Londonderry, *Narrative of the Peninsular War 1808–1813* (Colburn, London, 1829). Two volumes

Wall, Capt A., *Diary of the Operations in Spain under Sir John Moore* (RAI, Woolwich, 1896)

Wellington, A., Duke of, *Dispatches of Field Marshal the Duke of Wellington* (ed. Gurwood), (London, 1830s and 1840s). Twenty volumes

Wilson, Sir, R., *Campaigns in Poland in 1806 and 1807* (Worley Publications Reprint 2000 of Egerton, London 1810 original)

Wollocombe, R.H. (ed.), *With the Guns in the Peninsula, Journal of Captain William Webber RA* (Greenhill Books, 1991)

PRINTED SECONDARY SOURCES

Adolfo de Castro, D., *Cádiz en la Guerra de la Independencia* (Revista Medica, Cádiz, 1862)

Alfaro Guixot, J.M., *El Castillo de Hostalric* (Fundación Privada Cultural, 2007)

Alfaro Guixot, J.M., *El Castillo de San Fernando de Figueras* (Fundación Privada Cultural, 2007)

Alinson, A., *History of Europe, During the French Revolution* (Blackwood, Edinburgh, 1847). Twenty volumes

Amaral, M., *The Portuguese Army at the Commencement of the Peninsular War* (Tribuna, 2007–8)

Aragón Gómez, J., *Chiclana Bajo el Gobierno de José Napoleón, 1810–1812* (Fundación Vipren, 2007)

Arcon Domínguez, J.L., Sagunto, *La Batalla por Valencia* (SIMTAC, 2002). Two volumes

Arteche, J.G., *Guerra de la Independencia* (Madrid, 1868). Fourteen volumes

Ascoli, D., *A Companion to the British Army, 1660–1983* (London, 1984)

Askwith, Gen W.H., *List of Officers of the Royal Regiment of Artillery from 1716 to 1899* (Clowes & Sons, London, 1900)

Banks, A., *A World Atlas of Military History 1860–1945* (Seeley Service & Co, 1978)

Beatson, Maj Gen F.C., *With Wellington in the Pyrenees* (Donovan, London, 1993)

Bradford, E., Gibraltar, *The History of a Fortress* (Granada, 1971)

Butler, Capt L., *Wellington's Operations in the Peninsula, 1808–1814* (Reprint of 1904 original, Naval & Military Press undated). Two volumes

Buttery, D., *Wellington Against Masséna, The Third Invasion of Portugal 1810–11* (Pen & Sword, 2007)

Chandler, D.G., *The Campaigns of Napoleon* (Weidenfeld & Nicolson, 1967)

Chandler, D.G., *Dictionary of the Napoleonic Wars* (London, 1979)

Chappell, M., *The King's German Legion (1)* (Osprey, 2000)

Chappell, M., *Wellington's Peninsula Regiments (1)* (Osprey, 2003)

Chartrand, R., *Bussaco 1810* (Osprey, 2001)

Chartrand, R., *Fuentes de Oñoro* (Osprey, 2002)

Chartrand, R., *Spanish Army of the Napoleonic Wars 1793–1815 (1), (2), & (3)* (Osprey, 1999)

Chartrand, R., *The Portuguese Army of the Napoleonic Wars (1), (2) & (3)* (Osprey, 2000)

Chartrand, R., *Vimeiro 1808* (Osprey, 2001)

Cierva, de la, R., *Historia Militar de España* (Planeta, 1884), volume VII

Clyde, R., *From Rebel to Hero: The image of the Highlander, 1745–1830* (East Linton, 1995)

Coss, E., *All for a Shilling a Day: The British Army under Wellington* (University of Oklahoma Press, 2010)

Craufurd, A., *General Craufurd and his Light Division* (Naval & Military Press, Undated, reprint of the original)

Crumplin, M., *Men of Steel: Surgery in the Napoleonic Wars* (Shrewsbury, 2007)

Delaitre, F., *Baron Charles Delaitre Général D'Empire* (L'Esprit du Livre, 2008)

Dempsey, G., *Albuera 1811, The Bloodiest Battle of the Peninsular War* (Frontline Books, 2008)

Detaille, E., *L'Armée Française* (Waxtel & Hasenauer, 1992)

Diaz Capmany, C., Pedler, R. & Reay, J., *El Setge de Roses de 1808* (Ayuntamiento de Roses, 2008)

Díaz González, J., *El Castillo de San Lorenzo del Puntal, La marina en la Historia de Cádiz* (Instituto de la Historia y Cultura Naval - No. 19, Madrid, 1992)

Díaz Torrejón, F.L., *José Napoleón en el sur de España* (Cajasur Córdoba, 2008)

Duffy, C., *Siege Warfare* (Routledge & Kegan Paul, 1979)

Duncan, Capt F., *History of the Royal Regiment of Artillery* (Murray, London, 1873). Two volumes

Ellicott, D., *Bastion Against Aggression* (Gibraltar during the Peninsular War) (Gibraltar Society, 1968)

Esdaile, C., *The Duke of Wellington and the Command of the Spanish Army 1812–14* (London, 1990)

Esdaile, C., *The Peninsular War, A New History* (Penguin, 2002)

Esdaile, C., *The Wars of Napoleon* (London, 1995)

Esdaile, C., *Peninsular Eyewitnesses: the Human Experience of War in Spain and Portugal, 1808–1814* (Barnsley, 2008)

Esposito, V. & Elting, J., *A Military History & Atlas of the Napoleonic Wars* (Greenhill, 1964)

Fletcher, I, and Poulter, R., *Gentlemen's Sons* (Tunbridge Wells, 1992)

Fletcher, I., *Badajoz 1812* (Osprey, 1999)

Fletcher, I., *Bloody Albuera* (Crowood Press, 2000)

Fletcher, I., *Fields of Fire, Battlefields of the Peninsular War* (Staplehurst, 1994)

Fletcher, I., *Galloping at Everything* (Stackpole, 1999)

Fletcher, I., et al, *The Peninsular War, Aspects of the Struggle for the Iberian Peninsula* (Spellmount, 1998)

Fletcher, I., *Salamanca 1812* (Osprey, 1997)

Fletcher, I., *The Lines of Torres Vedras 1809–11* (Osprey, 2003)

Fletcher, I., *The Waters of Oblivion, The British Invasion of the Rio de la Plata 1806–07* (Spellmount, 2006)

Fletcher, I., *Vittoria 1813* (Osprey, 1998)

Fortescue, J.W., *A History of the British Army* (Naval & Military Press, 2004 reprint). Twenty volumes

Gates, D., *The Spanish Ulcer* (Pimlico, 2002)

Glover, M., *The Peninsular War, a concise military history* (Penguin, 2001)

Glover, M., *Wellington's Peninsular Victories* (Windrush Press, 1998)

Glover, M., *Wellington as a Military Commander* (Penguin, 2001)

Gordon, I., *Admiral of the Blue, The Life and Times of Admiral John Child Purvis 1747–1825* (Pen & Sword, 2005)

Gould, R., *Mercenaries of the Napoleonic Wars* (Donovan, 1995)

Griffith, P., *French Artillery* (Almark, 1976)

Griffith, P., et al, *Modern Studies of the war in Spain and Portugal 1808–1814* (Greenhill, 1999)

Guedalla, P., *The Duke* (Hodder & Stoughton, 1931)

Guinot Rodríguez, E. & Selma Castell, S., *El Partimoni Historic de Petres* (Maral, 2001)

Guscin, M., *Moore 1761–1809* (Arenas, 2000)

Hall, C., *British Strategy in the Napoleonic War 1803–15* (Manchester University Press, 1992)

Hall, C., *Wellington's Navy, Sea Power & the Peninsular War 1807–1814* (Chatham Publishing, 2004)

Hall, J., *The Biographical Dictionary of the British Officers Killed & Wounded 1808–1814* (Greenhill, 1998)

Haythornthwaite, P., *Corunna 1809* (Osprey, 2001)

Haythornthwaite, P., *Napoleonic Cavalry* (Cassell, 2001)

Haythornthwaite, P., *Napoleonic Infantry* (Cassell, 2001)

Haythornthwaite, P., *Napoleon's Military Machine* (Spellmount, 1988)

Haythornthwaite, P., *The Armies of Wellington* (Brockhampton, 1994)

Haythornthwaite, P., *The Peninsular War* (Brassey's, 2004)

Haythornthwaite, P., *Uniforms of the Peninsular Wars 1807–1814* (Arms & Armour Press, 1995)

Haythornthwaite, P., *Weapons & Equipment of the Napoleonic Wars* (Poole, 1979)

Haythornthwaite, P., *Wellington's Military Machine* (Spellmount, 1989)

Haythornthwaite, P., *Who was Who in the Napoleonic Wars* (Arms & Armour Press, Undated)

Head, M., *French Napoleonic Artillery* (Almark, 1970)

Hibbert, C., *Corunna* (London, 1961)

Hofschroer, P., *Leipzig 1813* (Osprey, 1993)

Holmes, R., *Tommy: The British Soldier on the Western Front 1914–1918* (London, 2004)

Holmes, R., *Redcoat: The British Soldier in the Age of Horse and Musket* (Harper Collins, 2001)

Horward, D., *Napoleon and Iberia, The twin sieges of Ciudad Rodrigo and Almeida, 1810* (Greenhill Books, 1984)

Howard, M., Dr, *Wellington's Doctors* (History Press, 2008)

Howarth, D., *A Near Run Thing* (Collins, 1971)

Hughes, B.P., *British Smoothbore Artillery* (Arms & Armour Press, 1969)

Hughes, B.P., *Firepower* (Arms & Armour Press, 1974)

Humble, R., *Napoleon's Peninsular Marshals* (Great Britain, 1974)

Keegan, J., *A History of Warfare* (Pimlico, 1994)

Keegan, J., *The Face of Battle* (Cape, 1976)

Kennedy, P., *The Rise and Fall of British Naval Mastery* (London, 1976)

Kiley, K., *Artillery of the Napoleonic Wars 1792–1815* (Greenhill Books, 2004)

Konstam, A., *The Napoleonic Era (A Historical Atlas)* (London 2003)

Lachouque, H., Tranie, J. & Carmigniani, J.C., *Napoleon's War in Spain* (Arms & Armour Press, 1982)

Lawford, J., *Wellington's Peninsular Army* (Osprey, 2000)

Laws, Lt Col, M.E.S., *Battery Records of the Royal Artillery, 1716–1859* (RAI, Woolwich, 1952)

Leslie, J.H., *The Services of the Royal Regiment of Artillery in the Peninsular War 1808–1814* (Hugh Rees, 1908)

Lluesma Espanya, J.A., *Sagunt* (Ayuntament de Sagunt, 2007)

Longford, E., *Wellington* (Abacus, 2004)

Mandarin, Capt A.H., *The Salamanca Campaign 1812* (Naval & Military Press, Reprint undated)

Martínez Lainez, F., & Sánchez de Toca, J.M., *Tercios de España* (EDAF, 2006)

Maughan, S.E., *Napoleon's Line Infantry & Artillery* (Windrow & Greene, 1997)

Militaria, *Revista de Cultura Militar*, Numero 7, 1995

Moliner, A. (ed.), *La Guerra de la Independencia en Espana 1808–1814* (NABLA, 2007)

Muir, R., *Triunfo de Wellington: Salamanca 1812* (Ariel, 2003)

Myatt, F., *British Sieges of the Peninsular War* (Spellmount, 1987)

Navas Ramírez-Cruzado, J., *Libertad y Victoria* (Arenas, 2004)

Nichols, A., *Wellington's Mongrel Regiment* (Staplehurst, 2005)

Norris A. H. & Bremner R. W., *The Lines of Torres Vedras* (British Historical Society of Portugal, 1986)

Nosworthy, B., *With Musket, Cannon and Sword* (New York, 1996)

Oliver, M., & Partridge, R., *The Battle of Albuera 1811* (Pen & Sword, 2007)

Oman, Sir C., *A History of the War in the Peninsular* (Greenhill, 1995, Original Print 1902). Seven volumes

Ontalba Juárez & Ruiz Jaén, *La Batalla de Ocaña* (Diputacion Toledo, undated)

Paget, J., *Wellington's Peninsular War* (London, 1990)

Parkinson, R., *The Peninsular War* (London, 1973)

Partridge, R, and Oliver, M., *Battle Studies in the Peninsula May 1808 – January 1809* (London, 1998)

Partridge, R, and Oliver, M., *Napoleonic Army Handbook the British Army and Her Allies* (London, 1999)

Partridge, R, and Oliver, M., *Napoleonic Army Handbook the French Army and Her Allies* (London, 2002)

Pivka, O, V., *Armies of the Napoleonic Era* (David & Charles, 1997)

Priego Lopez, J., *Servicio Historico Militar*, Guerra de la Independencia, 1808

Rathbone, J., *Wellington's War, His peninsular dispatches* (Book Club, 1984)

Reid, S., *Quebec 1759* (Osprey, 2003)

Reynaud, J.L., *Contre-Guerrilla en Espagne 1808–1814* (Economica, 1992)

Roberts, A., *Napoleon & Wellington* (Weidenfeld & Nicolson, London, 2001)

Robertson, I., *Wellington Invades France* (Greenhill, 2003)

Rogers, H.C.B., *Artillery Through the Ages* (Military Book Society, 1971)

Rogers, H.C.B., *Wellington's Army* (London, 1979)

Ross, Sir H., *Memoir of* (Trotman, 2008)

Saint-Cyr, Gen, G., *Journal Des Operations De L'Armée De Catalogne en 1808 et 1809* (Paris, 1865)

Sañudo Bayon, J., *La Albuera 1811* (Almena, 2006)

Sañudo Bayon, J., Stampa Pineiro, L. & Arcon Domínguez, J.L., *Batallas Campales de 1808* (SIMTAC, 2008)

Sañudo, J., *Base de Datos sobre las Unidades Militares en la Guerra de la Independencia* (Ministerio de Defensa CD, 2007)

Sarrazin, Gen, *History of the war in Spain and Portugal* (Colburn, 1815 – Reprinted Trotman, 1999)

Smith, D., *Napoleon's Regiments, Battle Histories of the Regiments of the French Army, 1792–1815* (London, 2000)

Soriano Izquierdo, J., *Batalla de Bailen 19 Julio de 1808* (La Paz, 2006)

Soriano Izquierdo, J., *Documentos Para el Bicentenario de Bailen 1808 – 2008* (Ademanda, 2007)

Soult, N., *Las Memorias Del Mariscal Soult, Las Tropas Napoleonicas en Galicia 1808–1809* (Arenas, 1999)

Southey, R., *History of the Peninsular War 1807–1811* (Murray, London, 1827). Four volumes

Strachan, H., *The Politics of the British Army* (Clarendon Press, 1997)

Sun Tzu, *The Art of War* (Hodder & Stoughton 1981)

Technigraf Editores, *Batalla de la Albuhera, Edicion Facsimil* (Technigraf, 2008)

Thiers, M.A., *Histoire du Consulat et de L'Empire* (Paulin, Paris, 1845). Twenty volumes

Todman, D., *The Great War: Myth and Modern Memory* (London, 2005)

Urban, M., *The man who broke Napoleon's codes* (Faber & Faber, 2001)

Vale, B., *The Audacious Admiral Cochrane* (Chrysalis Book Group, 2004)

Various, *Bicentenario de la Guerra de la Independencia (1) & (2)* (Revista Ejercito de Tierra Espanol, 2009, No. 805 & 811)

Various, *Los Arapiles Encuentro de Europa* (Diputacion Salamanca, 2002)

Various, *Los Arapiles La Batalla y su Entorno* (Diputacion Salamanca, 2004)

Various, *Talavera 1809, La Batalla, La Ciudad, sus Gentes* (Talavera, 2009)

Vela, F., *Bailén 1808*, (Almena, 2007) Volumes 1 and 2.

Verdera Franco, Soraluce Blond, López de Prado Nistal & Carril Cuesta, *La Capitanía General en la Historia de Galicia* (A Coruña, 2003)

Vincenti, J.P., *Resting Place of General Moore* (Arenas, 2000)

Weller, J. A. C., *Wellington in the Peninsula 1808–1814* (Greenhill, 1962)

Wilkinson-Latham, R., *British Artillery on Land & Sea 1790–1820* (Charles & Abbot, 1973)

Winter, F., *The First Golden Age of Rocketry* (Smithsonian Institution Press, 1990)

Worley Publications, *Atlas of the Peninsular War 1808–1814* (Worley Publications, 2000)